STANDARD LOAN

Plea~ ~urn or renew thi~

ACCOUNTING INFORMATION SYSTEMS

ESSENTIAL CONCEPTS AND APPLICATIONS

THIRD EDITION

JOSEPH W. WILKINSON
Arizona State University

MICHAEL J. CERULLO
Southwest Missouri State University

JOHN WILEY & SONS, INC.

NEW YORK • CHICHESTER • BRISBANE • TORONTO • SINGAPORE • WEINHEIM

Acquisitions Editor	Susan Elbe
Marketing Manager	Wendy Goldner
Production Coordinator	Elm Street Publishing Services, Inc.
Senior Designer	Laura Nicholls
Assistant Manufacturing Manager	Mark Cirillo
Senior Illustration Coordinator	Anna Melhorn
Cover Art	Marjory Dressler

This book was set in 10/12 Novarese by University Graphics, Inc. and printed and bound by R. R. Donnelley & Sons/Willard. The cover was printed by Phoenix Color Corporation.

Recognizing the importance of preserving what has been written, it is a
policy of John Wiley & Sons, Inc. to have books of enduring value published
in the United States printed on acid-free paper, and we exert our best efforts to that end.

Library of Congress Cataloging in Publication Data:
Wilkinson, Joseph W.
     Accounting information systems: essential concepts and
applications / by Joseph W. Wilkinson and Michael J. Cerullo.—3rd
ed.

        p.   cm.
     Includes bibliographical references and index.
     ISBN 0-471-05592-1
     1. Accounting—Data processing.   2. Management information
systems.   1. Cerullo, Michael J. (Michael Joseph), 1940–   .
II. Title.

HF5679.W523   1997
657'.0285—dc20   96-24713
                                                           CIP

Printed in the United States of America

10 9 8 7 6 5 4 3 2 1

SUMMARY

After a design for a new system is specified, the system must be justified as being technically, economically, and operationally feasible. Then proposals are requested from suppliers for the needed system resources. After evaluating the proposals and selecting the suppliers, the soliciting firm undertakes the varied activities necessary to complete the detailed design and to implement the new system.

Information is an economic resource. Information economics, the study of costs and benefits of information, states that added information should be gathered for any purpose so long as its added benefit (value) exceeds its added costs. Relevant costs for determining economic feasibility include costs of acquiring new information system resources, costs of developing the system, and costs of operating and maintaining the new system. Benefits of a new system include tangible benefits, such as cost savings and revenue increases, and intangible benefits, such as better and more timely information. Computations for economic feasibility are based on methods involving net present value, payback period, and the benefit-cost ratio.

In selecting system hardware and software, options to be considered include purchasing versus leasing, single vendors versus multiple vendors, in-house systems versus outsourcing computing services, in-house software development versus commercial software packages. Proposals should be solicited from relevant suppliers of computer resources. Then these proposals should be evaluated, using such techniques as the benchmark problem, simulation model, and weighted-rating analysis.

Systems implementation begins with plans and controls being established, managers and employees being informed, and the project team being reorganized. Project control techniques such as Gantt charts and PERT diagrams may be applied. Major activities include personnel selection and training, physical site preparation, detailed system design, software development, program testing, system testing, standards development, documentation, file conversion, and system conversion. An implemented system should be followed up and undergo postimplementation evaluation. Detailed systems design usually involves such structured design techniques as decision tables, Warnier-Orr diagrams, structure charts, and structured English.

APPENDIX TO CHAPTER 20

NETWORK DIAGRAMS

Two major project planning and control techniques, PERT (Program Evaluation and Review Technique) and CPM (Critical Path Method), incorporate network diagrams. Our discussion follows the terminology of PERT. To simplify the discussion, we will ignore the feature of PERT that requires three time estimates for each activity.

Nomenclature

Figure 20-16 presents a simple network diagram for a hypothetical project. The key features of the diagram are

1. **Activities:** tasks to be completed in the course of the project. Nine activities (labeled A, B, C, E, F, G, H, I, and J) appear in the figure, together with the "dummy" activities labeled D and K. Each activity requires an estimated time for completion (e.g., four weeks in the case of activity A).
2. **Events:** milestones (points in time) representing the completion of one or more activities *and* (except for the terminal event) the beginning of one or more following activities. Seven events, numbered from 1 through 7, appear in the figure.
3. **Paths:** routes through the network from the initial event to the terminal event (i.e., from event 1 to event 7). Six paths can be traced through the figure: A–G–K; A–H; A–F–I; B–E–I; B–D–J; and C–J.
4. **Critical path:** the path with the greatest overall total time. In this example, A–F–I is the critical path, since $4 + 4 + 5$, or 13 weeks, is the greatest time required to complete the project by any path shown.
5. **Overall project time:** the time required to complete all activities within the project. The time along the critical path (13 weeks in this example) is equal to the overall project time.

Diagram Development

Developing or constructing a network diagram involves two basic steps: estimating activity times and linking activities together. Estimating activity times requires knowledge of such factors as the available resources and the exact nature of the activities. It is also necessary to judge the productivity of each resource in achieving the tasks involved in each activity.

Linking activities together requires close knowledge of their relationships. The planner needs to be aware of those activities that necessarily precede other activities, those activities that necessarily follow other activities, and those activities that can be performed concurrently.

Computational Procedure

After developing a network diagram, the next objective is to compute the overall project time and critical path.

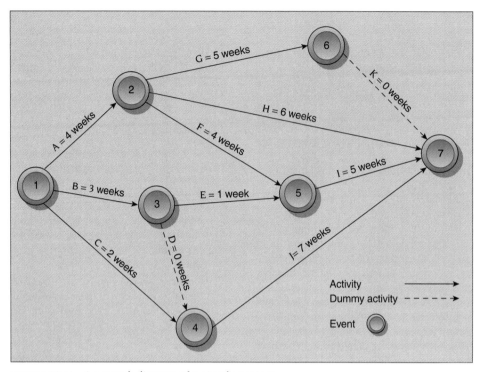

FIGURE 20-16   A network diagram of a simple project.

Although the values of these key factors are readily apparent in a simple diagram such as Figure 17-15, they are not so apparent in the more complex diagrams usually encountered in real-world projects. A systematic procedure is therefore desirable.

One suitable procedure consists of these steps:

1. Determine the earliest time when each event in the network can take place.
2. Compute the overall project time.
3. Determine the latest time when each event can occur within the constraint of the overall project time.
4. Compute the critical path.

Figure 20-17 shows the application of this procedure to the network portrayed in Figure 20-16. The specific values derived by each of the above steps are discussed next.

Determine the Earliest Times

Each event has an earliest time (ET). An ET for a particular event may be defined as the sum of activity times along a path from the beginning point of a project to the event. When more than one path leads to an event, the ET is the *largest* time required by any of the paths.

Consider event 5 in Figure 20-17. Two paths, A–F and B–E, lead to the event. Path A–F is composed of 4 weeks + 4 weeks = 8 weeks. Path B–E is composed of 3 weeks + 1 week = 4 weeks. The larger time of 8 weeks is thus the ET for event 5, as denoted by the 8 in the square symbol.

A question that might be asked at this point is, Why not allow a particular event to have an ET for each path leading to the event? For instance, why not assign 4 weeks as a second ET at event 5, since path B–E requires only 4 weeks to complete the B and E activities? The answer is as follows: Each event in a network diagram represents a termination point as well as a commencement point; progress cannot begin on any activities *beyond* an event until *all* preceding activities have been completed. Thus, activity I cannot begin until activities A and F as well as B and E are completed; 8 weeks after the project begins is therefore the earliest time that activity I can begin.

Dummy activities, such as activities D and K in Figure 20-17, also must be considered when determining earliest times. A *dummy activity* is a constraint or imaginary activity rather than a real activity; that is, it requires *zero* time and use of resources. However, a dummy activity is needed to show more fully the relationship between activities and to allow the proper ET to be determined at a particular event. For instance, a dummy activity is needed to constrain the beginning of the equipment installation until after the ordered hardware and software arrive, even though the physical preparation activity will

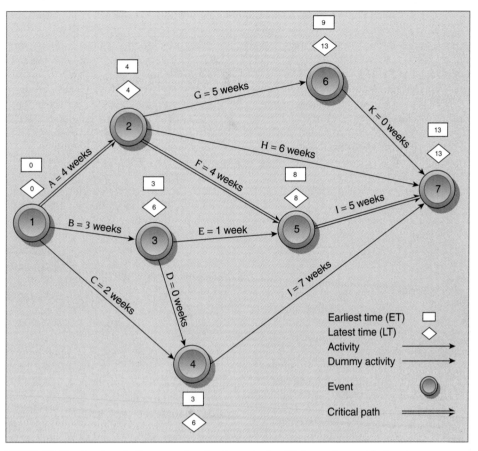

FIGURE 20-17   A network diagram of a simple project, with key values added.

be completed at an earlier date. Similarly, in Figure 20-17, activity J cannot begin until after activity B is completed. Thus, dummy activity D is drawn between activity B and event 4, with the result that the ET at event 4 will be 3 weeks + 0 weeks = 3 weeks, rather than 2 weeks.

Compute the Overall Project Time

The overall time to complete all the activities within a project is the ET of the terminal event. In Figure 20-17 the overall project time is 13 weeks, the ET of event 7.

Determine the Latest Time

Each event has a latest time (LT). An LT for a particular event may be defined as the latest time that an event can take place without delaying the completion of the overall project. When more than one path leads from a particular event toward the terminal event, the LT is the *smallest* of the LT values for the respective paths.

Let us consider the LTs for events 4, 3, and 2 in Figure 20-17. To determine each of these LTs, we begin by setting the LT for event 7, the terminal event, at 13 weeks,

the overall project time. Then, to find the LT for event 4, deduct 7 weeks from 13 weeks, thereby obtaining 6 weeks. Since only one path leads back to event 4, 6 weeks is the only possible LT. To find the LT for event 3, next deduct 0 (the time for activity D) from 6 weeks, thereby obtaining 6 weeks. However, this is not the only possible LT for event 3, since the path E–I also leads back to the event. For this path the LT is 13 weeks − 5 weeks − 1 week = 7 weeks. Because 6 weeks is *smaller* than 7 weeks, the LT for event 3 should be 6 weeks. Finding the LT for event 2 means comparing the LTs for three paths.

LT via path G–K is 13 − 0 − 5 = 8 weeks
LT via path H is 13 − 6 = 7 weeks
LT via path F–I is 13 − 5 − 4 = 4 weeks

Since 4 weeks is the smallest value, it represents the LT for event 2.

Compute the Critical Path

The critical path of a network is the path whose activity times equal the overall project time. For Figure 20-17 the critical path is A–F–I, as seen earlier. In a complex network, however, the critical path seldom can be spotted by knowledge of the overall project time alone. Thus, a more operational definition for the critical path is as follows: The critical path is the path formed by events at which the ETs are equal to the LTs.

In Figure 20-17 the ET equals the LT at events 5 and 2. Conversely, the ET and LT at events 3, 4, and 6 are not equal. Thus, the critical path ranges from event 1 to event 2 to event 5 to event 7.

The critical path is so named because the activities it encompasses are critical or bottleneck activities. If any of these activities is delayed (i.e., its time is lengthened), the overall project time will be lengthened. On the other hand, activities not on the critical path are not critical. Any such noncritical activity might be delayed (up to a point) without the overall project time being affected. For instance, in Figure 20-17, activity G might be delayed for up to 4 weeks without affecting the overall project time of 13 weeks.

The notion of *slack time* is generally introduced into network computations to denote the extent of allowable delay. The slack time of a noncritical event is the difference between its ET and LT.* For instance, the slack times for events 3, 4, and 6 in Figure 20-17 are 3, 3, and 4, respectively. Incidentally, the slack times for events along the critical path are zero, since the ET and LT for each event are equal. Thus, the critical path may alternatively be defined as the path along which the slack times are zero.

REVIEW PROBLEM WITH SOLUTION

PRECISE MANUFACTURING COMPANY, THIRD INSTALLMENT

Statement

After the new sales order system design is approved, the project team prepares a report that shows the system to be economically feasible. The team also prepares a request for proposals from computer hardware and software suppliers. On receiving several proposals, the team and information systems manager evaluate those proposals that are sufficiently responsive to the firm's needs. They present their recommendations to the steering committee in December 1997. After due consideration the steering committee approves the project for implementation. The information systems manager believes that the period of 11 months, which was originally estimated, is too short. Thus he extends the period for

*Slack times may alternatively be measured in terms of activities if the ETs and LTs are determined for activities rather than events.

a full year, so that the new completion date is December 31, 1998.

To provide better control over the implementation process, the information systems manager divides the phase into major activities such as detailed design, training, and so on. These activities and related times are shown in the network diagram on page 919. Activity times appear in parentheses after the activity labels and are stated in weeks. Events appear at the beginning and end of each activity, starting with event 1 and finishing with event 11. Event 11 marks the cutover point. By means of this network diagram, the project leader guides and controls the activities of her project team during the next year. The work of the project generally progresses in a smooth manner. Only one significant delay is encountered: the ordered hardware and software arrive a month late. Consequently, the equipment installation activity is completed approximately a month behind schedule. However, since adequate slack time is available, the overall project time is not lengthened.

Required

a. Prepare a Gantt chart that reflects the time schedule originally established for the project in the First Installment (Chapter 18).

b. Verify the critical path shown in the network diagram and compute the slack times for the various events.

Solution

a. Gantt chart: See page 919.

b. The critical path shown in the diagram is equal to the project time of 52 weeks, or the cumulative times of the activities along the path $(3 + 16 + 17 + 8 + 8 = 52)$. This total time is greater than the time along any other path from event 1 to event 11. For instance, the total time along path $1-2-5-11$ is computed as $3 + 4 - 14 = 21$ weeks. The "slack" times are as follows.

Event	ET (weeks)	LT (weeks)	Slack Time (weeks)
1	0	0	0
2	3	3	0
3	2	32	30
4	16	27	11
5	19	38	19
6	19	19	0
7	16	27	11
8	36	36	0
9	21	32	11
10	44	44	0
11	52	52	0

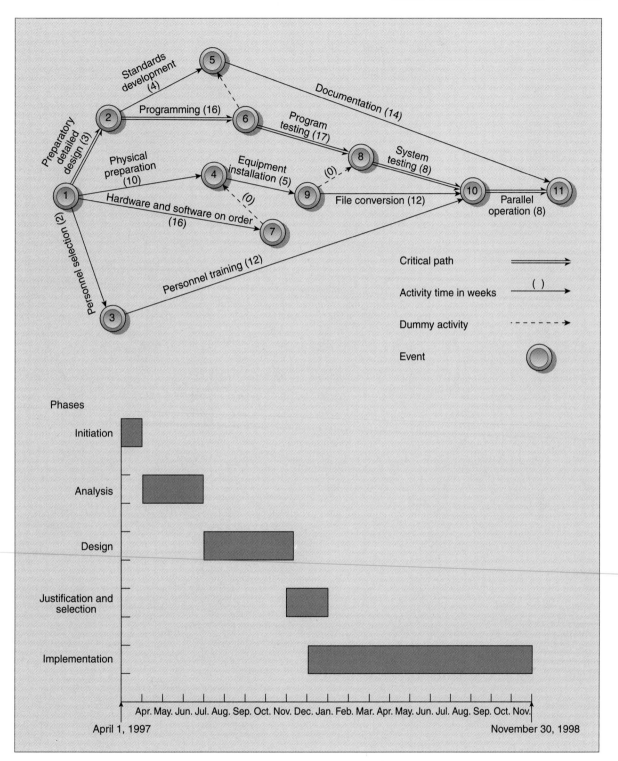

TABLE 1   Present Value of $1

Years	5%	6%	8%	10%	12%	14%	15%	16%	18%	20%	22%	24%	25%
1	0.952	0.943	0.926	0.909	0.893	0.877	0.870	0.862	0.847	0.833	0.820	0.806	0.800
2	0.907	0.890	0.857	0.826	0.797	0.769	0.756	0.743	0.718	0.694	0.672	0.650	0.640
3	0.864	0.840	0.794	0.751	0.712	0.675	0.658	0.641	0.609	0.579	0.551	0.524	0.512
4	0.823	0.792	0.735	0.683	0.636	0.592	0.572	0.552	0.516	0.482	0.451	0.423	0.410
5	0.784	0.747	0.681	0.621	0.567	0.519	0.497	0.476	0.437	0.402	0.370	0.341	0.328
6	0.746	0.705	0.630	0.564	0.507	0.456	0.432	0.410	0.370	0.335	0.303	0.275	0.262
7	0.711	0.665	0.583	0.513	0.452	0.400	0.376	0.354	0.314	0.279	0.249	0.222	0.210
8	0.677	0.627	0.540	0.467	0.404	0.351	0.327	0.305	0.266	0.233	0.204	0.179	0.168
9	0.645	0.592	0.500	0.424	0.361	0.308	0.284	0.263	0.225	0.194	0.167	0.144	0.134
10	0.614	0.558	0.463	0.386	0.322	0.270	0.247	0.227	0.191	0.162	0.137	0.116	0.107

TABLE 2   Present Value of $1 Received Annually for N Years

Years (N)	5%	6%	8%	10%	12%	14%	15%	16%	18%	20%	22%	24%	25%
1	0.952	0.943	0.926	0.909	0.893	0.877	0.870	0.862	0.847	0.833	0.820	0.806	0.800
2	1.859	1.833	1.783	1.736	1.690	1.647	1.626	1.605	1.566	1.528	1.492	1.457	1.440
3	2.723	2.673	2.577	2.487	2.402	2.322	2.283	2.246	2.174	2.106	2.042	1.981	1.952
4	3.546	3.465	3.312	3.169	3.037	2.914	2.855	2.798	2.690	2.589	2.494	2.404	2.362
5	4.330	4.212	3.993	3.791	3.605	3.433	3.352	3.274	3.127	2.991	2.864	2.745	2.689
6	5.076	4.917	4.623	4.355	4.111	3.889	3.784	3.685	3.498	3.326	3.167	3.020	2.951
7	5.786	5.582	5.206	4.868	4.564	4.288	4.160	4.039	3.812	3.605	3.416	3.242	3.161
8	6.463	6.210	5.747	5.335	4.968	4.639	4.487	4.344	4.078	3.837	3.619	3.421	3.329
9	7.108	6.802	6.247	5.759	5.328	4.946	4.772	4.607	4.303	4.031	3.786	3.566	3.463
10	7.722	7.360	6.710	6.145	5.650	5.216	5.019	4.833	4.494	4.192	3.923	3.682	3.571

KEY TERMS

acceptance testing   (909)
benchmark problem technique   (900)
benefit-cost ratio   (894)
coding   (908)
cutover   (909)
decision table   (911)
desk checking   (908)
detailed structure chart   (913)
detailed systems design   (906)
direct conversion approach   (909)
facilities management firm   (897)
file conversion   (909)
Gantt chart   (902)
information economics   (887)
intangible benefit   (890)
modular conversion approach   (910)
net present value   (892)
network diagram   (903)
one-time cost   (888)
parallel operation approach   (909)
payback period   (894)

phased conversion approach   (910)
postimplementation review and evaluation   (910)
recurring cost   (888)
service bureau   (896)
simulation model technique   (901)
string testing   (908)
structured English   (913)
structured programming   (908)
system conversion   (909)
system testing   (909)
tangible benefit   (890)
time-sharing service center   (896)
user signoff   (910)
Warnier-Orr diagram   (912)
weighted-rating analysis technique   (901)

REVIEW QUESTIONS

20-1. What are several alternative information system changes that involve the acquisition of computer resources?

20-2. In what ways can accountants be useful in the system development phases following conceptual systems design?

20-3. What are the steps required to justify and select resources for a newly designed information system?

20-4. Describe the information economics concepts that concern information and information system resources.

20-5. List several one-time and recurring costs in system development projects.

20-6. Contrast and identify tangible and intangible benefits in system developments.

20-7. Identify several approaches that may be employed to estimate costs and benefits related to system development projects.

20-8. What are the relevant factors in the net present value method?

20-9. Construct the computations under the net present value, payback period, and benefit-cost ratio methods.

20-10. What acquisition options are available to designers of information systems?

20-11. What types of outside computing services are available?

20-12. What are the benefits and drawbacks of outside computing services?

20-13. What are the benefits and drawbacks of acquiring commercial software packages?

20-14. Describe the procedure for selecting computer hardware and software.

20-15. What should be included in a request for proposal, including the cover letter?

20-16. Contrast the benchmark problem, simulation model, and weighted-rating analysis methods.

20-17. What are several preliminary actions that should be taken prior to the beginning of implementation activities?

20-18. Contrast the Gantt chart and network diagram, with respect to both their characteristics and their abilities to provide effective control over systems projects.

20-19. Briefly describe several typical implementation activities.

20-20. Identify the types of features that are included in a set of detailed system specifications.

20-21. Contrast the direct, parallel operation, modular, and phases approaches to system conversion.

20-22. What are the purposes of a postimplementation evaluation?

20-23. What are the similarities and differences between a program flowchart and decision table?

20-24. What are the similarities and differences between a data hierarchy diagram and Warnier-Orr diagram?

20-25. What are the components of a detailed structure chart?

20-26. What are the relationships of structured English (1) to other structured detailed design techniques and (2) to program code?

20-27. What are the steps in developing a network diagram?

20-28. What are three important quantitative results provided by a network diagram?

DISCUSSION QUESTIONS

20-29. Discuss the respective contributions that a systems analyst and accountant can make in the procedure that determines whether an information system is feasible. Also discuss the desirability of having these persons closely coordinate their efforts during the procedure.

20-30. Contrast the benefits that Infoage can expect from an improved inventory management system with those that it can expect from an improved budgetary control system.

20-31. What criteria should apply in the selection of decision support software?

20-32. Does a firm ever complete in-house the design and implementation of a new information system?

20-33. Discuss the hidden costs traceable to employee fears and uncertainties concerning a new information system.

20-34. A systems analyst has just developed a design for a new production information system. She is justly proud of the design, since it is innovative and well structured. However, the production manager and his employees are very critical of the new system and refuse to use it properly. Discuss.

20-35. Discuss the matters that should be examined during a postimplementation review and evaluation of a recently implemented electronic data interchange network.

PROBLEMS

20-1. Ann Strong, the single proprietor of a small public accounting firm, has seen her business grow appreciably during the past year. Thus, she has opened a second office and added two other professional accountants to the firm, plus three additional staff persons in the branch and two others in the main office. Because of the added activity she has decided that a client/server network may be suitable. Alternatively, separate stand-alone microcomputers might be the more desirable acquisition. Together with the other professional accountants, she performed an analysis of the firm's requirements and developed new designs based on each of the alternative computer configurations.

Required

a. Describe the steps that Ann should take to determine the feasibility of each alternative system, with special attention to economic feasibility but also considering other types of feasibility.

b. Assuming that the client/server network appears to be feasible and preferable to stand-alone microcomputers, briefly describe the various steps that Ann should take in selecting the system and implementing it.

c. One of the other professional accountants has considerable experience in consulting with clients that are in need of new computer systems and networks. In what activities is he likely to be most helpful during the selection and implementation phases?

20-2. Identify each of the following items as one of these choices:

1. One-time tangible cost.
2. Recurring tangible cost.
3. Intangible cost.
4. Tangible benefit.
5. Intangible benefit.

a. Replacement of magnetic tapes for backup.

b. Improved sales forecasts due to better data stored in the data base.

c. Training of users of a new computer system.

d. Reduction of bad debts by 20 percent.

e. Loss in employee productivity due to poor morale caused by a new information system.

f. Software needed for data communications within a client/server network.

g. Improved data-base maintenance, including updates of tables, which saves one-half the time of two accounting clerks.

h. Salary of a data-base administrator.

i. Time required by three systems analysts and two programmers to perform systems testing of a newly installed computer system.

j. Better after-sales service to customers due to a new on-line computer system.

20-3. The Pence Company of Ellensburg, Washington, a local grower and distributor of produce, is investigating the economic feasibility of acquiring a small computer system to aid in processing transactions and providing information for managers. It has gathered the following data.

Purchase price of hardware and software	$85,000
Other one-time costs, such as costs pertaining to design and implementation	$40,000
Annual before-tax savings in operating costs	$38,000
Salvage value of the computer system in five years	$22,000
Salvage value of presently owned processing devices	$0
Expected economic life of the computer system	5 years
Required after-tax rate of return	15 percent

Required

a. Compute the net present value of the returns from the proposed investment in the computer system, ignoring the effects of taxes.

b. Compute the payback period, ignoring the effects of taxes.

c. Compute the benefit-cost ratio, ignoring the effects of taxes.

d. Compute the net present value of the after-tax returns, assuming that (i) the marginal income tax rate is 34 percent, (ii) all one-time costs are depreciated over the economic life according to the straight-line method, and (iii) the book value of the presently owned processing devices is zero. Ignore the investment tax credit.

e. Compute the payback period under the assumptions stated in **d.**

f. Compute the benefit-cost ratio under the assumptions stated in **d.**

g. Evaluate the economic feasibility of the proposed investment in the computer system, based on the results obtained in the preceding parts.

20-4. The Jarvon Company of Lincoln, Nebraska, is a distributor of cosmetics. Because of continued growth and the need to compete effectively, the management has assigned you to conduct a feasibility study. Your first step is to gather data concerning the present processing system, which consists of manual processing and limited processing on an outdated computer system. For instance, payroll, the general ledger accounting, and inventory record keeping are handled by the computer system.

You next study the needs of the firm in the areas of purchasing, billing, and inventory management. On the basis of your investigation you specify a particular system design. After management approves the overall design, you estimate the costs and benefits that are to be expected from its installation.

Your design contemplates the purchase of a modern disk-oriented computer system (software as well as hardware) for approximately $140,000. The system is expected to have a $50,000 salvage value at the end of its five-year economic life. However, maintenance costs for the computer system will be $9000 per year higher than those for the present computer system.

Several significant benefits are expected to be achieved with the new computer system. Purchasing costs are expected to be reduced from current levels by $20,000 in each of the first three years and by $30,000 in the last two years. Savings in billing costs are expected to be $10,000 in the first year and to increase by $5000 in each of the following years. Improved inventory management is expected to reduce processing and stockout costs by $10,000 in each of the next five years. In addition, the reduction in inventory is estimated to average about $100,000 over the five-year period.

The controller provides you with the following figures: a 20 percent required rate of return (after income taxes); a 34 percent marginal income tax rate; and a 10 percent inventory carrying cost rate. He also tells you that the salvage value (and also the book value) of the current computer system is $10,000 and that all costs related to the study and installation of the new system should not exceed $30,000. The straight-line method of depreciation is employed with respect to newly acquired assets.

Required

Compute (a) the net present value and (b) the benefit-cost ratio of the proposed new computer system. Be careful to include tax effects, such as (1) the savings stemming from the depreciation tax "shield," (2) the added taxes, if any, resulting from the gain on the sale of the present computer system, and (3) the added taxes resulting from net yearly savings. Assume that the cost for design and installation is to be amortized over the economic life of the investment.

20-5. Magruder Industries manufactures automobile components that are sold worldwide. The firm has three large production facilities and has been debating the benefits of implementing computer-integrated manufacturing (CIM) in one of these factories. A net present value analysis of this investment has been prepared, and summarized results of the analysis are shown below.

Ray Cooper, vice-president of production, is heading the committee charged with investigating the CIM project and is concerned that this analysis is shortsighted. He sees many benefits of CIM that have not been included in the analysis. He also believes that the firm

should view this project as a change in long-range strategy rather than just another investment project. After discussions with the vice-president of marketing, Cooper and Liz Austin, corporate controller, have compiled the following list of benefits with suggestions as to how they might be quantified.

- Increased manufacturing flexibility. The equipment can be easily programmed for process and design changes and from one product line to another. Conceptually, it is as efficient to make one unit of product as to make a large quantity. This provides for more reliable and flexible production scheduling, reduced set-up costs, and reductions in the amounts of required work-in-process and finished-goods inventories. Cooper and Austin believe that the projected operational savings should be increased ten percent to include these efficiencies.

- Improved product quality. CIM reduces the risk of production by making output more uniform and decreasing rework and scrap. In addition, processes can be more easily refined to improve quality. Historically, scrap and rework costs have averaged $150,000 annually at Magruder. Cooper and Austin believe that by the beginning of Year 3, these costs will average only $50,000.

- Less required floor space. As computer-controlled equipment replaces conventional equipment and the need for inventory storage is reduced, 3000 square feet of floor space will be released for other uses. The current plan envisions using this floor space with a current annual cost of $14 per square foot, for new research facilities, precluding the need for additional rental cost. However, this benefit has not been included in the net present value analysis.

- Increased customer satisfaction. Increased flexibility provides incentive for product improvements and new product development and provides the firm with the capability to respond more quickly to customer demands. In addition, improved product quality and turnaround times will increase customer acceptance of Magruder's products. While these benefits may not be realized initially, Cooper and Austin believe that revenues will increase as a result of these factors. Therefore, they have suggested that the analysis be revised to include a conservative estimate of $800,000 in additional annual contribution beginning in Year 6.

Cooper and Austin believe that there are significant risks of not purchasing the equipment. For example, Magruder could lose market share if the competition automates and reaps the benefits. However, they have not factored this into the revised net present value analysis.

Magruder uses a 12 percent discount rate (present value tables below) and has a 40 percent effective tax rate. For the purpose of analysis, all tax effects and cash flows from equipment acquisition and disposal are considered to occur at the time of the transaction while those from operations are considered to occur at the end of each year.

	Year(s) Affected	Annual Cash Flow Amount
CIM investment	Current	$(6,000,000)
Working capital	Current	(600,000)
Gain on equipment disposal (net of tax)	Current	20,000
Operational savings (net of tax)	1–10	600,000
Depreciation tax shield	1–10	240,000
Salvage (net of tax)	10	200,000
Recovery of working capital	10	600,000

Required

a. Compute the net present value of the proposed new CIM system, using the revised estimates developed by Cooper and Austin.

b. Discuss which benefits are intangible, or at least not clearly tangible.

c. In what ways might the risks of not investing in a CIM system be incorporated into the economic feasibility analysis?

(CMA *adapted*)

20-6. Novus Financial Corp. of Riverwoods, Illinois, is a consumer finance firm that services about 400,000 customer accounts.* Recently it decided to replace its mainframe-based legacy systems, written in COBOL, with a client/server architecture and relational data base. The two main applications to be replaced were its (1) loan origination system and (2) loan-servicing and collection system. Its first step was to evaluate the possibility of outsourcing the project to such computer service consultants as EDS and Perot Systems, rather than assigning the project to its in-house information systems department. It finally decided to do the development in house, although it did use consultants to aid in selecting a suitable relational data-base package. Next it had to consider whether to acquire commercial software packages for its two main applications. Its decisions differed. For the loan origination system, it acquired Creditrevue, an application package developed by Credit Manage-

ment Solutions, and modified the code (which was written in a fourth-generation language). For the loan-servicing and collection system, it developed a customized system in-house, since management felt that this area is the most competitive.

Required

a. What were likely to be the reasons for not outsourcing the systems development to outside consultants? Why did the firm decide, on the other hand, to use outside consultants to aid in selecting the data-base package?

b. What were the benefits to the firm in acquiring a commercial software package for the loan origination application?

c. What were the benefits to the firm in developing a customized loan-servicing and collection system in-house?

20-7. Dial Corporation, whose main office is in Phoenix, Arizona, recognized a few years ago that its highly centralized management structure did not meet the needs of a diverse and growing firm.* Upon changing its organization structure, the management discovered that its current information system, based on a centralized mainframe-based computer network architecture, was no longer satisfactory in serving its decentralized management. Working with outside consultants, Dial's MIS department identified two feasible distributed processing architectures. One alternative involved the use of midrange computers, while the other emphasized servers and microcomputer users (clients). Each alternative was evaluated by means of a point-scoring (weighted-rating analysis) procedure, considering such factors as security, related software, training, flexibility, availability of vendors, and functionality. The more flexible client/server network architecture was selected.

The development and changeover to this new distributed network was found to require three to five years to implement. After lengthy discussions, management realized that its MIS department was not sufficiently large to both develop a new system and operate the current system satisfactorily. Thus, it decided to outsource the mainframe operations during the developmental period to Andersen Consulting. In performing its outsourcing services, Andersen Consulting would transfer the major files and programs to its Dallas mainframe and process data from there. Both batch and on-line processing from all of Dial's sites would be supported. Its mainframe and supporting equipment are state-of-the-art and upgraded periodically. It would also maintain all other systems

*Jeff Moad, "Shock Therapy Cures Fossilitis," *Datamation* (June 1, 1994), pp. 57–59.

*Michael A. Robinson, "Decentralize and Outsource: Dial's Approach to MIS Improvement," *Management Accounting* (September 1991), pp. 27–31.

hardware and software on the premises of Dial and provide user services and support. The contract called for charges based on a set rate per central processing unit (CPU) hour and gigabyte of storage required, plus reimbursement of telecommunications costs and software costs.

Required

a. Describe the nature of outsourcing to be provided by Andersen Consulting, and discuss the benefits and drawbacks of this outsourcing agreement.

b. During its development Dial's MIS department recommends that commercial software packages be acquired to process its basic accounting applications on the client/server network. What are the benefits of this choice, as well as the drawbacks?

c. In developing the client/server network, Dial must decide on a wide variety of hardware. The MIS department recommends that the various hardware components be selected from several vendors. What are the benefits of this choice, as well as the drawbacks?

20-8. Many small and medium-sized firms have decided that computerized data processing would be beneficial to their needs. They are confronted with several alternatives, however. They may buy or lease a small or medium-sized computer system, subscribe to a commercial time-sharing service, or utilize a local service bureau or a facilities management firm. Discuss which of these alternatives appears to be suitable to each of the following firms:

a. A small but rapidly growing contractor that needs consolidated financial statements pertaining to the operations of its several divisions.

b. An independent automotive supply house that needs to maintain an inventory consisting of over 50,000 parts by placing weekly orders with suppliers.

c. An engineering research center ("think tank") that needs to keep track of costs incurred against various contracts, to prepare periodic cost reports, and to provide computational facilities for its engineers.

d. A medium-sized public utility that needs to prepare customers' bills on a daily basis (known as cycle billing), as well as to prepare payrolls, maintain the general ledger, keep track of costs incurred in new construction and maintenance operations, and provide monthly reports to managers.

e. A medium-sized bank that is acquiring several small but growing local banks and needs to merge their processing operations as quickly as possible into a set of uniform systems.

20-9. The following are results of benchmark problems run on configurations A, B, and C.* The benchmark problems run on each configuration are representative sample workloads, which test for both input-output and internal processing capabilities of each configuration. The monthly rental, based on projected usage of at least 176 hours per month, is $30,000 for configuration A, $34,000 for configuration B, and $32,000 for configuration C.

Benchmark Results: CPU Times (in Seconds) for Compilation and Execution of Different Programs

	Type of Problem		
Vendor	Process-Bound Problem	Input-Output-Bound Problem	Hybrid Problem
A	400.5	640	247.5
B	104.9	320	260.3
C	175.4	325	296.8

Required

a. On the basis of the three benchmark problems, decide which vendor's (supplier's) configuration is preferable.

b. Compute cost-effectiveness indices by dividing the total benchmark time of each configuration by that vendor's monthly payments. How do these computations affect the results?

20-10. The Kenmore Company has determined that a new interactive computer system is economically feasible with respect to its accounting transaction processing applications. It has requested and received proposals from three suppliers of hardware and software. The system evaluation team assigns the following weights and ratings to the relevant factors:

		Supplier		
Factor	Weight	X	Y	Z
Hardware performance	20	8	7	9
Software suitability	15	9	6	7
Hardware features	10	7	8	7
Software features	10	8	6	5
Overall price	15	7	9	8
Support by supplier	20	8	10	8
System reliability	10	10	9	10

*Adapted from John G. Burch and Gary Grudnitski, *Information Systems: Theory and Practice*, 4th ed. (New York: Wiley, 1986). Used with permission.

Required

a. Compute the total evaluations of the suppliers, using the weighted-rating analysis technique, and explain the results.

b. Describe the uncertainties involved in using the data provided.

c. What other techniques might aid in making the final selection?

Required

a. Assume that one of the user managers disagrees with the weights. She believes that performance should be weighted higher, perhaps 10; she also states that assistance, training, and documentation is extremely important and deserves at least a weight of 12. An accounting manager, on the other hand, believes that security (under special features) is critical and deserves a weight of 10, and that backup facilities also should be weighted

Factor	Weight	Supplier		
		Able	Baker	Charlene
Ease of use	(12)	10	8	10
Compatibility to variety of hardware	(10)	7	9	8
Software support by supplier	(10)	7	10	8
Price of package	(9)	8	10	6
Reliability	(8)	9	6	10
Query language facility	(8)	8	9	8
Training provided by supplier	(6)	6	8	8
Performance (speed)	(6)	10	8	10
Documentation	(5)	5	9	7
Data definition facility	(5)	10	7	8
Reputation of supplier	(5)	8	8	10
Enhancements	(4)	7	5	9
Ease of installation	(4)	7	5	9
CODASYL compatibility	(4)	10	8	10
Flexibility to accommodate changes	(4)	5	6	8

20-11. The Tootle Corporation of Newark, New Jersey, has decided to acquire a data-base management system. After receiving proposals from three suppliers, the feasibility study team employs a weighted-rating analysis as its chief means of evaluation. In preparing to apply this evaluation technique, it assigns weights to the relevant factors to be considered and then rates each supplier on each of the factors on a scale from 1 to 10. The results are listed in the accompanying table, with the numbers in parentheses being the weights.

Required

a. Perform a weighted-rating (point-scoring) analysis and explain the results.

b. As a user of relational data-base management system packages, such as Paradox or Access, what additional factors would you consider?

c. If the software being considered was a general ledger accounting package, how would the factors change, if at all?

20-12. Refer to Figure 20-8.

as high as 8. Discuss the usefulness of the weighted-rating analysis method in light of such disagreements.

b. Recompute the table in Figure 20-8 after changing the values of factors to reflect the views of both managers in **a** above. To compensate for the increases, lower the values for compatibility, range of capabilities, and reputation by 6, 6, and 8 points, respectively. How do the changes affect the relative evaluations of vendors A and B?

c. Recompute the requirements-cost indexes if each vendor's system is expected to cost $1 million.

d. If the computer systems being evaluated in Figure 20-8 are client/server networks, what additional factors (if any) should be included?

20-13. A savings and loan association has decided to undertake the development of an in-house computer system to replace the processing it currently purchases from a time-sharing service. The internal auditors have suggested that the systems development process be planned in accordance with the systems development life cycle concept.

The following nine items have been identified as major systems development activities that will have to be undertaken:

   a.   System test.

   b.   User specifications.

   c.   Conversion.

   d.   System planning study.

   e.   Technical specifications.

   f.   Postimplementation review.

   g.   Implementation planning.

   h.   User procedures and training.

   i.   Programming.

Required

a. Rearrange these nine items to reflect the sequence in which they should logically occur. If certain items would likely occur roughly at the same time, bracket those items.

b. An item not included in the list is file conversion. List the key steps involved in this activity.

c. Describe the results that the postimplementation review should achieve.

d. Describe the ways that the three final system conversion approaches would be applied in this situation.

(CIA *adapted*)

20-14. Artists' Delights, Inc., of Lawrence, Kansas, is a manufacturer of paints, brushes, and other art supplies. Although the firm has prospered for a number of years because of its quality products, it currently is experiencing several problems. For instance, it is having difficulty in keeping its catalog up to date, in conducting low-cost and efficient production operations, in maintaining adequate inventories, and in making prompt deliveries of ordered goods. Since the president recognizes that most, if not all, of these problems are related to the firm's information system, he has authorized the director of information systems to undertake a systems development investigation.

The director forms a steering committee, which in turn establishes several project areas. It assigns the highest priority to the inventory area and approves the organization of a project team. After analyzing inventory operations and management, the team recommends that a computer-based system be considered as a replacement for the present manual information and processing system. On the concurrence of the steering committee, a feasibility study then is undertaken. Based on costs and benefits developed during this study, a computer-based information system is found to be feasible.

At this point the steering committee asks the director to prepare plans that reflect the activities necessary to acquire a computer-based system and to put it into operation. If the plans appear reasonable, the steering committee likely will give its approval to proceed.

The director thus sits down and ponders. He is aware that the present information system has many deficiencies, including weak standards and documentation. He also recognizes that few employees have experience with computers. Because of these deficiencies he intends to acquire well-documented software packages for the first applications to be implemented on the anticipated computer system. However, he does want to develop the programs for the other applications, which he hopes can be in process later this year.

Required

Prepare an appropriate list of implementation activities for the director to submit to the steering committee. Arrange the activities in approximate chronological order.

20-15. Dorothy Sadfoss is a systems analyst for the Brookside Manufacturing Company of Boulder, Colorado. Since Dorothy is a hard-working and intelligent graduate of a nearby university, she was recently given a challenging assignment: developing a new purchase-ordering system for the firm.

Having been exposed to the latest forecasting techniques (in a senior-level course she took two years ago), she decided that they should provide the foundation for her design of the purchasing system. Consequently, she developed a sophisticated ordering model that incorporated exponential smoothing forecasts, economic order quantities, quantity discount analysis, and supplier evaluation features. As a result, the system would automatically produce a purchase order that needed only to be approved by a buyer and the purchasing manager before being mailed to the supplier.

On presenting her new design to her superior and then to higher management, Dorothy was accorded a puzzled reception. However, after she pointed out such benefits as reduced inventory costs and fewer stockouts, the reception became quite warm and approval was granted.

She then turned to the implementation of her new purchase ordering system. After writing the necessary programs and conducting extensive tests, she presented the system to the buyers at a special meeting. (The purchasing manager could not attend, since he was out of town. However, he had been informed the previous week by the president that the new system had the approval of top management and that he was to allow Dorothy complete freedom in putting the new system into effect.) At the meeting, several buyers were impressed, especially since the new system involved the use of microcomputers. A few buyers seemed a bit dubious, but Dorothy assured them of the benefits.

When the new system was completely installed, Dorothy met again with the buyers to explain the use of new forms and the sequence of steps necessary to operate the installed computers. She also left some operating instructions, which she had written the previous weekend, consisting of about 20 typed pages. (She had meant to develop some diagrams and other instructional aids to show at the meeting, but the implementation schedule was rather tight and she did not have time.) At the end of the same day the president issued a bulletin in which he stated that the new system would require the services of one-half the current number of buyers. For the present all buyers would be kept; however, at the end of the month only those buyers who appeared to have adjusted most easily and enthusiastically to the new system would be kept in their positions. Others would be transferred to new positions (if available) and completely retrained in their duties or would be helped to find employment outside the firm.

Required

Discuss people-related problems caused by actions taken and not taken by Dorothy and the president during the development and implementation of the new purchase ordering system. Suggest specific steps which, if taken during this period, would have rendered the new system more operationally feasible.

20-16. Mickie Louderman, the new assistant controller of Pickens Publishers, was assigned to develop a new AIS. She began to develop the new system at Pickens by using the same design characteristics and reporting formats that she had developed at her former firm. She sent details of the new accounting information system to the departments that interfaced with accounting, including inventory control, purchasing, personnel, production control, and marketing. If they did not respond with suggestions by a prescribed date, she would continue the development process. Louderman and John Richards, the controller, determined a new schedule for many of the reports, changing the frequency from weekly to monthly. After a meeting with the director of computer operations, she selected a programmer to help her with the details of the new reporting formats.

Most of the control features of the old system were maintained to decrease the initial installation time, while a few new ones were added for unusual situations; however, the procedures for maintaining the controls were substantially changed. Louderman appointed herself the decisive authority for all control changes and program testing that related to the AIS, including screening the control features that related to batch totals for payroll, inventory control, accounts receivable, cash deposits, and accounts payable.

As each module was completed by the programmer, Louderman told the department to implement the change immediately, in order to incorporate immediate labor savings. There were incomplete instructions accompanying these changes, and specific implementation responsibility was not assigned to departmental personnel. Louderman believes that each operations person should "learn as they go," reporting errors as they occur.

Accounts payable and inventory control were the initial areas of the AIS to be implemented; several problems arose in both of these areas. Louderman was disturbed that the semimonthly runs of payroll, which were weekly under the old system, had abundant errors and, consequently, required numerous manual paychecks. Frequently, the control totals of a payroll run would take hours to reconcile with the computer printout. To expedite matters, Louderman authorized the payroll clerk to prepare journal entries for payroll processing.

The new inventory control system failed to improve the carrying stock level of many items, causing several critical raw material stockouts that resulted in expensive rush orders. The primary control procedure under the new system was the availability of ordering and usage information to both inventory control personnel and purchasing personnel by direct access terminals so that both departments could issue purchase orders on a timely basis. The inventory levels were updated daily, so the previous weekly report was discontinued by Louderman.

Because of these problems, system documentation is behind schedule and proper backup procedures have not been implemented in many areas. Louderman has requested budget approval to hire two systems analysts, an accountant, and an administrative assistant to help her implement the new system. Richards is disturbed by her request since her predecessor had only one part-time employee as his assistant.

Required

a. List the steps Mickie Louderman should have taken during the design of the AIS to ensure that end-user needs were satisfied.

b. Identify and describe three areas where Ms. Louderman has violated the basic principles of control during the implementation of the new AIS.

c. By referring to Mickie Louderman's approach to implementing the new AIS,

   (1) identify and describe the weaknesses.

   (2) make recommendations that would help her improve the situation and continue with the development of the remaining areas of the AIS at Pickens Publishers.

(CMA *adapted*)

20-17. Mariposa County's accounting information system has a number of accounting applications written in

COBOL and RPG for use on its mainframe. Because the programs are 25 years old, they are difficult to maintain by the County's systems analysts. Users are also unhappy, since the programs are not very user-friendly and do not have adequate features for information retrieval.

The County had recently hired a new information systems director who was experienced with more up-to-date technology. Thus, the decision was made to convert to a client/server architecture and to replace the accounting applications. Since the information systems professional staff is quite limited, the County manager agreed that the new accounting software should be selected from commercial packages. After discussions with a couple of vendors, the county chose an accounting package marketed by Financial Whizzes.

The implementation was arbitrarily scheduled to be completed in about nine months, since that coincided with the beginning of a new fiscal year. However, due to inexperience with client/servers and related software on the part of the project team, the date was not met. Another problem was the immaturity of the accounting package, which contained a number of bugs. Furthermore, the users were not sufficiently trained in the new package and hence were inefficient in its use. Finally, the results obtained by the new package were often incorrect, as determined when certain key transactions were reprocessed manually.

Required

a. Describe the steps that should have been taken during the selection of software, the preimplementation period, and the implementation period.

b. What other options should have been considered in addition to commercial software?

c. What system conversion approach was apparently employed, and what alternative approach should have been selected instead? Why?

20-18. The Greenspray Company of St. Johns, Newfoundland, is a retailer of fishing supplies. Recently it acquired a minicomputer system. One of the high-priority applications is to have a program that evaluates wholesalers from whom Greenspray might purchase supplies for resale. The criteria that the program is to apply are as follows.

   a. A quality rating from 1 to 3 for each wholesaler; 1 represents the highest rating.

   b. Percentage of times in the past each wholesaler has been late in delivering orders.

   c. Whether each wholesaler's prices have been stable or unstable.

   d. Whether each wholesaler is in an economically undepressed ("well-off") area or a depressed area.

   e. Whether or not each wholesaler has suggested new products from time to time.

The decision rules according to which actions are to be applied by the program are as follows.

   a. If the quality rating is 1, award the wholesaler 20 percent of the business.

   b. If the quality rating is 2, and the wholesaler is not more than 10 percent late, award him 15 percent of the business.

   c. If the quality rating is 2 and the wholesaler is more than 25 percent late, reject him.

   d. If the quality rating is 2 and the wholesaler is between 10 and 25 percent late, award him 10 percent of the business, but only if prices have been stable.

   e. If the quality rating is 3 and the wholesaler is not more than 5 percent late, award him 10 percent of the business, but only if he is in a depressed area and if he has been good at suggesting new products.

Required

a. Compute the total number of possible rules that would be listed within a "full" decision table of the limited entry form.

b. Prepare a "collapsed" decision table that shows the logic needed to write a program for the selection of wholesalers by the Greenspray Company.

(SMAC *adapted*)

20-19. Prepare a Warnier-Orr diagram pertaining to a purchase order. Included should be data elements such as: purchase order date, purchase order number, supplier data (number, name, address), terms, product data (number, description, expected unit price, quantity ordered), desired delivery date, shipping mode, and buyer name.

20-20. The detailed structure chart on page 930 pertains to the process of determining when and how much to reorder in a purchasing procedure.

Required

Prepare a segment of structured English that reflects the process shown in the detailed structure chart. Refer to Figures 20-14 and 20-15 for guidance. Note that the small diamond shown in the detailed structure chart indicates that a computation is made, with the result yielding a value that is either positive or negative. A negative value leads to a computation of the economic order quantity. A positive value causes the process to move to the next inventory item.

20-21. Thrift-Mart, Inc., is a chain of convenience grocery stores in Washington, D.C. Elvira Jones, the

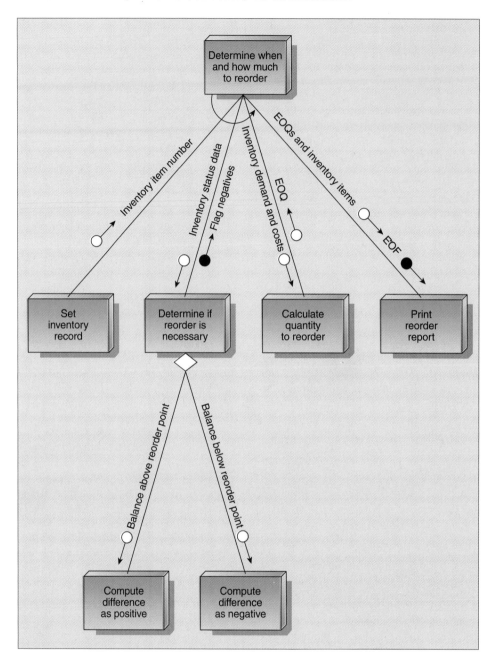

development manager for the chain, has been assigned the project of finding a suitable building and establishing a new store. Her first step is to enumerate the specific activities to be completed and to estimate the time required for each activity.

Activity Designation	Description of Activity	Expected Activity Time (weeks)
1 to 2	Find building	3
2 to 3	Negotiate rental terms	2
3 to 4	Draft lease	5
2 to 5	Prepare store plans	4
5 to 6	Select and order fixtures	1
6 to 4	Accept delivery of fixtures	6
4 to 8	Install fixtures	3
5 to 7	Hire staff	5
7 to 8	Train staff	4
8 to 9	Receive inventory	2
9 to 10	Stock shelves	2

She then asks you to develop suitable planning and control mechanisms, based on the listed data. She tells you that the activity designations refer to the bounding events for each activity. For instance, event 1 refers to the beginning of the search for a building and event 2 refers to the completion of the search.

Required

a. Prepare a network diagram to aid in coordinating the activities.

b. Determine the overall project time and the critical path of the project.

c. Prepare a Gantt (bar) chart to monitor and control the progress of the 11 activities listed, assuming that the project will begin on March 1. Use the diagram prepared in **a** as a guide.

d. Verify that the ending date on the Gantt chart reconciles with the overall project time determined in **b.**

e. Elvira would like to finish the project two weeks earlier than the schedule indicates. She believes that she can persuade the fixture manufacturer to deliver the fixtures in four weeks instead of six weeks. Would this step achieve the objective of reducing the overall project time by two weeks?

f. The project cannot be implemented successfully unless the required resources are available as needed. What information does Elvira need to administer the project in addition to that shown by the diagrams prepared in the previous requirements?

(CMA *adapted*)

20-22. Whitson Company, of Vancouver, B.C., has just ordered a new computer for its financial information system. The present computer is fully utilized and no longer adequate for all the financial applications Whitson would like to implement. The present financial system applications must be modified before they can be run on the new computer. Additionally, new applications that Whitson would like to have developed and implemented have been identified and ranked according to priority.

Sam Rose, manager of data processing, is responsible for implementing the new computer system. Sam listed the specific activities that had to be completed and determined the estimated time to complete each activity. In addition, he prepared a network diagram to aid in the coordination of the activities. The activity list and the network diagram are presented below and on page 932.

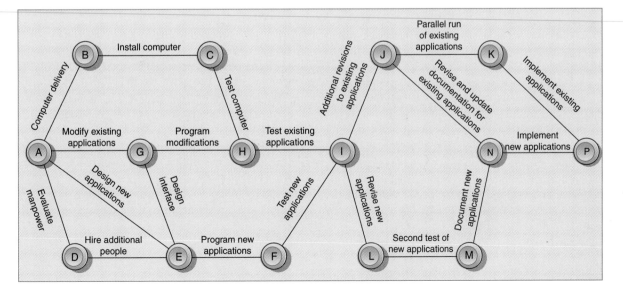

Activity	Description of Activity	Expected Time Required to Complete (in weeks)
AB	Wait for delivery of computer from manufacturer	7
BC	Install computer	2
CH	General test of computer	3
AD	Complete an evaluation of manpower requirements	2
DE	Hire additional programmers and operators	2
AG	Design modifications to existing applications	3
GH	Program modifications to existing applications	4
HI	Test modified applications on new computer	2
IJ	Revise existing applications as needed	3
JN	Revise and update documentation for existing applications as modified	2
JK	Run existing applications in parallel on new and old computers	2
KP	Implement existing applications as modified on the new computer	1
AE	Design new applications	9
GE	Design interface between existing and new applications	3
EF	Program new applications	6
FI	Test new applications on new computer	2
IL	Revise new applications as needed	3
LM	Conduct second test of new applications on new computer	2
MN	Prepare documentation for the new applications	3
NP	Implement new applications on the new computer	2

Required

a. Determine the number of weeks that will be required to implement fully Whitson Company's financial information system (i.e., both existing and new applications) on its new computer, and identify the activities that are critical to completing the project.

b. Whitson Company's top management would like to reduce the time necessary to begin operation of the entire system.

(1) Which activities should Sam Rose attempt to reduce in order to implement the system sooner? Explain your answer.

(2) Discuss how Sam Rose might proceed to reduce the time of these activities.

c. The general accounting manager would like the existing financial information system applications to be modified and operational in 22 weeks. Determine the number of weeks that will be required to modify the existing financial information system applications and make them operational.

(CMA *adapted*)

20-23. *Datacruncher Office Equipment, Inc. (Continuing Case)*

Required

For the systems project that you have selected or been assigned to undertake, perform the following steps:

a. Describe the types of benefits and costs that will be involved in an economic feasibility analysis; identify each benefit as either tangible or intangible in nature.

b. List the factors that will be considered in a weighted-rating analysis that aids in the selection of needed hardware and software.

c. List the activities that should be included in the implementation phase.

d. Describe the system conversion approach that appears to be most suitable for the improved system.

CASE A

DATACRUNCHER OFFICE EQUIPMENT, INC.

(A CONTINUING CASE)

STATEMENT

Datacruncher Office Equipment, Inc., of Dallas, Texas, is a manufacturer of varied machines and devices for the modern office. Among its products are copy machines, terminals, printer units, key-to-tape units, microfilm readers, microcomputer systems, time-stamping machines, and addressing devices. The firm distributes its products nationwide through 150 franchised dealers who also handle the products of competitiors. In addition, the firm sells direct to large and medium-sized business firms and other organizations having substantial data processing requirements. The firm also provides service to its customers. About 600 customers receive statements at the end of a typical month for sales or service.

Datacruncher was started in the late 1970s. The founders were four employees—two salespersons and two engineers—from a long-established office machines manufacturer. They foresaw the growing importance of the office in the modern firm. Their vision has been amply rewarded, since their firm has enjoyed an explosive growth. Of course, vision alone was not sufficient to generate this growth. A sound knowledge of the office equipment market and skillfully designed products were the essential ingredients.

The firm's growth is reflected by several measures. Sales have reached $70 million during this year just ended; this amount represents a 20 percent increase over last year's sales. The number of managers and employees has climbed to almost 1100 as of this year-end. Approximately 500 suppliers provide materials and parts for the 120 products that the firm manufactures. The physical facilities consist of the home office building and production plant, located just off an express parkway in Dallas, plus three regional sites in San Francisco, St.

Louis, and Philadelphia. Each regional site contains a sales office and a warehouse. A finished-goods warehouse is attached to the plant in Dallas.

Besides growth in sales the firm's founders have emphasized the need to increase the firm's share of the office equipment market and the return on total assets. To achieve these objectives, they have stressed aggressive salesmanship, new-product development, prompt deliveries of ordered products, minimized production and inventory costs, and prudent cash management.

ORGANIZATION

Datacruncher is organized as a corporation and has 2500 stockholders. The board of directors consists of the four founders plus four outside directors. The four founders occupy top positions in the firm: Bill Dixon is the president, Bert Sanders is the vice-president of marketing, Judy Hollis is the vice-president of engineering, and Jim Marshall is the vice-president of production. The first two were formerly salespersons; the last two were engineers. Other high-level managers include Harry Myler, vice-president of administration; Charles Dauten, vice-president of finance; Barbara Fulton, controller; and Tim Baker, director of information systems.

FINANCIAL STATUS

The income statements for the last two years (as shown in Exhibit A-1) reflect the sales growth mentioned earlier. They also show, however, that net income has grown less rapidly than net sales. In fact, net income for this year has declined from last year's net income. There are indications that this decline stems from two factors:

EXHIBIT A-1

Datacruncher Office Equipment, Inc.
Statement of Income
For the Years Ended December 31, 1996 and 1997

	1997	1996
	(thousands of dollars)	
Revenues		
Sales, dealers	$35,812	$30,654
Sales, direct	27,343	21,870
Service	7,327	6,236
Total revenues	$70,482	$58,760
Cost of goods sold	49,934	39,375
Gross profit on sales	$20,548	$19,385
Operating expenses		
Selling and distribution expenses	$11,284	$ 9,532
Administrative (including accounting and data		
processing) expenses	2,302	1,875
Research and engineering expenses	1,346	1,473
Interest expense	1,372	1,013
Other expenses, including depreciation	741	733
Total operating expenses	$17,045	$14,626
Net income before income taxes	$ 3,503	$ 4,759
Provision for income taxes	1,191	1,618
Net income	$ 2,312	$ 3,141
Assets		
Current assets		
Cash	$ 516	$ 2,178
Accounts receivable, net	12,022	9,518
Inventories		
Raw materials and parts	5,674	4,852
Work-in-process	6,923	5,107
Finished goods	9,547	7,321
Prepaid expenses	547	695
Total current assets	$35,229	$29,671
Fixed assets	$12,184	$11,380
Less: Accumulated depreciation	7,132	5,939
Net fixed assets	$ 5,052	$ 5,441
Other assets	$10,636	$ 6,991
Total assets	$50,917	$42,103
Equities		
Current liabilities		
Notes payable	$ 5,731	$ 1,880
Current maturities of long-term debt	682	595
Accounts payable	4,619	3,751
Accrued expenses and taxes	6,978	4,826
Total current liabilities	$18,010	$11,052
Long-term debt	$ 7,100	$ 6,400
Stockholders' equity		
Common stock, no par value		
Authorized 1,000,000 shares;		
outstanding 650,000 shares	$ 9,858	$ 9,858
Capital surplus	2,610	2,610
Retained earnings	13,339	12,183
Total stockholders' equity	$25,807	$24,651
Total equities	$50,917	$42,103

(1) rising costs in production, inventory, and other areas; and (2) necessary reductions in the prices of certain products to combat the new products of competitors.

The balance sheets for the last two years (also shown in Exhibit A-1) indicate that the firm's financial position is basically sound. However, there are certain adverse signs, such as a shrinking cash balance.

PROCEDURES

Four broad activities at the operational level can be identified as the revenue cycle, the production cycle, the expenditure cycle, and inventory management. Other activities include engineering design, market research, personnel and payroll, cash management, and general ledger accounting. Processing of transactions pertaining to the first four preceding activities, plus payroll and general ledger accounting, is aided by two computers. One of these computers is located within the accounting function, the other within the production function. Magnetic disks are employed for on-line storage of files. The following sections describe briefly the current processing, including key documents, outputs, and files. (In addition, Exhibit A-2 contains measures of activity relating to the following procedures.)

EXHIBIT A-2   Measures of Activity

DOCUMENT VOLUMES PER MONTH

Sales orders	2000
(with an average of 6 items per document)	
Cash receipts	1950
Purchase requisitions	1000
Purchase orders	1000
(with an average of 8 lines per document)	
Back orders	260
Production orders	105
Shipping reports	1980
Bills of lading	1980
Materials requisitions	475
Move tickets	355
Stock transfer notices	240
Receiving reports	960
(with an average of 7 lines per document)	
Disbursement vouchers	1010
Check vouchers (other than payroll)	830

NUMBERS OF ACTIVE RECORDS IN KEY FILES

Accounts receivable	1850
Accounts payable	517
Finished-goods inventory	120
Work-in-process inventory	170
Raw-materials and parts inventory	11,960
Bills of materials	120
Employee earnings	1098
General ledger	92

OTHER MEASURES OF ACTIVITY

Number of new customers per month	20
Number of inquiries from customers per day	70
Number of adjustments (e. g., sales returns, purchases, returns, write-offs) per month	160
Number of days (on the average) between the time that a purchase order is mailed and materials or parts are received	15
Number of days (on the average) required to process a sales order	12
Percentage of products rejected during production inspections during current year	5
Number of dealers accounting for 75% of sales by all dealers	40

Revenue Cycle Salespersons periodically visit the dealers and prospective business firms and other organizations in their sales regions. As they obtain orders, they mail or phone in the orders to their regional sales offices. Each sales office then records the orders on a register and prepares formal sales orders in quadruplicate. The original of each order is mailed to the customer, whereas the last copy is filed by customer name. At the end of each day the batch of orders (consisting of the middle two copies of all orders prepared that day) is mailed to the home office.

When received in the sales order department, the orders are reviewed for completeness and accuracy by sales order clerks and numbers are assigned. The orders are then forwarded to the credit department for a credit check. When credit is approved for the amounts of the orders, one copy of each order is sent to the inventory control department and the other copy to the billing department.

By reference to computer printouts of product status, inventory control clerks determine whether or not sufficient inventory is available to fill each order. If sufficient inventory is available at the warehouse in the region where the customer resides, one copy of the order is mailed there. If sufficient inventory is not available in the regional warehouse but is available in the main finished-goods warehouse in Dallas, the copy of the order is routed there instead. In either case the goods are picked and readied for shipment, based on the order. A shipping report and bill of lading are prepared and the order is shipped. A copy of the shipping report is enclosed with the shipment as a packing slip, and another copy is returned to the billing department. If sufficient inventory is not available to fill the order in its entirety, the inventory control clerk prepares a back order, which he or she routes to the production planning and control department.

On the receipt of a shipping report, a billing clerk pulls the department's copy of the sales order from a file, verifies that the product numbers and quantities match, and notes the shipping date and prices on the order copy. Next he or she sends the order copy (together with the other orders processed that day) to the data preparation section in the accounting data processing department. The orders then are keyed onto magnetic tape, edited, sorted, and processed against the accounts receivable and finished-goods inventory (product) master files. Sales invoices are generated as outputs from this processing, together with an open sales invoice file on magnetic disk.* Two copies of each sales invoice

are mailed to a customer, two other copies are sent to the sales order department and the appropriate regional sales office, and a fifth copy is filed alphabetically.

All cash receipts from customers are received in the mail room at the home office. There they are opened and listed on a special form. Then the checks are routed to the cashier, together with a copy of the list. The cashier prepares a bank deposit slip in duplicate, endorses the checks, and delivers the deposit to the bank the next morning. A copy of the deposit slip is returned to a file in her office. Another copy of the listed receipts is sent to the credit department, where a clerk enters the customer numbers that correspond to the listed names and addresses. The clerk forwards the list to the data preparation section, which keys the receipts data onto magnetic tape. The transaction data are then sorted and processed against the accounts receivable master file once each day. At the end of the month the accounts receivable master file is processed to produce an accounts receivable aging schedule, which is sent to the credit manager, and statements, which are mailed to customers.

Production Cycle Products are manufactured either for inventory or to fill back orders. The overall production level generally is based on a sales forecast made by the marketing function. However, back orders occur because of out-of-stock conditions, and they must be fitted into the schedule. In fact, back orders are given priority in order to pacify unhappy customers.

Production operations are triggered when the production planning and control department receives production authorizations or back orders. The production authorizations are prepared by comparing forecasted sales levels with current levels of finished-goods inventory on hand and are issued jointly by the production superintendent and the inventory control manager.* Back orders are prepared, as described earlier, on the basis of orders that cannot be filled. The production planning and control department then obtains the bills of materials from the engineering function and explores the production requirements to determine materials and parts requirements. With the materials and parts requirements in hand, a production planning clerk checks a computer printout of materials and parts inventory on hand. If the materials and parts on hand are adequate for a particular product, the clerk schedules a production run (based on available labor and machines). As each scheduled date nears, the clerk sends the affected production authorizations and back orders to the data preparation section of the production data processing department. There the production requirements data are keyed onto magnetic tape, sorted by product number,

---

*Sales due to services rendered are also reflected in sales invoices. The service details, including amounts, appear on service reports forwarded to billing by the service department. The amounts charged to customers must of course be processed against the accounts receivable master file.

---

*Needed levels of product are related to the rates at which products are being sold, which in turn are tied to the sales forecast.

and processed to produce numbered production orders, materials requisitions, and move tickets. Files used in this processing run (all on magnetic disk) are the bill-of-materials file, the operations list file, the open production order file, and the work-in-process inventory master file.

Copies of the materials requisitions are sent to the materials storeroom, which then delivers materials and parts to the designated production departments. Copies of the production orders and the move tickets are sent to the first production department involved in the manufacturing process (usually the fabricating department). Copies of production orders are also sent to the cost accounting department, and copies of materials requisitions are kept in the data processing department for inventory processing. As work is completed on an order in a department, a move ticket is returned to the production planning and control department. At the end of each day, all returned move tickets are batched and forwarded to the data preparation section. There the move ticket data are keyed onto a magnetic tape, sorted by production order number, and processed to produce a daily production status report. The open production order file is updated during the processing.

In separate daily processing steps, the materials requisitions are batched, keyed onto a magnetic tape, sorted by material-part number, and processed to update the raw-materials inventory master file. Then the materials requisitions are re-sorted by production order number and processed (together with labor job-time tickets forwarded from work centers and sorted in a like manner on a separate magnetic tape) to update the work-in-process inventory master file.

When a production order has progressed through the fabrication and assembly departments, the units of completed product are inspected. Those units that pass inspection are released to the finished-goods warehouse, and copies of the order release are sent to the production planning and control department and the cost accounting department. From the central warehouse the finished products are shipped, via stock transfer notices, to the three remote warehouses as needed to replenish stocks. The production planning and control department records the completion and then sends the releases to the data preparation section. There they are keyed onto a magnetic tape, sorted by product number, and processed against the finished-goods and work-in-process inventory master files, as well as the open production orders file. A completed production orders report is also printed; it includes the costs charged to each order.

When the materials and parts needed to manufacture particular products are not available, the production planning and control clerk prepares purchase requisitions. These requisitions are sent to the purchasing department.

Expenditure Cycle   A wide variety of expenditures, ranging from utilities to insurance, are necessary. Expenditures for raw materials and parts, as well as subassemblies, are particularly significant, since the products manufactured by the firm require a high level of precision. Thus the procedure pertaining to the purchases of such items and the disbursements for them is another of the critical transaction cycles within Datacruncher.

Purchases are initiated by either production planning and control clerks or inventory control clerks. The former clerks issue purchase requisitions when they note that materials and parts are not adequate for upcoming production runs, whereas the latter clerks issue similar documents when their experience suggests that the on-hand quantities of particular items have declined to reorderable levels. On the basis of these purchase requisitions, buyers in the purchasing department select suppliers who are known to be reliable and enter their codes on the requisitions, together with acceptable prices for the items to be ordered. The requisitions are then forwarded to the data preparation section in the production data processing department. There they are keyed onto a magnetic tape, sorted by supplier number, and processed to produce purchase orders. During subsequent runs, the raw-materials inventory master file and the open purchase order file are updated. The purchase orders are then signed by the purchasing manager and mailed to the suppliers. Copies of the purchase orders are forwarded to the receiving department and the accounts payable department, and a fourth copy is filed by supplier name in the purchasing department.

When ordered materials and parts arrive at the receiving dock, receiving clerks pull the purchase order copies from their file. Then they count or weigh the items and prepare receiving reports. The items are next transferred to the materials storeroom and the initialed copies of the receiving reports are sent on to the accounts payable department and filed. Another copy of each receiving report is sent to the data preparation section of the data processing department, and a third copy is filed numerically in the receiving department. In the data preparation section, the receiving reports are keyed onto a magnetic tape, sorted by material-part number, processed to update the raw-materials inventory master file, resorted by purchase order number, and processed to update the open purchase order file.

When suppliers' invoices arrive in the accounts payable department, clerks pull the receiving reports and purchase orders from the file and compare the documents. After completing their vouching of the invoices, they prepare disbursement vouchers, record them in a voucher register, and file all the documents together by payment due date.

Each day other clerks pull the vouchers due for payment that day and send them to the data preparation section of the accounting data processing department.

There the payment data are keyed onto magnetic tape, sorted by supplier account number, and processed to produce check vouchers and a check register. The accounts payable master file is also updated during this run; in effect, each affected supplier's account is credited to reflect the obligation and debited to reflect the payment.

Inventory Management   Three inventory files are maintained by the firm. The raw-materials inventory master file is updated to reflect orders for materials and parts, as well as receipts from suppliers and issues into production. The finished-goods inventory master file is updated to reflect the newly manufactured products and the sales of products to customers. The work-in-process inventory master file is updated to reflect the start in production of each production order, the issues of materials into production, the charges of labor (from job-time records) into production, the application of overhead to production, and the completion of production.

An actual cost accounting system is employed. Direct materials and direct labor costs are posted to the work-in-process inventory records from the raw materials requisitions and the job-time records. Overhead costs are compiled from the documents pertaining to indirect labor, utilities, and other production-related costs and allocated to the jobs at the end of each month. Direct labor hours is the activity base for allocating these actual overhead costs.

PROBLEMS

A number of specific problems have become apparent. Some of these problems relate to the procedures described earlier, whereas other problems arise from weaknesses in the organizational structure and in financial planning. Many of these problems stem from the fact that the founders have focused on selling and engineering. They have not given as much attention to the areas of accounting, finance, production, and inventory management. Most of the problems also arise from the rapid growth in sales.

Some of the more significant problems, in addition to those noted earlier, should be mentioned. Interest costs are relatively high, as are costs in production and distribution. Back orders are fairly numerous, even though inventory levels have been rising. Promised delivery dates on customers' orders are often missed, even though lead times of two weeks or more often are allowed. Processing backlogs are sustained in several of the accounting departments. These backlogs lead to a variety of ill effects; for instance, purchase discounts are frequently lost and numerous errors are introduced into the transaction data. The percentage of products that do not pass inspection is rather high, perhaps at least in part because of fairly obsolete production equipment and a high labor turnover. Production schedules are difficult to keep up to date, and production jobs often fall behind their schedules. In fact, production clerks keep extremely busy "pushing" jobs, monitoring their progress, and answering phone calls from concerned customers and salespersons. Also, production rates tend to fluctuate, so that production employees are idle at times and required to work overtime at other times. This problem stems in part from rush back orders; however, it also arises from sales forecasts that prove to be quite inaccurate and from planning procedures that are relatively weak. For instance, the budget process is fairly rudimentary. Budgets are not tied to carefully established cost standards, are not developed in detailed formats, and are not revised to reflect changed conditions. Finally, the reports provided to managers are rather inadequate; most are of the status variety, such as the weekly materials-and-parts status report, the daily product-status report, and the monthly report of budgeted costs versus actual costs.

INITIATION OF SYSTEMS DEVELOPMENT

These problems, and their effects on the firm's financial status, have been of concern to the founders for some time. Their view is that at least some of the problems are aggravated by an inadequate accounting information system. Recently, in fact, they created the position called director of information systems and hired Tim Baker, because they strongly felt that corrective measures were necessary. Perhaps, they thought, he could harmonize and update an accounting information system that is rather uncoordinated and obsolete at present.

After hearing the news concerning the decline in net income for this year, the founders decide to take further action. They appoint a steering committee and announce a long-range systems development program. They ask the committee to develop a strategic systems plan, in which a number of systems projects are identified. Within a couple of months the committee develops the requested plan.

Note: Requirements for this continuing case are found at the ends of the problem sets for Chapters 11, 12, 14, 15, 16, 17, 18, 19, and 20.

CASE
B

DRESS ACE! INC.*

STATEMENT

Dress Ace! Inc. was a small clothing manufacturer, operating with a subcontracted workforce and selling the finished goods to a variety of wholesalers and boutiques. It consisted of five individuals, outlined in the figure below.

The owner was also responsible for the purchase of raw materials and the selling operation.

The owner had become aware that, over the past few months, despite increasing sales and a constant dollar mark-up on finished goods, the firm seemed to have very little cash in the bank. He asked you to examine the efficiency of the accounting controls operating within Dress Ace! Inc.

Upon questioning the owner, you discovered that the accounting system operated as follows:

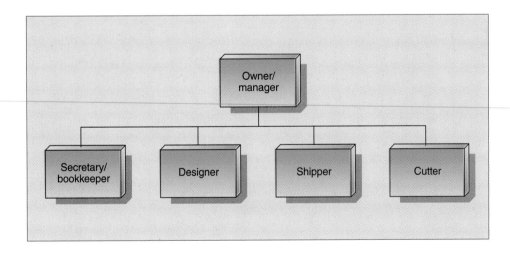

*This case was prepared by Elizabeth Bedirian (student), Concordia University, Montréal, Québec, and Roger Collins, University College of the Cariboo, Kamloops, British Columbia, Canada, as the basis for class discussion rather than to illustrate either effective or ineffective handling of a managerial situation. Distributed by the Accounting Education Resource Centre, The University of Lethbridge, © 1994. All rights reserved to the author and to the Accounting Education Resource Centre. Permission to use the case in classes of instruction, without restriction, is provided to subscribers of the journal. Reprinted from the *Journal of Accounting Case Research* with the permission of Captus Press Inc., North York, Ontario, Canada, and the Accounting Education Resource Centre of the University of Lethbridge, Alberta, Canada.

THE ACCOUNTS RECEIVABLE DEPARTMENT

Once the designer developed several sample styles, which have been approved by the owner, the salesperson (a commission agent: i.e., self-employed) went off with the new line of clothing and attempted to obtain purchase orders from various customers; thus a potential for accounts receivable was set up. Purchase orders, an internal order containing the supplier name, location, and description of goods and quantities requested, were received and filled out by the shipper. The shipper then brought the order to the bookkeeper, who used it to prepare an invoice.

The invoice, which was prenumbered, consisted of three detachable copies: one went to the customer, one was kept for accounting records, and one was included in the customer's individual file. Once the invoice was made out, one copy was sent to the customer, and the other two were filed away. Invoices were accumulated and at the end of the week, entered into the sales journal, and finally entered into the accounts receivable auxiliary ledger by the bookkeeper.

Payments to the accounts were often received by mail and sometimes delivered in person. The owner opened the mail and gave the checks, which were to be deposited in the firm account to the bookkeeper who prepared the deposit slip. Once the checks were deposited, the bookkeeper transferred the amounts from the deposit slip into the auxiliary ledger of accounts receivable to reduce the customer's account (Figure 1). Occasionally, the owner would check the accounts receivable auxiliary and

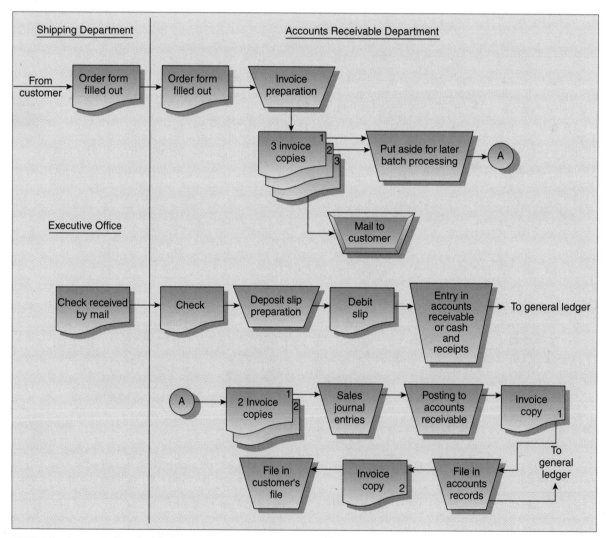

FIGURE 1　Accounts Receivable Department—Operating Presently.

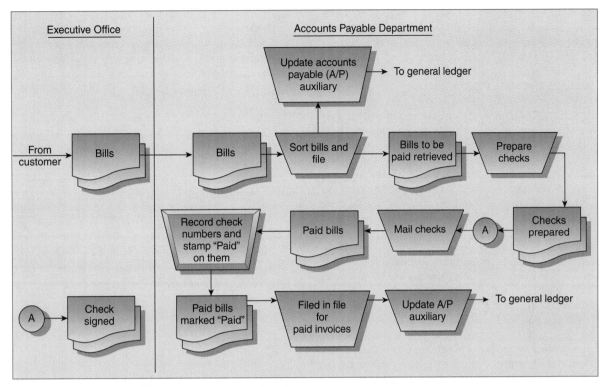

FIGURE 2   Accounts Payable Department—Operating Presently.

the sales journal to discover how monthly sales of the current year compared to previous years.

THE ACCOUNTS PAYABLE DEPARTMENT

Invoices from suppliers were received daily by mail. Once again, the owner took the responsibility of opening the mail and giving the bills to the bookkeeper so she could sort them out in alphabetical order in separate files.

About once a month, the bookkeeper ran through the billing and picked out those that were due to be paid. She first made sure the shipping memos were attached to the bills. The bookkeeper prepared the checks and the owner signed them. They were then dispatched.

To keep control of payments, the bookkeeper took the invoices that had been paid and recorded the amount, the date of payment, the check number with which the payment was made, and finally stamped "PAID" on them. These invoices were then transferred to a permanent file.

Payments to contractors were administered by the bookkeeper although the owner verified the contractors' check amounts and signed them. The bookkeeper sometimes held on to these checks before handing them out to the contractors (who usually picked up their checks the same day or sometimes a day later).

Finally, the salesperson was paid on commission. The bookkeeper prepared the appropriate amount and the owner verified it. Once again, the bookkeeper held on to the check until the salesperson picked it up. All other expenses were paid out in a similar fashion (Figure 2).

INVENTORY DEPARTMENT

The owner was responsible for the ordering of goods worth more than $50. When the goods arrived at the factory, the shipper was responsible for verifying the number of items entering the factory. He signed a shipping memo showing the amount of goods received. The driver kept one copy and the shipper kept another. The shipper's copy went back to the owner's office, where he verified the number received against the number ordered, and the order form and shipping memo were filed together.

Similarly, finished goods coming in from the contractors were counted and a shipping memo signed indicating the number of garments of each type received. One copy went into the office file of accounts to be paid, and one was kept with the contractor. The contractor was not always present when the goods were being counted. Sometimes the goods arrived in packages of dozens and only the number of packages was counted, not the individual items. It was only when the goods were prepared to be shipped to their destinations that they were transferred from the old packs to new ones; each garment was then individually counted. Any missing garment was reported on the memo that would then be deducted from the contractors' pay.

Other goods entering the factory were returns from customers. These were usually received through a mailing service and anyone at Dress Ace! signed for them, although this usually meant the shipper. The shipper counted the garments received and verified the number against the request for a credit memo. The request for a credit memo form went to the bookkeeper, who then prepared a credit memo according to the number of items the shipper claimed to have received.

Goods leaving the factory included any shipments of orders made for boutiques. The shipper counted the number of items to be shipped according to an order received. The number of items was reported on the order forms that went to the bookkeeper who then billed the boutiques, and here the accounts receivable cycle began.

Finally, goods in stock were basically of three types: finished goods, raw materials, and work-in-process. There were only three people working in the storage area: the cutter, the shipper, and the designer. No supervisor, aside from the owner, who was not always available, was present.

The firm's cost of sales was calculated by conducting a physical count of the inventory at the year-end and deducting the value as determined from the sum of the inventory at the start of the year and the purchases made in the course of it.

Required

a. Prepare a systems plan for investigating the current system and developing a new system, identifying the various projects that should be undertaken as modules. Include an outline of the phases in the systems development life cycle.

b. Identify the problems that exist in the current systems.

c. For each of the modules identified in **a** above,

(1) Draw a data-flow diagram of the processes.

(2) Draw a computer system flowchart of an improved system.

(3) Prepare an entity-relationship diagram. Then draw the tables needed if a relational data base is chosen.

(4) Suggest internal controls that are needed.

(5) Prepare formats of reports that will provide information to appropriate managers.

APPENDIX
A

···

COMPUTER HARDWARE, SOFTWARE, AND DATA COMMUNICATIONS TECHNOLOGIES

···

In this Appendix we review the following three topics:

- Computer hardware, the physical equipment of computer systems.
- Computer software, the instructions that guide the processing jobs and direct the actions of computer hardware.
- Data communications, the means of electronically transferring information from one computer to another.

The main purpose of this survey is to describe technical material related to the above three topics in order to recall the options available to systems designers and users. If you have already taken a course in computer technology, a survey of computer hardware, software, and data communications would represent a review of familiar material. It is strongly suggested that you refer to one of the many available textbooks on computer technology for photographs and working details.

COMPUTER HARDWARE

Figure A-1 lists the variety of hardware that may be found in present-day computer systems. As the figure indicates, the term "computer hardware" encompasses an extremely wide range of processors, storage devices and media, input-output devices, and data communication devices.

PROCESSORS

Basic Units The heart of a computer is its processor, which consists of a control unit, an arithmetic-logic unit, and a primary storage unit. These basic components are collectively known as the *central processing unit* (CPU). Figure A-2 shows these units and the flows of data, information, and control among them and connecting input and output units.

The *control unit* directs and coordinates the actions of all the other components. It instructs the input unit concerning when and what data to enter, the primary storage unit where to store the data, the arithmetic-logic unit what operations to perform and where to put the results, and the output unit what information to provide on which medium.

The *arithmetic-logic unit* performs all operations specified by the control unit. As the name implies, these operations include calculations (e.g., additions, subtractions, multiplications, divisions) and logical operations (e.g., comparisons of numbers).

The *primary storage unit*, also called main memory, serves as a repository. Data received from input devices, from instructions in computer software, and from arithmetic-logic operations are all brought together (at least temporarily) in this unit. Each item of data is stored at a specific location having a unique address. This unit also provides the required area in which instructions from computer software are executed. The larger the capacity of the primary storage unit, the more easily it can perform these assigned functions.

Most present-day primary storage units contain two basic types of memory: random access memory and read-only memory. *Random access memory* (RAM) allows data and instructions to be stored and retrieved. Thus it enables the above-mentioned functions to be performed. The term "random access" refers to the ability of the processor to access any address in the memory in

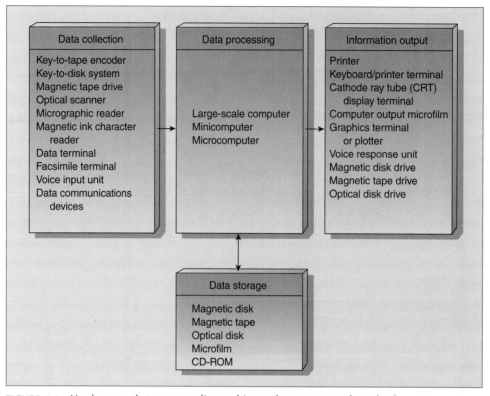

FIGURE A-I   Hardware and storage media used in modern computer-based information systems.

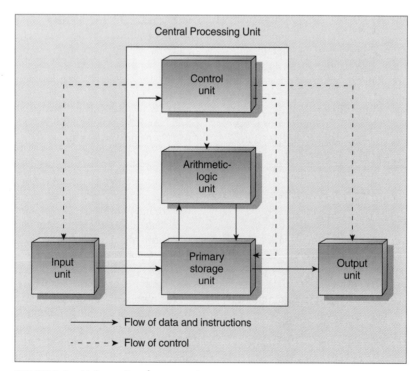

FIGURE A-2   Major units of a computer.

a direct manner. One of two types of RAM chips can be purchased for a computer's memory: static RAM chips, or SRAM, and dynamic RAM chips, or DRAM. SRAM chips are preferable to DRAM chips because of their faster processing speeds. However, SRAM chips are used mainly in caches (defined below) due to their higher costs. Memory size can be increased by installing a *single in-line memory module* (SIMM) containing more chips onto the motherboard.

Read-only memory (ROM) only allows data and/or instructions to be retrieved (i.e., read from). It does not allow new data and/or instructions to be stored; thus it cannot be altered by users or programmers. Its contents usually consist of microprograms, also called microcodes or firmware, that are permanently fixed ("burned" or "hardwired") on a silicon chip by the computer manufacturer. These microprograms can be executed more quickly than instructions that are executed in RAM. They also improve security and reliability, which result from their unchangeable nature. The *basic input-output system* (BIOS) program is contained in ROM. When the computer is turned on, the BIOS loads the operating system into memory and completes the *power-on self-test* (POST), a series of built-in diagnostics. *Programmable read-only memory* (PROM) is similar to ROM, except that a programmer or user enters the data or instructions. Afterward, the entered material cannot be altered. An *erasable programmable read-only memory* (EPROM) chip can be altered and realtered.

Cache memory is a type of high-speed memory that can greatly shorten the time in accessing data. It is used in processors for all sizes of computers. Because cache memory is quite expensive, it is limited to storing frequently referenced data and instructions.

Various technologies have been tapped in the construction of primary storage during the computer era. Magnetic cores, tiny ferrite rings that can be magnetized in two opposite directions, were principally used in earlier decades. Semiconductors, on-off circuits mounted in silicon chips, are currently in wide use. They are smaller and have faster access times than magnetic cores, and their costs are competitive. New technologies will in time replace the current one. For instance, gallium arsenide chips or diamond chips are likely to replace silicon chips. Magnetic bubbles or charged-couples may replace semiconductor circuits. Optics (light directed) may replace magnetics.

Additional storage is provided by *secondary storage devices*. Examples of secondary storage devices are magnetic tape and magnetic disk. While secondary storage devices increase the overall capacity of a computer system, the data and programs that they store must be transferred into the primary storage unit for processing. Thus, the processing is slowed somewhat when they are used.

Processor Capabilities Computer processors may be differentiated by such measures as processing speed and memory capacity. Both measures are prominently displayed in advertisements appearing in computer journals; buyers are keenly interested in comparing processors.

Processing speed may be measured by the cycle time, that is, the time required to execute a typical instruction. Cycle time may range from a fraction of a *millisecond* (one-thousandth of a second) for a relatively slow processor, to a *nanosecond* (one-billionth of a second) or more for a fast processor. A massively parallel computer's cycle time is measured in *picoseconds* (one-trillionth of a second). Processing speed may also be measured by million cycles per second (megahertz).

In order to increase processing speeds, computer manufacturers focus on several factors involved in the processing of a single instruction. Three time-related factors are *access time* (the time required to retrieve data from primary storage for processing), *execution time* (the time required to perform a single computation), and *transfer rate* (the speed with which data can be moved from one place to another within primary storage, or from a secondary storage device to primary storage). Another factor is *word size*, the width of the data block that can be moved and manipulated within the processor. Word size is limited by the capacities of the registers used in the calculations and the buses (conduits) that carry the data between components. Word sizes for current processors range from 16 bits to 128 bits.

Because cycle times and megahertz clock speeds are difficult measures to reduce to anything meaningful, a more easily understood measure of processing speed is needed. One such measure is *million instructions per second* (MIPS), which reduces cycle times, megahertz clock speed, execution time, transfer rate, word size, and bus speed to a common denominator. This measure can easily be computed by using a simple MIPS program. Thus a computer operating at 1 MIPS means that, on average, one million integer (whole number) computations per second can be performed. Mainframe computers using the Alpha chip have a MIPS rating of 400. MIPS ratings for the common microcomputer chips are examined in Appendix B. To overcome the MIPS limitation of only testing integer operations, the *million floating point operations per second (megaflops)* measures a computer's power to perform operations on both integers and nonintegers. Another very widely used measure of microcomputer performance is the *Norton Benchmark* computing index. An index is computed in relation to the Intel 8088-based chip used in the IBM PC-XT, which is assigned a base weight or index of 1.0. The computer being tested is compared with the overall speed of several widely employed computers. For example, the computing index for an Intel 386DX-33 (the computer being tested) is 35.9; this is compared with two benchmarks: the Intel 486DX-66, which has a computing index of 141.7, and an Intel 486DX-50, which has an index of 59.5. All three computed indexes are in relation to the IBM PC-XT's base weight of 1. Thus, the Intel 486DX-66 is about 4 times faster (141.7/35.9) than the Intel 386DX-33 and the Intel 486DX-50 is about 1.7 times faster (59.5/35.9) than the Intel 386DX-33 microcomputer.*

Primary storage (memory) capacity is the quantity of data and programs that can be stored in the primary storage unit. Since programs can be processed more quickly when both programs and data can fit into primary storage, a greater capacity can improve performance. The basic unit of data is the binary digit, or bit. A *bit* can have a value (state) of either zero or one. Bits in turn are combined in groups of eight to form *bytes*, which are used to represent characters. The primary storage capacity for processors is typically measured and expressed in *kilobytes* (thousands of bytes) or *megabytes* (millions of bytes). Data are stored, using bits, according to a particular format. Three available formats are binary coded decimal (BCD), extended binary coded decimal interchange code (EBCDIC), and American Standard Code for Information Interchange (ASCII). ASCII is the form in which data are transmitted over communications lines.

Computer processors may possess a variety of features that enable them to perform more efficiently. Among these enhancing features are overlapping, multiprogramming, boundary protection, virtual storage, multitasking, and time sharing. They function in cooperation with the software that guides the processors (i.e., the operating systems). Most are especially relevant when more than one user shares the processor.

Overlapping enables a computer system to perform processing, input, and output operations simultaneously. This feature improves the computer system's throughput, that is, the quantity of work processed in a given period of time. Without overlapping, a processor remains idle during much of the time, since it is waiting for data to be entered or for information to be outputted. Overlapping involves the use of devices known as channels, controllers, and buffers, which serve as interfaces between a processor and connected input-output devices.

Multiprogramming enables the processor to execute two or more programs (sets of instructions) concurrently. Each program is allowed to execute instructions for a short time, and then the next program in order takes its turn. This rotation continues for an individual program until it has executed all its instructions. When integrated with the overlapping feature, multiprogram-

ming further improves throughput. It also shortens the average turnaround time (the time between the start and finish of execution) for shorter jobs or applications. (Without multiprogramming, a computer system executes each program in the order received; thus long programs tend to delay the completion of short programs.)

Boundary protection prevents the programs and data of several applications from interfering with each other. It consists of dividing or partitioning the primary storage space. By means of a technique known as interleaved storage access, each partitioned area can be controlled separately. Thus the data of one application may be accessed or retrieved from one partitioned area while the data related to a second application are being entered into a separate area.

Virtual storage involves a technique of program swapping that allows users to view primary storage as being virtually unlimited. By means of this feature, programs are divided into segments called *pages*. Pages are stored in secondary storage (such as magnetic disks) and moved into primary storage only when needed for execution. Virtual storage is particularly useful when very lengthy programs are to be processed and when multiprogramming is employed. It allows the processor to be used more efficiently. Figure A-3 illustrates the virtual storage technique.

Multitasking, a variation of multiprogramming, allows a single processor to process several applications or jobs concurrently.

Time-sharing is the capability of a single processor to handle the applications or jobs of multiple users, who are connected to the processor via terminals. In an effective time-sharing system, each user is served so promptly that the user may feel that he or she has the exclusive attention of the system. A time-sharing system is often called a multiuser system. As in the case of virtual storage, time-sharing is usually accompanied by the multiprogramming feature.

---

*For other performance measures, see Martin A. W. Nemzow, *Computer Performance Optimization* (New York: McGraw-Hill, 1994).

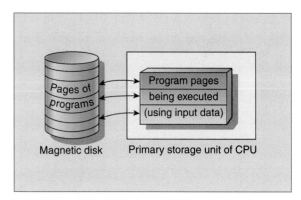

FIGURE A-3   Virtual storage technique.

SECONDARY DATA STORAGE DEVICES AND MEDIA

Because of the limited capacity of primary storage, secondary storage is typically needed in a computer system. Thus devices are usually attached on-line to the processor to provide additional storage capacity. These devices, often known as drives, control storage media. The media in turn contain data for use in processing and for preparing reports and answering inquiries. When needed for processing or for outputs, the data are transferred from their secondary storage locations to the primary storage unit.

Among the secondary storage media employed by current computer systems are magnetic tapes, magnetic disks, optical disks, magnetic drums, magnetic cards, and data cells. Only the first two media listed are in wide use today, although the third holds great promise for the future.

Magnetic Tapes *Magnetic tapes* are stored on reels or in cartridges. They are viewed as off-line storage media, since individual reels or cartridges are kept in vaults or other repositories until needed for processing. Then they are mounted on the tape drives that are connected on-line to the computer. Magnetic tapes store data as magnetized bits, which are arrayed along channels to tracks to form bytes, that is, coded characters. Nine-track tapes are in most common use, although seven-track tapes are also available. One of the tracks provides bit positions for check or *parity bits*, bits that enable the computer system to check the accuracy of the characters stored and transferred.

Figure A-4 depicts how a file of data may be arranged on a magnetic tape. Groups of characters form data elements, such as customer numbers or names. Data elements in turn are collected together to form *records*, and records are grouped into *blocks*. For instance, a record may contain the data concerning a customer, whereas a block contains the data for several (e.g., four as in Figure A-4) customers. An *interblock gap* (IBG) at each end of a block separates the block from its neighbors. Thus a block is a physical unit that a processing program handles when moving data into and out of primary storage. Records are blocked to store data more efficiently. Also, the blocked records of a file can be processed more quickly than unblocked records. (If blocking is so advantageous, you might ask: Why not simply treat an entire field as a single block? This treatment is not possible, since the size of a block is limited by the buffer space in primary storage.) To continue our description of a data file on magnetic tape, a special record, called a *header label*, is placed at the beginning of a file when the file is created. The header label identifies the field and its date of creation, so that a computer operator can verify that the proper tape is being used. At the end of the file is placed a *trailer label*, which contains a count of the number of records and other totals of data within the records. Finally, an end-of-file mark is inserted after the trailer label, since a file may not occupy an entire reel of tape.

Magnetic tapes can hold huge quantities of data. For instance, a typical reel of tape, measuring one-half inch by 2400 feet, may contain several thousand characters of data per inch of length, and perhaps as many as a billion characters of data in total. Tape cartridges may be clustered in mass storage systems to contain over a trillion characters in total. In addition to their huge storage capacities, magnetic tapes have other advantages:

1. Fast transfer rates, which allow data to be moved within computer systems at speeds of several hundred thousand characters per second to over one million characters per second.

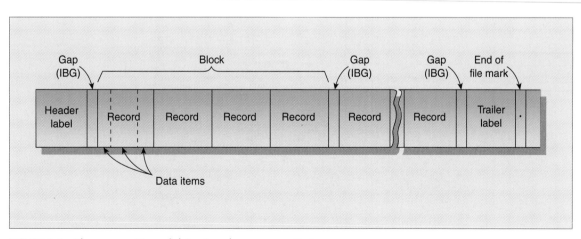

FIGURE A-4 The composition of data stored on a magnetic tape.

2. Relatively low cost, as compared to magnetic disks.

3. Reliability, with very few errors or losses of data occurring during transfers.

4. Reusability, since data can be erased or written over many times. (However, magnetic tape follows the principle of *nondestructive read-out*, in which stored data can be "read" from the tape into the primary storage unit any number of times without the reading action causing the data on the tape to be erased.)

5. Portability, since magnetic tape reels or cartridges can easily be moved or mailed to other locations.

These advantages cause magnetic tapes to be frequently used in applications involving large volumes of transactions and large numbers of records in master files. For instance, magnetic tape may be suitable for the processing of payroll transactions in many firms. It is also often used to store duplicate files that provide duplicates or "backups" to active files stored on other media. These backup files may be transported, for reasons of security, to other locations.

Two forms of magnetic tape used with microcomputer systems are tape cassettes and tape cartridges. These tape forms not only can hold large quantities of data but also can be loaded very quickly. For example, a standard tape cartridge holds 250 or more megabytes of data and can be loaded relatively quickly.

Magnetic Disks *Magnetic disks* represent the principal current alternative to magnetic tapes. They have supplanted magnetic tapes in most applications. Not only do they offer most of the advantages of magnetic tapes, but magnetic disks provide the highly important additional feature of direct access. That is, any record of data stored on a magnetic disk can be accessed by the computer system and immediately transferred to the primary storage unit. (Hence, a magnetic disk is called a *direct-access storage device.*) This direct-access feature is made possible by means of permanent *addresses* assigned to all locations on a magnetic disk where data may be stored. By contrast, data stored on a magnetic tape, which does not have permanent addresses, can feasibly be accessed only by scanning for the data from the beginning point of the tape.

Most magnetic disks are assembled into stacks of metal platters, called disk packs. Locations on a disk pack are physically accessed by means of an access mechanism containing read-write heads, which move back and forth while the disk pack rotates at a high speed. Each recording surface is divided into hundreds of concentric tracks. In turn, the corresponding tracks of all the disk recording surfaces of a disk pack form a *cylinder*. Related data are often stored on the tracks that make up a cylinder in order to reduce the access times. Figure A-5 illustrates these features.

Certain types of disk packs are fixed, whereas others are removable. Fixed disk packs are continuously on-line; consequently, the inconvenience of removing and mounting is avoided. Thus fixed disk packs provide yet another advantage over magnetic tapes, which must normally be mounted before each processing activity and removed thereafter.

Fixed magnetic disks have become common fixtures in microcomputers. However, a hard disk in a microcomputer consists of a single platter, either 5¼ or 3½ inches in diameter. It may be mounted on a *Winchester drive* or in an expansion slot within the microprocessor. If a removable disk is desired, it is inserted within a box-like device, which in turn is attached internally or externally to the microprocessor. One very popular device is the Jaz drive (from Iomega Corp.).

Mainframe hard-disk drive storage capacity ranges into the *terabytes* (trillions of bytes). The storage capacity of newer microcomputer hard-disk drives is measured in either megabytes or *gigabytes* (billions of bytes). The in-

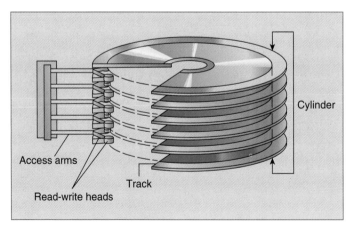

FIGURE A-5 Features of a magnetic disk pack.

terface standard is a method of connecting the hard-disk drive to the processor. Common microcomputer disk drive interface standards are *enhanced device system interface* (EDSI), *small computer system interface* (SCSI), and *integrated device electronics* (IDE). Presently, SCSI drives are the fastest ones available. Whichever drive standard is used, the *mean time between failure* (MTBF) averages over 250,000 hours. That is, the hard-disk drive's running time averages 250,000 hours before breakdown. MTBF for very early hard-disk drives averaged 20,000 hours.

Magnetic disks have three drawbacks. Even though hard disk prices have decreased significantly in recent years, they are still more expensive than magnetic tapes having equal storage capacity. They are less portable than tapes. Finally, data stored on magnetic disks are often lost through *destructive read-in*; for instance, data entered to update the balance of an account will be written back into the same physical location. Thus a previous balance is wiped out when a transaction is posted and a new balance is computed. Because of this overlay approach, special data backup procedures are needed to provide an adequate audit trail.

Optical Disks The *optical disk* is a secondary storage medium that has transparent, rigid optical recording surfaces. It is also called a *laser disk*, since laser beams burn microscopic spots onto the surfaces. These spots are electronic representations of data characters or images, which can be read and retrieved by the laser beams. Most currently available optical disks do not allow burned spots containing data to be erased or modified. Such disks are thus called WORM (write once, read many) storage media or devices. They generally store data and images pertaining to a firm's transactions and activities, such as source documents and schedules. Erasable versions of optical disks are also available, thus further enhancing their appeal.

Optical disks can contain massive quantities of data at a much lower cost than can magnetic disks. For instance, a single 12-inch optical platter can store over 2 gigabytes (2 billion bytes). They are also easily removable from their disk drives, so that other disks can be inserted as needed. The main drawback of optical disks (apart from the WORM limitation) is that data cannot be retrieved as quickly as from magnetic disks.

One version of optical disks, known as CD ROM (*compact disk read-only memory*), is exploding in terms of usage. CD ROM disks are inserted into drives that are internally or externally attached to microcomputers. Available in 8-inch and 5¼ inch sizes, CD ROM disks generally store 400 or 600 megabytes of data. However, storage capacities of seven gigabytes or more are becoming available, as are CD ROM recordable disks, which also allow data to be written on the recording surface. CD ROM access time (about 140 milliseconds) is very slow compared to hard disk access time (9–11 milliseconds).

One of the most promising applications of optical disks is related to image processing. Examples of such applications are the capture of credit card transaction images by American Express, and images of turned-in tickets by several airlines.

Other Storage Media Additional storage media that are employed within computer systems are magnetic diskettes, microfilm, and optically scannable documents. A diskette, or floppy disk, consists of a circular piece of material coated with magnetic oxide and covered with a protective jacket. Most diskettes are available in two sizes: 5¼ inch and 3½ inch; however, 3½-inch floppy drives predominate the market. They are inserted into the disk drives of microcomputers via slots in the microprocessor. Both sizes of diskettes come in either *double density* (DD) or *high density* (HD). DD drives are found on older models of microcomputers. The storage capacities in bytes of both densities are given below:

Size	DD	HD
5¼ in.	360 KB	1.20 MB*
3½ in.	720 KB	1.44 MB†

Identifying features:
*One circular hub, instead of two.
†Two square holes, one on the lower left side and one on the lower right side.

Microfilm provides a means of storing archival records and reference data that are not subject to change. It is very popular because of its low cost, although the devices for displaying the data (called *computer-output microfilm*, COM) can be fairly expensive. Also, microfilm forms are extremely compact and portable.

Optically scannable documents are paper forms whose data can be read only by optical character-recognition devices. They are widely used as source documents and as turnaround documents. (A *turnaround document* is an output document that is returned to the system as an input document. For example, bills can be mailed to customers as two-part forms, with one part being returned later to the billing firm with the payment.) Another medium, *punched cards*, were widely used in early computer systems; however, they are very seldom used today.

INPUT DEVICES (OFF-LINE)

A modern computer system can accept data from a wide variety of devices and generate output information on an equally wide variety of devices. Input data and output information handled by these devices appear on various media or in alternative modes, ranging from paper documents to spoken words. Input-output devices can be critical components in the design of effective computer-based information systems. Off-line input devices are particularly suitable for those applications involving large volumes of transactions. They enable batches of transactions to be prepared for efficient and speedy entry. Thus off-line input devices can help prevent or reduce the state known as *input-output bound*, in which a processor is forced to sit idle much of the time waiting for data to process. In this section we survey several off-line input devices, ranging from key-to-tape encoders to optical character-recognition devices.

Keying Input Devices Two devices that are designed for continuous keying operations are key-to-tape encoders and key-to-disk systems. These off-line devices key data onto storage media, from which the data are later read into a computer system. Thus they may be described as data-preparation devices. They are particularly useful when large volumes of input data are to be prepared for processing.

Key-to-tape encoders transcribe data onto magnetic tapes. Usually they include CRT screens, so that the data-entry clerks can visually view the data being transcribed and make corrections when necessary. Key-to-tape encoders may be used as stand-alone units or may be grouped into key-to-tape systems involving several units or stations and small computer processors. Key-to-tape systems allow transaction data to be validated as they are keyed. After the data have been completely keyed onto magnetic tapes, the tapes are then mounted on tape drives for entry into the computer system.

Key-to-disk systems consist of a number of keyboard stations, at which data-entry clerks prepare data for entry. Although similar to a key-to-tape system, a key-to-disk system may be used to transcribe transaction data onto magnetic tapes or magnetic disks. It also generally includes more stations and performs more validating and editing steps. Transactions containing input data errors can be shunted into an error-correction procedure. The system gains its name from the fact that the data are temporarily stored on a magnetic disk while being validated. A key-to-disk system has more capacity than a key-to-tape system, and it tends to enhance the productivity of the data-preparation activity. However, this type of input system tends to be more costly per station than a key-to-tape encoder system.

Character-Recognition Devices Three major types of devices can recognize and read characters from documents or other hard-copy forms. These devices are optical character-recognition devices, magnetic ink character-recognition devices, and image-reading devices. They are well suited for the handling of data from large batches of documents. In the case of the first two devices, the data are often read from the documents onto magnetic

tapes or disks. Then the data on these media are transferred into the computer system. The reason for this added step is that the data transfer rates of character-recognition devices are much slower than from magnetic tape or disk drives.

Optical character-recognition (OCR) *devices* read characters from documents, whether handwritten, typed, or computer generated. For example, they are used to read sales data from credit transaction flimsies, and cash payment data from credit statement stubs. Less sophisticated OCR devices, known as mark-sense readers, are able to sense marks entered in pencil. The main drawback to OCR devices is that current models are limited in the types of character fonts they can read and paper they can handle; imperfections in written characters and paper cause documents to be rejected and, hence, to require reprocessing.

Magnetic ink character-recognition (MICR) *devices* read documents that are encoded with magnetic ink. MICR devices are universally employed at bank processing centers to read checks into computer systems. These devices have a much lower rejection rate than OCR devices.

Image-reading devices convert images into electronic impulses. Then the images may be stored on suitable media, such as microfilm, magnetic disks, or optical disks. Alternatively, the images may be transmitted to remote facsimile (FAX) devices and converted back into facsimiles of their original hard-copy forms. The images are often of source documents, such as checks; however, they may be of photographs, blueprints, handwritten notes, and so on.

INPUT DEVICES (ON-LINE)

Most input devices in use today provide data directly into computer systems. Figure A-6 shows an array of on-line input devices, as well as the on-line storage media already discussed and the on-line output devices to be discussed next. Note that the OCR device and image reader are included as input devices, since they may serve as either off-line or on-line devices. We will omit them in the following discussion, however, since they have already been covered.

On-line input devices capture data directly into the computer system at the point where transactions originate. That is, they employ the approach known as *source data automation* (SDA). The advantage of capturing data at the earliest feasible time is that input errors and data-entry costs are reduced, and more timely processing is possible.

Terminals On-line devices known as *terminals* are widely used for both input and output operations. Terminals enable users to interact directly with the processing system, in most cases; they also allow data to be entered

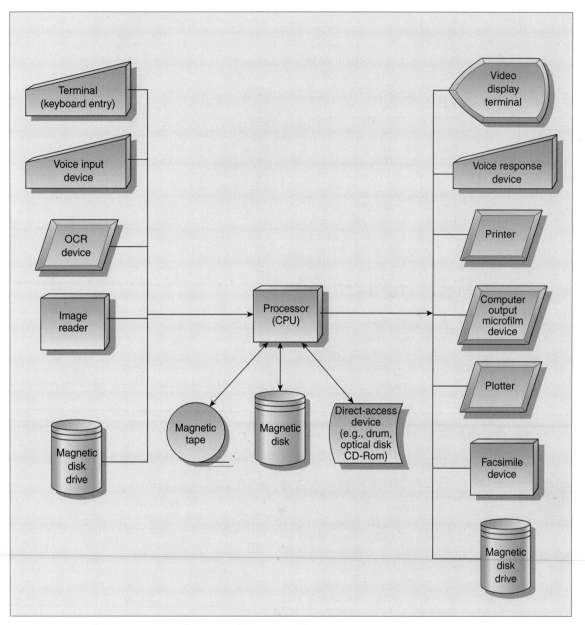

FIGURE A-6   On-line input-output devices and storage media.

by a variety of methods and information to be obtained in a variety of modes.

Terminals range widely in capabilities and functions. At one end of the spectrum are *intelligent terminals*, which can process and store data to a limited degree. In effect, they can serve as microcomputers or they can serve as input-output devices for mainframe computer systems. Intelligent terminals are often used in transaction processing systems, where they may edit data and perform tasks such as checking the credit of customers who place

sales orders. Then they may transmit the data to the mainframe computer for storing in the central data base. At the opposite end of the spectrum are *"dumb" terminals* that simply accept data and produce outputs. Most terminals, such as those described in the following paragraphs, fall somewhere between these two extremes.

Video display terminals, also known as cathode-ray tube (CRT) terminals, incorporate screens that display information in soft-copy form. Also, this type of terminal allows data to be entered by such alternative methods as:

(1) a light pen that "writes" on a light-sensitive screen, (2) a fingertip touch that makes selections on a touch-sensitive screen, (3) a penpad that accepts handwriting via a stylus, and (4) a mouse that gives commands through movements and clicks. These alternative methods of data entry render the video display terminal more user-friendly and tolerant of varied forms of data. With the addition of graphics boards, this type of terminal can display graphs and charts in color. The greatest drawback of this type of terminal is that a separate printer or plotter is needed if hard-copy outputs (e.g., managerial reports) are desired.

Audio input/response terminals, also called voice terminals, allow voice interactions with computer systems. These terminals usually function in conjunction with telephones to accept voice commands. For instance, a bank depositor can orally request the current balance in his or her account, or a retail store clerk can request the credit status of a customer. Voice terminals also usually provide answers to such inquiries orally. At the present time this type of terminal is limited to relatively brief inquiries and commands. Within a few years, however, voice commands are likely to become a widely accepted way of inputting data into computer systems.

Specialized single-function terminals include the following:

1. *Data-collection terminals*, like those used at product workstations and in the vehicles of police officers, route salespersons, construction supervisors, and delivery persons. For instance, a data-collection terminal at a production workstation will typically be used to collect labor hours worked on production jobs. The data may be entered by alternate methods. Thus the job number may be keyed in, the number of the employee performing the labor may be entered by inserting the employee's badge in a reader slot in the device, and the time may be entered by pressing a special function lever.

2. *Point-of-sale terminals*, like those used at checkout counters in retail stores. The method of entering sales data may consist of keying the item numbers of the merchandise and sales quantities into keyboards on the terminals. More likely, however, the data entry method involves the use of an optical scanner (as discussed below).

3. *Automated teller machines*, such as those mounted outside banks.

4. *Reservations terminals*, like those in airports and motels.

OTHER ON-LINE INPUT DEVICES

Although terminals are the most common means of on-line data entry, other devices include OCR devices, image readers, and disk drives. On-line OCR devices scan data from source documents or universal product codes, convert the data into electronic signals, and route the signals to the computer processor. The OCR scanners, which may be fixed or hand-held, often function in unison with terminals (such as point-of-sale terminals). On-line image readers scan drawings, photographs, or handwritten documents and transmit the images into a computer system for processing or storage. Magnetic or optical disk drives transfer data from the drives into a computer system for processing or display.

OUTPUT DEVICES

Among the output devices used in a computer system are printers, computer output microfilm devices, plotters, and terminals.

Printers   These output devices provide hard copy on paper stock. Two categories of printers are available: *impact printers*, which print one line or character at a time, and *nonimpact printers*, which may print an entire page at a time. Line impact printers are high-speed printers used in medium-sized or large computer systems. Character impact printers, which include dot matrix and daisywheel printers, are typically used in microcomputer systems. Although dot matrix printers do not produce printed characters that are as sharp as those from daisywheel printers, they operate much faster. Moreover, dot matrix printers with 24-pin printheads can approach the quality of even the best daisywheel printers.

Nonimpact printers—which include such types as thermal, electrostatic, laser xerographic, and ink jet—offer several advantages over impact printers. In addition to performing at high speeds, they operate quietly and can produce high-quality graphics as well as text and tables. *Laser printers*, shown in Figure A-7, are gaining in popularity within microcomputer systems. They incorporate a laser device, a photosensitive drum, and a paper-handling mechanism. The printer operates by shining short bursts from a laser beam onto the drum, which thereby becomes sensitized. Next the drum is rotated through a toner bath to pick up the ink (toner) on the sensitized areas. This ink is then transferred to paper moving under the drum. A typical laser printer produces high-quality printing at about 4–12 pages per minute.

Computer Output Microfilm Devices   Microfilm is a widely used medium. *Computer output microfilm (COM) devices* provide outputs on various microfilm forms. Instead of working from hard-copy input documents, however, a COM device transfers data from the primary storage unit of a processor or from a secondary storage medium such as magnetic tape. The resulting microfilm form may then be displayed on microfilm readers (viewers) or retrieval terminals. The COM devices provide two significant ad-

FIGURE A-7   A laser printer, together with a Macintosh microcomputer. (Courtesy of Apple Computer, Inc, photo by John Greenleigh.)

vantages. First, they generate output at an extremely high rate of speed, perhaps exceeding 32,000 lines per minute. Second, the microfilm form is very compact and hence relatively inexpensive to produce and store.

Plotters   Devices that convert coded digital data into designs or graphs are known as *plotters*. They may use either mechanical pens or electrostatics to produce the outputs.

Terminals   The major means of providing outputs via terminals is through displays on screens. However, terminals that provide audio responses are being employed in an increasing variety of applications. Also, their vocabularies are expanding.

OTHER OUTPUT DEVICES

Facsimile (FAX) *devices* reproduce transmitted images of source documents and other materials back into facsimiles of their original hard-copy forms. These devices, which are in effect terminal-type image readers, enable needed information to be speedily and accurately dispatched to distant points in an inexpensive manner. *Cellular telephones* allow voice inputs and responses to be transmitted to and from moving vehicles. Magnetic disks accept and store input data or the results of processing.

Often they are used for *spooling*, that is, storing data temporarily, which is to be printed in hard-copy form at a later, more convenient time.

COMPUTER SOFTWARE

Computer software is the programmed instructions that enable a computer to run applications and perform other tasks. Figure A-8 indicates that computer languages are the building blocks for software development. Using these computer languages, programmers prepare systems software, operating systems, utility programs, and application programs.

COMPUTER PROGRAMMING LANGUAGES

Computer programming languages have evolved through four generations. The first generation consists solely of machine languages, the second of symbolic languages, the third of procedure-oriented languages, and the fourth of problem-oriented languages. Although languages from all four generations are still being utilized, the first generation was introduced at the advent of computer technology; the fourth generation came into being during the 1970s and has grown to the present time.

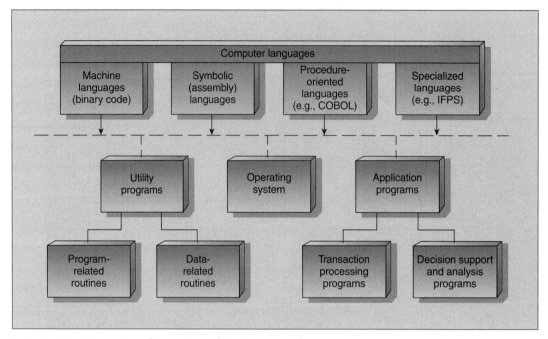

FIGURE A-8 An overview of computer software.

First Generation Each type of computer follows (executes) instructions expressed in a machine language that is unique to it. *Machine languages* employ a binary code composed of zeros and ones. As one can imagine, developing programs in machine language is a slow, tedious, and error-prone task. Thus human programmers develop (write) programs in a higher-level language, which is then converted into machine language by special software.

Second Generation The higher-level languages closest to machine language are known as *symbolic* (assembly) *languages*. They utilize mnemonic codes for instructions and even symbolic codes for storage locations. For instance, the instruction to add numbers may be represented by ADD rather than 010, and the location where the total is stored may be named SUM. Since these codes are easier to remember, programs can be written faster and with fewer errors.

Third Generation Still higher-level languages are known as *procedure-oriented languages*. They are also called *compiler languages*, since compilers are needed to translate programs written in the languages (source programs) into machine language programs (object programs). Examples of procedure-oriented languages are BASIC, COBOL, FORTRAN, and PASCAL. Procedure-oriented languages enable instructions to be expressed by alge-

braic or English-like statements. Thus they are simpler to learn and easier to use than assembly languages. COBOL (Common Business Oriented Language) is of particular interest to accountants, since it is suited to transaction processing applications, relatively easy to understand, and well documented. However, COBOL, like all procedure-oriented languages, is less efficient and hence slower to execute than assembly languages.

Fourth Generation Although procedure-oriented languages are still in widespread use, they are being challenged by fourth-generation languages, specialized software packages (4GLs), and object-oriented programming languages. These *problem-oriented languages* are powerful software languages and tools that function at even higher levels than the procedure-oriented languages. In fact, they are designed to be so user-friendly that users having no previous exposure to computers can employ them effectively. For instance, they do not require statements to be arranged procedurally. Instead, they allow the developer to focus more directly on the problem to be solved and less on the procedure by which it is to be solved. Examples of 4GLs are FOCUS, Express, and Interactive Financial Planning System (IFPS). Fourth-generation languages are also found in various types of applications development tools, such as spreadsheet packages, data-base management packages, and expert systems software. These packages are discussed in Appendix B. Object-oriented programming languages, such as Smalltalk and C^{++}, are described in Chapters 3 and 20.

OPERATING SYSTEMS

An *operating system* is a master program that controls all aspects of a computer's operations. A modern operating system automates and expedites many of the control, coordinating, and "housekeeping" tasks performed by people in earlier computer systems. Common mainframe operating systems include Digital Equipment Company's VMS and ULTRIX, and IBM's VSE, MVS, and VM. Operating systems for IBM microcomputers and IBM compatibles include Windows 95, Windows NT, OS/2 Warp, DOS, and UNIX. The ProDOS and System 7 operating systems control Apple Company's microcomputers. Microcomputer operating systems are described further in Appendix B.

Compared to microcomputer operating systems, mainframe operating systems cost significantly more, handle larger volumes of data, process data faster, and control complex communications networks. Although mainframe and microcomputer operating systems differ in the manner in which specific tasks are performed, the following list of functions is reasonably typical:

1. **Controlling the movement of data and programs within and between the primary and secondary storage units.** A supervisor program performs this function in both mainframe and microcomputer operating systems. A microcomputer's supervisor is called a "kernel." A supervisor also coordinates the execution of all the other programs.

2. **Loading or "booting" the computer system and then passing control to the supervisor.** A load program performs this task for mainframe and microcomputer operating systems.

3. **Retrieving and loading programs and data and interpreting instructions.** A mainframe operating system uses a job control language (JCL) program to perform these procedures. These same functions are accomplished in a Windows-based microcomputer operating system by pointing to and selecting on-screen graphical icons with a mouse. DOS is a nongraphical user system that requires users to run applications by typing commands.

4. **Assigning and managing the particular input and output devices to the various jobs being run by the computer system.** Whereas mainframe operating systems manage all devices using input-output programs, microcomputer operating systems sometimes do not, relying instead on programs called *drivers*. Drivers are supplied by software developers

to manage particular models of displays and printers.

5. **Determining the sequence and scheduling the data processing jobs involving application and utility programs.** A mainframe operating system uses a scheduling program to automatically run programs. Scheduling programs are not needed with microcomputer operating systems since users are responsible for manually running one or two jobs at a time.

6. **Monitoring performance.** A mainframe operating system's monitoring program can generate logs and statistics pertaining to job and equipment performance. Microcomputer operating systems rarely incorporate these features.

7. **Assigning primary storage locations to data and programs and "remembering" the locations of all applications and utility programs that are stored on secondary storage devices.** Both large and small operating systems provide these functions in library/memory or device driver programs.

UTILITY PROGRAMS

Utility programs are under the control of the operating system. They are normally written in symbolic languages, since they are expected to operate efficiently on a particular computer system.

One category of utility programs is data oriented. Examples include routines that transfer data from one storage medium to another, sort data, and manage data within a data base. Sometimes utility routines may be incorporated into application programs. Another category of utility programs may be described as program oriented. Examples are diagnostic routines, which help programmers to find programming errors, and compilers, which were identified earlier. Further examples of microcomputer utility programs are given in Appendix B.

APPLICATION PROGRAMS

Application programs perform specific functions, such as generating payroll checks, preparing financial statements, and developing budgets. For instance, a set of application programs may pertain to sales transactions. One program might verify and edit sales data when entered for processing. A second program may update the accounts receivable and inventory files to reflect the sales data. A third program may print the sales invoices and related reports. Other application programs pertain to information processing activities such as sales forecasting, cash budgeting, and inventory control. Still other application programs broadly aid activities such as word processing and financial analysis. Further examples of microcomputer-based application programs are illustrated in Appendix B.

DATA COMMUNICATIONS

DATA COMMUNICATIONS HARDWARE

A data communications network also requires a variety of specialized hardware and software components. Most of these hardware components, briefly described below, are listed in Figure A-9. Figure A-10 shows these network components together with a central processor and on-line secondary storage unit.

Terminals The varied types of terminals are the primary interfaces between a communications network and the users. As we have noted, "dumb" terminals send and receive data only within the network. At the other end of the terminal spectrum, intelligent terminals can edit and format data for transmission, process data against files, communicate with other components in the network, and so on. In effect, they can serve as workstations. For instance, *remote job entry* (RJE) *stations* are terminals that allow the entry of batched data from remote points within a network.

Modems Modulator-demodulator coupler units, known as *modems*, are devices that interface between a sending point and receiving point in a communications network. As Figure A-11 portrays, a pair of modems converts signals from the digital (discrete) form to the analog (continuous wave) form and back again. They are necessary because voice telephone lines, the major type of communications medium, can handle only analog signals.

Modems vary in several respects. First, they differ in the ways they connect to the communication lines. *Acoustical coupler modems*, almost extinct, used with dial-up terminals, connect through touch-tone telephones that are placed into couplers. *Hard-wired modems*, and the terminals to which they are attached, are connected through permanent wiring. Second, they differ with respect to *baud rates*, the speeds at which they transmit data. Common baud rates are 2400, 4800, 9600, 14,400, and 28,800 bits per second (bps). Third, they differ by mode of transmission. Asynchronous modems transmit on a character-by-character basis, whereas synchronous modems transmit blocks of characters. The latter mode

---

"Dumb" terminals

Intelligent terminals

Remote job-entry (RJE) terminals

Acoustical coupler modems

Hard-wired modems

Wireless modems

Fax modems

Channels

Peripheral device controllers

Front-end processors

Multiplexers

Concentrators

Servers (disk, print, processor, communications, data base, transaction processing)

Network controllers (including private branch telephone, PBX, exchanges)

Gateways, bridges, routers

FIGURE A-9   Hardware components used in data communications networks.

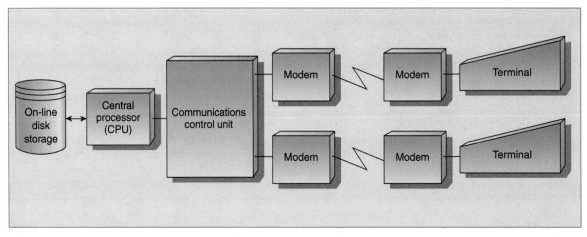

FIGURE A-10   A data communications network.

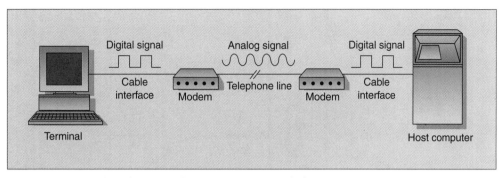

FIGURE A-II   Use of modems in a data communications linkup.

allows faster transmission, but requires more expensive equipment. When telephone lines are inaccessible, *wireless modems* connected to cellular telephones can transmit messages directly over the airwaves from laptop computers. *Fax modems* are similar to conventional modems except that they can also transmit and receive faxes.

Certain communications lines allow digital transmission and hence do not require modems. However, digital transmission is relatively expensive and has other shortcomings.

Communications Control Units   As terminals, other input-output devices, and storage devices are added within a communications network, control mechanisms are needed. Among the hardware control units employed in computer systems and networks are channels, controllers, front-end processors, multiplexers, and concentrators.

A *channel* serves as a data pipeline between input-output devices and/or storage devices and the central processor. It relieves the central processor of the need to communicate directly with the peripheral devices, and it also makes adjustments for differences in transfer speeds between the processor and the devices. In effect, a channel is a small specialized computer.

A *controller* is a control mechanism that is linked to a channel. Its circuitry maintains direct contact with a particular type of device, translating and routing coded signals from the processor to each individual device, and vice versa. Figure A-12 depicts channels and controllers for three types of peripheral devices. It also shows the location of a buffer, a storage area that holds small quantities of data awaiting processing within the primary storage unit of the central processor. The feature known as overlapping, described earlier, is achieved through the use of the control mechanisms shown in the figure.

A *communications control unit* known as a *front-end processor* relieves the central processor of functions such as editing data, detecting and correcting errors in transmitted data, and routing messages among terminals and the central processor. It can be viewed as a sophisticated channel that allows the processor to perform more efficiently.

A *multiplexer* combines the data signals from multiple terminals into a composite signal for transmission to a single point. Figure A-13, on page 965, illustrates the effect of multiplexing. Without a multiplexer, 10 modems and five communication lines would be needed in the pictured network. Consequently, the costs of eight modems and four communication lines are saved. Another benefit is increased overall transmission speed, since a multiplexer can transmit at very high speeds compared to the typical terminal rate.

A *concentrator* performs multiplexing, plus certain functions performed by a front-end processor. Because it can more effectively utilize a shared communication line, it is able to control more terminals.

Other Data Communications Devices   Local-area networks (LANs), discussed in Chapter 17, are being installed in increasing numbers. Among the specialized hardware devices needed in such networks are servers, network controllers, gateways, bridges, and routers. *Servers* are devices that enable services to be shared by several workstations. Examples are disk servers, print servers, processor servers, communications servers, data-base servers, and transaction processing servers. *Network controllers* control the various workstations and ensure that messages are properly routed. They are switching devices; in fact, private branch telephone exchanges (PBXs) can be used as network controllers. Both servers and network controllers are types of communications control mechanisms.

Another type of useful LAN hardware is a communications device that interfaces between a LAN and either another LAN or a wide-area network. A *gateway* connects together LANs that employ different protocols, for example, token passing and CSMA/CD protocols. (Protocols prescribe the rules by which LAN workstations communicate to each other.) A *bridge* joins similar or dissimilar LANS together, such as two EtherNet LANs or an EtherNet LAN and a Token Ring LAN. A *router*

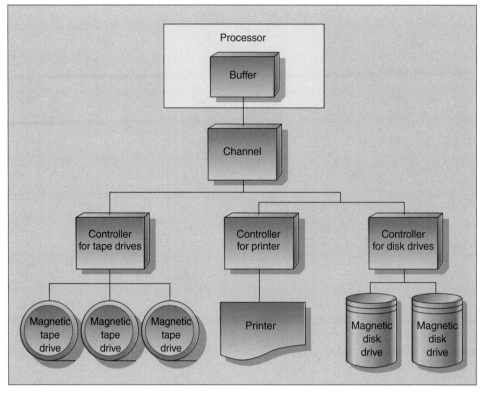

FIGURE A-12   Communications control devices.

connects two similar LANs together, each of which uses a different protocol or standards.

DATA COMMUNICATIONS MEDIA

The communications media for transmitting data within a network can assume any of several forms. Traditional electrical lines consist of insulated copper or aluminum wires, called *twisted pairs*. In addition to carrying voice messages, they can transmit data via analog signals. *Co-axial cables* can support a wider variety of devices and carry thousands of data transmissions simultaneously. *Fiber optics cables*, composed of numerous glass or plastic filaments, transmit data by means of concentrated light waves. Although thinner and less expensive than coaxial cables, fiber optics cables allow speeds of hundreds of millions of bits per second (bps). This medium also can carry an incredible number of messages simultaneously, is virtually free of electrical interference, and thus can transmit data with more reliability and security. Not surprisingly, fiber optics networks are being rapidly installed by communications firms such as AT&T. Wireless networks communications media include satellite transmission, line-of-sight microwave data transmission (both ground-hugging and ground-to-satellite-to-ground) and cellular radio. Microwave transmission has also grown in popularity in recent years because it allows

data to be transmitted at very high rates of speed. Cellular radio is a recent ground-hugging form of microwave data transmission. Two media that are likely to become important in the future are modulated laser light beams and helical waveguides (hollow tubes).

COMMUNICATION CHANNEL FACTORS AND OPTIONS

Moving data from one point to another involves more than a particular communication medium, however. Among the factors to be considered (assuming the use of communications lines) are the grade of line, transmission mode, type of transmission, protocol, and type of line service. Each factor offers certain options to the user of the network. These options are listed in Figure A-14, on page 966, and are summarized in the following paragraphs.

Grade of Line   Communication lines are graded according to their speed of transmission. Voice-band lines, such as twisted-pair telephone lines, transmit at relatively low rates (e.g., up to 28,800-plus bps) and are used mainly by terminals and microcomputers. Broad-band lines transmit at high to very high rates (up to 50 million bps). These lines, which include coaxial cables and fiber optics cables, carry data from input-output devices to

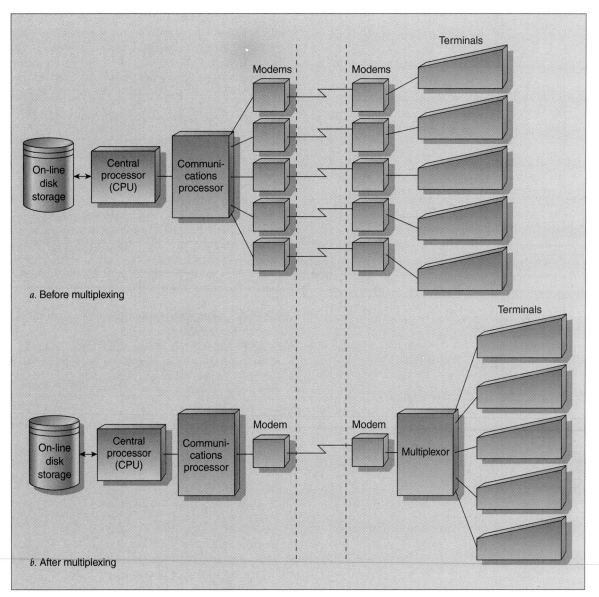

FIGURE A-13   A data communications network before and after multiplexing.

mainframe computers, as well as from computer to computer, or from communications processor to computer.

Type of Transmission   One aspect of transmission relates to the directions of transmission. *Simplex transmission* involves transmission in one direction only. *Half-duplex transmission* allows transmission in both directions, but not at the same time. *Full-duplex transmission* allows transmission in both directions at the same time. Real-time processing requires full duplex, whereas less demanding applications may be able to use half-duplex or simplex.

Another aspect of transmission relates to the wave form of the data signal. *Analog transmission* is a sinusoid

wave form, the form that most present-day communications lines are designed to carry. It must be converted to the digital pulsed form by modems for use by computers. *Digital transmission* is the pulsed data form that computers can recognize and use. It requires no modems for conversion. Also, it allows data to be transmitted faster and more reliably. However, communications lines designed to transmit digital forms are relatively expensive and not yet in widespread use.

Still another aspect of transmission relates to the number of communication channels used to transmit a message. *Serial transmission* consists of sending an entire message over a single channel, one character after another. *Parallel transmission* consists of sending portions of

Factor	Options
Grade	Voice-band
	Broad-band
Transmission type	Simplex
	Half-duplex
	Full-duplex
	Analog
	Digital
	Serial
	Parallel
Transmission mode	Asynchronous
	Synchronous
Type of line service	Public switched lines
	Private leased lines
	WATS lines
	Public data networks
	Proprietary networks

FIGURE A-14   Options to be selected with respect to communications lines.

a message over separate communications channels. The latter is faster but more expensive.

Mode of Transmission   *Asynchronous transmission* involves a character-by-character transmission, since each character is preceded by a start bit and is followed by a stop bit. *Synchronous transmission* involves continuous transmission. Instead of marking each character with start and stop bits, it transmits blocks of characters comprising entire messages. The latter mode of transmission is faster; however, it requires more expensive equipment, such as synchronous modems and processors.

Type of Line Service   The three basic types of available service for communications lines are *private* (leased) *lines*, *public* (switched, dial-up) *lines*, and *wide-area telephone service* (WATS) *lines*. Distinguishing features of the three types are listed in Figure A-15.

Communications carriers and computer manufacturers have developed *public data networks*. Examples are Accunet (marketed by AT&T) and Telenet (marketed by General Telephone and Electronics Co.) These networks can supplement or replace the public or private lines described in the figure. These networks are available to subscribers on a fee basis. In addition to the timely and efficient transmission of data and graphics over great distances, a public data network provides services such as error detection and correction, electronic mail, teleconferencing, and access to commercial data banks. A network of this type may employ switching technologies such as message switching, packet switching, or time-division circuit switching.

Private data networks, called *proprietary networks*, can also be developed. A proprietary network may be developed by the using firm or may be leased for private use from a commercial developer. An example of a network

	Private Leased Line	Public Switched Line	WATS Line
Use	Available only for use by paying customer	Employs public telephone lines; requires dialing for connection and service	Employs public telephone lines; requires dialing for connection and service
Rate	Fixed with respect to time used; variable with respect to distance	Variable with respect to time used	Fixed for a minimum number of hours per month; variable above the minimum
Advantages	Least expensive at high volumes and short distances	Least expensive at low volumes and relatively long distances	Tends to be least expensive at certain intermediate volumes and distances
	No waiting for service, hence generally faster transmissions	Flexible; can access system from any telephone	Flexible; can access system from any telephone
	Lower error rate		

FIGURE A-15   Types of services in communications lines.

for private lease is *Systems Network Architecture* (marketed by IBM Corporation).

Protocol A *protocol* prescribes the manner by which data are transmitted from one computer to another. In effect, it is the set of rules or procedures applied by the communications software to move data throughout one or more data communications networks. One rule concerns the way in which each message is packaged in an "envelope," so that it does not become intermixed with other messages and arrives safely at its destination. Included in a typical envelope (besides the message) might be a message number, to and from addresses, end-of-message mark, and error check. Figure A-16 illustrates a message envelope. For instance, an envelope could contain a message consisting of a sales order transaction and be identified by 5621 (a sequential message number), 07216 (the disk address to which the message is directed), 27 (the number of the terminal from which the message is being transmitted), and characters that represent the end-of-message mark and allow the message to be checked for transmission errors.

Two basic protocols are known as token passing and carrier sense multiple access/collision detection (CSMA/CD). Token passing involves the use of a unique token (special signal), which allows a message envelope to move only when its transmitting device has retrieved the token. Since only one message envelope is moving through the network at a time, collisions between envelopes are avoided. CSMA/CD requires a transmitting device (e.g., a terminal) to listen for traffic in its channel and to transmit only when the channel is free.

DATA COMMUNICATIONS SOFTWARE

Special communications control programs operate under the broad control of the network's operating system. This type of software enables data and programs to be transmitted from one device in the network to another. For instance, electronic mail may be transmitted by a manager from one terminal in the network to the private file of another manager. Microcomputers may be converted into terminal emulators, from which data may be entered into the network for processing or storage in an integrated data base.

Network Operating System Examples of *network operating systems* (NOSs) employed in dedicated server networks are Netware (from Novell), LAN Server (from IBM), and VINES (from Banyon). The most popular peer-to-peer NOSs are LANtastic (from Artisoft), Personal NetWare (from Novell), and Windows NT (from Microsoft).

Data Communications Programs *Data communications programs* may be maintained by a host computer within the network; most likely, however, they are assigned to specialized computers or controllers called network servers. Certain communications software may also be placed within a network's communications processors, such as the front-end processor or multiplexers. All such communications programs are designed to move data and programs throughout the network as efficiently and speedily as possible, maintain security and data accuracy, and keep useful records of system activity.

Middleware A main category of software used in networks, especially LAN-based client/server computing platforms, is middleware. Middleware is a collection of software that enables LAN-based client/server setups to run as a seamless unit, even though the network contains many kinds of hardware and software purchased from different vendors. There are numerous categories of middleware, and within each category several vendors offer a "hodgepodge" of different software products. Examples of categories of middleware software include remote procedure calls, conversational, message routing services, remote data-base access, directory services, time services, and security services. *Remote procedure calls software* synchronize requests and responses from diverse multivendor protocols and workstations operating in different locations. *Conversational software* synchronizes the updating of data bases in multiple locations. *Message routing services software* handles the sending of messages among multivendor platforms. *Remote data-base access software* enables users to access remote data bases in real-time. *Directory services software* provides a directory of users and servers on the network. *Time services software* enables users to synchronize clocks so that transactions and data bases are correctly updated. *Security services software* provides security among multivendor protocols and workstations.

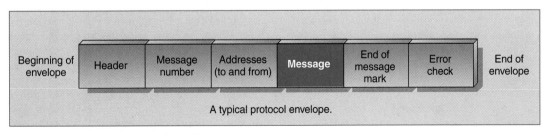

A typical protocol envelope.

FIGURE A-16   A typical protocol envelope.

APPENDIX
B

MICROCOMPUTER SYSTEMS

DISTINCTIVE HARDWARE FEATURES

As a member of the computer family, a microcomputer consists basically of a central processing unit, input-output devices, and secondary storage devices. All of these units and devices have been covered in Appendix A. However, several distinctive features concerning the central processing unit might be noted.

At the heart of the central processing unit is the *microprocessor*. It is constructed on a single silicon chip, which may be less than one square inch wide and one or more inches long. Thanks to very large scale integration, this chip contains several million logic gates (i.e., transistors, circuits, and electronic components). Together with switches and a connected clock, it performs the control and arithmetic-logic functions. The chip also contains registers, called *cache memory*, that store relatively small quantities of data for very fast access. In addition, recently designed processor chips incorporate a math coprocessor, which can perform significantly faster than the principal microprocessor.

Microprocessors are designed by chip manufacturers. Four microprocessor chips found in many microcomputers are the Intel P6, Motorola 68040, Motorola/IBM/Apple PowerPC, and MIPS Technologies R4000. However, new chips are continually under development; consequently, more powerful versions of the four chips are being installed in newer microcomputers. Other chips able to emulate Intel chips are being developed by the Open Microcomputer Systems Initiative, a European project involving a large number of firms and universities. As mentioned in Appendix A, the performance of microcomputer chips is measured by factors such as word size, bus, and clock frequency speed. For instance,

the Intel P6 has a word size of 32 bits and a clock frequency speed up to 200 megahertz (million cycles per second). Because this chip also integrates both a math coprocessor and cache memory, it can perform about twice as many million instructions per second (MIPS) as the most powerful P5 chip. Figure B-1 shows the average MIPS speed of the Intel 8000 series of chips. As displayed, the average number of MIPS has increased from 0.5 for the 8086 chip to an estimated 350 for the P7 chip, a speed improvement of 700 times! The Motorola, PowerPC, and MIPS Technologies chips' clock frequency speed and MIPS performance rating are similar to the Pentium chips. All newer chip designs have the ability to perform parallel processing and three-dimensional graphics.

The microprocessor chips are mounted on a main circuit board, often called a *motherboard*, *planar board*, or *system board*. Also on this board are primary storage (main memory) chips. In addition, the motherboard provides connection points (i.e., interfaces, ports, controllers) for a variety of input-output and storage devices. Figure B-2, on page 970, shows a motherboard for an Intel Pentium Processor. Among the connections that it provides are a *serial port* (i.e., a communications link), a *parallel port* (i.e., a printer or plotter link), a pointing device interface (i.e., a mouse or light pen link), and a disk controller (i.e., a link to a diskette drive). In addition, the motherboard usually contains modules for special capabilities, such as the graphics module shown in the figure. Furthermore, the board contains expansion slots (shown in the lower left corner of the figure) and plug-in pins for devices such as add-in memory boards, terminal keyboards, timers, oscillators, accelerator cards, clock/calendars, and voice synthesizers.

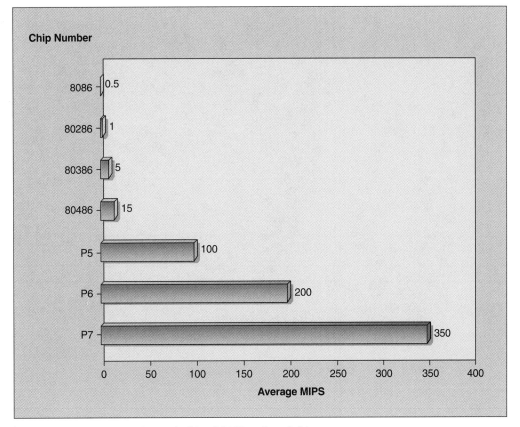

FIGURE B-1   Average MIPS speed of Intel 8000 series of chips.

Notes:

The chip number is usually followed by a second number, which is the clock speed. Thus 486/66 means a 80486 chip running at 66 megahertz (MHZ). Each microprocessor chip comes in several clock speeds, for example, 486/25, 486/33, 486/66. Faster clock speeds are more expensive but perform more math operations.

MIPS is an abbreviation for million of instructions per second. It is the average number of integer calculations executed in one second. In the above figure only, MIPS is based on the fastest clock speed for each chip number.

The 386 and 486 chips come in DX and SX versions. The SX is a scaled-down version of the DX, running at a slower clock speed.

The 80586 and all subsequent Intel chips were renamed Pentium, or P for short. The anticipated date of introduction for the P7 chip is 1999.

On the typical motherboard all of the various components receive their electrical power (in the form of digital electronic pulses) via one or more system bus bars and connectors. Figure B-3 depicts a bus bar and a variety of likely components for a dedicated microcomputer having communications capability. Multiple buses are being increasingly used, since the newer microprocessor chips are designed to take advantage of their features. A *bus* is a pathway that transfers electronic signals between computer components. This common bus pathway allowed numerous firms to manufacture IBM clones and hundreds of software firms to develop thousands of IBM compatible software packages. The most common bus is *Industry Standard Architecture* (ISA), which carries 16 bits of data along the pathway at once. To overcome this relatively slow transfer speed, *Extended Industry Standard Architecture* (EISA), a 32-bit bus, was developed. *Micro Channel Architecture* (MCA) is a 32-bit bus that is exclusive to the IBM PS/2 family of microcomputers.

The two bus architectures ISA and EISA are multiple bus architectures that transfer data relatively slowly between computer components. To partially overcome this limitation, a *local bus* video adapter can be plugged into an expansion slot inside the microcomputer to provide

FIGURE B-2 A view of the motherboard of a microcomputer. (Courtesy of Intel.)

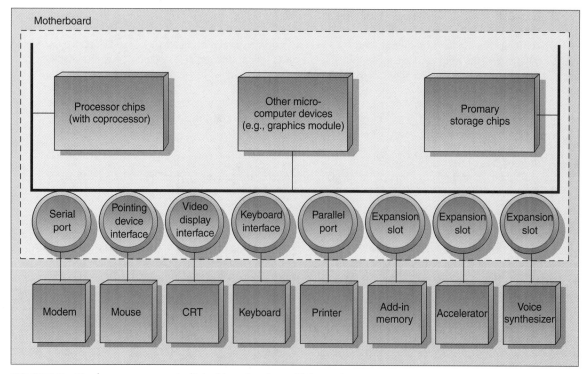

FIGURE B-3 Hardware components linked by a bus bar within a microcomputer.

Accounting Software*

ABS Accounting	Macola Progression Series
ACCPAC 2000	M·A·S 90 Evolution/2
BusinessWorks	One-Write Plus
CYMA Accounting	Peachtree
CYMA PAS+	Platinum Series Accounting
DAC Easy	Ready-to-Run Accounting
Great Plains Dynamics	Real-World Accounting
LIBRA Signature	SBT Pro Series
LIBRA Perspectives	Solomon Series

Spreadsheet Software

Commander Prism	Paradox
DS LAB	Quattro Pro
Excel	Supercalc
Improv	TM/1
Lotus 1-2-3	

Financial Modeling and Decision Support Software

Criterium	IFPS
Encore! Plus	Javelin Plus
Expert Choice	SAS
Express	Statistix
Focus	SPSS

Data-Base Management System Software

Access	Oracle
Dbase	Paradox
Fox Pro	

Expert Systems Software

EXSYS	Personal Consultant
KDS	Visual Expert
Level-5	VP-Expert
OPS5	1st Class Fusion

Neural Network Software

ModelQuest	Brainmaker
Autonet	Neural Works Professional

Wordprocessing Software

MS Word	WordPerfect
Professional Write Plus	Word Pro

*The above accounting software packages range from low-end packages such as DAC Easy and Peachtree, which can be used by "Mom and Pop" businesses, to high-end packages such as Solomon, which can be used by very large firms. For example, Koch Industries, headquartered in Wichita, KS, and the second largest privately held U.S. firm, with worldwide revenues of about $24 billion, recently switched its accounting software off mainframes to the LAN-based client/server Solomon IV accounting modules.

FIGURE B-4   Examples of IBM compatible application software packages.

almost instantaneous transfer of data between memory and the monitor.

Although most microprocessors are built into housings that are intended to stay in one location, a fast-growing part of the microcomputer market is directed toward portables. Portable microcomputers range from suitcase models weighing 10 or more pounds to palm-size models weighing less than one pound. Most of the portable microcomputers are called *laptops*, since you can use them in your lap. The most recent entries are called notebook PCs. Portable microcomputers generally have built-in liquid crystal display screens, rather than cathode-ray tube screens. The screens may provide color displays for an added price. Certain advanced models of portable microcomputers provide input devices known as *notepads*, which can accept data written by hand using a stylus. A more advanced version of a notepad is a *personal digital assistant* (PDA). A PDA is a hand-held input-output device that allows wireless data and file transfers, paging, faxing or E-mail services. Users can write or tap on the PDA's screen with a special pen to transmit sales orders, inventory data, and other information directly to a firm's mainframe or to microcomputers in a local-area network.

APPLICATIONS SOFTWARE PACKAGES

The advent of microcomputers has led to an explosion of application software packages. Although many firms develop their own special programs, using such third-generation languages as COBOL and BASIC, most firms rely heavily if not exclusively on software packages developed outside. Thus a number of software vendors have come into existence. Among the more familiar names are Microsoft, Novell, Borland, and Computer Associates International, Inc. These software development firms prepare accounting applications, electronic spreadsheets, financial modeling and decision support systems, data-base management systems, expert systems, neural net systems, and wordprocessing systems. Examples of particular software packages in each category are listed in Figure B-4. All of these types of packages, plus a variety of others, which are surveyed in the following sections, aid users in creating, developing, and running specific AIS-related tasks.

Before undertaking our survey, however, we should remember that such applications must function under the control of an operating system. Examples and characteristics of operating systems for IBM compatible microcomputers are shown in Figure B-5. Operating systems for the Apple family of computers include System 7 (from Apple Computer, Inc.) and ProDOS (from Apple Computer, Inc.). Application software packages are writ-

ten to comply with the specifics of a particular operating system. Thus operating systems used by a variety of microcomputers tend to engender a wide variety of applications software packages. The *Windows* 95 operating system (from Microsoft Corp.) employs a graphical user interface (GUI), which allows the use of a mouse to select icons to run software packages. The Windows NT (from Microsoft Corp.) and OS/2 Warp (from IBM Corp.) operating systems provide a GUI similar to Windows 95. DOS (versions from Microsoft Corp. and IBM Corp.) is a command language operating system that requires the user to type keyboard commands to run software packages.

ACCOUNTING APPLICATION PACKAGES

Most accounting application packages focus on common transactions. For instance, a typical set of packages covers transactions affecting the general ledger, accounts receivable, accounts payable, inventory, and payroll. Each of these packages verify and edit entered transaction data, update established master files, process the data, and produce various documents and reports. They normally include subsidiary ledgers for customers, suppliers, and employees. Designers of such packages normally use a modular approach, with the various modules being integrated into the general ledger module.

Microcomputer-based accounting application packages are used by firms of all sizes, from small business firms to large organizations having widespread operations. Since the users of these packages are typically data-entry or accounting clerks, the designers attempt to render the packages as user-friendly as possible. Menus, account prompts, forced balancing of transaction amounts, simplified reports, and thorough audit trails are among the accommodating devices employed. Tutorials and easy-to-understand manuals are often provided.

An enormous number of accounting packages are currently available from a variety of software vendors. *The CPA Software News*, a monthly publication, is an excellent source that has feature articles and reviews on the latest accounting software.* In addition, accounting software reviews can also be located on the World Wide Web, which is part of the Internet.

Figure B-6, on page 974, shows the main menu for the general ledger module of the MSA Accounting System (from Management Science America, Inc.).

ELECTRONIC SPREADSHEETS

The software package known as an *electronic spreadsheet* has become the most popular accounting and business ap-

---

*This publication is available from *Software News*, 110 N. Bell, Suite 300, Shawnee, OK 74801.

Name	Characteristics
Windows 95	Introduced in 1995, it is an amalgamation of Microsoft DOS and the Windows 3.1 graphical user interface (GUI) package. Currently, one of the most popular microcomputer OSs in use. The first version of this OS was named Windows 95. The latest version can be identified by the last two digits, which indicate the year the version was introduced. Can run two or more programs at once. Includes a number of built-in security features.
DOS (Disk Operating System)	The most popular OS from 1981–1995. There are Microsoft and IBM versions of DOS. MSDOS 6 and PCDOS 7 were the last versions manufactured. Millions of copies are in use. Non-graphical user interface. To simplify its use, DOS is often run with the Windows 3.1 GUI software package already installed on the microcomputer. No built-in security features.
OS/2 Warp	Developed by IBM, operating system/2 (OS/2) has a very small share of the total microcomputer OS market. OS/2 will run DOS and Windows 3.1 programs, but not any Windows 95 programs. Effectively runs multiple programs concurrently. Built-in access controls to safeguard a user's data. OS/2 is compatible with IBM's other OSs.
UNIX/XENIX	Runs on all sizes of computers. Comes in several versions. Not popular in the PC environment. Used extensively on the Internet—a global web of computer networks.

FIGURE B-5 Examples of operating systems (OS) software for IBM compatible microcomputers.

plication since the first version, VisiCalc, burst on the scene in 1978. Since that date Lotus 1–2–3 (from IBM Corp.), Paradox (from Borland International Corp.), Quattro Pro (from Borland International Corp.), and others have appeared. (These names, and others to be mentioned in later sections, are registered trademarks.) An electronic spreadsheet is a menu-driven set of commands that allow the construction of multicolumn worksheets on the screen of a video display terminal or microcomputer. It enables accountants and others to develop worksheets with a large number of rows and columns, to perform powerful computer-aided functions, to display the results, and to store the results in computer-readable files.

The electronic spreadsheet has four attributes that enable it to be an effective business planning tool:

1. It displays data in a form (i.e., columnar worksheet) that is familiar to accountants and other financially oriented persons.

2. It eliminates the onerous chore of manual calculating, since it performs calculations such as footing, cross-footing, and extensions. At the same time, it does require users such as accountants to act as programmers to gain desired results.

3. It allows accountants and other users to ask "what if" questions and to obtain complete recalculations very quickly. Thus an accountant who is preparing a forecast may change a sales estimate from an increase of 1 percent per month to 3 percent per month. The spreadsheet formulas will then automatically recalculate the expected sales levels. If the sales forecast is part of a budgeted income statement, the spreadsheet will also recalculate the expected net income amounts and all intervening expense amounts.

4. It enables templates to be constructed and repeatedly used in solving various problems. A template is a program that (a) models the relationships

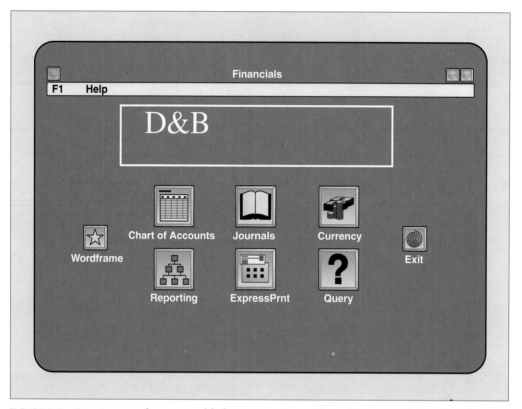

FIGURE B-6   A main menu for a general ledger accounting package. (Courtesy of Dun & Bradstreet Softwares, Inc.)

among factors, (b) details the procedural steps by which values are manipulated on the spreadsheet, and (c) expresses the format of the output. For instance, a template may be created by an accountant to prepare consolidated financial statements; this same template may be used at the end of each accounting period. Spreadsheet templates are extremely useful in planning and forecasting situations, since they allow users to ask "what if" questions and obtain quickly recalculated answers. Figure B-7 displays a template for calculating budgeted income statements.

FINANCIAL MODELING AND DECISION SUPPORT SOFTWARE

Financial modeling software packages allow users to build customized models by employing powerful instructions and functions. A financial model has the primary purpose of enabling managers and other users to project future business activity or to aid in solving problems. Financial modeling software represents an alternative to electronic spreadsheets. Both allow calculations and other manipulations of data and clearly present the results in tabular or graphical forms. Both provide a programming language that enables the user to create software instructions or to construct models. Both offer special functions and macro commands.

In many situations, however, financial modeling software packages are distinctly preferable to electronic spreadsheets. Financial modeling software enables decision makers and model builders to construct models with English-like statements. Not only do these statements provide more understandable documentation but they facilitate the logical development. Thus fewer logic errors are found in financial models than in electronic spreadsheet programs. Also, financial models are more flexible and reusable, since the data are stored in files or data bases rather than in referenced cells. Finally, more manipulative techniques may be employed with the typical financial modeling software package. In addition to "what if" statements, both goal-seeking commands and sensitivity analyses may be more easily performed. Thus financial modeling software is more suited to complex and recurring problems.

Certain microcomputer-based financial modeling software packages, such as ENCORE! PLUS (from Ferox Microsystems, Inc.), emphasize the use of English-like

	A	B	C	D	E	F
1	Account		Budget	Actual	Variance	Variance
2	Name		Amount	Amount	(Dollars)	(Percent)
3						
4	Sales		....	....	0	0
5	Cost of sales		....	....	0	0
6	Gross margin		0	0	0	0
7	Operating exp.		....	....	0	0
8	Nonoper. exp.		....	....	0	0
9	Total expenses		0	0	0	0
10	Net income		0	0	0	0
11						
12						
13						
14						

Notes: 1. Letters mark columns; numbers mark rows.
2. The spaces denoted by ...... indicate amounts to be entered, whereas the spaces marked by 0 indicate amounts to be computed by the spreadsheet software.

FIGURE B-7   A template of a budgeted income statement.

commands. Other packages, such as IFPS (from Comshare, Inc.), provide a variety of user-friendly menus and built-in functions for developing models. Still others, such as JAVELIN PLUS (from Information Resources, Inc.), store both data and program logic in a multidimensional data base, from which a variety of two-dimensional views can be displayed for the user.

DECISION SUPPORT SOFTWARE

Decision Support System (DSS) software packages, such as Criterium (from Sygenex) and Expert Choice (from Analytic Science Corp.), aid managers in making decisions concerning semistructured or unstructured problem situations. DSSs are thoroughly examined in Chapter 16. Other DSS software packages, such as SAS (from SAS Institute), Statistix (from Analytical Software), and SPSS (from SPSS, Inc.), enable users to look for patterns among data items or to use samples to make estimates and decisions about a population of data. DSS statistical software packages contain routines to do basic statistics, such as summary descriptive statistics as well as sophisticated analyses like linear regression. Summary statistics about mean, median or mode, frequency distributions, histograms, and scatter diagrams can be prepared. Linear regression models can analyze historical patterns among data items to compute predicted values and determine, through a series of tests, if the forecasted values can be utilized to make meaningful decisions.

DATA-BASE MANAGEMENT SYSTEMS

From the viewpoint of a microcomputer user, an application is any data-oriented use to which the microcomputer system may be put. One such application is data management. A software package that enables users to manage data and files is known as a data-base management system (DBMS). DBMS packages for microcomputers have become quite important, since they enable nonprogrammers to process and manage data without writing computer programs.

DBMS packages for the microcomputer environment range widely in capabilities. A simple, file-oriented package allows nonprogrammer users to develop mailing lists and keep track of records. A more complex, data-oriented package allows users to build multiple files to desired specifications, keep the files up-to-date, sort data elements quickly within the files, summarize values of data elements, and construct special reports according to desired formats.

Currently popular data-base management software packages include Access (from Microsoft Corp.), an object-oriented package; Oracle (from Oracle Corp.); Dbase (from Borland International Corp.), and Paradox (from Borland International Corp.). Each of these packages, store data in tables in accordance with the relational model.

Various periodicals (e.g., PC Week, PC Magazine, Byte, and Computer Shopper) provide evaluations of data-base management software packages. In addition, evaluative articles appear in these periodicals on a regular basis.

EXPERT SYSTEMS SOFTWARE

Popular *expert systems software* include Level-5 (from Information Builders, Inc.), VP-Expert (from WordTech Systems, Inc.), Personal Consultant (from Texas Instruments, Inc.), Visual Expert (from Softsell), and 1st Class Fusion (from 1st Class Expert Systems, Inc.). An expert system is a computer program that arrives at a decision by evaluating the answers to questions provided during a consultation. It fully supports the making of decisions by both nonmanagerial and managerial users that meet certain criteria. The nature, characteristics, advantages, limitations, and applications of expert systems in accounting, tax, and auditing are more thoroughly explored in Chapter 16.

NEURAL NETWORK SOFTWARE

Popular *neural network software* packages include Model-Quest (from AbTech Corp.), Brainmaker (from California Scientific Software), and Neural Works Professional (from NeuralWare, Inc.). Conventional manual or statistical approaches to uncovering patterns in data relationships may not discover obscure but meaningful patterns in data. Neural network software can be used to find these significant patterns and test the relevancy of the relationships. Neural networks are well suited for applications in detecting credit card fraud and financial statement fraud, in financial analysis, in predicting bankruptcy, and in predicting which investments to buy and/or sell. Differences between expert systems and neural networks and their applications in accounting are examined in Chapter 16.

WORDPROCESSING SOFTWARE

Wordprocessing software packages are among the most frequently used microcomputer software. *Wordprocessing* is the preparation of letters and other textual materials. Wordprocessing provides the ability to draft the text on a video screen and to edit and format the text easily and quickly. It stores the results on a diskette or hard disk, from which the results may be printed as many times as desired. Currently available wordprocessing systems include WordPerfect (from Novell, Inc.), Word (from Microsoft Corp.), Professional Write Plus (from Software Publishing Corp.), and Word Pro (from Novell, Inc.). Wordprocessing packages enable users to check documents for misspelled words and to use a thesaurus to find synonyms. A word can be highlighted and a list of words similar in meaning will be displayed, enabling the user to select an alternate word that improves readability.

OTHER PACKAGES

A large selection of optional *utility software packages* help users to perform a variety of tasks, facilitating the operation of the microcomputer. Figure B-8 shows seven categories, specific examples of utility packages, and main uses of the utilities found in a particular category. *Desktop publishing packages*, such as Pagemaker (from Aldus Corp.), Corel Draw (from Corel Corp.), and Ventura Publisher (from Corel Corp.), enable users to format and print professional-quality newsletters and other textual materials. This type of software is particularly useful for projects that emphasize visuals such as pictures and graphs in color. Its use is also necessary when sophisticated typographical control and features such as registration and crop marks are involved. One feature that facilitates the use of desktop publishing packages, as well as other types of microcomputer software packages, is known as split-screening or windowing. Windows are areas of a video display screen that are devoted to separate views. In the case of desktop publishing systems these views may be different documents, pages, or columns under development.

A *graphics system* displays financial and other information in graphical forms. It involves a wedding of microcomputer hardware and software. Graphics are best displayed on special graphics terminals or on color microcomputers containing graphics cards. Alternatively, graphics displays may be transformed into hard-copy graphs by means of plotters, certain types of printers (e.g., laser, color ink-jet, dot matrix), or film-recording devices. Graphics software packages are needed to transform tabular data into such graphical forms as pie charts, bar graphs, line graphs, and flowcharts. Examples of microcomputer-based graphics packages are Harvard Graphics (from Software Publishing Corp.), Freelance and Powerpoint (both from Microsoft Corp.), 3-D Graphics (from Intex Solutions, Inc.), and PCcrayon (from PCsoftware). Two major types of graphics packages are available. *Presentation graphics* generate high-quality graphs to be used in presentations and publications. The graphs are generally developed by transforming tabular data into the graphical forms. Often they appear in color and some present three-dimensional views. *Freehand graphics* allow users to draw or "paint" pictures or graphs by means of light pens. These packages are pixel oriented, in that the user can manipulate images bit by bit.

A *multimedia package* is an extension of desktop publishing and graphics software. In essence, it enables users to combine and present text, graphics, animation, and audio via a video display system. Images as well as text can be stored on magnetic or optical disks and retrieved for display as needed. For instance, J. C. Penney stores the pages of its merchandise catalog, including pictures, which are retrieved by marketing and merchandising employees to aid in the publishing process.

Category and Examples	Uses
Access and Data Security Watchdog On-Guard	Provides access and security to data stored on hard disks.
Data Protection and Recovery Norton Utilities PC Tools	Collection of programs that can recover erased files, identify problems with computer hardware, recover from an accidental format of a hard or floppy disk, and repair defective disks.
Disk Compression Stacker SuperStor	Doubles the storage capacity of hard disks.
File Managers and Disk Organizers Windows DOS Norton Desktop Xtree	Runs concurrently with DOS and/or Windows 95 to manage disks. Enables users to easily rename, sort, copy, format, erase, and view files, without having to memorize DOS commands.
Memory Managers Qemm 386Max	Increases the amount of DOS free memory by relocating some programs into high memory.
Software Backup Norton Backup Fastback Plus	Provides fast backup of hard disk files to floppy disks.
Virus Protection Norton Antivirus Central Point Anti-VIrus Viruscan	Prevents viruses from writing onto hard or floppy disks. Protects and removes numerous viruses.

FIGURE B-8 Common categories, examples, and uses of IBM compatible microcomputer utility software packages.

Even more software packages are available for use by firms. *Time-management packages* allow using firms to record the hours worked by employees and other data concerning their activities. *Electronic calendars* enable employees to keep track of appointments, meetings, and other events. *Electronic mail* software transmits written messages via data communications networks to recipients who have electronic storage "mailboxes." *Voice mail* software transmits spoken messages to the telephones of recipients, assuming that the telephones serve as terminals of a data communications network. *Videotext* software transmits data or images (e.g., documents, pictures, graphics) interactively to receiving points, which may be microcomputers, television sets, or telephones. Firms can also receive data and images from other firms or from outside services, such as Dow Jones.

Integrated software packages do not fit into a single application category. Instead, they combine two or more functions and provide facilitating interfaces among them. Thus users can easily switch from one application to another. Also, data can easily be transferred from one application to another. For instance, packages such as Microsoft Office and Framework combine an electronic spreadsheet, a DBMS, a graphics package, and a word-processing package. The disadvantage exhibited by these integrated packages is that each function tends to have less power and flexibility than higher quality packages that focus on a single function.

REFERENCES

CHAPTER 1

BEDFORD, NORTON. "Future Accounting Education: Preparing for the Expanding Profession." *Issues in Accounting Education* (Spring 1996), pp. 168–195.

CASTELLANO, F. JOSEPH, ROEBM, A. HARPER, and HUGHES, T. DONALD. "The Deming Philosophy." CMA *Magazine* (February 1995), pp. 25–28.

ELLIOTT, ROBERT K. "The Third Wave Breaks on the Shores of Accounting." *Accounting Horizons* (December 1991), pp. 61–85.

FRIEDLANDER, PHILIP. "Developing IS Professionals." *Information Systems Management* (Summer 1995), pp. 79–80.

JENSEN, DANIEL L., ed. *Information Systems in Accounting Education*. Columbus: Ohio State University, 1985.

JOSEPH, GILBERT W. "Why Study Accounting Information Systems?" *Journal of Systems Management* (September 1987), pp. 24–26.

KEEGAN, DANIEL P., and PORTIK, STEPHEN W. "Accounting Will Survive the Coming Century, Won't It?" *Management Accounting* (December 1995), pp. 24–29.

MOCK, THEODORE J. "Report of the AAA Committee on Contemporary Approaches to Teaching Accounting Information Systems." *Journal of Information Systems* (Spring 1987), pp. 127–156.

PORTER, M. E., and MILLAR, V. E. "How Information Gives You Competitive Advantage." *Harvard Business Review* (July-August 1985), pp. 149–160.

RUSSELL, GRANT. "The Ethical Dilemma at Northlake." CMA *Magazine* (March 1993), pp. 13–15.

ZAHRA, A. SHAKER, NASH, SARAH, and BICKFORD, J. DEBORAH. "Transforming Technological Pioneering Into Competitive Advantage." *Academy of Management Executive* (Vol. 9, No. 1, (1995), pp. 17–30.

CHAPTER 2

DAVEPORT, H. THOMAS, and BEERS, C. MICHAEL. "Managing Information About Processes." *Journal of Management Information Systems* (Summer 1995), pp. 57–80.

DELANY, ED. "Strategy Consultants—Do They Add Value?" *Long Range Planning* (December 1995), pp. 99–106.

DRUCKER, PETER F. "The Coming of the New Organization." *Harvard Business Review* (January-February 1988), pp. 45–53.

DRUCKER, PETER F. "The Information Executives Truly Need." *Harvard Business Review* (January-February 1995), pp. 54–62.

LEIFER, RICHARD. "Matching Computer-Based Information Systems with Organizational Structures." MIS *Quarterly* (March 1988), pp. 63–73.

LIN, W. THOMAS, and HARPER, WILLIAM. "A Decision-Oriented Management Accounting Information System." *Cost and Management* (November-December 1981), pp. 32–36.

PREECE, STEPHEN, FLEISHER, CRAIG, and TOCCACELLI, JAMES. "Building a Reputation Along the Value Chain at Levi Strauss." *Long Range Planning* (December 1995), pp. 88–98.

CHAPTER 3

ADELMAN, SID, and ECIMOVIC, DUSAN. "Assessing New Technologies." *Internal Auditor* (June 1994), pp. 46–49.

Advanced Technology Supplement, Module 13. Systems Auditability and Control Report. Altamonte Springs, Fla.: The Institute of Internal Auditors Research Foundation, June 1994, Chapters 2, 3, and 5.

"Annual Report on Information Technology." *Business Week* (June 26, 1995), pp. 85–94.

BERSON, ALEX. *Client/Server Architecture*. New York: McGraw-Hill, 1992, Chapters 1–6.

BORTHICK, A. FAYE, and ROTH, HAROLD P. "Understanding Client/Server Computing." *Management Accounting* (August 1994), pp. 36–41.

BURCH, JOHN G. *Cost and Management Accounting: A Modern Approach*. St. Paul, Minn.: West Publishing Company, 1994, Chapters 1–3.

CERULLO, MICHAEL J., and CERULLO, VIRGINIA. "Key Information Technologies Relevant to Auditors." *Internal Auditing* (Fall 1992), pp. 59–70.

Emerging Technologies, Module 11. Systems Auditability and Control Report. Altamonte Springs, Fla.: The Institute of Internal Auditors Research Foundation, June 1994, Chapters 1–6.

HOFFMAN, GERALD M. *The Technology Payoff*. Burr Ridge, Ill.: Irwin Professional Publishing, 1994, Chapters 1–3.

HOLLANDER, ANITA SAWYER, DENNA, ERIC L., and CHERRINGTON, J. OWEN. *Accounting, Information Technology, and Business Solutions*. Chicago, Ill.: Richard D. Irwin, 1996.

LAUDON, KENNETH C., and LAUDON, JANE PRICE. *Management Information Systems*, 3rd ed. New York: Macmillan Publishing Company, 1994, Chapters 1, 6, and 9–10.

ORFALI, ROBERT, HARKEY, DAN, and EDWARDS, JERI. *Essential Client/Server Survival Guide*. New York: Van Nostrand Reinhold, 1994, Chapters 1–4.

TAYLOR, DAVID A. *Business Engineering with Object Technology*. New York: John Wiley and Sons, Inc., 1995, Chapters 1–3.

WARREN, J. DONALD, JR., EDELSON, LYNN W., and PARKER, XENIA LEY. *Handbook of IT Auditing*. 1996 ed. Boston: Warren, Gorham, and Lamont, Chapters A1–A2.

CHAPTER 4

BURCH, JOHN G. *Systems Analysis, Design, and Implementation*. Boston, Mass.: Boyd and Fraser Publishing Company, 1992, Chapter 2.

FITZGERALD, JERRY. "Data Flow Diagrams for Auditors: Part One." EDPACS (October 1987), pp. 1–11.

GIBSON, MICHAEL L., and HUGHES, CARY T. *Systems Analysis and Design*. Boston, Mass.: Boyd and Fraser Publishing Company, 1994, Chapters 2 and 5.

SUMMER, MARY, and RYAN, TERENCE. "The Impact of CASE: Can It Achieve Critical Success Factors?" *Journal of Systems Management* (June 1994), pp. 16–21.

The Visible Analyst Workbench for Windows: Tutorial on Structured Methods and the Repository. Waltham, Mass.: Visible Systems Corporation, 1994, Tutorials 1–7.

CHAPTER 5

BAKER, M. WILLIAM. "Shedding The Bean Counter Image." *Management Accounting* (October 1994), pp. 29–31.

BOER, GERMAIN. *Classifying and Coding for Accounting Operations*. Montvale, N.J.: National Association of Accountants, 1987.

COLE, JR., C. RAYMOND, and HALES, LEE H., "Automation" *Management Accounting* (January 1992), pp. 39–43.

DAVIS, LEILA. "On-Line Applications Grow Up." *Datamation* (January 1, 1990), pp. 61–63.

HOFMAN, J. DEBRA, and ROCKART, F. JOHN. "Application Templates: Faster, Better, and Cheaper Systems." *Sloan Management Review* (Fall 1994), pp. 49–59.

KUMAR, VIJAY. "Current Trends in Transaction Processing Systems." *Journal of Systems Management* (January 1990), pp. 33–37.

CHAPTER 6

ARMITAGE, HOWARD, and McCARTHY, WILLIAM E. "Decision Support Using Entity-Relationship Modeling." *Journal of Accounting and EDP* (Fall 1987), pp. 12–19.

ELLINGEN, C. DANA. "Database Design." *Database* (February 1991), pp. 90–93.

ELMASRI, RAMEZ, and NAVATHE, SHAMKANT B. *Fundamentals of Database Systems.* Redwood City, Calif.: Benjamin/Cummings, 1989.

GAYDASCH JR., ALEXANDER. *Effective Database Management.* Englewood Cliffs, N.J.: Prentice-Hall, 1988.

GOSLING, D. H. "Data Architecture: A Blueprint for Managing Your Business." *CMA Magazine* (October 1993), pp. 17–23.

HEINTZ, TIMOTHY J. "Object-oriented Databases and Their Impact on Future Business Database Applications." *Information and Management* (1991), pp. 95–103.

HOVEN, JOHN VAN DEN. "Data Base Management." *Information Systems Management* (Summer 1995), pp. 69–72.

LOEFFEN, DOROTHY. "The Data Warehouse." *CMA Magazine* (November 1995), pp. 16–17.

MEADOR, JO GUASASCO. "Data Bases That Put the Business First." *Financial & Accounting Systems* (Fall 1990), pp. 34–40.

NORMAN, RONALD J. "Object-Oriented Systems Analysis: A Methodology for the 1990s." *Journal of Systems Management* (July 1991), pp. 32–34.

RADDING, ALAN. "Building a Better Warehouse." *Info World* (November 20, 1995), pp. 57–62.

RAM, SUDHA. "Intelligent Database Design Using the Unifying Semantic Model." *Information and Management* (1995), pp. 191–206.

REUBER, A. REBECCA, and LEPAGE, MARY T. "From Data Modeling to Management Decisions." *Financial and Accounting Systems* (Summer 1990), pp. 5–10.

TOMAN, H. GREGORY. "The Amazing Data Connection." *Journal of Accountancy* (May 1994), pp. 63–68.

WALTZ, J. TIMOTHY, YEN, DAVID (CHI-CHUNG), and LEE, SOOUN. "Object-oriented Database Systems: An Implementation Plan." *Industrial Management & Data Systems*, vol. 95 no. 6 (1995), pp. 8–17.

CHAPTER 7

ALBRECHT, W. STEVE, McDERMOTT, EDWIN A., and WILLIAMS, TIMOTHY L. "Reducing the Cost of Fraud." *Internal Auditor* (February 1994), pp. 28–34.

American Institute of Certified Public Accountants. SAS No. 78: *Consideration of Internal Control in a Financial Statement Audit: An Amendment to SAS No. 55*, 1995.

American Institute of Certified Public Accountants. SAS No. 55, *Consideration of the Internal Control Structure in a Financial Statement Audit*, 1988.

CERULLO, MICHAEL J., and McDUFFIE, R. STEVE. "Anticipating Accounting's Natural Disasters." *Financial and Accounting Systems* (Fall 1991), pp. 32–35.

CERULLO, MICHAEL J., and SHELTON, F. A. "EDP Security and Controls Justification." *Internal Auditing* (Fall 1989), pp. 13–30.

CERULLO, MICHAEL J., McDUFFIE, R. STEVE, and SMITH, L. MURPHY. "Planning for Disaster." *CPA Journal* (June 1994), pp. 34–38.

Committee of Sponsoring Organizations of the Treadway Commission. *Internal Control: Integrated Framework*, Vol. 1 of 2. New York: Coopers & Lybrand, 1994.

RATLIFF, RICHARD L., and BECKSTEAD, STEPHEN M. "How World Class Management is Changing Internal Auditing." *Internal Auditor* (December 1994), pp. 38–44.

WARREN, J. DONALD, JR., EDELSON, LYNN W., and PARKER, XENIA LEY. *Handbook of IT Auditing*, 1996 ed. Boston, Mass.: Warren, Gorham, and Lamont, Chapters A3 and D1.

WELLS, JOSEPH T., et al. *Fraud Examiners Manual*, 2nd ed. Austin, Texas: Association of Certified Fraud Examiners, 1993, Volume 1, Sections 1 and 2.

CHAPTER 8

CERULLO, MICHAEL J. "Application Controls for Computer-Based Systems." *Cost and Management* (June 1982), pp. 18–23.

GELINAS, ULRIC J., JR. and ORAM, ALLAN E. *Accounting Information Systems*, 3rd. ed. Cincinnati, Ohio: South-Western Publishing Company, 1996, Chapters 6 and 7.

MOSCOVE, STEPHEN A., SIMPKIN, MARK G., and BAGRANOFF, NANCY A. *Accounting Information Systems: Concepts and Practice for Effective Decision Making*, 5th ed. New York: John Wiley, 1997, Chapters 8 and 9.

ROMNEY, MARSHALL B., STEINBART, PAUL JOHN, and CUSHING, BARRY E. *Accounting Information Systems*, 7th ed. Reading, Mass.: Addison-Wesley, 1997, Chapters 13 and 14.

WU, FREDERICK H., and SAFRAN, RONALD A. "A Practical Approach for Evaluating EDP Controls." *CPA Journal* (October 1987), pp. 58–69.

CHAPTER 9

MENKUS, BELDEN. "Introduction to Computer Security." *Computers and Security* (November 1992), pp. 121–127.

ROMNEY, MARSHALL B., STEINBART, PAUL JOHN, and CUSHING, BARRY E. *Accounting Information Systems*, 7th ed. Reading, Mass.: Addison-Wesley, 1997, Chapter 14.

WOLFE, CHRISTOPHER, and WIGGINS, CASPER E. "Internal Control in the Microcomputer Environment." *Internal Auditor* (December 1986), pp. 54–60.

CHAPTER 10

American Institute of Certified Public Accountants. SAS No. 78: *Consideration of Internal Control in a Financial Statement Audit: An Amendment to SAS No. 55*, 1995.

American Institute of Certified Public Accountants. Statement on Auditing Standards No. 48: *The Effects of Computer Processing on the Examination of Financial Statements*. New York: AICPA, 1984.

ARENS, ALVIN A., and LOEBBECKE, JAMES K. *Auditing: An Integrated Approach*, 6th ed. Englewood Cliffs, N.J.: Prentice Hall, 1997, Chapters 9 and 10.

BRAITHWAITE, TIMOTHY. "A Methodology for CASE, Security, and Control." *EDPACS* (August 1990), pp. 1–12.

CERULLO, MICHAEL J., and CORLESS, JOHN C. "Auditing Computer Systems." *CPA Journal* (September 1984), pp. 18, 20, 22, 24, 26–28, 30, 33.

GROOMER, S. MICHAEL, and MURTHY, UDAY S. "Continuous Auditing of Database Applications: An Embedded Audit Module Approach." *Journal of Information Systems* (Spring 1989), pp. 53–69.

MOELLER, ROBERT R. *Modern Computer Security, Audit and Control*. New York: John Wiley, 1988.

WARREN, J. DONALD, JR., EDELSON, LYNN W., and PARKER, XENIA LEY. *Handbook of IT Auditing*, 1996 ed. Boston: Warren, Gorham, and Lamont, Chapter A5 and Part E.

WEBER, RON. *EDP Auditing: Conceptual Foundations and Practice*, 2nd ed. New York: McGraw-Hill, 1988.

CHAPTER 11

BANT, JOHNSON. "Why Your Company Needs Three Accounting Systems." *Management Accounting* (September 1984), pp. 39–46.

GELINAS, ULRIC J., JR., and ORAM, ALLAN E. *Accounting Information Systems*, 3rd. ed. Cincinnati, Ohio: South-Western Publishing Co., 1996, Chapter 13.

HALL, JAMES A. *Accounting Information Systems*. St. Paul, Minn.: West Publishing Co., 1995, Chapter 7.

CHAPTER 12

CORCORAN, T. CATE. "New Order-Entry System Tames a Bear of a Sales Process." *Info World* (November 20, 1995), p. 72.

CUSHING, BARRY E., and ROMNEY, MARSHALL B. *Accounting Information Systems*, 7th ed. Reading, Mass.: Addison-Wesley, 1997, Chapter 17.

GELINAS, ULRIC J., JR., and ORAM, ALLAN E. *Accounting Information Systems*, 3rd ed. Cincinnati, Ohio: South-Western Publishing Co., 1996, Chapters 8 and 9.

HALL, JAMES A. *Accounting Information Systems*. St. Paul, Minn.: West Publishing Co., 1995, Chapter 4.

CHAPTER 13

CUSHING, BARRY E., and ROMNEY, MARSHALL B. *Accounting Information Systems*, 7th ed. Reading, Mass.: Addison-Wesley, 1997, Chapter 18.

GELINAS, ULRIC J., JR., and ORAM, ALLAN E. *Accounting Information Systems*, 3rd. ed. Cincinnati, Ohio: South-Western Publishing, 1996, Chapters 10 and 11.

HALL, JAMES A. *Accounting Information Systems*. St. Paul, Minn.: West Publishing, 1995, Chapter 5.

LEE, L. HAU., and BILLINGTON, COREY. "The Evolution of Supply-Chain-Management Models and Practice at Hewlett-Packard." *Interfaces* (September-October 1995), pp. 42–63.

PAVLINKO, JEAN L. "Paperless Payables at Lord." *Management Accounting* (July 1993), pp. 32–34.

CHAPTER 14

BAKER, M. WILLIAM, FRY, D. TIMOTHY, and KARWAN, KIRK. "The Rise and Fall of Time-Based Manufacturing." *Management Accounting* (June 1994). pp. 56–59.

CUSHING, BARRY E., and ROMNEY, MARSHALL B. *Accounting Information Systems*, 7th ed. Reading, Mass.: Addison-Wesley, 1997, Chapters 18 and 19.

GELINAS, ULRIC J., JR., and ORAM, ALLAN E. *Accounting Information Systems*, 3rd ed. Cincinnati, Ohio: South-Western Publishing, 1996, Chapters 11, 12, and 14.

GRANT, M. ROBERT, KRISHNAN, R., SHANI, B. ABRAHAM, and BAER, RON. "Appropriate Manufacturing Technology: A Strategic Approach." *Sloan Management Review* (Fall 1991), pp. 43–54.

HALL, JAMES A. *Accounting Information Systems*. St. Paul, Minn.: West Publishing, 1995, Chapters 6 and 7.

HANKS, F. GEORGE, FREID, A. MICHAEL, and HUBER, JACK. "Shifting Gears at Borg-Warner Automotive." *Management Accounting* (February 1994), pp. 25–29.

JURIS, ROBBIN. "Managing Human Resources On-line." *Computer Decisions* (January 14, 1986), pp. 44–52.

Payroll/Personnel. Atlanta, Georgia: Management Science America, 1989.

WALKER, B. KENTON, and ZINSLI, TERRY. "The Coors Shenandoah Experience." *Management Accounting* (March 1993), pp. 37–41.

CHAPTER 15

BELASCO, JAMES A., and STAYER, RALPH C. *Flight of the Buffalo*. New York: Warner Books, 1993.

BURCH, JOHN G. *Cost and Management Accounting: A Modern Approach*. Saint Paul, Minn.: West Publishing, 1994, Chapters 1–3.

CERULLO, MICHAEL J., and CERULLO, VIRGINIA. "Information for Managerial Decision Making." *International Journal of Management* (September 1987), pp. 467–476.

DRUCKER, PETER F. "The Information Executives Truly Need." *Harvard Business Review* (January-February 1995), pp. 54–62.

ENZWEILER, ALBERT J. "Improving the Financial Reporting Process." *Management Accounting* (February 1995), pp. 40–43.

HACKATHORN, RICHARD. "Data Warehousing Energizes Your Enterprise." *Datamation* (February 1, 1995), pp. 38–42.

HOFFMAN, GERALD M. *The Technology Payoff*. Burr Ridge, Ill.: Irwin Professional Publishing, 1994.

Improving Business Reporting: A Customer Focus. New York: American Institute of Certified Public Accountants, 1994.

KAPLAN, ROBERT S., and NORTON, DAVID P. "The Balanced Scorecard—Measures That Drive Performance." *Harvard Business Review* (January-February 1992), pp. 71–79.

ROBBINS, STEPHEN P., and COULTER, MARY. *Management*, 5th ed. Englewood Cliffs, N.J.: Prentice-Hall, 1996, Chapters 6 and 15.

ROTHSTEIN, LAWRENCE R. "The Empowerment Effort That Came Undone." *Harvard Business Review* (January-February 1995), pp. 20–31.

WALLACE, PEGGY. "Building a Data Warehouse." *Infoworld* (February 21, 1994), pp. 56–57.

WALLACE, PEGGY. "Data Warehouse Options Abound." *Infoworld* (March 14, 1994), pp. 49–50.

CHAPTER 16

ALAVI, MARYAM. "Group Decision Support Systems." *Journal of Information Systems Management* (Summer 1991), pp. 36–41.

Audit and Security Issues with Expert Systems. New York: American Institute of Certified Public Accountants, 1992.

BROWN, CAROL E., COAKLEY, JAMES, and PHILLIPS, MARY ELLEN. "Neural Networks Enter the World of Management Accounting." *Management Accounting* (May 1995), pp. 51–57.

CERULLO, MICHAEL J., and GREER, OLEN. "Using

Decision Support in the Basic Accounting Information Systems Course." *Journal of Accounting and Computers* (Fall 1992), pp. 27–47.

HARRIS, JEANNE. "Is Your EIS too Stupid to be Useful?" *Chief Information Officer Journal* (May-June 1993), pp. 52–56.

LAUDON, KENNETH C., and LAUDON, JANE PRICE. *Management Information Systems*, 3d ed. New York: Macmillan, 1994, Chapter 17.

PORT, OTIS. "Computers That Think Are Almost Here." *Business Week* (July 17, 1995), pp. 68–71, 73.

SMITH, L. MURPHY, McDUFFIE, R. STEVEN, and FLORY, STEVEN M. "A GAAP-Based Expert Prototype for Business Combinations." *Financial and Accounting Systems* (Summer 1991), pp. 17–22.

VIJAYARAMAN, BINDIGANAVALE S., and OSYK, BARBARA A. "An Empirical Study on the Usage of Intelligent Technologies." *Journal of Computer Information Systems* (Fall 1994), pp. 35–40.

WARMOUTH, MICHAEL T., and YEN, DAVID. "A Detailed Analysis of Intelligent Executive Information Systems." *Journal of Computer Information Systems* (Spring 1995), pp. 99–111.

YELLEN, RICHARD E. "Introducing Group Decision Support Software (GDSS) in an Organization." *Journal of Systems Management* (October 1993), pp. 6–8.

CHAPTER 17

Advanced Technology Forum: Audit, Control, and Security Issues in Networks. Cleveland, Ohio: Ernst and Young, 1993.

CERULLO, MICHAEL J. "Internal Controls for Stand-alone Microcomputers." *EDP Auditor Journal* (October 1991), pp. 59–67.

COLBERG, THOMAS P., et al. *The Price Waterhouse EDI Handbook*. New York: John Wiley and Sons, 1995.

CORRIGON, PATRICK H. *LAN Disaster Prevention and Recovery*. Englewood Cliffs, N.J.: PTR Prentice-Hall, 1994.

KANTER, ANDREW. "Making On-Line Services Work for You." *PC Magazine* (March 15, 1994), pp. 111–114, 116–118, 120, 122, 126, 128, 143–144, 148–150, 153–155, 158.

McCUSKER, TOM. "How to Get More Value from EDI." *Datamation* (May 1, 1994), pp. 56, 58, 60.

ORFALI, ROBERT, HARKEY, DAN, and EDWARDS, JERI. *Essential Client/Server Survival Guide*. New York: Van Nostrand Reinhold, 1994.

RENAUD, PAUL E. *Introduction to Client/Server Systems*. New York: John Wiley and Sons, 1993.

SCHULTHEIS, ROBERT A., and BOCK, DOUGLAS B. "Benefits and Barriers to Client/Server Computing." *Journal of Systems Management* (February 1994), pp. 12–15, 39–41.

SHELDON, TOM. LAN Times Encyclopedia of Networking. Berkeley, Calif.: Osborne/McGraw-Hill, 1994.

SOLOMON, ELINOR HARRIS. "Electronic Funds Transfer: Challenges for the Computer Age." Bankers Magazine (January-February 1993), pp. 69–77.

CHAPTER 18

BALLOU, H. ROGER. "Reengineering at American Express: The Travel Services Group's Work in Progress." Interfaces (May-June 1995), pp. 22–29.

BORTHICK, FAYE, and ROTH, P. HAROLD. "Accounting for Time: Reengineering Business Processes to Improve Responsiveness." Cost and Management (Fall 1993), pp. 4–14.

BOYNTON, ANDREW C., and ZMUD, ROBERT W. "Information Technology Planning in the 1990's: Directions for Practice and Research." MIS Quarterly (March 1987), pp. 59–72.

CARON, J. RAYMOND, JARVENPAA, L. SIRKKA, and STODDARD, B. DONNA. "Business Reengineering at CIGNA Corporation: Experiences and Lessons Learned from the First Five Years." MIS Quarterly (September 1994), pp. 233–249.

CURLE, HOWARD A., JR. "Supporting Strategic Objectives: Building a Corporate Information Technology Architecture." Information Strategy: The Executive's Journal (Fall 1993), pp. 5–12.

DAVENPORT, THOMAS H. "Saving IT's Soul: Human-Centered Information Management." Harvard Business Review (March-April 1994), pp. 119–131.

DAVENPORT, THOMAS H., HAMMER, MICHAEL, and METSISTO, TAUNO J. "How Executives Can Shape Their Company's Information Systems." Harvard Business Review (March-April 1989), pp. 130–134.

FRAMEL, E. JOHN. "Information Value Management." Journal of Systems Management (December 1993), pp. 16–41.

GOTLIEB, LEO. "The Evolution of the Information Systems Function." CMA Magazine (November 1995), pp. 23–26.

HOPLIN, P. HERMAN. "Integrating Advanced Information Systems and Technology in Future Organizations." Industrial Management & Data Systems, vol. 94, no. 8 (1994), pp. 17–20.

KAUTZ, KARLHEINZ, KUHLENKAMP, KARIN, and ZULLIGHOVEN, HEINZ. "What Is Prototyping?" Information Technology & People (1992), pp. 89–95.

KING, V.R., and SETHI, V. "Developing Transnational Information Systems: A Case Study." OMEGA, vol. 21, no. 1 (1993), pp. 53–59.

LEDERER, ALBERT L., and MENDELOW, AUBREY L. "Information Systems Planning: Top Management Takes Control." Business Horizons (May-June 1988), pp. 73–78.

LEDERER, ALBERT L., and GARDINER, VERONICA. "Meeting Tomorrow's Business Demands Through Strategic Information Systems Planning." Information Strategy: The Executive's Journal (Summer 1992), pp. 20–27.

LEIFER, RICHARD. "Matching Computer-Based Information Systems with Organizational Structures." MIS Quarterly (March 1988), pp. 63–73.

LEVINSON, NANETTE S. "Interorganizational Information Systems: New Approaches to Global Economic Development." Information & Management (1994), pp. 257–263.

MORISON, ROBERT F. "Beyond Centralized and Decentralized IS: Virtual Centralization." Information Strategy: The Executive's Journal (Spring 1991), pp. 5–11.

REUBER, A. REBECCA. "Planning for Information Resource Management." CMA Magazine (April 1991), pp. 17–21.

TENG, T. C. JAMES, GROVER, VARUN, and FIEDLER, D. KIRK. "Business Process Reengineering: Charting a Strategic Path for the Information Age." California Management Review (Spring 1994), pp. 9–31.

CHAPTER 19

BENTO, M. ALBERTO. "Systems Analysis: A Decision Approach." Information and Management (1994), pp. 185–194.

BURCH, JOHN. "The Case for Object-Oriented Financial Systems Development." Financial and Accounting Systems (Summer 1991), pp. 35–40.

BURCH, JOHN. "To Predict Business Contribution, Look at Systems Design Quality." Information Strategy: The Executive's Journal (Spring 1992), pp. 17–22.

CERULLO, MICHAEL J. "Designing Accounting Information Systems." Management Accounting (June 1985), pp. 37–42.

DEAN, ROBERT L., and JOHNSON, DALE. "Designing an Information System for a Health Care Organization." Journal of Systems Management (January 1991), pp. 23–31.

GARCEAU, LINDA, JANCURA, ELISE, and KNEISS, JOHN. "Object-Oriented Analysis and Design: A New Approach to Systems Development." Journal of Systems Management (January 1993), pp. 25–32.

GAVURIN, STUART. "Where Does Prototyping Fit in IS Development?" Journal of Systems Management (February 1991), pp. 13–17.

GRANT, DON. "CASE Tools: In the Systems Development Environment." CMA Magazine (October 1993), pp. 25–28.

KERR, JAMES M. "The Information Engineering

Paradigm." Journal of Systems Management (April 1991), pp. 32–36.

LIN, CHANG-YANG. "Systems Development with Application Generators: An End User Perspective." Journal of Systems Management (April 1990), pp. 32–36.

CHAPTER 20

AMEEN, A. DAVID. "Evaluating Alternative Computer Acquisition Strategies." ASM/Journal of Systems Management (September 1990), pp. 15–20.

BACON, C. JAMES. "The Use of Decision Criteria in Selecting Information Systems/Technology Investments." MIS Quarterly (September 1992), pp. 335–353.

CARTER, K. WILLIAM. "To Invest in New Technology or Not? New Tools for Making the Decision." Journal of Accountancy (May 1992), pp. 58–64.

DRTINA, E. RALPH. "The Outsourcing Decision." Management Accounting (March 1994), pp. 56–62.

GIBSON, MICHAEL L., SYNDER, CHARLES A., and CARR, HOUSTON H. "CASE's Place in Financial Systems Management." Financial and Accounting Systems (Spring 1991), pp. 15–20.

HEIDKAMP, M. MARTHA. "Reaping the Benefits of Financial EDI." Management Accounting (May 1991), pp. 39–43.

KESNER, M. RICHARD, and PALMISANO, F. PETER. "Transforming the Global Organization: Integrating the Business, People, and Information Technology at Camp Dresser & McKee, Inc." Information Strategy: The Executive's Journal (Winter 1996), pp. 6–15.

LACITY, C. MARY, and HIRSCHHEIM, RUDY. "The Information Systems Outsourcing Bandwagon." Sloan Management Review (Fall 1993), pp. 73–86.

LEDERER, ALBERT L., MIRANI, RAJESH, NEO, BOON SIONG, POLLARD, CAROL, PRASAD, JAYESH, and RAMAMURTHY, K. "Information System Cost Estimating: A Management Perspective." MIS Quarterly (June 1990), pp. 159–176.

LUTCHEN, MARK D. "How to Implement Technology Solutions Worldwide." Price Waterhouse Review (1992), pp. 7–13.

POLAKOFF, C. JOEL. "Computer Integrated Manufacturing: A New Look at Cost Justifications." Journal of Accountancy (March 1990), pp. 24–29.

ROBINSON, A. MICHAEL. "Decentralize and Outsource: Dial's Approach to MIS Improvement." Management Accounting (September 1991), pp. 27–31.

SOUZA, EILEEN. "The Impact of CASE on Software Development." Journal of Information Systems Management (Winter 1991), pp. 17–24.

PREFACE

Accountants interact with the accounting information systems of business and government enterprises as users, evaluators, and designers. They *use* accounting information systems when retrieving data to prepare reports for managers and financial statements for external parties. They *evaluate* accounting information systems when reviewing internal controls during audits. They *design* accounting information systems when devising charts of accounts or proposing the addition of specific controls within transaction processing systems.

This textbook is intended for undergraduate accounting majors (as well as graduate business students) who will soon be assuming the responsibilities of professional accountants. Most of these students are currently majoring in accounting, but some may be majoring in computer information systems or another business discipline and minoring in accounting. Presumably students using this textbook will have completed courses in (1) elementary financial and managerial accounting and (2) fundamentals of computer hardware, software, and applications.

The purpose of this extensively modified textbook is to provide students with a body of knowledge that includes the following:

1. A broad awareness of the concepts of accounting information systems, especially those pertaining to systems, information, managerial decision making, control, accounting models, and information technology.

2. A familiarity with the basic components of accounting information systems, such as inputs, outputs, processing procedures, data bases, and controls.

3. An introduction to a wide range of systems analysis and design techniques, with particular attention to system flowcharts, data-flow diagrams, and data modeling.

4. An understanding of the steps involved in comprehensive systems development, as well as the ability to apply the appropriate techniques in conducting a reasonably complex systems development project.

5. A selective exposure to emerging and exciting developments in information technology, including client/server systems, decision support systems, expert systems, neural networks, electronic data interchange networks, Internet, computer integrated manufacturing, structured systems development tools (including CASE tools), and computerized audit-assist software tools.

In compiling the body of knowledge from which the above-mentioned results will accrue, we have drawn heavily upon such authoritative sources as the 1986 Report of the American Accounting Association Committee on Contemporary Approaches to Teaching Accounting Information Systems and the Committee of Sponsoring Organizations of the Treadway Commission.

ORGANIZATION

The third edition is organized into five parts. The parts are weighted to emphasize several major issues, including key roles of accountants, uses of information, risk exposures and accounting controls, transaction processing systems and cycles, and the systems development life cycle.

Part I introduces the basic concepts pertaining to accounting information systems, computer technology, data and information processing, and data bases.

Part II surveys risk exposures, the internal control structure and related control systems, general and application controls for accounting information systems, plus computer-based auditing approaches and techniques.

Part III examines basic transaction processing systems that are incorporated within the general ledger and financial reporting, revenue, expenditure, and product conversion cycles.

Part IV introduces decision-making concepts, managerial reporting, and decision-oriented information systems for management, as well as computer-based wide-area and local-area networks.

Part V traces the phases that make up the systems development life cycle, i.e., planning, analysis, design, selection, and implementation.

The final section provides two cases that are suitable for assignment as student system term projects.

KEY CHANGES TO THE THIRD EDITION

This edition reflects several significant changes.

1. Topics concerning documentation techniques and data bases have been significantly expanded, with greater attention given to data-flow diagrams and entity-relationship diagrams and their development.

2. Recommendations made by the Committee of Sponsoring Organizations of the Treadway Commission have been given prominent attention; general controls, application controls, and security measures have received greater coverage; and computer-based auditing techniques, such as test decks and generalized audit software packages, have been expanded.

3. Emerging developments involving expert systems, neural networks, electronic data interchange networks, and client/server systems have been discussed and illustrated more extensively.

4. Systems development life cycle chapters have been placed in the last section of the textbook, so that the array of system components and architectures may be introduced without interruption. However, the three chapters composing this part are self-contained and may be assigned at any point in the course. The first chapter within this part, Chapter 18, includes expanded coverage of the varied approaches to systems development.

5. Many of the important concepts discussed throughout the book are illustrated by two hypothetical but typical firms—Infoage, Inc., and Ann Strong, CPA/CMA.

6. More illustrations of applications in real-world firms have been sprinkled throughout the chapters. These vignettes, introduced by the word *Spotlighting*, appear in shaded boxes.

7. Many new questions and problems have been added to the chapters. The questions and problems cover most of the key concepts introduced within the chapters. Some of the later problems in the chapters may be used for group assignments both within and outside of the classroom.

8. Requirements for two continuing cases—a small business students select and Datacruncher Office Equipment, Inc.—that appear at the end of most chapters have been revised and expanded.

CONTINUING CHAPTER FEATURES

Each chapter includes the following learning aids:

1. A brief introductory statement of objectives and a concluding summary.

2. A variety of figures and diagrams to clarify the concepts and techniques described.

3. A comprehensive set of review and discussion questions.

4. One or two problems that review the important points covered in the chapter. Throughout several chapters the review problems are based on continuing cases involving the Campus Bookstore and Precise Manufacturing Company.

5. Numerous problems that may be assigned as homework or discussed in class. Certain problems, indicated by a computer icon, may be assigned to be solved by using microcomputers.

6. A list of suggested readings, arranged by chapter, is included at the end of the textbook.

SUPPLEMENTS

We are indebted to Professor Vasant Raval of Creighton University for preparing the supplemental materials. The following supplements to the third edition are available from the publisher:

● A Solutions Manual, prepared by Vasant Raval, contains suggested answers to discussion questions; solutions to the problems; and solutions to the comprehensive cases.

● An Instructor's Resource Guide, by Vasant Raval, which includes information about the end-of-chapter problem material; guidance on selecting and assigning problems; lecture outlines and tools; and a comprehensive test bank (also available computerized).

● AIS PowerPoint Presentations, prepared by Marianne Bradford of the University of Mississippi. These presentations are divided into twelve key topics of AIS, and are designed to support and guide lectures and presentations.

It is our intention to also make portions of the supplements available via the Internet.
   For the growing number of instructors who wish to include significant hands-on assignments, two useful supplements are now available:

1. LOTUS 1-2-3® *and Database Software Applied to* AIS *Cases* by W. Ken Harmon and James P. Borden. New York: John Wiley, 1992.

2. *Projects for Accounting Systems*, second edition, by Robert M. Harper, Jr. Fresno, Calif.: BIP, 1996.

ACKNOWLEDGMENTS

We wish to acknowledge the very helpful suggestions provided by the following reviewers: James Borden, Villanova University; Eleanor Fillebrown, University of New Haven; Paul Goldwater, University of Central Florida; David Olsen, University of Akron; William Sailors, Western Washington University; Andrew Schiff, University of Baltimore; and Ram Sriram, Georgia State University.

We have appreciated the continuing support of Karen Hawkins, our editor, and her assistant, Cecilia Anderson. During the production process Charlotte Hyland, Ingrid Mount, and Anna Melhorn have been conscientious in assisting us to develop a final product with which we can be pleased; in order to meet tight deadlines they have employed gentle but effective prodding when necessary. Susan Elbe and Wendy Goldner have been helpful in focusing our attention on the needs of the students who will encounter the textbook in future classes.

Four professional accounting groups have graciously permitted the use of problem materials from past professional examinations: the American Institute of Certified Public Accountants, the Institute of Management Accounting of the National Association of Accountants, the Institute of Internal Auditors, and the Society of Management Accountants of Canada.

In particular, we wish to thank our wives, Sharon and Jenny, who have provided gracious support and to whom we dedicate this edition.

Finally, we want to express gratitude to all other individuals and organizations who have been of help—some in very significant ways. Responsibility for any errors and omissions that may appear, however, must rest with us alone.

Joseph W. Wilkinson
Tempe, Arizona

Michael J. Cerullo
Springfield, Missouri

CONTENTS

CHAPTER

1

THE STUDY OF ACCOUNTING

INFORMATION SYSTEMS

THE LEARNING OBJECTIVES FOR THIS CHAPTER ARE TO ENABLE YOU TO:

1. Appreciate the importance of information and accounting to organizations of all types, as well as the impact of information technology.

2. Understand the nature and purposes of an accounting information system, its relationship to other information systems within an organization, and the variety of users of its outputs.

3. Describe the major characteristics and functions of an accounting information system.

4. Recognize the roles of accountants with respect to accounting information systems and the importance of ethics to professional accountants.

INTRODUCTION

You have been involved with accounting information systems most of your life. When you bought candy as a child or textbooks as a college student, you entered into accounting transactions. If you sold lemonade in an earlier time, or sold back your textbooks in a more recent time, you engaged in other types of accounting transactions. If you have received a bill from a department store or a monthly statement from a credit card organization, you have received **accounting information.**

Thus all of us have our very own *accounting information systems* (AISs). We may be involved with them only to the extent described above. On the other hand, we may employ them to a greater degree and in a more formal manner. For instance, we could keep careful records and prepare financial statements. All transactions might be recorded on columnar paper (which we call our accounting books). From these recorded transactions we might draw up statements monthly (or quarterly or yearly) that (1) compare our revenues against our expenses for the period and (2) reflect the status of what we own and what we owe as of the end of the period. (As you know, these statements are called income statements and balance sheets, i.e., statements of financial position). If we are interested in planning ahead, we might also prepare budgets. To maintain control over the accuracy of our bank accounts, we might prepare bank reconciliations when the bank mails us our monthly bank statements.

You may have encountered firsthand other AISs than your own. Maybe you have worked during past summers for a business organization or enterprise (which we will henceforth call a *firm*), or maybe you are currently working part-time for a firm. If so, you have likely seen a more formal and complicated AIS than the one that you may maintain for yourself. As you probably suspect, all organizations—not-for-profit institutions as well as profit-oriented business firms—must maintain AISs. Our focus in this textbook will be on the AISs that pertain to business firms. Nevertheless, we should remember that an AIS is needed by every entity. As we will see, all AISs (ranging from the most simple to the most complex) exhibit the same set of essential features.

REASONS FOR STUDYING ACCOUNTING INFORMATION SYSTEMS

As an accountant, you will be closely involved with AISs during your entire career. Not only will you be a *user* of these AISs but you may also have more demanding roles. Perhaps you will be expected to evaluate AISs an an *auditor*. Furthermore, you may possibly become a *developer* of such systems, either in a full-time position or as an occasional member of systems development teams.

The next reason for their study is that modern-day AISs have become increasingly difficult to understand. Almost all business firms have microcomputers and larger computers as integral parts of their information systems. Users, auditors, and developers of these systems must be aware of numerous aspects of computer technology. As information has become more vital, the management of data and the preparation of needed reports have become more complex and varied functions. You need to acquire the knowledge and skills that will enable you to apply computer-based AISs in effectively achieving these functions. Otherwise, you are likely to be much less productive in employing your accounting knowledge and skills.

Modern-day information systems are also rapidly changing and improving. They are implementing concepts from areas of study such as systems and information theory. They are incorporating new developments from fields like communications and control. You should be aware of these developments and others that are just emerging, since they will be increasingly common in the future. Furthermore, with adequate knowledge and skills concerning computer-based information systems, you should be in a position to take advantage of the opportuntities that they offer.

Still another reason for studying accounting information systems is that they are intimately involved in all other accounting courses. For instance, in financial accounting courses you make journal entries based on transaction data. In the AIS course you learn where the data come from and what steps are involved in processing the data to generate needed information. Furthermore, you discover what resources are needed to produce information that is timely, accurate, cost-effective, and in a form that is most appropriate for the users.

THE IMPORTANCE OF INFORMATION TO MODERN ORGANIZATIONS

Information has been critical to individuals and organizations throughout recorded history. Since the start of the agricultural and industrial ages, part of the needed information has been provided by accounting systems. During the agricultural age, farmers used rudimentary accounting systems to determine their costs of producing crops for sale. By comparing these costs against the revenues received in the marketplace, they ascertained how much they profited or lost from each season's crop. During the industrial age, corporations manufactured or purchased goods for sale. Although the processes they performed and the types of costs they incurred differed significantly from those encountered by farmers, they likewise compared their expenses against their revenues to measure each period's profit or loss. Although their accounting systems were somewhat more sophisticated, most of the systems employed during the industrial age were still manually based and historically oriented.

We have now entered the *information age*. Modern organizations, such as business firms, function in a vastly altered environment. They must treat information as a *valued resource* in order to prosper. Much more information must be generated than the historical profit or loss incurred during each accounting period. A steady stream of information is needed to enable firms to make sound planning decisions and to control their operations. Firms that use information effectively can take advantage of their opportunities and thus gain ground on their competitors.

TRENDS IN INFORMATION AND INFORMATION SYSTEMS

Recent years have witnessed rapid changes and developments with respect to information systems and the information that they deliver. Perhaps the most important trends concern the focus on strategic information, information technology, information infusion and services, service-oriented industries and organizations, globalization, user involvement, and information-oriented professionalism.

The Focus on Strategic Information   Information for a firm ranges from current bank balances and daily purchases to last year's sales and next year's expected profit. Much of the information arises from routine and day-to-day events, as we noted in the opening paragraph, and is called accounting information. However, some of the most important information needed by a firm is strategic in nature, since it relates to the vital long-term well-being of the firm. Strategic information includes nonaccounting as well as accounting information. Examples of information useful for strategic purposes include shares of the market for products sold by the firm, likely new products to be marketed, products of competitors and prices they charge, expected increases in numbers of likely customers, and expected long-term interest rates. In order to develop strategies for survival, firms are finding it necessary to devote greater attention to the acquisition of such information. That is, firms are learning that information can be an important *strategic resource* as well as a necessity for day-to-day operations. This realization is affecting the development of the information systems used to collect and process the needed strategic information.

Information Technology   The information age has been accompanied by **information technology,** the application of computers and related technologies to the generation and communication of information. Information technology has enabled firms to automate their processing of data and information, so that most processing is performed without the direct involvement of humans. Automated or computer-based information systems can perform a variety of functions extremely quickly and accurately. Moreover, each processing step can be performed at a much lower cost by computers than by humans. These benefits have been realized by firms since the mid-1950s. Almost every firm, regardless of size, has one or more computers today.

In recent years information technology has expanded its impact. Very large computers with complex processing features have been built and often connected in wide-spread networks. In some cases these computer networks link together the computers of two or more firms. New applications have been fostered by information technology, including automated offices, flexible manufacturing operations, computer-assisted audits, and decision support systems.

Information technology is increasingly important in strategic terms.* Firms are effectively employing information technology to change the ways they operate,

*This discussion is based on Michael E. Porter and Victor E. Millar, "How Information Gives You Competitive Advantage," *Harvard Business Review* (July-August 1985), pp. 149–160.

SPOTLIGHTING

INFORMATION TECHNOLOGY USED BY AN INTERNATIONAL FIRM
at Microtronics Systems*

Information technology is being incorporated by firms both large and small and by firms in most countries around the world. Microtronics Systems is a small business firm having 65 employees and based in Singapore, the capital of one of the "four tigers of the Pacific Rim." It designs and manufactures made-to-order electronic industrial control systems and automation products for local and foreign client firms. It also distributes these systems and components through offices in Malaysia and Thailand and agents in other parts of the world.

For several years Microtronics used microcom-

puter-based accounting software to aid in processing orders and preparing reports. With sales growing by 50 percent per year, however, it was necessary to review its automation needs. With the assistance of a consultant and the Singapore-sponsored Small Enterprise Computerization Program, several design proposals were evaluated. The system that best suited the growing needs was a minicomputer software package that integrates manufacturing and accounting activities and generates useful management information. After carefully defining the requirements of the system, a project team modified, installed, and tested the software over the period of a year. Management is encouraged that the new system will significantly improve efficiency and will aid decision making.

*Guy Grant Gable and K. S. Raman, "Government Initiatives for IT Adoption in Small Businesses." *International Information Systems* (January 1992), pp. 90–91.

---

enabling them to gain advantages over their competitors. They do so by applying the technology to their "value chains," the stream of activities by which values are created in the products or services they offer. For instance, firms are able to reduce their costs throughout the value chain, to differentiate their products or services from those of competitors, or to develop new products or services. In some cases information technology changes the structures of entire industries or spawns completely new business activities. Automated teller machine networks, increasingly used by banks, are dependent on information technology.

Information Infusion and Services Although the application of information technology is vital to the health of most modern firms, knowledge concerning new methods as well as technologies is also important. Progressive firms continuously monitor emerging developments. By doing so they can evaluate the usefulness of new methods and technologies and employ those that promise strategic advantage.* During the 1990s numerous firms have incorporated such methods as total quality management, just-in-time (JIT) inventory management, and computer-integrated manufacturing. They have installed such technologies as electronic data interchange (paperless) networks, electronic mail (E-mail) systems, and multimedia presentation systems.

The information age has also fostered expanded information services. For instance, many new publications have been introduced during the 1990s that pertain to particular industries, interests, and methodologies. The information systems field alone has witnessed dozens of new publications, such as *Information Strategy: The Executive's Journal*, which is referenced in a nearby footnote. In particular, a number of new information services are being provided by computer on-line electronic

---

*John R. Dixon, "Information Infusion Is Strategic Management," *Information Strategy: The Executive's Journal* (Fall 1991), pp. 16–21.

networks, such as the *Dow-Jones News/Retrieval Service* that offers financial information. Some of the electronic services can be personalized to the interests and needs of individual managers.

Service-Oriented Industries and Organizations During most of the years of this century, merchandising and manufacturing firms received the greatest attention. Now service-oriented firms have become dominant in the U.S. economy. The sector that provides services ranges from financial institutions to health maintenance organizations, from telecommunications companies to universities. Service-oriented firms tend to be labor-intensive, to have few if any inventories, and to focus on service outputs. Thus the information systems that they need differ significantly from those needed by product-oriented firms.

Globalization of Organizations and Services An increasing number of firms have become huge diversified multinational organizations that face global competition. Not only must such firms deal with more complex logistical problems, but they must accommodate widely diverse consumer demands, local customs, and legal obligations. Rapid and reliable communications networks are needed that span the globe and reach into hundreds of countries. Of course, the huge multinational firms are not alone in being affected by globalization. This internationalism trend has increased competitive pressures on firms of all sizes; thus, it has compelled firms to expand their computer networks and information systems to improve their competitive postures.

User Involvement As the number of computers has grown in many firms, managers and others have discovered new needs that they desire the computer systems to meet. These increased demands have often caused backlogs, since the computer information systems professionals have been overwhelmed and not able to respond promptly. Thus managers and other users within firms have had to learn to fulfill their own information needs. This information fulfillment has come through *end-user computing*. The end-user computing approach has been aided by "user-friendly" computer software packages, such as Excel and Paradox.

Information-Oriented Professionals Various professionally trained persons from several fields have focused on providing information to users. Those of primary interest to us are managerial and systems accountants and auditors. Others that work closely with the information systems of firms include computer information system analysts and industrial engineers. One mark of professionalism is the increasing number of professional certifications, such as the Certified Management Accountant, Certified Information Systems Auditor, and Certified Computing Professional.

WHAT IS AN ACCOUNTING INFORMATION SYSTEM?

All of the trends mentioned above have a bearing on accounting information systems. Although the linkages and implications will only become clear as we move through successive chapters, we can begin our journey by looking separately at the terms "accounting," "information," and "system." Then we can compile a definition and set of purposes for the AIS.

ACCOUNTING

As you have learned from previous accounting courses, **accounting** has several facets. First, it is an *information system* in its own right. That is, it employs various systemic

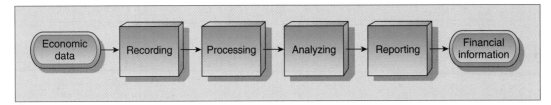

FIGURE 1-1   Operations within the accounting activity.

operations to generate relevant information. Among the operations that it encompasses are (1) recording economic data, (2) processing and analyzing these data, and (3) presenting quantitative information in financial terms. Figure 1-1 portrays this set of operations within the accounting activity. Second, accounting is the "language of business": it provides the means by which the key affairs of a business firm are expressed and summarized. Finally, accounting may be viewed as financial information needed for the overall functioning of an entity (such as a business firm). Certain key financial information, for instance, reflects the results of operations during accounting periods and the status of assets and equities at the ends of accounting periods. A variety of users, of whom some are within the entity and some reside outside the entity, employ this information for various purposes.

INFORMATION

In the broadest sense, **information** is intelligence that is meaningful and useful to persons for whom it is intended. Information has value to firms and their managers, as we have noted, because it is necessary for making sound decisions and inducing desired actions. Much of the information needed by firms is accounting information, since it is particularly useful in meeting these needs. Accounting information is the output of AISs and is financially oriented. Among the many examples of accounting information are income statements provided to a firm's managers and bills sent to a firm's customers. Information in the income statements may lead the managers to make decisions concerning which expenses to reduce. Bills mailed to customers should induce them to pay the owed amounts by the stated due dates.

Usually information is derived from the processing of data. **Data** are the raw facts and figures and even symbols that together form the inputs to an information system. Figure 1-2 shows the relationship of data and information by means of an I-P-O diagram. That is, data become information through three stages. In the input stage (I), data of concern to a firm arise from various sources, such as external events. For instance, a sale may create such data as the quantity of a product sold and the

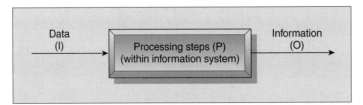

FIGURE 1-2   Information derived from data.

unit price of the product. Data may also arise from operations inside the firm. For example, raw materials may be issued into production, and employees may expend hours of work on production jobs. Still other data may be created by managers, as when they establish standard costs for elements of production. When the data inputs are entered into an information system, such as the AIS of a firm, the processing stage (P) takes place. Thus, the quantity of product sold will be multiplied by the unit price to determine the extended amount of a sale. The processed data in the output stage (O) become information outputs, which are then communicated to the appropriate users. The processed data pertaining to a sale, formally reflected on a bill or invoice, become information to the firm's accounts receivable department and also to the customer involved in the sale.

SYSTEM

A **system** is a unified group of interacting parts that function together to achieve objectives and purposes. The world is brimming with systems, those that are natural and those made by humans. The Mississippi River and the solar system are natural systems, whereas a clock and a freeway network are human-made systems. Each system has a boundary that separates it from its environment. Most systems are open, in that they accept inputs from their environments and provide outputs to the environments. Most are also tangible, in that they employ physical resources such as materials and personnel. Figure 1-3 presents a generalized view of a tangible system.

Because systems are complex and numerous in the business as well as natural world, we will revisit them later in this chapter and in Chapter 2. In particular, we will be concerned with the fact that a system contains interdependent parts called subsystems.

THE COMPOSITE NATURE OF AN ACCOUNTING INFORMATION SYSTEM

The preceding descriptions of accounting, information, and system enable us to develop a workable definition of an AIS. An **accounting information system** is a unified structure within an entity, such as a business firm, that employs physical *resources and*

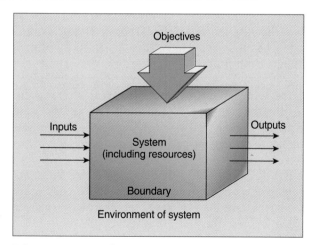

FIGURE 1-3   Basic characteristics of a tangible open system.

other components to *transform economic data into accounting information*, with the *objective* of satisfying the information needs of a variety of *users*.

FEATURES OF TYPICAL ACCOUNTING INFORMATION SYSTEMS

The above definition of an AIS, like all definitions, is rather vague and lifeless. To bring the concept of an AIS to life, we will describe the features of AISs in two business firms. Figure 1-4 provides brief backgrounds of these hypothetical, but typical, firms with the names Infoage, Inc., and Ann Strong, CPA/CMA. We have selected two organizations in order to illustrate a major point: that while the features of AISs assume somewhat differing appearances from organization to organization, all AISs have common characteristics. The illustrations—which build upon the prior discussions of information, data, and systems—emphasize the purposes and users of information, the functions performed during transformation, and the components/resources employed.

INFOAGE, INC.

Infoage, Inc., is a Seattle corporation with two revenue activities. Its principal activity is selling microcomputers and accessories to small businesses and individuals. It also provides services related to the selection and installation of microcomputer systems. George Freeman is the president, Diane Varney is the treasurer and controller. Mike Barker is the marketing manager, Jack Dyson is the inventory manager, Jane Thomson is the systems services manager, and Ralph Cannon is the office manager. Roughly five dozen employees support these managers at the main office. In addition, Infoage has two retail sales outlets in the area, each headed by an outlet manager who supervises eight employees. Sales are made on credit or for cash. Services are billed at the end of an engagement or periodically during extensive engagements. Each of the managers in the corporation has assigned responsibilities that involve planning, control, and directing operations.

The AIS/MIS maintained by Infoage is computerized, both in the main office and in the outlets. Ralph Cannon is responsible for its development and operation. While the computers in the main office and in the warehouse are linked together into a peer-to-peer network, they are not electronically connected to the microcomputers in the outlets. Daily operations, such as purchasing merchandise for resale, are performed according to prescribed procedures. Most of the records and files are stored in the computer system, although historical records and correspondence are kept in file cabinets. A variety of computer-generated outputs are produced by the AIS/MIS, including sales and payroll reports.

ANN STRONG, CPA/CMA

Ann Strong is the single proprietor of a small public accounting firm. After six years of experience with a Big-Six public accounting firm, she opened a three-room office in Des Moines, Iowa, to provide specialized services. Primarily she offers consulting services involving financial analysis and systems analysis. However, to gain new business she also performs tax, audit, and write-up work on occasion. Although Ann is the only professional in her small firm, she does employ a secretary (Janet Li) and a bookkeeper (Tad Malcolm).

The AIS used by Ann is relatively simple. One microcomputer located in the workroom is used by all three persons. In addition, Ann takes a portable notebook computer with her when she goes on engagements to clients. Also, Ann and Janet keep desk drawers reserved for bills, checks received, correspondence, and copies of other documents and reports. A file cabinet contains the records of clients, suppliers, taxes, and so on. Some outputs, such as bills to clients and financial statements, are prepared on the microcomputer. Other outputs (e.g., paychecks) are prepared by hand.

FIGURE 1-4 Two illustrative business firms and their AISs.

PURPOSES AND USERS OF INFORMATION

The primary objective of any AIS, as the definition notes, is to provide accounting information to a wide variety of users. The users may be **internal users,** such as managers, or **external users,** such as customers. Within this broad objective are three purposes. Each purpose is closely interwined with the users of the AIS, so both should be viewed together.

First Purpose: To Support the Day-to-Day Operations In order to operate from day-to-day, a firm conducts a number of business events called **transactions.** Infoage, Inc., is involved daily in receiving computers and accessories at its warehouse next to the main office and in selling the merchandise. Ann Strong makes appointments with clients and performs paid services for the clients. **Accounting transactions** are events or transactions that represent exchanges having economic value. Of the example transactions noted above, the sale of merchandise and the payment for service performed are accounting transactions. Accounting transactions are formally captured by the AIS for processing. Most nonaccounting transactions, such as receiving merchandise, lead to accounting transactions. Thus, they are also captured and processed by the AIS. Other nonaccounting transactions and nontransactional data are handled by a related information system within the firm, as we will see.

Transaction processing consists of processing accounting and nonaccounting transactions through key accounting records by means of procedures. As you have learned in earlier accounting courses, accounting records consist primarily of journals and ledgers; however, they also include source documents, registers, reference tables, and various other records. Transaction processing is fairly standardized among firms for like transactions, such as sales. For instance, the billing of customers by Infoage and Ann Strong will have similarities, since similar accounting records will be employed. On the other hand, the details of the procedures usually differ, depending on the system design. Also, while basic types of accounting transactions tend to be reasonably common among firms, there are differences. Infoage requires the basic set of accounting transactions typical to most merchandising firms: sales of products and services, purchases of merchandise and supplies and services, receipts and disbursements of cash, and payroll disbursements to employees. Ann Strong needs all these transactions except those involving products.

Transactions are processed by means of **transaction processing systems (TPSs),** which are subsystems of the AIS. Each TPS encompasses the steps for a particular type of transaction. In some cases a TPS groups the steps into *applications*. Thus the TPS involving sales transactions for Infoage is subdivided into order taking, billing, and accounts receivable. Being subsystems, the TPSs of a firm are closely interrelated. Figure 1-5 shows the relationships among the TPSs used by Infoage's AIS.

Users of outputs from transaction processing systems range from managers and employees within the affected firms to a variety of parties external to the firm. With respect to Infoage, the external users and the information output documents or reports they receive include:

- Customers who receive sales invoices or bills.
- Suppliers who receive purchase orders and then (upon payment) checks.
- Employees who receive paychecks.
- Banks that receive (on request for bank loans) financial statements.

Second Purpose: To Support Decision Making by Internal Decision Makers An equally important purpose is to provide information for decision making. Decisions must be made pertaining to planning and controlling a firm's operations. This second purpose

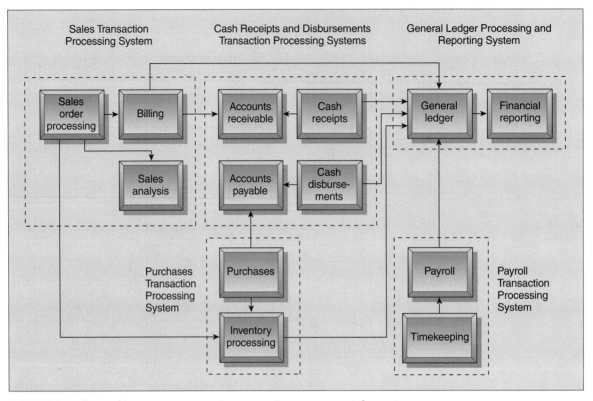

FIGURE 1-5   Relationships among transaction processing systems at Infoage, Inc.

is aided by activities that may be broadly labeled as **information processing.** For instance, Ann Strong uses her AIS for a vital information processing task: projecting expected revenues for the coming year. In doing so she employs a forecasting method (a type of decision model). With the expected revenue amount in hand, she can do her necessary planning. She might, for example, need to hire another employee to handle some of the added workload. Through the transactions it processes, the AIS usually provides some of the information needed in such decision making. In Ann's decision situation, for example, the AIS provided the trend of revenues for past years and the current level of revenues. Other data needed in the decision-making process—usually nonfinancial quantitative and qualitative data—must be acquired from nontransactional sources. Figure 1-6 diagrams the relationship between information processing and transaction processing.

The managers of a firm are the primary decision makers who use the outputs from information processing. Infoage therefore contains several decision makers, in contrast to Ann Strong's firm. In sizable firms certain key employees may also be involved in making decisions. For instance, a cost accountant may need a report concerning the actual costs of producing a new product to aid her in recommending control-type decisions to a production manager.

Third Purpose: To Fulfill Obligations Relating to Stewardship   Every firm must fulfill its legal obligations. Certain important obligations consist of providing mandatory information to users who are external to the firm. Firms that are incorporated and publicly owned have greater obligations, as do firms in regulated industries such as public utilities. They may be required to provide information to *stakeholders*—persons

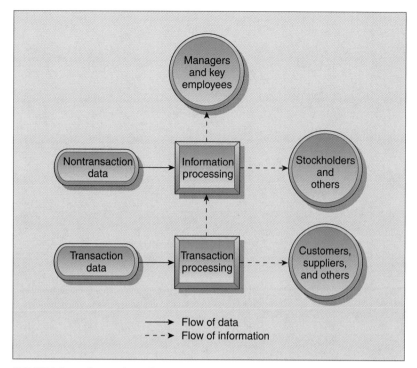

FIGURE 1-6   Relationship of transaction processing to information processing.

having a stake in the welfare of a firm. Stakeholders include owners, creditors, labor unions, regulatory commissions, financial analysts, industry associations, and even the general public. While not a large firm, Infoage has owners called stockholders, and thus it periodically issues financial statements to them. It also must provide payroll tax withholding reports and income tax withholding reports to the appropriate government agencies. Even a firm as small as Ann Strong's must provide reports concerning payroll taxes, and as a single proprietor, she must submit tax returns to the Internal Revenue Service.

FUNCTIONS IN TRANSFORMING DATA INTO INFORMATION

Earlier we observed data being transformed into information during input, processing, and output stages. An effective AIS performs several key functions throughout these three stages. Figure 1-7 shows these functions to be data collection, data processing, data management, data control (including security), and information generation. As the figure indicates, these functions are akin to interrelated subsystems. Each function can in turn be subdivided into several steps.

Data Collection   The **data collection** function (performed during the input stage) involves steps such as capturing the transaction data, recording the data onto forms, and validating and editing the data to assure their accuracy and completeness. If the data elements are quantitative, they may also need to be measured before recording. If the transactions are captured at a point remote to the point where they are to be processed, the data will need to be transmitted.

Consider sales transactions made by Infoage. When a customer places an order, the facts concerning the credit sale are captured by a salesperson at one of the

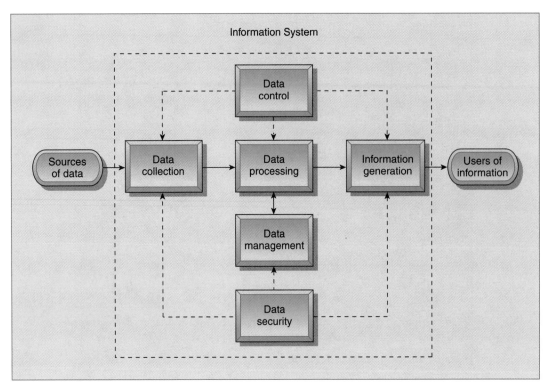

FIGURE 1-7 Functions of an AIS (Adapted with permission from "Report of the Committee on Accounting and Information Systems," in *Committee Reports: Supplement to Vol. XLVI of the Accounting Review* [Evanston, Ill.: American Accounting Association, 1971], p. 290).

outlets. The salesperson records on a sales order form the pertinent data, such as the customer's name and the desired products and quantities. Then the salesperson transmits the order to the main office by fax machine. There a salesclerk validates the name and address of the customer by reference to a file.

Data Processing   The **data processing function** (performed during the processing stage) involves steps like the following:

- Classifying, or assigning collected data to preestablished categories.
- Transcribing, or copying/reproducing the data onto another document or medium.
- Sorting, or arranging data elements according to one or more characteristics.
- Batching, or gathering together groups of transactions of a similar nature.
- Merging, or combining two or more batches or files of data.
- Calculating, or performing addition, subtraction, multiplication, and division operations.
- Summarizing, or aggregating quantitative data elements.
- Comparing, or examining items from separate batches or files to find those that match or to determine how they differ.

For example, a clerk at Infoage begins the processing of sales transactions by listing product codes next to descriptions in order to classify the product data. When the products have been received by the customers, the key data are entered into the computer system. The computer system then performs the following processing steps for each sale, being guided by instructions called a **computer program:** The quantities sold are multiplied by the unit sales prices to calculate the amount owed by the customer for each product. The extended amounts are summed. The sales invoice is next formatted into a record within the computer system.

At the end of each day, the computer program batches the invoice records and sorts them by customer numbers. Then, it summarizes the quantities of each product sold and lists the totals on a sales recap record. Finally, the computer program compares today's totals with yesterday's totals and records each increase or decrease on an analysis record.

Data Management   The **data management** function consists of three steps: storing, updating, and retrieving. *Storing* involves placing data in repositories called files or data bases. Data must often be stored for future reference; also, data that have been processed into information may be held temporarily until needed by users. *Updating* involves adjusting stored data to reflect newly occurring events, operations, or decisions. *Retrieving* consists of accessing and extracting data, either for further processing or for reporting to users.

In the case of sales transactions at Infoage, a clerk stores data concerning new customers in records within the computer system. When sales have been made to customers, the customers' accounts in the stored records are updated. For instance, a computer program adds the amount of a sale (e.g., $100) to the previous balance in the customer's account (e.g., $900), thereby deriving the updated balance owed by the customer (e.g., $1000). At the end of each month, a clerk accesses all of the customer records in the computer system and retrieves the appropriate data to prepare needed information for managers.

Data Control   The **data control** function has two basic aims: (1) to safeguard and secure the firm's assets, including data, and (2) to ensure that the captured data are accurate and complete and processed correctly. A variety of techniques and procedures are employed in an effective AIS to maintain adequate control and security. One technique employed by Infoage is to validate input data by checking the sales and other transaction data against reference records stored in the computer system. Another technique is to require employees to enter passwords each time they turn on their microcomputers to begin processing for the day.

Information Generation   The **information generation** function includes such steps as interpreting, reporting, and communicating information. It supports the outputs from both transaction processing and information processing. For instance, sales invoices are printed by Infoage each day, together with sales summaries. In addition, each month a computer program prepares an aged accounts receivable report, which analyzes the customer account balances according to their overdue status, and sales analyses. The invoices are mailed to customers, while the other reports and analyses are communicated to the appropriate managers.

RESOURCES/COMPONENTS

Since an AIS is tangible, it requires physical resources and related components. We may classify these resources and components as processor, data base, procedures, and input/output devices. Control and security devices could also be included, but they have been discussed under the control function. Not included are the input data, output information, and users. These components meet at the boundary of the AIS, that is, they *interface* with the AIS.

Processor The physical means by which data are transformed may be called a *processor.* In Infoage the processing function is essentially represented by the computer system. In Ann Strong's firm more of the processing is performed manually by the secretary and bookkeeper, so they represent processors. Most firms today perform processing with a mixture of human and automated processors. We should note, however, that processors are not solely represented by computers. They often include such devices as calculators, typewriters, and cash registers.

Data Base Broadly speaking, the *data base* consists of all stored data. Ann Strong and Infoage are both typical, in that their data are stored partly in a computer system and partly in such storage devices as file cabinets and desk drawers. (We should note that in its narrow sense the term "data base" refers only to data stored in a computer system.)

Procedures Particular sequences of steps performed within one or more of an AIS's functions are known as **procedures.** They may be performed manually or by means of the instructions in computer programs, as we have seen.

Input/Output Devices Although the data and information are not resources to an AIS, the physical means of handling or storing them can be included. At Infoage the data are initially stored on paper forms or documents and then entered into the computer system via microcomputer keyboards. Similarly, outputs are printed on hard-copy forms by printers. For instance, paychecks are printed by Infoage on pre-numbered blank-form stocks. A variety of other devices are available, as described in Appendix A at the end of the book.

Miscellaneous Resources An AIS requires other resources that should be noted. For instance, many employees of a firm perform certain AIS functions, such as recording data. Fixed assets may be needed to house the system. Various supplies are needed, such as printer ribbons. Finally, funds must be budgeted in order to maintain and develop an AIS.

INFORMATION SYSTEMS WITHIN A FIRM

The AIS is not the only system within a firm that is concerned with data and information. In fact, the AIS is a subsystem of a broader information system that encompasses all information generating activities. Other component information systems include the management information system, decision support systems, expert systems, and executive information systems. In this section we shall survey these types of information systems, suggest relationships among them, and identify key subsystems.

While our discussion will be brief, much additional coverage will be given to the management information system as well as to the AIS in following chapters. Also, Chapter 16 is devoted to decision support systems, expert systems, and executive information systems.

MANAGEMENT INFORMATION SYSTEM

As the name implies, the **management information system (MIS)** serves the managers of the firm with their information needs. It is as important to a firm's well-being as the AIS.

Purpose and Scope   The sole purpose of an MIS is to aid the managers of a firm in making decisions related to their responsibilities. That is, the MIS provides information needed to plan and control the activities of the firm, ranging from organizing the firm's personnel and setting policies to taking corrective actions when raw materials are wasted. It spans all the managerial levels of a firm, ranging from the president to the lowest supervisor. The MIS employs all types of data, including nontransactional data; it disseminates nonfinancial as well as financial information.

MIS Subsystems   Like all systems, the MIS contains subsystems. Perhaps the most useful set of subsystems it incorporates are functional information systems. (Since subsystems have all the characteristics of systems, the terms are interchangeable.) Functional information systems are so-named because they support key organizational functions, to be discussed in Chapter 2. They interact with each other by passing data and information among themselves. While functional information systems vary among different types of firms, four found in a manufacturing firm pertain to marketing, finance, human resources, and production. Figure 1-8 lists examples of data captured by these subsystems and information provided to managers.

Relationships with Other Component Systems   The relationship between the MIS and the AIS is complex and somewhat controversial. Some view the AIS as being a subsystem of the MIS, since the data accepted by the MIS have a broader scope. On the other hand, the AIS serves a wider range of users. Through its **financial accounting subsystem,** the AIS serves external users not accommodated by the MIS. Also, the AIS serves managers through its **managerial accounting subsystem,** in part directly and in part by providing information to the functional information systems of the MIS. Thus, our view is that the MIS and AIS are overlapping systems, with each having assigned missions that are particular to it.

   The MIS also has relationships with the decision support systems, expert systems, and executive information systems to be discussed next. We may view these systems as being subsystems of the MIS, since it provides most of the information needed by these systems. Some of the information they need, however, may originate in the AIS and be passed through the MIS.

Function supported	Data	Information
Marketing	Sales, customer preferences, demographics, competitors' prices, market size	Sales analyses and forecasts
Finance	Cash balances, interest rates, credit markets, bank requirements	Cash-flow projections, payment analyses, accounts receivable aging analyses
Human resources (personnel)	Payroll totals, benefits lists, salary schedules, skill needs	Payroll analyses, personnel projections
Production	Raw materials levels, standard costs for materials and labor, production rules	Production schedules, materials requirements productivity levels, product cost analyses

FIGURE 1-8   Functional information subsystems within the MIS, together with typical data inputs and information outputs.

Figure 1-9 portrays the suggested relationships just described. As we can see, all of the component information systems communicate information directly to the managers of a firm, providing them with portions of their information needs.

Computerization of the **MIS**   Traditionally all information systems were **manual systems,** in that people performed the processing tasks. In most firms the AIS was the first component system to be automated, so that the processing was **computer-based**. Examples of computer-based transaction processing systems in the business world date from the 1950s. The second wave of automation has involved the information processing tasks performed by the MIS. Computerization of those tasks that provide decision-oriented information is still taking place in most firms. As we noted earlier, a recent trend has been toward providing more information to aid in making strategic decisions.

DECISION SUPPORT SYSTEMS

A **decision support system (DSS)** is a computer-based information system that aids managers in making ad hoc decisions that involve significant uncertainty. It allows

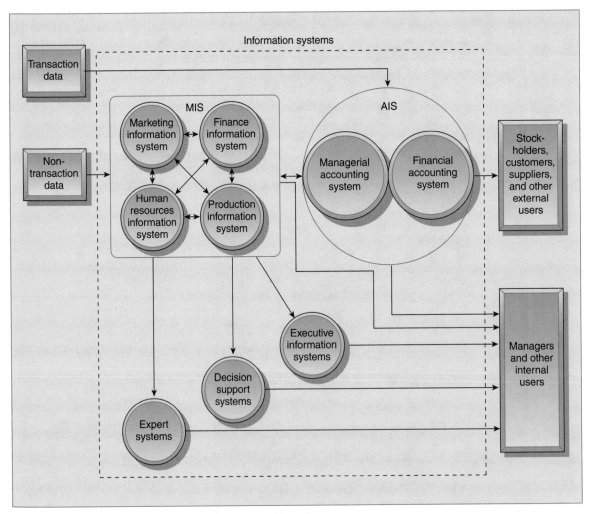

FIGURE 1-9   The component information systems within a firm.

SPOTLIGHTING

INFORMATION TECHNOLOGY THAT PROVIDES COMPETITIVE ADVANTAGE*
at American Airlines

A number of business firms have shown that information technology can be used effectively to obtain clear advantages over competitors. Well-publicized success stories include:

- American Airlines, whose SABRE reservation system transformed marketing and distribution practices in the airline industry.

- American Hospital Supply, whose ASAP order-entry and inventory-control system revolutionized the ordering patterns of hospitals.

- United Service Automobile Association, whose Automated Insurance Environment outperformed its insurance industry rivals in providing quality service at reduced costs.

- Mrs. Fields Cookies, whose Retail Operations Intelligence System enabled the firm to build and operate a nationwide chain of retail outlets that was more efficient than other food chains.

American Airlines' SABRE system offers perhaps the most interesting experience, partly because it began relatively early and has undergone several improvements. SABRE was introduced in 1963, at the dawn of computer networks. It started with a central computer, which was connected to a data base of airline flight records and to "dumb" terminals located in scattered airline reservation of-fices. In the first year it made 40 thousand reservations. The most significant improvement, made in 1976, was to install terminals also in the offices of travel agents. By 1990 the number of reservations had climbed to 45 million and the service had become worldwide. During a "fare war" as many as 1.5 million fares have been handled per day. Services other than airflight reservations have been added to the system. Now an airline passenger can also obtain tickets and boarding passes and reserve hotels and rental cars. Moreover, it has become, in effect, an electronic travel supermarket, since it links to other services such as Broadway shows and packaged tours. Because it quickly became the world's leading computerized reservations system, other airlines requested and were allowed to include their flights in the system.

As we can see, the SABRE system has [provided] and is providing a convenient and very welcome service to airline passengers. Consequently, American Airlines has gained several major benefits. First, the system has enabled the airline to increase its market share of passenger miles flown. Second, it generated handsome additional revenues by charging other airlines for the privilege of linking to the system. Third, it reduced overall reservations labor costs, since the travel agents performed the actual booking services. Fourth, the system provided a base of data that supports a variety of decisions—ranging from planning flights and scheduling flight crews to reordering spare parts and scheduling aircraft maintenance.

*Max D. Hopper, "Rattling SABRE—New Ways to Compete on Information." *Harvard Business Review* (May–June 1990), pp. 118–125.

---

the decision maker to perform manipulations with one or more decision models, using data that are mostly gathered by the MIS. DSSs may be subdivided into non-intelligent DSSs and intelligent DSSs. An intelligent DSS enables the decision maker to incorporate rules of thumb into decision models, thereby refining the decision process.

EXPERT SYSTEMS

An **expert system (ES)** is a knowledge-based and computer-based information system that fully supports the making of decisions. It employs specialized computer programs to process data and rules in order to produce clear-cut decisions affecting problem areas. These decisions—the output information—are provided directly to the users (usually managers) to execute. The decisions are usually sound, since the rules (stored in a knowledge base within the expert system) have been established by persons who are expert in the problem areas.

EXECUTIVE INFORMATION SYSTEMS

An **executive information system (EIS)** provides managers (i.e., executives) with information that is tailored to their needs and interests. Since an EIS is computer-based and interactive, the information is generally very timely. Managers for whom EISs are designed can easily access the information, analyze it in various ways, generate graphs, and perform other manipulations.

AISs AND THEIR SUBSYSTEMS

As Figure 1-9 shows, two key subsystems of an AIS are the financial and managerial accounting systems. They are discussed further when we consider the roles of accountants later in this chapter. Other sets of subsystems are the transaction processing systems shown in Figure 1-5 and the AIS functions shown in Figure 1-7. Still another useful set of subsystems are transaction cycles, which are discussed in Chapter 5. Typical transaction cycles are the revenue cycle, the expenditure cycle, the general ledger cycle, the resources-management cycle, and the production cycle.

OTHER INFORMATION SYSTEMS

Modern firms have incorporated various specialized information systems. Certain examples, such as point-of-sales systems and computer-integrated manufacturing systems, are related to particular types of industries. Other examples, such as automated offices, may be applied by firms of all types.

All of the information systems discussed thus far have been formal in nature, since they have been structured to accommodate specific tasks. We may also identify **informal information systems,** which exist in firms to satisfy informational needs not met by formal information systems. Information obtained by managers at conferences, through periodicals, and via telephone conversations represents typical gleanings of the informal information system.

CONCLUSION

Each of these types of information systems serves purposes that are similar yet different. Firms employ information systems as required to fulfill their total information needs. In a typical firm we will find an intermingling of the systems. Smaller firms are likely to emphasize the AIS, since they tend to be simpler, with the managers gathering more of their decision-making information informally. Medium-sized firms, being more complex and having more than one level of management, tend to require more formalized MISs as well as AISs. Large firms, being extremely complex and having several levels of management often scattered to numerous sites, tend to emphasize decision support and expert systems as well as MISs and AISs. Also, firms employ a mixture of computer-based and manual processing within their transaction and information processing activities. As a generalization, we may say that the medium and large firms emphasize computerization to a higher degree than small firms. However, most small firms have acquired at least one microcomputer. Figure 1-10

A SMALL CHURCH

The Peaceful Community Church uses simple single-entry transaction processing systems for handling its cash. All collections and disbursements are manually recorded on summary sheets. At the end of each quarter, a statement of cash receipts and disbursements is prepared by hand.

A SMALL LANDSCAPING SERVICE

Greenthumb Landscapers uses a manual double-entry transaction processing system for handling its sales and accounts receivable. All sales, which are on credit, are recorded on sales tickets. At the end of each month, the sales tickets are posted to individual customer account cards by a mechanized accounting machine. Any payments received during the month are also posted to the account cards in order to reflect the current outstanding balances. Then the account cards are photocopied and mailed as monthly statements to the customers. At the end of each quarter, a local public accountant prepares financial statements on the accrual basis for the firm.

A MEDIUM-SIZED MANUFACTURER

The Jiffy Manufacturing Company uses a minicomputer-based TPS to maintain its production job costs. Data concerning materials used and labor employed are entered into the minicomputer via terminals at various production floor workstations. These data are processed to yield the material and labor costs for each job in production; then the processing program computes and adds the related costs for overhead. Cost accounting statements are printed at the end of each day.

This same minicomputer is also used as the nucleus of the production information (processing) system. Various control and planning reports are prepared by the system for the production managers. For instance, data concerning actual job costs are compared with standard costs and presented in cost variance reports.

AN EDUCATIONAL INSTITUTION

Old Winsockie University has several computer systems. One mainframe computer is used to support academic research performed by faculty and graduate students, as well as assigned projects in computer science and engineering courses. A local-area network of microcomputers also supports the academic program. It enables numerous undergraduate students in a variety of courses across the campus to be introduced to computers and to learn a variety of software packages. Most of the accounting courses require "hands-on" assignments involving general ledger, spreadsheet, and data base packages.

A second mainframe computer is employed in administrative duties. In addition to basic transactions, such as purchases and payroll, it handles transactions that are unique to schools. For instance, students can register at terminal sites located around the campus and can check out books at the university library. The computer system prepares outputs related to these latter applications, such as course schedules for the registered students, class listings for the instructors, and overdue book notices.

The administrative computer is also used to aid university administrators in their planning responsibilities. For example, it stores a budget-modeling program and key planning data. The vice-presidents, deans, and department chairs can access this decision-support system in developing the most suitable operating budget plan for the coming year.

A NATIONAL CPA FIRM

CrackerJack, a large national public accounting firm, has a number of local offices across the country. Each office has microcomputers on the desks of the staff members, local partner, and managers. All of the hours worked by the staff and professional accountants are keyed into the microcomputers daily. At the end of each week a program prepares billable time summaries and paychecks. At the end of each month and quarter other programs prepare bills for clients, accrual-basis financial statements, and various analyses. The partner and managers use other computer programs to develop time schedules for the various accountants and to keep track of progress on the respective client engagements. Since their microcomputers are

FIGURE 1-10 A variety of information systems applications in organizations of varying sizes and types.

linked to the other offices and to the head office, they send and receive electronic mail from offices. In addition, they access public data bases to which the firm subscribes, such as the National Automated Accounting Research System (NAARS), which contains financial data concerning 4200 publicly traded firms.

Each professional accountant in CrackerJack, in addition, has his or her own microcomputer, to be used in fulfilling assigned responsibilities. For instance, auditors are given portable microcomputers (e.g., "laptops"), which they carry to the clients' premises. Stored in the microcomputers are the audit programs, results of past audits, client financial statements, and other needed records.

FIGURE 1-10   (continued)

supports these comments by illustrating briefly several transaction and information processing applications in firms of varying size.

ROLES OF ACCOUNTANTS WITH RESPECT TO AN AIS

As a student preparing for a career in business, you can expect to become acquainted with a variety of real-world firms. In fact, you are likely to encounter many types other than those described in Figure 1-10. As an accountant, you will also interact with the AIS and its information products in each such firm. These interactions generally consist of (1) using, (2) evaluating, and (3) developing the AIS. Thus, you may assume roles such as (1) user, (2) evaluator, and/or (3) developer. In turn, these roles are conducted within the contexts of specific positions to which you may be appointed. Six familiar positions assumed by accountants are financial accountant, tax specialist, managerial accountant, accounting manager, auditor, and systems developer. The close relationships among these positions and roles are portrayed in Figure 1-11. Our discussion of these relationships is most conveniently organized around the positions.

FINANCIAL ACCOUNTANTS

Financial accounting is the field of accounting that is mainly concerned with generating financially oriented historical (i.e., *scorekeeping*) information. For a firm this information is cast in the form of balance sheets, income statements, cash-flow statements, and other financial statements. As we have seen, numerous parties external to the firm need some or all of these financial statements for legitimate uses. Because of these external users, especially the investors and creditors, the financial accounting information system must prepare financial statements in accordance with generally accepted accounting principles (GAAP). Financial accountants are responsible for assuring that the financial statements are in full accord with the financial accounting model (assets = equities) as well as GAAP.

TAX SPECIALISTS

Tax accounting has the purposes of developing information that reflects the tax obligations of an entity and of aiding the making of decisions having tax implications. It therefore provides outputs to two types of users. External taxing authorities, such as the Internal Revenue Service, receive income, property, sales, and other forms of

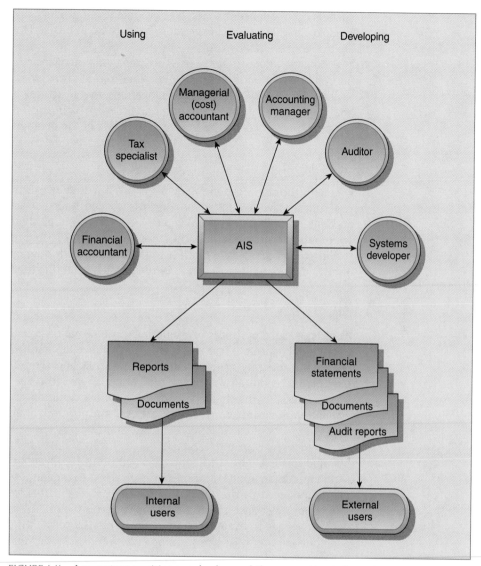

FIGURE I-II   Accountant positions and roles and the accounting information system.

tax returns. The firm's managers, who must make decisions, receive various tax reports and analyses. Tax specialists make use of the firm's AIS to prepare the tax returns and to obtain data for tax planning. When tax laws change, they need to recommend revisions to the AIS that enable it to process the information needed for compliance.

MANAGERIAL ACCOUNTANTS

Managerial accounting, also called cost accounting, has the purpose of providing financial information to the internal users of a firm. This information may be *attention-directing*, in that it aids in controlling various operations and activities of the firm. Alternatively, it may be *decision-oriented*, in that it aids the planning process. Much of the information may be prepared through the use of control and decision models, such as cost-variance models, cost-volume-profit models, and cash-flow forecasting models. Since the results from these models are to be used by managers, the models are not constrained by GAAP.

Managerial accountants use the managerial accounting system to develop the information for their firm's managers. They frequently must evaluate and recommend revisions to the AIS, particularly concerning the structures of the decision models and the formats of the reports and analyses. In doing so, managerial accountants are primarily guided by the information needs of the managers.

ACCOUNTING MANAGERS

Generally the chief accounting manager in a firm is known as the controller. Managers reporting to the controller may include a head financial accountant, a head cost accountant, and a budget manager. These managers guide the activities of the accountants discussed earlier. Thus they use the AIS to obtain information for controlling the accounting activities, evaluating the performances of the staff accountants, and planning the direction of the firm's accounting function.

AUDITORS

Auditing has the purposes of evaluating the information products of an AIS or various operational aspects of the AIS itself. For instance, an audit might evaluate the reliability and integrity of information from an AIS and the adequacy of the internal controls incorporated within the AIS. Although varied types of audits may be performed, perhaps the financial audit is the most common. In this type of audit the evaluation is based on reviews of the AIS and its control environment and procedures, on tests of the existing controls, and on substantive tests of the accounting records.

Auditors evaluate the adequacy of features (e.g., internal controls) incorporated within an AIS. In addition, some auditors attest to the fairness of the financial statements produced by the AIS. Although auditors are primarily concerned with evaluation, they must of course make extensive use of the AIS. Also, they may recommend design changes to the AIS, especially with respect to the internal controls. A knowledge of computer-based processing and systems can be very helpful in this regard. In fact, auditors who are very familiar with computer-based systems and related auditing techniques (often called EDP auditors) are greatly in demand.

SYSTEMS DEVELOPERS

Accountants are increasingly serving as designers and developers of AISs. Systems design is the key phase within the **systems development cycle.** It consists of devising specifications for an AIS that best fit a firm's current and expected circumstances. The design may involve an improvement to an existing AIS or may pertain to the initial AIS for a new firm. Preceding systems design are two phases: systems planning and systems analysis. Systems planning consists of laying the foundation for a new or revised AIS. Systems analysis involves defining the problems facing the current AIS and determining the requirements for the new or improved system. After a system design is accepted, it is installed and put into operation during a systems implementation phase.

Accountants may be engaged in systems development in various capacities. Internal systems designers (or systems analysts, as they are sometimes called) are employees of the firms whose systems they analyze and design. Accountants in this role may be assigned on a permanent basis to the information systems department of the firm. More often, accountants assume the role of full-time systems developers by being assigned to a system design project team. For instance, an accountant in the cost accounting department may be assigned to a production control design project team, together with systems analysts from the information systems department and a production planner from the production department. When the project is completed, the accountant returns to his or her responsibilities in the cost accounting department. Still another way in which accountants can participate in systems development is in a consulting capacity. Systems consultants are often members of public accounting firms, where they may be called consulting services specialists. They help client firms to evaluate all aspects of their AISs, including controls and data bases as well as reports. They also design new or improved AISs, recommend suitable computer systems, install the computer systems, and train personnel in their use.

EXTENDED SYSTEMS-RELATED ROLES

The systems-related roles of accountants extend beyond the AIS. In fact, accountants in all of the positions described above interface with the MIS. For instance, the controller of a firm will acquire and use information from the MIS in making key decisions relating to the accounting function. Those in positions such as managerial accountant, auditor, and systems developer also become involved in improving and developing the MIS as well as the other decision-oriented information systems. Some of the ways they might become involved are as follows:

1. Assisting the accounting managers, such as the controller, in deciding on information needed from the MIS for specific decisions.
2. Assisting nonaccounting managers, such as the treasurer, in developing models that will aid in making finance decisions.
3. Evaluating computer-based security and control measures to be incorporated in the MIS.
4. Assisting high-level managers in obtaining needed information for decision support systems to be employed in strategic decisions, as well as interpreting results obtained from the systems.
5. Serving as experts when expert systems are being developed to deal with accounting-related applications and decisions.

ACCOUNTANTS AS SYSTEMS-ORIENTED PROFESSIONALS

In addition to having a degree in accounting, two additional marks of a truly professional accountant are (1) obtaining a certification and (2) abiding by a code of professional ethics.

PROFESSIONAL CERTIFICATIONS

As an accountant specializing in information systems, you will have a choice among several certifications. Very possibly you may decide to obtain more than one, since the field of information systems spans more than accountants. Several certifications you might consider, and the administering professional associations, are listed in Figure 1-12.

Each of the certifications requires that you pass a written uniform examination and complete a stated period of professional experience. Most also have an education requirement, such as a stated number of courses or hours in accounting, and a requirement that you become a member of the administering professional association.

PROFESSIONAL ETHICS

A person cannot be viewed as a professional unless he or she adheres to high standards of ethical conduct or behavior. **Ethics** is a set of moral principles or values. Thus, ethical behavior consists of making choices and judgments that are morally proper and then acting accordingly. Ethics can govern an organization, such as a business firm, as well as individuals. In the context of an organization, an underlying ethical principle is that each person in the organization has responsibility for the welfare of others within the organization, as well as for the organization. Consequently, the managers of a firm should make decisions that are fair to the employees as well as gainful to the firm.

At either the personal level or the organizational level, ethics embodies the essence of integrity and morality. Ethics goes beyond the observance of human laws and customs, even beyond the trait of technical honesty. For instance, the actions of a person could be described as within the realm of legality, while at the same time the person exhibits unethical behavior.

Importance of Ethics to Accounting Professionals   Professional accountants have a greater degree of responsibility than many others who interact within the business world. In their roles as financial accountants or auditors, they are responsible for the reliability of financial statements to external users such as owners, government agencies, and the public. As tax specialists, they are responsible for the reliability of tax documents to government agencies (and ultimately all taxpayers) as well as the firms to which the tax documents pertain. As managerial accountants, they are responsible for the reliabilty of information provided to managers. As systems developers and consultants, they are responsible for the soundness and integrity of their services to managers. Those consultants who are members of public accounting or management consulting firms have the added responsibilities related to client relations.

- Certified Management Accountant, administered by the Institute of Certified Management Accountants, an affiliate of the Institute of Management Accountants.
- Certified Public Accountant, administered by the American Institute of Certified Public Accountants.
- Certified Internal Auditor, administered by the Institute of Internal Auditors.
- Certified Information Systems Auditor, administered by the Information Systems Audit and Control Association.
- Certified Computing Professional, administered by the Institute for Certification of Computing Professionals, an affiliate of the Data Processing Management Association.
- Certified Management Consultant, administered by the Association of Consulting Management Engineers.

FIGURE 1-12   Certifications relevant to accountants, together with the administering associations.

Because they must work closely with managers at various levels within a firm, professional accountants tend to encounter ethical problems more frequently than other employees. They are in position to observe unethical acts performed by managers, even at the highest level. For example, managers might manipulate financial information to give false or misleading pictures of the health of the firm or its prospects; they might employ highly questionable methods to compute their bonuses; they might alter the purchasing procedures so that goods are diverted to their use. Managers might also ask accountants to suppress information that is unfavorable, either to the managers or to the firm.

In sum, the unethical acts of managers, together with the unethical acts of other responsible parties such as professional accountants, can have serious repercussions on a firm. On a broader scale, unethical behavior may pervade numerous firms throughout the business world. In addition to financial losses it may cause investors, creditors, government bodies, and the public, an unethical climate can lead to mistrust and doubts concerning an entire economy. Thus, it is imperative to the economic health of a nation that high ethical standards be established and fostered.

Standards of Ethical Conduct   Unethical acts are not always easy to identify, and the appropriate actions in response to such acts are often not obvious. To provide guidance, various professional associations have promulgated standards of ethical conduct. One set of standards specifies that systems-oriented accountants involved in consulting services should (1) gain professional competence, (2) exercise due professional care, (3) plan and supervise the work performed, (4) obtain sufficient relevant data to support reasonable recommendations, (5) maintain integrity and objectivity, (6) understand and respect the responsibilities of all parties, and (7) disclose any conflicts of interest.*

AIMS AND DIRECTIONS OF THIS TEXTBOOK

As an accountant, you should be aware of the body of knowledge and current practices relating to accounting information systems. A major aim of this textbook is therefore to survey the relevant concepts and the most useful applications of a typical AIS. While delving into these applications, we will focus on such key functions as collecting, processing, storing, retrieving, controlling, and auditing data. Because of the impact of information technology, we will concentrate on those applications that incorporate computers. Because any information system is subject to becoming outdated, we also discuss the phases that span the planning, development, and management of a new or improved AIS.

Of course, every topic that touches an AIS cannot be exhaustively explored in a textbook of moderate size. Therefore, we have selected several topical areas in which to devote our greatest attention: accounting internal controls, transaction cycles, data bases (especially the relational model), and system development techniques (especially system flowcharts and data-flow diagrams). Later chapters should amply clarify the meanings of these topics and the uses of the related techniques.

It is hoped that this textbook will help you to appreciate the importance of an effective AIS to the modern firm. If it serves its purpose well, it will also enable you to use, evaluate, and develop those specific AISs that you encounter throughout your career.

---

*Management Advisory Services Executive Committee, "Statement on Standards for Consulting Services No. 1," *Journal of Accountancy* (November 1991), pp. 164–165.

SUMMARY

In this information age, information is a valued resource. Recent years have seen a focus on strategic information, rapid developments in information technology and related services, the rise of a service-oriented economy, globalization of organizations, greater user involvement in information system development, and more information-oriented professionalism.

An accounting information system (AIS) for an entity is a unified structure that employs physical resources and other components to transform data into accounting information, with the objective of satisfying the information needs of a variety of users. Three major purposes of an AIS are (1) to support day-to-day operations, (2) to support decision making by internal decision makers, and (3) to fulfill obligations relating to stewardship. These purposes incorporate five major functions: data collection, data processing, data management, data control (including security), and information generation. Each function involves several steps. The resources and components of an AIS include a processor, data base, procedures, input/output devices, employees, plant assets, supplies, and funds.

The overall information system of a firm encompasses several systems in addition to the AIS. The management information system serves the managers with most of their information needs, using various subsystems such as the marketing and finance information systems. Three other decision-oriented systems are decision support systems, expert systems, and executive information systems.

Accountants use, evaluate, and develop AISs and also MISs. Although individual accountants generally perform all three roles, the degree to which they perform each depends on their areas of responsibility. These areas include financial accounting, tax accounting, managerial accounting, auditing, and systems development. Accountants also are recognized as professionals, especially when they obtain certification and join one or more professional associations. As professionals, accountants are expected to observe standards of ethical conduct.

REVIEW PROBLEM WITH SOLUTION

CAMPUS BOOKSTORE, FIRST INSTALLMENT

Statement

The Campus Bookstore occupies two levels in a building adjacent to the campus of a large state university. On the lower level are textbooks and other books; on the upper level are sundry nonbook articles and supplies.

Tom Long, who is the sole owner of the bookstore, personally directs all operations. Lois Sutton is in charge of merchandising on the upper level; Don Burgess manages the merchandising activities on the lower level. The remaining personnel consist of one accountant, three bookkeepers, four merchandise order clerks, one inventory manager, one cashier, two stock clerks, four checkout clerks, and one custodian. Temporary personnel are added during peak periods, such as at the beginnings of semesters.

The building occupied by the bookstore is leased. However, the four cash registers, store fixtures, desks and related office furniture, typewriters, desk calculators, dollies, and two small vans are owned.

Merchandise for resale is purchased from over 200 suppliers. Store supplies, ranging from accounting spreadsheets to cleansing powders, are acquired from several other suppliers. Textbooks are bought subject to return privileges, since estimated course sizes do not always materialize. On the other hand, the bookstore buys used textbooks from students at the end of each semester; these used textbooks are then resold to other students or sold to used-book wholesalers.

All merchandise is sold on a cash basis. Funds are also raised by short-term bank loans at the beginning of each semester.

Required

a. Describe the purposes of the bookstore's AIS.

b. Identify key transactions conducted by the bookstore.

c. Identify the varied users of the bookstore's AIS outputs.

d. Identify the resources of its AIS.

e. Identify several useful products (i.e., reports) that might be generated by its AIS.

Solution

a. The two major purposes of the bookstore's AIS are (1) to process transactions in order to provide information for its various operations and to meet legal obligations, and (2) to process information that is useful for decision making.

b. The key transactions processed by the bookstore are (1) cash sales to bookstore customers, (2) purchases from suppliers, (3) returns of purchased textbooks to suppliers, (4) cash disbursements to suppliers and others, (5) payroll payments to employees, and (6) loans from banks. Note that the cash receipts transaction is combined with the sales transaction since sales are not made on credit.

c. The users of the outputs from the AIS include (1) the managers of the bookstore, (2) the employees of the bookstore, (3) the customers (who are primarily students), (4) the suppliers, (5) the banks, (6) the used-book wholesalers, (7) Tom Long (as owner), and (8) governmental agencies who have responsibility with respect to taxes.

d. The resources of the bookstore's AIS consist of the fixed assets, merchandise, supplies, employees, data, and funds from revenues and loans.

e. Among the reports that might be usefully provided to the bookstore's managers by information processing are (1) balance sheet, income statement, and cash-flow statement; (2) reports of actual costs versus budgeted costs for each level; (3) reports of sales and profits for each level and each product line; (4) reports of the status of each merchandise item in stock; and (5) budgets for each level.

KEY TERMS

accounting (5)
accounting information (1)
accounting information system (AIS) (7)
accounting transaction (9)
auditing (22)
computer-based (16)
computer program (13)
data (6)
data collection (11)
data control (13)
data management (13)
data processing function (12)
decision support system (DSS) (16)
ethics (24)
executive information system (EIS) (18)
expert system (ES) (17)
external users (9)
financial accounting (20)
financial accounting subsystem (15)
informal information system (18)
information (6)
information generation (13)
information processing (10)
information technology (3)
internal users (9)
management information system (MIS) (14)
managerial accounting (21)
managerial accounting subsystem (15)
manual system (16)
procedure (14)
system (7)
systems development cycle (22)

tax accounting (20)
transaction (9)
transaction processing (9)
transaction processing system (TPS) (9)

REVIEW QUESTIONS

1-1. Why should accountants study accounting information systems?

1-2. Identify several recent trends and developments relating to information and information systems.

1-3. How do the terms *accounting, information,* and *system* clarify the meaning of an AIS?

1-4. What are the three purposes of an AIS?

1-5. Who are the users of an AIS, and which users are supported by each of the three purposes?

1-6. Contrast transaction processing and information processing.

1-7. Identify the five major functions of an AIS and the several steps within each function.

1-8. What are several physical resources and components employed by an AIS?

1-9. What is the purpose and scope of the MIS, as well as its relationship with the AIS and other component information systems within a firm?

1-10. Discuss the roles of accountants and how these roles relate to the AIS.

1-11. Contrast scorekeeping, attention-directing, and decision-making information.

1-12. Identify the major phases in the systems development cycle.

1-13. What are several typical roles of accountants, beyond the AIS?

1-14. What are three marks of a professional accountant?

1-15. What types of certification are available to systems-oriented accountants?

1-16. Why are the standards of ethical conduct imperative to the accounting profession?

1-17. Identify several areas of ethical responsibility for accountants.

DISCUSSION QUESTIONS

1-18. Has the influence of accountants changed since the advent of computers? If so, in what ways?

1-19. Accounting has been defined as "the art of recording, classifying, and summarizing, in a significant manner and in terms of money, transactions and events which are, in part at least, of a financial character, and interpreting the results thereof."* Compare and contrast this definition with the one given in the chapter. Is it consistent with the chapter discussion?

1-20. In what ways might financial statements prepared for the management of a firm differ from financial statements published in annual reports? Can financial statements based on historical information be useful to either internal managers or external parties in their decision making?

1-21. To what extent must a manager rely on intuition and the informal information system, rather than the formal information system, when making decisions? How does the level of the manager within the firm and the type of decision influence the answer?

1-22. What topics should be studied by accountants so they can acquire a common body of knowledge relating to accounting information systems?

1-23. Describe a computer-based MIS for a medium-sized business firm in the year 2000; include in your description the types of information it will provide and the decisions it will support.

1-24. Ann Strong is asked by a medical group client to evaluate a new expert system that has been offered by a systems software firm. The purpose of the expert system is to aid in diagnosing the ills of patients. Discuss whether Ann should accept this engagement.

1-25. If Ann Strong performs an audit for a department store client, can she ethically also accept an engagement with the client to improve its AIS? Discuss this situation in terms of objectivity and independence.

1-26. Describe several strategic decisions that must be made from time to time by a higher-level manager of Infoage, Inc.

1-27. In what ways is the AIS for a nonprofit organization, such as a university, different from the AIS for a manufacturing firm? In what ways are the two AISs similar?

PROBLEMS

1-1. Below is a list of topics that may be covered in a course concerning accounting information systems. Group the topics into three categories—I, II, and III—according to their relative importance to accountants and hence the degree of attention that you believe they will receive in this course. Category I is those topics of greatest importance, while Category III is those of least importance.

*Committee on Terminology, "Review and Resume," *Accounting Terminology Bulletins*, No. 1 (American Institute of Accountants, 1953), p. 9.

a. Internal accounting controls
b. Computer programming
c. Processing of basic transactions
d. Computer networking technology
e. Expert systems
f. Journal entries for routine and nonroutine transactions
g. Data-base processing
h. Computer system architectures
i. Managerial reports
j. Decision support systems
k. Forms design
l. Auditing of computer systems
m. Flowcharting of accounting procedures
n. Reports for governmental bodies, such as tax returns and Form 10-Ks
o. Structure charts and other detailed design techniques

1-2. Annual reports provide information to a variety of users. These users may be either internal or external to the issuing firm. Identify each of the following users as internal or external and describe the extent to which the annual reports are likely to fulfill the information needs of the user with respect to the firm.

a. Creditor bank.
b. Securities and Exchange Commission.
c. Accountant in the general ledger department.
d. Shareholder.
e. Labor union representing employees of the firm.
f. Vice-president of finance.
g. Prospective investor.
h. Customer.

1-3. An AIS supports (1) day-to-day operations, (2) decision making, and (3) stewardship obligations. Identify which type or types of support each of the following outputs provides, and briefly explain how:

a. Annual budgets.
b. Payroll tax withholding reports.
c. Sales transactions.
d. Annual reports to shareholders.
e. Cost variance analyses.
f. Purchase orders.
g. Cash-flow forecasts.
h. Financial statements.
i. Shipping registers.
j. Bank reconciliations.
k. New-product evaluation models.
l. Income tax returns.

1-4. As an accounting student who will be graduating soon, you are currently considering two job offers: one from a Big-Six public accounting firm and one from a large semiconductor manufacturing firm. It so happens that the semiconductor firm is a client of all the services offered by the public accounting firm.

    a. Assume that you accept the offer of the public accounting firm. Identify the position (e.g., financial accountant, auditor) that you would personally prefer. Then describe the roles that you would assume and interactions that you would likely have with the AIS of your firm and also with the AIS of the client firm.

    b. Assume that you accept the offer of the semiconductor manufacturer. Identify the position that you would personally prefer. Then describe the roles that you would assume and the interactions that you would likely have with the AIS of your firm. Also, contrast your roles with those of (i) the auditor and (ii) the systems development consultant from the public accounting firm that provides services to your firm.

1-5. You have just been hired as an accounting intern in a merchandising firm, similar to but larger than Infoage, Inc. At the completion of your internship, you will be asked to select the field in which you desire to specialize. When the time for selection arrives, you determine that the final choice will be from one of the two following pairs:

    1. Financial accountant or internal auditor.

    2. Managerial accountant or systems developer.

Required

a. Compare the roles within each pair, identifying their similarities as well as differences.

b. Contrast the two pairs with respect to their primary and unique relationships to the AIS of your firm.

1-6. Ann Strong's public accounting firm is briefly described in Figure 1-4. Reread the description provided, and also read the Review Problem at the end of the chapter.

Required

a. Identify the key transactions conducted by the public accounting firm.

b. Identify the varied users of the public accounting firm's AIS outputs.

c. Identify the resources and components of the AIS.

d. Identify several useful reports that are likely to be generated by the AIS of the firm, both for Ann and for the clients.

1-7. Figure 1-10 provides examples of information system applications in a variety of business firms and not-for-profit organizations. For each example, list (a) one additional type of transaction processing system and (b) one type of system that would support information processing.

1-8. An inventory clerk for an appliance dealer manually transforms data from input documents into a daily report. The input documents contain the code numbers and quantities of merchandise items received from suppliers and sold to customers. Each individual document refers *either* to a receipt *or* to a sale, although some of the documents may contain the code number and quantity for more than one item of merchandise. About 100 documents are given to the clerk each day in unsorted batches. The daily report shows the *dollar amounts* of merchandise received and sold, in terms of both (a) individual merchandise items *and* (b) totals of merchandise items involved in the day's transactions. The merchandise items are arranged in code number order, and each is identified on the report by its descriptive title. To aid in the processing, the clerk has available a reference file that lists the descriptive titles, item code numbers, and unit prices for all coded merchandise items.

Required

Prepare a list, in appropriate order, of the specific processing steps that must be performed by the inventory clerk in transforming the inputs into the desired output.

1-9. A procedure consists of a series of steps involving the several functions of an AIS. For each of the following procedures, list data collection, data processing, data management, data control, and information generation steps that are needed. Assume that the procedure is performed manually. Begin each step with a verb (e.g., record, calculate, retrieve).

    a. A procedure used by a campus bookstore to purchase merchandise on credit for resale. (*Hint: See the Review Problem*)

    b. A procedure used by a service station to sell gasoline and other products to customers for cash.

    c. A procedure used by a shoe store to pay bills owed to suppliers.

1-10. Below are a variety of applications in which real-world firms have effectively employed information resources and technology. Identify at least one benefit that each application appears to provide to the adopting firm.*

---

*Most of these applications are drawn from "Towards a Theory of Strategic Use of Information Resources: An Inductive Approach," by Rajiv Sabherwal and William R. King (*Information and Management*, 1991, pp. 204–207), although each application has been described more fully in other sources referenced by the article.

a. American Hospital Supply Corporation, a leading manufacturer and distributor of health-care products, has established direct computer links with hospitals, thereby simplifying their ordering of supplies.

b. Citicorp has installed user-friendly automated teller machines in wide-spread networks.

c. Delta Airlines employs a reservation system that, in addition to making reservations, monitors sales patterns and fare changes of its competitors.

d. Digital Equipment Corporation uses an expert system to help configure computer systems ordered by customers.

e. Federal Express Corporation uses data-base software to track all letters and parcels handled by the firm through each delivery step.

f. Merrill Lynch & Co. provides a Cash Management Account, which combines the information pertaining to all of a customer's securities accounts into one computerized monthly statement.

g. Procter & Gamble Co. uses terminals and phones to capture and log complaints from customers.

h. Metpath, a large clinical laboratory, keeps records of patient data on file and offers financial processing services through billing and accounts payable applications, thus achieving differentiation in an otherwise commodity service.

i. St. Petersburg Junior College has developed a multimedia simulation—employing graphics, video moving images, and sound—for interactive use by veterinary students.

1-11. Ethics is important to accounting professionals. Briefly explain why each of the following actions is likely to be unethical.

a. While being interviewed for a position as an auditor of computer systems, Sherry states that she is very familiar with computers—even though she has only played games on a computer at home.

b. In the course of an audit, Jack discovers that an employee has signed false purchase orders to a nonexistent supplier. When confronted, the employee offers to pay for Jack's vacation if he does not report the discovery, and Jack accepts.

c. Jane, a managerial accountant, overhears a manager discuss the upcoming sale of the firm to a competitor. Although she realizes the planned sale is confidential, she tells her friends within the firm, who rapidly spread the news.

d. Mark, the controller of an electronics firm, includes the revenue from several sales in this year's income statement, even though the products have not been shipped by year's end and thus the sales are incomplete. All managers are paid a bonus on the basis of revenues.

e. Doretta, an accounting manager for a small manufacturer, disagrees with new restrictive credit policies established by the top managers, since she believes that sales will be reduced too severely. Thus she relaxes the credit policies when large orders are received from customers.

1-12. Infoage, Inc., is described briefly in Figure 1-4. You are a member of a public accounting firm who has been engaged to analyze the firm's activities and to recommend improvements, especially with regard to the information systems. During the early part of your engagement, you decide to prepare a background report.

Required

Drawing on the material provided in Figure 1-4, plus the examples scattered throughout the chapter, include the following in the background report:

1. The major organizational functions.

2. The internal and external users of information.

3. The major types of accounting transactions.

4. The components of the AIS/MIS.

5. The functional components of the MIS, plus examples of information that each is likely to provide.

6. One possible application of a decision support system.

CONTINUING CASE

Select a small firm in your locality, such as a florist shop, building contractor, delivery service, accounting firm, or bank branch. This selected firm will be the basis for a series of requirements related to material presented in this and selected following chapters. By completing these requirements, you should gain a better understanding of an organization and its AIS.

For Chapter 1, prepare a report that contains brief descriptions of the following:

a. The firm's location, history, and products or services it provides.

b. The major purposes, functions, and resources of its AIS.

c. The key accounting transactions processed by its AIS.

d. The internal and external users of information from the AIS.

e. The relationship of the AIS to the MIS of the firm.

f. Several key reports prepared by the AIS or MIS.

g. The steps in a key procedure, involving the input, processing, and output stages.

CHAPTER 2

THE BUSINESS ENVIRONMENT AND THE AIS

THE LEARNING OBJECTIVES FOR THIS CHAPTER ARE TO ENABLE YOU TO:

1. Describe the essential characteristics of business firms, their key subsystems, and their environments.

2. Discuss organizational structures that are suitable for business firms, including the functions to be performed and the levels of management.

3. Identify the types of processes performed by business firms within their operational systems.

4. Discuss information needed by business firms and its flows within their organizational structures.

5. Identify the varied events that business firms encounter when conducting their range of activities.

6. Describe the steps composing financial and managerial accounting cycles within business firms.

INTRODUCTION

An AIS does not exist in a vacuum; rather, it is an integral part of the firm that it serves. As such, it has close relationships with the firm's organizational structure and set of physical operations or processes. Furthermore, many of the business and accounting events that are captured and processed by the AIS arise within the environment of the business firm. On the output side, the information generated by the AIS flows to users who reside either within the firm's organizational structure or in its environment. This information, which derives from the processed events, must have value to each of the users who receive it. Unless an accountant clearly understands all these relationships, in specific business settings, he or she cannot help develop the AISs that fully meet the needs of users.

BUSINESS SETTINGS

A business firm can be viewed as a system. In this section we survey the system characteristics that it exhibits. We also review its major subsystems and the key aspects of its environment. We should emphasize that our discussion pertains to all organizations, not-for-profit as well as profit-oriented. However, illustrations will relate primarily to our two typical firms, Infoage, Inc., and Ann Strong, CPA/CMA.

BUSINESS FIRMS AS SYSTEMS

Several characteristics of a system were mentioned in Chapter 1. To understand the underlying nature of firms, we can begin our survey by making a more complete list of characteristics and defining key system-related terms.

Objectives   The **objectives** are the goals or motivating forces. A firm such as Infoage, Inc., has such primary objectives as maximizing its sales and the profits of computer-related products, as well as gaining the greatest market share within the Seattle area. It also has an objective of providing superior services related to microcomputer systems. Ann Strong also focuses on the service objective, since providing desired services in a superior manner should lead to satisfactory income and longevity.

Environment   The surroundings that lie beyond a firm's boundary compose its **environment.** Infoage's environment includes its customers, suppliers, competitors, government agencies, and the market for computers.

Constraints   The **constraints** are the internal or external restrictions that define the configuration and capabilities. One type of constraint is the **boundary** that separates the system, such as a firm, from its environment. Infoage is constrained by its market area, which presently is the metropolitan area of Seattle. In addition, it is restricted by limited resources, such as funds and trained sales personnel.

Controls   The **controls** are the means of regulation. They enable a system such as a firm to monitor operations and processes, so as to identify and correct deviations from plans. Thus controls help to achieve the stated objectives. Infoage takes frequent inventory counts of its on-hand computers and accessories and compares the counts with stock records. Ann Strong prepares time schedules for the projects she undertakes for clients and compares the actual times with these schedules.

Input-Process-Outputs   The inputs to a business firm include **resources** needed to conduct operations and produce outputs. Infoage requires such resource inputs as merchandise, the labor of employees and managers, facilities such as the main office and sales outlets, funds such as payments from customers, and data. Most of these resources are similar to—but more extensive than—those required by the AIS. The process consists of all the procedures to convert the inputs into outputs. Processes in business firms will be discussed in detail later. The outputs include information and tangible results. Both Infoage and Ann Strong generate a variety of information outputs, ranging from financial statements to billing statements. They differ in other outputs, however: Infoage produces sales of products and installed microcomputer systems for customers; Ann Strong's firm generates most of its outputs for clients, ranging from audit reports and tax returns to systems analysis reports.

Often the information outputs are reentered or fed back as inputs; that is, a firm may employ **feedback** as a means of increasing the degree of control. For instance, Infoage gathers information concerning the performance of its merchandise suppliers; this information is fed back to Mike (the manager who purchases the merchandise), in order to aid him in selecting suppliers.

Subsystems   Finally, every system has interdependent **subsystems.** One of the reasons that a firm such as Infoage is so complex is that it has numerous overlaid sets of subsystems. Its varied facilities, such as the main office and sales outlets, represent one set, while the employees and managers represent another. With respect to the latter, each person is a separate subsystem within the firm and interacts with others, through both the formal organization and the "grapevine." Another reason for a firm's complexity is that people may behave in unpredictable ways.

Subsystems, which have all the characteristics of systems, are linked to each other through couplings or shared boundaries called **interfaces.** Figure 2-1 shows a set of subsystems within a manufacturing firm that interface with each other in order to exchange inputs and outputs. Each subsystem shown in the figure is a functional activity of the firm. By referring back to Figure 1-9, you can see that each functional activity is supported by a component MIS.

Conclusion Firms are very complex systems with environments, constraints, controls, resource inputs, multiple processes, at least two types of outputs, and numerous subsystems. Figure 2-2 summarizes several of the key characteristics. It also shows an important set of subsystems, to be discussed next.

MAJOR SUBSYSTEMS OF FIRMS

Every business firm fits into a framework called a **systems hierarchy.** Figure 2-3 depicts this hierarchy. In certain respects it represents an alternative view of Figure 2-2. Our present focus is on the three major subsystems of a firm: the organizational structure, the information system, and the operational system. Each of these major subsystems can be factored into numerous sub-subsystems, as will be illustrated later. A brief illustration portrayed by the figure is the subdivision of the information system into transaction processing and information processing systems. This particular subdivision is a more summarized view of the AIS, MIS, and other component information systems shown in Figure 1-9.

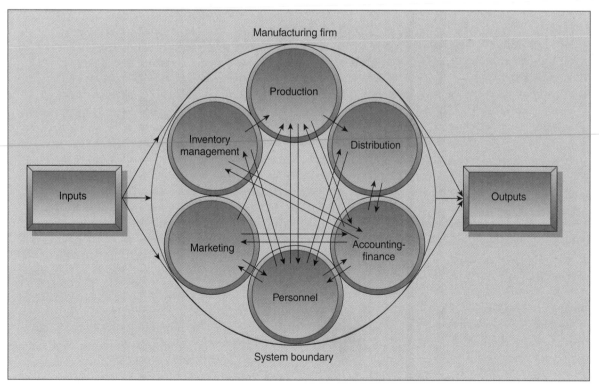

FIGURE 2-1 Coupled-subsystems in a manufacturing firm.

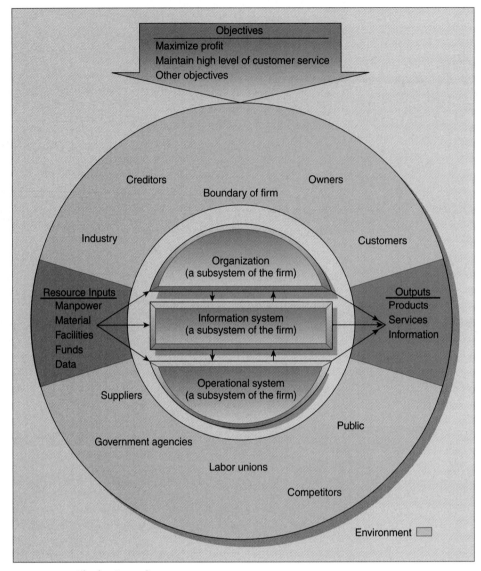

FIGURE 2-2   The business firm as a system.

ENVIRONMENTS BEYOND BUSINESS FIRMS

Beyond any firm lies an environment that is economic, social, technical, and political in nature. It contains the sources of resources and various data as well as facilities and funds. For example, one type of data received by Infoage consists of Department of Commerce summaries concerning the economy. The environment also encompasses all of the external users of information, as well as the products and/or services provided. In some cases the outputs also include resources, as when Infoage pays dividends to its owners.

The environment beyond a firm is extremely influential. It not only presents problems and challenges but also provides opportunities. Problems that Infoage faces are possible shortages of merchandise and the appearance of new competitors. Opportunities include the chance to acquire merchandise at a reduced price because of a manufacturer's overproduction.

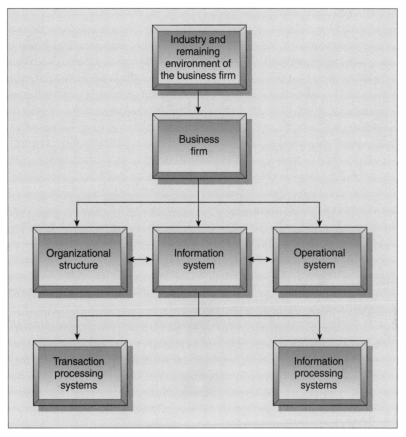

FIGURE 2-3   A hierarchy of systems.

The environments of business firms vary enormously, particularly among different industries. These variations have considerable impacts on the needed resources. Let us consider just a few of the many differing situations. For firms in capital-intensive industries, the facilities resource is of paramount concern. By contrast, the labor resource is critical for firms in labor-intensive industries. In financial institutions like banks, the funds resource is most important, whereas a retailing institution like a grocery chain is concerned about merchandise. The AISs for these firms must emphasize the records that reflect the dominant resources. In a more general sense, the AIS for any firm should reflect the specific needs of the firm.

The burden of legal obligations also varies among firms and industries. Firms in highly regulated industries, such as large public utilities, are obligated to generate numerous reports to meet their legal obligations. Their required reports concern such matters as payroll taxes, worker's compensation, new issues of capital stock, and requests for rate increases. On the other hand, small unregulated firms such as photography shops need prepare few reports other than tax returns.

Environmental differences can be at least as significant to firms as their organizational structures and operations. Firms must therefore align their strategies and resource levels to cope with these differences. In highly competitive and dynamic industrial situations, such as faced by Infoage, firms need to be responsive to changing conditions. Soundly designed information systems, amply supported by information technology, can be vital to the firms' continued success and competitiveness.

ORGANIZATIONAL STRUCTURES

The **organizational structure** is the means by which the managers of a firm direct and coordinate the set of activities and operations. It specifies the relationships among the tasks to be performed; it also distributes the degrees of authority and responsibility assigned to the various managers. In effect, the organizational structure can be viewed as a management system, since it encompasses the managers who perform the planning and control for the firm. An **organization chart** is a diagram that depicts an organizational structure. It contains boxes, or nodes, representing **responsibility centers** where the responsible managers reside, plus the lines that relate the responsibility centers to each other.

In this section we briefly review alternative organizational structures, identify the relationships of the organization structure to the AIS, and illustrate how information needs are affected by an organizational structure.

HIERARCHICAL STRUCTURES

Traditionally organizations have been structured in a hierarchical manner. Under this type of arrangement, the activities and operations of a firm are subdivided, with the levels of management being arrayed vertically. Clear lines of authority are typically established, with the manager at each subordinate responsibility center reporting to one designated superior center. Explicit **spans of management,** reflecting the number of subordinates reporting to each manager, also can easily be identified.

Figure 2-4 illustrates the features of the relatively simple hierarchical structure presently employed by Infoage. Only two managerial levels are necessary, since the firm is relatively small and entrepreneurial. All of the managers report directly to the president, who thus has a span of management of seven. Because of its "flat" structure, Infoage has considerable flexibility. That is, it can respond quickly to changing conditions. However, if Infoage is to grow appreciably, it will need to modify its structure.

Functional Structure of a Manufacturing Firm   Figure 2-5 illustrates a more complex hierarchical structure for the hypothetical Tractors Manufacturing Company.

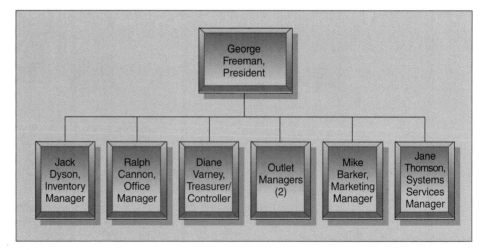

FIGURE 2-4   An organization chart for Infoage, Inc.

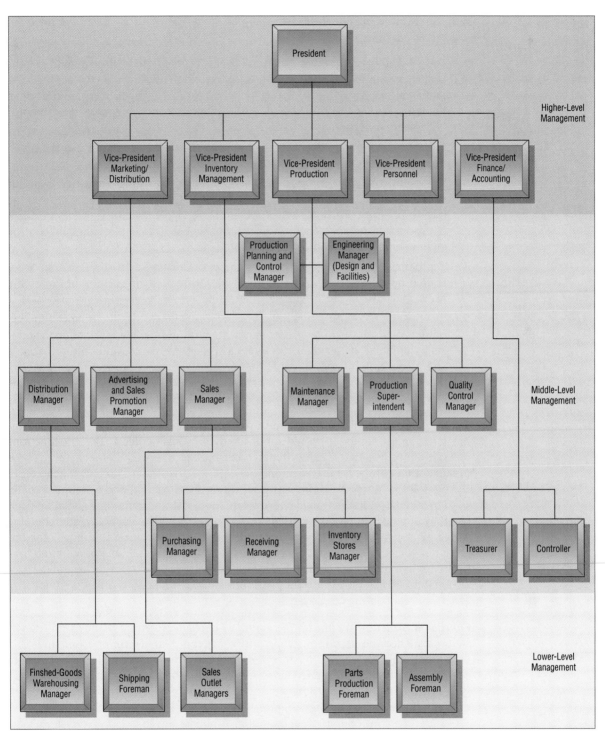

FIGURE 2-5   An organizational structure for the Tractors Manufacturing Company.

Reporting to the president are five vice-presidents, who in turn head five major *organizational functions*:

1. The marketing/distribution function obtains orders from customers and fills the orders efficiently. It assigns these two objectives to two line managers—the sales manager and distribution manager—who report directly to the vice-president. Providing support to the sales effort is a staff manager in charge of advertising and sales promotion.

2. The inventory management function purchases, receives, and stores the materials resource in an efficient manner.

3. The production function converts raw materials into finished goods. Value is added by producing useful physical outputs, i.e., what the economists call the creation of form utility. Because of the function's complexity, the vice-president of production requires such staff positions as production planning and control, engineering, quality control, and maintenance.

4. The personnel (or human resources) function ensures that the firm's labor resource needs are met and also that the job-related needs of employees are likewise met.

5. The finance/accounting function is in effect two functions. The finance function obtains funds at the lowest costs and disburses funds efficiently. It often includes such subfunctions as cash receipts, cash disbursements, and credit checking. The accounting function records the physical operations, produces output documents, summarizes the financial status and results of operations, and prepares other financial reports.

An organizational structure should fit the unique needs of a specific firm. Thus, in a functional structure it should subdivide the firm's activities so that the functions have subobjectives that mesh with and contribute to the overall objectives. In some manufacturing firms, for instance, the overall objectives might be better achieved if the production function encompasses inventory management and warehousing.

Functional structures divide responsibilities and accommodate growth. When carefully arranged to group together compatible specialties, such as credit checking with cash receipts, they provide a high degree of specialization that promotes operational efficiency. When highly centralized, as in Figure 2-5, functional structures facilitate tight managerial control. However, they can impede the horizontal flows of information across functions. They also are slow to adapt to changes and not very effective in motivating employees.

Functional Structure Within the Accounting Function   Figure 2-6 shows an organization chart for the accounting function of Tractors Manufacturing Company. This illustration links to Figure 2-5, since it details the subfunctions under the authority of the controller. In addition to portraying two additional managerial levels within a typical firm, Figure 2-6 provides us an initial view of several departments we will encounter many times in later chapters.

Under the controller are four staff units—budgeting, cost analysis, system analysis, and tax reports—and two line subfunctions—cost accounting and general accounting. Cost accounting records and processes costs and resources (materials and labor) employed in production. Through its six units, the general accounting subfunction records accounting transactions, maintains account balances, and generates output documents. In summary, both accounting subfunctions are responsible for conducting day-to-day record-keeping duties.

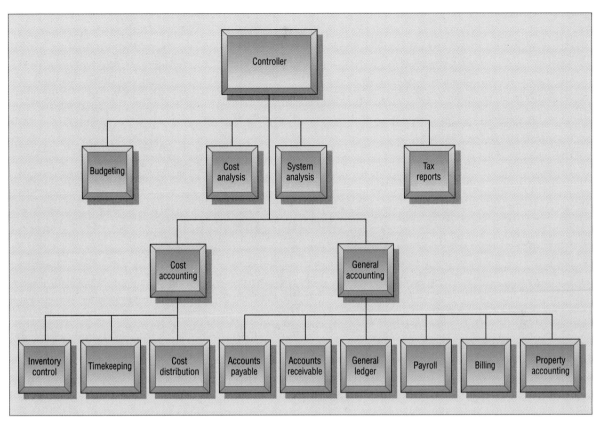

FIGURE 2-6   An organization chart of the accounting function of Tractors Manufacturing Company.

Product Line Structure   When a firm expands to offer new product lines or to open new markets, the functional structure becomes less advantageous. Usually it does not provide the means by which top management can coordinate the new activities effectively and control their development. Consequently, alternative structures have become feasible for many large firms.

Figure 2-7 portrays an organization structured according to divisions, where each division focuses on a product line. Three product lines form the firm's divisions, each headed by a division manager. Each division in turn is subdivided into functions (not shown), such as production, marketing, and administrative services. Certain services, however, are retained at the corporate level.

Organizations may alternatively be segmented according to geographical territories (for example, East and West), markets served (for example, industrial and home consumer), and projects (for example, 727 aircraft development and 757 aircraft development). By focusing on such segments, these alternative structures enable an organization to be more responsive to that segment's needs. They also reduce the coordination problem of functional structures, although at the cost of duplicated functional services.

Matrix Structure   The **matrix organizational structure** blends the functional and project-oriented structures. Thus Tractors Manufacturing Company could undertake the development of two new products, bulldozers and trenchers. It could establish a project manager in charge of each of these developments. Employees attached to the projects would be those already assigned to functions, such as accountants and

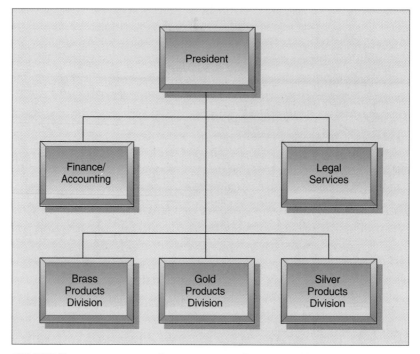

FIGURE 2-7   An organizational structure according to product lines.

engineers. The term *matrix* can be seen to apply if we visualize the two projects as horizontal strips that are laid over the vertical functions. Each project has access to all of the needed functional skills without duplication. However, because each attached employee reports to two or more superiors, it is possible that confusion will result.

Decentralized Structure   In a **decentralized organizational structure,** a considerable degree of authority is delegated to middle-level and lower-level managers within the structure. Decentralization can be employed with any of the organizational structures already discussed. It seems to work well with such structures as those arranged by product lines or other segments. Decentralization can powerfully motivate the managers throughout an organization, especially if appropriate evaluative measures are devised. For instance, the divisional managers in Figure 2-7 could be given responsibility for the profit of their divisions, together with the resources to achieve the profit objective. Because the decision-making authority is at a lower level, decisions can be made and responses taken in a more timely and effective manner.

NETWORKED STRUCTURES

An increasing number of firms recognize that they face changeable processes and environments. They have become concerned that hierarchical structures, being relatively rigid, cannot easily adapt to changes. Moreover, each firm's organizational needs are different. To deal with these situations, firms are turning to approaches having such labels as resource dependency theory, reengineering, and contingency theory. For instance, *contingency theory* suggests that a firm's organizational structure should be contingent on the current and expected environmental conditions (e.g., industry, resources, external parties) and internal processes that it uniquely encounters.

A firm can better cope with these ever-changing conditions and processes by adopting a flexible structure. A **networked structure** represents an interconnected but nonhierarchical structure that is both flexible and fluid. Figure 2-8 diagrams a hypothetical networked structure for a business firm. It shows several ongoing projects and tasks, each being performed by a team of employees and headed by a manager. All projects and tasks are linked via communication networks, so that information can be shared and decisions made quickly. In fact, certain members could be assigned to more than one project or task, since communication is so easy. As a project or task is completed, the members are reassigned elsewhere.

Networked structures enable projects and tasks to be completed faster and more economically, while new projects can quickly be established to meet arising challenges. While they do not completely replace hierarchical structures, networked structures may be superimposed on traditional structures that have been reduced to minimal functions.

RELATIONSHIPS BETWEEN THE ORGANIZATION AND AIS

The organizational structure has significant impacts on the information system and its component, the AIS. Several critical relationships exist that should be understood by systems developers.

First, the organizational structure dictates many of the key flows of information generated by the AIS (and MIS). These *vertical flows* carry information needed by managers to carry out their responsibilities.

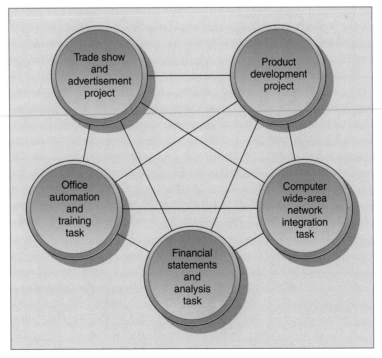

FIGURE 2-8   A networked organizational structure.

SPOTLIGHTING

RELATIONSHIPS BETWEEN THE ORGANIZATION AND AIS
at Texas Instruments*

Texas Instruments, a large computer technology firm headquartered in Dallas, can be viewed as having three organizational focuses: (1) the product organization, (2) the functional organization, and (3) the business process organization. Each organizational focus has implications for the AIS and the information it provides to users. To monitor the product organization, the AIS must identify the resources required by each product, such as a computer chip, and the activities involving the product during its life cycle. Such techniques as activity-based costing are useful in matching the resources and activities with the products. Information must be provided to the personnel in the respective functions, such as design, marketing, and accounting. An accounting method that aids in controlling the performance of organizational functions is responsibility accounting.

The organizational focus receiving increased attention at Texas Instruments is that relating to the formal and informal business processes. The firm has identified six major business processes, including order fulfillment and product development. The AIS can aid in supporting these processes by measuring key success factors, such as cycle time reduction, quality improvement, and cost reduction.

It has become clear that all three views should be linked, so that the business processes and functional units can best support the products and the strategies related to product development. The highest level concerns are to improve market share and profitability of the products. These concerns have a greater priority than such subgoals as reducing the time required to complete monthly closings of accounting ledgers. Accountants and others throughout Texas Instruments are expected to subordinate their subgoals in favor of product-oriented objectives.

*Alan Vercio, "What Organization Are You Accounting For?" *Management Accounting* (December 1993), pp. 39–42.

Second, the organizational structure determines the *horizontal flows* of transaction data that are handled by the AIS personnel in the various processing steps. Figure 2-9 illustrates this relationship for transactions related to purchases of and payments for merchandise. It is clear from the diagram that the AIS must align its various record-keeping steps to match the organizational departments. The figure also emphasizes the roles of various parties within the organization. For instance, employees in departments such as receiving and stores physically handle the inventory, while the cashier handles cash. In contrast, employees in the inventory control and accounts payable departments maintain the records only, since they are within the accounting function. Finally, the figure shows that the physical operations are also related to the processing steps.

Third, the social counterpart of the formal organizational structure interacts with and closely resembles the informal information system, also known as the "grapevine."

INFORMATION NEEDS WITHIN ORGANIZATIONAL STRUCTURES

Within an organizational structure managers reside in responsibility centers. The managers incur costs and (in some centers) generate revenues. Information pertaining to these costs and revenues provide a basis for evaluating the managers when comparing budgeted amounts allotted to the centers.

In functional structures the managers perform specialized activities, such as marketing, manufacturing, or accounting. They need information to aid them in planning

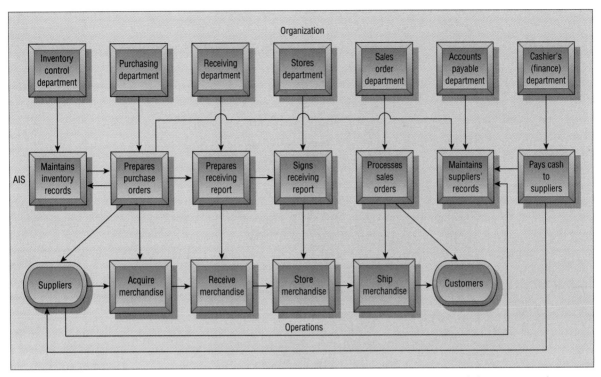

FIGURE 2-9   Relationships among the organizational structure, the information system, and the operational system.

and controlling such activities. For instance, Mike Barker, marketing manager of Infoage, needs information relating to which products to sell, how much to price each product, what discounts and terms to allow customers, how much and where to advertise, and what market research (if any) to conduct. Diane Varney, treasurer and controller, needs information relating to how much cash to acquire for short-term needs and from what sources, what credits and collections policies to establish, what accounting procedures and records to establish, and what budgets to develop for planning and control.

Alternative organizational structures emphasize other information needs. When product-oriented structures are employed, for example, detailed information concerning products would be particularly critical. Product information might range from sales and profits for each product to its life cycle and activity-based costs.

OPERATIONAL SYSTEMS

The **operational system** of a firm is its collection of primary physical processes. These processes (also called business processes, operations, or activities) form a chain through which resources are transformed into the products and/or services that a firm provides. Since each primary process adds value to the final output, the collective processes can be called a **value chain.** Figure 2-10 shows the operational system, and hence the value chain, for a firm such as Tractors Manufacturing Company. Four primary processes—acquiring materials, producing finished goods, storing finished goods, and shipping finished goods—represent the chain from suppliers to customers.

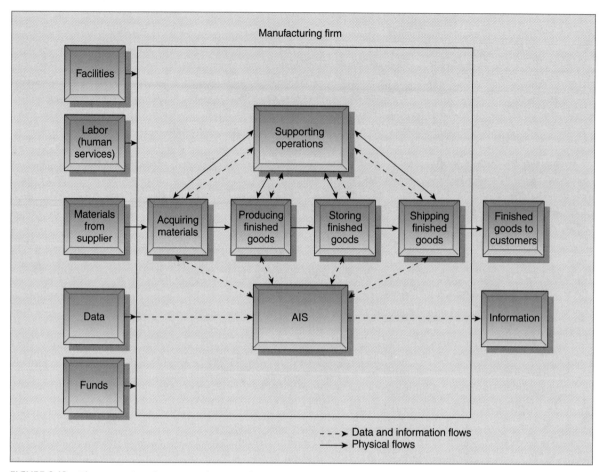

FIGURE 2-10 The operational system of a manufacturing firm.

Since the processes are interdependent and integrated, they may be viewed as subsystems. Subsystems (like systems) can be subdivided if desired. For instance, acquiring materials could be divided into ordering materials, receiving materials, and storing materials. The process of shipping goods can include selling the goods and servicing the goods after sales. By subdividing the processes, we can examine each more closely and observe its interfaces with the others. This technique, an integral part of the *systems approach*, can be useful when analyzing the operational system (or the AIS) for improvements. The analysis can be enhanced by carefully considering the value that each subsystem provides to a firm's overall operational system, i.e., its value chain.

The value chain of a firm can be expanded to form a value system. In the manufacturing firm, the chain could reach out to include the suppliers and customers. For instance, value could be added by establishing direct communications links to key suppliers. Ordered materials could be received just in time for the production process, thereby reducing storing costs.

A number of activities or operations support the primary processes. These supporting activities are performed by many of the organizational functions shown in Figure 2-5, including finance, accounting, personnel, advertising, and the production staff departments. Taken together, these supporting activities enable a firm to administer their resources. Through the aid of information technology, both the primary and supporting activities can be administered more efficiently and timely.

The AIS, as shown in both Figure 2-9 and Figure 2-10, has two close relationships to the operational system. First, it monitors and records the various processes. Consequently, managers can keep abreast of the status of physical activities and the levels of available resources. Second, it triggers actions within the operational system. For example, it generates the purchase orders that trigger the delivery of materials by suppliers.

The organization is also closely related to the operational system, since the employees and managers of the organization conduct and supervise the physical activities. In addition, they make the myriad of decisions affecting all the processes and related resources. In doing so, the employees and managers are aided by information captured by and stored in the AIS.

INFORMATION SYSTEMS AND VALUED INFORMATION OUTPUTS

The information system, including the AIS, is the final major subsystem within a firm to be considered. We begin by exploring the economic nature of information and qualities of information captured by the AIS. Then we survey the key decision processes to which managers apply information, the role of the information system in creating valued information, and the flows of information to the managerial users.

ECONOMIC NATURE OF INFORMATION

Information, being derived from processed data, represents the finished goods of an information system. Being a resource, information has both benefits and costs. The **value of information** is the difference between the benefits and costs. Information value is related to the effectiveness of decision making. It is based on the common-sense concept that the more information of value given to a decision maker, the less risk he or she has of making a bad decision.

In a more precise but still qualitative sense, a piece of information has value if it reduces a user's *uncertainty* concerning a particular decision situation. Conversely, it has no value if it does not produce any new intelligence to the user. Information value can vary appreciably, not only among different pieces of information but also among users. A manager with a technical background may understand a specification concerning a machine and find it very helpful in making a production decision; another manager who is nontechnical may find the information incomprehensible and hence of no value.

While this qualitative definition gives us a clearer view of information value, it does not help us to apply the concept. We therefore need to consider quantitative approaches. The *information economics* approach tells us that additional information should be gathered for use in making a decision as long as the value of the next piece of information exceeds the costs. (These costs are typically related to collecting, processing, storing, and communicating the information to the user.) As Figure 2-11 indicates, this means that a piece of information has value as long as its marginal benefits exceed its marginal costs. A way of implementing this concept is known as the "expected value of perfect information" approach. In this approach the payoff (benefit) of "perfect information" is compared with the costs of the information.

QUALITIES OF INFORMATION

The value of information, and hence the soundness of decisions, can be affected by qualities that attach to the information. As shown in Figure 2-12, useful **information**

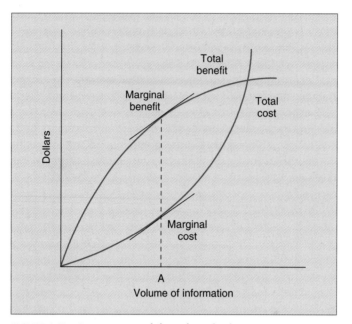

FIGURE 2-11   Components of the value of information.

qualities are relevance, accuracy, timeliness, conciseness, clarity, quantifiability, and consistency. Each is discussed, with reference to managerial decisions, in Chapter 15. When these qualities are inadequate, the symptoms listed in Figure 2-13 are likely to occur.

Preferably all of these information qualities would be maximized in any situation. Since this ideal condition can seldom if ever be achieved, *trade-offs* are necessary. A common tradeoff is between accuracy and timeliness. For instance, the president of Infoage may insist on having the financial statements on his desk one day after the end of the period. In order to gain this degree of timeliness, the president must

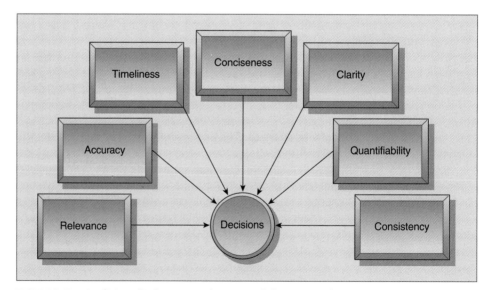

FIGURE 2-12   Qualities of information that can aid decision making.

SPOTLIGHTING

INFORMATION NEEDS*

Much has been written about the information that executives or managers need to be effective. A variety of accounting-oriented approaches have increased the availability of useful information. An example is activity-based costing, which identifies the costs of performing activities in both manufacturing and service-oriented industries.

Professor Drucker, a long-time business author, suggests the key types of information that are needed by profit-oriented businesses. Certain of these types of information are accounting-oriented, while others are qualitative. All are broad-gauged and critical to the long-term success of businesses.

• Total costs incurred throughout the value chain—including the costs of suppliers and dis-

tributors as well as the costs of manufacturing products. Firms that have successfully measured the total economic cost stream and applied the results include General Motors, Toyota, Sears, and Wal-Mart.

• Total factor productivity, which measures the value added at each stage in the chain and by all factors of production.

• Innovations, as reflected by performance in some critical competencies (e.g., miniaturization of electronic parts) or by spending on research.

• Return on proposed capital expenditures, as measured by such yardsticks as discounted cash value.

• Value of human resources, especially employees and managers.

*Peter F. Drucker, "The Information Executives Truly Need." *Harvard Business Review* (January-February 1995), pp. 55–62.

---

sacrifice a degree of accuracy. The accountants would not have had time to post all accounting adjustments and to verify all of the accounts.

INFORMATION RELATING TO MANAGERIAL FUNCTIONS

Information needed by the managers of a firm, as has been emphasized, pertains primarily to decisions. In addition to being affected by the organizational responsibilities of managers, decisions and hence information needs are affected by key

---

• An overload of unfiltered and unprocessed information, often presented in extremely detailed reports.
• Reports used to monitor and control operations distributed monthly or quarterly.
• Tables of figures and dense text that are hard to decipher, often with undefined terms and jargon.
• Sketchy listings of summarized amounts, often with incomplete identifying headings and explanations.
• Forecasted amounts that are expressed in qualitative terms (such as "sales are expected to increase significantly next year") or that are not supported by sound forecasting methods.
• Financial statements and related analyses that are received a month or so after the ends of the accounting periods.

FIGURE 2-13 Symptoms of inadequacies in the qualities of information provided to managers.

managerial functions. In this section we briefly look at the nature and types of two key functions—planning and control—and their impact on information needs.*

Planning The **planning** function consists of deciding among alternative courses of action and then determining how to put the decision choices into effect. Planning within a firm is tied directly to its objectives. For example, Infoage sets an objective of earning 10 percent greater profits from sales next year. It then must decide which courses of action will help to achieve this profit target. Perhaps it should hire more salespersons for the outlets or consider opening a new outlet.

Since planning involves looking into the future, the key information needed for any planning activity must involve forecasts; it must also focus on the differences among the alternatives. We can better understand planning by a firm if we look at two component planning processes: strategic planning and tactical planning.

Strategic planning is the high-level process of deciding on the strategies and resources necessary to achieve the firm's enduring objectives. *Strategies* provide specific means by which to attain the objectives. For instance, Infoage may adopt a low-price, high-volume strategy in order to achieve its objective of maximizing profits from sales. *Resource-allocation decisions* are ad hoc strategic decisions with long-range time horizons and broad scopes. Information used in making strategic decisions should look more than a year into the future, be summarized rather than detailed, and draw heavily on environmental sources. Thus when Infoage plans for a new outlet, it must consider expected overall profits from the outlet for several years in the future and look at such factors as construction costs, customer preferences, and competing stores in the area of the selected site. Managers at the highest level of an organization do strategic planning, as indicated in Figure 2-14.

Tactical planning is the process of translating strategic planning decisions into specific, more immediate operational plans. For example, Infoage's broad marketing policies are converted into detailed selling and advertising plans. Tactical decisions have shorter time horizons, are narrower in scope, and tend to employ less environmental information. Managers at the middle levels of an organization do much of the tactical planning, as Figure 2-14 suggests.

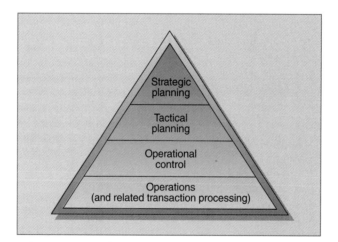

FIGURE 2-14 Levels of managerial decision-making activity and underlying operations.

---

*The process of making decisions and the specific information to be reported to managers are discussed in Chapters 15 and 16.

Control   The managerial function of **control** consists of ensuring that plans are being followed as intended to achieve a firm's objectives. To provide effective control, managers need attention-directing information. That is, they must have *feedback* concerning how well the plans are currently being carried out. This feedback is usually provided through reports that compare actual results with planned results. Upon receiving feedback, managers must make appropriate decisions when necessary and take corrective actions. Two processes involving feedback control in a firm are operational control and management control.

Operational control is the process that promotes efficiency in operations. Decisions made to ensure operational control focus on the tasks performed by the operational system. Thus they involve short-range time spans and are narrow in scope. Most of the information needed for control is found within the firm. Lower-level managers usually make operational control decisions, as Figure 2-14 shows. For instance, Infoage's shipping supervisor assigns shipping employees to each day's scheduled work. He can quickly determine when shipments fall behind schedule and take quick remedial actions.

Management control is the process of ensuring that managers acquire and use resources efficiently and effectively. It focuses on managerial performance rather than operational tasks. Management control extends throughout the organizational structure of a firm and tends to affect managerial behavior. One control technique that Infoage might employ, for instance, is to establish an operating budget that allocates resources to each managerial responsibility center. Periodic budgetary control reports would compare the budgeted amounts for various objects and activities against the actual amounts expended. If Jack Dyson, the inventory manager, exceeds his budgeted amount for a period, an explanation and perhaps a corrective action is in order.

ROLE OF THE INFORMATION SYSTEM IN CREATING VALUE

The information system of a firm, including the AIS, can add significant value to the firm and its outputs. Following are several benefits that it provides:

1. Increased efficiency of the physical processes, hence reduced costs of operations. In the case of Infoage, the information system can help to make sure that merchandise is shipped to the outlets as soon as needed, so that no sales are lost. It can also help to reduce the inventory of merchandise carried in the warehouse.

2. Increased accuracy and currency of the records pertaining to the various entities, such as customers and suppliers. By enhancing these two key information qualities, the information system helps management to achieve its objective of service. Thus when a customer calls to discuss his or her account balance, the firm can respond knowledgeably.

3. Improved quality of products and services. Ann Strong, for example, can provide better consulting services by having an information system that stores reference materials. Thus she can refer to a stored data bank of information concerning a useful systems analysis technique to apply in a particular engagement. In the case of a manufacturing firm, the information system can monitor the quality of products in the manufacturing process and reject those that do not meet specifications.

4. Enhanced quality of planning and control. Infoage, for instance, has improved its budget planning and control process through the aid of its information system.

SPOTLIGHTING

ORGANIZATIONAL STRUCTURE AND PLANNING
at State Farm Insurance Company*

State Farm is one of the largest insurance companies in the United States. Its organizational structure basically consists of a corporate office, 25 regional offices, and more than 16,000 independent agents spread across the country. The corporate office, located in Bloomington, Indiana, provides overall support and management through broad functions such as marketing, services, accounting, and data processing. Each regional office, headed by a regional vice president, contains four primary functions: service, underwriting, claims, and marketing. In turn, each of these functions spreads its activities among such lines of business as auto, property and casualty, fire, health, and life insurance.

The major planning process focuses on the upcoming year. It begins with the president's forecast, which is provided to the organization during the latter part of the preceding year. The forecast lists objectives pertaining to marketing and the major operations. It includes desired performance levels

with respect to loss ratios and earned premiums (two of the key success factors). All of the major functions and the regional offices develop their proposed annual plans based on the forecast, working closely with their subordinate organizational units (e.g., departments). Meetings are held with representatives of the units and resource allocation decisions are made. Unit managers also meet their individual employees and help them to set performance objectives. The proposed plans of the various units are consolidated to form the firm's annual operating plan (budget).

Other significant planning revolves around various projects to be undertaken. Approved projects are fitted into the annual plans. If the projects are long-range in scope, they are tied to the firm's strategic planning process. An example of a project assigned to the data processing function concerned a new class system for unisex ratings for the auto insurance line of business. Once a decision has been made to undertake a project, controls are established during its life. For example, a computerized project reporting system accepts data concerning projects and generates monthly summary reports for each project. Project coordinators review the reports and make decisions to take corrective actions when necessary.

---

*Carol Csanda, "A Tactical Review of the Planning and Control Process within Data Processing at State Farm." In *Management Information Systems: Planning, Evaluation, and Implementation*, John S. Chandler and H. Peter Holzer (eds.), Oxford: Basil Blackwell, 1988, pp. 76–87.

Information technology can be instrumental in all of the improvements described above. Recent advances have made it possible for technology to be applied to the value chains of firms and aid in strategic planning.

On the other hand, information system design and the use of information technology must be governed by information economics. Consider the decision concerning whether or not to install additional technology, perhaps point-of-sale terminals and scanning devices, in Infoage's outlets. To justify this installation, the quantified benefits from the new hardware should be shown to exceed the expenditure for the hardware and its installation. Consider another example: the addition of internal controls into Infoage's system to improve the accuracy of information. The decision should be based on a comparison of (1) the benefit gained from the added accuracy against (2) the direct cost of operating the control plus the indirect cost due to the loss of processing efficiency.

Accountants should be closely involved in these values relating to the information system and especially the AIS. In fact, they can take a proactive role through periodic evaluations. To do so, they can develop checklists of questions relating to the efficiency and effectiveness of the AIS. Among the questions that might be included are,

Are the reports provided to managers understandable, with clear headings, classifications, explanations, graphs, and so on?

Are all key internal controls installed, and are redundant controls whose costs exceed their benefits excluded?

COMMUNICATION OF INFORMATION

After being processed, information needed for decision making must be communicated to the managerial users. Let us consider the levels on which information is communicated and the flows of the information throughout the organization.

Levels of Communication Communication occurs on a technical level, a semantic level, and an effectiveness level. On a technical level, the objective is to convey accurate and complete information. On a semantic level, the objective is to convey information that the receiver (user) can clearly understand. On an effectiveness level, the objective is to stimulate desired results, such as sound decisions. Achieving perfect communication on all three levels is difficult because of **noise** (undesired effects). A well-designed information system, however, can overcome much of the noise.

Consider an example. Pat, a tax practitioner, has a microcomputer-based AIS. He enters data relating to a client's taxable transactions into the AIS. By means of a suitable tax preparation software package, the AIS produces the required tax returns. After reviewing the returns, Pat drives with the returns to the client, who signs the returns and then mails them to tax authorities (e.g., the Internal Revenue Service). In this example, Pat and his AIS represent sources of the information, while Pat's auto delivery is the channel of transmission and the client is the receiver of the prepared tax returns. In turn, the client becomes the source of the signed returns, while the postal service is the channel and the tax authority becomes the ultimate receiver of the returns.

Let us observe effects on the three levels of communication. The information sources function well on a technical level if the returns are based on accurate and complete data and are processed properly, reviewed carefully, and then delivered intact to the client. On the semantic level, however, communication may not be satisfactory if the completed returns are simply handed to the client. Since tax returns can be complicated documents to many taxpayers, they may cause confusion and thus create "noise" in the communication process. Consequently, it may be necessary for Pat to explain how the taxable amount was computed. Satisfaction on the effectiveness level may also require more than merely handing the returns to the client. It may be necessary for Pat to help the client estimate earnings for this year, so that the client can be stimulated to make sound tax decisions. In developing the information for such decisions, Pat will be aided by data from the returns, plus other tax-related data from the client's past years and special tax planning software.

Flows of Information Accounting transactions, many of which originate outside the firm, flow horizontally through various organizational units. Business events, including some of the accounting transactions, also flow horizontally through the physical processes of the operational system. Information arising from these transactions and events flows vertically upward to the responsibility centers at the various managerial levels. Usually this information based on transactions and events tends to be more summarized as it rises to higher levels of management. After decisions and plans are made by the managers in the responsibility centers, the implementing instructions flow downward in the form of schedules, benchmarks such as standard costs, budget levels, and so on. Then this information can be used in the operational and management control processes.

Nontransaction data, informal information, and other types of incipient information originate outside the firm and are captured in large part by the management information systems, decision support systems, or executive information systems. They are used in various ways to aid in making decisions, as we will see in Chapter 16.

BUSINESS EVENTS AND TRANSACTION CYCLES

In this section we survey business events and typical transaction cycles for business firms. The following section looks at standardized subsystems of transaction cycles, the financial and managerial accounting cycles.

BUSINESS EVENTS

Business events, also called transactions, are the steps within the physical and financial processes of firms. Examples of business events are ordering merchandise, receiving merchandise, storing merchandise, and paying for merchandise. External events, such as a sales event, take place between the firm and external parties. Internal events, such as storing merchandise or inspecting a part on the production line, take place entirely within the firm. Taken together, they comprise in essence the primary and supporting activities of the operational system. That is, business events comprise the activities that the management of a firm plans for, directs, and controls.*

It is important to distinguish business events from accounting (i.e., AIS) steps and functions. Thus, recording transactions, posting transactions to a ledger, and preparing reports are *not* business events. On the other hand, accounting transactions—such as paying for merchandise—do represent business events. In fact, the collection of accounting transactions forms a subset of business events.

Useful data elements concerning a business event include:

1. The nature of the event and when it occurred (e.g., a credit sale of March 18, 1998).
2. Which "agents" (e.g., customer X and salesperson Y) were involved.
3. What kinds of resources were involved and in what quantities (e.g., 100 units of product Z).
4. Where the event took place (e.g., outlet B).

TRANSACTION CYCLES

For convenience of analysis, we may group the business events of a firm into process sequences called **transaction cycles** (or transaction processing cycles). The sequence of events that begins with ordering merchandise and ends with payment for the

---

*Eric L. Denna, J. Owen Cherrington, David P. Andros, and Anita Sawyer Hollander, *Event-Driven Business Solutions* (Homewood, Ill.: Business One Irwin, 1993), p. 93. Other concepts from the same chapter in this reference are included in this discussion of business events.

merchandise is an example of a basic transaction cycle. Each transaction cycle typically has one or more key accounting transactions and resources on which it centers. The grouping is called a cycle, since processing of like events or resources recurs in a cyclical manner. The collected transaction cycles for a firm depend on the type of activity conducted by the firm. Figure 2-15 diagrams four transaction cycles pertaining to a typical merchandising firm. (We may recall from Figure 1-5 that transaction processing systems employed within an AIS may be arranged differently. Conceptually, however, the transaction cycle view provides a more logical basis for discussion.)

Revenue Cycle   The **revenue cycle** encompasses two key business events or transactions: sales and cash receipts. In the sales transaction for the assumed merchandising firm, a customer's order for merchandise gives rise to a sales invoice document. The merchandise is shipped to the customer. In the cash receipts transaction, a check or currency is received from the customer.

Expenditure Cycle   The **expenditure cycle** encompasses two key business events or transactions: purchases and cash disbursements. The purchases transaction consists of acquiring resources or services (e.g., merchandise, parts, supplies, utility services).

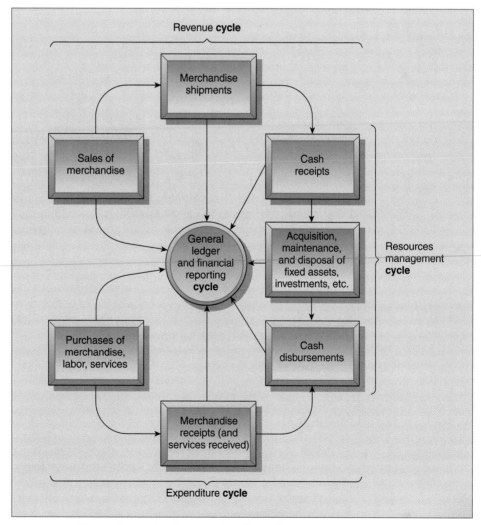

FIGURE 2-15   Transaction cycles for a merchandising firm.

If merchandise is involved, it is received and stored until needed. In the disbursements transaction, a check payment is prepared and delivered to the supplier.

Resources-Management Cycle   The **resources-management cycle** consists of all the activities related to the physical resources of a firm. Thus it includes such business events as the following:

1. Acquiring funds from all sources (including owners), investing the funds, and disbursing funds to recipients.
2. Acquiring, maintaining, and disposing of facilities (fixed assets).
3. Acquiring, storing, and selling inventory (merchandise).
4. Acquiring, maintaining, and paying personnel (such as employees, managers, consultants, and other outside parties).

Since in this grouping each resource has its own cycle, the resources-management cycle is actually a series of cycles. These cycles appear to overlap, as Figure 2-15 shows, with the revenue and expenditure cycles. To avoid this apparent overlap, we define the funds resource cycle to include only the funds acquired from bank loans, bond issues, stock issues, contributions from owners and others, and disposal of plant assets.

The grouping of events within the resources-management cycle and the other two cycles has not been fully standardized. Certain authors define a separate finance cycle, which essentially corresponds to the funds resource cycle described above. Others include the events relating to acquiring facilities and employee services within the expenditure cycle.

General Ledger and Financial Reporting Cycle   At the center of the aforementioned cycles is the **general ledger and financial reporting cycle.** This cycle is unique in that the processing of individual transactions is not its sole or even its most important function. Also, it incorporates accounting-related processing steps rather than business events. (It is included in this section in order to complete the discussion of transaction cycles.) The primary inflows to this cycle arise as outputs from the other transaction cycles. In addition, the cycle encompasses the nonroutine and adjustment-type transactions that occur during or at the end of each accounting period.

Other Transaction Cycles   The set of transaction cycles just described is modified for firms that do not merchandise products. For instance, manufacturing firms add a production or conversion cycle. A bank requires demand-deposit and installment-loan cycles. A government agency does not make sales and therefore dispenses with the revenue cycle. It is clearly important for an accountant to be well aware of the business processes of a firm before attempting to define an appropriate set of transaction cycles.

ACCOUNTING TRANSACTIONS AND CYCLES

After this survey of business events and transaction cycles, we can see that the accounting transactions form subsets within the transaction cycles. Also, in the general ledger and financial reporting cycle, the accounting processing can be fitted into the context of transaction cycles. In this section we consider two accounting cycles, with emphasis on the financial cycle.

OVERVIEW OF TWO ACCOUNTING CYCLES

The **financial accounting cycle** is portrayed in Figure 2-16. It consists of several transformations:

1. The transformation of raw data concerning an economic event into a transaction, reflected in measured amounts and in recorded form on a source document.

2. The transformation of a recorded transaction, via a chart of accounts, into classified and coded data ready for processing.

3. The transformation of coded transaction data into an accounting entry (in a journal) having equal debits and credits.

4. The transformation of the accounting entry into posted amounts in ledger accounts, based on the classification performed in step 2.

5. The transformation of ledger account balances, via such processing steps as sorting and summarizing, into various financial outputs such as trial balances, income statements, and balance sheets.

The transformations listed above are repeated during each accounting period, so that the process can be viewed as a cycle. We should note again that only accounting transactions follow this sequence; other business events are processed by differing procedures.

A contrasting **managerial accounting cycle** is pictured in Figure 2-17. This cycle may be viewed as a separate sequence related to the activity of information processing. Alternatively, it can be considered as overlapping with the financial

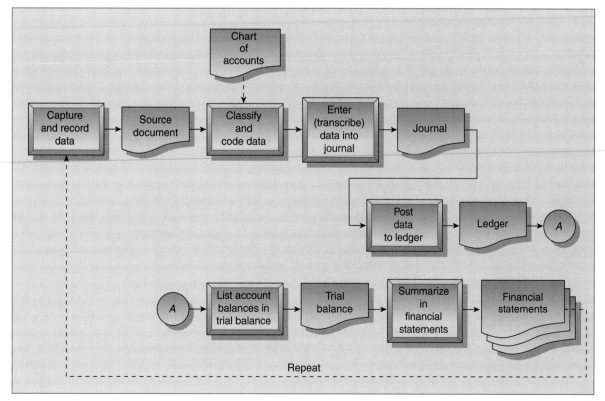

FIGURE 2-16   The financial accounting cycle.

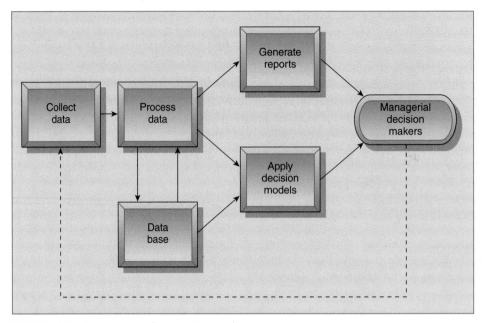

FIGURE 2-17   The managerial accounting cycle.

accounting cycle. It includes data collection, processing, and storage steps. It also results in financial outputs, such as reports and analyses for managers. Rather than being engaged in day-to-day transaction processing, however, the managerial accounting cycle focuses on the information needed for managerial decision making. Two paths may be followed in providing this information. One path generates periodic reports used primarily for operational and management control functions. The other path involves the use of decision models in the creation of useful information; thus it aids in strategic and tactical planning. As the dashed line in Figure 2-17 indicates, these steps are repeated cyclically and decision results are fed back for later use. For instance, standard cost information is fed back for use in periodic variance control reports.

STEPS IN THE FINANCIAL ACCOUNTING CYCLE

To clarify the transformations that occur in the financial accounting cycle, we will discuss each step in terms of the accounting records. This discussion assumes that the processing is performed by a manual AIS.* Because the steps and accounting reappear in all transaction cycles, they are illustrated in the second Review Problem at the end of this chapter.

Prepare Source Documents   Most transactions are initially recorded on forms called **source documents.** An example of a source document is the sales invoice shown in Figure 2-18. In addition to providing written details of transactions, source documents can do the following:

1. Authorize succeeding transactions. For instance, an order from a customer authorizes the transactions involving the shipping of the ordered merchandise and the billing for the merchandise.

*Changes to the cycle when a computer-based AIS is employed are described in Chapters 5 and 11.

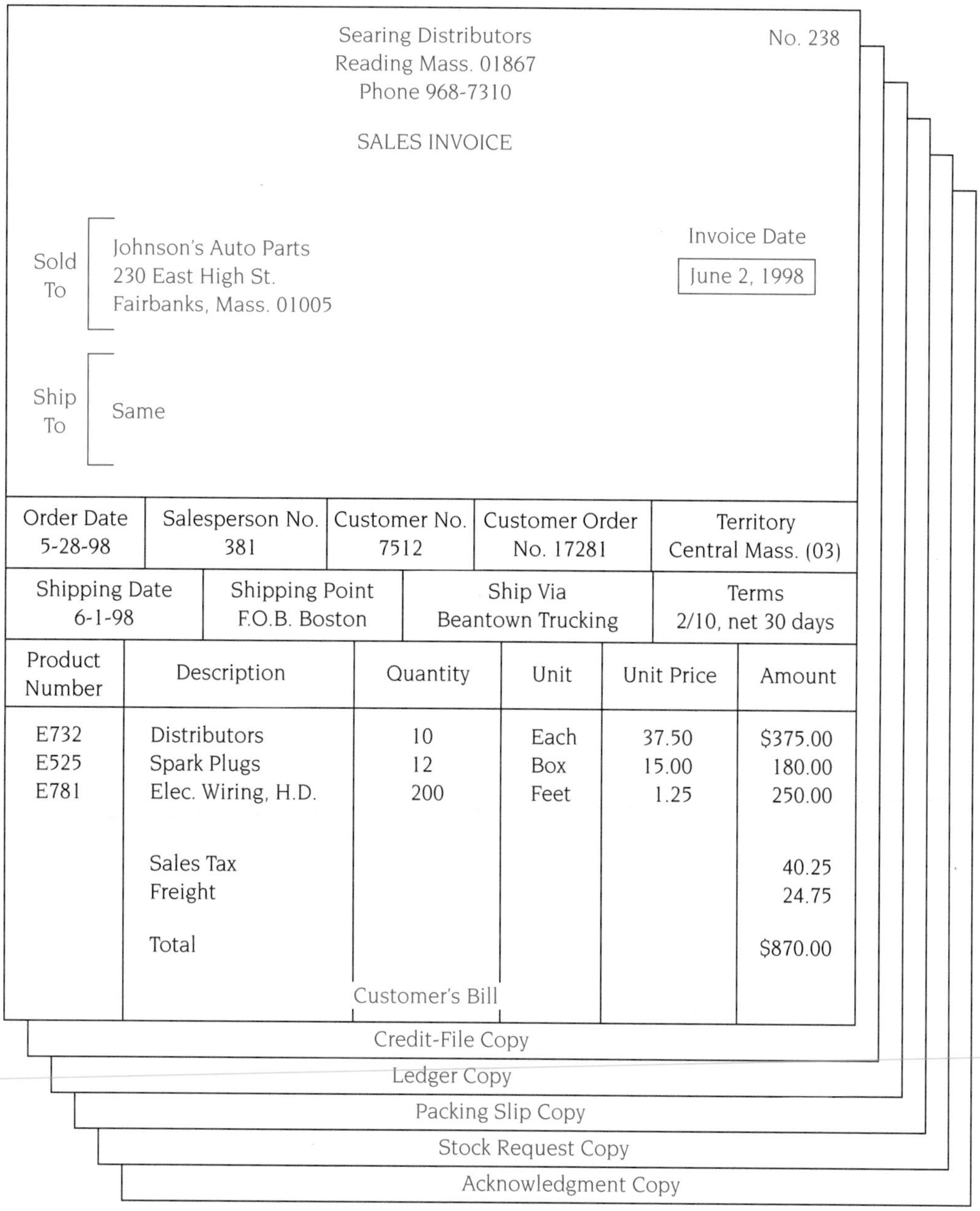

```
                    Searing Distributors              No. 238
                    Reading Mass. 01867
                      Phone 968-7310

                       SALES INVOICE
```

Sold To	Johnson's Auto Parts 230 East High St. Fairbanks, Mass. 01005	Invoice Date June 2, 1998
Ship To	Same	

Order Date 5-28-98	Salesperson No. 381	Customer No. 7512	Customer Order No. 17281	Territory Central Mass. (03)
Shipping Date 6-1-98	Shipping Point F.O.B. Boston		Ship Via Beantown Trucking	Terms 2/10, net 30 days

Product Number	Description	Quantity	Unit	Unit Price	Amount
E732	Distributors	10	Each	37.50	$375.00
E525	Spark Plugs	12	Box	15.00	180.00
E781	Elec. Wiring, H.D.	200	Feet	1.25	250.00
	Sales Tax				40.25
	Freight				24.75
	Total				$870.00

Customer's Bill
Credit-File Copy
Ledger Copy
Packing Slip Copy
Stock Request Copy
Acknowledgment Copy

FIGURE 2-18   A sales invoice.

2. **Trigger desired actions.** Thus a sales invoice such as shown in the figure initiates the payment of cash by the customer.

3. **Reflect accountability.** For example, suppliers' invoices are initialed by those accounting employees who check the invoices for accuracy.

4. **Provide data for outputs and reference.** Thus sales invoices are stored in a repository, so that they can be available for preparing sales analyses or for reviewing a sales history. As we will note later, well-designed source documents contain identifying codes, so that they may be traced via the audit trail.

Enter Extracted Transaction Data After being prepared and coded, the source documents serve as the basis for entering the key data into a journal. Figure 2-19 shows the entry of data from a sales invoice into a journal, often called the accounting record of original entry. Among the data extracted from the source documents are the dates of the transactions, the types of transactions, and the amounts affecting the ledger accounts. For each transaction the credit amounts must equal the debit amounts. For instance, a loan received from a bank in the amount of $1000 would be reflected in a journal entry as a debit of $1000 to the Cash account and a credit of $1000 to the Notes Payable account.

The two main types of journals are the general journal and special journal. A **general journal** has a generalized columnar format that allows any type of accounting transaction to be recorded. A **special journal**, on the other hand, accepts transactions of a particular type. Thus a sales journal (as portrayed in Figure 2-19) accepts sales transactions. Special journals are widely used in manual systems because they enable transactions occurring in high volumes to be efficiently recorded and posted. They typically handle most of the transaction load of a firm, leaving for the general journal only the nonroutine transactions and end-of-period adjustments. Other than sales journals, the most frequently used special journals accept cash receipts, purchases, and cash disbursements.

A **journal voucher (JV)** is a form that contains a single transaction. In most firms it has replaced the general journal, for two reasons: (1) it is easier to process than journal pages, and (2) it provides better control and accountability.

A **register** is a record that may serve as an alternative to a journal or as a chronological log of nonaccounting events. For instance, the receipt of ordered merchandise from a supplier is a nonaccounting event, as is the shipment of merchandise to a customer.

Post to Ledgers After transactions have been journalized, the debit and credit amounts are posted to ledgers. A ledger is an accounting record that summarizes the status of the accounts in financial terms. Its distinguishing feature is a column for the current balance of the account. During the posting step the balance of each affected account is raised or lowered to reflect the transaction amounts.

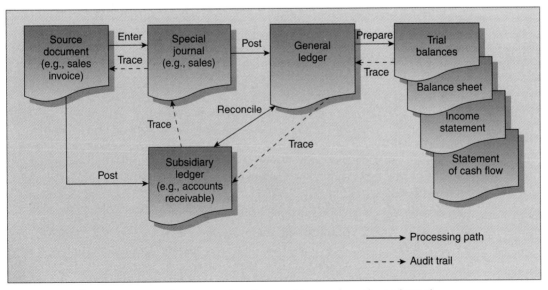

FIGURE 2-19 Flows from transaction processing steps and traces along the audit trail.

Two types of ledgers exist: a general ledger and a subsidiary ledger. A **general ledger** contains the summary financial data concerning the status of all the asset, liability, revenue, and expense accounts established by a firm. A **subsidiary ledger** contains the detailed records pertaining to a particular account in the general ledger. Two examples are the accounts receivable and accounts payable subsidiary ledgers. These ledgers hold the records affecting a firm's customers and suppliers, respectively. The sum total of all balances in a subsidiary ledger should equal the balance of the related account in the general ledger. Thus the general ledger account that is supported or detailed by the subsidiary ledger account is called a **control account.**

As Figure 2-19 indicates, two postings take place when subsidiary ledgers are employed. Totals from the columns of the special journal, as summed periodically (perhaps daily), are posted to the accounts in the general ledger. Transaction amounts from the source documents are posted to the affected records in the subsidiary ledger.

Prepare Trial Balances   During an accounting period, a firm enters and posts a variety of accounting transactions. Each account balance in the general ledger reflects at the end of the accounting period the net effects of all posted transactions. The status of the accounts must be summarized for various users. Before doing so, however, it is prudent to verify that the debits and credits have been posted accurately and completely. Thus a listing of all general ledger account balances, called a **trial balance,** is prepared. The specific purpose of a trial balance is to ascertain that the total of all debit account balances is equal to the total of all credit account balances. Normally three end-of-period trial balances are needed:

1. A preadjusting trial balance, which is prepared after all the entries of an accounting period have been posted.

2. An adjusted trial balance, which is prepared after adjustments have been recorded and posted to the general ledger accounts. These adjustments, called **adjusting entries,** are journal entries made to recognize accruals, deferrals, and errors in previously posted transactions.

3. A postclosing trial balance, which is prepared after the accounts are readied for the next accounting period. The closing process consists of entering and posting **closing entries,** which has the effect of closing the temporary accounts (i.e., the revenue and expense accounts).

Prepare Financial Statements and Other Accounting Reports   The final step in the financial accounting cycle is to produce the outputs needed by the wide array of internal and external users. The most familiar outputs are the financial statements: balance sheet, income statement, and statement of cash flows. Other outputs based on transaction data include monthly statements for customers and quarterly payroll statements concerning employees' earnings.

Outputs for the benefit of the firm's managers are generated in cooperation with the managerial accounting cycle. Chief among these outputs are financial statements in more detail than those provided to external parties. Also, managers may desire breakdowns of revenues by various segments such as product lines, markets, and geographical areas. They may need performance reports concerning the results achieved by the various responsibility centers throughout the organization.

CONTROLS

A variety of controls underlie transaction processing. In addition to the trial balances already noted, important controls include the chart of accounts, reconciliation of the ledgers, and the audit trail.

A coded **chart of accounts** is a listing of the general ledger accounts and their codes. It enables transaction data to be classified and coded precisely and concisely. Therefore, a chart of accounts tends to reduce confusion and the likelihood of making errors in recording data.

A subsidiary ledger provides control by separating a set of detailed accounts into a separate accounting book. To manifest this control, however, it is necessary to ensure that the total of the balances in the subsidiary ledger equals the balance in the account within the general ledger that controls this ledger. Periodic comparisons and reconciliations, as indicated in Figure 2-19, offer the needed assurance.

An **audit trail** is a set of references included on the key accounting records. It links together the steps in the processing procedure, normally using codes based on the source documents and accounting records. Examples of references are the assigned numbers of source documents and page numbers in journals. A complete audit trail enables each transaction to be traced from the source document to the financial outputs, and vice versa. In Figure 2-19 the dashed line traces the trail from the financial statements back to the source documents. By following this trail, an auditor can locate the journals and source documents that support the balances in the balance sheet, for example. Also, accountants can more easily correct errors in transactions and managers can more quickly obtain answers to their inquiries.

SUMMARY

A business firm is a system that has objectives, constraints, controls, inputs, processes, outputs, an environment, and interdependent subsystems. Beyond a business firm lies an environment that is economic, social, technical, and political in nature. Variations in the environments of firms have impacts on needed resources and legal obligations. Three major subsystems of a firm are the organizational structure, operational system, and information system.

The organizational structure is the means by which managers direct and coordinate the firm's activities and operations. Traditional organizational structures are hierarchical in appearance. Hierarchical structures may be centralized or decentralized. The activities are often divided into such functions as finance, marketing, and personnel to gain the benefit of specialization. Alternatively, the activities may be segmented according to product lines, geographical territories, markets served, or projects under development. A matrix organizational structure blends the functional and project orientations. A newly emerging type of structure, the networked structure, is more flexible than the hierarchical and is more motivating to employees. The organization structure is related to the information system through vertical flows of information to the managers, through horizontal flows of transactions across organizational units, and through the social or informal components. Information needs of managers are determined in part by the organizational division of responsibilities.

The operational system incorporates the primary physical processes of the firm, which add value to the products or services. Supporting processes are needed to facilitate the operations. The operational system is related to the information system, since the latter monitors the operations and triggers certain key actions.

Information has value if it reduces a decision maker's uncertainty concerning a decision and yields greater marginal benefits than marginal costs. The expected value of perfect information can sometimes be used to quantify the costs and benefits. Qualities that can give value to information include relevance to the decision in question, accuracy, timeliness, conciseness, clarity, quantifiability, and consistency. Managerial decisions for which information is needed may be classified according to the functions of strategic planning, tactical planning, operational control, and management control. The information system can add value in various ways, such as by improving the value of information used in managerial decision making. Information flows upward to aid in making decisions related to planning, then flows downward to implement the planning decisions and provide control. Information is communicated to users, such as managers, on the technical, semantic, and effectiveness levels.

A variety of business events take place relative to a firm's physical and financial processes. Several key aspects of each event should be recorded for later use. Business events can be grouped into transaction cycles. Four cycles for a typical merchandising firm are the revenue, expenditure, resources-management, and general ledger and financial reporting cycles.

The financial accounting cycle is the standardized procedure by which accounting transactions, a subset of business events, undergo several transformations. Steps in the cycle consist of preparing source documents, entering extracted transaction data, posting to ledgers, preparing trial balances, and preparing financial statements and other accounting reports. The managerial accounting cycle, by contrast, represents the information processing steps needed to provide decision-oriented information to managers.

....

REVIEW PROBLEMS WITH SOLUTIONS

CAMPUS BOOKSTORE, SECOND INSTALLMENT

Statement

The Campus Bookstore (described in the Review Problem at the end of Chapter 1) utilizes an AIS in which the bookkeeper, clerks, cashiers, and managers perform all the activities. In other words, the system is essentially a manual system, although some equipment is used. Sufficient records are maintained to control the cash received, the obligations to suppliers, the levels of merchandise and supplies, and the payments to suppliers and employees.

Required

By reference to the Review Problem in Chapter 1 and the foregoing brief statement,

a. Describe the bookstore in terms of its system characteristics.

b. Briefly describe the operational system of the bookstore.

c. Briefly describe the organizational structure of the bookstore, including the functions that are incorporated.

d. Identify the accounting records that are likely to be used.

e. Discuss the steps involved in processing sales transactions.

Solution

a. The bookstore is a member of a systems hierarchy. Above the firm is its environment, consisting of students and other customers, suppliers, the university campus, the city and other governmental bodies, the bank, and so on. Subsystems within the bookstore include the upper- and lower-level operations, the employees and organizational structure, the AIS, the fixtures and equipment, and so forth. The bookstore has the objectives of earning profits on the sales of merchandise and of providing satisfactory service to all customers. Its inputs consist of the various resources, while its outputs are the merchandise sold and information to outside parties. Finally, it has a number of constraints and controls, such as the physical boundary of the building, the available funds from the owner and sales and bank, the sales seasons that are governed by the university's semesters, the controls over merchandise inventory and repurchases of used textbooks, and so on.

b. The operational system consists of such operations as acquiring merchandise, receiving merchandise, storing merchandise, selling merchandise, returning unsold textbooks, and buying used textbooks from students. These primary operations receive support from such operations as hiring employees, installing fixtures, picking up needed supplies from local firms, cleaning the bookstore, and repairing the various equipment and vans.

c. The organizational structure is a hierarchy with three levels. At the top is the bookstore owner. Reporting to Tom Long are the two merchandise managers, accountant, inventory manager, and cashier. In turn, the merchandise managers direct the salesclerks, checkout clerks, and merchandise order clerks; the accountant directs the three bookkeepers; and the inventory manager directs the stock clerks and custodian. Among the functions around which the personnel are organized are sales, purchasing, accounting, finance, and inventory management. A personnel function is also needed to handle various responsibilities concerning managers and employees.

d. The accounting records that are likely to be used include a general journal, cash receipts journal (which includes all cash sales for new merchandise as well as used textbooks), purchases journal, purchase returns journal (to handle textbook and other merchandise returns), cash disbursements journal, payroll register, general ledger, accounts payable ledger, cash disbursements ledger, employee earnings records, fixed asset records, and inventory ledger or records (for individual merchandise and supply items). It is important to note that the journals and ledgers are unique to this firm, since it has a particular set of circumstances and needs.

e. The steps involved in sales transaction processing are likely to be as follows: First, the salesclerk aids the customer in selecting merchandise. Then, the checkout clerk receives the merchandise from the customer, rings up items on the cash register from price tags, totals the item amounts, adds the sales tax, and informs the customer of the total due. The customer then gives the cashier currency, a check, or a credit card. In the last two cases the cashier then verifies the validity of the check or credit card in some manner. Finally, the checkout clerk bags the merchandise, inserts the cash register receipt, and gives the bag to the customer. At the end of each day the cashier reconciles the cash in the register drawer with amounts listed on a tape locked in the cash register.

Sales Journal — Page 32

Date		Customer Name and Account Number	Sales Invoice Number	Amount
June	2	Johnson's Auto Parts #7512	238	870.00
	2	Royal Auto Parts #6158	239	567.50
	2	Automotive Sales #4779	240	1009.00
	2	B & S Auto Supply #5211	241	223.75
	2	Parts Mart #3835	242	818.00
	2	Thomas Motor Exch. #4138	243	1351.25
	2	Fox Auto Service #2816	244	654.50
			Posted 12/50	5494.00
				√ √

Name Johnson's Auto Parts **Account Number** 7512
Address 230 East High St.
Fairbanks, Mass. 01005

Date		Explanation	Document Number	Debits	Credits	Balance
June	1	Balance forward				750.00
	2	Sale	S238	870.00		1620.00
	2	Payment	R525		750.00	870.00

General Ledger

Account Accounts Receivable **Account Number** 12

Date 1998		Description	Post. Ref.	Debits	Credits	Balance
June	1	Balance forward				21214.00
	1	Sales	SJ31	4828.00		26042.00
	1	Cash receipts	CR40		5132.00	20910.00
	2	Sales	SJ32	5494.00		26404.00
	2	Cash receipts	CR41		4591.00	21813.00

Cash Receipts Journal — Page 41

Date		Received from	Remittance Number	Other Credits Acct. No.	Other Credits Amount	Accounts Receivable (credit)	Sales Discount (debit)	Cash (debit)
June	2	Fox Auto Service #2816	520			520.00	10.40	509.60
	2	A-1 Auto Parts #1913	521			989.00		989.00
	2	Republic Sales Co. #7008	522			450.00	9.00	441.00
	2	Dividend-West Corp.		86	2000.00			2000.00
	2	Del's Auto Electric #3496	523			1230.00	24.60	1205.40
	2	Flint's Distributors #4653	524			652.00		652.00
	2	Johnson's Auto Parts #7512	525			750.00	15.00	735.00
					2000.00	4591.00	59.00	6532.00
		Posted				12	51	10
					√	√	√	√

FIGURE 2-20 Illustrative accounting entries and postings made by Searing Distributors.

Then the cashier prepares a bank deposit slip and takes the funds to the bank.

SEARING DISTRIBUTORS

Statement

Searing Distributors sells a variety of automotive parts and supplies to automobile repair shops, garages, and supply houses. The firm currently utilizes a manual AIS to process all of its transactions, including sales and cash receipts. Among the accounting records employed in Searing's AIS are a sales journal, cash receipts journal, general journal, accounts receivable subsidiary ledger, and general ledger. Monthly the balances from the general ledger are arrayed in a trial balance; then financial statements, such as an income statement, are prepared.

Required

Describe and illustrate the flow of selected sales and cash receipts transactions through the financial accounting cycle during June 1998. Begin with the sales transaction recorded on the sales invoice shown in Figure 2-18. Assume amounts and dates and customer data for additional transactions.

Solution

The first step is to enter the amount of $870 into the single column sales journal shown in Figure 2-20. Other sales for June 2 are also entered into the special journal. At the end of the day, the batch of entries totals $5494. Each entry in the batch is posted to the appropriate account in the accounts receivable subsidiary ledger. For instance, in Figure 2-20 the amount of $870 is posted to the account record for Johnson's Auto Parts. (The code S238 refers to the number of the sales invoice and constitutes part of the audit trail.) After these amounts are posted, the posted amounts are computed. If the batch total is determined to equal $5494, it agrees with the precomputed total in the sales journal. Then the total is posted from the sales journal to accounts 12 and 50 in the general ledger. (The check marks indicate that the posting has been done.) Figure 2-20 shows the results of this posting, which includes the code SJ32 as the posting reference (part of the audit trail). The account numbers involved in the posting are based on the *coded chart of accounts*, a summary version of which appears in Figure 2-21.

Cash receipts transactions are processed in a similar manner. For instance, on June 2 Johnson's Auto Parts remits an amount of $735, which is entered in the cash receipts journal (shown in Figure 2-20). As the entry indicates, the transaction has been recorded on a remittance advice numbered 525. After the entered amounts in the cash receipts journal are totaled, each payment by a customer (shown in the Accounts Receivable col-

Account Codes	Major Account Groupings
10–19	Current assets
20–22	Investments
23–29	Plant assets
30–39	Current liabilities
40–44	Long-term liabilities
45–49	Owners' equity
50–54	Revenues
55–59	Cost of sales
60–69	Selling expenses
70–79	Administrative expenses
80–84	Financial management expenses
85–89	Other revenues and expenses

FIGURE 2-21 A coded chart of accounts, in summary form, used by Searing.

umn) is posted to the appropriate accounts receivable record. In Figure 2-20 we can see that the payment has been posted and represents the amount of a sale that was made prior to June. if the posted total agrees with the precomputed total in the cash receipts journal (i.e., $4591), then all amounts in the various columns of the cash receipts journal are posted to the appropriate accounts in the general ledger. (Note that extra columns have been provided in the cash receipts journal, since all cash receipts are entered into the journal. For instance, an amount of $2000 has been received from a dividend paid by West Corp.; it is posted as a credit to account 86, Other Income.)

On June 30 a trial balance is prepared, as shown in Figure 2-22, from the balances of accounts in the general ledger. (In this illustration only the adjusted trial balance is shown.) Since total debits equal total credits, the financial statements can be prepared. Figure 2-23 shows the income statement, which begins with the gross sales amount of $96,000 shown in the trial balance.

Nonroutine transactions are entered into the general journal. Figure 2-24 shows two such entries. The amount of $4000 in the first entry can be traced to the notes receivable account in the trial balance. (See Figure 2-22.)

KEY TERMS

adjusting entry (59)
audit trail (60)
boundary (of a system) (32)
business event (52)
chart of accounts (60)
closing entry (59)
constraint (of a system) (32)
control (function) (49)
control (of a system) (32)

Searing Distributors
Trial Balance
June 30, 1998

Account Number	Account Title	Debit	Credit
10	Cash	$ 7,717.00	
11	Notes receivable	4,000.00	
12	Accounts receivable	22,838.00	
13	Merchandise inventory	12,337.00	
14	Supplies inventory	1,260.00	
18	Prepaid insurance	300.00	
20	Inestment in long-term securities	3,000.00	
23	Land	1,500.00	
24	Building	90,000.00	
25	Accumulated depreciation—building		$ 22,500.00
26	Office equipment and furniture	18,000.00	
27	Accumulated depreciation—office equipment and furniture		8,400.00
30	Notes payable		2,500.00
31	Accounts payable		6,710.00
33	Taxes payable		4,320.00
40	Long-term notes payable		5,000.00
45	Capital stock		80,000.00
46	Retained earnings		23,650.00
50	Sales of merchandise		96,000.00
51	Sales discounts	1,246.00	
52	Sales returns and allowances	654.00	
55	Purchases	40,020.00	
56	Purchase returns and allowances		1,268.00
57	Freight-in	1,376.00	
61	Sales salaries	22,087.00	
62	Travel expense	3,842.00	
63	Freight-out	2,671.00	
71	Administrative salaries	17,925.00	
72	Utilities expense	200.00	
74	Office supplies expense	75.00	
76	Depreciation expense	550.00	
81	Interest expense	290.00	
82	Bad-debt expense	460.00	
86	Dividend revenue		2,000.00
	Totals	$252,348.00	$252,348.00

FIGURE 2-22   Trial balance prepared by Searing.

control account   (59)
decentralized organizational structure   (40)
environment (of a system)   (32)
expenditure cycle   (53)
feedback   (32)
financial accounting cycle   (55)
general journal   (58)
general ledger   (59)
general ledger and financial reporting cycle   (54)
information qualities   (45)

interface (of a system)   (33)
journal voucher (JV)   (58)
management control   (49)
managerial accounting cycle   (55)
matrix organizational structure   (39)
networked structure   (41)
noise   (51)
objective (of a system and firm)   (32)
operational control   (49)
operational system   (43)

Searing Distributors
Income Statement
For the Month Ended June 30, 1998

Sales		$96,000
Less: Sales discounts, returns, and allowances		1,900
Net sales		$94,100
Less: Cost of goods sold		38,300
Gross profit on sales		$55,800
Operating expenses		
Selling expenses	$28,600	
Administrative expenses	18,750	
Financial management expenses	750	
Total operating expenses		48,100
Net operating income		$ 7,700
Plus: Nonoperating revenues		2,000
Net income		$ 9,700

FIGURE 2-23   Income statement prepared by Searing.

General Journal — Page 75

Date		Account Names and Description	Posting Reference	Debit	Credit
June	16	Note receivable	11	4000.00	
		Land	23		4000.00
		To record the exchange of an unimproved lot for a note from John Broder.			
June	30	Depreciation expense	76	300.00	
		Accumulated depreciation—office equipment and furniture	25C		300.00
		To record depreciation expense for the month.			

FIGURE 2-24   General journal used by Searing.

REVIEW QUESTIONS

2-1. Why is the business environment important to the study of an AIS?

2-2. What are the several characteristics that suggest a business firm to truly be a system?

2-3. What are the three major subsystems of a business firm?

2-4. What are the types of resource inputs to and outputs from a business firm?

2-5. In what significant ways do the environments of business firms tend to differ?

2-6. Why is the environment of a business firm so influential in the design of the firm's AIS?

2-7. What are the key features of a hierarchical type of organizational structure?

2-8. Briefly discuss several major functions within the organizational structure of a manufacturing firm.

2-9. In what ways may an organization's activities be segmented?

2-10. What are the relative advantages of a functional type of organizational structure?

2-11. What are the relative advantages of a product line type of organizational structure?

2-12. Identify several features of the organizational structure of the accounting function of a typical firm.

2-13. What are the relative advantages of centralized and decentralized organizational structures?

2-14. What are the advantages of networked structures over hierarchical organizational structures?

2-15. What are the relationships of the organizational structure of a firm to its information system, including the AIS?

2-16. Contrast the primary operational processes and supporting operations of a firm.

2-17. What are the relationships of the operational system of a firm to its information system?

2-18. What is the qualitative concept of the value of information?

2-19. Identify two quantitative approaches to determining the value of information and the means of determining whether additional information should be gathered for a decision maker.

2-20. What are the qualities of information that add to its value?

2-21. Describe the two planning activities and two control activities for which managers make decisions, and list several features of information needed for making each type of decision.

2-22. What are several benefits that the information system can provide?

2-23. What are the three levels of communicating information to users such as managers?

2-24. What are the basic flows of information within a firm that provide the information for planning and control?

2-25. What are several facets of a business event that should be captured for later use?

2-26. What are several typical transaction cycles for a merchandising firm?

2-27. Identify a special transaction cycle for each of several types of firms.

2-28. Contrast the financial accounting cycle and managerial accounting cycle.

2-29. What are the key records that are employed in the financial accounting cycle?

2-30. Contrast three types of trial balances.

DISCUSSION QUESTIONS

2-31. Discuss the following types of firms with respect to their system characteristics:
   a. An electric utility.
   b. A paper-products manufacturer.
   c. A bank.
   d. A wholesale grocer.
   e. A college bookstore.
   f. A brokerage house.

2-32. Give one example of how an understanding of a firm and its environment aid in the design of an accounting information system?

2-33. Indicate how differences in their firms' environments may lead to differences in the information systems of the following pairs:
   a. A grocery chain versus an integrated steel producer.
   b. A retail jeweler versus a passenger airline.
   c. An oil refiner versus a bank.
   d. A toy manufacturer versus a public utility.
   e. A governmental agency versus a public accounting firm.

2-34. Describe the ways in which an accounting information system can facilitate the acquisition, use, and reporting of the following types of resources:
   a. Materials
   b. Labor
   c. Funds
   d. Facilities

2-35. Describe how the concept of a systems approach could aid in the design of an AIS.

2-36. Discuss the concept of the organization as a management system.

2-37. Discuss the similarities and differences between the physical processing of materials resources and the paperwork processing of data.

2-38. Discuss the value chains for the following types of firms:
   a. A construction firm.
   b. A management consulting firm.
   c. A health-care organization.

2-39. Discuss how the AIS of Infoage can add value to the firm.

2-40. Ann Strong is continually looking for new clients. Discuss the costs and values involved in her efforts to obtain relevant information concerning possible clients.

2-41. Discuss the ways that information technology can improve the qualities of information that Infoage needs.

2-42. Discuss at least one trade-off concerning qualities of information, other than the trade-off between accuracy and timeliness.

2-43. How do the information needs of external users differ from the information needs of managers?

2-44. What are the possible drawbacks of providing too much information to a manger? Too little information?

2-45. How do flows of informal information differ from flows of formal information in a firm?

2-46. A merchandising firm whose organization is structured according to sales territories sells several product lines in all its territories. Discuss the needed changes to its information system if the firm decides to add

    a. A new sales territory.

    b. A new product line.

2-47. It has been said that business events are the foundation of a firm's data base. Discuss.

2-48. What data elements of an event might usefully be captured in each of the following cases:

    a. The initiation of a consulting engagement by Ann Strong with a new client.

    b. The sale of products by a multinational firm.

    c. The admittance of a new patient into a health-care organization.

2-49. Identify various accounts in the general ledger that may suitably be used as control accounts rather than detailed ledgers maintained by a medium-sized merchandising firm. Explain how logical candidates for detailed ledgers are determined.

2-50. What advantages do students gain when they begin their study of transaction processing systems by focusing on manual rather than computer-based examples?

2-51. Why do specific sets of transaction cycles and types of events differ from firm to firm?

PROBLEMS

2-1. Identify several key subsystems of each of the following types of organizations, and then describe each organization in terms of its characteristics as a system:

    a. A merchandising firm such as Infoage, Inc.

    b. A bank.

    c. A public accounting firm such as Ann Strong's.

    d. A university.

2-2. An accounting supervisor leaves a memo for one of his employees that states "You are being reassigned, effective Monday, to our accounting unit in Kansas City." The memo is typed on Friday and misplaced, so that the employee does not receive it until Tuesday. In the meantime, the supervisor has gone on vacation.

Required

Discuss the ways that the communication is impaired in this situation on all three levels (technical, semantic, and effectiveness), as well as the noise that is present.

2-3. A Fortune 500 firm has experienced increased competition in recent years, resulting in declining sales and profits. In order to reduce costs, the firm has had a couple of layoffs, which have reduced the employee head count by 25 percent. Now, rumors have circulated that a planned merger is in the works. Although these rumors have substance, since discussions have been held with several possible candidates, top management is concerned about poor morale and productivity. Thus a notice is posted on the bulletin board by the cafeteria, where some of the employees eat lunch. The notice reads in part: "No merger is planned, in spite of rumors. Discussion of such matters by employees is a violation of the spirit of firm policy and is inimicable to the perpetuation of our continual success and profitability."

Required

a. Describe the inadequacies in communication relating to the merger possibilities.

b. Identify several improvements that could be made with respect to the communication.

2-4. The Pullen Company is a medium-sized merchandising firm that is owned and managed by Jack Pullen. Reporting to Jack are four managers: Linda Scudder, controller; George Clark, sales manager; Bill Henry, warehouse/distribution manager; and Barbara Rhodes, office manager. Within the accounting department are managers in charge of general accounting, budgets, and systems. Within the sales department are managers in charge of advertising, retail store sales, and direct sales. Within the warehouse/distribution department are managers in charge of purchasing, receiving, shipping, and warehouse operations. Finally, under the office manager are the personnel manager, credit manager, and cashier.

Required

Draw the organization chart for the Pullen Company.

2-5. Two major types of firms are integrated oil companies and electric utilities.

Required

a. Draw operational diagrams, similar to the diagram shown in Figure 2-10, for these two types of firms, given the following key activities:

(1) Integrated oil company: oil exploration, drilling, production, refining, storage, and marketing.

(2) Electric utility: generation, transmission, and distribution of electricity, as well as the construction of new facilities.

b. Expand these operational diagrams by including outside entities such as suppliers and customers. Explain why these extended operational systems are value chains, and suggest how they may add value to the chain of each firm.

2-6. The accounting information system of an organization should add significant value to the organization by providing benefits to its users. However, the types of benefits may vary among organizations. Contrast the value—and hence the benefits—that the AIS of Infoage, Inc., provides with the value provided by the AIS of a law firm.

2-7. The Internal Revenue Service (IRS) has been implementing a plan to adapt electronic data interchange technology to tax filling. Under this plan tax returns that are completed by authorized tax preparers would be electronically transmitted from the offices of the tax preparers to a branch of the IRS. The returns would be processed at the branch. When refunds are involved, the amounts can be returned via paper checks to the taxpayers. Alternatively the refund amounts can be transmitted electronically (deposited) to the taxpayers' bank accounts.

Required

a. Draw a diagram showing a value chain that portrays the activities and parties identified above, allowing for the alternative handling of refunds and for the likelihood that many taxpayers will prepare their own returns and mail them as they have done traditionally.

b. Discuss why the addition of the electronic links allows the tax filing procedure to be described as a value-added network.

2-8. The Brown Company of Coral Gables, Florida, is a medium-sized regional distributor. Over the past 10 years its sales have increased more than 100 percent; however, its profits have not kept pace with the growth in sales. The lag in profits began about the time the founder died, five years ago. He had managed largely on instinct, or "by the seat of his pants," as he put it. His successors apparently have not had his intuitive sense about the business, and they have blamed the slower growth of profits on inflation.

Other ominous signs have recently appeared. For instance, the firm borrowed funds at high rates of interest two years ago to build a warehouse. The intentions were to obtain higher sales penetration in the area surrounding the warehouse and to reduce shipping costs. However, inventory costs and operating costs at the warehouse have been higher than expected; also, the monthly payments on the loan have proved to be quite burdensome. Furthermore, the firm has been paying its suppliers immediately on receipt of invoices, apparently because of pride rather than necessity. As a result, the firm is currently encountering a cash squeeze in addition to the profit decline mentioned earlier.

Required

Describe specific information that, if more accurate and available in a timely manner, would have helped to avert the firm's current problems.

2-9. Marval Products of the Bronx, New York, manufactures and wholesales several lines of luggage in two basic types: soft-side and molded. Each luggage line consists of several different pieces, each of which is available in a variety of sizes. At least one line is a complete set of luggage designed to be used by both men and women; however, most of the lines are designed specifically for either men or women. Certain of the lines also include matching attaché cases. Luggage lines are discontinued and introduced as tastes change or as product improvements are developed.

The firm also manufactures luggage for large retail firms, in accordance with each firm's unique specifications. Luggage in this category is marketed under the retail firms' private labels, rather than under the Marval label.

Marval has been in business for 10 years and has increased its annual sales volume manyfold.

Required

a. Identify strategic and tactical decisions that must be made periodically by Marval with respect to new and/or existing products.

b. Identify in detail the information that Marval needs during its annual review of long-term product strategy.

c. Identify in detail the information that Marval needs to prepare its sales forecast for the annual budget.

d. Marval is currently organized by means of a centralized functional structure. Identify alternative organizational structures for Marval, and briefly describe the advantages and drawbacks of each.

e. Describe the information flows that occur in relation to the development of product strategy and the preparation of the sales forecast.

(CMA *adapted*)

2-10. Keepwell Association, a health maintenance organization (HMO), provides medical services to a large number of subscribers in metropolitan Minneapolis. The subscribers (patients) call for appointments and enter the reception room at the appointed time. When they check in, their files are "pulled" and they are assigned to available physicians on the staff.

When a particular subscriber sees the assigned physician, several options are possible: he or she may be (1) treated and sent home; (2) treated and also given a prescription to be filled at Keepwell's pharmacy; (3) given a written authorization to receive medical tests and/or X rays at Keepwell's laboratory; (4) referred, via a written authorization, to a specialist such as a surgeon or allergist. In all cases the attending physician notes the action in the subscriber's file.

In addition to general medical services, Keepwell also provides preventive dental services and eye examinations. Subscribers call those offices directly for appointments. Separate dental and eye examination files are maintained for subscribers who make use of such services.

Payments for services take two forms. Each subscriber pays a flat fee of $15.00 at the time of each visit. He or she also pays a monthly charge, consisting of a predetermined base amount plus added charges for services not covered in the contract. A billing department prepares and mails monthly statements to all subscribers; it ascertains the amount of each statement by reference to the subscriber's contract and to notices received from the various service areas concerning uncovered services.

Required

Identify all significant system characteristics in Keepwell's operations.

2-11. The current organization chart for the Smithers Merchandising Corp. of Kansas City appears below in the accompanying diagram. Since the firm has grown rapidly from a small, family-owned enterprise to a large corporate distributor of high-quality electronics components, the president is concerned that the organization is in need of an overhaul. Accordingly, he asks you to *analyze the chart and the firm's activities and then to prepare a new chart that reflects sound organizational standards and practices.* The new chart can include additional organizational units that you feel are needed.

In the course of your analysis of Smithers' activities, you discover the following facts:

a. Credit losses have been high.

b. Merchandise for resale has often been acquired because of its ease in handling and its accessibility to warehouses, rather than with the considerations of purchasing economy or marketability in mind.

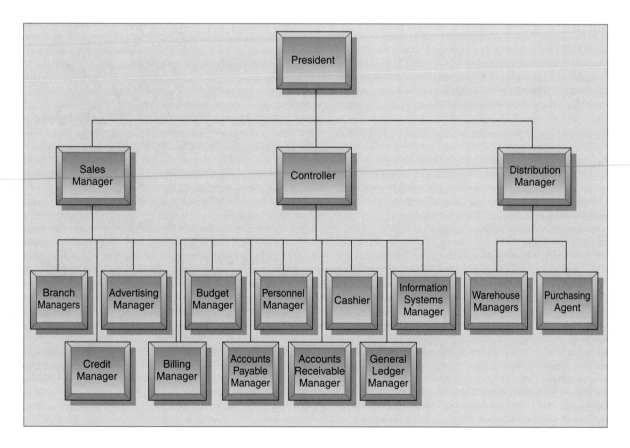

c. The distribution manager and sales manager have often complained that they do not receive the reports that they need in order to manage.

d. Customers' bills are not mailed until a couple of weeks after orders are shipped, since the sales manager insists on approving prices charged to each customer.

e. Cash shortages have been detected from time to time.

f. Employee turnover has been rather high; terminating employees have indicated that salaries and employee benefits are below par and that paychecks are frequently a day or so late.

2-12. Contronics Inc. is a large electronics-component manufacturer in San Antonio, Texas. It has grown substantially in the last four years. As the firm has expanded its operations, the duties and responsibilities of the accounting department have also increased. The size of the controller's staff has increased, and the department has added more responsibility centers as the department has expanded.

Each responsibility center manager reports directly to William Smart, the company controller. An organization structure in which all subordinates report directly to a single supervisor is referred to as a flat organization. The organization chart presented represents the controllership function of Contronics Inc.

Each manager of a responsibility center supervises a moderate-sized staff and is responsible for undertaking the tasks assigned to the position to accomplish the designated objectives for the individual responsibility center. The managers depend on William Smart for direction in coordinating their separate activities.

Required

a. Identify and explain briefly how a flat organization structure, such as the one employed by Contronics Inc. in its accounting department, might benefit downward and upward communication between the controller and his subordinates.

b. Identify and explain briefly the downward and upward communication problems that can result from the flat organization structure in Contronics' accounting department.

c. Redraw the organization chart of the controllership function to reflect sound organizational standards and practices; add one or more staff units that should facilitate the communication process of Contronics' controllership function.

(CMA *adapted*)

2-13. Refer to the Review Problem pertaining to Searing Distributors. Sales invoice no. 238 is mailed to Johnson's Auto Parts as a part of a credit sale. The review problem shows the processing of this sales invoice among other sales, plus the subsequent cash receipt

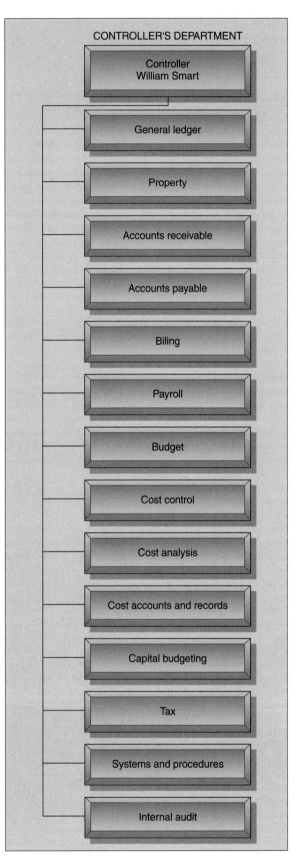

CONTROLLER'S DEPARTMENT

Controller
William Smart

General ledger

Property

Accounts receivable

Accounts payable

Biling

Payroll

Budget

Cost control

Cost analysis

Cost accounts and records

Capital budgeting

Tax

Systems and procedures

Internal audit

reflected by remittance no. 525. This problem focuses on the processing by Johnson's Auto Parts of companion transactions.

Required

a. Sales invoice no. 238, when received by Johnson's Auto Parts, will be seen as a supplier's invoice. What functions does it serve at Johnson's Auto Parts when used in processing?

b. What accounting records does Johnson's Auto Parts employ in processing the sales invoice at Searing Distributors?

c. Describe the journal entries that Johnson's Auto Parts makes in its records to reflect the entries relating to the purchase and related payment.

2-14. Special journals may be designed in differing formats, as the examples in the Searing review problem illustrate. Design a purchases journal in two formats. In both designed formats include additional needed columns, such as a column for the supplier's invoice number. Also, mark each amount column as pertaining to a credit or debit account.

    a. A format having a single amount column from which totals are posted to the accounts payable and purchases general ledger accounts.

    b. A format having amount columns for accounts payable, merchandise purchases, freight-in, supplies, and other debit amounts.

2-15. A check register and cash disbursements journal, though serving essentially the same purpose, generally have somewhat different formats.

    a. Design a check register for use in a voucher system that employs disbursement vouchers. Include columns for the amount paid, payee, check number, disbursement voucher number, and date.

    b. Design a cash disbursements journal that provides amount columns for cash (credit), accounts payable (debit), other debit amounts, and purchase discounts (credit). Include other needed columns.

2-16. Design a multiple-column sales journal that reflects all sales made by the Easyway Co., which maintains its records manually. The firm makes both credit and cash sales. It needs to record freight, which is prepaid, and a sales tax. Credit sales are to be entered from numbered sales invoices, and daily cash sales are entered in total from a cash register tape. Totals are to be posted to the appropriate general ledger accounts on a daily basis.

2-17. Design a supplier's accounts payable ledger record, post the following data, and reflect the balance after each posting:

Larry's Supply Mart (No. 37285)
39873 South Plymouth Ave.
Cleveland, OH 44101
Terms: 2/10, n/30

CREDIT PURCHASES: $2000 on October 10, posted from invoice 2191.
$3400 on November 19, posted from invoice 3374.

DEBITS: $2000 on October 19, posted from check CD5832.
$1600 return of goods on November 23, posted from credit memo CM638.

The beginning balance on October 1 was zero.

2-18. Design a raw materials inventory ledger record for a manufacturing firm that maintains a perpetual inventory system. The firm desires to reflect balances in terms of both quantities and dollar amounts for each inventory item. The record should also contain columns that show quantities received from suppliers and issued to production, as well as the unit price of the item in each transaction.

Post data for item number M2389, connecting rod, which has a reorder point of 100 units. On March 1 the quantity on hand is 170 units; the unit price is $10. Issues for the month were as follows: 80 units on requisition 1432 dated March 3, 100 units on requisition 1476 dated March 14, 90 units on requisition 1497 dated March 23, and 150 units on requisition 1525 dated March 28. Receipts for the month, all at a unit price of $10, were as follows: 200 units on receiving report RR3462 dated March 10 and 200 units on receiving report RR3503 dated March 27.

2-19. *Note:* This problem can be solved by means of an electronic spreadsheet package on a microcomputer, such as Lotus or Excel.

Bellevue Repair Service was organized by Charles Bellevue on August 1, 199X. Following are its account balances, listed in random order, as of August 31. Assume that adjusting entries have already been made and posted.

Advertising expense	$ 600
Cash	7,500
Rent expense	1,000
Service trucks	38,800
Tax expense	200
Accounts receivable	13,600
Insurance expense	460
Revenue from repairs	46,000
Salaries and wages payable	2,600
Accounts payable	3,700
C. Bellevue, Capital	75,000
C. Bellevue, Drawing	2,000
Accumulated depreciation—equipment	600
Accumulated depreciation—service trucks	2,000
Utilities expense	700

Miscellaneous expense	540
Parts and supplies on hand	8,900
Prepaid insurance	1,500
Depreciation expense	2,600
Parts and supplies expense	5,700
Salaries and wages expense	11,800
Equipment	34,000

Required

a. Prepare a trial balance from the given account balances.

b. Prepare an income statement for the month of August and a balance sheet as of August 31.

2-20. An audit of AIMS Manufacturing, a medium-sized firm, revealed the following about its growth:

1. AIMS was started in 1950 as a supplier of brass and bronze electrical connectors, which are still produced in the firm's own foundry and machined in its machine shop. The products are sold directly to electric utilities and to electrical contractors through electrical wholesale distributors. In the 1960s AIMS built an aluminum foundry on the same site and began producing a line of aluminum connectors to complement its then current product line. These new products are sold to the same customers through existing distribution channels.

2. In early 1983, because of expertise in the foundry business, AIMS bought an iron foundry, which was located approximately 150 miles away in a neighboring state. This new acquisition produced products primarily for Original Equipment Manufacturers (OEMs). These products are designed and engineered by the customer and are produced according to customer specifications. Recreational horseshoes and weight sets, lawnmower housings, fence components, and manhole covers are some of the biggest OEM product lines.

3. An examination of the most recent income statement shows that electrical products represent approximately 60 percent of the net sales: the remaining sales are from OEM products. None of the products produced at the original site are sold to OEMs nor are any of the iron products sold to electrical customers.

4. AIMS currently utilizes a functional organizational structure with four vice-presidents in the areas of marketing, engineering, production, and administration, each reporting directly to the president. The responsibilities of the four vice-presidents are as follows:

Marketing—sales (electrical and OEM), marketing and advertising (all products), marketing research.

Engineering—product design and testing (electrical), research and development (electrical), production engineering (electrical and OEM).

Production—three foundries (two at the original site and one at the new site), two machine shops (one at each site), shipping and receiving (at both sites); one centralized production planning and control unit and one quality control unit.

Administration—data processing, purchasing, personnel, accounting.

Required

a. List three advantages and three disadvantages of using a functional structure for this organization.

b. If the firm decided to change its organizational structure, which type would be most appropriate? Justify your answer.

c. If the firm chooses a new, decentralized structure, which functions (or subfunctions) should be decentralized and which should be retained at the corporate level? Justify your answer.

(CIA *adapted*)

2-21. Sovera Enterprises, an expanding conglomerate, was founded 35 years ago by Emil Sovera. The firm's policy has been to acquire businesses that show significant profit potential; if a business fails to attain projected profits, it is usually sold. Presently, the firm consists of eight businesses acquired throughout the years; three of these businesses are described below.

LaBue Videodiscs produces a line of videodisc players. The sale of videodisc players has not met expectations, but the management of LaBue believes that the firm will succeed in being the first to develop a moderately priced videodisc recorder/player. Market research predicts that the first firm to develop this product will be a star.

Ulysses Travel Agencies also showed potential, and the travel industry is growing. However, Ulysses' market share has declined for the last two years even though Sovera has contributed a lot of money to Ulysses' operations. The travel agencies located in the midwest and eastern sections of the country have been the biggest drain on resources.

Reddy Self-Storage was one of the first self-storage firms to open. For the last three years, Reddy has maintained a large market share while growth in the self-storage market has slowed considerably.

Ron Ebert, chairman of Sovera, prepared the agenda for the firm's annual planning meeting where the present businesses were evaluated and strategies for future acquisitions were formulated. The following statements of strategy for each of the subsidiary companies discussed were formulated as the basis for the master plan.

- *LaBue Videodiscs*. Sovera's discretionary resources are to be employed to support the growth of this business. The future officers of Sovera are to be developed here.
- *Ulysses Travel Agencies*. An orderly disposal of the least profitable locations is the initial objective. Once the disposals are complete, an acceptable profit and growth strategy for the remaining locations will be formulated.
- *Reddy Self-Storage*. The strategy for this company is to maintain efficient operations and maximize the generation of cash for use in the further development of Sovera's other firms.

These strategy statements were part of the strategic plan presented to Sovera's board of directors. The directors' only debate was whether Sovera should sell the entire Ulysses organization rather than parts of it. However, the board approved all three statements as presented and circulated them to managers throughout the three units as the corporation's "new marching orders."

Required:

a. Identify corporate policies and practices needed for strategic planning to be effective.

b. Identify at least four general characteristics that differentiate the three businesses identified above, and describe how these characteristics influenced the formation of a different strategy for each business.

c. Discuss the likely effects of the three strategy statements on the behavior of the top management and middle management of each of the three businesses.

(CMA *adapted*)

2-22. Grayson Corp. manufactures sophisticated instruments that are primarily used on military aircraft and ships. Martin Grayson founded the firm in the 1980s when he received a patent on a laser-directed aiming device for military equipment. Since that time, several new products have been developed and patented. Owing to the government's increase in defense spending, the firm grew significantly throughout the 1980s. In recent years, however, critical problems have arisen due to the effects of adjusting to the end of the "cold war." The sales department has complained that some of the products are not receiving the attention they deserve from the production and research departments. The latest technology has not been incorporated into the products in time to meet deadlines imposed by customers. Also,

there has been decreased efficiency in the allocation and use of resources.

The firm is currently divided into four separate areas of responsibility—sales, finance and administration, production, and research. Grayson serves as president and also continues to manage the research and development activities. He has appointed a task force to evaluate the organizational structure, which may be the cause of the lack of coordination among departments and the increasing inefficiencies. He has specifically asked that the matrix and networked organizational structures be considered.

Required

a. Discuss how the matrix structure might be applied to Grayson Corp.

b. Identify the benefits and weaknesses of the matrix structure with respect to Grayson Corp.

c. Discuss how the networked structure might be applied to Grayson Corp.

d. Identify the benefits of the networked structure as contrasted with the matrix and functional structures. What difficulties do you foresee in applying the networked structure?

(CMA *adapted*)

CONTINUING CASE

With respect to the small firm that you selected in Chapter 1, complete the following requirements:

a. A brief description of the firm in terms of its system characteristics.

b. A brief description of the firm's environment, such as the industry of which it is a member, its physical facilities and other resources, and its employees.

c. A listing of its transaction cycles and the component transaction processing systems.

d. A diagram of the primary operations and business processes, with a brief discussion of the value added by these operations and processes.

e. A chart of the current organization.

f. A listing of key information needs relating to strategic planning, tactical planning, management control, and operational control.

g. A description of the processing of basic transactions through the financial accounting cycle, including copies of the source documents and outputs relating to one of the transactions.

CHAPTER
3

INFORMATION TECHNOLOGY
AND THE AIS

INTRODUCTION

Information technology (IT) concerns the use of computer and related technologies to manage the information resource. The financial impact of IT is enormous, since information-related costs may amount to as much as 10 percent of sales. In this chapter we briefly review the components of computer technology. Next we consider the major information systems architectures that serve as the essential ingredients in the development of communications networks and the accounting information system (AIS) of a modern firm. Then we review major hardware, software, and telecommunication technology trends that will affect the way accounting and information-related applications are developed. Finally, we examine the expected improvements in the AIS brought about by IT.

This survey of information technology can be prefaced by answering two questions: Why is IT important to accountants? What is the impact of IT on the AIS?

IMPORTANCE OF INFORMATION TECHNOLOGY TO ACCOUNTANTS

With each passing year, information technology becomes more tightly interwoven with the fabric of business. Harvard Business School scholar Warren McFarlan suggests a simple thought experiment that reveals an organization's dependency on information technology: If information systems should fail, then how long would it take until the corporation *is unable to conduct business? In decades past, the answer was often measured in days or even weeks. In the next millennium, the answer will be measured in hours or even min-utes. Information technology is rapidly taking hold of the daily operations of business.**

Computers are at the heart of IT. Computer technology is an essential ingredient in the AIS of most modern firms. Although computers do no more than manipulate bits and digits, they greatly enhance the capabilities of information systems. As such, computers represent a means of managing information. In fact, a new term—**information resource management**—reflects the impact of computerization. In order to treat information effectively as a valuable resource, information resource management strongly suggests that computer technology be integrated into the modern AIS. Thus, to use, evaluate, and develop a modern AIS, accountants must be familiar with computer-based IT. Although a thorough technical knowledge is not necessary, an accountant should understand the various options that are available. Assuming that you intend to be an accountant, you will therefore want to be aware of the various devices for entering data, processing data, communicating data from place to place, and generating information. You will also be more effective in your responsibilities if you appreciate the varied types of software that are employed in operating an AIS and in processing the applications that it handles. Furthermore, you will be able to protect a computerized system against problems to which it is subject. For instance, you might prevent loss of valuable accounting records stored in the AIS or provide ways of ensuring that entered data are accurate.

Computers are important to accountants for personal as well as for business reasons. They can greatly extend the capabilities of individual accountants. Compared with manual methods, computers enable accountants to perform many of their duties more quickly, accurately, consistently, and easily. For example, accountants may use computers, together with electronic spreadsheet software packages, to analyze financial statements and to develop budgets. Tax accountants use special tax software to prepare tax returns.

Very likely as an accounting student you are already acquainted with computers, especially the friendly versions known as microcomputers. In fact, you may use a microcomputer to perform accounting homework assignments; perhaps, during your "free time" (what little there is) you use the microcomputer to hone your skill in playing chess or "surfing the net." Thus you are probably familiar with the four reasons why microcomputers are so revolutionary: (1) low cost for the benefits reaped, (2) versatility in quickly and accurately performing a wide range of processing tasks, (3) ease of use without the need to know how to program, and (4) total control of the processing machine by the individual user.

In summary, you, as an accountant, have a double incentive to learn more about IT. On the one hand, it can be essential to the efficient functioning of your firm's AIS. On the other hand, it can aid you in being a more effective accountant.

EFFECTS OF INFORMATION TECHNOLOGY ON THE AIS

When a computer system is installed in an AIS, no major activities are added or deleted. The AIS still collects, processes, and stores data. It incorporates controls over the accuracy of data. It generates reports and other information. However, computerizing an AIS often changes the character of the activities. Data may be collected

---

*Systems Auditability and Control Report, Module 11, *Emerging Technologies*, Altamonte Springs, Fla.: The Institute of Internal Auditors Research Foundation, June 1994, p. 11-3.

by special devices. Fewer paper accounting records may be employed. In some instances even source documents are dispensed with. Many if not all of the processing steps are performed automatically. The outputs are neater, in more varied forms, and often more numerous. More outputs can be generated on demand by any user. Moreover, the outputs can be distributed to other persons connected via a local-area network of interconnected microcomputers. Additional controls can be incorporated that enable the computer itself to check the accuracy of data.

More important than these surface changes, however, are the improvements in performance that computer technology, when properly implemented, provides:

1. Faster processing of transactions and other data.
2. Greater accuracy in computations and comparisons with data.
3. Lower cost of processing each transaction.
4. More timely preparation of reports and other outputs.
5. More concise storage of data, with greater accessibility when needed.
6. Larger range of choices for entering data and providing outputs.
7. Higher productivity for employees and managers (when they learn to use computers effectively in their routine and decision-making responsibilities).

These improvements have caused computers to be chosen by an increasing number of firms for an ever-widening range of applications. Prime candidates for computerization take advantage of several of the improvements. Thus high-volume accounting transaction processing applications are generally among the first to be computerized. Computerization enables large volumes of transactions to be processed more quickly, accurately, and inexpensively. Applications involving insurance policies, motor vehicle records, and veterans' records have also been automated at an early stage. Such applications concern huge quantities of data that need to be stored and accessed frequently by clerks and managers. Other applications that are ideally suited to computerization include those that involve:

1. Extensive manipulation and analysis of data, as in sales analysis applications.
2. Continuous monitoring of processes and timely preparation of reports, as in inventory control and quality control applications.
3. Complex and flexible interactions between decision models and data bases and managers, as in strategic decision applications.

Figure 3-1 compares the tasks that are more suitably performed manually with those more suitably performed by computer technology.

VERSATILITY OF COMPUTERS IN BUSINESS SETTINGS

Organizations can employ computers in a variety of ways to perform such tasks as listed in Figure 3-1. To set the stage for our survey of information technology, we will briefly describe the roles of computers in varied business settings. Because of the ever-increasing use of microcomputers in the business world, we will give microcomputers the greatest attention.

In a very small business firm a microcomputer may be the sole automated processing device. The office clerk may use packaged application programs to process a variety of transactions during the course of a day. At times when the microcomputer

Suitable Tasks to Be Performed Manually	Suitable Tasks to Be Performed by Computer
Processing exceptional and infrequently occurring transactions	Collecting and processing large volumes of routine transactions
Setting objectives and making policies involving considerable judgment	Storing large quantities of data and information
	Monitoring and controlling continuous processes
Finding new problems that need solutions	Answering specific inquiries based on stored data
Supervising employees	Preparing complex analyses and extensive reports
Fostering social communications (i.e., grapevine)	Helping managers to gather data and understand the relationships concerning all types of decisions
Making complex strategic decisions	

FIGURE 3-1 Suitable tasks to be performed by manual and computer-based information systems.

is not being used by the clerk, the manager might use the same microcomputer to prepare a budget or retrieve customer information.

In a very large firm a number of microcomputers will likely be located in individual departments, sales offices, warehouses, accounting areas, and executive suites. Some may serve as stand-alone microcomputers, unconnected to other microcomputers. These stand-alone microcomputers are used to process data in the same manner as microcomputers in small firms. However, a large firm usually has larger computers, such as mainframe computers, that perform the processing tasks involving high volumes of transactions or complex computations. Often the outputs from these larger computers, or portions of the outputs, are used by one or another of the microcomputers as data for performing analyses or preparing summaries. These data from computer outputs are often keyed into the microcomputers. Since keying is a slow and error-prone process, an alternative means of transferring data are preferred.

Many large firms have found such an alternative through the use of **micro-to-mainframe** connections, electronic links (together with special communications software) that enable data to be transferred between a microcomputer and a mainframe computer.

Micro-to-mainframe connections allow data to flow either from the microcomputer to the mainframe computer (called **uploading**) or from the mainframe computer to the microcomputer (called **downloading**). Multiple micro-to-mainframe connections create a computer network.

As a member of a micro-to-mainframe connection, a microcomputer functions as a **terminal emulator.** That is, it imitates a terminal by providing a means of accepting data for transmission to the mainframe computer or receiving outputs from the mainframe computer. With appropriate software the microcomputer can serve as an intelligent terminal by also editing entered data and/or uploading entire files.

Alternatively, a microcomputer within a computer network may function as a *user workstation*, a center where processing tasks are performed. If it contains a hard disk, it may even function as a server workstation, such as a *file server*, in which role it provides application software and data files to multiple microcomputer users in the network and also remains available for processing tasks (e.g., running spreadsheet applications), posting and receiving electronic mail, teleconferencing, checking electronic calendars and appointment schedules, and sharing expensive laser printers. When used appropriately within computer networks, microcomputers foster *cooperative processing*, the allocation of processing tasks so that the best capabilities of all computer resources are employed.

SPOTLIGHTING

A STAGE BY STAGE DEVELOPMENT OF COMPUTER-BASED APPLICATIONS

On acquiring computer hardware and software, a firm typically progresses through several stages of applications development. Recall from the discussion in Chapter 1 that a firm can automate data processing (DP) applications and management information systems (MIS) applications.

FIRST STAGE: DP APPLICATIONS

First-stage applications focus on narrow unintegrated applications that are oriented toward the processing of routine transactions. Typical applications in this stage are general ledger accounting, payroll processing, and inventory record keeping. The output of this stage is summary reports and document outputs to accounting and nonaccounting departments. In addition, the prepared financial statements represent primary information to external users, such as investors and creditors. Top-level managers also analyze the statements to determine if their strategies, policies, and plans have been completed effectively and efficiently.

SECOND STAGE: MORE INTEGRATED DP AND LIMITED MIS APPLICATIONS

Second-stage applications still focus on transaction processing. However, they are more integrated. Thus a firm might combine its accounts receivable, sales order entry, and inventory record keeping applications to create an integrated credit sales processing application. Applications at this stage still generate financial statements, summary reports, and other document outputs. Also, decision-oriented information is provided to lower-level managers. For example, by-product reports prepared from the AIS sales processing application may notify the inventory and purchasing managers of the need to replenish orders. Other information from the same application may help the credit department in making decisions concerning credit approvals and collections.

THIRD STAGE: HIGHLY INTEGRATED MIS APPLICATIONS

Third-stage applications are very integrated and broad based. They tend to cut across two or more organizational functions, such as marketing, inventory management, and accounting. A goal of third-stage applications is to automate MIS tasks in each major organizational unit, thereby providing decision-making information to middle- and upper-level managers. For example, each organizational unit's computer may be networked (connected) to the other organizational units' computers. This interconnected network of computer systems can generate reports and information to support middle- and upper-level management decisions.

In the third stage, the accounting department often receives requests for special projects that provide support in making decisions such as developing for the:

1. Treasurer a computerized cash-flow report to assist in managing working capital.
2. Marketing vice-president a DSS application that provides a graphical ranking of alternatives to aid in selecting new products.
3. Distribution manager a DSS application to select a location for a new warehouse.
4. Advertising manager an expert system to select the media in which to advertise.

The middle- and upper-level managers' information needs for all third-stage decisions must be obtained from sources other than routine transaction processing.

During stage three, financial statements, summary reports, and document outputs are still prepared, as well as decision-making information for lower-level managers.

Most firms are still developing second-stage and third-stage applications. Very few firms are nearing completion of the third stage. Emerging developments in the areas of data modeling, decision support systems, expert systems, neural networks, and computer networks will continue to be helpful to firms as they continue their efforts in developing sophisticated computer-based applications in the coming years.

COMPONENTS OF INFORMATION TECHNOLOGY

With these uses of computers in mind, we can undertake a nontechnical review of IT components. The main components are hardware and software. These components are often combined to form telecommunication networks. Technical details have been placed in Appendix A at the end of this textbook. If any terms mentioned in this section are unfamiliar to you, please refer to the appendix.

COMPUTER HARDWARE

Computer hardware comprises the physical equipment of computer systems. A specific collection of hardware composing one particular computer system is known as a **hardware configuration.** For instance, a hardware configuration may consist of a mainframe processor, keyboard terminal, printer, and magnetic disk. Many hardware devices are **on-line devices,** in that they are connected directly and continuously to the computer. The data terminal, for example, is an on-line device. Those devices used to prepare input-output media while disconnected from the computer, on the other hand, are called **off-line devices.** An example is the key-to-tape encoder. Computer hardware encompasses an extremely wide range of processors, storage devices and media, input and output devices, and data communication devices.

COMPUTER SOFTWARE

Computer software embodies the instructions that guide the processing jobs and direct the actions of computer hardware. Software development may be undertaken by the using firm, in which case it is labeled *customized software*. Alternatively, software may be developed by software firms or computer manufacturers. In this latter instance it is termed *packaged* or *canned software*. Computer software includes the programs and routines—sets of instructions that guide the hardware of a computer system in performing its varied operations and functions. **Computer programming languages** such as COBOL, C++, Visual Basic, Pascal, and Java, are the building blocks for software development. Using these computer languages, programmers prepare systems software, including operating systems, utility programs, and programs that are employed in applications.

The software that manages and coordinates the various hardware components and all assorted programs of a computer system is called the **operating system**. When the computer is turned on (booted), the operating system, such as Windows 95 or UNIX, is the first program to load into memory. **Utility programs** include a series of routines that aid in the functioning of a computer system and the applications that it executes. They are used to manage computer files, identify problems with hardware, provide disk compression, detect computer viruses, manage memory, and back up files. The specific data and information processing tasks are performed in a computer-based system by **application programs.** Such programs enable accountants to use wordprocessors to prepare written documents, spreadsheets to develop budgets, accounting software to prepare financial reports and statements, data-base management systems to query data bases, and expert systems to give advice.

TELECOMMUNICATIONS

Many modern firms have facilities—plants, warehouses, sales offices—at more than one location. Communications among these remote locations have traditionally been

SPOTLIGHTING

A BRIEF HISTORY OF THE COMPUTER REVOLUTION

Modern computer hardware and software did not develop overnight. Instead, they are the product of mechanical and electrical innovations that date back several centuries. In fact, the first known computational device was the abacus, which was devised in ancient times. It is still used in some countries. The first real mechanical calculator, however, was invented by Blaise Pascal in the mid-seventeenth century. Not many years later Gottfried von Leibnitz improved Pascal's calculator by including multiplication, division, and square roots to the addition and subtraction functions. Then, in the nineteenth century Charles Babbage developed the difference machine, which could perform calculations without human intervention. Paralleling these hardware developments were two forerunners to computer programs, both devised in the nineteenth century. Joseph Jacquard used holes punched in cards to provide instructions to textile looms, and Herman Hollerith adapted the use of punched cards to process data gathered in the 1890 U.S. census.

All of these early inventions set the stage for an explosive series of developments in the twentieth century. William Burroughs developed a key-driven adding machine that was a best seller in the early decades. Accounting machines that performed varied record-keeping functions were developed in the 1920s and 1930s. Many of these machines were electromechanical in nature, since they employed punched cards to contain the data. Electromechanical machines were specialized to handle particular data processing tasks. Typical machines were card punches, punched card readers, punched card sorters, punched card collators, and punched card accounting (printing) machines. Then, the first automatic electronic calculator, the Mark I, was designed during World War II. It was quickly followed by ENIAC, the first all-electronic computer, which was developed at the University of Pennsylvania. Two computers, the EDVAC and EDSAC, were developed that utilized the stored-program concept, that is, that instructions comprising the programs are stored inside the computer itself.

These experimental computers gave rise to four generations of commercial computers. The first generation, from 1951 to 1956, began with the UNIVAC I. Like all first-generation computers, it utilized vacuum tubes to control internal operations and punched cards to enter data. Instructions to operate these computers were written in the ones and zeros of machine language or in symbolic languages. Late in the first generation General Electric Corporation installed the first large-scale business application.

The second generation, from 1959 to 1964, saw a change from vacuum tubes to transistors. Also, magnetic cores were used as the primary storage medium. Magnetic tapes came into use. Higher-level languages such as FORTRAN and COBOL came into use. An increasing number of business applications were designed and put into use by firms in a variety of industries. Several major mainframe computer manufacturers—including IBM, Univac, Honeywell, Burroughs, and General Electric—engaged in tight competition.

Third-generation computers, during the period from 1965 to 1971, contained integrated circuits rather than transistors. Minicomputers and remote terminals were also introduced. Magnetic disks were widely used.

The fourth generation, which began around 1972 and continues until today, has seen several significant developments. Large-scale integrated circuits, thousands of logic gates on a single silicon chip, packed more processing capability into a smaller space. The other major hardware development is the rise of microcomputers. On the software side, new user-friendly fourth-generation languages have become widely accepted.

The fifth generation, which began in the mid-1990s, introduced computers that can perform at a more advanced level. They are able to undertake tasks that approach artificial intelligence and even to "learn" from past experiences.

conducted by mail and telephone calls. In recent years an increasing number of firms have connected their remote locations via data communication systems. The hardware components that make up data communication systems usually include communications links, terminals and microcomputers, modems, and communication control units. Data communication systems require the variety of software needed by any hardware configuration, plus such special software as communications programs.

A **computer network** is a data communication system that enables firms to share information and programs by linking computers and other devices such as printers. Among the categories of computer networks are wide-area networks (WANs), local-area networks (LANs), third-party networks, and client/server networks. Each category represents an information system architecture and will be discussed further in the next section.

As noted earlier, computers can be used in extremely versatile ways when linked within networks. They enable accounting applications to be moved off mainframes, information to be disbursed instantaneously throughout an organization and to other organizations, and data to be collected in "warehouses." Uses such as these are discussed in Chapters 16 and 17.

INFORMATION SYSTEM ARCHITECTURES

An **information system architecture** may broadly be defined as the structural arrangement of hardware and data communications components of an information system. In addition to its physical design dimension, an architecture may also pertain to software, concepts, or capabilities—such as relevant industry standards for database software and guidelines or rules for sharing data and information among users. Our survey of architectures focuses on hardware and ranges from single and multiple computer processors to client/server networks. Other architectures will appear in later chapters.

HIERARCHY OF SINGLE COMPUTER PROCESSORS

The typical computer today employs a single processor. Although a number of single computer processor categories could be specified, the three most clearly defined—in terms of overall performance and size—are mainframes, minicomputers, and microcomputers.

Mainframes are the large-scale computer processors. They often serve as the centers of complex configurations or as the flagships of computer networks. However, the number of installed mainframes has decreased as the number of networks and client/server computing platforms has dramatically increased. Processors in this category have processing speeds in the hundreds of MIPS (million instructions per second). Their primary storage capacities may be measured in dozens of megabytes, and their word sizes are typically 64 bits or greater.

Minicomputers, also called midrange computers, are the medium-scale computer processors. Although smaller than mainframes, they can accommodate multiple users and can even control networks of microcomputers. They are suitable as the sole computers in small firms and as key elements in computer networks of large and medium-sized firms. Minicomputers provide processing speeds and primary storage capacities similar to mainframes, and word sizes of 32 or 64 bits.

Microcomputers are the small-scale computer processors, although they are as powerful as present-day minicomputers and yesterday's mainframes. Microcomputers have been improving so rapidly that any statement concerning them is likely to be out of date before print. However, they provide processing speeds of millions of instructions per second, primary storage capacities from 640 kilobytes to 64 or more megabytes, and word sizes of 16 or 32 bits. A separate appendix pertaining to microcomputer systems, Appendix B, has been included at the end of this textbook. In addition to the distinctive hardware features embedded in microcomputers, Appendix B discusses application software packages for microcomputers.

MULTIPLE PROCESSOR CONFIGURATIONS

An increasing number of computer systems are being constructed with more than one processor, so that **multiprocessing** can be performed. These multiple processor configurations include coupled processor systems, parallel processing systems, and distributed processor systems.

A **coupled processor system** consists of two or more processors that share a common primary storage unit. Each processor, which is incorporated in a separate unit, enables more than one program to be processed simultaneously. In some cases specialized computers are used to perform functions such as input-output or data communications. All of the processors within the coupled arrangement, however, are under the control of a supervisor computer. Thus the configuration is relatively inexpensive, when compared with the use of several totally separate computers. In addition, coupled processor systems can provide "built-in backup." If one of the processors fails, one of the others can take over the processing task. Thus coupled processor systems are often called fault-tolerant systems. Figure 3-2 shows a coupled processor system involving two processors.

A **parallel processing system** consists of clusters of microprocessors that are incorporated into a single powerful computer. In **massively parallel supercomputers,** these clustered microprocessors can number into the thousands, involving extremely complex patterns of interconnections. They allow many segments of a program to be executed in parallel simultaneously. Even computer systems having multiprogramming capabilities can only process the multiple resident programs in

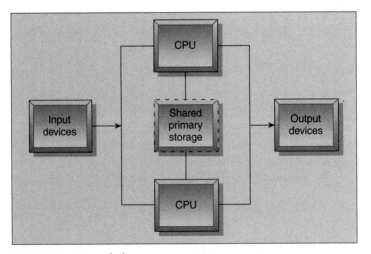

FIGURE 3-2   A coupled processor system.

a concurrent manner. Parallel processing systems are therefore assigned to manage the most complex processing tasks and huge bases of data. For instance, they may be used in scientific applications and for major tasks such as forecasting the weather conditions for a nation.

A **distributed processor system** is a computer network consisting of two or more interconnected computers. Being a type of network, it is more logically discussed in the next section.

INTERNAL COMPUTER NETWORKS

Computer networks that are restricted to individual firms are known as internal networks. Two basic categories of internal networks are wide-area networks and local-area networks. These networks are differentiated on the basis of the areas that they span. An in-depth discussion of networks is presented in Chapter 17.

A **wide-area network (WAN)** is formed among computers and interconnected devices that are geographically distant from one another. Two wide-area network architectures are centralized networks and distributed networks.

A **centralized WAN** concentrates all application processing at one geographical location. Typically all hardware, software, and data processing personnel are located at the corporate headquarters of a firm using a centralized network. The data processing staff supports users at remote locations by analyzing, designing, and implementing requested applications. Remote locations maintain peripheral devices such as terminals and printers, together with the communications hardware and software that support these peripherals.

A **distributed WAN** places fully functioning computers at each remote site within the geographically distributed network. Each remote site processes its own applications, thereby reducing processing demands on the central computer facility. Computers at each remote site can be interconnected by data communications hardware and software to other remote sites and to the central computer facility to form an enterprisewide network. All sites in such a network are able to share files, printers, and data with other sites.

A **local-area network (LAN),** a type of distributed network, is created when the linked computers are grouped within a limited geographical area. This local area may be a single building, a cluster of buildings, or a department within the firm. A LAN can be connected to other LANs and/or to WANs via hardware devices known as gateways or bridges. Although computers of all sizes may be included in a LAN, most tend to be microcomputers.

EXTERNAL COMPUTER NETWORKS

External computer networks are those that are established by third parties for commercial use by a variety of customers, including individual firms. One group of external networks, *public data networks*, provide data services to subscribers. Examples are Accunet, marketed by AT&T Communications Co., and Telenet, marketed by General Telephone and Electronics Co. They enable firms to augment their own internal networks and to connect with other firms. For instance, a firm can conduct electronic data interchange transactions with its key suppliers. Another group of external networks may be called *public information data bases*. Examples in this group are CompuServe and Dow Jones News/Retrieval. These networks enable firms to access a wide variety of valuable information. Still other networks, most notably the Internet, can serve both functions.

Although the details of the architectures underlying external networks are not of concern to us, we should be aware of the difference between open and closed system architectures. **Open systems architecture** refers to the condition in which the internal computer network of a firm is able to "talk" to an external network. That is, the design specifications of the computers in a firm's network are publicly available to the third-party vendors who operate the external networks. Thus, they can develop add-on hardware and software products that allow computers in both the internal and external networks to communicate effectively when linked together. For instance, in 1981 IBM allowed other computer manufacturers to duplicate the ISA bus architecture of its microcomputer. **Closed systems architecture,** on the other hand, refers to design specifications that are *proprietary* trade secrets and not publicly available. Thus, third-party vendors have been prevented from developing add-on products without purchasing expensive licenses. Mainframe computer architectures, including those of IBM, have traditionally been proprietary.

CLIENT/SERVER ARCHITECTURE

In contrast to the previously described architectures, a client/server architecture is not a physical hardware structure. **Client/server (C/S) architecture** is a *logical* model of computing that takes place within a *physical* computer network such as a LAN. Processing is performed either at a client workstation, at one or more *servers*, or at both the client and servers. A client is a microcomputer or workstation accessed by users, whereas a server is a centrally located microcomputer, workstation, minicomputer, or mainframe. The majority of servers are dedicated data-base servers that act as central repositories, thus enabling clients to share data and files, conduct database searches, and update the data base. Popular client/server applications include transaction processing, decision support, and data analysis.

Client/server computing is one of the fastest growing areas of information technology, with many mission-critical accounting systems already converted or in the process of being converted to this environment.* A technology subcommittee of the American Institute of Certified Public Accountants (AICPA) has identified client/server computing as one of the top information technologies that will have a significant impact on accountants and businesses.† This architecture provides the technological support for the "empower the employee" paradigm, the thrust toward decentralization, and the fundamental shift of computing from mainframes to microcomputers. A large number of firms are employing or evaluating client/server architecture as a way to provide more flexible computing to the end user.**

To appreciate the rapid movement toward the client/server architecture, consider the traditional approach to processing. Assuming the presence of a LAN, an entire application is typically processed at the user's desktop computer. Only simple tasks, such as sharing files stored on hard disks and printing reports, are assigned to special workstations. For example, when a user requests access to a file stored on another workstation's hard disk, the file is transferred to the user's computer where further operations on the data are performed. Thus, under the traditional approach a LAN provides only limited service to its users (clients).

Cooperative client/server computing is the most commonly employed mode of the client/server architecture. It facilitates the optimal sharing of computing resources, since the client and server(s) jointly (and cooperatively) perform the pro-

---

*Systems Auditability and Control Report, Module 13, *Advanced Technology Supplement*, Altamonte Springs, Fla.: The Institute of Internal Auditors Research Foundation, June 1994, p. 13-21.
†"IT Division Research Group Lists Top Technologies," *Journal of Accountancy* (June 1994), pp. 97–98.
**Advanced Technology Supplement*, Module 13, p. 13-2.

cessing of an application. Each processes those parts of the application for which it is best suited.

TRENDS IN INFORMATION TECHNOLOGY

In this section, we survey IT trends related to computer hardware, software, and telecommunications that will impact the accounting profession and business organizations.

COMPUTER HARDWARE TRENDS

Computer hardware has dramatically improved over the past four decades in the following respects:

- **Size.** An early-day computer the size of a moving van had less computing power than a present-day microchip half the size of a dime.
- **Speed.** The time required to process a single computation has dropped from 20 milliseconds to 50 nanoseconds.
- **Storage capacity.** The primary storage unit has grown from a capacity of a few thousand characters to capacities (for larger computers) of more than 100 million characters.
- **Reliability.** The earliest computers frequently made errors, whereas present-day computers are much more likely to be error-free.
- **Cost.** Processing costs per million instructions have declined from over one dollar to less than one cent.
- **Options.** The early-day computers provided very few choices with regard to processing features, input-output devices, and secondary storage devices and media. Present-day computers provide the numerous choices identified in this chapter.

Hardware trends should continue in the same direction for all of the aforementioned facets. Computer hardware should become even faster, smaller, more reliable, and more user-friendly. The capacity of transistors in microprocessor chips should increase from today's 2.4 million to an estimated more than 15 million in 2005. Thus the least expensive microcomputers should be able to process more than 500 MIPS, whereas supercomputers are likely to process trillions of computing operations per second.

As silicon chips reach their maximum capacity and speed limits in the early twenty-first century, scientists should have developed molecules of DNA digital chips to store information and carry out operations. These so called **"molecular" computers** will be composed of trillions of "living" molecules able to do billions of operations at once. A molecular computer would represent the ultimate parallel processor and would be 100,000 times faster than today's supercomputers.* On the horizon **super-supercomputers** will combine tens of thousands of microprocessors together to execute more than one trillion mathematical computations per second!

Optical disks are likely to be the dominant secondary storage medium, storing billions of bits of data each. **Voice-input terminals** will become prevalent, and graphics will be displayed in three dimensions. Even reliability is likely to improve. Diagnostic devices are expected to be incorporated into future computer models; when

---

*Sharon Begley and Gregory Beals, "Computing Is in Their Genes," *Newsweek* (April 24, 1995), p. 57.

an element is about to fail, the diagnostic device will signal the user that the element should be replaced. Fifth-generation computers will be able to perform logical inferences, recognize patterns, and "learn" from past processing experiences. Because they will mimic human brain processes, these computers are likely to be named neurocomputers.

Accountants will feel the impact of future hardware developments. Improvements in microcomputers should increase their productivity in their various activities. For example, auditors will be able to apply computer-based audit techniques more thoroughly. Managerial accountants and consultants will be able to develop more realistic financial models and to employ sophisticated analytical techniques. Also, the increased hardware options will allow the development of AISs that can provide more useful information for decision making. To make effective use of these hardware developments, accountants will need to devote an increasing number of their scarce hours in keeping abreast of changes. One way to do so is to be a regular reader of periodicals such as PC *Week*, PC *Magazine*, and *Datamation*.

COMPUTER SOFTWARE TRENDS

Software has become more "user friendly," packaged, and specialized. As a consequence, users are developing new programs to meet their needs. Programmers are spending less time writing programs from "scratch"; instead, they are often involved in modifying software purchased from commercial sources. Users, such as accountants, are able to obtain a variety of software packages that are designed to suit their particular needs. In addition to general ledger and transaction processing packages, these specialized packages include spreadsheets, financial modeling, and audit-assist packages. Most of these packages are compatible with the computer processors provided by a variety of hardware manufacturers.

Software has assumed an increasingly important role in the eyes of management and information systems specialists. Thus, the overall cost for software in the typical current computer system is higher than the overall cost for hardware. These comparative costs are the reverse of what they were in the earlier days of the computer age.

The current computer software trends are likely to continue. Software will be even easier to develop, use, and maintain. Several current developments are likely to exhibit significant impacts on software. Two of the more important are CASE (Computer-Assisted Software Engineering) tools and object-oriented software tools. Automated software development tools such as CASE (examined in Chapters 4 and 19) will enable software instructions to be generated automatically from system analysis diagrams.

Systems professionals will employ object-oriented techniques to develop applications much more quickly. Rather than focusing on program instructions and data collection, **object-oriented (OO) software** models real-life things—called *objects*—such as a customer, an income statement, or a mailing list.

To provide a simple example of how the OO approach works, consider the Windows 95 operating system, which is an object-oriented system. Assume that the controller recently completed the quarterly income statement and wants to send the statement to the recipients via a LAN. One icon button displayed on the controller's screen may represent an income statement, and another icon may depict a mailing list. Each object is a self-contained computer program module giving instructions that tell how to manipulate its data and send or respond to messages. To send the income statement, the controller may draw a line connecting the two objects. The income statement will be routed according to the mailing list object's programming code, which includes detailed instructions that specify how to send messages automatically.

Object-oriented software builds systems following a *modular* approach. Rather than applications developed from scratch, they are developed from predefined objects that are linked to other objects to form more complex systems. Each object's program is *reusable*, meaning it can be used in other applications without additional programming.

Other emerging software developments include the following:

1. **Natural language packages** are becoming available that enable users to employ everyday English in requesting needed information.

2. Software packages are becoming extremely specialized. For instance, application software packages are likely to be developed on an almost customized basis (e. g., by specific industry, size, accounting methods).

3. **Neural network software** is becoming available. This intelligent software will enable auditors, for instance, to predict with a high degree of accuracy which firms are likely to remain ongoing concerns.

4. **Voice-activated software** will permit users to enter words and numbers into a computer orally—rather than by typing, clicking a mouse, or touching a screen. This software will then translate the speech into typed text.

5. **Virtual reality (VR) software** is expected to change the way users interact with computers. VR software creates an artificial computer-generated three-dimensional image representation of an object that users will accept as real. The object may represent a product, concept, or process. The VR software then enables users to manipulate and test the illusory object they have created on the screen, pinpointing problems prior to commercial development or use.

6. **Geographic information systems (GIS) software** will capture, organize, analyze, and present complex geographic data. The results will be precisely displayed on a map. GIS software interacts with an orbiting satellite and a data base. It will enable management to evaluate sales performance in different regions, for example, by displaying a map on the screen showing the exact location of sales. Other business applications of GIS include detailing the location of customers, judging the results of an advertising campaign, and analyzing plant location decisions.

TELECOMMUNICATION TRENDS

Following are four significant telecommunication trends:*

- Digital technology.
- Optical fiber transmission.
- Wireless telecommunications.
- Intelligent networks.

Analog telephone service is slowly being replaced with a digital connection through the phone lines. This emerging worldwide digital transmission network offered by local telephone companies is known as **integrated services digital network (ISDN).** It can efficiently send large quantities of data, voice, and image

---

Emerging Technologies, Module 11, p. 11-91.

transmissions at the same time through the phone lines in a binary format at speeds of 1.5 million bits per second or more. Compare this to wide-area analog phone lines that can efficiently transmit up to 56 thousand bits per second.*

Optical fiber transmission provides digital connections to large areas not covered by the local telephone switching systems. Its outlook is quite promising because (1) most intra-city and inter-city copper lines have been converted to high-speed optical fiber cables and (2) a uniform standard for building fiber optics digital transmission equipment is being devised. This standard is called **synchronous optical network (SONET).** The integration of ISDN with SONET will result in rapid corporate acceptance of videoconferencing, electronic data interchange, telecommuting, and other wide-area applications requiring real-time access.

Wireless telecommunications enable voice, data, and video to travel over networks wire-free by radio waves and by other means. The growing availability of inexpensive cellular telephones, laptops, notepads, pagers, and personal digital assistants[†] is tied to the projected growth of a variety of wide-area wireless applications. For example, off-site employees, such as executives and sales personnel, can employ their wireless devices to instantaneously transmit messages to headquarters, receive E-mail, update inventories, check product prices, or conduct electronic data interchange by sending customer orders.

Intelligent networks enable telephone companies to *program* their networks of switches and routing devices so that they can rapidly and efficiently create new services for customers.

The convergence of the above four emerging trends should have a significant impact on the development of telecommuting, the creation of virtual organizations, the extensive use of groupware tools, and the maturing of the information superhighway. **Telecommuting** enables employees to do work at home or in the field, instead of at headquarters, as long as they have the computing devices necessary to perform the work. **Virtual organizations** are created when work teams of co-workers contact each other over networks instead of interacting face-to-face. **Groupware** consists of software that facilitates E-mail, computer conferencing, and videoconferencing. Groupware allows co-workers to collaborate on projects anywhere and anytime and to make decisions jointly. The **information superhighway,**** a major component of which is the Internet, is a web of interconnected publicly accessible networks located all over the world. This vast global network of networks revolutionizes the development of electronic commerce, enables individuals to freely exchange information, and redefines how individuals, groups, and companies interact. For instance, it enables accountants to connect to bulletin boards encompassing diverse accounting topics and to access a wide range of data bases containing timely information concerning customers, competitors, financial affairs, and the environment.

STATE-OF-THE-ART INFORMATION TECHNOLOGY AND THE AIS

The aforementioned trends in hardware, software, and telecommunications are likely to significantly affect the nature of the typical AIS of the future. In this concluding

---

*A potential alternative to ISDN is two-way cable, offered by cable TV companies. Cable TV lines are cheaper and faster than ISDN. However, at this time, it is uncertain if two-way cable will succeed due to certain technical considerations.

†These separate products will be combined into a pocket-sized device called a personal wireless communicator. These communicators will usher in a new communications revolution early in the twenty-first century.

**The information superhighway is sometimes referred to as "cyberspace," the "infobahn," or the "IWay."

section we first survey the limitations exhibited by an automated AIS that incorporates traditional technology. Then we suggest the improvements to the AIS that state-of-the-art information technology should provide. Because these improvements will not be easy to achieve, we end by noting the most severe difficulties to be expected.

LIMITATIONS OF THE TRADITIONAL COMPUTERIZED AIS

Most modern-day firms employ computers in their AISs. The advantages are so overwhelming, as we observed early in this chapter, that automation cannot be ignored. However, current systems in many firms are constructed with outdated technology and are ineffectual in many respects.

Infoage, Inc., one of the typical firms that we have been following, can serve to illustrate the limitations of outdated technology. Until a few years ago Infoage had a traditional AIS that is still found in many firms. Its AIS was built around a mainframe computer. The basic transaction processing systems, called *legacy systems*, were designed using a third-generation language such as COBOL. The data bases consisted of data files that stored financial data (e.g., receivables, payables, payroll) separate from the operational data (e.g., orders, inventories, and shipments).

The following are some of the major limitations exhibited by Infoage's AIS:

1. The systems personnel had to spend a large portion of their time on systems maintenance. Very little time was left for value-added services, such as improving old systems or developing new systems. Consequently, the AIS could not easily respond to changing business conditions.

2. The financial and operational data were not integrated; thus, it was difficult to generate reports involving both financial and nonfinancial information.

3. Moreover, the accounting transaction processing systems—which accumulated the financial data—were organized by a "stovepipe" approach and focused on the chart of accounts classification. Thus, the files related to these applications were unintegrated, and the multidimensional aspects of transactions were ignored.

4. The business processes and accounting procedures were not analyzed and improved before being converted from manual to automated form. As a result, the inefficiencies were simply embedded in the automated system.

5. The legacy systems were not designed to generate timely decision support information. Needed data could not be easily and directly accessed by end users. When new reports were required, computer programmers had to write programs over extended time periods to extract the requested information.

IMPROVEMENTS DUE TO STATE-OF-THE-ART INFORMATION TECHNOLOGIES

Currently available and expected future developments in hardware, software, and telecommunications were described in the previous section. These developments have led to such technologies as client/server platforms (systems), relational database management systems, data warehouses, groupware, decision support systems, electronic data interchange networks, and electronic funds transfer systems.

Firms that update their technologies can reap significant benefits. Infoage, for instance, converted its mainframe system a few years ago to a computer network with on-line data files. As a result, the managers and employees in the main office have (1) easier and faster access to certain needed information and (2) more effective communication among departments in the main office and the warehouse.

By converting to state-of-the-art technologies, such as those listed above, firms can achieve even greater improvements in performance. We can illustrate this assertion by briefly considering two technologies: data warehouses and LAN-based client/server systems. (These technologies are discussed at greater length in Chapters 15 and 17, respectively.)

A *data warehouse* is a data base containing information to support decision-making activities of end users. It enables firms to make information easily accessible to key workers attached to the network. For instance, end users can work with flexible analysis and reporting tools, such as groupware, to quickly locate information, generate scheduled or on-demand reports, and make more informed decisions. A data warehouse provides information to consumers with access to both financial and non-financial information that enables them to:*

1. Perform their assigned tasks.

2. Make decisions about how to organize and control their work.

3. Monitor, control, and allocate the required resources.

4. Understand their roles in the firm.

5. Use their power to enhance enterprise performance as well as their individual performance.

A LAN-based *client/server* system can be an advantageous platform for a firm's accounting applications, as described earlier. Specific benefits that can be expected by a typical firm include the following:

1. Improved productivity of the accounting staff, since many paper accounting documents are eliminated and the staff is freed to complete important value-added tasks.

2. Less required training and support, since a graphical interface and available customizing tools enable the accounting staff to employ the packages' functions quickly and easily.

3. Immediate updating of accounting files as transactions are entered.

4. Reduced time to generate and distribute financial reports and analyses, since useful information can be distributed over the network via E-mail. For example, a member of the accounting staff could prepare a cost center expense summary report and electronically distribute the report over the network to the appropriate manager.

5. Improved customer service. For example, a firm can provide its customers with on-the-spot, up-to-date information on product prices and scheduled delivery times. To ensure that ordered merchandise is delivered to customers when promised, the shipping function can be easily monitored.

6. Simplified accounting cycle, resulting in faster end-of-period closings.

7. Simplified data-entry process, with both real-time processing and batch direct processing accommodated.

8. Flexibility in maintaining and modifying applications software to meet a wide range of changing requirements without major reprogramming.

As these examples show, information technology can be very important to the well-being of all firms. Firms must be prepared to change their information systems

---

*Ibid., p. 112.

SUMMARY • 91

to incorporate new developments as they occur. Those firms that are subject to rapid, frequent, and unpredictable changes must, in addition, focus on achieving as great a stability as possible by managing information through the intelligent use of technology.*

DIFFICULTIES ENCOUNTERED WITH RESPECT TO INFORMATION TECHNOLOGIES

While information technologies can significantly improve the functioning of automated AISs, various obstacles may impede the achievements. Developing such technologies as data warehouses and client/server platforms can be very complex undertakings; thus, they are likely to be extremely costly and time consuming. Certain costs tend to be unanticipated, such as those related to testing, network and systems maintenance, end-user retraining, and security.

Even when the technology has been fully implemented, other hidden costs and problems may arise. Because LAN-based hardware and software tend to be less reliable than mainframe hardware and software, both data warehouses and client/server systems tend to crash frequently, sometimes for extended periods. Also, managers may block the flows of information throughout the organization, preferring to hoard the information for their exclusive use. Even if information is allowed to flow freely, employees may not understand how to employ it or share it on a peer-to-peer basis to aid in making decisions related to their job functions.

Certain obstacles to incorporating technologies within the AIS may be beyond the control of a firm. Some countries may be slow in updating regulations concerning telecommunications, for instance. Outdated regulatory constraints can restrict the ability of the firm in offering advanced services to its customers.† Countries may also be delinquent in installing enabling technologies, such as fiber optics cables for better telecommunications.

Finally, the most advanced technologies may not be suitable for many firms, especially those that are small and/or that have cash-flow problems. The added values of such technologies as LAN-based client/server systems and data warehouses may not be sufficient for such firms. In any case their benefits as well as hidden costs are difficult to measure and hence to justify on an economic basis. Consequently, each firm should carefully weigh the available technologies in light of its needs and resources.

*Andrew C. Boynton, "Achieving Dynamic Stability Through Information Technology," *California Management Review* (Winter 1993), pp. 58–77.
†Catherine Arnst, "The Networked Corporation," *Business Week* (June 26, 1995), p. 87.

SUMMARY

Accountants should grasp the essentials of information technologies (IT), since these technologies are dramatically improving AIS performance in many firms. The main components of IT are computer hardware, computer software, and telecommunications. Computer hardware includes processors, input-output devices, storage devices and media, and data communications equipment. Computer software includes operating systems, utility programs, and application programs. Tele-communications hardware and software connects computer hardware into local-area and wide-area networks, facilitating the sharing of resources such as programs and data files.

Information systems architectures include single computer processors, multiple computer processors, internal computer networks, external computer networks, and client/server systems. Single computer processors are mainframes, minicomputers, and microcomputers.

Multiple processor configurations include coupled processor systems and parallel processing systems. Internal computer networks include centralized wide-area networks, distributed wide-area networks, and local-area networks. External computer networks include public data networks and public information data bases.

Client/server systems are an emerging type of distributed network that optimally splits applications processing between user workstations (called the clients) and one or more other computers (called servers). The physical foundation of this computing model is the local-area network.

Hardware trends have been dramatic with respect to computer size, speed, storage capacity, reliability, cost, and available options. Over the past decades software has become more "user-friendly," packaged, and specialized. It also has become more costly relative to hardware. Trends in computer-based applications have been toward greater integration of transaction processing applications and greater emphasis on generating decision-making information. Four major telecommunications trends are digital technology, optical fiber transmission, wireless communications, and intelligent networks. These trends are accelerating the development of telecommuting, virtual organizations, groupware software, and the information superhighway.

Many accounting information systems, although automated, are traditional in that they employ mainframe computers and unintegrated data bases. Their limitations can be diminished or eliminated by judicious utilization of a variety of information technologies. However, the implementation of state-of-the-art technologies can be difficult and costly. Thus each firm must carefully consider the degree of technology that is suitable for it.

KEY TERMS

application program (79)
centralized wide-area network (WAN) (83)
client/server (C/S) architecture (84)
closed system architecture (84)
computer hardware (79)
computer network (81)
computer programming languages (79)
computer software (79)
cooperative client/server computing (84)
coupled processor system (82)
distributed processor system (83)
distributed wide-area network (WAN) (83)
downloading (77)
geographic information systems (GIS) software (87)
groupware (88)
hardware configuration (79)
information resource management (75)

information superhighway (88)
information system architecture (81)
integrated services digital network (ISDN) (87)
intelligent network (88)
local-area network (LAN) (83)
mainframe (81)
massively parallel supercomputer (82)
microcomputer (82)
micro-to-mainframe (77)
minicomputer (81)
molecular computer (85)
multiprocessing (82)
natural language package (87)
neural network software (87)
object-oriented (OO) software (86)
off-line device (79)
on-line device (79)
open systems architecture (84)
operating system (79)
optical fiber transmission (88)
parallel processing system (82)
super-supercomputer (85)
synchronous optical network (SONET) (88)
telecommuting (88)
terminal emulator (77)
uploading (77)
utility program (79)
virtual organization (88)
virtual reality (VR) software (87)
voice-activated software (87)
voice-input terminal (85)
wide-area network (WAN) (83)
wireless telecommunications (88)

REVIEW QUESTIONS

Note: These questions incorporate material found in Appendixes A and B at the end of the textbook.

3-1. Why is information technology of particular importance to accountants?

3-2. What are the effects of information technology on the AIS?

3-3. What are the advantages of computers when used in an AIS?

3-4. What are the characteristics that render an application suitable for computerization?

3-5. What are several roles in which microcomputers may serve in business firms?

3-6. Describe the features of a current microcomputer processor.

3-7. Discuss software packages for microcomputers pertaining to accounting applications, electronic spreadsheets, financial modeling and decision support, data-base management, expert systems, neural network, wordprocessing, and others.

3-8. What is computer hardware? What are its main components?

3-9. Contrast on-line and off-line devices.

3-10. What are the various components composing a computer processor?

3-11. Contrast several types of memory used in computer processors.

3-12. In what ways may processor performance be measured?

3-13. Describe several enhancing features that enable computer processors to perform more efficiently.

3-14. Contrast the features and relative advantages of magnetic tape, magnetic disk, and optical disk storage media.

3-15. Identify forms of storage media other than those discussed in question 3-14.

3-16. Describe several types of off-line computer input devices.

3-17. Describe several types of terminals and other on-line input devices.

3-18. Describe several types of printers and other computer output devices.

3-19. Define computer software.

3-20. What is the function of an operating system?

3-21. How do operating systems differ from application and utility programs?

3-22. What are several typical functional programs in an operating system?

3-23. Contrast the several generations of computer programming languages.

3-24. What is the nature of telecommunications?

3-25. Identify the basic components of data communications.

3-26. Why have telecommunications networks grown in recent years?

3-27. How is telecommunications related to local-area networks?

3-28. What is information system architecture?

3-29. Contrast the three sizes of computers.

3-30. Briefly describe several configurations to which multiple computer processors are incorporated.

3-31. What is a distributed processor system?

3-32. What is a wide-area network?

3-33. What is a centralized WAN?

3-34. What is a distributed WAN?

3-35. What is a local-area network?

3-36. How does open system architecture differ from closed system architecture?

3-37. What is client/server architecture? How is this concept related to a LAN?

3-38. In the client/server model, we refer to "clients" and "servers." Define both of these terms.

3-39. What is cooperative client/server computing?

3-40. Discuss the several trends in computer hardware over the past four decades.

3-41. What is a molecular computer?

3-42. What are super-supercomputers?

3-43. Discuss several continuing trends in computer software.

3-44. What is the function of a natural language package?

3-45. What is virtual reality and why is it important to accountants?

3-46. Discuss several continuing trends in telecommunications.

3-47. What are the four developments that will significantly increase in the future due to the trends identified in 3-43?

3-48. What are several limitations of present-day automated AISs?

3-49. Discuss how various state-of-the-art information technologies can overcome the limitations identified in 3-48.

3-50. What difficulties or obstacles may impede the development of state-of-the-art accounting information systems?

DISCUSSION QUESTIONS

3-51. What level of understanding should accountants have concerning computer hardware and software and telecommunications?

3-52. Do you think that Infoage's accounting information system is completely computerized? Why or why not?

3-53. Should the double-entry method of recording transactions be retained when computers are introduced into the AIS of a firm?

3-54. An owner of a small firm argues that a computer system for her firm would never pay for itself and that she would lose control over the firm's operations to the computer. Discuss.

3-55. Discuss the likely effects that a newly installed computer system will have on the scope and complexity of a firm's AIS.

3-56. What specific improvements in reports are most

easily achieved when computers are incorporated into an AIS?

3-57. What are some of the difficulties in implementing the client/server model of computing?

3-58. When a firm moves its mainframe accounting applications to a client/server environment, what problems would it encounter?

3-59. The implementation of LAN-based client-server AIS software often results in the elimination of paper accounting documents and reports. Reports are sent across the network and displayed on a screen. How will the elimination of many paper documents and reports affect the work of accountants?

3-60. If Infoage, Inc., were to implement a client/server network in the near future, what types of applications would probably be implemented on the network?

3-61. What qualifications would Ann Strong need to audit a LAN-based client/server setup? What problems may she encounter in such audits?

3-62. On the basis of past trends and emerging developments, discuss the likely features of an AIS in a large progressive firm in the late 1990s.

3-63. Do you think that the trends in hardware, software, and telecommunications will continue at the same pace as they have in the past?

···

PROBLEMS

Note: Certain problems require knowledge found in Appendixes A and B at the end of the textbook.

3-1. Indicate which of the following system-related tasks can best be performed primarily by computers, which primarily by humans, and which by both computers and humans.

   a. Making decisions concerning the location of new retail outlets.

   b. Making routine decisions concerning the ordering of inventory.

   c. Processing large volumes of business transactions.

   d. Making decisions concerning the promotion and/or termination of accountants.

   e. Preparing income tax returns.

   f. Preparing journal entries for very complex types of accounting transactions.

   g. Answering queries from customers concerning the status of their catalog orders.

   h. Determining the causes of large unfavorable variances that appear in a weekly E-mail report.

   i. Making recommendations for specific mutual funds to purchase.

   j. Calculating financial ratios and analyzing financial results based on the calculations.

   k. Selecting accounting software packages.

3-2. For each of the following types of organizations, identify a key computer system (e.g., reservation systems for an airline) and the needed software for it.

   a. Airline companies

   b. Insurance companies

   c. Banks

   d. Hospitals

   e. Retailing companies

   f. Utilities

   g. Publishing/Television companies

   h. Manufacturing companies

   i. Automotive companies

3-3. Accountants must become well-versed in evolving telecommunication technology trends. These trends include (1) digital technology, (2) optical fiber technology, (3) wireless communications, and (4) intelligent networks.

Required

Discuss how each of the four telecommunication technology trends will affect

a. Auditors.

b. Management advisory services specialists.

c. Tax accountants.

d. Management accountants.

3-4. For each of the following situations, indicate why the firm is not effectively using information technology (IT). What changes could have been made to employ IT to achieve significant improvements?

   a. Employees of a large aerospace and defense manufacturer use 47 brands of stand-alone microcomputers.

   b. A large tire and rubber wholesaler installed a mainframe computer 15 years ago. During the last 15 years, the MIS department has automated general ledger, accounts receivable and billing, purchasing, fixed asset, payroll, and inventory applications.

   c. A medium-sized electric utility firm's computer steering committee determines the applications to automate. The committee is composed of the MIS manager, the chief information officer, and department heads from the MIS department.

   d. One of the world's largest automobile manufacturers has lost 6 percentage points in market share in the last five years to other manufacturers. Its prices average 3 percent lower than its main competitors.

e. A chief information officer of a semiconductor firm responding to a survey pertaining to client/server computing stated that in no way would he ever recommend that his firm move to a client/server environment. The reasons given were lack of industry-wide standards, architectures, tools, and control and security measures.

f. The 12 salespersons for a tool-and-die shop call the home office to confirm customer orders and to verify that the raw materials for the job are in-stock.

g. A $2 million children's-book publisher receives orders and payments from customers via U.S. mail. However, the firm has lost several major customers to more technologically advanced firms.

h. A product-design-and-development firm's designers use a traditional drawing board to redraw parts before they are sent to a parts maker.

i. An installer of burglar-alarm systems recently filed for bankruptcy. Its sales staff had a difficult time obtaining lists of potential customers interested in installing alarm systems.

j. A sports franchisor uses warehouse workers to search its warehouse for needed inventory, such as sports jackets. However, the process is slow since the firm stocks 12,000 different items; it often loses out on sales because the workers can not locate the item fast enough to make overnight deliveries.

k. A sheet metal fabricator mails blueprints between its designers and customers. As a result, lead time required to complete a job order is 18 weeks.

l. A large, well-known southern university's academic Department of Accounting secretaries are using a dedicated Wang word processing package; faculty members are using an assortment of wordprocessors, including Leading Edge, Volkswriter, WordPerfect 5.1 for DOS, MS Word 4.0 for DOS, Wordstar, and PFS Write.

3-5. You have just joined a public accounting firm. On the first day you are assigned a microcomputer to aid you in performing your designated duties. Describe the specific tasks that the microcomputer can aid you in performing, as well as the types of software packages that might be employed, if your position is:

a. Auditor.

b. Management advisory services specialist (i.e., systems consultant).

c. Tax specialist.

3-6. There are distinct advantages to using different types of computer systems that meet the various processing needs of the users. While it is known that many firms are racing ahead to install microcomputers, mainframe computers continue to provide certain advantages that the smaller systems cannot match. In recent years, several billions of dollars have been invested in used computer systems, primarily mainframes. Also, manufacturers are moving ahead with introducing mainframes that use parallel processing technology, linking microcomputers into a powerful coordinated whole.

Required

a. Identify
   (1) The advantages of mainframe computer systems.
   (2) The disadvantages of mainframe computer systems.

b. Identify
   (1) The advantages of microcomputers.
   (2) The disadvantages of microcomputer systems.

c. Identify factors and/or actions that have been taken to prolong the lives of mainframe computer systems.

d. Identify the reasons why firms may not want to retire their mainframe computer systems.

(CMA *adapted*)

3-7. Jim Mitchell is the assistant controller employed by Eastman Company, a large publishing firm. The firm presently processes all accounting applications on a mainframe computer system. Recently, top management made a decision to move the accounting applications to a client/server computing environment. One of the first steps in the project will be to link the stand-alone microcomputers throughout the firm to a number of local-area networks. Jim is the accounting department's representative on the computer steering committee that is developing and implementing the new system.

Required

a. Describe the features of client/server computing as they would affect Eastman Company.

b. Identify and explain how Eastman Company's move to client/server computing can improve the accounting information system.

c. Identify and explain several of the risks to Eastman Company of moving the accounting applications to a LAN-based client/server architecture.

3-8. In recent years, there has been explosive growth in electronic communication. Microcomputers, pen notebooks, fax machines, on-line services, wireless communications, electronic mail, teleconferencing, videoconferencing, and sophisticated management information and decision support systems and groupware have changed and altered the way information is received, processed, transmitted, and used by decision makers.

With increasingly more powerful computers available every two or three years and more powerful software programs available on a regular basis, the full impact of computerization on organizations has not yet been felt. Although the development of computer applications is directed as being "user friendly" or "user oriented," the integration of computers into the organization has had both positive and negative effects on the employee and the traditional AIS.

Required

a. Describe the benefits that firms and their employees can receive from electronic communication.

b. (1) Explain why an employee might resist the introduction of electronic communication systems.

(2) Explain the steps an organization can take to alleviate the employee's resistance to electronic communication.

c. Discuss both the positive and negative impact on an organization's traditional AIS caused by the introduction of an electronic communication system.

d. It has been said that electronic communication systems enable firms to do business anywhere and anytime, getting a jump on competitors who do not utilize such technology. Do you agree? Explain your answer.

e. Will the proliferating use of electronic communication systems mean that mainframe computer systems will decrease in importance during the next five to 10 years, eventually being replaced by networks of personal computers?

(CMA *adapted*)

3-9. How can firms use the following information technologies to create a competitive advantage?

    a. E-mail
    b. Virtual corporation
    c. Telecommuting
    d. Videoconferencing
    e. Client/server architecture
    f. LANs
    g. Geographic information systems
    h. Microcomputers
    i. Object-oriented software development
    j. Wireless communications
    k. The Internet

3-10. You are a CPA working for a large CPA firm specializing in management consulting assignments for a variety of clients in different industries. Indicate which information technology(s) you would recommend to solve the following systems problems and state the benefits of choosing the particular IT.

a. One of a firm's major long-term decisions is where to locate new retail outlets. Once a site is selected, a lease is signed and construction of the facility begins. Each outlet takes about three months to complete. The firm is adding about 250 outlets annually at an average cost of $1,450,000 per outlet. The firm's computer-based information system rarely provides relevant information to make these types of decisions.

b. A Fortune 500 insurance firm processes its accounting applications at a centrally located mainframe computer located in Providence, Rhode Island. The accounting programs were written 35 years ago using the COBOL programming language. Currently, programmers spend most of their time maintaining these COBOL programs. About 10 percent of their time is spent on new systems development activities.

c. A large Midwest state university enrolls 25,000 full-time students. The university's security force issues parking tickets to violators who do not display valid stickers. Two handwritten copies of the ticket are prepared—one is attached to the violator's windshield and the other is kept by the security officer. The officer turns in his or her batch of tickets at the end of the day to the data processing department. Data-entry personnel key in each ticket using on-line terminals. However, numerous errors are made by the data-entry clerks.

d. A firm has an automated inventory system maintained on a mainframe computer system. Inventory reorder reports are prepared weekly. As a result, the retailer keeps four and a half weeks of inventory on hand in the warehouse to avoid shortages.

e. A firm's engineering staff is scattered in 57 geographic locations around the country. Frequently, the engineers must travel to meetings to collaborate on projects and make joint decisions.

f. A law firm composed of 35 partners uses the Commerce Clearing House and Research Institute of America's weekly updated three-ring binder law library reference manuals to conduct legal research.

g. Residential and commercial customers of the Vermont Telephone Company primarily employ copper telephone wires to make local and long-distance calls within the state.

h. Rockyville Meat Distributing Company's 450-person salesforce periodically calls on customers, who place orders with a sales rep for various meat products. At the end of the week, the sales rep calls in all customer sales orders to the home office where they are processed on the firm's mainframe computer.

i. Federal Atlantic Department Stores, Inc., which sells merchandise similar to Sears Roebuck Company, has its marketing personnel based in New York City, Philadelphia, Pittsburgh, and Washington, D.C. The marketers are using fax machines and telephones when they collaborate to make complex decisions and presentations.

3-11. You are a CPA working for a large CPA firm specializing in management consulting assignments for a variety of clients in different industries. Indicate which information technology(s) you would recommend to solve the following systems problems and state the benefits of choosing the particular IT problems for each of the following clients.

a. A small retail firm with sales of $2,000,000 uses five stand-alone microcomputers to process its accounting applications. It wishes to develop automated decision-making applications to support its two key managers in making a variety of decisions.

b. A large regional telephone firm employing 16,000 workers shares information, such as requests for personnel files, by sending requests through the mail. However, such requests are not passed around to the employees fast enough.

c. A large construction firm's Environmental Division gathers legal regulations about states where the firm faces potential environmental problems. It collects regulations by conducting standard library research or browsing various newspapers maintained by the library.

d. Rochester General Technologies' 55 computer programmers use COBOL to develop accounting and business applications software programs. However, changes or expansions of these applications (software) requires costly rewriting of the COBOL programs. The firm's programmers have a 14-month backlog of COBOL applications that need to be rewritten.

e. Students at the nation's American Medical Association's 126 approved medical schools dissect human cadavers to gain a firsthand understanding of human anatomy.

f. The Laurel Gazette, a weekly newspaper sold in Laurel, Mississippi, with a circulation of 75,000 newspapers, recently has had trouble signing on potential advertisers. The firm cannot pinpoint exact newspaper circulation and income potential in order to run special promotions.

g. A large firm annually batch processes 640,000 invoices on a mainframe computer. Many duplicate payments are made and many vendor discounts are overlooked.

h. A large health-care group located in Boston, Massachusetts, with 15 clinics and 110,000 members uses a centralized mainframe computer to process all data for the 15 suburban Boston clinics.

i. A New York City bank with 365 branch offices located throughout the city uses a third-party service to fax information directly to the bank's 365 branches. Each branch office periodically transports the scheduled faxes to the service firm's centralized location.

3-12. What adverse effects do you feel the following environments could have on the utilization of information technology in each of the following firms?

a. A Fortune 500 company's MIS department reports to the corporate controller, who is five years away from retirement.

b. A Midwest bank's data processing department of 12 full-time employees is headed by a manager who acquired an associate degree in computer programming 16 years ago from a local two-year college.

c. Most of the general managers of a multibillion dollar pharmaceutical firm are computer illiterate.

d. The internal audit function has not been assigned a role during a systems development project in which several mainframe accounting applications are being moved to a new client/server network. Several mainframe accounting applications will be moved to the client/server network.

e. A regional public accounting firm's partner in charge of management consulting, as well as his 10-person staff, is not familiar with applications of artificial intelligence.

f. A health-maintenance organization uses computers throughout the firm. Presently, it is not using external on-line services.

g. A food processing manufacturer's top managers are not involved in the strategic computer planning process.

h. A small hardware retail store has used the DAC Easy accounting software package for 10 years. It is still using the original DOS version of the package.

i. A printing shop is using an IBM compatible 80286 processor, running at 12 megahertz. The PC has one 5¼ inch floppy and a 30 megabyte hard disk.

j. A Fortune 1000 surgical supply firm makes extensive use of local-area and wide-area networks and groupware software. Even though all employees use the networks, they rarely share information with colleagues.

k. Thirty percent of a firm's employees telecommute from their homes. However, the 2400-bits-per-second data transfer rates over their residential phone lines to the local telephone company are very slow.

l. A small automobile paint shop is currently using DOS 3.0.

3-13. Jackalope Plumbing Company, a medium-sized plumbing firm, currently employs 25 persons at Goose Egg, Montana. The firm services a population of about 30,000 inhabitants in a three-county region. For the last two years, Ron Quincy, owner-manager, has noticed that labor, office, and clerical expenses have been increasing at an annual rate of 10 percent. Revenues, on the other hand, have been rising at an annual rate of 6 percent. Ron feels that this increase in expenses can be attributed to increasing supplies, inflation, and a tight labor market for master plumbers. Ron wants to implement cost controls to improve the firm's efficiency and productivity. Consequently, he retained a CPA to study the firm's problems and make recommendations. At the conclusion of the engagement, the CPA recommended the purchase or lease of a microcomputer, a laser printer, the Windows 95 operating system, and a spreadsheet package. The latter software would be used to prepare budgets, financial statements, and monthly variance analysis reports, which would aid in controlling costs.

However, Ron tabled the CPA's report. He argued that his firm is too small to justify the hardware and software costs, that the computer will have an unfavorable impact on the employees, and that his current manual system, with some modifications, is satisfactory.

Required

a. Is Jackalope Plumbing Company too small to effectively use a microcomputer?

b. Are Ron Quincy's arguments for not using a microcomputer valid?

c. Briefly indicate what information technologies a small firm, such as Jackalope, can economically justify to reduce costs and improve the productivity of its employees.

d. Discuss the positive and negative impacts a microcomputer can have on the firm's AIS.

3-14. Heathcliff Thornski is a buyer for the Screw-Up Tool and Die Company of Columbia, South Carolina. On August 1 he received a requisition from the materials control department pertaining to part number XTPO311K34. The firm had just received a contract, due to begin January 1, that would require a quantity of these parts. Since the parts were not needed for five months, Heathcliff put the requisition in his "to be done in the future" file. After all, the part was a fairly common steel gadget that could be obtained from a dependable supplier on very short notice; ordering early would unduly increase the investment in inventory. Besides, Heathcliff was very busy at the moment.

In fact, Heathcliff was busy during the rest of the year. His "to be done in the future" file grew and grew.

Suddenly, on December 15, several steel-fabricating firms were struck by their unionized employees. Among the struck firms were Screw-Up's principal suppliers of steel parts.

When January arrived and work began on the contract mentioned above, usage of part number XTPO311K34 jumped from 100 units per month to 1000 units per month. Naturally, the available supply of the parts was soon exhausted. Heathcliff tried to obtain the parts, but he could locate only a few for a premium price. Production thus stalled on the contract. As a result of failing to complete the contract by the scheduled date, the firm suffered a very substantial loss.

Required

Describe the ways that a computer-based information system could help prevent such catastrophes as that described, as well as improve other purchasing-related activities.

3-15. The Ute Savings and Loan Association of Salt Lake City has over 50 branches throughout Utah at which members' savings are deposited or withdrawn. It also has a mortgage department that converts the deposited funds into mortgage loans to home buyers and builders. Currently the firm uses a small computer system located at the main office to prepare payroll, to update savings and loan accounts, and to prepare routine accounting reports. However, the controller of Ute believes that the computer system is not adequate for the current and future needs of the firm.

Required

Propose in broad terms a new computer system that might better serve Ute's needs. Include in your proposal the following:

a. A description of the system, including the hardware components needed to operate the system.

b. A description of desirable applications, both those that involve transaction processing and those that aid managerial decision making.

c. A list of needed software required to run the applications identified in (b) above, including:

    (1) Absolutely essential or core software.

    (2) Utility programs.

    (3) Transaction processing software.

    (4) Software to support decision making.

    (5) Telecommunications hardware/software.

3-16. The Gripper Brake Company is a small New Orleans manufacturer of brakes, brake linings, and other parts of braking systems. It sells approximately 100 different sizes and varieties of brake products to garages and retail outlets of motor vehicle products in 10 states. With a work force of 30 employees and three managers, Gripper generated sales revenues last year of $8 million. Moreover, John Hartley, the owner and manager of Gripper, foresees rapid growth in sales during the coming years.

Mr. Hartley, however, has become aware that the firm is already suffering growing pains. For instance, it is having difficulty in processing the increasing number of sales orders and in delivering orders to customers by promised dates. When customers inquire about the status of their orders, clerks often must spend hours tracking down the answers. Critical parts and materials needed in manufacturing the ordered products are frequently out of stock. Losses from bad debts have been increasing at an alarming rate.

These problems lead Mr. Hartley to seek help from Jeff Harris, the firm's public accountant. After a careful investigation, Jeff recommends that the firm acquire its own computer system. On agreement from Mr. Hartley, he investigates further and proposes two alternatives in terms of hardware components: (a) a minicomputer system, or (b) five stand-alone microcomputer systems.

Required

a. If you were Mr. Hartley's public accountant, which one of the two alternatives would you recommend? Describe the hardware components that appear to be suitable for the alternative that you recommended.

b. After installing the selected computer system, Gripper acquires software application packages that perform general ledger accounting and that process sales orders. What other essential types of software packages should be purchased by Gripper, in conjunction with purchasing the accounting software?

c. Describe other software application packages that would aid Gripper in solving its current and future problems.

 3-17. *Note: This problem can be solved by means of an electronic spreadsheet package on a microcomputer.*

The firm of Wu & Wright, CPAs, has just acquired an electronic spreadsheet package for use on its microcomputer.* As their first application the partners decide to prepare an income statement template, to enter data of

---

*Problem 3-17 is adapted from an application in Frederick H. Wu, "Teaching Managerial (Cost) Accounting with Electronic Spreadsheet Software." In *Issues in Accounting Education*, 1984, Sarasota, Fla.: American Accounting Association, 1984. Used with permission.

a client firm into the income statement, and to determine the effects on net income resulting from changes in certain factors.

They begin by inserting the diskette containing the spreadsheet package into disk drive A and turning on the computer. After obtaining the logo of the package, they stroke the indicated key and obtain the control panel. This panel displays the rows and columns of the worksheet. (To be more precise, it displays a "window"—the first few rows and columns of the complete worksheet—plus a menu of commands.)

Then with the aid of the electronic spreadsheet manual and the menu, they develop a template for an income statement as follows.

Documentation for Template

a. Amounts indicated by . . . . are to be entered by user.

b. Amounts indicated by 0 are to be calculated by formulas that have been stored in the memory of the spreadsheet software package.

c. The stored formulas are

(1) Cost of goods available for sale = beginning finished goods + cost of goods manufactured. (The formulas for this and following relationships are expressed by the software in terms of cells; e.g., C12 is C9 + C10.)

(2) Cost of goods sold = cost of goods available for sale − ending finished goods.

(3) Gross margin = sales − cost of goods sold.

(4) Selling and administrative expenses = sales commissions + sales salaries + shipping expenses + administrative expenses.

(5) Net income = gross margin − selling and administrative expenses.

(6) Sales commissions = 0.05 × sales.

(7) Shipping expenses = $\frac{1}{30}$ × sales.

Required

Access the electronic spreadsheet package available on your school's microcomputer system, in accordance with your instructor's directions. Then perform the following.

a. Prepare the template, including the underlying formulas.

b. Enter these data into the template: ABC Company; 1998; 1,500,000 (for sales); 100,000 (for beginning finished goods); 900,000 (for cost of goods manufactured); 150,000 (for ending finished goods); 100,000 (for sales salaries); and 100,000 (for administrative expenses).

c. Print the income statement based on these data.

d. Change the sales amount in the template to 2,100,000, and print the resulting income statement.

Template No. 1: Income Statement
....

Income Statement
For the Year Ended Dec. 31, . . .

Sales		$..........
Less Cost of Goods Sold:		
Finished Goods, Jan. 1	$..........	
Cost of Goods Manufactured	....	
Cost of Goods Available for Sale	$ 0	
Finished Goods, Dec. 31	....	
Cost of Goods Sold		0
Gross Margin		$ 0
Less Selling and Admin. Expenses:		
Sales Commissions	$ 0	
Sales Salaries	....	
Shipping Expenses	0	
Administrative Expenses	....	0
Net Income		$ 0

3-18. Specify the most suitable input or output device for each of the following transaction processing situations.

a. A public utility needs to employ a specialized means of handling turnaround documents returned by customers with their payments.

b. An insurance firm having numerous branches needs to transmit policy data from its regional offices for timely processing by a mainframe computer located at its home office.

c. A bank needs to employ a specialized means of inputting its large volume of checks for processing each day.

d. A grocery store chain desires to capture barcoded data on grocery and sundry items of merchandise and to transmit these data to a central computer so that each sales transaction can be automatically and immediately completed.

e. A stock exchange desires to provide the latest stock prices to security representatives in brokerage offices who enter requests via special telephones with keyboard attachments.

f. A construction firm desires to process its weekly payroll from time records in which the hours worked have been mark-sensed in pencil.

g. A university desires to employ a specialized means of handling registration forms filled in by students and returned for computer processing.

h. An automobile salvage dealer (one who buys old or wrecked automobiles and salvages key parts) is tired of answering numerous telephone inquiries every day concerning the availability of parts for specified models; instead, the dealer prefers that personalized answers be provided by a computerized system.

i. A large transportation firm having more than 3000 prime and subsidiary accounts posts batches of journal vouchers each month to the general ledger, which is maintained on magnetic tape.

j. A wholesaler desires to record its numerous sales of merchandise on media that can be entered quickly in batches for processing by its computer system.

k. An automobile manufacturer receives from its dealers orders that have been directly entered into a computer system and transmitted immediately to the manufacturer's order department at its home office.

l. A steel manufacturer prefers to eliminate the use of time cards for recording attendance times of employees; instead, it plans to assign badges containing employee numbers as bar codes, which would interface with an input device to the computer system.

m. A small business proprietor needs to obtain cash on Saturday to pay for emergency repairs to the firm vehicle.

n. A management consultant desires to include high-quality colored graphics in her report to a client firm.

3-19. Assume the availability of these computer-based storage media: magnetic tape, internal magnetic hard disk, external Jaz drive, optical disk, microfilm, and primary storage. Indicate which storage medium (or media, if more than one) is preferable for each of the following situations. Briefly state why the selected medium is preferred.

a. A brokerage firm desires to retain records of the complete daily stock quotations as taken from the financial newspapers.

b. A credit card firm desires to keep its members' account records readily available so that updates can be made and inquiries can be quickly answered.

c. A private research institute needs to retain files concerning its completed projects; the files are not subject to updating, but they need to be frequently referenced in a timely manner.

d. A bank needs to keep available a series of amortization tables; these tables require relatively little storage space, but they need to be frequently accessed by a computer program that determines interest payments due from debtors.

e. A railway firm needs to record transactions pertaining to movements of its freight cars so that it can update the master file (which contains 10,000 records) on a daily basis.

f. A department store needs to record the amounts owed by customers on bills, which are mailed to the customers and returned by them (with payments) for processing.

g. A telephone company desires to retain copies of all checks and drafts that it issues for occasional reference by accounting clerks.

h. A hospital needs to back up all its patient-related records, which are stored on magnetic disk.

i. A defense industry contractor needs to store backup information about secret plans for a new strategic bomber.

3-20. Mason's Department Stores, Inc., of Mississippi owns two stores: a large store located in Jackson and a small store in Columbus. It recently upgraded its computer system and added a network that links the two stores. The new configuration consists of the following hardware: (a) a mainframe computer, (b) six magnetic disk drives, (c) three magnetic tape drives, (d) three printers, (e) one plotter, (f) one image-reading device, and (g) 30 point-of-sale terminals. In addition, communications hardware consists of several controllers and channels at the Jackson store, where the computer and most of the other hardware items are located, and a multiplexer at the Columbus store. The only other hardware consists of two modems at the ends of a coaxial line between the mainframe computer and the multiplexer. In the Columbus store are 10 of the point-of-sale terminals mentioned earlier.

Required

Draw a hardware configuration diagram that includes the network described in the problem statement. Employ as many controllers and channels as necessary to complete the configuration of the hardware devices located at the Jackson store.

3-21. Sparr Manufacturing Company of Evanston, Wyoming, installed a minicomputer five years ago and spends about $450,000 annually for hardware, software, and personnel costs. The firm has automated purchasing, payroll, inventory, labor cost analysis, accounts receivable, billing, and general ledger applications. Dr. Elmer Sparr, the firm's president, is unhappy with the information and reports produced by the computer system. He does not feel that the computer's potential is being fully utilized and is dismayed at the number of errors contained in reports. In a meeting with David Creach, manager of the data processing department, Dr. Sparr is told that many of the problems are due to the unreliability of the firm's minicomputer. David also indicates that some of the firm's other problems relate to the poor quality of the instructional computer materials available to the data processing personnel. The meeting is concluded with the decision to purchase hand-held scanners that input data directly into the computer system and to purchase better quality instructional materials. The firm's computer steering committee is given the authority to carry out the decisions.

About six months later, Elmer Sparr is not satisfied with the progress being made by David Creach. He decides to hire a management consultant to help the firm solve its data processing problems. During the course of his study, the consultant learns that David Creach received a certificate in computers by completing a one-year course at the Denver Institute of Computers, a community college. The firm's three other data processing employees were also recruited from the Denver Institute by Mr. Creach. Also, the firm's computer steering committee is composed of the three data processing employees and Mr. Creach, who serves as chair. The firm's top management is not involved with the computer system; Dr. Sparr, for example, stated he is too busy. Besides, he stated, the data processing department employs four experts who can handle all aspects of computer operations, including applications to automate. Finally, David Creach told the consultant that, within a year, the computer steering committee will recommend the purchase of a new minicomputer system; the system will increase annual operating costs to about $600,000. Mr. Creach stated that the new minicomputer will decrease input errors, result in more accurate and comprehensive reports, and provide decision-making information to the firm's top managers.

One month after beginning the assignment, the consultant submitted a lengthy report to Elmer Sparr outlining the steps the firm should take to solve its problems.

Required

a. One recommendation contained in the consultant's report resulted in the prompt dismissal of the data processing staff, including Mr. Creach. Why do you think that Dr. Sparr terminated the staff?

b. Are David Creach and his staff automating applications to produce relevant management information?

c. What other recommendations, relating to the data processing staff, information technologies to be implemented, and so on, may have been included in the consultant's report?

CONTINUING CASE

With respect to the small firm that you selected in Chapter 1, complete the following requirements:

a. If the firm currently uses a computer-based accounting information system,

(1) Draw a hardware configuration diagram of the system.

(2) Would you say that the firm's accounting staff is computer literate? Explain your answer. How involved is the accounting staff with the computer system?

(3) Identify the variety of applications utilizing the system. Also, describe one of the key applications. Suggest additional applications that appear to be feasible.

(4) Is the firm using information technology for strategic applications? Explain your answer.

(5) How, if at all, has information technology improved the firm's accounting information system? Has the firm encountered any problems with information technology? Discuss.

b. If the firm does not use a computer-based accounting information system,

(1) List the reasons why the firm should purchase a computer system.

(2) Propose a system that appears to be feasible and the applications that it should handle.

(3) Draw a hardware configuration diagram of the proposed system.

CHAPTER 4

AIS DEVELOPMENT AND DOCUMENTATION TOOLS

THE LEARNING OBJECTIVES FOR THIS CHAPTER ARE TO ENABLE YOU TO:

1. Describe common documentation techniques used to portray an AIS and their importance to various persons.

2. Describe documentation pertaining to data storage for a typical AIS.

3. Discuss the steps in preparing logical data-flow diagrams and system flowcharts relating to transaction processing systems.

4. Describe documentation pertaining to inputs and outputs, including hard-copy documents, forms, reports and display screens.

5. Describe emerging documentation techniques used to portray an AIS.

INTRODUCTION

Documentation consists of written materials that clearly describe procedures, forms, and other aspects of an ongoing system. These materials require early attention in a textbook about the accounting information system (AIS). In fact, in Chapter 2 we discussed and illustrated examples of documentation such as source documents, accounting journals and ledgers, and charts of accounts. Documentation spans all aspects of an AIS, ranging from inputs to data storage to outputs. Furthermore, documentation is as important to computer-based systems (if not more so) as it is to manual systems.

IMPORTANCE OF SYSTEMS DEVELOPMENT AND DOCUMENTATION

Documentation is important chiefly because it communicates knowledge about an AIS. It informs a variety of persons who interact with the AIS about its objectives, components, and operations. Interested persons include users, evaluators, and developers of the AIS. Accountants have a particular interest, since they can serve in any of these three roles. Persons with differing backgrounds, however, also draw on documentation for a variety of reasons. Several specific benefits of documentation are as follows:

1. Prescribed procedures can be performed more reliably, efficiently, and consistently by users of the AIS such as cost accountants, shipping clerks, and computer operators. Documentation also aids in the training of newly employed users.

2. Weaknesses and deficiencies in transaction processing systems and internal controls can be spotted more easily. Evaluators such as internal auditors, external auditors, and accounting managers may be able to prepare their own documentation or review documentation prepared by others.

3. Systems flows and components can be visualized more clearly and hence can be designed more carefully and soundly. Among those who may employ documentation as a design aid are systems analysts, accountants, industrial engineers, and programmers.

COMMON AIS DEVELOPMENT AND DOCUMENTATION TECHNIQUES

Figure 4-1 lists many common documentation tools needed to describe fully the transaction processing systems within an AIS. At the center of the figure are the documentation techniques pertaining to procedures. Several of these techniques, such as **data-flow diagrams (DFDs)** and system flowcharts, provide a pictorial view of procedures. Techniques related to data storage, inputs, and outputs are also listed. Those pertaining to data storage include layouts of records within files, descriptions of individual data elements, and data models. Those pertaining to inputs and outputs include formats of source documents, screens for entering and displaying data, and formats for reports. Several of these techniques are described and illustrated in the following sections of this chapter, whereas all will appear in one or more places throughout the remaining chapters.

Two of the techniques, logical data-flow diagrams and system flowcharts, receive the most attention for three reasons. First, even though they portray data flows through the various transaction cycles differently, both are often employed during analysis and design phases. Both techniques supplement each other and model important aspects of the AIS. A logical DFD is a newer documentation tool that uses a few symbols to draw pictures depicting logical data flows of business processes

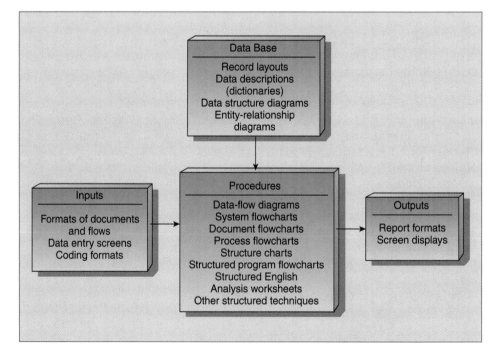

FIGURE 4-1   Types of documentation for an AIS.

and determining information needs requirements. Thus a logical DFD is user-friendly and accountants and systems developers can jointly prepare them. A system flow-chart, which is an older, traditional documentation tool, can be employed in the analysis and design phases to portray the current, modified, or new AIS. Several chapters are devoted to surveys of transaction cycles, so you can expect to see many examples of both techniques.

Second, since logical data-flow diagrams and system flowcharts are often used together by many businesses, accountants and auditors as well as systems analysts are called on to prepare and to interpret them, especially during the analysis and design phases of development. DFDs are more popular than system flowcharts because they can be used in structured systems development and are incorporated into practically all computer-assisted software engineering tools (described below). The third reason for devoting attention to these techniques is that skill is required for their preparation. You cannot easily draw examples of either without practice. Thus we will illustrate a step-by-step approach for preparing both logical data-flow diagrams and system flowcharts. You will then be able to develop the needed skill at this early stage in the course, without the need to consider the remaining portions of the AIS.

Before undertaking our detailed development of logical data-flow diagrams and system flowcharts, however, we will first examine data storage.

DATA STORAGE

Data can be stored in various types of structures. Traditionally data have been stored in **files**—collections of related records. Each record in turn contains a group of fields, with each field being reserved for a specific data element. Finally, data elements are composed of characters such as letters, numbers, and special symbols. Presently, however, firms are employing alternative structures or data sets for storing data. We shall explore these alternative structures in Chapter 6. At this point we will introduce three types of documentation related to stored data: record and table layouts, data dictionaries, and conceptual data models.

RECORD LAYOUTS

A **record layout** shows the respective fields that make up a record and the sequence in which they appear. It also specifies the number of characters allowed in each field, such as two character positions for the year. Furthermore, the layout identifies the attribute of the data element (e.g., a feature such as price or size) to be contained in the field. Figure 4-2a depicts a record layout for a stockholder file. Each stockholder is identified by an account number, which appears in the leftmost field. Among the attributes listed in the record are the name and address of the stockholder, as well as the number of shares owned. Figure 4-2b shows an alternative format for a customer accounts receivable file, plus illustrative data for customer number 1158.

Additional features concerning a record may be included in a record layout. One such feature is the mode of each data element, that is, the degree of permanency. For instance, the customer number is of numeric mode and is permanently assigned to a customer; the customer name is of alphabetic mode and is relatively permanent; the account balance is of alphanumeric mode (since it contains a special-character decimal point) and varies with each sales or payment transaction.

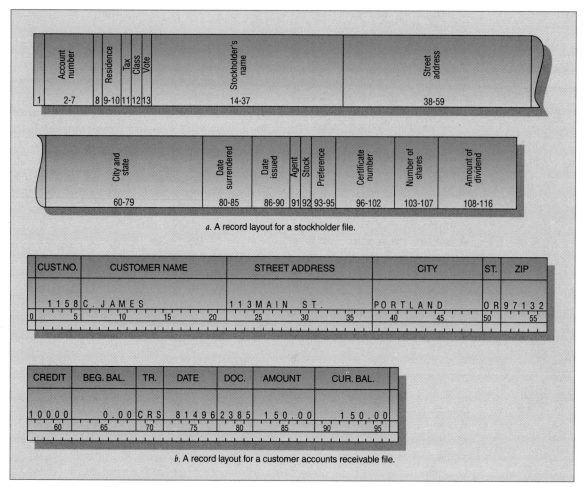

a. A record layout for a stockholder file.

b. A record layout for a customer accounts receivable file.

FIGURE 4-2   Record layouts. (a) A record layout for a stockholder file. (b) A record layout for a customer accounts receivable file.

DATA DICTIONARIES

If a firm does not store its data in files, record layouts are not suitable. Thus we need a type of documentation that focuses on the data elements themselves. A **data dictionary** serves as a reference or repository containing facts about the structure of the data elements employed in applications. This directory enables users to access and maintain the data stored in data bases. Figure 4-3 portrays a segment of a data dictionary for a manufacturing firm. As the illustration indicates, each entry in a data dictionary defines a variety of relevant characteristics pertaining to a data element. For instance, one column in the dictionary specifies the various records in which a data element appears. Thus the dictionary provides a cross-reference to record layouts. Even more aspects may be included if useful. In a computerized system the data dictionary is often stored within the system itself, such as a data-base management program, or in a separate data dictionary software package.

ENTITY-RELATIONSHIP MODELS

Record layouts and data dictionaries present the needed details concerning stored data. A broader and more conceptual view of a firm's data is also very useful. Such

Precise Manufacturing Co.								
Data Dictionary								
Item Code	Name of Element	Element Description	Field Size	Mode of Characters	Records in Which Found	Source	Number of Appearances	Outputs in Which Used
01	Customer order number	The code on the customer order that identifies the order	5	Numeric	Open order, sales history, back-order record	Customer order	500–600 daily	Sales invoices, back orders, production orders, shipment records
02	Customer number	The code assigned to identify a customer	6	Numeric	Customer, open order record	Customer number list	10,500–12,000	Sales analysis by customer, list of outstanding orders, aging report, sales invoice
03	Customer name	The first name, middle initial, and last name of a customer	25	Alphabetic	Customer record	Initial customer order	10,500–12,000	New business report, credit flash report, sales invoice, back order, shipment record

FIGURE 4-3   A portion of a data dictionary.

a view can be provided by a model, a means of representing some aspect of reality. For instance, a balance sheet is a model that represents the financial condition of a firm at a point in time.

A **data model** portrays the key entities that have impact on a firm and the relationships or associations among the entities. An **entity** is an object that really exists and is identifiable—such as an agent, event, or resource. Students served by a college or university are examples of agents, whereas acts of registering for upcoming semesters are events. Since students must perform the act of registration, a relationship clearly exists. A class is an example of a resource; that is, it is an object of value since students need to enroll for classes via registration in order to subsequently graduate. There is also a clearcut relationship between the registration event and classes. Figure 4-4 contains a type of data model, called an **entity-relationship (E-R) diagram,** that graphically depicts the above entities and relationships. According to convention, rectangles represent entities and diamonds represent relationships. Each rectangle can also be denoted by the attributes of the entity. By reference to a data model, such as an E-R diagram, a system designer can design the detailed repositories of data, for example, records or tables. E-R diagrams can be easily constructed to model the information needs of the entire enterprise or segments of the enterprise, such as divisions or departments, as well as those of the individual managers. The E-R diagram portrayed in Figure 4-4 will be expanded in Chapter 6 to encompass other entities and relationships related to the student registration system. As we shall see, the expanded E-R diagram shall be very useful in designing a data base for our registration system.

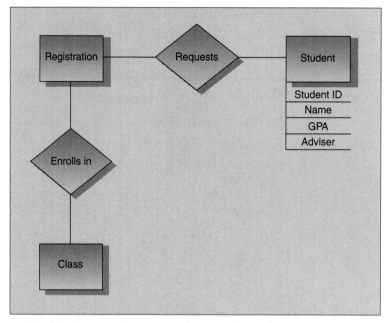

FIGURE 4-4   An example of a partial entity-relationship diagram for a student registration processing system.

PROCEDURAL FLOWS

Data models provide a static view of the data used by a firm. By contrast, flows of data through procedures present a dynamic view because data are "moving" between processes. Narrative descriptions are often used to document procedural data flows. Many firms maintain procedures manuals that are full of such descriptions. They are useful, since narratives of all sorts have been familiar to us since our earliest school days. However, narratives should be supplemented by pictorial techniques. As mentioned earlier, two very suitable techniques for depicting data flows are logical data-flow diagrams and system flowcharts.

Both logical DFDs and system flowcharts are used to graph the flow of data through transaction processing systems (TPSs). TPSs can be designed to process data in a batch processing or immediate processing mode. Batch processing is a delayed processing mode that accumulates transactions for a designated period of time before the transactions are processed. An example would be a payroll processing system. An immediate processing system is a real-time processing mode that captures and processes each transaction as it occurs. An example would be a hotel or motel reservation system. Both processing modes are thoroughly explored in Chapter 5.

Accountants and auditors can use procedural flow documentation in several ways. First, they can gain an overall understanding of each of the transaction cycles and their interrelationships. Second, they can determine if the TPSs are operating efficiently or inefficiently. They can spot weaknesses in processing steps and determine how the system can be improved. Third, they can determine where risks are likely to occur within the system and judge if the implemented internal controls will prevent or detect these undesirable events. Fourth, they can employ the diagrams to train new accounting staff to operate the TPSs.

DATA-FLOW DIAGRAMS

A **logical data-flow diagram** shows the flows of data through a transaction processing system without regard to the time period when the data flows or the processing procedures occur. This technique portrays data flows independent of any physical devices used to transform the data. Since data flows are emphasized, it is similar to a system flowchart. However, the two techniques differ significantly. We should be aware of these differences, since both techniques can be very useful in developing and documenting an AIS. After learning to draw a logical DFD, it should be easier for you to acquire the skill of preparing a system flowchart.

Distinctive Features A logical DFD emphasizes the specific data and *what* is being done to them. The diagram reveals the data flows into and out of processes, the rules to process data, the stores of data, and the external entities. Because of this simplified focus, only four symbols are needed. In contrast, a system flowchart clearly indicates *how* data are being processed, for example, manually or with the aid of computers. A system flowchart is a physical data-flow model since it shows the physical elements required to transform data into outputs. For example, a system flowchart may portray the storage media as being file cabinets or magnetic disks and the input method as being documents on hard copy or data-entry screens.

The two techniques also differ with respect to their roles. A logical DFD is better suited for analyzing processes and data flows. Logical DFDs are prepared during the systems analysis stage to portray flows and processes of existing systems or systems in the developmental stages. They can also be employed during the early phases of systems design to depict how the flows and processes of existing systems have been modified. That is, a logical DFD allows accountants and analysts to visualize the essential flows and processes without being concerned about the physical design features. On the other hand, a system flowchart is mainly used to document the physical elements of an AIS, either the system that is currently in use or a newly designed system.

Symbols The four needed symbols are shown in Figure 4-5. A *rectangle* represents an entity that is a source or destination of data that resides outside the system being diagrammed and therefore is not subject to further analysis (note that it has no relation to the entity in an entity-relationship diagram). Examples of sources (and also destinations) are customers, suppliers, banks, and managers. A *circle* (also called

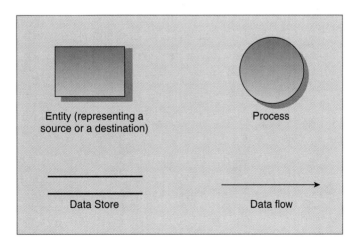

FIGURE 4-5 A set of symbols for data-flow diagrams.

bubble) represents a process that transforms data inflows into data outflows. An example is the process of handling incoming cash receipts. A pair of *parallel lines* represents a data store, that is, a place where data can be kept. An example is a file of cash receipts transaction data. A *curved line* having an arrowhead represents a data flow.* It may connect together any of the above symbols, but at least one end of the flow will generally be connected to a process.

Example of a Logical Data-Flow Diagram A logical "DFD" is in reality a hierarchical set of diagrams. Each diagram in the set is a decomposition (in effect, an "explosion") of the preceding diagram. In other words, each succeeding diagram provides a greater degree of detail concerning a process. Logical DFDs within a set may delve deeper and deeper until extremely detailed views appear.

Our example of a registration process will consist of only three levels, as depicted in Figures 4-6, 4-7, and 4-8.

The diagram in Figure 4-6 is called a **context diagram.** It is the top level of a set of logical DFDs, since the process is encompassed within a single circle. The four entities shown in the diagram are *outside* the scope of the process being documented. Two of the entities (student and registration clerk) serve as both sources and destinations with respect to data involved in the registration process. Two of the entities (the instructor and registrar) are only destinations (i.e., recipients of data and information) from the process. Neither of these entities is a source of data. Notice that the type of data involved in each flow is written along the flow line. Also note that *no* data stores appear on this diagram, since they are incorporated within the process itself.

The logical DFD in Figure 4-7 shows certain details of the registration process. It contains four subprocesses, numbered 1.0, 2.0, 3.0, and 4.0. (Because of the zeros

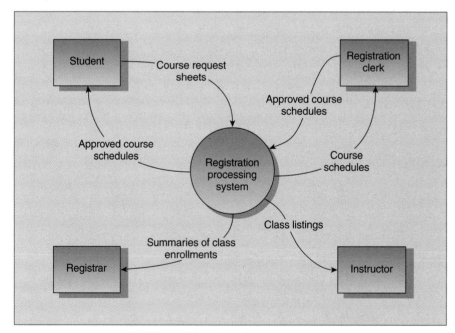

FIGURE 4-6   A context-level logical data-flow diagram for a registration processing system.

---

*A straight flow line can also be used to prepare DFDs. We prefer the curved line, which is primarily used throughout this textbook.

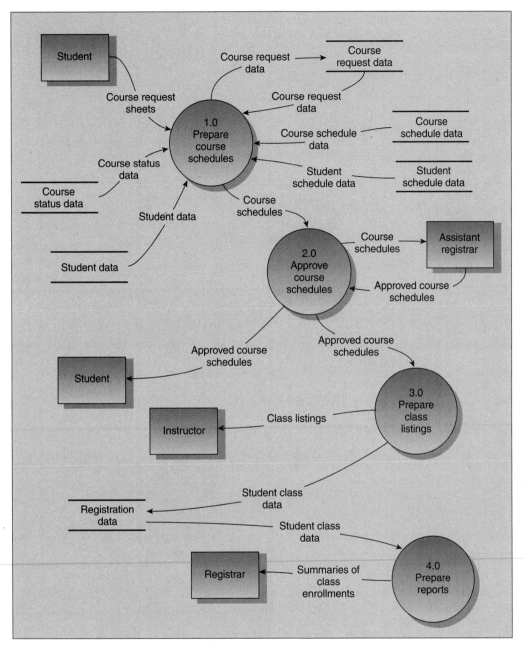

FIGURE 4-7 A logical data-flow diagram (level-zero) relating to the class registration process.

following the decimal points, this level just below the context diagram is called the level-zero DFD.) Included with the subprocesses are six data stores (student, course status, course request, course schedule, student schedule, and registration data) and a variety of data flows.

The logical DFD in Figure 4-8 is a level 1 diagram that explodes process 1.0 in Figure 4-7—"Prepare course schedules." It includes sub-subprocesses shown by bubbles coded 1.1, 1.2, and 1.3. The outputs of process 1.0—"Course schedules"—are inputs into subprocess 2.1 and the outputs of subprocess 1.3 serve as inputs into process 2.0.

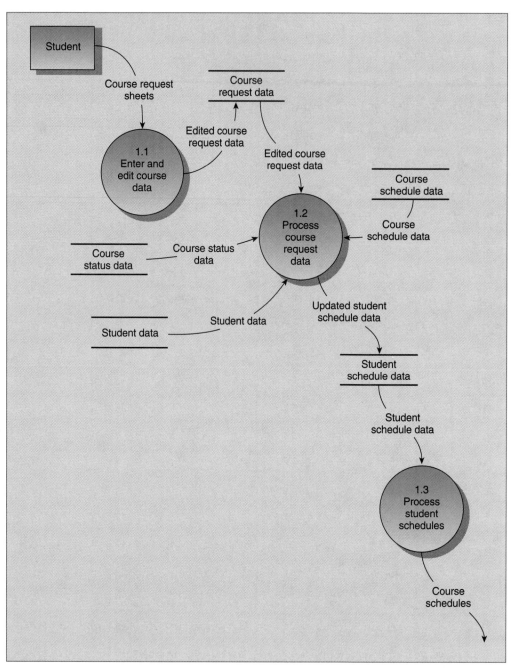

FIGURE 4-8   A level 1 logical data-flow diagram for preparing course schedules for the student registration system.

Additional logical DFDs can be prepared to show more details concerning each process. For instance, a level 2 diagram of process 1.3—"Process student schedules" would show sub-sub-subprocesses denoted by bubbles coded 1.31, 1.32, 1.33, and so on.

Guidelines for Construction   Guidelines that should be helpful when you prepare your first logical DFD include the following:

1. Begin with a context diagram, as shown in Figure 4-6, that shows the interactions of the selected process with the outside entities. Include all interactions as separate data-flow lines, even though there may be more than one flow from the process to an outside entity, or vice versa. On the other hand, include in the context diagram only those outside entities that are directly involved in data flows to or from the process. The process symbol in Figure 4-6 should not contain any number, such as 0.0; the name of the system should be inside the process symbol. Label a process with an *action verb* and all other symbols with *nouns*.

2. Then decompose the context diagram into a logical DFD at the zero level. Within each process symbol, above the writing, number each process, beginning with 1.0, 2.0, etc. Verify that the data flows are *balanced* between the context diagram and the level-zero diagram. That is, make sure that all of the data flows in the context diagram also appear in the level-zero diagram. Thus there should be two flows between the student and registration clerk entities and the subprocesses in the level-zero diagram depicted in our example above. This is the case, if you count the flows to the student and registration clerk entities appearing in the level-zero diagram.

3. "Explode" the subprocesses in the level-zero diagram into successively more detailed sub-subprocesses in level 1 diagrams, level 2 diagrams, level 3 diagrams, and so on. Continue the balancing of data flows between successive levels, for example, between the level-zero diagram and its set of "exploded" diagrams at level 1. (To check that the diagrams are balanced, first verify that all of the outside entities have been carried to the lower level, e.g., from level-zero to level 1. Then count the data flows between each outside entity and the subprocesses in the diagrams.)

4. Do not incorporate too many details into any single diagram. For instance, limit each detailed diagram to only a few bubbles, probably not more than six or seven.

5. Code the sub-subprocesses carefully in each detailed diagram, so that they can be identified easily with their "parent" subprocess. For instance, if three subprocesses are coded as 1.0, 2.0, and 3.0, the sub-subprocesses for 1.0 would be 1.1, 1.2, 1.3, and so on; the sub-subprocesses for 2.0 would be 2.1, 2.2, 2.3, and so on; and the sub-subprocesses for 3.0 would be 3.1, 3.2, 3.3, and so on. In turn, those for 1.1 would begin as 1.11, 1.12, and 1.13.

6. In instances where multiple entities function in the same manner, use a single encompassing label to represent all. For instance, the reference to "student" in our example means all students.

7. Where multiple entities function differently, use separate boxes. For instance, assume that a process involves both credit and cash customers, and that the processing steps relating to credit customers are different from those of cash customers. Separate boxes, labeled "credit customer" and "cash customer," should be employed.

8. Do not allow data-flow lines to cross over each other. To avoid crossovers, repeat an entity box or data-store symbol as necessary in a single DFD. Note that in Figure 4-7 the "student" entity appears twice.

9. Show only normal processing sequences in a single DFD. That is, avoid exceptional situations or show them as a separate set of DFDs.

10. Show process bubbles that progress generally from left to right and from top to bottom in a single DFD. Thus in Figure 4-7 the first bubble (1.0) appears near the upper left and the last bubble (4.0) appears near the lower right.

Physical Data-Flow Diagrams   To summarize, the logical DFD just illustrated is a logical representation of data flows that focuses on processes. It is not concerned with the technology required to implement the processes. A variation of this type of representation, called a **physical data-flow diagram,** specifies *where* or by *whom* the processes are performed. It also may indicate the particular technology used to perform the processing. Based on our registration processing example, a physical DFD may include bubbles containing "registration site," which performs process 1.0 (in conjunction with the data processing department), and "assistant registrar's office," which performs processes 2.0, 3.0, and 4.0. The data flows may specify that course request sheets are delivered by students, approved course schedules are entered via an on-line device, and so on. We will not offer any examples of physical DFDs, since system flowcharts are a widely accepted means of presenting the same aspects.

Relationship of DFDs to E-R Diagrams   Many accountants may start a structured systems development project by working with users to construct a logical data model, usually an E-R diagram. The E-R diagram may model an entire business or a subset of the business. This approach enables accountants to model the AIS's data requirements and then develop a set of logical DFDs to determine the processing to be performed on the data. Or, other accountants may begin a systems project in the reverse order by preparing the logical DFDs to model the AIS's processes. Then, they determine the data needed to implement the processes by developing the E-R diagram(s). Either of the two approaches is acceptable; most computer-aided software engineering (CASE) tools (examined in a subsequent section) accommodate either approach.

To illustrate the first approach, the E-R diagram portrayed in Figure 4-4 models a subset of a university's data needs and shows only a "portion" of the data needs of its registration processing system. One entity identified, called student, represents a data store or file requiring the four attributes or data elements shown. A more complete E-R diagram of the process (see Figure 6-14) would identify all of the entities and data stores required to generate student course schedules, as well as any other processing requirements of the registration system. As the set of logical DFDs is developed, we would refer back to the E-R diagram to identify the data stores required to implement the various registration processes. Note that the level-zero logical DFD pictured in Figure 4-7 shows six data stores or files: registration, student, course status, course request, course schedule, and student schedule data. As the level-zero logical DFD is prepared, we would refer to a "complete" E-R diagram of the registration system to determine the data stores needed to process student course schedules. These data stores would then be incorporated into the evolving level-zero logical DFD.

SYSTEM FLOWCHARTS

Placing System Flowcharts in Perspective   Flowcharts are pictorial representations of transaction processing systems that portray flows of some type. The main categories of flowcharts are document, program, process, and system. A **document flowchart** emphasizes the hard-copy inputs and outputs and their flows through organizational units, from "inception to final disposition." Sometimes they are used by auditors and accountants when analyzing a current system for weaknesses in controls and reports. They are still employed to portray manual processing systems and are illustrated in the appendix to this chapter. Program flowcharts, which depict program instructions, are described below. They have been replaced with structure charts and Structured English (both discussed below). A process flowchart, which is no longer widely employed, emphasizes the procedural steps that occur in transaction processing systems. It is therefore useful to review present procedures for possible improvements.

Purposes Of greatest interest to accountants are **system flowcharts**—diagrams that pictorially portray the physical flows of data through sequential procedures. They picture transaction processing systems or major subsystems, highlighting relationships among the elements within TPSs. That is, they provide answers to questions such as:

1. What inputs are received, and from whom?
2. What outputs are generated, and in what form?
3. What is the next step in the processing sequence?
4. What files and accounting records are affected?
5. Which accounting and organizational controls are employed (assuming that they can be pictorially portrayed)?

A **computer system flowchart,** our major concern in this section, focuses on the computer-based portions of transaction processing systems, including computer runs or steps and accesses of on-line files. The most important use of a computer system flowchart is to document a current procedure or a proposed improved or new procedure.

Flowcharting Symbols The building blocks for a system flowchart are a set of symbols, most of which are generally accepted by accountants and analysts. Figure 4-9 displays the set of standard symbols to be used in this textbook. These symbols have been adopted by the American National Standards Institute (ANSI), an international standards agency. Flowcharting symbols may be grouped as input-output symbols, processing symbols, storage symbols, flow symbols, and miscellaneous symbols. All of the symbols in the figure can be found on a flowcharting template (available in most bookstores) or in a computer-assisted flowchart package.

1. **Input-output symbols.** The top symbol in the leftmost column represents data on source documents or information on output documents or reports. The second and third symbols reflect the entry of data by keyboards or other on-line means and the display of information on terminal screens or other on-line devices. (Note: The term "on-line" refers to devices that are connected directly to a computer system.) The last two symbols in the column, involving punched cards and punched paper tape, are rarely used in modern-day systems.
2. **Processing symbols.** Symbols are available to indicate the processing of data by clerks (trapezoid), noncomputerized machines (square), and computers (rectangle). The decision symbol (diamond) is used to indicate when alternative processing paths exist. For instance, in a flowchart showing sales transaction processing, a decision symbol may be placed at the point just after a credit check.

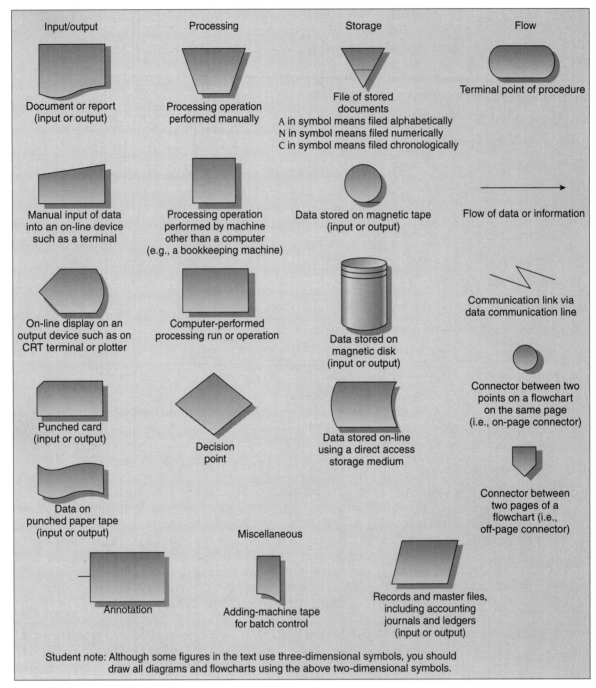

FIGURE 4-9   A set of standard symbols for system flowcharting.

If an ordering customer's credit is found to be satisfactory, one path may lead to continued processing of the order. Alternatively, if the credit is not satisfactory, another path might lead to the writing of a rejection letter.

3. **Storage symbols.** The top symbol (a triangle) is used to show documents and/or records being stored in an off-line storage device, such as a file cabinet or hold-basket. Remaining symbols are available to show data being stored on computerized media. The bottom symbol pertains to any on-line storage device, including a magnetic disk.

4. **Data and information flow symbols.** The five symbols in the rightmost column provide direction throughout a flowchart. The oval terminal symbol marks a beginning or ending point within the flowchart being examined, such as the receipt of an order from a customer. Often a beginning or ending point is also a link to an adjoining procedure. The flow line shows the flow of data or information, usually in written form. The communication link symbol (the one that looks like a lightning bolt) represents the electronic flow of data from one physical location to another. Finally, two connector symbols are available to provide further linkages. The on-page connector (circle) is used within a single page of a flowchart, while the off-page connector (like a home plate) links two pages of a multipage flowchart.

5. **Miscellaneous symbols.** The annotation symbol (open-ended rectangle) can be connected to any symbol within a flowchart; its purpose is to provide space for a note concerning the procedure. For instance, it could indicate how often a particular processing step takes place, or who performs it. The remaining two symbols are useful in flowcharts portraying transaction processing through the accounting cycle. The parallelogram, for instance, is a specialized symbol that adds clarity to journalizing and ledger posting steps.

Guidelines for Construction   Good flowcharts result from sound practices consistently followed. Sound practices should be grounded on the following guidelines:

1. Carefully read the narrative description of the procedure to be flowcharted. Determine from the facts the *usual* or *normal* steps in the procedure, and focus on these steps when preparing the flowchart.

2. Choose the size of paper to be used. Use either regular size (8½ × 11 in.) or an extra-large size.

3. Select the flowcharting symbols to be used. Generally the symbols should be drawn from those listed in Figure 4-9. Although other symbols are available and may appear in the template or flowchart software package, the variety of symbols used should be limited for clarity.

4. Prepare a rough flowchart sketch as a first draft. Attempting to draw a finished flowchart during the first effort usually results in a poor final product.

5. Review your sketch to be sure that the following have been accomplished:
   a. The flows begin at the upper left-hand corner of the sheet and generally move from left to right and from top to bottom.
   b. All steps are clearly presented in a sequence, or a series of sequences. No obvious gaps in the procedure should be present.
   c. Symbols are used consistently throughout. Thus, the symbol for manual processing (an inverted trapezoid) should appear each time that a clerk performs a step in the procedure.

d. The dispositions of all documents and reports are shown. In fact, the final "resting place" of every copy of every prepared document should be specified. Typical dispositions include placing documents in files, sending documents to outside parties such as customers, forwarding documents to connecting procedures (such as a general ledger procedure), and distributing reports to managers. If the disposition consists of destroying a document, this action may be represented in the manner shown in this diagram:

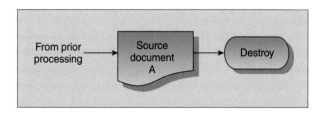

e. The "sandwich" rule is consistently applied. This rule states that a processing symbol should be sandwiched between an input symbol and an output symbol, in the manner shown in this diagram:

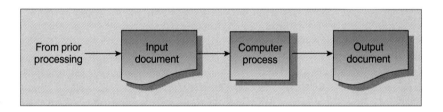

f. When a document crosses an organizational line within the flowchart, the document is normally pictured again in the new organizational unit. However, the repetition is not necessary in some instances if the organizational units are adjacent.

g. All symbols contain brief but specific labels written inside the symbols. For instance, "Sales invoice" might appear inside a document symbol. (Do not simply write "Document" inside a document symbol, since the shape of the symbol indicates its nature.) When lengthy labels are needed, draw the symbols sufficiently large to contain the labels completely. (That is, the size of a symbol may vary without affecting its meaning.)

h. Multiple copies of documents are drawn as an overlapping group and are numbered in the upper right-hand corners; these numbers remain with the copies during their flows through the procedure.

i. Added comments are included within annotation symbols and are attached to appropriate symbols, such as the processing symbols to which the comments are related.

j. Ample connections (cross-references) are provided. The symbols used in forming the connections depend on the situation. Thus if two sheets are needed to contain the flowchart, the flows between pages are formed by off-page connector symbols. In those cases where the procedure being flow-charted links to an adjoining procedure, the connection can be formed by a terminal symbol as follows:

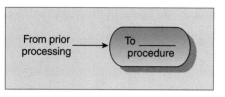

k. Exceptional occurrences, such as back orders, are clearly noted. They may appear as (i) comments within annotation symbols, (ii) separate flowcharts, with references to the main flowchart, or (iii) decision branches. The last alternative may be illustrated as follows:

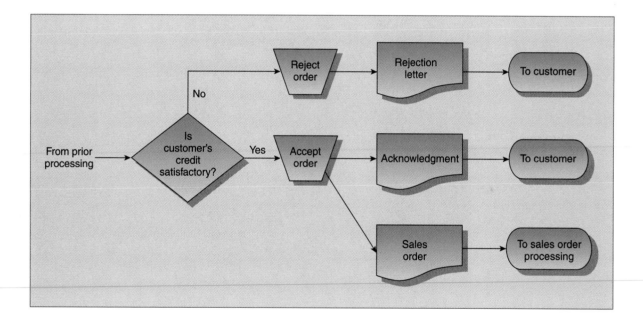

6. Special presentation techniques are adopted when their use increases both the content and clarity of the procedure. An apt illustration of this rule is the portrayal of batch control totals in computer-based batch processing systems. As described earlier, batch control totals are generally computed from key data in each batch of transactions prior to processing runs. Then during each processing run the totals are recomputed and compared to the precomputed totals. These run-to-run comparisons may be performed at the direction of the computer processing programs, and the results may be shown on printed exception and summary reports. If the results show differences in the totals, the differences must be located before processing can continue. This batch control procedure may be diagrammed as follows, where the dashed lines indicate the run-to-run comparisons with the precomputed totals.

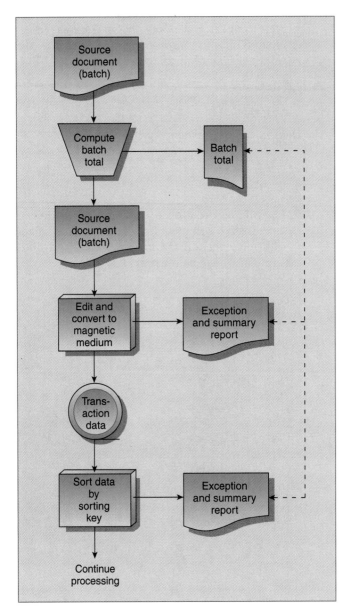

7. Complete the flowchart in final form. A finished flowchart should be neatly drawn and uncrowded. Normally it also should contain a title, date, and the name(s) of the preparers.

Example of a Computer System Flowchart Figure 4-10 shows a computer system flowchart for preparing course schedules for college students. It assumes the use of on-line input and the batch processing approach and is based on the following narrative:

Each student at Branson State University brings a completed course request sheet to an on-line registration site. There a registration clerk enters the student's identification number, plus the schedule line numbers (e.g., 1,2,3,6,9) that identify the particular section of courses being requested by the student. The course data are edited on entry and then stored in an on-line request file (on magnetic disk). On course assignment day, the data processing department

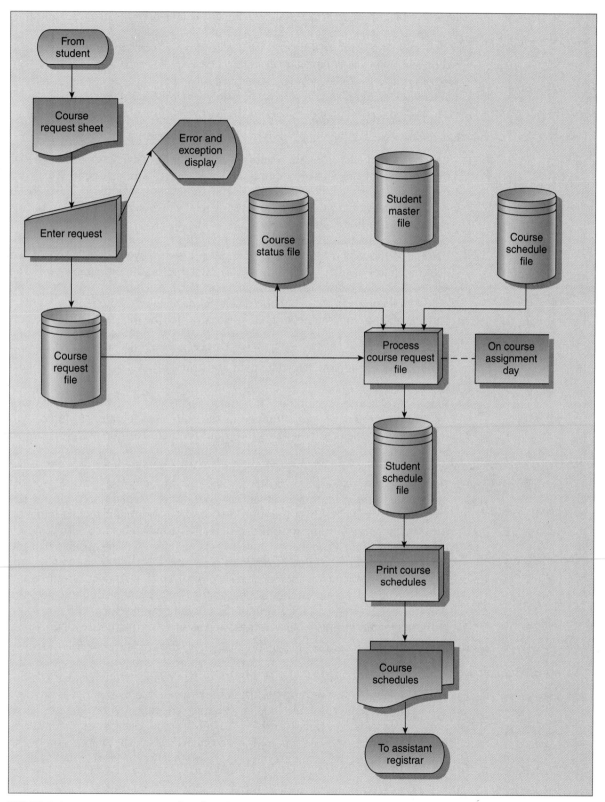

FIGURE 4-10 A computer system flowchart for preparing student course schedules.

processes the course request data to produce course schedule listings. (In preparing these listings the computer program refers to a course schedule that contains descriptive data concerning the courses, to a class status file that shows the number of vacancies remaining in each course section, and to the student file that contains descriptive data—name, address, and so on— concerning students. It also increases the count by one in each course section to which the student is added.) The course schedules are then sent to the assistant registrar.

To illustrate the preparation of this flowchart, we subdivide our task into three major segments. Each is discussed in the following numbered sections.

1. ***Conversion and edit of course request sheets.*** This flowchart segment begins at the registration site with the terminal symbol labeled "From student." This symbol is connected by a flow line to a document symbol. Inserted in this second symbol is the notation "Course request sheet," which serves as input into this module of the flowchart. The second flow line connects an on-line data-entry device, such as a terminal or microcomputer. This device is connected to a monitor and as the registration clerk keys in data, it is displayed over the screen. We use the on-line display symbol to portray the monitor. Simultaneously with the keying in of each course request, a magnetic disk file is being created. Note that a flow line connects the magnetic disk symbol, labeled "Course request file." The final step in this segment of the flowchart is for the registration clerk to edit the displayed data for errors. Errors are corrected and rekeyed into the on-line entry device to create a corrected "Course request file," which is the output for this module of the flowchart. The data are stored on this disk file until course assignment day.

2. ***Processing of course request file.*** This course segment is located in the data processing department and is performed by the computer operator. To indicate to the computer operator that the processing runs are to take place on course assignment day, an annotation symbol is attached to the computer processing symbol. The first run also uses the computer processing symbol and is labeled "Process course request file." Note that the four properly labeled disk symbols are on-line to the computer and that flow lines from each disk file connect to the processing symbol. Each of the four files serves as the input to this updating run. The processing of the four files generates the magnetic disk output file for this segment of the flowchart—"Student schedule file." Please observe that the registration system's computer program accesses the "Course status file," updates the count by one in each course section to which a student is added, and writes the updated count in the "Course status file." This new count replaces the previous count stored on the file. A bi-directional flow line (one with arrows on both ends) symbolically represents these accessing, updating, and writing actions.

3. ***Printing course schedules.*** In this brief segment, the student schedules are also printed out on course assignment day. The "Student schedule file" serves as the input into this flowchart segment and a flow line connects the file to the "Print course schedules" processing run. The output generated by this run is denoted by the document symbol and labeled "Course schedules." A flow line pointing from the processing symbol to the document symbol designates the latter as being an output. The last part of the flowchart depicts the disposition of the course schedules. The terminal symbol indicates that they are sent to the assistant registrar.

Other examples involving the preparation of computer system flowcharts appear in Chapter 5. Other computer-oriented symbols not illustrated in the above example will be explained and used.

Conversion from a Logical DFD to a Computer System Flowchart Logical DFDs can aid in preparing a system flowchart. For example, assume that a system flowchart is needed of the current registration system. Figure 4-7 reveals by means of a logical DFD that process 1.0—"Prepare course schedules"—is subdivided into the three subprocesses depicted in Figure 4-8. Also, three data files are seen as required to process the course request data. Furthermore, updated student schedule data provides the input into subprocess 1.3—"Process student schedules"—from which course schedules are generated. Armed with this information, as well as information about the type of technology employed in the registration system, the computer system flowchart portrayed in Figure 4-10 can be easily prepared.*

STRUCTURE CHART

Processing steps within a computer system flowchart have traditionally been detailed by means of one or more program flowcharts. **Program flowcharts** contain the detailed programming instructions to implement a system, such as printing output documents or updating a particular master file. Program flowcharts have largely been replaced in recent years with structure charts and structured English. A **structure chart** portrays the hierarchy of levels and interrelationships within a system. A high-level structure chart is used by computer programmers to determine the overall structure of the program modules required to operationalize a system. Figure 4-11 shows

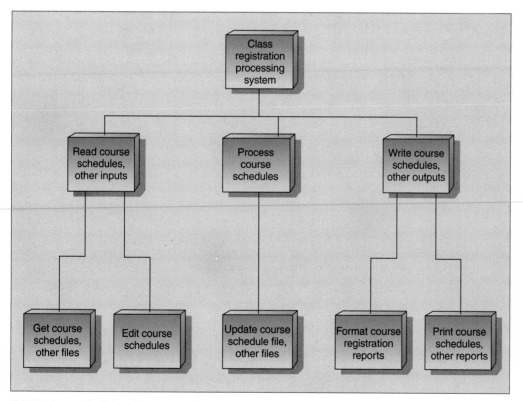

FIGURE 4-11   A high-level structure chart for the course registration system.

*Conversely, a computer system flowchart of the current AIS prepared early in the analysis helps accountants and analysts to prepare a logical DFD of the current AIS. Also, logical DFDs prepared during the design phase portray a new or modified AIS; they can likewise be converted to a computer system flowchart to depict the physical aspects of implementing the new or modified AIS.

a high-level structure chart for the class registration processing system. It can be derived from the data-flow diagrams portrayed in Figures 4-6 through 4-8. Submodules at the second level depict the three independent program modules involved in operationalizing the class registration processing system. In turn, submodules at the third level show more detailed program modules related to the activities at the second level.

A low-level structure chart, prepared during the detailed design phase, enables a computer programmer to create source code subroutines that implement the registration system. It is prepared from the leveled DFDs for the registration system (these diagrams are not shown). The source code subroutines are frequently written in **Structured English,** which are English-like statements generated from a low-level structure chart. These statements are then converted to detailed source programming code instructions.

INTERRELATIONSHIPS AMONG DIAGRAMS AND FLOWCHARTS

In summary, a variety of diagrams and flowcharts are currently used in practice. As Figure 4-12 indicates, they range from the broad to the very detailed. The newer

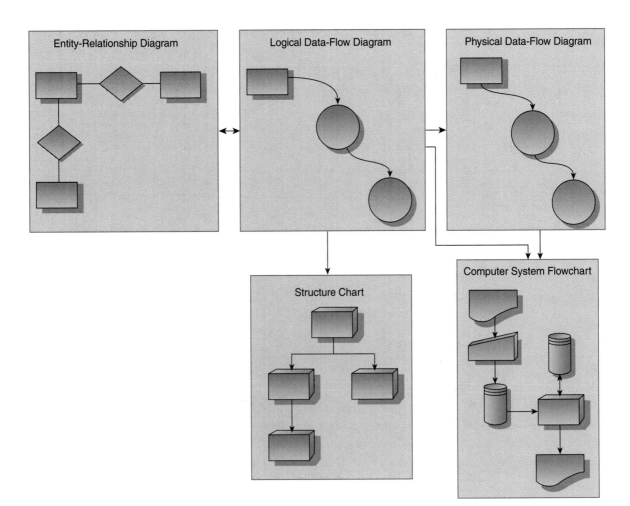

FIGURE 4-12   Interrelationship among diagrams and flowcharts.

structured systems development process utilizes all the diagrams shown, except for the computer system flowchart, which is an older nonstructured technique. Figure 4-12 also depicts the interrelationships among the various types of diagrams and flowcharts. The double arrow between the E-R diagram and logical DFD means that either diagram can be prepared before the other, depending on individual preferences. The flow line from the bottom of the logical DFD indicates that a structure chart is derived from a leveled set of logical DFDs. The flow line from the logical DFD to the physical DFD or to the computer system flowchart means that either one can be generated from the logical DFD.* Finally, it is also possible to prepare a computer system flowchart from a physical DFD.

INPUTS/OUTPUTS

Data are normally entered into an AIS by means of paper (hard-copy) forms or computer terminal (soft-copy) screens. Thus input documentation consists principally of the hard-copy or soft-copy formats that are designed to contain the transaction data.

HARD-COPY DOCUMENTS AND FORMS

Most hard-copy documents are source documents, such as the sales invoice illustrated in Chapter 2. Other forms, such as accounting records and registers, also fall into this category. Well-designed documents and forms are particularly helpful in capturing transaction data. Moreover, well-designed inputs aid the smooth functioning of transaction processing systems, since they clearly document the essential data needed during the processing steps.

Hard-copy documents and forms should be designed only after a careful analysis. If documents or forms are in use at present, a **form analysis sheet** like that shown in Figure 4-13 can be employed. In addition, a list of relevant questions can be referred to. Figure 4-14 provides a list that is suitable either when replacing an existing form or when developing an entirely new form. In essence, this checklist reflects the qualities that a form should have:

1. Exhibit a clear purpose.
2. Be easy for the preparing employee to fill in.
3. Minimize the number of data-entry errors.
4. Enable the data to be easily absorbed by users or entered into the system for processing.
5. Minimize the combined costs of printing, preparing, and using.

PREFORMATTED DATA-ENTRY SCREENS

Transactions increasingly are being entered into computerized systems via on-line video display terminals (CRTs). In many instances the transactions are keyed directly onto **preformatted data-entry screens,** usually by reference to hard-copy source

---

*It should be noted that while the normal process is to progress from logical to physical diagrams, some analysts may prefer to construct physical DFDs or computer system flowcharts before the logical DFDs.

The HIJ Company
Sales Order   No. 2653

Date Received 3-16-97	Customer's Order Number 1738-6	Salesperson K. Brown

Sold to
Handy Warehousing Co.
718 South Desert
Phoenix, Arizona 85208

Ship to
Handy Warehouse No. 5
6100 No. College Drive
Tempe, Arizona 85282

F.O.B. Destination	Routing Via Western Rail Lines	Terms Net 30 Days

Product number	Quantity ordered	Unit of measure	Description	Unit price
26-B	10	50 gal. dr.	Cleaning Solvent	76.50
75-A	5	Unit	Steel Brush	8.75
106-D	50	Yard	Heavy Duty Hosing	5.07

Form No. HIJ162

Form Analysis Sheet

Title: Sales order   Form Number HIJ162

Purpose: To record on a firm form the receipt of an order, so that shipment of the order can be assured.

Point of origin: Sales order department when customer's order received.

Source of data: Customer's order by letter, telegram, or call; salesperson's order slip.

Method of preparing: Typed

Average lines of data: 11   Frequency of use: Daily

Annual quantity used: 2500   Peak weekly volume: 130

Size of form: 6½ × 8½ in.   Cost of preparing 100 forms: $145.00

Disposition—   Original: Sales order department
                 Copy 1 : Shipping department
                 Copy 2 : Billing department
                 Copy 3 : Acknowledgment to customer
                 Other copies: None

Other forms using data: Sales invoice, shipping order

Transcription onto machine-readable media: Magnetic tape
Files affected: Inventory, customer, open orders, various reference files
Volume of errors per week: 20   Approval signatures required: None
Data added after form originated: Back order number, if any; unit costs; freight cost
Use of form for internal checking and control: Initialed by clerks who review for completeness and who enter in register; compared with shipping report
Remarks: No spaces for priority, delivery date scheduled, unit costs, special instructions

FIGURE 4-13   A sales order document and related form analysis sheet.

What is the purpose of the form?

What is the source of the information?

Who are the users of the form?

Has a title been established?

Has an identification number been assigned for control purposes?

Are the information items adequate to meet the purpose, with all unnecessary items omitted?

Are clear but brief instructions provided, when necessary, for use by the preparer?

Is a space provided for the date?

Is related information grouped together?

Is there a logical flow of the information items (e.g., from left to right and from top to bottom) to minimize backtracking?

Is the quantity of information to be entered kept at a minimum by such devices as check boxes and preprinted descriptions?

Is adequate space provided for entering needed information?

Are key information items stressed by heavy type or distinctive color?

Are the margins adequate?

Is standard-size paper (8½ × 11 in.) used?

Is the vertical spacing appropriate for the machines used to enter the items?

Are such technical features as perforations, scoring, type size, and paper weight suited to the intended use?

Are adequate copies prepared for distribution and filing, and are they prebound in multi-copy sets?

Are copies color-coded to reduce mistakes in distribution?

FIGURE 4-14   A checklist for forms design.

documents. Figure 4-15 displays a preformatted screen that is suitable to savings institutions. Its purpose is to aid tellers in keying journal entries into a computer system from hard-copy deposit slips.

Key principles of forms design apply to screen design. Thus a data-entry screen should have a clear purpose and a logical arrangement. In fact, the screen should look very much like the related source document. Thus it should provide clear but concise labels. It might also provide boxes or underscores to denote needed characters or words.

On the other hand, screens are "electronic forms." Therefore, they should take advantage of special features that can aid the humans who use the screen. That is, the computer system can be instructed (programmed) to

1.   Enter standard data items (e.g., the date of the transaction).

2.   Perform needed computations (e.g., compute totals).

3.   Respond with ("echo") clarifying data (e.g., customer names that correspond to entered customer numbers).

4.   Move cursors automatically to places where data elements are to be entered.

5.   Highlight special areas, error messages, and so on.

6.   Prompt the user with questions (e.g., "Another deposit?").

7.   Provide a HELP function that the user can access.

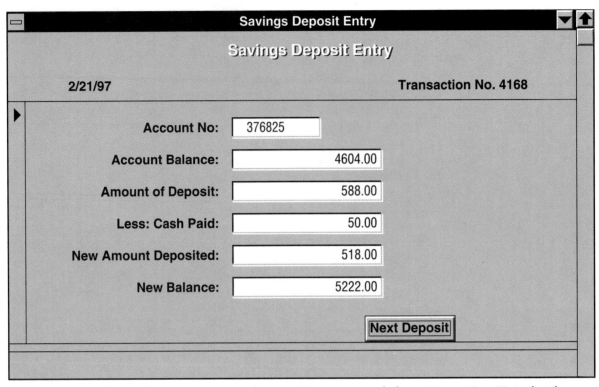

FIGURE 4-15   A preformatted screen for entering data pertaining to one cash deposit transaction. (Note that the date, terminal number, transaction number, and prior account balance are entered automatically by the computer system after the account number is entered manually. In addition, the net amount deposited and the new account balance are computed automatically after the amount of deposit and cash paid amount are entered manually.)

Data-entry screens should fit into an integrated framework of screens. **Menu screens** can be employed to provide listings of options. All screens within the framework should present consistent formats. For instance, the headings and data such as the date and transaction number should be placed in the same relative locations on the screens.

REPORTS AND DISPLAY SCREENS

Most outputs from computer-based systems appear as hard copies or as soft-copy screen displays. The formats of these outputs represent another key type of systems documentation. Information needs of managers and external parties are often met by generating a variety of hard-copy reports and other outputs. These systems outputs aid in making the necessary planning and control decisions and in meeting the firm's other responsibilities. A large number of specific reports and output displays fitting into one or more categories are generated by a typical firm. Thus on the basis of occurrence, reports may be identified as scheduled, demand, and event-triggered. **Scheduled reports** are issued at predetermined intervals of time, such as daily or weekly. **Demand reports** appear only when requested or demanded by managers; they are **ad hoc reports** in that they are intended to respond to specific problems. **Event-triggered reports** are triggered by events such as shortages of inventory or breakdowns of machines. Reports may also be classified on the basis of conciseness. Thus **detail reports** provide an abundance of data, whereas **exception reports** provide only highlighted data. For example, a detailed inventory status report might list pertinent facts concerning all of the inventory that a firm stores; an exception report would list only those inventory items whose on-hand balances are below established reorder points.

Perhaps the most useful classification plan is according to the main purpose of the report. **Stewardship reports** are intended to disclose the custodianship of the resources entrusted to management. They are prepared for the eyes of stockholders, prospective investors, creditors, and others. **Legal compliance reports** are intended to fulfill requirements specified by laws. Examples are Form 10-K reports filed with the Securities and Exchange Commission and income tax returns filed with the Internal Revenue Service. **Operational reports** reflect past events (e.g., sales) and/or current status (e.g., account balances). Most operational reports, such as sales summaries and inventory status reports, are largely based on transactions. They are mainly used by the employees and lower-level managers of a firm in conducting operations. **Control reports** aid managers in controlling the acquisition of resources needed in operations and their ongoing use. These reports also are often based on data from transactions. However, they must include benchmarks that provide means of comparison. Examples of control reports are (1) production control reports that compare actual costs with standard costs and (2) inventory control reports that com-

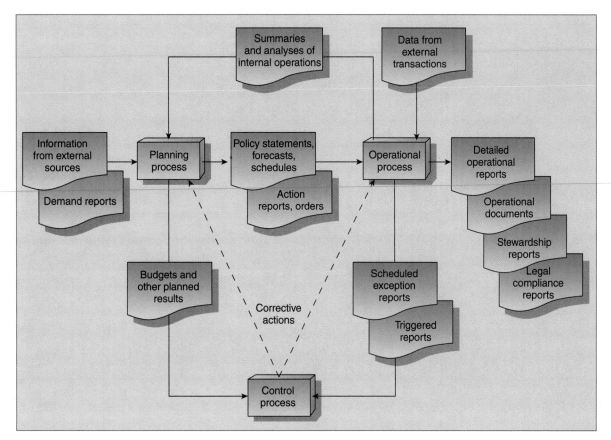

FIGURE 4-16   Reports related to the planning, control, and operational processes.

pare actual quantities on hand with established reorder point quantities. **Planning reports** aid managers in making decisions concerning the firm's future need for resources. These reports are least dependent on transaction data. Examples are (1) budgets and (2) analyses of alternative choices (e.g., an analysis of alternative products newly developed for marketing). The relationships of these types of reports to the underlying processes of a firm are depicted in Figure 4-16. An example of a report format appears in Figure 4-17.

In terms of volume, the dominant type of output for a typical firm is the source document produced during transaction processing. Examples of output source documents are purchase orders and checks. Generally speaking, the checklist in Figure 4-14 applies as fully to the design of output documents as to input source documents. Figure 4-18 illustrates this point via a monthly statement, that is, an output document, for a customer. This document satisfies one main purpose: clearly informing the customer of the current account balance and the transactions leading to this balance.

As in the case of inputs, terminal and microcomputer screens are increasingly being employed to display outputs. These outputs may take the forms of responses to specific on-line inquiries. Alternatively, they may be elaborate ad hoc reports that are constructed with the help of report-generation software. Both types of outputs are called screen displays.

Screen displays should be designed in a manner that enables the user to locate needed information quickly and easily. An effective screen display arranges the

Maxy Sales Corp. Sales Report (Thousands of Dollars) July 1997									
	Product line								
	A			B			Total		
Regional Sales Office	Budget	Variance Over (Under) Budget	Percent Variance	Budget	Variance Over (Under) Budget	Percent Variance	Budget	Variance Over (Under) Budget	Percent Variance
Western: sales contribution	$6,000 2,000	($500) (167)	(8.3) (8.3)	$10,000 1,000	$400 40	4.0 4.0	$16,000 3,000	($100) (127)	(0.6) (4.2)
Eastern: sales contribution	$9,000 3,000	($200) (67)	(2.2) (2.2)	$14,000 1,400	($100) (10)	(0.7) (0.7)	$23,000 4,400	($300) (77)	(1.3) (1.8)
Northern: sales contribution	$7,500 2,500	$100 33	1.3 1.3	$12,000 1,200	$600 60	5.0 5.0	$19.500 3,700	$700 93	0.8 2.5
Total: sales contribution	$22,500 7,500	($600) (201)	(2.7) (2.7)	$36,000 3,600	$900 90	2.5 2.5	$58,500 11,100	$300 (111)	0.5 (1.0)

FIGURE 4-17 A managerial report format.

Arvin

STATEMENT

ArvinAir Division

Arvin Industries, Inc.
500 South 15th Street
Phoenix, Arizona 85034

TO:

ACCOUNT NUMBER

STATEMENT DATE

INVOICE DATE	INVOICE NO.	CUSTOMER NO.	CUSTOMER LOCATION	TERMS	LINE CODE	DUE DATE	AGE CODE	DAYS OVERDUE	INVOICE AMOUNT

AMOUNTS OVERDUE (AGED IN DAYS)

AMOUNT CURRENTLY DUE WITHIN NEXT 30 DAYS CODE A	1 – 30 DAYS OVERDUE CODE B	31 – 60 DAYS OVERDUE CODE C	61 – 90 DAYS OVERDUE CODE D	90+ DAYS OVERDUE CODE E	TOTAL AMOUNT DUE CURRENT AND OVERDUE ITEMS

TO ASSIST YOU IN YOUR CASH PLANNING THE FOLLOWING IS AN AGING OF FUTURE DUE AMOUNTS

DUE IN 31 – 60 DAYS	DUE IN 61 – 90 DAYS	DUE IN 91 – 120 DAYS	DUE IN OVER 120 DAYS	TOTAL FUTURE DUE CODE F	ACCOUNT BALANCE

PLEASE REMIT TO:

LINE CODE:

INV = INVOICE
C/B = CHARGE BACK
C/M = CREDIT MEMO
LPC = LATE PAYMENT CHARGE
OAP = ON ACCOUNT PAYMENT
U/D = UNRESOLVED DEDUCTION

CUSTOMER COPY

FIGURE 4-18   A monthly statement. (Courtesy of Arvin Industries.)

131

information items logically and meaningfully for the user. Figure 4-19 shows a screen display that meets this standard. Key descriptions appear at the top of the display. Details are balanced throughout and organized into columnized groupings. Labels are expressed clearly and concisely in bold letters. The amount of information is limited and focused.

The screen display in Figure 4-19 is tabular in format. Graphical formats, however, are becoming very popular. Managers and other users find that graphs convey information more meaningfully. Figure 4-20 shows graphs displayed on a microcomputer screen. Powerful graphics software packages that can produce graphs quickly from tabular data are now available.

EMERGING DOCUMENTATION TECHNIQUES

Until recently, most documentation was manually prepared during the AIS software development process. In recent years two computer-aided development tools have been utilized more frequently by firms to automate portions of the systems development process: computer-aided flowchart software and computer-aided software engineering tools.

COMPUTER-AIDED FLOWCHART SOFTWARE

Instead of manually drawing data models or flowcharts using a plastic flowcharting template, the process can be automated by using dedicated flowchart software packages. Several such packages include Flow Charting 4 (from Patton and Patton Software Corp.), ABC Flowcharter (from Micrografx, Inc.), EasyFlow (from HavenTree Software, Ltd.), and allCLEAR (from CLEAR Software). These powerful, easy-to-use packages enable users to create, edit, and print high-quality flowcharts. Basically, a template of shapes is selected, shapes are properly positioned on a blank screen, and flow lines and text are added. Editing the flowchart involves such tasks as adding/deleting/moving text and/or shapes, resizing the symbols (if necessary), and aligning the chart.

COMPUTER-AIDED SOFTWARE ENGINEERING TOOLS

The structured systems development approach is a systematic, top-down, disciplined method for graphically portraying an information system (see Chapter 18). In a large minority of the firms, the documentation required for structured systems development (refer back to Figure 4-1) is still prepared manually. This approach is inefficient, slow, costly, and often fails to satisfy user expectations. For example, backlogs of requests for new software development and modifications to existing software may not be completed for months or years. Consequently, user requirements often change by the time the development process is completed, resulting in information systems of inferior quality. In recent years many firms have employed **computer-aided software engineering (CASE)** tools as a strategy to automate portions of the tedious clerical tasks required to perform a structured systems development. CASE tools, if properly used, can boost productivity of the systems development staff by reducing the time and cost to produce high-quality documentation for new systems. Less time is spent on maintaining systems and more time is spent on developing more effective systems.

CASE tools can automate the preparation of entity-relationship diagrams, data dictionaries, data-flow diagrams, structure charts, business forms, and screen and report displays, and automatically generate some of the source programming code.

```
ICP02                NEW PURCHASE ORDER (STOCK ITEMS)                854
   DATE-02/04/97              TIME-13:15:50              TERM ID-AT01


- - - - - - - - - - - - - - - - - - - - - - - - - - - - - - - - - - - -

  PURCHASE AGENT: 01                    VENDOR NAME1: SUNSHINE OFFICE SUPPLY
  SHIP TO:                              VENDOR NAME2:
  TAX CODE:        T                    ADDRESS:      14137 W. OAK PLACE
  TERMS:          10                    CITY/STATE:   MORRISON, CO 80465
  FOB POINT:      OUR PLANT                    SHIP VIA: BEST WAY

- - - - - - - - - - - - - - - - - - - - - - - - - - - - - - - - - - - -

  LN  WSE   ITEM CODE QUANTITY - ORDERED VENDOR - PRICE  DUE - DATE PROJ/CO/CODE ACT

  01  100   1016            25          20000       05/05/97   0105 1500
  02  200   1010            20           5000
  03  200   1017            30
  04  200   1024
  05
  06
  07
  08
  09
  10
  11
  12

        PURCHASE ORDER NUMBER: 000010          VENDOR NUMBER: 500777
```

FIGURE 4-19   A screen display. (Courtesy of Dun & Bradstreet Software Services, Inc.)

FIGURE 4-20   Graphical displays on a microcomputer. (John Greenleigh/Courtesy of Apple Computer, Inc.)

As a result, the systems development process is standardized and systems developers can prepare more comprehensive and consistent documentation. CASE tools are further explored in Chapter 19.

SUMMARY

Documentation communicates knowledge concerning procedures and other system components to users, systems analysts, accountants, auditors, and other interested parties. Pertinent documentation techniques include record layouts, data dictionaries, data models, data-flow diagrams, system flowcharts, structure charts, formats of source documents, reports, screen entry forms, and screen displays.

Documentation should be complete. Illustrated examples should be included to improve its understandability. Its effectiveness is also enhanced if the various components are well designed. Thus record layouts and data dictionaries should clearly show the details concerning data elements. Entity-relationship diagrams model the associations among data employed in applications. These diagrams can serve as the basis for preparing data-flow diagrams (DFDs), which graphically depict the data flows involved in processes or procedures. Both logical and physical DFDs should employ four standard symbols to reflect entities, data flows, processes, and data storage. They should also follow established guidelines, such as the decomposition into successively more detailed views of the processes.

Although a logical DFD is similar in several respects to a computer system flowchart, there are also important differences. One notable difference is that a computer system flowchart reflects the specific details concerning the implementation of particular processes and procedures, including certain physical aspects of the system. In documenting a procedure, the flowchart should employ a consistent set of symbols, clearly portray a sequence of steps in a procedure, show connections to other flowcharts, show the final dispositions of all documents and reports, incorporate adequate labels and added comments, and so on. It should focus on the normal flows, although it may recognize any exceptional occurrences. Logical DFDs and computer system flowcharts serve as a guide for preparing structure charts. An AIS produces a variety of documents, forms, and reports. Each one of these outputs should have clear purposes and be easily prepared.

Although most of this documentation is manually prepared, many firms have begun to employ computer-assisted flowchart software and computer-aided software engineering (CASE) tools to automate portions of the process.

APPENDIX TO CHAPTER 4

DOCUMENT (SYSTEM) FLOWCHART FOR A MANUAL PROCEDURE

Nature

A document flowchart shows the detailed path of hard-copy input and output documents through organizational units, from origination to disposition. It is primarily employed during systems analysis and early design to portray manual procedures. Accountants can use document flowcharts to pinpoint weaknesses in internal controls and paper flows as the documents move through business processes. In this section, we illustrate the preparation of a document flowchart which blends the features of a system flowchart with those of a process flowchart. This blended flowchart can be called a document system flowchart.

Symbols

Only certain symbols are needed to prepare a document system flowchart. They are the terminal, manual processing, document, annotation, on-page connector, file, and records and master files symbols.

Example

The following narrative describes the purchasing procedure for the Easybuy Company:

A clerk in the accounting department periodically reviews the inventory records in order to determine which items need reordering. When she notes that the quantity on hand for a particular item has fallen below a preestablished reorder point, the clerk prepares a prenumbered purchase requisition in two copies. The original is sent to the purchasing department, where a buyer (1) decides on a suitable supplier by reference to a supplier file and (2) prepares a prenumbered purchase order in four copies. The original copy of the purchase order is signed by the purchasing manager and mailed to the designated supplier. The second copy is returned to the inventory clerk in the accounting department, who pulls the matching requisition copy from a temporary file (where it had been filed chronologically), posts the ordered quantities to the inventory records, and files the purchase requisition and order together. The third copy is forwarded to the receiving department, where it is filed numerically to await the receipt of the ordered goods. The fourth copy is filed

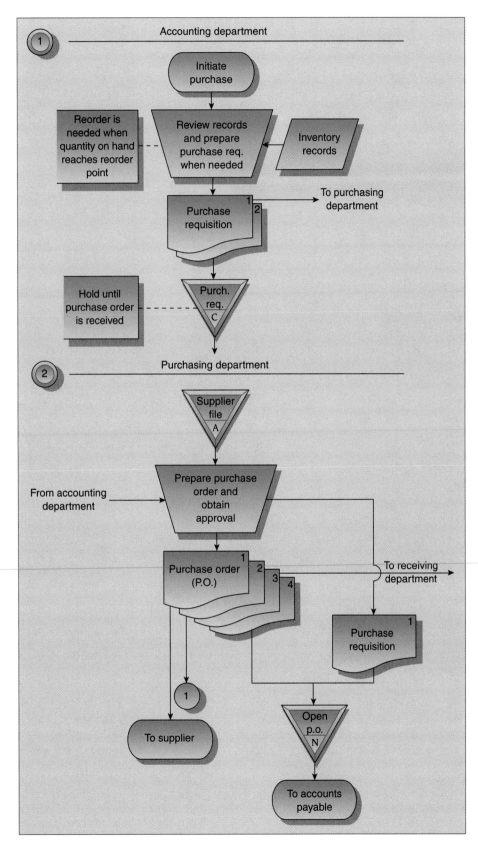

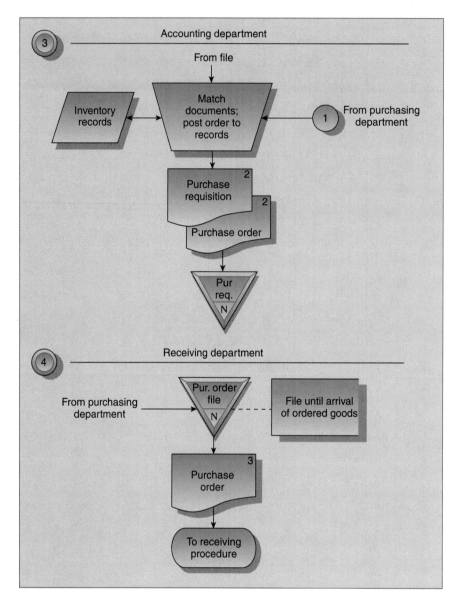

numerically, together with the original copy of the purchase requisition, in an open purchase order file. When the invoice from the supplier arrives, this last copy will be entered into the accounts payable procedure.

Several features of the purchase procedure should be noted. It involves manual processing of transactions, it moves among three departments, and it generates documents having several copies. In order to plan a flowchart of this type, we begin by deciding that three organizational units are to be involved in the procedure. Then we section a sheet of paper (or the computer screen, if a flowchart package is used) into three columns, which we label "Accounting Department," "Purchasing Department," and "Receiving Department."

There are many similarities between preparing computer system and document system flowcharts. Thus we will limit our discussion to important concepts not illustrated in the example to prepare a computer system flowchart. For convenience we subdivide our work into four key steps or functions. Each is briefly discussed in the following numbered sections and shown on pages 135–136.

1. **Preparation of the purchase requisition.** Note that a flow line connects an accounting record symbol, labeled "Inventory records," to the manual processing symbol. This connection from the inventory records to the manual processing symbol denotes that inventory data are used during the preparation of the purchase requisition. A flow line from the manual processing symbol to the document symbol indicates that a purchase requisition, in two copies, is

an output from the processing step. (Note that when multiple copies of a form are prepared, they are numbered and shown in an offset manner.)

The final function of this flowchart segment is to show the disposition of the two copies of the purchase requisition. A flow line pointing to the right directs copy 1 to the purchasing department, whereas a downward flow line indicates that copy 2 is filed in a folder. The letter C in the file symbol means that copy 2 is arranged chronologically (by date) within the file. (Note that it is not necessary to show a processing symbol that specifies a filing action between the document and the file.)

2. **Preparation of a purchase order.** Two flow lines lead to the processing symbol, one from the first copy of the purchase requisition and the other from the supplier file. Based on data from these two sources, a buyer in the purchasing department prepares a purchase order in four copies. Another "output" flowing from the processing symbol is copy 1 of the purchase requisition. Since it entered the processing symbol, as noted by the flow line from the accounting department, it must also leave the processing symbol. As the segment shows, it is then deposited in the open purchase order file. (An important rule of document flowcharting is to show the final disposition of every copy.)

The remainder of this flowchart segment depicts the disposition of the four purchase order copies. An alternate way to show the disposition of copy 1 would be to add a column on the flowchart labeled "Supplier" and show the flow of copy 1 to that column. (However, a column is necessary only if processing steps are to be shown within the column.) Copy 2 terminates with an on-page connector labeled "1." The receiving department will continue the disposition of copy 2. Copy 4 is filed together with copy 1 of the purchase requisition. The terminal symbol below the file indicates that the filed copies will be used in the accounts payable procedure. (Note that a column has not been allotted on this flowchart for the accounts payable department, since the department is not involved in the processing being portrayed.)

One additional flowcharting convention is illustrated in this segment. When flow lines cross, a "jumper" (⌒) denotes the crossover.

3. **Updating of the inventory records.** Two inputs, copy 2 of the purchase requisition and copy 2 of the purchase order, enter into the processing. The former is pulled from the file folder, while the latter arrives from the purchasing department. (Note that the on-page connector in effect links to the on-page connector shown in the previous segment.)

As the last step in this segment, the two documents leave the processing symbol and flow into a file. Note that when two or more documents move together, a single flow line is sufficient.

4. **Filing of the receiving department's copy of the purchase order.** In this brief segment, copy 3 of the purchase order is placed temporarily into a file maintained in the receiving department. On the arrival of the ordered inventory goods, the copy is withdrawn (pulled) and entered into the receiving procedure.

Figure 4-21 combines the four segments just described into a manual document system flowchart of the purchases procedure. As we shall learn, it is possible for multicolumn document-type flowcharts to portray computer systems. However, in most situations they are less useful than when manual systems are to be portrayed.

KEY TERMS

ad hoc report (129)
computer-aided software engineering (CASE) (133)
computer system flowchart (115)
context diagram (109)
control report (129)
data dictionary (106)
data-flow diagram (DFD) (104)
data model (107)
demand report (128)
detail report (129)
documentation (103)
document flowchart (114)
entity (107)
entity-relationship (E-R) diagram (107)
event-triggered report (129)
exception report (129)
file (105)
form analysis sheet (125)
legal compliance report (129)
logical data-flow diagram (109)
menu screen (128)
operational report (129)
physical data-flow diagram (114)
planning report (130)
preformatted data-entry screen (125)
program flowchart (123)
record layout (105)
scheduled report (128)
screen display (130)
stewardship report (129)
structure chart (123)
Structured English (124)
system flowchart (115)

REVIEW QUESTIONS

4-1. Which individuals need documentation of transaction processing systems?

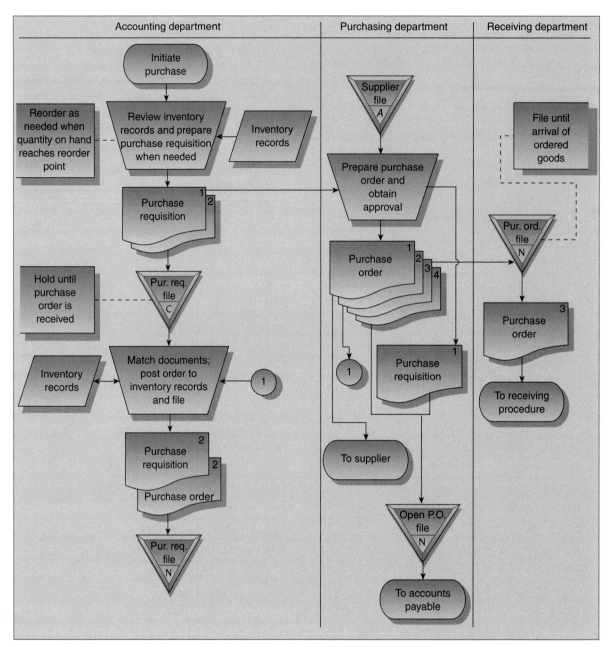

FIGURE 4-21   A document system flowchart of a manually performed purchases procedure.

4-2. How are the foregoing individuals benefited by effective documentation?

4-3. List the various types of documentation applied to transaction processing systems within an AIS.

4-4. What are CASE tools?

4-5. What portions of the structured system development process can be automated with the use of CASE tools?

4-6. What are the components of a typical record layout?

4-7. What characteristics pertaining to data elements should appear in a data dictionary?

4-8. Describe the major features of an entity-relationship diagram.

4-9. What is a logical DFD?

4-10. Define the term "entity" as used in entity-relationship models and data-flow diagrams.

4-11. Identify the various symbols that may be used in preparing data-flow diagrams.

4-12. List several guidelines for preparing logical data-flow diagrams.

4-13. Distinguish between a logical DFD and a physical DFD.

4-14. How is a logical DFD related to an E-R diagram?

4-15. What elements are highlighted in a computer system flowchart?

4-16. Identify the various symbols that may be used in preparing a computer system flowchart.

4-17. Identify several typical steps that are likely to appear in a computer system flowchart.

4-18. List several guidelines for preparing system flowcharts.

4-19. Contrast the purpose and features of a computer system flowchart and those of (1) a logical data-flow diagram and (2) a physical data-flow diagram.

4-20. What is a structure chart? How is it related to (1) a logical data-flow diagram and (2) computer system flowchart?

4-21. What are the benefits of using a software package to prepare various types of data models and flowcharts?

4-22. What are the attributes of a well-designed form?

4-23. What questions should be asked when designing a form?

4-24. What additional concerns apply to the design of a screen for the entry of transaction data?

DISCUSSION QUESTIONS

4-25. Is it beneficial to prepare more than one type of flowchart or diagram of the same transaction processing system?

4-26. Why should Ann Strong become familiar with such documentation techniques as entity-relationship diagrams, data-flow diagrams, system flowcharts, report formats, and record layouts? How can she employ these techniques in her practice?

4-27. Why are logical data-flow diagrams and system flowcharts so important as documentation of transaction processing systems?

4-28. Discuss the interrelationships among entity-relationship diagrams, logical data-flow diagrams, physical data-flow diagrams, computer system flowcharts, and structure charts.

4-29. George Freeman, president of Infoage, approached Diane Varney, treasurer and controller, about the possibility of using CASE tools to automate aspects of new AIS development. Diane made the following comments: "Despite its many benefits, most firms have found it very difficult to implement CASE tools. Its obstacles include high cost, resistance from systems personnel, unacceptable learning curves, and minimal gains in productivity." Please state the reasons why you would agree or disagree with Diane.

PROBLEMS

Note: Certain problems for this chapter require knowledge found in the Appendix at the end of this chapter.

4-1. Design a record layout for a student master file. Include at least ten data elements, beginning with the student identification number. Do not include transcripts. Arrange the data elements within the record, specifying field lengths and modes for the respective elements. (Modes may be numeric, alphabetic, or alphanumeric.)

4-2. Draw a context diagram for a situation involving the registration of students for classes at a university, where the outside entities are students (who prepare and submit course request forms and receive approved course schedules), instructors (who receive class listings of registered students), and the registrar (who receives summaries of class enrollments).

4-3. Draw a context diagram for a situation involving the processing of purchases transactions, where the external entities are suppliers (who receive purchase orders and ship ordered goods with packing slip), the inventory control department (which prepares requisitions relating to needed goods), the storeroom (which accepts received goods from the receiving department together with receiving reports), the cash disbursements department (which receives approved suppliers' invoices, together with supporting purchase orders and receiving reports) and management (which receives purchase analysis reports from purchasing).

4-4. Draw a context diagram for a situation involving the processing of payroll transactions, where the external entities are employees (who receive paychecks and earnings statements and submit time cards signed by supervisors), managers (who receive labor distribution summaries and earnings reports), the personnel department (which receives a payroll register prepared from a computer processing run, and submits personnel action forms to interested parties), government agencies (which receive payroll tax reports), and the bank (which receives a payroll transfer check deposited into the firm's account to pay the current period's payroll, a deposit slip, and a cash amount withheld from employees for payroll taxes that agrees with the total payroll).

4-5. Draw a context diagram for a situation involving a credit-checking system, where the external entities are customers (who prepare and submit credit applications, sales data, and customer inquiries, and receive order acknowledgments), the credit manager (who receives reports), the sales order department (which submits sales orders for credit checking and receives approved sales orders and rejected sales orders), and the credit agency (which prepares and submits credit files and receives updated credit information).

4-6. Draw a context diagram for a situation involving an audit process, the output of which is an audit report attesting to a firm's set of financial statements. For purposes of this problem, assume that the outside entities include the auditee (who submits various types of financial data to the auditors), the audit committee (which receives audited financial statements, an audit report, and a letter of reportable conditions), the board of directors (which receives audited financial statements, an audit report, and a letter of reportable conditions), and the public (which receives audited financial statements and an audit report).

4-7. Refer to Problem 4-3. Prepare a level-zero data-flow diagram in good form that articulates with (links to) the context diagram. The subprocesses are as follows: prepare purchase requisition for needed goods, place order for goods, receive and count goods, place goods in storeroom, vouch invoice and approve for payment, and prepare reports. Needed data stores include supplier data, open purchase order data, and receiving report data.
Hint: See Figures 4-7 and 13-2 for assistance.

4-8. Refer to Problem 4-4. Prepare a level-zero data-flow diagram in good form that articulates with (links to) the context diagram. The subprocesses are as follows: edit time cards, prepare paychecks, distribute paychecks to employees, and prepare payroll reports and statements. Needed data stores include employee earnings records and employee master records.

4-9. Refer to Problem 4-5. Prepare a level-zero data-flow diagram in good form that articulates with (links to) the context diagram. The subprocesses are as follows: prepare sales orders for customer orders, check credit rating, approve credit, approve sales order, and prepare reports. Needed data stores include sales order data and credit history data.

4-10. Refer to Problem 4-6. Prepare a level-zero data-flow diagram in good form that articulates with (links to) the context diagram. The subprocesses are as follows: conduct audit planning, conduct a preliminary review of internal controls, conduct a detailed evaluation and testing of controls, perform an analytical and substantive review, and prepare reports on findings. For purposes of this problem, assume that needed data stores include prior years' working papers data, financial ratios data, and financial data (related to the revenue, expenditure, conversion, and payroll cycles).

4-11. Refer to Problem 4-10. Prepare a level-1 data-flow diagram for subprocess 1.0—conduct audit planning—that articulates with (links to) the level-zero diagram. For purposes of this problem, assume that the sub-subprocesses are as follows: determine scope and objectives of the audit, study prior years' audit working papers (if available), prepare a preliminary audit program, obtain an understanding of the firm's business, and perform preliminary analytical procedures. Assume that needed data stores include prior years' audit data, financial ratios data, and financial data (related to the revenue, expenditures, conversion, and payroll cycles).
Hint: See Figure 4-8 for assistance.

4-12. Note: Requirement b may be performed by the use of a microcomputer-based data-base software package such as Paradox or Access.

a. Locate from a college or university a form for entering the courses that students request to take each semester. The form would show all necessary information concerning the student and the courses, including name, ID number, major department, the course numbers and descriptions, the times of the courses, and the room locations of the courses.

b. Design a simplified form (screen) to capture registration data on-line. Identify data elements that the system can "echo" back to the user.

c. What other methods of data capture might be possible in the student registration application?

4-13. Draw segments of computer system flowcharts that depict each of the activities described. Assume that all files are maintained on magnetic disk, unless otherwise indicated.

a. An unsorted cash receipts file is sorted by customer number.

b. An employee at a remote site keys in inventory data that is transmitted directly to the home-office computer.

c. A shipping notice is generated from a shipping file and sent to the billing department.

d. A sales order file (on magnetic tape) and a cash receipts file (on magnetic tape) are used to update a master sales order file (on magnetic tape).

e. A sales order file and a cash receipts file are used to update a master sales order file.

f. An accounts receivable aging report is prepared from an accounts receivable master file. The report is reviewed by the controller and filed chronologically.

g. Payroll transactions (on magnetic tape) are sorted by employee identification number.

h. A cash receipts file is used to prepare a deposit slip.

i. A rejected sales order file is sorted by sales order

number. The sorted file is used to prepare a rejected sales order report.

j. During a computer processing run, selected data fields are extracted from an inventory master file. The data in the extracted file are used to prepare an inventory reorder list.

k. Daily, invoices received from suppliers are visually scanned for accuracy by an accounts payable clerk. Using his or her terminal, the clerk enters the batch of invoices into the computer system.

4-14. Draw segments of computer system flowcharts that depict each of the activities described. Assume that all files are maintained on magnetic disk.

a. A data-entry clerk keys in monthly sales data to generate a sales transactions file. During a processing run, this file is used to update the customer master file.

b. An updated sales master file is used to prepare a weekly sales report by region and a weekly sales report by salesperson. The latter report shows each salesperson's weekly gross sales and weekly gross margin. One copy of each report is filed for future reference, another copy is distributed by the internal auditor to the regional sales managers, and a final copy is mailed to each salesperson.

c. An accounting clerk enters the weekly sales transactions directly into the computer system. A list of the weekly transactions is then printed out and visually checked for errors. All errors are corrected and reentered into the computer to produce a corrected sales transactions file.

d. An error and summary report is generated during an accounts receivable input run. An accounting clerk checks the report containing credit sales transactions for exceptional items, keys in corrections, and updates the master customer file.

e. Su Bee Company processes its accounting applications on a minicomputer system, which is maintained in a separate data processing department. The firm employs a real-time system to process sales orders. Customer orders are received from salespersons in the field, by telephone, or by fax machine. Salespersons use their laptop computers to transmit orders directly to the minicomputer. Order-entry clerks immediately complete a preformatted sales order form displayed on a computer monitor as orders are received over the telephone. After the order is visually checked for correctness, a send icon button displayed on the bottom of the sales order form is "clicked" with a mouse to transmit the order to the minicomputer. The order-entry clerks also follow the same procedure for entering fax orders.

f. An order-entry clerk transmits each sales order over the local-area network to a printer located in the warehouse, where it is printed off-line. Using the sales order data, a warehouse worker packs the order, fills in a preformatted packing slip displayed on the computer screen, and E-mails it directly to the customer's computer.

4-15. J. B. Means, a retail chain based in Buffalo, uses the following procedure to produce routine reports concerning its charge customers. Customer records are maintained in a sequential accounts receivable master file on magnetic disk. Each day the account balances are updated from sales and cash receipts transaction files; any customer whose balance exceeds the credit limit is listed on a credit notification report. At the end of each month the daily transaction files are merged and re-sorted; then they are used together with the master records to print the monthly statements for customers.

Required

Draw a computer system flowchart that portrays the steps required to produce a non-routine report that lists the data item customer name, arranged alphabetically within ZIP codes.

4-16. Draw segments of document system flowcharts that depict each of the activities described:

a. Manually prepares invoices in five copies by reference to a customer's order and pricing file.

b. Manually sorts purchase orders by assigned numbers and then files.

c. Manually compares the purchase order and receiving report with the pertinent supplier's invoice, marks the invoice approved, and files all documents together in chronological order in an open-to-pay file.

d. Manually posts a batch of check vouchers to the accounts payable subsidiary ledger, re-sorts the batch by suppliers' names, and files in suppliers' folders.

e. Receives cash payments (checks) from customers in the mail room, manually records the payments on a remittance listing, transmits one copy of the listing and the checks to the cashier, who manually (1) prepares a deposit slip in two copies by reference to the checks, (2) compares the total on the slip with the total on the remittance listing, (3) transmits the checks and deposit slips to the bank, and (4) files the remittance listing by date.

f. Receives a batch of shipping notices in the billing department, manually matches the shipping notices to customers' orders pulled from the orders file, and prepares sales invoices in four copies by means of a posting (accounting) machine.

(Copies 1 and 2 are sent to the customer, copy 3 is sent to accounts receivable, and copy 4 is filed numerically with corresponding copies of the order and shipping notice.)

g. Manually enters a batch of suppliers' invoices received today into an invoice register, computes a batch total, posts the invoices to the accounts payable subsidiary ledger, and verifies that the total of the posted amounts equals the predetermined batch total.

4-17. A partially completed document system flowchart appears below. The flowchart depicts the charge sales activities of the Bottom Manufacturing Corporation of Lansing, Michigan.

A customer's purchase order is received and a six-part sales order is prepared therefrom. The six copies are initially distributed as follows:

Copy no. 1—Billing copy: to billing department.

Copy no. 2—Shipping copy: to shipping department.

Copy no. 3—Credit copy: to credit department.

Copy no. 4—Stock request copy: to credit department.

Copy no. 5—Customer copy: to customer.

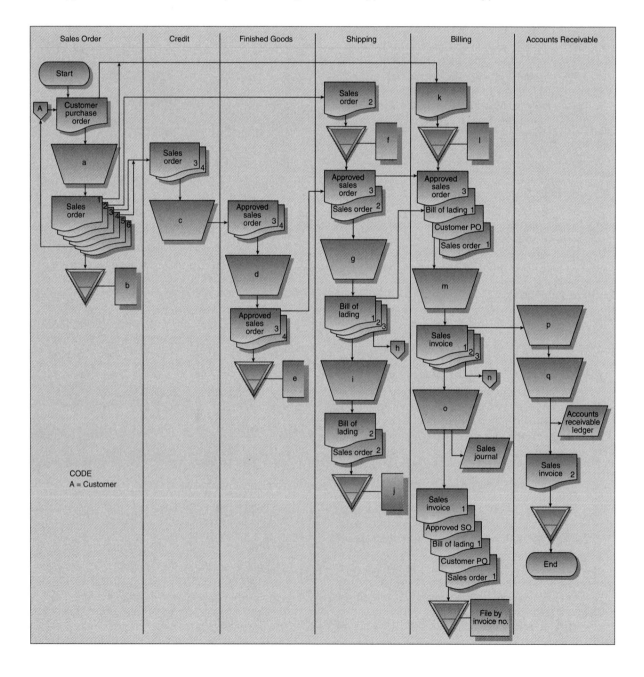

Copy no. 6—Sales order copy: file in sales order department.

When each copy of the sales order reaches the applicable department or destination, it calls for specific internal control procedures and related documents. Some of the procedures and related documents are indicated on the flowchart. Other procedures and documents are labeled with the letters *a* to *q*.

Required

Complete the flowchart by listing the names of documents or procedures represented by letters *a* to *q*.

(CMA *adapted*)

4-18. Liberty Container Company uses a microcomputer system to process its payroll transactions. All transaction and master files are maintained on magnetic disk. Time cards serve as the primary input into the payroll system. Every two weeks the timekeeper collects the time cards, reviews them for accuracy, makes corrections, and sends them to the payroll department. The payroll clerk keys the information contained on each time card directly into the microcomputer system. As a transaction is entered, it is displayed over the monitor so that the payroll clerk can edit the entry for correctness. Transactions containing errors are corrected and reentered into the system. The payroll transactions file is then sorted by employee social security number. The sorted payroll transactions file is used to update the employee master payroll file. The final computer processing run is a report preparation run, which generates the payroll outputs. The following outputs are generated during the output run: paychecks, earnings statements, and a payroll register. The paychecks and earnings statements are distributed by the supervisor to the employees. The payroll register is reviewed by the controller and filed for later reference.

Required

Prepare a computer system flowchart of the payroll procedure described.

4-19. A newly employed accountant prepared the computer system flowchart on page 144 from the following information: Schneider Bailey Company, headquartered in Chicago, uses stand-alone microcomputers located in the accounting department to process all accounting applications. Files are stored on magnetic disk, which are *accessed and updated in a batch mode*. As a batch of source documents is received from a user department, an accounting clerk computes a batch total. The accounting clerk delivers the batch of source documents and batch transmittal slip to the assistant controller, who completes the remaining steps in the procedure to generate the application's outputs.

The data on each source document and the amount of the batch total are entered over the microcomputer's keyboard. Next, an edit run detects errors in the source documents data; the output of this run is an error and summary report. The assistant controller compares the amount of the batch total with the amount shown in the error and summary report, notes discrepancies, and reenters any corrections. During an updating (or posting) run, the corrected source documents (transactions) file is used to update the master file. A report preparation run generates three copies of a report. Copy 1 is sent to management, copy 2 is filed by date, and copy 3 is sent to the controller for review.

Required

Assume that you have been employed by Schneider Bailey Company for one year and during this period have prepared numerous computer system flowcharts. One of your responsibilities is to supervise and train the accountant who prepared the poorly constructed flowchart.

a. Prepare a list of the errors in the flowchart on page 144.

b. Based on the narrative given in the problem and the flowchart prepared by the staff accountant, prepare a revised computer system flowchart, following established flowchart guidelines.

4-20. A cash sale procedure in a small department store involves several steps. First, the sales clerk prepares a prenumbered sales slip as a triplicate set. The original and second copy, together with the payment, are presented to the cashier by the salesclerk. The cashier validates the original copy and gives it to the customer. The third copy of the sales slip is retained in the sales book; when the sales book has been depleted of sales slip sets, it is filed in the sales office.

At the end of each day the cashier prepares a sales summary, counts the cash, and prepares a deposit slip in duplicate. He or she next takes the cash to the bank, where one copy of the deposit slip is retained and the other is validated to reflect the amount deposited. Then the cashier turns over the validated deposit slip, second copies of the sales slips, and the sales summary to the firm's accountant. The accountant compares these documents and accounts for all numbered sales slips. Then he or she gives the sales summary to the general ledger clerk, who posts the sales totals to the appropriate accounts and files the sales summary chronologically. The accountant files the sales slips numerically and the deposit slip chronologically.

Required

Prepare a document system flowchart of the procedure described.

4-21. Design a suitable format of a form to be used by a depositor of Thrift Savings and Loan. The form should

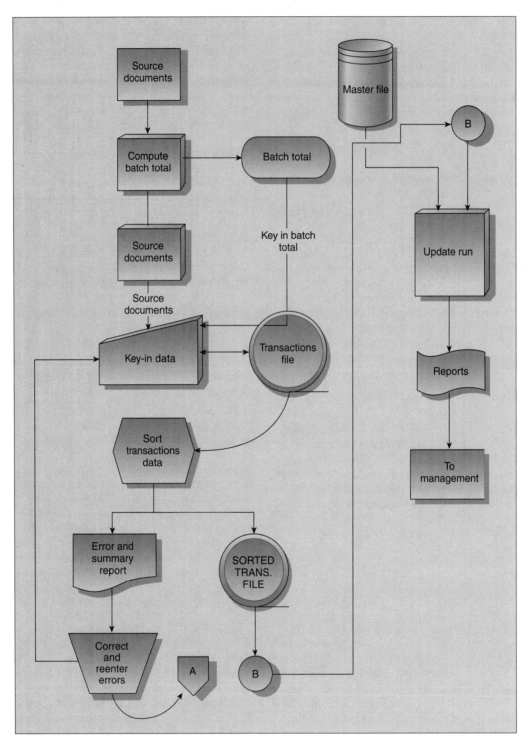

accommodate either a deposit or a withdrawal of funds from a savings account. When filled in, it is given to the teller together with the depositor's passbook. The form should allow checks or currency to be deposited and allow cash to be returned to the depositor from the total of deposited checks if desired.

4-22. The Good Shepherd Hospital employs an on-line patient transaction processing system, including video display terminals. Design a preformatted data-entry screen to aid the receptionist in admitting a patient to the emergency room. Data to be entered include the patient's name, address, age, medical insurance plan;

the means by which the patient was delivered to the hospital; the code for the suspected type of injury or illness; the attending physician; the time of arrival; and so on. Allow space for the description of the injury or illness to be "echoed" on the entry of the code.

4-23. Design formats of queries or reports that will provide needed information to the responsible managers.

   a. Query to review the activity and status of each merchandise item.

   b. Report of projected requirements for cash during the four quarters of the coming year.

4-24. Refer to Problem 4-15. J. B. Means, a retail chain based in Buffalo, uses the following fixed-length master records to retain data concerning its charge customers:

Data Element	Field Size (Characters)
Account number	10
Customer name	35
Customer address	40
Customer ZIP code	5
Credit limit	10
Account balance, beginning of month	10
Account balance, current	10

Required

a. Design a format for a routine monthly report concerning the firm's charge customers.

b. Design a monthly statement for a customer and enter sample data.

c. Design a record layout for the master record. Identify each data element in the master record in relation to the printed element(s) in the monthly statement. For instance, enter a circled A under the account number field in the record layout, and also a circled A next to the assumed value for the account number (e.g., 01234567) in the statement.

d. Draw record layouts for the sales and cash receipts records, including only those data elements needed to identify the transactions and affected customers and to provide the amounts and dates that will appear in the monthly statement. Identify each data element from the record layouts to a related or derived item in the monthly statement.

4-25. Down and Out is a not-for-profit organization in Victoria, British Columbia. Its accounting information system uses the general ledger to summarize and report variances between actual and budgeted amounts. The general ledger master file is actually split into two files: (1) a header file that contains relatively permanent data concerning each account in the chart of accounts and (2) a balance file that contains the total outstanding commitment, the budgeted amount, and the actual amount for each account. In addition, a general ledger transaction file contains transaction data pertaining to commitments and actual expenditures.

The following steps are involved in the expenditures procedure: When a purchase order is issued, the committed amount of the expenditure and the appropriate numbered general ledger account that it affects are recorded. After purchase orders have been batch processed, summary amounts for the accounts involved in the purchases are computed and entered into the general ledger transaction file. Then the commitment balances in the general ledger master file are updated.

When supplier invoices are received, they are vouched and marked to reflect the accounts against which the amounts apply. Then the invoices are batch processed, and the summary amounts affecting each account are posted to the general ledger balance file. This updating step reduces the commitment balance and increases the actual expense balance.

For each of the 13 periods in the organization's fiscal year, the accounting manager receives a report summarizing each of the following: (1) the total commitment amount, (2) the actual expense amount, (3) the budgeted expense amount, and (4) the variance for each project in progress. Furthermore, another report is provided that shows a detailed breakdown of the expenses pertaining to each project.

Required

a. Prepare record layouts for the general ledger header file and balance file.

b. Prepare a format of the summary report described.

                    (SMAC *adapted*)

CONTINUING CASE

With respect to the small firm that you selected in Chapter 1, choose one of the transaction processing cycles and complete the following requirements:

a. Describe tools and techniques that the firm employs to document the transaction processing cycle.

b. Prepare a context-level data-flow diagram for the transaction processing cycle. Convert the context-level diagram into a level-zero DFD. For one of the subprocesses depicted on the level-zero DFD, prepare a level 1 DFD.

c. Determine the source documents used in the cycle.

d. Determine the reports produced from the cycle.

e. Prepare a system flowchart showing the preparation of reports in the cycle.

CHAPTER
5

··

COMPUTER-BASED
TRANSACTION PROCESSING

··

THE LEARNING OBJECTIVES FOR THIS CHAPTER ARE TO ENABLE YOU TO:

1. Review the transaction cycles for a typical firm.

2. Contrast the two alternative modes of entering data into computer-based systems.

3. Distinguish between the two basic approaches to processing transactions in computer-based systems, as well as the possible variations within these two approaches.

4. Discuss the storage of data in files and records.

5. Identify the methods of organizing, storing, maintaining, and accessing records within computer-based files.

6. Describe typical outputs from transaction processing systems.

7. Devise codes that facilitate the storage and processing of transaction data.

INTRODUCTION

A fundamental task of any accounting information system (AIS) is to process the transactions affecting its organization. Transaction processing involves three stages: data entry, data and file processing, and output preparation. This chapter surveys alternative approaches to transaction processing in computer-based systems. Because of its importance to transaction processing, we also introduce coding of transaction data. However, the controls relating to transaction processing in computer-based systems are deferred until Chapters 7 through 9.

IMPORTANCE OF TRANSACTION PROCESSING TO ACCOUNTANTS

Accountants are greatly interested in transaction processing systems. Accountants' responsibilities directly involve accounting transactions, which represent many of the key events affecting a firm. As a professional accountant, you very likely will prepare reports and analyses whose information derives in large part from transaction processing. Understanding the alternative ways of processing transactions and storing the data in files should be very useful, in at least two respects. First, you will be able to recognize the limitations of currently installed transaction processing systems with which you must cope. Second, you will be able to recommend new or improved processing approaches and storage methods that should fully satisfy the current needs of users and provide the best value (benefits minus costs).

TRANSACTION PROCESSING AT INFOAGE, INC.

We can best visualize aspects of transaction processing through examples drawn from Infoage, Inc., with particular attention to the firm's service activities. To set the stage, we should first consider overall views of transaction processing. Figure 5-1 lists the transaction cycles employed by Infoage. Since Infoage is a merchandising and service firm, the transaction cycles include those pertaining to revenues from product sales and services, expenditures for merchandise and supplies and services, employee services, fixed assets, funds, and the general ledger. In addition to the major business events of each cycle, the figure includes key accounting steps (such as postings to ledgers) and accounting documents and records.

Figure 5-2 presents a context diagram pertaining to the service activities of Infoage. (As we recall, Infoage employs computer processing with respect to these activities.) The circle in the diagram encompasses the system involved in providing

Cycle	Included Business Events and Accounting Steps	Key Accounting Records
Revenue	Ordering products or scheduling services Shipping products or performing services Billing for products or services Posting to accounts receivable Preparing customers' statements Receiving cash payments	Sales or service order Record of service Sales invoice Sales journal Sales transaction file Cash remittance Cash receipts journal Cash receipts transaction Accounts receivable master file
Expenditure	Requisitioning needed products or services Ordering products or services Receiving products or services Posting to accounts payable Remitting cash disbursements	Purchase requisition Purchase order Purchases journal Supplier's invoice Purchases transaction file Disbursement voucher Check voucher Cash disbursements journal Cash disbursements transaction file Accounts payable master file
Resources management	Hiring employees Performing employee services Acquiring fixed assets Acquiring funds Paying employees Disposing of fixed assets Disbursing funds for fixed assets, investments, repayment of loans, and so on Preparing payroll reports, asset analyses, and so on	Personnel action records Time and attendance records Capital investment proposal Payroll register Paycheck Fixed assets register Fixed assets change form Sources and uses of funds statement
General ledger and financial reporting	Compiling accounting transactions Posting to general ledger Generating financial reports	Journal voucher Journal voucher file General ledger analysis General ledger master file Trial balance Balance sheet Income statement

FIGURE 5-1 Transaction cycles for Infoage, Inc.

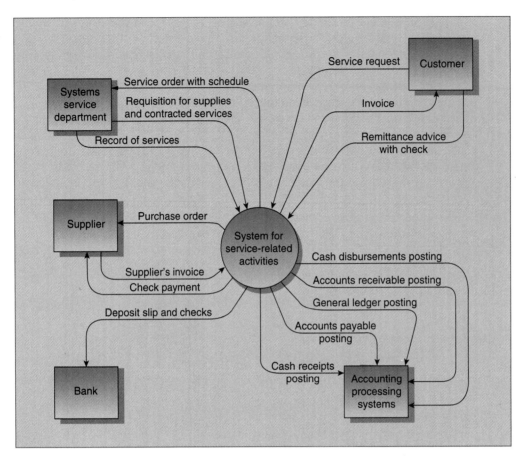

FIGURE 5-2 Context diagram for Infoage's service-related revenue and expenditures.

services to customers, including the acquisition of supplies and subcontractors and other outside services. It shows the major flows of data between the service-oriented system and the relevant entities that are external to the system. Three of these external entities are in the environment of Infoage, while two are entities within the firm. The entity labeled "accounting processing systems" could alternatively be labeled "accounting department." Note that all affected flows and entities are not included within the large circle representing the system under study. For instance, those related to selling products, as well as hiring and paying service employees, are excluded.

INPUTTING TRANSACTION DATA

Most transactions are initiated by specific business events, such as an order from a credit customer or a receipt of merchandise. Various agents, ranging from customers and purchasing managers to governmental agencies and banks, trigger the events. In computer-based systems the triggering agents may include instructions in computer programs. For instance, the replenishment of materials may be triggered by a reordering computer program that compares the quantities on hand against reorder points. Some transactions are not initiated by events, however. For example, the accrual of interest is triggered by the passage of time.

Transactions also may vary in terms of source and time. Thus they may arise at the main offices of firms or at sites remote to the main offices. Transactions occur on distinctive dates and at specific times of day, while *types* of transactions occur at differing frequencies. Thus, Infoage's systems services manager, Jane Thomson, accepts a request for service from a client at noon on June 3. Requests are usually received by phone or visits at the main office, and 10 requests are received per week on the average.

Furthermore, the nature of the input arising from a specific transaction has distinguishing aspects. First, the input consists of data relating to the type of transaction. A request for service may include the client identification, which may be numeric (e.g., 4876) or alphanumeric (e.g., CL780); the client name, which is alphabetic; and the requested service, which may be expressed by an alphabetic phrase or a code. Second, the input is communicated in some form. Often the form is a hard-copy source document. However, it may be a spoken message, as in the service request example. Alternatively, it may be transmitted electronically, as when an order is entered at a remote terminal and transmitted to a firm's sales department.

Inflows of transactions must be handled by a firm's AIS in some manner, so that the data can be entered for processing. When firms have computer-based systems, they employ an off-line approach, an on-line data-entry approach, or a mixture of the two.

OFF-LINE INPUT OF DATA

The term **off-line** refers to input devices not directly connected to a computer. As described in Appendix A at the end of this book, off-line devices include key-to-tape encoders, key-to-disk systems, and character-recognition devices such as optical character recognition (OCR) readers. In an off-line approach, transaction data are first captured on source documents. Certain data—such as identification data—are recorded as codes, as we discuss later in this chapter. Generally the source documents pertaining to a group of like transactions are gathered into a batch. Then the batched transactions are transcribed into computer-readable form, using an off-line device. For instance, Infoage batches and transcribes the orders for product sales it accepts from credit customers. A trained data-entry clerk employs a key-to-disk system that converts the data from the sales orders to a magnetic tape. The records on magnetic tape are then entered into the computer system for processing.

Before the data are ready for processing, however, they should be checked for errors and omissions. In the case of off-line input systems, checking or verifying can occur at two points. After the data are keyed, they may be verified by a separate key-verification step. Then, as the data elements are entered, they may be verified by an edit program. Detected errors and omissions are typically listed on sheets known as *error* or *edit listings*.

In some cases transaction data need not be recorded separately on source documents. For example, Infoage has designed the sales invoices (bills) it mails to be turnaround documents. A **turnaround document** is a document containing data prepared by the firm and returned by an external party to be used as direct input into the computer system. Thus customers return the top portion of the invoices with their payments. These turnaround documents are read by an optical character recognition device directly into the computer system, to be processed as cash remittances. Turnaround documents are useful, since they reduce the keying workload and the possible errors in entering data.

ON-LINE INPUT OF DATA

The term **on-line** refers to devices that are directly and continuously connected to a computer system. As described in Appendix A, on-line devices primarily consist of terminals of various types. In addition, OCR scanners, image readers, and magnetic disks can serve as on-line devices when hooked into systems. In *on-line data entry* the data from individual transactions are entered directly into a computer system as they occur. At Infoage, for instance, service orders are entered via a terminal in the systems services department. Figure 5-3 shows the preformatted screen for a service order, together with data for a sample transaction. The service transaction data are keyed into the system by reference to a handwritten service request document. After being entered, the system prints a confirmation copy of the service order to mail to the client.

On-line data entry permits certain variations to the procedure just described:

1. Source documents are not always prepared before transaction data are entered. For example, data could be entered into the on-line screen portraying the service order directly, perhaps during a telephone or face-to-face conversation with the client.

2. Data may be entered by means other than keying. Manually, the data might be entered via voice-input devices or light pens. Thus the receiving clerk at Infoage's warehouse might enter coded data concerning received goods through a voice-input terminal. In some situations data may be captured and entered into a computer system by means of such automated devices as optical scanners. Most

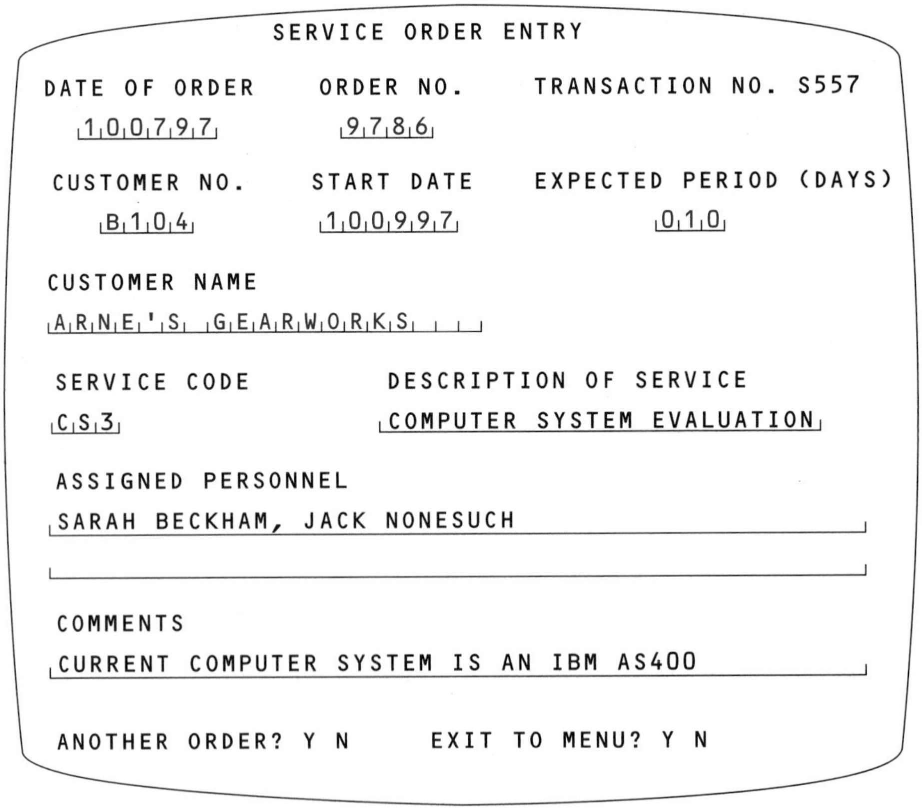

```
                    SERVICE ORDER ENTRY

   DATE OF ORDER      ORDER NO.      TRANSACTION NO.  S557
     1 0 0 7 9 7       9 7 8 6

   CUSTOMER NO.       START DATE     EXPECTED PERIOD (DAYS)
     B 1 0 4           1 0 0 9 9 7          0 1 0

   CUSTOMER NAME
    A R N E ' S   G E A R W O R K S

   SERVICE CODE              DESCRIPTION OF SERVICE
    C S 3                     COMPUTER SYSTEM EVALUATION

   ASSIGNED PERSONNEL
    SARAH BECKHAM, JACK NONESUCH


   COMMENTS
    CURRENT COMPUTER SYSTEM IS AN IBM AS400


   ANOTHER ORDER?  Y N     EXIT TO MENU?  Y N
```

FIGURE 5-3   A preformatted data entry screen for Infoage's service orders.

grocery stores currently employ scanners at their checkout counters to process sales transactions. Since the scanners are connected to point-of-sale terminals, the data are in computer-readable form and captured at the point where the transaction arises; thus they embody the concept of *source data automation.**

3. Data may be entered directly by parties outside the firm who originate transactions. Depositors who use automated teller machines (ATMs) to obtain cash are an example, as are customers who use push-button telephones to order products or to make exchanges among mutual funds.

4. Data may be captured and entered from remote sites, rather than at the site where the main computer is located. Either individual transactions or batches of transactions may be entered via terminals located at remote sites. Thus, if Infoage had communications links between its main office and sales outlets, each day's batches of orders relating to credit sales of products could be entered on-line from the outlets. This approach is sometimes called *remote job entry* or *remote batch processing*. (Currently the sales orders are delivered by car or mailed from the sales outlets to the main office, both methods being part of the off-line approach for inputting sales orders.)

Most on-line data entry involves using terminal keyboards, a meticulous and error-prone task for humans. Edit programs are therefore normally used. In addition, the entry process should be designed to reduce the workload and provide memory aids to the users of data-entry terminals. Four widely used approaches are menus, dialogue prompts, graphical user interfaces, and preformatted screens.

1. **Menus** are numbered listings of options by which users can quickly and clearly specify desired actions. Figure 5-4 shows a set of menus, arranged at three levels, which allow a salesclerk to specify that she needs to enter a sales order.

2. **Dialogue prompts** consist of questions or suggestions displayed by a computer software application to a user. For instance, if a salesclerk takes an order by phone, a series of questions may be displayed, beginning with:

   IS THE PERSON PLACING THE ORDER A NEW CUSTOMER?

   If the clerk answers "Y" (for yes), questions follow to acquire information concerning the customer's creditworthiness. If the clerk answers "N" (for no), questions follow to ascertain the customer number and the particulars of the order.

3. **Graphical user interfaces (GUIs)** allow users to make selections—such as application programs and data files—by pointing to pictorial views (icons) with a device such as a mouse. For example, a salesclerk can "click" on a sales-entry program to begin a sales order entry.

4. **Preformatted screens** are displayed formats or masks of transaction documents, which are to be filled in by the relevant users. Figure 5-3 is an example of a preformatted screen. It can be linked to a set of menus, such as those shown in Figure 5-4, so that it automatically appears upon entering a desired data-entry option.

Sound design principles of screens were discussed in Chapter 4. For example, codes should be employed to the greatest possible extent, since they reduce key strokes. Also, the application software should provide as much data as feasible. For instance, the transaction number should be automatically assigned, and the current date should appear when the screen is displayed. In addition, descriptive data should be "echoed" upon the entry of codes, so that the data-entry clerk can verify the

---

*See Appendix A for a description of source data automation.

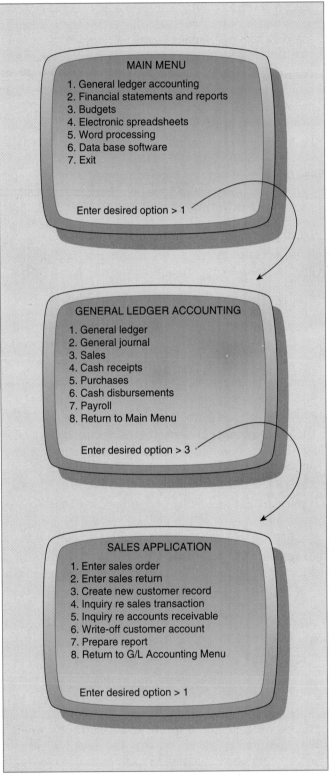

FIGURE 5-4   Menus that aid in the selection of options in an immediate processing system.

correctness of the code. Two echoed descriptions appear in Figure 5-3 upon the entry of related codes: the customer name and the description of service.

RELATIVE ADVANTAGES OF DATA-INPUT APPROACHES

Assuming that transactions are batched, the off-line data-input approach offers two advantages: economy and productivity. Batch-oriented hardware and software are less expensive than the hardware and software required by the on-line approach. The handling of large batches of transactions by well-trained clerks is inherently more productive than the intermediate handling of transactions by clerks who have other tasks. Furthermore, by batching transactions batch-total control can be employed.

The on-line data input approach offers greater timeliness, flexibility, and simplicity. Transactions are generally entered into the computer system as they arise. Those containing errors can usually be corrected immediately by the entry clerk, so that they do not need to be suspended. Transactions can be flexibly captured wherever they arise. They can often be entered without the transcription of data from source documents. If the person giving rise to a transaction (such as a customer) is present, he or she can confirm the accuracy of the input.

PROCESSING TRANSACTION DATA

After the transactions have been entered, further options exist. The transactions may be processed (a) periodically or immediately, and (b) in a sequential or direct fashion. Furthermore, the outputs may be provided periodically or immediately.

Figure 5-5 shows this series of options, together with the options pertaining to data entry. Note that the options listed on the left are those associated with traditional batch input/processing and routine accounting applications. The options listed on the right in the figure, however, are being increasingly employed. They are being demanded to satisfy the faster pace of modern business operations and to meet the needs of insistent users of information.

In this section we emphasize the differences between the periodic and immediate processing approaches, as well as key variations. Some applications within a firm may be better served by the periodic approach, while other applications are likely to be better handled by the immediate approach.

PERIODIC PROCESSING APPROACH

Periodic processing, also called *delayed* or *batch processing*, involves the processing of data from groups of like transactions at periodic intervals. This approach has traditionally been employed by firms with minimal computer resources, but it is also adaptable by firms that have computer-based systems. Furthermore, this approach may be combined with either the off-line or on-line entry of data.

Transactions are accumulated until the batch of transactions is sufficiently large or until a designated time arrives. For instance, a batch may consist of all sales transactions received by 3:00 P.M. Then the batch is processed, usually by posting the transaction data to one or more files. The periods of time between successive postings, which may range from hours and days to months, are called *processing cycles*.

Applications involving large volumes of routine transactions are apt candidates for the periodic approach. In addition to its payroll application, for example, Infoage employs the periodic processing approach for (1) billings of credit sales of products, (2) payments to suppliers relating to purchases of merchandise and supplies, and (3) distributions of employee time spent on service jobs.

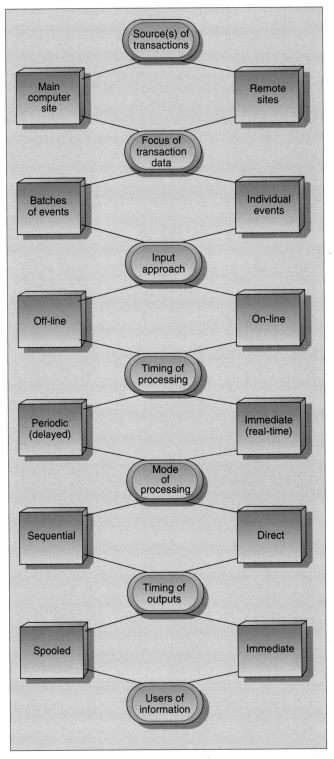

FIGURE 5-5   Options in computer-based transaction processing.

The critical step in routine transaction processing is the posting of data from a batch of transactions to one or more files, such as an accounts receivable file (in effect, a subsidiary ledger). This step is called **updating.** It may be performed sequentially from batched input, sequentially from on-line input, or directly from either type of input.

Sequential Updating from Batched Inputs   To update a master file sequentially within a computer-based application, the processing program starts at the beginning master file record. It reads every record in the file, changing data in each record affected by a transaction. We can best understand **sequential updating** within the context of batch-oriented sales and billing applications employed by Infoage.

Figure 5-6 shows the key steps via a data-flow diagram. Sales for services rendered, first recorded on service orders, are transcribed onto sales invoices. These

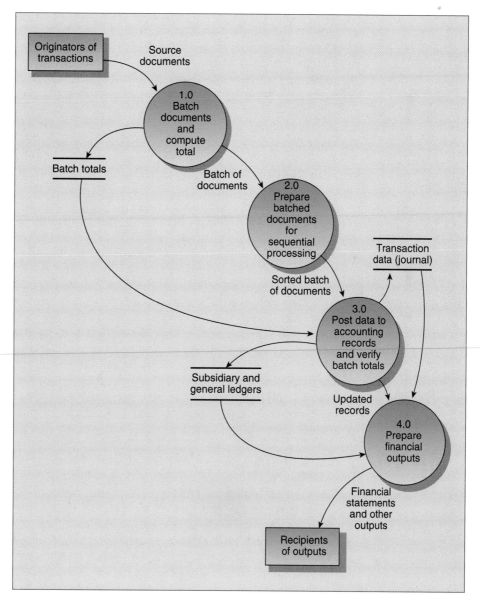

FIGURE 5-6   Data-flow diagram showing generalized batch sequential processing of transactions.

transaction-oriented source documents are then batched. Batch control totals, such as the billed amounts, are computed. The sales invoices are next sorted in the same order as the records in the ledgers to be updated. In this application the **sort key** used by Infoage is customer number, since the file to be affected is the customer accounts receivable file. Transaction records are then posted to the records in the customer accounts receivable file, thereby updating the customers' account balances. The batch totals should be checked to verify that the postings are accurate and complete. Also, the totals are posted to the general ledger. Finally, sales summaries and other financial reports are prepared from sales invoice data. The sales invoices are mailed to customers, while financial reports are delivered to managers.

Figure 5-7 shows a system flowchart that includes certain physical features of a computer-based application. For our example, we choose the application involving product sales by Infoage. Batch totals have been computed from shipping documents prepared in the shipping department. The shipping data are converted or transcribed by a data-entry clerk by means of an off-line device. Data from each document, such as customer number and name, are stored in a record on magnetic disk. Either magnetic tape or removable magnetic disks may be employed as the storage medium; Infoage previously used the former, as shown in the figure, but now has converted to the latter. The master file *prior* to updating is stored on one disk (or tape) and an entire new master file *after* updating is created on another disk (or tape). Each block of transaction records is then entered into the computer processor. On being entered the transaction data are validated by an edit procedure within the credit sales billing program. Next the data are sorted and then sequentially posted to the accounts receivable master file.

Several additional actions occur as a part of the updating program, or **run.** Shipping data, together with data from the customer records in the master file and a pricing file, are used to compute amounts of sales and to prepare sales invoices. A listing of the sales transactions (i.e., a journal) is printed and totals from this journal computed by the application program. The computed totals, printed on the listing or on a separate report, are compared with the predetermined batch totals. Data from the transactions are also summarized and copied onto a magnetic tape, together with the batch totals.

Periodically the summarized transaction data are posted to the affected accounts in the general ledger, as are adjusting journal entries. Various outputs are generated from the general ledger and subsidiary ledger, ranging from financial statements to accounts receivable aging reports.

The advantages of sequential processing are tied to those of the off-line data-input approach. That is, it provides economy, efficiency, and the availability of the batch-total control.

Sequential Updating After On-line Data Entry Transactions may be processed sequentially after the data are entered by on-line devices such as terminals, as Figure 5-8 shows. This sequential processing approach provides essentially the same advantages as sequential processing after batched data entry. In addition, it allows errors in the transactions to be corrected and data to be stored within the system at the earliest possible time. On the other hand, it is not quite as economical.

Consider the service orders entered on-line by Infoage. The service order data are first validated (edited) while being entered via a screen like that shown in Figure 5-3. Transaction data are accumulated temporarily on an on-line magnetic disk. In the case of Infoage's service orders, data concerning orders are stored while the orders are being filled. Orders are priced (in a step not shown), so that invoices can be prepared. Periodically the invoice data are posted to the accounts receivable master file in a manner similar to the posting steps described earlier.

Disadvantages of Sequential Processing Perhaps the most serious disadvantage is that the records in the master files become out of date, except just following an updating run. Consequently, most reports from a periodic processing application are

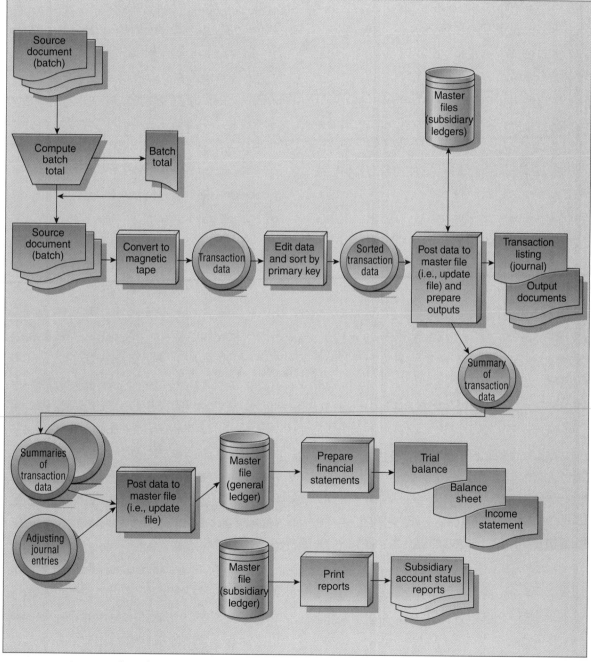

FIGURE 5-7   Computer-based sequential processing of batched transactions.

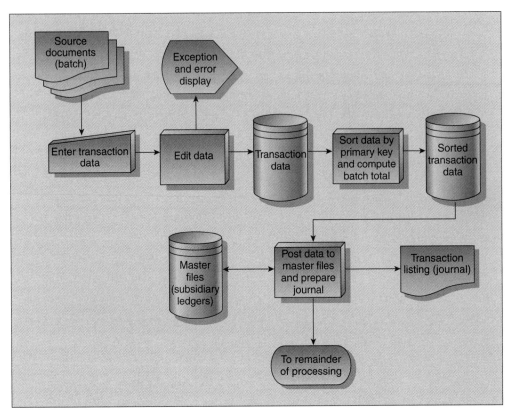

FIGURE 5-8   Computer-based batch processing of transactions with on-line inputs.

tied to the processing cycles. A second disadvantage, if transactions are batched before entry, is that the errors detected in transaction data cannot easily be corrected at the time of their entry. They must be corrected and reentered, either in a separate run or during the next processing cycle. A third disadvantage is that the processing step of sorting must be performed before updating a master file. Finally, all records in the master file must be read during the updating step, thus increasing the processing time when only a few records are affected.

Direct Updating   Instead of processing a batch of transactions sequentially against an entire master file, each transaction in the batch can be posted directly to the affected records. Infoage uses the direct updating approach with respect to its service orders. Each day the employees involved in performing service activities charge their time to various service orders. They enter their time via on-line terminals at the end of each day. Then, during the evening shift the batch of time transactions is posted directly to the service order records stored on-line.*

Direct updating with batched transactions allows the sorting step to be eliminated. Also, individual records can be retrieved at any time to determine the status of data (such as service orders). However, direct updating is feasible only if the master files are stored on a direct-access storage medium and should only be considered when the batches are quite small.

---

*As each service order is completed, the accumulated times are used in preparing the sales invoice mentioned in the previous section; the invoice amount is based in part on the time charged as costed by the hourly service rates.

Contrasts with Manual Processing Figure 5-9 displays a flowchart of periodic processing within a manual processing system. We may assume that the figure reflects the way that Infoage processed batches of sales orders before the present computer system was installed. If we compare this figure with Figure 5-7, we can see these similarities between manual and computer-based sequential processing:

1. Key steps such as computing batch totals, sorting transactions, posting to subsidiary and general ledgers, and preparing financial outputs.

2. The outputs generated (although their timing may differ).

3. The use of batch totals. Figure 5-10 illustrates, in a simplified format, how postings to the general ledger are compared to postings to the subsidiary ledger records in order to verify completeness and accuracy.

Computer-based sequential processing has several distinctions with respect to manual processing. It is faster and more accurate. Data are stored on magnetic media

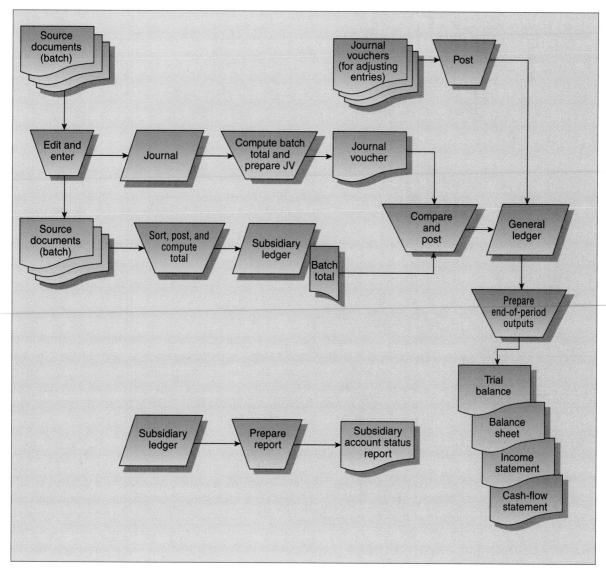

FIGURE 5-9   Periodic processing of batched transactions within a manual system.

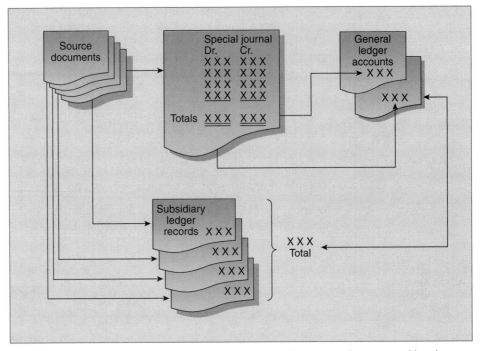

FIGURE 5-10   Comparison of batch totals to verify completeness and accuracy of batch processing.

in compressed form, rather than on hard-copy records. In addition, the journal is produced as a by-product of the posting step in computer-based processing, such as in Infoage's sales order application. The main purpose of a journal in computer-based systems is to provide a human-readable link in the audit trail. Finally, many of the processing steps (including input validation) are combined and performed automatically, whereas in manual systems all of the steps are performed by human clerks located in various organizational units.

IMMEDIATE PROCESSING APPROACH

Immediate processing—often called *real-time processing*—consists of processing each transaction as it arises and is captured. Data from each transaction are entered via an on-line device and posted immediately and directly to the affected record in one or more master files. Thus the stored data in the master files, which are continuously on-line, are kept in an up-to-date status. Immediate (real-time) processing applications are interactive, in that they involve direct interactions between humans and computer-based systems.

An increasing number of applications covering a wide range of activities employ the immediate (real-time) processing approach. For instance, Ann Strong charges her time spent on clients' engagements and prepares invoices for clients by this approach. Infoage handles all time and costs relating to service orders by means of the immediate processing approach. It also employs this approach to deal with receipts of merchandise as they arrive at the warehouse, with shipments of ordered products, and with other transactions where timeliness is an important factor. Applications in other firms that are suited to this approach include airline reservations, custom manufacturing, and hospital patient care.

SPOTLIGHTING

AN IMMEDIATE PROCESSING SYSTEM
*at Helene Curtis Industries, Inc.**

A Chicago-based cosmetics maker, Helene Curtis, recently changed its strategy of being a low-cost manufacturer to being a supplier with excellent service to retailer customers. To foster this new strategy, the firm developed transaction processing systems for on-line order entry and finished-goods inventory. It also added a 300,000-square-foot automated warehouse. Immediate transaction processing is performed by a dedicated Stratus computer system, which is designed to accommodate on-line applications very efficiently and reliably. Also supporting the processing is a DB-2 relational data base system. Tom Gildea, vice-president of business information services, feels that the new system provides "quick response" to its retailer customers. When the new warehouse is fully tied into the new processing systems, the firm's shipping costs are expected to decrease by 25 percent.

*Leila Davis, "On-Line Applications Grow Up." *Datamation* (January 1, 1990), pp. 61–63.

Example of Immediate (Real-Time) Processing Let us survey the steps that Infoage employs in its application involving the immediate processing of open service orders. Figure 5-11 shows the steps in pictorial form.

As time and cost data arise, they are entered via a terminal in the systems services department. Often the time data are phoned in from service job locations; cost data are usually obtained from documents, such as invoices from outside contractors or supply houses. The data-entry step is performed as described earlier in the section entitled On-Line Input of Data. Menus are employed in this application to access the appropriate preformatted screen pertaining to service order updates. Underlying the preformatted screen is the service order update application program, which has been loaded by the operating system into the primary storage unit and initialized. As the time or cost data are entered, they are edited by the edit routine portion of this program. If errors or omissions are detected, the edit routine notifies the clerk by a message displayed on the screen. For instance, if a nonexistent service order number is entered, the edit routine spots the error by reference to a listing of current service orders and flags the error on the screen. After all errors and omissions are corrected, the data are accepted and readied for processing.

The key processing step is to update the service order file. Thus the time or cost data from a transaction are posted to the service order file, thereby increasing the accumulated cost of the affected order. For instance, if a service representative charges four hours of time to service order number 9786 (shown being initiated in Figure 5-3), and the hourly charge is $30.00, an amount of $120.00 is added to the cost previously accumulated against the order.

Other steps may occur when a transaction undergoes immediate processing. The transaction may be inserted in a transaction log in order to provide a complete audit trail. Stored with the key data of the transaction would be the assigned transaction number and the number of the terminal or other input device where the transaction was entered. One or more outputs can be printed, such as hard copies of service orders and/or reports concerning the status of all open service orders. Moreover, stored data may be accessed at any time. For example, if Infoage's service manager needs to see the up-to-date status of any service order or transaction during the day, she can readily access the desired item and view it on her screen.

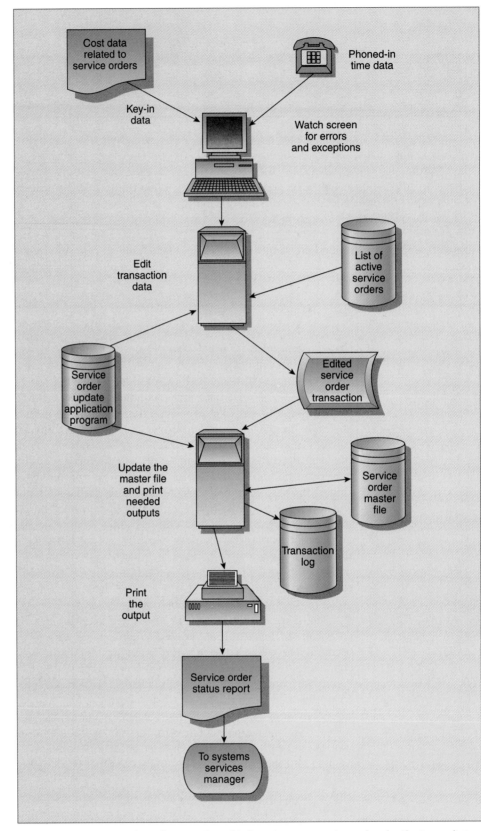

FIGURE 5-11 Computer-based processing of Infoage's open service orders by the immediate processing approach.

Immediate (Real-Time) Processing Variations In an *integrated immediate processing system*, a variety of applications can affect multiple files that are continuously on-line. For instance, Infoage employs the same system to accommodate its receipts and shipments of products as it uses to process service order transactions. When one of these types of transactions arises, a transaction code must be entered with the transaction data, in order to specify the application program that is needed. The transaction code for a service order transaction is SOC.

Certain immediate processing applications, involving on-line real-time systems, are designed to control physical or business processes by timely responses. Business processes controlled by on-line real-time systems include credit checks at checkout stands, reservations of airline tickets, and purchases of shares listed on stock exchanges.

Contrasts with Computer-Based Periodic Processing Immediate processing applications, as distinct from many sequential periodic processing applications, always employ direct processing. Whereas sequential processing applications are unintegrated, most immediate processing applications are highly integrated, using application programs that direct all processing steps pertaining to individual transactions.

The relative advantages and disadvantages of each approach are summarized in Figure 5-12. In contrast to those pertaining to periodic processing, discussed earlier, the immediate processing approach offers better service to users. Since records are updated immediately and are readily accessible, up-to-date information is available in a timely manner. The data are accurate and complete, since transactions are checked thoroughly on being captured and detected errors are corrected. Since processing is focused on individual transactions, no sorting or transcribing is necessary. If applications are integrated, a greater array of information can be made available to users.

Periodic Processing Approach	Immediate Processing Approach
Advantages	
Improves efficiency of processing, especially when large batches are processed sequentially.	Provides up-to-date information that is available in a timely manner.
Enables use of batch totals for better control of accuracy and completeness of processing.	Eliminates the need for the unproductive sorting and transcribing steps.
Requires less expensive computer hardware and software.	Enables transactions to be edited as soon as they are captured and any errors to be corrected without delay.
Disadvantages	
Allows records in master files to become out of date, except just after a processing run.	Requires relatively expensive computer hardware and software.
Delays the correction of errors in transactions and the processing of the affected transactions until the next processing cycle.	Does not enable transaction data to be supported by the batch-total control.
Requires the unproductive step of sorting to be performed prior to the updating run.	Causes the audit trail to be more complex and difficult to maintain.
	Involves slower entry of data, especially when keying is required.

FIGURE 5-12 The differences between the periodic processing approach with sequential updating and the immediate processing approach.

The main disadvantage of the immediate processing approach is the relatively costly computer hardware needed. The needed terminals, desktop computers, disk storage units, and other devices are likely to be more expensive than the devices required in periodic applications. Because the software must perform more functions, it is likely to be more complex. Another disadvantage is that transaction data cannot be supported by certain controls, especially batch totals. In addition, reliable and thorough audit trails are more difficult to maintain. Finally, entering data will be slower if human clerks are expected to key in the data and respond to error messages.

These disadvantages are diminishing. For instance, prices for direct-access storage and other on-line computer hardware are steadily declining. Also, powerful client/server transaction processing servers are becoming available, which greatly enhance immediate processing capabilities. Thus more and more applications are being converted to the immediate processing approach.

MANAGING FILES

Data arising from transactions and other sources must be stored in a reservoir. This stored base of data includes identification data, dates, quantities, dollar amounts, explanations, instructions, and so on. Much of the data have traditionally been stored in a variety of structures called files. A **file** of data may be defined as a collection of data elements that have been organized into records. All applications involving transaction processing employ one or more files. Certain files contain the transactions, other files are updated by the transactions, and still other files contain data needed in the processing steps. These and other types of files maintain the data needed by a firm for conducting its operations, reporting to various interested users, and making key decisions.

Because of their close involvement with transaction processing, accountants should be aware of effective means by which to manage files. That is, they should understand the basics related to storing data in files, maintaining files, and retrieving data from files. Accountants need to recognize several alternative file structures, i.e., methods by which files are organized and accessed in computer-based systems. Moreover, they can profit by knowing how to choose among these file structures under varying conditions.

FILE STORAGE

An understanding of files begins with the range of file types, the characteristics within the types of files containing data, storage media, and the differences between logical and physical storage.

Types of Files Most files exist for the purpose of storing data. The following are four common types of data files:

1. **Master files,** which contain records pertaining to entities (e.g., people, places, or things) such as customers, departments, and products. An accounting-related master file is the general ledger.
2. **Transaction files,** which contain records pertaining to events currently being processed, such as sales and receipts of goods.
3. **History files,** also called archive files, which contain records pertaining to completed transactions, such as past sales.

4. **Reference files,** which contain tables or lists of data needed for making calculations or checking the accuracy of input data, such as product price tables and customer lists.

Other data files are derivative in nature. Like the history file, an *open document file* is derived from the transaction file. An example is the open purchase order file, which is composed of records from the purchase order transaction file still awaiting the arrival of corresponding supplier invoices. A *report file* is derived from records within master or transaction files. For instance, data may be periodically extracted from the inventory master file to prepare an inventory status report. A *backup file* is a copy of a current file, generated so that the original file can be re-created if lost. A *suspense file* is a collection of those records of a transaction file that appear to contain erroneous or questionable data.

Several types of files contain information that is not intended to be used in processing or to be summarized in reports. Examples are *program files*, *text files*, and *index files*.

Storage Media   When its information system was noncomputerized, Infoage kept its filed data in folders, tubs, in/out baskets, and file drawers. Much of the data were duplicated on multiple copies of forms and documents and stored in several different places. Certain data were abbreviated or even omitted on the forms, since such shortcuts were understandable to Infoage's experienced clerks. In general, an air of informality permeated the management of its files.

In Infoage's current computerized AIS, much of the data are stored on magnetic tapes, magnetic disks, and optical disks. Appendix A describes the characteristics of each storage medium.

Computerized file storage and management require formalized procedures that must be strictly followed. The identity and location of each element of data must be precisely specified. Each file management step must be carefully programmed. In return for the inconvenience and costliness of these requirements, however, computer-based storage provides important benefits to Infoage. Large quantities of relevant data are stored very compactly. Data are stored efficiently, since the duplications of records are reduced. In addition, the data stored in computerized files can be accessed as quickly as, or more quickly than, the records stored in file cabinets.

Logical Versus Physical Storage   From the point of view of users, a record contains data elements pertaining to a single focus of interest. For instance, each record in Infoage's computerized customer master file concerns a particular customer. Because these records have meaning and relevance to users within Infoage, they represent **logical records.**

Data contained in logical records must necessarily be physically stored. In computer systems the term **file organization** refers to the methods by which the data in logical records are stored on physical storage media. When stored on magnetic tape, the physical characteristics dictate that logical records be arranged in a sequential fashion one after the other. When stored on magnetic disks, the logical records are stored within sectors along circular tracks. The records may be physically adjacent to each other (i.e., sequenced) or may be scattered in a manner that appears to be random.

Files stored on physical media can be viewed to be structured as a collection of **physical records.** In some cases there is a one-to-one correspondence between the logical and physical records. For instance, each service order prepared by Infoage is a logical record. When in the form of a hard-copy source document, the physical and logical records correspond. When stored in computer-based systems, the physical and logical records often differ. Thus logical records that are sequentially stored on magnetic tapes or disks may be grouped into blocks. The physical record in such a case consists of logical records contained between successive interblock gaps.

In summary, logical records and files are intended to serve the informational needs of users, since users view data in logical terms. Physical arrangements of records and files, on the other hand, should be selected to make the best use of the capabilities of the physical storage medium.

Characteristics of Files Data files, especially master and transaction files, contain a finite number of logical records. Each **record** consists of a series of **fields** that are identical (or, at least, very similar) in layout. Each field provides the location for a **data element,** the smallest unit of data having intrinsic meaning. Figure 5-13 lists the data elements that might be found in two types of records in a merchandising firm like Infoage. Composing each data element, in turn, are bytes of data representing **characters,** usually numbers or letters. The *data hierarchy* within a file therefore moves downward from file to record to data element to character.

Let us look more closely at fields and data elements. Among the characteristics of particular interest are the lengths of fields and records, data attributes, data values, data modes, and record keys.

1. **Field length.** Each field spans a number of character positions. In a file containing *fixed-length records*, the fields and thus the number of positions in every record of the file are identical. A file in which all of the records are fixed in length is called a **flat file.** By contrast, in a file containing *variable-length records*, the fields differ from record to record. Consider the sales transaction record in Figure 5-13, for example. The two fields relating to a product sold—the product number and quantity—may vary in number from sale to sale, depending on how many products are involved in a sale.

2. **Data attributes.** The **attribute** of a data element is the relevant facet concerning the entity or event being represented. The customer number and account balance are two attributes of the accounts receivable record, as shown in the partial record layout presented in Figure 5-14.

3. **Data value.** The **value** of a data element is its specific quantitative content in a single occurrence. In Figure 5-14 the value of the customer number is shown to

Accounts Receivable Master Record	Sales Transaction Record
Customer account number	Sales document number
Customer name	Customer account number
Customer address	Date of order
Credit limit	Date shipped (or to be shipped)
Balance beginning of year	Customer name
Current account balance	Customer purchase order number
	Salesperson number
	Sales territory number
	Product number*
	Quantity sold*
	Amount of sale

*These elements will be repeated to reflect each product sold in the transaction.

FIGURE 5-13   Data elements within the records of two types of files.

Occurrence of value:	23861	Eric Peters	} {	1550.00
Attribute:	Customer number	Customer name		Account balance
Field size:	5	16		8
Degree of permanency:	Fixed	Fixed		Variable
Data mode:	Numeric	Alphabetic		Alphanumeric
Record key type:	Primary	Secondary		Secondary

FIGURE 5-14   Added features of an accounts receivable record.

be 23861, whereas the account balance is $1550.00. The former value provides identification, while the latter value reflects current status.

4. **Data mode.** The **mode** of a data element is the type of data represented by its value. Two commonly used data modes are numbers and letters. A third data mode is alphanumeric—letters, numbers, and special characters such as hyphens and decimal points. All three modes are illustrated in Figure 5-14. A further type of data element, not illustrated, is the **flag**—a symbol or character used for control purposes. For instance, a flag may be set by a computer program to indicate a record that is to be purged or archived at a certain date.

5. **Record keys.** Certain data elements within a record can serve as sort keys. Two types of keys found in a typical record of a master or transaction file are a primary key and one or more secondary keys.

   A **primary key,** also called a record key, is the attribute that uniquely identifies a specific record of an entity or event. The customer number 23861 uniquely identifies the record shown in Figure 5-14 as pertaining to Eric Peters. Primary keys are generally numeric codes, although they may be of other modes. The alphanumeric code ACC330A may identify a specific accounting class. Primary keys may be called sort keys, since they are used to arrange the records of transaction and master files for sequential batch processing applications.

   A **secondary key** is an attribute other than the primary key. It represents an alternative way by which to sequence the records within a file. The customer name in Figure 5-14 may be viewed as a secondary key. Another secondary key in the record (not shown) might be the ZIP codes within the addresses of customers. Customers may be sorted by ZIP codes in order to facilitate the mailing of promotional materials and notices.

MAINTENANCE OF FILES

The function known as **file maintenance** includes the updating activity. Updating, or posting, consists of making routine and relatively temporary changes to the data values in stored records. As shown in Figures 5-7, 5-8, and 5-11, updating generally occurs to records in master files. File maintenance also involves three other activities: (1) adding new records to a file, (2) changing fixed or relatively permanent values within records, and (3) deleting records from a file. A related activity, although not normally viewed as file maintenance, consists of merging the records of two or more files into a single combined file. For example, a customer master file and an accounts receivable file may be merged to form a customer accounts receivable master file.

Master files are usually the focal point of file maintenance because they contain current data values, such as account balances. However, history files and reference files also must be continually maintained to reflect ongoing additions and changes. New transactions, organized into transaction files, are typically the source of data involved in the maintenance function.

Let us return to the computerized processing of product sales by Infoage, for a closeup view of file maintenance. Figure 5-15a portrays the details of a file mainte-nance run within its sequential batch processing application. To simplify the illus-tration, we assume (1) that the records are not blocked, (2) that no more than one transaction affects a particular customer, and (3) that only one product is involved per sale.

As Figure 5-15a shows, the prior accounts receivable master file and sales order transaction file are inputs to the file maintenance run. Since the accounts receivable master file has been arranged according to customer numbers, it has been necessary to sort the sales order transaction file into the same arrangement. The computer program begins by reading the first transaction record (with a customer number of 11050) into primary storage. It then reads each record in turn from the master file, comparing the customer number from the transaction record with the customer num-ber from the master record. Each time a match occurs, some maintenance action is to be taken. After taking a designated action, the program continues the matching process until all the transactions have been processed.

Each of the four transaction records shown in Figure 5-15a requires a different type of maintenance action. The record for customer 11050 involves an update, as detailed in Figure 5-15b. The record for customer 11055 is to be deleted; thus no record appears in the updated master file of Figure 5-15a. The record for customer 11058 involves a change in the credit limit; this change would be reflected in the updated master file. Finally, a record is to be added for a customer having the as-signed number of 12580; this new record appears in the updated master file.

Several outputs are generated as a result of the file maintenance run. In addition to the sales invoices and Daily Invoice Register, an exception and summary report lists any transaction errors encountered by the file maintenance program, as well as computed batch totals.

RETRIEVAL OF STORED RECORDS

Users such as accountants need to retrieve data from stored records to meet their responsibilities. Application programs also often retrieve data, such as stored unit prices, while processing transactions. The term **file access** refers to the method by which data are located and retrieved from the records of a file. The two major file access methods are sequential access and direct access.

Sequential Access As we have seen, the **sequential-access method** requires each record in a file to be scanned, beginning with the first record in the file. Consider a master file having records with primary key values that begin 102, 126, 127, 138, and so on, with each record immediately following the preceding record. If a particular record is desired, its location within the file determines how fast it can be accessed. Thus, record 126 can be accessed very quickly. However, the last record in the file (say, 998) requires a more lengthy search. On the average, one-half of the records in the file must be scanned sequentially to locate a desired record.

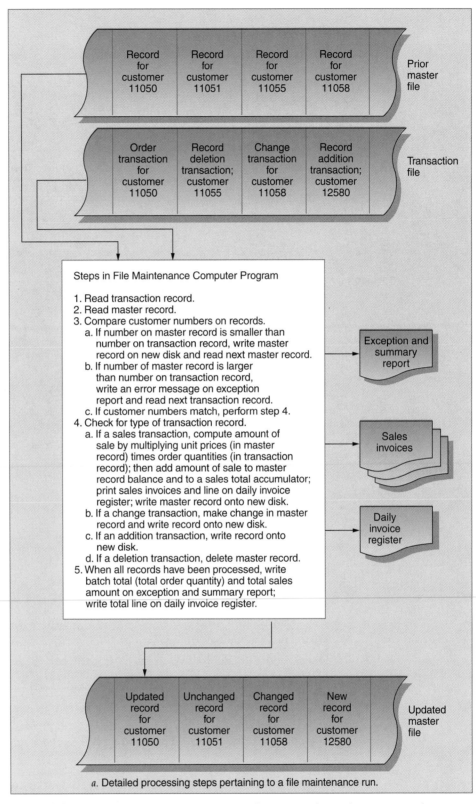

a. Detailed processing steps pertaining to a file maintenance run.

FIGURE 5-15   Details of the updating run for an illustrative sales and invoicing application for Infoage. (*Note*: Certain data elements, such as the sales date, have been omitted from the records in the interest of simplicity.)

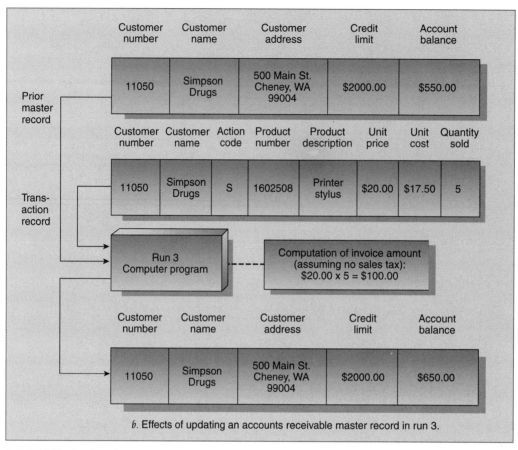

b. Effects of updating an accounts receivable master record in run 3.

FIGURE 5-15   (*continued*)

The sequential-access method is consequently inefficient for finding individual records. However, it can be a very effective method when many of the records in the file are involved, as the following two examples show:

- An auditor desires to review the file of sales invoices prepared by Infoage this week, to see that all sales invoices are accounted for. The sales invoices are arranged by sales invoice numbers in ascending order, since they are prenumbered by the computer program as they are prepared. The auditor accesses the computerized sales invoice transaction file and scans all of the sales invoices, beginning with the first sales invoice record.

- The credit manager requests the computer system to provide an accounts receivable schedule for his review, with all credit customers and their balances listed in ascending order of customer numbers (the primary key of the accounts receivable file).

Direct Access   We use the term **direct access** to denote any method that involves the accessing of desired records in some way other than by an exhaustive search through all of the records of a file. Two significant methods by which records are accessed directly involve indexes and randomizing procedures. They are discussed below. Other methods, such as those employing binary searches and linked lists and inverted lists, are described in the appendix to this chapter. All of these methods require direct-access storage media, such as magnetic disks.

1. The index as an accessing device is widely applied through the **indexed sequential file.** This type of file combines a sequential arrangement of records with an index that cross-references the primary key values of the records. The index enables individual records to be retrieved quickly, while the file retains the benefits of sequential processing. Thus a sequentially arranged accounts receivable master file with an index can efficiently process batches of sales and payments transactions; between processing cycles individual customer records can be accessed quickly to answer inquiries or to make changes to relatively permanent data values.

   Figure 5-16 shows a portion of an index and the sequentially arranged blocks of records to which the index refers. The index contains values for primary keys of sequential records. Cross-referenced to each listed key value is the disk address pertaining to the first record in each physical block. The records relate to the customers within an accounts receivable master file. When a user has an inquiry concerning a specific customer, he or she enters the primary key value of the desired customer's record. The computer file management software first scans the primary keys listed in the index. If the value is 136, the search program scans the records at the disk address (06004) until number 136 is found.

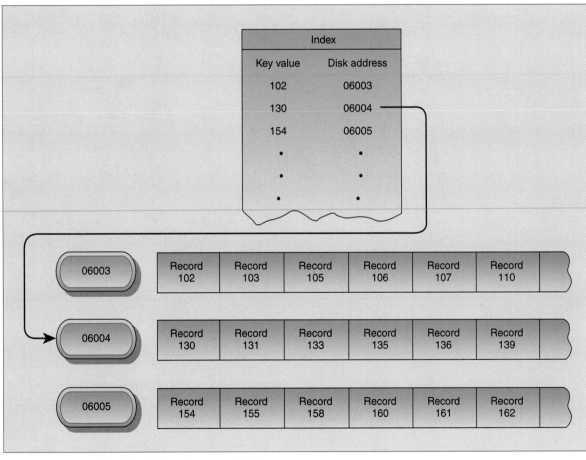

FIGURE 5-16   A portion of an indexed sequential file.

2. **Randomizing** is an accessing procedure in which computations are performed to generate addresses of individual records. When the records of a file are located throughout a direct-access storage medium by means of a randomizing procedure, the file is described as a **random file.** Figure 5-17 portrays the records of a random file. Although they appear to be stored in no apparent order, the records are readily accessible. The randomizing procedure, called a *hashing scheme*, transforms the primary key of a record into a disk address. For instance, the primary key value of 218 may be converted into the disk address 10204. The record is stored at this computed address; it is accessed by performing the same set of computations. A hashing scheme provides a random file with its major advantage: fast access. Computational procedures are performed more quickly by computers than the table look-up procedures required with indexed sequential files.

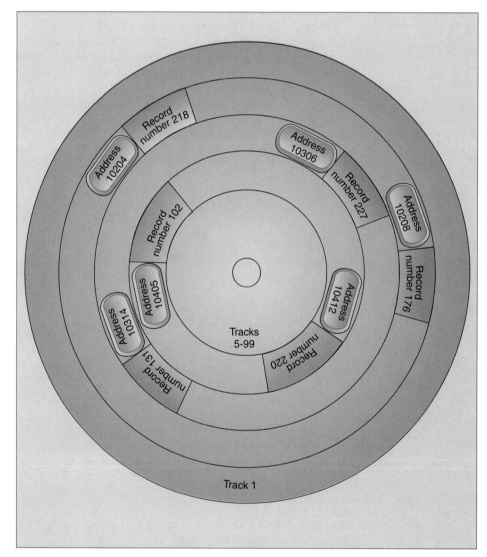

FIGURE 5-17   Records stored by the random method on a magnetic disk. (Notes: (1) For simplicity, the disk is assumed to have only one recording surface and 99 tracks. (2) The records, as well as the tracks, are greatly magnified in the figure. Many more records than shown, for instance, would fit around one track.)

DESIGN CONSIDERATIONS FOR RECORDS AND FILES

Managing files and records involves answering such questions as follows:

- How should the records be structured?
- What type of file organization and accessing method (e.g., indexed sequential, random) should be employed?
- How long should records be retained?

Answers to these questions depend in part on the requirements of the particular applications being designed. They also are affected by storage requirements, efficiency in file maintenance, and accessibility of the stored data. These criteria will become clearer if we briefly consider each question in relation to selected applications.

Establishing Record Structures   The structure of a record is defined by its content, arrangement, modes of data fields, lengths of fields, and keys. We can observe these features by referring again to Figures 5-13 and 5-14. The contents of the accounts receivable master record and the sales transaction record are determined by the circumstances of the credit sales application. Rules for arranging data elements within these records cannot be hard and fast. However, generally the primary keys are placed in the first fields of the records, while balance amounts or amounts of transactions are placed in the last fields. Transaction records are usually arranged somewhat in accordance with the placement of the elements on the source documents (e.g., sales invoices). The modes and lengths of fields depend on the nature of the data placed therein, while the keys are generally expressed as codes.

An important design matter concerns the extent to which records should be consolidated. Infoage has split the records for its credit sales application into two files: an accounts receivable master and a sales transaction. It would be possible to combine these two files, so that all customer-related data are contained in a single file. However, the resulting records would likely be unwieldy, especially in the cases of those customers involved in numerous sales.

Alternatively, Infoage could further split the accounts receivable master into two files: an abbreviated accounts receivable master record containing only the account number and balance, and a customer master record containing the account number and the remaining data elements. Since the accounts receivable master file is smaller, each update run can be completed more quickly. This advantage must be compared to the drawback of separating the data that pertain to each customer.

Selecting File Organization and Accessing Methods   The methods of physically organizing and accessing records have been embodied in three major types of master files: sequential files, indexed sequential files, and random files. In order to select the most appropriate type for a particular situation, a firm such as Infoage must consider several file-related measures. These measures include file size, activity ratio, file volatility, response time, and up-to-dateness.

1. **File size** is determined by multiplying the number of records in the file by the length of each record.
2. The **activity ratio** measures the busyness of a file, since it is computed by dividing the number of records affected during a file maintenance run by the total number of records in a file. If 1,000 records are affected in a file of 10,000 records, the activity ratio is 10 percent. Generally, the higher the activity ratio, the greater the efficiencies gained from processing batches of data sequentially.

Measure	Sequential File (on Magnetic Tape)	Indexed Sequential File	Random File
Size of file	Very large	Large	Limited
Activity ratio	High	Moderate	Low
Up-to-dateness	Relatively unimportant	Important	Very important
Fast response time	Relatively unimportant	Important	Very important
File volatility	Low	Moderate	High

FIGURE 5-18   Comparison of conditions that favor the use of the respective file methods.

3. **File volatility** refers to the frequency with which records are added and deleted over a period of time, such as a day or a week. The records in the guest file of a motel are very volatile, for instance. Applications that encounter high file volatility require frequent access to individual records.

4. The **response time** is the time that elapses between the request for information and the receipt of that information.

5. The *up-to-dateness*, or currency, of stored data depends on the promptness with which transactions are processed against the files that they affect. Data in sequential files are least likely to be up-to-date, since lags occur between successive file processing runs.

Figure 5-18 lists those conditions that favor the use of the three file organization and access methods. In summary, a random file on a direct-access storage medium is most suitable when up-to-dateness and fast response times are important, the activity ratio is low, the file volatility is high, and the file is relatively limited in size. A sequential file (on magnetic tape) is most suited to the opposite set of conditions. An indexed sequential file is a good choice when both processing efficiency and rapid accessibility are paramount.

Determining Record Retention and Management   The term **records management** pertains to the creation, maintenance, and retention of the records from transactions and other business activities. In addition to designing needed records and forms, effective records management consists of such actions as (1) determining when records should be transferred from active files to inactive files, such as history files, (2) deciding how long records should be retained in an inactive file before being destroyed, and (3) establishing the manner of storing inactive and backup files. Inactive files are often needed for reference and to meet legal obligations, while backup files are needed for security. Inactive and backup files are often stored on microfilm or magnetic tape in a records storage center, with each container cataloged, clearly marked, and dated. As each scheduled disposal date arrives, the affected records are pulled and destroyed.

GENERATING OUTPUTS

Transaction processing applications generate various outputs for a variety of users. These outputs range from documents, such as sales invoices and paychecks, to reports, such as financial statements and sales analyses. Although some reports are detailed responses concerning specific entities (e.g., customers) or events (e.g., sales), most are summaries of transactions (e.g., customers' monthly statements). They may be generated periodically or on an ad hoc basis. Often they are formatted to aid managers in planning activities or providing control over operations.

As noted in Chapter 4, outputs are presented and handled in a variety of ways. They may appear in narrative, tabular, or graphical formats. They may be provided on paper (hard copy), microfilm, or screen displays (soft copy). Alternatively, outputs may be stored temporarily, or **spooled,** on a magnetic or optical medium; at a later time the outputs could be printed off-line. In some cases an output is transferred electronically via a communications network to another computer system, where the output is stored until displayed or printed by the receiving system.

As the key products of information systems, reports and other outputs deserve considerable attention. Thus they are discussed extensively in Chapters 15 and 16, as well as in the several transaction processing chapters of Part III.

CLASSIFICATION AND CODING OF TRANSACTION DATA

CLASSIFICATION VERSUS CODING

Classification is the act of grouping into classes—such as classes of data. Classification plans are designed to achieve specific objectives. For instance, a chart of accounts is a plan that classifies the financial accounts of a firm. It is one of several plans employed by a typical firm in order to satisfy the information needs of users. Charts of accounts are discussed in Chapter 11.

Coding is the assignment of symbols, such as letters and numbers, in accordance with a classification plan. Effective codes provide unique and concise identities to the entities and events involved in transactions. Therefore, they ease the entry of data, enhance processing efficiency, speed the retrieval of data from files, and aid the preparation of reports. Consider an example related to sales transactions: The letter code CS may be used to identify the type of transaction; the number code 711 can identify the sales invoice issued in a specific sales transaction; the number code 1346 can identify the particular customer named John Henry Johnson of Akron, Ohio; and the alphanumeric code XQ7 can specify a particular type of transmission involved in a sale.

ATTRIBUTES OF CODES

In addition to satisfying the informational needs of users, a coding system that supports a firm's classification plan should

1. Uniquely identify objects such as particular customers and sales.

2. Be as concise and simple as possible, in order to aid the memory of users and minimize the cost of using and maintaining it.

3. Allow for expected growth, so that it will not need to be changed in the foreseeable future. For instance, a growing firm with nine product lines should allow two digits (assuming a numeric code) for product line codes.

4. Be standardized throughout all functions and levels within a firm, so that reporting systems can be fully integrated.

The presence of computer-based systems further influences the selection of codes. For example, they encourage the use of codes that are numeric and fixed in length. They also require the use of special codes, such as passwords, ciphers, transaction codes, and action codes. Passwords and ciphers (encrypted messages) facilitate the security of data within computer systems. *Transaction codes* identify types of transactions. In effect, they designate the specific application programs to be used in processing on-line applications. *Action codes* identify specific operations pertaining

> ## SPOTLIGHTING
>
> ### A CODING SYSTEM
> ### *at Bell Communications Research, Inc.**
>
> A large organization such as Bell Communications requires a consistent coding system for identifying its extensive array of equipment. Two separate group codes identify the specific items of equipment and the locations of the items.
>
> A CLEI code, for specific items, has four segments: a four-character field for the basic function of the equipment, a three-character field for one or more key features, a single-character field for reference, and a two-character field for complementary data. An example of this code is
>
> ### DLMO 52B B RA
>
> where
>
> > DLMO represents a miniaturized dial, long-line circuit,
>
> ---
>
> *Germain Boer, *Classifying and Coding for Accounting Operations* (Montvale, N.J.: National Association of Accountants, 1987), pp. 57–63. The term "CLEI" is a trademark of Bell Communications Research.
>
> 52B indicates that the term has interrupted-ringing supply capability, a particular power-supply arrangement, and no motor start lead,
>
> B (in position 8) specifies the source drawing,
>
> RA refers to computer-based operations support systems using the item.
>
> The location code has three segments: a four-character field for place, a two-character field for state, and a five-character field for building and other location identifiers. An example is
>
> ### DNVR CO MAF24
>
> where
>
> > DNVR stands for Denver,
> >
> > CO stands for Colorado,
> >
> > MAF24 specifies a main distributing frame on the second floor of the main building.

to file maintenance or data retrieval. For instance, they may specify the addition of new master records or the display of stored records.

CODING SYSTEMS

A variety of coding systems have been devised. Familiar examples are (1) bar codes, such as those used to identify merchandise items, (2) color codes, such as those used to distinguish copies of multicopy forms, and (3) cipher codes, such as those used to protect confidential messages. However, the codes most widely useful to business firms are based on alphabetic, numeric, and alphanumeric characters. Four coding systems that use these characters are mnenomic, sequence, block, and group coding systems.

Mnemonic Coding System A code of this type provides visible clues concerning the objects it represents. For instance, AZ is the code for Arizona and WSW-P175R-14 represents a white sidewall radial tire of a specific size. Thus, a **mnemonic code** is relatively easy to remember. On the other hand, its applications are more limited than those of the other three coding systems.

Sequence Coding System The simplest type of code is the **sequence coding system,** which assigns numbers or letters in consecutive order. Sequence codes are applied primarily to source documents such as checks and sales invoices. A sequence code can facilitate document searches, such as a search for a particular sales invoice.

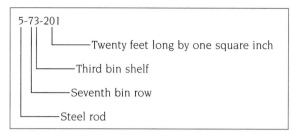

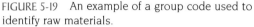

FIGURE 5-19   An example of a group code used to identify raw materials.

Furthermore, a sequence code can help prevent the loss of data, since gaps in the sequence signal missing documents.

Sequence codes are inflexible, however. New entities or events can be added only at the end of the sequence. Moreover, a sequence code generally is devoid of logical significance. For instance, a specific sequence code assigned to a customer does not identify the sales territory within which he or she resides, nor the customer class to which he or she belongs.

Block Coding System   A third coding system partially overcomes these drawbacks. A **block coding system** assigns series of numbers within a sequence to entities or events having common features. Consequently, a block code designates the classification of an individual entity or event.

Block codes have varied applicability within a firm. Customer numbers, for instance, may be blocked by sales territory. To illustrate, customers in the southern sales territory may be assigned numbers ranging from 1 to 4999, whereas customers in the northern sales territory may be assigned numbers from 5000 to 9999. In other applications, products may be blocked by product line, employees by department. An important use of block codes is to designate blocks of numbers for the major account groupings within charts of accounts.

While a block is reserved for individual codes, it is not necessary to assign every possible number within a block. In fact, one advantage of a block code is that unassigned numbers are usually available to be assigned to new items (e.g., products) as they are added to the firm's scope of activity.

Group Coding System   The group code is a refinement of the block code, in that it provides added meaning to the users. That is, a **group coding system** reveals two or more dimensions or facets pertaining to an object. Each facet is assigned a specific location, called a *field*, within the code format. Code segments (i.e., subcodes) appear within the respective fields, thus identifying the facets pertaining to a particular object.

An example of a group code for an entity should clarify this description. Raw materials stored for use by a metal products manufacturer may be coded according to the format in Figure 5-19.

SUMMARY

Transaction processing systems of a typical organization may be grouped to form cycles. Typical cycles involve revenues, expenditures, the management of resources, and the general ledger.

Two approaches to inputting transaction data are off-line input, which provides economy and productivity, and on-line input, which provides timeliness and flexibility. In the off-line approach, data are captured on source documents in batches, transcribed by off-line devices into computer-readable form, and then entered for processing. In the on-line approach, data from individual transactions are entered directly into the computer system as they occur.

Two major approaches to computer-based transaction processing are periodic processing, which provides efficient processing and batch-total controls, and immediate processing, which provides up-to-date records that are readily accessible to users. Periodic processing generally consists of computing batch totals of transactions, entering and sorting the batches of transactions, posting the data to sequentially organized records in master files, and generating printed outputs. The immediate processing approach consists of entering single transactions, via on-line input devices; posting the transactions directly to the records in the master files; and generating outputs as needed. It allows data to be edited and corrected upon being entered and eliminates the need for sorting transaction records.

Data arising from transactions must be managed—stored, maintained, and retrieved—as needed. Data are stored in master, transaction, history, open document, report, backup, suspense, or reference files. Files are stored on physical media, ranging from paper forms to magnetic and optical disks. The data files are arranged in a hierarchy that consists of logical records, data elements, and characters. Each logical record is organized into a series of fields. Data elements, whose values are placed within the fields, reflect attributes of entities or events. Data elements also have modes and may serve as primary or secondary keys within records. File maintenance involves the activities of updating, adding new records to a file, changing fixed or relatively permanent values within records, and deleting records from a file. Retrieval of stored data involves the accessing of records within a file, either sequentially or by a direct-access method. In deciding which types of files to employ in an application, it is necessary to consider such measures as file size, activity ratio, volatility, response time, and up-to-dateness of stored data.

A variety of outputs for users are generated by transaction processing applications. The outputs may be documents or reports, detailed or summary, periodic or ad hoc, tabular or graphical, hard copy or soft copy, immediate or delayed.

Sound classification and coding techniques can improve the efficiency of data storage, processing, and retrieval of information. A sound coding system satisfies the information needs of users, employs unique identifiers, allows for expected growth, and is concise and sim-

ple. Four coding systems that use alphanumeric characters are the mnemonic, sequence, block, and group coding systems.

APPENDIX TO CHAPTER 5

SELECTED ACCESS METHODS

Three access methods—involving binary searches, linked lists, and inverted lists—were briefly mentioned in Chapter 5. Because they can be useful to a complete data retrieval strategy, we will examine them in this appendix. Certain problems in the following pages draw upon the methods described here.

Binary Searches

Binary search is a direct-access method that can be employed in locating records arranged via a primary key within a sequential file. It is a much more efficient search procedure than the sequential-access method, however. Binary search consists of first checking the value of the primary key of the record at the midpoint of the file being searched. After determining in which half of the file the desired record resides, the method then checks the midpoint of that half. This procedure continues until the record is located.

Linked Lists

A **linked list** is a connected chain of logically related data. It is formed by means of pointers that are embedded within the records of the file or files to which the list pertains. Since the records of the file are normally arranged according to their primary keys, the linked list pertains to one of the secondary keys.

Pointers are data elements whose values specify ("point to") the physical storage addresses where associated data are stored. In contrast to the other data elements of a record, a pointer provides *direction* rather than *content*.

We can observe the use of linked lists through a real estate example. Figure 5-20 shows the fields composing a record relating to sales of houses. The primary key is the listing number of the houses available for sale; secondary keys include such attributes as the city where each house is located, its asking price, its number of bedrooms, the number of square feet it contains, and the date of construction. Figure 5-21 portrays the portion of a flat file relating to the homes-for-sale records, with

Listing number	Realtor name	Street address	City where located	Asking price	Number of bedrooms	Number of square feet	Date of construction

FIGURE 5-20   A record layout of the key data elements relating to a home for sale.

Listing number	Realtor name	Street address	City where located	Asking price	Number of bedrooms	Number of square feet	Date of construction	Pointer field (city)
1			Phoenix					
2			Mesa					
3			Phoenix					
4			Tempe					
5			Mesa					
6			Mesa					
7			Phoenix					
8			Tempe					
9			Phoenix					
10			Tempe					
11			Mesa					

Linked list

FIGURE 5-21   Linked lists relating to the cities where houses for sale are located.

data included within the city field. Attached to the records is a field that would contain the values of pointers forming chains (linked lists) for the city attribute. No actual values have been entered, but loops have been drawn in black to show the chain pertaining to Phoenix. Two other chains pertaining to Tempe and Mesa are drawn in blue. Because each chain links identical values of an attribute (e.g., Phoenix) within a single file, this linkage is known as an **attribute chain.**

In addition to forming attribute chains, linked lists can form pointer chains to serve the following purposes:

1. Linking newly added records to indexed sequential files and overflow records to random files.

2. Linking together sequentially (via the primary keys) the various records that have been stored randomly in a random file. Thus a file of work order records can be processed sequentially by beginning with the first record and tracing the pointers from record to record.

3. Linking together various secondary keys of a file in desired order, so that analytical reports can be prepared more easily. For instance, the customer num-

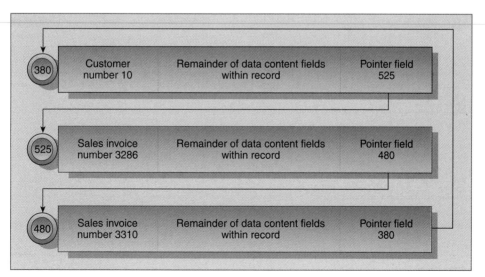

FIGURE 5-22   Embedded pointer ring list for an occurrence involving a customer and two sales invoice records.

bers in sales records can be linked to enable analyses of sales to be generated.

4. Linking records from one file to records of another file, for example, the records of customers to records of their sales invoices.

Pointer chains or lists can exhibit several variations. Thus, pointers in a *simple list* point to the next record in the list, and the pointer field contains an end-of-list symbol. A *ring list* is similar to a simple list, except that the chain is connected by including the disk address of the first record within the pointer field of the last record. Figure 5-22 illustrates a ring list that chains a customer record with the records of two sales invoices pertaining to the customer. (The values in the circles are the disk addresses of the records.)

Inverted Lists

An **inverted list,** also called an inverted file, consists of data arranged according to one secondary key within the records of a sequential file. It is an index that is created *in addition to* the records that make up the sequential file, so that the records containing desired values can quickly be accessed. Each of the values in the index is in effect a pointer to a disk address.

Let us return to the real estate example. Figure 5-23 depicts two inverted lists, based on the city and asking

City where located	Disk storage addresses of records in Figure 5-20

Asking price	Disk storage addresses of records in Figure 5-20

FIGURE 5-23   Inverted lists pertaining to the homes-for-sale records.

price attributes. Each inverted list contains the addresses on the direct-access storage medium where the records relating to a particular occurrence are stored. For instance, the city inverted list would show Phoenix, Tempe, and Mesa. On the same line with Tempe might be these three disk addresses—12682, 13256, and 13890—which represent the locations of the records having listing numbers of 4, 8, and 10 (see Figure 5-21). Thus, if a real estate agent requests a list of all houses for sale in Tempe, the retrieval program simply determines the locations of the applicable records by reference to the inverted list and displays the requested data.

When two or more inverted lists—each focused on a secondary key—are involved, the request is called a **multiple-key inquiry.** For instance, a request involving both inverted lists in Figure 5-23 might be, What are the

Disk Address	Customer Number	Customer Name	Credit Limit (000$)	Current Balance ($)
1000	100	Waters, John	2	715.00
1100	101	Jacobs, Paul	4	3010.00
1200	104	Adams, Steve	3	0.00
1300	106	Trimble, Shirley	2	1497.50
1400	107	Baker, Trevor	4	50.00
1500	110	Early, Kristin	3	882.75
1600	112	Malcolm, Doris	2	100.00

Credit Limit	Disk Addresses
2	1000, 1300, 1600
3	1200, 1500
4	1100, 1400

FIGURE 5-24   Records in an accounts receivable master file and an inverted list based on the credit limit secondary key.

addresses of houses for sale in Tempe that are priced at $100,000 or under? By adding an inverted list focused on "number of bedrooms," the request could be further narrowed to, What are the addresses of houses for sale in Tempe having three bedrooms that are priced at $100,000 or under?

Another example should clarify the construction of inverted lists. Figure 5-24 shows, in the upper part, several records of an accounts receivable master file arranged according to customer numbers. Each record contains three attributes that can serve as secondary keys: customer name, credit limit, and current balance. The lower part of the figure shows an inverted list pertaining to the credit limit attribute. All values of the credit limit—$2,000, $3,000, and $4,000—are listed in the left column, expressed as numbers 2, 3, and 4. Each value has been cross-referenced to the disk addresses at which the records are located. For instance, the $2,000 credit limit is cross-referenced to disk addresses 1000, 1300, and 1600, since those are the locations of the three records having that limit of credit. Assume that a user, say a clerk in the credit department, makes a request for those customers having a credit limit of $2,000. The database software will (1) scan the inverted list, (2) retrieve the records located at addresses 1000, 1300, and 1600, and (3) display the names John Waters, Shirley Trimble, and Doris Malcolm.

REVIEW PROBLEM WITH SOLUTION

CAMPUS BOOKSTORE, THIRD INSTALLMENT

Statement

The Campus Bookstore (described in the Review Problem at the end of Chapter 1) begins to develop applications identified in the Second Installment. For example, the accounting system manager guides the development of a cash sales application, using point-of-sale terminals. Linked to this application is an inventory record-keeping and reordering application. Other applications that are given high priority include general ledger accounting, purchases, and cash disbursements processing.

Required

By reference to this statement (and facts in the previous installments),

a. Describe a suitable batch-oriented computerized cash disbursements transaction processing application. The bookstore does not employ the voucher system of handling suppliers' invoices.

b. Prepare a computer system flowchart for the entry of payables data and the daily processing steps in the cash disbursements application. Assume that the sup-

plier's (accounts payable) master file is stored on magnetic disk.

c. Discuss the considerations in selecting the logical file organization method and storage medium for the supplier's master file.

Solution

a. A cash disbursements transaction batch processing system would likely involve these steps: Suppliers' invoices that have been approved for payment would be filed in accordance with the purchase discount period. Each day those invoices reaching the end of the purchase discount period are pulled from the file. Batch totals of this day's invoices are computed on a calculator. For example, separate batch totals might be computed for the net amounts to be paid and the account number of the suppliers being paid, as well as the count of the invoices in the batch being processed. An accounting clerk next keys the pertinent data from each invoice in the batch onto magnetic tape, using the key-to-tape encoder. During this conversion step the encoder edits the data for errors and omissions. Any invoices found to contain errors are returned to the accounts payable clerk for correction. After transcribing all invoices, the clerk compares the batch totals computed by the encoder with the precomputed batch totals. She or he reconciles any differences.

Following these data-preparation steps, the bookstore's computer operator mounts the magnetic tape containing the invoice payment data onto an input tape drive. The operator first sorts the transaction data in accordance with the arrangement of the supplier master records (i.e., by supplier account numbers). Then the operator performs a sequential processing check printing and updating step (or "run"). This step consists of (i) printing each check; (ii) posting the check amount to the supplier's account, thus reducing the account payable balance; and (iii) printing a listing of cash disbursed (i.e., the cash disbursements journal).

Although these are the basic steps in the application, several other steps should be noted. Batch totals are automatically computed by the system during both the sort and update steps. These totals are compared to the precomputed batch totals. Also, at the end of each day the computer operator copies all the data from the magnetic disks, which contain (among other files) the supplier master file, onto magnetic tape. This tape, together with the transaction tape, are stored to provide backup. Furthermore, added reports are likely to be prepared on a periodic basis. For instance, a listing of open accounts payable amounts is printed by the computer system at the end of each month.

b. A computer system flowchart appears on the following page. Note that it pertains to the second paragraph of the written description.

c. In the problem statement the supplier's master file was specified as being stored on a magnetic disk. This storage medium affords several benefits. The individual accounts payable records can be accessed directly, since magnetic disk is a direct-access storage medium. Thus, a batch of payables transactions can be posted to the accounts without the need for sorting beforehand. Also, a particular supplier's account may be displayed on a monitor screen by an accounts payable clerk at any time he or she needs to see the up-to-date status of an account. If other master files, such as the general ledger, are also stored on magnetic disk, they may be posted

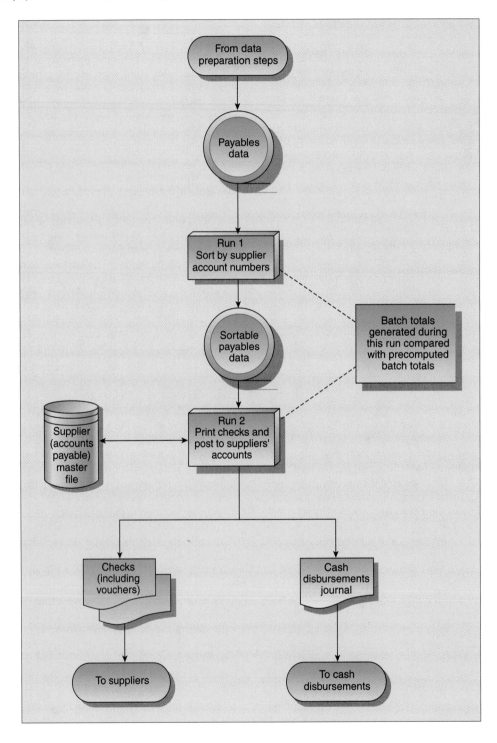

during the updating process. Consequently, the sum of the amounts posted to the accounts payable master file can be immediately reconciled to the precomputed batch totals and to the total posted to the accounts payable control account in general ledger.

The particular logical file organization method to employ depends on the uses to be made of the supplier master file. Very likely an indexed sequential file will be the preferred choice in the case of the cash disbursements application. An indexed sequential file allows a batch of payables transactions to be processed efficiently against sequentially organized supplier (accounts payable) records, and it also allows the accounts payable clerk to access any record quickly as needed. The indexed sequential file is generally preferable to the random file in this type of application, since the volatility of suppliers is likely to be low and the response time in accessing records is not critical.

KEY TERMS

activity ratio   (173)
attribute (of a data element)   (166)
attribute chain   (179)
binary search   (178)
block coding system   (177)
character   (166)
classification   (175)
coding   (175)
data element   (166)
dialogue prompt   (151)
direct access   (170)
field   (166)
file   (164)
file access   (168)
file maintenance   (167)
file organization   (165)
file size   (173)
file volatility   (174)
flag   (167)
flat file   (166)
graphical user interface (GUI)   (151)
group coding system   (177)
history file   (164)
immediate processing   (160)
indexed sequential file   (171)
inverted list   (180)
linked list   (178)
logical record   (165)
master file   (164)
menu   (151)
mnemonic code   (176)
mode (of a data element)   (167)
multiple-key inquiry   (180)

off-line   (149)
on-line   (150)
periodic processing   (153)
physical record   (165)
pointer   (178)
preformatted screen   (151)
primary key   (167)
random file   (172)
randomizing   (172)
record   (166)
records management   (174)
reference file   (165)
response time   (174)
run   (156)
secondary key   (167)
sequence coding system   (176)
sequential-access method   (168)
sequential updating   (155)
sort key   (156)
spooled   (175)
transaction file   (164)
turnaround document   (149)
updating   (155)
value (of a data element)   (166)

REVIEW QUESTIONS

5-1. What are the basic transaction processing cycles of a merchandising firm?

5-2. What is the importance of transaction processing to accountants?

5-3. Contrast the off-line and on-line approaches to data entry.

5-4. Identify three methods of interactive assistance provided by the system to users of on-line data entry.

5-5. Contrast the characteristics of periodic and immediate processing of transactions.

5-6. What are the relative advantages and disadvantages of periodic transaction processing?

5-7. Identify several variations of periodic processing.

5-8. Contrast the advantages of computer-based periodic processing with manual processing of transactions.

5-9. Identify several variations of the immediate processing approach.

5-10. What are the relative advantages and disadvantages of immediate processing of transactions?

5-11. What are the three major functions within the management of data?

5-12. What are the major types of data and nondata files?

5-13. Contrast logical and physical data records.

5-14. What is the hierarchy of data?

5-15. Describe the composition of a logical record.

5-16. What are four activities in file maintenance?

5-17. Contrast the sequential and direct methods of accessing data.

5-18. What are several methods of direct access?

5-19. Contrast the sequential, indexed sequential, and random files.

5-20. Describe the situations for which each of the three files listed in Question 5-19 are best suited.

5-21. What are several design considerations when establishing the structure of a record?

5-22. Contrast the classification and coding of data.

5-23. What are the attributes of a sound coding system?

5-24. Describe four coding systems, and provide suitable applications for each coding system.

DISCUSSION QUESTIONS

5-25. Contrast the impacts of computerization on the collection and processing of nontransaction data and transaction data.

5-26. Suggest applications for which on-line input but delayed batch processing would be suitable in a typical firm.

5-27. Discuss the value of the immediate processing approach in relation to the frequency of reporting.

5-28. Describe the trade-offs involved in choosing between alternatives in each of the following pairs of situations:

   a. (1) Inputting transaction data via a terminal at a sales office and transmitting the data to a central sales order department via data communications facilities.

       (2) Collecting transaction data by clerks at a sales office and mailing the data to a central sales order department.

   b. (1) Processing transactions one by one against relevant files as soon as they are captured.

       (2) Processing transactions in batches once a day.

   c. (1) Preparing a desired managerial report each Friday.

       (2) Preparing a desired managerial report one-half hour after it is requested.

5-29. Discuss the advantages of maintaining the general ledger on a magnetic disk.

5-30. The steps involved in updating records in files appear to be the same, regardless of whether the records pertain to customers or to suppliers or to general ledger accounts. Can one general-purpose updating program therefore be used?

5-31. How is a telephone directory that has an index at the top of each page an example of an indexed sequential file?

5-32. Discuss the trade-offs involved in designing a classification plan and a coding system for a firm such as Infoage, Inc.

PROBLEMS

5-1. Identify the transaction cycle within which each of the following business events or accounting steps takes place, and state which source documents and/or accounting records are likely to be involved:

   a. Posting credit sales made to customers (by a distributor).

   b. Ordering products from a supplier (by a distributor).

   c. Preparing the monthly balance sheet and income statement (by a department store).

   d. Registering students in classes for the upcoming semester (by a university).

   e. Posting books received from suppliers (by a retail bookstore).

   f. Printing paychecks for employees (by a legal services firm).

   g. Issuing raw materials into the production process (by a manufacturer).

   h. Acquiring new road building equipment (by a construction firm).

   i. Recording time worked by professional accountants on clients' engagements (by a public accounting firm).

5-2. Figure 5-2 shows a context diagram pertaining to Infoage's service-related revenue and expenditure activities. By reference to this figure, prepare context diagrams concerning the following:

   a. Infoage's revenues derived from its sales of products.

   b. Infoage's expenditures relating to its sales of products.

5-3. Figure 5-6 shows a data-flow diagram pertaining in generalized terms to the batch sequential processing of transactions. With slight modifications it may be used as a guide in preparing flows of specific transactions. Illustrate this assertion by drawing diagrams at level-zero concerning:

   a. Infoage's processing of sales invoices, with the originator being the billing department, the recipients of the sales invoices being the credit customers, and the recipient of sales reports being the sales manager.

b. A hospital's processing of cash disbursements, with the originator being the cashier, the recipients of checks being the suppliers of supplies and services, and the recipient of cash distribution reports being the treasurer.

5-4. Describe a suitable data-entry approach and related input device for each of the following situations, given that a computer system with on-line files is available. Note alternative approaches and/or input devices if the choice is not clear cut.

a. Batches of checks from depositors to be processed by a bank overnight.
b. Individual sales made to customers by salesclerks in a department store.
c. Collected copies of credit card slips to be processed by a credit-card center.
d. Collected copies of the top portions of monthly bills, returned to a public utility with checks from customers.
e. Times worked by factory employees on separate job orders in production.
f. Requests placed via telephones by investors involving transfers of amounts among mutual funds within a funds "family" such as Vanguard.

5-5. A grocery chain located in a large metropolitan area has a main office, plus a distribution center that services its dozen stores. All of the facilities are linked by a computer network, with a mainframe computer in the main office building. Sales are made by means of point-of-sale terminals.

Required

Describe a suitable data-input approach and input device for each of the following types of transactions:

a. Sales to customers.
b. Payroll preparation for employees.
c. Purchases from suppliers.
d. Cash disbursements to suppliers.
e. Daily shipments of merchandise from the distribution center to all stores.
f. Emergency replenishment of merchandise from the distribution center to one of the stores.

5-6. *Note: This problem may be solved with the aid of a data-base software package such as Paradox or Access.*

Assume that your university employs an on-line computerized registration system. Design the format of a preformatted data-entry screen to aid a clerk at an on-line campus computer site in entering the data from a handwritten course request form that you hand her. Assume that the computer system stores descriptive information concerning students and courses. Thus only the identification numbers need be entered and the system can retrieve the related descriptive information. Identify any other items that the system should automatically display on the screen.

5-7. A savings and loan branch employs on-line terminals for use of the tellers. The terminals are connected to a computer system that includes a data base with records of all depositors.

Required

a. Design a preformatted data-entry screen to aid the tellers in entering deposit and withdrawal transactions. Include a menu within the screen to allow the teller to select "Deposit," "Withdrawal," "New Depositor," or "Exit." Provide for the retrieval of the depositor's name and current account balance on the screen upon the entry of the depositor's account number. Identify any other items that the system should automatically display on the screen.

b. Revise the data-entry screen in **a** above to include explicit dialogue prompts, in the form of questions and directions. Assume that a separate screen is used for new depositors.

5-8. *Note: This problem may be solved with the aid of a data-base package such as Paradox or Access.*

The Good Shepherd Hospital employs an on-line patient servicing system, including terminals for data entry and a data base with records of the patients. The system is employed to admit patients and maintain their records during stays in the hospital. When new patients are admitted, the system must capture needed data concerning the patients as well as facts surrounding the admission event. To speed the process, codes are assigned whenever possible. When codes are employed by the entering clerk or nurse, descriptive terms are "echoed" by the system on the screen.

Required

Design a preformatted data-entry screen to aid the receptionist in admitting a patient to the emergency room. Data to be entered include the patient's name, address, age, medical insurance plan (if any); the means by which the patient was delivered to the hospital; the suspected type of injury or illness; the attending physician; the time of arrival; and so on.

5-9. Among the processing approaches that can be employed via computer-based systems are the following:

a. Immediate processing.
b. Periodic processing, with on-line data entry and sequential updating.

c. Periodic processing, with batched data entry and sequential updating.

d. Periodic processing, with batched data entry and direct updating.

Required

With respect to each of the following applications, specify which of these approaches is likely to be the most suitable and state your reasoning. If an alternative approach also appears to be suitable, briefly explain why.

a. Preparing a weekly payroll by a merchandiser.

b. Reserving seats on scheduled airline flights by a travel agent.

c. Preparing monthly statements for credit customers by a department store.

d. Maintaining credit histories of individuals and businesses by a centralized credit bureau.

e. Producing goods to fill customers' special and rush orders by a manufacturer.

f. Posting monthly adjusting journal entries by a retailer.

g. Processing and shipping catalog orders received by a mail-order house.

h. Maintaining the records of patients in a hospital.

i. Producing cement for inventory by a concrete manufacturer.

j. Maintaining the records of policyholders by an insurance firm.

k. Generating and transmitting purchase orders by an automobile manufacturer.

l. Preparing checks for suppliers by a contractor.

m. Checking out customers by a branch of a grocery chain.

n. Registering students for courses at a university.

5-10. The computer system flowchart depicted on page 187 reflects the sales and cash receipts procedure for the Boomer Sales Corporation. Unfortunately, the accountant who was preparing the flowchart was suddenly called to another assignment.

Required

Complete the flowchart by labeling the symbols.

(CPA *adapted*)

5-11. The computer system flowchart shown on page 188 depicts a newly proposed procedure pertaining to the receipts of ordered goods for the Frost Company. Your assistant, a new accountant, has drawn most of the symbols for the procedure. Now she asks your assistance in completing the flowchart, recognizing that it may be incomplete.

In order to complete the flowchart, both of you review the procedure, which states in part: After updating the master inventory file to reflect the receipts, the records containing receipts data are stored until the end of the day. Then they are printed as prenumbered receiving reports and delivered to the storeskeeper with the received goods. Records of the receiving reports are also stored on-line to facilitate the audit trail.

5-12. Auto Barn is an automotive parts retailer in a midwestern city. It supplies its three outlets from a central warehouse. The firm sells about 6000 separate merchandise items, with payment by cash or credit card. Because of its low prices and varied merchandise, sales have been growing rapidly. However, two other automotive part retailers have just entered the city and promise to provide stiff competition. To meet this competition, Auto Barn must add even more merchandise items to its line and reduce paperwork costs. It also needs to improve service. One way to do so is by keeping all parts continually available in the outlets. Another way is by aiding customers by locating desired parts quickly. For instance, when a customer wants an air filter for a 1990 Camry, a clerk should be able to determine quickly the stock number and its shelf location. To achieve these goals and thus effectively meet the new competition, Auto Barn has decided to acquire a new computer system.

Required

Describe at least three alternative computer-based processing approaches that Auto Barn might employ to maintain its inventory. Identify the relative advantages of each approach. State which of the approaches appears most likely to achieve the benefits specified above.

5-13. Figure 4-10 shows a computer system flowchart for preparing student course schedules based on the immediate processing approach, together with batch processing of outputs. In order to solve this problem, please refer to the accompanying figure and textual description. This problem concerns alternative procedures that may be employed in preparing student course schedules.

Required

Revise the flowchart to reflect each of the following procedures:

a. Students submit course request sheets to a registration site. The sheets are accumulated by batches, totals computed, and the data keyed onto magnetic disks. The data are entered from the disks into the computer system, with appropriate edit checks being performed. The course request records are sorted according to student name and processed, with new student schedule records being established. The course status records and schedule are accessed directly, with data concerning available courses being copied into the student schedule

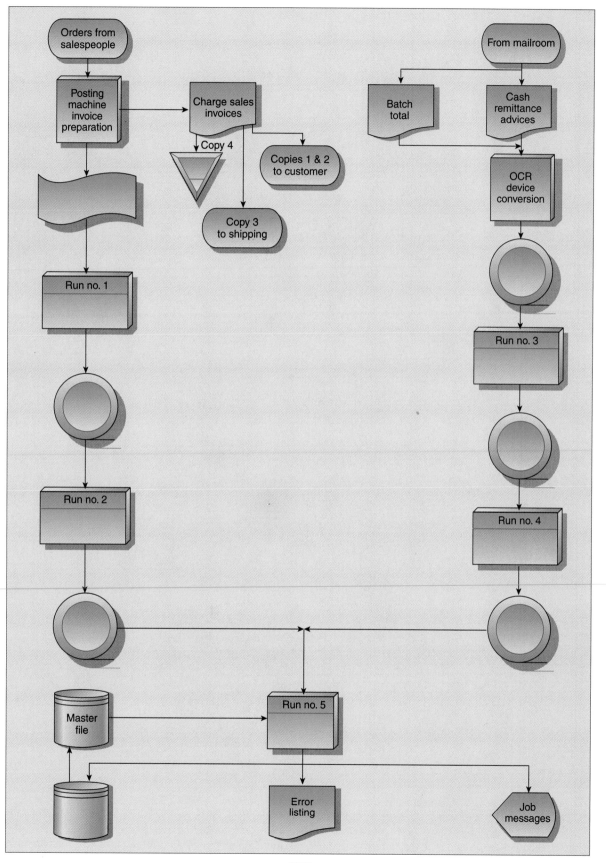

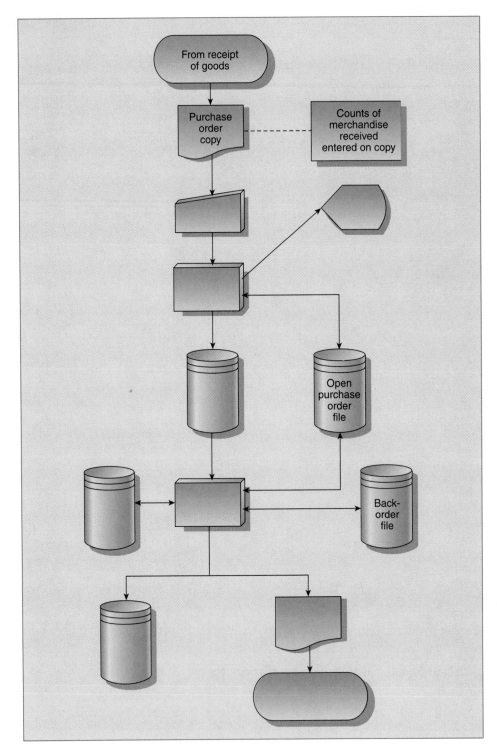

records. (If a course is filled to capacity, a notation to that effect is noted in the student schedule record.) After all course request records have been processed, the course schedules are printed as in the current procedure and mailed to the students.

b. Students submit course request sheets to a registration site. The sheets are accumulated by batches, totals computed, and the data keyed onto magnetic tapes. The data are entered from the tapes into the computer system, with appropriate edit checks being performed.

The course request records are first segmented by requested courses, with the student number attached to each course segment. Then the segments are sorted by course number. The segments are processed sequentially against the course status and schedule files. Data from the on-line files are added to the segments, with the course status record being changed to reflect the increased enrollment each time a student is added. (If a course is filled to capacity, a notation to that effect is placed in the segment record.) After all course segments have been processed, they are re-sorted according to student number and combined into new student schedule records. Finally, these schedule records are printed and mailed to the students.

c. After scanning the printed course schedule, students use a touch-tone telephone to enter their requests for courses. Any errors in entry are announced to the students by means of audio response. The requests are immediately processed by the registration system, with responses to the requests again provided via an audio device. Course schedules are immediately printed at a designated registration site and held for students to pick up.

5-14. The Mobile Insurance Co. of Birmingham, Alabama, issues automobile insurance policies. Currently the firm has about 20,000 policies in force. Transactions affecting these policies are processed on a computer system with magnetic disk storage.

Policy processing involves several steps. Transaction data pertaining to billing, payments, renewals, new policyholders, canceled policyholders, and changes in status are first recorded on standardized source documents. After batch totals are computed, the documents are forwarded by the initiating departments to the input preparation section so that the data therein can be keyed onto magnetic tape. The transaction data are next edited in a computer run and then sorted by policyholder number. Then they are processed against the policyholder master file in order to update the records. During this updating run a transaction listing (journal) is prepared. Also, data are extracted from the policyholder records concerning those policyholders who are due to pay premiums or to renew policies. A magnetic disk onto which the extracted data have been spooled is later processed to print premium notices and renewal notices. Batch totals are computed during the edit, sort, and update runs and printed on an exception and summary report for comparison with the predetermined totals.

Required

a. Draw a computer system flowchart of the described policy maintenance procedure.

b. Draw an alternative computer system flowchart that shows a policy maintenance procedure employing the on-line entry and immediate processing of individual policy changes. However, the procedure should continue to print all policy notices once a day as a batch.

c. Explain the relative advantages and drawbacks of the alternative computer system for this application. What is another alternative that may be an even better choice in this situation?

5-15. Identify each of the following files according to their types, i.e., master, transaction, history, reference.

   a. A file of general ledger accounts for a contractor.
   b. A file that contains all past diagnoses and treatments of patients in a hospital.
   c. A file that contains all current prices charged by a merchandising firm for its products.
   d. A file of jobs currently in progress by a manufacturer.
   e. A file of amounts paid to suppliers today by a retailer.
   f. A file of services performed for patients this month by a physician.
   g. A file that contains the trade discount rates allowed to customers by a distributor.
   h. A file of income tax regulations promulgated by the Internal Revenue Service.
   i. A file of times charged by a consultant for services performed for clients this week.

5-16. For each of the following files, identify the likely primary key; also, list three likely secondary keys and their modes, plus sample data values.

   a. General ledger
   b. Accounts receivable
   c. Accounts payable
   d. Inventory
   e. Cash receipts
   f. Purchase orders
   g. Patient
   h. Cash disbursements
   i. Work order

5-17. Longevity Life Insurance Company of Omaha has 30,000 policyholders, each of whom has one life insurance policy type (e.g., term, ordinary life, endowment). It maintains a master file of policyholders on magnetic disk. Weekly it processes an average batch of 800 transactions (including both billings and payments) against the policyholder master file, in order to update the account balances. During the week policy clerks process via on-line terminals an average of 500 renewals, new policyholders, cancellations, and changes in policy type or status of policyholder data.

Required

a. Prepare a layout for a fixed-length record in the policyholder master file, incorporating a reasonable set of data elements and including the mode of each data element. Identify the primary key and three secondary keys. Also specify the length of each field.

b. List needed data elements in a fixed-length record that services both billing and payment transactions.

c. Describe the relative advantages of using indexed sequential versus random file organizations for the master file.

d. Describe and illustrate codes that identify (i) each type of transaction and (ii) each policy.

e. Briefly describe the data that might be contained in the following types of files useful to this application: (i) reference file, (ii) history file, (iii) report file, and (iv) suspense file.

5-18. Assume that an accounts receivable master file contains records having fields for customer numbers and current balances, and that the values in the records for the 12 customers are as follows:

Customer Number	Current Balance
128	100.00
156	2452.00
194	776.00
205	3381.00
234	629.00
257	00.00
288	343.00
297	5710.00
312	30.00
364	1002.00
377	220.00
399	2010.00

The following sales transactions and changes occurred during a recent processing cycle, where the transaction codes are S for sale, D for deletion of the customer record, and A for addition of a new customer.

Customer Number	Transaction Code	Amount
288	S	40.00
377	S	35.00
156	S	138.00
257	D	
234	S	204.00
321	S	80.00
288	S	129.00
210	A	200.00
377	S	40.00
205	S	450.00
368	A	
128	S	30.00

Required

Show the contents of the accounts receivable master file after the transactions have been sorted by customer numbers and processed sequentially against the master file. Use Figure 5-15 as a guide in the processing steps. If the customer number on a transaction does not match a number in the master file, the transaction should appear as an error on an exception and summary report. Specify if any of the above transactions would so appear.

5-19. A master file is stored on a magnetic tape as a sequential file. The file is made up of 100 fixed-length records with primary key values ranging from 100 to 199. These records are not blocked. An identical file is stored on a magnetic disk. Its sequentially organized records are grouped into blocks of four and located at disk addresses 0820 through 0844.

Required

a. Describe the procedure by which the computer system accesses the record stored on magnetic tape whose key value is 157.

b. What advantages are provided by the file stored on the magnetic disk?

c. Prepare an index to convert the file on magnetic disk to indexed sequential, using the key value of the first record in each block to represent the block of logical records. Then describe the procedure by which the computer system accesses the same numbered record (157).

d. Assume that the file on magnetic disk is changed to a random structure. The hashing scheme consists of dividing the key value of a record by 13 and using the first four digits of the remainder as the disk address. For instance, the disk address for the record having the key value of 100 is 6923, based on the division of 100 by 13. Describe the procedure by which the computer system would access the record having the key value of 157. Include the computed disk address.

5-20. Refer to Figure 5-16.

a. Describe the procedure for accessing the record with a key value of 161.

b. Describe the procedure for processing, by the direct method, a batch of transactions affecting records with key values of 155, 103, 131, 161, 107, 110, and 135.

c. Describe the procedure for processing the transactions in b by the sequential method.

d. A new record with the key value of 134 is to be added to the master file. Describe in general terms where the record would be located and how it would be accessed.

5-21. Each of the following situations involves the use of one or more master files. Select the method (sequential, indexed sequential, or random) by which the file(s) in each situation are best physically organized. Explain the reasons for your choices. You may assume additional facts, if necessary, to reinforce your justifications.

a. A large life insurance firm with approximately 2 million policyholders maintains a single policy-holder master file, which is updated twice weekly to reflect premium payments, to add new policy-holders, to delete canceled policyholders, to reflect changes to permanent data, and to print overdue premium notices. Approximately 1 million records are affected during each processing run.

b. An automotive and truck parts supplier maintains a 10,000-record inventory master file. An average of 2500 records are updated daily to reflect sales and receipts, and approximately 30 parts are either added or deleted daily. An inventory reorder list is printed daily to notify buyers when parts on hand have declined to their reorder points; however, parts clerks need to be able to check the status of parts on hand at any time during the day, since customers often want to know how many units of particular parts are available when they call to place orders.

c. A manufacturing firm produces goods on orders received from customers. Approximately 100 orders are in production on any given day, and these orders are maintained as records in a work-in-process master file. Each record must be accessed frequently in order to post data concerning production steps completed and to enable managers and planners to discover current order status. A five-second response time is considered tolerable. On the average, about 10 orders are begun and 10 completed daily.

d. The water department in a city with approximately 75,000 residents maintains a resident account master file. Once a month all the records in the file are updated to reflect water usage; bills are also prepared at that time, as well as a listing of residents and amounts billed.

e. A motel chain employs a room reservation system, in which all rooms of each member motel represent the available inventory. Each time a room is reserved, a new record is created in the name of the person making the reservation. This record is then changed to reflect occupancy on specific dates, to add food and phone charges, to prepare the bills, and then to delete the records when occupants leave. On the average, travelers occupy a room for one and one-half nights.

5-22. The Phoenix Board of Realtors' Multiple Listing Service (MLS) maintains a listing of houses for sale in the Phoenix metropolitan area. The listing for each house includes the data in the collection of ten records in the table below. To provide faster service to buyers, MLS has decided also to maintain inverted files. Then, when buyers ask to see houses having certain desired features, the computer system can quickly retrieve the requested data.

Required

a. Prepare inverted files based on the four attributes that can serve as secondary keys. The records shown are stored on a magnetic disk and located at consecutive disk addresses, beginning with 250. (Thus, the record having MLS number 10 is located at address 259.) In preparing the inverted file for asking price, use a range that begins from $99,999 to (but not including) $105,000.

b. Describe the procedure for obtaining the answers to the following inquiries, and show how the answers might appear on a video display screen.

(1) What are the addresses of the houses for sale in Mesa?

(2) Which houses in Tempe, identified by address, are priced below $120,000?

MLS Number	Address	Area	Asking Price (000$)	Number of Bedrooms	Date of Construction
1	2340 Cricket Dr.	Tempe	119	4	1990
2	1504 Indian St.	Phoenix	103	4	1985
3	4328 Sunset Rd.	Mesa	104	4	1984
4	2264 Robson Dr.	Mesa	102	3	1989
5	1720 Terrace Ave.	Tempe	139	5	1995
6	116 Mountain Dr.	Phoenix	130	5	1986
7	3101 Gilbert Rd.	Mesa	106	3	1988
8	1730 Brown St.	Phoenix	132	4	1991
9	2525 College Ave.	Tempe	144	5	1996
10	5150 Vista Dr.	Mesa	127	4	1993

(3) Which houses in Phoenix, identified by address, have four bedrooms and were constructed since 1990?

c. List three more inquiries, involving at least two inverted files, that can be answered by the set of inverted files.

Hint: Refer to the appendix at the end of the chapter.

5-23. Supplier records for a firm are listed in the flat file below. They contain such data elements as the supplier number, supplier name, address, date of last purchase, and so on. In addition, a single pointer field appears as the last field in the records. Addresses at which the records are stored on a magnetic disk are also listed alongside the records in the flat file.

Required

a. Insert the appropriate pointer values in the pointer field to form a linked list, if the purpose of the linked list is to enable the preparation of a report arranged by date of most recent purchase, with the latest date listed first.

b. Prepare an inverted list that contains the values relating to the months of most recent purchase.

		SUPPLIER RECORDS		
Disk Address	Supplier Number	Date of Most Recent Purchase	Remainder of Record Content	Pointer Field
010	1000	10/3		
020	1001	9/6		
030	1002	9/17		
040	1003	8/30		
050	1004	10/7		
060	1005	9/21		
070	1006	9/14		
080	1007	10/2		
090	1008	9/11		
100	1009	9/28		
110	1010	9/5		

5-24. Resort Hotels, a luxury hotel chain in the Virgin Islands, recently computerized its front desk operations. It installed a software package that provides "management by exception" reports. These reports reflect only those activities that vary significantly from established plans. One report shows the variation of the actual room rates charged to guests from standard room rates. The columns in this report are, from left to right: room number, guest's name, type of room, number of guests (adults, children), room rate (charged, standard), and comments. This particular report would be used by the front desk manager to be aware of pricing practices by the front desk personnel, so that he can approve or disapprove of specific cases.

Required

a. Assume that two files—a guest file and room file—are used to prepare this report. List the data elements that would likely appear in the records of each file.

b. Guests and rooms are clearly related. Describe two methods by which the relationship may be reflected in the files.

Hint: A third file may be employed in one of these two methods.

c. Reports are also needed to show: (1) the number of days that guests have occupied their rooms, grouped by one day, two days, etc., and (2) the rooms that are unoccupied, listed by room numbers. Describe in detail two ways of facilitating the preparation of each report. Assume that the software package can accommodate inverted lists and linked lists.

d. Describe one additional report that can be provided by using the files and explain how it will be useful to the front desk manager.

(SMAC *adapted*)

5-25. Specify the most suitable type of coding system for each of the following situations:
   a. Numbering payroll checks.
   b. Identifying airports on baggage claim checks.
   c. Identifying categories of expenses incurred during business operations.
   d. Identifying key aspects (e.g., salesperson) of a sales transaction.

5-26. Devise block codes for the following situations:
   a. The courses of a university that has both undergraduate and graduate programs. (Each course is to be identified by the department prefix, such as ACC, followed by a number within the block code.)
   b. The jersey numbers to be assigned to football players for a university (e.g., 10–19 for quarterbacks).
   c. The major groups of accounts (e.g., assets) in a chart of accounts.

5-27. Devise combinational group codes for the following entities that contain at least three fields:
   a. A checking account depositor in a national bank.
   b. A patient admitted to a hospital.
   c. A consumer of a gas and electric utility.
   d. A project undertaken by a construction firm that builds highways, bridges, airports, apartment buildings, and so on.

5-28. Price-Anders Consulting, a worldwide consulting firm specializing in information systems development, requires a code by which to classify its engagements so that they may be easily accessed for future reference. Several facets are to be included in the code. These facets are the nature of the engagement, the industry of the client being served, the office through which the engagement is performed, the person in charge of the engagement, the client being served, the key technique employed (if any), and the year in which the engagement is conducted.

Required

a. Design a combinational group code that includes the above facets. Letters as well as numbers may be employed. In order to establish field sizes, assume that the firm has 94 offices and expects to expand further, that there are 3820 clients in 64 industries, and that 23 basic types of services can be provided with the aid of about the same number of key techniques. The persons in charge can be represented by the three initials of their names, while the year would be specified by four digits.

b. Illustrate the designed code for an engagement in which the office in Tokyo (number 29) conducted a feasibility study (F) for Fuji Electronics (client number 2883) in 1992, using the discounted cash flow technique (DCF). The electronics industry is assigned number 9. The consultant in charge was Samuel Wan Kuo.

5-29. The Speedy Bike Company of Cambridge, Massachusetts, sells bicycles to bike shops, department stores, and discount stores throughout the country. It employs eight salespersons, each of whom covers several states. Because sales trends are extremely important to its success, the firm carefully records considerable data concerning each sale and stores the data, in coded form, within a sales data base. Any manager can retrieve desired data, via interactive terminals, from this data base by means of English-like commands. Software within the system can select data, arrange data, and compute totals as specified by the commands.

Each sales transaction, broken down according to product characteristics, is stored according to the following format. (The transaction code is omitted.)

Product number 1*	Wheel size 2–3	Color 4	Style 5	Sales terrritory 6–7

Outlet 8–10	Salesperson number 11	Date 12–16	Blank 17	Quantity 18–20

*Digit position(s) pertaining to each field.

Codes, on a selected basis, are as follows.

Product number: 1, single speed; 2, three-speed; 3, five-speed; 4, ten-speed standard; 5, ten-speed deluxe.

Color: 1, blue; 2, red; 3, green; 4, tan; 5, black; 6, orange; 7, yellow.

Style: 1, male; 2, female.

Salesperson: 1, Jake; 2, Julie; 3, Sam; 4, Cindy; 5, Mac; 6, Marsha; 7, Rick; 8, Trish.

Following is the set of transactions for the first day of May:

```
2262214310705012 005
4261114310705012 021
3263108181205012 010
4275108181205012 003
4262222057405012 090
4261110263105012 030
3263110571105012 020
1244116208605012 004
5262116208605012 006
4261216433605012 012
```

Required

On the basis of this very limited sample, specify the responses that the system would provide to a manager who enters the following commands:

a. NAME PRODUCT THAT HAD MOST UNIT SALES.

b. NAME WHEEL SIZE THAT HAD LEAST UNIT SALES.

c. LIST COLORS THAT HAD NO UNIT SALES.

d. LIST TWO TOP SALESPERSONS IN ORDER OF UNITS SOLD AND UNIT SALES OF EACH.

e. LIST UNIT SALES BY TERRITORY AND TOTAL.

5-30. Valpaige Co. of Omaha is an industrial machinery and equipment manufacturer with several production departments. The firm employs automated and heavy equipment in its production departments. Consequently, Valpaige has a large repair and maintenance (R & M) department for servicing this equipment.

The operating efficiency of the R & M department has deteriorated over the past two years. Further, repair and maintenance costs seem to be climbing more rapidly than other department costs. The assistant controller has reviewed the operations of the R & M department and has concluded that the administrative procedures used since the early days of the department are outmoded due in part to the growth of the firm. The two major causes for the deterioration, in the opinion of the assistant controller, are an antiquated scheduling system for repair and maintenance work and the actual cost system to distribute the R & M department's costs to the production departments. The actual costs of the R & M department are allocated monthly to the production departments on the basis of the number of service calls made during each month.

The assistant controller has proposed that a formal work order system be implemented for the R & M department. The production departments would submit a service request to the R & M department for the repairs and/or maintenance to be completed, including a suggested time for having the work done. The supervisor of the R & M department would prepare a cost estimate on the service request for the work required (labor and materials) and indicate a suggested time for completing the work on the service request. The R & M supervisor would return the request to the production department which initiated the request. Once the production department okays the work by returning a copy of the service request, the R & M supervisor would prepare a repair and maintenance work order and schedule the job. This work order provides the repair worker with the details of the work to be done and is used to record maintenance hours worked and the materials and supplies used.

Production departments would be charged for actual labor hours worked at a predetermined standard rate for the type of work required. The parts and supplies used would be charged to the production departments at cost.

The assistant controller believes that only two documents would be required in this new system—a repair maintenance service request initiated by the production departments and the repair maintenance work order initiated by the R & M department.

Required

a. Prepare a document (system) flowchart to show how the assistant controller's proposed work order system would coordinate the maintenance service request and the repair maintenance work order among the production, R & M, and accounting departments. Assume that the procedure does not involve computer processing. Number the various copies of the docments and trace the copies through the procedure.

b. Prepare a computer system flowchart of the proposed work order system if the documents are prepared by the aid of preformatted screens and the immediate processing approach is employed.

c. Design a preformatted screen for the repair maintenance work order.

d. Design a group code to aid in analyzing maintenance service work orders. Identify all fields in the code and illustrate the code for a work order involving an overhaul of heavy equipment in the assembly production department that is scheduled for the third week of September 1997.

(CMA *adapted*)

CONTINUING CASE

With respect to the small firm that you selected in Chapter 1, complete the following requirements:

a. A list of the documents employed in transactions.

b. Examples of input forms, including at least one hard-copy form and one preformatted screen.

c. A list of all files employed in transactions, organized by type and storage media.

d. A description of a computer-based application involving the immediate processing approach. If no applications currently involve this approach, select an application for which the approach is suitable, describe its use, and explain why the approach is suitable.

e. A description of a computer-based application involving the periodic processing approach. If no applications currently involve this approach, select an application for which the approach is suitable, describe its use, and explain why the approach is suitable.

f. A description of selected codes employed for entities and transactions.

CHAPTER
6

....

DATA AND DATA-BASE
MANAGEMENT

....

THE LEARNING OBJECTIVES FOR THIS CHAPTER ARE TO ENABLE YOU TO:

1. Describe the importance of effective data and data-base management to accountants and other users.

2. Discuss the data-base approach to data management and the advantages it offers over the file-oriented approach.

3. Identify the phases in developing an integrated data base for a firm.

4. Describe the technique of data modeling via entity-relationship diagrams.

5. Contrast several logical data structures that are suitable to data-base systems.

6. Detail the features of a relational data-base system, including normalization.

INTRODUCTION

....

In this information age the data resource has assumed increasing importance. As a key source of the information needed for operations and decision making, it can be critical to the success of a firm. When relevant data are uncollected or lost or inaccessible, a firm can suffer severe economic consequences. As a result, the management of many firms has recognized the need to devote careful attention to managing the data resource.

In Chapter 5 we surveyed the roles of files in transaction processing. We learned that managing files involves three major functions: (1) creating the records and files into which data are stored, (2) maintaining the files through such activities as updating current records and adding new records, and (3) retrieving the data that are stored in the records of the files. A fourth function, we observed, was to dispose of or archive data no longer currently useful.

Our aim in this chapter is to sharpen our view of bases of data and data management by today's firms. We use the term **data base** to mean the collected data sets that are organized and stored as an integral part of a firm's computer-based information system. In turn, we define the term **data sets** as flexible data structures, including groupings of data that are logically related as well as the files with which we are familiar. The three major functions associated with file management remain the same, although now we will call them **data management.** Much of this chapter attempts to show how data management can be achieved more effectively through a combination of information technology and data modeling. In particular we will learn how to develop **data-base systems** that integrate data bases through the hardware and software of varied computer-based architectures.

ROLES OF ACCOUNTANTS IN DATA MANAGEMENT

Accountants have deep concerns with data-management functions. On the input side they are concerned that all the relevant data involving transactions are stored, kept up-to-date, and well protected from loss or unauthorized alterations. On the output side they are concerned that needed data can be quickly retrieved from its storage locations and converted into valued information. Thus, although accountants do not have primary responsibility for data-base design, they do have active roles to play.

Accountants can be heavily involved in the development of data bases. They often serve as members of data-base design teams. They may also provide information to evaluate the feasibility of a new data base. A most important service is to identify the information needs of information customers, in particular the managers and firm that they support. Accountants are concerned that both the financial and the managerial reports contain timely information in understandable formats. They may also be involved with providing data for decision support systems and expert systems that aid managers in making key decisions. In addition, accountants have a responsibility to ensure that every data base incorporates adequate internal controls and security measures.

As a professional accountant, you would be least concerned with the physical design aspects of data bases, such as details of indexes and pointers. However, you would need to know the logical contents of data sets, as incorporated into the data dictionary, and the overall organization of the data bases. You also should be familiar with the characteristics and relative advantages of various data-base systems. In fact, you likely will be expected to have considerable skill in using such data-base packages as Access or Paradox, in order to view stored data and perhaps also to process transactions.

DEFICIENCIES OF THE FILE-ORIENTED APPROACH

The **file-oriented approach,** described and illustrated in Chapter 5, is the traditional manner of storing data. In this approach each computer application maintains its own set of files. Each application has a limited number of users, who are involved in processing specific types of captured data and employing the outputs for their specialized needs. This group of users, who might consist of the employees and managers of a department or function, view the data as "owned" by them.

Two applications under the file-oriented approach are pictured in Figure 6-1. If the file structures and related records are well designed and are maintained on-line, the file-oriented approach can be both efficient and effective. The data in records can be kept up-to-date; the needs of each application and its users can be met, especially when the needs remain unchanged. However, this approach has several severe deficiencies with respect to managing and controlling the collected data for a firm.

Data Redundancy Since each application within the file-oriented approach maintains its own files, those files needed by more than one application must be duplicated. Figure 6-2 shows duplicate inventory master files being maintained by sales and purchases transaction processing systems. Also, the same data elements often appear in more than one file. Thus the numbers of inventory items (and perhaps their descriptions) are likely to be repeated in the inventory master file, the open

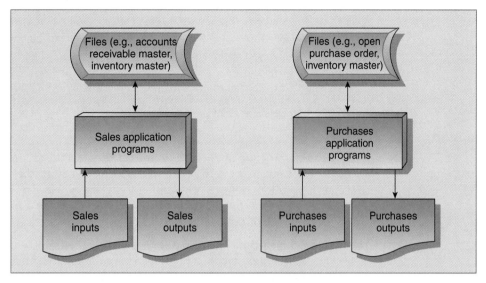

FIGURE 6-1　Two applications within the file-oriented approach.

purchase order file, and the supplier file. Data redundancy leads to increased costs due to the added storage space. Even heavier costs, however, are incurred because data concerning the same transactions must be entered more than once to update duplicate files.

Data Inconsistency　As a consequence of redundant files and data elements, the characteristics of data elements and their values are likely to be inconsistent. For example, the inventory item number may be assigned the name ITEM in the sales

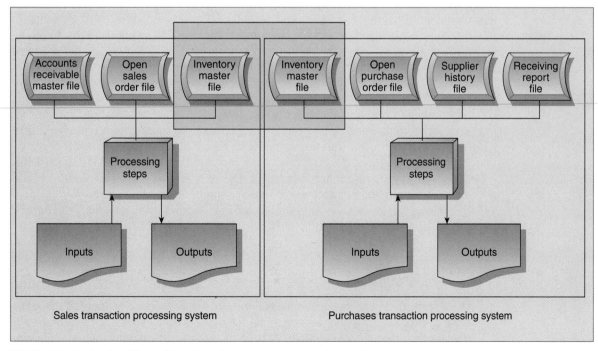

FIGURE 6-2　Redundant file in file-oriented transaction processing applications.

- Data redundancy. The same data elements appear in more than one file.
- Data inconsistency. The values of duplicated data elements are not identical.
- Inaccessibility of data. Inquiries that were anticipated when designing files cannot be answered quickly.
- Inflexibility. Needed changes to applications are difficult to make.

FIGURE 6-3   Deficiencies of the file-oriented approach.

application program and INVNO in the purchases application program. The quantity on hand of inventory item B43 might appear as 100 in the file maintained by the sales application; however, the value for the same item may appear as 10 in the file maintained by the purchases application, since that file has not yet been updated to reflect a receipt of 90 units.

Inaccessibility of Data   Information available under the file-oriented approach generally consists of reports that have been preprogrammed. An example of such a report is the inventory status report arranged according to the inventory item number (i.e., the primary key). Ad hoc reports usually cannot be provided quickly upon request, since new programs must be written. If the reports are to be based on data from more than one application, the task is even more difficult. Since files are not integrated across applications, duplicates of the affected files would first need to be collected into a new application. This step may not be feasible, since organizational functions in charge of applications are often reluctant to share the files and data that they "own."

Inflexibility   Changes to current file-oriented applications cannot be made easily, nor can new developments be realized quickly. In fact, both tend to be quite time-consuming and costly. The main reason for this inflexibility is that the application programs are closely dependent on (1) the data that they access, and (2) the physical media on which the data are stored. Generally the programs directly incorporate the record structures and data names within the files used in the applications. Programs must often be written with the nature of the physical storage media in mind, as well as the location of the records on the media and the file organization method being used. Thus, each change tends to involve extensive and detailed reprogramming. Also, since reprogramming is necessary each time a revision is made to a file (e.g., a lengthened field) and each time a new report is needed, the changes can become quite numerous. Furthermore, each change usually requires the attention of experienced programmers, who are scarce resources in most firms. Still another reason for inflexibility is that an autonomous file represents the only type of data structure employed in the file-oriented approach. The only way to combine logically related data is to create mammoth records that are cumbersome to process.

These four deficiencies are summarized in Figure 6-3. They are sufficiently serious that an alternative approach is needed to the file-oriented approach.

THE DATA-BASE APPROACH

Most firms that develop new systems and applications elect to employ the **data-base approach,** a broader approach that recognizes data as a valued resource to be managed for the use and benefit of multiple applications, organizational units, and users. At the center of the data-base approach is an integrated data base, which maintains data for the applications and users. Figure 6-4 shows the data base that combines the separate sales and purchases applications of Figure 6-1. As we see in the figure, a key component of the data-base approach is a **data-base management system (DBMS)**—special software that manages the data management functions related to the data base.

The data-base approach applies whenever an integrated data base is established to serve two or more applications, organizational units, or types of users. Examples of integrated data bases to be established at Infoage, Inc., might focus on customers, human resources (employees), and fixed assets. Alternatively, integrated data bases might focus on transaction cycles, such as the revenue cycle and the expenditure cycle. The possibilities are endless and depend on the needs to be served. For instance, Merrill Lynch has a customer data base, which serves its cash management account system and varied brokerage services; American Airlines has flight and customer data bases, which serve its reservations system and customer services systems; McKesson Robbins (a wholesaler) has an inventory management data base that serves its order-entry, purchasing, and distribution systems.

The scope of the data-base approach is quite elastic. While it may only span two applications, such as shown in Figure 6-4, it can extend to the activities and entities of an entire organization or firm. A data base that spans an entire enterprise is often called a *data warehouse* and is established to serve the needs of corporate decision makers. It may be formed by extracting data from application-oriented or production data bases throughout the firm.

Implementing an enterprise data base or data warehouse is a very challenging undertaking. Nevertheless, a few progressive firms are accepting the challenge. Corning, Inc., a leading manufacturer of fiber optics, is designing what it calls a

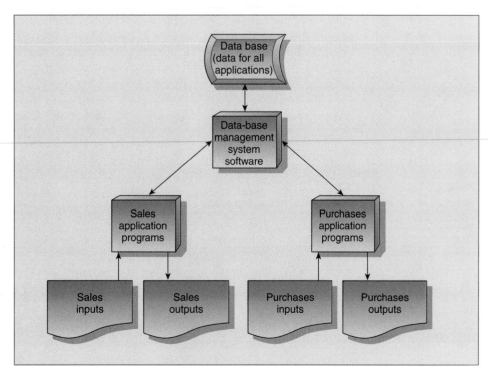

FIGURE 6-4   An illustration of the data-base approach, with the sales and purchases applications being linked by an integrated data base.

"Data-Centered Architecture" whose scope is enterprise-wide and is based on such key aspects as orders, products, and equipment. When completed the data-base system should provide accurate data that are highly accessible to users in all functional areas. It should also provide the flexibility to meet the rapidly changing demands of the optical-fiber industry, so that the system can quickly adapt to new products, production processes, orders, and so on.*

CHARACTERISTICS OF THE DATA-BASE APPROACH

Among the typical characteristics of the data-base approach are data independence, data standardization, one-time data entry and storage, data integration, shared data ownership, and centralized data management.

Data Independence   Critical to the data-base approach is the characteristic of **data independence**—the separation of the data from the various application programs and other accesses by users. Data independence is achieved by interposing the data-base management system (DBMS) software between the data base and the requests for data (e.g., by application programs). Figure 6-5 depicts this separation. Because of data independence, application programs do not need to specify the location of the data structures containing needed data. The programs need only to state needed data elements by names; the DBMS then "looks up" the data in an on-line dictionary and retrieves the data for the programs to use.

In addition to separating the data from application programs, the DBMS also isolates the logical view of data from the physical view. The **logical view** of data is the perspective that users have of the data stored within the data base and the relationships among the data elements. A "blueprint" or view of the logical organization of an entire data base is generally called a **schema.** The term *physical view*, also called the internal view, refers to the actual arrangement of data on the physical storage media, as well as the physical means of integrating the data. As we recall from Chapter 5, data are physically integrated through pointers and indexes as well as by contiguous (e.g., sequential) placement of records.† Only the DBMS needs "knowledge" of both the logical and physical views.

Data independence enables changes to be made much more easily, quickly, and less expensively in the data-base approach than in file-oriented systems. Changes

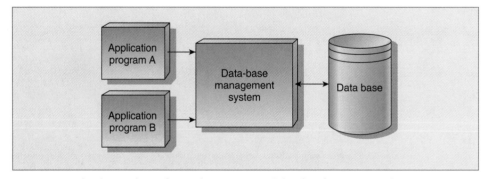

FIGURE 6-5   The data-independence characteristic of the data-base approach.

---

*Andrew C. Boynton, "Achieving Dynamic Stability through Information Technology," *California Management Review* (Winter 1993), pp. 69–70.
†Note that the logical and physical views correspond roughly to the logical and physical records discussed in Chapter 5.

affecting data need be made in the DBMS alone, rather than in all the application programs that use the data. A change in the size of the ZIP code field from five to nine digits, for instance, is entered once—even if 20 programs include ZIP codes in output reports. Also, changes in the physical storage of data can be made independent of the logical view or application programs. Thus data may be physically stored in the most efficient manner possible.

Data Standardization Data elements within a data base have standard definitions. For instance, the data element representing the amount of a sale has only one name, meaning, and format. Thus stored data are compatible with every application program that accesses the data base.

One-Time Data Entry and Storage Individual values of data, such as the amount of a sales transaction, are entered into a data base from only one source. Each data element is thus processed only once by direct access. Generally the entered and processed elements are stored in only one location, unless duplicate elements are needed to provide cross-references or faster retrieval. Consequently, redundancy is reduced and inconsistencies among data elements are effectively eliminated. As a result, processing time is minimized, storage requirements are reduced, and data integrity is enhanced.

Data Integration As we have noted, data are organized by means of flexible and logically-related structures called data sets. For instance, a data set might consist of the records from two or more files that are linked together. It might be a collection of two-dimensional tables. Alternatively, it could be a multidimensional structure that consists of the income statements for a firm over 10 years, segmented by the several divisions of the firm and by the several product lines that the firm produces.

Data sets in the data-base approach also integrate the data pertaining to a broad range of activities and entities. Integrating data sets offers two benefits. It enables all affected data sets to be updated simultaneously by entered data elements. As a result, the data sets are synchronized and the data they contain are consistent and highly reliable. Integrated data sets also enable users to obtain needed data more easily and quickly from the data base. Because they often cut across broad areas of a firm, a wide variety of users' needs can be met from the same data base. Comprehensive reports that require data from several areas, such as budgets and product analyses, can be provided more easily.

Shared Data Ownership Related to data integration is the characteristic of shared data ownership. All data within a data base are "owned in common" by the users. Thus users from the accounting function as well as those from marketing and production may draw on the same data base.

Shared ownership, however, does *not* mean that every user's logical view extends to the overall schema of a data base. Instead, a typical user needs access only to that portion of the schema that enables him or her to fulfill assigned responsibilities. The portion of the schema that is of interest to a particular user and reflects the user's view is called a **subschema.** It includes both data content and the relationships among the elements of data. To use an analogy, a schema is like the map of a city, while a subschema is the portion of the map that contains an individual's neighborhood and other points of interest. Like the schema, the subschemas are maintained by the DBMS.

Figure 6-6 illustrates the relationships of subschemas for three Infoage employees with the firm's proposed schema (i.e., collection of logical user views), DBMS,

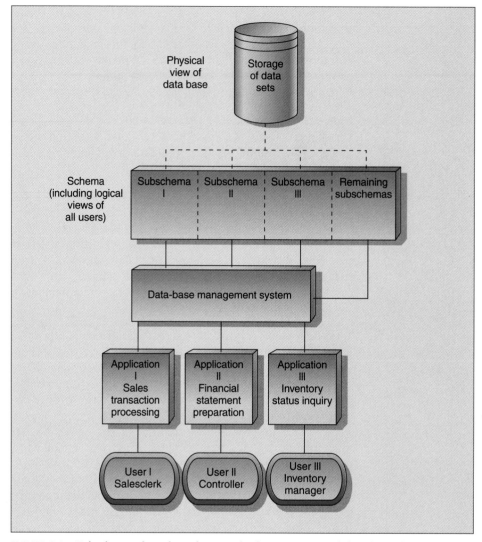

FIGURE 6-6   Subschemas for selected users of Infoage's proposed data base.

and physical view. These three subschemas illustrate the interaction of users with a data base. First, a salesclerk accesses her subschema to process a sales order, which will be achieved by an on-line processing program developed by programmers. Second, the controller obtains financial statements, based on data within his or her subschema. Third, an inventory manager determines the status of an inventory item by reference to his inventory-oriented subschema.

Shared ownership of data prevents functions from blocking the free flow of data to qualified users. At the same time, the subschema concept simplifies the logical view for each individual user and provides appropriate protection against unauthorized uses of the data base. Shared ownership also means that more than a single user may have access to any data element. Thus the subschemas of certain users—such as the controller and inventory manager in the above illustration—may frequently overlap. We should also note that users may extend to parties outside a firm. For instance, a depositor in a bank may have access to a subschema consisting primarily of his or her accounts and related transactions.

Centralized Data Management The DBMS controls and maintains data on a continuous basis. It stands guard over the data base and presents the logical view to users and application programs. Also, the DBMS generally provides data security through such measures as passwords.

Data and the data base are managed centrally by a person known as the **database administrator (DBA).** The DBA has overall responsibility for the data resource and for maintaining the DBMS. Among the functions performed by the DBA are defining data requirements, establishing data structures, and upholding such features of the data-base approach as standardized data elements. The duties of the DBA are discussed more fully in Chapter 18.

BENEFITS OF THE DATA-BASE APPROACH

Through the characteristics just described, we can see that the data-base approach overcomes or significantly corrects the shortcomings of the file-oriented approach. Data redundancies are reduced through the one-time entry and processing of data, as well as by the integration of data sets. Inconsistencies are eliminated, since all data sets affected by transaction data are updated simultaneously. Increased flexibility is provided through data independence and standardization. Accessibility is improved, due to both the sharing of data by users and the extensive relationships among the data. Each of these benefits enables the using firm to achieve the significant results listed in Figure 6-7.

RELEVANCE TO MANAGERS AND ACCOUNTANTS

The greatest benefit of the data-base approach is the ability to provide various managers with information they need, even though much of the needed information may be scattered throughout the data base. For example, a vice-president may need an analysis that draws on production, marketing, and accounting data. Often information is needed that users cannot anticipate when the data base is established. For instance, a president may need information bearing on a proposed merger or joint venture with a competitor. A soundly designed data base with adequate scope can be expected to organize and display this needed information in a timely manner.

Characteristic(s)	Benefit(s) Provided	Result(s) Achieved
Data independence Data standardization	Increased flexibility	Application programs can be changed more easily, more quickly, and less expensively.
One-time data entry Data integration	Reduced redundancy; eliminated inconsistencies	Storage space is conserved, processing time is minimized, and data are highly reliable.
Data integration Shared data ownership	Improved accessibility	Needed information can be obtained faster and more easily; a wider variety of users and their needs can be served.
Centralized data management	Improved data security and coordination	Unauthorized persons are prevented from accessing stored data; data resources are kept updated and available to meet specified requirements of users.

FIGURE 6-7 Correlation of data-base characteristics with the benefits they provide and the positive results the benefits achieve.

SPOTLIGHTING

DATA-CENTERED REPORTING
*at Asea Brown Boveri**

Asea Brown Boveri (ABB) is a global organization composed of over 1300 operating units scattered around the world and headquartered in Switzerland. Its major segments are involved in power distribution and transmission, environmental control, and financial services. One of its most difficult problems is obtaining useful information without stifling local initiative and responsiveness.

The answer discovered by the organization was to develop a centralized reporting system. Thus, it designed a data-based vertical information system called ABACUS (Asea Brown Boveri Accounting and Communication Systems). This financial data-

collection and managerial reporting system is data based and report oriented. It is not intended to serve the accounting processing needs of the operating units. Instead, it collects data from the various operating units concerning sales and profit results and other financial matters on a continuous basis. Then, the information-generating portion of the system provides the senior management of the umbrella organization with a wide array of relevant information—ranging from regional trends, economic fluctuations, and product and process performance to the results achieved by the various profit centers in the different countries. The major benefits have been to speed and improve decision making, especially concerning products and processes.

---

*Andrew C. Boynton, "Achieving Dynamic Stability through Information Technology," *California Management Review* (Winter 1993), p. 68.

The data-base approach is entirely consistent with the accounting equation and should not cause concern to accountants. Since the approach is employed only in computer-based systems, trial balances are not needed to verify the accuracy of postings. Consequently, redundant double-entry procedures are not necessary. Debits and credits can be associated with the accounts to which they pertain, even though each transaction amount is entered only once. Financial statements in accordance with generally accepted accounting principles can be prepared. Linkages can be employed that enable desired accounting or managerial reports to be prepared very quickly from stored data.

Figure 6-8 illustrates the way that a data-base system might handle transactions. A clerk enters a sales transaction by selecting a menu option and keying in the amount of $100, plus other pertinent data. The system then records the $100 (together with other pertinent data concerning the sale) at a single location within the data base; the sales amount is linked to the affected accounts through pointers. When a cash payment is received, a similar procedure is followed. At any time a balance sheet and income statement can be prepared by means of a programmed procedure that accumulates the transactions that affect the various general ledger accounts.

DRAWBACKS OF THE DATA-BASE APPROACH

As with any significant technological advance, the data-base approach exacts certain penalties or costs. Consequently, it is necessary to compare the costs with the benefits before choosing the approach for any particular situation.

Costliness The hardware and software required by the data-base approach are relatively elaborate. Needed hardware usually includes a processor with a large primary

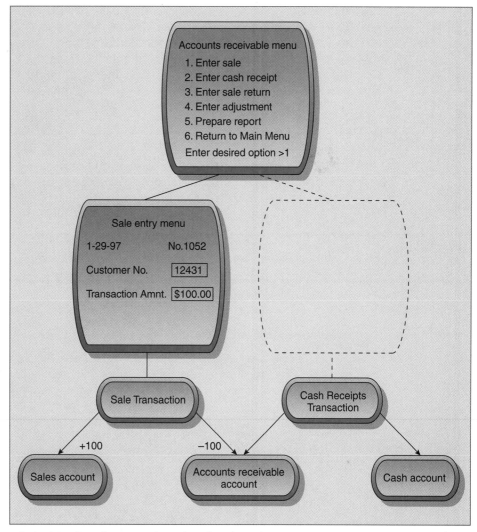

FIGURE 6-8 Sample transactions that show how the accounting equation is maintained via the data-base approach. (Note: To simplify the illustration, other data concerning the sale, as well as the entry for the cash receipt, are omitted.)

storage, direct-access secondary storage devices, and terminals. Needed software includes the DBMS in addition to the application programs. These resources might cost many thousands of dollars in a mainframe computer environment.

Costliness is being overcome, however. When firms migrate from computer mainframes to microcomputers (either stand-alone or networked) or to client/server environments, the costs of both hardware and software are usually low. For instance, a DBMS that is suitable for microcomputer networks costs only a few hundred dollars and is accessible to numerous users.

Initial Inertia Because it is radically different from the file-oriented approach, the data-base approach generally creates complications and resistances. Systems development personnel encounter difficulties in working with an unfamiliar technology. Functional managers exhibit possessiveness with respect to "their" functions' data and resist giving the data to a central data group.

Vulnerability Because a common data base is highly integrated, it is highly vulnerable. A breakdown in hardware or software has a much more severe effect than in a system that has insulated applications and files. If the system and its data base become inoperable for any reason, the applications will cease functioning. Also, extensive data can be lost through errors in programming, foolish or fraudulent acts of users, or destructive acts (e.g., viruses) of unauthorized parties.

DATA-BASE DEVELOPMENT

Data bases can be constructed or developed for a great variety of purposes, such as cataloging books in libraries and storing medical histories in hospitals. Our focus is on the data base for a typical firm—for example, Infoage. Among the questions that must be answered in constructing a data base for such a firm are:

- What data management perspective should be adopted?
- What phases should make up the development process?
- How can the data be organized, both logically and physically, to best serve a variety of users?

EVENTS AS A DATA PERSPECTIVE

A firm's *business events* include both the external economic events affecting the firm, plus its collective internal events or processes. These events constitute the firm's essential and dynamic operations. The firm's managers are responsible for planning and controlling these operations. Thus, events represent perhaps the most sound and enduring perspective for the organization and management of data.

Business events, as we have noted, encompass accounting transactions for which journal entries are made. However, they extend beyond accounting transactions to include operations and activities not entered into the accounting records. Examples of nonaccounting events are the receipt of sales orders and the placement of purchase orders.

In order to achieve its overall objectives, a firm must undertake events that affect resources. It must acquire and employ resources having economic value such as merchandise, facilities, and cash. A firm must also deal with various agents, both external and internal. External agents include customers and suppliers. Internal agents include employees, organizational departments, and functions. For example, Infoage purchases (an event) merchandise inventory (a resource) from a supplier (an agent). It is assisted in this event by a buyer in the purchasing department.

All of the events experienced by a firm, the resources that it employs, and the agents with whom it deals make up its **entities.** These entities thus represent a generalized data framework for its accounting information system.* Figure 6-9 lists a number of entities for Infoage. Note that although accounting transactions appear as events, the processing steps such as posting or updating accounting records are omitted. Nor are accounting records such as accounts receivable ledgers included as separate resources. These accounting "artifacts" simply reflect the status of events,

---

*This data-oriented framework is described and illustrated in William E. McCarthy, "The REA Accounting Model: A Generalized Framework for Accounting Systems in a Shared Data Environment," *The Accounting Review,* July 1982. Some authorities add locations, such as branch outlets and plants, to the term *entities.* Our view is that locations are a special type of resource, especially if owned or leased by the firm in question.

Events	Resources	Agents
Sales order	Cash	Customer
Sale	Merchandise inventory	Supplier
Cash receipt	Building (e.g., warehouse)	Creditor
Purchase	Furniture and fixtures	Stockholder
Obligate to pay	Prospective customer list	Salesperson
Cash disbursement—supplier	Consultant's expertise	Buyer
Cash disbursement—employee		

FIGURE 6-9   Selective entities that pertain to Infoage.

resources, and agents. Thus, they are more soundly incorporated in data sets pertaining to them, e.g., to sales, merchandise inventory, and customers.

Just as the events encompassed by this framework extend beyond accounting transactions, the data perspective concerning each event may be extended. Several dimensions—nonfinancial as well as financial—may be recorded. Thus data concerning each sale might include the region where sold, the salesperson, the type of customer, the products sold, and other data that are useful for sales analysis. Similarly, multiple values might be included in financial events. For example, recorded data relating to fixed asset transactions might include the current values and future expected values of the assets as well as their historical values.

A key feature of the events perspective is that data concerning each individual event should be stored separately in disaggregated form. Events (e.g., sales orders) can thereby be summarized only when needed by particular users and in accordance with their needs. It is not strictly necessary to store the balances of accounts in the various accounting ledgers. Outputs can be produced at any time by assembling the required data from the various interrelated records, tables, or other structures in which they are stored. For instance, summaries of sales can be generated from the collected sales transactions; even financial statements can be provided by reference to the transactions affecting the general ledger accounts.

The events perspective and the features that it implies are not yet adopted by many firms. It represents a change of considerable magnitude from the traditional double-entry accounting transaction approach. Nevertheless, the events perspective is increasingly seen as being necessary to meet rapidly changing information needs of users in this information age.*

PHASES IN DATA-BASE DEVELOPMENT

Developing an integrated data base is a complex project. As in the case of any complex development project, it should be accomplished in phases. Five reasonable phases are planning and determining requirements, modeling the conceptual view, specifying the logical view, selecting the data-base software, and implementing the physical data base.

Planning and Determining Data Requirements   The main purpose of planning is to identify the scope and ascertain the feasibility of a data base. The scope may be a

---

*This change is part of the new wave of accounting, sometimes called the "third wave," which is evolving to meet the time-accelerated demands of the information age. In addition to the data-base approach and expanded events perspective, the new wave also involves the incorporation of value-added aspects of information technology. As we observed in Chapter 1, the first two waves of accounting supported the agricultural and industrial ages.

firm's overall activities or some portion thereof. Assuming that a data base is technically viable, feasibility focuses on (1) whether the benefits of a proposed data base are greater than its costs and (2) whether the data base will be effectively used. Planning can be best achieved if the top management of the firm first clarifies the firm's objectives and strategies. Next, management should evaluate the firm's strategic position with respect to its industry and competitors and develop a long-range strategic plan. On the basis of this organizational plan, and perhaps as a part of it, analysts should prepare a broad, high-level diagram of the firm's entire array of operational activities.

Called an *enterprise diagram*, this broad diagram shows many of the firm's entities, especially the key agents and processes (collected events), and their relationships. It provides a comprehensive slice of reality concerning the firm. Figure 6-10 depicts

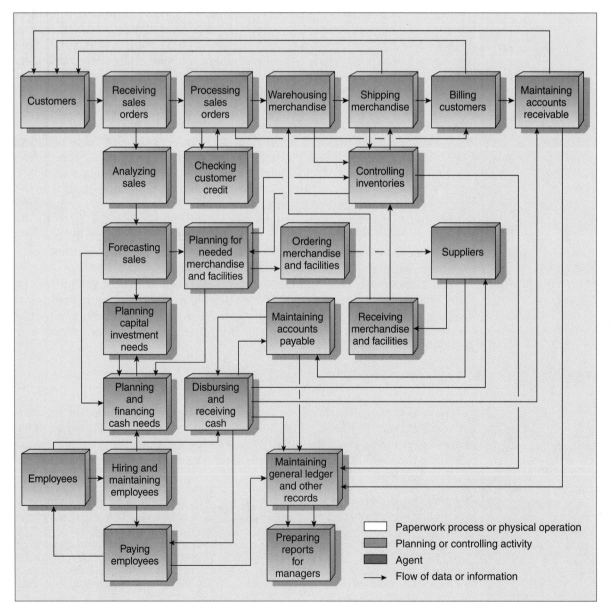

FIGURE 6-10   Enterprise diagram of daily operations and related planning and control activities for Infoage.

an enterprise diagram for Infoage, focusing on the processes related to product sales (but omitting those involved in revenues from services).*

Data requirements include all data needed (1) to reflect the firm's operations and relationships and (2) to provide the myriad users with the information they need to meet their responsibilities. One of the first actions of the designated data-base design team should be to talk with key users, ranging from clerks who operate application programs, to accountants who generate financial reports, to managers who make decisions at all organizational levels.

Modeling the Conceptual View   After data requirements are determined, they should be organized or modeled. While the enterprise diagram provides a beginning, it is too unstructured to be operationally useful. **Data modeling** is a technique of formalizing the data requirements into a conceptual model according to a set of rules. Several data modeling techniques are available, but the most widely used technique leads to a conceptual data model called an **entity-relationship (E-R) diagram.**

An E-R diagram provides an understandable picture of the data base to users, thus allowing better communication between the users and data-base designers. It also identifies the "data nodes" around which a firm's base of data can reasonably be grouped.

The basic arrangement or segment of an E-R diagram is shown in Figure 6-11. Entities I and II are shown as rectangles, while the relationship between them is indicated by a diamond. These two symbols, plus connecting lines, are the only symbols needed to portray an E-R diagram. To develop a full E-R diagram, we assemble a number of E-R segments.

Users such as accountants should definitely be involved in the construction of E-R diagrams, so that they can be assured that the needed data are incorporated. In addition, users can aid in clarifying the constraints, conditions, and policies (i.e., organizational rules) under which the firm functions. For instance, a firm may have a policy that it can acquire several types of merchandise from a single supplier, but it cannot acquire any particular item from more than one supplier. This constraint must be reflected in the E-R diagram. Thus E-R diagrams will differ from firm to firm, even with respect to the same area, e.g., purchasing activities.

An E-R diagram does have limitations. Since it is conceptual or abstract, it does not specify any features (e.g., data locations) of the physical data base. Also, it does not show flows of data within a procedure, as does a system flowchart or data-flow diagram. Instead of showing dynamic data flows, it provides a snapshot of relevant data relationships at a single point in time.

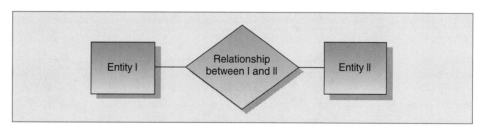

FIGURE 6-11   The basic symbols and arrangement of an entity-relationship diagram.

---

*An enterprise diagram is in effect a block diagram. There is no standard form of this diagram, so various alternatives are acceptable. For instance, a functional decomposition diagram (similar to the high-level structure chart shown in Figure 4-11) may be employed, especially if annotated to indicate the entities involved.

In sum, data modeling is an essential phase in the development of a sound data base. A comprehensive E-R diagram presents a framework of data relationships pertaining to the entire firm. Alternatively, it could focus on a single transaction cycle or organizational function. Within the E-R diagram each segment encompasses a group of data elements that are likely to be needed by one or more users. Thus, segments can be said to represent user views (or a portion of user views).

Specifying the Logical View After constructing the E-R diagram and identifying the needed data attributes for each entity, it is necessary to specify the logical view. The first step within this phase is to select the logical data structure that is most suitable for implementing the conceptual model. Among the logical data structures from which we would choose are the tree, network, relational, or object-oriented structures.

The second step is to construct the schema and subschemas, the logical views, that reflect the selected logical data structure. This step is achieved by mapping from the conceptual model to the logical views. Figure 6-12 contrasts the logical views

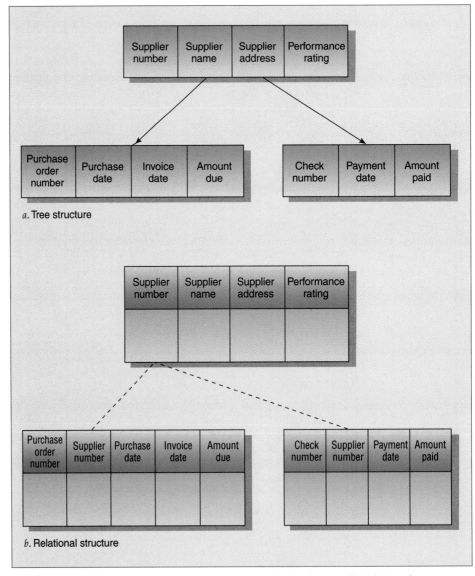

FIGURE 6-12　Alternative forms of a logical view. (*a*) Tree structure. (*b*) Relational structure.

based on alternative data structures. Although the example has been simplified so that only a single subschema is involved, the logical views have differing appearances. The view in Figure 6-12*a* appears as a **data structure diagram,** also called a Bachman diagram. It is similar in appearance to an E-R diagram, except that it omits the diamonds and adds arrowheads to the links. The view in Figure 6-12*b* appears as a collection of tables. Logical views and logical data structures are discussed further in a later section.

During this phase the data elements composing the data base are fully described via a data dictionary, similar to the one illustrated in Figure 4-3. In addition, the primary and secondary keys of the data sets are designated.

Selecting the Data-Base Software After constructing a schema, plus representative subschemas, the next step is to select a particular DBMS to fulfill the logical design. Most firms purchase commercial DBMS packages, rather than developing their own. Generally a commercial package is constructed to reflect one of the logical data structures. For instance, DBMS packages that reflect the relational data structure include DB/2 from IBM, Ingres from Relational Technology, ORACLE from Oracle Corp., Access from Microsoft Corp., and Paradox from Borland International, Inc.

A commercial DBMS typically provides the following basic components and capabilities:

1. A **data definition language (DDL)** that provides the means of describing the physical aspects of the data and logical structure of the data base to the DBMS. These specifications are usually provided via an on-line data dictionary.

2. A **data manipulation language (DML)** that provides the commands (e.g., SORT, GET) by which users can access and manipulate data within the data base. These commands often appear within the application programs employed by users.

3. A **query language** that enables users to query and manipulate the data base without the need for application programs. Two query languages that are widely employed by DBMSs of the relational type are structured query language (SQL) and query-by-example (QBE). Such query languages are designed especially for the retrieval of data by users with no programming knowledge.

4. A **data-base control system (DBCS)** that controls the various components of the DBMS.

In addition to the capabilities provided by the components mentioned above, many DBMS packages allow users to (1) analyze data and create ad hoc or customized reports, (2) create and display graphs, (3) create customized applications via host programming languages, (4) import and export data and images from other packages, (5) perform on-line data editing, (6) purge obsolete data, (7) back up data, (8) maintain other security measures, and (9) interface with communications networks.

In selecting a suitable DBMS commercial package, a firm should decide which capabilities are needed. However, it must also consider such other factors as cost, efficiency, response times to user requests, extent of in-house expertise, and so on.

Implementing the Physical Data Base Among the decisions that must be made in this phase include the type of hardware and storage, the locations of data on the storage medium, and the access methods to employ. Users, such as accountants, have scant interest in the physical aspects of a data base. For instance, the access methods (e.g., pointers, indexes, hashing schemes) are transparent (invisible) to them.

After the physical aspects have been decided, a number of implementation activities must take place. For example, data must be loaded from the previous repositories into the new data base and then tested for correctness. These activities involved in the implementation phase are similar to those for any system development project. General systems development activities are discussed in Chapter 20.

After the implementation is completed, the data base can be said to be operational. Both the implementation and operational phases should be directed by a data-base administrator. Large organizations may split the role into two parts: a technical data-base administrator and a data resources manager. The former is concerned with the DBMS and the physical data base. The latter deals with the logical views of data and the management of data as a resource.

DATA MODELING VIA THE ENTITY-RELATIONSHIP DIAGRAM

Because of their critical role in developing a sound data base, it is necessary to consider how E-R diagrams are constructed. This introductory discussion will be limited to the basic steps, using an expanded E-R diagram relating to the student registration example in Chapter 4.* Based on the developed E-R diagram, we can compile the set of records or tables composing the desired data base.

A step-by-step procedure for constructing an E-R diagram consists of establishing and integrating the entities and relationships, assigning cardinalities, and specifying the data attributes. While this is not the only possible procedure, it provides the easiest way to learn data modeling.

ESTABLISH THE ENTITIES AND RELATIONSHIPS

To begin construction of an E-R diagram, we must clearly establish the scope of processes to be modeled and make a list of the affected entities. Our scope will be the student registration system, for which the key entities are as follows: students and registration clerk (agents), semester registration (event), and semester class. The class may be viewed as a resource since it is of value to students. In addition, the registration system can include the fee payment (event), cash (resource), and cashier (agent). However, in the interest of simplicity we will ignore these added entities.

Next, we construct several segments of an E-R diagram, each showing two entities linked by a relationship as in Figure 6-11. Each segment should include entities that have a direct relationship to each other. Figure 6-13 arrays four segments that may be formed to express direct relationships within the registration activity. The top segment expresses the relationship between students and the event of their registering for classes. The second relationship reflects the link between students and the classes in which they are enrolled. The third segment shows the relationship between the registration event and the resource called *class*. The fourth segment indicates that the registration event is aided by the agents known as registration clerks.

Within the diamonds, which indicate relationships, we may place either a descriptive verb or the linked entity names. In the first segment the verb "requests" in the relationship diamond specifies that the student (an agent) initiates the event. In the third segment the linked names "Student/class" express a relationship between students and classes.

---

*Data modeling with E-R diagrams can lead to very elaborate models when the scope is broad and organizational rules are complex. It is underpinned by principles of semantics and is as much an art as a science. Thus, our presentation of the topic must be simplified. For a full discussion of data modeling, with numerous examples of E-R diagrams, see G. Lawrence Sanders, *Data Modeling* (Danvers, Mass.: Boyd & Fraser Publishing Co., 1995).

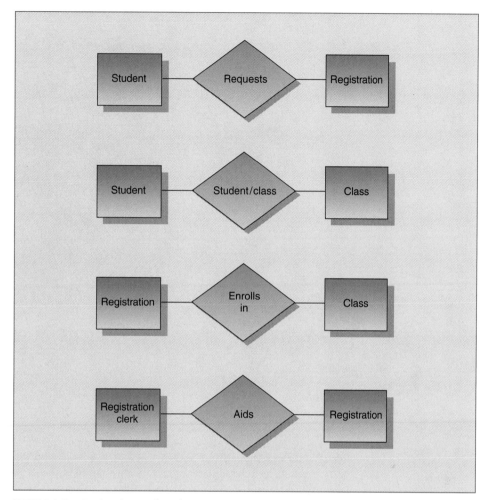

FIGURE 6-13 Basic relationships between entities in the student registration illustration.

Each of these four relationships is of interest to one or more users of the data base being designed. That is, each expresses a user view (or a portion of a user view). For instance, the first, third, and fourth relationships (segments) express views of interest to the registration office, while the second segment designates a view of interest to instructors and academic departments.

INTEGRATE THE ENTITIES AND RELATIONSHIPS

These individual relationships, or user views, need to be integrated to form the structure of the E-R diagram. Figure 6-14 shows how the integrated views might appear.

Integration consists of locating common entities within the relationships of Figure 6-13 and superimposing them. For instance, the first and second relationships are combined by overlapping the boxes marked "Student," the second and third relationships are combined by overlapping the "Class" boxes, and the third and fourth relationships are combined by overlapping the "Registration" boxes. The resulting E-R diagram consists of an event (registration) that links the resource (class) to two agents (student and registration clerk). It also reflects the association between a key agent (student) and the resource (class).

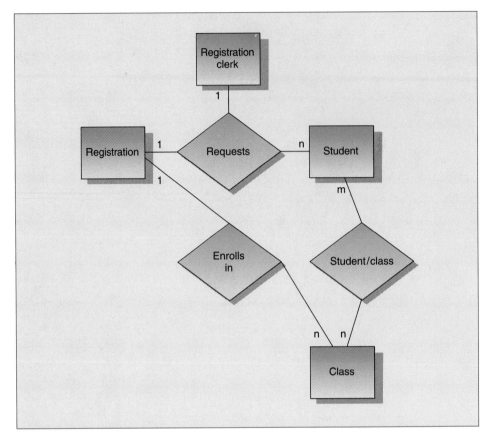

FIGURE 6-14 An entity-relationship diagram pertaining to the student registration illustration. (Note: The relationship reflected by the boxes and diamond at the top is as follows, from right to left: Student requests registration in one or more classes. The registration clerk aids by placing the request via the computer system.)

ASSIGN CARDINALITIES OF THE RELATIONSHIPS

Cardinality refers to the numerical relationship between entities within an E-R diagram. For instance, in Figure 6-14 the 1 by the registration event (entity) and the n by the student entity indicate a 1-n (one-to-many) relationship between the two. Cardinalities are important in designing a data base. They aid in determining the links needed among the files or tables composing the data base. The cardinality of a relationship depends on specific circumstances, such as the organizational constraints and rules affecting an organization.

Three types of cardinality can be assigned:

1. **One-to-one (1:1) relationship,** which exists when one occurrence of an entity is related to one and only one occurrence of a linking entity. This cardinality occurs least frequently; in fact, no one-to-one relationships appear in Figure 6-14. An example would be the relationship between a firm and its incorporation event.

2. **One-to-many (1:N) relationship,** which exists when one entity can have more than one (many) occurrence of a linking entity. For instance, the registration event allows students to enroll in several classes; also, registration involves many students. Note that even though a particular student may register for only

one class, the typical situation is that students will register for more than one class. Thus the one-to-many rather than the one-to-one relationship is appropriately indicated.

3. **Many-to-many (M:N) relationship,** which exists when linking entities can each have more than one occurrence of the other. For example, a student may enroll in more than one class, while each class may have more than one student. Complex processes usually incorporate many-to-many relationships; however, when too many such relationships exist, the data base can become unwieldy.

SPECIFY THE DATA ATTRIBUTES

Specific data elements should be associated with each entity in an entity-relationship diagram. These data elements are the attributes of the entities, as determined by the needs of the users. For example, attributes of a student are the student number, name, and address, plus such other data elements as the student's class standing, date of birth, declared major, and cumulative grade point average.

This completes our discussion of data modeling. In the two following sections we describe how the E-R diagram can be used (1) to map the schema from selected logical data structures and (2) to convert a schema to the tables in a relational data base.

LOGICAL DATA STRUCTURES

In the file-oriented approach, the principal data structure is the flat file composed of fixed-length records. Although flat files are usually retained in integrated data bases, more elaborate data structures have been developed. These logical data structures, which emphasize the associations of related data elements, can be classified as tree, network, relational, and object-oriented.

TREE STRUCTURE

The **tree structure,** also called the *hierarchical structure*, expresses hierarchical relationships among stored data. A fully developed tree structure looks a bit like an upside-down tree. Instead of branches, a tree structure consists of data nodes and paths. The data nodes are usually records or data elements and the paths are pointers that explicitly link from one file to another.

The tree structure is relatively simple. It is best suited to a situation in which the focus of concern is a single entity, such as an employee or a job order or an inventory item. Because of the explicit links established by pointers, a DBMS can rapidly access data within a tree structure.

At the top of the structure is the *root node.* In using a tree structure to retrieve data, the only means of entry is through the root node. Extending downward from the root node are explicit access paths that connect to data nodes at one or more lower levels.

Example Figure 6-15 illustrates a simple tree structure, consisting of two levels. The root node is a record of the type found in a customer accounts receivable master file. It thus contains a collection of data elements relating to the customer as an entity, beginning with the customer number as the primary key. The data node at the lower level is a record of the type found in a sales invoice transaction file. The

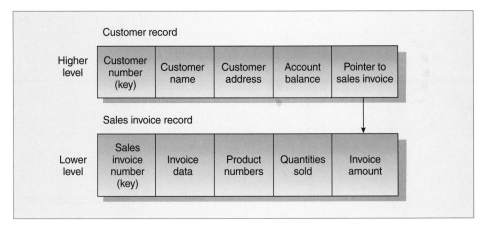

FIGURE 6-15   A set of two record types.

relationship rule is that a single customer can have one or more sales, and hence sales invoices. The pictured structure allows the following questions to be answered: What are the details of sales made to a particular customer? What is an analysis of sales, broken down according to customers?

An example of a specific occurrence appears in Figure 6-16. A sales manager who desires to know the details of sales made to Nancy P. Ragsdale would enter the customer number 5638 into his or her microcomputer, plus a code for a sales inquiry. The DBMS would access Ms. Ragsdale's record, probably by means of an index that cross-references customer numbers. Then it would locate the two relevant sales records by means of the embedded pointers. The application retrieval program would

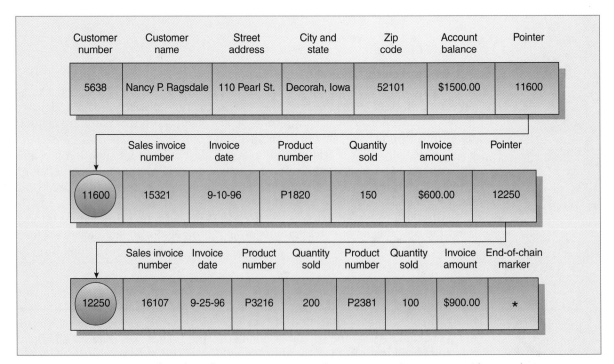

FIGURE 6-16   An occurrence based on the set in Figure 6-15, showing a specific customer with two sales.

receive the data concerning the sales from the DBMS and display the results on the screen of the user's monitor. The disk addresses (11600 and 12250), being of no interest to the user, are transparent to him or her.

NETWORK STRUCTURE

Like the tree structure, the **network structure** establishes explicit access paths or links among data nodes. In contrast to the tree structure, however, the network structure (1) allows any data node to be linked to any other node, (2) allows entry at more points than a single root node, and (3) requires at least one subordinate data node to have two or more owner nodes. Consequently, a network structure offers a more realistic structuring of the complex relationships encountered by the typical firm. It allows a greater variety of information to be accessed quickly.

Simple Network Example In Figure 6-17 an additional record has been added to the set shown in Figure 6-15. The resulting diagram thus shows two record types, the customer and salesperson, to be *owners* of the sales invoices, called *members*. In a network diagram the arrows point from the owner records to member records.

The structure reflects the recognition that the salesperson who makes a sale is related to the sales data. This relationship is due to the fact that a salesperson is paid a commission based on the amount of the sale. Since the sales invoice record has more than one owner record, the structure fulfills the criteria for being a network. Also, being an owner record within a network, the salesperson record can serve as another entry point. Furthermore, it has a one-to-many relationship with the sales invoice record. As a consequence, the structure enables a user to inquire about recent sales made by salesperson 287. Upon accessing the record for salesperson 287, the network DBMS would then follow embedded pointers to access data from the sales invoices that reflect recent sales.

Complex Network Example Figure 6-18*a* portrays a network structure pertaining to students and classes. This diagram is a mapping of the many-to-many relationship shown in the E-R diagram in Figure 6-14. Since student records and class records are owner records, both can serve as entry points for particular data retrieval purposes. Entering via student records enables course schedules to be quickly printed for enrolled students (one group of users); entering via class records enables class enrollment lists to be quickly printed for instructors (another group of users). Figure 6-18*b* shows simplified occurrences of this many-to-many relationship. For instance, Able's course schedule would specify Math 100 and English 100. Conversely, the Math 100 class has two students: Able and Charlene.

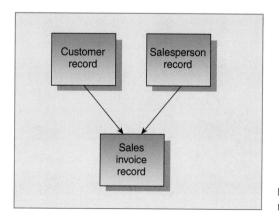

FIGURE 6-17 Examples of a simple network structure.

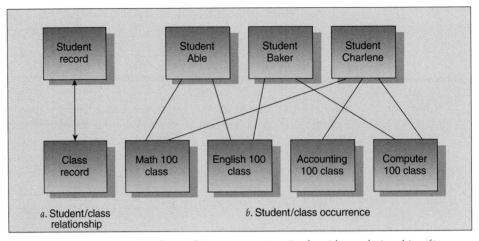

a. Student/class relationship   *b.* Student/class occurrence

FIGURE 6-18 Many-to-many relationship structures. (*a*) Student/class relationship. (*b*) Student/class occurrence.

A network that contains one or more many-to-many relationships is known as a *complex network*. It may be contrasted with the *simple network* shown in Figure 6-17, which contains one-to-many relationships only. Many-to-many relationships in a network DBMS cannot be implemented as diagrammed in Figure 6-18*a*. Instead, they must be converted into equivalent one-to-many relationships by means of *intersection records*. By forming a linkage between two entities with a many-to-many cardinality, an intersection record enables the DBMS to enter the structure via either record type and to gain access to data in the other record. Stated another way, an intersection record is an index that provides cross-reference data. In Figure 6-19 the student/class record is an intersection record that converts the many-to-many relationship shown in Figure 6-18*a* to two one-to-many relationships. This intersection record contains two fields, one for student identification number (e.g., 3456) and one for class code (e.g., ACC 100).

Logical View for the Student Registration Illustration Look again at the E-R diagram in Figure 6-14. If a network is selected as the data structure, the next step is to map the schema. This consists of (1) identifying the record types of interest and (2) specifying the paths. Figure 6-20 shows the data structure diagram that reflects a simplified network schema for the student registration data base. The student, class, and

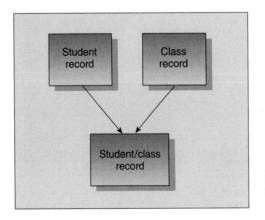

FIGURE 6-19 Two one-to-many relationships derived from the many-to-many relationship in Figure 6-18*a*.

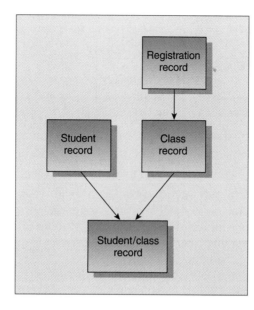

FIGURE 6-20 A data structure (Bachman) diagram that portrays a network logical view (schema) for the student registration illustration.

registration records are owner records, while the student/class record is a member (as well as an intersection) record. The class record is a member record as well as an owner record.

User views or subschemas may be carved from the schema in Figure 6-20. For instance, a subschema for an instructor might consist of the class, student/class, and student records, with their linkages. A subschema for the registrar might consist of the registration and class records, with their linkage. Note that these two subschemas overlap, in that both include the class record.

RELATIONAL STRUCTURE

The **relational structure** uses tables, rather than linked data nodes, as the means of reflecting the overall logical view within a data base. These tables, or *relations*, are two-dimensional data structures. Each table resembles a flat file. However, they are more sophisticated than files. Being constructed according to the rules of a mathematical branch called relational algebra, tables can be manipulated in a variety of ways. They thereby enable users to create a multitude of user views, so that information needs can be satisfied as they arise.

Logical View for the Student Registration Illustration Assume that the relational structure is selected instead of the network in the student registration illustration. As in the case with the network logical view, constructing the relational logical view involves two steps: (1) determining the needed set of tables and (2) establishing the means by which they are associated or linked. The tables needed in a relational data base generally correspond to the records incorporated in a network data base. Thus, four tables are needed to reflect the main entities and the basic relationship between students and classes. For a soundly designed data base, each table should be simplified and focused with respect to the attributes that it contains. Tables and the data they contain are associated in a relational data base by means of implicit links, rather than explicit access paths. (These links are described later).

Table Composition A **table** is composed of rows (called *tuples* in relational algebra) and columns. Each row is of equal length and is similar to a record in a flat file, in

Student number	Student name	Class standing	Cumulative GPA
186531829	Molly Bloom	Junior	2.97
293652565	George Stucky	Sophomore	3.16
296831432	William Rose	Senior	2.58
334527647	Jennifer Olum	Junior	3.21

FIGURE 6-21   A student table in a relational data base.

that it contains the attribute values of one instance of the entity to which the table pertains. An important property of the table is that each row in a table must be unique. Each column contains the values of one attribute of the entity. The range of values that can appear in a column are called the *domain* of the attribute. Usually the values that appear in the leftmost column are the table or primary keys.

Figure 6-21 shows a table of students. Each row contains the values of four attributes pertaining to a particular student, e.g., Molly Bloom. Each column contains the values for one attribute that are within a prescribed range. For instance, the cumulative grade point average (GPA) can range from zero to 4.0. The student number is the primary key for this student table; in the figure the student listings are arranged by student number in ascending order.

Advantages   The relational structure offers several advantages to business firms. Tables are easy for users such as managers and accountants to understand. The structure is extremely flexible, since any table can serve as a point of access for retrieving data, and since there are no explicit links among tables. Thus a greater variety of information requests from users can be satisfied than with the network structure. Users can often obtain answers to inquiries that were unanticipated when the tables were constructed. Most relational DBMSs allow English-like commands or menus to be employed when requesting information. Thus the data base is readily accessible to nonprogrammer users, in contrast to the tree or network structured data bases. Finally, it is not necessary to rebuild portions of the structure to include new relationships, as is the case with tree and network structures. For these reasons relational DBMSs are being used exclusively in microcomputer systems and client/server systems and are rapidly displacing tree and network DBMSs in mainframe computer systems.

Drawbacks   One serious drawback of the relational structure is its relative inefficiency. Underlying physical structures consume huge quantities of storage space; thus they cannot respond as quickly to inquiries as either tree or network structures. Also, more redundancy tends to appear in the logical structures, due to the need for duplicate data that provides the implicit links mentioned earlier.

Since access times for retrieving data tend to be slower, the relational structure is less suitable for high-volume transaction processing applications. While these limitations become quite noticeable when large data bases are involved, they should diminish as faster processing speeds become available. Also, upgrades of relational DBMSs (e.g., DB/2) are incorporating features of the network structure, so that transaction processing will be faster and more efficient.

Because relational data bases have become so prevalent, their features deserve more attention. Thus expanded coverage is provided in the final section of this chapter.

OBJECT-ORIENTED DATA-BASE STRUCTURES

The relational structure has been implemented for less than two decades. During this period its data retrieval features and user-friendliness have been improved through upgrades. However, its tables are limited in various respects concerning the data they organize. Thus an **object-oriented data base** is emerging as a possible contender. It is more than a new type of data structure, hence the use of the term *data base*. Currently, object-oriented data bases are still undergoing development and refinement, and only the more technically sophisticated firms are applying the concepts in actual data bases. Nevertheless, its basic features should be examined, so that we can be aware of likely future improvements in data-base management.*

Object-Oriented Data Modeling   The object-oriented data base is a collection of **objects,** tangible or intangible things that can be uniquely classified. In the context of a business firm, objects can include customers, departments, contracts, reports, documents, ledger accounts, and so on. Objects are grouped into **object classes,** with each member of the class having the same set of attributes. Objects and object classes are similar to entities, in that they can represent the enduring aspects of a firm. However, they are broader in scope. Thus objects and object classes enable data models to be developed that are richer in detail, reflect multiple interrelationships, and hence provide more realism.

Classes of objects can be modeled by a technique similar to the E-R diagram. Figure 6-22 portrays an object-oriented data model for a selective portion of an academic institution's data base.[†] It consists of a nested structure of object classes, called *class hierarchies*. Superclasses are at the top of the hierarchies, with classes and subclasses being linked below. As we can see, this object-oriented data model is similar to a tree or network data structure, in that it is navigational. That is, it retrieves data to answer inquiries by traversing along predefined paths. Instead of moving from owner records to member records, the object-oriented data model moves among linked class nodes.

In Figure 6-22 each class node contains the name and attributes of a class. (It also contains methods, to be discussed later.) The names of classes are university-person, student, staff, faculty, university, academic department, undergraduate, graduate, course catalog, and class enrollment. Movement within the class hierarchies is downward from superclass (e.g., university-person) to class (e.g., student, staff, faculty), and then to subclass (e.g., undergraduate, graduate). In addition, classes form sidewise associations, such as the association of university-person with university, and faculty with academic department.

Although each class node contains the attributes pertaining to the class, only a sampling is shown in the figure. Thus the attributes for university-person are shown to be social security number, name, address, and phone number. Values of the attributes are stored for all instances, e.g., for each member of the university community.

Advantages of Object-Oriented Data Bases   In addition to the increased realism and richness that it offers, an object-oriented data base provides important advantages.

---

*For an extended discussion of developing a useful object-oriented data base and accounting system, see Pai-Cheng Chu, "An Object-Oriented Approach to Modeling Financial Accounting Systems," *Accounting, Management, and Information Technology* (January-March 1992), pp. 39–56.

[†]Certain aspects have been omitted from the figure, such as the cardinalities of relationships among classes.

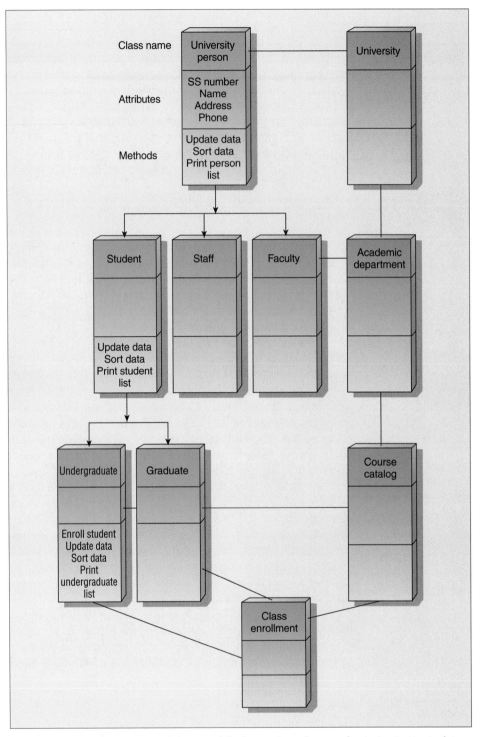

FIGURE 6-22   An object-oriented data model of a portion of an academic institution's data base.

These advantages are mainly due to the features of encapsulation and inheritance that are embodied in object-oriented data bases.

1. *Encapsulation* consists of storing procedures or operations, called *methods*, with the data to which the methods relate. It thus brings together the data attributes and operations pertaining to objects and object classes. Figure 6-22 shows a sprinkling of methods in the bottom portion of selected class nodes. The methods shown represent programmed instructions for updating the data pertaining to university-persons, including undergraduate students. Because of encapsulation, the application programs that access the data base can be greatly simplified. Thus programming errors are likely to be reduced.

2. *Inheritance* allows subclasses to inherit methods and/or data from higher classes within a class hierarchy. For example, the student, staff, and faculty classes can inherit the "updating the data" methods from the university-person superclass. (Thus in Figure 6-22 it is redundant to show methods in the student and undergraduate class nodes.) The major advantage of the inheritance feature is that programmed instructions are reusable. Libraries can be maintained of programs relating to commonly used classes. These standardized programs, which would be fully tested and applied, can thereby greatly reduce reprogramming efforts. They can be as useful to the information age as standard machine parts have been to the industrial age.

Object-Oriented Implementation   After an object-oriented data model has been developed and accepted, much of the design effort is completed. It is not necessary to map a schema or to devise tables, since object-oriented software is available. Suitable software programming languages include Smalltalk and C++, while object-modeling technology includes Access Object Oriented Data Base from Microsoft. Of course, certain implementation activities must be performed for the object-oriented data base to become operational. It is necessary to select the object-oriented language and hardware, code and test the software modules, and load data into the data base.

RELATIONAL DATA BASES

In the introduction to relational data structures, we discussed the composition of a single table and the reasons why relational data bases have become so popular. This expanded treatment of relational data bases considers the construction of multiple tables, the retrieval of data from relational tables, and the normalization of tables that function with each other in a relational data base.

CONSTRUCTING MULTIPLE TABLES IN A RELATIONAL DATA BASE

A relational data base consists of multiple tables, in some cases hundreds or even thousands. Each table is composed of fixed-length rows and two or more columns, with the primary key column being in the leftmost position. One trait of a primary key is that it provides uniqueness to the data with which it is associated. Thus each row of a table (which contains the values of an instance) is guaranteed to be unique, due to the value of its primary key. To the right of the primary key, the remaining columns contain relevant attributes. In fact, a table can best be described in terms of its attributes. Assume that a customer table has the following attributes: customer

SPOTLIGHTING

DATA MANAGEMENT
at Playtex Apparel*

Playtex Apparel, a global manufacturer of intimate apparel, has the leading market position in the industry in the United States and several European countries. To increase its market share in all countries, it realized in 1992 that it needed to react more quickly to market trends. Its system at that time involved an arrangement with a service bureau, which had become overwhelmed with queries. Turnaround time to answer a query was about two weeks.

To provide faster responses, and hence better decision support, Playtex installed a relational data-base product called Red Brick Warehouse, which functions under the control of a Hewlett-Packard 9000 server located in Stamford, Conn. The resulting data-based system provides much improved support, quickly transmitting information to users that best meets their needs. For example,

sales users can receive sales data broken down by customer, market, retail class, product type, style, and color. Users in all areas can make ad hoc queries, such as, "Who were the top ten customers by sales amounts?" For greater user friendliness, a front-end query package (Data Prism from Brio Technology) provides a graphical interface and handles structured query language (SQL) commands.

Playtex decided that its transaction processing needs are significantly different from the decision support needs. Thus, for transaction processing it installed an Oracle relational data-base management system. It processes all new orders, shipments, billing, account maintenance, and product maintenance applications. Also installed was a client/server system that links to a wide-area network. Thus, transaction processing is performed faster and more efficiently, and clerical users can access individual transactions and entities very easily.

*Sandra Tucker, "At Playtex Apparel, Two Database Management Systems Are Better Than One," *Network Computing* (September 1993), pp. 114–115.

---

number, customer name, customer address, and current account balance. Using relational notation, this table might be described as follows:

`CUSTOMER (CUST-NO., CUST-NAME, CUST-ADD, CURBAL)`

Note that the primary key is underlined and all attributes are expressed in terms of the programmed variable names they have been assigned.

How can a designer determine the attributes to include within a table? There is no easy answer, but several guidelines can be offered. The attributes should all directly relate to the entity that the table concerns; any attribute not dependent on the entity should be excluded. A table should therefore be simple and focused. Technically speaking, it should be normalized (as we show later). If the data base is being converted from a network structure to a relational structure, the data elements in the records provide a starting point. Since the users best understand their data needs, they should be interviewed.

A user can access any table in a relational data base through commands given to the DBMS. Moreover, a significant advantage of the relational data base is flexibility—the ability to gain access to the data in two or more tables easily and without the need for explicitly specified paths. Data in two or more tables are accessed by means of implicit links. Two types of links are (1) foreign keys and (2) cross-reference tables that implement relationships. A **foreign key** is the primary key of one table, which is inserted or embedded in a column of another table that is logically associated with the first table. A *relationship table*, akin to an intersection record, provides cross-references because it contains the primary keys of two tables.

Linkages through foreign keys are illustrated in Figure 6-23. This figure is a logical view or subschema for such users as accounts receivable personnel. It shows three tables: a customer table, a sales invoice table that contains data in the header portions of invoices, and an invoice line-item table that contains the data in the bodies of invoices. Data concerning the header are placed in a separate table from the line-item table. Two separate tables are desirable, since the header table deals with sales made to customers (events) and the line-item table concerns items of inventory that are sold (resources).

Two foreign keys appear in the figure. The customer number, which is the primary key of the customer table, is inserted as a foreign key in the sales invoice table. Similarly, the sales invoice number, the primary key of the sales invoice table, is inserted as a foreign key in the invoice line-item table.

Since the customer table and sales invoice table are linked by the common customer number columns, their data may be joined together for accessing by a user.

CUSTOMER TABLE

Customer number (key)	Customer name	Customer address	Current account balance
1001	Jane Grett	816 Western Ave., Fort Worth, TX	1500.00
1002	Tom Moon	1272 College Dr., Pittsburgh, PA	670.00
(A) 1004	Kathy Popel	6050 Three Sisters Way, Bend, OR	895.00

SALES INVOICE TABLE

Sales invoice number (key)	Customer number (foreign key)	Invoice date	Shipping date	Total sale amount
250	1576	11/03/97	11/06/97	1025.00
(B) 251	(A) 1004	11/04/97	11/06/97	535.00
252	1891	11/04/97	11/07/97	728.00

INVOICE LINE ITEM TABLE

Line number (key)	Sales invoice number*	Item number	Unit price	Quantity sold
1	250	34A	50.00	10
2	250	16B	100.00	5
1	251	27B	40.00	6
2	(B) 251	35C	80.00	1
3	251	14D	100.00	2

*Sales invoice number is a foreign key as well as being part of a concatenated primary key.

FIGURE 6-23 A logical view, consisting of three tables, in a relational data base, with implied linkages between.

The sales invoice and line-item tables may also be joined. Consequently, a user can quickly have access to all sales data pertaining to a customer. To see this, follow the linkage for customer number 1004 (marked by a circled A) to the linkage for the sales invoice pertaining to that customer (marked by a circled B). This latter linkage shows that three items were sold on invoice 251, and that the quantities involved were 6, 1, and 2, respectively.

Two additional points are worth noting:

1. The foreign key is inserted in the table that is subordinate to the table containing the linking primary key. In network structure terminology, the foreign key is in the member table (e.g., the sales invoice table), while the linking primary key is in the owner table (e.g., the customer table).

2. Sometimes the primary key must be a combination of two separate keys in order to provide unique values. This type of combined key is called a *concatenated key*. An example appears in the invoice line-item table, where the primary key consists of the line number plus the sales invoice number. Using either number alone would not yield unique values for all rows. Note that the item number could replace the line number as a part of the primary key.

CONSTRUCTING TABLES FOR THE STUDENT REGISTRATION ILLUSTRATION

Figure 6-24 represents the set of tables composing the logical view of a relational structure for the student registration activity. Only the column headings with the attribute names are shown, but you can visualize data being stored in rows within each table. The four tables parallel the four records in the logical view of a network structure, as shown in Figure 6-20. Attributes that appear in the tables are suggestive only. Most likely you could specify additional attributes, e.g., student address, class enrollment limit, registration clerk name.

Both types of links are illustrated. The student number appears as a foreign key in the registration table. The student/class table provides cross-referencing ties between the student and class tables, tables that correspond to two owner records in the network schema.

Users can retrieve a variety of needed information from this relational schema. For instance, a student can receive a list of the classes for which he or she is enrolled; an instructor can receive a list of the students taking a particular class; the registrar can obtain lists of registered students and total number of enrolled semester hours.

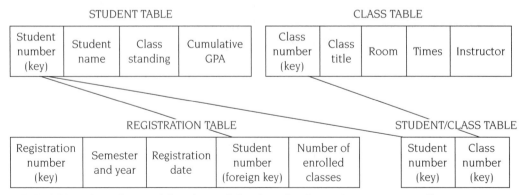

FIGURE 6-24   A logical view of the relational data base for the student registration illustration.

RETRIEVING DATA FROM RELATIONAL TABLES

A relational DBMS greatly facilitates the retrieval of stored data. In part this retrieval facility is due to the flexibility of the tables composing the data base. Another reason is because a relational DBMS supports three powerful manipulative and retrieval functions. These functions are performed by **relational operators,** which specify particular operations to be performed in order to create new tables. The relational operators are stated in commands or inquiries entered by users of the relational data base.

We can call these three basic relational operators by the names JOIN, SELECT, and PROJECT, although actual names may vary from DBMS to DBMS. A JOIN creates a new table by joining the values of rows and columns extracted from two tables, using the common columns created by primary and foreign keys. A SELECT creates a new table by extracting the values of certain rows from a table. A PROJECT creates a new table by extracting the values of certain columns. While a JOIN is the most powerful operator, the other two are extremely useful in providing precise information requested by users.

Example Involving Relational Operators   An extended example should clarify the retrieval capabilities that these relational operators afford. A manufacturing firm has installed a human resources relational DBMS. It consists of the four tables shown in Figure 6-25. Three of the tables concern employee, skill, and job entities. These

Skill

Skill No.	Skill Description	No. of Vacancies
10	Lathe operator	0
20	Carpenter	1
30	Arc welder	0
40	Lab technician	0
50	Truck driver	2
60	Mechanic	0

Employee

Employee No.	Employee Name	SSN	Age
1000	Brown	xxx-xx-xxxx	23
2000	Smith	"	26
3000	Kimble	"	30
4000	Jones	"	32
5000	White	"	45
6000	Green	"	39
7000	Black	"	37

Employee/Skill

Employee No.	Skill No.
1000	30
2000	40
3000	50
3000	60
4000	10
5000	20
6000	60
7000	20
7000	30

Job

Job No.	Skill No.	Job Description	Accum. Cost
100	20	Lab facility	30000
100	40	Lab facility	30000
100	50	Lab facility	30000
100	60	Lab facility	30000
200	10	Filter system	14500
200	30	Filter system	14500
200	60	Filter system	14500

FIGURE 6-25   Tables in a skill/employee relational data base. (Based on an example in Dan C. Kneer and Joseph W. Wilkinson, "DBMS: Do You Know Enough to Choose?" *Management Accounting* (September 1984), pp. 34–38. Copyright © 1984 by National Association of Accountants, Montvale, N.J. All rights reserved. Reprinted with permission.)

entities may be classified as an agent, a resource, and an event, respectively. Two linkages are provided: (1) A foreign key in the job table (skill number) that allows the job table to be joined with the skill table. (2) An employee/skill table that contains the primary keys of the employee and skill tables.

Let us assume that the personnel manager needs answers to a variety of concerns. Thus, she enters via the user interface the following inquiries, specifying the data elements to be displayed on her monitor and the order in which they are to be arranged:

1. Which employees, identified by number, possess skill number 30?
2. Who are the firm's employees, identified by number and name?
3. Which employees, identified by number *and* name, possess skill number 20?
4. Which skills, identified by number and description, are assigned to job 200, identified by description?
5. Which skills, identified by description, are possessed by employee Kimble?

Figure 6-26 displays the new tables created in response to these inquiries. Each is discussed by reference to its inquiry number.

Inquiry 1. The upper-left table is created by the SELECT operator, which extracts the requested rows from the employee/skill table.

New Table Based
on Inquiry 1

Skill No.	Employee No.
30	1000
30	7000

New Table Based
on Inquiry 2

Employee No.	Employee Name
1000	Brown
2000	Smith
3000	Kimble
4000	Jones
5000	White
6000	Green
7000	Black

New Table Based
on Inquiry 3

Skill No.	Employee No.	Employee Name
20	5000	White
20	7000	Black

New Table Based
on Inquiry 4

Job Description	Skill No.	Skill Description
Filter system	10	Lathe operator
Filter system	30	Arc welder
Filter system	60	Mechanic

New Table Based
on Inquiry 5

Employee Name	Skill Description
Kimble	Truck driver
Kimble	Mechanic

FIGURE 6-26 Responses to inquiries generated by using the data base in Figure 6-25.

Employee number	Employee name	Skill number	SSN	Age
1000	Brown	30	XXX-XX-XXXX	23
2000	Smith	40	"	26
3000	Kimble	50	"	30
3000	Kimble	60	"	30
4000	Jones	10	"	32
5000	White	20	"	45
6000	Green	60	"	39
7000	Black	20	"	37
7000	Black	30	"	37

Notes: 1. The PROJECT operator extracts the left three columns as requested, and moves the skill number column to the leftmost position (in accordance with the wording of the request). 2. The SELECT operator extracts the data from the sixth and eighth rows, based on skill number 20 listed in the request.

FIGURE 6-27   The temporary table formed by the JOIN in Inquiry 3, from which the requested data are obtained via PROJECT and SELECT operators.

Inquiry 2. The upper-right table is created by the PROJECT operator, which extracts the requested first two columns from the employee table.

Inquiry 3. The middle-left table is created by first using a JOIN operator to form a new temporary table from the employee and employee/skill tables. It is necessary to join the tables in order to bring together all three of the data elements—employee number, employee name, and skill number—in the inquiry. This resulting newly created table is shown in Figure 6-27. It has the same number of rows (nine) as in the employee/skill table, and the same number of columns (five) as in the employee table. That is, a table created by a JOIN assumes the larger of both the number of rows and columns. Thus the resulting table is somewhat redundant in that it repeats certain data (e.g., employee names when they have more than one skill). Note, however, that the common columns (i.e., the employee number) only appear once. From the new table a PROJECT operator extracts the three relevant columns and a SELECT operator extracts the two relevant rows, as indicated by shading in Figure 6-27.

Inquiry 4. The middle-right table is created by first using a JOIN operator to form a new table from the skill table and job table. A temporary table is created, based on the skill number. From this table a PROJECT operator extracts the three relevant columns and a SELECT operator extracts the three relevant rows for the requested table. As requested, the table lists the job description (filter system), rather than the job number.

Inquiry 5. The bottom table is created by first using the JOIN operator twice to combine the skill and employee/skill tables and then to combine this newly formed table with the employee table. Using the second temporary table, a PROJECT operator extracts the two relevant columns and a SELECT operator extracts the two relevant rows for the resulting table.

Query Languages for a Relational Data Base   The three relational operators just illustrated represent the minimum functions that are supported by a relational data base. In effect, they are a subset of a larger interface by which users can manipulate data. Two types of user interfaces, called *query languages*, are structured query language (SQL) and query-by-example (QBE). Both allow users of relational data bases to retrieve data based on specified questions (which are called inquiries or queries). In addition, they allow users to insert data into table rows, to delete data from tables, to create new table columns, to perform computations, to create reports, and so on. Two brief examples of inquiries or queries based on a student table should clarify the differences between these two query languages.

SQL requires the use of commands, such as SELECT, to specify the terms of the inquiry. If a user wants a listing of all students who are seniors and majoring in accounting—with columns including the student numbers, names, and grade point averages—the following SQL expressions might be entered on a query screen:

```
SELECT    SSN, NAME, GPA
FROM          STUD.TABL
WHERE     STANDING = SENIOR
          AND MAJOR = ACCOUNTING
```

QBE employs gridlike query windows, into which users enter examples of the form of the desired answer. The result is displayed in a special table, sometimes called a *dynaset*. If the abovementioned student listing is needed, the following headings would be entered in columns within the query window:

```
SSN    NAME    GPA    STANDING    MAJOR
```

On a criteria line in the query window the user would enter "SENIOR" within the STANDING column and "ACCOUNTING" within the MAJOR column.

NORMALIZING TABLES IN A RELATIONAL DATA BASE

Certain rules should be followed when mapping from an E-R diagram to the tables composing a relational data base. We have already referred to the rules of table composition. Other rules, such as restricting the focus to single entities, also apply. When all the appropriate rules have been followed, a table is said to be normalized. Our examples in Figures 6-23 and 6-24 showed sets of normalized tables, although they were not described as such.

Definition   **Normalization** is a process of decomposition, by which data structures are transformed into tables having the following characteristics:

1. Each row is fixed in length. For instance, the table does not allow repeating groups, such as the data that pertain to several lines in a body of a sales invoice. To meet this condition, it was necessary in Figure 6-23 to separate the invoice line items from the sales invoice header data.

2. Each row contains values that are unique. Usually the leftmost column contains a primary key, such as a customer number, that satisfies the uniqueness requirement.

3. All of the attributes are functionally dependent on (pertain directly to) a single entity, such as a customer or a sale.

4. All of the attributes are independent of other attributes in the table (except the primary key). Assume, for instance, that an inventory table includes the name of the sole supplier from which the inventory item is acquired. If in addition all the other data are brought into the table concerning that supplier, such as address and phone number, the table becomes unnormalized.

The underlying design of a relational data base should be based on normalized tables. They reduce redundancy in the data base and enable data to be updated easily. They also facilitate changes within tables, e.g., the addition of a new student in a student table.

Conversely, unnormalized tables are generally undesirable. They tend to increase the degree of redundancy and the difficulty of updating and making changes. Also, audit trails can sometimes be disrupted if unnormalized tables are employed.

The job table in Figure 6-25 reflects the degree of redundancy that is typical of an unnormalized table. The job number, job description, and accumulated cost are repeated several times. We can normalize the table by splitting it into two tables. One table will focus exclusively on jobs if the skill number column is eliminated. In addition to the job number column, this table is limited to job description and accumulated cost columns. It is thereby reduced to two rows. The other table focuses on the relationship between jobs and skills and includes job numbers and skill numbers. It is needed for cross-referencing since each job requires more than one skill.

Unnormalized tables are not always to be avoided, however. On occasion they can be useful. Consider class lists, which are needed several times a semester for each class in a university. These outputs require that two or more normalized tables be joined in order to draw together the needed data. If the unnormalized table based on join operations is retained in the data base, the times required to generate the class lists can be shortened. The overall time saving can be significant if numerous outputs and tables with many rows are involved.

Student Registration Illustration Due to its importance, we will trace through an extended example of normalization based on student registration. Our illustration begins with an extremely unnormalized table and concludes with a set of normalized tables.* Figure 6-28 shows a portion of an unnormalized table for students and the

Student number (key)	Student name	Class standing	Cumulative GPA	Course number	Course title	Course room
123456789	CD White	Junior	2.88	ACC200	Cost accounting	BA212
234567891	SP Adams	Sophomore	3.17	BUS300	Communications	BA350

Course time	Course instructor	Instructor's department	Course number	Course title	Course room
MW10:00	Monroe	Accounting	ENG300	English literature	LA162
MW11:00	Pugh	Business	MAT250	Calculus I	LA210

Course time	Course instructor	Instructor's department
MW2:00	Hart	English
TTH8:00	James	Engineering

FIGURE 6-28   An unnormalized table containing data relating to student courses.

---

*When we refer to normalized tables, we mean the *third normal* form, as defined by E. F. Cobb. See C. J. Date, *An Introduction to Database Systems*, 4th ed., Addison-Wesley: Reading, Mass., 1986, p. 99. Although some authorities prefer the Boyce-Codd normal form, which is quite similar but does involve the elimination of one additional redundant situation, the third normal form is widely employed. We should also note that while normalization is most frequently applied to relational data bases, its concepts also pertain to tree and network structures.

Student number (key)	Course number (key)	Student name	Class standing	Cumulative GPA	Course title	Course room	Course time	Course instructor	Instructor's department
123456789	ACC200	CD White	Junior	2.88	Cost accounting	BA212	MW10:00	Monroe	Accounting
123456789	ENG300	CD White	Junior	2.88	English literature	LA162	MW2:00	Hart	English
123456789	MGT370	CD White	Junior	2.88	Organizations	BA330	TTH9:00	Engle	Management
234567891	BUS300	SP Adams	Sophomore	3.17	Communications	BA350	MW11:00	Pugh	Business
234567891	MAT250	SP Adams	Sophomore	3.17	Calculus I	LA210	TTH8:00	James	Engineering

FIGURE 6-29   A student-course table in first normal form.

courses (classes) in which they are enrolled. It includes repeating groups (number, title, and room for each enrolled course), redundant data (title and room for each course enrolled in by each student), and dependency on a nonkey entity (assigned department depends on the course instructor and not the student). Instead of a single focus on students (the entity of concern), the table has a blurred focus that includes data concerning courses and instructors.

Our first step in moving toward normalization is to eliminate the repeating groups, with the result shown in Figure 6-29.* This table now has fixed-length rows. However, two difficulties have been introduced. First, the student number is no longer a unique identifier of each row. It is necessary to add the course number to the student number in order to gain uniqueness. Thus, the concatenated student number–course number becomes the primary key. Second, redundancy is increased. Thus, we cannot stop with this table form.

The next step is to establish separate tables for students and courses, as shown in Figure 6-30. As a consequence, the student table contains only data that are functionally dependent on the student number; thus it is normalized. (Refer back to Figure 6-24, where the student table contains the same data.) Also, the degree of redundancy concerning students and courses has been reduced. Again, however, two

Course number (key)	Course title	Course room	Course time	Course instructor	Instructor's department
ACC200	Cost accounting	BA212	MW10:00	Monroe	Accounting
ENG300	English literature	LA162	MW2:00	Hart	English
MGT370	Organizations	BA330	TTH9:00	Engle	Management
BUS300	Communications	BA350	MW11:00	Pugh	Business
MAT250	Calculus I	LA210	TTH8:00	James	Engineering

Student number	Student name	Class standing	Cumulative GPA
123456789	CD White	Junior	2.88
234567891	SP Adams	Sophomore	3.17

Student number	Course number
123456789	ACC200
123456789	ENG300
123456789	MGT370
234567891	BUS300
234567891	MAT250

FIGURE 6-30   A set of student-course tables in second normal form.

---

*In technical terms, the table has been cast into first normal form.

Course number (key)	Course title	Course room	Course time	Course instructor

Student number (key)	Student name	Class standing	Cumulative GPA		Student number	Course number

Course instructor (key)	Instructor's department
Monroe	Accounting
Hart	English
Engle	Management
Pugh	Business
James	Engineering

FIGURE 6-31   A set of student-course tables in third normal form.

difficulties arise. First, the association between students and their courses has been lost. A student number–course number relationship table must therefore be added.* Second, the course table still contains a so-called transitive dependency, i.e., the attribute "Instructor's department" is not dependent on the course number, the primary key of the table. Hence, the course table is not yet in normalized form.

The final step is to split the course table into a course table and an instructor table, as shown in Figure 6-31. To retain the linkage between tables, the instructor number is kept in the course table as a foreign key. This change has eliminated all remaining anomalies, so that updates, additions, and deletions can easily be made and no needed data are lost. For instance, if an instructor does not teach any courses during a semester, his or her data are not deleted from the data base. If a new course is added to the curriculum but not yet offered, it can be entered into the data base at once. The resulting tables, shown in Figure 6-31, are now normalized, i.e., expressed in third normal form. They make up a data base that can flexibly meet the varied needs of users, even though the number of tables has been increased from one to four.

*Note that if grades are to be added to the data base, they must be inserted into the relationship table rather than either the student table or the course table.

SUMMARY

Data management consists of creating a data base, maintaining the data sets within a data base, and retrieving data from the data base. It is of great importance to accountants, who are concerned with the processing of transaction data, with the preparation of outputs, and with the security and accuracy of stored data. A new "events" perspective concerning data management holds promise of revolutionizing the management of data and the generated information.

The traditional file-oriented approach has severe shortcomings. Since the files are tied to individual ap-plications, redundancy in files and data generally occurs. Redundancy leads to inconsistencies and hence to loss of data reliability. Other likely shortcomings are inflexibility and relative inaccessibility. An alternative approach, known as the data-base approach, can reduce or overcome these shortcomings. It features data independence, data standardization, one-time data entry, data association and integration, shared data ownership, and centralized data management. Its benefits therefore include reduced redundancy, eliminated inconsistencies, increased flexibility, and improved accessibility. On the other hand, the drawbacks of the data-base approach are increased cost, complexity, and vulnerability to loss of data.

In developing a data base it is suggested that the "events" perspective be adopted, with entities representing the main points of focus. Five development phases are planning and determining needs, modeling the conceptual view, specifying the logical view, selecting an appropriate DBMS, and implementing the physical data base. Modeling the conceptual view, a critical phase, consists of establishing the entities and relationships and integrating them via an entity-relationship diagram, determining the cardinalities (one-to-one, one-to-many, many-to-many) between the pairs of entities, and specifying the needed attributes. The logical view is known as the schema, which incorporates overlapping subschemas. The data-base management system is the software that stores, maintains, and retrieves data from an integrated data base. It serves as the buffer between the application programs (and their users) and the data base, and it communicates directly with the operating system in accomplishing its purposes. Principal components of a DBMS are the data definition language (with data dictionary), data manipulation language, query language, and data-base control system.

Four logical data structures are the tree, network, relational, and object-oriented structures or data bases. The first two may be depicted by data structure diagrams, whereas the last two are shown as linked tables or nodes. The tree structure forms hierarchical arrangements from root nodes and expresses one-to-many relationships. The network structure forms interconnected arrangements in which multiple data nodes (records) serve as entry points and at least one member record has two or more owner records. A complex version of the network structure includes at least one many-to-many relationship, which must be implemented via an intersection record.

The relational structure does not explicitly predefine relationships among its tables or data elements. Instead, the relationships or links are implied by means of foreign keys or relationship tables. The object-oriented structure is more broadly based than the relational structure, since it can reflect classes and class hierarchies. It also incorporates such features as encapsulation of methods with data and inheritance of methods and data within class hierarchies. While the tree and network structures emphasize the rapid retrieval of data, the relational and object-oriented structures offer extreme flexibility and the familiarity of tables. Thus a greater number of ad hoc requests can be answered by these structures than by the tree or network structures. In addition, the object-oriented data base provides the most realistic and comprehensive view of reality. Certain rules apply in establishing the structures. For instance, tables in the relational data base should be established by means of a normalization procedure. Unnormalized tables can cause problems in using and making changes to the data base.

KEY TERMS

data base (195)
data-base administrator (DBA) (203)
data-base approach (198)
data-base control system (DBCS) (211)
data-base management system (DBMS) (199)
data-base system (196)
data definition language (DDL) (211)
data independence (200)
data management (195)
data manipulation language (DML) (211)
data modeling (209)
data set (195)
data structure diagram (211)
entity (206)
entity-relationship (E-R) diagram (209)
file-oriented approach (196)
foreign key (224)
logical view (of data) (200)
many-to-many (M:N) relationship (215)
network structure (217)
normalization (230)
object classes (221)
object-oriented data base (221)
objects (221)
one-to-many (1:N) relationship (214)
one-to-one (1:1) relationship (214)
query language (211)
relational operator (227)
relational structure (219)
schema (200)
subschema (201)
table (219)
tree structure (215)

REVIEW PROBLEM WITH SOLUTION

ROSEBUD COLLEGE

Statement*

Rosebud College employs a data base related to its students and the classes that are offered to the students.

*This problem is based on James F. Smith and Amer Mufti, "Using the Relational Database," *Management Accounting* (October 1985), pp. 43–50, 54. Copyright 1985 by National Association of Accountants, Montvale, N.J. All rights reserved. Used with permission.

The records pertaining to the students and classes are accessed by a DBMS that uses a network structure. The schema for this data base is similar to that portrayed by the data structure diagram shown in Figure 6-19. However, each student record contains only the student number and the pointer fields shown below, whereas each class record contains only the class number and pointer fields.

Student number	Pointer to student data	Pointer to student/ class record

Additional data relating to students and classes are maintained in separate records. Included as additional data are student names, class standings, GPA, class title, time, days, classroom numbers, and instructor names.

In the terms of network structures, the student number and class number records "own" the member records containing the additional data; they also serve as entry points, since their embedded pointer fields contain pointers that allow access to the additional data. For instance, a pointer in the record for student number 1 may contain the value 974, which represents the disk address of the record that holds the name, class standing, and GPA of student number 1. Similarly, a pointer in the record for class number ENG 100 may contain the

value 692, which represents the disk address of the record that holds the title of the class and other data pertaining to ENG 100.

In addition to the pointers described in the preceding paragraph, embedded pointers are needed to traverse throughout the network structure. Thus, the student number record also contains a pointer to a student/class intersection record (as seen in the portrayed record layout). Other pointers must appear in the class number record and student/class record. By means of such pointers, the DBMS can follow paths A, B, C, and D as shown in the following diagram. Path A allows the retrieval of data concerning student number 1, while path B allows the retrieval of data concerning class coded ENG 100, path C allows the retrieval of all classes taken by student number 1, and path D allows the retrieval of all students taking ACC 200.

Required

a. Specify the additional pointer fields that are needed to allow the accesses shown in the diagram below.

b. Identify the types of outputs that the data base can provide.

c. Assume that Rosebud changes to a relational structure. Identify the tables that would be needed and list the attributes in relational notation.

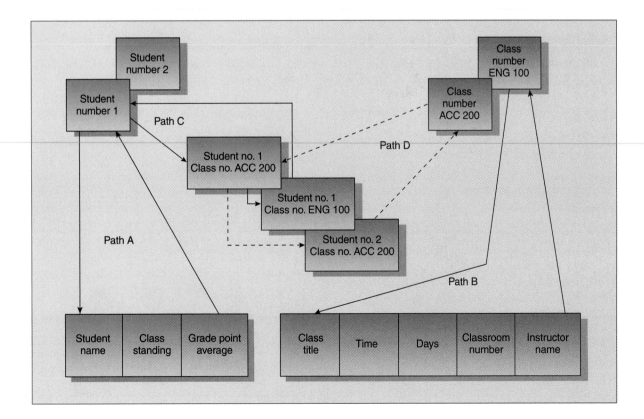

d. Assume that an instructor table is to be added. List at least four attributes in relational notation.

e. Assume that grades are to be included in the data base. Draw the column headings for the table that would include the grades.

Solution

a. Needed pointer fields are (i) class number record—pointers to class data and the student/class records; (ii) student data record—pointer back to the student number record; (iii) class data record—pointer back to the class number record; (iv) student/class record—pointers to the next record having the same student number, to the next record having the same class number, back to the student number record, and back to the class number record.

b. Outputs include (i) complete data concerning particular students; (ii) complete data concerning particular classes; (iii) class lists that show all enrolled students; (iv) course schedules that show all classes currently being taken by particular students; (v) list of students taking more than five classes; (vi) list of classes having more than 30 students; (vii) list of students by class standing, arranged alphabetically; (viii) list of classes, arranged according to times and days, and so on.

c. STUDENT (<u>STUDENT-NO</u>, STUDENT-NAME, CLSTD, GPA)

CLASS (<u>CLASS-NO</u>, CLASS-TITLE, TIME, DAYS, CLROOM, INST-NAME)

STUDENT/CLASS (<u>STUDENT-NO, CLASS-NO</u>)

d. INSTRUCTOR (<u>INST-NAME</u>, OFFICE-NO, PHONE-NO, DEPARTMENT, RANK)

e.

Student number	Class number	Grade

REVIEW QUESTIONS

6-1. What are the three major functions of data management?

6-2. Why do accountants need to understand data management fundamentals?

6-3. What is the "events" approach, and why is its use advantageous in computer-based transaction processing systems?

6-4. What are several shortcomings of the file-oriented approach?

6-5. What features characterize the data-base approach?

6-6. What are the benefits of the data-base approach?

6-7. What are the drawbacks of the data-base approach?

6-8. Describe the rationale for using the "events" perspective in developing an integrated data base.

6-9. Briefly describe the five phases in developing a data base.

6-10. What are the three types of entities encountered by a firm?

6-11. How is data modeling useful in the development of a data base?

6-12. What are several steps in the process of data modeling?

6-13. What are the three cardinalities that describe relationships between the entities of a data base?

6-14. What are the four types of logical data structures?

6-15. How does the data structure diagram relate to the entity-relationship diagram, and what does the former portray?

6-16. What are the major functional components of a data-base management system?

6-17. What are typical activities during the implementation phase of a data-base development project?

6-18. Contrast a flat file, tree structure, network structure, relational structure, and object-oriented data base.

6-19. Describe the considerations in selecting among the logical data structures for a data base.

6-20. Under what conditions is a relational data base the best choice?

6-21. Explain how desired data are retrieved from a relational data base when the data are located in more than one table.

6-22. Describe the steps in normalizing tables for a relational data base.

DISCUSSION QUESTIONS

6-23. In what situations might a firm find the file-oriented approach to be preferable to the data-base approach?

6-24. What are the benefits and drawbacks to the development of a single overall data base that includes all of a firm's data? What are feasible alternatives to this overall data base?

6-25. Very few firms develop their own data-base management software. Instead, they buy or lease commercial DBMS packages. Discuss the advantages and disadvantages to Infoage of buying a commercial DBMS package.

6-26. Briefly describe applications for which a relational data base could be particularly useful to Ann Strong. For what applications might a network data base be most helpful to Infoage?

6-27. Why are control and security problems likely to be more severe in a data-base environment than in a file-oriented environment?

6-28. Why is a data-base administrator so important in a data-base environment and what are his or her most important tasks?

6-29. How does a data dictionary relate to the data definition language? What are the purposes of a data dictionary and what key data does it contain?

6-30. Discuss the improvements of the object-oriented data base over the relational data base. Also, discuss the obstacles in replacing network and relational data bases with object-oriented data bases.

6-31. Certain data-base management software, such as DB/2 from IBM, have recently been transformed into a combination network/relational structure. Why was this done, and will it reduce the comparative advantages of the object-oriented data base?

PROBLEMS

6-1. Mariposa Products, a textile and apparel manufacturer, acquired its own computer in 1986. The first application to be developed and implemented was production and inventory control. Other applications that were added in succession were payroll, accounts receivable, and accounts payable.

The applications were not integrated as a result of the piecemeal manner in which they were developed and implemented. Nevertheless, the system proved satisfactory for several years. Generally, reports were prepared on time, and information was readily accessible.

Mariposa operates in a very competitive industry. A combination of increased operating costs and the competitive nature of the industry have had an adverse effect on profit margins and operating profits. Ed Wilde, Mariposa's president, suggested that some special analyses be prepared in an attempt to provide information that would help management improve operations. Unfortunately, some of the data were not consistent among the reports. In addition, there were no data by product line or by department. These problems were attributable to the fact that Mariposa's applications were developed piecemeal and, as a consequence, duplicate data that were not necessarily consistent existed on Mariposa's computer system.

Wilde was concerned that Mariposa's computer system was not able to generate the information his managers needed to make decisions. He called a meeting of his top management and certain data processing personnel to discuss potential solutions to Mariposa's problems. The consensus of the meeting was that a new information system that would integrate Mariposa's applications was needed.

Mariposa's controller suggested that the firm consider a data-base system that all departments would use. As a first step, the controller proposed hiring a data-base administrator on a consulting basis to determine the feasibility of converting to a data-base system.

Required

a. Identify the characteristics that constitute a system under the data-base approach.

b. List the benefits and drawbacks to Mariposa Products of converting to the data-base approach.

c. What steps should be taken in converting to the new system?

d. What are several key duties of the data-base administrator?

(CMA *adapted*)

6-2. The Bunting Construction Co. of Dayton, Ohio, is a building contractor and materials supplier. Its annual sales for last year were $105 million. For a number of years the firm has used computers to process transactions and prepare reports and documents. It currently employs a large mainframe computer to perform both batch and on-line processing. For instance, it processes most of the accounting applications, such as payroll, by the batch mode and maintains the relevant files on magnetic tape. On the other hand, it employs on-line processing, via terminals, to dispatch loads of materials to customers and to keep track of the status of construction projects.

Over the years the firm has developed and acquired over 150 application programs, and it maintains approximately 200 files. These programs and files are documented in a variety of styles; some documentation was prepared by programmers no longer with the firm, and some was acquired from software suppliers when packages were purchased. Many of the programs have not been changed significantly in several years. According to the information systems manager, the time required to make changes is very lengthy; he has not been able to spare programmers to spend this needed time in program maintenance, since he has been "pushed" to provide new programs. For instance, he has recently supervised the writing of several new engineering and bidding programs. As a consequence, the programs tend to be inefficient and unintegrated. In addition, many of the data items appear in several files and are used in a variety of programs. Often these data items (e.g., raw materials item numbers) are assigned a different name in each program.

The operations manager of Bunting recently raised a disturbing problem at a meeting of top managers. He complained that although he could make inquiries concerning individual projects via his terminal, he could not obtain certain reports—such as lists of overdue projects, cost overruns, and expected receipts of materials—in a timely manner. Other managers agreed that they likewise had difficulty in obtaining ad hoc demand reports from the information system. As a consequence of these comments, the president directed the controller to investigate the feasibility of moving to the data-base approach.

Required

a. What benefits would Bunting gain by moving to the data-base approach?

b. What steps should be taken in the process of converting to the data-base approach?

c. How would a DBMS be selected, and what are several desirable components that it should contain?

d. If Bunting decides to convert only a portion of the files and programs to the data-base approach initially, which areas of activity would be the best candidates?

(CMA *adapted*)

6-3. Organizations of all types have developed data bases. One of the first actions they often take is to list the relevant entities, such as appear in Figure 6-9 for Infoage, Inc. Each type of organization is likely to have some of the same entities as found in Infoage. However, it is likely to have certain entities that are peculiar to its type of operations and activities. List several entities for each of the following types of organizations, grouped according to events, resources, and agents.

    a. Hospital

    b. University

    c. Public accounting firm

    d. Construction contractor

    e. Professional football club

    f. Brokerage firm

6-4. Ann Strong is considering the acquisition of a data-base software package for her public accounting firm. She intends to use the package to aid in maintaining data concerning services provided to clients on various engagements, billing of clients, purchases of supplies and services, accounts payable, cash disbursements, and budgeting. Providing services to clients includes such activities as scheduling engagements and keeping a log of the times worked on various specialties (e.g., tax, financial analysis consulting).

Required

a. Identify the phases that are desirable in developing the data base and acquiring the data-base software package. Be specific in describing each phase and state its importance in obtaining a sound data-base system.

b. Describe the components and capabilities of a desirable data-base software package; list several microcomputer-based data-base software packages that are likely to be on a "short list" of candidates.

c. Describe several inquiries and reports for which the information can be quickly retrieved by the data-base software package. Identify those inquiries and reports that could not be easily accommodated with a file-oriented system. Specify how each inquiry and report can aid Ann Strong in planning or controlling the firm's activities.

6-5. Morgan Electrical Supplies Inc. distributes electrical components to the construction industry. Morgan began as a local supplier 15 years ago and has grown rapidly to become a major competitor in the north central U.S. As the business grew and the variety of components to be stocked expanded, Morgan acquired a computer and implemented an inventory control system. Other applications, such as accounts receivable, accounts payable, payroll, and sales analysis were gradually computerized as each function expanded. The inventory system, due to its operational importance, has been upgraded to an on-line system while all the other applications are operating in batch mode. Over the years, Morgan has developed or acquired more than 100 application programs and maintains 150 files.

Morgan faces stiff competition from local suppliers throughout its marketing area. At a management meeting, the sales manager complained about the difficulty in obtaining immediate, current information to respond to customer inquiries. Other managers stated that they also had difficulty obtaining timely data from the system. As a result, the controller engaged a consulting firm to explore the situation. The consultant recommended installing a data-base management system (DBMS), and Morgan proceeded on this course, employing Jack Gibbons as the data-base administrator.

At a recent management meeting, Gibbons presented an overview of the DBMS using the chart presented on the following page. Gibbons explained that the data-base approach assumes an organizational, data-oriented viewpoint as it recognizes that a centralized data base represents a vital resource. Instead of being assigned to applications, information is more appropriately used and managed for the entire organization. The operating system physically moves data to and from disk storage, while DBMS is the software program that controls the data definition library that specifies the data structures and characteristics. As a result, both the roles of the application programs and query software and the tasks of the application programmers and users are simplified. Under the data-base approach, the data are available to all users within security guidelines.

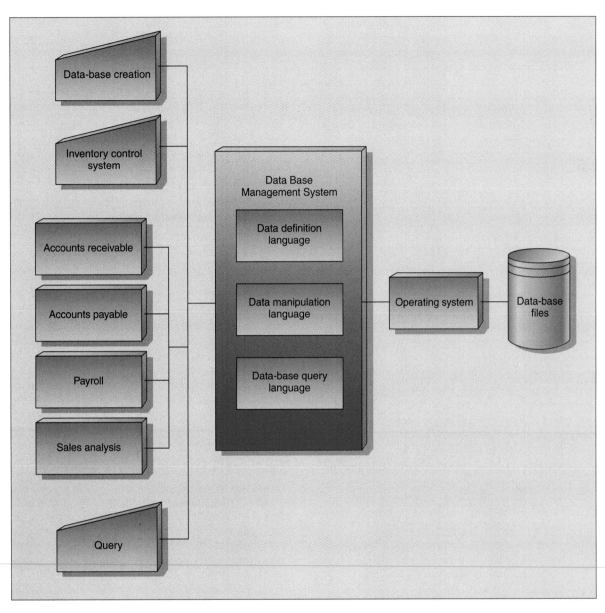

Required

a. Describe the duties and responsibilities of Jack Gibbons, the data-base administrator.

b. Assume that all of the applications described in the problem except payroll are approved for inclusion within the recommended data base. Describe the phases by which the data base will be developed, being as specific as the problem statement allows.

c. Describe two inquiries to which the data base can provide prompt answers for the use of each of the following:

    (1) sales manager

    (2) construction firm (customer)

    (3) controller

    (4) inventory manager

(CMA adapted)

6-6. TempClerk is a temporary clerical help agency. Because it has 1000 employees and 300 clients and is growing rapidly, it decides that a data-base system is needed to control its operations and provide adequate information. Prospective employees are interviewed and tested for clerical skills before being hired. Skills include word processing, typing, bookkeeping, filing, and stenography. Each skill has four levels: beginner, semiskilled, skilled, and expert. Clients request a specified number of employees and the skills and skill levels needed. Employees are paid weekly after their days of work have been verified with the clients at which they are assigned. They are paid at rates determined by the skill and its level. Clients are charged a daily rate (which includes overhead as well as employee costs) and billed weekly. Employees are evaluated after each job by the clients. Based on evaluations over the course of six months, an employee's skill level can be increased or the employee may be promoted to supervisor. If the ratings are poor, the employee may be fired.

Required

a. A data-base project team is formed during 1997. Describe the several phases of data-base development in this situation, being as specific as the facts in the problem statement allow. Identify in each phase the decisions that must be made by the developers.

b. Assume that a relational data-base structure is selected. One important table is the employee table. List several other entity tables that would be needed, plus at least one relationship table. (Recall that entities can include intangible resources as well as agents and events.) Identify the primary table key and any foreign keys that would appear in each listed table.

c. Briefly describe three reports that would be useful to the manager of the agency in (1) planning or (2) controlling the activities of the agency. Draw the format of one report and specify its effective features. All of the reports should be based on data in the data base.

6-7. Refer to Figures 6-14 and 6-24.

    a. Expand the entity-relationship diagram in Figure 6-14 to include the payment of fees by students to the university cashier. Add the relationships, if the fee payment is viewed as being a single event involving all registered students.

    b. Map the additional entities on the entity-relationship diagram to the relational data-base structure diagram shown in Figure 6-24.

6-8. Refer to Figure 6-25.

    a. Redraw the Job table to show the two normalized tables described within the chapter.

    b. Prepare an entity-relationship diagram from which the tables in the skill/employee relational data base have been mapped.

    c. Prepare a Bachman diagram that reflects the network structure that could be mapped from the entity-relationship diagram.

6-9. Sunvalley Hospital has rooms for 200 patients, who are assigned to beds upon admission. One or more physicians order treatments for a particular patient, with one or more treatments (e.g., operation, therapy) being ordered for any given patient. Each treatment is provided by a nurse and other hospital employees and its costs are recorded by office employees. A patient is billed for

treatments, including medical items (e.g., supplies, medicines, wheelchairs), with the bills usually being paid by third-party insurers.

Required

a. Identify the entities in this situation, grouped by agents, events, and resources.
Hint: Group all employees as a single entity.

b. Prepare an entity-relationship diagram, showing the cardinality of relationships as well as the linked entities.

c. Specify three data attributes for each entity.

d. Draw the fields of one intersection record that would be needed if a network structure were selected.

e. Draw the headings of one relationship table that would be needed if a relational structure were selected. Do not portray the same many-to-many relationship that was shown in **d** above.

6-10. Square O Markets operates 50 convenience stores in the Denver metropolitan area. It sells 2000 items on a cash basis. All of the stores are supplied by a single warehouse, which in turn receives goods that have been ordered by the purchasing department. The firm has a computer-based AIS, which handles the various accounting applications. Three of the most important applications are store sales, inventory management, and purchasing. Each application maintains its own set of files.

Sales have grown steadily during the past few years. However, sales might have been significantly better if stores had not often been out of stock on popular items. Also, inventory management has been rather inefficient. An outside consultant hired by the president has blamed most of the problems on a lack of integration among the key applications and inadequate information for inventory planning and control. His chief recommendation is to move to a data-base approach and to acquire data-base software.

On approval of his recommendation, the consultant is engaged to design an appropriate data base. He begins by surveying the relevant operations and interviewing such parties as store clerks and managers, the warehouse manager, the manager of inventory control, the purchasing manager and buyers, plus selected customers and suppliers. The consultant learns that four key master files are the warehouse inventory file, the inventory-by-store file, the supplier file, and the accounts payable file. Key inconsistencies exist between the two inventory files. For instance, in one file the inventory item number is designated as INVNO, while in the other file it is labeled ITEMNO. On the other hand, both files refer to the quantity on hand by the label QOH, although the quantity on hand of an item at the warehouse does not correspond to the quantity on hand at a particular store or at all of the stores. Thus, separate application programs must be employed in processing each of the inventory files.

The consultant also discovers that each item is provided by any of several selected suppliers, while a single supplier may provide more than one item to the firm.

Required

a. List the entities, grouped by the three application areas. If an entity overlaps two or more areas, include it in all applicable areas.

b. Prepare an entity-relationship diagram pertaining to the store sales and inventories maintained by the stores and warehouse. Exclude the purchasing application.

c. Describe three reports that could be provided by the implemented data base to aid in tracking sales at the stores, controlling warehouse inventories, and replenishing inventories at the stores in order to prevent stockouts.

d. Explain how an on-line data dictionary, generated by the data-base software, aids in maintaining the three application areas and in serving users.

6-11. The data structure diagram below reflects a four-level tree structure that links customer-related data. Prepare a set of tables for a relational structure that corresponds to the tree structure, similar to the correspondence shown in Figure 6-12. Refer to Figure 6-16 for the data elements that are likely to be contained in the

customer and sales invoice records. However, you will need to modify the sales invoice record in preparing the sales invoice record (which contains the header data) and the invoice line-item record (which contains the data found in the body of the invoice). Be sure to include common columns (with foreign keys) in the two tables composing the sales invoice records. Also, explain why the separation of the sales invoice records into two tables is necessary and desirable in a relational data base.

6-12. Draw a data structure diagram that models each of the following situations. Then illustrate the physical implementation of a specific occurrence by means of pointers in a chain. An example appears in Figure 6-16. Note that individual data elements need not be shown, except for the pointers in the linked structures.

a. Supplier records in the accounts payable file point to their purchase orders in the open purchase order file.

b. Customer records within the accounts receivable master file point to their sales invoice records *and* to their remittance advice records maintained in separate transaction history files. (Use *two* pointer fields in the customer record.)

c. Employee records within the employee master file point to their skills records in the skills inventory file.

d. Skills records within the skills inventory file point to the employee records in the employee master

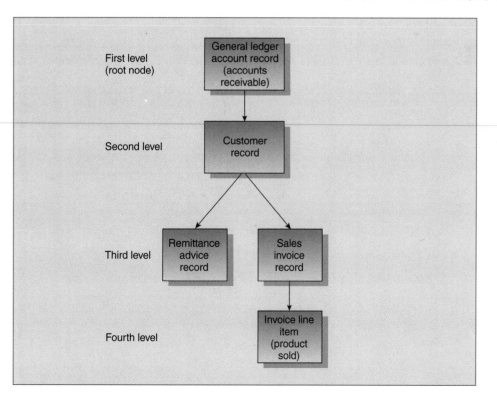

file possessing such skills. (Note that the skills records are now the parent records and the employee master records are now the children records.)

e. Skills records within the skills inventory file point to the employee records in the employee master file possessing such skills; department records within the department master file (containing such data items as the department number, department name, department manager, and responsibility center code) *also* point to the employees assigned to the departments. (Use *two* pointer fields in the employee record, one for the skill list and one for the department list.)

6-13. The data structure diagram below reflects a network data base for a firm such as Infoage, Inc.

Required

a. Expand the network structure to include additional relationships pertaining to the supplier, including the general ledger account and transactions involving purchase obligations and cash disbursements. Also, include a record for the general ledger itself, which links to each of its accounts. Furthermore, show in the expanded structure an intersection record that implements the many-to-many cardinality shown in the diagram below.

b. Draw the entity-relationship segments that link

(1) suppliers and merchandise inventory items

(2) suppliers and purchases

(3) cash disbursements and cash.

6-14. Southeastern State University intends to acquire a DBMS to integrate its data concerning students, classes, instructors, registration, classrooms, and grades. Among the reports and documents that the data base is to produce are semester class schedules (showing the numbers and names of all classes offered, plus their times, rooms, and instructors); class rosters (where each shows the class number and name, instructor, and classroom number, plus the students enrolled by social security numbers, names, and majors); student class schedules (where each shows the numbers and names of classes being taken by a student, plus the times, rooms, and instructors); classroom schedules (where each shows the times a room is occupied and the related classes); and semester grade reports (where each shows the grades earned by a student for the respective classes taken).

Required

a. Prepare an entity-relationship diagram that reflects the various entities identified in the problem statement and that specifies the types of relationships. Also, list any assumptions that underlie the diagram.

b. Prepare a data structure diagram based on the network structure, which is to facilitate the preparation of the listed reports. Note that three entry points are required.

c. Revise the data structure diagram in **b** to show all many-to-many relationships converted into one-to-many relationships with intersection records.

d. The class schedule for Melody Dunson, student number 684, is requested. Draw the pointer chain of the ring type that shows how the records are accessed, if the student's record is located at disk address 350 and the four classes she is taking (coded ACC221, CIS 302, ART 101, and MAT 201) are located at disk addresses 520, 260, 490, and 730, respectively.

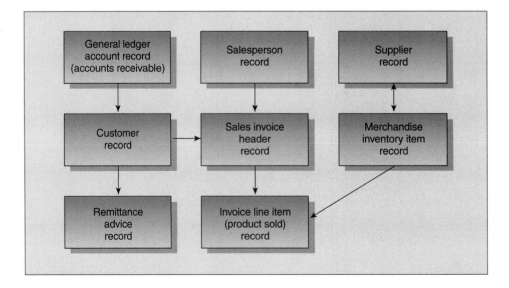

e. Prepare an SQL expression similar to the one shown in the chapter to request a listing of the students who are majoring in accounting, have a grade-point average above 3.00, and either have senior standing or are older than 20. The student records are maintained in a data set called STDREC and contain the student number, GPA, name, address, and related data.

f. The university administration indicates an interest in various ad hoc reports and inquiries in addition to the listed reports and documents. Prepare the headings for a set of tables that would be needed if the data base were converted to a relational structure.

6-15. Pronto Auto Rental is a nationwide firm that rents cars, trucks, vans, and other vehicles. Rented cars include both foreign and domestic makes, but all other vehicles are solely domestic makes. Each vehicle is assigned an alphanumeric code, with the first field of the code being the type of vehicle, the second field being the country of manufacture, the third field being the manufacturer, the fourth field being the year of manufacture, and the fifth field being a unique number. All vehicles that it rents are also serviced and maintained by Pronto. Thus, the firm's two major activities are rentals and maintenance. The maintenance activity is divided into the major components of the vehicles, e.g., engines, transmissions, bodies. Because so many makes must be maintained, service manuals from the manufacturers are critical references.

Information desired by the management of Pronto include analyses of vehicles on hand, of rentals, and of maintenance of the various components. This information cannot be easily provided by the current relational data base. However, the management has heard that an object-oriented data base would organize the data and provide other advantages over the relational data base.

Required

a. Draw a model of an object-oriented data base for Pronto, if the focus is on vehicle rentals and maintenance.

b. Describe several analyses that the object-oriented data base could easily provide to Pronto's management.

c. Discuss advantages, other than the accessibility of information, that the object-oriented data base could provide to Pronto.

 6-16. Note: *This problem may be solved with the aid of a data-base software package such as Paradox or Access.*

Refer to the four tables in Figure 6-25, which compose a relational data base. Separate the Job table into two normalized tables, labeled Job and Job/skill. Also, add the following two tables to the data base:

Department

Dept. no.	Dept. name	Phone no.
1	Alpha	(520)965-3810
2	Beta	(520)965-4727

Department/skill

Dept. no.	Skill no.
1	10
1	20
1	30
2	40
2	50
2	60

Required

a. Considering the data base *before* the addition of the two new tables, list three inquiries (other than those in the chapter example) that could be answered from the data. Then draw the newly created tables that provide the answers, and describe how the new tables were formed.

b. Using the added department and department/skill tables, develop the new tables to answer the following inquiries and describe their formation:

(1) Which departments (by number) provide each of the required skills (by number and description)? Assume that skills 10, 20, 30, 40, 50, and 60 are required and that no employee has a skill used in both departments.

(2) Which skills and employees (by number) are currently employed in the Beta department?

(3) Which departments and skills (by name) are involved in job number 100?

c. Explain how the procedure for creating new tables is changed in **b** (2) when employee names and skill descriptions, respectively, are needed.

 6-17. Note: *This problem can be solved with the aid of a data-base software package such as Paradox or Access.*

The following three tables are maintained in a purchasing data base:

PARTS

Part No.	Pname
P107	BOLT
P113	NUT
P125	SCREW
P132	GEAR

SUPPLIERS

Supp. no.	Sname
S51	ABC Co.
S57	XYZ Co.
S63	LMN Co.

PRICES

Part no.	Supp. no.	Price
P107	S51	0.59
P107	S57	0.65
P113	S51	0.25
P113	S63	0.21
P125	S63	0.15
P132	S57	5.25
P132	S63	7.50

Required

a. Draw the segment of an entity-relationship diagram from which the tables have been mapped.

b. Draw the new table that is created and answer each of the following inquiries. Specify the series of SELECT, PROJECT, and JOIN operators that will create each new table.

(1) Which suppliers, by name, provide part 113?

(2) Which suppliers, by name, provide gears?

(3) Which suppliers, by name, provide more than three parts?

(4) Which parts, by name, are provided by only one supplier?

(5) Which suppliers, by name, have which parts (by name and number) that are priced below $0.50?

(*Courtesy of International Business Machines Corporation*)

6-18. Refer to the relational tables in Figure 6-23. Show the columns of data, together with column headings, that would be displayed when each of the following SQL inquiries are entered via an on-line terminal. Assume for the purposes of this problem that all of the rows in the tables are shown in the figure.

a. SELECT   SALES INVOICE
               NUMBER, ITEM
               NUMBER, QUANTITY
               SOLD
    FROM   INVOICE LINE ITEM
               TABLE
    WHERE   QUANTITY SOLD > 5

b. SELECT   SALES INVOICE
               NUMBER, TOTAL SALE
               AMOUNT
    FROM   SALES INVOICE TABLE
    WHERE   SHIPPING DATE = 11/
               06/97

c. SELECT   CUSTOMER NAME,
               SALES INVOICE
               NUMBER, ITEM
               NUMBER, QUANTITY
               SOLD
    FROM   CUSTOMER TABLE
    WHERE   SHIPPING DATE = 10/
               6/97 AND ITEM
               NUMBER = 14D

d. SELECT   CUSTOMER NAME,
               CURRENT ACCOUNT
               BALANCE
    FROM   CUSTOMER TABLE
    WHERE   CUSTOMER NUMBER >
               1000
    ORDER BY   CURRENT ACCOUNT
               BALANCE, DESC

(*Note:* ORDER BY refers to sorting, DESC refers to descending order.)

6-19. The table on page 245 is in a relational data base for inventory activities. It is unnormalized, since the table contains data with respect both to inventory items and to suppliers.

Required

a. Convert the table to tables in third normal form, showing the headings for each table plus the primary and foreign keys.

b. A user (e.g., the inventory manager) needs a report showing the inventory items (by descriptions) provided by each of the firm's suppliers (by names). If all tables in the data base are in third normal form, explain the operations by which the data-base software provides this report.

c. Assume that the table on page 245 is still used, rather than the tables in third normal form that you prepared in **a** above. Inventory item 348J is discontinued. What happens to the data concerning Bluebell Merchandisers if that is the only item the supplier provides? What is the drawback, if the firm expects to acquire other items from Bluebell Merchandisers in the near future?

6-20. The following descriptions of tables in a relational data base are not in a suitably normalized form. Specify the columns, using relational notation and assumed data names, of the two or more tables that represent suitable normalization in each case. Also under-

Inventory Table

Inventory Item No.	Description	Unit Cost	Reorder Point	Quantity on Hand	Supplier Number	Supplier Name	Supplier Address
145P	Table	50.00	25	58	28	Sam's Mart	3978 Market
203G	Chair	20.00	46	76	21	The Showroom	450 So. Ray
298M	Lamp	24.00	30	49	21	The Showroom	450 So. Ray
348J	Desk	99.00	10	14	30	Bluebell Mdse.	35 Spence
372P	Sofa	245.00	23	36	22	Morton's, Inc.	559 Loyd

line the primary key for each table, as well as any foreign keys needed to provide common columns between tables. Include relationship tables when necessary, with both columns of each such table viewed as foreign keys.

Required

a. The job table in Figure 6-25.

Hint: The current table would be specified as follows in relational notation and with assumed data names:

$$JOB \ (JOB-NO, \ SKILL-NO, \\ JOB-DESCR, \ ACCUM-COST)$$

Also see Problem 6-8 for the normalized tables.

b. An inventory table containing these columns: item number, item description, quantity on order, quantity on hand, supplier number, supplier name, supplier address. (Each inventory item may be supplied by more than one supplier.)

c. A sales order table containing these columns: order number, order date, expected delivery date, customer number, customer name, customer billing address, customer shipping address, product number, product description, unit of measure, quantity of product, expected unit price. (More than one product can be included on a single order.)

Hint: Begin with a customer table.

d. A production department table containing these columns: department code, department name, name of manager in charge, number of work order in progress, quantity of items in work order, scheduled time to move order to next department, expected shipping date of completed order. (More than one work order is often in progress within a single production department.)

e. An employee table containing these columns: employee number, employee name, address, grade level, department, year of employment, salary. (The salary is based solely on grade level; roughly a dozen grade levels are in use, and more than one employee may have the same grade level.)

6-21. The Bluegrass Plumbing Supply Co. of Lexington, Kentucky, wholesales a variety of plumbing supplies to plumbing contractors throughout several states.* To increase sales and improve profits, it feels that it needs to improve service in processing orders, to sharpen purchasing and receiving operations, and to reduce inventory investment. Thus, the firm designs a new system pertaining to purchasing and inventory control. To implement this new system, it acquires computer hardware, including terminals and magnetic disk storage. It also purchases a data-base management system.

The newly designed system employs three key files: a product (finished-goods inventory) master file, a supplier master file, and an outstanding purchase orders file. These files are accessed via terminals by employees concerned with sales order processing, purchasing, and receiving.

When an order from a customer is received, a sales order clerk checks via a terminal to see whether the quantity shown in the inventory record is adequate to fill the order. If so, the quantity on hand is reduced to reflect the order; if not, the clerk checks to see if a purchase order is outstanding and when goods are due.

Each day, buyers in the purchasing department place purchase orders by entering (via terminals) the transaction code, the numbers of products being ordered, the order quantities, the anticipated unit prices, the supplier numbers, and the anticipated due dates. The computer system then retrieves the proper supplier record—which contains such data as the supplier name, mailing address, and other header data that normally appear in a purchase order—and prepares the purchase order which has a computer-assigned number; finally, it places a copy of the order in the open purchase order file.

When ordered goods arrive at the receiving dock and have been counted, a receiving clerk enters the transaction code, the purchase order number, the product numbers, and the quantities received. The computer system then verifies that the purchase order is valid and that the quantities agree with those on the order. If the

*Adapted from *Information Systems in Management* by James A. Senn. ©1978 by Wadsworth Publishing Co., Inc. Reprinted by permission of Wadsworth Publishing Co., Inc., Belmont, Calif. 94002.

clerk enters an acceptance code, the system prepares a receiving report and also increases the quantity-on-hand balance in the inventory record to reflect the received goods.

On request of the purchasing manager, the system prepares a list of products that have fallen below their reorder points, together with their optimal reorder quantities. This list is used as the basis for making ordering assignments to the buyers.

Required

a. List the data elements that should appear in each of the three files.

b. Prepare a data structure diagram that reflects a reasonable network schema for the data base.

c. Prepare and discuss separate data structure diagrams that reflect the subschemas for (i) an order processing clerk, (ii) a buyer, (iii) a receiving clerk, and (iv) the purchasing manager. In other words, isolate the portion of the schema that can satisfy the needs (e.g., to make an inquiry, to update a file, to prepare a report) of each of these four users. For instance, if the schema is in essence a structure involving three record types, a subschema may consist of two of these three record types. In fact, it may consist only of certain selected data elements from the records.

CONTINUING CASE

With respect to the small firm that you selected in Chapter 1, complete the following requirements:

a. An overview diagram of the major activities and entities related to the firm.

b. An entity-relationship diagram concerning one major area other than the revenue or expenditure cycles, e.g., the employee or human resource activities, including payroll.

c. A discussion of the advantages of a data base to this firm, including the various uses to which the data base can be put.

d. A brief description of the data-base software package that the firm currently uses (or would suitably select for use if none is currently in use).

e. A description of problems in using the data base, especially relating to controlling and securing the data and making changes (or that would likely be encountered if no data base is currently in use).

CHAPTER 7

RISK EXPOSURES AND THE INTERNAL CONTROL STRUCTURE

INTRODUCTION

Control is a concept that is relevant to every system. Controls are particularly important to accounting information systems. In this and the following three chapters we will examine many aspects of controls and audits within the context of a business organization. Chapters 7–9 span control processes, control objectives, control systems, control classifications, risk exposures, feasibility considerations, and the varied controls that are needed to counteract the risk exposures. Chapter 10 will cover audits of information systems. Mastering the major control and audit topics will enable you to apply this knowledge to the remaining parts of the text.

NATURE OF CONTROL

The process of control is one of management's basic functions. Management must establish and maintain control over its firm's operational system, organization, and information system. The decisions that are made by management in doing so are crucial to the firm's success. Effective control decisions enable a firm to employ its resources efficiently, to fulfill its legal responsibilities, and to generate reliable and useful information. Because the control process is employed within an entity such as a business firm, it is often referred to by accountants and auditors as **internal control.**

Since our focus is on the accounting information system (AIS), we need to become familiar with **controls**—measures and practices whose purposes are to counteract exposures to certain risks. An integral part of a firm's AIS is a framework of controls. The overall purpose of this control framework, which spans all of the firm's transactions, is to provide reasonable assurance that objectives will be achieved. Thus it also encompasses the firm's operations and system of management.

Because these controls and security measures are internal to the firm and are closely interwoven, the control framework is called its **internal control structure (ICS).*** This structure is the means through which the process of internal control functions. If the ICS is strong and sound, all of the operations, physical resources, and data will be monitored and kept under control. Information outputs will be trustworthy. On the other hand, a weak and unsound ICS can lead to serious repercussions. The information generated by the AIS is likely to be unreliable, untimely, and perhaps unrelated to the firm's objectives. Furthermore, the firm's resources may be vulnerable to loss through theft and carelessness.

IMPORTANCE OF THE CONTROL PROCESS AND CONTROL MEASURES TO ACCOUNTANTS

Internal control, as a process and a structure, is of great concern to accountants. As key users of the AIS, they need to know which control practices are in effect. Therefore, accountants often take active roles in developing and reviewing control frameworks. They work closely with system designers during the development of information systems, to ensure that the planned control measures are adequate and auditable. For instance, accountants/auditors make sure that totals will be balanced and reconciled properly and that audit trails are clearly established. During audits they determine the adequacy of measures that facilitate the internal control process, so that they can assess the reliance to be placed on the ICS when performing subsequent auditing program steps. Developing and evaluating control frameworks are skills in which accountants can and are expected to excel.

CONTROL PROCESSES

A control process both monitors and regulates. In brief, the process consists of (1) measuring actual results against planned accomplishments, and (2) taking corrective actions when necessary. These corrective actions are the decisions that keep the firm moving toward its established objectives.

ELEMENTS OF A CONTROL PROCESS

Examined in detail, a typical **control process** consists of six elements:

1. A factor being controlled, called the characteristic or performance measure.
2. An operating process that gives rise to the characteristic.
3. A sensor element that detects the actual state of the operating process.
4. A planned accomplishment, or benchmark, against which the actual state of the characteristic is to be compared.
5. A planner who sets the benchmark.
6. A regulator element that compares the actual state of the characteristic against the benchmark and feeds back corrections to the operating process.

---

*Internal control structure may also be referred to as internal control.

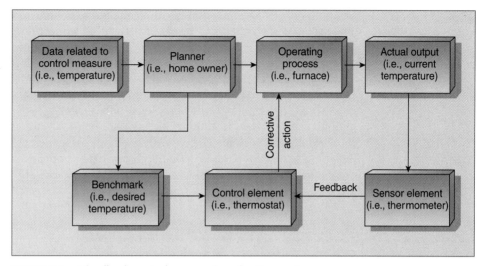

FIGURE 7-1   A feedback control process for a heating system.

Figure 7-1 portrays the control process and illustrates it in terms of a household heating system. The overall purpose of a heating system is to control the temperature, which is the characteristic or performance measure. A homeowner begins the process by setting the thermostat reading for the desired temperature (the benchmark). He or she chooses a setting that is determined by personal objectives, such as comfort and economy. Then an automatic process takes over. As the furnace (the operating process) generates heat, the thermostat's thermometer (the sensor element) detects the actual temperature. Next the thermostatic mechanism (the regulator element) compares the actual temperature (fed to it by the sensor element) with the benchmark temperature. When the actual temperature rises above the preset temperature, the control element notifies the activating mechanism in the thermostat to shut down the furnace. Later, when the actual temperature drops below the preset temperature, the information feedback leads to the furnace being turned on again.

A central feature of the control process is **feedback.** As the foregoing heating system example shows, feedback is an information output that returns ("feeds back") to a regulator element and then to the operating process as an input. Feedback therefore provides the means for deciding when collective action (e.g., turning off the furnace) is necessary.

LEVELS OF CONTROL PROCESSES

An entity such as a business firm may employ a variety of control processes. For example, as both Infoage and Ann Strong's consulting firm grow in size and complexity, the number of needed control processes (and controls) is likely to increase. Presently, since Ann Strong's firm is much smaller than Infoage, her firm requires fewer and less sophisticated controls to effectively operate the business. Moreover, these processes may vary in sophistication. The heating system is an example of a first-order feedback control process or system, if the benchmark is assumed to remain unchanged after being set. For example, a budgetary control system implemented at Infoage compares actual revenues and expenses with forecasted revenues and expenses and is an example of a first-order feedback control process. By contrast, a second-order feedback control system employs a benchmark that adjusts to meet changing environmental conditions. For example, Diane Varney, treasurer and controller of Infoage, installed a flexible budgeting system in which the budget values are adjusted with changing levels of activity. Assume that only 90 percent of the products budgeted for the year are sold. Diane's system allows her to adjust the cost budgets to reflect the level of sales achieved so that meaningful variances can be computed and proper corrective action can be taken. A third-order feedback control system attempts to predict future conditions and results. Based on such predictions, the system anticipates future problems and suggests corrective actions *before* the problems occur. Several third-order feedback control systems, also known as **feed-forward control systems,** are typically used by business firms. One example is a cash planning system designed by Diane Varney. Based on periodic cash forecasts, she may anticipate seasonal cash shortages by arranging for bank loans before the shortages actually occur.

EXAMPLE OF CONTROL PROCESSES

The AIS is central to a firm's control processes, since it can serve as both a monitor and a regulator. We can see how it functions through the example of inventory control systems. The inventory control process begins when Jack Dyson, Infoage's inventory manager, decides how much to carry of each inventory item. Let us assume that Jack decides to carry at least 50 computers for sale at Infoage's two retail sales outlets. When the quantity on hand drops to 50 (the reorder point), he purchases 25 more computers from a wholesale store across town the same day. Infoage's AIS keeps track of the inventory level by deducting the quantity of each sale from the on-hand quantity shown on an inventory record. Thus the AIS serves as a monitor and provides feedback information to Jack via a first-order feedback control system. Figure 7-2 shows the elements in Infoage's inventory control feedback system.

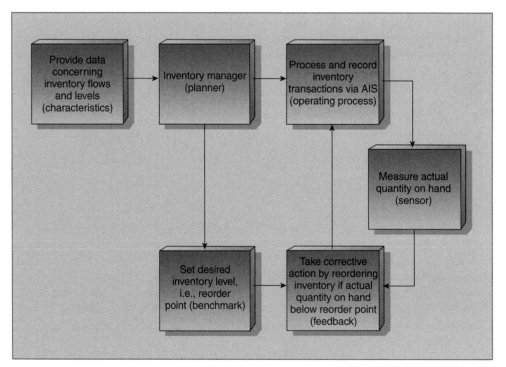

FIGURE 7-2   A first-order inventory feedback control system, relating to the flow and level of a single inventory item at Infoage, Inc.

Now assume that Infoage recognizes that the sales of computers face seasonal fluctuations. More computers are sold in October, November, and December, when customers begin their Christmas shopping in earnest. Thus Jack adjusts the level of minimum inventory by referring to sales for the same month last year and adjusts the reorder quantity by reference to the current on-hand quantity. Now Infoage's AIS provides added feedback information that is affected by changing conditions; thus it acts as a second-order feedback control system.

Finally, assume that computers can be obtained more cheaply from a mail-order wholesaler doing business in the next state, but the lead time is two weeks. Also, Infoage's sales have grown substantially but fluctuate more significantly from week to week. Jack now employs a reorder point that is affected by the expected demand in the weeks ahead, as well as by the lead time. Infoage's AIS automatically informs him when the reorder point has been reached. Then, the AIS computes the economic reorder quantity, which also depends in part on the expected sales demand for the coming weeks. Because it provides inventory information that anticipates future needs, the AIS now acts as a feedforward control system.

INTERNAL CONTROL STRUCTURE

Since the ICS is the vehicle through which the AIS employs an array of controls, it deserves prominent attention. In this section we provide a view of the ICS developed by the **Committee of Sponsoring Organizations of the Treadway Commission** (known as **COSO**), survey the control objectives that the COSO report recommended, and present a comprehensive systems model of the ICS as it applies to financial reporting objectives and nonfinancial objectives.

COMMITTEE OF SPONSORING ORGANIZATIONS OF THE TREADWAY COMMISSION

Before the issuance of the COSO report, the major accounting bodies involved in assessing and evaluating the internal control process viewed an entity's internal control system in diverse ways. Internal controls were defined differently, the objectives to be achieved by the ICS were not standardized, and the components making up the internal control system varied. The COSO report provided consensus in these three areas.

INTERNAL CONTROL OBJECTIVES

COSO's landmark study, titled Internal Control—Integrated Framework, is rapidly becoming widely accepted by the major U. S. accounting bodies as the authority on internal controls.* The study defined internal control as a "process, effected by an entity's board of directors, management, and other personnel, designed to provide reasonable assurance regarding the achievement of **control objectives** in the following categories:

---

*For example, COSO's recommendations have been incorporated by the American Institute of Certified Public Accountants (AICPA) into SAS No. 78—Consideration of Internal Control in a Financial Statement Audit: An Amendment to SAS No. 55. New York: AICPA, 1995. This statement conforms to the COSO recommendations.

- Effectiveness and efficiency of operations.
- Reliability of financial reporting.
- Compliance with applicable laws and regulations.*

The second control objective, concerning the reliability of financial reporting, is dependent on the transaction processing portion of the AIS. As discussed in a later section, several subobjectives must be accomplished to fulfill this objective. The first and third control objectives pertain to the operational system of a firm. In essence, their purposes are to ensure (1) that the firm is in compliance with relevant laws and regulations and (2) that operations are performed (a) *effectively*—in a manner best to achieve the firm's broad goals and (b) *efficiently*—in a manner that does not waste resources.

In striving to achieve these objectives, the ICS incorporates a variety of established procedures. For instance, Diane Varney of Infoage matches the actual cash on hand and in the bank to the amount reflected in the cash budget account; she also matches the customer number on a cash remittance advice to the number of an account in the accounts receivable master file.

Control objectives are not easily achieved, however. One difficulty arises from the changes faced by a modern firm, ranging from the ever-changing tax laws to rapidly developing technology. Another difficulty derives from the array of risks to which the ICS and its firm is exposed. A third difficulty, related to the first, concerns the use of computer technology within the control structure. For example, both Infoage and Ann Strong must implement additional internal controls unique to the computer environment, as well as other internal controls for the manual portions of their AISs. A fourth difficulty may be traced to the human factor, since control objectives are accomplished through people. For example, George Freeman, president of Infoage, and his subordinate managers may establish policies, procedures, rules, and benchmarks that are unclear and unwise. Infoage's employees may not follow procedures consistently or may make incorrect comparisons. A final difficulty relates to the costs of controls. For instance, how does Diane Varney decide whether the benefits of installing an additional internal control procedure into an accounting application are worth the cost involved?

FINANCIAL-ORIENTED VIEW OF THE INTERNAL CONTROL STRUCTURE

The five interrelated components and other considerations of the ICS are depicted in Figure 7-3. These components are as follows:

- Control environment
- Risk assessment
- Control activities
- Information and communication
- Monitoring

All firms need each of the components of the ICS to ensure strong control over their activities. The extent to which each component is implemented is influenced by the size and complexity of the firm, type of industry, management philosophy, and corporate culture. For example, in smaller firms, such as Ann Strong's, the five com-

---

*Committee of Sponsoring Organizations of the Treadway Commission, *Internal Control: Integrated Framework*, volume 1 of 2, 1994, p. 3.

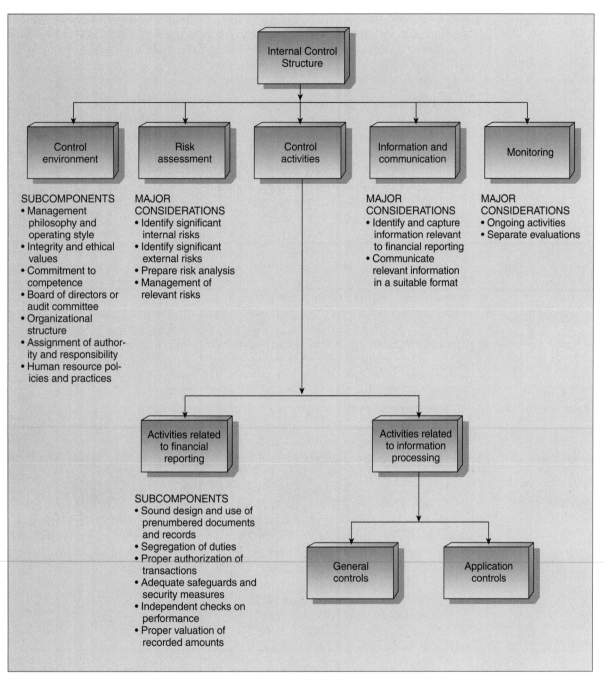

FIGURE 7-3 Components and major considerations of the internal control structure.

ponents may be implemented informally. Larger firms require a more formal structure to ensure that its objectives are satisfied.

We present a "systems" model of the ICS based upon the concepts of the COSO report. In this model all components of the ICS interact to help achieve enterprise-wide objectives. First, we take a financial-oriented view of the five components of the ICS that helps ensure that reliable financial statements and reports are prepared. Then, we examine the aspects of the ICS that help achieve a firm's nonfinancial operations and compliance objectives. During this survey we should be aware that the five components often overlap. That is, an operation's objective may overlap with and help to achieve certain financial reporting objectives. Likewise, a financial reporting objective may overlap with and aid in achieving certain compliance objectives, and so on.

Control Environment Component   Every size organization should devise a strong internal control environment. The control environment "sets the tone of an organization, influencing the control consciousness of its people. It is the foundation for all other components of internal control, providing discipline and structure."* It is the overall attitude and awareness of the board of directors, audit committee, managers, owners, and employees concerning the importance and emphasis of internal control in the firm. The internal control environment is composed of the seven subcomponents portrayed in Figure 7-3. A weak control environment is a "red flag" that often indicates weaknesses in the other components of the ICS. We examine each subcomponent below.

Management should strive to create an environment or culture that minimizes the occurrence of fraudulent financial reporting and other wrongdoing. First, **management philosophy and operating style,** a subcomponent of the control environment, requires certain positive management actions. These actions include setting an example of ethical behavior by following a personal code of ethics, establishing a formal corporate code of conduct, stressing the importance of internal controls, and treating personnel fairly and with respect. Some key questions to assist in assessing this factor are provided in Figure 7-4. The importance of management integrity is emphasized in the next subcomponent.

Integrity and ethical values is a second subcomponent of the control environment. From all indications, it appears that ethical and unethical behaviors of managers and employees can have a pervasive impact on the entire ICS, creating an atmosphere that can significantly influence the validity of the financial reporting process. Every public or nonpublic firm should prepare a written code of corporate conduct that determines the appropriate tone of management, subordinates, and employees. Management should take a *proactive* approach to ensure that all employees are fully aware of these standards and their assigned responsibilities. Thus managers should require subordinate managers and employees to read the code and sign the last page, indicating that they understand it. Furthermore, all managers should act as strong role models, strictly following the standards in their own daily behavior. Management that follows strong ethical principles when confronted with a difficult decision sends a strong positive message to all employees. A small firm such as Ann Strong's may develop only a very brief written statement. However, Ann could orally communicate acceptable behavior in staff meetings, in one-on-one meetings, and in dealings with her clients.

Management should establish enlightened policies that encourage long-term goals and delineate fair human resource practices. Many managers—knowingly or unknowingly—provide their subordinates with strong incentives to engage in questionable behavior. For instance, employees may be pressured to meet unrealistic short-term performance goals, with the consequence that they may "pad" the figures on reports. In one large firm, several managers created millions of dollars of fictitious journal entries to inflate the ending inventory, resulting in a much larger income than otherwise would have been reported. When apprehended, they revealed that

---

*Ibid., p. 23.

Management Philosophy and Operating Style
- Does management emphasize short-term profits and operating goals to the detriment of long-term goals?
- Is the management group dominated by one or a few individuals?
- What type of business risks does management take and how are these risks managed?
- Is management conservative or aggressive toward selecting from available alternative accounting principles?

Organization Structure
- Is an up-to-date organization chart prepared, showing the names of key personnel?
- Is the information systems function separated from incompatible functions?
- How is the accounting department organized?
- Is the internal audit function separate and distinct from accounting?
- Do subordinate managers report to more than one superior?

Assignment of Authority and Responsibility
- Does the company prepare written employee job descriptions defining specific duties and reporting relationships?
- Is written approval required for changes made to information systems?
- Does the company clearly delineate to employees and managers the boundaries of authority-responsibility relationships?
- Does the company properly delegate authority to employees and departments?

Human Resource Policies and Practices
- Are new personnel indoctrinated with respect to internal controls, ethics policies, and corporate code of conduct?
- Is the company in compliance with the Americans with Disabilities Act? The Equal Employment Opportunity Act?
- Are grievance procedures to manage conflict in force?
- Does the company maintain a sound employee relations program?
- Do employees work in safe, healthy environments?
- Are counseling programs available to employees?
- Are proper separation programs in force for employees who leave the firm?
- Are employees who have access to cash and other negotiable instruments bonded? (A fidelity bond indemnifies a firm when it incurs losses of insured assets, due to events such as fraudulent activities of bonded employees.)

FIGURE 7-4   An example of key questions to aid in evaluating certain subcomponents of the internal control environment.

they were under extreme pressure from top management to produce short-term "bottom-line" results. Undesirable behaviors can be reduced or eliminated by removing the incentives and temptations, that is, through an emphasis on ethics.

A third subcomponent of the control environment is **commitment to competence.** Firms must recruit competent and trustworthy employees to encourage initiative and creativity and to react quickly to changing conditions. Thus the recruiting department should staff all positions with personnel who have the knowledge and skills to accomplish a job at a satisfactory level of performance.

The **board of directors or audit committee** is a fourth subcomponent of the control environment. A properly functioning board of directors should appoint an audit committee of outside directors. The audit committee's role is to actively

---

1. Establish an internal audit department.

2. Review the scope and status of audits.

3. Review audit findings with the board and ensure that management has taken proper action recommended in the audit report and letter of reportable conditions.

4. Maintain a direct line of communication among the board, management, external auditors, and internal auditors and periodically arrange meetings among the parties.

5. Review the audited financial statements with the external auditors and the board of directors.

6. Require periodic quality reviews of the operations of the internal audit department to identify areas needing improvement.

7. Supervise special investigations, such as fraud investigations.

8. Assess the performance of financial management.

9. Require a review of compliance with laws and regulations and with corporate codes of conduct.

FIGURE 7-5   Key functions performed by audit committees.

oversee the firm's accounting and financial reporting policies and practices and to act as a liaison between the board and the external and internal auditors. An audit committee can significantly contribute to the early detection of control deficiencies and other irregularities by performing the key functions shown in Figure 7-5.

A fifth subcomponent of the control environment is **organizational structure,** which identifies the framework of formal relationships for achieving firm objectives. Principal responsibilities and reporting relationships are often depicted in an organization chart. Some key questions to assess this factor are shown in Figure 7-4.

Another subcomponent of the control environment is **assignment of authority and responsibility.** Authority is the right to command subordinates on the basis of rank or formal position. Responsibility is one's obligation to perform assigned duties and to be held accountable for the results attained. Methods of assigning authority and responsibility can have a significant impact on accomplishing objectives. Examples of key questions to aid in assessing this factor are shown in Figure 7-4.

Human resource policies and practices is the seventh and final subcomponent of the control environment to be examined. This factor involves a consideration of policies regarding the recruitment, orientation, training, motivation, evaluation, promotion, compensation, counseling, discharge, and protection of employees. Sound human resource policies and practices can significantly aid a firm to achieve efficient operations and to maintain data integrity. Some key questions to help assess personnel policies and practices are presented in Figure 7-4.

To summarize, all seven subcomponents should be assessed and evaluated before a valid conclusion can be reached on the overall effectiveness of the control environment.

Risk Assessment Component   All firms, regardless of size, structure, or industry, face significant internal and external risks. If possible, top management should be directly involved in conducting the risk assessment. A precondition to the risk assessment is the establishment of objectives. The **risk assessment** component of the ICS consists of (1) the identification and analysis of relevant risks that may prevent the attainment of objectives and (2) the formation of a plan to determine how to manage the risks.* The subject of business risk assessment is examined in the risk exposures

---

*Ibid., p. 33.

section of this chapter. Audit risks relevant to the preparation of financial statements are addressed in Chapter 10.

Control Activities Component A firm should develop specific **control activities**—policies and procedures—to help ensure that management directives are properly carried out. To fulfill objectives, control activities are implemented to address specific risks identified during risk assessment. One subcomponent of control activities relates to the achievement of financial reporting objectives and includes the representative items portrayed in Figure 7-3. These items are further discussed in Chapter 8. Another category of control activities relevant to achieving financial reporting objectives, but not depicted in Figure 7-3, is performance reviews. Such reviews include the following:

- Comparing budget to actual values.
- Relating different sets of data—operating or financial—to one another, together with analyses of the relationships and investigative and corrective actions.
- Reviewing functional performance, such as a bank's consumer loan manager's review of reports by branch, region, and loan type for loan approvals and collections.[*]

A third subcomponent of control activities presented in Figure 7-3, divided into general and application controls (examined in Chapter 8), helps ensure the reliability and integrity of information systems that process both financial and nonfinancial information.

The control activities implemented at both small and medium-sized firms are similar. For example, both Infoage and Ann Strong should implement general and application controls for the manual and computerized portions of their information processing systems. The control process will be more formal at Infoage than at Ann Strong's firm. Since Infoage has more employees, the firm can develop an effective separation of duties. Further, a small firm may find that many control activities are not required because the owner-manager is involved in all aspects of the firm's operations. Thus, Ann Strong can overcome any incompatible duties among her employees by exercising a great deal of owner control. For instance, she can authorize all transactions, sign all checks, prepare bank reconciliations, supervise employees that use the microcomputer, review sales made to her major customers, and analyze key financial statement relationships.

Information and Communication Component Information must be identified, processed, and communicated so that appropriate personnel may carry out their responsibilities. A properly functioning information system helps ensure that responsibilities are achieved. One major information system, the AIS, helps attain financial reporting objectives. The AIS "consists of the methods and records established to record, process, summarize, and report entity transactions (as well as events and conditions) and to maintain accountability for the related assets, liabilities, and equity."[†]

The following subobjectives ensure that the AIS's methods and records result in reliable financial reporting:

1. All transactions entered for processing are valid and authorized.
2. All valid transactions are captured and entered for processing on a timely basis and in sufficient detail to permit the proper classification of transaction.

---

[*]Ibid., pp. 49–50.
[†]AICPA, SAS No. 78, pp. 11–12.

3. The input data of all entered transactions are accurate and complete, with the transactions being expressed in proper monetary terms.

4. All entered transactions are processed properly to update all affected records of master files and/or other types of data sets.

5. All required outputs are prepared according to appropriate rules to provide accurate and reliable information. For example, ensure that financial statements such as income statements are prepared from complete and up-to-date records and in accordance with generally accepted accounting principles.

6. All transactions are recorded in the proper accounting period.

Information must be effectively communicated throughout the organization to all appropriate personnel. A properly functioning AIS communicates information in standard written reports, policy manuals, accounting and financial reporting manuals, and memoranda. Information can also be communicated orally, graphically, and electronically. The actions of management, such as maintaining open channels of communication, provide accounting and other personnel with a means of communicating significant information upstream.

Monitoring Component   The purpose of **monitoring,** the final component of the ICS, is to assess the quality of the ICS over time by conducting ongoing activities, separate evaluations, or a combination of the two. **Ongoing monitoring activities,** such as supervision of employees, are conducted daily, and **separate monitoring activities,** such as audits, are performed periodically. Small firms, such as Ann Strong's consulting firm, are more likely to employ ongoing monitoring activities. Since she is closely involved in the daily business operations, Ann can quickly spot deviations in critical processes and uncover inaccuracies in the reports she receives. Ann is also familiar with correspondence with regulators and with complaints received from vendors and customers that may indicate a breakdown in the control process over time. Infoage can also informally conduct ongoing monitoring activities since it is a small firm with a flat organization structure. The president of Infoage and his key managers can perform similar ongoing monitoring functions as those performed by Ann Strong. Infoage's president could also assign Diane Varney, treasurer and controller, to perform separate evaluations of internal controls. Since Infoage employs no internal auditor, the firm may hire an external auditing firm to conduct more in-depth, separate evaluations of the ICS and to audit the financial statements.

Ongoing and separate monitoring activities include internal and external auditing. Evaluating the internal control structure and accounting records can best be done by auditors. Thus **internal auditors** are often assigned to a permanent organizational function within the firm. The internal audit function is an independent appraisal activity that examines and evaluates the adequacy and effectiveness of the control system and promotes effective and efficient operations. **External auditors** perform periodic independent verifications or audits of the accounting records underlying the financial statements. External auditors also provide written reports containing recommendations for strengthening the ICS.

NONFINANCIAL-ORIENTED VIEW
OF THE INTERNAL CONTROL STRUCTURE

This section examines the compliance and operations objectives of the ICS. We must remember, however, that some controls overlap, satisfying both financial and nonfinancial objectives. An operations control can help meet financial reporting objectives; a financial reporting control can ensure compliance. Since the preceding section outlined the basic framework of the ICS, much of the discussion is relevant to this section. The nonfinancial-oriented view considers the same five components of the ICS, except that we concentrate on the factors relevant to achieving each component's operations and compliance objectives.

A strong control environment maintained by general management influences the attainment of operations and compliance objectives. For these nonfinancial managers, each component of the control environment depicted in Figure 7-3 is related specifically to engineering, production, and marketing managers' areas of responsibility.

With respect to risk assessment, significant nonfinancial objectives, such as performance goals, market share goals, safeguards against losses of resources, and adherence to laws and regulations, should be identified. The four major considerations included in a risk assessment as delineated in Figure 7-3 are related to these objectives.

Regarding the information and communication component of the ICS, management must improve the financial reporting system to capture and process not only financial information but also pertinent nonfinancial information and communicate it to appropriate personnel. Examples of nonfinancial information include information about product defect rates, orders filled, accident statistics, competitors' product releases, number of customer complaints, and percent of products returned. Financial and nonfinancial reporting systems, as well as ways to improve the reporting process, are covered in Chapter 15.

Control and monitoring activities important to the attainment of nonfinancial goals include management control and operational control systems. External auditors limit their reviews of nonfinancial controls to those that influence the presentation of external financial reports, such as budgets and performance reports. Internal auditors are equally concerned with all aspects of control.

Management Control Systems The **management control** process focuses on managerial performance, rather than on technical operations. Management control systems involve developing control and monitoring activities to evaluate performance and supervise the firm's activities on an ongoing basis. Their purpose is to encourage compliance with the firm's policies and procedures and with laws and regulations. Policies are the strategies or guidelines by which the overall goals and objectives are to be achieved; procedures are the prescribed steps by which specified tasks are accomplished. If the policies and procedures are soundly developed, resources should thereby be acquired and used effectively and efficiently. As the term implies, management control is exercised through the actions of managers. These activities usually follow the organizational structure of a firm, since the managers function through responsibility centers. For example, Infoage's organization chart (refer to Figure 2-4) shows seven organization units or departments with a manager responsible for the operation of each unit. Management control is exercised by each of the seven managers to ensure that the unit's resources are used effectively and efficiently in achieving objectives.

Consider, for instance, budget preparation for each of Infoage's seven units. A budget is a control activity employed to satisfy an entity's financial and nonfinancial objectives. Through comparisons with actual performance, the budgeted amounts can help to detect inefficiencies, losses, and other unfavorable results in Diane Varney's department, Jane Thomson's department, and so on. A budget can be prepared to track production processes and major marketing thrusts in Mike Barker's department—to measure the extent to which operations' goals are being attained. Actions taken by individual managers at Infoage to analyze and follow up on such reporting represent management control activities.

Other management control and monitoring activities include review of reports by Infoage's managers to identify trends such as data on new business, competitors' product releases, market share percentages, and customer complaint trends, and to relate the results to economic statistics and targets. For example, an outlet manager at Infoage receives a report on the dollar amount of new business obtained by his assistant manager, and depending on the materiality of any unfavorable variances, suitable corrective action is taken.

An organization's operations and internal controls are often affected by forces outside its control. Another management control activity is to monitor compliance with legislation and external regulatory agencies, such as bank regulatory agencies. For example, many firms must comply with the provisions of the Foreign Corrupt Practices Act, Americans with Disabilities Act, Family and Medical Leave Act, and others. Penalties for noncompliance can result in stiff fines and jail sentences.

Operational Control System   The process or system that promotes effectiveness and efficiency in performing day-to-day operating tasks is called **operational control.** Operational control systems within typical firms are the inventory control system, the credit control system, the production control system, and the cash control system. For instance, a credit check of a customer ordering microcomputers from Infoage is a central control within the credit control system; it also is a key control in Infoage's sales transaction processing system. Similarly, a bank reconciliation prepared by Diane Varney's accounting staff is an important part of the cash control system; it also is a key control in Infoage's cash receipts and cash disbursements transaction processing systems.

Operational control systems are also concerned with controlling individual employees. For example, operational employees such as the two data-entry clerks at Infoage should be rotated among jobs and shifts. Employees in key positions of trust at Infoage such as the two outlet managers should be required to take periodic vacations, to subject their activities to review by substitutes. In addition, the two outlet managers should be well supervised, so that they are encouraged to follow established policies and to avoid irregularities. Diane Varney should closely observe and review the actions of the accountants and bookkeepers working in her department. Finally, employees should be terminated only in accordance with reasonable and well-publicized policies. Lax or nonexistent policies in operational control areas can have a significant negative impact on the entire financial reporting process, possibly resulting in widespread theft, errors, embezzlement, fraudulent financial statements, and conflicts of interest.

For the controls provided by the internal control structure to be adequate, they should counteract all the significant risks to which a firm is exposed. We now turn our attention to the subject of risk exposures.

RISK EXPOSURES

Every entity, such as a business firm, faces risks that reduce the chances of it achieving its control objectives. **Risk exposures** may arise from a variety of internal and external sources, such as employees, customers, computer hackers, criminals, and acts of nature. Figure 7-6 lists these sources. Risks change over time due to circumstances, including the hiring of new employees, the introduction of new highly sophisticated technology, corporate restructurings, and operations in foreign countries.

- Clerical and operational employees, who process transactional data and have access to assets.
- Computer programmers, who prepare computer programs and have knowledge relating to the instructions by which transactions are processed.
- Managers and accountants, who have access to records and financial reports and often have authority to approve transactions.
- Former employees, who may still understand the control structure and may harbor grudges against the firm.
- Customers and suppliers, who generate many of the transactions processed by the firm.
- Competitors, who may desire to acquire confidential information of the firm, such as new product plans.
- Outside persons, such as computer hackers and criminals, who have various reasons to access the firm's data or its assets or to commit destructive acts.
- Acts of nature or accidents, such as floods and fires and equipment breakdowns.

FIGURE 7-6 Sources of risk to which a firm is exposed.

In order to design sound control systems, accountants and system designers should be able to assess the risks that affect a firm's objectives. Risk assessment consists of identifying the relevant risks, analyzing those risks in terms of the extent of exposure, and managing risks by proposing effective control procedures.

TYPES OF RISKS

Among the system-related risks, other than poor decision making and inefficient and ineffective operations, that confront the typical firm are the following:

Unintentional Errors Errors may appear in input data, such as in customer names or numbers. Alternatively, they may appear during processing, as when clerks incorrectly multiply quantities ordered (on customers' orders) times unit prices of the merchandise items. These errors often occur on an occasional and random basis, as when a clerk accidentally strikes the wrong key on a terminal keyboard. However, errors may occur consistently. For instance, an incorrectly written computer program may produce computational errors each time the program is executed. In any of these situations, the erroneous data will damage the accuracy and reliability of a firm's files and outputs. Unintentional errors often occur because employees lack knowledge owing to inadequate training; they may also occur when employees become tired and careless or are inadequately supervised.

Deliberate Errors Deliberate errors constitute **fraud,** since they are made to secure unfair or unlawful gain. These irregularities may appear in input data, during processing, or in generated outputs. For instance, a clerk may increase the amount on a check received from a customer or underfoot a column of cash receipts. Either type of error damages the accuracy and reliability of files and/or outputs. Additionally, deliberate errors may also conceal thefts (and hence losses) of assets. For example, a manager may enter a misstatement in a report or financial statement. This type of error could mislead and thereby injure stockholders and creditors.

Unintentional Losses of Assets Assets may be lost or misplaced by accident. For example, newly received merchandise items may be put into the wrong warehouse bins, with the result that they are not found by pickers when filling orders. Data as well as physical assets may be lost. For instance, the accounts receivable file stored on a magnetic disk may be wiped out by a sudden power surge.

Thefts of Assets Assets of a firm may be stolen by outsiders, such as professional thieves who break into a storeroom in the dead of night. Alternatively, assets may be misappropriated through embezzlement or defalcation, that is, taken by employees who have been entrusted with their care. For instance, a cashier may pocket currency received by mail, or a production worker may carry home a tool. Employees who embezzle often create deliberate errors in order to hide their thefts. Thus, the cashier who pockets currency may overstate the cash account.

Breaches of Security Unauthorized persons may gain access to the data files and reports of a firm. For instance, a "hacker" may break into a firm's computerized files via a distant terminal, or an employee may peek at a salary report in an unlocked file drawer. Security breaches can be very damaging in certain cases, as when competitors gain access to a firm's confidential marketing plans.

Acts of Violence and Natural Disasters Certain violent acts cause damage to a firm's assets, including data. If sufficiently serious, they can interrupt business operations and even propel firms toward bankruptcy. Examples of such acts are sabotage of computer facilities and the willful destruction of customer files. Although violent acts are sometimes performed by outsiders such as terrorists, they are more often performed by disgruntled current employees and vengeful ex-employees. Also, violent acts can arise from nonhuman sources, such as fires that engulf computer rooms, short circuits that disable printers, and natural disasters such as hurricanes and tornadoes that destroy computer resources.

DEGREE OF RISK EXPOSURE

To combat risks effectively, the degree of risk exposure should be assessed. Exposure to risk is affected by factors such as the following:

1. **Frequency.** The more frequent an occurrence, the greater the exposure to risk. A merchandising firm that makes numerous sales is highly exposed to errors in the transaction data. A contractor that bids on custom projects is exposed to calculating errors. A department store with numerous browsing shoppers has a significant exposure to merchandise losses from shoplifting.

2. **Vulnerability.** The more vulnerable an asset, the greater the exposure to risk. Cash is highly vulnerable to theft, since it is easily hidden and fully convertible. A telephone may be vulnerable to unauthorized use for long-distance calls, especially if it is left untended in a remote office.

3. **Size.** The higher the monetary value of a potential loss, the greater the risk exposure. An accounts receivable file represents a high-risk exposure, since it contains essential information concerning amounts owed and other matters that affect credit customers.

When two or more of the foregoing factors act in unison, the exposure to risk is multiplied. Thus, an extremely high exposure occurs in the case of a firm that conducts numerous sales for cash, with each sale involving a sizable amount. As might be imagined, this situation requires more extensive controls than a situation in which the exposure to risk is slight.

PROBLEM CONDITIONS AFFECTING EXPOSURES TO RISK

The exposures to risk faced by a firm can be heightened by various internal conditions. Perhaps most serious are weaknesses in one or more of the control systems. Weaknesses may be caused by an inadequate selection of controls. Thus thefts are abetted when the organizational structure is weakened by an inadequate segregation of duties. Control system weaknesses may also occur because of breakdowns. For instance, a manager may sign a purchase order authorizing the purchase of merchandise, but does not carefully study the document. Other problem conditions involve collusion, lack of enforcement, and computer crime.

Collusion   A frustrating condition of which a firm must be aware is internal **collusion:** the cooperation of two or more employees for a fraudulent purpose. For instance, an employee who has custody over inventory may remove inventory items from the storeroom, while another employee who keeps inventory records deducts the removed items from the records; the consequence to the employer is lost inventory and covered tracks. Collusion may also involve an employee and a nonemployee. This situation is known as external collusion. Either type of collusion is difficult to counteract, even with soundly designed control systems.

Lack of **Enforcement**   Still another troubling condition is lack of enforcement. Thus a firm may have adequate management policies and control procedures, but may overlook irregularities. For instance, an employee who has committed embezzlement may not be prosecuted on being detected, perhaps so the firm may avoid embarrassment over its weak security measures. Such lack of action by a firm may encourage other potential wrongdoers.

Computer Crime   A relatively recent risk of heightened proportions is computer crime. Because of its prominence, we shall delve into this problem in more detail.

COMPUTER FRAUD AND CONTROL PROBLEMS RELATED TO COMPUTERS

Computer systems present special risk exposures and problems of control. After surveying these exposures and problems, we shall examine the impacts computer systems have on controls. In the following two chapters, we emphasize the controls that are needed when computer systems are installed.

IMPORTANCE OF COMPUTER FRAUD

Offenses involving computer-based systems have grown in quantity and seriousness in recent years. **Computer fraud** poses very high degrees of risk, since all three factors—frequency, vulnerability, and size—tend to be present. A computer-based system may process hundreds of transactions per hour, with each transaction being subject to error or fraudulent activity. A computer and its stored data are often vulnerable to unauthorized access as well as to damage. To make matters worse, fraudulent activities—by either authorized or unauthorized persons—are very difficult to detect. Also, the average loss per incident of computer fraud is significantly larger than the average fraud loss when manual systems are involved. Huge quantities of data and lightning-fast processing speeds magnify the payoff from computer fraud. Individual losses from computer fraud can easily exceed two or more millions of dollars.

A famous case uncovered as early as 1973 illustrates the magnitude that computer fraud can assume. Equity Funding Corporation, an insurance holding firm in Los Angeles, employed its computer system to create over 63,000 fictitious insurance policies with assumed values of hundreds of millions of dollars. In addition to reporting grossly inflated assets in its 1972 year-end financial statements, the

SPOTLIGHTING

COMPUTER FRAUD
at First Fidelity Bank*

The senior vice-president for information systems and technology of First Fidelity Bank of Newark, New Jersey, Robert Venezia, was accused of embezzlement in October 1990. Mr. Venezia established two shell business firms, Universal Business Supplies and American Leasing Co., which submitted invoices regularly for payment, based on apparently legitimate (but really fictitious) supplies and services. As a senior manager of the bank, Mr. Venezia was allegedly authorized to approve payments for routine invoices. The computer system then processed checks for the two shell firms. Over a period of 11 years he was allegedly able to accumulate $6.2 million through payments received

on such routine invoices. Although repeated audits and bank examinations were performed, the auditors and examiners did not detect the spurious invoices or question the payments of relatively small amounts. They apparently accepted the invoices because they were approved by an authorized person.

This situation illustrates the dangers of computer crime committed by insiders. In order to counteract fraudulent actions by insiders, auditors must test the trustworthiness of transactions and data within files. In this particular instance, they should have verified that all frequently used suppliers had legitimate operations and places of business. They should not assume that payable transactions are valid just because the invoices have been approved.

*Belden Menkus, "More Attention Needs to be Paid to Insider Computer Criminals." EDPACS (February 1991), pp. 9–11.

higher-level managers of the firm embezzled millions of dollars by selling the policies to reinsurers.

COMPUTER CRIMES

A **computer crime** is defined as any type of criminal act in which the computer is directly or indirectly involved. Sabotage of computer facilities is classified as a direct computer crime, and unauthorized access of stored data is an indirect computer crime because the presence of the computer created the environment for committing the crime. The Equity Funding case is an indirect computer crime, since the computer was used to create the fictitious insurance policies and to conceal the crime by storing the fake data on magnetic media.

The type of person who commits computer crimes seems to have a profile that is similar to that of white-collar criminals, except that as a group, white-collar criminals are older. He or she tends to be intelligent and without a previous criminal record. The person is seldom prone to violence toward others. Generally, however, he or she has a personal problem for which computer fraud appears to be the answer. Since the computer can be viewed as an inanimate object without human feelings, the perpetrator can treat any planned manipulation as a challenge rather than as an illegal action. A typical profile is presented in the appendix to this chapter.

> **Theft of computer hardware and software.** The latter, known as software piracy, is quite prevalent. It involves making unauthorized copies of programs and software packages, usually from diskettes.
>
> **Unauthorized use of computer facilities for personal use.** This crime may be committed by a "hacker," who breaks into a computer system via a remote terminal or microcomputer, or by an employee who runs his or her own programs on the firm's computer.
>
> **Fraudulent modification or use of data or programs.** In most fraud cases the perpetrator intends to steal assets, such as cash or merchandise. For instance, a purchasing agent may enter unauthorized purchase transactions via a terminal and have merchandise sent to his home. A programmer employed by a bank may modify a withdrawal program in a manner that causes withdrawals against his or her personal account to be charged to an inactive account.

FIGURE 7-7 Examples of types of computer crimes.

OTHER COMPUTER-RELATED MISCHIEF AND CONTROL PROBLEMS

In addition to fraud, computer systems are subject to each type of risk exposure listed in the previous section. Unintentional errors in transactions and losses of assets, as well as breaches of security and acts of violence, can and do occur on a frequent basis. Figure 7-7 lists a few of the many actual occurrences.

Furthermore, computer programs themselves are vulnerable to a variety of mischievous software techniques that can cause significant damage. These techniques travel under such colorful names as viruses, worms, trapdoors, and Trojan Horses.

Other important aspects of noncomputer fraud, computer fraud, and viruses, including several pertinent examples, are covered in the appendix to this chapter.

REASONS WHY COMPUTERS CAUSE CONTROL PROBLEMS

Computer-based information systems manipulate and transcribe data with impeccable accuracy. In spite of this significant advantage, computers do introduce severe problems of control. The major reasons for such problems can be traced to the following inherent characteristics of computer-based systems.

Processing Is Concentrated   In manual systems the processing is done by clerks in various departments, thereby providing for adequate segregation of duties. Employees can cross-check each other's work, thus detecting processing errors. In computer-based systems the processing is often concentrated within self-contained computer facilities. Certain organizational units are bypassed during processing operations.

Consequently, less opportunity exists for detecting errors and fraudulent events such as unauthorized transactions, changes in programmed instructions, and thefts of assets.

Audit Trails May Be Undermined   Portions of the audit trail are more likely to be fragmented or eliminated in computer-based systems than in manual systems. Source documents may not be used, for instance, when sales orders are received via telephones and entered directly through terminals. Journals or other records may not be maintained when transactions or adjustments are posted directly to ledgers (master files). These shortcuts improve processing efficiency but cause partial losses of the audit trail. One consequence is that fraudulent acts are less likely to leave traces that can be detected.

Human Judgment Is Bypassed   Computers perform programmed instructions blindly; that is, they exercise no judgment. Thus fewer opportunities exist for persons to spot errors and questionable data or to observe processing steps. Without special programmed controls and reviews of processed results, transaction errors and irregularities in data can easily escape detection.

Data Are Stored in Device-Oriented, Rather Than Human-Oriented, Forms   Data stored in computer-based systems are oriented to the characteristics of magnetic or optical media. These characteristics differ radically from the paper-oriented and hence human-oriented media familiar to users. First, the data are invisible. Although this characteristic does not cause a serious problem, it is necessary for users to take specific steps to retrieve the data in readable form. The necessity for data retrieval increases opportunities for errors and often frustrates users. Second, stored data (except for read-only memory) are erasable. Thus, valuable data, such as accounts receivable records, may be lost. Third, data are stored in compressed form. A single magnetic disk can hold as much data as several file cabinets. Thus damage to a single device can cause the loss of a tremendous quantity of valuable data. Finally, stored data are relatively accessible. This condition is particularly acute in the cases of on-line computer systems and computer networks, since persons can access data from various points where terminals and on-line microcomputers are located. Thus knowledgeable but unauthorized persons may more easily gain access to vital files.

Computer Equipment Is Powerful but Complex and Vulnerable   As a result of its processing power, a computer-based system can disseminate errors throughout files and reports more quickly. Because of its complexity, a computer system tends to be confusing to many employees, both at the clerical and the managerial levels. Such confusion can cause employees to make errors. It also may lead employees to resist questioning computer output or suggesting improvements in computer systems, including improved control procedures. Complexity in computer hardware also causes a system to be vulnerable to breakdowns. If the breakdowns are not quickly repaired, serious interruptions to business operations may occur. Furthermore, computer hardware is often placed in fixed locations, thus rendering it relatively vulnerable to disasters such as fires, floods, and vandalism.

Figure 7-8 summarizes these control problems caused by computerization. The second and third columns in the figure contrast key characteristics of manual systems with those of computer-based systems. The two columns on the right list the added exposures to risks faced by computer-based systems and the types of controls and security measures needed to offset the risk exposures.

Element or Activity	Manual System Characteristics	Computer-Based System Characteristics	Computer-Based System Risk Exposures	Computer-Based System Compensating Controls
Data collection	Data recorded on paper source documents. Data reviewed for errors by clerks	Data sometimes captured without use of source documents. Data often not subject to review by clerks	Audit trail may be partially lost. Errors, accidental or deliberate, may be entered for processing	Printed copies of source documents prepared by computer system. Edit checks performed by computer system
Data processing	Processing steps performed by clerks who possess judgment. Processing steps spread among various clerks in separate departments. Processing requires use of journals and ledgers. Processing performed relatively slowly	Processing steps performed by CPU "blindly" in accordance with program instructions. Processing steps concentrated within computer CPU. Processing does not require use of journals. Processing performed very rapidly.	Errors may cause incorrect results of processing. Unauthorized manipulation of data and theft of assets can occur on larger scale. Audit trail may be partially lost. Effects of errors may spread rapidly throughout files	Outputs reviewed by users of computer system; carefully developed computer processing programs. Restricted access to computer facilities; clear procedure for authorizing changes to programs. Printed journals and other analyses. Editing of all data during input and processing steps
Data storage and retrieval	Data stored in file drawers throughout the various departments. Data stored on hard copies in human-readable form. Stored data accessible on a piecemeal basis at various locations	Data compressed on magnetic media (e.g., tapes, disks). Data stored in invisible, erasable, computer-readable form. Stored data often readily accessible from various locations via terminals	Data may be accessed by unauthorized persons or stolen. Data are temporarily unusable by humans, and might possibly be lost. Data may be accessed by unauthorized persons	Security measures at points of access and over data library. Data files printed periodically; backups of files; protection against sudden power losses. Security measures at points of access

FIGURE 7-8 Control problems caused by computerization.

Element or Activity	Manual System		Computer-Based System		
	Characteristics		Characteristics	Risk Exposures	Compensating Controls
Information generation	Outputs generated laboriously and usually in small volumes Outputs usually in hard-copy form		Outputs generated quickly and neatly, often in large volumes Outputs provided in various forms, including soft-copy displays and voice responses	Inaccuracies may be buried in impressive-looking outputs that users accept on faith Information stored on magnetic media is subject to modification (only hard copy provides permanent record)	Reviews by users of outputs, including the checking of amounts Backups of files; periodic printing of stored files onto hard-copy records
Transmission of data and information	Usually transmitted via postal service and hand delivery		Often transmitted by communications lines	Data may be accessed or modified or destroyed by unauthorized persons	Security measures over transmission lines; coding of data; verification of transmitted data
Equipment	Relatively simple, inexpensive, and mobile		Relatively complex, expensive, and in fixed locations	Business operations may be intentionally or unintentionally interrupted; data or hardware may be destroyed; operations may be delayed through inefficiencies	Backup of data and power supply and equipment; preventive maintenance of equipment; restrictions on access to computer facilities; documentation of equipment usage and processing procedures

FIGURE 7-8 (*continued*)

FEASIBILITY OF CONTROLS

Building an effective and feasible internal control structure is not a simple task. It involves more than assembling all of the controls and security measures that come to mind. Audit and cost issues need to be considered.

AUDIT CONSIDERATIONS

A typical AIS undergoes periodic audits. Normally the internal control structure receives particularly close scrutiny during such audits, as we will discuss in Chapter 10. Thus the internal control structure should be designed to be fully auditable. For instance, certain analyses and reconciliations can be generated on a routine basis for use by the auditors. Generally auditors should be consulted during the system design phase, so that all of the needed controls are considered beforehand. Adding controls after the system is designed usually tends to be more costly and difficult.

COST-BENEFIT CONSIDERATIONS

Incorporating a control into an information system involves a cost. If every conceivable control were included within an organization structure, the total cost would likely be exorbitant. Thus, a firm should conduct a **cost-benefit analysis,** in which the following key question is posed: Will the addition of a specific control provide expected benefits (e.g., value) that exceed the cost of the control? If the answer is yes, and there is **reasonable assurance** that the control will achieve specified objectives, the control is a desirable action. The broadest benefit provided by a control usually consists of reducing risk exposures or undesirable events, that is, reducing the risks of failing to achieve one or more of the objectives pertaining to the internal control structure. Specific benefits may be either quantitative or qualitative in nature. Examples are (1) to reduce the losses due to thefts of assets, (2) to improve the reliability of information provided to management, and (3) to improve the reputation of the firm.

Cost of a control includes one-time costs, recurring costs, additional losses caused by control failure, and opportunity costs. Normally, only the first three costs are quantified when a cost-benefit analysis is prepared. One-time costs include the installation of security devices and the training of clerks; recurring costs may be for supplies and salaries for new employees needed to implement the control. An example of an additional cost caused by the failure of a control to prevent or detect a risk exposure is illustrated in step 6 of the cost-benefit analysis presented in Figure 7-9. An opportunity cost arises from the reduced efficiency in transaction processing caused by the added control; reduced efficiency may or may not translate into lost income.

When the cost of a control exceeds its expected benefits, and the control is nevertheless installed, overcontrol exists. For instance, a control might be installed that detects certain errors that are missed by complementary controls. However, the costs from these errors may not be as great as the costs of maintaining the added control.

Before undertaking a cost-benefit analysis, management must set objectives. Without objectives, management cannot identify the risks that may prevent the objectives from being achieved. A cost-benefit analysis involves the interrelated phases of completing (1) a risk analysis and (2) a value of controls analysis. The seven steps in the two phases are illustrated in Figure 7-9 (the first five steps are related to risk analysis and the last two to value of controls analysis.)

1. **Determine specific computer resources subject to control.** These resources consist of people, hardware, software, supplies, files, site-housing the computer, etc.

2. **Determine all potential threats to the company's computer system.** Threats fall into one of four categories: Acts of nature, accidental nonhuman threats, nonintentional human threats, and intentional human threats.

3. **Assess the relevant risks to which the firm is exposed.** That is, rank the risks as to their likelihood of occurrence. For example, omissions may occur many times in one day, while a hurricane may occur once in 25 years. Thus, a firm's geographical location must be considered when rank-ordering risks.

4. **Measure the extent of each relevant risk exposure in dollar terms.** For instance, if the exposure is the possible loss of an asset, the value would be the amount needed to replace the asset.

5. **Multiply the estimated effect of each relevant risk exposure by the estimated frequency of occurrence over a reasonable period, such as a year.** This step will provide the expected loss per year for each risk exposure. Thus, the *expected loss per year* is computed as follows: the expected loss from a single occurrence of the risk exposure is multiplied by the expected number of occurrences of the risk per year. The resulting product is the potential loss that can be incurred by not reducing or avoiding a particular risk. Alternatively, it is the benefit to be gained by avoiding the risk or improving the reliability of information.

6. **Compute the cost of installing and maintaining a control that is to counteract each relevant risk exposure.** This step involves the following substeps: (1) Determine key controls that reduce exposure to each relevant individual risk. (2) Compute one-time and recurring costs of the control measures selected. (3) Determine the reliability percentage of each control. For example, a control expected to have a 95 percent reliability means that the control will fail to prevent or detect risk exposures about 5 percent of the time. (4) The total costs of the controls equal the one-time cost plus the operating costs plus the additional cost (loss) due to failure of the control (i.e., expected loss from the risk exposure $\times$ .05 = loss due to control failure. To illustrate the last factor, assume that an entity estimates the annual loss from embezzlement of cash to be $10,000 if no controls are implemented. However, the firm's accountant prepares a monthly bank reconciliation that reduces the risk of cash embezzlement by 95 percent, or an average of $9,500 annually. Because the bank reconciliation may fail to detect embezzlement 5 percent of the time, this results in an additional cost due to control failure of about $500).

7. **Compare the benefits against the costs of each control.** On a broader level, this comparison should be employed for the group of controls pertaining to individual transaction processing systems and to the activities of the firm as a whole.

FIGURE 7-9   The seven steps to conducting a cost-benefit analysis.

Cost-benefit analyses are difficult to apply. None of the factors is easy to measure. Also, in many situations several controls may be needed to mitigate a particular risk. However, new analytical techniques are being developed. For instance, a technique known as **reliability analysis** calculates reliability by measuring the error probabilities related to a process such as transaction processing.

FORCES FOR THE IMPROVEMENT OF CONTROLS

During earlier periods many an AIS was deficient with respect to controls and security measures. Often the system was intended primarily to provide the needed day-to-day documents and reports and to satisfy legal obligations. In recent decades, however, various forces have arisen to encourage the improvement of internal control systems. Perhaps the most influential forces have been managers, professional associations, and governmental bodies.

NEEDS OF MANAGEMENT

The managers of most firms have recognized their vital stake in adequate internal control structures. On the one hand, they have become aware of the huge losses and damages that can occur to the costly assets entrusted to their care. Newspapers and the other media have publicized the increasing instances of white-collar crime, as well as overt thefts of merchandise and other portable assets. Managers have noted that the average loss from each crime has also been rising dramatically. On the other hand, they have grown concerned about the accuracy and reliability of the information they receive. Being primary users of information from their AISs, they appreciate the potential for making poor decisions owing to inaccurate and incomplete information. Furthermore, with the increasing dependence on computer systems, they have gained a realization of the seriousness of security breaches.

ETHICAL CONCERNS OF PROFESSIONAL ASSOCIATIONS

Professional accounting associations such as the American Institute of Certified Public Accountants (AICPA), the Institute of Management Accountants (IMA), the Institute of Internal Auditors (IIA), and the Information Systems Audit and Control Association (formerly the EDP Auditor's Association) have had a code of ethics or code of professional conduct in force for many years. These codes are self-imposed and self-enforced rules of conduct. One of the most important goals of a code of ethics or conduct is to help professionals choose among alternatives that are not clear-cut. Included in professional association codes are rules pertaining to matters such as independence, technical competence, and suitable practices during audits and consulting engagements involving information systems. The certification programs of these associations increase awareness of the codes of ethics and are essential in developing professionalism.

The codes of conduct have been expanded and clarified by various pronouncements, such as Statements on Auditing Standards issued by the AICPA. Particular attention has been given to internal controls. In spite of these pronouncements, a number of regulatory agencies have criticized the accounting profession for failure to uncover fraudulent financial reporting and other widespread wrongdoing. These frauds often involve millions of dollars in losses to stockholders, who frequently file class-action lawsuits against public accounting firms. Numerous firms have been found guilty of negligently violating the professional code of conduct, resulting in the payment of large fines.

Recently, professional accounting associations at both the national and state levels have established ethics committees to assist practitioners in the self-regulation process. The committees provide members with continuing education courses, advice on ethical matters, investigation of possible ethics violations, and instructional booklets covering a variety of ethics case studies. Some ethics committees provide a "hot line" to advise members on ethical and moral dilemmas encountered in the workplace. Another goal of ethics committees is to encourage the instruction of ethics in accounting curriculums.

Professional computer associations, such as the Data Processing Management Association (DPMA) and the Association for Computing Machinery (ACM), have recently developed codes of ethics, ethics committees, and certification programs. The codes of these professional computer associations address issues such as obligations to the professional association, to the profession, to colleagues, to clients, to the employer, and to society. Thus, Jane Thomson, Infoage's systems services manager, should consider becoming a Certified Computing Professional (CCP).

The major professional computer and accounting associations each follow a different code of ethics, which can create dilemmas when a member belongs to two or more associations. Having analyzed this weakness, the computer associations have formed a joint committee to study the feasibility of developing a universal code of ethics for all computer professionals.

ACTS AND RULINGS OF GOVERNMENTAL BODIES

Investigations by government agencies such as the Securities and Exchange Commission (SEC) have revealed illegal activities within American firms that were not detected by their internal control structures. As a result, Congress passed the **Foreign Corrupt Practices Act** in 1977. In addition to prohibiting certain types of bribes and hidden ownership, this act requires subject corporations to devise and to maintain adequate internal control structures. Managers of these corporations are legally as well as ethically responsible for establishing and maintaining adequate internal control structures. They are expected to establish a level of "control consciousness," so that employees are not inclined to subvert the control structures. Those managements that knowingly circumvent the act's requirements are subject to criminal penalties. It is not surprising that many managements have taken significant actions. For instance, many corporations now maintain sizable internal audit departments.

The part of the act pertaining to internal control structures states that corporations subject to the Securities Exchange Act of 1934 shall

(A) *make and keep books, records, and accounts, which, in reasonable detail, accurately and fairly reflect the transactions and dispositions of the assets of the issuer (corporation); and*
(B) *devise and maintain a system of internal accounting control sufficient to provide reasonable assurance that*
   (i) *transactions are executed in accordance with management's general and specific authorization.*
   (ii) *transactions are recorded as necessary (I) to permit preparation of financial statements in accordance with generally acceptable accounting principles applicable to such statements, and (II) to maintain accountability for assets.*
   (iii) *access to assets is permitted only in accordance with management's general or specific authorization.*
   (iv) *the recorded accountability for assets is compared with the existing assets at reasonable intervals and appropriate action is taken with respect to any differences.*

Subsequent to the Foreign Corrupt Practices Act, the SEC has issued rulings pertaining to internal control structures. In time it may issue a ruling that requires auditors to make formal reports concerning their evaluations of the internal control structures of client firms.

In 1984 Congress passed the Computer Fraud and Abuse Act (as amended in 1986). Under this law it is a crime to knowingly, and with intent to defraud, gain unauthorized access to data stored in the computers of federally regulated financial institutions, the federal government, or computers operating in interstate or foreign commerce. This law applies to corporations as well as to individuals.

The **Financial Fraud Detection and Disclosure Act** has been recently introduced in Congress. If passed, this act would mandate the fraud-related responsibilities of auditors. It is designed to bolster the public's confidence in the U.S. financial reporting process. Auditors would be required to give earlier public notification of management fraud and other illegal activities. Also, the law would require a firm to include in its annual report a description of the internal control structure established by management. This description would enable outside parties to analyze and evaluate the system's effectiveness.

SUMMARY

Control is a monitoring and regulatory process that helps a firm achieve its objectives and fulfill its plans. Elements in the control process are a performance measure, an operating process, a sensor, a benchmark, a planner, and a regulator. A central feature is feedback. Although objectives of all firms regardless of size can be conveniently categorized as either financial or nonfinancial, the two categories often overlap. Financial objectives are concerned with producing reliable financial reports and with safeguarding assets. An entity's nonfinancial objectives are designed to promote operational effectiveness and efficiency and to encourage compliance with management's policies, procedures, laws, and regulations. These objectives are often difficult to achieve owing to business complexity, risk exposures, human factors, costs, and the presence of computers. The process is implemented within a firm through an internal control structure. The interrelated components of an internal control structure promulgated by the Committee of Sponsoring Organizations of the Treadway Commission (COSO) are the control environment, risk assessment, control activities, information and communication, and monitoring. All five components must be assessed and evaluated to ensure that an entity's objectives are attained. Control measures established within an entity's accounting system achieve primarily financial reporting and safeguarding of assets objectives. Management and operational controls that achieve operations and compliance objectives may also contribute to the achievement of financial objectives. Thus, controls frequently overlap, satisfying both financial and nonfinancial objectives. Among the risks that the accounting system counteracts in all firms regardless of size are unintentional errors, deliberate errors, thefts of assets, breaches of security, and acts of violence. The degrees of these risks are affected by such factors as frequency of occurrence, vulnerability of the assets, and size of the potential losses. When computers make up a part of the accounting system, the degrees of risk can be very high. Computers concentrate processing, undermine audit trails, bypass human judgment, store data in devices rather than on paper, and incorporate powerful but complex and vulnerable equipment. Thus, compared to manual systems, significant changes in controls are necessary. However, whether manual or computer-based, the underlying concepts of control are similar—both types of systems strive to attain the same financial and nonfinancial objectives, and to achieve the objectives through an effective internal control structure.

Building an effective and feasible internal control structure requires that audit, cost, ethical, and human factors be considered. Internal control structures are undergoing improvements, partly as a result of forces such as the needs of management, the concerns of professional associations, and the acts and rulings of government bodies.

APPENDIX TO CHAPTER 7

FRAUD AND VIRUSES

Two closely related types of crimes receiving widespread media coverage are noncomputer fraud and computer fraud. Another crime making headlines is a type of sabotage known as computer viruses.

Fraud is defined as any intentional or deliberate scheme that one person uses to gain an unfair advantage over another person by resorting to lying, trickery, surprise, cunning, cheating, or any other unfair means. The major elements of fraud include a misrepresentation of a material point, which is believed and acted upon by a victim who suffers damages. **Financial fraud** is any intentional or deliberate act a wrongdoer commits to deceive other persons who in turn suffer a financial loss.

Crimes Classified as Frauds

Fraud is a very broad term used to describe a wide assortment of crimes, including the following, many of which result in financial losses:

1. **Misrepresentation of material facts.** This fraud offense involves the making of deliberate false statements to induce a victim to part with money or property.* Misrepresentation cases include making false statements or false claims that are often prosecuted under the U.S. Criminal Code statute covering wire

---

*Joseph T. Wells, et al., *Fraud Examiners Manual*, 2nd ed. Austin, Texas: Association of Certified Fraud Examiners, 1993, p. 2.201.

and mail frauds. For example, this statute was used to convict television evangelist Jim Bakker of defrauding tens of millions of dollars from his television viewers who purchased a lifetime share in a theme park based on the facts Bakker presented to them during his television shows. Many external auditors have been found guilty of misrepresentation, such as issuing a false audit report, falsely stating that the audit was conducted in accordance with generally accepted auditing standards, and violating the competency standard of fieldwork that requires all audits to be performed by duly qualified auditors.

2. **Failure to disclose material facts.** As a result of failing to disclose material facts, the victim is misled or deceived. Accountants, lawyers, management, and the board of directors all have an agency relationship involving a special position of trust. These agents must fully disclose material facts to those parties who rely on the facts to make decisions. For example, an external auditor may be held liable for failing to report to the corporate audit committee a material misrepresentation on a financial statement.

3. **Embezzlement. Embezzlement** is a very common fraud committed by persons who have legal possession of another's property. The essence of embezzlement is that it is committed *after* a person has been entrusted with or legally comes into possession of the property. Thus a bookkeeper who handles cash has a fiduciary duty to his or her employer to account for all cash and to record the cash in the appropriate books of account. The bookkeeper commits the crime of embezzlement if he or she confiscates cash.

4. **Larceny. Larceny** is wrongfully taking away someone's personal property with the intent to convert the property to one's personal use. Larceny differs from embezzlement since the intent to commit the crime and the carrying away of the property occur simultaneously. In a larceny the lawbreaker was never legally entrusted with the property. Under most criminal statutes, embezzlement and larceny are types of **theft.**

5. **Bribery. Bribery** is giving or receiving anything of value "to influence" an official act. The thing of value—cash, gifts, loans, paying off credit card debt, travel, or entertainment—is promised or given before the act is completed. That is, the thing of value influences the decision. For example, if a vendor gives a purchasing agent free tickets to the Super Bowl, the agent may feel indebted to make unnecessary future purchases from the vendor.

6. **Illegal gratuity.** An **illegal gratuity** is giving or receiving anything of value "for or because of an official act" that has already taken place. The distinction

between a bribe and illegal gratuity is that a bribe is given before the official act takes place, whereas in an illegal gratuity, the thing of value, such as a gift, is awarded to an official for performing the desired duties.

Major Types of Frauds

Major types of frauds reported by respondents to a survey conducted by KPMG Peat Marwick, a Big-Six public accounting firm, are shown in Figure 7-10. Misappropriation of funds occurs most frequently, followed by check forgery and credit card fraud. Surprisingly, respondents reported that check manipulation frauds, accounts receivable manipulation, altered expense accounts, and false financial statements were frauds that occurred least frequently. Although false financial statements fraud occurred in only 1 percent of the responding firms, the losses from such frauds often amount to millions of dollars, as opposed to misappropriation of funds, such as cash, whose losses may amount to hundreds of dollars.

All frauds are intentional, not accidental, and involve three phases. First, a wrongful act is committed. For example, a bookkeeper steals cash from his or her employer. Second, the person committing the wrongful act attempts to conceal or hide the act. For instance, the bookkeeper could create a fictitious journal entry debiting an expense account and crediting cash. The debit to an expense, particularly miscellaneous or consulting expenses, is harder to trace since no movement of assets, such as inventory, is involved. When the expenses are closed at year end, the fraud becomes very difficult to discover. The third element of a fraud is conversion. That is, the item taken is used for the personal benefit of the person committing the crime. The bookkeeper could use the illegally obtained funds to purchase a new BMW automobile.

Classification of Frauds

Two types of frauds are committed within organizations—internal and external frauds. **Internal frauds** are committed by the managers or employees of a firm. Examples of internal frauds include creation of fictitious journal entries and preparation of phony inventory tickets to inflate ending inventory, thus falsely increasing income. Others include larceny, embezzlement, and the creation of fraudulent financial statements. **External frauds** are committed against the firm by nonemployee parties. Our main concern is with internal frauds, since most of them are related to the accounting system. A properly functioning internal control structure will prevent or detect material internal frauds.

Methods of Concealing Frauds

Financial frauds are concealed in one of two ways. **On-book frauds** involve concealing the fraudulent activity

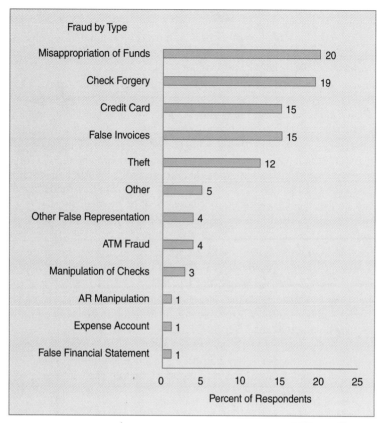

FIGURE 7-10 Types of frauds. Source: Adopted from "Fraud Survey Results," KPMG Peat Marwick, 1993. Used with permission.

in the normal accounting records. An auditor searching for this type of fraud would find evidence in the firm's journals and ledgers. Unauthorized cash could be drawn from the firm's bank account, recorded as a credit in the regular books and records, and the theft could be disguised as a debit to a regular business expense. On-book frauds, therefore, leave a visible audit trail of forged or altered documents, and the preparation of fictitious journal entries to conceal the scheme. On-book schemes are easy to apply, but leave a trail of incriminating evidence.

Off-book frauds are not concealed in the normal accounting records. These frauds are maintained off the books and are more difficult to uncover since no visible audit trail exists. Such schemes are frequently employed by firms that generate large cash sales, for example restaurants and bars. In these types of firms, a bartender may record half the cash sales in the cash register and pocket the other half. The stolen cash does not appear anywhere in the firm's books. This off-book scheme is known as skimming. As fraudulent schemes become more complex, they will sometimes exhibit the characteristics of both on- and off-book schemes.

Computer Frauds

Due to the proliferation of microcomputers and computer networks, and to the increasing computer knowledge of millions of microcomputer users, computer fraud is expected to significantly increase in both frequency and amount of losses. Computer frauds exhibit the same characteristics as noncomputer frauds, except that the perpetrator uses a computer to help commit the fraud, often over long distances. Also, the average dollar loss is much greater than in manually committed frauds. Computer frauds involve the same six types of frauds discussed above; they are often committed internally by management and employees and are concealed using either on- or off-book schemes. Computer frauds can be committed at breathtaking speeds over long distances and are easier to conceal since the evidence of the crime is maintained on magnetic tape or disk files. These files are often encrypted or coded so that an auditor investigating the crime could not use the coded file as evidence unless the files were decrypted. Unfortunately, decrypting a file involves a special key or password that is only possessed by the perpetrator, who is unlikely to

- A self-employed computer expert discovered the daily code that authorized funds to be transferred from a large bank to other banks. One day, five minutes before closing time, he called the wire room, gave the correct authorization code, and transferred $10 million into a bank account opened under his alias.
- A technician who helped design the computerized ticket system for a major league baseball club stayed around the office one day to show staff workers how to operate the system. Later, club officials discovered that he had also used that day to print 7000 tickets, which he illegally sold through ticket brokers.
- Automated teller machines (ATMs) installed by a large New York bank were the means of an ingenious fraud. Persons posing as bank employees would stop depositors in the middle of ATM transactions and direct them to other ATMs, explaining that the ATMs being used were inoperative. Then these persons would withdraw funds from the abandoned ATMs that had been opened (but not closed) by the depositors.
- A number of unauthorized persons obtained the password into the files of the largest credit bureau in the country. From home computers they were thereby able to view the credit reports of millions of credit card users.
- In a case similar to the preceding one, the "414 gang" (a group of young computer "hackers") broke into the highly sensitive files of the Los Alamos National Laboratory.
- Two executives of a nationwide firm pleaded guilty to the theft of Social Security numbers. The executives used a microcomputer to illegally access a federal government computer containing the Social Security data.
- In a case widely publicized in *The Wall Street Journal*, hackers from a European country gained unauthorized access to hundreds of university and military defense computers. The illegally obtained data was reportedly sold to the former KGB.

FIGURE 7-11   A sampling of reported computer crimes.

reveal it. A sampling of reported computer crimes, many of which are in fact types of computer frauds, is given in Figure 7-11.

Firms Vulnerable to Fraud

Some firms are more vulnerable to fraud than others. In particular, organizations with weak internal control environments are susceptible to frauds, computer frauds, and other types of computer crimes. Poor personnel practices and policies, such as hiring untrustworthy, in-

competent, and unethical managers and employees, is a major factor contributing to internal management and employee fraud. A typical profile of persons who commit fraud and computer crimes is presented in Figure 7-12. Dominance by one or two managers, as was often true in the savings and loan scandals, allows these managers to override the internal controls and commit frauds amounting to tens of millions of dollars. A list of factors that increase a firm's exposure to fraud appears in Figure 7-13. These indicators of possible fraud are called "red flags."

- Male, white, 19–30 years old (persons committing fraud tend to be older)
- First-time offender
- Modified Robin Hood syndrome (i.e., keep for thyself)
- Bright, well-educated, highly motivated
- Accepts challenges and likes to play computer games
- Disgruntled, frustrated
- Bragger
- Identifies with own technology far more than with employer's business

- Often employed in data processing or accounting field
- Frequently suffers from financial pressures (e.g., expensive tastes, habits, drugs, high living costs)
- Feels exploited by employer and wants to get even; feels employer can afford the loss
- Does not intend to hurt anyone
- Sees self as a borrower, not as a thief

FIGURE 7-12   Typical profile of persons who commit fraud and computer crimes.

• Many disgruntled and disloyal employees	• No controls in computer programs
• Poor employee/management relations	• Poor or nonexistent documentation
• Management lacks ethical values and integrity	• Advanced on-line computer systems
• One or two dominant top managers	• No internal audit department
• Code of conduct not in force or not being followed	• No internal auditor involvement in systems development
• Inadequate personnel policies and practices	• Understaffed accounting department
• Inadequate planning, control, and performance evaluation systems	• Fast expansion of business
• Reengineering (downsizing) in progress	• Cash-flow problems
• Lack of separation of duties	• Numerous adjusting entries

FIGURE 7-13   Factors contributing to increased risk exposure to fraud.

Uncovering Fraud

Predication is defined as the totality of circumstances that would lead a reasonably prudent person to believe that a fraud has occurred, is occurring, or will occur. Figure 7-14 points out factors (i.e., violations of internal controls, internal auditor findings, anonymous letters, and notification by police of possible wrongdoing) that may trigger the initial fraud investigation.

A **Certified Fraud Examiner** (CFE) is often contacted to conduct a scientific fraud investigation. The CFE's first step is to gather and analyze the relevant data to determine if predication is sufficient to proceed further. Sufficient predication is the basis for creating a hypothesis of a specific fraud. That is, the CFE, based on an evaluation of the initial fraud indicators, decides whether enough evidence exists to proceed further. The next step is to test the hypothesis by gathering sufficient evidence through interviews, document examinations, and observation. At the conclusion of evidence gathering, the CFE prepares a written report that does or does not support the allegation of fraud or is inconclusive. If warranted, the case is turned over to an attorney, who works closely with the CFE to prosecute the case.

Fraud and Computer Crime Prevention Safeguards

With the massive number of cases of insider theft, fraud, embezzlement, and other crimes reported in the media, management should take proper action to prevent, detect, and deter these risk exposures. Firms should establish and enforce a strong written code of professional conduct. Ethical principles should receive increased attention throughout the organization. Sound personnel policies and controls, such as reference checks on employment applications, need to be enforced. The corporate audit committee should be independent of management and should closely monitor stakeholders' interests. A properly developed internal audit function, adequately staffed, can significantly reduce the proba-

bility of fraud and other computer crimes. Internal auditors should complete training courses on fraud and computer crime, such as those offered by the Association of Certified Fraud Examiners of Austin, Texas. Also, internal auditors and other accountants involved in the audit function should be encouraged to become Certified Fraud Examiners (CFE). A CFE is trained in criminology, legal elements of fraud, interrogation and investigative matters, and financial transactions. These and other safeguards and controls are listed in Figure 7-15. While such crimes can never be eliminated, organizations that adopt the safeguards shown in this figure can dramatically reduce their vulnerability.

COMPUTER VIRUSES AND RELATED RISKS

A potentially significant risk exposure to information stored on microcomputers and local-area networks (LANs) is a computer virus. A **computer virus** is a computer program that is designed to copy or attach itself to other computer programs and causes either the display of prankish messages or the destruction of data, such as erasing all the files on a hard disk. Frequently, viruses are introduced into a microcomputer or a LAN when an infected floppy disk is copied onto a hard disk. Once attached to a program on a hard disk, a computer virus can remain dormant and undetected for long periods. Usually the virus will carry out its intended function when it is activated by the computer's internal clock. If the microcomputer is part of a LAN, the virus can rapidly spread to all microcomputers in the network.

Thousands of known virus strains exist and new strains appear almost daily. Most viruses have static or unchanging structures that render them relatively easy to detect and destroy with the use of vaccine programs. A **vaccine program** checks for, finds, and removes most types of viruses. More recent viruses with dynamic structures, called **polymorphic viruses,** are much more difficult to detect and destroy. Every time a polymorphic virus copies onto another program, it randomly scrambles

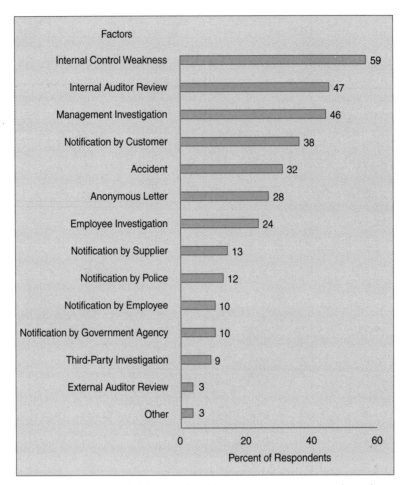

FIGURE 7-14   Factors that initiate fraud investigations. Source: Adopted from "Fraud Survey Results," KPMG Peat Marwich, 1993. Used with permission.

the original program code creating a new virus strain that is invisible to many current vaccine programs.

A second category of maliciously written computer programs has viruslike characteristics, but they are not true viruses. These computer programs are usually written to perform one or more destructive operations, and

go by names such as Trojan Horses, logic bombs, and worms. These nonviruses are usually placed illegally into a particular software package. The malicious nonvirus programs may be written by dishonest programmers who want to get even with their employers or to commit a computer crime. A **Trojan Horse** is an unauthorized pro-

---

- Separation of duties
- Increased role of internal audit and audit committee
- Strong personnel policies and controls
- Corporate code of conduct
- Management exhibits strong ethical values
- Professional certifications (such as Certified Internal Auditor and Certified Fraud Examiner)
- Internal auditors trained in fraud prevention and detection

- Programming controls
- Preparation of good documentation
- Auditor involvement in systems development
- Embedded audit routines
- Close supervision
- Proactive philosophy (i.e., active fraud investigations, immediate dismissals, reporting of violations to proper authorities, civil suits for recovery of losses)

FIGURE 7-15   Safeguards to prevent, detect, deter fraud and computer crimes.

• Purchase and use anti-virus software • Test all software before copying onto the hard disk • Write-protect floppy disks, hard disks • Prepare backups on read-only disks of all programs and data files • Only use well-respected national bulletin board services that screen all programs for viruses	• Do not download software from unknown public bulletin boards • Be leery of demo programs received in the mail from unknown sources • Shut down computers when not in use • Do not copy pirated software • Exercise common sense

FIGURE 7-16   Security and control measures to safeguard against computer viruses.

gram code hidden inside an application program that performs a valid function, such as the payroll program. For example, the unauthorized code may activate each pay period to produce a check for the programmer's mother-in-law. This hidden code enables the programmer to conceal an ongoing computer fraud. Like a virus, a **logic bomb** is a small program inserted into another program to cause some type of destructive operation. For instance, a programmer threatened with dismissal from his job might plant a logic bomb into a computer program to destroy all of the accounting data. The programmer could set the logic bomb to automatically go off ("explode") shortly after his termination date. A logic bomb is designed to perform only one function. A **worm** is similar to a logic bomb, except that when activated, it replicates itself by generating random digits until the entire hard disk's memory is filled, bringing the system down.

Security and control measures to safeguard against computer viruses and some related viruslike programs include anti-virus software that checks for, finds, and destroys viruses. As mentioned, many vaccine programs are not very effective for polymorphic viruses. Also, all software should be tested before copying the data onto a hard disk. Other safeguards are listed in Figure 7-16.

Three examples should show the havoc that mischiefs can reap, as well as the extent of their spread:

1. Bulgarian computer hackers have developed a computer virus known as the Dark Avenger. It attacks and destroys both computer programs and data. This particular virus is sophisticated, since it contains several perverse features. Dark Avenger operates on a delay cycle, infecting only once in every 16 operating cycles. It modifies part of its structure after a certain number of executions, to frustrate virus detector software.*

2. Robert Tappan Morris, the son of the chief scientist of the U.S. National Security Agency, has been found guilty of creating the Internet Worm. This viruslike program disabled 600 computers that were connected to the Internet (a nationwide network of networks examined in Chapter 17). He claimed that there was no malicious intent; rather, it was simply a misguided stunt gone wrong.[†]

3. A fired employee of the USPS & IRA Company planted a virus that destroyed 168,000 sales commission records. Like Morris, this person was eventually convicted of committing this destructive act.[‡]

REVIEW PROBLEM WITH SOLUTION

CAMPUS BOOKSTORE, FOURTH INSTALLMENT

Statement

The Campus Bookstore (described in the Review Problem at the end of Chapter 1) has been pleased with its new minicomputer system. However, the manager has become a bit apprehensive after talking with the auditors from the public accounting firm that reviews the bookstore's operations and financial statements. They have advised him that the bookstore's assets and information are exposed to a variety of risks. They suggest that the internal control structure of the bookstore be reviewed as soon as possible, to determine what changes may be needed in the controls and security measures as a result of the minicomputer system.

Required

a. Identify the three component systems composing the bookstore's internal control structure, and illustrate by means of the cash control system, the budgetary control system, and the general ledger control system.

b. Discuss the risks to which the assets and information of the bookstore are exposed; give examples of each type of risk. Also, identify high-risk and low-risk exposures.

---

*"Existence of Powerful New Computer Viruses Confirmed." EDPACS (April 1991), p. 17.

[†]"Internet Worm Planter Conviction Upheld on Appeal." EDPACS (June 1991), p. 18.
[‡]Jeffrey A. Hoffer and Detmar W. Straub, "The 9 to 5 Underground: Are You Policing Computer Crimes?" Sloan Management Review (Summer 1989), p. 41.

c. Describe the changes in accounting controls that have been made necessary or desirable by the new minicomputer system, assuming that the internal control structure has been adequate for a manual system.

Solution

a. The first of the component control systems is the operational control system, which promotes efficiency in operational tasks. An important operational task is to maintain an adequate supply of cash to meet operational needs. In order to control cash, the bookstore manager (planner) first sets a minimum bank balance (benchmark) with respect to the level of cash (performance measure). This benchmark is set at a level that is (1) sufficiently high to prevent the bookstore from depleting its funds and entailing bank charges, and (2) sufficiently low to minimize idle cash deposits. Periodically the cash control system compares the actual amount of cash on hand with the minimum balance. When the actual amount on hand falls to or below the minimum balance, the system takes corrective action by borrowing an amount to replenish the account balance. Conversely, when the actual amount on hand rises significantly above the minimum, the system either repays a previous loan or invests the excessive amount. This cash control system, which is operated manually by the bookstore manager or the bookkeeper, may be aided by means of third-order feedback mechanisms such as cash forecasts.

The second component control system is the management control system, which encourages compliance with the bookstore's policies and procedures. An important tool of management control is a budgetary control system. The process begins with policies and revenue and cost benchmarks being set by the bookstore manager (planner). These policies and benchmarks are embodied in annual operating budgets for the three major responsibility areas: the upper-level and lower-level sales areas and the central administrative activities area. During the budget year revenues are accumulated and expenses are incurred. Monthly budget control reports that compare these actual results against the budgeted amounts and computed variances are prepared. The area managers are evaluated on the basis of the feedback provided by these reports. When necessary, corrective actions are taken.

The third component control system is the accounting control system, which has the objectives of safeguarding the bookstore's assets and ensuring the accuracy and reliability of the bookstore's data and information. An important means for providing accounting control is the use of the general ledger system. A key device in this system is the trial balance, which helps to ensure posting accuracy by verifying that total debit account balances equal total credit account balances. Another feature of the system that helps to ensure posting accuracy is the reconciliation of control accounts in the general ledger with the accounts in subsidiary ledgers. A feature that helps to safeguard assets is the reconciliation of physical counts of assets on hand (e.g., inventory) with the balances in general ledger accounts. Other control features include the use of coded accounts and the audit trail.

b. The bookstore is subject to risks with respect to its assets and information. Among these risks are the following.

(1) Unintentional or deliberate errors can be made in recording and processing transactions and related events such as sales, purchases, merchandise receipts, payroll, and cash disbursements. For instance, a clerk might enter an incorrect quantity to order on a purchase order, or might mismultiply the number of hours worked by an employee times the hourly rate of pay.

(2) Deliberate errors can be made in counting assets or in preparing reports or records. For instance, a clerk might deliberately undercount a receipt of merchandise and keep some of the items. A sales manager might inflate the sales amounts on a sales report.

(3) Assets may be stolen by outsiders or by employees. For instance, a customer may shoplift a paperback book or a sweater. A stock clerk may carry merchandise out the back door. (See comments regarding deliberate errors.)

(4) Security may be breached. For instance, a stock clerk may see a budget sheet on the bookkeeper's desk and repeat the key amounts to a friend.

(5) An act of violence may be committed. For instance, a customer may deface textbooks on a shelf.

High-risk exposures faced by the bookstore include theft and damage of merchandise, which is easily available on shelves and racks. Other high-risk exposures are the theft of cash by the cashiers. Low-risk exposures include accidental errors. Although accidental errors may occur fairly frequently, they are not likely to be sizable. Also, breaches of security are likely to be low-risk exposures, since information is not often easily available to unauthorized persons, especially when the system involves manual processing.

c. The minicomputer system should have the following impacts on the accounting controls currently in place.

(1) A variety of new controls will need to be incorporated into the computer programs that process the transactions, since fewer of the errors on source documents are likely to be detected by the clerks and cashiers.

(2) A greater number of analyses and listings of transactions will need to be provided for review by the managers and employees, since most of the files will be stored on computer-readable media and parts of the manual system audit trail will be lost.

(3) Careful procedures will need to be established to ensure that computer programs are not changed without proper authority.

(4) Security measures will need to be introduced to ensure that unauthorized users are not able to access confidential computerized files and data and to modify records concerning assets.

(5) Backup procedures will need to be established to ensure that computerized files and records are not accidentally lost as a result of human errors or equipment breakdowns.

(6) Maintenance procedures will need to be established and disaster prevention devices will need to be installed to prevent breakdowns or damages to the computer equipment.

(7) Procedures manuals and other documentation, as well as adequate training, will be needed to provide the clerks and other employees with the references and knowledge to operate the minicomputer system properly.

(8) Organizational changes will be needed to prevent employees from having opportunities to acquire bookstore assets fraudulently.

(9) Physical restrictions will be needed to prevent unauthorized persons (employees or outsiders) from obtaining access to computer facilities or records.

cost-benefit analysis (269)
embezzlement (274)
external auditors (258)
external frauds (274)
feedback (249)
feedforward control system (250)
financial fraud (273)
Financial Fraud Detection and Disclosure Act (272)
Foreign Corrupt Practices Act (272)
fraud (261)
human resource policies and practices (256)
illegal gratuity (274)
integrity and ethical values (254)
internal auditors (258)
internal control (247)
internal control structure (ICS) (248)
internal frauds (274)
larceny (274)
logic bomb (279)
management control (259)
management philosophy and operating style (254)
monitoring (258)
off-book frauds (275)
on-book frauds (274)
ongoing monitoring activities (258)
operational control (260)
organizational structure (256)
polymorphic virus (277)
predication (277)
reasonable assurance (269)
reliability analysis (270)
risk assessment (256)
risk exposure (260)
separate monitoring activities (258)
theft (274)
Trojan Horse (278)
vaccine program (277)
worm (279)

KEY TERMS

assignment of authority and responsibility (256)
board of directors or audit committee (255)
bribery (274)
Certified Fraud Examiner (CFE) (277)
collusion (263)
commitment to competence (255)
Committee of Sponsoring Organizations of the Treadway Commission (COSO) (251)
computer crime (264)
computer fraud (263)
computer virus (277)
control activities (257)
control objectives (251)
control process (248)
controls (247)

REVIEW QUESTIONS

Note: Certain questions require knowledge found in an Appendix at the end of this chapter.

7-1. What is the nature of control as it pertains to a business firm?

7-2. Why is the internal control structure so important to accountants?

7-3. Why is the topic of internal control so important to accountants?

7-4. Identify the elements of a control process.

7-5. Contrast first-order, second-order, and third-order feedback control systems.

7-6. What are the three objectives of an internal control structure?

7-7. Identify several control subobjectives that follow from the control objective of assuring accurate and reliable information.

7-8. Identify several difficulties in achieving the control objectives.

7-9. Briefly discuss the five components of the internal control structure.

7-10. Contrast the management control and operational control systems.

7-11. Identify several sound human resources practices that aid a firm in achieving efficient operations and maintaining data integrity.

7-12. What are several audit practices that should provide sound evaluation of the internal control structure and accounting records?

7-13. Identify several types of AIS-related risks confronting a typical firm.

7-14. What are three factors that influence the degree of risk exposure?

7-15. Refer to Question 7-14. What other problem conditions within a firm affect the degree of risk exposure?

7-16. Why has computer fraud become such a serious problem?

7-17. Identify several types of computer crimes.

7-18. What are several conditions introduced by computer-based systems that cause control problems?

7-19. Discuss the audit, cost, and human factors that should be considered in designing a feasible internal control structure.

7-20. List several steps in applying a cost-benefit analysis.

7-21. What is the principle of reasonable assurance?

7-22. How may the ethical climate of a firm be strengthened?

7-23. Discuss the forces that are influencing the improvement of the internal control structures.

7-24. Distinguish between fraud and computer fraud.

7-25. Contrast embezzlement and larceny.

7-26. Distinguish between on-book and off-book frauds.

7-27. What is predication? Give an example.

7-28. What is a computer virus? Illustrate using an example.

7-29. Distinguish between nonpolymorphic and polymorphic computer viruses.

DISCUSSION QUESTIONS

7-30. Discuss the control process for each of the following:
   a. Quality control
   b. Budgetary control
   c. Production cost control
   d. Credit control

7-31. Respond to a manager who says that her firm does not need internal control measures over the assets, since the firm has only one employee, who is highly trusted.

7-32. Discuss the costs that a particular accounting control might impose on a firm, including the possible adverse effect on processing efficiency.

7-33. What are examples of high-risk exposures and low-risk exposures within a typical firm?

7-34. Which errors, either accidental or deliberate, must be eliminated or reduced when an AIS is converted from manual processing to computer-based processing?

7-35. When a firm converts from a manual AIS to a computer-based AIS, in what ways does the conversion help or hinder (a) an accounting employee who is intent on embezzling funds, (b) a competitor who is intent on accessing confidential files, and (c) a disgruntled ex-employee who is intent on disrupting data processing operations?

7-36. How would the specific control activities implemented in Ann Strong's firm differ from those implemented at Infoage?

7-37. How would ongoing and periodic monitoring activities differ between small and medium-sized firms?

7-38. Discuss how the unethical behaviors of managers can have a negative impact on the internal control structure.

7-39. Provide an example of how an operational control can help meet financial reporting objectives and a financial reporting control can help meet compliance objectives.

7-40. Identify examples of pairs of risk exposures that are interrelated, in that one exposure in a pair tends to cause or heighten the degree of the other.

7-41. An effective internal control structure should deter persons from committing fraudulent acts by removing opportunities or by promptly exposing acts where opportunities do exist. However, certain behavioral tendencies may undercut this presumption. Discuss.

7-42. It has been stated that a firm with a strong internal control structure will always succeed in achieving its financial and nonfinancial objectives. Do you agree or disagree with this position?

7-43. How do the roles and responsibilities for internal control differ among the following parties?

   a. Manager

   b. Board of directors

   c. Internal auditors

   d. External auditors

   e. Chief financial officer

7-44. Discuss the pressures on external auditors to accept unrealistic valuations of real estate and other assets owned by client firms, as well as the countervailing influences that are available to aid them in resisting such pressures.

PROBLEMS

Note: Certain problems require knowledge found in the Appendix at the end of this chapter.

7-1. Jane Huston opens a shoe store and hires two employees. She also asks you, a public accountant, to prepare financial statements for her at the end of each month. You agree, but suggest that she needs an adequate internal control structure to make the venture a success. She tells you that internal controls are not critical to the operations of a very small firm, such as the shoe store. Also, she replies that she cannot afford more costly outlays and that she does not want to offend the two employees with elaborate precautions. She says her employees are family-oriented, ethical, and honest and therefore would not steal from the firm.

Required

a. Explain to Jane why a sound internal control structure is as critical to a very small firm as it would be for a much larger firm.

b. Present the response you would offer to her argument that controls would be too costly.

c. Present the response you would offer to her other argument that her employees would not steal from the firm.

d. Point out the difficulties in establishing an effective internal control structure in her shoe store.

e. Would you recommend that she formally implement all five components of the internal control structure? Explain your answer.

f. Describe several independent checks that the public accountant could design into the system to reveal if the internal controls were operating as intended. These checks would not be revealed to Jane Huston and her employees.

(Hint: *For example, the public accountant could design a particular account so that it always has a zero balance at the end of the month.*

A nonzero balance would indicate that the internal control system is not properly functioning to prevent or detect certain errors.)

7-2. The Bronco Manufacturing Company produces wood products to order. Each job order is begun when a customer places a sales order and credit is approved. The order moves through three departments—fashioning, assembly, and finishing—during the production process. On completion of a job order the products are shipped and the customer is billed.

Required

a. Describe the operational control system, including the control process, relating to credit approval.

b. Describe the operational control system, including the control process, relating to the time scheduling of job orders.

c. Describe the operational control system, including the control process, relating to the costs of job orders.

d. Describe management control systems that may be employed with respect to the three production departments.

e. Describe accounting control activities relating to the processing of sales transactions.

7-3. Mike Smith, CPA, has been engaged to audit the financial statements of Reed and Sons, Inc., a publicly held retailing firm. Before assessing control risk, Mike is required to obtain an understanding of Reed's control environment.

Required

a. Identify additional control environment factors (excluding the factor in the example illustrated below) that establish or enhance the effectiveness of specific policies and procedures.

b. For the control environment factors identified in **a,** describe the components that could be of interest to the auditor.

   Use the following format:

   Management Philosophy and Operating Style

   Management philosophy and operating style characteristics may include the following: management's approach to taking and monitoring business risks, management's attitudes and actions toward financial reporting, and management's emphasis on meeting budget, profit, and other financial and operating goals.

(CPA *adapted*)

7-4. The internal control environment is composed of the following seven subcomponents:

- Integrity and ethical values.
- Commitment to competence.
- Board of directors or audit committee.

- Management philosophy and operating style.
- Organization structure.
- Assignment of authority and responsibility.
- Human resource policies and practices.

The absence of which one of these subcomponents allowed the following undesirable events to occur? What recommendations would you make to correct these weaknesses?

  a. Due to budget cuts, employees rarely attended firm continuing education or professional development courses to improve their skills.

  b. A firm pressured its managers to meet unrealistic short-term performance targets. To meet the goals, the managers often engaged in questionable financial reporting practices.

  c. The manager of internal auditing reported to the controller. Consequently, many of internal audit's recommendations were ignored.

  d. Top management often took an aggressive posture toward the selection of accounting principles.

  e. Top managers were the only employees given the power to negotiate contracts, enter into joint ventures, and offer discounts to customers. However, the firm often missed many potential opportunities.

  f. Prospective employees were not required to fill out detailed employment applications.

  g. A firm was unable to reduce product defects to a satisfactory level. Thus it did not achieve a high level of customer satisfaction.

  h. Top management's philosophy toward alternative financial reporting practices was never questioned or scrutinized. As a result, liberal accounting practices were frequently followed, which artificially inflated net income.

7-5. The internal control structure is composed of the following five components:

- Control environment.
- Risk assessment.
- Control activities.
- Information and communication.
- Monitoring.

The absence of which one of these components allowed the following undesirable events to occur? What recommendations would you make to correct these weaknesses?

  a. Salespersons made false statements to potential customers concerning the capabilities of a newly introduced laptop computer.

  b. A firm failed to properly supervise its warehouse personnel. As a result, employee theft of small

tools was five times greater than the industry norm.

  c. A firm with $23,000,000 in annual sales went out of business because it was unable to process its critical accounting applications for an eight-week period during its busiest season. The shutdown was caused by an unanticipated natural catastrophe. This type of natural catastrophe occurs once every five years on average in this region of the country.

  d. A cost accountant learned that the plant manager was systematically overstating inventory. However, the accountant failed to report the suspected impropriety. The firm did not have open channels of communication for reporting such information to higher organizational levels.

  e. A large firm implemented a variety of accounting expert systems throughout the organization. Most of these accounting applications were developed by end users who failed to consider enterprisewide policies regarding system development. As a result, most of the expert systems were scrapped within two months of implementation.

  f. In the most recent fiscal year, a firm's internal audit function failed to identify a major weakness in the internal control system. As a result, the firm received a qualified audit opinion from its external auditors. The internal auditors also overlooked several significant internal control structure weaknesses in earlier years. The internal audit function was subsequently outsourced.

  g. A well-known Fortune 500 high-tech firm's main product failed to carry out arithmetical operations to an acceptable level of precision. When the matter was brought to the firm's attention, top management denied that the product was defective and initially refused to provide customers with free replacements.

  h. A performance report revealed that budgeted monthly sales for a particular laptop computer were $150,000 less than actual sales. However, the report did specify why the laptop became unsalable.

7-6. Refer to Problem 7-4. The absence of which one of the seven subcomponents of the control environment allowed the following undesirable events to occur? What recommendations would you make to correct these weaknesses?

  a. A high-tech firm's employee turnover rate was three times greater than the industry average.

  b. Employees were not held accountable for their actions and engaged in a number of dishonest acts.

c. A Fortune 1000 firm provided new employees with a one-time, two-week, formal training course. They were not given any subsequent on-going training to further their skills.

d. Top management's bonus was dependent on the firm's annual net income. Consequently, top managers took significant business risks to maximize income.

e. A firm's key strategy was to achieve 100 percent customer satisfaction for its services and products. However, the firm ignored the recommendations made by lower-echelon employees on ways to increase customer satisfaction, relying instead on the recommendations made by top management. The top managers rarely interacted with the firm's customers.

f. The chief executive officer of a small firm did not play a significant role in determining the corporate culture of his firm. As a result, many questionable practices developed throughout the organization.

g. Due to limited travel funds, a firm seldom required on-site interviews of prospective new employees.

h. A firm did not establish appropriate reporting relationships. As a result, reports were inappropriately sent to many of the firm's managers.

7-7. Refer to Problem 7-5. The absence of which one of the five components of the internal control structure allowed the following undesirable events to occur? What recommendations would you make to correct these weaknesses?

a. A firm maintained an elaborate 300-page corporate code of conduct. However, firm officials never periodically asked employees if they understood and compiled with the code. Consequently, widespread violations of the corporate code were common.

b. The three regional managers of a large midwest manufacturing firm rarely received guidance from their district manager on what constituted acceptable business practices. Thus, the regional managers often inflated the year-end inventory to overstate income so that they would more likely receive acceptable performance evaluations.

c. A firm revamped its mainframe AIS applications, moving them to a local-area network–based client/server computing environment. However, the firm experienced frequent crashes and major security and control problems that were not present in the mainframe environment.

d. A firm's top management rejected a plan to implement a code of conduct for its employees.

e. A production manager failed to question a report that differed significantly from actual operations.

f. A firm's board, audit committee, and internal auditors assumed a minimal role in the areas of financial reporting and corporate controls.

g. An outside supplier of raw materials gave the purchasing agent a gift for her recent $10,000 order. However, the purchasing agent indicated that firm policy prevented her from accepting gifts. The supplier had been unaware of the firm's ethical standards.

h. The president of a midsize New England bank personally made unsecured loans of large amounts to relatives. As a result, the bank wrote off several of these loans, incurring bad debts of $150,000.

7-8. The Alert Company is a closely held investment services group that has been very successful over the past five years, consistently providing most members of the top management group with 50 percent bonuses. In addition, both the chief financial officer and the chief executive officer have received 100 percent bonuses. Alert expects this trend to continue.

Recently, the top management group of Alert, which holds 35 percent of the outstanding shares of common stock, has learned that a major corporation is interested in acquiring Alert. Alert's management is concerned that this corporation may make an attractive offer to the other shareholders and that management would be unable to prevent the takeover. If the acquisition occurs, this executive group is uncertain about continued employment in the new corporate structure. As a consequence, the management group is considering changes to several accounting policies and practices that, although not in accordance with generally accepted accounting principles, would make the firm a less attractive acquisition. Management has told Roger Deerling, Alert's controller, to implement some of these changes. Deerling has also been informed that Alert's management does not intend to immediately disclose these changes to anyone outside of the immediate top management group.

Required

a. Evaluate the nature of changes the top management group is considering.

b. Evaluate Roger Deerling's responsibilities as a management accountant.

c. Identify the steps Roger Deerling should take to resolve the situation descirbed above.

d. Discuss social and ethical responsibilities that a firm should consider before taking defensive actions such as those described above.

(CMA *adapted*)

7-9. It has been suggested that all large organizations develop written codes of conduct in order to promote business ethics.

Required

a. Identify eight elements that should be included in a corporate code of conduct.

b. List steps that can be used to review the adequacy of a firm's business ethics efforts.

(CIA *adapted*)

7-10. Jiffy Express is an overnight air-freight delivery service. It guarantees delivery of letters and packages to points throughout the United States by 10 A.M. the day following pickup. The reputation of Jiffy is directly related to the reliability of this service. Thus, it maintains pools of vans for local pickup and delivery as well as a large fleet of planes. Because time is of the essence, Jiffy has installed an on-line computer-based information system, with terminals located at its offices in all metropolitan centers. In addition to owning its various offices, the firm has its own garages for overnight parking. Moreover, it services both its vans and planes in rented facilities.

Required

Discuss the various high-risk exposures faced by Jiffy, and specify the factors that accentuate the risk in each case.

7-11. Colleges and universities have installed complex networks of computers and microcomputers in recent years. Although the specifics of the networks differ from university to university, they generally serve two major purposes: academic and administrative. They also are subject to a variety of abuses.

Required

a. Identify at least a dozen risks, abuses, and crimes to which a typical university computer network is exposed. Assume that a single network, involving one mainframe and numerous microcomputers, serves both academic and administrative purposes.

b. Why do you suppose that colleges and universities and other not-for-profit institutions traditionally have weak internal conrol structures?

7-12. Hot & Shot, CPAs, has just installed a new minicomputer system. This system includes eight terminals that are directly connected to the minicomputer, as well as an on-line magnetic disk unit, one magnetic tape cartridge unit, two printers, and one plotter. The firm intends to use the system to perform internal applications, such as billing and budgeting, as well as to prepare tax returns and financial analyses for clients. Each of these applications involves the use of software packages that are to be acquired from an outside software firm. It is anticipated that most of the packages will need to be modified by the single programmer that the firm employs.

Required

Discuss the several control problems that are introduced by the new minicomputer system, assuming that the firm has never used computers before. Illustrate these control problems, where suitable, by reference to the billing and financial analysis applications.

7-13. Identify a risk exposure that each of the following control procedures or practices is intended to prevent or detect. For each item give an example of what might occur if the control were not in place, and list one or more factors that could cause the risk exposure to be relatively high.

   a. Assigning one employee to handle the merchandise in the warehouse and another employee to maintain the inventory records.

   b. Storing the inventory within a fenced area that is kept locked.

   c. Requiring all disbursements (except petty transactions) to be made by check.

   d. Counting the inventory on hand periodically and comparing the count of each item to the inventory records.

   e. Requiring all returns of sold merchandise to be listed on a special credit memorandum form that is prepared and signed by a manager.

   f. Mailing a monthly statement to each customer, showing the details of all transactions and the balance owed.

7-14. Identify a risk exposure that each of the following control procedures or practices is intended to prevent or detect. For each item give an example of what might occur if the control were not in place, and list one or more factors that could cause the risk exposure to be relatively high.

   a. Preparing reconciliations of all bank accounts on receipt of the bank statements.

   b. Maintaining comprehensive manuals that show detailed steps of all the accounting procedures.

   c. Requiring a clerk who receives ordered merchandise to prepare and sign a form that separately lists all the items and quantities received.

   d. Listing all the cash remittances received daily by mail and comparing the total to the deposit slip.

e. Depositing all cash received daily intact in the bank.

f. Having auditors examine the financial statements once a year.

7-15. The Arcade Co. of Orlando, Florida, has established a new division that will manage a chain of video-game arcades in 40 locations throughout several southern states. The locations will be divided into two regions under regional managers. Each location will be assigned a local manager. As many as 60 machines will be available at certain locations, although the average per location will be 35 machines.

Management intends to minimize the number of operating and accounting employees in order to reduce costs. However, it plans to hire sufficient maintenance personnel to minimize downtime of machines. The resident manager will be required to collect, count, and deposit the quarters from machines in a local bank. Each machine uses an internal mechanical meter for internal control. Access to the mechanical meters and quarters in each machine will be by means of a master key. Weekly, the resident manager reconciles the count of quarters with the count displayed on the mechanical meters. After the two counts are reconciled, the mechanical meters are reset to zero. Validated deposit slips are to be mailed to the corporate office by the resident manager. Bank statements are to be mailed by the bank directly to the corporate office.

Required

Identify the specific risk exposures that are inherent in the operations of the new division. Group the risk exposures according to the four activities with which accounting controls are concerned (i.e., execution of transactions, recording of transactions, access to assets, and recorded accountability for assets); for each risk exposure suggest one or more offsetting accounting control activities.

(CIA *adapted*)

7-16. Contrary to standard practice, a bank loan officer charged certain customers a 1 percent origination fee on commercial loans. The fee was to be paid by check, made payable to the bank. The fee was shown on the customer's loan documentation, but not on the bank's copy of loan documentation.

The loan officer would then take the customer's check to a teller and state that the customer wanted a cashier's check for the same amount made payable to a certain firm. The loan officer subsequently deposited the cashier's check in an account established for the fictitious firm at another bank. Funds were later transferred back to the loan officer's personal account at his employer's bank.

Required

a. Identify four elements of a legal definition of fraud.

b. Describe the aspects of fraud present in this case that correspond to the elements of fraud.

c. Describe three factors that allowed this fraud to occur.

d. Identify two audit procedures that would have disclosed this fraud.

(CIA *adapted*)

7-17. Internal auditors must be alert for errors, irregularities, and fraud. Errors are generally considered unintentional acts, while irregularities refer to intentional acts, including fraud. Preventive, detective, and corrective controls can be designed to limit errors and irregularities. Of these three types of controls, preventive controls generally are the most cost-effective. Following are three situations in which fraud was suspected or detected by internal auditors.

Situation 1: Many employees of a firm that manufactures small tools pocket some of these tools for their personal use. Since the quantities taken by any one employee were immaterial, the individual employees did not consider the act as fraudulent or detrimental to the firm. As the firm grew larger, an internal auditor was hired. The auditor charted the gross profit percentages for particular tools and discovered higher gross profit rates for tools related to industrial use than for tools related to personal use. Subsequent investigation uncovered the fraudulent acts.

Situation 2: A controller set up a fictitious subsidiary office to which he shipped inventories and then approved the invoice for payment. The inventories were sold and the proceeds deposited to the controller's personal bank account. Internal auditors suspected fraud when auditing the plant's real estate assets. They traced plant real estate descriptions to the assets owned and leased, and could not find a title or lease for the location of this particular subsidiary.

Situation 3: The manager of a large department was able to embezzle funds from his employer by carrying employees on the payroll beyond actual termination dates. The manager carried each terminated employee for only one pay period beyond the termination date so the employee would not easily detect the additional amount included on the W-2 reporting of wages to the Internal Revenue Service. The paymaster regularly delivered all checks to the department manager who then deposited the fraudulent checks to a personal checking account. An internal auditor discovered the fraud from a routine tracing of sample entries in the payroll register to the employees' files in the personnel office. The sample included one employee's pay record whose personnel file showed the termination date prior to the pay period audited. The auditor investigated further and discovered other such fraudulent checks.

Required

Referring to the three situations presented above, describe the recommendations that an internal auditor (or fraud examiner) should make in each situation to prevent similar problems in the future.

(CMA adapted)

7-18. An organization's director of maintenance has sole custody of the vehicles and related replacement parts. The director's spouse is in charge of the inventory control section of the Controller's office. Both of them come from families that had low to moderate incomes, but they have risen rapidly in the organization. The two are highly regarded by nearly everyone in the organization. They are generous; their peers have come to expect nice presents for special occasions such as birthdays and anniversaries.

Both are tireless workers. They are often the last to leave work at night and the first to arrive in the morning. When they work late, they often allow the security guards to leave early.

To some, however, they seem to be somewhat paradoxical. On one hand, they follow their conservative roots. They have saved enough to purchase a light, twin-engine airplane, a 40-acre farm, and nice automobiles for both of their teenaged children. On the other hand, they demonstrate some very excessive tendencies. They often fly their airplane the 1000 miles from their home to a resort for gambling weekends. Friends who have accompanied them report that they seldom win.

Management views these trips as justifiable rewards for their hard work. They are so busy taking care of the organization's interests that they never have time to take the two weeks' vacation they earn each year.

Although it is a relatively large, privately held organization, an internal auditing department is a recent addition. While conducting a survey to become familiar with the organization and to determine the required staffing level for the new department, the new director of internal auditing became somewhat skeptical when these facts came to light.

Required

a. What are the two major classifications of frauds?

b. What are the major methods for concealing fraud?

c. List six indicators of potential fraud that the new audit director might recognize in the above scenario.

d. Do the director and his spouse fit the typical profile of white-collar criminals?

e. Describe the steps that should be taken to determine if a fraud is taking place.

f. Describe several major safeguards to prevent or deter fraud.

(CIA adapted)

7-19. The studies conducted by the National Commission on Fraudulent Financial Reporting revealed that fraudulent financial reporting usually occurs as the result of certain environmental, institutional, or individual influences and opportune situations. These influences and opportunities, present to some degree in all firms, add pressures and motivate individuals and firms to engage in fraudulent financial reporting. The effective prevention and detection of fraudulent financial reporting requires an understanding of these influences and opportunities, while evaluating the risk of fraudulent financial reporting that these factors can create in a firm. The risk factors to be assessed include not only internal ethical and control factors, but also external environmental conditions.

Required

a. Identify two situational pressures in a publicly owned firm that would increase the likelihood of fraud.

b. Identify three corporate circumstances (opportune situations) when fraud is easier to commit and when detection is less likely.

c. For the purpose of assessing the risk of fraudulent financial reporting, identify the external environmental factors that should be considered in a firm's:

   (1) industry.

   (2) business environment.

   (3) legal and regulatory environment.

d. List several control procedures or measures that top management should incorporate to reduce the possibility of fraudulent financial reporting.

(CMA adapted)

7-20. The first conviction of a computer "hacker" under the Computer Fraud and Abuse Act of 1986 occurred in 1988. There have been other cases of computer break-ins reported in the news, as well as stories of viruses spreading throughout vital networks. Though these cases make the headlines, most experts maintain that the number of computer crimes publicly revealed represents only the tip of the iceberg. Firms have been victims of crimes but have not acknowledged them in order to avoid adverse publicity and not advertise their vulnerability.

Although the threat to security is seen as external, through outside penetration, the more dangerous threats are of internal origin. Management must recognize these problems and commit to the development and enforcement of security programs to deal with the many types of fraud that computer systems are susceptible to on a daily basis. Several types of computer systems fraud are (1) input manipulation, (2) program alteration, (3) file alteration, (4) data theft, (5) sabotage, and (6) theft of computer time.

Required

a. How do computer systems frauds differ from non-computer systems frauds?

b. For each type of fraud identified above, explain whether it is an on-book or off-book scheme, and explain how each one is committed.

c. For each of the above frauds, the computer system is only "indirectly" involved in committing the act. Give several examples of computer systems frauds where the computer is "directly" involved in committing the act.

d. Identify a different method of protection for each type of fraud, describing how the protection method operates. The same protection method should not be used for more than one type of fraud, that is, six different methods must be identified and described.

(CMA *adapted*)

7-21. Randy and John had known each other for many years. They had become best friends in college, where they both majored in accounting. After graduation, Randy took over the family business from his father. His family had been in the grocery business for several generations. When John had difficulty finding a job, Randy offered him a job in the family store. John proved to be a very capable employee. As John demonstrated his abilities, Randy began delegating more and more responsibility to him. After a period of time, John was doing all of the general accounting and authorization functions for checks, cash, inventories, documents, records, and bank reconciliations. (1) *John was trusted completely and handled all financial functions.* No one checked his work.

Randy decided to expand the business and opened several new stores. (2) *Randy was always handling the most urgent problem . . . crisis management is what his college professors had termed it.* John assisted with the problems when his other duties allowed him time.

Although successful at work, John had (3) *difficulties with personal financial problems.*

At first, the amounts stolen by John were small. John did not even worry about making the accounts balance. But John became greedy. "How easy it is to take the money," he said. He felt that he was a critical member of the business team, (4) *and that he contributed much more to the success of the firm than was represented by his salary.* It would take two or three people to replace me, he often thought to himself. As the amounts became larger and larger, (5) *he made the books balance.* Because of these activities, John was able to purchase an expensive car and

take his family on several trips each year. (6) *He also joined an expensive country club.* Things were changing at home, however. (7) *John's family observed that he was often argumentative and at other times very depressed.*

The fraud continued for six years. Each year the business performed more and more poorly. In the last year the stores lost over $200,000. Randy's bank required an audit. John confessed when he thought the auditors had discovered his embezzlements.

When discussing frauds, the pressures, opportunities, and rationalizations that cause/allow a perpetrator to commit the fraud are often identified. Symptoms of fraud are also studied.

Required

For each question numbered 1 through 7, identify the numbered and italicized factors (from the case) as being one of the symptoms, pressures, opportunities, or rationalizations given.

1. Number 1, "John was trusted completely . . ." is an example of a(n):
   a. Document symptom.
   b. Situational pressure.
   c. Opportunity to commit.
   d. Physical symptom.

2. Number 2, "Randy was always handling the most urgent . . ." is an example of a(n):
   a. Opportunity to commit.
   b. Analytical symptom.
   c. Situational pressure.
   d. Rationalization.

3. Number 3, "difficulties with personal financial problems" is an example of a(n):
   a. Behavioral symptom.
   b. Situational pressure.
   c. Rationalization.
   d. Opportunity to commit.

4. Number 4, "and that he contributed much more . . ." is an example of a(n):
   a. Rationalization.
   b. Behavioral symptom.
   c. Situational pressure.
   d. Physical symptom.

5. Number 5, "he made the books balance" is an example of a(n):
   a. Physical symptom.
   b. Analytical symptom.
   c. Lifestyle symptom.
   d. Document symptom.

6. Number 6, "He also joined an expensive country club" is an example of a(n):

   a. Rationalization.

   b. Lifestyle symptom.

   c. Behavioral symptom.

   d. Physical symptom.

7. Number 7, "John's family observed that he was often argumentive . . ." is an example of a(n):

   a. Rationalization.

   b. Lifestyle symptom.

   c. Behavioral symptom.

   d. Physical symptom.

(CIA *adapted*)

7-22. The purchasing clerk responsible for maintaining the purchases journal set up a fictitious on-book payment scheme. The clerk periodically enters fictitious acquisitions into the purchases journal. The nonexistent vendor's address is given as a post office box, which is rented by the clerk. The clerk forwards notification of the fictitious purchases for recording in the accounts payable ledger. Payment is ultimately mailed to the post office box. The purchasing clerk deposits the check in an account established in the name of the nonexistent vendor.

Required

a. Describe the type and nature of the risk exposure illustrated by this situation.

b. Would the scheme be classified as a larceny, theft, or embezzlement? Explain your answer.

c. Distinguish between on-book and off-book plots. Why is the purchasing clerk using the on-book approach to conceal the diversion of cash? Which of the two plots is more difficult to prevent or detect?

d. Identify in broad terms several control procedures that could be useful in detecting this on-book purchasing fraud or in preventing similar occurrences in the future.

e. Describe how an off-book purchases fraud could be committed. Identify several control procedures that could be useful in detecting the off-book purchasing fraud or in preventing similar occurrences in the future.

(CIA *adapted*)

7-23. A computer "hacker," who was known among friends as Terminus, was also an industrial spy. After admitting to five felonies, he was sentenced to one year in prison. His illegal activities began by his receiving the software code for an advanced computer operating system, which he knew was stolen from the developer firm. Then he distributed the stolen code on the black market. Next, he placed a Trojan Horse, designed to trap and save passwords, in the code's log-on procedure. He made this modified code available to other hackers by setting up a home page via the Internet's World Wide Web. Finally, he inserted the modified code into the system of his employer at the time, thereby obtaining the passwords pertaining to sensitive files and using the passwords to access information in the file.

Required

a. Discuss the nature of the risk exposures illustrated by this situation.

b. What are the similarities and differences between a Trojan Horse and a computer virus?

c. Identify in broad terms several control procedures and security measures that might be employed to protect against such activities.

7-24. After undertaking a data security review, a firm adopts plastic cards that are needed for accessing the computer terminals owned by the firm. These cards are then given to those employees whose duties require them to use the terminals. The cost of the cards is $100,000. The probability that unauthorized persons will be able to access the system is thereby reduced from 25 percent to 5 percent. What reasons have likely been used by management to justify the $100,000 investment?

7-25. The Northwestern Division of the PVT Supply Company has the following inventory.

- Pipe ($600,000 average balance)—stored in an unfenced, unguarded yard.
- Valves and tools ($300,000 and $100,000 average balances, respectively)—stored in an unguarded warehouse, which is attached to the division's sales office.

All personnel have access to the inventory area through the adjoining offices.

The Northwestern Division was opened as a test market area two years ago and has grown rapidly, although it still represents only 5 percent of PVT's total operations. For various reasons (initially, the tentative nature of operations, and then, their rapid growth), the firm did not install the same physical controls to safeguard the inventory at its Northwestern Division that it had established at its three other divisions. Such controls are now being considered.

The identified risk is that inventory with a total value of $1 million is not safeguarded. Such an amount is "significant" and a major loss would interrupt the division's business; nevertheless, the asset is not material to PVT's total financial position and results of operations. In the most recent physical inventory, the division determined that it had incurred a 7 percent inventory shrinkage ($70,000) in one year. This is related primarily to certain valves, tools, and smaller diameters of pipe that are readily marketable. Historically, inventory shrinkage at the other divisions has been only one half of 1 percent; therefore, "normal" shrinkage would have been $5000. The division suspects theft, but since it has no proof, it cannot recover under its theft insurance. The annual cost to install the controls at the Northwestern Division that are in place at other PVT divisions is estimated as follows.

Hire a night watchman:

Salary	$12,000
Taxes and fringe benefits @ 20%	2,400
Build a 10-foot-high chain-link fence around the pipe yard ($5000 ÷ 10 years = $500 annual cost)	500
Build a special enclosed area (with separate locks) within the warehouse for storing tools and smaller, more expensive valves; assign one of the workers already on the payroll (no incremental cost) exclusive access to the area and responsibility for filling orders for these items. (Cost to build enclosed area: $1000 ÷ 10 years = $100 annual cost)	100
Install separate locks on the warehouse so that access (through the office or from outside) can be limited to authorized personnel ($200 initial cost; annual cost nil)	—
Total	$15,000

The proposed controls will not result in any costs of lost sales resulting from a reduction in customer service if (1) the other divisions' abilities to service their customers are not affected by having similar controls and (2) the Northwestern Division believes its experiences will be similar. If this is not the case, the division should consider costs of lost sales in its cost-benefit analysis.

Required

Discuss the desirability of installing the controls and security measures pertaining to the pipe, valves, tools, and warehouse.*

CONTINUING CASE

With respect to the small firm that you selected in Chapter 1, complete the following requirements:

a. How does the firm define internal control? Determine the firm's internal control objectives. How do the definition and objectives of internal control differ from the recommendations made in the Committee of Sponsoring Organizations (COSO) report?

b. Determine the major components of the firm's internal control environment. How do these components differ from the recommendations made in the COSO report?

c. If the firm employs a corporate code of conduct, determine its major provisions.

d. How does the firm handle ethical violations?

e. For one major transaction processing cycle, identify several major exposures to risk that the firm faces with respect to assets and data.

f. Determine whether the firm uses a cost-benefit analysis to determine which controls to implement in the AIS. If such an analysis is utilized, determine how the firm computes costs and benefits.

g. Determine whether any fraudulent activities have been committed by the firm's employees. How did the firm deal with the perpetrators of these suspect activities?

---

*Courtesy of Arthur Young & Co., CPAs. Adapted with permission from *Evaluating Accounting Controls: A Systematic Approach.* Copyright © 1980 by Arthur Young & Company.

CHAPTER
8

GENERAL CONTROLS AND
APPLICATION CONTROLS

THE LEARNING OBJECTIVES FOR THIS CHAPTER ARE TO ENABLE YOU TO:

1. Identify several plans for classifying controls and security measures.

2. Describe general controls that pertain to the manual processing portions of accounting information systems.

3. Describe general controls that pertain to the computer-based portions of accounting information systems.

4. Describe transaction controls that pertain to both manual and computer-based accounting information systems.

5. Contrast controls needed in various computer-based systems environments, including those involving batch-processing, on-line processing, and data bases.

INTRODUCTION

In this chapter, we will discuss the *control activities component* of the internal control structure pertaining to information processing systems. The first section of this chapter presents several generally acceptable alternative ways of classifying control activities. The second part of the chapter covers general controls that pertain broadly to all accounting information systems. Then, we look at the application controls that directly impinge on the input, processing, and output stages of transaction processing applications. When appropriate, we distinguish those controls that pertain to manual processing, to computer-based processing, or to both.

Accountants, including auditors as well as those involved in systems design, need a thorough knowledge of control activities in accounting infor-

mation systems. If you intend to pursue an accounting career, you are likely to come into contact with both manual systems and computer-based systems. You should be aware of the specific controls that pertain to both.

CONTROL CLASSIFICATIONS

Controls may be classified by objectives, by settings, by risk aversion, and by systems architectures. Figure 8-1 shows these four classification plans. As the figure indicates, the plans represent alternative ways of presenting and arranging the total array of available controls over information processing systems found in the authoritative literature. For instance, general and application controls, a category under the settings classification

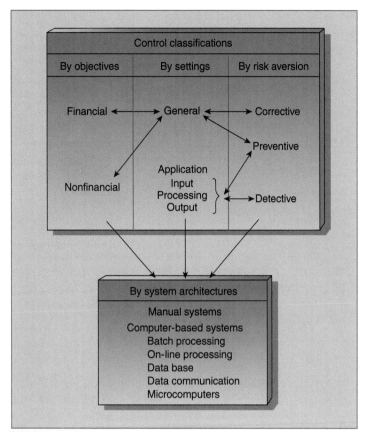

FIGURE 8-1 Plans for classifying controls.

plan, encompass financial controls and nonfinancial controls (under the objectives classification plan). Also, general controls include corrective controls and preventive controls, and application controls embody preventive and detective controls (under the risk-aversion classification plan). Controls from all three classification plans shown in the upper box of the figure are employed within the various systems architectures, shown in the lower box of the figure.

CLASSIFICATION BY OBJECTIVES

Two major control categories under the objectives classification plan are the financial and nonfinancial controls. Financial controls can also be categorized as financial reporting controls, and nonfinancial controls can also be categorized as compliance controls and operations controls.

CLASSIFICATION BY RISK AVERSION

Controls may also be classified according to the ways that they combat the risks to which a firm and its information are exposed. **Preventive controls** block adverse events, such as errors or losses, from occurring. For example, a manual of processing procedures prepared by Diane Varney, treasurer and controller of Infoage, is a preventive control. Preventive controls tend to be passive in nature. **Detective controls** discover the occurrence of adverse events. They are more active than preventive controls. An example of a detective control is key verification of data typed onto a magnetic medium by a clerk. Certain detective controls cause further processing to be temporarily halted, as when Infoage's accounts payable bookkeeper detects an input error by visually verifying the transaction's accuracy as displayed on the computer's monitor. **Corrective controls** lead to the righting of effects caused by adverse events, usually by providing needed information. For example, information to the effect that the level of an inventory item is too low may trigger a suitable request in Infoage's inventory management system that more inventory be ordered. In some instances corrective controls may anticipate adverse events, as when Infoage's management purchases insurance coverage against the theft of assets. Corrective controls are generally more active than detective controls.

CLASSIFICATION BY SYSTEMS ARCHITECTURE

As indicated by Figure 8-1, systems architectures include manual systems and the following types of computer-based systems: batch processing, real-time, data base, data communications, and stand-alone microcomputer. The first three of these types of systems have already been discussed; the latter two are covered in Appendixes A and B, respectively.

CLASSIFICATION BY SETTINGS

One of the most useful groupings of information processing systems' control activities is into the two broad groupings of general controls and application controls.* **General controls** are those controls that pertain to all activities involving a firm's accounting information system and resources (assets). These controls include those encompassed by the internal control environment, plus the other components of the internal control structure; many such controls were described in Chapter 7. The general controls covered in this chapter are found under the control activities component of the internal control structure. **Application controls** relate to specific accounting tasks or transactions; hence, they may also be called transaction controls. Application or transaction controls roughly parallel the accounting system. Another group of controls does not fit comfortably into either category. These controls, which we shall call **security measures,** are intended to provide adequate safeguards over access to and use of assets and data records.

These three categories of controls are intertwined, especially in computer-based information systems. An appropriate balance of controls in all three categories is needed for an internal control structure to function effectively.

GENERAL CONTROLS

The following are the primary general control groupings over information processing systems:

1. Organizational controls.
2. Documentation controls.

---

*Information processing controls must be implemented to ensure that an organization achieves both its financial and nonfinancial objectives.

3. Asset accountability controls.
4. Management practice controls.
5. Data center operations controls.
6. Authorization controls.
7. Access controls.

However, we will treat authorization controls as a separate category of application controls, since they are a bridge between organizational and transaction controls. Also, access controls more comfortably fit into the security controls category, and their discussion will be deferred to Chapter 9.

ORGANIZATIONAL CONTROLS

A firm's organizational structure represents an underlying control because it specifies the work relationships of employees and units. The central *control objective* when designing the organizational structure is to establish **organizational independence.** When properly provided through a careful and logical segregation of assigned duties and responsibilities, organizational independence results in a complete separation of incompatible functions. It involves two or more employees or organizational units in each procedure, who can be assigned to check on the work of one another. Thus errors made by one employee or unit will be detected by another. No single employee is able to commit a fraudulent act in the normal course of duties and then to hide the deed. Fraud under such an arrangement can be perpetrated only by means of collusion. Thus the chance for fraudulent activities to occur is greatly reduced, since most persons who might consider fraud are afraid of being socially rejected if they propose the idea to a co-worker. Collusion by related persons can be prevented by employment rules that prohibit nepotism, that is, not hiring a relative of an employee.

Although very important to organizational control, the segregation of duties is usually not sufficient. Most firms also depend on the diligence of independent reviewers. To be truly effective, these reviewers or monitors must stand apart from the procedures themselves. A typical large- or medium-sized firm has several types of reviewers, including the board of directors, higher- and lower-level managers, and internal and external auditors.

To understand the concept of organizational independence, we should review its application in various types of systems. We will begin with manual systems, since they present the most familiar situations.

Manual Systems   Authorizing, record-keeping, and custodial functions should be organizationally separated in manual systems. Thus, employees who handle assets, such as cash and inventory, should not authorize transactions involving those assets or keep the records concerning them. For instance, if an accountant is allowed to handle cash receipts and also keep the accounts receivable records, the accountant can easily conceal a theft. Figure 8-2 shows a logical division of duties in handling sales and cash receipts transactions. Not only are numerous units involved in the procedure, but the functions mentioned above are separated. The sales order department originates and authorizes sales transactions, while the credit department authorizes the credit terms on which the sales are made; record keeping is performed by the billing and accounts receivable departments; and custodial duties are handled by the warehouse, shipping, and cash receipts departments.

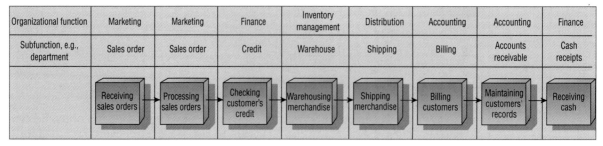

Organizational function	Marketing	Marketing	Finance	Inventory management	Distribution	Accounting	Accounting	Finance
Subfunction, e.g., department	Sales order	Sales order	Credit	Warehouse	Shipping	Billing	Accounts receivable	Cash receipts
	Receiving sales orders	Processing sales orders	Checking customer's credit	Warehousing merchandise	Shipping merchandise	Billing customers	Maintaining customers' records	Receiving cash

FIGURE 8-2   Organizational independence with respect to the revenue cycle.

The concept of organizational independence also prohibits the combining of duties in those cases where assets are endangered or adequate checks are not applied. Several examples are as follows: A clerk who is assigned the duty of handling a petty-cash fund should not also handle cash received from customers, since the funds might become commingled and later lost. A buyer who prepares a purchase order should not also approve the prepared form; instead, the purchase order should be signed by the purchasing manager. An accountant who prepares a journal voucher should present the completed form to an accounting manager for signature. An accounting clerk who performs key steps in a procedure, such as posting cash receipts, should not perform a check on the procedure, such as preparing a bank reconciliation.

Computer-Based Systems   Organizational independence should also be maintained in computer-based systems, although adjustments are necessary. As with manual systems, the authorizing, custodial, and record-keeping functions are to be separated. (In fact, most computer-based systems involve significant amounts of manual processing.) Our discussion of organizational controls in computer-based systems will first consider the needed segregation between user departments and the information systems function; then, we will look at needed segregation of responsibilities within the systems function itself.

The information systems (IS) function has responsibilities relating to processing and controlling data (i.e., record keeping). Thus it should be organizationally independent of (1) all departments that use data and information, (2) those departments that perform operational and custodial duties, and (3) those persons who authorize transactions. All transactions and changes to master records and application programs should be initiated and authorized by user departments. For instance, sales transactions should be initiated by the sales order department, with the sales orders being processed within the information systems function. Changes to sales application programs should be initiated by sales management. Furthermore, errors in transactions should be corrected by user departments. All assets (except computer and data processing facilities) should reside under the control of designated operational departments. Thus merchandise to fill customers' orders are stored in a warehouse department.

Sometimes it may appear that complete separation of these functions is not possible. For example, when a computer-based system automatically approves an order from a customer, on the basis of credit guidelines built into a sales application program, it may seem that the information systems function is authorizing the transaction. However, the authorizing function is in reality performed by the person, perhaps the credit manager, who established the guidelines.

The IS function has the overall purpose of providing information-related services to other departments within a firm. In those many firms having computer-based systems, they have taken over the array of record preparation, record-keeping, and processing activities traditionally performed by several accounting departments. That is, the presence of computers centralizes duties that should be segregated. To achieve organizational independence, it is necessary to subdivide several key responsibilities within the organizational structure of the IS function itself.

Figure 8-3 displays an organization chart of an IS function that is reasonably typical for a firm employing centralized computers. The major segregation of responsibilities is between (1) systems development tasks, which create systems, and (2) data processing tasks, which operate systems. The **systems development function** is concerned with analyzing, designing, programming, and documenting the various applications needed by user departments and the firm as a whole. Not only is this function responsible for new computer-based applications but also it must make changes in existing applications as needed. Furthermore, it aids users via an information center. The **data processing function** has responsibility for ensuring that transaction data are processed and controlled and the related files and other data sets are properly handled. These two major functions are separated—both organizationally and physically—for a very sound reason. If the same individuals had both (1) detailed knowledge of programs and data and (2) access to them, they could make unauthorized changes. Thus, systems analysts and programmers should not be allowed to operate the computer or to have access to "live" programs or data. Furthermore, computer operators and other data processing personnel should not have access to the documentation concerning programs (nor to various assets such as inventory and cash).

As Figure 8-3 shows, the IS function also includes other functions, such as technical services and data-base administration. (Various other groups, such as planning staff and the steering committee, are discussed in Chapter 18.) **Technical services** has responsibilities with respect to computer-related areas such as data

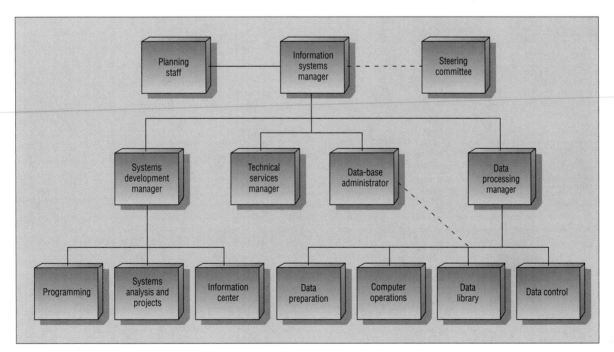

FIGURE 8-3 Organizational independence within the information systems function of a firm using computer-based processing.

communications, systems programming, and decision modeling. **Data-base administration** is concerned with all aspects of the data resources. The data-base administrator must establish and define the schema of the data base, control the use of the data base via appropriate security measures, and control all changes in data and programs that use the data base. As indicated by Figure 8-3, the data-base administrator should have functional authority over the data library. However, he or she should not have direct access to "live" data or programs.

In Figure 8-3 the organizational arrangement of the data processing function concerns batch processing, since the typical firm employs this mode of processing for, at least, some of its accounting applications. These units are repeated in Figure 8-4, which shows the flow of batched data during batch applications. A high degree of segregation is needed to reduce the risks of alteration to "live" data or programs. For instance, without adequate segregation a computer operator could make changes to his personnel records at will and escape detection, or a programmer could alter a computer program and not be caught.

Figure 8-5 illustrates how a suitable division of responsibilities provides needed segregation of duties in the course of a batch processing application. For on-line processing applications, the division of duties is simplified. As Figure 8-6 shows, the user departments enter the transactions via terminals. The transactions are checked

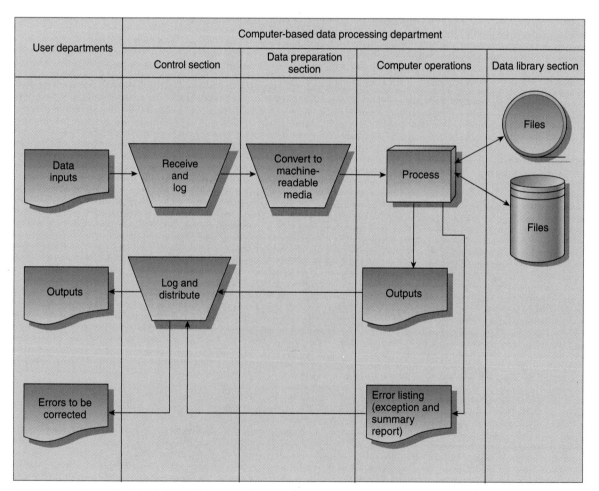

FIGURE 8-4   Flow of batched data within several units of an organization(s) using computer-based processing.

1. The **data control unit** serves as an interface between the various user departments and computer operations. It records input data (including batch totals) in a control log, follows the progress of data being processed, and distributes outputs to authorized users. As a part of its control responsibilities, it maintains the control totals pertaining to master files as well as transaction files and reconciles these totals to updated totals shown on exception and summary reports. Finally, it monitors the correction of detected errors by the user departments. The data control unit must be independent of computer operations, since it helps to ensure that processing is performed correctly and that data are not lost or mishandled.

2. The **data preparation unit** prepares and verifies data for entry into processing.

3. **Computer operations** processes data to produce outputs. Its duties include loading data into input devices, mounting secondary storage devices such as magnetic tapes and magnetic disk packs, and performing operations as prescribed by run manuals and computer console messages. (A console is the portion of the computer, usually a visual display screen and keyboard, that allows communication between the operators and the computer.) One duty that computer operators should not perform is correcting errors detected during processing, since the corrections may introduce new undetected errors. Computer operations should be physically as well as organizationally separated from the other units, so that persons such as the librarian and data control clerks do not have direct access to the computer.

4. The **data library unit** maintains a storage room, called the library, where the data files and programs are kept. A librarian issues these files and programs to operators when needed for processing and keeps records of file and program usage. Thus the files and programs are better protected when not being used.

FIGURE 8-5 An example of segregation of duties in a batch processing application.

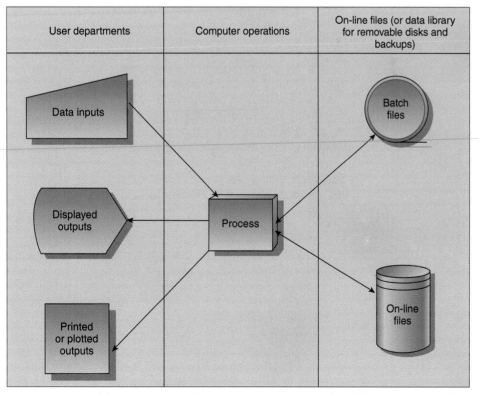

FIGURE 8-6 Simplified organizational separation in a computer-based system using on-line processing.

by computer edit programs for accuracy and then are processed against on-line files. Outputs may be printed or displayed on printers, plotters, or terminals located in the departments of the recipients. The data control and data library tasks as well as data processing are thus performed by the computer system hardware and software.

DOCUMENTATION CONTROLS

An accounting information system (AIS) is a complex mixture of procedures, controls, forms, equipment, and users. If the instructions and guidelines for operating such a system are inadequate, the system is likely to function inefficiently. If and when breakdowns occur, the disruptions to operations are likely to be quite harmful. Consider the situation in which a system analyst has designed and installed a computer-based accounting application, but has neglected to prepare computer flowcharts that describe the programs. If a "bug" develops in one of the programs, the repairs to the program would be difficult and time-consuming.

Documentation consists of procedures manuals and other means of describing the accounting information system and its operations. It also should include those aspects of a firm that have impact on the AIS, such as policy statements, organization charts, and job descriptions. Documentation is an important cog in the internal control structure. It helps employees to understand and interpret policies and procedures. Thus data processing clerks are more likely to perform their AIS-related tasks correctly and consistently. Systems analysts and programmers can redesign transaction processing systems more easily and reliably, especially when the original designers may have left the firm. Auditors are able to examine the internal control system more quickly and thoroughly. Consequently, another general control objective is to prepare complete and clear documentation and to maintain it in an up-to-date condition.

Manual Systems   Documentation for manual systems should include all of the following components: source documents, journals, ledgers, reports, document outputs, charts of accounts, audit trail details, procedural steps, record layouts, data dictionaries, and control procedures. Numerous examples should be provided, such as typical accounting entries and filled-in source documents. Procedures should be documented by narrative descriptions, system flowcharts, and data-flow diagrams. Equally important are those elements that are related to the effective operation of the AIS. Clear policy statements encourage employees to adhere to management's policies. An organization chart and job descriptions inform employees of their roles and responsibilities with respect to data processing.

Computer-Based Systems   All of the documentation appropriate to manual systems is likewise needed in computer-based systems. Even the most automated system contains some manual processing steps and involves interactions with human users and clerks. However, additional documentation is needed because of the presence of complex hardware and nonvisible programs.

Computer-related documentation concerns the computer system itself and the persons who interface with it. In the former category are the overall system standards, system application documentation, program documentation, and data documentation. In the latter category are operating documentation and user documentation. Also, the contents of each type of documentation will differ as circumstances dictate. Figure 8-7 itemizes the array of documentation needed in a computer-based system. These types of documentation are more fully discussed in Appendix 1 to this chapter.

System Standards Documentation
   Systems development policy statements
   Program testing policy statements
   Computer operations policy statements
   Security and disaster policy statements

System Application Documentation
   Computer system flowcharts
   Data-flow diagrams
   Narrative descriptions of procedures
   Input/output descriptions, including filled-in source documents
   Formats of journals, ledgers, reports, and other outputs
   Details concerning audit trails
   Charts of accounts
   File descriptions, including record layouts and data dictionaries
   Error messages and formats
   Error-correction procedures
   Control procedures

Program Documentation
   Program flowcharts, decision tables, data structure diagrams
   Source program listings
   Inputs, formats, and sample filled-in forms
   Printouts of reports, listings, and other outputs
   Operating instructions
   Test data and testing procedures
   Program change procedures
   Error listings

Data Documentation
   Descriptions of data elements, including names, field sizes, and so on
   Relationships of specific data elements to other data elements

Operating Documentation
   Performance instructions for executing computer programs
   Required input/output files for specific programs
   Setup procedures for specific programs
   List of programmed halts, including related messages and required operator actions,
      for specific programs
   Recovery and restart procedures for specific programs
   Estimated run times of specific programs
   Distribution of reports generated by specific programs

User Documentation
   Procedures for entering data on source documents
   Checks of input data for accuracy and completeness
   Formats and uses of reports
   Possible error messages and correction procedures

FIGURE 8-7   Types of documentation needed in computer-based systems.

Control of Documentation   A system should be in place to ensure that documentation is not only prepared and kept up-to-date but also properly secured and controlled. One employee, called a data librarian in a large firm, is usually responsible for the control, storage, retention, and distribution of documentation. To improve control, all copies of documentation are numbered. No employee should be permitted to remove documentation from the premises without authorization; if such use is allowed, a proper check-out procedure should be enforced. Duplicate copies of documentation should be prepared and at least one copy stored in a fireproof container at a remote location. Photocopying documentation without special permission should be prohibited. Confidential documentation should be prepared on a special type of chemically treated paper that does not allow the contents to be photocopied.

Computer-Generated Documentation   In larger companies the computer is an underutilized tool that can be employed to automatically prepare much of an application's documentation. Computer-assisted software engineering (CASE) and other special software packages can replace handwritten documentation with computer-generated documentation, thereby cutting costs and increasing productivity. CASE and related tools can partially or totally automate the preparation of data-flow diagrams, structure charts, program code, data dictionaries, modeling diagrams, decision tables, and user manuals.

ASSET ACCOUNTABILITY CONTROLS

A firm's assets are the productive resources that it possesses. These valued assets are subject to losses from theft, waste, pilferage, accidents, damage, and bad business decisions. Harmful business decisions include selling a firm's products at too low a price, extending credit to bad risks, and failing to retain key personnel or preventing patent infringement or incurring unforeseen liabilities.* Another risk is that the assets will be valued incorrectly in the financial statements, perhaps as a result of miscounting the quantities. Thus, one of the objectives of the internal control process is to protect a firm's assets from these risks.

Restricting access to assets is achieved through various security measures, which are discussed in the next chapter. Specific **asset accountability controls** that aid in ensuring that assets are properly valued in the accounting records include the use of subsidiary ledgers, reconciliations, acknowledgment procedures, logs and registers, and reviews and reassessments. These controls are equally needed in manual and computer-based systems. However, because of the added computation power of computers, controls such as reconciliations can be performed more frequently in computer-based systems.

Accounting Subsidiary Ledgers   Subsidiary ledgers can be maintained for assets such as accounts receivable, inventory, plant assets, and investments. Amounts reflected in these ledgers are based on postings from transaction documents. The total of all balances in a particular subsidiary ledger should be equal to the balance in the corresponding control account in the general ledger. Since the postings are performed independently of each other, the use of a subsidiary ledger provides a cross-check on the correctness of the control account, and vice versa.

Reconciliations   A **reconciliation** consists of comparing values that have been computed independently. Thus a comparison of the balance in a control account with

---

*Committee of Sponsoring Organizations of the Treadway Commission, *Internal Control: Integrated Framework*, volume 1 of 2, 1994, p. 37.

the total of balances in a corresponding subsidiary ledger is an example of a reconciliation. Reconciliations can also involve comparisons of physical levels of resources with the quantities or amounts reflected in accounting records. For instance, each item of a physical inventory should be counted periodically. These physical counts can then be reconciled with the quantities shown in the accounting records. If differences appear, they may signal the need to adjust the quantities in the accounting records to reflect the physical realities. Another important reconciliation, the bank reconciliation, compares the balance in the bank account with the cash balance in the general ledger.

In accordance with the principle of organizational independence, reconciliations should be prepared only by employees or managers not otherwise responsible for the processing of related transactions. For instance, no employee of Infoage involved in the processing or handling of cash receipts or cash disbursements should prepare a bank reconciliation. Instead, it should be prepared by the treasurer and controller, Diane Varney.

Acknowledgment Procedures In various transactions, employees are called on to acknowledge their accountability for assets. For instance, when merchandise arrives from Infoage's suppliers, the clerks in the receiving department of the warehouse count the incoming goods, prepare a receiving report, and sign the report. In doing so they acknowledge accountability for the goods. When the merchandise later is moved to the storeroom, Infoage's storeskeeper recounts the goods and signs for their receipt. Through this acknowledgment procedure, he or she accepts the transfer of accountability for the goods.

Logs and Registers Receipts, movements, and uses of assets can be monitored by means of logs and registers. For example, cash receipts are logged on remittance listings (i. e., registers). Later the amounts recorded on deposit slips are reconciled to the amounts of these remittance listings, to ensure that all receipts are deposited intact. Files of data on magnetic tapes are noted on logs as they are moved from the data library into the computer room, and vice versa. When an employee uses a computer system from a terminal, the access can be recorded on a console log. Logs and registers thus help a firm to account for the status and use of its varied assets.

Reviews and Reassessments **Reviews** by outside parties provide independent verification of asset balances and, hence, accountability. For instance, an auditor may verify that the fixed assets reflected in the accounts actually exist and are properly valued. A customer who receives her monthly statement will likely verify that the amount owed is correct.

Reassessments are reevaluations of measured asset values. For example, Infoage's accountants make periodic counts of the physical inventory and compare the counts to the inventory records. If necessary, the quantities and amounts in the records may be adjusted downward to reflect losses, breakage, and aging.

MANAGEMENT PRACTICE CONTROLS

Some of the most severe risk exposures that a firm faces are related to possible deficiencies in management. For instance, Diane Varney may improperly define the necessary competence and skill levels required for a payroll accountant to succeed at Infoage and hire a marginally qualified employee. Consequently, the payroll accountant may commit excessive errors. If Diane dismisses the payroll employee, Infoage will incur significant additional costs of screening, hiring, and training a new

COMPUTER OPERATING PROCEDURES
at Avery Dennison Corporation*

Avery Dennison's main data center is located near Cleveland. It has four AS/400 systems, which are connected by a token ring local-area network to workstations that support 500 users. Financial, marketing, distribution, and manufacturing applications are processed by the facilities within the data center. Until recently the center was plagued by a variety of problems: slow response to breakdowns in communications; excessive time to back up data and difficulty in keeping track of backup tapes, erroneous scheduling of batch processing runs, and excessive time in processing and reprocessing applications. These problems have led to poor use of computer operators' time, to lost back up files, to improperly prepared and distributed managerial reports and summaries, to break-

downs in security within the data center, and so on.

Although these effects appear to relate mainly to operational matters, in reality most also affect the internal control structure, including the reliability of information provided to users and the safety of the data resource. Consequently, the manager of the data center recently began to install automated hardware and software to reduce the cumbersome and error-ridden manual procedures. For instance, an automated monitoring system has been installed to detect communications problems, high-speed and high-density cartridge tape drives that have autoloading and automatic labeling features have been acquired, and an automatic job scheduling system has been implemented. In addition, all data center staff are receiving continuous training, procedures are being standardized and fully documented, and relations with users are being actively cultivated.

---

*William C. Stief, "Automating the AS/400 Data Center at Avery Dennison Corporation." *Journal of Systems Management* (February 1992), pp. 23–24.

---

payroll accountant. In addition, Diane may make the same mistakes in hiring the replacement payroll accountant and the cycle may be repeated.

A wide variety of general controls are needed to counteract management-related risks. Most of the controls are those identified as being a part of the internal control structure, such as human resource policies and practices, commitment to competence, planning practices, audit practices, and management and operational controls. In addition, this category is sufficiently broad to encompass organizational and documentation controls already discussed. A final grouping of management practice controls are **application system development controls,** which include system change procedures, and new system development procedures. These controls are examined in Appendix 2 to this chapter.

DATA CENTER OPERATIONS CONTROLS

A final group of general controls may be described as **data center operational controls.** These controls pertain mainly to computer-based systems and may be subdivided into (1) computer operating procedures, and (2) computer hardware and software checks.

Computer Operating Procedures Computer operations are subject to a variety of problems and abuses. For example, operations might be poorly scheduled, with the result that needed computer parts are not ordered in time to keep the production line running.

Sound and well-controlled computer operations are based on close supervision, careful planning, and organized procedures. Thus supervisory personnel, such as the manager of data processing and shift supervisors, should actively observe and review the actions of computer operators. Procedural manuals concerning all aspects of computer operations should be prepared and provided to the computer operators, together with the appropriate console run books. Data processing schedules should be prepared as far in advance as feasible and revised as necessary. Preventive diagnostic programs should be employed to monitor the hardware and software functions, so that existing or potential problems may be detected. In a medium-sized firm, such as Infoage, Diane Varney should prepare a variety of daily or weekly reports to control the accounting department's microcomputer operations. Suggested reports Diane should prepare include microcomputer utilization reports and employee productivity reports. To be most effective, these reports should compare actual times against standard times. In addition, large firms can prepare computer facilities utilization reports and computer run-time reports. For instance, the last-named report can compare actual run times, as shown in the console log, against standard times shown in the data processing schedule.

Computer Hardware and Software Checks   Though modern computer hardware is generally reliable in operation, malfunctions can occur. Thus a variety of hardware and software checks are built into computer systems. They ensure the reliability of computations, manipulations, and transfers of data within the systems.

APPLICATION (TRANSACTION) CONTROLS

Those controls that pertain directly to the transaction processing systems are called **transaction or application controls.** The overall objectives of application controls are to help ensure that all transactions are legitimately authorized and accurately recorded, classified, processed, and reported. Application controls are generally subdivided into input, processing, and output controls, as Figure 8-8 suggests. However, as mentioned, we will treat authorization controls as a separate category, since they are a bridge between general and application controls.

Figure 8-8 also identifies **control points,** screens or junctures within a transaction processing system where specific transaction processing controls are needed. For instance, the point at which a transaction is recorded represents a control point. Each type of transaction has a unique pattern of control points. Thus the control points for a cash receipts transaction differ in certain details from those for a purchases transaction.

Before discussing application controls, we should understand that general and application controls are interrelated. General controls are needed to ensure the proper functioning of application controls that depend on computer-based processing.* For instance, application controls such as computer matching and edit checks examine data as they are entered on-line. These controls provide immediate feedback when something does not match, or is incorrectly formatted, so that user departments can make corrections. If general controls are determined to be inadequate, we may not be able to depend on application controls, which display error messages or indicate what is wrong with the data, or produce error and exception reports for subsequent follow-up. Thus, general controls are required to support the functioning

---

*Ibid., p. 54.

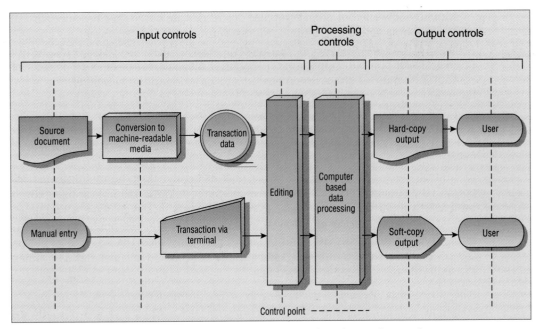

FIGURE 8-8   Subdivisions of transaction (application) controls and typical control points.

of transaction controls, and both groups of controls are needed to ensure the accuracy and completeness of data processing applications.*

AUTHORIZATION CONTROLS

Unauthorized transactions can lead to lost assets. For instance, fictitious checks result in a drain on the cash asset. Authorizations enforce management's policies with respect to the varied transactions flowing into the general ledger system. They have the objectives of assuring (1) that transactions are valid and proper, (2) that outputs are not incorrect due to invalid inputs, and (3) that assets are better protected. Because authorizations are granted by persons not involved in the processing, authorizations enhance the concept of organizational independence.

Authorizations may be classified as general or specific. A **general authorization** establishes standard conditions under which transactions are approved and executed. For instance, management sets criteria by which credit sales are to be approved. Ann Strong establishes the criteria for approval in her firm. At Infoage a formal credit approval process would be enforced. When a customer of Infoage purchases a microcomputer, he or she can pay cash or apply for credit. When the customer applies for credit, the credit department manager either approves or disapproves the application according to the criteria of the general authorization. A **specific authorization** pertains to a particular event, with the conditions and parties specified. For example, a cashier at Infoage who has general authorization to sign checks may need additional authorization to sign a $25,000 check that repays a bank loan. Such authorization may be obtained from Diane Varney or George Freeman.

Authorizations are generally reflected through transaction documents. Thus copies of a sales order prepared by a clerk in the sales order department authorize goods

---

*Ibid., p. 55.

to be released from the warehouse and to be shipped. This specific authorization derives from management's general authorization granted through the established sales procedure. To take another example, the write-off notices signed by a designated Infoage manager authorize amounts owed by certain customers to be cleared from their accounts. Again, the power of such notices to authorize derives from management's general authorization embodied in the established bad-debt/write-off procedure.

In manual systems and computer-based batch processing systems, authorizations may appear as signatures, initials, or stamps on transaction documents. For on-line computer-based systems, the authorizations are usually verified by the computer system.

Whatever form they take, authorizations should be verified before processing proceeds. Before Infoage's cashier prepares checks for suppliers, he or she reviews invoices for the initials indicating that the invoices have been vouched and authorized for payment. When transactions are entered in batches for computer processing, the data control clerks review the batched documents. When transactions are entered on-line, perhaps without the support of source documents, authorizations are immediately verified. One generally adopted verification procedure involves passwords. If a user provides the proper password, he or she is presumed by the security module to be authorized to enter forthcoming transactions or to change data. Verification instructions also may be built directly into the application programs. Thus requisitions authorizing more inventory of microcomputers and other devices to be purchased may be prepared by Infoage's inventory reorder program only when the program determines that the need for inventory meets management's reorder policies.

INPUT CONTROLS

Transactions should be recorded accurately, completely, and promptly. The proper amounts should be reflected in the proper accounts and within the accounting periods during which the transactions occur. All erroneous data should be detected, corrected, and resubmitted by user departments for processing. For example, assume that Infoage is using an integrated accounting software package to automate applications such as accounts receivable and payable, billing, cash receipts and disbursements, purchases, inventory control, payroll, and sales order processing. Adequate **input controls** would detect errors such as omitted employee time records, omitted customer numbers on sales orders, and unreasonable order quantities. Other input controls at Infoage ensure, where necessary, that all captured data are converted into computer-readable form and are transmitted over communications lines.

Input controls are especially important to on-line computer-based information systems. Errors in data are quickly spread through such systems and can be quite difficult to detect after leaving the input stage. A single erroneous transaction, for instance, might affect several files and cause undesired results. Consider an unreasonably large quantity of brand X microcomputers on one of Infoage's sales orders. It could cause the quantity on hand for the brand X microcomputer to drop below the reorder point. If an automatic purchasing procedure is built into the application, this situation could lead to the preparation of a purchase order even though a sufficient number of brand X microcomputers may actually be on hand. Thus, Diane Varney should establish controls to ensure that input errors are definitely detected and corrected at the point of entry.

Input controls are logically grouped according to the data-collection steps. Thus we will discuss controls pertaining to recording, batching, converting, editing, and transmitting data.

Recording of Transactions   Transaction data are recorded onto source documents in all manual systems and in most computer-based processing systems. For example, to minimize errors in processing data, Infoage's source documents should be carefully structured. Diane should design source documents so that blocked spaces provide clearly defined entry areas for all key items. She should also make sure that codes, such as account numbers and transaction codes, are widely employed to reduce the size of data elements. Spaces should be provided for necessary authorizations. Infoage's documents should be sequentially prenumbered, so that transactions can be easily traced via clear audit trails. Prenumbering also aids in detecting the loss of transaction data, thus helping to ensure that input data are complete. In addition, Infoage's incoming source documents should be listed in document registers when appropriate. Document registers such as invoice registers reinforce the prenumbering feature, especially if responsible Infoage employees check off the document numbers after processing.

Fictitious transactions and altered transaction records, as we noted previously, can lead to losses of assets. To preclude the preparation of fictitious transactions on source documents, Infoage's blank forms should be under lock and key. If the blank source documents are also prenumbered, the custodian (presumably Ralph Cannon, Infoage's office manager, or another supervisor) can easily determine when copies are missing. Tampering with key transactions, especially those involving cash at Infoage's two retail outlets, can be limited through measures such as the use of controlled tapes that are locked in cash registers.

On-line computer systems offer several features that facilitate the entry of complete and accurate data:

1. Menu screens that allow data-entry clerks and users to select the appropriate transaction screen by simply entering the numbers or letters of desired options.

2. Preformatted screens that display formats of input documents or a series of prompting questions.

3. Bar codes, preprinted documents, or badges that enter product codes, employee codes, and other data via scanners or terminals.

4. Automatic data entry and echoing routines within the computer system. For instance, the computer system can automatically provide the transaction date, as well as a preassigned document number. It also can echo descriptive data such as the customer's name on the entry of the customer's number by a clerk.

Batching of Transaction Data   When transactions are processed in batches, control totals should always be computed and maintained. **Batch control totals** help prevent the loss of transactions and the erroneous posting of transaction data. They also help to prevent unauthorized transactions from being introduced during the processing steps.

The batching procedure in computer-based systems is detailed in Figure 8-9, an expanded version of Figure 8-4. First, a clerk runs batch totals on an adding machine tape. Next the clerk prepares a prenumbered batch transmittal sheet, such as appears in Figure 8-10. Then the clerk forwards the transmittal sheet with the batched documents to the data control section. There, a control clerk logs the batch number and control totals on a **batch control log.** This log enables transactions to be traced from their point of receipt or preparation into the computer operations area. After the transaction data have been keyed and verified, the newly computed totals are checked against the original batch control totals. This comparison should be made by a supervisor or control clerk. The transaction file is then delivered for processing.

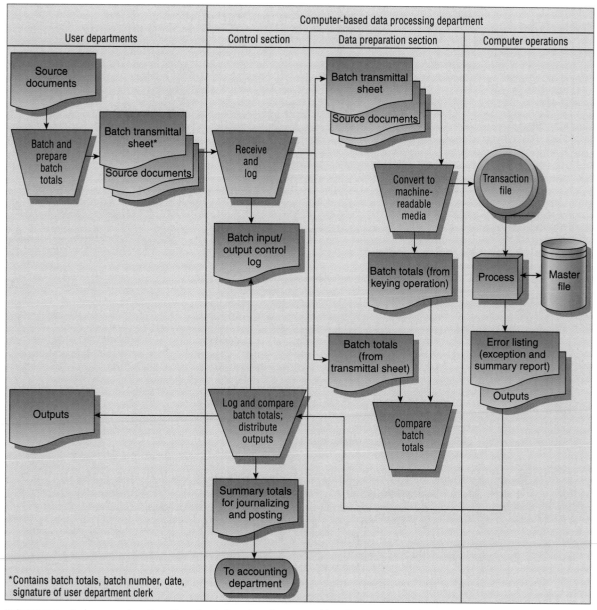

FIGURE 8-9 A document system flowchart showing the uses of batch controls within a computer-based data processing system.

All outputs from processing are returned to the control section, which enters the batch in the control log as completed. It also verifies that the totals derived from computer operations agree with the batch control totals originally calculated. This verification consists of checking the **exception and summary report** (also called the error listing), on which the computer will have printed the control totals. If a discrepancy exists, the control section must investigate for unprocessed or incorrectly processed transactions.

Often a computer is programmed to print the difference between the two sets of totals. A nonzero difference would then indicate a discrepancy. For instance,

BATCH TRANSMITTAL SHEET

Batch No. 175

Date_____

Originating Dept. Code ☐☐☐☐

Transaction data type ☐☐☐

Number of documents ☐☐☐

Name of field	Type of total	Control total

Prepared by:	Approved by:	Logged by:	Verified with totals from data preparation by:

FIGURE 8-10   A batch transmittal sheet.

assume that the precomputed total is 362589, and the following appears at the bottom of the error listing:

```
BATCH TOTAL FROM TRANSMITTAL SHEET    362589
TOTAL COMPUTED DURING PROCESSING      361076
DIFFERENCE                              1513
```

The difference of 1513 must be resolved before the outputs can be released.

When differences have been resolved, the control section distributes the outputs to the user departments. It also transmits summary transaction totals for posting to the general ledger. For instance, several payroll and labor distribution registers are generated during payroll and labor-time processing. The originals of these registers are forwarded to the user departments in this application. In addition, copies of these registers are also sent to the general ledger department for posting.

Three types of totals are used in the control of batches:

1. An **amount control total,** the total of the values (e.g., dollars, hours, units) in an amount or quantity field.

2. A **hash total,** the total of the values (e.g., employee numbers, transaction codes) in an identification field.

3. A **record count,** the total number of source documents, and hence transactions, being processed in a batch.

The amount control and record count have intrinsic meanings. For example, an amount control total drawn from the hours-worked field of Infoage's employee time records reflects the total hours worked by the employees represented in the batch. On the other hand, a hash total (e.g., the total of all of Infoage's employee numbers in a batch of time transactions) has no intrinsic meaning; it is simply the total of a set or "hash" of identification numbers.

Several batch control totals should normally be completed for each batch of transactions. For a batch of sales transaction documents, for example, five totals might be computed: the total quantity of items ordered, the total dollar sales amount, the total of the customers' numbers, the total of the unit prices of all items ordered, and the total count of sales transaction documents.

Batch control totals need not be limited to transaction documents. They may also be applied to master files. Thus in Infoage's customer accounts receivable master file, the total of all account balances represents an amount control total. In addition, the total of all Infoage's customer account numbers is a hash total, and the total number of the firm's master records is a record count. Batch control totals pertaining to a master file are normally stored in the trailer label (e.g., the last record) of the file.

Conversion of Transaction Data   In manual systems, transaction data often must be transcribed or copied from one source document to another, or from a source document to a document register. Thus a clerk may copy data from a customer's order onto a formal sales order form, or from a supplier's invoice onto an invoice register. In batch processing systems, transaction data are generally converted from source documents onto computer-readable media by off-line devices. In on-line processing systems the data are generally "converted" by keying or scanning directly from source documents into the computer system. Whichever type of system is employed, conversion is often a major source of errors.

Converted transaction data therefore need to be verified. In manual systems, verification is typically performed visually by clerks. For instance, a sales order clerk who receives a customer's order first checks the data for valid customer and product codes. Then after copying the data onto a sales order form, the clerk (or, preferably, a second clerk) visually reviews the completed form for accuracy and completeness.

In computer systems, verification may be performed by visual means, by means of keying devices, or by means of edit computer programs. **Visual verification** may consist of comparing data from the original source documents, such as customers' orders, against the converted data. If a batch of transactions has been converted off-line, the documents would be compared with printed listings of the converted data. If a transaction has been entered via a terminal, the document would be compared against the displayed data on the screen. **Key verification** consists of rekeying (reentering) the data and comparing the results of the two keying operations. Preferably, key verification is performed on special verifying keyboards by operators other than those who do the original keying. Errors are indicated by lights or some other means of signaling. Since key verification is an expensive and nonproductive process, only critical fields (e.g., customer numbers, sales amounts) should be so verified. The third type of verification, using edit computer programs, will be discussed next.

Editing of Transaction Data   The numerous transactions that enter the typical computer-based system do not normally undergo the close scrutiny of trained clerks, as they would in manual systems. Also, many of the transactions are likely to be originated by persons for whom data entry is not a primary duty. For instance, a storeskeeper in a remote warehouse may enter shipping transactions via a terminal. In such situations, visual verification is not sufficient and key verification is not appropriate.

Fortunately, the logical capabilities of computer systems enable a wide variety of input errors to be detected. Thus each computer-based transaction processing system can and should incorporate logical data error-detecting **edit tests.** The editing procedure has the purpose of screening and comparing all incoming data against established standards of validity. Those data that pass all edit tests are viewed as being valid and are then admitted to processing. Those data that fail one or more edit tests are viewed as being invalid and are diverted into an error-correction procedure. For computer systems these edit tests are the *most* important means of ensuring input accuracy.

Because of severe problems caused by errors reaching the processing stage and beyond, edit tests should be applied as early as possible. In batch processing systems an edit program is generally run, often in combination with a conversion run, just after the transactions are batched. In on-line processing systems each transaction is generally edited as soon as it is entered at a terminal. However, not all edit tests can be applied during the input stage. Certain tests must be deferred until immediately after a processing step is completed. For instance, a test to verify that the correct master record has been updated cannot be applied until after updating occurs.

Edit tests are often called **programmed checks,** since they are in effect validation routines built into applications software. A variety of programmed checks are applied in a typical transaction processing system. Among the conditions that can be validated with respect to transaction data are the following. (The validating programmed checks follow the conditions in parentheses.)

- Identification numbers are valid (validity check).
- Quantities and amounts are reasonable in size or are within specified ranges (reasonableness check, limit check, range check).
- Numbers do not appear in fields reserved for words; letters do not appear in fields reserved for numbers (field check).
- Logically related data elements are compatible in quantities or amounts (relationship check).

These conditions and accompanying programmed checks, plus others, are described and applied in Chapters 11 through 14.

You may better understand the use of programmed checks by reading the spotlight illustration of the widely adopted edit test known as the check digit. The **check digit,** more correctly called the **self-checking digit,** is a redundant numeral character added to an identification number. It has the sole purpose of detecting incorrectly recorded numbers.

Transmission of Transaction Data   Transaction data must often be transmitted from the point of origin to the processing center. Increasingly, transmission involves the use of data communications facilities. In these instances, all of the programmed checks noted earlier are necessary. Certain programmed checks such as the following should also be considered:

- An **echo check,** which consists of transmitting data back to the originating terminal for comparison with the transmitted data. For instance, if the customer number is transmitted in a sales transaction, the customer name and address could be echoed back (returned) on the screen of the originating terminal. Pre-

SPOTLIGHTING

AN ILLUSTRATION OF A CHECK DIGIT

Assume, for example, that Infoage's payroll clerk transposes two digits in an employee number, writing 3578 instead of 3758. If both numbers have been assigned to employees, the error would not be detected by an edit test such as a validity check. However, if a self-checking digit were incorporated into the number, the error should be detected by the edit program when the number is entered into the computer system. In order to employ this edit test, we will add a self-checking digit to each four-digit employee number, thus converting it into a five-digit number. To determine the value of the self-checking digit for each particular employee number, we apply an algorithm based on the four digits. For instance, we might use the algorithm in the box in the next column (a variant of the modulus-11 technique),* to obtain the self-checking digit 3 to append to 3758.

Validation consists of *recomputing* the self-checking digit, using the same algorithm by which it was predetermined, and then comparing the result to the keyed-in value. If the correct number, 37583, is

Four digits of employee number:	3	7	5	8
Weighting factors:	5	4	3	2
Digit products:	15	28	15	16
Sum of digit products:				74
Next higher multiple of 11:				77
Check digit (difference):				3
Complete employee number:				37583

entered as a part of a transaction, the algorithm will generate a 3 as the self-checking digit. Since this digit is the same as the last digit on the entered number, the number is accepted as correct. If the incorrect number 35783 is entered, the self-checking digit generated by the algorithm would be 5.[†] Since this digit is not the same as the last digit on the entered number, the number would be rejected as incorrect.

---

*As shown in the box, the Modulus-11 technique means to subtract the sum of the digit products from the next highest multiple of 11, which is 77.

[†] $|(3 \times 5) + (5 \times 4) + (7 \times 3) + (8 \times 2)| = 72$. The next highest multiplier of 11 is 77: $77 - 72 = 5$.

---

sumably the sender could visually verify that the name and address match with the number.

- A **redundancy check,** which involves the transmission of additional data to aid in the verification process. For a sales transaction, the sender might enter the first few letters of a customer's last name in addition to the number. A programmed check could then verify that the two items match.

- A **completeness check,** which consists of verifying that all required data have been entered and transmitted. If the sender of a sales transaction, for instance, omitted the number of an ordered merchandise item, the completeness check in the edit program could notify the sender to retransmit or could refuse to accept the transmission until the missing element was entered.

PROCESSING CONTROLS

Controls over the processing of transactions should ensure that the data are processed accurately and completely, that no unauthorized transactions are included, that the proper files and programs are included, and that all transactions can be easily traced. **Processing controls** can be grouped under manual cross-checks, processing logic checks, run-to-run controls, file and program checks, and audit trail linkages.

Manual Cross-Checks   In manual systems and even in computer-based systems various cross-checks can be performed. One type of check involves one person checking the work of others. For instance, Ann Strong could check the work of Tad Malcolm, her bookkeeper. She could double-check his computations on the billing invoices before they are sent to clients, noting any amounts that appear to be abnormal. Also, at Infoage a clerk in the billing department may check the computations appearing on sales invoices before they are mailed to customers. A supervisor at Infoage in the general ledger department may verify the postings performed during the day by the general ledger clerk.

Another type of check is a reconciliation, as when documents from different sources are compared. Thus copies of sales orders may be compared with notices of goods shipped in order to ascertain that no orders are overlooked. Still another type of check is a form of acknowledgment. For example, the cashier at Infoage may check to see that each invoice being paid contains a stamp reflecting acknowledgment that the invoice has been vouched.

Processing Logic Checks   Several of the programmed checks needed in the input stage of a computer-based system are also applicable to the processing stage. For instance, a check on the reasonableness of hours worked by Infoage's employees may be applied during the input stage. It may also be applied during the processing stage with respect to the computed gross earnings for Infoage's employees. In addition, a **sequence check** is appropriate when sequential processing is performed. Its purpose is to detect when records are not in proper order. For example, the sequence check may be applied to a field of sorted time records for each of Infoage's employees. If the records are arranged by employee numbers and begin with numbers 3476, 3401, and 3498, the middle record would be detected as out of order. A sequence check would be applied before the records are used in preparing Infoage's payroll, so that processing delays due to out-of-order records can be avoided.

Run-to-Run Controls   As was noted previously, batched data should be controlled during processing runs, so that no records are omitted from or no unauthorized records are inserted into a transaction file. The processing programs thus should compute and print batch totals with respect to each run, usually on an exception and summary report. For example, totals may be printed after the edit run, sorting run, update run, and report preparation run. These totals then should be balanced against the predetermined batch totals. When data are processed on-line, proof account activity listings, also called file change reports, should be prepared at the end of each day. These reports show, for each general ledger account, the beginning account balance, all transaction activity, and the ending account balance. The change in each account balance should be reconciled to the total of the transactions, as determined from source documents or other sources. For instance, cash receipts that are entered on-line by one of Infoage's accounting clerks and posted to the cash account can be balanced against totaled listings of remittance advices.

File and Program Changes   Although very useful, batch control totals have limitations. They cannot ensure that transactions are posted to the proper master files, or that individual postings are made to the proper accounts. To ensure that transactions are posted to the proper master files, processing programs should verify that the master files are correct before processing begins. These checks are made by reference to the header labels, which show the dates as well as the names of the files. If an incorrect or outdated file is mounted with respect to either the input file or the output file, a warning message should be displayed on the computer console or the program should be inhibited from processing data. To ensure that transactions are posted to proper accounts, the processing program should employ a matching check.

Processing programs should periodically be checked for validity. One approach that is used is to employ test data to see that expected results are obtained. Another approach is to reprocess actual data with the program and to compare the results against previously generated reports.

Audit Trail Linkages Fostering the audit trail is an important objective of processing controls. A clear audit trail is needed to enable individual transactions to be traced, to provide support to changes in general ledger account balances, to prepare financial reports, and to correct transaction errors or lost data.

Among records needed to provide a clear audit trail for users are input-output control logs, transaction logs, and transaction listings. Processing procedures should require that a printed transaction listing be prepared (1) during each file-updating run by batch processing systems, and (2) at the end of each day by on-line processing systems. In addition, each transaction in a listing should be identified by a unique and sequentially assigned transaction reference number. These transaction numbers should be posted to the general ledger account records and also should be recorded on source documents pertaining to the transactions. Figure 8-11, which illustrates the audit trail for a computer-based system, shows how source documents can be easily located by tracing back from a proof account activity listing, which is discussed below.

OUTPUT CONTROLS

The outputs provided by an information system should be complete and reliable and should be distributed to the proper recipients. **Output controls** that have these objectives consist mainly of reviews and distribution logs or registers.

Reviews of Processing Results Recipients of processed outputs include managers, employees, customers, creditors, and auditors. In the act of using the outputs, these recipients perform reviews that tend to verify the accuracy of the results. Several examples should demonstrate how widespread this review activity can be for a typical firm, such as Infoage, Inc. Diane Varney often reviews the deposit slips prepared by the cashier before the day's cash receipts are taken to the bank. Customers of Infoage review the monthly statements they receive before remitting the amounts due. Creditors review the financial statements and key accounts before extending credit to

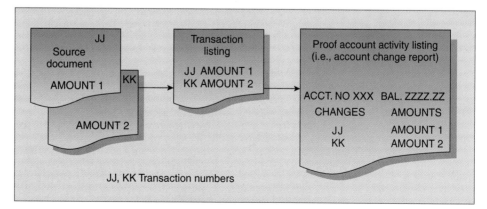

FIGURE 8-11 An audit trail for a computer-based system.

Infoage. If Infoage's bank required the firm to obtain a financial audit, the external auditors would review the financial statements before releasing their written professional opinions.

Reviews are particularly important when computer files have been affected. Thus, proof account activity listings, which are generated to reflect changes made to master records, should be reviewed by user departments. These listings should contain all changes to the accounts, including changes due to file maintenance runs. A listing showing the effects of changes to selling prices, for instance, might be sent to the sales department for review. Another output, the exception and summary report (i.e., error listing), should be reviewed by the data control group. As a part of the review, a control clerk might reconcile the final batch totals reflected in the outputs to the precomputed control totals. In addition, the clerk should balance the new control totals of key fields in the master records, as shown in the trailer label, against the control totals of these fields before updating. Other reports that should be reviewed include those based on the console log and change log.*

Controlled Distribution of Outputs The outputs generated during processing should be distributed only to proper users. Distribution can be controlled by means of **distribution registers.** By reference to the registers, the control group should distribute the outputs directly and in a timely manner, recording the distribution in the control log. On receiving the outputs, the users should carefully review their contents by

Control Stage \ Control Purpose	Preventive	Detective	Corrective
Input	Properly authorized transactions Well-designed and controlled source documents, e.g., prenumbered forms Sound conversion control techniques, e.g., key verification of input data	Batch control totals Adequate input edit tests (programmed checks), e.g., field checks	Sound error correction procedures Complete audit trail
Processing	Sound file maintenance procedures Adequate preventive-type programmed checks, e.g., label checks, sequence checks, matching checks	Run-to-run verifications Adequate detective-type programmed checks, e.g., limit checks, sign checks	Complete audit trail
Output	Distribution log of authorized users	Reconciliation of computed totals with predetermined control totals Reviews of outputs and tests to source documents by users	Reviews of logs and procedures by internal auditors Reviews of error-correction statistics

FIGURE 8-12 Application controls arranged by two classification plans.

*See Chapter 9 for definitions of *console log* and *change log*.

comparing any computed results against the input data and assessing their reasonableness.

SUMMARY OF TRANSACTION (APPLICATION) CONTROLS

Figure 8-12 summarizes the array of input, processing, and output controls described in the preceding pages. Because a transaction control framework should incorporate controls that prevent, detect, and correct errors and omissions, the figure organizes the controls according to those three purposes.* Numerous examples of the controls appear in Chapters 11 through 14.

CONTROLS IN DIFFERING TYPES OF COMPUTER SYSTEMS

Our survey of controls will be clearer if we briefly contrast the differences among three types of computer systems: batch processing systems, on-line processing systems, and data-base systems. In addition to highlighting the specific input, processing, and output controls that particularly apply to each type of system, we will compare the error-correction procedures for batch and on-line processing systems.

BATCH PROCESSING SYSTEMS

Distinctive Controls   Among the controls, both general and transaction, that are distinctive in batch processing computer-based systems are the following:

- Batch control totals, plus batch transmittal sheets.
- Key verification of critical data input fields.
- A data control group, which maintains a batch input-output control log and distribution log.
- A data librarian, which maintains a data library check-out log.
- Programmed edit checks, such as a sequence check and a run-to-run batch-total check.
- File and program checks, such as header label check and matching check.
- Printed transaction listings and proof account activity listings.
- A grandparent-parent-child backup procedure (when magnetic tape files are used). This backup procedure is discussed in Appendix 1 to Chapter 9.

Error-Correction Procedure   A sound **error-correction procedure** for batch processing applications should ensure that detected errors are corrected and reentered for processing. It would consist of the following steps, assuming that the errors are detected by edit checks:

1. Flagging the erroneous transactions and suspending their processing.
2. Recording the erroneous transactions by fully explanatory error messages on exception and summary reports or error listings.
3. Entering the erroneous transactions on a file of suspended transactions called a suspense file and adjusting the batch control totals accordingly.

---

*Krish N. Bhaskar, W. Thomas Linn, and Richard Savich. "An Integrated Internal Control Framework to Prevent and Detect Computer Frauds," *The EDP Auditor Journal*, Vol. 2 (1987), pp. 42–49.

4. Recording the suspended transactions, that is, the contents of the suspense file on periodic printed listings.

5. Returning the erroneous transactions, together with reasons for rejection, to the user departments for correction by supervisors.

6. Reentering corrected transactions for reediting and processing.

7. Deleting each corrected transaction from the suspense file.

8. Periodically investigating any erroneous transactions that have not been reentered for processing within a specified period of time.

9. Periodically printing statistical reports that reflect the number of times each type of error has occurred, the average lengths of time to correct the various types of errors, and so on.

Steps 1, 2, 3, 4, and 7 can be performed by the edit or processing programs; step 9 can be performed by system software. Steps 5, 6, and 8 would be monitored by the control group. Thus a control clerk might enter each erroneous transaction in an error log. Dates would be entered in the log as each transaction is returned to the user and then later resubmitted for processing.

ON-LINE PROCESSING SYSTEMS

Distinctive Controls General and transaction controls distinctive to on-line processing systems are as follows:

- Access or identification codes plus passwords for the users.
- Restricted functions on terminals used to access and change data.
- On-line terminals placed in secure locations. A built-in terminal check such as a terminal alarm should ring when someone tampers with the locking device. Periodic monitoring of the terminal area should be conducted on a random basis.
- On-line menu screens, dialogue prompts, and preformatted screens.
- **Single-transaction controls** implemented to control entering of individual transactions. For example, enhanced programming edit checks, such as checks for the completeness of data entered and checks that "echo" back descriptive data (e.g., customer names) when codes (e.g., customer numbers) are entered. Other single-transaction controls include instructions, serial numbering, and dual recording of transactions.
- **Group-transaction controls** implemented to ensure that groups of transactions entered during given time periods are accurate and complete. Transaction logging, including system-assigned transaction numbers, terminal numbers, dates and times, and authorization codes, is an example of a group transaction control. Others include time control totals, generation of duplicate data files, and periodic dumping backup procedures, plus before-and-after images of records being updated or otherwise changed.
- Lockout procedures to prevent errors in updating master files when two or more users attempt to access the records simultaneously.
- On-line data and program logs.

Batch control totals are generally not applicable to on-line processing systems. However, balance or logical batch controls, akin to the traditional batch controls, can be developed on occasion. In a savings and loan firm, for instance, the daily deposits and withdrawals entered from each terminal can provide balance controls. Thus, the amounts deposited today via a specific terminal can be accumulated by a computerized balancing routine and the total printed out at the end of the day. This balancing total can then be reconciled to today's total deposits shown on deposit slips (the application's source documents) collected by the terminal's teller.

Error-Correction Procedure   Almost all errors are detected in on-line processing applications by means of edit checks. When an error is detected during data entry, the edit program notifies the entering clerk via an error message or flag on the screen of his or her monitor. The clerk must immediately correct the error or omission before the program will accept additional data concerning the transaction. The corrected data element is reedited and successive elements are then edited as entered until all required transaction elements have been accepted. At that point the program may ask the clerk to confirm the transaction by striking a function key. When the clerk does so, the program enters the transaction into the system for processing.

Some errors will not be detected until the data are stored in the data base. Changes to data already in the data base should be made only by authorized persons; these changes can be controlled by requiring such persons to use specially assigned passwords. In addition, the proof account activity listings should clearly identify changes to each account balance. All changes should also be recorded on change logs and be reviewed by user departments and internal auditors.

DATA-BASE SYSTEMS

All of the distinctive controls pertaining to on-line processing systems are also applicable to data-base systems, including the corrections to stored data as described in the preceding paragraph. In addition, the following controls are particularly relevant to an integrated data base:

- Data-base management software that controls all accesses to data.
- Layered passwords that restrict access by users to precisely designated data sets and files and even to individual data elements.
- Thorough documentation, with particular emphasis on an up-to-date and comprehensive data dictionary that is on-line.
- A data-base administrator (DBA) who has adequate authority with respect to standardization of data elements and sets, assignment of passwords, and maintenance of change procedures concerning data and the data-base management system.
- The DBA should report to senior management and not to the director of data processing.
- A backup to the DBA could take over when the DBA is unavailable.
- Sound security modules that are protected from unauthorized access.
- Authorization and approval of all major in-house and manufacturer modifications to the data-base management system (DBMS) software.
- The DBA should be closely monitored, supervised, and closely controlled. Do not allow the DBA to operate computer equipment. Escort the DBA when he or she is in the computer room. The DBA should not be allowed to initiate transactions without obtaining approval from proper officials.
- The internal auditor should perform an annual audit of the DBA and the DBMS controls implemented by the DBA.

Control Data Element	Validity Check	Relationship Check	Limit Check	Completeness Check	Error Correction
Student number	X	X		X	X
Code for major field of study	X	X		X	X
Course number	X			X	X
Requested semester hours			X	X	

FIGURE 8-13   A controls matrix for student registration on-line data entry.

DOCUMENTATION OF CONTROL COVERAGE

After our survey of controls in this and the preceding chapter, we can appreciate the difficulty in evaluating the adequacy of an internal control structure. However, we can be helped by diagramming techniques. Instances of such aids are document system flowcharts that shown control points, and control-oriented flowcharts. Another aid is a controls matrix, as shown in Figure 8-13. The example in the figure includes several edit checks that are desirable in an on-line student registration application. It cross-references these checks to the particular data elements that are entered via a terminal when a student requests his or her courses for the upcoming semester.

SUMMARY

Controls may be classified in a variety of ways: as controls for manual systems and controls for computer-based systems (in several architectures); as preventive, detective, and corrective controls; and as general controls and application controls. Drawing primarily on the general and application controls classification plan, general controls are discussed under the headings of organizational controls, documentation controls, asset accountability controls, management practice controls, data center operations controls, and authorization controls. And, application controls are discussed under input, processing, and output controls. Security measures are discussed in Chapter 9.

Access controls, an additional category of general controls, are more appropriately discussed as security controls in Chapter 9. Organizational controls center on the concepts of divided responsibilities and independent reviews. Authorizing, record-keeping, and custodial functions should be organizationally separated. In firms having computer-based systems, the systems development and data processing functions, as well as the outside user and custodial departments, should be sepa-

rated. For batch processing applications, the data processing function should have separate computer operations, data control, and data library units. Documentation controls consist of procedures manuals and various records that describe the AIS and its operations. In computer-based systems, documentation pertains to systems standards, system applications, programs, data, computer operations, and user instructions. Asset accountability controls ensure that assets are properly valued in the records; they include the use of subsidiary ledgers, reconciliations, acknowledgment procedures, logs and registers, and reviews and reassessments.

Management practice controls pertain to system change procedures, and new systems development procedures. Data center operations controls pertain to computer operating procedures and computer hardware and software checks. Application controls provide reasonable assurance that all transactions are properly authorized and accurately recorded, classified, processed and reported. In addition to the authorization controls, application controls consist of input, processing, and output controls. Input controls include those that relate to steps such as recording data, batching data, converting data, transmitting data, and editing data. Specific input controls include well-designed source documents, key verification, batch control totals, and a variety of programmed edit checks. Processing controls include additional programmed checks, run-to-run controls, file and program checks, and audit trails. Output controls include reviews of outputs and distribution registers.

Various types of computer systems, such as batch processing and on-line processing, and data-base systems employ distinctive general controls and transaction controls. Included in these controls are error-correction procedures that are needed to ensure that detected transaction errors are corrected as early as possible during the handling of transaction data.

APPENDIX 1 TO CHAPTER 8

Types of Computer Documentation

Systems standards documentation consists of policy statements pertaining to systems development and other system-related matters. For instance, a systems development standard might describe suitable methods and procedures for analyzing, designing, and implementing information system modules. One firm's standard might specify, for example, the use of techniques such as data-flow diagrams and entity-relationship diagrams.

System application documentation includes the purpose of the application and descriptive materials such as computer system flowcharts, input-output descriptions, error procedures, and the components needed for manual as well as computer-based systems. This type of documentation is of primary interest to systems analysts, systems users, and auditors.

Program documentation includes program flowcharts or other logic diagrams, source program listings, printouts of inputs and outputs, record layouts or data structures, and information pertaining to operations, testing, changes, and errors. Program documentation is usually organized around individual programs and packaged into run manuals. In the case of applications programs, program documentation may be combined with system application documentation. It is of primary interest to programmers; however, data-base administrators have concerns with respect to data manipulation language verbs that alter data. Auditors may also need to review program documentation to detect unauthorized changes to programs, as reflected in program listings and printouts of outputs.

Data documentation includes the descriptions of data elements stored within the firm's data base, including their relationships. This type of documentation, usually incorporated within a data dictionary, is of particular importance to database administrators and auditors. It is also of interest to application programmers, but only insofar as it relates to the data elements required by the programs that they develop or change.

Operating documentation includes all of the performance instructions needed to execute computer programs, plus instructions for distributing the outputs. Operating documentation, generally organized into console run books, is of primary interest to computer operators, since they need very explicit directions. Note, however, that operating documentation does not contain program flowcharts and listings, since operators should not be informed of the detailed logic of the programs that process data.

User documentation includes instructions for entering data on source documents, information relating to the formats and uses of reports, and procedures for checking for and correcting errors in data. User documentation is of primary interest to user-department clerks and managers. Large firms should prepare each major type of documentation discussed. On the other hand, small or medium-sized firms, such as Infoage, Inc., and Ann Strong, CPA/CMA, that employ microcomputers to process most applications, require only a subset of the documentation listed in Figure 8-7. Diane Varney, treasurer and controller of Infoage, and Ann Strong should ensure that their firms prepare the following minimum level of documentation: problem statements, narrative descriptions of procedures, source documents, flowcharts, source-code listings, test data, program and systems change approvals, details concerning audit trails and internal controls, operating instructions, sample printouts, and user instructions. To evaluate if the documentation is acceptable, a person, other than the preparers, should find the instructions clear and easy to follow when running a job.

APPENDIX 2 TO CHAPTER 8

Management Controls: Application System Development Controls
System Change Procedures

Changes in a computer-based information system most often pertain to application programs or the schema of the data base. Both types of changes should follow clearly defined and sound procedures to prevent unauthorized manipulations and possibly well-meaning but injurious errors and mishaps. For instance, a programmer could incorporate into a program a feature that benefits him or her personally or that violates management policy.

If the change pertains to an application program, it should be initiated by a user-department manager, who explains the needed change in writing. The requested change should then be approved by the systems development manager (or by a committee of high-level managers if the modification is sufficiently large). After approval the change or addition would be assigned to systems personnel, usually a maintenance programmer, in the case of an application program. This programmer should use a working copy of the program, rather than the "live" version currently in use. The new or revised design is next tested jointly by systems personnel (including persons not involved in the design) and the user. Documentation should be thoroughly revised to reflect the change or addition. Finally, the documented change or addition and test results should be approved by the systems development manager and should be formally accepted by the initiating user.

New System Development Procedures

The design and development of new computer-based applications require controls similar to those needed for system changes. Each request for development of new systems or modifications to existing ones should be initiated by either a user-department manager or a higher-level manager. Assume, for example, that Infoage's credit manager desires a modified credit approval system to replace the current, outdated approval system. The credit manager would initiate a written request and submit it to Diane Varney. Diane Varney or a computer steering committee, if one exists at Infoage, would then authorize the development of the modified credit approval system. The credit department personnel and accounting personnel next would work together to clarify information needs, to define systems requirements, and to develop necessary change specifications. After implementing the designed system, they would jointly test all portions of the system, manual as well as computerized. Finally, the documentation concerning the design and test results would be reviewed and approved by Infoage's credit manager.

....

REVIEW PROBLEM WITH SOLUTION

Campus Bookstore, Fifth Installment

Statement

The Campus Bookstore (described in the Review Problem at the end of Chapter 1) continues to develop its new minicomputer system. In response to his concerns expressed in the Fourth Installment, the manager requests that the auditor from the bookstore's public accounting firm prepare a report that recommends specific general controls for the new system.

Required

Identify (a) organizational, (b) documentation, (c) asset accountability, (d) management practice controls, and (e) data center operations controls that the auditor would likely propose for incorporation into the new computer-based AIS.

Solution

a. Organizational controls include
   (1) Supervision and reviews of reports by the store manager and the managers on the two levels.
   (2) Periodic reviews by the bookstore's public accountant.
   (3) Adequate organizational separation between the authorizing, record-keeping, and custodial functions. Consider, for instance, the purchases transaction procedure. A purchase would be authorized by the signature of a merchandise manager on a purchase order. The goods would be received and stored under the custody of the inventory manager. The records concerning the receipt and storage of the goods would be maintained by one of the bookkeepers. Similar segregations of functions would be established for the cash receipts, cash disbursements, payroll, and fixed asset transactions.
   (4) Careful division of duties within the accounting function, in order to avoid incompatibilities. One sound division would consist of having the first bookkeeper maintain the inventory and purchases and fixed asset records, as well as prepare checks (including paychecks) for signature; having the second bookkeeper maintain the accounts payable records and employee earnings records; having the third bookkeeper maintain the purchase returns, sales returns, and general ledger; and having the accountant reconcile the bank statement and prepare the financial statements. Note that the cashier would handle the received cash, make entries in the cash receipts journal, and prepare the bank deposit slip.
   (5) Further organizational separation to accommodate the needs of the new minicomputer system. Thus, if a system analyst-programmer is hired, he or she should be organizationally separate from the actual operations of the computer system. Also, the operators of the minicomputer system (to be hired shortly) should be separated from the various users of the system, such as the merchandise managers, and from a data control clerk (to be hired).

b. Documentation controls should include all the accounting records involved in the transactions, in addition to policy statements, organization charts, and so on. With the introduction of the minicomputer system, new documentation will be needed, such as system standards, descriptions of all computer-based applications, programs, and related flowcharts and so forth; descriptions of all data items; operating instructions for all programs to be run by computer operators; and documentation to aid users in accessing the minicomputer system.

c. Asset accountability controls include the accounts payable subsidiary ledger plus records concerning the merchandise inventory and fixed assets, periodic physical counts of the merchandise and reconciliations with the records, monthly bank reconciliations, reconciliations of cash received daily with the recorded listings of the receipts, acknowledgment and logging of all receipts and storage of all merchandise and supplies, and periodic reviews of all records pertaining to the various assets of the bookstore.

d. Management practice controls of particular importance include primarily systems development controls. These controls establish procedures for required changes and additions to the AIS to be initiated in writing by a manager, to be approved by the bookstore manager, to be developed by the systems analyst programmer (or outside consultant) and tested apart from the "live" system, and to be accepted by the initiating manager.

e. Data center operations controls include properly scheduling the running of applications so that required reports arrive on time to the bookstore's managers, close supervision of all operations personnel, the use of diagnostic utility programs to monitor the hardware and software and to generate an on-screen report of potential problem areas, the preparation of daily performance reports to monitor operations personnel, and the preparation of weekly reports to control the bookstore's computer operations.

KEY TERMS

amount control total (310)
application control (294)
application system development controls (304)
asset accountability control (302)
batch control log (308)
batch control total (308)
check digit (312)
completeness check (313)

computer operations (299)
control point (305)
corrective control (294)
data-base administration (298)
data center operational controls (304)
data control unit (299)
data documentation (321)
data library unit (299)
data preparation unit (299)
data processing function (297)
detective control (293)
distribution registers (316)
documentation (300)
echo check (312)
edit tests (312)
error-correction procedure (317)
exception and summary report (309)
general authorization (306)
general control (294)
group-transaction controls (318)
hash total (310)
input control (307)
key verification (311)
operating documentation (321)
organizational independence (295)
output control (315)
preventive control (293)
processing control (313)
program documentation (321)
programmed check (312)
reassessment (303)
reconciliation (302)
record count (310)
redundancy check (313)
review (303)
security measure (294)
self-checking digit (312)
sequence check (314)
single-transaction controls (318)
specific authorization (306)
system application documentation (321)
systems standards documentation (321)
systems development function (297)
technical services (297)
transaction or application control (305)
user documentation (321)
visual verification (311)

REVIEW QUESTIONS

Note: These questions incorporate material found in Appendixes 1 and 2 of this chapter.

8-1. In what ways may controls be classified?

8-2. Contrast preventive, detective, and corrective controls.

8-3. Contrast financial and nonfinancial controls.

8-4. Which functions should be organizationally separated to provide adequate independence?

8-5. Identify several parties that provide independent review of transaction processing activities.

8-6. How may a small firm compensate for the lack of adequate organizational independence?

8-7. Describe the modifications that are necessary to achieve adequate organizational independence when a firm acquires a computer system.

8-8. Identify the roles of the various organizational units within the data processing function when batch processing is performed.

8-9. Identify the various types of documentation needed by a firm having a manual system.

8-10. What additional documentation is needed when a firm employs computer-based transaction processing?

8-11. By what two key means are the assets of a firm safeguarded?

8-12. What control procedures are available for achieving asset accountability?

8-13. Identify and define management practice controls.

8-14. Describe a sound procedure for making changes to application programs.

8-15. What control procedures should be established with respect to data center operations?

8-16. Describe several checks that computer manufacturers build into their hardware and software.

8-17. Identify the various control points within a typical transaction processing system where specific controls are needed.

8-18. What are the overall objectives of application controls?

8-19. Contrast general and specific authorizations.

8-20. Contrast the objectives of input, processing, and output controls.

8-21. What means are available for minimizing errors when the on-line input approach is used?

8-22. Explain how batch control totals help to prevent the loss of data during the processing of batches of transactions.

8-23. Contrast the three types of batch control totals.

8-24. Describe two types of verification that may be performed during the conversion of data.

8-25. Identify a variety of conditions that programmed checks are designed to confirm in computer-based sys-

tems, as well as the names of the corresponding programmed checks.

8-26. Describe how a self-checking digit validates the accuracy of identification numbers.

8-27. Identify three programmed checks that are important when transmitting data over data communications facilities.

8-28. Discuss several controls that are pertinent to the processing phase.

8-29. Describe the linkages necessary to establish a clear audit trail in a computer-based AIS.

8-30. Discuss several controls that are pertinent to the output phase.

8-31. List the controls that are distinctive to (a) batch processing systems, (b) on-line processing systems, and (c) data-base systems.

8-32. Contrast the error-correction procedures suitable for (a) batch processing, (b) on-line processing, and (c) data-base systems.

DISCUSSION QUESTIONS

8-33. What depth of computer knowledge should be possessed by accountants concerning (a) computer hardware and software controls, (b) general controls, and (c) application controls?

8-34. Are the general control activities maintained by Infoage likely to differ significantly from the general control activities maintained at Ann Strong's firm?

8-35. Assume that Infoage and Ann Strong's firm have identical financial and nonfinancial objectives. Would you expect their application control over information processing systems to be different?

8-36. What are the features of on-line processing systems that create difficulties in establishing a sound control framework?

8-37. Provide examples of preventive, detective, and corrective controls for (a) batch processing systems, (b) on-line systems, and (c) data-base systems.

8-38. What steps should be taken to locate an error when totals computed during a processing run do not match the predetermined batch control totals?

8-39. How can the audit trail be maintained when source documents are not used in a specific application?

8-40. Is it possible to incorporate too many programmed checks into an application edit program?

8-41. Assume that Ann Strong's firm uses a popular microcomputer accounting software package to process transactions and generate monthly financial statements and reports. What kinds of application controls do you think should be incorporated into such packages? What additional controls over processing are needed if Ann determines that the software package has few, if any, programmed checks?

PROBLEMS

8-1. To which general control objective does each of the following specific control procedures relate?

a. Undertaking periodic counts of the physical inventory and comparing the counts to the inventory records.

b. Ensuring that all adjusting entries are formally approved.

c. Preparing a manual concerning the approved procedure for processing sales returns or reversals, and revising the manual when procedural changes occur.

d. Examining endorsements on all paychecks for a designated period, and further investigating paychecks with second endorsements.

e. Performing a surprise count of the imprest petty-cash funds (by an auditor).

f. Engaging external auditors to examine the financial statements for this year.

g. Performing preventive maintenance on the mainframe computer.

h. Investigating unusually high performance by a newly hired salesperson whose compensation is based solely on commissions.

i. Investigating dramatic changes in an employee's living conditions and spending patterns.

8-2. To which general control objective does each of the following specific control procedures relate?

a. Assigning one employee to approve suppliers' invoices for payment and another employee to prepare the disbursement checks.

b. Assigning separate employees to approve the credit of customers, to ship the ordered goods, and to prepare the sales invoices.

c. Performing a cutoff test to ensure that sales revenue is recorded in the year it is earned (by an auditor).

d. Requiring the accounts payable manager to request changes to the payables programs and to "sign off" on the changes that are made.

e. Investigating all adjustments to the perpetual inventory records.

f. Requiring a production department supervisor to sign a form that indicates he has received the partly finished goods pertaining to a job in progress.

g. Checking that all invoices are on preprinted forms or letterheads and not on plain paper.

h. Requiring the cashier to take a vacation each year.

i. Reconciling all the bank account balances to the cash account balances as soon as the bank statements are received.

8-3. The Y Company has three clerical employees who must perform the following functions.

a. Maintain the general ledger.

b. Maintain the accounts payable ledger.

c. Maintain the accounts receivable ledger.

d. Prepare checks for signature.

e. Maintain the cash disbursements journal.

f. Issue credits on returns and allowances.

g. Reconcile the bank account.

h. Handle and deposit cash receipts.

Assuming that the employees are able, the firm requests that you assign these functions to the three employees in such a manner as to achieve the highest degree of internal control. It may be assumed that the employees will perform no accounting functions other than the ones listed and that any accounting functions not listed will be performed by persons other than the three employees.

Required

State how you would distribute these functions among the three employees. Assume that with the exception of the nominal jobs of the bank reconciliation and the issuance of credits on returns and allowances, all functions require an equal amount of time.

(CPA adapted)

8-4. Identify each of the following general controls as being predominantly preventive, detective, or corrective in nature. Briefly explain each selection.

a. Rotation of employee duties.

b. Adequate supervision of employees.

c. Hardware echo check.

d. Adequate segregation of duties.

e. Physical inventory count and reconciliation.

f. Careful review of job and personal qualifications of personnel applicants.

g. Standardized procedure for changing computer programs.

h. Bank reconciliations.

8-5. What general control(s) would be most effective in preventing or detecting each of the following errors or undesirable practices?

a. A storeroom clerk discovers that a particular part is out of stock, even though the accounting records show that 90 units are on hand.

b. A purchasing manager orders goods that are not needed from a supplier firm, of which he happens to be an owner.

c. A cashier steals $50 in currency received by mail from a customer; she conceals the theft by preparing a credit memorandum that reduces the balance of the customer's account by $50.

d. A petty-cash custodian removes $100 from the petty-cash fund for personal use but replenishes the amount with cash received from customers that day.

e. A partner working for a regional CPA firm increased his travel expenses by altering restaurant receipts.

f. An accounting clerk was misappropriating customer payments. She covered the shortage by making adjustments to receivables accounts.

g. The board of directors failed to disclose to stakeholders material fraud committed by three executives.

h. A receiving clerk and delivery driver colluded to steal large amounts of inventory. The clerk prepared a receipt for the inventory, which was later sold by the delivery driver. The cash proceeds were split by the thieves.

i. An employee in the cosmetics department receives cash payments from customers for merchandise, fails to ring up some sales, and takes the cash proceeds.

j. A purchasing agent gives extra business to a vendor in exchange for kickbacks, sexual favors, and free vacations.

k. In order to boost his year-end bonus, a controller increased his firm's income by creating fictitious sales booked to phantom customers.

l. A division manager obtained access to the electronic counting devices used to record the physical inventory. He systematically overstated the ending inventory by increasing the item counts stored in the metering devices. As a result, the division reported a higher income.

8-6. What general control(s) would be most effective in preventing or detecting each of the following errors or undesirable practices?

a. A clerk in the personnel department lists a phantom employee in the personnel records; when the signed paychecks are received from the cashier for distribution, this clerk takes the paycheck for the fictitious employee, cashes it, and keeps the proceeds.

b. A salesperson collects $500 cash on account from a customer and pockets the proceeds.

c. A storekeeper takes inventory items home at night. When the shortages become apparent during physical inventory, he claims that the receiving department did not deliver the goods to the storeroom.

d. An unusually large number of adjusting entries were being made to the cash, receivables, and inventory accounts.

e. An accounts payable clerk prepares and submits an invoice from a fictitious supplier having the name of her mother, writes a check to the "supplier," and mails the check to her mother's address; the daughter and mother later split the proceeds.

f. Several employees were padding the hours worked on their time cards to receive pay for overtime hours never worked.

g. An accountant was stealing payments made by customers by writing off the receivables against the allowance for doubtful accounts.

h. Controls were frequently being overridden by an accountant who handled the cash transactions.

i. An employee was pocketing payments made by certain customers and was covering the shortage by debiting long-term notes receivable and crediting accounts receivable.

j. Six firms control the worldwide supply of raw materials used to manufacture a particular product. The top managers of these firms conduct secret meetings to fix the raw materials price charged to customers.

k. A firm intentionally failed to write down to current value obsolete microcomputers. Consequently, assets were overstated and revenue was not properly matched with expenses.

l. An employee was stealing customer payments. He covered the shortage by failing to post the payments to the customer accounts.

8-7. What general control(s) would be most effective in preventing or detecting each of the following errors or undesirable practices?

a. An accounts receivable clerk pockets $100 in currency received by mail from a customer but nevertheless posts the amount of the receipt to the customer's accounts receivable account.

b. A cashier who receives currency and checks over the counter from customers keeps a portion of the receipts for her own use.

c. A general ledger clerk posts to the accounts receivable control account a credit pertaining to a return of merchandise from a customer; however, the clerk forgets to post the debit to the sales return account.

d. A firm's bank prepares a debit memorandum for an NSF (Not Sufficient Funds) check, but the bank clerk forgets to mail a copy of the memo to the firm.

e. The disbursement voucher forms were modified substantially and given to the payables clerks at the beginning of a week with no explanation. As a result, most of the vouchers for the week were incorrectly prepared and the corresponding checks were delayed, causing the loss of several purchase discounts.

f. A treasurer suddenly left the country with bearer bonds owned by his firm and worth one-half million dollars. The firm was not able to recover the bonds.

g. A firm that is keenly interested in merging with another firm presents its financial statements for the past several years; however, the controller of the other firm seriously questions whether the statements have been prepared in accordance with generally accepted accounting principles.

8-8. What general control(s) would be appropriate to prevent, detect, or minimize the adverse effects from each of the following occurrences?

a. A programmer modifies her firm's microcomputer-based operating system, thereby accidentally eliminating password protection over certain confidential files. She used a well-known utility program to make the modifications.

b. A firm recently moved several important mainframe accounting applications to a client/server network. The director of internal auditing recently was made aware of the move when the system crashed and the firm was unable to process its accounting applications.

c. A firm that performs periodic batch processing runs frequently has difficulty in assuring that invalid transactions are corrected and resubmitted for processing, and that batch totals are verified after each processing run.

d. An accountant developed a forecasting model using a popular spreadsheet program. However, when the accountant was terminated, his successor had to develop a new model because he could not understand the old model's logic.

e. A firm's data security manager co-owned a janitorial service with his wife's relatives. The manager would periodically throw into his wastebasket sensitive reports, passwords, disks, and magnetic tape files. When emptying the data security manager's wastebasket, the relatives would retrieve the discarded items and place them in a separate section of a large trash bin located on the outside of the building. Late at night, the data security manager would retrieve the trash bag containing the items. He eventually sold

these items to competitors for large sums of money.

f. The throughput of a firm's main computer system drops sharply for three consecutive weeks, although the computer operators seem to be continually busy.

g. A programmer for a local bank modifies the program that computes interest amounts on savings account balances. His modification, known as the "salami fraud," consists of accumulating into his account a fraction of a cent from each interest computation (which previously had been rounded in the depositor's favor).

h. A programmer for a small firm assists the computer operator during rush periods. One day during the processing of checks, he substitutes bogus vouchers and overrides the control in the program designed to prevent the payment of unauthorized vouchers.

i. A computer operator makes corrections to several data errors that are detected during the processing of the payroll program. However, in making the corrections she actually introduced new errors that caused the printed paychecks to reflect incorrect amounts.

j. Unknown to a bank's management, four years ago the data processing manager won the "hacker of the year" award from the International Computer Hacker's Association (ICHA). The data processing manager, who has worked at the bank for two months, frequently reads sensitive information contained on personnel and payroll files. He also works as a part-time consultant to other banks in the region.

8-9. What application (transaction) controls would be appropriate to detect and/or prevent each of the following occurrences?

a. A payroll accountant keyed in 94 hours instead of 49 hours in the hours-worked field.

b. A salesperson entering a sales order via her terminal for 100 microcomputer keyboards mistakenly keys in the product number for microcomputers.

c. A data-entry clerk incorrectly entered the letter *r* instead of the digit 4 as the last data item in a customer identification number field.

d. On his way to the payroll department, the timekeeper lost 10 employee time cards when they accidentally fell out of a file folder.

e. A reel of magnetic tape containing the current cash receipts transactions was moved to the section of the tape library reserved for "scratch" tapes. A data-entry clerk mounted this tape on a tape drive and reformatted it for use in another application. It took the firm four hours to reconstruct the day's cash receipts transactions.

f. A salesperson using her microcomputer, which was interconnected to a local-area network, accessed the server containing payroll data and printed out a list of the salaries of the firm's sales personnel.

g. An unauthorized employee took the executive payroll printout from output bins accessible to all employees. He subsequently sold the printout for a large sum of money.

h. The computer operator mounts the magnetic tape containing the cash disbursements, rather than the cash receipts, thereby incorrectly updating the accounts receivable master file.

i. A data-entry clerk inadvertently entered part number 820015 as 820510 (an invalid number).

8-10. What application (transaction) controls would be appropriate to detect and/or prevent each of the following occurrences?

a. A sales order is coded with an incorrect and nonexistent customer number. The error is not detected until the file updating run, when no master record is located to match the number.

b. A data-entry clerk correctly entered the debit of a $5000 transaction for the purchase of fixed assets. However, she forgot to enter the offsetting credit.

c. A programmer working for a large mutual fund firm gained unauthorized access to the computer program to calculate investors' monthly interest from bond investments. He then inserted a program routine into the main program to accumulate roundoff errors into a secret account, which he later accessed.

d. During the inventory updating run, an issue transaction containing an incorrect quantity is posted to the inventory item record, thereby reducing the on-hand balance in the record to a negative number.

e. A payment from a customer in the amount $55.10, and properly listed on a remittance advice, is keyed in by a data preparation clerk as $551.00.

f. A programmer increased the monthly salaries of several co-workers by using his networked microcomputer that was on-line to the mainframe computer containing the payroll files.

g. Using a preformatted screen display, a salesperson in the field entered a sale as $5.77. The correct amount on the sales invoice was $57.77.

h. An unauthorized employee inadvertently received a report indicating that the firm was about

to downsize and terminate 15 percent of the workforce.

i. A programmer made unauthorized modifications to a payroll program.

8-11. What application (transaction) controls would be appropriate to detect and/or prevent each of the following occurrences?

a. Data-entry personnel made an unusually large number of errors when entering data from source documents on-line.

b. A computer operator was unable to determine if the cash receipts updating run had been performed.

c. A data-entry clerk using a terminal on-line to a mainframe entered the quantity 317 as 3x7.

d. A buyer in the purchasing department attempts to initiate a purchase transaction affecting the supplier master file, using her user's code to access the on-line computer system.

e. The last few records on a payroll master file were omitted during an update run because the batch processing program failed to read to the end-of-file marker.

f. A computer operator has been selling one copy of the inventory report, which contains confidential operating information, to a competitor.

g. A programmer who gained unauthorized access to the payroll program inserted a routine into the program to double his pay rate.

h. On September 7, 1997, an accounting clerk prepared an invoice dated September 67, 1997. The invoice was part of a batch of invoices sent to the data-entry department.

8-12. Presented below is a list of internal controls, labeled *a–q*. These controls are commonly implemented in a firm's AIS. Below this list is a definition or description of a variety of internal controls, labeled 1–16. Match each number with the letter of the control that best fits the definition or description. You may use a control more than once. For some definitions or descriptions, more than one correct answer is possible.

a. Application controls
b. Backup
c. Character check
d. Compatibility test
e. Detective controls
f. Distribution log
g. Encryption
h. Fire controls
i. Hash totals
j. Internal control structure

k. Output controls

l. Personnel controls

m. Range test

n. Reasonableness test

o. Redundant data check

p. Separation of duties

q. Sequence check

1. Two identifiers are entered for each transaction, for example, the inventory part number and an item description. A program matches the part number with the item description and if the two items do not match, an error was made in entering the transaction.

2. For items like inventory, the balance must always be zero or positive. A negative balance triggers an error notation.

3. This test determines whether a data field contains only proper characters. For example, assume that a five-character field should contain all numbers, but that one of the characters in the field is a letter. An error message would indicate that an incorrect character exists in the field.

4. A test that specifies both a lower and upper limit, for example, employees should be between the ages of 21 and 65.

5. A check applied to various data items to determine if the relationships among the data elements are normal or expected.

6. A test to ensure that numbers entered during input match a list of acceptable numbers stored in a master file.

7. The adding of nonmonetary amounts whose total is meaningless, except for control purposes.

8. A check of a person's password against a table of codes that indicate the transactions the person is authorized to process.

9. This output control ensures that reports are distributed to personnel authorized to receive them.

10. An internal control to prevent an individual from accessing a file that he or she is unauthorized to access.

11. A process to ensure that the organization's financial and nonfinancial objectives are attained.

12. Procedures to identify errors and irregularities after they have occurred.

13. When a catastrophe destroys accounting data and files, this control ensures continuation of processing.

14. Controls that must be implemented for each automated accounting application.

15. A test to determine if the relationship described is a logical occurrence.

16. A control that scrambles the contents of a file to make it unreadable to an unauthorized user.

8-13. Presented below is a list of internal controls, labeled *a–q*. These controls are commonly implemented in a firm's AIS. Below this list is a definition or description of a variety of internal controls, labeled 1–15. Match each number with the letter of the control that best fits the definition or description. You may use a control more than once. For some definitions or descriptions, more than one correct answer is possible.

a. Access controls

b. Access log

c. Callback

d. Corrective controls

e. Documentation

f. Error log

g. Field-size test

h. General controls

i. Input controls

j. Internal label check

k. Organization controls

l. Overflow test

m. Programming controls

n. Read-back

o. Record count

p. Rounding error test

q. Sequence check

1. After a data-entry clerk enters a transaction on-line, it is displayed on the monitor, compared with the original transaction, and errors are corrected.

2. A test to determine if the capacity of a memory field has been exceeded.

3. A test to ensure that rounding errors are properly controlled.

4. A check to ensure that files to be updated have matching identification numbers.

5. A count of the quantity of items transmitted or delivered to the computer department for processing.

6. The rekeying of incorrect data displayed on a monitor.

7. A control to ensure that a programmer does not operate the computer.

8. A device that shows all accesses, both authorized and unauthorized, to the computer system, as well as any changes made to the files.

9. Internal controls that affect the AIS applications processed by a computer system.

10. Controls to prevent an unauthorized individual from retrieving or modifying data stored in a computer system.

11. Controls to ensure that data is accurate and complete prior to processing the data further.

12. Instructions containing information about how to operate an automated AIS.

13. A check used in batch sequential processing systems before an updating run to ensure that the record key values are in the proper order, usually ascending or descending.

14. A report generated at the end of a batch processing run that lists any exceptional items.

15. After a remote computer makes a connection with another computer, this control ensures that the remote device is authorized to transmit and receive data.

8-14. The city of Paige, Utah, recently acquired a private water firm. As a result, the city has had to develop a new monthly water billing system. It first made an inventory of the customers receiving water from the firm and devised meter-reading routes. Preprinted customer lists have been prepared for each route, showing customer account number, address, and last meter reading. Each meter reader will simply record the current reading in the last column on the list. When the recording is complete, each meter reader will submit the original of the list to the billing department and retain the duplicate.

After reviewing the lists, the billing department will submit them to the data-preparation section, which will convert the meter-reading data to magnetic tape. Then computer operations will process the data against the customer files (on magnetic disks), generating water bills that are calculated by reference to residential or commercial rate files. During the billing processing, an exception report will reflect all accounts for which consumption differed from the previous month by more than 40 percent. A billing register, showing current billings receivable and customer details, will also be printed. Then the bills will be mailed to the customers. City regulations require that all exceptions be cleared within two weeks of the report date; then the exception report is destroyed.

Required

a. Identify the various risks to which the new billing system is exposed, such as the types of errors that may arise, and the omissions in its design.

b. Identify any control weaknesses in the design as described above.

c. Identify specific transaction controls that are needed in the proposed procedure, organized by authorization, recording, batching, conversion, editing, processing, and output controls. Include under batching three types of batch totals that might be used and the data elements on which they would be employed (if applicable). Also include under editing controls several programmed checks that should be employed and the elements of data to which the checks should be applied. Employ a controls matrix similar to Figure 8-11 to list these programmed checks.

(CIA *adapted*)

8-15. Self-checking digits are employed by a firm to validate its identification numbers. The algorithm used is known as the modulus-11 system and involves the following steps:

   a. Assign weights to each digit in the number (except the check digit), using 2 as the weight for the lowest-order (right-most) digit, 3 for the next-lowest-order digit, and so on.

   b. Multiply each digit by its weight.

   c. Sum the products.

   d. Divide the sum by 11.

   e. Subtract the remainder from 11; the result is the self-checking digit. (If there is no remainder or if the result is 10, the self-checking digit is zero.)

Required

a. Verify the correctness of the self-checking digit for each of the following employee numbers where check digit is the right-most digit:

(1) 45675   (2) 33693

Solution to (1):

$$2 \times 7 = 14$$
$$3 \times 6 = 18$$
$$4 \times 5 = 20$$
$$5 \times 4 = \underline{20}$$
$$72$$

$$6 \text{ R}6$$
$$11\overline{\smash{)}72}$$
$$11 - 6 = 5$$

Thus, 5 is the self-checking digit.

b. Verify that the following five-digit product number, recorded by a salesperson, contains an incorrect self-checking digit: 73256. What is the correct self-checking digit for this number, assuming that the remainder of the digits were recorded correctly?

c. Determine the digit that should be attached to customer number 28346 in order to provide the self-checking feature.

d. Each of the following customer numbers (all of which contain self-checking digits) were entered via a salesperson's terminal as a part of sales order data. Which should be rejected by the computer system as invalid?

   (1) 357920

   (2) 186252   (3) 243760

e. Recompute the self-checking digits that should be attached to the customer numbers listed in **d** above, using the modulus-11 variation method illustrated in the chapter. Employ weights of 6, 5, 4, 3, and 2 for the five digits composing each integral number. See the second Spotlighting box in the chapter for a description of Modulus 11.

8-16. Gose Hotels of Reno, Nevada, utilizes an on-line computer system to maintain room reservations. Operators key data concerning each reservation into on-line terminals. Included in each entry are the name of the person making the reservation, the code of the hotel for which the reservation is being made, the reservation dates, the expected time of arrival, and special requests (e.g., a roll-away bed). The system then updates the room master file and creates a new record for the traveler. All files are maintained on magnetic disks.

Required

Give specific descriptions of general controls and application controls needed to provide an adequate control framework for this system. Relate any programmed checks you describe to specific elements of data being entered by the operators.

8-17. Recently, the Central Savings and Loan Association of Jefferson City, Missouri, installed an on-line computer system. Each teller in the association's main office and seven branch offices has an on-line terminal. Customers' mortgage payments and savings account deposits and withdrawals are recorded in the accounts by the computer from data input by the teller at the time of the transaction. The teller keys the transaction code and proper account by account number and enters the information in the terminal keyboard to record the transaction. The accounting department at the main office also has terminals. The computer is housed at the main office.

In addition to servicing its own mortgage loans, the association acts as a mortgage servicing agency for three life insurance firms. In this latter activity the association maintains mortgage records and serves as the collection and escrow agent for the mortgagees (the insurance firms), who pay a fee to the association for these services.

Required

List specific general controls and application controls needed to provide an adequate control framework for this system. Relate any programmed checks you describe to specific elements of data being entered by the tellers.

(CPA *adapted*)

8-18. Babbington-Bowles is a Toronto advertising agency. It employs 625 salespersons whose responsibilities require them to travel and entertain extensively.

Salespersons, who earn both salaries and commissions, receive paychecks at the end of each month. Formerly, the paycheck for each salesperson included reimbursement for expenses. These expense reimbursements were based on expense reports submitted by the salespersons, approved by supervisors, and computer-processed in batches.

Although this procedure was satisfactory to the firm, it displeased the salespersons. They were forced to wait a month (sometimes two) for the reimbursement, which often amounted to several thousand dollars. Thus, they requested permission to submit expense reports with receipts directly to the accounting department, and to receive reimbursement very promptly thereafter.

To provide this service, the accounting department would need a video display terminal and small on-line printer. The accounting clerk would enter the salesperson's name into the terminal, together with the requested expense amounts and account numbers to which the amounts would be charged. An on-line program would process the data and, if valid, print a check on presigned blank-check stock kept in the printer. Assume that the firm's computer system contains an on-line file pertaining to salespersons' expense reimbursements and earnings, as well as an on-line general ledger file.

Required

a. List several general controls that are needed in the proposed expense-reimbursement procedure.

b. Identify specific transaction controls that are needed in the proposed procedure, organized by authorization, recording, editing, processing, and output controls. Include under editing controls several programmed checks that should be applied (including transmission and processing logic checks) and the elements of data to which the checks should be applied. Employ a controls matrix similar to Figure 8-13 to list these programmed checks.

(SMAC *adapted*)

8-19. A wholly owned real estate investment subsidiary, despite its $10 million in assets, operates out of the main office of the parent. The parent firm administers all purchasing, payroll, and personnel functions. The subsidiary's board of directors consists entirely of selected officers of the parent.

The real estate investment subsidiary's activities consist primarily of buying, developing, and selling real estate, with some development projects involving joint ventures with contractors. Day-to-day operations are handled by the president and two vice-presidents. The president also acts as liaison with the parent; each vice-president has additional projects to manage.

All invoices and itemized statements requiring direct payment or reimbursement to contractors or vendors are delivered to one of the two vice-presidents for review and approval. After approval, the staff accountant prepares checks and then obtains the signature of one of the vice-presidents on the checks. After signing, the checks are returned to the staff accountant for mailing, and supporting documents are filed. All blank checks are kept by the staff accountant.

All customer payments on notes and accounts receivable originating from the sale of real estate are sent to one of the two vice-presidents and then forwarded to the staff accountant, who records the payment and prepares the deposit slip. The deposit may be given to the parent's accounting department or to a teller of the parent.

If the subsidiary experiences a cash shortage, a promissory note is prepared by the staff accountant and signed by the president or one of the vice-presidents. The staff accountant submits the promissory note to the parent and awaits receipt of the funds. The staff accountant is responsible for billing customers and advising management when payments are due. The staff accountant reconciles the bank statement once a month on receipt.

The staff accountant prepares monthly financial statements, including the accrual of interest receivable and the capitalization of certain interest charges. These financial statements are prepared to reflect the substance of both joint ventures and subsidiary operations. The board of directors reviews the financial statements.

Required

Identify specific areas in which segregation of duties is inadequate.

(CPA *adapted*)

CONTINUING CASE

With respect to the small firm that you selected in Chapter 1, complete the following requirements:

a. List several specific general controls that the firm has implemented into its AIS.

b. If the firm uses an accounting software package, list the program controls that have been implemented into the package. Do you feel that these program controls are adequate to control the processing of transactions? What additional programming controls do you feel should be implemented into the software package?

c. Does the firm have adequate segregation of incompatible duties? Cite several examples.

d. Identify the various types of documentation prepared by the firm. Evaluate the comprehensiveness and quality of this documentation. Determine if the documentation is adequately controlled.

e. Identify the major types of output controls that the firm has implemented into the AIS.

f. If the firm employs a data-base management system, determine the distinctive controls implemented into the data-base environment.

CHAPTER
9

SECURITY FOR
TRANSACTION/INFORMATION
PROCESSING SYSTEMS

THE LEARNING OBJECTIVES FOR THIS CHAPTER ARE TO ENABLE YOU TO:

1. Describe security measures that pertain to physical noncomputer resources.
2. Examine security measures for computer hardware facilities.
3. Discuss security measures for data and information.
4. Describe the features of computer contingency and disaster recovery planning.

INTRODUCTION

This chapter continues the survey of controls that are suited to accounting information systems. Specifically we consider security measures that protect a firm's resources. The resources of a firm include its cash, marketable securities, inventory, facilities, and data and human resources (i.e., intellectual capital). They are threatened by most of the risk exposures described in Chapter 7.

IMPORTANCE OF SECURITY

Assets such as cash and inventory may be stolen or lost, and facilities such as a copy machine may be damaged or destroyed. Data or information may be accessed and read or even changed by unauthorized persons, with possible adverse consequences. For example, a competitor who acquires a firm's confidential product plans could effectively counteract those plans. Computer facilities might be damaged or destroyed by fires, by floods, by hurricanes, by accidental misuse, or even by sab-

otage. Human resources must be protected from a variety of risk exposures, including natural or human-made disasters, riots, freak accidents, and sabotage by disgruntled employees. Computer security in particular is becoming a matter of increasing concern to organizations of all sizes, both public and private. Risks due to security lapses have heightened, partly because of the complexity of computer systems and intra- and interorganization networks. Publicized losses in recent years, however, are causing firms to take more effective actions in improving security for both their computer systems and their other resources.

Every size organization must define, identify, and isolate the most frequently occurring hazards that threaten its hardware, software, data, and human resources. After isolating common hazards, the organization should complete a risk assessment and analysis, as described in Chapter 7. Since security measures cannot completely protect against all possible threats, only the most cost-effective controls for the relevant or significant risks should be implemented.

VARIETY OF SECURITY MEASURES

In order to safeguard its resources, an individual firm should employ a variety of security measures. Through adequate security measures, the firm can provide day-to-day protection of its computer facilities and other physical facilities, maintain the integrity and privacy of its data files, and avoid serious damage or disastrous losses. Certain security measures are directed against acts of nature, whereas others are intended to inhibit human actions. Some security measures are highly technical and sophisticated, especially when providing security for centralized data bases and data communications networks. Certain security measures are *preventive* in nature, in that they prevent unauthorized access to resources. For instance, a password could be used to prevent one of Infoage's bookkeepers from intentionally accessing unauthorized data, such as the executive payroll file. Other measures are *detective*, such as closed-circuit television that observes an intruder in a restricted area. Still others are *corrective*, in that they enable lost data to be reconstructed or lost facilities to be recovered. An example of a corrective data security measure is the periodic preparation of backup files for all of Infoage's microcomputers linked to its local-area network. Finally, some measures represent limitations, in that they restrict losses that occur in spite of prevention and detection defenses. An instance of a limiting measure is adequate insurance coverage on Infoage's office microcomputers, which enables the firm to recover financial losses in case of fires, floods, sabotage, and accidents.

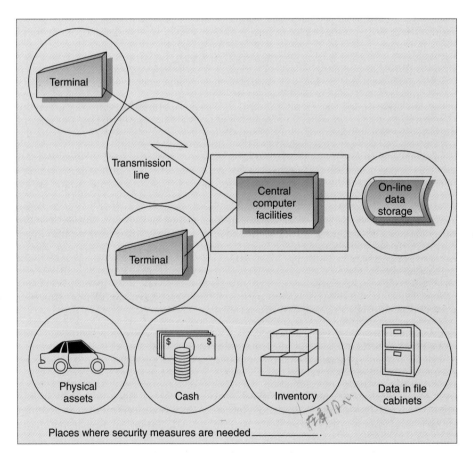

FIGURE 9-1 Resources needing protection by means of various types of security measures.

Security measures focus on physical security and data/information security. For convenience physical security can be divided into two categories: (1) security for all physical resources except the computer facilities, and (2) security for computer hardware facilities. Figure 9-1 portrays the types of noncomputer resources, computer facilities, and data reservoirs that need protection.

In the following sections we will survey a substantial number of security measures, using the broad framework of physical noncomputer resources, computer hardware facilities, and data/information. Within each of these three categories the specific security measures are discussed according to their several key purposes:

1. Protection from unauthorized access.
2. Protection from disasters.
3. Protection from breakdowns and interruptions.
4. Protection from undetected access.
5. Protection from loss or improper alteration.
6. Recovery and reconstruction of lost data.

A seventh purpose establishes a mechanism to monitor the previous six. Figure 9-2 lists these categories and purposes, together with typical security measures. As shown in the figure, not all purposes are relevant to all categories.

SECURITY FOR PHYSICAL NONCOMPUTER RESOURCES

Security measures needed for physical resources such as cash and inventory do not depend on the extent to which the AIS is automated. Thus they apply as much to resources in firms that have manual systems as to firms that have computer systems.

PROTECTION FROM UNAUTHORIZED ACCESS

The major category of security measures for physical resources is known as *access controls*. These controls or measures have the purpose of restricting entry to unauthorized persons, generally to circumvent theft or vandalism. Access controls include security guards, receptionists, fenced-in areas, grounds lighting, burglar and fire exit alarms, motion detection alarms, locked doors, closed-circuit television monitors, safes, locked cash registers, locked file cabinets, and lockboxes in post offices. A complementary measure is close supervision of employees who handle assets, such as Infoage's or Ann Strong's mailroom clerks who open mail containing currency and checks. Supervision is a relevant security measure for all size firms.

Large firms having sufficient cash resources and expensive mainframe computers may find that a large number of these security measures are needed to adequately protect their resources. A medium-sized firm such as Infoage would find many of these measures too costly to implement, such as guards, receptionists, fenced-in areas, and television monitors. Other security measures such as safes and vaults, insurance coverage, locked boxes, and burglar and fire exit alarms are within the security budget of Infoage. Some of these latter measures may be cost justifiable for Ann Strong's consulting firm. Before she can decide what security devices are needed, Ann should determine if the relevant risks identified require such measures and if they are cost-effective. Still another useful measure for all size firms, including Infoage and Ann Strong's, is to affix nonremovable labels to facilities such as office equipment, microcomputers, and production machinery. If, in spite of these measures, certain valuables are stolen, what recourse does a firm have? All size entities

Purpose of Security Measures	Physical Noncomputer Resources in Both Manual and Computer-Based Systems	Hardware Facilities of Computer-Based Systems	Data in Computer-Based Systems
1. Protect from theft or access by unauthorized persons	√ Security guards √ Receptionists √ Fenced-in areas √ Grounds lighting √ Burglar alarms √ Fire exit alarms √ Motion detector alarms √ Locked doors √ Television monitors √ Safes and vaults √ Locked cash registers √ Locked boxes √ Close supervision √ Insurance coverage √ Logs and registers	√ Security guards √ Receptionists √ Electronic scanning devices √ Motion detection devices √ Locked doors √ Restricted entry policy √ Television monitors √ Locked terminals √ Inaccessible terminals √ Card-activated locks √ Employee badges √ Passwords √ Segregated test terminals √ Log-in/log-out visitors √ Photograph visitors √ Escorts when in sensitive areas	√ Electronic scanning devices √ Locked doors, terminals, stacks of blank forms √ Principle of least privilege access √ Off-line data library √ On-line data and program storage partitions √ Encoded data √ Paper shredders √ Passwords √ Limited terminal functions √ Automatic lockouts √ Callback procedures √ Zero disking √ Keyboard locks
2. Protect from natural environment or disasters	√ Sprinkler systems √ Fireproof vaults	√ Air conditioning √ Humidity controls √ Waterproof floors, walls, and ceilings √ Proper water drainage facilities √ Underfloor water detectors √ Water pumps, sump pumps √ Fireproof vaults √ Fireproof construction √ FM 200 gas spheres √ Portable fire extinguishers √ Ionization fire alarm systems √ Smoke exhaust systems √ Plastic covers to protect equipment √ Fire hazard inspections √ Auxiliary power supplies (i.e., diesel generators and batteries) √ Accessible power-off switches √ Insurance coverage √ Prudent location √ Disaster contingency and recovery plans √ Isolation of computer site	

FIGURE 9-2 A list of selected security measures for physical resources, computer facilities, and data.

3. Protect from breakdowns and business interruptions	√ Preventive maintenance √ Backup equipment √ Insurance coverage	√ Preventive maintenance √ Backup hardware systems √ Graceful degradation √ Insurance coverage	
4. Detect attempted access or change			√ Access logs √ Control logs √ Access control software √ System and program change logs
5. Protect from loss or alteration			√ Library log √ Transaction logs √ Tape file protection rings √ Write-protect floppies and hard disks √ External file labels √ Internal file labels √ Read-only memory √ Batch control logs √ Lockouts
6. Reconstruct lost files			√ Activity log √ Vital records plan √ Backup procedures √ Off-premise storage √ Reconstruction procedures √ Rollback and recovery procedures √ Checkpoints
7. Monitor security measures	√ Internal security group √ Annual internal audit of security measures	√ Internal security group √ Annual internal audit of security measures	√ Internal security group √ Annual internal audit of security measures

FIGURE 9-2 (*continued*)

can consider measures that protect the *value* of physical assets, such as fidelity bonds for employees who have access to cash and negotiable instruments.

PROTECTION FROM DISASTERS

Another category of security measures protects physical resources from destruction due to natural causes. *Sprinkler systems* are available to put out fires that may break out in Infoage's merchandise warehouse, for instance. A *fireproof vault* maintained by Infoage protects cash and valuable papers from fire. In some instances, a security measure serves two purposes. For example, Infoage's fireproof vault that is carefully positioned in a secured area can also prevent access to unauthorized personnel.

PROTECTION FROM BREAKDOWNS AND INTERRUPTIONS

A third category of security measures protects resources from breakdowns and business interruptions. *Preventive maintenance* of automobiles, office machinery, production machinery, and other assets is a prime example. Preventive maintenance measures are used by all size firms. If breakdowns occur, business interruption and backup measures can provide support.

MONITOR SECURITY MEASURES

A final category is composed of security measures that monitor the accomplishment of the other six objectives shown in Figure 9-2. A *corporatewide security program* provides assurance that control objectives are accomplished in an efficient and effective manner throughout the organization. A *formal security group* should be formed in large organizations. Ann Strong and Infoage should also develop a security program, except that such a program in these small and medium-sized firms is likely to be more informal. In large firms, management should prepare a *written security policy* that may include the appointment of a security administrator. The administrator heads a security group formed to recommend and implement effective security procedures. Infoage may appoint an employee to serve in this capacity on a part-time basis. Ann Strong should perform this function for her firm. Since Ann's firm is very small, this additional duty should only require her to spend a few hours per month on administering security policies. If a firm has an internal audit department, it should perform an *annual security audit*.

These monitoring measures are also applicable to computer hardware facilities and data/information.

SECURITY FOR COMPUTER HARDWARE FACILITIES

The computer system and related equipment, such as off-line input-output devices, require protection from the same types of risks to which noncomputer physical resources are exposed. Many of the same types of security measures are applicable.

PROTECTION FROM UNAUTHORIZED ACCESS

To reduce the risk from exposures, in large organizations the computer facilities center should be as *isolated* as possible. The center's location should not be advertised, nor should it be visible from the street. In all size organizations, physical access to computer facilities should be restricted to authorized persons. In mainframe computer systems found in large firms, typically only personnel such as computer operators, librarians, data processing supervisors, and information systems management should have access to the computer facilities. Unauthorized personnel—such as accountants, clerks, and visitors—should be denied access to the main computer room and to other areas that do not pertain to their responsibilities; otherwise, the hardware will be needlessly exposed to possible damage. Even systems analysts, programmers, and the data-base administrator should not be allowed access. Although they are less likely to damage the hardware accidentally, they would have the opportunity to alter programs and data with which they are familiar.

Among the effective means of restricting access to centralized computer rooms and similar facilities are

- Security guards and receptionists posted at strategic entry points.
- Electronic scanning devices to prevent employees from removing disks and magnetic tapes, and from bringing metals, such as magnets, into the center.
- Motion detectors to alert security to the presence of unauthorized persons.

- Locked doors to the computer room and other key entry points, which are opened only by means of magnetic-coded cards.
- Closed-circuit monitors that are viewed from central locations.
- Color-coded identification badges that must be worn at all times.
- Log-in/log-out of all visitors.
- Escorts of all visitors.
- Alarms that sound when forced entry occurs.

When terminals are employed as part of an AIS, the restrictions on physical resources must be modified. As we will learn when discussing data security, it is necessary to allow data clerks, accountants, and others in all size firms to have access to the system via terminals or microcomputers. However, it is feasible to limit their use to (1) authorized activities, (2) specified terminals, and (3) designated time periods. For instance, firms employing programmers may be allowed to use terminals only for the purpose of testing programs, and they may be assigned specific test terminals to use.

In entities using terminals connected to a mainframe computer, the terminals may also be physically restricted to nonclerical employees and nonemployees. The terminals should be disconnected and locked at the end of each working day, to render them secure against night custodial employees. The terminals can be placed behind counters or locked doors to keep them out of reach of visitors and unauthorized employees. In addition, the terminals can be controlled by security software that detects all attempts to access the system (this software is discussed later in this chapter) and that locks a terminal after a specified number of unsuccessful attempts (say, three). This measure should detect hackers and others who try to guess the passwords.

Many of the above security measures are also relevant in smaller firms, such as Infoage or Ann Strong's firm, that utilize only one or a few microcomputers. Infoage and Ann Strong's firm can prevent unauthorized access by incorporating a few other inexpensive measures, such as supervising closely, locking the microcomputers in a specially designed cabinet when not in use, locking the keyboard, using card activated locks, and securing floppy disks.

PROTECTION FROM DISASTERS

Computer facilities are subject to a variety of disasters. Most are likely to arise from acts of nature, but some are caused by human actions. Large firms utilizing expensive mainframe computers can spend huge sums to protect against disasters, both natural and human-made.

To protect against fire, floods, power outages, and natural disasters, the mainframe computer facilities of large firms should be environmentally controlled. Sites that house the major mainframe computer facilities should be air conditioned and humidity controlled.

To protect against water damage, a commonly occurring risk exposure, the data center should be constructed of waterproof floors, walls, and ceilings. In addition, the computer center should have proper water drainage facilities. Underfloor water detectors, water pumps, and sump pumps should be placed in the center. Also, computer centers can be constructed on high terrain, to minimize the threat of floods.

Sites housing mainframe computer facilities should be constructed of fireproof materials and should contain a fireproof vault to serve as the data library. Smoke detectors and fire alarm systems should be installed, together with FM 200 gas-based automatic extinguisher systems.* FM 200 is nontoxic, environmentally safe, and does not damage equipment since no residue of the gas remains after it has extinguished a fire. Ionization fire alarms detect fires before any smoke is visible and should be placed at strategic locations throughout the sites. Portable fire extinguishers should be located throughout the center and employees should know where they are located and how to operate them. Regular fire hazard inspections should be conducted.

Uninterruptible power systems are also very desirable and include diesel generators for mainframes. These auxiliary power supplies ensure that electrical power is continually available and is maintained within tightly regulated voltage limits. Smaller firms such as Infoage and Ann Strong's do not require very many expensive security measures to adequately protect their microcomputers from the natural environment or disasters. Such firms do not need a bombproof, riotproof, or fireproof building to protect their PCs. For these size firms, portable fire extinguishers, ionization fire alarm systems, plastic covers to protect the equipment, insurance coverage, and disaster recovery and contingency plans should provide more than adequate protection at a reasonable cost.

To protect against human violence, such as vandalism or sabotage, large computer facilities can be placed in inconspicuous locations that are not inviting or known to possible vandals or saboteurs. Devices such as antimagnetic tape storage holders may be used by all size firms to shield data storage units from the effects of magnets. Perhaps the most effective measures are to keep all unauthorized persons away from the computer facilities by means of the restrictive devices described previously. Also, any terminated employee (even a computer operator) should immediately be denied access to the computer room and other facilities. In a small firm such as Infoage, a terminated employee in a short time period can do a great deal of damage to computer disks and other equipment, unless he or she is removed immediately from the premises.

This array of protective security measures can be made more effective by careful planning. A **disaster contingency and recovery plan (DCRP)** (1) identifies all potential threats to the computer system, (2) specifies the needed preventive security measures, and (3) outlines the steps to be taken if each type of disaster actually strikes. It also identifies the resources that must be protected and the available techniques to minimize the disaster. Furthermore, the plan should assign responsibility for its implementation and should provide for follow-up reviews. Due to recent widespread natural disasters causing tens of billions of dollars in damages, the subject of contingency planning has become a very important area of study. We devote the last section of this chapter to a more in-depth review of the topic, as well as in Appendix 2 to this chapter.

PROTECTION FROM BREAKDOWNS AND INTERRUPTIONS

Since breakdowns and interruptions of a computer system can be disastrous, these risks would be covered by the disaster contingency and recovery plan. To be effective, however, the plan must be implemented. Thus, an employee should be assigned to administer the plan, either on a part-time or full-time basis, depending on the size of the firm and the value of resources needing protection. This person should as-

---

*The manufacture of Halon gas was banned by the Environmental Protection Agency as of January 1, 1994. However, firms can continue to use Halon, an environmentally unsafe fluorocarbon, until the inventories of the gas have been depleted, estimated to occur sometime early in the twenty-first century.

SPOTLIGHTING

SECURITY MEASURES FOR RISK MANAGEMENT
*at Aetna Life Insurance Co.**

M odern firms have become so dependent on their computer systems that breakdowns, natural disasters, and human violence can cause great losses and can create severe disruptions to operations. Recent examples include the following:

- A breakdown of American Airlines' Sabre reservation system in May 1989, as a result of a programming error, which eliminated access to reservation data on 1080 hard disks. For about 13 hours the entire reservation system was inoperable; as a result, American lost millions of dollars in potential revenue from bookings.[†]

- A fire in the headquarters building of First Interstate Bank in Los Angeles in May 1988. Before being brought under control, the fire destroyed the twelfth through the sixteenth floors, including many computer files and facilities. Smoke and water damage throughout all 62 floors was so severe that the entire building was closed for several months. Two thousand employees had to be relocated, and phone lines had to be rerouted.

- A flood in the $100 million computer facility of Household Finance Corporation in Chicago in 1987, which left two feet of water standing among mainframe computers.

In some instances, firms that have experienced disasters were prepared. For example, First Interstate Bank had previously developed its business crisis/resumption plan. As a consequence, the firm was able to function effectively after the devastating fire. Thus, even though the securities trading floor was completely destroyed, traders were able to operate in temporary quarters the very next day.

Aetna, an insurance giant located in Hartford, also has carefully planned for disasters. In fact, it has elevated the security issue to the level of business risk management, in which disaster recovery is secondary to business continuity. To ensure that business operations function without serious disruption, Aetna has established a department within its information systems function with the title Corporate Security/Risk Management. This department has four groups: IS security, physical site security, loss control, and insurance. Together these groups have conducted a risk analysis. First, they identified and prioritized the functions necessary for business continuity and the risks that affect them. Then, they identified the areas where protective controls were weak, such as the large computer installation in the commercial insurance division. Next they developed strategies to eliminate avoidable risks and to minimize those risks that cannot be removed. Finally, they specified the steps to take in case of a disaster that cannot be prevented. This risk management planning has been extended to the entire information systems function of the firm and has been approved by top management.

---

*Paul Tate, "Risk! The Third Factor." *Datamation* (April 15, 1988), pp. 58–64.
[†]Don Steinberg. "Rare Software Glitch Costs American Millions." PC *Week* (May 29, 1989), p. 61.

certain that a preventive maintenance program is put into effect and that adequate insurance coverage is acquired. In addition, he or she should make arrangements for backup system components (besides the backup power supply mentioned earlier). Thus, the plan administrator might arrange with another firm or a service bureau to provide computer service if a breakdown occurs.

Alternatively, duplicate computer facilities could be acquired by the firm. A less expensive approach is to acquire a computer system having the capability of "graceful degradation." That is, it is able to continue operations in the face of hardware problems, but at lowered efficiency.

SECURITY FOR DATA AND INFORMATION

The data/information resource of a firm is quite varied. It includes (1) data stored in files and data sets, both on-line and off-line; (2) application programs, whether stored on magnetic tapes in a data library or on magnetic disks under the control of the operating system; and (3) information, both in hard-copy reports and in computer formats. In addition, a data-base system maintains a data dictionary.

Various types of fraud and irregularities can occur in computer systems with respect to data and information. Stored data or information may be accessed, viewed by unauthorized persons, stolen, or lost. Stored programs as well as data or information may be accessed and improperly altered. Security measures that are designed to combat these types of fraud provide protection from (1) unauthorized accesses to data and information, (2) undetected accesses of data and information, and (3) losses or improper alterations of data and information. The measures providing these protections are generally preventive or detective in nature, although certain security measures are corrective in nature.

In the following sections we will survey a wide range of data-oriented security measures. However, every type of data-oriented security measure is not discussed at this point. For instance, a very serious risk concerns the entry of improper or erroneous data into stored files. The means of counteracting such risks were explored in the applications control section of Chapter 8.

PROTECTION FROM UNAUTHORIZED ACCESS TO DATA AND INFORMATION

Various means of restricting access are needed, since (1) unauthorized persons can range from employees to outside parties such as suppliers and industrial spies, and (2) the techniques for penetrating are numerous and sophisticated. For instance, a phone firm needs not only to prevent outside private detectives and hackers from accessing its private telephone conversations and unlisted phone numbers but also to prevent its own programmers and clerks from accessing confidential salary files. One such unauthorized person may use a random-number generator to search for codes that permit entry to the data base; another may "tap" the communications lines to gain access to transmitted data.

Two additional factors complicate the task of devising measures to restrict access to data and information. First, most persons granted access rights are authorized for only a portion of the data base. For example, a bank may allow depositors to access their checking account balances, but will not want the depositors to browse within the data base for the balances of other depositors. The same bank may allow bank tellers to access account balances of depositors but will likely not want the tellers to access the loan accounts of the other depositors. The second complication exists because of the various types of accessing actions. Among the actions that might be taken are reading a record or report, changing data within a record, adding a new record, and deleting a current record. For instance, the bank may authorize its tellers to read and change data within a depositor's record but not to add or to delete a depositor's record. Access restrictions are thus needed both (1) to prevent access to *all* data and information by unauthorized persons and (2) to restrict the *degree* of access by persons who have limited rights with respect to certain data and information.

Useful security measures that restrict access employ means such as isolation, authentication and authorization of users, limitations on terminal usage, encryption, and destruction. Many of these measures pertain to all types of computer system architectures, but we give special attention to on-line computer systems. They are especially vulnerable, since they can be accessed from a number of terminals and handle a variety of files and programs.

1. **Isolation.** Data and information that are confidential or critical to a firm's operations should be physically isolated to discourage unauthorized access. Thus key reference files, confidential files, programs, and program documentation should be kept in a secured off-line or on-line library when not in active use. Hard-copy printouts of programs could be kept in a locked file cabinet or vault, for instance. In on-line processing systems the master files and data sets of various users should be maintained in separate partitions on direct-access storage media and provided boundary protection. In data-base systems environments the data dictionary should be maintained under the control of the data-base administrator; it should remain inaccessible to all others except high-level systems managers and auditors. Programs that are currently being executed in primary storage should also be isolated from one another to prevent intentional or accidental modifications. Program isolation is achieved by means of the memory-protect feature of multiprogramming.

Programs being tested should be isolated from both the live programs currently in use (i.e., the production programs) and the live data base. This isolation may be achieved, without harm to testing effectiveness, by generating a separate copy of the data base for program testing.

2. **Authentication and authorization of users.** **Authentication** is concerned with identifying and proving authenticity of users during log-on procedures. Once a person has been identified as a legitimate or "trusted" system user, he or she is provided with **authorization privileges** to access particular services and resources. Authorized use and modification of data and information should be precisely established by key designated managers. **Access control lists (ACLs)** are tables that list authorized systems users and the extent of their authorizations; ACLs should be maintained by the data-base administrator. Figure 9-3 shows an ACL table of authorizations broken down by user, file, and type of access. In addition to files, ACLs may also be used to authorize particular programs, terminals, or other devices.

The **principle of least privilege access** should be enforced. For example, Infoage's accounts payable bookkeeper should be granted the absolute minimum access to those program modules, data, and files to perform his or her job function. He or she should not be allowed access to the entire accounting system. Accounts receivable and the general ledger software should be maintained on other networked microcomputers. The separation of records will prevent the bookkeeper from "snooping" into files that are not needed to perform his or her duties, thus taking away the temptation toward unethical or unlawful behavior.

Authorizations should be verified by sound identification techniques. When requesting access to data and information via on-line terminals, users should be required to enter passwords, badges, magnetic-striped cards, or "smart" (e.g., chip or optical scannable) cards. Another authentication system increasingly being utilized in data communication networks is known as Kerberos authentication and is described in Chapter 17. Security modules, embedded within the operating system, can then verify that the requesting person is an authorized user. For instance, when a

User number	User name	Inventory master file	Accounts payable master file	Purchase order file	
1234	B. White	R		W	
1286	P. Dane		RW		
1302	R. Rogers	RWCD			
1355	H. Powers		W		

Action codes:

R	Display (i.e., read) only
W	Write (e.g., update) only
RW	Display and write
C	Create new record
D	Delete current record

FIGURE 9-3 An access control list table.

production employee is ready to record her time spent on a job, she inserts her badge into a badge reader (a type of terminal) to identify herself to the security module. The security module, in effect a specialized software routine, compares the entered data (e.g., the employee number) against the stored authorization list.

Passwords   Of the available techniques for restricting access, the password technique is the most frequently employed. A **password** is a user authorization code. It has a two-fold purpose: (1) to allow access to authorized users, and (2) to restrict each user to the data or information and programs related to his or her responsibilities. Usually, the password is preceded by a unique user identification number, which the user first enters to gain access to the system itself. Then the user enters the password to à particular file or program. A security module verifies, by referral to a stored ACL authorization table similar to Figure 9-3, that the user having the unique code entered is authorized to use the designated file or program. If so, the user is allowed by the security module to undertake the types of actions indicated by the ACL table. For example, one of Infoage's retail outlet salesclerks might be allowed to read the inventory master file but not to write records therein. (In this case the file can be said to be "write-protected" from the clerk.)

A password procedure is most effective when it provides precise and tight security. Both of these attributes can be enhanced by the tiered approach, that is, by increasing the number of levels of password protection. Figure 9-4 illustrates a three-level password system that can identify authorized users down to the level of data elements. Gaining access to particular data elements requires the use of three passwords in a specific sequence. Users who do not know all three passwords cannot gain access, that is, are locked out. Security locks on individual data elements are normally reserved for the most sensitive elements, for instance, salary levels of individual employees or sales forecasts of product lines.

After a user has provided the correct series of passwords, the operating system security software may request other identifiers for access to highly strategic information critical to a firm's survival. Two specific methods of requesting other user identifiers are called the handshaking method and the math method. When the hand-

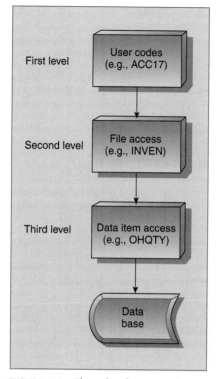

FIGURE 9-4 Three-level password security.

shaking method is employed, the security software establishes a monologue with the user, asking the user a series of random questions from a set stored in the system. For example, the system may display a message on the monitor requesting the spouse's maiden name and if answered correctly, the user is allowed access to the confidential file. When the math method is used, the computer generates a set of, say, six random digits. Assuming that the user knows the key, he or she would manipulate the numbers to generate a correct answer. For example, the security system may generate the digits 6, 5, 3, 2, 9, and 0. The user may sum the numbers and subtract the product from the next highest multiple of 10, in effect generating a type of check digit. In this case the six numbers sum to 25 and when deducted from the next highest multiple of 10, which is 30, generates 5. Assuming that the number 5 is entered into the system, the user will be permitted access to the requested confidential file.

Passwords are subject to abuse. Employees have been known to tape their passwords to terminals, to lend their passwords to friends, or to throw the passwords into a trash container. Browsing or scavenging through trash by hackers or other unauthorized users is one of the easiest ways to gain illegal access to a computer system. Thus passwords should be changed frequently, usually every 30 or 60 days. Sophisticated methods of identifying authorized users include electronic fingerprints, voice patterns, retina scans or other biometrical means. A new approach is for users to carry with them a credit-card size device that contains a small computer chip and clock. The chip randomly generates a new password about every five minutes that is in sync with the password generated by the computer. Such a device, if properly used, makes it almost impossible for an unauthorized person to illegally obtain the password and attain access to the system.

Automatic Lockout   Still other techniques may be used to keep unauthorized persons from accessing an on-line computer system. To prevent persons from guessing passwords, an **automatic lockup** feature causes the security module to lock a terminal after three attempts to enter the proper password. The security module might also automatically log a user off the screen after a short period (say, 15 minutes) during which a terminal stands idle. If this procedure is established, an unauthorized person cannot use a terminal when an authorized user leaves for any reason.

Callback Procedures   To thwart hackers and other outside parties who may discover passwords and attempt to gain access from outside a firm's premises, the system may employ a **callback procedure.** Under this procedure the security module automatically breaks the connection and dials back in order to verify that the person signing on is accessing the system from a terminal with an assigned and authorized number. An alternative method for preventing access from unauthorized terminals is to hardwire the authorized terminals to the mainframe computer through private or dedicated communications lines.

Keyboard Locks   When the computer is unattended, a **keyboard lock** can disable a computer keyboard, rendering it useless. Only when the key is turned on can the keyboard be reactivated. Also, disabling floppy-disk drives should prevent someone from using microcomputer access control software to bypass normal log-in scripts, thus rendering the micro vulnerable to unauthorized access. Finally, securing automatic boot or startup batch program files should prevent a person from overriding prescribed log-in procedures, thereby gaining unauthorized access to a network or stand-alone devices.*

3. **Usage Limitations.** Devices as well as users may be restricted with respect to usage. Thus terminals may be locked after working hours. They should also be placed in areas that are not easily accessible by unauthorized persons. Through internal security software controls, each terminal might be authorized to access data only from certain files, to enter only specified types of transaction data for processing against those files, to read but not to update, and so on. For example, a terminal in Infoage's warehouse may allow the warehouse worker to access the inventory master file, to enter data concerning movements of inventory items to the shipping department, and to read (but not update) the on-hand balances of inventory items. Limitations like these may be implemented by (1) assigning a number to each device, and (2) placing a device authorization table in on-line storage. Each time a user employs a particular terminal, the security module would check the device authorization table; if the terminal's number is matched with the user's password in the table, the terminal is permitted to access the specified file or program and perform the specified actions.

When used together, device authorization tables and user authorization tables provide an added degree of security. For instance, Infoage's warehouse worker might learn the passwords for accessing the payroll master file from a friend in the accounting department. However, the worker cannot access the file from the warehouse terminal if usage limitations are in effect.

4. **Encryption.** To counteract unauthorized wiretapping of communication lines, sensitive and confidential data may be protected by **encryption.** That is, data being entered at one point in an "untrusted" system (e.g., a remote terminal) may be encoded, transmitted in coded form, and then decoded on their arrival

Systems Auditability and Control Report, Advanced Technology Supplement, Module 13. Altamonte Springs, Fla.: Institute of Internal Auditors, 1994, p. 13-31.

at the receiving point (e.g., the firm's home office). Being in coded form, the data would not be understandable to a wiretapper, unless he or she breaks the key. If desired, data might also be stored in coded form. Currently, the two main types of encryption schemes are private and public.

Private Key Encryption   In the **private key encryption scheme,** the sender employs a private key to encode a message before transmitting it to a recipient. Since the private key is also held by the recipient, it is used to decrypt the message. Numerous inexpensive or free encryption programs are available to develop private encryption codes. For instance, for microcomputer and network users, Norton, Superkey, and Windows DOS utilities have developed relatively user-friendly encryption programs, but the key can be broken by a knowledgeable hacker who has at his disposal special code-busting software. For users demanding an unbreakable private algorithmic coding scheme, a program called pretty good privacy (PGP) can be downloaded free from the Internet.

Public Key Encryption   In the **public key encryption scheme,** two code keys are maintained by message recipients—a private key and a public key. A centralized computer maintains security over the public keys. Before a message is transmitted, the sender encodes the message with the recipient's publicly available key. The recipient can only decode the message using his private key. The **RSA public key encryption scheme** is highly secure and is the mostly widely adopted public key algorithm. Recently, the U.S. federal government proposed the so-called Clipper chip as the national standard public key encryption scheme. The government's plan would require that the Clipper chip be installed in every computer and that it would be used to transmit encrypted messages. However, since the government can use its key to decrypt any message, not just those of hackers, criminals, and other intruders, the proposed plan has created a great deal of controversy among businesses and individuals who prefer less government "snooping."

5. **Destruction.** To counteract unauthorized browsing, confidential data should be destroyed after their need has expired. For instance, hard-copy printouts might be fed to paper shredders or disintegration machines and then placed in **lockbox trash containers.** Disintegration shredders are preferred because they create a pulplike residue instead of narrow slices of paper that can be glued or taped together to form the original document. Confidential data on magnetic media should be erased after the results have been recorded elsewhere (unless the data include active account balances). Moreover, data in records and master files should be purged when no longer needed. A technique known as **zero disking** can be used to purge data and files. Zero disking prevents unauthorized persons from using a file rescue routine to recover erased data and files. When a file or data is erased using traditional operating system commands, only the reference to the file is erased, not the data itself. A person can easily recover the file by using a special utility routine found in, for example, Norton Utilities (for microcomputers only). However, Norton Utilities also has a special zero disking routine that overwrites the file with zeros, making it impossible to recover the file's contents.

PROTECTION FROM UNDETECTED ACCESS OF DATA AND INFORMATION

Preventing unauthorized access is not sufficient. All attempts to access the computer system and all authorized access should be monitored. Unwarranted activity can thus be investigated and halted before security breaches are effected. Two types of logs and a special kind of access control software facilitate this monitoring process.

Access Log An **access log,** generally a component of an operating system's security module, records all attempts to interact with the data base. This log reflects the time, date, code of the person attempting the access, type of inquiry or mode of access requested, and data accessed (if the access is successful). Thus it creates an audit trail, which should be reviewed by an internal auditor or security administrator for possible threats to the system's security. Mainframe operating systems and some microcomputer operating systems have built-in security features to automatically produce an access log. Stand-alone microcomputer security software packages can be purchased to interact with operating systems software to generate an access log.

Console Log The second type of log, known as a **console log** or an internal run log, is suitable for mainframe computers utilizing batch processing. It records all actions of the operating system and the computer operators. For instance, it shows the requests and responses made during processing runs and other activities. When displayed on a video monitor located near the central computer console, the log can be helpful to the operator in determining the causes of program halts and in entering instructions or data to resume processing. Also, the computer room supervisor can compare a hard-copy printout of this log to the computer operator's handwritten run log, to determine if unauthorized runs were made or improper actions taken.

Access Control Software **Access control software** can provide higher-level access controls than either access or console logs. Such software interacts with the computer's operating system to restrict and monitor access to data and files. These packages can also generate audit trails and activity logs listing attempted and unauthorized accesses for further follow-up by appropriate officials. **Access Control Facility 2 (ACF2)** and **Resource Access Control Facility (RACF)** are mainframe security programs. Watchdog and On-Guard are scaled-down versions of access control software packages utilized in a microcomputer environment.

System and Program Change Log Changes to programs, files, and controls can be monitored by a **system and program change log.** A systems development manager enters onto this log all authorized changes or additions. These entries should be reviewed by an internal auditor for adherence to prescribed procedures for changes.

PROTECTION FROM LOSS OR IMPROPER ALTERATION OF DATA AND INFORMATION

Two additional logs are useful in preventing the loss of data or information in computer systems.

Library Log A **library log** tracks the movements of data files, programs, and documentation that are used in processing or other activities. It includes the persons, such as the computer operators, who request the items, the times checked out and returned, and the identification of the items involved. A well-maintained library log can aid the data librarian in promptly reclaiming the items after uses, so that they can be returned to off-line storage in fireproof vaults. An on-line version of the library log can aid in tracking uses of data files and programs stored on direct-access storage devices.

Transaction Log A **transaction log** records individual transactions as they are entered into on-line systems for processing. This log, which is under the control of the operating system, provides a key part of the audit trail in an on-line processing system. It is especially crucial when source documents have not been previously prepared. Included in the transaction log would be the number of the terminal through which the transaction is entered, the time and date entered, the identification of the person entering the data, the identification of the person or entity affected by the transaction, the transaction code, and the amount involved. For added identification the system software typically assigns a number to each transaction. Periodically a hard-copy listing of the transaction log should be prepared.

Tape File Protection Ring   A **tape file protection ring** provides protection to a reel of magnetic tape. Only when it is inserted into the reel can the magnetic tape be written on; when the ring is removed, the data on the tape are protected from accidental writeovers.

Write-Protect Notch   Small firms can achieve the same type of protection with floppy and hard disks. When the **write-protect notch** on a 5¼-inch floppy is covered with an adhesive tab, the disk cannot be accidentally erased or overwritten. To write-protect a 3½-inch floppy, the sliding tab is moved so that the hole is uncovered. Similar protection for microcomputer hard disks is available by using special utility software.

File Labels   External and internal file labels provide protection to either a reel of magnetic tape or a disk pack and can be effectively used with all sizes of computers. An **external file label** is a gummed-paper label attached to a physical storage unit, such as a tape reel, to identify its contents. An **internal file label** is a message stored on a physical storage medium in computer-readable form. An *internal header label*, the first record in a file stored on magnetic tape or a direct-access storage device, contains the name and number of the file, the date it was created, and other identifying data. Before allowing a computer program to use data from the file in processing steps, the operating system checks the header label to be sure that the file is specified by the program. If not, the operating system alerts the computer operator via the computer console. An *internal trailer label*, the last record in a file, contains an end-of-file code plus control totals and record counts that pertain to data in the file. These totals and counts can be checked by the program to ensure that all data have been processed and that none have been lost.

Read-Only Memory   **Read-only memory (ROM),** a type of storage from which data can be read but not changed, provides security to the operating system, key programs, and critical data sets. Any software and data stored in ROM cannot be altered by new instructions, nor can new data be added. Thus, instructions stored in ROM are safe from unauthorized tampering by a programmer, operator, or other person who might access the system.

Lockout   Special protective measures are needed in the presence of a data base, since multiple users and programs can often access the stored data simultaneously. One necessary measure, called **lockout,** prevents two programs from accessing the same data concurrently. In effect, one of the programs is held in abeyance until the other program has completed its action (e.g., updating a record). If both of the programs were allowed to update the same record at the same time, it is likely that one set of data would be written over and lost.

RECOVERY AND RECONSTRUCTION OF LOST DATA

In spite of sound security measures, abnormal events sometimes cause data to be lost. Perhaps the hardware malfunctions, a fire or other natural disaster sweeps through the computer-based data processing facility, or a computer operator makes a serious error. When events of this kind cause data to be lost, there must be a means of recovery. Adequate recovery requires the protection of a firm's vital records.

Vital Records Program   A **vital records program** should be established to identify and protect those computer and noncomputer records crucial to operations, such as stockholder records, personnel records, customer records, IRS and SEC records, and inventory records.

Backup and Reconstruction Procedures   **Backup** consists of duplicate copies of the vital documents, files, data sets, programs, and related documentation. These backup copies should reflect all of the changes made in programs and documentation, as well as the up-to-the-moment status of data files. At least one set of backup copies should be stored at a fireproof location that is physically removed from the computer facilities. A clear policy should be established concerning how long data and program backup are to be retained.

A **reconstruction procedure** consists of using the backup to re-create lost data or programs. Various backup and reconstruction procedures have been devised, depending on the type of storage medium used to contain the files and data sets. The **grandparent-parent-child (G-P-C)** procedure is employed mainly by larger firms using mainframe computers when data files and programs are stored on magnetic tape. These firms employ batch processing for certain large-volume accounting applications. Smaller firms using microcomputers, such as Infoage and Ann Strong's, are likely to use the other backup approaches described below. The G-P-C procedure is illustrated in Appendix 1 to this chapter. A **periodic dump procedure** is needed when data files and programs are stored on magnetic disks. The G-P-C procedure is not suitable for backup because the overlay approach of updating files on magnetic disks destroys the previous data. Figure 9-5 shows the backup and reconstruction steps involved in the periodic dump procedure. In Figure 9-5a the files and data sets are dumped at the end of each day onto magnetic tape. (A magnetic disk could alternatively be used as the backup medium.) In addition, an activity log may be maintained on a continuous basis. An **activity log** contains images ("snapshots") of the elements in the data base that are changed by each transaction, plus the time of the transaction, the files affected, and other useful facts. For each element changed, the activity log shows both the value *before* the change and the value *after* the change. Since a single transaction may change (e.g., update) more than one file or data set, an activity log is needed to provide links from the backup file to the current status of the "live" data base.

The dumped data and the activity log, which constitute the backup, are stored in a site remote from the computer facility. If files or programs in the data base are lost, or if the storage media are damaged or shut down, this backup generally enables the data base to be reconstructed. The transaction log, discussed earlier, could also be employed if the activity log is incomplete.

Reconstructing a data base depends on the extent of damage incurred. If all or part of the data base is lost, its recovery involves a **rollforward procedure.** As shown in Figure 9-5b, this procedure begins with the most recent dump of the data base being loaded onto a new magnetic disk. Then the images from the activity log (and the transaction log, if needed) are processed against this data-base backup. When all intervening transactions have been reprocessed, the data base should be fully restored.

On occasion certain data in the data base may become invalid, perhaps because an updating program containing "bugs" has been used. In such instances the

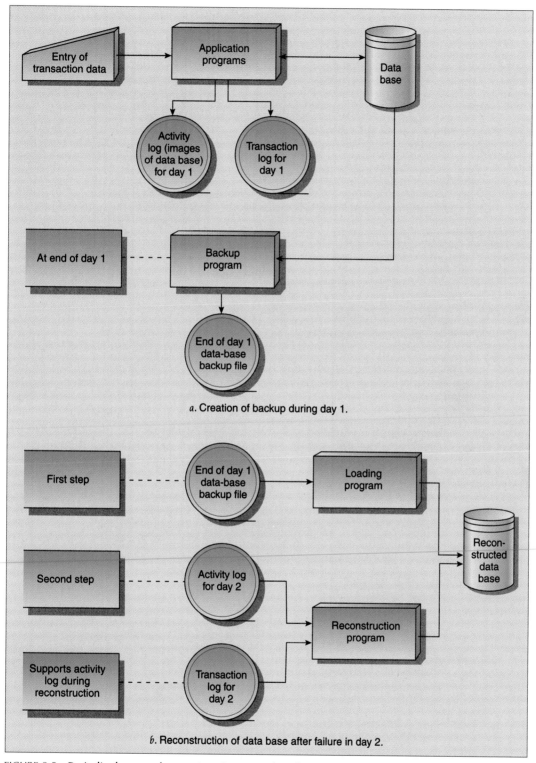

a. Creation of backup during day 1.

b. Reconstruction of data base after failure in day 2.

FIGURE 9-5   Periodic dump and reconstruction procedure for creating backup magnetic disk files. (*a*) Creation of backup during day 1. (*b*) Reconstruction of data base after failure in day 2.

recovery involves a rollback procedure. **Rollback** consists of removing the effects of erroneously processed transactions from the affected files. Then the activity log would be used to restore the data base to its proper state.

A recovery procedure useful for application programs involves the use of checkpoints. **Checkpoints** are points in a batch processing program at which snapshots are taken of the values of all data elements and program indicators. For instance, snapshots might be taken every 10 minutes during the running of an inventory processing program and transcribed onto a backup magnetic tape. If a temporary hardware failure occurs during the run, the processing can be resumed at the last checkpoint. Thus recovery from a failure can be achieved in a shorter time than if the program had to be restarted at the beginning.

Backup procedures for data communications networks often involve a method called fault tolerance. **Fault tolerance** is a procedure of ensuring uninterrupted operations by using redundant devices. Redundant devices include control units, servers, communications channels, and duplicate computer systems in remote locations that automatically take over processing when a failure is detected. Disk mirroring and disk duplexing, two important types of fault tolerant techniques used to back up data in network environments, are explained in Chapter 17.

DISASTER CONTINGENCY AND RECOVERY PLANNING

A disaster contingency and recovery plan is a strategy for recovering from natural and human-made disasters that affect not only a firm's computer processing capabilities but also its critical business operations. Studies show that the longer a major disaster interrupts a firm's critical operations, the more probable the firm will shut down permanently. With support from top management, a DCRP should enable a firm to respond to disasters without suffering irreparable damages. The basic concepts of a DCRP should be present in all firms, regardless of size or mode of processing—manual, computerized, or a combination of the two. Large firms should prepare a more formal and comprehensive plan, developing a separate plan in each of the five areas discussed below. The DCRP process is likely to be less formal, less structured, and less comprehensive in smaller firms such as Infoage or Ann Strong's. Diane Varney of Infoage should set up an internal task force to prepare the DCRP. Ann Strong can prepare a DCRP if she feels qualified or can hire a local consulting firm to assist in the plan's preparation.

COMPONENTS OF A DCRP

A comprehensive DCRP consists of five separate interrelated component plans: emergency, backup, recovery, test, and maintenance plans. The **emergency plan** provides guidelines to follow during and immediately after a disaster. A **backup plan** ensures that key employees, vital records, and alternative backup facilities are available to continue business and data processing operations. A **recovery plan** ensures that a skilled recovery team is formed to reconstruct and restore full operational capabilities. Key components of emergency, backup, and recovery plans are given in Appendix 2 to this chapter. The purpose of the **test plan** is to uncover and correct defects in the DCRP before a real disaster occurs. At random intervals a mock disaster, such as a fire, is simulated. The results are critiqued by test participants and management; gaps in the plan are identified and corrected. The final phase to the DCRP is to prepare a **maintenance plan,** which devises guidelines ensuring that the entire plan is kept up-to-date. Factors requiring revision of the DCRP include major changes in branch locations, key personnel, organization structure, vendor policies, hardware, and software. Any resulting updates to the DCRP are reviewed by appropriate organization officials before the DCRP is modified.

STRENGTHENING THE DCRP PROCESS

Firms often overlook a number of important factors when preparing a disaster contingency and recovery plan. Considering these important factors should result in the development of a more effective plan. These important factors include the following:

1. The recovery plan should be broadened to include not only recovery of computer operations but also ensure continuity of general business operations.
2. The internal audit department should be involved in all phases of the contingency planning process.
3. The human element should be considered. For example, at times of disaster the firm should provide assistance to employees and their families, such as locating temporary apartments and providing transportation to work.
4. The contingency plan should address relations with customers, vendors, and other service firms. For example, vendors and customers should be notified of the alternate business location and the length of time the firm will be operating at that site.
5. Managers and employees should be made aware of their responsibilities in the DCRP process. Thus, key employees should be given a complete copy of the contingency planning documents and a summary of the DCRP should be distributed to all employees.
6. The contingency plan should embrace telecommunications backup. For example, several means of maintaining communications should be investigated and incorporated into the plan.

SUMMARY

Security measures protect the physical assets, data assets, and human resources of a firm from a wide variety of risk exposures. In manual systems they restrict access to the assets, protect the assets from natural disasters, and protect the assets from breakdowns and business interruptions. In computer-based systems security measures also protect computer hardware and software from the natural environment, from unauthorized access, and from interruption. Furthermore, they protect data from unauthorized access, loss, and alteration; they monitor attempted accesses and changes; and they enable lost data to be reconstructed. These six objectives of security should be monitored by forming a security group and conducting an annual audit of the implemented security controls.

Earthquakes, floods, bombings, and other natural and human-made disasters occur regularly throughout the U.S. and the rest of the world. These disasters in-

evitably shut down business operations. The longer a disaster shuts down a firm's operations, the more likely it will never reopen for business. Thus, quickly recovering from a disaster is crucial to a firm's survival as a going concern. Studies have demonstrated time after time that a comprehensive disaster contingency and recovery plan must be prepared to survive a severe crisis. The plan provides guidelines that, if followed, enable a firm to minimize damage and restore both its computer operations and regular business operations.

APPENDIX 1 TO CHAPTER 9

ILLUSTRATION OF GRANDPARENT-PARENT-CHILD BACKUP PROCEDURE

Figure 9-6 pictures the G-P-C procedure when the processing cycle is one day in length. Over a three-day

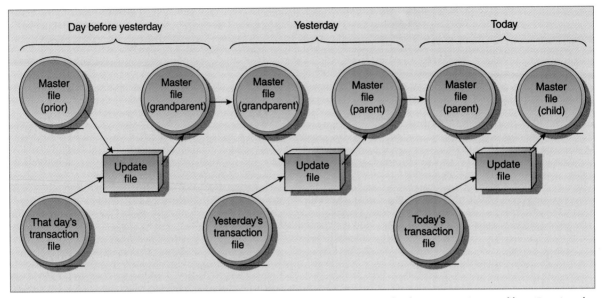

FIGURE 9-6 Grandparent-parent-child reconstruction procedure for creating backup magnetic tape files. (Reprinted by permission of the publisher from *Management Information Systems*, first edition by Raymond McLeod, Jr. Copyright © 1979 by Science Research Associates, Inc.)

period three generations of master files would be generated. All three generations of master files would be retained during this period, together with the transaction files. Furthermore, one generation would be kept at a site remote from the computer facility. If the "child" file were destroyed or if during later use it were found to contain errors, it would be reconstructed by reprocessing the "parent" file against the transaction file for today. If both the child and parent files were destroyed, they could still be reconstructed by reprocessing the "grandparent" file and the last two days of transaction files to create new files. Note that during tomorrow's processing run the grandparent file may be released to create tomorrow's child file.

....

APPENDIX 2 TO CHAPTER 9

KEY ITEMS TO INCLUDE IN EMERGENCY, BACKUP, AND RECOVERY DISASTER CONTINGENCY PLANS

Emergency Plan

An emergency plan should contain, as a minimum, the following considerations:

1. Prepare an organization chart, showing the chain of command involved in DCRP. A disaster recovery manager and a second in command should be designated to lead the DCRP, and they should appoint the key team members depicted on the chart.

2. Determine disasters that trigger the entire DCRP or only part of the plan. Conducting a risk analysis should identify the significant disasters unique to a particular industry and the firm's geographical location.

3. Determine who will contact fire, police, and other agencies.

4. Determine the personnel who will remain at headquarters to lock doors, power-down computers, and perform other vital duties.

5. Prepare a map of primary and secondary evacuation routes and post these throughout the organization.

6. Develop a method for communicating the "all-clear" signal that indicates when employees can return to headquarters or the temporary business location.

Backup Plan

Representative elements in a backup plan include the following:

1. Store duplicates of vital software, data, and records at appropriate off-premises locations.

2. Identify the key critical and noncritical full-time and part-time employees and temporary hires who will be involved in the backup operations.

3. Cross-train key employees to perform several duties. Oftentimes, after a disaster strikes, many key employees are injured or otherwise temporarily unable to perform their jobs.

4. Select the most appropriate type of backup system to quickly resume operations. Choose an alternate site for conducting regular business operations that is outside the area of anticipated destruction. Several options are available for resuming data processing operations. **Manual backup systems** may be feasible for small and medium-sized organizations that process low volumes of transactions. Decentralized firms with multiple compatible computer sites should airfreight critical jobs to an alternative firm location. A reciprocal arrangement can be made between two firms who contractually agree to provide backup for each other following a disaster. A third-party agreement to supply backup can be formed between the firm and a data processing service bureau, university or vendor's computer facility.

Other disaster recovery services include cold sites, hot sites, cooperative hot sites, and flying hot sites. A **cold site** is an alternate data processing facility equipped with all the necessary resources, except for personnel, files, and computer equipment. Following a disaster, a prearranged plan is activated to move the firm's personnel, vital files, and newly acquired or rented equipment to the cold site. A **hot site** is a fully staffed and equipped computer facility contracted to provide temporary and immediate off-site services to firms suffering disasters. Vital records are moved to this location and processed by the hot site's data processing staff and equipment. A **cooperative hot site** is similar to a hot site, except that the site is co-owned by two or more members who share operating expenses. A **flying hot site** is similar to a hot site, except that the site stores up-to-date copies of the firm's vital records and software.

Recovery Plan

Some key items to incorporate into a recovery plan are the following:

1. Appoint a recovery manager and a second in command. These officials should define specific assignments of key recovery team members.

2. Select an off-site facility to store backups and periodically inspect the facility.

3. Maintain liaison with insurance firms to facilitate the assessment of damages to resources destroyed in a disaster.

4. Arrange with vendors to have resources delivered to the alternate firm site and the backup facility.

5. Establish a timetable for the recovery operations.

6. Develop a strategy to ensure the strict control of applications processed at the backup site.

REVIEW PROBLEM WITH SOLUTION

CAMPUS BOOKSTORE, SIXTH INSTALLMENT

The Campus Bookstore (described in the Review Problem at the end of Chapter 1) continues to develop its new microcomputer system. In this installment the bookstore manager requests that the auditor from the bookstore's public accounting firm prepare a report that recommends security measures for the new system.

Required

Identify selected security measures that should help protect the computer facilities, assets, and information of the bookstore.

Solution

Security measures to protect the cash, inventory, and fixed assets should include (1) locked doors, (2) locked cash registers, (3) burglar alarms, (4) safes, (5) insurance coverage, and (6) sprinkler systems. Measures to protect the minicomputer facilities should include several of the above plus (1) air conditioning, (2) humidity controls, (3) FM 200 gas, (4) a disaster contingency and recovery plan, (5) passwords for all authorized users of terminals (including point-of-sale terminals), (6) preventative maintenance, and (7) an arrangement for a backup minicomputer system (this arrangement is often found in the backup plan, a major component of the disaster contingency and recovery plan). Measures to protect the data (in addition to passwords) include (1) limitations on the capability of terminals to access data files, (2) automatic lockouts on all terminals, (3) ROM, (4) internal file labels, (5) transaction logs, (6) console logs, (7) backup copies of all master files, and (8) a reconstruction procedure.

KEY TERMS

console log (348)
cooperative hot site (355)
disaster contingency and recovery plan (DCRP) (340)
emergency plan (352)
encryption (346)
external file label (349)
fault tolerance (352)
flying hot site (355)
grandparent-parent-child procedure (G-P-C) (350)
hot site (355)
internal file label (349)
keyboard lock (346)
library log (348)
lockbox trash containers (347)
lockout (349)
maintenance plan (352)
manual backup system (355)
password (344)
periodic dump procedure (350)
principle of least privilege access (343)
private key encryption scheme (347)
public key encryption scheme (347)
read-only memory (ROM) (349)
reconstruction procedure (350)
recovery plan (352)
Resource Access Control Facility (RACF) (348)
rollback (352)
rollforward procedure (350)
RSA public key encryption scheme (347)
system and program change log (348)
tape file protection ring (349)
test plan (352)
transaction log (348)
vital records program (350)
write-protect notch (349)
zero disking (347)

REVIEW QUESTIONS

9-1. What are the purposes of security measures in computer-based AIS?

9-2. Identify a variety of security measures that are suitable for a firm having a manual AIS.

9-3. Identify security measures that are suitable for protecting physical resources such as cash and fixed assets from theft, destruction, and breakdowns.

9-4. Identify security measures that are suitable for protecting computer hardware facilities from unauthorized access.

9-5. Identify security measures that are suitable for protecting computer facilities from disasters and breakdowns.

9-6. Identify security measures that are suitable for protecting data and information in computer-based systems from unauthorized access.

9-7. What factors complicate the task of devising measures to restrict access to data and information?

9-8. Identify security measures that are suitable for protecting a firm's data and information stored on computerized media from loss or improper alteration.

9-9. Distinguish between a private encryption key scheme and a public encryption key scheme.

9-10. What is the Clipper chip?

9-11. Define fault tolerance.

9-12. Identify security measures that can detect attempted accesses and changes of computerized data in (a) batch processing systems, (b) on-line processing systems, and (c) microcomputer systems.

9-13. Contrast security measures that facilitate recovery and the reconstruction of lost data in (a) batch processing systems, (b) on-line processing systems, and (c) microcomputer systems.

9-14. Define the following component plans that are included in a disaster contingency and recovery plan: (a) emergency plan, (b) backup plan, (c) recovery plan, (d) test plan, and (e) maintenance plan.

9-15. Distinguish between a cold site and a hot site.

9-16. What is a cooperative hot site?

9-17. What is the role of internal auditors in disaster contingency and recovery planning?

DISCUSSION QUESTIONS

9-18. What depth of knowledge should be possessed by accountants concerning (a) security measures and (b) application controls?

9-19. What is the relationship between security measures and general controls?

9-20. What are the features of on-line processing systems that create difficulties in establishing a sound control framework?

9-21. Discuss the likely effects of magnetic disk storage on data security and control.

9-22. Compare and contrast security measures needed by (a) Ann Strong's consulting firm, (b) Infoage, Inc., and (c) a large firm owning one or more mainframe computers.

9-23. What type of disaster contingency and recovery plan is needed by Ann Strong's consulting firm? How would this plan differ from one prepared by Infoage, Inc.?

9-24. Why do you think the human element is often ignored when firms prepare disaster contingency and recovery plans?

9-25. Why do disaster contingency and recovery plans mainly emphasize the recovery aspect of computer operations?

9-26. What is the relationship of risk analysis to disaster contingency and recovery planning?

PROBLEMS

9-1. Aidbart Company has recently installed a new on-line, data-base computer system. CRT units are located throughout the firm with at least one CRT unit located in each department. James Lanta, vice-president of finance, has overall responsibility for the firm's management information system, but he relies heavily on Ivan West, director of MIS, for technical assistance and direction.

Lanta was one of the primary supporters of the new system because he knew it would provide labor savings. However, he is concerned about security of the new system. Lanta was walking through the purchasing department recently when he observed an Aidbart buyer using a CRT unit to inquire about the current price for a specific part used by Aidbart. The new system enabled the buyer to have the data regarding the part brought up on the screen as well as each Aidbart product that used the part and the total manufacturing cost of the products using the part. The buyer told Lanta that, in addition to inquiring about the part, he could also change the cost of parts.

Lanta scheduled a meeting with West to review his concerns regarding the new system. Lanta stated, "Ivan, I am concerned about the type and amount of data that can be accessed through the CRTs. How can we protect ourselves against unauthorized access to data in our computer file? Also, what happens if we have a natural disaster such as a fire, a passive threat such as a power outage, or some active threat resulting in malicious damage—could we continue to operate? We need to show management that we are on top of these things. Would you please outline the procedures we now have, or need to have, to protect ourselves."

West responded by saying, "Jim, there are areas of vulnerability in the design and implementation of any automated system. Some of these are more prevalent in on-line systems such as ours—especially with respect to privacy, integrity, and confidentiality of data. The four major points of vulnerability with which we should be concerned are the hardware, the software, the people, and the network."

Required

a. For each of the four major points of vulnerability identified by Ivan West,

    (1) Give one potential threat or risk to the system.

    (2) Identify the action(s) to be taken to protect the system from that threat or risk.

b. Ivan West knows that he must develop a contingency plan for Aidbart Company's new system in order to be prepared for a natural disaster, passive threat, or active threat to the system.

    (1) Discuss why Aidbart should have a contingency plan.

    (2) Outline and briefly describe the *major components of a contingency plan* that could be implemented in the case of a natural disaster, passive threat, or active threat to the system.

(CMA *adapted*)

9-2. MailMed Inc. (MMI), a pharmaceutical firm, provides discounted prescription drugs through direct mail. MMI has a small systems staff that designs and writes MMI's customized software. Until recently, MMI's transaction data were transmitted to a service bureau for processing on its hardware.

MMI has experienced significant sales growth as the cost of prescription drugs has increased and medical insurance firms have been tightening reimbursements in order to restrain premium cost increases. As a result of these increased sales, MMI has purchased its own computer hardware. The computer center is installed on the ground floor of its two-story headquarters building. It is behind large plate glass windows so that the state-of-the-art computer center can be displayed as a measure of the firm's success and attract customer and investor attention. The computer area is equipped with FM 200 gas fire suppression equipment and an uninterruptible power supply system.

MMI has hired a small computer operations staff to operate this computer center. To handle MMI's current level of business, the operations staff is on a two-shift schedule, five days per week. MMI's systems and programming staff, now located in the same building, has access to the computer center and can test new programs and program changes when the operations staff is not available. As the systems and programming staff is small and the work demands have increased, systems and programming documentation is developed only when time is available.

Periodically, but not on a scheduled basis, MMI backs up its programs and data files, storing them at an off-site location.

Unfortunately, due to several days of heavy rains, MMI's building recently experienced serious flooding that reached several feet into the first-floor level and affected not only the computer hardware but also the data and program files that were on site.

Required

a. Describe the security weaknesses that existed at MailMed Inc. prior to the flood occurrence.

b. Describe at least five components that should be incorporated in a formal *disaster recovery plan* in order that MailMed Inc. can become operational within 72 hours after a disaster affects its computer operations capability.

c. Identify at least three factors, other than the plan itself, that MailMed Inc.'s management should consider in formulating a formal disaster recovery plan.

(CMA adapted)

9-3. What security measure(s) would be appropriate in preventing or detecting each of the following errors, natural disasters, or undesirable practices?

  a. A fire in an office area spread to the computer center of a firm. All the computer facilities and many files were destroyed.

  b. A computer hardware component malfunctioned during a processing run, causing many of the accounts receivable records to be lost. The records must be reconstructed manually from stored transaction documents and past monthly statements.

  c. A production-line employee walked into the tool room just before quitting time one day, put a small precision tool in his jacket pocket, and took it home.

  d. Two accountants posted adjusting journal entries concurrently from separate terminals to accounts in the firm's on-line general ledger file. Both entries affected a common general ledger account, so that one of the entries was written over and the account balance was not updated to reflect that entry.

  e. An inexperienced computer operator mounted the accounts receivable master file (a read-only file stored on magnetic tape) for the daily updating run. However, the operator inadvertently designated the tape drive on which it was mounted as an output drive and erased many of the customer records.

  f. A firm's computer facilities were extensively damaged by a hurricane. The firm, located in South Florida, was unprepared for the disaster. As a result confusion reigned, many of the firm's operations were crippled, and employee paychecks were delayed.

  g. The computer operator was running the payroll program when the processing was interrupted by a 45-minute power failure. All data in memory at the time the power failure occurred were lost.

  h. A magnetic tape containing yesterday's sales transactions was accidentally moved to the scratch-tape rack and could not be located.

  i. A computer printout of confidential personnel data was routed to the production manager by mistake.

  j. An employee payroll file, maintained on a removable magnetic disk, was destroyed by a small fire in the computer center. Paydays were consequently delayed.

9-4. What security measure(s) would be appropriate to prevent, detect, or minimize the adverse effects from each of the following computer crimes/frauds?

  a. A teenaged hacker broke into the data base of a military contractor from a home computer that was emulating a terminal. He viewed classified specifications of a new fighter plane.

  b. A disgruntled computer operator accessed master files through the main computer console and altered data in their header labels.

  c. A warehouse worker accessed the confidential salary file in the data base via a terminal located in the warehouse.

  d. A payroll clerk accessed her salary records from a terminal and increased her salary level.

  e. A group of computer information systems majors with microcomputers and modems illegally obtained the password to the university's mainframe computer file containing student grade records, accessed the file, and made several grade changes to their personal records.

  f. A repairman from an equipment servicing firm accessed a teller's terminal one weekend at a bank branch office where he was servicing typewriters and other office machines. He entered a fictitious deposit of $1000 to his personal checking account.

  g. Late one night, a computer-literate janitor, using a terminal, illegally gained access to several on-line accounting department files, browsed through the files, and made copies of two of the files. He sold the files for a large sum of money.

  h. A group of teenagers broke into the U.S. Defense Department's computer located in Washington, D.C., stole confidential data, and sold it to an unfriendly foreign government.

9-5. What security measure(s) would be appropriate to prevent, detect, or minimize the adverse effects from each of the following computer crimes/frauds?

  a. A computer programmer was fired for failure to satisfactorily perform his job responsibilities.

Sometime during the two-week notice period, he was transferred to a less sensitive job and his passwords and other identifiers were removed from the system. On April 1, exactly three months after the programmer was terminated, the mainframe computer's hard disks were erased and the computer crashed.

b. A firm's vital accounting data stored on hard disks were destroyed by a computer virus.

c. A small consulting firm processes all its applications on its sole microcomputer. The computer, kept on the accountant's desk, was apparently stolen during the previous night.

d. A terrorist broke into a computer center and detonated a plastic bomb, which did $2,000,000 damage to a mainframe computer system.

e. A visitor to the computer center of a nationwide publication carried away a diskette containing a list of subscribers. After using a service bureau to prepare a hard-copy printout, she sold the list to direct-mail advertisers.

f. A disgruntled employee planted a "time bomb" to systematically destroy all data and files maintained on 500 networked computers.

g. Users often discarded their passwords, identification numbers, disks, computer reports, and other items that they believed to be worthless, in the wastebasket. A computer-literate high school student, working as an office helper, stole the items from a trash container located outside the building. He made considerable sums of money selling the "trash" to his employer's competitors.

9-6. What security and other control measures would be appropriate to prevent, detect, or minimize the adverse effects from each of the following computer crimes/frauds?

a. A manufacturing firm's major competitor gained access to its on-line mainframe computer. The culprits then downloaded a secret patent on a new product, filed the patent with the proper authorities, and received the exclusive rights to develop the product.

b. A hacker, using a tape recorder, tapped into a telephone line of a bank used to electronically transmit funds to overseas locations. The recording was used to obtain the code needed to transfer the funds.

c. A trusted employee obtained permission from his supervisor to take his firm-issued laptop home each night to work on firm business. However, he in fact used the laptop to conduct a side business of selling deer antlers to the Orient.

d. One day during working hours, an employee of a large insulation firm located in Harrison, Arkan-

sas, illegally copied over $5000 of software packages. He sold these packages at substantially discounted prices to friends.

e. A programmer working for a large bank used his computer to access a customer's dormant account and siphoned $25,000 from the account.

f. A firm was charged with copyright violations for using unauthorized copies of software that employees had installed on the local-area network. Top management was unaware that these illegal copies were in use throughout the firm.

g. An executive employed by an insurance firm gained unauthorized access to the customer policy file. During a three-month period, she created 5000 fictitious insurance policies with a total value of $100,000,000. When the annual financial statements were prepared, assets were overstated by $100,000,000.

h. Hackers gained unauthorized access to the mainframe computer of the long-distance telephone carrier and downloaded a list of 25,000 telephone credit card numbers, which they sold on the street for $10 each.

i. An employee used his microcomputer to play games on firm time. When caught one day, he admitted that he had been playing computer games an average of two hours a day for the last six months. However, he stated that he always completed his job responsibilities before he played the games.

j. An ex-employee gained unauthorized access to his former employer's on-line data-base files, downloaded a top secret formula for a new soft drink, and sold the formula to a foreign competitor.

k. A vengeful computer programmer gained unauthorized access to the unattended terminal of the data-base administrator and planted a computer virus. Two days later, the virus wiped out the data stored on every microcomputer connected to the firm's local-area network.

l. During the electronic transmission of information between branch offices, an internal auditor discovered that, on several occasions, a major competitor had illegally accessed the firm's pricing data relating to new products.

9-7. What security and other control measures would be appropriate to prevent, detect, or minimize the adverse effects from each of the following noncomputer occurrences of fraud?

a. A bartender rang up one-half of the dollar amount of each sale and "skimmed" the other half, which he pocketed.

b. Rather than mail in a $1000 cash payment for

merchandise, the firm's cashier turned the funds over to the sales rep handling the account. The sales rep pocketed the cash.

c. A supplier unintentionally prepared duplicate copies of invoices for merchandise sold to a customer. The customer mistakenly paid both invoices and the supplier kept the cash. The supplier, pleased with making easy money, decided to extend the scheme to all its customers.

d. During an interrogation, an employee suspected of committing fraud confessed to embezzling $780,000 over a five-year period. However, the organization's written code of conduct did not indicate the specific action to be taken in fraud cases. As a result, the employee was not reported to law enforcement, but reprimanded and suspended without pay for a two-week period.

e. A university faculty member, while on official university business trips, altered restaurant receipts, thus overstating his expense reports. During the two-year period the professor used the scheme, he defrauded the university of $1500.

f. An accounting clerk added 10 hours of overtime to her time card for hours she never worked. She has performed this scheme many times during the last several months.

g. A purchasing agent frequently bought goods for the firm that were not needed by the firm and stole them for personal use.

9-8. What security and other control measures would be appropriate to prevent, detect, or minimize the adverse effects from each of the following noncomputer occurrences of fraud?

a. A vendor had provided a purchasing agent with expensive gifts, amounting to over $500,000 over a three-year period. In return, the purchasing agent favored this vendor's bids over many others.

b. A clerk working for a large retailer received $100 in cash from a customer for the purchase of a briefcase. She failed to ring up the receipt and pocketed the cash.

c. A bookkeeper took small amounts of cash from the imprest petty-cash fund. She concealed the theft by preparing fictitious receipts with a form creation program, and filling out the dummy receipts for the amount of cash taken.

d. A manager approved invoices for consulting services never performed and split the receipts with the consultant.

e. Last year, a salesperson accumulated 250,000 airline frequent flier miles while traveling on official firm business. He sold the frequent flier miles to

relatives and friends, without informing his employer.

f. A bookkeeper embezzled about $125,000 in firm funds by using a simple on-book fraud scheme. She debited miscellaneous expenses and credited cash for the funds taken.

g. A salesclerk working for an office supplies firm stole small, expensive items, such as pens and calculators, by placing them in a trash bin. His accomplice, the janitor, retrieved the items, which the two subsequently split.

9-9. The Landers Corporation has established the following procedures pertaining to its information systems function.

a. Access to the computer room where the mainframe is kept is limited to the firm's employees.

b. Access to the firm's 12 microcomputer data-base servers is restricted to the firm's managers, accountants, data processing employees, and the internal auditor.

c. The vault door of the disk and tape library is locked at night and opened each morning by the data processing manager or his assistant. The combination is known only to information systems personnel.

d. All on-line disk files are dumped to magnetic tapes every 30 days. The tapes are stored in the vault.

e. The grandparent-parent-child retention cycle is used for all batch sequential applications using magnetic tape files, with ancestors stored in the vault.

f. An administrative manager authorizes the development of applications, approves run schedules, and supervises the work of programmers, analysts, and operators. Another of her responsibilities is to review all program modifications.

g. The programmers and analysts have flexible work requirements and frequently work evenings or weekends to "debug" and test programs on the mainframe computer.

h. All systems development is initiated by the data processing manager. An informal mechanism exists to assess users' needs and to prioritize application requests. Priorities are determined by the data processing manager according to a long-range master plan initiated last year. The information systems function absorbs all costs of development work.

i. Each program is assigned to a programmer who is responsible for coding, testing, debugging, and documenting that program. Programmers tend to prepare very minimal and highly technical documentation; in order to run applications, computer operators often must obtain verbal instructions from the programmer who developed the program. The only copy of the documentation is kept in the vault.

Required

For each of the nine preceding procedures, identify the strengths and/or weaknesses present. For each strength, indicate why it is a strength; for each weakness, suggest a procedure to correct the deficiency.

(CIA *adapted*)

9-10. A preliminary survey of a firm's data-base system and EDP (information system) department reveals the following:

a. There are no restrictions regarding type of transaction or access to the on-line terminals.

b. All users and EDP personnel have access to the extensive system documentation.

c. Before being entered in the user authorization table, user passwords and access codes are established by user management and approved by the manager of computer programming.

d. The manager of computer programming establishes and controls the data-base directory.

e. User requests for data are validated by the system against a transactions-conflict matrix to ensure that data are transmitted only to authorized users.

f. System access requires the users to input their passwords, and terminal activity logs are maintained.

g. Input data are edited for reasonableness and completeness, transaction control totals are generated, and transaction logs are maintained.

h. Processing control totals are generated and reconciled to changes in the data base.

i. Output is reconciled to transaction and input control totals. The resulting reports are printed and placed in a bin outside the EDP room for pickup by the users at their convenience.

j. Backup copies of the data base are generated daily and stored in the file library area, access to which is restricted to EDP personnel.

Required

a. List all effective controls and security measures that are currently installed.

b. Evaluate the relative adequacies of the general and application (transaction) controls, and indicate significant omissions.

(CIA *adapted*)

9-11. KLM Electronics, a subsidiary of your firm, is a retailer of home electronic items. KLM has grown rapidly in the past three years. Starting with a single store, there are now six stores in four cities employing 150 people. The most distant store is 300 miles from the home office.

Each store has two personal computers serving as cash registers that operate on-line via phone lines back to the main office. When clerks enter sales data, a receipt is printed and a cash drawer opened. Other operations including payroll, accounts receivable, accounts payable, purchasing and inventory are also computerized. All buying is done centrally at the main office.

An employee recently quit and took a copy of the price book containing cost and price information on all 1000 items carried in the stores. For the first time, management has become aware of the need to provide security for sensitive information.

As a first step, you have been called in to perform an internal audit of information security. Top management has promised full cooperation in this effort.

Required

a. What important questions should be asked of management concerning information security?

b. Identify security risks posed by the use of the on-line sales terminals.

c. For each security risk identified in **b,** suggest a method for controlling the risk. Match the method of control to each particular risk.

(CIA *adapted*)

9-12. You are performing an operational audit of the management information system (MIS) department, which integrates planning, development, and computer operations. The MIS department has a staff of 100 people and an annual budget of $8,000,000.

The firm's 10-story, 60-year-old headquarters building is located in one of the older sections of South Miami, Florida. The building is adjacent to the South Miami Hotel and Kitchen, a facility providing food and lodging to about 500 homeless people daily.

The firm's data center is on the basement level of the building, next to the boiler room and rest rooms. Visitors are allowed to obtain permits from a receptionist located on the first floor to observe, through the "shatter-proof" glass walls, the impressive computer installation. The location also allows the visitors to view the computer operators mounting the disk packs or tapes and removing computer reports. The reports are placed in a container outside the data center; periodically, one of the accountants distributes the reports to the appropriate managers. Before they leave, visitors are required to discard their permits in a wastebasket outside the data center.

One morning in the cafeteria you overhear the following conversation between the payroll system supervisor and his manager.

"Russell did it again! The payroll checks had to be ready by 6 o'clock this morning, but the payroll system went down last night. Operations notified Russell, our super programmer, who came in at 3:00 a.m. Fortunately, the librarian had not locked the door to the disk and file library while he was taking a short break. This enabled Russell to pick up the right tape, mount it onto the computer himself, and fix the problem in 25 minutes with some changes to the program. Earlier, I had guaranteed the controller of the corporate accounting department that the system would be working like a charm. I am glad that the problem has been rectified, so that no one needs to be informed of the change. Documentation for the change will be made when Russell can free himself from his tight work schedule."

When you talk to the director of MIS, you note the following:

- Many of the legacy systems have been in place for 15 or more years. Maintenance and enhancements have been made where required. Users are still receiving reports produced by the same COBOL and RPG programs used since system implementation. Some of the reports that are produced weekly and monthly for management decision-making purposes are over 100 pages in length.

- A disaster contingency and recovery plan has been set up for the MIS department. The plan was prepared by the director of MIS and his staff. However, because of the high costs involved, it has never been audited, tested, or updated since it was prepared two years ago.

- The corporation has a backup site one block away, where documentation and backup disks and tapes are stored in duplicate. The backup site was selected for its proximity, which allows quick access by authorized staff and provides nearby storage.

Required

Identify the risks inherent in the operations of the MIS department, and for each risk recommend a compensating internal control.

(SMAC *adapted*)

9-13. The headquarters of Gleicken Corporation, a private firm with $3.5 million in annual sales, is located in Los Angeles, California. Gleicken provides for its 150 clients an on-line legal software service that includes data storage and administrative activities for law offices. The firm has grown rapidly since its inception three years ago, and its data processing department has mushroomed to accommodate this growth. Because Gleick-

en's president and sales personnel spend a great deal of time out of the office soliciting new clients, the planning of the facilities has been left to the data processing professionals.

Gleicken recently moved its headquarters facility into a remodeled warehouse on the outskirts of the city. While remodeling the warehouse, the architects retained much of the original structure, including the wooden-shingled exterior and exposed wooden beams throughout the interior. The minicomputer distributive processing hardware is situated in a large open area with high ceilings and skylights. The openness makes the data processing area accessible to the rest of the staff and encourages a team approach to problem solving. Before occupying the new facility, city inspectors declared the building safe; that is, it contains adequate fire extinguishers, smoke detectors, sufficient exits, and so on.

In an effort to provide further protection for its large data base of client information, Gleicken has instituted a tape backup procedure that is on a time-delay mechanism and automatically backs up the data base weekly, every Sunday evening, avoiding interruption in the daily operations and procedures. All the tapes are then labeled and carefully stored on shelves reserved for this purpose in the data processing department. The departmental operator's manual has instructions on how to use these tapes to restore the data base should the need arise. In the event of an emergency, there is a home phone list of the individuals in the data processing department. Gleicken has recently increased its liability insurance for data loss from $50,000 to the current $100,000.

This past Saturday, the Gleicken headquarters building was completely ruined by fire, and the firm must now inform its clients that all their information has been destroyed.

Required

a. Describe the computer security weaknesses present at Gleicken Corporation that made it possible for a disastrous data loss to occur.

b. (1) List the components that should have been included in the disaster contingency and recovery plan at Gleicken Corporation in order to ensure computer recovery within 72 hours.

(2) What factors, other than those included in the plan itself, should a firm consider when formulating a disaster contingency and recovery plan?

(CMA *adapted*)

9-14. Refer to Problem 8-17, the Central Savings and Loan Association of Jefferson City, Missouri.

Required

List specific security measures for this system.

9-15. Refer to Problem 8-16, Gose Hotels of Reno, Nevada.

Required

Give specific descriptions of security measures needed for this system.

CONTINUING CASE

With respect to the small firm that you selected in Chapter 1, complete the following requirements:

a. Determine the specific security measures the firm has implemented to protect its cash and fixed assets from theft, destruction, and breakdown. Evaluate the strengths and weaknesses of these security measures.

b. If the firm maintains a disaster contingency and recovery plan (DCRP),

    (1) Examine the major components of the plan and evaluate the DCRP's strengths and weaknesses.

    (2) Determine the person or persons responsible for preparing the plan and keeping it up-to-date.

    (3) Determine if the DCRP is audited. If so, who is responsible for conducting the audit?

    (4) If the plan is not audited, determine the reasons why it is not audited.

    (5) If the DCRP is tested, determine the types of tests conducted to spot loopholes in the plan.

c. If a disaster strikes, what type of backup facilities are available to run critical applications? Evaluate the strengths and weaknesses of these backup facilities.

d. Determine the procedures followed by the firm to back up its critical data and information. Evaluate the strengths and weaknesses of these procedures.

e. Determine the procedures followed by the firm to recover and reconstruct lost data. Evaluate the strengths and weaknesses of these procedures.

f. If the firm employs a local-area network or other type of network, determine

    (1) If passwords are used to control access to resources.

    (2) How often the passwords are changed.

    (3) The party or parties responsible for maintaining the passwords.

    (4) Any problems the firm has encountered in using passwords.

g. If the firm uses encryption techniques to prevent unauthorized access to sensitive data, determine the types of encryption schemes in use.

CHAPTER
10

AUDITING OF
INFORMATION SYSTEMS

THE LEARNING OBJECTIVES OF THIS CHAPTER ARE TO ENABLE YOU TO:

1. Describe the various types of audits and their purposes.

2. Discuss basic auditing considerations, including ethics and major audit standards and the effects of computerization.

3. Discuss the auditing process, especially with respect to financial audits and evaluation of the internal control structure.

4. Describe the three major approaches to audits of computer-based information systems, as well as audit techniques that are applied within each of the approaches.

5. Discuss changes in the auditing environment and emerging auditing techniques and tools to meet these changes.

INTRODUCTION

NATURE OF AUDITS

Although various types of audits are performed, perhaps the most typical audit focuses on the accounting information system (AIS) of a firm and the financial records. Other important audits focus on promoting effective and efficient firm operations. Before an audit can be undertaken, a thorough knowledge of the internal control structure and the specific internal controls and security measures discussed in Chapters 7 through 9 is essential. Auditing consists of a process in which a variety of approaches and techniques are applied. **Audits** are examinations performed to assess and evaluate an activity or object, such as whether the internal controls implemented into the AIS are working as prescribed by management, or whether the data processing function needs improvement.

Both external and internal auditing have become highly refined in America, owing in large part to the efforts of the major professional accounting associations. Another influence on auditing has been the federal Foreign Corrupt Practices Act of 1977. However, the auditing profession must continually strive to improve its techniques; otherwise, it will be unable to cope with the developments in information technology and the increasing demands by users of accounting information.

ROLES OF AUDITORS AND ACCOUNTANTS

Both accountants and systems analysts have roles to play with respect to auditing. Many accounting majors will accept positions as auditors and, as such, will be deeply involved in audit programs and processes. Those of you who become industrial or governmental accountants will need to rely on the information received from AISs. Thus you will be interested in helping auditors to evaluate generated information and to detect control weaknesses in the systems. Those of you who become involved in systems analysis and design will be expected to develop systems that provide reliable information. You will discover that you need to anticipate the problems and weaknesses that auditors are likely to detect during their audits.

Auditors are increasingly being used as advisors during systems development projects. In their roles as advisors, they might aid in establishing control objectives, selecting suitable controls and security measures, estimating costs of controls, and determining the most effective audit schedules and procedures.

TYPES OF AUDITS

Audits that may be performed within a typical firm are operational, compliance, project management and change control (formerly known as a system development audit), internal control, financial, and fraud audits. These types of audits are summarized in Figure 10-1.

Four types of auditors are involved in performing the listed audits. **Internal auditors,** who are employees of the firms being audited, usually perform management, compliance, operational, project management and change control, internal control, and fraud audits. **External auditors,** who are independent public accountants, typically perform financial audits. External auditors are appointed by the owners, for example the stockholders of a corporation, to examine the management's financial statements. In some financial audits the external auditors receive assistance from internal auditors; however, the external auditors are responsible for attesting to the fairness of the financial statements. A third type of auditor, the **government auditor,** also performs compliance audits or examines the records of firms under the supervision of government agencies. For instance, government bank examiners perform audits of banks; auditors employed by a state's auditor general may perform audits of school districts and state agencies. The fourth type of auditor is the **fraud auditor,** the newest type of specialist. He or she specializes in investigating fraud and works closely with internal auditors and attorneys. A majority of fraud auditors

---

- An **operational audit** is concerned with the efficiency and effectiveness with which all resources are being used to accomplish tasks, as well as the extent to which practices and procedures accord with established policies.
- A **compliance audit** is concerned with the extent to which laws, governmental regulations, controls, and other obligations to external bodies have been followed.
- A **project management and change control audit** (formerly known as a systems development audit) is concerned with the efficiency and effectiveness with which the various phases of the systems development life cycle are being conducted.
- An **internal control audit** is concerned with evaluating the internal control structure.
- A **financial audit** is concerned with the fairness with which financial statements present the firm's financial position, results of operations, and cash flows.
- A **fraud audit** is a nonrecurring audit conducted to gather evidence to determine if fraud is occurring, has occurred, or will occur, and to resolve the matter by affixing responsibility.

FIGURE 10-1   A summary of the major types of audits.

have accounting backgrounds and are either self-employed fraud investigators or work for various organizations. For example, a large number of fraud examiners are employed in the fraud investigation units of the FBI, large public accounting firms, the IRS, insurance firms, and large corporations.

Our main concern in the following sections is with the financial audit, a widely performed audit. The financial audit is centered on the attest function, a primary function performed by the external auditor. The operational audit of the data processing function, performed by internal auditors, will also be examined.

BASIC AUDITING CONSIDERATIONS

Before discussing the auditing process, approaches, and techniques, we should answer three questions:

- What is the role of ethics in auditing and what standards are needed?
- What are the effects of automation on audits?
- Why has the transaction cycle approach to auditing gained general acceptance?

ETHICS AND AUDIT STANDARDS

Need for Ethics   Every profession has a standard of professional conduct and practice. Professional codes of ethics state in written form the definable, practicable, and enforceable rules of conduct. Codes of ethics for auditors, such as Ann Strong, CPA and CMA, express the attitudes and principles that have been found to contribute to effective audits, that protect the interests of the owners of firms being audited as well as the public, and that encourage equitable and satisfactory client-auditor relationships.

Auditing codes of ethics also serve several very useful purposes. First, they are educational, in that they provide members of the auditing profession with guides to the kind of ethical behavior that historical experience has found to attract and justify the confidence of the public. Second, they serve as impersonal standards that auditors can use to support their decisions. Third, they narrow the areas in which an auditor must struggle with doubts.

In the field of auditing, the codes of ethics are called codes of professional conduct. Internal auditors follow the Standards for the Professional Practice of Internal Auditing (promulgated by the Institute of Internal Auditors), whereas external auditors, such as Ann Strong, observe the Statements on Auditing Standards (promulgated by the American Institute of Certified Public Accounts [AICPA]). These two sets of standards have many more similarities than differences.

Before leaving this broad discussion level, we should recall that independent consultants in the areas of management and information systems also have codes of ethics. The code that pertains to management consultants within CPA firms has been developed by the AICPA. It is similar in many respects to the auditors' standards.

Content of Standards   **Audit standards** prescribe professional qualities and conduct. They can be divided into two groups. One audit standard group specifies professional characteristics relating to adequate technical training and proficiency, independent attitude, and due care during audits. Exhibiting due care involves planning the work adequately, supervising assistants properly, and gathering sufficient evidence. The other audit standard group pertains to the scope of the audits. Although each type of audit has its own scope, the financial audit must include (1) an evaluation of the internal control structure to assess control risk as well as (2) a review of all the pertinent documents and records. Thus the financial audit encompasses the internal control audit.

Effect of Computerization on Standards When a firm installs a computer-based AIS, this act of computerization does affect the audit procedures to be applied. We will briefly survey the effects in the following section. On the other hand, standards remain unchanged regardless of changes in system technology. In other words, computerization has absolutely *no* effect on the generally accepted professional standards of auditing. Auditors are expected to exhibit proper professionalism, which includes having adequate technical training and proficiency. They also are expected to follow the same thorough auditing process. This process must include the evaluation of all existing internal controls, including those that are computer-oriented.

IMPACTS OF COMPUTERIZATION ON AUDIT PROCEDURES

As we noted in the preceding paragraph, audits that involve the AIS are affected by the method of processing.

> *The extent to which computer processing is used in significant accounting applications, as well as the complexity of that processing, may also influence the nature, timing, and extent of audit procedures.**

For instance, computer-based systems do not provide a visible audit trail. Audits of these systems may thus require frequent printouts of journals and ledgers and other file records. Real-time processing systems cause additional difficulties, in that they often function without the need for source documents. They also overwrite existing records during updates. Microcomputer systems, such as those employed by Infoage, Inc., and Ann Strong's firm, cause other problems. Microcomputer hardware devices can be easily stolen and can be easily accessed by unauthorized personnel. Also, microcomputer software packages often lack sufficient programmed checks. Computer networks transmit data over great distances and are especially vulnerable to unauthorized accesses and breakdowns. Since these conditions affect the internal control structure, they affect the conduct of audits.

Because of the complexity of computer-based processing, a special type of auditor—the computer information systems (CISA) auditor—is needed. CISAs possess special skills, such as thorough knowledge of computer hardware and software, database technology, data communications technology, and computer-oriented controls and audit techniques. Ideally, in the future all auditors should acquire many of the skills of the current CISAs. However, CISAs with an in-depth knowledge of computer technology will always be needed to assist in audits of complex computer systems.

TRANSACTION CYCLE APPROACH TO AUDITING

Our survey of transaction processing has been oriented to the cycles approach. The cycles approach is quite useful in auditing. By examining controls within the context of complete processes, the auditor gains a continuous view of the controls and, hence, a greater understanding of the control structure. Also, the cycles approach

---

*American Institute of Certified Public Accountants, *Statement on Auditing Standards No. 48: Computer Processing on the Examination of Financial Statements.* New York: AICPA, 1984, Sec. 1.09.

SPOTLIGHTING

THE FUTURE OF THE AUDIT FUNCTION*

Information technology causes great change to the value of financial audits. It provides alternative information sources to those who traditionally have relied on financial statements and dramatically changes all aspects of preparing, auditing, and using financial statements.

Although these changes pose serious threats to the economic viability of auditing, they also offer CPAs extraordinary opportunities to strengthen the audit function. The increasingly pervasive use of information technology and its growing power threaten auditors in several ways.

The first threat relates to the relative importance of financial statements to investors. Facilitated by information technology, other sources of relevant information are available; for example, investors can get up-to-the-minute data about firms through public and proprietary data bases without waiting for quarterly or annual reports. Moreover, information technology has created new ways for businesses to become more competitive (for example, continuous quality improvement, cycle-time reduction, and enhanced vendor and customer relationships), the effects of which are not reflected in financial statements. Thus, financial statements describe modern firms less well than they described industrial-era firms. Because the audit franchise is tied to financial statements, auditors'

"market share" for investor-related data has been declining.

Another threat derives from the fact that users are forced to look at a firm through a keyhole that permits only a small part of available information to be seen. The audit is also threatened by the fact that annual printed financial statements may be destined for history's scrap heap because information technology permits far more frequent and timely reports.

The role of information technology, fortunately, is two-edged. Not only does it present threats to traditional audits and auditors but it also creates opportunities. For example, a special committee on financial reporting recommended that firms increase their disclosures of nonfinancial information; these new types of information could be audited. In addition to reporting on nonfinancial information, auditors also could offer assurances on the quality of decision-making information and on the contents and relevance of information contained in data bases. A possible extended role created by information technology may enable CPAs to interpret financial statements and add qualitative information about a firm and its prospects. The American Institute of Certified Public Accountants has appointed a special advisory committee to lay out a future framework for the audit function and prepare the profession to seize its opportunities to serve the public better.

*Robert K. Elliott, "The Future of Audits," *Journal of Accountancy* (September 1994), pp. 74–82.

---

simplifies the audit review, since similar patterns of controls become apparent between cycles. For instance, nearly identical sets of controls exist in the revenue and expenditure cycles, given the same mode of processing.

AUDITING PROCESS

Figure 10-2 shows an overview of the five phases of a financial audit. The phases are (1) planning the audit, (2) preliminary review and assessment of the internal control structure, (3) completion of the review, which involves detailed evaluation and testing of controls, (4) analytical and substantive review, and (5) audit reporting. Each of these phases, including the type of risk related to each stage, is briefly reviewed in this section.

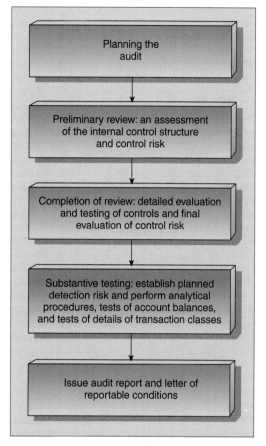

FIGURE 10-2   An overview of the phases of a
financial audit.

Figure 10-3 portrays the detailed steps that form the necessary **auditing process**
for performing a financial audit. Both internal and external audits are conducted
using the same five basic phases. However, the activities within the phases may vary
slightly because of the different objectives of the audits. The biggest difference is
found in the types of audit reports presented by internal auditors as opposed to
external auditors. To simplify the discussion, each of these phases is reviewed from
the external auditor's perspective.

INITIAL AUDIT PLANNING

The first step is to recognize the need for an audit and to establish its scope and
objectives. For instance, the scope of an audit might be the revenue transaction cycle.
Objectives for an audit of this kind will include those listed in Chapter 12, such as
determining that all sales are recorded and processed properly. Other steps during
this phase are to research information about the firm's industry, study prior years'
working papers, prepare a preliminary audit program, obtain an understanding of the
firm's business, and perform preliminary analytical procedures. **Analytical procedures** are tests to examine relationships among financial and nonfinancial data and
to investigate material inconsistencies. Evaluating material variations among key
financial ratios is an example of an analytical test.

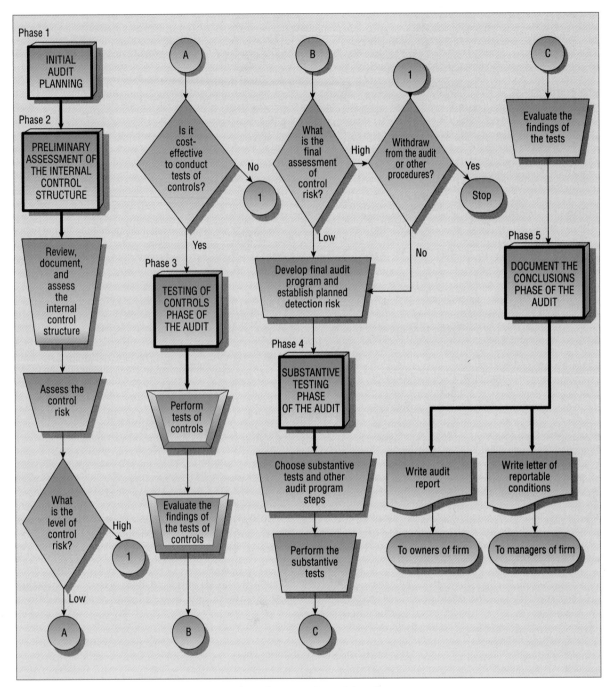

FIGURE 10-3   Steps composing the process of conducting a financial audit.

PRELIMINARY ASSESSMENT OF THE INTERNAL CONTROL STRUCTURE

As illustrated in Figure 10-3, **preliminary assessment** involves reviewing, documenting, and assessing the internal control structure (ICS); assessing initial control risk; setting the initial level of control risk; and establishing whether it is cost-effective to conduct tests of controls.

Review, Document, and Assess the ICS   The auditor begins by obtaining an understanding of the five components of the ICS. The extent of the understanding should be sufficient to assess the strengths and weaknesses in the ICS. Thus the auditor is required to employ a variety of fact-gathering techniques, such as review of records and documents, observation of activities, and interviews with key personnel.* These fact-gathering techniques simply suggest the presence or absence of an acceptable ICS. If the ICS is found to have significant deficiencies, such as a poorly designed AIS lacking key controls, the auditor may conclude that the client's financial statements are not auditable and withdraw from the audit engagement. If the auditor does not withdraw from the engagement, he or she may take into account the concept of offsetting controls. These offsetting controls are called compensating controls. A control weakness in one area may be offset by a control in another area. Compensating controls reduce the risk exposure; what were originally considered control weaknesses are no longer a problem.†

Assess and Set the Level of Control Risk   The previous step provides an overall (i.e., macro) view of the existing ICS. This step more intensely studies and evaluates the ICS by expanding on the facts obtained in the previous step. Now the auditor is ready to form a preliminary assessment concerning the operating effectiveness (i.e., adequacy) of the internal control structure. If it appears that the ICS provides a basis for reliance, the auditor should first identify the specific controls required to prevent or detect frequently occurring risk exposures. Second, particular controls placed in the AIS must be identified. Next, the auditor must judge if the implemented internal controls are the key controls, and that they are working as prescribed by management. Finally, the auditor must document each major control strength and weakness so that control risk can be assessed. Knowledge of the ICS points to the types of material errors or misstatements that can occur in financial statement assertions. (An **assertion** is an expressed account balance, transaction classification, or disclosure in the financial statements being examined. For instance, it might be asserted that the balance in the period-end accounts payable account is $39,400.)

Control risk is defined as the risk that material misstatements in assertions, leading to significant errors in the financial statements, will fail to be prevented or detected by the internal control structure. The level of control risk can be expressed numerically such as 100 percent, 70 percent, or 25 percent, or subjectively such as high, moderate, or low.

As shown in Figure 10-3, the next step in the preliminary review is for the auditor to seek an answer to the question, "What is the level of control risk?" A high or maximum level of control risk is assessed when the policies and control procedures within the ICS cannot be relied on; at this stage, the auditor may withdraw from the

---

*Older, manual check-off questionnaires are giving way to comprehensive automated expert systems audit software packages that assist in conducting and assessing the preliminary review. These packages are also useful in testing controls. For example, Expert Auditor (from Boden Associates) requires the auditor to complete a questionnaire on-line and to type in the main findings of the key personnel interviewed. The knowledge-based software automatically generates, based on the answers provided during the consultation, an audit findings report, a control strengths and weaknesses report, a compensating controls report, and a user actions required report.

†With respect to compensating controls, such controls can reduce the risk exposure in smaller firms. For example in smaller firms, such as Infoage and Ann Strong's, owner-manager supervision can offset shortcomings in segregation of duties. Also, users' review of the output can detect errors undiscovered by weak microcomputer application controls. A reliance on some compensating controls requires that these controls be tested and evaluated. The outcome of the evaluation would determine the amount of substantive audit techniques required to complete the audit.

audit engagement or rely on other procedures, such as the compensating controls previously discussed. A risk level below the maximum is assessed when the control procedures appear to be sufficiently sound and adequate to provide reasonable assurance that the transaction processing objectives can be achieved. Setting the level of control risk is the final step in the preliminary review. When the level is within an acceptable range, the auditor should prepare a preliminary audit program, indicating audit steps to test key control strengths.

Cost-Effectiveness of Testing Controls Even though initial control risk is within an acceptable range, the auditor may choose not to test controls because of the costs involved.* The audit may be completed by setting control risk at the maximum, and preparing a modified audit program expanding the amount of substantive testing procedures. For example, the auditor may omit testing of controls when the automated AIS is not complex and the volume of transactions is low. If the auditor decides that it is cost-effective to conduct tests of controls, as pointed out in Figure 10-3, he or she proceeds to phase 3 of the audit—controls testing.

TESTING OF CONTROLS PHASE OF THE AUDIT

The steps in the testing of controls phase are to perform tests of controls, to evaluate the findings of the tests, to resolve whether or not to rely on the controls, and to develop the final audit program.

Perform Tests of Controls Tests of controls may consist of observing the processing operations and the control-related activities, reprocessing transactions, and so on. If the control risk is assessed to be at or near the maximum level, the auditor bypasses tests of controls and determines the planned substantive tests to be performed within the audit program. On the other hand, if the control risk is judged to be below the maximum level, suitable tests of controls should be performed. The amount of testing of controls also affects the amount of the resultant substantive tests to be performed, as discussed below.

Tests of controls gather evidential matter concerning how effectively and consistently the current control procedures actually function. Their results document the basis for the conclusions of the auditor concerning the level of control risk. Several specific techniques for applying tests of controls within computer-based systems are discussed in later sections.

Evaluate the Findings of the Tests of Controls After obtaining the results of the tests of controls, the auditor is in a position to evaluate the operational effectiveness of the ICS. Evidence supporting audit findings for each transaction cycle is evaluated. For example, in the revenue cycle the controls documentation pertaining to sales, cash receipts, sales returns, and accounts receivable is analyzed. In effect, the evaluations represent the best judgments of the auditor concerning (1) the adequacy of observed controls and (2) the detectability of the results of the inadequacies.

Final Assessment of Control Risk Based on this evaluation, a specific level of control risk for each major transaction class can be assessed. The level of final control risk provides the basis for determining the level of planned detection risk, and the nature, timing, and extent of the substantive testing procedures. When the control risk is set at the maximum level, only substantive tests will be performed. The planned **detection risk** is the risk that a material misstatement in the financial statements or in an

---

*Other reasons to bypass testing of controls include the following: (1) substantive tests are more economical to complete, (2) last year's control risk was set at a low level, and (3) manual information systems predominate.

individual account balance will fail to be uncovered by substantive testing procedures. For instance, the lower the level of control risk for a major transaction class, the higher the planned detection risk and the fewer the substantive tests (i.e., program steps) that will be needed. The higher the control risk, the lower the level of planned detection risk and the more tests that will be needed.

Develop Final Audit Program   The last step in phase 3 is to develop the final audit program. An **audit program** is a list of specific procedures needed to achieve the audit objectives. In addition to stating the nature of the tests and procedures, it also clarifies their extent and when they will be performed.

SUBSTANTIVE TESTING PHASE OF THE AUDIT

As illustrated in Figure 10-3, the steps in the substantive testing phase include choosing substantive tests, performing the tests, and evaluating the test findings.

Choose and Perform Substantive Tests   **Substantive tests** constitute the bulk of the audit program. The purpose of substantive testing in a financial audit is to validate the financial statement assertions made by management. Three substantive tests are (1) performing final analytical procedures, (2) testing account balances, and (3) testing details of transaction classes. The amount of substantive testing is based on the final detection risk for each major transaction class. Based on the assessed detection risk, substantive testing evidence is obtained to the effect that the sample of transactions selected for testing is valid and processed in accordance with generally accepted accounting principles and that account balances are not materially misstated. Typical tests confirm the existence of various assets (e.g., inventory) and analyze the trends of key factors (e.g., inventory turnover). Specific substantive tests within computer-based systems are subsequently examined.

Evaluate Substantive Tests   As substantive tests are completed, the results should be summarized and evaluated. Acceptable test results mean that the likelihood of material errors and misstatements in the financial statement assertions is minimized. That is, the conclusions are within the selected level of detection risk. Unacceptable results call for additional sampling of transactions before the audit can be completed.

DOCUMENT THE CONCLUSIONS

The final phase of the audit is to write the audit report and issue a letter of reportable conditions. However, between the client's fiscal year-end and the date of the audit report, the auditor is required to review and report on material contingent liabilities and significant subsequent events, such as the settlement of litigation or the purchase of a subsidiary.

Writing the Audit Report   The final step is for the auditor to report the results of the audit to the proper parties. In the case of a financial audit performed by external auditors, the owners of the firm would receive the auditor's report, which expresses an opinion on the financial statements. The conclusions are documented in the audit report. The opening paragraph of an audit report specifically identifies the statements audited and declares that the financial statements are the responsibility of the firm's management and that the auditor's responsibility is to express an opinion on the statements. The second paragraph is the scope paragraph, which explains essentially what the auditor did in the process of examining the financial statements. The third paragraph, an opinion paragraph, states the findings of the examination and expresses an opinion. The opinion sums up the considered evaluation of a professional concerning the fairness with which the financial statements reflect the entity's

> - An **unqualified opinion** states that the financial statements present fairly, in all material respects, the financial status, results of operations, and cash flows of the firm being audited.
> - A **qualified opinion** is issued when a significant condition, such as departure from generally accepted accounting principles, prevents the issuance of an unqualified opinion.
> - An **adverse opinion** is given when the auditor concludes that the overall financial statements are so materially misleading that they cannot be relied upon.
> - A **disclaimer of opinion** means that the auditor refuses to express an opinion on the overall financial statements due to major restrictions placed on the scope of the audit or the failure to collect sufficient evidence.

FIGURE 10-4   A summary of the types of audit opinions.

financial position and results of operations. Depending on the audit findings, the auditor may issue an unqualified opinion, a qualified opinion, an adverse opinion or disclaim an opinion. These types of opinions are summarized in Figure 10-4.

Letter of Reportable Conditions   The auditor is required to write a **letter of reportable conditions** to the corporate audit committee, covering significant deficiencies in the design or operation of the firm's ICS, such as absence of appropriate segregation of duties.*

COMPUTER-BASED AUDITING APPROACHES AND TECHNIQUES

Among the techniques or tests applied by auditors are counting cash on hand, tracing transactions through the accounting cycle, observing the taking of physical inventories, and confirming the existence of assets. These techniques are suitable for financial audits of either manual or computer-based information systems. Additional techniques are applicable only to those information systems that employ computer-based processing of transactions. Though no single audit would employ all of these computer-oriented techniques, owing to the excessive costs entailed, each of the techniques can aid in tests of controls or substantive testing. However, they do not replace the use of system flowcharts, data flow diagrams, and questionnaires in reviewing the internal control structure.

Most of these computer-oriented techniques will be included in the discussion that follows. They are organized according to three key approaches to computer-based auditing: auditing-around-the-computer, auditing-through-the-computer, and auditing-with-the-computer.

AUDITING AROUND THE COMPUTER

The **auditing-around-the-computer approach** treats the computer as a "black box." Instead of looking inside the "black box," the approach focuses on its inputs and outputs. Underlying this approach is the following assumption: If the auditor can show that the actual outputs are the correct results to be expected from a set of

---

*Other deficiencies that should be noted in this letter include (1) inadequate provisions for safeguarding assets, (2) absence of appropriate authorization and approval of transactions, (3) evidence of intentional override of the ICS by those in authority, (4) evidence of failure to perform reconciliations, (5) evidence of fraudulent wrongdoing by employees or management, and (6) evidence of an insufficient control consciousness within the firm.

inputs to the processing system, then the computer processing must be functioning in a reliable manner.

Because the computer is ignored, an auditor using the around-the-computer approach does not need to understand computer processing concepts. He or she performs an audit as if a manual processing system were involved. Thus the techniques can be easily and economically applied.

A key technique under this approach involves tracing selected transactions from source documents to summary accounts and records, and vice versa. As Figure 10-5a shows, an auditor compares the actual printouts of results obtained by the computer processing with those previously computed by hand. Any differences are likely to reflect control weaknesses. The auditor ensures that the computer printouts are properly distributed, and that controls contained in programs appear to be reliable in detecting errors by observing user reconciliations of errors contained in the error and summary printout reports. A related technique is to trace rejected transactions from one or more batches, to determine if they were properly corrected and reentered for processing. These techniques are concerned with tests of controls and the evaluation of the control risk. Thus they should be performed prior to developing the audit program.

As noted in Figure 10-5a, the auditing-around-the-computer approach is a *non-processing* of data method. The auditor does not prepare simulated data transactions or use actual client files to process with the client's computer programs.

The auditing-around-the-computer approach is suitable only when three conditions are fulfilled:

1. The audit trail is complete and visible. That is, source documents are used for all transactions, detailed journals are printed out, and transaction references are carried forward from the journals to the ledgers and summary reports.

2. The processing operations are relatively straightforward, uncomplicated, and low volume.

3. Complete documentation, such as data-flow diagrams and system flowcharts, is available to the auditor.

These conditions are most likely found in independent batch processing applications, such as typical cash disbursements and payroll processing. Other types of applications, for instance, sales order processing systems, often fail one or another of the conditions. They may dispense with source documents, accept individual transactions at random times, or involve complicated processing. Tracing transactions in such systems can be a very difficult task for auditors.

Even when the three above-mentioned conditions are met, this approach cannot be viewed as sufficient. Its main shortcoming is that it does not allow the auditor to determine exactly how all conceivable types of transactions would be handled by the computer processing programs. In particular, it does not reveal how the edit programs of accounting applications would respond to a wide variety of transactions containing errors or lacking necessary data.

AUDITING THROUGH THE COMPUTER

As a result of the insufficiency of the auditing-around-the-computer approach, an alternative approach is needed for computer-based auditing. This alternative approach opens the "black box" and directly focuses on the processing steps and the programmed controls. It assumes that if the processing programs are soundly developed and incorporate adequate programmed checks, then errors and irregularities

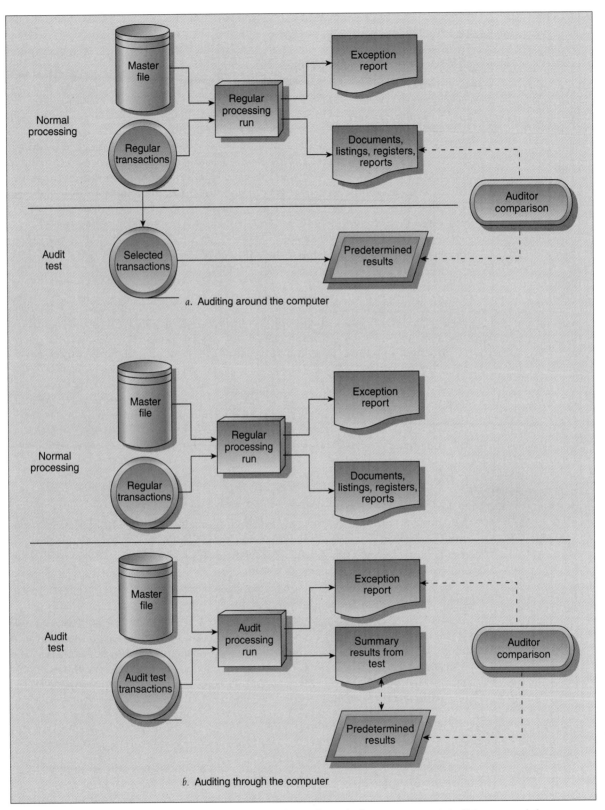

FIGURE I0-5   Auditing-around-the-computer versus auditing-through-the-computer. (*a*) Auditing-around-the-computer. (*b*) Auditing-through-the-computer.

are not likely to slip by undetected. As a result, the outputs can reasonably be accepted as reliable.

This **auditing-through-the-computer approach** should be applied with respect to all complex computer-based processing systems. It is particularly essential for an on-line processing application where the audit trail is impaired. When they are cost-effective and feasible, the around-the-computer approach and through-the-computer approach may be performed within the same audit; by doing so the auditor will gain greater assurance that the audit objectives are achieved.

Figure 10-5*b* contrasts the auditing-through-the-computer approach with the around-the-computer approach. To apply this technique, the auditor first observes the normal processing of a particular transaction or nontransaction processing application. Next, he or she prepares a collection of simulated test transactions pertaining to the application. Then, the test transactions are entered for processing. The results are printed on the routine output summary, with detected errors being listed on an exception report. The auditor then compares the summary output and listed errors against a list of expected results. Any differences represent possible control weaknesses or omissions. Extended illustrations of the auditing-through-the-computer approaches will be presented in subsequent sections of this chapter.

The auditing-through-the-computer approach embraces a family of techniques. Those in the widest use or having the greatest potential include the test data, integrated test facility, and embedded audit module techniques. Other auditing-through-the-computer approaches less frequently used or having lesser potential include program code checking, parallel processing, parallel simulation, and controlled processing. These techniques are examined in the appendix to this chapter. All auditing-through-the-computer techniques provide evidence concerning the level of control risk. The test data approach, integrated test facility, parallel simulation, program code checking, and parallel processing techniques are particularly useful in applying tests of controls.

Test Data Technique   The **test data technique** was the first auditing-through-the-computer approach developed to audit complex computer systems. All other through-the-computer techniques are variations of this method. The test data technique uses a set of hypothetical data to audit the programmed checks in both transaction and nontransaction processing programs. The technique is useful in auditing transaction processing applications, such as payroll, accounts receivable, accounts payable, cash disbursements, or inventory. It is also suitable for auditing nontransaction applications, such as spreadsheets, data-base management systems, or some types of decision support and expert systems.

An extended illustration and application of the test data technique for a payroll program is given in Figures 10-6 and 10-7. Preparing test data verifies that payroll transactions are accurately processed and that controls within pay programs prevent improper results, such as issuing exorbitant checks. However, it should be noted that it is nearly impossible to test every conceivable programmed check. As shown in Figure 10-6, the first two steps are to obtain payroll documentation and then evaluate the payroll programs to be tested. Proper documentation includes obtaining a copy of the latest program source listing, flowcharts, and the record layouts of payroll records contained on transaction and master files. Based on the record layouts, the third step is to determine valid and erroneous payroll program conditions to test. The pay program should process valid test transactions correctly and erroneous ones should be identified by the program controls, rejected, and written to an error and summary report.

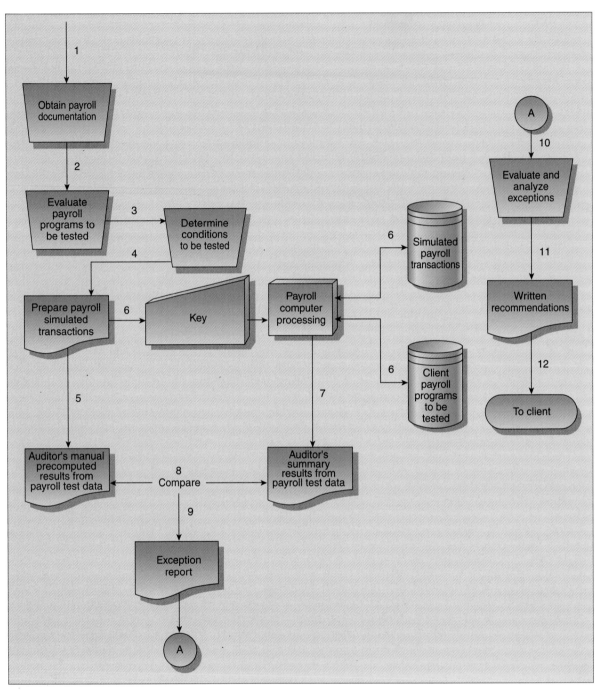

FIGURE 10-6 The test data approach for a payroll application.

For example, valid conditions would include computing gross pay, FICA, federal income taxes, gross and net pay, state income tax, and insurance withholding. Invalid conditions include

- duplicating payments,
- making unreasonable payments,

Test Code	Condition Being Tested	Transaction Data				Expected Result	Actual Result
		Employee Number (1)	Employee Name (2)	Department No. (3)	Hours Worked (4)		
1	Valid transaction	13251	SMITH, JOHN	1	40.0	$200 gross pay $7800 earnings year-to-date	
2	Invalid check digit in field (1)	13629	BLACK, CHARLES	1	40.0	Exception	
3	Out of sequence in field (1)	13543	ADAMS, STEVE	1	40.0	Exception	
4	Invalid composition in field (2)	13658	BR67N, RODNEY	1	40.0	Exception	
5	Invalid relationship between fields (1) and (3)	13752	JONES, PAUL	2	40.0	Exception	
6	Out-of-limit in field (4)	24313	KRAUSE, KEN	2	60.0	Exception	
7	No matchup with master in field (1)	25000	TINGEY, SHERMAN	2	40.0	Exception	

Explanation Code

a
b
c
d
e
f

Exception Report Messages

```
EMPLOYEE 13629 HAS AN INVALID CHECK DIGIT
EMPLOYEE 13543 IS OUT OF SEQUENCE
EMPLOYEE 13658 HAS INVALID CHARACTERS IN NAME FIELD
EMPLOYEE 13752 DOES NOT CORRESPOND WITH DEPARTMENT
EMPLOYEE 24313 EXCEEDS ALLOWABLE HOURS WORKED
EMPLOYEE 25000 HAS AN INVALID EMPLOYEE NUMBER
```

a. Check figure is computed by computer to be a 7.
b. Employee number should be arranged in sequence.
c. Only alphabetic characters should appear in the name field.
d. The left-most digit of the employee number should correspond with the department number.
e. A maximum limit of 56 hours worked has been established.
f. No master record is found with number 25000 in the master file.

FIGURE 10-7 Test transactions and expected results for a payroll program test.

- paying for excessive hours worked,
- leaving a mandatory data field blank (such as no employee number),
- typing an alpha character in a numeric field,
- typing in a negative employee number,
- adding a fictitious employee to the transactions, and
- attempting to pay the same employee twice.

After studying the record layouts and the conditions to be tested, the fourth step is for the auditor to prepare a collection of test transactions to include in his or her working papers. The fifth step is for the auditor to manually precompute the expected results. Figure 10-7 lists several test transactions prepared by the auditor for making the payroll tests; it also shows the results the auditor expects.

The sixth step is to enter the test transaction using a terminal; this step creates the simulated payroll transactions. Next, the simulated payroll transactions and the client's payroll programs are processed to generate the auditor's summary results, which are printed on a summary report (e.g., a weekly payroll register). The eighth step depicted in Figure 10-6 is to compare the payroll register with the auditor's manually computed results. The ninth step is to prepare an exception report listing detected errors. The tenth, eleventh, and twelfth steps are to analyze and evaluate the exceptions, and write a letter of reportable conditions to the board of directors covering any deficiencies in the ICS. Below the transaction data sheet in Figure 10-7 is the exception report that reflects the detected errors. Since no deviations appear between expected results and actual results, no control weaknesses apparently exist.

The test data technique is relatively simple to apply, since it does not require a high degree of computer expertise on the part of the auditor. Also, it normally does not interfere with the regular processing activities of the firm being audited. However, it does impose certain conditions and does possess several limitations.

Effective use of the test data technique depends on the following conditions:

1. A wide variety of possible input errors, logical processing errors, and irregularities are considered. Thus hypothetical data rather than actual data should be used.

2. A test master file, or a copy of the actual master file, is used during testing. Otherwise, actual file records are likely to be contaminated by test data.

3. Careful procedures are followed to preserve the auditor's independence. The auditor can either observe the processing of the test transactions on the client's computer or use a laptop computer to download the necessary computer programs and process the test transactions at his office.

Following the first approach requires the auditor to acquire the printed outputs immediately after processing. Also, the auditor should ascertain that the program used during testing is the actual "production" program used during normal processing. A convenient means of obtaining this assurance is to arrive unannounced at the processing site during the scheduled time for processing. When the processing is completed, the auditor then requests the operator to process the test transactions before removing the program, or else downloads it to the laptop.

The limitations of the test data technique are as follows:

1. Test data can be very expensive and time-consuming to develop, since the error possibilities are numerous even in relatively simple applications. As a consequence, auditors sometimes use the test data developed by programmers during the implementation phase.

2. The technique is static, in that it focuses on single points in time. When programs are changed frequently, the results quickly become obsolete.

3. The technique focuses on individual applications, rather than the overall set of transaction processing systems or data bases.

4. The technique is limited to transactions processed in a batch mode and to several types of nontransaction processing applications mentioned above.

5. The test data approach must be used in conjunction with other audit techniques to form an overall assessment of control risk.

Integrated Test Facility   An extended version of the test data technique is the **integrated test facility (ITF) or "minicompany" technique.** It enables test data to be continually evaluated when transactions are processed by on-line systems. There are several variations of the ITF. All variations of the ITF allow the auditor to create a minicompany or fictitious entity, such as a customer, employee, or department, and perform a wider variety of tests compared to the test data approach. Whichever variation of the ITF is used, the fictitious customer (e.g., the auditor) conducts business like other customers. For example, the auditor may purchase and receive merchandise, make merchandise returns, pay invoices, take discounts, and over/under/not pay invoices. In the role of auditor, he or she is able to continually monitor most aspects of the computer system's ICS, in addition to programmed controls. The auditor maintains an accounting system to track the test transactions, including any merchandise received or returned.

One variation of the ITF infrequently employed in practice combines into one data base the auditor's fictitious transactions and the client's real transactions. At the end of the period the auditor must prepare reversing journal entries to remove the test transactions, leaving only the real transactions in the data base. Sometimes it is very difficult to ensure that all of the auditor's simulated transactions have been removed from the client's data base.

A more common variation of ITF is portrayed in Figure 10-8. This second variation has many of the same features as the variation described above. However, variation two assumes that the auditor does not have products shipped to an outside address. The auditor creates fictitious transactions within selected departments to test programmed and other types of controls in particular accounting applications.

As illustrated in Figure 10-8, at some point in time the auditor's test transactions are entered into the computer system concurrently with actual (live) transactions. The test transactions consequently undergo the same processing steps and programmed checks as the actual transactions. Each test transaction, however, is identified with the processing programs by means of a code. This code causes the test transactions to be shunted into a special test facility (i.e., a collection of miniature files used to collect audit data concerning the various applications being tested). In the case of a sales transaction, for example, the transaction will be deposited in special ITF disk files for customers and sales orders. Since the test transactions are hypothetical, the ITF files also pertain to fictitious customers, orders, and so on.

As in the test data technique, the auditor obtains printouts of the summary records and the error reports. By comparing these printouts with predetermined results, he or she determines how effectively the programmed checks detect errors. Thus the auditor has a sound basis for evaluating the adequacy of built-in controls and other control measures.

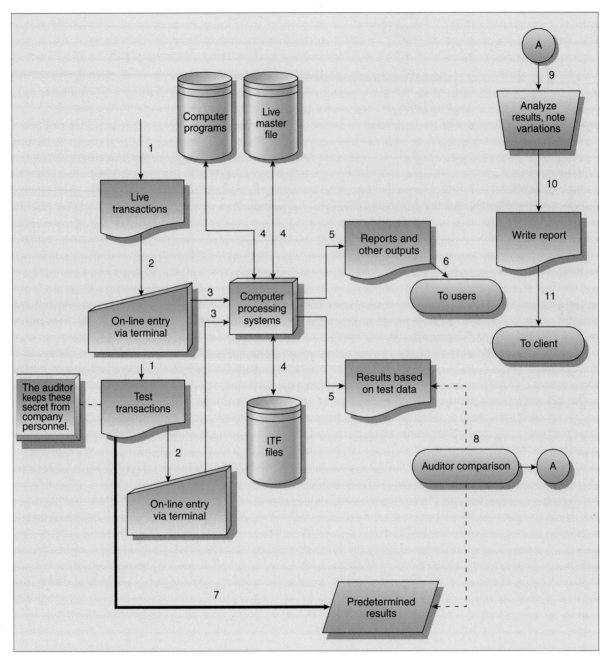

FIGURE 10-8   Integrated test facility technique.

After analyzing the ITF results and uncovering any significant ICS weaknesses, the auditor is required to write a letter of reportable conditions to the corporate audit committee within a reasonable time.

The ITF technique has the following advantages:

1. It allows test transactions to simulate live transaction processing more closely, since the test transactions are entered randomly and continually throughout the year.

2. Since the test and live transactions are entered together, the auditor is assured that the "production" programs are processing both in the same ways.

3. It enables on-line processing programs to be tested, while avoiding the contamination of live files.

4. It enables all on-line applications within a computer system to be tested in an integrated manner. Thus the technique allows a more comprehensive evaluation of input and processing controls.

The ITF technique has the following disadvantages:

1. It is very costly and time-consuming to apply.

2. It requires an in-depth knowledge of computer technology.

3. It may disrupt the client's operations. Depending on the variation of the approach used, it may be difficult to separate the auditor's test transactions from the client's live or actual transactions.

Embedded Audit Module Technique   An embedded audit module is a programmed module or segment that is inserted into an application program. Its purpose is to monitor and to collect data based on transactions, particularly those processed by on-line computer-based systems. The data are then used by the auditor in the tests of controls and the evaluation of control risk. In essence, this computerized technique enhances and extends the review of computer-generated documentation.

Figure 10-9 depicts the features of the **embedded audit module technique.** As

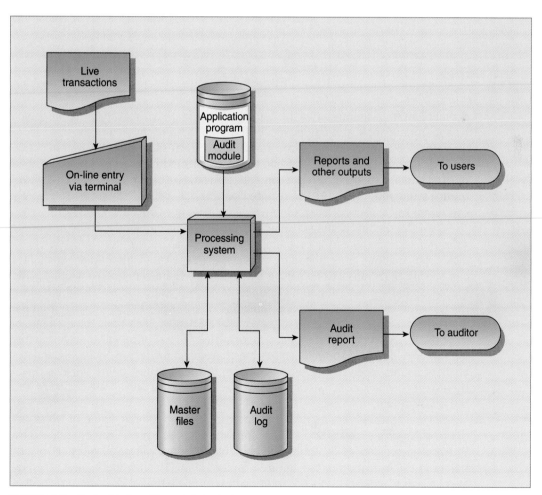

FIGURE 10-9   Embedded audit module technique.

SPOTLIGHTING

COMPUTERIZED AUDIT-ASSIST SOFTWARE
at Johnson & Johnson*

Johnson & Johnson is a multibillion-dollar health-care organization whose headquarters are in New Brunswick, New Jersey. In 1989 it acquired a custom-developed audit tool from Silvon Software to aid in auditing the IBM AS/400 minicomputer systems at its headquarters. The name given to the audit tool was System Management Tool (SMT).

SMT simplifies the review of controls and security that are integrated into the minicomputer systems. It provides a series of predefined on-line screen formats, which may be customized by the auditors. When the auditor signs on, a session with SMT begins by showing a main menu of about a dozen options. The options allow the auditor to display a variety of screens or to compare key information pertaining to the system or users. One screen displays all of the libraries (of files and programs) established by the various authorized users. Another screen displays all relevant details concerning a particular library, including its owner (user), size, creation date, last change and save dates, and password levels.

This audit tool also allows auditors to obtain snapshots of the contents of the system at any time, to retrieve and print detailed data, and to compare user authority data between different time periods. A benefit of the tool is to allow auditors to perform more complete audits of users of the system, as well as to search and retrieve desired information quickly. For instance, an auditor can ask the tool to show all users whose passwords have not been changed since a specified date.

*Salil Sarkar, "Auditing the IBM AS/400: The Johnson & Johnson Automated Approach," EDPACS (June 1991), pp. 1–6.

actual (live) transactions enter the computer system, they are edited and processed by appropriate application programs. In addition, they are checked by the audit modules that are embedded in the programs. When a transaction meets certain conditions or criteria that the auditor has set, it is selected by the module and copied onto an audit log. Periodically the contents of the log (usually called a **system control audit review file,** or **SCARF**) are printed out for review by the auditor. The SCARF can reveal key aspects of programming logic, including errors and omissions.

Consider the functioning of an audit module that is embedded within an on-line sales transaction processing program. The program has been written in EQUEL FORTRAN, which allows the embedding of query language capabilities. Thus, an auditor can specify that transactions having the following characteristics be captured and logged during a processing run: (1) amounts of credit sales above $5000 for which preapproved credit has not been obtained, (2) credit sales to customers not on the approved customer list, and (3) all sales above $10,000. Each week the contents of the SCARF are to be provided via a report writer; the auditor will then review the manner in which the captured transactions have been processed, including updates to the accounts receivable records. Analysis provided by the module will also reveal the extent to which policy violations (e.g., lack of credit approval) are occurring and the total amounts involved.

Several features relating to an audit module are available, some of which are optional. *Tagging* consists of placing identifying "tags" on the selected transactions. *Snapshotting* consists of capturing the contents of primary storage areas at specific points in the execution of the selected transactions. (This feature is also called *extended records.*) *Tracing* consists of capturing the complete trail of instructions executed during the processing of the selected transactions. *Real-time notification* involves the display of selected transactions on the auditor's terminal as they are captured by the audit module.

This technique has several advantages:

1. It enables data concerning transactions of audit interest to be easily captured, even when the audit trail is obscure.

2. It enables all processing to be monitored. For instance, intermediate and final processing results can be captured on the audit log; analyses can be provided concerning transaction errors and violations of policy.

3. It detects breaches of security as well as programming improprieties. For example, it can spot unauthorized attempts to access master files, enter spurious transaction data, or override processing parameters such as prices in a billing program.

Although this technique is gaining in popularity, it has certain drawbacks:

1. The time required to process transactions is increased, since the instructions contained in the audit module must also be executed.

2. An audit module should be embedded in an application program at the time the program is first written. Attempting to attach the module to the program later is quite expensive and not as satisfactory.

3. The security requirements for the computer system are heightened, since the audit module and log must be kept secure from all users of the computer system.

AUDITING WITH THE COMPUTER

A third approach involves using either mainframes or microcomputers to aid in performing the steps in detailed audit programs. This **auditing-with-the-computer approach** is used to automate much of the auditing process. Microcomputers are transforming the audit scene. They can now perform a number of audit functions, such as testing of controls and substantive tests.

Microcomputer Audit-Assist Software   Many auditors routinely carry portable microcomputers, such as notebook computers, into the offices where audits are to be conducted. For instance, Ann Strong might use a Lotus spreadsheet package to create a spreadsheet containing the financial statements of the firm she is auditing.

Certain noteworthy developments have resulted from the widespread use of microcomputers by auditors. Thus a number of specialized accounting, auditing, and tax software packages have been developed. One such package is the generalized audit software (GAS) package, which has been adapted for microcomputer use by the larger CPA firms. GAS is examined in more detail in the next section of this chapter. A computer-assisted flowchart package allows auditors to prepare flowcharts on the screens of their microcomputers, and to store the results on the hard disks.

Another development is the **template,** in effect a program and on-screen format that is constructed with the use of a spreadsheet package. Templates enable auditors to perform tasks that were formerly done manually. Templates are typically designed to aid in preparing trial balances, maintaining adjusting journal entries, evaluating sample results, scheduling and managing the time of auditors in field audits, performing reasonableness tests of expenses, and estimating expenses. Figure 10-10 displays a worksheet prepared by a large CPA firm to aid in summarizing and controlling accounts confirmation requests. (Many of the microcomputer software packages described in Appendix B at the end of the book can also be used to automate the audit process.)

```
*************************************************************************
SUMMARY OF CONFIRMATION COVERAGE          PREPARER:JP          VERSION 1.0
STORY SALES CO.                           RUN DATE:11/29/--
10/31/--
*************************************************************************
CONFIRM  ACCOUNT  DESCRIPTION         WP    BK VALUE  BK VALUE  AUDITED  OVER/UNDER
NO.      NO.                          REF     SENT      RECD     VALUE     STATED
-------  -------  -----------------  -----  --------  --------  -------  ----------
   1     200-13   HART SUPPLY        50-40  1500000   1500000   1200000   -300000
   2     200-24   JOHNSON LOCKS      50-41   980156    980156    980156         0
   3     200-46   C&D CO., INC.      50-42  2100450   2100450   2000000   -100450
   4     200-58   VAL-MART           50-43   357456              357456         0
   5     200-72   SMITHSON TECH. CO. 50-44  2575100   2575100   2575100         0
                                                                                0
                                                                                0
                                                                                0
                                                                                0
                                                                                0
                                            -------   -------   -------   -------
                                            7513162   7155706   7112712   -400450
*************************************************************************


RESPONSE RECAP           #.ITEMS    %.VALUE.
.............           .......    ........
CONFIRMS MAILED              5      7513162
CONFIRMS RECD               4      7155706
RESPONSE %              80.00        95.24


SUMMARY.OF.RESULTS       #.ITEMS    %.VALUE.
...............         .......    ........
ACCOUNT TOTAL             500     49852357
BOOK VALUE EXAMINED         5      7513162
AUDITED VALUE EXAMINED      5      7112712
% COVERAGE               1.00        15.07
RATIO OF AUDITED TO BOOK VALUE        .95
```

FIGURE 10-10 Microcomputer-assisted summary of accounts receivable confirmation request. (Courtesy of Coopers & Lybrand. *Software News-letter* (Fall 1983), Coopers & Lybrand.)

Audit Software A popular auditing-with-the-computer approach is to use audit software during the substantive testing of a firm's records and files. Audit software generally consists of a collection of program routines. Each program routine serves, in effect, as a "robot," in that it performs a mechanistic audit function like that traditionally assigned to junior auditors or clerical personnel. Because it is powered by a computer, however, an audit program routine can perform this function very quickly and accurately.

Audit software may be classified as specialized and generalized. **Specialized audit software** consists of one or more program routines that are customized to suit a particular audit situation. Because this type of software is quite expensive and time-consuming to develop, it is seldom used. **Generalized audit software (GAS)** consists of one or more program routines that are applicable to a wide variety of audit situations in most types of organizations. The two GAS packages most widely used are IDEA (Interactive Data Extraction and Analysis) and ACL (Audit Command Language).* Five of the Big-Six public accounting firms use ACL. The sixth firm employs IDEA, as well as a proprietary GAS package developed by its internal staff. Numerous other public accounting firms, governmental agencies, and corporate internal audit departments also use either IDEA or ACL.

IDEA is an interactive, menu driven microcomputer-based data analysis tool. It allows an auditor to analyze a client's data file by means of functions such as attribute sampling, histogram generation, record aging, file comparison, duplicate checking, and file printing. It is relatively powerful, flexible, and easy to learn; however, it does not allow an auditor to do custom programming for special situations. ACL allows most of the same functions to be performed. Moreover, it can perform somewhat more sophisticated analyses. For instance, ACL accepts more selection criteria during a data extraction operation.

Typical audit functions available in a GAS package, which are listed in Figure 10-11, may be described as follows.

1. **Extracting data from files.** A GAS package must have the ability to extract or retrieve data from a variety of file structures, file media, and record layouts, since it will be used in auditing various firms. After being extracted, the data are edited and then transferred to an audit work file. The stored data are available for use by other routines in the GAS package.

2. **Calculating with data.** Many audit steps involve addition, subtraction, multiplication, and division operations. For example, correctness of footings in journals may be verified by redoing the additions.

3. **Performing comparisons with data.** Comparisons may be performed to select data elements for testing, to ascertain consistency between elements, and to verify that certain conditions are met. A GAS package should provide logical operators such as EQUAL, LESS THAN, and GREATER THAN. For instance, all 30,000 items in an inventory file might be searched, in order to select for review those items having on-hand balances that are GREATER THAN 1000 units. Also, all customers' records might be searched, with those accounts having balances that are GREATER THAN their credit limits being listed for investigation.

---

*IDEA has been developed in the United States by the American Institute of Certified Public Accountants. ACL has been developed by ACL Services of Vancouver. These two packages were evaluated in use by Dresser Industries and reported in "Microcomputer Audit Software: Uses and Comparisons by Dresser Industries Internal Audit" by Marc A. Garcia in EDP *Auditor Journal* (1990), pp. 65–71.

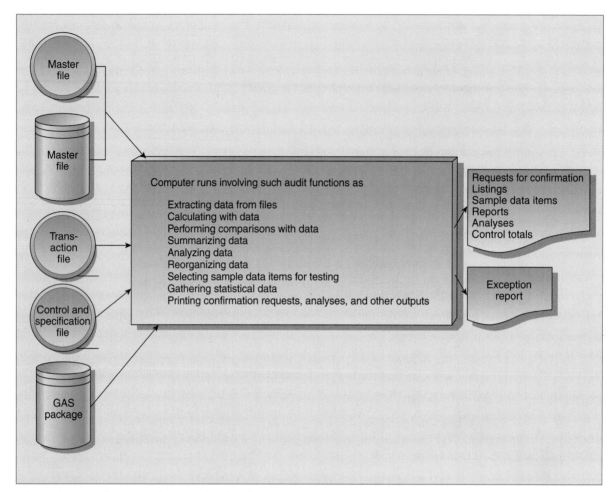

FIGURE 10-11 Applications of a generalized audit software package.

4. **Summarizing data.** Data elements must often be summarized to provide a basis for comparison. For example, detailed listings of salaries may be summarized for comparison with payroll reports.

5. **Analyzing Data.** Various data may be usefully analyzed, to provide a basis for reviewing trends or judging likelihoods. For instance, accounts receivable might be aged to provide a basis for judging the likelihood of their collection.

6. **Reorganizing data.** Data elements often need to be sorted or merged. For example, the various products sold by the firm might be re-sorted in ascending order of total sales quantities to aid the analysis of sales.

7. **Selecting sample data for testing.** In many audit steps the entire array of data cannot feasibly be tested. Thus samples must be drawn randomly from the array. For instance, a sample of customers might be selected randomly from the accounts receivable records, with the intention of confirming their account balances.

8. **Gathering statistical data.** An auditor often needs to gather or calculate statistical measures from an array of data. For example, the mean and median amounts of individual sales last month might be calculated to aid analysis.

9. **Printing confirmation requests, analyses, and other outputs.** For instance, the confirmation request forms and envelopes might be printed for those customers selected for testing.

The procedures for applying IDEA or ACL to a particular application are very similar, assuming that Windows 95 or another graphical user interface operating system is employed. They do not require a knowledge of computer programming, nor do they require the services of highly trained experts to gain access to the computer files. The use of either package begins with the auditor planning the audit objectives and work program. The result of this step is to specify the particular functions to be accomplished with the GAS. Then, the auditor uses the appropriate menu commands to directly access most micro, mini, or mainframe computer applications data file formats. This step is accomplished by either downloading the files into the auditor's laptop computer's hard disk or directly reading the other computer's files, without the need to convert or import the files. Thus the auditor gains total control over the processing of applications since the applications are run on the auditor's microcomputer. Having accessed the appropriate files, the actual audit and analysis of the data is the next step. The auditor performs each step listed in the application's audit program by selecting appropriate commands from the package's menu.

To illustrate, assume that an auditor is using ACL to perform substantive tests on a master file. One of the first steps in the audit program might be to total the relevant fields in the master file. The steps and screen displays to perform this function are presented in Figure 10-12. As illustrated, ACL's processing operations can be completely controlled through the utilization of a graphical user hierarchical menu interface. As the tests are conducted, the auditor applies his or her experience and judgment in handling and evaluating the outputs.

The advantages of a GAS package are that it

1. Allows an auditor to access computer-readable records for a wide variety of applications and organizations.

2. Enables an auditor to examine much more data than could be examined through manual means. In some situations 100 percent of the records or other data can be examined.

1. As illustrated, ACL's processing operations can be completely controlled through the use of a hierarchical menu interface or click on one of the buttons in the button bar. Each button corresponds to a menu command.

2. Selecting an item from the Main menu immediately changes the screen to the appropriate sub-menu.

FIGURE 10-12   An example of using ACL for Windows to total selected fields in a file. (Screen displays Courtesy of ACL Services.)

3. To select a file, simply select **Data** from the menu bar and choose the command **Select**. Note that the master file is selected.

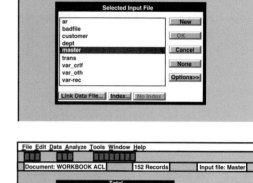

4. To work with data, simply select a menu option, such as **Analyze**, and then choose a command from the submenu, such as **Total**. This action displays the screen at right which shows the fields in the master file that can be totaled.

5. Select the fields to be totaled (in this example, three fields are selected).

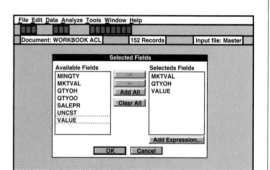

6. Because ACL is fully interactive, as soon as the OK button is clicked, ACL displays the results on screen. A printout can also be included in the audit working papers.

Other audit tests of the master file, such as reviewing samples of the records, verifying extended amounts against account records, and so on, are performed in a similar manner.

FIGURE 10-12 *(continued)*

3. Rapidly and accurately performs a variety of routine audit functions, including the statistical selection of samples.

4. Reduces dependence on nonauditing personnel for performing routine functions, such as summarizing data, thereby enabling the auditor to maintain better control over the audit.

5. Requires only minimal computer knowledge on the part of the auditor.

The main limitation of current GAS packages is that they do not directly examine the application programs and programmed checks. Thus they *cannot* replace the techniques that audit through the computer.

RECENT DEVELOPMENTS IN AUDITING

Auditors are facing rapid changes in computer-based systems. Four significant developments affecting audits are the following:

1. Integrated data bases that utilize data-base management systems and contain complex data structures.

2. Computer networks that connect multiple computers and terminals at various geographic locations by means of data communications lines.

3. Operational audits of data processing.

4. Artificial intelligence that introduces knowledge-based software into the audit process.

Each development is discussed separately in the following paragraphs. However, keep in mind that all four developments form part of today's audit environment and will become even more important tomorrow.

DATA-BASE AUDITS

Data-base systems complicate audits because of their data-base software (i.e., DBMS), complex data structures, on-line documentation, and accompanying data-base administration. During the preliminary review step, the auditor should examine a printout of the data dictionary and other printed documentation. The procedure for maintaining the data dictionary should be reviewed. During the detailed review step, the auditor should examine controls such as passwords, transaction log, activity log, and programmed checks.

During tests of controls, the following might be performed:

1. Tracing selected transactions through the system, using a system software utility.

2. Reviewing the console log and investigating selected entries.

3. Entering test transactions for processing, using an integrated test facility.

4. Monitoring transactions with an embedded audit module and entering selected transactions on an audit log.

Substantive testing should begin by retrieving data from the data base for review. After the data are transferred to the audit work file, the auditor may apply tests such as (1) reconciling batch totals to processed results, and (2) verifying changes in account balances between successive closing dates.

COMPUTER NETWORK AUDITS

During the review steps, the auditor estimates the exposures to risk that are posed by the communications lines and dispersed processing points. Exposures may exist because of unauthorized accesses to data, lack of audit trails, transmission and processing errors, and line distortions. Then the auditor reviews all of the installed controls and security measures. For instance, in the case of networks involving electronic transfers of funds, he or she might note controls relating to plastic debit cards and personal identification numbers (PINs).

Tests of controls might include (1) tracing a sample of transactions along the audit trail and (2) examining selected software changes for proper authorization, testing, and final approvals. Substantive testing could include surprise visits to remote processing sites, where a GAS package could be used to retrieve data from local files and to perform a variety of detailed tests.

Recent developments with respect to computer network audits are focusing on more thorough and integrated planning and on more sophisticated embedded audit modules. Auditors are able to view the results of transaction processing throughout such networks. They can retrieve the results from audit logs on command via microcomputers located in their own accounting offices.

OPERATIONAL AUDITS OF DATA PROCESSING

While the importance of operational auditing has been known for many years, internal audit departments have only recently performed such audits with regularity. One major type of operational audit involves auditing the data processing (DP) function. The **operational audit of data processing** systematically appraises the unit's effectiveness in achieving objectives and identifies conditions needing improvement. The two major areas of concentration are detecting inefficient operations—from the time and cost angles—and determining resource waste. This audit may include all DP activities or focus on only a few activities. Typical situations that may trigger DP operational reviews are systems that appear unresponsive to user needs, an increasing number of user complaints, and a high turnover in the data processing department. Like most audits, the operational audit of the DP function progresses through the following stages: audit planning, preliminary survey, detailed audit, and reporting.

During the planning stage, the internal auditor performs several important functions, such as becoming familiar with the operations of the DP department, determining the scope of the audit, and appraising risk exposures. The preliminary survey enables the internal auditor to interview key DP personnel, to observe operations, to study the problem areas identified, to form an assessment on the degree to which actual operations conform to described operations, and to develop an audit program.

During the detailed audit phase, representative activities to test and evaluate, depending on the audit's scope, include organization of the DP department, human resource practices and policies, computer operations, and application system operation. At the completion of the audit, a comprehensive report should be prepared; it is addressed to the corporate audit committee. The report should contain an opinion concerning the overall effectiveness and efficiency of the DP function and make recommendations for improvement. The internal auditor is required to follow up on reported audit findings and recommendations to ascertain that proper action is taken by the audit committee.

SPOTLIGHTING

THE IMPACT OF EXPERT SYSTEMS ON AUDITING FIRMS*

An investigation of large public accounting firms was undertaken to determine the most and least likely impacts of using expert systems as audit tools. A panel of experts, composed of those actively researching, developing, implementing, and using expert systems, concluded that expert systems are very likely to be widely available and used by auditing firms in the next decade. This conclusion was reached because of increased competition for auditing services, increasing complexity of audit tasks, firms' limited resources, and increasing pressures to boost quality while minimizing costs. The use of expert systems in audit firms will reduce risks; preserve expertise; save labor, time, and money; and provide a competitive advantage. Most likely impacts identified included productivity, expertise, and education impacts. Specifically, productivity impacts involve the use of expert systems

*Amelia Annette Baldwin-Morgan, "The Impact of Expert System Audit Tools on Auditing Firms in the Year 2001: A Delphi Investigation." *Journal of Information Systems* (Spring 1993), pp. 16–34.

for tasks that improve audit task decision quality and improve decision consistency for that particular task. Expertise impacts concern the use of an expert system for an audit task that provides documentation references for audit judgments and reasoning concerning the task, results in the distribution of expertise pertaining to the task within the auditing firm, and leads to an increased ability to handle complex analyses. Education impacts of expert systems in auditing firms result in changes in the education of auditors, particularly in-house training. In addition to the most likely audit impacts of expert systems, the least likely impacts identified included efficiency and external impacts. The efficiency impact least likely to occur in auditing firms included a reduction in the cost of audits because audit expert systems would not reduce staff time to perform an audit. The least likely external impact identified was that the development and use of expert systems for audit tasks would not lead to loss of prestige for firms relying heavily upon such systems.

ARTIFICIAL INTELLIGENCE IN AUDITING

Two branches of artificial intelligence (AI) having a significant impact on auditing are expert systems and neural networks. Expert systems are well established in the auditing area. In addition to providing assistance with audit tasks, these expert auditor systems serve as training aids for inexperienced auditors and as knowledge reservoirs. The applications for which expert auditor systems have been developed are discussed in Chapter 16.

Neural networks solve audit problems by recognizing patterns in data that may be too subtle or complex for auditors to discern. A neural network can solve a greater range of audit problems than an expert system. Chapter 16 also examines audit applications of neural networks.

SUMMARY

Audits of information systems examine the reliability of information generated and the efficiency and effectiveness of the systems. Among the types performed are management, operational, compliance, internal control, systems development, fraud, and financial audits. Audits are performed by both external and internal auditors and involve manual and computer-based systems.

Auditors are guided by codes of professional conduct,

which include standards concerning professional characteristics and the scope of audits. However, computerization does affect the audit procedures and techniques.

The auditing process includes steps such as initiating audit planning, reviewing and documenting the internal control structure, assessing the control risk, performing tests of controls, evaluating the findings of the tests of controls, developing the audit program, assessing the detection risk, selecting and performing substantive tests, and communicating the audit results in written reports. The two types of written reports are the audit report and the letter of reportable conditions.

The three major approaches to audits of computer-based systems are auditing-around-the-computer, auditing-through-the-computer, and auditing-with-the-computer. The first two of these approaches are mainly used for test of controls and involve techniques such as transaction traces, printout review, code review, parallel processing, test data, integrated test facility, parallel simulations, and embedded audit routines. The auditing-with-the-computer approach uses the power of the computer to assist in the completion of the audit. The main auditing-with-the-computer approach uses the generalized audit software (GAS) technique. A GAS package is a collection of program routines that perform audit functions such as extracting or retrieving data, calculating with data, performing comparisons with data, analyzing data, reorganizing data, selecting samples, gathering statistical data, and printing outputs. Microcomputer-aided auditing software packages have become widely used and include statistical packages, graphics software, GAS, and templates. Recent developments in auditing involve data-base systems, computer networks, operational audits of the DP function, and microcomputer-based expert audit systems.

··

APPENDIX TO CHAPTER 10

OTHER AUDITING-THROUGH-THE-COMPUTER-APPROACHES

This section examines auditing-through-the-computer approaches less frequently used or having lesser potential than the techniques discussed in the body of the chapter. During the early survey of the internal control structure, an auditor may review documentation prepared by the firm being audited. For instance, an auditor might review program flowcharts and narrative descriptions of applications and the underlying programs. Later in the auditing process, during the evaluation of tests of controls, computer-generated documentation can be reviewed. This type of documentation includes statistics concerning usage of computer resources, contents of data files, and evaluations of program controls in application programs. Such reviews can be revealing, in that they provide the auditor with a clearer picture of the interaction of the computer system and the processing software.

Program Code Checking

One such review is program code checking, which requires the auditor to obtain the latest version of the program he plans to evaluate, review the program documentation, and manually study the logic embodied in the programs line by line. The auditor identifies and tests by "inference" each program control contained in the source code. Sample transactions are traced through the program to judge whether the implemented controls appear to be functioning as written. A written report on weaknesses contained in the program and recommendations for improving the program are provided to the client. Limitations of this technique include the following:

1. Evaluates only a limited number of exceptions in the program.
2. Fails to test the "real" operation of the program.
3. Requires a reasonable degree of computer "literacy."
4. Demands considerable time to properly apply.

Parallel Processing

The parallel processing or controlled reprocessing approach, illustrated in Figure 10-13, requires two computer runs of the client's data, one by the client and a second or "parallel" run by the auditor. As shown on the left-hand side of the figure, the client enters the actual payroll transactions for the period ended May 14 onto a disk file. The data are run with the client's production payroll programs to generate the actual processing results. As shown on the right-hand side of the figure, during the course of the audit, the auditor dumps a copy of the client's actual payroll transactions for the period ended May 14 and production payroll programs to his computer. The auditor runs the payroll transactions with the payroll programs to produce test results, which are compared to the client's actual payroll results for the period ending May 14. The two processing results should agree since the two parallel processing runs used the same payroll transactions. An exception report is generated, any exceptions are evaluated and analyzed, and a written report containing findings is prepared and delivered to the client. The main disadvantage of parallel processing is that it is a narrow version of the test data approach. The client's payroll programs may contain only a limited number of programmed checks that correctly function for the particular pay period tested by the auditor. Thus, the auditor cannot conclude that the payroll programs will function correctly for all pay periods since he or she did not develop simulated transactions testing a variety of valid and invalid conditions.

Parallel Simulation Technique

As the term implies, the **parallel simulation technique** simulates the actual processing that a firm's system

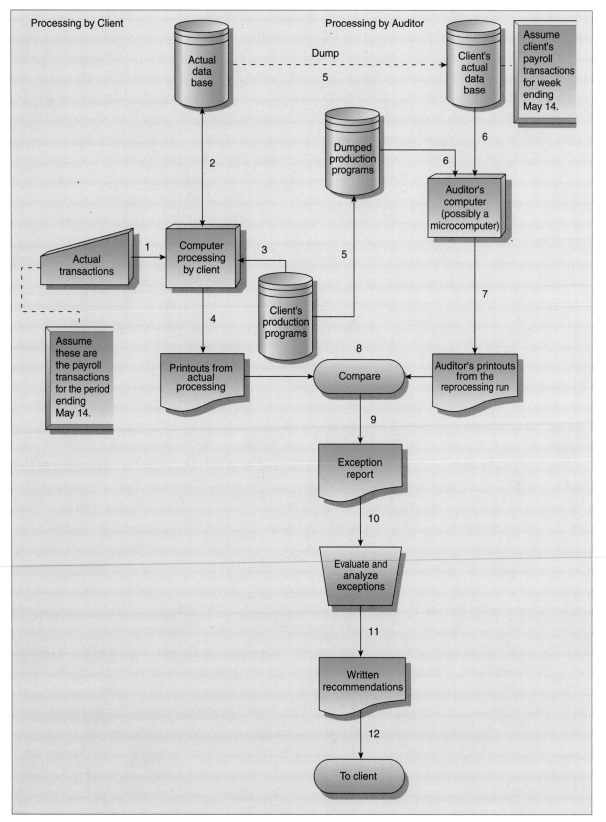

FIGURE 10-13   Parallel processing approach.

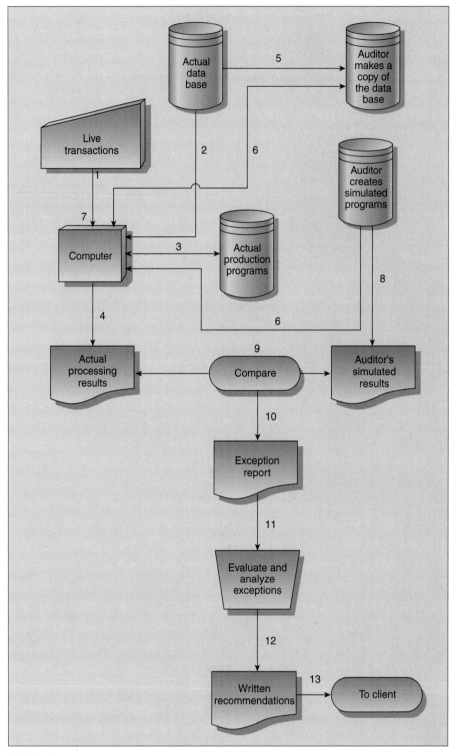

FIGURE 10-14   Parallel simulation approach.

performs. As shown in Figure 10-14, to employ this technique, the auditor copies the portion of the client's actual data base that the auditor will be testing. Then, the auditor must create or develop a program that is a model of one or more "production" programs used by the firm for processing applications. This program can be written by the auditor or by a consulting computer programmer retained by the auditor. In microcomputer environments, the auditor can often purchase a software package that models the client's production programs. For instance, the auditor could purchase a payroll package program to model the client's payroll program. Then the auditor reprocesses the same actual data that were processed earlier. Reports generated during the simulated processing runs are compared by the auditor with the reports generated during regular processing runs. Differences between the reports suggest that the "production" programs are not processing in accordance with desired specifications.

Since the parallel simulation technique validates the actual processing outputs, it may be used in substantive testing as well as in tests of controls. The technique has several drawbacks. Developing a simulation program is time-consuming and expensive and requires considerable programming expertise. After the test results are obtained, difficulties are often experienced in tracing differences between the two sets of outputs back to faults in the "production" programs.

Controlled Processing

The final auditing-through-the-computer procedure to be surveyed is the **controlled processing approach.** As depicted in Figure 10-15, at an unannounced time the auditor makes a surprise visit to the client's computer center and takes over the processing of actual application programs. The client's computer operators run the programs under the auditor's supervision. The auditor observes the resubmission of input containing errors, reviews error listings to determine if programmed controls are functioning, and observes the distribution of reports. The approach has limitations similar to the parallel processing approach.

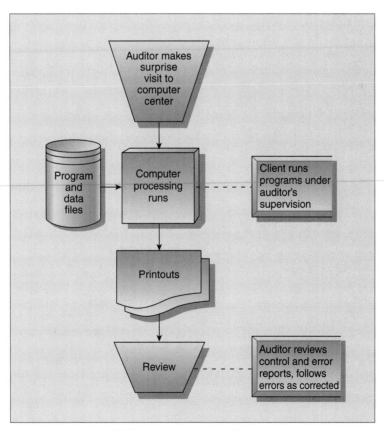

FIGURE 10-15   Controlled processing approach.

REVIEW PROBLEM WITH SOLUTION

MERLIN DISTRIBUTORS, INC.

Statement

Merlin Distributors, Inc., of Normal, Illinois, provides a variety of home appliances to consumers through retailers located in most states. Although it markets the appliances under its own name, it acquires the merchandise from several manufacturers. Its major operations consist of purchasing, receiving, storing, and distributing the appliance products. These operations have been growing in volume since the firm's inception two decades ago. All of the operations are conducted at a single site.

As sales and related inventory activities grew in volume, management recognized the need for data processing assistance. Thus, it first installed a computer system ten years ago. Although the system provided considerable assistance, it gradually became outdated. Consequently, last year the firm installed a late-model computer system. This new system includes a mainframe computer processor, magnetic tape and disk drives, high-speed printers, key-to-tape devices, and several terminals. It serves a redesigned information system that is organized around three processing areas: the revenue cycle (i.e., the sales and cash receipts systems), the inventory control system, and the general ledger system. Transaction processing primarily affects these areas and is performed in batch mode. However, authorized personnel can directly access data in magnetic disk files via the terminals.

You have just been designated the auditor in charge of an impending financial audit of the computerized inventory control system. This will be the first audit involving the new computerized system.

Required

a. Outline the auditing process that you plan to follow, assuming that you discover that the internal accounting controls relating to the computerized portion of the information system are sufficiently adequate to be relied on.

b. Describe audit techniques and procedures, especially computerized techniques, that will be useful in tests of controls. Assume that special audit instructions have been incorporated into the inventory program during its development.

c. List several specific audit objectives to be achieved during the substantive testing step.

d. Discuss how your firm's GAS package can be used with respect to each of the audit objectives listed in **c**.

Solution

a. The audit process to be followed consists of the following steps:

(1) Develop the audit objectives and scope, and then acquire adequate knowledge concerning management's philosophy and operating style, the organizational structure, the personnel policies and practices, the accounting information system, and relevant external influences.

(2) Perform a review of the internal control structure pertaining to the inventory transaction flows; document by means of such techniques as flowcharts and questionnaires.

(3) Assess the level of control risk.

(4) If the assessment in (3) indicates that the computer-oriented control structure can be relied on, devise and perform tests of controls.

(5) Evaluate, on the basis of the tests of controls, the operational effectiveness of the portion of the internal control structure relating to the inventory control system.

(6) Develop the audit program, including the audit objectives relating to the inventory control application and the substantive tests and procedures needed to achieve them.

(7) Perform the substantive tests with the aid of the GAS package.

(8) Prepare a letter of reportable conditions in which any discovered control weaknesses are described, plus the auditors' report to the owners.

b. Audit techniques and procedures that are suitable for tests of controls pertaining to the inventory control system include

(1) Reviewing evidence (e.g., signatures on system specifications) that the new system development of last year was approved by management throughout the various phases; observing actual procedures followed in the computer operations (e.g., noting whether a data librarian maintains close control over data files).

Computer-oriented techniques may also be used in testing for unauthorized program changes. One technique consists of comparing current inventory processing programs with previous versions of the same programs and tracing changes to signed authorizations. Another technique is controlled reprocessing, in which the same data are processed by the current program and a previous version of the program.

(2) Observing computer operations to determine that systems personnel do not have unre-

stricted access to computer programs or data files, that only authorized personnel have access to the computer facilities, and that passwords are necessary in order to gain access to the system via terminals; examining several passwords to see that they do not allow the holders to access files other than those related to inventory, and that they do not allow files to be modified.

(3) Observing that selected source documents are properly authorized and prenumbered, that batch control totals are properly maintained and logged, that the control group is organizationally independent of the user departments and computer operations, and that key verification is carefully performed; tracing a sample of erroneous transactions listed on computer error reports to the original source documents and to the corrected inputs.

A computer-oriented technique that may be used in testing input controls is the test data technique. It consists of processing test inventory transactions in order to determine whether the programmed checks are comprehensive and operating properly.

(4) Observing the processing in computer operations, the transfers of data from the library to operations, and the movement of output results and error reports from the computer facility back to the control group; tracing selected inventory transactions from source documents to the output reports, and vice versa; reconciling batch control totals shown on batch transmittal sheets to the totals shown on exception and summary reports and in the control log.

Computer-oriented techniques that might be used include (i) embedded audit modules to monitor transaction activity and (ii) traces of selected transactions to observe the functioning of the inventory application programs. The use of these techniques, however, assumes that they are already built into the programs before the audit begins.

(5) Observing the distribution of output reports to the users, verifying that the distribution is in accordance with the distribution manual or log; reviewing the reports and tracing selected batches and file balances to their entries in the reports.

c. Audit objectives to be achieved via substantive testing include the following:

(1) To verify that the quantities shown in the inventory records agree with the physical quantities on hand.

(2) To verify that the prices and extensions for the inventory items are proper, and that the balance in the inventory general ledger account is correct.

(3) To verify that the value of the inventory on hand has been adjusted to allow for reduced salability due to obsolescence, etc.

(Other objectives might be listed, but the preceding objectives are most frequently encountered.)

d. The GAS package may be employed with respect to each of the foregoing objectives as follows:

(1) After the physical inventory is taken, the cards containing the counts of the various items can be keyed onto magnetic tape and the data sorted by inventory item number. This tape file can then be compared against the inventory master file by the GAS package; when the two quantities for an item are not equal, the difference is listed on a report. If a count is missing in either file for an item, that fact is noted on the report. The auditor then investigates the differences and makes necessary adjustments to equalize the quantities.

(2) In preparing the test of inventory prices, the statistical sampling routine of the GAS package can be employed to select a sample of inventory items (each of which lists a current price). Then the auditor can vouch the prices to the suppliers' invoices. The calculating function of the GAS package can be used to recompute the extension for each item, as well as the total amount of the inventory on hand. Any differences will be printed on a report, which will then be investigated by the auditor.

(3) To aid the auditor in analyzing the salability of the inventory, the GAS package can scan all inventory items in the master file and print an analytical report. This report could indicate (i) obsolescence, by listing all items for which no recent sales have been made; or (ii) slow-moving inventory, by listing all items for which the quantity on hand appears excessive in relation to the quantities sold last year. Each item in the report could then be investigated by the auditor.

KEY TERMS

REVIEW QUESTIONS

Note: These questions incorporate material found in the appendix to this chapter.

10-1. What roles do accountants play with respect to auditing?

10-2. What types of audits may be performed within a firm?

10-3. Contrast an external auditor and internal auditor.

10-4. What useful functions do auditing codes of ethics or codes of professional conduct serve?

10-5. What are the general contents of audit standards?

10-6. What effects does computer-based processing have on audit procedures?

10-7. What effects does computer-based processing have on audit standards?

10-8. List and briefly describe the steps in the auditing process.

10-9. Contrast tests of controls and substantive tests.

10-10. Contrast the around-, through-, and with-the-computer approaches.

10-11. Why is the auditing-around-the-computer approach insufficient when performing audits of computer systems?

10-12. Describe techniques that fall under the auditing-through-the-computer approach.

10-13. What are the conditions that should be met when using the test data technique, and what are its limitations?

10-14. What are the advantages of the integrated test facility technique?

10-15. Describe several features that are available with the embedded audit module technique.

10-16. What are the advantages and drawbacks of the embedded audit module technique?

10-17. Describe the parallel simulation technique.

10-18. What audit-assist techniques have become widely used owing to the availability of microcomputers?

10-19. List and briefly describe typical audit functions provided by a generalized audit software (GAS) package.

10-20. Describe the steps performed in using a GAS package such as Audit Command Language (ACL) for Windows 95.

10-21. What are the advantages and limitations of current GAS packages?

10-22. Why must the auditor obtain audit evidence beyond the testing of internal controls?

10-23. Describe the steps involved in conducting an operational audit of the data processing function.

10-24. What recent developments in computer-based systems are affecting audits?

10-25. What steps and tests of controls are suitable when auditing data-base systems?

10-26. What steps and tests of controls are suitable when auditing computer networks?

10-27. How may expert systems be employed in the auditing process?

DISCUSSION QUESTIONS

10-28. Contrast the level and types of computer-related knowledge needed by a general auditor and a computer information systems auditor.

10-29. Why should an external auditor, whose primary responsibility is to express an opinion concerning the representations in financial statements, suggest improvements to the information system?

10-30. Why do audit techniques always seem to lag behind the developments in computer technology? Can this lag be overcome in the future?

10-31. During the course of a meeting between Diane Varney, treasurer and controller of Infoage, Inc., and George Freeman, president of Infoage, George asks Diane if she recommends an annual audit of the firm's financial statements. Diane tells him such an audit is not necessary. Do you agree?

10-32. Assume in Question 10-31 that Diane recommends an annual audit of Infoage's financial statements. After a few weeks, the firm receives bids from two audit firms: A large regional CPA firm and Ann Strong's firm. Who should be responsible for selecting the audit firm? Both bids are approximately equal. What factors should the firm consider in making the final selection?

10-33. Assume that Ann Strong is applying for a bank loan to expand her consulting practice. The bank requires an audit of Ann's financial statements to help it evaluate the loan application. What specific aspects of the five components of the internal control structure will be evaluated by the firm conducting the audit?

10-34. Do you think Ann Strong is qualified to conduct operational audits of the data processing department?

10-35. Do you feel that Infoage, Inc., should hire a full-time internal auditor?

10-36. Why is it becoming increasingly important for auditors to be consulted during the development phases of a new information system? Should the auditor ideally be a member of the systems development team? What other roles may the auditor assume?

10-37. Assume that an audit firm is about to conduct an audit of a small firm. How should the audit firm determine if the firm is auditable?

PROBLEMS

10-1. Davis Industries has been manufacturing small machine parts for ten years. Recently, management decided to establish an internal auditing function within the organization. Before submitting the proposal to the board of directors, the president, Tom Paulsen, wants to learn more about internal auditing. In particular, Paulsen wants to know what impact the internal auditing function will have on the external audit performed by the firm's independent accountant. Paulsen has asked Barbara Meiser, Davis's accounting manager, to prepare a report on the internal auditing function.

Required

a. Identify and describe the objectives of the internal auditing function.

b. Describe the ideal positioning and reporting responsibility of the internal auditing function within the organization.

c. What types of audits might the internal auditors be assigned to perform?

d. What types of audits will the external auditors likely perform, and what role (if any) would the internal auditors likely have in this type of audit?

e. Assume that the external auditors are satisfied with the competence of the internal auditing staff and with the firm's internal control structure. Identify and describe at least three coordinating efforts that occur between the internal auditing staff and the external auditor.

f. What benefits could Davis Industries derive from the addition of the internal auditing function?

(CMA *adapted*)

10-2. Glazer Enterprises is a holding firm that has purchased many firms in different industries in order to diversify. Glazer's most recent acquisition was Tanner Stores, a regional chain of department stores.

The audit committee of Glazer's board of directors has established a policy of having the internal audit function conduct a review of the operations of all new acquisitions. The primary purpose of this review is to determine the strength of each firm's internal control structure.

Such a review was conducted for Tanner Stores. The director of internal audit reported to Glazer's senior management and audit committee that he believed there were serious weaknesses in the control activities over cash receipts. As a consequence of the suspected poor controls over cash receipts, and the fact that cash receipts are part of the revenue cycle, the audit committee directed the internal audit manager to conduct an audit of the revenue cycle of Tanner Stores.

Required

a. What audit standards should be followed in performing the audit of the revenue cycle?

b. Discuss the means by which the internal auditors likely determined that serious weaknesses probably exist regarding cash receipts.

c. What are the audit objectives with respect to cash receipts?

d. The audit committee decided to expand the scope of the audit as a consequence of the suspected poor control activities over cash. What other course of action could have been taken?

(CMA adapted)

10-3. Sylvan Engineering is a regional distributor of tool, die, jig, and fixture components. The firm's primary customers, located in the upper Midwest, are the manufacturers of tooling for the automotive and machine tool industries. Sylvan has one location with a warehouse and administrative offices.

Sylvan Engineering uses a minicomputer system with two five-gigabyte disk drives, 14 networked microcomputers, and two printers. The computer department has a manager who reports to the vice-president for distribution and computer operations. The system is used for order processing, billing, accounts receivable and payable, inventory, sales analysis, and the general ledger. Most of the applications are interactive. Payroll has been outsourced to a data processing service bureau, and the fixed asset system is manual. All systems development is done by the equipment/software supplier.

Sylvan's external auditors have recently completed a review of the firm's internal control structure. Several weaknesses in the electronic data processing (EDP) general controls were noted and are presented below.

    a. The reconciliation of batch totals is performed by the EDP manager.

    b. All documentation, which consists of run manuals only, is prepared by the software vendor.

    c. A console log is produced daily but is not reviewed nor kept on file.

    d. Program changes are initiated by the EDP manager and implemented and tested by the software vendor. No formal approvals are required.

    e. User passwords are not used; all microcomputers can access any application that is on-line.

    f. Sylvan has no EDP steering committee and as a result no long-range EDP plan, no security committee, and no disaster contingency and recovery plan.

Required

a. Identify the criteria that would be used by the external auditor to determine whether the firm's internal control structure is adequate.

b. (1) Describe the review and evaluation steps or phases in the audit process.

    (2) Explain what the external auditor reviews to gather evidence during each of these steps or phases of an internal control structure study, assuming that the firm's information system is automated.

c. For the six weaknesses in Sylvan Engineering's EDP general controls that are noted in the auditor's report,

    (1) Recommend a corrective action to be taken by Sylvan Engineering.

    (2) Describe how each recommendation would prevent future problems.

(CMA adapted)

10-4. An internal auditor is preparing to audit a portion of her firm's automated payroll application. She designates the scope of the audit to include only the following: payroll computation, labor cost distribution, payroll taxes, and paycheck distribution.

Required

Indicate whether each of the following proposed audit procedures should or should not be included in the audit program. Justify any exclusions (e.g., this procedure is beyond the scope of the audit, this procedure does not provide useful audit evidence, etc.).

a. Review the computer programming related to payroll computations.

b. Review programmed checks incorporated into payroll programs.

c. Review a sample of time cards for overtime abuse schemes.

d. Review last year's pay rates with current pay rates.

e. Perform a reconciliation of time card hours to hours recorded on production time cards.

f. Conduct an analysis of payroll withholding taxes.

g. Determine whether checks are delivered to departmental timekeepers for distribution.

h. Perform a reivew of workers' compensation claims.

i. Distribute checks to employees on a sample basis and require positive identification of the payee.

j. Obtain a certificate from the timekeeper pertaining to employees who were absent when the auditor distributed paychecks and who are to be paid later in the usual manner.

k. Review personnel files to verify documents in payroll files.

l. Review procedures related to the signing of paychecks.

m. Review payments of employee benefit premiums withheld.

(CIA adapted)

10-5. Linder Company of Fresno, California, is completing the implementation of its new, automated inventory control and purchase order system. Linder's controller wants the controls incorporated into the programs of the new system to be reviewed and evaluated. This is to ensure that all necessary computer controls are included and functioning properly. The controller respects and has confidence in the system department's work and evaluation procedures, but she would like a separate appraisal of the control procedures by the internal audit department. It is hoped that such a review would reveal any weaknesses or omissions in control procedures and lead to their immediate correction before the system becomes operational.

The internal audit department carefully reviews the input, processing, and output controls when evaluating a new system. When assessing the processing controls incorporated into the programs of new systems applications, the internal auditors regularly employ the approach commonly referred to as auditing-through-the-computer.

Required

a. Identify specific application controls and programmed checks that should be incorporated in the programs of the new system.

b. Prepare a matrix that specifies the fields of data to be verified by the respective programmed checks listed in **a**, given that the following data items are entered relating to a purchase: transaction code, supplier name, supplier number, inventory item number, quantity ordered, unit of measure.
Hint: See the Review Problem.

c. Describe at least two techniques that can verify the proper functioning of controls by means of the through-the-computer approach.

(CMA *adapted*)

10-6. A retail organization has just implemented electronic data interchange (EDI) to issue purchase orders to major vendors. The client has developed a data base of "approved vendors." New vendors can be added only after a thorough review by the purchasing manager and marketing director. Only purchasing agents can issue purchase orders and the amount of purchase orders for a particular product line cannot exceed a budgeted amount specified by the marketing manager.

All purchases go to the distribution center where they are electronically scanned into the computer system. All incoming items must reference a firm purchase order and any items that do not contain such a reference will not be accepted. Prenumbered receiving slips are not used, but all receipts are referenced to the purchase order. Price tags are generated per the purchase order and for the quantities indicated by the electronically scanned-in receiving report. The number of price tags generated is reconciled with the number of products received.

The vendor sends an invoice to the retailer. The invoices are entered into the system by data entry clerks. The computer software is programmed to match the vendor invoice, the purchase order, and the receiving report.

If the three items are matched within a tolerance of 0.5 percent, the computer program schedules the items for payment at a time to take advantage of purchase discounts. A check is generated by the cash disbursements program and is electronically signed and mailed. If there is a discrepancy among the three documents, a report is printed and sent to the accounts payable department for investigation.

Required

a. What is the best audit approach to determine whether the control procedure to limit the amount of purchases for a particular product line was working properly during the past year?

b. Sometimes one control procedure by itself is not sufficient to achieve a particular control objective. One control objective for this system is to ensure that purchase orders are made only by authorized purchasing agents, to authorized vendors, for authorized goods. What combination of control procedures would be necessary to accomplish this objective?

c. The auditor desires to determine that the program is correctly approving items for payment only when the purchase order, receiving report, and vendor invoice match within the tolerable 0.5 percent. Which computerized audit techniques would provide the most persuasive evidence as to the correct operation of the program?

d. The auditor desires to test controls over computer program changes. The specific objective to be addressed in the following audit step is *that only authorized changes have been made to computer programs* (i.e., *there are no unauthorized program changes*). The organization uses an automated program library system and the auditor obtains copies of the table of contents of the program library system at various periods of time. The table of contents indicates the date a change was last made to the program, the version number of the program, and the length of the program. What audit procedures would best address the stated objective?

(CIA *adapted*)

10-7. Discuss the suitability of using the test data audit technique for each of the following situations.

    a. An internal auditor has been assigned the task of monitoring the performance of the firm's 110 retail outlets to identify high-risk locations.

    b. A firm's programming staff used the COBOL programming language to write a payroll application. The batch processing payroll system is used to generate paychecks, earnings statements, and other reports for both hourly and salaried employees.

    c. An accountant developed a small rule-based expert system application to provide advice in making journal entries to record exchanges of nonmonetary assets, such as land, property, and equipment. A number of the application's rules contain complicated formulas for making the necessary computations before the expert system can prepare the journal entries.

d. An accountant desires to recompute his client's lower of cost or market inventory calculation.

e. A firm uses a real-time sales processing system to generate a variety of sales analyses.

f. A large firm uses a mainframe computer to process all accounting applications. The firm uses the batch sequential processing mode to process most applications. On average, the accounting department processes 55,000 transactions per month.

g. A firm's programmers developed an accounts receivable application by using a data-base management system software package. The application's outputs include accounts receivable summary reports and aging schedules and customer monthly statements.

h. An end user developed an important spreadsheet application to compute the amount of commissions due to sales personnel.

i. Several of a firm's executives use an executive information system to periodically prepare a number of preformatted financial reports.

j. A large firm employs an enterprisewide LAN-based client/server setup to process transactions, generate financial statements, and produce managerial reports.

k. An external auditor desires to compute a number of key financial ratios to identify unusual relationships.

l. A small firm with annual sales of $1,000,000 is currently using an accounting software package (e.g., DACEASY) to generate financial statements and prepare other accounting reports.

m. An internal auditor desires to determine whether a check digit program module placed into an accounts receivable program is properly working. The check digit program uses the modulus-11 method to generate a check digit when customer account numbers are entered by data-entry personnel.

10-8. The Weimer Co. of Ames, Iowa, processes its payment transactions on a computer system. Batches of payment transactions are keyed onto magnetic disk from check vouchers, sorted by supplier number, and then checked by an edit run. Each payment transaction record contains the following data elements. The size of the fields containing the data and sample data values appears to the right of the data element names.

Data Element	Size of Field (in characters)	Sample Value
Supplier number	4	4569
Voucher number	5	20310
Voucher date	6	060393
Invoice date	6	052893
Invoice number	5	68732
Purchase order number	5	10500
Due date	6	070393
Check number	6	530000
Check date	6	070293
Amount	9	5000.00

The edit program has been designed to verify the input data and processing by the use of the following types of programmed checks: field check, completeness test, sign check, sequence check, validity check, limit check, and relationship check.

Required

a. Prepare a matrix that specifies the particular data elements to be verified by each of the programmed checks.

b. Prepare test transactions that each contain one error intended to determine that a programmed check is functioning properly. Each transaction should contain data in all the fields (except when the completeness of data is being tested). List the test transactions in the rows of a table that has columns pertaining to the ten fields of input data (with the column headings consisting of the data item names). In a separate table state the purpose of each transaction and show the expected result that should appear on an exception and summary report.

10-9. Refer to Problem 10-8. The Weimer Co. also processes its sales transactions on a computer system. Each sales order is entered via a terminal at a sales branch and stored on a magnetic disk at the home office to await further processing. As each sales order is entered, it is checked by an edit program. Each transaction involving a sales order should include the following data: user code, transaction code, customer number, sales branch number, salesperson number, expected shipping date, product number(s), and quantity (or quantities).

Required

a. Prepare test data that are to be used to check for the presence of needed programmed checks in the edit program. State the purpose of each test and show how an error detected by the test might be displayed on the screen of the auditor's terminal.

b. If the integrated test facility technique is employed in conjunction with the test sales transactions, describe the likely contents of the test facility and the report based on the contents.

10-10. An internal auditor for Consolidated Freight Company of Vancouver, British Columbia, has determined that an end user has implemented a major application on a spreadsheet. The spreadsheet takes input regarding projected freight deliveries from the mainframe computer and develops an optimal freight dispatching plan. When first used two years ago, the spreadsheet application helped reduce costs dramatically. However, freight costs have been increasing and no one, other than the developer, has reviewed the spreadsheet application.

The freight dispatching algorithm is complicated, but the internal auditor has researched the area and understands the algorithm and its correct computation. The internal auditor is considering three options to gain assurance on whether the spreadsheet application has properly implemented the freight dispatching algorithm. These options are (1) develop an independent spreadsheet, run test data through it and through the user's spreadsheet, and compare the results; (2) print out the logic of the freight dispatching algorithm and examine the logic line by line to determine if it has been correctly incorporated into the spreadsheet application; (3) develop a set of test data, manually calculate the expected results, run the test data through the user application, and compare the results.

Required

a. Discuss the merits and limitations of each one of the three options in verifying whether the freight dispatching algorithm has been properly implemented.

b. Assume the audit testing indicates that the spreadsheet application has correctly implemented the freight dispatching algorithm. What conclusion is justified from the audit evidence?

(CIA *adapted*)

10-11. Talbert Corporation hired an independent computer programmer to develop a simplified payroll application for its newly purchased computer. The programmer developed an on-line data-base microcomputer system that minimized the level of knowledge required by the operator. It was based on typing answers to input cues that appeared on the terminal's viewing screen, examples of which follow.

New employees routine.
  a. Employee name?
  b. Employee number?
  c. Social security number?
  d. Rate per hour?

  e. Single or married?
  f. Number of dependents?
  g. Account distribution?

Current payroll routine.
  a. Employee number?
  b. Regular hours worked?
  c. Overtime hours worked?
  d. Total employees this payroll period?

The independent auditor is attempting to verify that certain input validation (edit) checks exist to ensure that errors resulting from omissions, invalid entries, or other inaccuracies will be detected during the typing of answers to the input cues.

Required

a. Identify the input validation (programmed edit) checks that the auditor should expect to find in the payroll edit program with respect to each input cue. Note that in the cases of certain cues more than one check is needed and that the same check may be applied to more than one cue. When a check requires that the data response to a cue be compared to another response, identify the data item being compared.

b. For each input validation (programmed edit) check identified in requirement **a,** state the assurances that it should provide in the payroll application.

(CPA *adapted*)

10-12. A medium-sized manufacturing firm is converting from predominantly manual systems to an in-house computerized environment with on-line real-time capabilities. The chief internal auditor and an assistant internal auditor are in the process of evaluating the feasibility of generalized audit software (GAS) to assist in their audit responsibilities.

Required

For the procedures numbered 1 through 20, write the appropriate letter (a, b, or c) that best applies to these described choices:

a. Potentially useful for audit testing, and facilitated by using GAS.

b. Potentially useful for audit testing, but generally not easily adaptable to GAS.

c. Of little apparent audit value even if within capabilities of GAS.

The procedures are as follows:

  1. Selecting and generating audit confirmations.
  2. Processing test checks on programs generated by GAS.

3. Verifying that disbursements are supported by purchase orders and receiving documents.

4. Preparing employee earnings report for tax purposes.

5. Footing the cash receipts file on magnetic tape.

6. Taking a physical count of inventory.

7. Discovering if records are out of sequence.

8. Computing gross pay, FICA, deductions, and net pay.

9. Verifying if the limit test in the payroll program is working as prescribed.

10. Computing financial ratios and other analytical procedures.

11. Writing a computer program to age accounts receivable.

12. Confirming if duplicate payments have been made to suppliers.

13. Verifying that new vendors can be added to the vendor master file on magnetic disk.

14. Preparing a report showing the percentage of customer orders backordered.

15. Listing inventory items with a negative balance on hand.

16. Examining records for completeness.

17. Using parallel simulation techniques.

18. Testing for excessive gross pay.

19. Determining if the same invoice has been paid twice.

20. Checking to see if valid identification numbers have been entered into the file.

(CIA *adapted*)

10-13. Assume that a generalized audit software (GAS) package is used to generate a *listing* of the items shown below. Discuss the audit question(s) to be answered by an examination of each listed item.

a. Employee expense account reimbursements.

b. Vehicles in the motor pool with excessively high maintenance costs.

c. Inventory items with credit balances.

d. Duplicate payments made to the same vendor.

e. Employees and vendors with matching addresses.

f. Employees with no payroll tax withholdings.

g. Patterns of bids from vendors.

h. Cash refunds matched with salespersons' numbers for a six-month period.

i. All vendors who use a post office box number as the shipping address.

j. Vendors who have had a significant number of price increases during the past year.

k. Debits to fixed asset accounts.

l. Checks outstanding for over six months on a bank reconciliation.

m. Sales returns and allowances for the first two weeks of the new accounting period.

n. Purchases made from individual vendors.

o. Employees with overtime.

p. Dates of customers' payments matched with dates the customers' accounts were posted.

10-14. Boos & Baumkirchner, Inc., of Montgomery, Alabama, is a medium-sized manufacturer of products for the leisure-time activities market (camping equipment, scuba gear, bows and arrows, etc.). During the past year, a minicomputer system was installed, and inventory records of finished goods and parts were converted to computer processing. Each record of the inventory master file, which is stored on a magnetic disk, contains the following data elements.

Item or part number
Description
Size
Unit of measure code
Quantity on hand
Cost per unit
Total value of inventory on hand at cost
Date of last sale or usage
Quantity used or sold this year
Economic order quantity
Code number of major supplier

In taking the year-end inventory, the firm's personnel will use a penlike device to write the actual counted quantity onto the screen of a hand-held personal digital assistant (PDA). When all counts are complete, the counted quantity will be downloaded and stored on a file in the minicomputer's hard disk. Then the file will be processed against the master file, and quantity-on-hand figures will be adjusted to reflect the actual count. A listing will be prepared to show all quantity adjustments of more than $100 of value. These items will be investigated, and all required adjustments will be made. When adjustments have been completed, the final year-end balances will be computed and posted to the general ledger.

The external auditor who will supervise the physical inventory and conduct an audit of inventory has available a general-purpose audit software package that runs on his laptop computer. He will download the necessary inventory files from the firm's minicomputer to his laptop and perform the required audit test procedures.

Required

a. What major problems will the external auditor likely encounter in verifying inventory?

b. Describe the ways that a general-purpose computer audit software package can be used to assist in all aspects of the audit of the inventory of Boos & Baumkirchner, Inc. (For example, the package can be used to read the inventory master file and list items and parts with a high unit cost or total value. Such items can be included in the test counts to increase the dollar coverage of the audit verification.)

c. Can the external auditor employ the generalized audit software package to obtain an understanding of the firm's internal control structure? Explain.

d. What other audit tasks can the external auditor perform with his laptop computer when auditing the financial statements of Boos & Baumkirchner, Inc.?

e. What are some likely recent uses of microcomputers as audit tools?

(CPA *adapted*)

10-15. Recently, the Central Savings and Loan Association of Jefferson City, Missouri, installed an on-line computer system. Each teller in the association's main office and seven branch offices has an on-line terminal. Customers' mortgage payments and savings account deposits and withdrawals are recorded in the accounts by the computer from data input by the teller at the time of the transaction. The teller keys the proper account by account number and enters the information in the terminal keyboard to record the transaction. The accounting department at the main office also has terminals. The computer is housed at the main office.

In addition to servicing its own mortgage loans, the association acts as a mortgage servicing agency for three life insurance firms. In the latter activity the association maintains mortgage records and serves as the collection and escrow agent for the mortgagees (the insurance firms), who pay a fee to the association for these services.

Required

Describe the ways an embedded audit module within the deposit/withdrawal processing program might be used to aid in performing tests of controls pertaining to Central's internal accounting controls. In particular, specify the types of erroneous or irregular transactions that should be captured, as well as the characteristics of other transactions of special interest (e.g., withdrawals that are larger than a designated amount).

(CPA *adapted*)

10-16. Sun States Bank, a regional bank, uses an automated human resource system to facilitate management of bank personnel assigned to 12 regional bank offices as well as to the central bank operations center. Operating in a data-base environment, the human resource system manages fundamental personnel functions, from hiring through termination, including personnel administration, payroll, benefits, promotions, and retirements. In addition, it supports management's attainment of affirmative action and equal employment opportunity goals and staff development policies.

Managers at each of the 12 regional offices and functional managers at the bank operations center are authorized to initiate human resource actions. Multiple-copy documents initiated by regional managers are delivered to the human resource manager for approval prior to data conversion and batch-mode data entry via terminals at the bank operations center. Functional activities at the operations center are authorized to update selected on-line application systems within the data base without hard-copy input. Input documents are filed after data entry. The data base is updated during processing, and a variety of output reports are generated for the managers who initiated actions as well as for the human resource manager.

Required

a. What security risks does a data base pose?

b. How would the audit of a data base differ from the audit of AIS applications programmed in COBOL?

c. What concerns would the specific data base of Sun States cause an auditor, and what means and techniques are available to an auditor in combating these concerns?

d. Can the auditor use a generalized audit software package to conduct audit tests of the human resource data base?

e. Of what use are structured query language commands in auditing the human resource data base?

(CIA *adapted*)

10-17. Sportgarb, Inc., a nationwide sportswear retailer, is preparing to implement electronic data interchange (EDI) of invoices, purchase orders, and delivery schedules with its suppliers. The retailer has a single distribution center for all the stores, which transmit sales and inventory positions daily to the distribution center. When conversion is complete, EDI will be used to transfer all business documents between the retailer and its suppliers. If EDI is really successful, management wants to implement EDI in its other lines of business.

Management has asked the director of internal auditing to plan for auditing the sportswear division to (i) compare its performance with and without EDI and (ii) audit the new system after installation on a continuing basis. The director consulted the audit staff, who suggested considering the following techniques for the continuing audit:

a. Test data method
b. Integrated test facility
c. Parallel simulation
d. Snapshot and mapping

Before responding to management, the director wanted the audit staff to agree on the best approach and decided to prepare a memorandum to the audit staff as a basis for further discussion.

Required

a. What security risks does EDI pose?

b. Prepare a memorandum that suggests the most suitable technique or techniques to employ for a continuous audit and justifies the selection(s), that explains why the other techniques are not suitable, and that proposes data to use in comparing performance with and without EDI.

(CIA *adapted*)

10-18. Microtronics, Inc., is a private firm involved in genetic engineering. The firm was started in 1988 by Joseph Graham, a scientist, and is financed by a group of venture capitalists. Microtronics has had some successful research, and one of its products recently received approval from the Federal Drug Administration (FDA). Two other products have been submitted to the FDA and are awaiting approval. Because of these successes, the investors believe the time is right for preparing the firm for a public stock offering.

In preparation for the public offering, Microtronics is having its financial statements audited for the first time by an external audit firm. During initial discussions with the audit firm, the partner in charge of the engagement stated that the first step would be to review and test Microtronics' internal control structure. Graham, unfamiliar with auditing procedures, is concerned about the cost of this review and wonders if it is necessary.

Required

a. Explain the purpose of the external auditor's study and evaluation of the internal control structure in connection with the audit of Microtronics' financial statements.

b. Identify the process promulgated by the Committee of Sponsoring Organizations of the Treadway Committee (COSO) that an external auditor would use to determine if Microtronics' internal control structure is adequate.

c. There are two phases in the internal control structure review conducted by an external auditor.

    (1) What information should the external auditor obtain from a preliminary review of the internal control structure? What would the external auditor review to obtain evidence during this phase of the study? Upon completion of the preliminary review, list possible conclusions that the external auditor may reach.

    (2) What information should the external auditor obtain from a completion of review and testing of controls phase? What would the external auditor review and/or test to obtain evidence during this phase of the audit? Upon completion of this phase of the audit, list possible conclusions that the external auditor may reach.

d. How would you answer Graham's concern about the cost and necessity of this review? Should all firms be following the recommendations made in the COSO report?

e. How will flattened organizational structures, the empowerment of lower-level workers, and the implementation of client/server architectures change the internal control structure? The external audit?

(CMA *adapted*)

10-19. The Desmond Manufacturing Company of South Orange, New Jersey, recently installed an on-line computer system, primarily to monitor its production operations. Your public accounting firm performs the annual financial audit, and you have been assigned to audit the direct labor and materials collection and processing system.

In meeting with the production manager during your visit, you learn that the computer hardware used in this production system consists of a mainframe processor, terminals at the various production floor workstations and in the materials storeroom, magnetic disk drives, and a high-speed printer. The data collection and processing procedure is as follows: Data concerning labor hours worked on production jobs are entered via the production floor terminals by the production employees themselves. Data concerning direct materials charged into production are entered via the storeroom terminal by the storeskeeper. Labor and materials data are edited when entered and then stored temporarily. Late each afternoon the data are processed by a job costing program, and the relevant files (i.e., materials inventory, labor costs, and work-in-process inventory) are updated. Outputs from this processing include job cost reports, labor distribution reports, materials usage reports, cost variance reports, and exception and summary reports. Standard costs maintained in an on-line file are used to convert the labor times and material quantities to dollar values and to apply overhead.

Required

a. Outline the auditing process that you plan to follow, assuming that you discover that the internal control structure relating to the production labor and materials system is sufficiently adequate to be relied on.

b. Describe audit techniques that will be useful in tests of controls. Assume that special audit instructions have been incorporated into the job costing program during its development.

c. List several specific audit objectives to be achieved during substantive testing.

d. Discuss specific functions that your firm's GAS package can perform during substantive testing.

Hint: Refer to the Review Problem and to any standard auditing textbook during the preparation of the solution.

10-20. Discuss the ethical implications of each of the following cases.

Hint: You may wish to review the material on ethics in Chapters 1, 7, and 10 before solving the cases.

   a. During an audit of a manufacturing division of a defense contractor, the auditor came across a scheme that looked like the firm was inappropriately adding costs to a cost-plus government contract. The auditor discussed the matter with senior management, which suggested that the auditor seek an opinion from legal counsel. The auditor did so and, upon review of the government contract, legal counsel indicated that the practice was questionable, but did not offer the opinion that the practice was technically in violation of the government contract. Based on legal counsel's decision, the auditor decided to omit any discussion of the practice in the formal audit report that went to management and the audit committee, but did informally communicate legal counsel's decision to management.

   b. The internal auditing department encounters a scope limitation from senior management that will affect its ability to meet its goals and objectives for a potential auditee.

   c. Management has requested that the audit department conduct an audit of the implementation of its recently developed code of conduct for the data processing department. In preparing for the audit, the auditor reviews the newly developed code and compares it with several others for comparable firms' computer departments and concludes that the newly developed code has severe deficiencies.

   d. An internal auditor, recently terminated from a firm because of downsizing, has found a job with another firm in the same industry. While at the previous firm, the auditor conducted a great deal of research to identify "best practices" for management of the data processing department as part of an audit for that firm. Since most of the research was done at home and during nonoffice hours, the auditor retained much of the research and plans to use it in conducting an audit of the management of the data processing department at the new employer.

   e. During a regularly scheduled computer information systems audit of a major division, the CISA discovers a complicated programming algorithm that adds costs to a cost-plus program billing the government. The amount added accounted for 95 percent of the net income for the division for the most recent year. Upon further investigation, the CISA finds that only the marketing manager, the division manager, and the programmer know of the algorithm. The firm has a separate division to investigate fraud. The auditor communicates with management and the special investigation division. The investigation is turned over to that group. However, after a month, it becomes apparent that senior management has instructed the group to "not make waves" and to drop the investigation.

(CIA *adapted*)

10-21. Ted Brown was conducting an audit of the excess materials operation of a manufacturer. This operation was responsible for collection, selling, or otherwise disposing of scrap, salvage, and surplus materials resulting from the operations of the firm. The operation was under the direction of a former operating manager who, several years ago, had been guilty of poor judgment in the management of his department, and because of his proximity to retirement, he was placed in this material disposition function as a holding job until he reached retirement.

Brown was a certified internal auditor (CIA) with four years experience with the firm. He was planning to take courses on the subject of microcomputers. He was an older person and his former employer used entirely manual methods. However, he was beginning to have problems with his current audits as the firm was becoming entirely computerized. When employed, he had indicated more familiarity with computers than he actually had because he was, at that time, registered for a course at a local university—a registration that he had been forced to cancel because of illness.

The excess material department had recently been converted to a computer operation. In the audit program there was an element that required that the auditor, through a microcomputer, query the operation's data base as to various criteria relative to disposal of purchases to see if there were any relationships between purchases, types of material, bid procedures, location, and the like, that would lead one to believe that there might be improper disposals or arrangements. Brown believed that he could obtain adequate information through physical testing of the files. He did this and noticed that there was one buyer who consistently was the purchaser of excess quantities of the nickel pipe used in the firm. This element aroused the auditor's curiosity, and he reviewed the firm's purchasing of the nickel pipe. To his surprise, the amount of nickel pipe disposed of was 50 percent of that purchased during the last two years. The requirements for the pipe in the manufacturing process had not varied during this period.

He reviewed the purchase requisitions and purchase orders for pipe and noticed that they were signed by the same purchasing agent. He then looked at the surplus disposal orders and found that this agent signed these documents as well. He then decided to investigate the buyer of the "excess" pipe and found through a Dun & Bradstreet report that its address was a post office box and that its principal officer was a person with the same initials and last name as the manager of the excess material disposal unit.

Brown collected all of this evidence and asked the unit's manager to talk with him about it. The manager, when faced with the evidence, confessed that he and the purchasing agent had developed the scheme so as to help him, the manager, maintain his standard of living after he had been demoted. The agent was a distant relative of the manager. The manager asked Brown not to report the item for two weeks so that he could arrange for a second mortgage on his home and, thus, replace the funds he had taken from the firm. Brown, against his better judgment, and because of his sympathy for the older man, agreed. In his interim report, Brown indicated that he had completed the computer inquiry and that there were no suspicious findings. The manager had also made a counteroffer to Brown. He agreed to take Brown into the illicit arrangement if he would not report it at all. Brown said he would consider it as he was planning to buy a house and needed funds for a down payment.

After a month had passed and the manager had not made any restitution, Brown went to him to find out the status of his plans. The manager said he had decided not to make restitution and told Brown that if he reported the incident now that he, the manager, would go to top management and disclose Brown's action in withholding the audit finding and considering the illicit partnership.

Required

Using the following format, identify ethics principles violated and how they were violated.

Principle Violated	Explanation of Violation

(CIA *adapted*)

CONTINUING CASE

With respect to the small firm that you selected in Chapter 1, complete the following requirements:

a. Determine what, if any, types of audits are performed within the firm. Who is responsible for conducting any audits performed?

b. If no audits are performed within the firm, what types of audits would you recommend should be conducted?

c. If the firm uses a computer system, determine whether the auditing-around or auditing-through-the-computer or a combination of approaches are employed. How did the firm select the audit approach or approaches in use?

d. If the firm employs the auditing-through-the-computer approach, determine the specific types of through-the-computer approaches used. Evaluate the strengths and weaknesses of these approaches.

e. If the firm uses a generalized audit software (GAS) package,

  (1) Determine the name of the package.

  (2) List the audit functions performed by the GAS package.

CHAPTER
11

THE GENERAL LEDGER AND FINANCIAL REPORTING CYCLE

THE LEARNING OBJECTIVES FOR THIS CHAPTER ARE TO ENABLE YOU TO:

1. Discuss the attributes of transaction cycles and key considerations when designing the cycles for a particular firm.

2. Describe the central nature of the general ledger and financial reporting cycle and list its objectives and functions.

3. Contrast the characteristics and benefits of differing general ledger architectures.

4. Construct a coded chart of accounts for a business firm.

5. Identify the data sources, inputs, files, data sets, data flows and processing, risks and accounting controls, and outputs pertaining to the general ledger system.

6. Describe the nature of financial statements and the characteristics of the responsibility accounting system.

INTRODUCTION

We have seen that transaction processing is an essential activity performed with respect to an accounting information system (AIS). Consequently, this and the following three chapters explore several major transaction processing cycles and systems.

THE CYCLES APPROACH

In order to study transaction processing, we need a framework that is common to most organizations and that reflects their basic events and processes. A framework that best meets these requirements is the **cycles approach,** a plan of grouping business events according to the primary and supporting objectives of the organization. The grouped events are called transaction cycles because they tend to be repeated over and over, either within each accounting period or at the ends of successive accounting periods. As testimony to its usefulness, the cycles approach has been adopted by most of the accounting and auditing firms in the United States.

In Chapters 2 and 5 we briefly surveyed several common cycles, including the revenue cycle, expenditure cycle, resources-management cycle, and general ledger and financial reporting cycle. Among the distinguishing attributes of each of these cycles is that it

1. *Aids in achieving objectives related to the overall mission of an organization.* For instance, the revenue cycle has an objective concerned with obtaining an inflow of funds.

2. *Traces the acquiring and/or managing of needed resources.* For example, the resources-management cycle involves the management of funds, facilities, inventory, and personnel.

411

3. **Incorporates multiple transaction processing systems and business events.** For instance, the revenue cycle includes a sales transaction processing system and a cash receipts transaction processing system, each of which spans one or more business events. As we recall from Chapter 1, transaction processing systems represent an alternative scheme for classifying the subsystems within the AIS.

4. **Encompasses all events that logically follow from the beginning event.** That is, a cycle does not leave "dangling" events. Thus the expenditure cycle begins with the recognition that additional inventory items or supplies are needed and the acquisition of these items or supplies; it continues until the payments for these acquisitions are made and recorded.

DESIGN OF TRANSACTION CYCLES

When designing transaction cycles we should remember that organizations differ in numerous ways. They have different value-added activities, different policies and strategies, and they are governed by different accounting methods and principles.

Effects of Value-Added Activities   Each type of organization requires its own set of transaction cycles. The set for merchandising firms, just described, focuses on value-added activities that make goods conveniently available to customers. Figure 11-1 shows the key business processes and document flows that are included in the major cycles for a merchandising firm like Infoage, Inc. Such external entities as customers and suppliers and banks are included, plus stores of data relating to these entities.

Organizations other than those of the merchandise type have their own distinctive value-added activities. An organization such as a manufacturing firm has activities focused on producing goods. Thus it requires a production cycle, in addition to the cycles needed by a merchandising firm. Similarly, banks have demand-deposit cycles and hospitals have patient-care cycles that support their value-added activities.

Effects of Management Policies   Managers have responsibility for organizing the activities of their firms. The policies that they set can significantly affect the content of the transaction cycles. Consider the revenue cycle of a merchandising firm, for instance. It might establish a policy that goods will be shipped on consignment, with receipts being deferred until the goods are sold. Alternative policies could be to require cash payments before the goods are shipped, or to allow installment payments.

Even the number of transaction cycles conducted by a firm can be affected by managerial policies. For instance, a policy that all assets of the firm be leased will eliminate the need for a fixed assets cycle.

Effects of Accounting Methods and Principles   Both financial and managerial accounting influence the design of transaction cycles. This influence mainly arises from the information needs of users and stakeholders.

Generally accepted accounting principles dictate the way that financial accounting information is presented. In order to prepare the financial statements for external parties, the transaction cycles must capture and process needed data according to rules and principles specified by such accounting authorities as the Financial

FIGURE 11-1   An overview data-flow diagram of basic transaction cycles for a merchandising firm. (*Note:* Certain details have been omitted for the sake of clarity, such as (1) the data stores and flows relating to the merchandise and (2) the activities relating to investments and other resources-management cycles.)

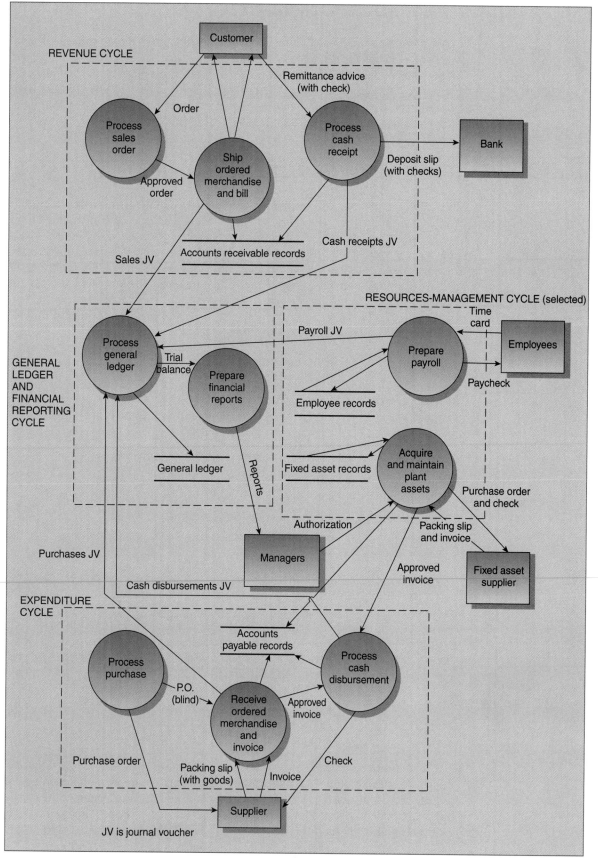

Accounting Standards Board. Such rules and principles range from the valuation of assets to the time that revenue is recognized.

Managerial decision making dictates the format and content of much managerial accounting information. Some of the information will appear as analyses and variance reports; other information may be based on the manipulation of decision models, such as discounted cash-flow models.

NATURE OF THE GENERAL LEDGER AND FINANCIAL REPORTING CYCLE

After careful consideration the **general ledger and financial reporting cycle** has been placed as the first chapter in Part III. The general ledger is the linchpin that ties together all of the component transaction processing cycles and systems. Necessary to *every* organization without exception, it provides the chart of accounts structure, which combines the financial and managerial sides of accounting. Furthermore, financial reporting includes the key financial statements, which present the current status and operating results of each organization. After surveying these pivotal features, we can better understand the functions and relationships of transaction processing systems employed by organizations of all types.

OBJECTIVES OF THE GENERAL LEDGER SYSTEM

The **general ledger system** performs the transaction processing for the general ledger and financial reporting cycle. A sound general ledger system has the following broad objectives:

1. To record all accounting transactions promptly and accurately.
2. To post these transactions to the proper accounts.
3. To maintain an equality of debit and credit balances among the accounts.
4. To accommodate needed adjusting journal entries.
5. To generate reliable and timely financial reports pertaining to each accounting period.

To achieve these objectives, the general ledger system employs a variety of resources in performing the periodic accounting functions centered on the general ledger. The manner in which these functions are performed depends in large part on the degree of information technology that is applied. However, the functions that are common to all organizations appear as processes in Figure 11-2. The data-flow diagram in this figure provides more details concerning the summarized general ledger and financial reporting cycle shown in the center of Figure 11-1.

FUNCTIONS OF THE GENERAL LEDGER SYSTEM

An overview of the general ledger system functions is as follows:

1. ***Collect transaction data.*** Transactions arise from sources such as sales events and purchase events. The high-volume types of transactions are handled by the operational processing systems, such as sales and purchase systems. These major component systems interface with the general ledger system in order to feed it their daily transactions. Thus they may be called *feeder processing systems*. Other

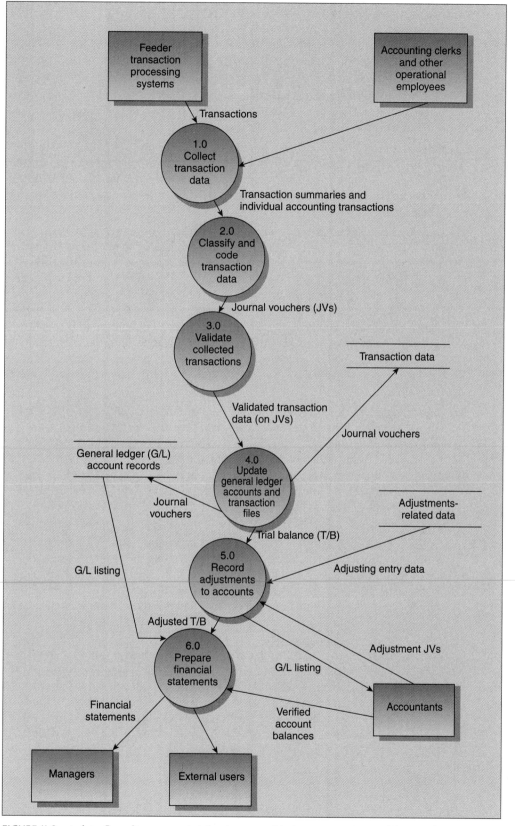

FIGURE II-2   A data-flow diagram pertaining to general ledger processing and financial reporting.

transactions arising individually are recorded by accounting clerks or managers, generally on specially designed hard-copy journal vouchers or preformatted screens.

2. **Classify and code transaction data and accounts.** Daily summaries of transactions, as well as individual transactions, are classified and coded according to a prescribed chart of accounts.

3. **Validate collected transactions.** To ascertain the accuracy of data, the collected transactions are necessarily validated by various control procedures. Each transaction can be subjected to checks on amounts, account names, authorization codes, and so on. Batches of transactions can be totaled and compared to predetermined batch totals.

4. **Update general ledger accounts and transaction files.** The ledgers represent master files within a firm's data base. A key step in processing is to update the ledger account balances through the posting of transaction data. Supporting these updated accounts are details of the transactions, which are kept in transaction files.

   At the end of each accounting period (which may be a month, quarter, or year) all of the period's transactions should have been posted. Each ending general ledger account balance should equal the beginning balance plus all transaction amounts increasing the balance, and minus all transaction amounts reducing the balance. An unadjusted trial balance is prepared to check that the total of accounts having debit balances equals the total of accounts having credit balances.

5. **Record adjustments to accounts.** Financial statements must be prepared at the end of each accounting period. However, if the accrual accounting system is employed, adjustments are needed to recognize revenues and expenses that are not reflected by the actual cash amounts received or disbursed during the period. After these adjustments are made, then an adjusted trial balance is prepared. Other outputs based on the general ledger are also prepared, such as changes to the various accounts during the period.

6. **Prepare financial reports.** The three primary financial statements are the income statement, balance sheet, and statement of cash flows. Information for the income statement is drawn from the adjusted revenue and expense account balances in the general ledger. After the revenue and expense accounts are closed to the retained earnings (or other owners' equity) account, the balance sheet showing assets and equities can be prepared. Finally, the statement of cash flows is prepared from the accounts, plus other cash-related transactions.

   While the most familiar financial outputs are the financial statements, numerous other reports and outputs are needed. Financial reports for managers include operating budgets and responsibility reports. Financial information for stockholders, usually provided in annual reports, includes descriptions of future undertakings and dividend rates as well as the financial statements. All financial outputs, and the underlying records, should be extensively reviewed by accountants before their release.

GENERAL LEDGER SYSTEM ARCHITECTURES

Like all of its transaction processing systems, a firm's general ledger system may be noncomputerized or computerized. These two basic system architectures affect the natures of the inputs, outputs, processing, data storage and retrieval, and other facets. In this section we will highlight the notable differences due to the architectures, especially as they affect the general ledger system. (However, many of these differences pertain to all of the transaction processing systems within the AIS.)

MANUAL GENERAL LEDGER SYSTEMS

In the past all firms used noncomputerized, or manual, general ledger systems. Many small firms (such as "Mom and Pop" businesses) still do. The major advantage of manual systems is their simplicity and lack of vulnerability. Users do not need to be trained in the details of accounting software packages. They can focus on the accounting essentials. Also, users do not need to be concerned about computer failures or wiped-out records.

The key data flows and processing steps for manual systems were described near the end of Chapter 2. Transaction data flow into journals from source documents. Data from source documents involving high-volume transactions, such as sales and cash disbursements, may be entered into special journals; all other transactions are entered into the general journal. Columns in the journals are summed to generate batch totals. Data from the source documents may also be posted to subsidiary ledgers. Totals accumulated from the postings to subsidiary ledgers are posted to the general ledger, after being compared with the precomputed batch totals. The financial statements are then manually prepared from the general ledger. Certain other reports and listings may also be prepared from the journals (and subsidiary ledgers, if any).

COMPUTERIZED GENERAL LEDGER SYSTEMS

Almost all firms, except the smallest, have computerized their transaction cycles, including their general ledger systems. The adopted computerized system architectures vary widely from firm to firm. These architectures may range from single

---

1. Transaction data may be captured by electronic devices and stored on magnetic media, rather than on hard-copy documents.

2. Transaction data can be verified by programmed edit checks, in order to detect and prevent errors, rather than by human clerks.

3. Added data may easily be captured, in order to identify transactions with individual employees or organizational units.

4. Transactions can be quickly posted directly to ledgers, rather than being laboriously entered into journals and then posted.

5. Transaction processing, including summarizing of journals and ledgers and computing trial balance totals, can be done faster and with fewer errors.

6. Financial statements and other financial summaries can be prepared at any time during the accounting period, rather than being delayed until the end of the period; furthermore, the ledgers can be kept in balance at all times.

7. Detailed listings of journals and ledgers, reflecting all individual transactions rather than summaries, can be printed for thorough review.

8. Required stewardship reports can be prepared quickly and easily from stored transaction data, using stored computer programs.

9. A wide variety of managerial reports and analyses can also be prepared from data stored in related files and tables, thereby providing managers and employees with useful information; in manual systems all reports must be laboriously prepared by clerks.

FIGURE 11-3   Benefits and differences of a computer-based general ledger system.

mainframe architectures to client/server architectures (as described in Chapter 3); they may employ periodic processing or immediate processing (as described in Chapter 5); they may incorporate application-oriented files or centralized data bases (as described in Chapter 6). Each of the computerized system architectures, however, differs in essentially the same ways from manual system architectures. Computerized system architectures also yield roughly the same benefits with respect to each of the transaction processing systems.

These differences and benefits of computerized general ledger systems are summarized in Figure 11-3 and illustrated in following sections. Because of the near-universality of computerized systems, our discussions in this and following chapters assume the presence of such systems. When certain aspects pertain to manual systems, as in the case of controls, we will flag the references.

CHART OF ACCOUNTS

Because of its central position within a general ledger system, we should first explore the chart of accounts and its development. As described in Chapter 2, a **chart of accounts** is a coded listing of the accounts—assets, equities, revenues, and expenses—pertaining to a firm. In addition to the account code, each listing in a sound chart of accounts describes the contents of an account, including the specific transactions that affect its balance. In relevant cases the description might refer to the accounting method employed. Thus a description of the purchases account could note the use of the periodic inventory method and refer to such transactions as purchases of merchandise and returns of purchases.

BROAD STRUCTURE OF THE CHART OF ACCOUNTS

Figure 11-4 shows the strategic place of the chart of accounts. The external and internal users of information essentially dictate the composition of the chart of accounts. Since their information needs are reflected through the financial statements and other financial reports, we must first develop these outputs in order to design the chart of accounts. Consider that the balance sheet of Infoage is to include the status of accounts receivable, and its income statement is to show the sales for the period. Its chart of accounts must therefore assign those accounts and their account numbers (such as 110 and 300) to two records within the general ledger. If sales analyses are also needed, the chart of accounts will provide additional detail. For instance, the chart of accounts for Infoage breaks down the sales account into sales by the various outlets through which the firm sells. These outlet sales accounts would then be combined in presenting the total sales on the income statement.

After the general ledger accounts have been specified, a designer considers the need for *control accounts*—general ledger accounts that control accounts in a subsidiary ledger. For example, Infoage needs an accounts receivable subsidiary ledger that supports the accounts receivable control account in its general ledger. Such a subsidiary ledger can be viewed as an integral part of the general ledger system.

Finally, as Figure 11-4 illustrates, journal vouchers, special journals, and source documents are affected by the previous sequence of design steps. Thus, journal vouchers should provide fields for entering the account numbers, while special journals (like the sales journal) need to provide posting references to ledger accounts. Source documents like sales invoices are coded with their individual document numbers, which enable users to trace transactions to their sources when the numbers are entered into journals and posted to ledgers.

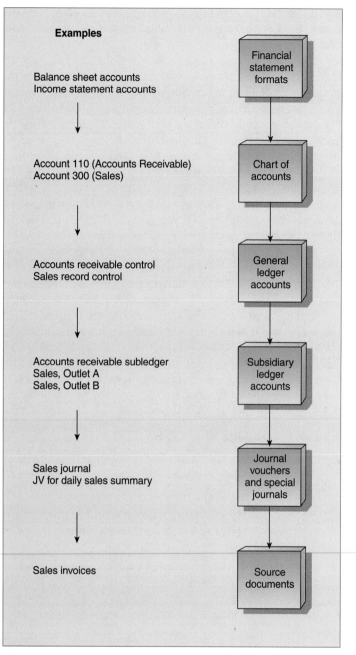

Examples

Balance sheet accounts
Income statement accounts
↓

Account 110 (Accounts Receivable)
Account 300 (Sales)
↓

Accounts receivable control
Sales record control
↓

Accounts receivable subledger
Sales, Outlet A
Sales, Outlet B
↓

Sales journal
JV for daily sales summary
↓

Sales invoices

Financial statement formats
↓
Chart of accounts
↓
General ledger accounts
↓
Subsidiary ledger accounts
↓
Journal vouchers and special journals
↓
Source documents

FIGURE II-4   Sequence in designing the components of the accounting cycle.

SCOPE AND CLASSIFICATIONS WITHIN THE CHART OF ACCOUNTS

In serving the varied needs of users, a chart of accounts has objectives relating to scope and classifications. Both objectives play key roles in the design process.

A chart of accounts provides adequate *scope* if all users are considered. Thus in addition to the key stakeholders—stockholders and managers—a firm must consider the accounts required by governmental agencies such as the Internal Revenue Service and the Securities and Exchange Commission. All firms are affected by payroll taxes, particularly with respect to withholding requirements. Certain types of firms, such as public utilities, have their accounts constrained by the Federal Power Commission and by state utility regulatory bodies.

The chart of accounts of a firm should provide sufficient *classifications* to allow extensive analyses of transaction data. For instance, sales transactions may include data concerning the region where the sales took place as well as the product lines sold. Through subsidiary ledgers, credit sales transactions provide data concerning the customers to whom sales were made. Expense transactions can include the responsibility centers that incurred the expenses (e.g., credit department) as well as the categories of expenses (e.g., supplies).

As a general rule, the number of accounts within a chart of accounts will be greater than the number of lines appearing in financial statements. Also, the needed accounts (as well as subsidiary ledgers) tend to increase as a firm grows, its transactions multiply, and new departments and other organizational divisions come into being.

The need for accounts is also affected by the accounting principles adopted by a firm. For instance, a firm that adopts the periodic inventory method requires a Purchases account. A firm that decides to use the allowance method for establishing bad debts expense needs an Allowance for Doubtful Accounts account.

Finally, account classifications should also reflect the activities and customs of the industries in which the firms reside. Firms that manufacture goods need three inventory accounts, whereas firms that provide services need supplies accounts only. Service firms, however, must focus on the performance and pricing of services, rather than products. Not-for-profit organizations are very concerned with cost accounts but may not need revenue accounts.

CODING THE CHART OF ACCOUNTS

Coding is as important as classification when designing a chart of accounts. Consider, for instance, the adverse effects due to not coding the numerous transactions that a firm must handle:

1. Each transaction will take longer to record. Writing or keying the descriptive title "Accounts Receivable" is more time-consuming than simply noting 110, the account number.

2. More errors will occur in processing transactions. Assume that payments from customers are credited in the Accounts Receivable ledger by reference to their names. The wrong account may be posted, as in the cases when payments are received from John Smith and more than one customer has that name.

3. Analyses based on transaction data will be more difficult to perform. Assume that an automobile parts firm desires to analyze its sales of each of its parts (e.g., fuel filter for 1996 Fords) by each of its parts dealers (e.g., Scott Toyota in Scottsdale, Arizona). Sorting on these parts descriptions and dealer names can be awkward at best.

As we observed in Chapter 5, *codes* provide unique and concise identifiers. These identifying codes relate to the transactions processed by a firm as well as to such entities as customers and products. Both block codes and group codes are typically employed.

Block Account Codes   The coding system used to form the broad framework within a chart of accounts is of the block type. A block account code designates ranges of

Account Code	Account Categories
100–199	Current assets
200–299	Noncurrent assets
300–399	Liabilities
400–499	Owners' equity
500–599	Revenues
600–699	Cost of sales
700–899	Operating expenses
900–999	Nonoperating expenses

FIGURE 11-5   Brief chart of accounts.

sequenced numbers representing significant account classifications. Figure 11-5 shows the outline of a chart of accounts that is block coded. In this example the asset accounts are assigned the block of numbers from 100 through 299.

As we can see in the figure, each major block can incorporate subordinate blocks. Thus, current assets are represented by the numbers 100 through 199. Figure 11-6 lists the block of accounts spanned by expense accounts constituting the administrative category. The particular accounts, and the details they represent, are based on the various needs of internal and external users of the financial outputs. Note that the first listed account, coded 850, is a control account over the remaining administrative accounts.

An advantage of block account codes is that new accounts or subdivisions of current accounts can be inserted. For instance, the Depreciation account (888) could be subdivided into Depreciation—building (888), Depreciation—office equipment (889), and Depreciation—furniture and fixtures (890).

Group Account Codes   A group coding system can provide added meaning to individual account codes. Moreover, the meaning can be ordered hierarchically in a descending manner. That is, the left-most digit can represent a major category (e.g., asset), the middle digit an intermediate classification (e.g., fixed asset), and the right-most digit a minor classification (e.g., type of fixed asset). For example, the account code 112 may refer to the type of fixed asset known as buildings.

850	Administrative expenses control
852	Officers' salaries
855	Office salaries
859	Overtime premium
861	Unemployment insurance expense
863	FICA expense
870	Office supplies
871	Office repairs
872	Telephone and telegraph
873	Postage
881	Dues and subscriptions
883	Donations
884	Travel
888	Depreciation
891	Insurance
892	Taxes
899	Miscellaneous administrative expense

FIGURE 11-6   Expense accounts.

General ledger account codes can be combined with other codes when recording transactions. For instance, when recording transactions that involve direct labor expense, we might also record the responsibility center that incurs the expense. Thus, if the direct labor expense account is coded 762, and the production department incurring the expense is coded 1333, the debit amount would be identified by the code 762-1333. Such group coding structures, which can reflect several meaningful facets concerning the transactions, are very useful when preparing analyses of the transaction data.

Consider the illustrative group coding structure having fields that identify the subsidiary ledger accounts and responsibility centers as well as the general ledger accounts. The generalized format for this group coding structure, beginning with the general ledger account code, would appear as follows:

$$AAA-BBBB-CC$$

If Infoage employs this coding format, it might record 121-5634-00 to identify the debit amount of the transaction, and 820-1738-08 to identify the credit amount. The 121 and 820 refer to the general ledger accounts entitled Accounts Receivable and Sales. The 5634 refers to the customer account against which the credit sale is charged, and the 1738 refers to the salesperson whose account is credited in the commissions payable ledger. The 08 refers to the sales outlet (responsibility center) where the sale is made. Finally, the 00 indicates that the Accounts Receivable account spans the entire organization, rather than being applicable to a particular responsibility center.

DATA SOURCES AND INPUTS

SOURCES

The general ledger system receives inputs from a wide variety of sources. Figure 11-7 illustrates the inputs into Infoage's general ledger system. Feeder transaction processing systems provide data via source documents, which are entered into special journals. Summary totals from these entries are posted to the general ledger, as well as those subsidiary ledgers in use.* Summary totals are recorded on *journal vouchers*, which serve as the posting media. Adjustments and nonroutine transactions are entered onto journal vouchers, from which they are posted to the general ledger.

Transactions that are posted to the general ledger of a firm may be classified as routine, nonroutine, adjusting, reversing, and closing entries. These major types are subdivided as follows:

1. **Routine external transactions** arise during an accounting period from exchanges with independent parties who are in the environment. A typical routine external transaction is a credit sale.

2. **Routine internal transactions** arise during an accounting period from internal activities. An example within a manufacturing firm is the transfer of raw materials inventory to work-in-process inventory.

3. **Nonroutine transactions** arise, usually on an occasional basis and externally, during an accounting period from nonroutine activities. An example is the debit to fixed assets to reflect the exchange of a truck for capital stock (which would be credited).

---

*The subsidiary ledgers shown are illustrative only. Others likely to be found in many firms include inventory, fixed assets, and employee earnings subsidiary ledgers.

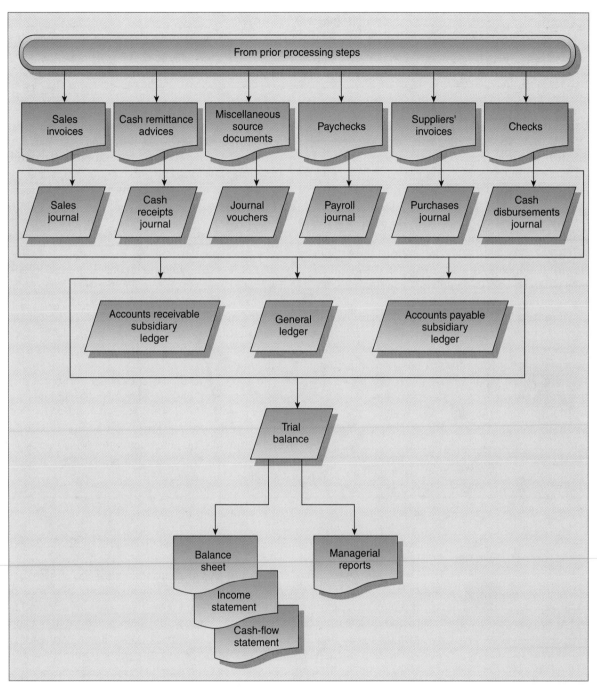

FIGURE II-7   Sources of inputs and their flows through the general ledger system of Infoage.

4. **Adjusting entries** usually recur at the ends of accounting periods (although some are nonrecurring and take place during the periods). Four types of adjusting entries are accruals, deferrals, revaluations, and corrections.

   a. **Accruals** are recurring entries that arise from the passage of time and reflect accumulated amounts as of the ends of accounting periods. For instance, Infoage may provide services that are not billed or paid by the end of an

SPOTLIGHTING

YEAR-END ACCOUNTING CLOSINGS
at General Mills*

In 1984 General Mills, a multidivision corporation based in Minneapolis, appointed a special design team from its Financial Reporting and Information Services function. The mission of the team was to develop an automated system to aid the closing and consolidation of the ledgers and other accounting records at the end of each fiscal year. This new automated system was to replace a time-consuming and error-prone manual process involving 110 separate reporting entities throughout the firm. Generally the manual process required nine person-weeks to complete, including substantial overtime at expensive rates.

The automated system resulting from the design effort is organized around a customized accounting package that employs Lotus spreadsheets and a network of microcomputers. It has streamlined the year-end adjusting and closing process, as well as the preparation of consolidated statements.

The procedure begins well before year-end, when accountants in the firm establish templates

for the current year's financial statements. To assure that the statements are sound, the accountants review issuances from the Financial Accounting Standards Board. Then, at year-end each of the reporting divisions and subsidiaries enter their financial data and journal entries into the spreadsheet ledgers, being guided by user-friendly menus. The edit program built into the system checks the entries for accuracy and generates error messages when necessary. As the data from the various reporting units are consolidated, the edit program checks for internal consistency and accuracy in the 83 supporting schedules to the financial statements. For instance, the cost of purchases used amount in the inventory schedule is compared to the amount in the cost of goods sold schedule.

In addition to the balance sheet and profit and loss statement and accompanying schedules for managers, the Form 10-K is prepared for the SEC and the financial section of the annual report for stockholders. The microcomputer-based consolidation software package that prints these outputs is called Micro Control.

*Earl E. Robertson and Dean Lockwood, "Tapping the Power of the PC at General Mills." *Management Accounting* (August 1994), pp. 46–47.

accounting period. The adjusting entry would show a debit to Accrued Fees Receivable and a credit to Service Fees Revenue.

b. **Deferrals** are recurring entries that also arise from the passage of time, but reflect amounts not yet due or earned. For instance, Infoage may receive revenue for which services are still unearned at the end of an accounting period. At the time of the receipt, the entry would show a debit to Cash and a credit to the liability account Unearned Service Fees. The adjusting entry at the end of the accounting period, to reflect the portion earned, would show a debit to Unearned Service Fees and a credit to Service Fees Revenue.

c. **Revaluations** are nonrecurring entries that arise when the value of a physical asset is found not to correspond to the values reflected in the accounting records, or when an accounting measurement method is changed. An example of the former is the adjustment of the inventory value when the physical inventory shrinks, due to pilferage or obsolescence. An example of an accounting change is the change in inventory cost-flow assumptions from the first-in first-out (FIFO) method to the last-in first-out (LIFO) method.

d. **Corrections** are entries that reverse the effects of errors, thus restoring affected accounts to their proper balances.

5. **Reversing entries** are entered at the beginning of accounting periods in order to reverse the effects of adjusting entries made at the ends of the previous periods. An example is the entry made on January 1, 1997, to reverse an entry made on December 31, 1996, that accrues payroll expense.

6. **Closing entries** transfer the amounts in all temporary accounts to the appropriate owners' equity account, leaving the temporary accounts with zero balances.

FORMS OF INPUT

Journal Voucher   The primary source document to the general ledger system is the **journal voucher (JV).** This input form, which has largely replaced the general journal sheet, abstracts pertinent details to support postings to the general ledger. A single journal voucher generally concerns either:

1. A nonroutine, adjusting, reversing, or correcting transaction, such as a transaction to amortize an annual portion of patent costs.

2. A summarization of a batch of routine transactions. Figure 11-7 shows a journal voucher used by a firm similar to Infoage to reflect the total of a batch of cash disbursements. If the illustrative firm employs a manual system, the journal voucher would be prepared manually by a clerk (such as Jean Nelson at Infoage) after computing the total of cash disbursements listed in the check register.

As Figure 11-8 reveals, a journal voucher should include such data as a journal voucher date, the account codes for the general ledger accounts to be posted, the debit and credit amounts, and an authorization signature or initials. A number assigned to the journal voucher serves to enhance the audit trail.

Computer-Oriented Inputs   Although the journal voucher format shown in Figure 11-8 is often used as a source document in computer-based systems, it is also likely to assume alternative forms. Two variations are the batch-entry form and the on-line preformatted screen.

JOURNAL VOUCHER					
				No. 6212	
				Date June 19, 1997	
Account Code	Account Titles	Accounts to Be Debited		Accounts to Be Credited	
204	Accounts payable-control	64,720	50		
101	Cash			64,720	50
Explanation of entry:					
To record the daily total of cash disbursed.					
Prepared by:		Approved by:		Posted by:	
Jean Nelson		*Shirley Hagan*		*Audrey Rule*	

FIGURE 11-8   A journal voucher.

Batch Entry Journal Voucher					
Date	Batch No.	Batch Total		Trans. Code	Voucher No.

Account description	Acct. no.	Debit	Credit
	Totals		

FIGURE II-9   A batch-entry journal voucher used by Infoage. (Note: More than one sheet is often needed to contain a batch of journal entries; hence, the totals at the bottom of a sheet generally differ from the batch total.)

The **batch-entry journal voucher** replaces the special journal. In effect, it serves as a combined special journal and journal voucher. Data from transactions are entered manually onto a blank form, such as the one in Figure 11-9 that Infoage employs for its sales made through its various outlets. Then the entered data are keyed onto disk or tape transaction files. Note that the totals line on the form contains batch totals, which can be verified by a programmed check in the general ledger entry program.

Alternatively, the various application programs compile lists of transactions during daily processing and print these as batch summary listings. The totals from these listings are then used in preparing journal entries, either by data clerks or by a journal-entry program; the journal entries will later be posted to the general ledger.

A preformatted **data-entry screen** can be used in on-line computer systems to enter transaction data interactively. Infoage employs the screen in Figure 11-10a to enter individual nonroutine journal entries in a user-friendly manner. The screen design portrayed in the figure allows complex transactions having multiple debits or credits to be entered. In addition, batches of transactions may be entered, with previous transaction data being scrolled up as the screen is filled. Running totals of entered transactons are computed by the entry program and shown on the screen.

To appreciate the widespread popularity of on-line data entry, consider these benefits that it confers to the entry of transactions into a general ledger system:

1. User-friendly techiques provide quick access to the screen. Menus, such as the main- and detailed-level menus shown in Figure 11-10b, are one technique; mouse-activated icons are another.

2. When the screen appears, the fields for entering data are preformatted and the cursor is positioned at the first field.

3. Certain fields, such as the journal voucher number and date, are filled automatically by the general ledger data-entry program.

4. Most of the data fields, other than amount fields, employ codes—thereby reducing the number of needed input strokes.

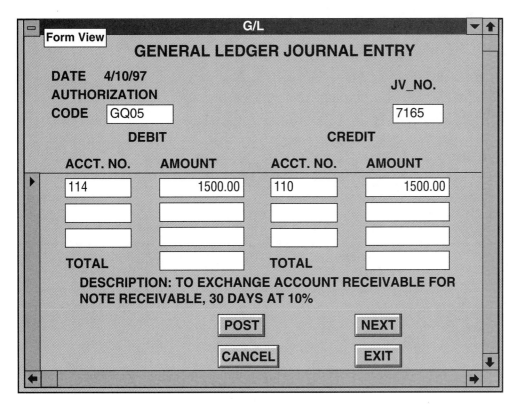

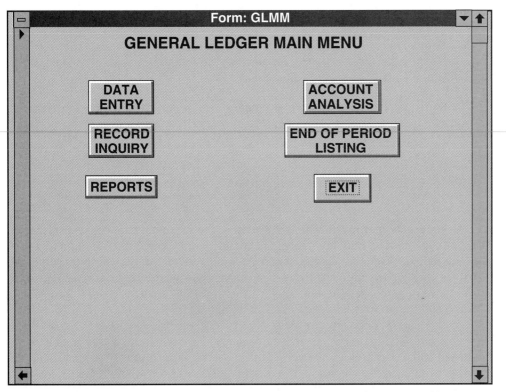

FIGURE 11-10   Screens relating to journal entries. (*a*) A journal-entry screen employed by Infoage. (*b*) Two menus used to access the journal-entry screen.

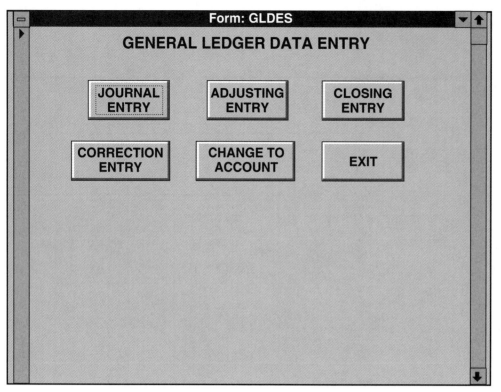

FIGURE 11-10   (b) (Continued)

5. Entered data are checked for accuracy by means of programmed checks. A zero-balance check, for instance, verifies that the total debit amount for each transaction equals the total credit amount.

Data may be entered onto a preformatted on-line screen from a hard-copy journal voucher or entered directly. In either case an authorization code field may be included in the header portion of the screen.

DATA BASE

The **general ledger master file** is the heart of the accounting data base. Each record shows the current status of a single general ledger account, plus a summary of the transactions affecting the account. One record is needed for each account within the firm's chart of accounts. Figure 11-11 displays the layout of a general ledger record employed by Infoage. The file of which this record is a part is stored on magnetic disk, and the primary key is the account number.

This central depository of data within the general ledger system is subject to numerous variations. For instance, a separate chart of accounts file may be established to contain the account descriptions and classifications. If a relational data base is employed, each account would be reflected as a row in a table. Transaction data may be maintained in detail files or tables, perhaps showing the totals of debits

Account number	Account description	Account classification (asset, liability, revenue, expense)	Account balance, beginning of year	Total debits, year-to-date	Total credits, year-to-date	Total debits, current month	Total credits, current month	Current account balance	Dr. or Cr.

Note: Lengths of fields and modes of data elements are omitted for simplicity, although they are necessary for complete documentation.

FIGURE 11-11   A record layout for the general ledger master file of Infoage.

and credits for each month during the current year, as well as the amounts budgeted for each month. In larger firms general ledger accounts may be maintained for such organizational units as divisions and departments, with the units identified by codes.

Among the files (or tables) that a computerized data base might contain are the following:

- **Current journal voucher file.** This transaction file contains all of the significant details concerning each transaction that has been posted to the general ledger during the current period. In addition to individual nonroutine transactions, it includes summary vouchers pertaining to daily routine transactions and adjusting entries. In each record would be the journal voucher number (the primary key), date of the transaction, initials of the preparer, accounts debited and credited and the corresponding amounts, and a description of the transaction. The number of the originating source document or the batch number—if any—would likely be included, in order to facilitate the electronic audit trail.

  In effect, the journal voucher file is a summary of all the journals for the current period. It can be printed as the general journal upon appropriate commands to the general ledger system. To provide continuity, a firm may store these printed journals as a journal voucher history. Alternatively, it may retain journal vouchers of past months and years in a separate on-line file.

  As in the case of the general ledger master file, alternatives may be considered with respect to the journal voucher file:

  1. Assuming the presence of an on-line processing system, a transaction code could replace the accounts being debited and credited and the description, so that only the amounts need be entered. For example, the write-off of receivables accounts due to long-term delinquency might have the following journal entry format to write off customers' accounts deemed uncollectible:

     Dr. Allowance for Doubtful Accounts   XXX
        Cr. Accounts Receivable   XXX

     This journal-entry format would be called by the data-entry program upon entering a transaction code, say 79.

  2. In a data-base system, the journal voucher records can be linked to the affected accounts in the general ledger master file. Furthermore, detailed line-item records for the respective debits and credits can be linked to the journal voucher records through the journal voucher number. Figure 11-12 shows how these linkages might appear within the relational data-base schema that Infoage is considering. A relationship table is used to provide the cross-references between the line items and the accounts they affect. Also, only the

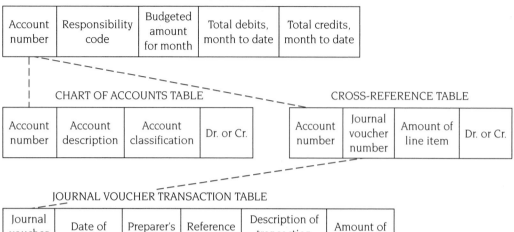

GENERAL LEDGER MASTER TABLE

Account number	Responsibility code	Budgeted amount for month	Total debits, month to date	Total credits, month to date

CHART OF ACCOUNTS TABLE

Account number	Account description	Account classification	Dr. or Cr.

CROSS-REFERENCE TABLE

Account number	Journal voucher number	Amount of line item	Dr. or Cr.

JOURNAL VOUCHER TRANSACTION TABLE

Journal voucher number	Date of transaction	Preparer's initials	Reference number	Description of transaction (or trans. code)	Amount of transaction

FIGURE 11-12 Linked tables within a general ledger relational data base being considered by Infoage.

current month's transactions are included in the current tables. Earlier data are maintained in a general ledger history table linked to the general ledger master table (and described next). Furthermore, beginning and ending account balances are not needed in a relational structure, since they can be calculated quickly from the accumulated given transaction amounts.

- **General ledger history file.** The general ledger history file contains the actual data concerning general ledger accounts for each month for the past several years. It can be used to generate past financial statements and related financial trend information.

- **Responsibility center master file.** The responsibility center master file contains the actual revenues and costs for the various divisions, departments, work centers, and other responsibility centers within a firm. It is used in the preparations of responsibility reports for managers, which are discussed later in this chapter. A reference file, called a cost allocation file, may also be maintained to provide the factors for allocating incurred costs (e.g., administrative costs) to responsibility centers.

- **Budget master file.** The **budget master file** contains the budgeted amounts of assets, liabilities, revenues, and expenses allocated to the various responsibility centers of the firm. The budgeted values may be broken down on a monthly basis for the following year, whereas the budget period may extend for five or more years into the future. Together with the responsibility center master file, the budget file provides the basis for the preparation of responsibility reports.

- **Financial reports format file.** This file contains the information necessary for generating the formats of the various financial reports. Included are factors such as the report headings, all needed column headings, all side labels (for instance, descriptions of accounts and subtotal and total lines), spacing and totaling instructions, and the like.

The relationships between the above-mentioned files and financial reports are shown in Figure 11-13. These reports, which are discussed later, are prepared as needed by means of output preparation programs.

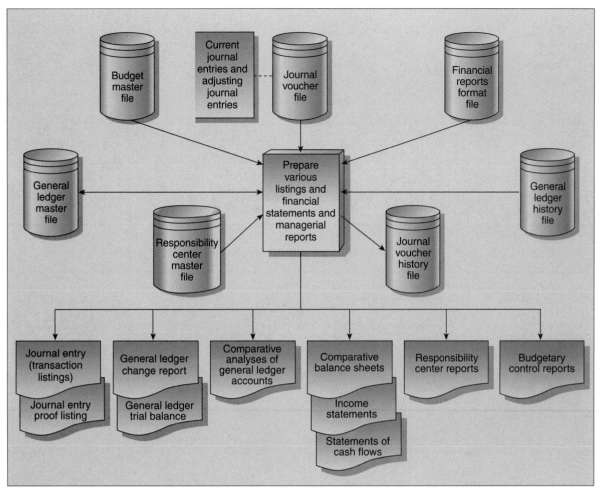

FIGURE 11-13   System flowchart showing period-end preparation of outputs relating to the general ledger.

DATA FLOWS AND PROCESSING

Processing within the general ledger system can be divided into daily processing and end-of-period processing. Both processing activities begin after the transactions have been captured, usually using the types of forms described earlier, and edited. The edited data are stored temporarily, typically on magnetic disks.

Computerized general ledger processing systems may employ either the periodic approach or the immediate approach. We examined each of these approaches in Chapter 5 and contrasted the processing steps in two figures. Many variations are feasible. In the two following sections we describe the processing system employed by Infoage. In effect it combines features of both approaches. You are likely to understand the processing more fully if you turn back to Chapter 5 and review Figures 5-7 and 5-8. You might also include Figure 5-9, which shows the key processing steps for a manual system, in your review.

DAILY PROCESSING OF TRANSACTION DATA

Figure 11-14 shows the processing of transaction data during an accounting period. Daily the sales, cash receipts, purchases, cash disbursements, payroll, and plant

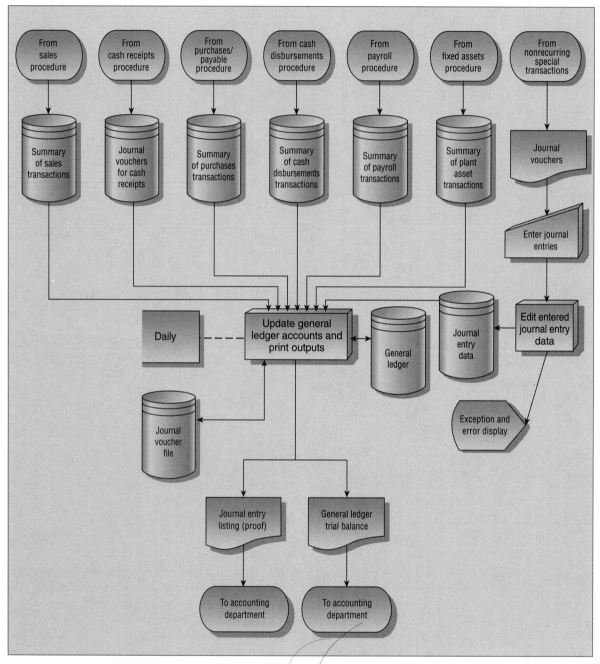

FIGURE II-I4   The computer-based general ledger processing procedure used by Infoage.

asset applications handle volumes of transactions. The individual routine transactions are captured on source documents, which are then converted off-line and entered in batches by transaction type.* These batches are processed to update the subsidiary ledger master files, as discussed in Chapter 5. As a part of this processing

---

*The procedure employed by Infoage varies slightly from the generalized procedure portrayed in the dataflow diagram of Figure 11-2. However, the essential aspects do not vary.

the application programs summarize the transaction amounts, by type of transaction, and store the summary data on magnetic disks. At the end of each day, the application programs post the summary amounts to the affected accounts in the general ledger. As nonroutine transactions arise, they are entered by accountants via on-line input devices from manually prepared journal vouchers. The debit and credit amounts of the individual transactions are temporarily stored and then posted to the general ledger accounts at the end of the day.

Service orders, not shown in the figure, are entered on-line. Transaction amounts are accumulated daily, with the summary amount being temporarily stored as a separate type of revenue transaction. At the end of each day, the summarized amount is posted to the general ledger accounts. Thus, Infoage processes its service order transactions in a hybrid manner; that is, it combines steps from the processing of other routine transactions and the processing of its nonroutine transactions.

After all daily postings have been made, the general ledger system generates a journal-entry listing and a trial balance. These outputs enable the accountants to verify the correctness and accuracy of the postings without delay. For instance, they can trace the summary amounts on the journal-entry listing back to predetermined batch totals for each of the types of transactions. Also, the journal listing serves as an integral part of the audit trail. Another output is an error listing of all transactions found to contain errors; this output can be used to monitor the corrections of the errors by the users.

END-OF-PERIOD PROCESSING OF ADJUSTING JOURNAL ENTRIES

Figure 11-15 shows a periodic approach for processing adjusting journal entries at the end of each accounting period. Two groups of journal entries are involved, standard entries and nonrecurring adjusting entries. The standard adjusting journal entries, which are recurring and whose amounts have been predetermined by accountants, are stored in an on-line file on a continual basis. At the end of the period, a special computer program transfers them to the journal-entry data file. The nonrecurring adjusting journal entries are entered by accountants at the end of the period, using manually prepared journal voucher coding forms. After being edited for errors, the adjusting journal entries are merged with the standard recurring adjusting entries on the journal-entry data file. The amount batch total is modified to include the amounts of both groups of journal entries.

Because the general ledger accounts are stored on a magnetic disk and organized as an indexed sequential file, Infoage employs the direct approach. Its updating program posts the debit and credit amounts from each of the journal entries in turn to the affected accounts. When the posting is complete, the program computes the totals of the debits and credits posted. These totals appear on a journal-entry proof listing; they are checked by accountants against the exception and summary report prepared as a part of the processing. Another output from the processing is an adjusted trial balance, which is also reviewed for correctness. Finally, another end-of-period program (not shown) produces and posts closing entries and prepares a postclosing trial balance and financial statements.

Alternatively, the adjusting entries could be posted to the general ledger accounts in a sequential fashion. To employ this approach, a processing program would first split the collected journal entries into their individual debits and credits, with each portion of a split entry being tagged by the identifying journal-entry number. A separate sort run would sort the split portions according to general ledger account numbers. Then the individual debits and credits would be posted in a following run

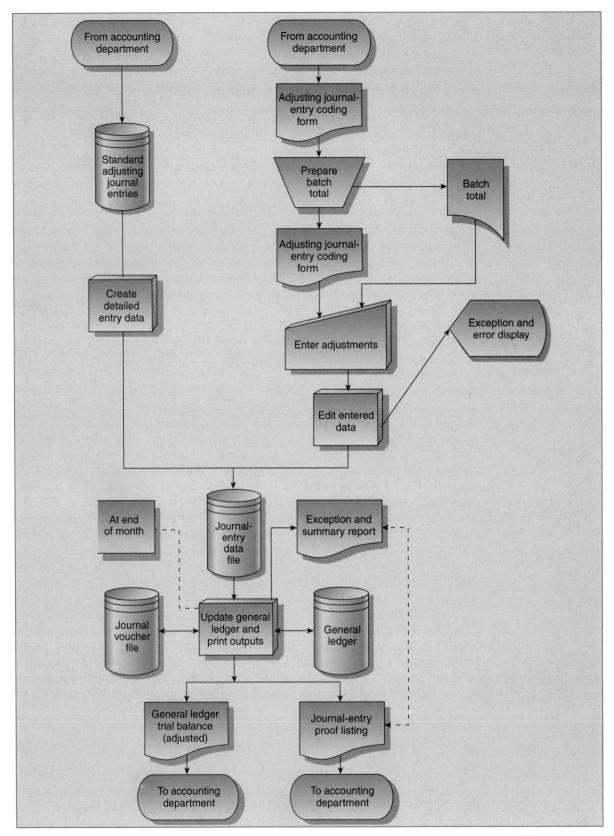

FIGURE II-I5   A computer system flowchart of a month-end general ledger processing procedure used by Infoage.

to the affected accounts. As we can see, this approach is more cumbersome and time-consuming. Since the number of adjusting entries is not large, the inherent efficiency of sequential processing would not be realizable.

PROCESSING IN CLIENT/SERVER NETWORKS

Many firms acquire accounting software packages from commercial software vendors to process their transactions. Such packages offer time and cost savings in development, which can be compelling when firms change to a new computing environment such as client/server. Two examples can illustrate the benefits of acquiring an accounting software package.

American Greetings Corporation moved its general ledger and financial reporting system from an IBM 3090 mainframe computer to a client/server package called Commander FDC (marketed by Comshare Inc.). The manager of accounting services has been pleased with the results, since the financial and managerial reports are now available five days sooner after each month-end close. The package allows transactions to be entered quickly from a variety of sites and the data to be consolidated in appropriate formats and delivered to the recipients at their respective locations.[*]

Sara Lee, a large consumer-oriented firm with such products as pastries and hosiery, also moved recently from a mainframe environment to a client/server computing network. It selected SQL Financials (marketed by a firm with the same name), due to its proven ability to expedite this type of migration and in order to exploit the capabilities of the network platform. The package enables the firm to handle complete requirements in the basic accounting modules and to deliver sound budgets and forecasts.[†]

INTERNAL CONTROLS

RISK EXPOSURES

The general ledger is exposed to a variety of risks, which can lead to inaccurate financial statements and related reports. For instance, the assets may be overstated and the liabilities may be understated. In addition to financial and judicial losses arising from unreliable reports, risk exposures can have such adverse consequences as "leaks" of important financial data to competitors and added costs from reconstructing transaction data.

Commonly occurring risks to which the general ledger is exposed include the following:

1. Journal entries that are incorrectly prepared in some way, such as unequal debits and credits or amounts (e.g., depreciation expense) based on inaccurate computations.

2. Journal entries that are posted incorrectly to the general ledger, either with respect to the debit/credit amounts or the accounting period.

3. Transactions that are not recorded as journal entries or that are not posted to the general ledger, due to some event such as losing the source documents.

---

[*]The Lee, "New Life for Old General Ledgers," *Datamation* (September 1, 1993), pp. 55–56.
[†]"SQL Financials: Customers Define Value," *Datamation* (June 15, 1995), pp. 51–53.

4. Journal entries that are not authorized properly, whether due to oversight or to fraudulent intent.

5. Balances of control accounts that become out of balance with the totals of balances in the subsidiary ledgers.

6. Imbalances between the accounts containing debit balances and those containing credit balances.

7. Accesses to data in the general ledger by unauthorized persons.

8. Defects or breaks in the audit trail that links the general ledger balances with the underlying source documents.

GENERAL CONTROLS

A number of internal controls are suitable for counteracting these risk exposures to the general ledger. For instance, trial balances are useful in detecting inequalities between postings of debits and credits, so that the errors can be corrected. Prenumbered source documents facilitate the audit trail and aid in detecting lost documents.

Our framework for discussing these control activities follows that established in Chapter 8. In this section we consider general controls, which are categorized as organizational, documentation, asset accountability, management practice, data center operations, authorization, and access. The next section discusses the categories within application controls.

Organizational Controls   The function of posting journal vouchers to the general ledger should be separate from the functions of preparing and approving journal vouchers, maintaining custody over the physical assets, and preparing the trial balances. If a manual system is employed, the record-keeping functions with respect to journals and subsidiary ledgers should also be segregated from the above functions.

Documentation Controls   Complete and up-to-date documentation should be available concerning the general ledger and financial reporting cycle. Included in the documentation should be a fully descriptive chart of accounts, a manual of general ledger procedures, copies of journal vouchers and other source documents, flowcharts, record layouts, and reports such as appear in Figure 11-13.

Asset Accountability Controls   Subsidiary ledgers should be maintained for all accounts having sufficient volume. The totals of balances in all established subsidiary ledgers should be reconciled periodically to the general ledger account balances. Also, the totals of batched journal vouchers should be precomputed and then compared and reconciled during the processing steps (e.g., from run to run).

Management Practice Controls   Sound policies and practices should be established and followed with respect to human resources employed in the general ledger area, to operational budgeting and responsibility accounting, and to auditing of general ledger activities. Procedures regarding systems development and changes should be in force and well documented. For instance, new general ledger accounts should undergo a sound change procedure.

Data Center Operations Controls   Computer processing schedules should be clearly established, including those relating to end-of-period procedures. Information system and accounting personnel should be actively supervised and their work reviewed. Operational reports and listings concerning general ledger processing should be generated for review by accountants.

Authorization Controls Journal vouchers, as the key source documents to the general ledger procedure, should be authorized by knowledgeable managers in the departments where the transactions arise. For instance, a nonroutine transaction involving the disposal of obsolete office equipment in the main office of Infoage would be approved by Ralph Cannon, the office manager. Likewise, corrections to transactions, adjusting entries, and closing entries should be authorized by appropriate accounting managers. In Infoage such authorizations would normally be the responsibility of Diane Varney or a subordinate accounting manager.

Access Controls A variety of access controls and security measures are needed, especially in the presence of on-line computer systems and networks. The following are illustrative (although not complete):

1. Passwords are required before clerks can access the records in the general ledger system and enter journal entries.
2. Special terminals are reserved for the entry of journal voucher data.
3. Access logs are maintained by the system to monitor all accesses and entries.
4. Transactions involving journal entries are logged upon entry.
5. All general ledger records are frequently dumped onto magnetic tape for backup.

APPLICATION CONTROLS

The following control procedures are applicable to general ledger transactions and financial reports. They are arranged by input, processing, and output categories.

Type of Edit Check	Typical Transaction Data Items Checked	Assurance Provided
1. Validity check	General ledger account numbers; transaction codes	The entered numbers and codes are checked against lists of valid numbers and codes stored within the computer system.
2. Field check	Transaction amounts	The amount fields in the input records are checked to see if they contain the proper modes of characters for amounts (i.e., numeric characters). If other modes are found, such as alphabetic characters or blanks, an error is indicated.
3. Limit check	Transaction amounts	The entered amounts are checked against preestablished limits that represent reasonable maximums to be expected. (A separate limit is set for each account.)
4. Zero-balance checks	Transaction amounts	The entered debit amounts are netted against the entered credit amounts, and the resulting net amount is compared to zero. (A non-zero net amount indicates that the debits and credits are unequal.)
5. Completeness check[a]	All entered data items	The entered transaction is checked to see that all required data elements have been entered.
6. Echo check[a]	General ledger account numbers and titles	After the account numbers pertaining to the transaction are entered at a terminal, the system retrieves and "echoes" back the account title; the person who has made the entry can visually verify from reading the titles that the correct account numbers were entered.

[a]Applicable only to on-line systems.

FIGURE 11-16 Programmed checks that edit and validate journal-entry data. *Note:* When entered data do not match or otherwise meet the expected conditions or limits, alerting messages are displayed by the edit program on the input screen in the case of an on-line data-entry system.

Input controls include the following:

1. Preparing prenumbered and well-designed journal vouchers that are approved by appropriate persons. For instance, a journal voucher reflecting the declaration of a dividend by Infoage would be prepared in the treasurer's office and approved by Diane Varney, the treasurer.

2. Validating data on journal vouchers, in order to provide assurance that errors and omissions are detected before processing. In the case of computer-based general ledger systems, the validation is performed by programmed edit checks as the journal voucher data are being entered. Figure 11-16 lists several suitable data-entry checks.

3. Correcting detected errors before the journal-entry data are posted to the general ledger. The error-correction procedure should be appropriate to the type of processing system being employed.

Type of Edit Check	Typical Transaction Data Items Checked	Assurance Provided
1. Internal label check[a]		The internal header label of the file to be updated (posted to) is checked before processing begins to ascertain that the correct general ledger master file has been accessed for processing.
2. Sequence check	General ledger account numbers	The transaction file, which has been sorted so that the amounts in the various journal vouchers are ordered according to account numbers, is checked to see that no transaction item is out of sequence.
3. Redundancy matching check[b]	General ledger account numbers and titles	Each transaction debit and credit is checked to see that its account number matches the account number in the general ledger record it is to update. Then the account titles in the transaction record and master file record are also matched, thus providing double protection against updating the wrong file record.
4. Relationship check[b]	Transaction amounts and account numbers	The balance of each general ledger account is checked, after the transaction has been posted, to see that the balance has a normal relationship to the account. If the balance in an account balance that normally exhibits a debit balance (e.g., accounts receivable) appears as a credit, the abnormality will be flagged by the check.
5. Posting check[b]	Transaction amounts	The after-posting balance in each updated account is compared to the before-posting balance, to see that the difference equals the transaction amount.
6. Batch control/total checks[a]	Transaction amounts	The amounts posted are totaled and compared to the precomputed amount total of the batch being processed; also, the total number of transaction items processed is compared to the precomputed count of the transactions.

[a]Although not true edit checks, these listed checks are programmed, and they help to assure that updated data will be accurate.
[b]These checks are also applicable to the posting step in on-line computer-based systems.

FIGURE 11-17 Programmed edit checks that validate batched data during posting (updating) runs.

4. Compiling *standardized adjusting journal entries* on a magnetic disk file (or on a hard-copy listing in the case of manual systems). A preestablished standing file of such recurring adjustments can facilitate the end-of-period processing and reduce possible errors from reentering the data each period.

5. Precomputing batch control totals, such as those pertaining to standardized adjusting journal entries and nonroutine entries. These precomputed batch control totals will be compared to posted totals during the processing phase.

Processing controls include the following:

1. Posting journal-entry data to the general ledger accounts, with checks being performed before and after the posting. Figure 11-17 lists a variety of programmed checks that are feasible when the journal-entry data are batched. Certain of the listed checks are also applicable to on-line systems in which data from journal vouchers are posted individually. Also, some of the validation checks listed in Figure 11-16 may be repeated. For example, the zero-balance check may be applied after posting to verify its accuracy.

2. Summing the amounts posted to general ledger accounts, and then comparing the posted totals to the precomputed batch control totals. Figure 11-18 shows a display screen in which the totals have been compared by a general ledger processing program. Note that the example indicates a difference of $1000, which must be investigated by an accountant in the general ledger department.

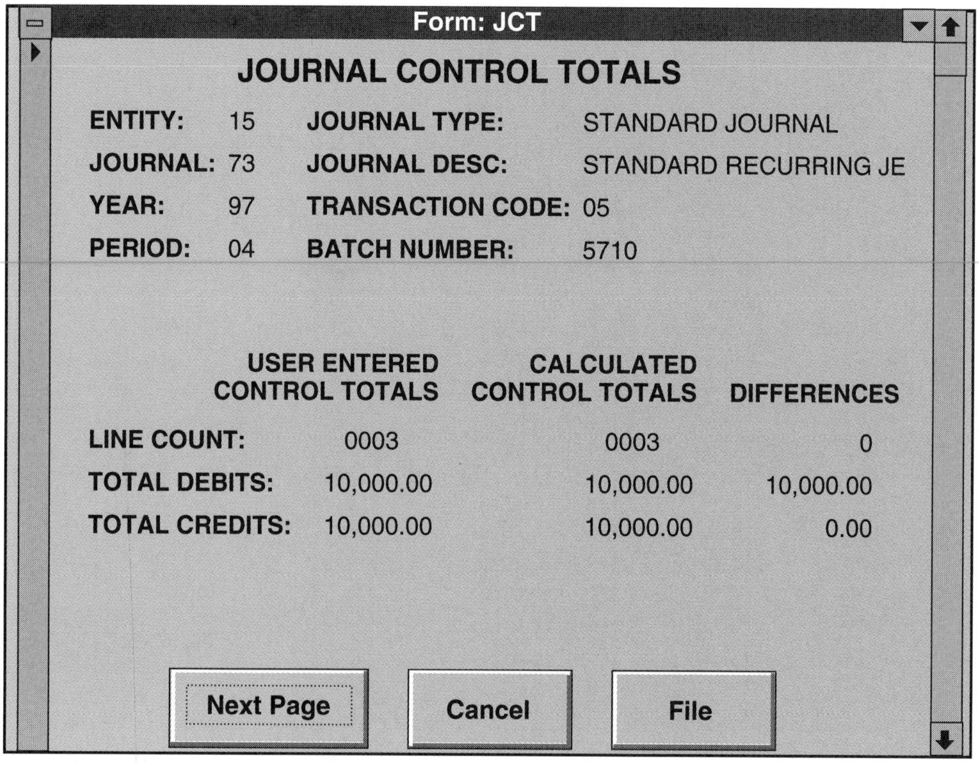

Form: JCT

JOURNAL CONTROL TOTALS

ENTITY:	15	JOURNAL TYPE:	STANDARD JOURNAL
JOURNAL:	73	JOURNAL DESC:	STANDARD RECURRING JE
YEAR:	97	TRANSACTION CODE:	05
PERIOD:	04	BATCH NUMBER:	5710

	USER ENTERED CONTROL TOTALS	CALCULATED CONTROL TOTALS	DIFFERENCES
LINE COUNT:	0003	0003	0
TOTAL DEBITS:	10,000.00	10,000.00	10,000.00
TOTAL CREDITS:	10,000.00	10,000.00	0.00

Next Page   Cancel   File

FIGURE 11-18   A display screen used to verify batch control totals relating to entered journal entries.

3. Establishing and maintaining an adequate audit trail. Examples of cross-references that provide a clear audit trail are journal voucher numbers that appear on journal listings, such as shown in Figure 11-19.*

Output controls include the following:

1. Preparing frequent trial balances, with any differences between total debits and credits being investigated.
2. Maintaining a log or file of journal vouchers by number, and periodically checking to make certain that the sequence of numbers is complete.
3. Printing period-end listings and change reports for review by accountants before the financial statements are prepared. Figure 11-20 depicts a general ledger change report with beginning and ending account balances, plus changes that occurred to each account during the period. Note that the report includes control totals at the bottom relating to the trial balance and transaction count. This type of report represents another means of providing a complete audit trail.

General Journal

Northcreek Industries   Time 15:52:00   Date 4/30/97   Page 1   37402
Journal—GJ001   Batch—1   Posting date 4/30/97

Reference Date	Reference Number	Description	Account Number	Debit	Credit
4/04/97	JV4-01	Deposits	1010	3,556.52	
4/04/97	JV4-01	Deposits	1110		3,056.52
4/04/97	JV4-01	Deposits	1140		123.00
4/04/97	JV4-01	Deposits	1130		377.00
4/09/97	JV4-02	Travel advances	1010	10,000.00	
4/09/97	JV4-02	Travel advances	1560		10,000.00
4/14/97	JV4-03	City power	6110	1,675.42	
4/14/97	JV4-03	City water	6120	30.00	
4/17/97	JV4-04	Central loan	2030	1,200.00	
4/17/97	JV4-04	Central loan	1010		1,200.00
4/22/97	JV4-05	Trash collection	6260	47.25	
4/22/97	JV4-05	Security service	6270	237.00	
4/22/97	JV4-05	Utility bills	1010		1,989.67
4/30/97	JV4-06	FET Transfer to bank	1010		3,250.00
4/30/97	JV4-06	FET Transfer to bank	2150	3,250.00	
4/30/97	JV4-07	Dep land improve	1720		318.54
4/30/97	JV4-07	Dep land improve	6020	318.54	
4/30/97	JV4-08	Dep buildings	1730		1,500.00
4/30/97	JV4-08	Dep buildings	6030	1,500.00	
4/30/97	JV4-09	Dep machinery & equip	1750		309.39
4/30/97	JV4-09	Dep machinery & equip	6050	309.39	
4/30/97	JV4-10	Dep auto & truck	1760		153.23
4/30/97	JV4-10	Dep auto & truck	6060	153.23	
4/30/97	JV4-11	Dep office equip	1740	150.00	
4/30/97	JV4-11	Dep office equip	6040		150.00
				22,427.35	22,427.35

FIGURE 11-19   A general journal listing. (Courtesy of IBM Corporation.)

*The general journal listing is illustrative only. Certain of the journal entries may perhaps more logically be entered via special journals.

GENERAL LEDGER

CLIENT 00125   PAGE 14   DECEMBER 31, 19XX

SAMPLE COMPANY

MO DAY YR	ACCT.	DESCRIPTION	REFERENCE	DEBITS	CREDITS	NET CHANGE	NEW BALANCE
11-30-xx	5130	ACCOUNTING & LEGAL	BALANCE	4750.00			
12-05-xx	5130	DEC. RETAINER	10131	450.00		450.00	5200.00
				450.00			
11-30-xx	5140	SALARIES	BALANCE	20769.83			
12-20-xx	5140	DEC. PAYROLL	12332	1885.12		1885.12	22654.95
				1885.12			
11-30-xx	5150	INSURANCE	BALANCE	1125.00			
12-15-xx	5150	ALLTOWN INSURANCE	652	105.10		105.10	1230.10
				105.10			
11-30-xx	5160	OFFICE RENT	BALANCE	3323.33			
12-15-xx	5160	CORRECT NOVEMBER ERROR	J12		23.33		
12-31-xx	5160	DEC. RENT	0012	300.00		276.67	3600.00
				300.00	23.33		
11-30-xx	5170	OFFICE SUPPLIES	BALANCE	895.26			
12-02-xx	5170	K & C FORMS	6736	33.75			
12-17-xx	5170	JACKS STATIONERY	J211A	51.25			
				85.00		85.00	980.26

········· CONTROL TOTALS ·········

PRIOR PERIOD BALANCE TOTALS	523,721.12	523,721.12	.00
CURRENT PERIOD TRANSACTIONS	33,968.22	33,968.22	.00
TRIAL BALANCE TOTALS	557,689.34	557,689.34	.00
TRANSACTION COUNT CURRENT PERIOD		453	

FIGURE II-20 A general ledger change report. (Courtesy of the American Institute of Certified Public Accountants, Inc.)

4. Reviewing financial reports and other outputs for correctness and reasonableness. These reviews should especially involve the managers of the functions and departments in which the journal entries originate.

5. Auditing general ledger procedures.

FINANCIAL REPORTS

Several of the financial-oriented outputs typically resulting from general ledger processing were portrayed in Figure 11-13. These financial reports can be classified as general ledger analyses, financial statements, and managerial reports.

GENERAL LEDGER ANALYSES

Examples of two analyses prepared as control devices—the **general journal listing** and the **general ledger change report**—in this chapter are shown in Figures 11-19 and 11-20. Another control-oriented analysis, the trial balance, was presented in Figure 2-21.

Other analyses are mostly provided to managers to aid them in evaluating performance or current status. Two examples are (1) an analysis of the allocations of expenses to the respective cost centers of a firm, and (2) a comparative analysis of account balances for the current period with those for the same period last year.

FINANCIAL STATEMENTS

The most important financial statements are the balance sheet, income statement, and statement of cash flows. These statements, which are primarily based on information in the general ledger, are provided to various stakeholders outside the firm. In addition to stockholders or other owners, they are made available to government agencies, creditors, prospective owners, and financial analysts. Most versions of these statements are prepared and disseminated to fulfill legal obligations. Thus, the AIS must incorporate rules and procedures which ensure that financial statements and derivative reports conform to generally accepted accounting principles. (Applicable rules and procedures are disclosed in footnotes to the statements where appropriate.) Furthermore, since the array of financial reports includes income tax returns and other tax reports, the AIS must also comply with federal and state and local tax regulations.

Often the financial statements are accompanied by additional information that is useful to the recipients. For example, they may be accompanied by comparative statements for previous years, by budgetary amounts, and by detailed schedules. Figure 11-21 shows a comparative balance sheet and income statement for the United Industries Company, with columns comparing budget and actual amounts. Variances within the income statement appear as both dollar amounts and percentages and pertain to the current month as well as to the year-to-date.

MANAGERIAL REPORTS

Many of the reports and analyses received by managers are generated from the same data used to prepare financial statements. However, financially oriented reports for managers tend to be much more detailed and analytical than those for outside stakeholders. Two categories of managerial analyses and reports are those based on general ledger accounts and those focused on responsibility centers.

```
UNITED INDUSTRIES                        BALANCE SHEET              AS OF 12/31/97      PAGE
COMPANY C000  GLR0100  REQ 8             CORPORATION                RUN DATE 01/01/98  21:35:49

BEGINNING    PCT     PRIOR      PCT                        CURRENT      CURRENT    PRIOR YR
OF YEAR      CHG     MONTH      CHG                        BALANCE      BUDGET     BALANCE
..........   ....    .........  ....   ASSETS:            .........    .........  .........
                                       CURRENT ASSETS:
1,044,500    46.4    1,028,899  48.6    CASH              1,529,480    598,000    1,044,500
  922,000   -15.7      841,020  -7.6    ACCOUNTS RECEIVABLE 776,580          0      922,000
 -117,582   -10.2     -104,122   1.3    ALLOW DOUBTFUL ACCT -105,942     -2,500    -117,582
  908,000    36.2      732,820  68.8    NOTES RECEIVABLE  1,237,180    200,000      908,000
   62,100    16.8       58,940  23.1    INTEREST RECEIVABLE  72,580      5,000       62,100
  972,000    73.3    1,026,207  64.2    INVENTORY         1,685,259    210,000      972,000
   19,645   131.4       28,158  61.4    OFFICE SUPPLIES      45,462      5,000       19,645
  113,450   137.6      168,482  60.0    PREPAID INSURANCE   269,578     25,000      113,450
.........    ....    .........  ....     TOTAL ...         .........    .........  .........
3,924,113    40.4    3,780,404  45.7    CURRENT ASSETS    5,510,577  1,040,500    3,924,113
                                        FIXED ASSETS:
8,346,400    72.7    8,368,314  72.3    MACHINERY        14,419,310  2,015,000    8,346,400
-6,513,500   71.0   -6,541,080  70.2    ACC DEPR - MACH -11,138,600 -1,583,600   -6,513,500
1,560,000   100.0    1,560,000 100.0    BUILDINGS         3,120,000          0    1,560,000
  -50,000   220.0      -80,000 100.0    ACC DEPR - BLDGS   -160,000          0      -50,000
  891,000    85.5      899,550  83.8    OFFICE EQUIP      1,653,433    250,000      891,000
 -256,390    21.6     -273,430  14.1    ACC DEPR - OFF EQUIP -311,990  -10,000     -256,390
1,175,000   100.0    1,175,000 100.0    LAND              2,350,000          0    1,175,000
.........    ....    .........  ....     TOTAL ...         .........    .........  .........
5,152,510    92.7    5,108,354  94.4    FIXED ASSETS      9,932,153    671,400    5,152,510
.........    ....    .........  ....     TOTAL ...         .........    .........  .........
9,076,623    70.1    8,888,798  73.7    ASSETS           15,442,730  1,711,900    9,076,623

                                         LIABILITIES:

  857,800
        0
1,358,800   UNITED INDUSTRIES                     INCOME STATEMENT          AS OF 12/31/97      PAGE
  164,200   COMPANY C070  GLR0120  REQ 9          CORPORATION               RUN DATE 01/01/98  21:35:49
        0
  153,200   ........... CURRENT MONTH ...........          ........... YEAR-TO-DATE ...........
.........    ACTUAL    BUDGET   BUDGET    PCT                  ACTUAL    BUDGET   BUDGET     PCT
2,534,000    AMOUNT    AMOUNT   VARIANCE  VAR                  AMOUNT    AMOUNT   VARIANCE   VAR
........     .........  .........  .........  .....             .........  .........  .........  .....
  463,900                                       INCOME:
1,500,000                                       SALES INCOME:
.........   1,931,600 1,500,000  431,600  22.3   SALES       2,624,650 1,500,000 1,124,650  42.8
1,963,900     -26,860   -22,500   -4,360  16.2   SALES RETURNS & ALL -34,630 -22,500 -12,130 35.0
.........   .........  .........  .........  -22.4  TOTAL ...  .........  .........  .........
4,497,900   1,904,740 1,477,500  427,240   5.0   SALES INCOME: 2,590,020 1,477,500 1,112,520 42.9
                                                 OTHER INCOME:
1,010,000     315,968   300,000   15,968   0.0    INTEREST INCOME 345,994 300,000  45,994  13.2
2,000,000           0         0        0   0.0    DIVIDEND INCOME     0       0        0    0.0
        0                                  17.4   CURRENCY GAIN/LOSS 1,367    0    1,367  100.0
.........      36,360    30,000    6,360          MISC INCOME    48,680   30,000   18,680  38.3
3,010,000   .........  .........  .........  -6.3  TOTAL ...     .........  .........  .........
1,568,723     352,328   330,000   22,328         OTHER INCOME   396,041  330,000   66,041  16.6
9,076,623   .........  .........  .........  -49.9 TOTAL ...     .........  .........  .........
.........   2,257,068 1,807,500  449,568         INCOME        2,986,061 1,807,500 1,178,561 39.4
            .........  .........  .........  .....             .........  .........  .........

                                                 EXPENSE:
                                                 COST OF GOODS SOLD:
              -29,052         0  -29,052 100.0    CHANGE IN INVENTORY -83,081    0  -83,081 100.0
              544,160   300,000  244,160  44.8    PURCHASES     974,980  300,000  674,980  69.2
                    0         0        0   0.0    PURCHASES I/C      0       0        0    0.0
               12,592    15,000   -2,408 -19.1    PURCH RETURNS & ALL 8,126 15,000 -6,874 -84.5
                    0         0        0   0.0    PURCH RET I/C      0       0        0    0.0
               22,360    15,000    7,360  32.9    FREIGHT        35,780   15,000   20,780  58.0
             .........  .........  .........  .....  TOTAL ...    .........  .........  .........
              550,060   330,000  220,060  40.0    COST OF GOODS SOLD 935,805 330,000 605,805 64.7
                                                 OPERATING EXPENSES:
               99,760    75,000   24,760  24.8    DEPR - MACH   146,130   75,000   71,130  48.6
              110,000    80,000   30,000  27.2    DEPR - BLDGS  140,000   80,000   60,000  42.8
               39,908    37,500    2,408   6.0    INSURANCE      44,474   37,500    6,974  15.6
               24,496    15,000    9,496  38.7    MISC OPERATING EXP 42,138 15,000 27,138 64.4
             .........  .........  .........  .....  TOTAL ...    .........  .........  .........
              274,164   207,500   66,664  24.3    OPERATING EXPENSES 372,742 207,500 165,242 44.3
                                                 GENERAL EXPENSES:
              789,980   685,500  104,480  13.2    RENT EXPENSE  942,530  685,500  257,030  27.2
              581,556   557,000   24,556   4.2    ADMIN SALARIES 614,443 557,000  57,443   9.3
              274,736   274,000      736   0.2    OFFICE SUPPLIES 272,178 274,000 -1,822 -0.6
              106,000   101,000    5,000   4.7    INCOME TAXES  111,000  101,000   10,000   9.0
               23,316    22,500      816   3.5    STATE AND LOCAL TAXES 27,968 22,500 5,468 19.5
               22,500    22,500        0   0.0    BAD DEBT EXPENSE 22,500 22,500     0     0.0
              295,908   284,500   11,408   3.8    INTEREST EXPENSE 309,474 284,500 24,974  8.0
               20,960    13,600    7,360  35.1    DEPR - OFF EQUIP 34,480 13,600  20,880  60.5
               11,400    10,000    1,400  12.2    DATA PROC EXPENSE 12,800 10,000   2,800 21.8
              106,720    92,000   14,720  13.7    MKTG EXPENSE  133,160   92,000   41,160  30.9
              477,172   475,500    1,672   0.3    MISC EXPENSE  480,416  475,500    4,916   1.0
           -3,666,400  -265,000 -3,401,400 92.7   EXPENSE    -3,655,260 -265,000 -3,390,260 92.7
             .........  .........  .........  .....  TOTAL ...    .........  .........  .........
             -956,152 2,273,100 -3,229,252 337.7  GENERAL EXPENSES -694,311 2,273,100 -2,967,411 431.0
             .........  .........  .........  .....  TOTAL ...    .........  .........  .........
             -131,928 2,810,600 -2,942,528 2230.4 EXPENSE       614,236 2,810,600 -2,196,364 -357.5
```

FIGURE 11-21 Comparative financial statements. (Courtesy of Data Design Associates.)

Account-Oriented Analyses Analyses based on major but individual general ledger accounts are often provided to managers. Examples include analyses of *sales*, broken down by products or markets; analyses of *cash*, broken down by types of receipts and expenditures; analyses of *accounts receivable*, broken down by customers and ages of amounts due. Analyses such as these aid managers in planning, decision making, and controlling operations. We shall see several illustrations of account-oriented analyses in following chapters.

Responsibility-Oriented Reports An important group of managerial reports provides information to aid in evaluating performance. Reports of this type have kinship with the financial statements of Figure 11-21—which show the top managers of United Industries Company how well the firm is performing with respect to budgeted expectations. However, the reports in which we are interested are mostly intended for managers below the top level, are more detailed than financial statements, and are oriented toward assigned responsibilities. Together they make up a reporting system known as responsibility accounting.

A **responsibility accounting system** consists of reports that compare actual financial performance results with planned budgetary amounts for the *responsibility centers* of a firm. The reports are correlated, in that they feed accountability information upward through the various managerial levels. At each level the reports summarize or filter the results of lower managerial levels. Thus the entire set of reports forms a

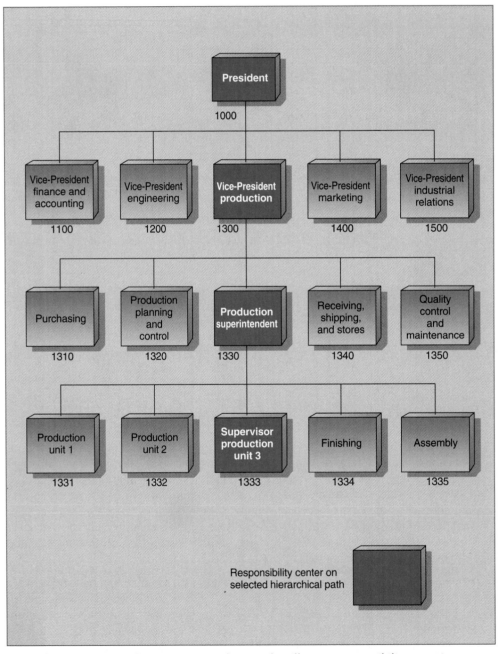

FIGURE 11-22   A portion of an organization chart used to illustrate responsibility reporting.

SPOTLIGHTING

FINANCIAL REPORTING
*at Sun Microsystems**

Six years after being founded in 1982, Sun Microsystems had moved into the Fortune 500. Its rapid growth caused difficulties in many areas, including the preparation of adequate and timely financial reports. As in many firms during the 1980s, Sun Microsystems was using electronic spreadsheet software to prepare consolidated financial reports. Each year, however, the spreadsheet-based system became more complex. For instance, 128 spreadsheets were required in 1988 to produce 74 spreadsheets of output. Much of the data had to be entered by hand, consuming days of effort.

In order to cope with this increasing workload, Sun Microsystems acquired a financial reporting software package known as Control. This application package was employed to set up a financial reporting system for Sun Microsystems called CORONA (Corporate Reporting On Anything). Much of the data used by CORONA is fed directly from the firm's operational data base, especially the files containing the general ledger and budget. Instead of assigning control over the package to the MIS or controller's function, reports are developed directly by users, such as accountants, financial analysts, and managers.

Among the financial reports that have been obtained through the use of CORONA are the following:
- Detailed income statements, broken down by product group and organizational territories (i.e., east, central, west).
- Revenue and gross margin analyses.
- Analyses of operating expenses by division and organizational territories.
- Actual monthly operating results versus plan (budget) and forecast, by division.
- Monthly product margin analysis, detailing units, revenue, discount and discount percentage, and standard margin percentage.
- Budgetary schedules based on financial planning and modeling.

Although it has been in use for only a few years, the new financial reporting software package has yielded several significant benefits. It has saved more than 500 hours of report preparation time each year. More importantly, it has allowed the firm to generate reports that fully meet its financial reporting requirements and to develop management reports in a more timely fashion. For instance, a user can obtain needed reports within one day, even if the reports have never been requested before. Under the previous reporting system newly requested reports would not be available from the MIS function in less than two to four months.

*Mitchell A. Levy, "Sun Microsystems Automates Financial Reporting." *Management Accounting* (January 1990), pp. 24–27.

pyramid linking together all managerial levels and units within the organizational structure.

An effective responsibility report traces inefficiencies to individual cost or revenue components and motivates the responsible manager to take corrective actions. Assume that the responsibility center is one of the retail sales outlets operated by Infoage. The responsibility report provided to the outlet manager would list the revenues and such controllable costs as salaries of the clerks, wholesale prices of merchandise, supplies, and so on. In the key column of the report would appear the variances between the actual and budgeted revenues and between the actual and budgeted controllable costs. (Costs not controllable by the manager, such as depreciation expense on the outlet building, would not be included.)

A responsibility accounting system is illustrated by two figures. Figure 11-22 shows a portion of an organization chart for a manufacturing firm. Responsibility

Cost Summary for President

Month: October	This Month		Year-to-Date	
		(Over) Under		(Over) Under
Cost	Budget	Budget	Budget	Budget
President's office*	$ 36,600	$200	$ 366,000	$1,000
V.P.–finance and accounting	52,700	300	527,000	(600)
V.P.–engineering	25,300	(100)	253,000	(900)
V.P.–production	244,000	(3,860)	2,440,000	(45,659)
V.P.–marketing	120,000	(850)	1,200,000	(7,640)
V.P.–industrial relations	12,600	—	126,000	500
Total controllable costs	$491,200	$(4,310)	$4,912,000	$(53,299)

*Includes insurance, taxes, staff salaries, depreciation other than factory equipment, and miscellaneous items.

Cost Summary for Vice President–Production

Month: October	This Month		Year-to-Date	
		(Over) Under		(Over) Under
Cost	Budget	Budget	Budget	Budget
Vice-President's office*	$ 30,800	$(200)	$ 308,000	$500
Purchasing**	3,500	310	35,000	(878)
Production planning and control	3,200	(480)	32,000	(4,280)
Production superintendent	192,430	(3,855)	1,924,300	(45,161)
Receiving, shipping, and stores	3,370	(85)	33,700	(660)
Quality control and maintenance	10,700	450	107,000	3,820
Total controllable costs	$244,000	$(3,860)	$2,440,000	$(45,659)

*Includes employee benefits, overtime premium, payroll taxes, staff salaries, and miscellaneous items.
**Includes material price variance.

Cost Summary for Production Superintendent

Month: October	This Month		Year-to-Date	
		(Over) Under		(Over) Under
Cost	Budget	Budget	Budget	Budget
Superintendent's office*	$ 20,500	$200	$ 205,000	$(500)
Production unit 1	57,200	(1,650)	572,000	(14,855)
Production unit 2	21,760	710	217,600	(1,960)
Production unit 3	36,930	1	369,300	(696)
Finishing	15,240	376	152,400	(2,050)
Assembly	40,800	(2,740)	408,000	(25,100)
Total controllable costs	$192,430	$(3,855)	$1,924,300	$(45,161)

*Includes depreciation—factory equipment, staff salaries, and miscellaneous items

Cost Summary for Supervisor, Production Unit 3

Month: October	This Month		Year-to-Date	
		(Over) Under		(Over) Under
Cost	Budget	Budget	Budget	Budget
Direct materials	$16,000	$150	$160,000	$1,210
Direct labor*	17,500	(276)	175,000	(3,172)
Supervision and staff salaries	1,500	—	15,000	—
Supplies	300	10	3,000	100
Setup for jobs	560	(35)	5,600	(318)
Rework	420	52	4,200	490
Heat, light, and power	200	15	2,000	(55)
Maintenance	350	(20)	3,500	117
Other costs	100	5	1,000	(68)
Total controllable costs	$36,930	$1	$369,300	$(696)

*Labor rate variance = $18; labor efficiency variance = $(294).

FIGURE 11-23 Four levels of responsibility reports.

centers at four managerial levels are shaded. Figure 11-23 presents the set of cost-oriented responsibility reports for the shaded centers. Each report links to (articulates with) the one above by means of "rolled-up" total controllable costs. (The arrows on the left sides of the reports trace these roll-ups.) Note that the roll-up of totals keeps the reports for each of the managers quite concise, with the details being relegated to those at the lowest levels.

Since every cost must be the responsibility of some manager, the report to the president contains all of the costs incurred by the firm. The president also has responsibility for the revenues of the firm, but they have been omitted to simplify the report. We might remember, though, that the president would also receive a report similar to that shown in Figure 11-21.

A sound coding system is critical to the success of a responsibility accounting system. Costs (and revenues) must be gathered and coded by responsibility centers. Figure 11-22 illustrates responsibility center codes based on a hierarchical group coding scheme. For example, all costs coded 1333 will be compiled for the report to be received by the foreman of production unit 3. If the code 761 is the general ledger account code for direct labor, the code 761-1333 attached to a cost of $500 would identify the cost as being direct labor incurred by cost center 1333. All costs incurred during a month with the same code would be totaled and listed as one of the items on the supervisor's report.

Financial Reporting and Information Technology   Improvements in financial reporting can be achieved by the application of information technology. Managers can instantaneously access all needed information electronically on their desktop computer screens, thus avoiding the need to handle hard-copy reports. They can also transmit messages and data in a matter of seconds to other managers at distant points around the world. When more information is wanted, managers can "drill down" to obtain finer levels of detail. They can employ spreadsheet templates that are customized for their cost and revenue items to produce required reports; furthermore, they can incorporate graphs and videos into such reports in order to magnify their impact.

SUMMARY

A framework for studying transaction processing is known as the cycles approach. Transaction cycles incorporate all of the transaction processing systems composing a firm's AIS, encompass all events logically following from key beginning events, trace the acquisition and management of needed resources, and relate to the overall mission of a firm. Designing transaction processing systems for a particular firm requires the consideration of the effects of its value-added activities, management policies, and accounting principles and practices.

A general ledger system of a firm is involved in collecting transaction data, classifying and coding transactions, processing transaction inflows, storing and retrieving transaction data, maintaining internal controls, and generating financial reports. The general ledger system, which supports the general ledger and financial reporting cycle, is at the center of such transaction-oriented cycles as the revenue cycle, expenditure cycle, and resources-management cycle.

General ledger systems may be manual or computerized. Manual systems are simple, but most have been replaced by computerized systems because of the many benefits they offer. Computerized systems differ in their architectures, ranging from mainframe to client/server, from periodic processing to immediate processing, and from file-oriented to data base.

The chart of accounts is a coded listing of all the classified accounts of a firm. Charts of accounts vary widely among firms, since they must satisfy the needs of both external and internal users. They cannot be specified, in fact, until the contents of financial statements and reports are developed. Often a chart of accounts embodies block coding and/or group coding. Its general ledger account codes are frequently linked to codes relating to organizational units and subsidiary ledger accounts.

The general ledger system receives routine recurring and nonrecurring transactions, nonroutine transactions, adjusting entries, reversing entries, and closing entries. The inputs are normally on general ledger journal vouchers, which in computer-based systems may be transferred to batch-entry or data-entry screens. The entered data, in journal-entry form, are then posted to the general ledger to update the accounts during the accounting period. At the end of each accounting period, standard and nonstandard adjusting journal entries are posted. The exact methods of processing vary, usually being variations of periodic or immediate processing approaches. The data base includes files such as the general ledger master file, chart of accounts master file, general ledger history file, responsibility center master file, budget master file, financial reports format file, current journal voucher file, and journal voucher history file.

A variety of general and application controls are needed to offset a number of risks to which the general ledger is exposed. These controls include organizational segregation, adequate documentation, reconciliations involving general ledger account balances, prenumbered journal vouchers, access controls, programmed edit checks, and accounting-oriented listings and change reports. Financial reports typically include financial statements and such managerial reports as budgetary control and responsibility reports.

....

REVIEW PROBLEM WITH SOLUTION

CAMPUS BOOKSTORE, SEVENTH INSTALLMENT

Statement

The Campus Bookstore (described in the Review Problem at the end of Chapter 1) has just received documentation, prepared by consultants, for its newly designed computer-based transaction processing systems. The accounting system manager begins his review of the documentation with the general ledger system. As stated in the Review Problem to Chapter 8, this documentation ranges from source documents to system flowcharts and reports. One item of particular importance to the general ledger system—a coded chart of accounts—is incomplete, since the accounting system manager is most knowledgeable concerning needed accounts.

To aid in completing the chart of accounts, the accounting system manager scribbles these notes of relevant facts about the bookstore: The major product lines are textbooks, other books, and sundry items. Payments are generally made to the over 200 suppliers within 10 days, in order to receive 2 percent discounts. Utilities

(heat, water, electricity, telephone) are paid within 30 days. All managers and employees are paid on the first and fifteenth of each month, with deductions made for federal and state income taxes, social security tax, federal and state unemployment taxes, the pension plan, medical insurance, and various miscellaneous items. Paychecks are written on a special bank account after funds are transferred from the regular checking account. Each of the four cash registers is provided with a change fund. Payments for returns of sale items are made from a cash register. The accounting period is one month, and financial reports are prepared at each month-end. (Other notes are omitted, since they appeared in earlier review problem statements.)

Required

a. Present the chart of accounts that the accounting systems manager is likely to prepare. Include a suitable code.

b. Develop an account code format for the accounts payable subsidiary ledger.

c. Provide illustrative journal entries for a routine transaction, a nonroutine transaction, a standard (recurring) adjusting transaction, and a nonrecurring adjusting transaction that would be posted to the general ledger.

d. Identify several controls that are to be maintained over data entry and processing relative to the general ledger.

e. Design the format of a report that shows gross profits on sales, broken down according to product lines.

f. Briefly describe how the chart of accounts would need to be expanded to enable the preparation of responsibility reports for the upper and lower levels of the bookstore.

Solution

a. The chart of accounts that follows is based on the following assumptions.

    (1) Sales and gross margins are to be computed for the three product lines. However, no responsibility reports for the upper and lower levels of the bookstore are presently required.

    (2) The periodic method of recording purchases and inventory is employed. If the perpetual method were assumed to be employed, the Purchases and Purchase Returns and Allowances accounts would not be included. (In reality, the perpetual method is likely to be used in a computer-based system, with the purchases and returns data being maintained apart from the chart of accounts.)

(3) The net method is employed with respect to purchase discounts, and hence a Purchase Discounts Lost account is shown. If the gross method is assumed to be employed, Purchase Discount accounts for the three product lines would be needed.

(4) The coding scheme employs three-digit blocks for the major areas (e.g., assets). Within these blocks the middle digit has meaning, and thus the individual accounts can be viewed as being group coded. For instance, within the asset block (in which the first digit is a 1), a middle digit of 0 means a cash account.

Assets (100–199)

101	Cash on Hand
102	Cash in Bank—General
103	Cash in Bank—Payroll
104	Change Fund
110	Inventory—Textbooks
111	Inventory—Other Books
112	Inventory—Sundries
113	Supplies
120	Prepaid Expenses
130	Leasehold Improvements
131	Allowance for Amortization—Leasehold Improvements
132	Furniture and Fixtures
133	Allowance for Depreciation—Furniture and Fixtures
134	Noncomputerized Office Equipment
135	Allowance for Depreciation—Noncomputerized Office Equipment
136	Computer Hardware and Software
137	Allowance for Depreciation—Computer Hardware and Software
138	Motorized Vehicles
139	Allowance for Depreciation—Motorized Vehicles
140	Other Assets

Liabilities and Capital (200–299)

201	Notes Payable—Bank
210	Accounts Payable
220	Sales Taxes Payable
221	Employee Income Taxes Payable
222	FICA Taxes Payable
223	Federal Unemployment Taxes Payable
224	State Unemployment Taxes Payable
225	Pension Expense Payable
226	Medical Insurance Withholdings Payable
227	Other Withholdings Payable
230	Salaries and Wages Payable
240	Lease Payable
250	Accrued Expenses Payable
260	Accrued Interest Payable
270	Tom Long, Capital
271	Tom Long, Drawing

Revenues (300–399)

310	Sales—Textbooks
311	Sales—Other Books
312	Sales—Sundries
320	Sales Returns and Allowances—Textbooks
321	Sales Returns and Allowances—Other Books
322	Sales Returns and Allowances—Sundries

Cost of Sales (400–499)

410	Cost of Sales—Textbooks
411	Cost of Sales—Other Books
412	Cost of Sales—Sundries
420	Purchases—Textbooks
421	Purchases—Other Books
422	Purchases—Sundries
430	Purchase Returns and Allowances—Textbooks
431	Purchase Returns and Allowances—Other Books
432	Purchase Returns and Allowances—Sundries
440	Freight In—Textbooks
441	Freight In—Other Books
442	Freight In—Sundries

Expenses (500–599)

500	Expenses—Control
510	Salaries and Wages—Clerical and Sales
511	Salaries—Professional
512	Salaries—Managerial
513	Employee Welfare Expense
520	Advertising
530	Rent Expense
540	Heating Expense
541	Water Expense
542	Electricity Expense
543	Telephone Expense
550	Repairs and Maintenance Expense
551	Janitorial Supplies
552	Office Supplies
553	Insurance Expense
554	Legal and Accounting Expense
555	Donations
556	Tax Expense
560	Amortization of Leasehold Improvements
561	Depreciation of Furniture and Fixtures
562	Depreciation of Noncomputerized Office Equipment
563	Depreciation of Computer Hardware and Software
564	Depreciation of Motorized Vehicles
570	Interest Expense

580   Purchase Discounts Lost
590   Miscellaneous Expenses

b. An account code format for the accounts payable subsidiary ledger would also be an identification code for suppliers. Since the bookstore has over 200 suppliers, a sequential numeric code must contain at least three digits in order to be a unique identifier. However, a meaningful code may need more digits. Among the facets that could be incorporated into a supplier·code are (i) the year in which the first purchase from the supplier was made, and (ii) the product line(s) provided by the supplier. With these two facets, plus a sequential code, the format might be ABCCC, where A is the last digit of the year of first purchase, B represents the product line(s) provided, and CCC is the next sequential number assigned. An example code would be 34165, where 3 refers to 1993, and 4 stands for the provision of textbooks and other books.

c. Illustrative journal entries are as follows.

(1)   Routine transaction:

Sales Returns and		
Allowances	XXX	
Cash		XXX

To record returns and allowances on cash sales for (date).

(2)   Nonroutine transaction:

Cash	XXX	
Notes Payable—Bank		XXX

To record the receipt of cash in exchange for a _____ -day, _____ percent note payable to the _____ Bank.

(3)   Standard (recurring) adjusting transaction:

Amortization of Leasehold		
Improvements	XXX	
Allowance for Amortization—		
Lease-hold Improvements		XXX

To record amortization of leasehold improvements for one month at _____ percent.

(4)   Nonrecurring adjusting transaction:

Miscellaneous Expenses	XXX	
Inventory—Sundries		XXX

To record the write-down of inventory damaged by floodwaters and not covered by insurance.

d. The general ledger controls for the bookstore are expected to include those described in this chapter that pertain to computer-based systems.

e. The format of the specified report is as follows.

Campus Bookstore
Gross Profits on Sales by Product Lines
For the Month Ended _____

	Textbooks	Other Books	Sundries
Sales	$........	$........	$........
Less: Sales Returns and Allowances	....	....	....
Net Sales	$........	$........	$........
Cost of Sales:			
Beginning Inventory	$........	$........	$........
Purchases, Net	....	....	....
Goods Available	$........	$........	$........
Less: Ending Inventory	....	....	....
Cost of Sales	$........	$........	$........
Gross Profit on Sales	$........	$........	$........

f. Both the upper and lower levels of the bookstore represent responsibility centers, since they are headed by individual managers. Responsibility reports for these managers should show the revenues and expenses that are directly assignable to their centers. The revenues can be easily assigned on the basis of the chart of accounts that has been designed in **a.** The manager of the upper level is responsible for the revenues from the sundries line, whereas the manager of the lower level is responsible for the revenues from all book sales. Expenses, however, cannot be collected and assigned by use of the chart of accounts alone. For instance, all salaries and wages for sales and clerical personnel are charged to a single account. In order to assign expenses directly to each center, it is necessary to expand the chart of accounts. A simple means of expansion is to add a digit for the responsibility center (e.g., 1 for the upper level) when coding an expense. (Not all expenses should be so coded, however. When preparing responsibility reports no joint expenses, such as the salary paid to Tom Long, should be allocated to individual centers.)

KEY TERMS

accrual (adjusting entry) (423)
adjusting entry (423)
batch-entry journal voucher (426)
budget master file (430)
chart of accounts (418)
closing entry (425)
correction (adjusting entry) (424)
cycles approach (411)

REVIEW QUESTIONS

11-1.   Why is the cycles approach useful in the study of transaction processing?

11-2.   What are the distinctive aspects pertaining to the design of transaction cycles in a particular firm?

11-3.   What are the objectives of the general ledger and financial reporting cycle?

11-4.   What are the typical functions of the general ledger system?

11-5.   What are the differences and benefits of a computerized general ledger system over a manual system?

11-6.   What information should a chart of accounts provide?

11-7.   What factors dictate the classification of accounts?

11-8.   Describe the applications of block and group codes to charts of accounts.

11-9.   What additional facets may logically be linked to general ledger account codes in order to create an expanded chart of accounts?

11-10.   What are several sources of inputs to the general ledger system?

11-11.   What types of transactions affect the general ledger?

11-12.   How are the forms of input likely to differ between manual and computer-based general ledger systems?

11-13.   What are the benefits of on-line data entry to the general ledger system?

11-14.   Describe the several variations to which the general ledger master file is subject in computer-based systems.

11-15.   Describe the other files that are likely to be found in a general ledger data base.

11-16.   Describe the daily processing of transactions in an on-line computer-based general ledger system.

11-17.   Describe the processing of adjusting journal entries at the end of an accounting period when the transactions are processed in batches.

11-18.   What are the risks to which the general ledger activity is exposed?

11-19.   Identify several of the general controls that may be employed to counteract the risks to which the general ledger is exposed.

11-20.   What input, processing, and output controls are suitable in a general ledger application?

11-21.   Identify programmed edit checks that are appropriate during the data entry and updating steps of a general ledger system.

11-22.   What types of analyses are needed in order to review the general ledger activity during an accounting period?

11-23.   What types of financial statements should be generated by the general ledger system?

11-24.   What are the features of the responsibility accounting system that provide useful financial performance results to the managers of a firm?

11-25.   What additional facets may logically be linked to general ledger codes in order to create an expanded chart of accounts?

11-26.   Describe the hierarchical group coding scheme that may be employed with respect to the responsibility centers of a firm.

DISCUSSION QUESTIONS

11-27.   Contrast the general ledger accounts needed by a manufacturing firm with those needed by a merchandising firm such as Infoage.

11-28.   What are the advantages of having a general ledger that is continually on-line and of processing each accounting journal entry as entered to update the general ledger immediately?

11-29.   Describe the differences in general ledger accounts needed by a not-for-profit organization and a merchandising firm such as Infoage.

11-30.   Describe the differences in general ledger accounts needed by Ann Strong's accounting firm and Infoage, Inc.

11-31.   Discuss modifications that are likely to be needed when a general ledger software package is acquired.

11-32.   Describe transaction-oriented cycle(s) that are unique or special for each of the following types of organizations:

a. Manufacturing firm.

b. Bank.

c. Hospital.

d. University.

e. Municipality.

f. Electric utility.

g. Insurance firm.

PROBLEMS

11-1. Dodger Software, Inc., is a financial software development firm that specializes in accounting software packages. Its central product is an integrated software package named AccountInfo, which contains modules pertaining to general ledger, accounts receivable, accounts payable, payroll, and fixed assets. It is now considering the addition of modules to this integrated package, with three possible candidates being job order accounting, project management, and currency conversion.

Required

a. Discuss the extent to which each of these possible modules represents a transaction cycle, including the range of firms for which they would be applicable.

b. If Dodger decides to develop a job order accounting module, describe the features that need to be considered in its design, recognizing that the module's success depends on its being usable by numerous firms having somewhat differing circumstances.

11-2. Prepare an overview data-flow diagram of the transaction cycles for Ann Strong's public accounting firm.

Hint: Use Figure 11-1 as a guide.

11-3. Archer's Sportswear chain has several outlets in the Milwaukee, Wisconsin, area. It sells sportswear to customers, who pay by cash or credit card. The chain has traditionally maintained its general ledger system manually, although it processes sales by means of a point-of-sale system. Recently the president was approached by a salesperson from CYMA Systems, Inc., who suggested that Archer's consider the acquisition of Professional Accounting Series Plus, an accounting software package. After comparing this package with several others, the president agreed to acquire the general ledger module.

Required

a. What are the key functions that any general ledger system must provide to a firm such as Archer's?

b. Refer to Figure 11-2. Give an example based on each of the six processes shown that pertains to Archer's activities.

c. Describe the advantages of a computerized general ledger package to Archer's, especially in comparison to its current manual system.

d. If Archer's installs a computer system based on the client/server architecture and encompassing both its general ledger and sales transactions, what additional benefits are likely to be achieved?

11-4. Ann Strong, CPA/CMA, has a single proprietorship that is quite simple in certain respects. She leases her office and all furniture and fixtures. Only the computers are owned. The only liability is a long-term note owed to the bank. Only a single responsibility center can be said to exist. However, four sources of revenue exist: consulting, tax, audit, and other.

Required

a. Prepare a coded chart of accounts for Ann Strong's firm. The code should be of the block type. Provide a separate account for each revenue source.

b. Assume that Ann buys a desk for herself. Insert accounts to accommodate this addition.

c. Show how the chart of accounts would be modified if the revenue sources were treated as a separate field, with only the revenue control account appearing in the basic chart of accounts.

11-5. Design a five-digit group code for fixed assets. The code should be of the hierarchical type and based on the ledger account codes. Thus, the left-most digit should designate the broad category of assets, and the remaining digits should specify increasingly narrow categories. Illustrate your code format by coding drill presses owned by a firm, assuming that the firm employs three types of drill presses.

11-6. Refer to the Review Problem. A transaction code has been selected with the following format: AAA-B-CCCCC, where AAA is the general ledger account to be debited or credited, B is the responsibility center (1 means upper level, 2 means lower level), and CCCCC is the subsidiary ledger account number. For the purposes of this problem, assume that the only subsidiary ledger is accounts payable, and that only suppliers of merchandise are maintained in the ledger. Assign codes to both the debit and credit portions of the following transactions, using the above format and the chart of accounts provided in the solution to the Review Problem. When a part of the coding format is not applicable, assign zeros in place of significant digits.

a. A valid and correct invoice is received from supplier number 52471 relating to the purchase of 9 dozen university-inscribed sweatshirts.

b. A check is prepared and mailed to supplier number 84237 relating to the purchase of 100 textbooks for an accounting course.

c. A valid and correct bill is received from the bookstore's accountants for general auditing services, and a check is duly prepared and mailed.

d. A valid and correct bill is received from the electric utility, and a check is duly prepared and mailed. Separate meters are employed to measure usage on each level so that amounts can be fairly allocated.

11-7. The Mountainair Public Service Company of Fort Collins, Colorado, serves approximately 195,000 gas and electric consumers throughout a portion of the state. The firm's operations and maintenance activities are divided into five districts, each headed by a manager. Within each district are from 7 to 20 offices, each headed by a supervisor.

As a public utility, Mountainair employs the uniform chart of accounts prescribed by the Federal Power Commission. Thus, codes in the 100s pertain to assets, in the 200s to liabilities, in the 400s to revenues, in the 500s and 600s to operating expenses associated with electricity, in the 700s and 800s to operating expenses associated with gas, and in the 900s to selling and administrative expenses.

However, the controller of Mountainair feels that the coding system might usefully be expanded. For instance, he would like a coding system that would enable the preparation of the following reports.

Balance sheet.

Income statement, by types of revenues.

Responsibility report for each supervisor, showing the types of expenses charged to his or her office, broken down by those that are controllable by the supervisor and those that are noncontrollable overhead.

Responsibility report for each district manager, showing the totals of expenses incurred by each supervisor within his or her district.

Operating statement showing expenses by district and office.

Required

a. Design and illustrate a coding system that will enable the preparation of these reports while retaining the coding prescribed by the Federal Power Commission.

b. Design a customer code that will be useful to the firm in analyzing sales. Note that some customers are residential, others are commercial, and still others fall into special categories such as public street lighting and school lighting; some use gas only, some use electricity only, and some use both.

11-8. Pitman Auto Sales and Service has just been established as a sole proprietorship in Blacksburg, Virginia. It plans to sell three lines of cars: Econs, Meds, and Quals. In addition to new-car sales, it has set up service, parts, and used-car sales departments, each under the supervision of a manager. The firm owns its buildings, land, furnishings, and service equipment. Some of the expenses that it expects to incur are salaries for salespersons and mechanics and for the office force (including managers), utilities, advertising, supplies, taxes, gas and oil, insurance, telephone, and various administrative items. Since it will not handle financing of sales contracts, its receivables will be due from financing agencies. Its inventories of cars and parts, as well as its suppliers, likely will be rather numerous.

Required

Design a coded chart of accounts, together with a group coding format that extends the chart of accounts to include subsidiary ledgers and responsibility centers. In addition to providing control over inventories and suppliers' accounts, the group code should enable the following reports to be prepared:

a. A balance sheet and income statement for the firm.

b. A report that reflects gross profits on sales related to each line of new cars, used cars, parts, and service.

c. An expense report that shows total expenses, plus a breakdown of the direct expenses chargeable to each department.

11-9. Merchandise Unlimited, Inc., records those daily and end-of-period transactions that affect the general ledger on numbered journal vouchers. Each journal voucher is entered by Joan Campbell and approved by Martin Turner. Selected general ledger account codes are as follows: Cash in Bank, 101; Accounts Receivable, 120; Prepaid Rent, 163; Capital Stock, 280; Rent Expense, 547.

Required

Draw journal voucher forms and enter the data to show how each of the following selected transactions would appear after being recorded by Joan Campbell. (Assigned journal voucher numbers appear in parentheses.)

a. Payments received from credit customers on October 12 and deposited in the bank total $12,435.20. (569)

b. Additional capital stock is issued and sold at par value for $10,000 on October 27; the full amount in cash is received the same day from several large acquirers. (598)

c. One month's prepaid rent of $2400 has expired on October 31. (617)

11-10. Your firm employs an on-line general ledger system. When you sign onto the system, the menu shown below appears on the video display screen. Draw the appearance of the data-entry screen after you press the number 1 and then enter the following transaction on September 15, 1997. A dividend of $5.00 per share is declared on the capital stock, payable on September 30 to stockholders of record on August 29. (Outstanding shares of capital stock total 10,000; account codes for Dividends Payable and Retained Earnings are 2780 and 2900, respectively.)

```
┌──────────────────────────────────────────────┐
│       GENERAL LEDGER MAIN MENU                 │
│   1. INPUT OF JOURNAL ENTRY                    │
│   2. CORRECTION OF PREVIOUS                     │
│      JOURNAL ENTRY                             │
│   3. CHANGE OF PERMANENT DATA IN               │
│      ACCOUNT RECORD                            │
│   4. INQUIRY INTO ACCOUNT RECORD               │
│   5. MONTH-END STANDARD                        │
│      ADJUSTING JOURNAL ENTRIES                 │
│   6. MONTH-END CLOSING ENTRIES                 │
│   7. FINANCIAL STATEMENT                       │
│      PREPARATION                               │
│   8. GENERAL LEDGER LISTING                    │
│      PROOF REPORTS                             │
│   9. MANAGERIAL REPORTS MENU                   │
│  10. EXIT FROM GENERAL LEDGER                  │
│      SYSTEM                                     │
│         ENTER DESIRED NUMBER >                 │
└──────────────────────────────────────────────┘
```

11-11. Note: *This problem can be solved with the aid of a data-base package such as Paradox or a presentation package such as Powerpoint.*

Your firm, the same as mentioned in Problem 11-10, acquires a graphical user interface (similar to Windows) and purchases a compatible general ledger system. Design a data-entry screen for accounting entries and enter the transaction described in Problem 11-10.

11-12. A firm has recorded on June 17, 1997, the following cash receipts on a batch-entry journal form, which has been assigned the batch number of 2871:

Document No.	Description	Acct. No.	Debit	Credit
R/A 452	Paul's Bakery	3211		420.00
R/A 582	Sam's Shoes	2862		110.00
R/A 639	Mod Clothes	4497		2486.00
R/A 661	Jumping Jacks	7202		664.00

The transaction code CR, which represents cash receipts transactions, has also been entered on the form. Assume that this firm does not offer purchase discounts.

Required

a. Describe how the cash receipts computer program would process this set of data on being entered via an on-line terminal.

b. Show how the data would appear on a batch-entry journal voucher.

c. Show how the summary general ledger transaction would appear if recorded via a preformatted journal voucher form on a computer terminal screen for on-line entry. The journal-entry number is 2348, and the authorization code is CRPX8. Assume general ledger account numbers where needed, defining these numbers below the screen format. Use Figure 11-10a as a guide, or modify it to reflect a graphical user interface.

11-13. Identify the type of each of the following journal entries.

a.
Cash	XXX	
Notes payable—		
bank		XXX

To record the receipt of cash in exchange for a _____ -day, _____ percent note payable to _____ Bank.

b.
Amortization-leasehold improvements	XXX	
Allowance for amortization-leasehold		
improvements		XXX

To record amortization for (period)

c.
Accounts receivable—trade	XXX	
Sales—major appliances		XXX
Sales—other merchandise		XXX
Sales—parts and accessories		XXX
Sales—service		XXX

To record sales of all lines for (date).

d.
Furniture and fixtures	XXX	
Paid-in capital		XXX

To record the donation of office furniture and fixtures by the president on the first day of incorporation.

11-14. Refer to the Review Problem. Prepare examples of journal entries pertaining to routine internal, routine external, nonroutine, accrual, deferral, revaluation, and reversing transactions.

11-15. As a provider of computer merchandise and services, Infoage, Inc., encounters a wide range of accounting transactions. For each of the following transactions, (1) identify the type and (2) show the journal entry:

a. Common stock in the amount of $800,000 is sold at par for cash.

b. Consulting services in the amount of $9000 that were provided in 1997 are still unbilled and unpaid as of the end of the year.

c. Suppliers' invoices for merchandise totaling

$22,345 are vouched and approved as valid obligations. Infoage records merchandise purchases according to the perpetual inventory method. It does not consider allowed purchase discounts upon the recording of the obligations.

d. Physical inventory is taken in the warehouse. It is discovered that certain inventory items have deteriorated, so that they will need to be sold at severe discounts. The loss in sales value amounts to $3800. This entry will leave only recoverable costs as a balance.

e. A consulting contract called for an advance payment of $20,000 during 1997 for services to be performed. At the end of the year, services in the amount of $8500 are still unearned.

f. Merchandise amounting to $12,300 in sales is returned by credit customers in the same month in which sold.

g. Supplies for use in the main office were inadvertently entered as inventory upon recording their obligations. Supplies are normally recorded as an expense. The amount involved is $1800.

h. Furniture and fixtures for the main office have depreciated this year in the amount of $4000.

11-16. The Deckman Company is a wholesale distributor of beers and wines. It sells on credit to retail establishments such as grocery chains. Merchandise is obtained by credit purchases from bottlers and wineries. Other transactions involve cash receipts and disbursements, payroll, inventories, and fixed assets. Certain of the transactions, such as those involving cash and payroll, are processed in batches. Other transactions are processed by the on-line approach. All master files are maintained on magnetic disk files. The firm has several video display terminals for entering data and obtaining output displays.

Required

a. Describe the master and transaction files that are needed by Deckman, if budgets are not used and no separate responsibility centers are established. Draw a record layout of the general ledger master file, assuming that Deckman prepares financial reports only at year-end.

b. Show sample data that might appear in the general ledger account Accounts Payable if the balance of the account is $5900. Assume codes and other amounts as necessary.

c. If Deckman establishes a budgetary control system, describe how and where the budgetary data might be stored.

d. Assume that Deckman converts to a data-base system, using the network structure. Draw a Bachman (data

structure) diagram that portrays the network for the general ledger system.

11-17. Infoage, Inc., decides to convert to a relational data base, using the structure portrayed in Figure 11-12.

Required

a. Show how the data for the transaction portrayed in Figure 11-10a would appear in the tables of the relational data base. Limit the rows in the master tables to the two accounts involved. Assume that the preparer's initials correspond to the authorization code and that no reference number is involved in this transaction. The responsibility code is FIN. Assume values to complete the records.

b. Redesign the general ledger table to eliminate the budgeted amount field; then establish a responsibility center/budget table that contains the description of each responsibility center and the manager in charge, plus the budgeted amounts for each month of the year. Link this latter table to the general ledger table via the responsibility code. Show data for the responsibility center/ budget table pertaining to merchandise sales, which are under the control of the marketing department. Assume monthly budgeted amounts for sales.

11-18. The Brassila Corporation performs all of its transaction processing on computers by the batch approach. Its sales, purchases/payables, cash receipts and disbursements, payroll, and fixed assets transactions are gathered into batches, batch-totaled, and then transcribed onto magnetic disks from the source documents. Then, as the individual transactions are processed daily or weekly to update the subsidiary ledgers, the summary data (i.e., total amounts affecting the various general ledger accounts) are transferred or extracted onto account distribution tapes. These account distribution tapes are merged daily with each other and with a daily tape containing entries for all nonroutine transactions originally recorded that day on journal vouchers. The resulting tape is sorted according to general ledger account numbers and then processed to update the accounts in the general ledger. Batch totals of the account distribution tapes are not computed.

At the end of each month, a tape containing all adjusting journal entries is processed to update the general ledger, just after the last day's tapes are processed. Then the firm performs computer processing runs that (a) close all temporary accounts and produce a magnetic disk containing all financial statement data pertaining to actual and budget values for the month and (b) print balance sheets and income statements that compare actual and budgeted values. The subsidiary ledgers, general ledger, and budget are maintained as separate files on magnetic disks throughout the month.

Required

a. Prepare a computer system flowchart that reflects the daily and monthly processing of the general ledger, as described above.

b. Prepare a revised computer system flowchart that reflects daily and monthly processing of the general ledger, employing only magnetic disk files and the immediate processing approach.

11-19. Below are several error risks to which the general ledger is exposed.

  a. The credit portion of a nonroutine transaction is inadvertently omitted when the transaction is entered for processing.

  b. The debit amount of a nonroutine transaction contains an inadvertent transposition on entry of the transaction.

  c. A nonroutine transaction is entered twice inadvertently.

  d. The cashier forgot to enter the accrual of the interest on the note payable last month.

  e. A nonexistent number of an accounts payable account is entered during the posting of cash disbursements, and hence the accounts payable ledger is out of balance with the general ledger account.

  f. A nonexistent number of a general ledger account is entered during the entry of a nonroutine transaction, and hence the debits do not equal the credits in the general ledger.

  g. A nonstandard adjusting entry is prepared and entered by the cashier to conceal the theft of cash.

Required

Identify one or more transaction controls that should have prevented or detected each of the errors, assuming the errors take place in:

a. An AIS that employs manual processing of transactions.

b. A computerized AIS that employs immediate processing of transactions.

Hint: Certain of the controls will be identical in both types of systems.

11-20. Refer to Problem 11-16. List the programmed checks that can perform appropriate validations in the following situations, and specify examples of data elements that each programmed check is intended to verify. Assume that journal vouchers contain journal voucher (JV) numbers, general ledger account numbers, account descriptions, debit amounts, credit amounts, and debit or credit (i.e., DR, CR) designations. In addition, assume that transaction codes are included when an on-line system is employed.

  a. Batches of journal vouchers being posted sequentially to general ledger accounts during batch processing runs.

  b. Data on journal vouchers, pertaining either to summarized transactions or to nonroutine individual transactions, being entered individually via on-line terminals and being posted immediately to the general ledger accounts.

11-21. *Note: This problem can be solved by using a microcomputer-based spreadsheet software package such as Lotus or Excel.*

The budget and actual values pertaining to the January 1998 income statement for Hargreaves, Ltd., are as follows:

	Budget	Actual
Sales	$10,000	$9,500
Cost of Goods Sold	6,500	5,600
Gross Profit on Sales	$ 3,500	$3,900
Selling Expenses	$ 500	$ 450
Administrative Expenses	1,400	950
Total Expenses	$ 1,900	$1,400
Net Income before Taxes	$ 1,600	$2,500
Estimated Income Taxes	240	300
Net Income	$ 1,360	$2,200

Required

Prepare a report for management in good form that reveals the performance of the firm during January.

11-22. The Mecom Co. of Las Cruces, New Mexico, produces sports equipment. Each manager in charge of a department or higher responsibility center receives a monthly performance report. Last month (June) the costs pertaining to the fabricating department within the production function were as follows:

	Actual	Budgeted
Raw materials	$ 6,600	$ 7,000
Direct labor	12,800	12,000
Supplies	650	700
Utilities	1,680	1,600
Depreciation of departmental equipment	1,000	1,000
Depreciation of plant— allocated	6,000	6,000
Production administration cost—allocated	5,200	4,000
Indirect labor	3,400	3,000
Salary—department head	2,000	2,000

Each department manager is responsible for decisions concerning equipment needed in his or her department.

Required

a. Prepare the monthly performance report for the fabricating department in June, based on sound concepts of responsibility reporting.

b. Explain where any costs that are omitted from the report in **a** above would be reported, or if they should not be reported.

c. The fabricating department is the second production department in the manufacturing process, and the general ledger account number for factory utilities is 623. What specific combined account code would have been used to charge the $1680 for June if a hierarchical group code is employed for responsibility centers?

11-23. The Brown Printing Company of Fairfax, Virginia, accounts for the services it performs on a job-cost basis. Most jobs require a week or less to complete and involve two or more of Brown's five operating departments. Actual costs are accumulated by job. To ensure timely billing, however, the firm prepares sales invoices based on cost estimates.

Recently, several printing jobs have incurred losses. To avoid future losses, management has decided to focus on cost control at the department level. Since labor is a major cost element, one proposal is to develop a departmental labor cost report. This report is to be issued by the payroll department as one of the biweekly payroll outputs. The report is to be sent to an accounting clerk for comparison with the labor cost estimates of each department. If the actual total department labor cost in a payroll period is not significantly more than the estimated amount, the accounting clerk is to send the report to the department supervisor. However, if the accounting clerk concludes that a significant variance exists, the report will be sent to the assistant controller, who will investigate the cause, if time is available, and will recommend corrective action to the production manager.

Required

a. Identify the features of the described procedure for controlling labor costs that are in accord with the concepts of responsibility accounting. Also, identify the violations of sound management control principles.

b. To ensure the accuracy of financial reports, the controller requires that a general ledger change report be prepared at the end of each month. Discuss the matters of concern for the accountants who review this report with respect to these accounts:

(1) Sales

(2) Direct labor cost

(3) Indirect labor cost

(4) Work-in-process inventory

(CIA *adapted*)

11-24. SharpEdge, Inc., is a manufacturer of cutlery and hand tools that are sold to retail hardware stores. SharpEdge also manufactures a line of industrial-quality tools that are sold to commercial establishments. The firm's single manufacturing plant and corporate headquarters are located in the Midwest. Regional sales offices and firm-owned warehouses are located on the East and West coasts and in the South.

SharpEdge initiated a new monthly closing and reporting procedure for calendar year 1997. The books are always closed on a Friday. In addition, each quarter consists of two four-week months and one five-week month; the five-week month is always the middle month of the quarter. Thus, each month for internal reporting purposes is not necessarily the end of the calendar month, and each four- or five-week reporting month may include days from two calendar months. The monthly reports and schedules are to be prepared and ready for the executive management meeting, which is held on the Friday following the monthly closing date. Prior to these changes, SharpEdge closed its books on the last day of each month, and the executive management meeting was not scheduled until all data were compiled. This frequently resulted in the executive management meeting being held as late as three weeks after the closing date.

When the new closing procedure was implemented, SharpEdge's accounting department had to implement some artificial cutoffs in order to ensure that the monthly reports would be completed for the executive management meeting. The schedule that was implemented is outlined as follows:

- Sales data from the regional offices are telexed to headquarters on the Monday morning following the closing date. Rather than wait for data regarding returned sales as was previously done, gross sales data are submitted by the regional offices. The gross sales are adjusted for returns during the closing procedures for the next month.

- Cash receipts are deposited daily. However, a lockbox system is employed for the eastern, western, and southern regional sales offices, and this lockbox report is not received at corporate headquarters until Monday afternoon for the preceding week. Thus, the last week's cash receipts from these three regions are estimated. The cash receipts for the midwestern region are available through the Thursday immediately preceding the Friday closing date.

- Hourly personnel (all manufacturing and clerical support in the administrative offices) are paid weekly. The payroll is run on Wednesday and distributed on Thursday for the prior week. Thus, actual payroll data for these people are not available for the last week of each month. Administrative personnel are paid monthly on the last calendar day of the month; however, each monthly salary is known and is included as of the monthly closing even if the payment date is after the designated monthly closing.

- The manufacturing records are updated on Thursday of each week after the payroll is completed. Thus, the actual manufacturing data are not available for the last week of the monthly period.

- All payments on account are paid out of corporate headquarters. All payables are entered into the accounting system each week on Wednesday. The payables represent all transactions that have been received from Wednesday of the prior week through the following Tuesday. Thus, three days of payables are not recorded during the last week of each monthly period.

Required

a. SharpEdge has elected a quarterly reporting period consisting of two four-week periods and one five-week period. Discuss the advantages of this type of schedule.

b. The accounting department of SharpEdge, Inc., must make several adjustments to accommodate the new monthly reporting and closing procedures. Explain why SharpEdge's top management is likely to accept these limitations in the monthly operating reports and results.

c. For each of the data constraints described in the question, discuss how errors in the estimates implemented by SharpEdge's accounting department could affect the current asset and/or current liability account balances on the firm's Statement of Financial Position.

(CMA *adapted*)

11-25. *Datacruncher Office Equipment, Inc. (Continuing Case)* In each of the remaining chapters of this textbook the last problem will consist of requirements pertaining to the Datacruncher Office Equipment, Inc., Case A at the end of the book. This comprehensive case will enable you to simulate the experience of analyzing and designing an improved accounting information system for a manufacturing firm. Generally the requirements at the end of each chapter will relate to material discussed in that chapter, although the requirements below extend to matters discussed in earlier chapters of the book.

Required

a. Prepare a coded chart of accounts for Datacruncher, based on the description and financial statements provided in the case statement.

b. Prepare an organization chart for Datacruncher, based on the description provided in the opening paragraphs of the case statement.

c. Prepare a report that surveys the environment of Datacruncher, drawing on sources in your school's library and elsewhere. The survey should include relevant information concerning the office equipment industry, the major resources needed, and the principal legal requirements.

CHAPTER
12

THE REVENUE CYCLE

THE LEARNING OBJECTIVES FOR THIS CHAPTER ARE TO ENABLE YOU TO:

1. Describe the objectives, functions, organizational units, and decisions that pertain to a firm's revenue cycle.

2. Identify the revenue cycle's data sources and forms of input.

3. Identify files and data structures that are needed within the data base for the revenue cycle.

4. Describe the steps and approaches employed in processing the transaction data flows through the revenue cycle.

5. List needed internal controls for the revenue cycle.

6. Describe a variety of operational and managerial reports and other outputs that may be generated by the revenue cycle.

INTRODUCTION

Business firms and many not-for-profit organizations depend on revenues from customers for their continued existence. Revenues arise because the business firms and organizations determine the needs of certain customers or clients and find ways to serve these needs. Some business firms and organizations provide products, others provide services (like Ann Strong), and still others (like Infoage, Inc.) provide both.

All of the events, or functions, involved in selling goods and services and reaping cash therefrom make up the revenue cycle. Revenue cycles tend to be similar for all types of firms, from merchandising firms to manufacturing firms to service firms. In all firms the entity of prime concern is the customer. However, details differ with respect to the ways that the products or services are delivered and the timing of the payments by the customers.

Two subsystems within the accounting information system (AIS) perform the processing steps composing the revenue cycle: (1) the sales processing system and (2) the cash receipts processing system. This chapter discusses the components that are suitable to these two processing systems.

OVERVIEW

OBJECTIVES OF THE CYCLE

The essential purpose of the revenue cycle is to facilitate the exchange of products or services with customers for cash. Typical objectives within this broad purpose are to (1) record sales orders promptly and accurately, (2) verify that the customers are worthy of credit, (3) ship the products or perform the services by agreed dates, (4) bill for products or services in a timely and accurate manner, (5) record and classify cash receipts promptly and accurately, (6) post sales and cash receipts to proper customers' accounts in the accounts receivable ledger, and (7) safeguard products and cash until shipped or deposited. As byproducts, the revenue cycle captures information relating to sales, customers, and receivables.

FUNCTIONS OF THE CYCLE

Functions pertaining to product credit sales, services, and cash sales differ somewhat. For product credit sales, they include obtaining the order from the customer, checking the customer's credit, entering and processing the sales order, assembling the goods for shipment, shipping the goods, billing the customer, receiving and depositing the cash payment, maintaining the receivables record, posting transactions to the general ledger, and preparing the needed financial reports and other outputs. For services, the functions of assembling and shipping goods are replaced by the function of performing the ordered services. For cash sales, the function of maintaining the receivables records is unnecessary. The functions pertaining to a credit sale of a product are shown in Figure 12-1 and described in the following survey.

Obtain Order from Customer Orders from customers may be obtained in various ways. A customer may mail or wire a purchase order; the customer might phone in an order or might enter the merchandising firm's store and buy one or more items from a salesperson. Alternatively, a salesperson (an employee or an independent broker) may travel to the customer's premises and obtain the order directly. In each instance a **customer order** is customarily expressed in writing. The written order often appears on a form, such as the customer's purchase order or the salesperson's order blank. Figure 12-2 shows a form used to enter a customer order. If the selling firm has a computer system, the order may alternatively be "written" in electronic form via a computer input device. The final step is to determine that the order is valid. For instance, a sales order clerk in one of Infoage's outlets may verify that the customer is a reputable banking firm in a nearby city.

Check Credit When the order pertains to a sale on credit, it is often subject to a credit check. If an order is received from a repeat credit customer, the firm will

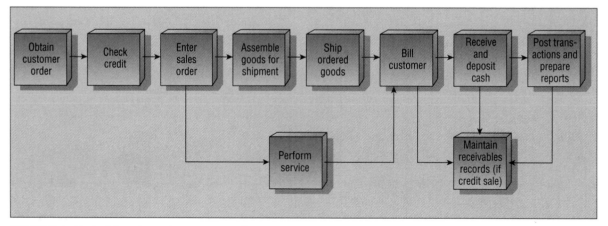

FIGURE 12-1 Typical functions of a revenue cycle.

PRODUCTS / PARTS
CUSTOMER ORDER

Sold To:*   Ship To:*
No. [ ][ ]—[ ][ ][ ][ ]   No. [ ][ ]—[ ][ ][ ][ ]

Order No:* _____   Date:* _____

Sold to:
Name: _____ / _____

Address: _____ / _____ Zip: _____

Ship to:
Name: _____ / _____

Address: _____ / _____ Zip: _____

Sman: (Products) _____   Terms: _____   B/O# _____

Page Qn:* _____   Ship From: (Products) __   Cust Date: _____

PO# _____   How to Ship:: _____   Date:* _____

: _____ / _____

Item #	Charge Description		Override		Special Instructions
	Quan.*	Model/Part No.*	Price	Disc	
1					
2					
3					
4					
5					
6					
7					
8					
9					
10					
11					
12					
13					
14					

Note: *Denotes Required Entries!

Special Price Approval_____   Order Taken By_____

Computer Form No. T-100   PC-3-76026

FIGURE 12-2   A customer order. (Courtesy of Arvin Industries.)

normally have credit information concerning the customer in its data base. The information will be summarized in the form of a credit rating (e.g., excellent, good, poor) or a credit limit (e.g., a cumulative $5000 of automatic credit). If an order is from a new customer, or if the customer applies for a credit card, the firm may refer to a credit bureau to ascertain the applicant's creditworthiness. In the case of a customer (new or old) who has a special situation, the credit manager will typically be expected to make a judgment.

Enter Sales Order   Orders that have been approved for credit are next entered into the sales processing procedure. Sales order entry usually involves two steps: (1) determining that the ordered products (or services) are available and (2) preparing a formal sales-entry document.

Determining the availability of ordered products is often a simple task. If the order concerns products carried by a merchandising firm such as Infoage, the salesclerk may simply check the back room of the sales outlet. If the products are stored in a warehouse, the clerk might check the inventory records to ascertain the status. He or she might also ask the warehouse clerk to reserve the ordered quantities. If the products are to be manufactured to order, the clerk would request a scheduled completion date from the production planning department.

Formal **sales orders** are usually prepared in multiple copies from customers' orders. They are prenumbered for more effective control. Three document preparation procedures are available: prebilling, incomplete prebilling, and separate order and billing. In the **prebilling procedure** the sales invoice (bill) is completely filled in, including prices and extensions and total, as soon as the order is approved. This procedure reduces the paperwork but is only feasible if all data are known, including the availability of ordered quantities. In the **incomplete billing procedure** a combined sales order–invoice is prepared at the time the order is approved. This document shows quantities but not price extensions, freight charges, and so on. After the order has been shipped, the document is completed and used as the sales invoice. In the **separate sales order and invoice procedure** the invoice is prepared as a separate document only after the goods have been shipped. The sales order in this case is used only as a shipping order. Although this procedure requires an additional document, it may be necessary when the availability of inventory cannot be determined or when ordered goods are often out of stock and must be back ordered.

Regardless of the procedure used, a copy of the formal sales order is generally sent to the customer as an **order acknowledgment** and to confirm the shipping date. Other copies are used to initiate processing steps and to store data concerning the transaction.

Assemble Goods for Shipment   Goods that are ordered must be physically moved to the shipping dock. Often this function involves picking the goods from a warehouse, using a **picking list** or a copy of the sales order as the authorizing document. The quantities of goods picked are noted on the picking list. Then the goods are moved to the shipping dock. (In the case of expensive goods or special made-to-order goods, this function may consist of acquiring the goods from suppliers or producing the goods within the firm's manufacturing facilities.) Since the picking activity reduces the inventory of available goods, the quantities should be noted in the appropriate inventory records.

Ship Ordered Goods   Unless the customer is to pick up the ordered goods at the shipping dock, the goods must be physically distributed to the customer. Before being distributed, the goods are generally packaged with a **packing slip** (often a copy of the sales order) enclosed. The goods are then shipped by means of the firm's own delivery vehicles, by a parcel service, by the U.S. postal service, or by an independent common carrier. In the last case, the carrier is selected (often in accordance with the customer's instructions), the packages are weighed and labeled, and the charges are established.

Documents that reflect shipments usually include a **shipping notice** or report. When common carriers are used, bills of lading must be prepared. A **bill of lading** is a standard document that is intended for the agents of the common carrier, informing them that goods are legally on board, that the freight charges have been paid, and that the consignee is authorized to receive the goods at the destination.

Bill Customer Billing should normally await the time at which the customer physically has the ordered goods in his or her possession. Otherwise, it is very likely that mistakes will be made and corrections will be necessary. For instance, ordered goods may be out of stock and the order cannot be filled. When the customer address is at a distance from the firm's warehouse or store, most firms view the time of possession to be when the goods have been shipped.

On receiving a copy of the shipping notice, an assigned person prepares a sales invoice. (An example of a sales invoice appears as Figure 2-18.) To complete the billing step, the sales invoice is presented to the customer for payment. It is the key document in the sales transaction system, since it provides the amount of the transaction to the accounting cycle and serves as the posting medium.

The sales invoice may be delivered in various ways: in person, via the postal service, or through an electronic data interchange network. The terms stated on the invoice specify the due date of the payment; often they allow a cash discount for payment by an earlier date.

The typical billing procedure related to product sales is subject to wide variations, depending on the type of sale and industry. At one extreme are cash sales made by retailing establishments, in which cases customers pay immediately and are given receipts in place of invoices. At the other extreme are long-term contractual sales, as in the case of construction projects; the customers pay periodically on the basis of a series of progress billings.*

A widespread billing practice involves credit sales at retail establishments. The retailer accepts credit cards serviced by an independent financing firm; it forwards the sales slip ("flimsy") to the financing firm and immediately receives cash in return. The financing firm then bills the customer via a monthly statement.

Receive and Deposit Cash Payment Cash remitted by customers may be received through the mail or over the counter. Each cash payment is recorded immediately upon receipt. Accompanying each payment should be a **remittance advice,** a document that contains the cash amount and the payer's name. An example of a remittance advice is shown in Figure 12-3. It is the counterpart to the sales invoice, since it also serves as the posting medium to the accounting records. Many remittance advices, such as the example, can be described as *turnaround documents,* since they incorporate portions of the sales invoices that are returned by the customers with their cash payments.

All remitted amounts should be listed on a **deposit slip** during the same day and delivered intact to the firm's bank. Figure 12-4 shows a deposit slip. The coding at the bottom of the slip refers to the account number and bank code.

---

*Between these extremes are sales of recurring services, such as utilities and insurance. Customers are billed periodically on the basis of the service provided. The periods may range from monthly for utilities to semiannually or annually for insurance. Sometimes cycle billing is employed, in which case a portion of the customer base is billed each working day. For instance, a particular utility customer may receive a bill on the tenth of each month.

OMEGA'S SPECIALTIES

Billing Date 03-03-97		Payment Due Date	04-03-97
Account No.			
2396-852-078		Balance Due	280.59

Omega's Specialties
PO Box 5566
Paul Emerick   Hayward CA
1520 Evergreen Ave.   94540-5566
Patagonia AZ 85624   Amount Paid $ _____

Detach and return this portion with your check

FIGURE 12-3   A remittance advice, which represents the return portion of a sales invoice or monthly statement.

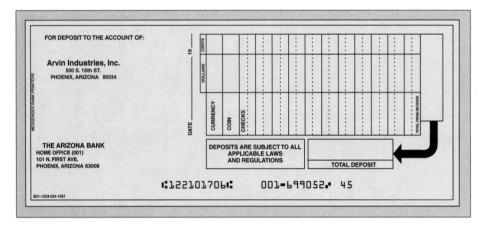

FIGURE 12-4   A deposit slip. (Courtesy of Arvin Industries.)

An alternative means of receiving cash is through a *lockbox collection system*. Customers mail cash remittances to a post office box. The firm's bank opens the boxes daily, deposits the remittances to the firm's accounts, and prepares a detailed listing.

Maintain Accounts Receivable   A separate accounts receivable record is maintained for each active credit customer. Each billed sale amount is debited to the account, whereas each cash remittance is credited to the account. An outstanding balance appears in the account as long as all sales have not been paid in full.

Either of two methods may be employed in adjusting the balance to reflect payments made by customers. The **balance forward method** applies a payment against the outstanding balance, rather than against a specific invoice. This method, which is generally employed when monthly statements are mailed to customers, merges all invoice amounts of previous months and simply shows a "balance forward." The **open invoice method,** on the other hand, matches each payment with a specific invoice. It continues to show all invoices as "open." Thus, disputed invoices are more easily isolated.

Post Transactions to General Ledger   Summarized sales and cash receipts transactions are posted to the general ledger. This function represents the interface between the revenue cycle and the general ledger system discussed in Chapter 11.

Prepare Needed Financial Reports and Other Outputs   A variety of outputs are generated as byproducts of the above-mentioned revenue cycle functions. One example already mentioned is the monthly statement for customers. Summaries of sales and cash receipts, akin to journal listings, are also needed. Financial reports ranging from the accounts receivable aging schedule to sales analyses are typically viewed as necessary. Displays of individual accounts and other specific information are also available when data are stored in on-line files.

Other Related Functions   Several functions supplement the major functions composing the revenue cycle. Supplemental functions of interest include paying salespersons' commissions, costing products being sold, acquiring cash from sources other than customers, handling sales returns and allowances, collecting delinquent accounts, and processing back orders. The first two functions are discussed in later transaction cycle chapters, and sources of cash are discussed in Appendix 2 to Chapter 14. Thus, we limit our brief descriptions to the last three supplemental functions.

- **Handling sales returns and allowances.** Sales returns arise when unsatisfied customers send back all or part of the ordered goods. Sales allowances are adjustments in prices granted to customers as compensation for damaged goods, shortages, or specified deficiencies. In either case **credit memos** (memoranda) are prepared to formalize the agreements reached. However, they are only issued when evidence is presented that the returns have actually been received or that the allowances are warranted. Figure 12-5 presents a prenumbered credit memo. When completed and approved, this credit memo will serve as the posting medium to reduce the balance in the customer's accounts receivable account.

- **Collecting delinquent accounts.** Most customers pay their outstanding balances, or make installment payments, upon receiving statements. Collection procedures

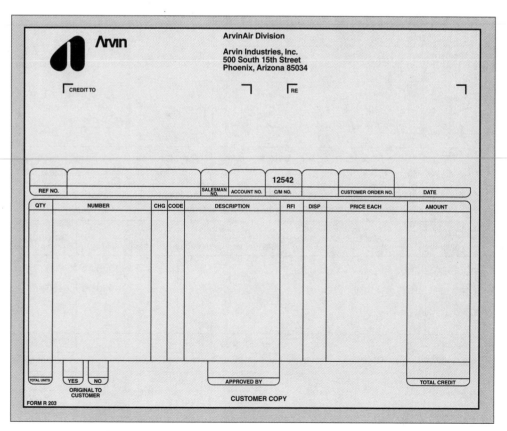

FIGURE 12-5   A credit memo. (Courtesy of Arvin Industries.)

are unfortunately necessary, however, in the case of slow-paying customers. Generally these procedures begin with second notices of balances due. Then delinquency notices are likely sent. If payments are still not received, the firm may hire a collection agency, factor the receivables with a financing agency, or eventually write off the balance. The last action involves the preparation of a write-off notice.

- **Processing back orders.** Back orders are necessary when insufficient quantities of inventory are on hand to fill all orders. Back ordering involves the preparation of a **back-order** form, showing the customer who ordered, the order number, the quantity needed, and the date requested. This form is sent to the selected supplier, and the ordered quantities are posted to inventory records. When the back-ordered items arrive, they are immediately shipped to the customer and the quantities on order in the inventory records are reduced. Since customers are generally not billed for back-ordered items until they are shipped, a new sales invoice is also prepared for the back-ordered items and mailed to the customer.

The original sales invoice should notify the customer of the items that have been back ordered. Figure 12-6 depicts a sales invoice to Hamill Company, showing that back-order number 3128 has been placed with Universal Computer by Infoage, Inc.

Invoice Date: 10/20/97 Cust. Order No.: B1738 Our Order No.: 10–4132 Cust. Acct. No.: 12260	INFOAGE, INC. 6000 Lakeshore Dr. Seattle, WA 98195 Phone (206) 543-1217 SALES INVOICE		No. 62138

	Hamill Company		
Sold to:	123 Couger Ave. Pullman, WA 99164	Ship to:	Same

Terms 2/10, net 30	How Shipped Husky Trucking	Date Shipped 10/17/97	Date Ordered 10/15/97	Salesperson H. Able

Back Order No. 3128	Back Order Date 10/16/97	Back Ordered From Universal Computer	Posting Date 10/20/97

Product No.	Description	Quan. Ordered	Back Ordered	Quan. Shipped	Unit Price	Amount
300100	Tobe Notebook Computer	8	3	5	1200.00	$6000.00
512364	Putz 500 Inkjet Printer	10	4	6	250.00	1500.00

	Amount
Subtotal	$7500.00
Freight	70.00
Sales Tax	450.00
Total Amount Due	$8020.00

FIGURE 12-6 A sales invoice showing items shipped and back ordered by Infoage, Inc.

RELATIONSHIPS TO THE ORGANIZATION

The concept of organizational independence requires that the several revenue cycle functions and related responsibilities be segregated among multiple organizational units. The array of responsibilities is mainly under the direction of the marketing/ distribution and finance/accounting organizational functions, as Figure 12-7 portrays. Thus the revenue cycle involves the close interaction of the marketing information system and the accounting information system (AIS).

Marketing/Distribution   Marketing management has the objectives of (1) determining and satisfying the needs of customers and (2) generating sufficient revenue to cover costs and expenses, replace assets, and provide an adequate return on investment. As Figure 12-7 shows, the top marketing manager is often a vice-president, whose responsibilities typically involve market research, product development and planning, sales, promotion and advertising, customer service, and shipping and transportation. Each of these organizational subfunctions, usually headed by a separate manager in medium- and large-sized firms, deserves brief attention.

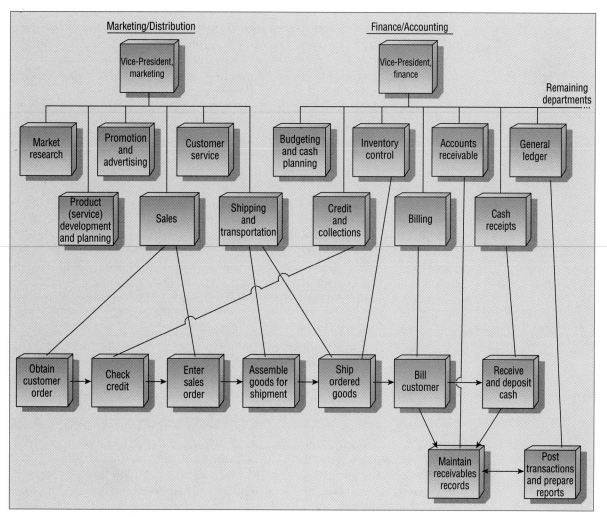

FIGURE 12-7   Relationships of organizational units to revenue cycle functions.

Market research focuses on the markets for the firm's products or services. It studies the customers and potential customers, including their attitudes, preferences, and spending power. Market research studies often provide critical information for promoting new products and determining pricing practices.

Promotion and advertising heightens the market's awareness of the firm's products or services. It establishes and executes the promotional strategies, such as direct mailings, telemarketing, and dealer incentives. It also determines the advertising mix, as among newspapers and television. Advertising personnel also may write the advertising material or may coordinate with an advertising agency. The function must be aware of the advertising and promotional costs, as tracked by the AIS, in order to remain within budget limits. Also, it gathers information concerning the relative effectiveness of the respective channels employed.

Product (or service) development and planning focuses on the product lines (or services), including styling, packaging, and performance. It also plans for the introduction of new products (or services) and for the elimination of unprofitable ones. Thus it must follow closely the sales and profitability of each product line (or service).

Sales concentrates on the selling effort, usually through a sales force. It is interested in sales forecasts, in current sales performance (including profitability), and in expenses incurred in selling activities. Its representatives also enter sales orders for processing.

Customer service handles customer needs before and after the sale of the product. A high level of customer service can lead to customer satisfaction and repeat business. Much of the service consists of providing information, such as delivery schedules and special product features and warranties. Other services may involve dealing with complaints and providing needed maintenance.

Shipping and transportation provides the distribution support for the marketing function. It may be under the direct sales organization or may be a separate organizational function. The major concern of shipping and transportation is to assure that ordered goods are delivered to customers promptly, in good condition, and in accordance with customer specifications.

Finance/Accounting The objectives of financial and accounting management relate broadly to funds, data, information, planning, and control over resources. With respect to the revenue cycle, the objectives are limited to cash planning and control, to data pertaining to sales and customers' accounts, to inventory control, and to information pertaining to cash and sales and customers. For instance, with respect to cash planning and control, the objectives are to maintain an optimal level of cash (neither too low nor too high) and to safeguard cash from loss or theft.

The top financial manager in many firms is the vice-president of finance. Two managers often report directly to this top manager: a treasurer and a controller. The treasurer has such responsibilities in the finance area as budgeting and cash planning, credit and collections, and cash receipts. The controller has such responsibilities in the accounting area as billing, inventory control, accounts receivable, and general ledger. (Both the treasurer and controller have other responsibilities that are irrelevant to the revenue cycle.)

The responsibilities of each may be summarized as follows: *Budgeting and cash planning* aids in developing short-range and long-range budgets and cash forecasts. *Credit and collections* develops credit and collection policies and administers the policies with respect to individual customers. *Cash receipts*, an arm of the cashier, deposits cash received and maintains the related records. *Billing* prepares the sales invoices. *Inventory control* maintains the records pertaining to inventory balances. *Accounts re-*

SPOTLIGHTING

DECISION-ORIENTED SYSTEMS IN MARKETING

Frito-Lay collects sales data daily on 200 grocery products, using hand-held computers operated by its 10,000 salespersons. The collected sales data are uploaded nightly from each hand-held computer to a central computer. When summarized, this sales data is promulgated to marketing managers via an executive information system (EIS). Weekly sales summaries and analyses are also distributed through the EIS. Based in part on the daily and weekly data, marketing managers make decisions concerning pricing and product promotions and transmit these decisions to the salespersons via their hand-held computers.*

In recent years decision support systems (DSS) have aided managers in making a variety of marketing-oriented decisions. Excelan, a marketer of circuit boards and software, modeled the buying behavior of prospects and customers within a market-based DSS. Through the model the managers detected a shift in customers' buying behavior from a technical focus to an office automation focus. This discovery pointed the managers toward new

target markets and the need for retraining the marketing employees. Grede Foundries, a Milwaukee producer of castings for original equipment manufacturers, developed a DSS that models a "perceived quality index." This index links sales orders, services delivered, preselling and postsale support, prices paid, discounts, selling costs, servicing costs, and other factors. It yields a much more complete and realistic measure of customers' reactions than the previous measure of returned sales. By careful analysis of the index's readings, managers gain insights into needed improvements in services and changes in prices.†

Expert systems have been employed to capture the experience gained by Mrs. Fields in marketing her cookies. An expert system module called Daily Production Planner first projects the quantity of dough that likely should be prepared for a full day's baking and sales. It monitors hourly sales and suggests changes in production quantities. At the end of the day the expert system measures performance against projections and recommends future production and sales strategies. The Broadway, a chain of department stores, employs its Area Sales Manager Expert System Consultant to analyze store-specific sales data (e.g., current versus last year versus average) to pinpoint areas of concern and to recommend strategies that the store managers should adopt.**

*James T.C. Teng, Varun Grover, and Kirk D. Fiedler, "Business Process Reengineering: Charting a Strategic Path for the Information Age," *California Management Review* (Spring 1994), p. 27.
†Rowland T. Moriarty and Gordon S. Swartz, "Automation to Boost Sales and Marketing," *Harvard Business Review* (January-February 1989), p. 103.
**Harvey P. Newquist III, "Experts at Retail," *Datamation* (April 1, 1990), pp. 54–55.

ceivable maintains the accounts of individual customers. *General ledger* maintains the ledger of all balance sheet and income statement accounts, from which financial reports are prepared.

MANAGERIAL DECISION MAKING

Marketing and financial managers must make decisions affecting the effectiveness of selling and collecting cash receipts. The aims of their decision making are (1) to maximize the revenues and profits of their firm while providing long-term satisfaction to their customers and (2) to optimize the use of the revenue-related resources of the firm. Among the decisions that must be made, especially at the tactical and strategic levels, are those listed in Figure 12-8. Much of the information needed to make such decisions derives from the AIS. For instance, information based on sales transactions aids in making decisions concerning products and markets. Additional

Marketing Decisions

1. Which types of markets and customers are to be served?
2. Which specific products are to be provided to customers, including new products to be introduced?
3. What prices are to be charged, and what discounts are to be allowed?
4. What after-sales services are to be offered?
5. What channels of distribution are to be employed?
6. What advertising media are to be employed, and in what mix?
7. What organizational units are to be incorporated within the marketing function?
8. What marketing plans and budgets are to be established for the coming year?

Financial Decisions

1. What criteria are to be employed in granting credit to potential customers?
2. What collection methods are to be employed in minimizing bad debts?
3. What accounts receivable records are to be maintained concerning amounts owed by customers?
4. What sources, other than receipts from sales, are to be employed in obtaining needed funds for operations?
5. What financial plans and cash budgets are to be established for the coming year?

FIGURE 12-8   Types of managerial decisions pertaining to the revenue cycle.

information, however, must be obtained—such as external information concerning competitors and other facets of the environment. Examples of needed information are listed in Chapter 15.

In addition to relevant information, decision making is aided by specialized systems that incorporate decision-modeling capabilities. A vignette on the previous page presents several examples of real-world decision-oriented systems.

DATA ENTRY

SOURCES

Data used in the revenue cycle are mainly based on inputs from customers. Customers initiate both the sales and cash receipts transactions. For product sales, other sources include the salespersons, the customer reference and credit records, the inventory records, the finished goods warehouse, the suppliers (and/or the firm's production function), the shipping department, and the common carrier. In some cases a financing agency or bank may also be a source of data.

FORMS OF INPUT

Most of the source documents involved in the revenue cycle have been identified in our discussion of cycle functions. Figure 12-9 summarizes the documents needed by merchandising firms, especially those that employ manual processing systems. Accountants are particularly concerned with the sales invoice, credit memo, remittance advice, and write-off notice, since they initiate entries into the accounting cycle.

Most of the above-mentioned hard-copy documents are also likely to be used in firms employing computer-based processing. Documents provide visible and tangible evidence and are necessary for certain users. For instance, sales invoices in hard-

Customer order. Either the customer's purchase order or a form prepared by a salesperson of the selling firm.

Sales order. A formal, multicopy form prepared from the customer order.

Order acknowledgment. Usually a copy of the sales order sent to the customer to acknowledge receipt of the order.

Picking list. Either a copy of the sales order or a separate document sent to the warehouse for use in picking the ordered goods from the bins.

Packing slip. A copy of the sales order or picking list enclosed with the goods when they are packaged for shipping order.

Bill of lading. A shipping document intended for the agents of the common carrier that is to transport the products.

Shipping notice. Often a copy of the sales order or a separate shipping document that serves as proof that the goods were shipped.

Sales invoice. The document that is sent to the customer to reflect the amount of a sale.

Remittance advice. A document that shows the amount of the cash receipt from a customer.

Deposit slip. The document that accompanies deposits of cash in the bank.

Back order. A document prepared when insufficient quantities are in inventory to satisfy sales orders.

Credit memo. A document that allows a credit to a customer for a sales return or for allowance on a sale.

Credit application. A form prepared when a new customer applies for credit, showing detailed data pertaining to the applicant's current financial condition and earning level.

Salesperson call report. A form used to describe a call made by a salesperson on a prospective customer and to indicate the result of the call.

Delinquent notice. A notice sent to a customer who is past due on his or her credit account balance.

Write-off notice. A document prepared by the credit manager when an account is deemed to be uncollectible.

Cash register receipts. A form used by a retailer to reflect cash received.

FIGURE 12-9 Documents pertaining to the revenue cycle.

copy form are clear evidence to most retail customers and are necessary when customers are not electronically linked to the selling firms.

When computer-based systems are present, however, data from hard-copy forms are often transcribed onto computer-readable media. Certain input documents may be redesigned to aid this purpose. For example, the sales order document in Figure 12-10 has been modified to accord with the data fields in the computerized records and to be a more user-friendly input form. Data-entry clerks can more quickly enter the necessary data elements from the structured boxes, with fewer transcription errors.

As we observed in Chapter 5, transaction data may be transcribed onto magnetic tapes or disks for entry as batches into computer processing systems. Increasingly, however, transaction data are being entered with the aid of on-line preformatted screens. Many firms employ such screens to enter data concerning sales orders, sales returns, and cash receipts transactions—individually or in batches.

Figure 12-11 displays the on-line entry of a batch of cash receipts with the aid of a preformatted screen. Before and while the data are being entered manually from the cash remittance forms, an underlying data-entry computer program assists in several ways. The date and batch number are entered when the preformatted screen

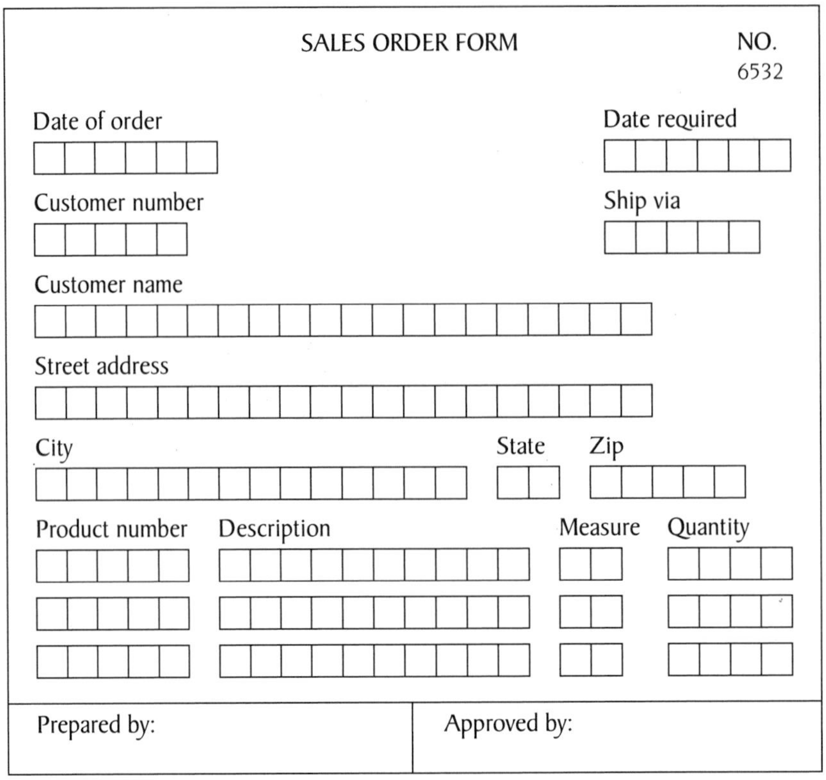
SALES ORDER FORM
NO. 6532
Date of order
Date required
Customer number
Ship via
Customer name
Street address
City
State
Zip
Product number
Description
Measure
Quantity
Prepared by:
Approved by:

FIGURE 12-10 A source document for manually recorded data.

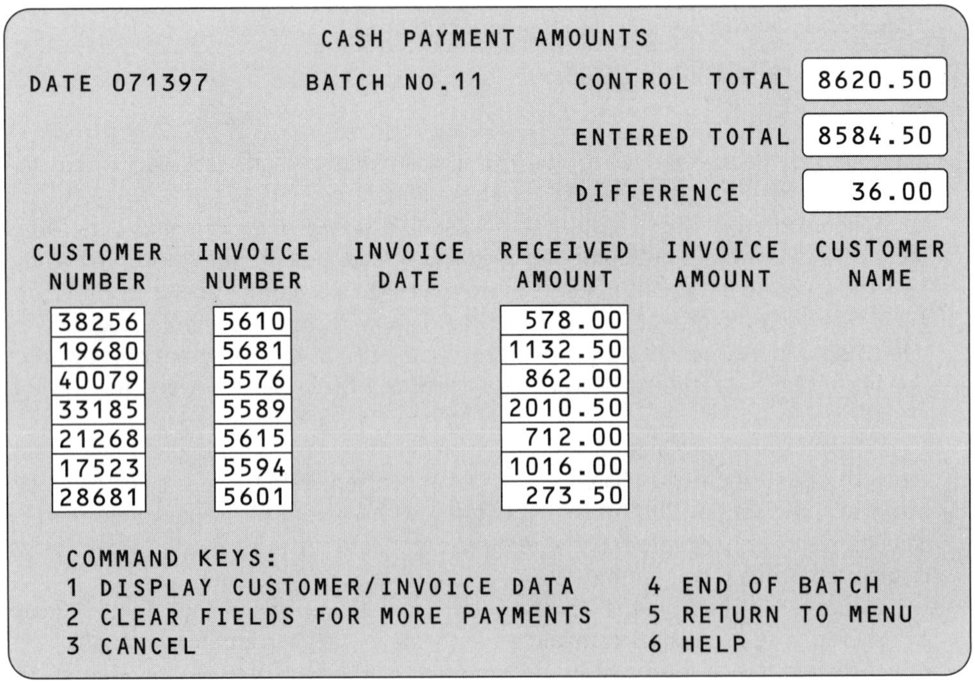

FIGURE 12-11 On-line entry of cash receipts.

is accessed. Entered customer and invoice numbers are checked for validity. The blank columns for invoice date, invoice amount, and customer name are filled in when command key number 1 is pressed. Data for these columns are retrieved from the open sales invoice and customer files, which the program searches by reference to the entered customer and invoice numbers. Also, the total of all payment amounts entered is computed and placed in the box labeled Entered Total; in addition, the Entered Total and previously computed Control Total are compared by the program, and the difference is displayed.

A common example of paperless entry occurs when you place an order for tires over the counter at Discount Tire Co., Inc. The order taker enters the data directly onto a preformatted sales invoice form. The processing program extends the amounts of ordered items and computes the total amount owed. When data have been entered by a paperless method, hard copies of documents can easily be generated. Thus, the order taker at Discount Tire strikes a key and a hard copy of the invoice is immediately printed.

TRANSACTION CODING

Codes are essential for identifying key aspects of sales and cash receipts transactions. An example in Chapter 5 suggested that codes may be assigned to customers, sales territories, salespersons, and product types when recording sales transactions. Codes such as these reduce the quantity of data to enter and provide unique identifiers. They also facilitate the preparation of sales analyses. Based on the above-mentioned example, two analyses could show (1) amounts of sales made to customers within each sales territory, and (2) amounts of sales made of the various products by each salesperson.

Codes that describe transactions should be group codes, since they encompass several characteristics. In turn, the code for each characteristic could incorporate several features. For instance, a particular customer code might be R9174248, based on the format

ABBCCCCD

where A represents the class or type of customer.

> BB represents the year the customer became active.
> CCCC represents the specific customer identifier.
> D represents a self-checking digit.

Immediate processing applications often employ codes that identify transactions. For instance, transaction codes may be entered together with the remaining data for transactions, so that the system knows which application program to select. Transaction codes may be developed for sales, sales returns or allowances, and the other prospective types of transactions. Of course, they are not needed if preformatted screens are accessed via menus or mouse clicks.

DATA BASE

The data base supporting the revenue cycle of a firm that sells merchandise (products) contains data pertaining to revenue-related resources (merchandise inventory, cash), key events (order, sale, cash receipt), and principal agents (customers). It also reflects the relationships among these basic entities. Depending on the nature of a firm's procedure, additional data might be stored concerning associated events (such as credit checking, shipping goods, and depositing receipts) and agents (such as salespersons, carriers, and cashiers).

In a broader perspective, the data base would be marketing-oriented. Beyond the data listed above, the data base would contain much of the information needed for making marketing decisions—information pertaining to markets, customers, competitors, and so on.

Data may be stored in files and/or data structures. Both forms of storage will be briefly surveyed.

FILES

Figure 12-12 lists the master, transaction, open document, and other files needed by a merchandising firm like Infoage, which currently employs the file-oriented approach for its revenue cycle. The master files focus on credit customers. It is possible to consolidate all of the data elements concerning a customer in a single master file. However, to reduce the size of records and thereby improve processing run times during updates, customer-related data are often placed in two master files. The **accounts receivable master file** contains data elements such as shown in the record layout of Figure 12-13. (In the case of firms that use the open invoice method, data concerning unpaid invoices would also need to be included.) The **customer master file** contains such data elements as listed in Figure 12-12.

If a firm sells products (merchandise), as does Infoage, it is necessary to include a **merchandise inventory master file.** Suggested data elements are also listed in Figure 12-12.

DATA STRUCTURES

When a firm converts to the data-base approach, the contents of the revenue cycle data base will be very similar to those in the above-mentioned files. However, there are significant differences. The data are organized as structured records or normalized tables (relations). Furthermore, these data structures are primarily focused on the key entities and relationships identified at the beginning of this section. To determine the related data structures, it is necessary to develop a conceptual and logical view. You may find a review of the related material in Chapter 6 to be helpful.

Entity-Relationship Diagram of the Revenue Cycle   The conceptual view of Infoage's revenue cycle is depicted by the entity relationship diagram in Figure 12-14. The diagram has been simplified, in that it overlooks the credit-checking event, the back-ordering event, and such adjustment events as sales returns. It also combines the shipping and billing events into the event labelled "Sale."*

---

*As described earlier, the two key events of the revenue cycle in a merchandising firm such as Infoage are the sale and cash receipt. These events are accounting transactions that are reflected in accounting records such as journals and ledgers. The other events—such as placing the order, checking a customer's credit, shipping, and billing—are nonaccounting events that do not result in entries in accounting records. Some data modelers combine these events into the two key events. For instance, our example incorporates the shipping and billing events into the sales event. However, certain nonaccounting events are sufficiently important to appear as separate entities in an E-R diagram. Our view is that the order event is particularly important when sales are made for credit, since the status of open sales orders is vital information to management.

MASTER FILES

The *customer master file* contains records pertaining to individual credit customers. Its primary and sorting key is the customer number. Each record of this file contains customer data, including the shipping and billing addresses, telephone number, past payment performance, credit rating, trade discount allowed, and sales activity.

The *accounts receivable master file* contains records that also relate to credit customers, including at least the customer identification (usually the customer account number) and the current account balance.

The *merchandise inventory master file* contains records concerning the various products that the firm sells (and therefore is sometimes called the product master file). Each record contains such data elements as the product (inventory item) number, description, warehouse location code, unit of measure code, reorder point, reorder quantity, unit cost, quantity on order, date of last purchase, and quantity on hand. Since Infoage maintains its inventory on the perpetual basis, the current balance is also included. The primary and sorting key is the inventory item number.

TRANSACTION AND OPEN DOCUMENT FILES

The *sales order file* contains the order number, the order date, the account number of the customer involved in the sale, the name and addresses (shipping and billing) of the customer, the name of the salesperson, the expected delivery date, and the data concerning each ordered item (i.e., inventory item number, description, and quantity ordered). The primary key is the sales order number.

The *open sales order file* consists of the orders that have not yet been shipped and billed. When an order is shipped and billed, it is transferred to a closed orders file.

The *sales invoice transaction file* contains records that provide the details of sales transactions posted to the accounts receivable records. Infoage stores these records both on magnetic disk and as hard copies. The contents of the record on magnetic disk at Infoage contain the billing date, customer number, sales order number, terms, shipping document number, product codes, unit prices, quantities, and transaction amount. (Infoage does not include the customer name and address and product descriptions, since they are stored in the order and customer files.) The primary key is the sales invoice number. Each record remains in an open sales invoice file until the end of the accounting period.

The *cash receipts transaction file* contains data relating to the payments from credit customers. Since Infoage processes cash receipts by computer, the record layout is stored on magnetic disk and contains the customer's account number, sales invoice number against which the payment is being applied, date of payment, and amount of payment. It also includes a code to identify the record as a cash receipt transaction. Furthermore, each transaction is assigned a cash receipts transaction number by the system.

OTHER FILES

The *shipping and price data reference file* contains such shipping data as freight rates and common carrier routes and schedules, plus current prices of all products and trade discounts.

The *credit reference file* is used to check and record approvals of the credit of customers.

The *salesperson file* contains the salesperson number, salesperson name and address, date hired, and commission rate.

The *sales history file* contains summary data from sales order–invoices. In Infoage the records pertaining to sales orders and invoices are transferred to this file when they are removed from the open files. These records are retained in the history file for a reasonable period. For instance, Infoage has decided to maintain a history file extending back for five years. Records older than five years are purged from the computer file. (However, printed copies of sales orders and invoices are retained for a longer period.) Data from this file are used to prepare sales forecasts and analyses.

The *cash receipts history file* contains summary data from cash remittances.

The *accounts receivable report file* contains accumulated and detailed records of the sales and cash receipts transactions for the current accounting period. Its main purposes are to facilitate the preparation of monthly statements for customers and to enhance the audit trail.

FIGURE 12-12 Files maintained within Infoage's revenue cycle.

Customer account number	Customer name	Credit limit	Balance beginning of year	Year-to-date sales	Year-to-date payments	Current account balance

Note: Although the lengths of fields and modes of data elements are necessary for complete documentation, they have been omitted for the sake of simplicity.

FIGURE 12-13   A layout of an accounts receivable record for Infoage, Inc.

We will briefly examine the diagram, with an emphasis on the relationships among entities. Please keep in mind that the relationships reflected pertain specifically to Infoage's policies and procedures (sometimes called organizational rules and constraints). For convenience, the one-to-many relationships are first considered and then the many-to-many. Also, we will discuss only those relationships pertaining to sales, i.e., those within the dashed lines on the figure.

1. **One-to-many (1:n) relationships.** Orders for goods are received from customers by salespersons (either in the sales outlets or in the main office). Each customer may place one or more orders, but each order is received from only one customer; hence the relationship is a one (customer) to many (orders). When orders are filled by being shipped and then billed, they become sales. Consequently, one customer can be involved in many sales. Also, since an order may require back ordering, more than one sale may result from a single order. Thus, three one-to-many relationships appear within the dashed-line borders.

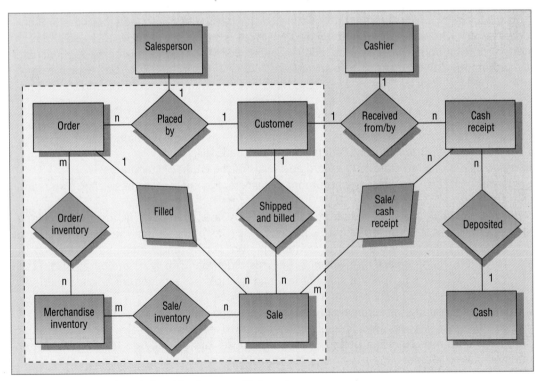

FIGURE 12-14   An entity-relationship diagram of Infoage's revenue cycle.

2. **Many-to-many (m:n) relationships.** Each sales order and sale may involve more than one item of merchandise (product), while each product may be involved in more than one order and sale. Hence, two many-to-many relationships exist with regard to the sales portion of the cycle. These relationships are signaled in two ways in Figure 12-14: (1) by the order/inventory and sales/inventory labels in two diamonds, and (2) by the m:n notations between the entity boxes. In order to implement a sound data structure, it will be necessary to create intersection records or relationship tables that reflect these relationships.

Logical View of Revenue Cycle Data Structures The logical view is determined by "mapping" from the entity-relationship diagram to a data structure diagram. If the network structure is selected, for instance, the mapping would yield records that correspond to the entities and relationships in the entity-relationship diagram. If the relational structure is selected, the mapping involves tables rather than records. Focusing on the portion of the entity-relationship diagram enclosed within the dashed lines, the following six entities and relationships (listed on the left) yield six tables:

Customer	Customer/accounts receivable table
Merchandise inventory	Merchandise inventory table
Order	Sales order header table
Sale	Sales invoice header table
Order/inventory	Ordered items table
Sale/inventory	Sold items table

Figure 12-15 depicts the logical view in the form of linked tables. Each table contains the attributes suitable to Infoage's sales/receivables situation.* Dashed lines connecting the tables indicate the implied linkages that may be achieved via common columns.

For instance, the primary or table key in the customer/accounts receivable table (i.e., customer number) allows the table to be joined to the sales order header table and the sales invoice header table through foreign keys in those tables. In turn, the ordered items table and sold items table are linked to their respective header tables.

Let us focus for a moment on the ordered items and sold items tables. Because each order and sale can involve more than one product, the problem of repeating fields (product numbers and quantities) arises. To normalize the orders and sales, it is necessary to remove these columns from their orders and sales invoice header tables. We recall from Chapter 6 that these line-item tables are relationship tables. In addition to containing line-item data, each has a primary key that is concatenated. The primary key for the ordered items table consists of sales order number and product number, while the key for the sold items table consists of the sales invoice number and product (item) number. These concatenated keys can be related directly to the line-item data of concern. For example, the quantity of each product ordered appears in the same row as the identifying product number and sales order.

---

*Back orders are omitted, while customer identification and accounts receivable data are combined in a single customer table. Accounts receivable ledger accounts are "accounting artifacts" and cannot be viewed as entities in themselves. Also, note that the customer/accounts receivable table omits the current account balances, since these values can be computed from the transaction and data and thus are not needed in the data-base approach.

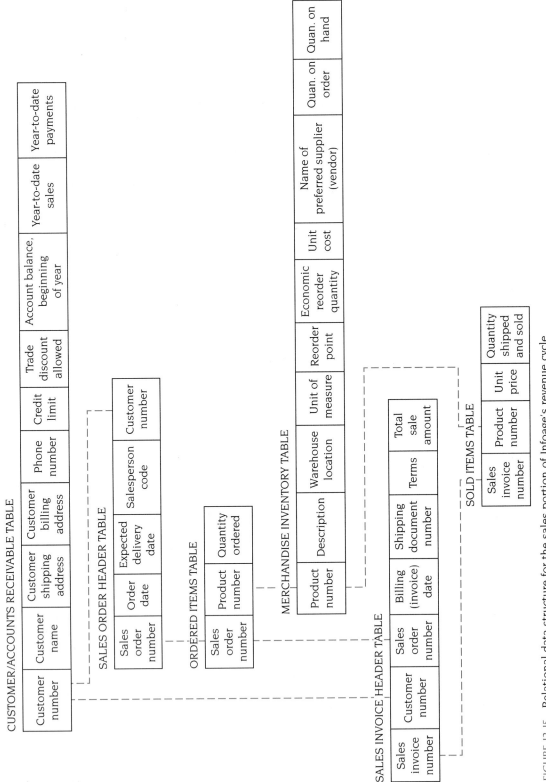

FIGURE 12-15 Relational data structure for the sales portion of Infoage's revenue cycle.

Relationship tables facilitate the preparation of useful reports, since they provide a cross-referencing capability. For instance, the merchandise inventory table and ordered items table can be joined via the product number. Thus, a data-base user could generate a report of all items ordered and their quantities. The report might include the description of each item as well as the extent to which it reduces the inventory on hand.

Given the attributes listed in Figure 12-15, we can observe how processing is performed. For example, refer to sales invoice 62138 (shown in Figure 12-6) which is issued to customer number 12260 and pertains to order number 10-4132 for products numbered 300100 and 512364. In order to print this document, Infoage's sales application program would join (via the implied links) the customer table to the order-related tables and invoice-related tables. From these tables would be extracted the data concerning the quantities ordered and quantities shipped. The resulting table would be joined with the merchandise inventory table to extract the product descriptions and to update the quantities on hand. Several calculations would be performed in preparing the invoice, such as multiplying the unit price times the quantity of units shipped and sold of each product. The extended amounts would be summed and freight and sales tax added to arrive at a total sales amount.* In addition, the row in the customer/accounts receivable table would be updated to increase the year-to-date sales to customer 12260 by the total sale amount of $8,020.00.

Although not shown in Figure 12-15, the cash receipts table would normally be part of a revenue cycle data base. Thus, when payments are received from customers, they can be processed to reduce the current account balances in the accounts of affected customers. Through the linkage to the sales invoice table, they can also be matched to the appropriate invoices if the open invoice method is employed.

DATA FLOWS AND PROCESSING

Figure 12-16 presents an overview of the processing steps and related documents for the revenue cycle. The figure shows that the accounts receivable processing activity serves as the connecting linchpin between the sales and cash receipts processing systems.

In this section we emphasize the computer-based processing of sales and cash receipts transactions. These types of transactions may be processed by the periodic (batch) approach, by the immediate (on-line) approach, or by some variation of the two approaches. The procedural approach to be described in this section is a redesign being considered for the processing of Infoage's product sales and related cash receipts. It essentially combines the immediate (on-line) input approach with the periodic (batch) processing approach and assumes the presence of on-line files, which have been organized as a network data-base structure.

If you are not familiar with business procedures, it may be helpful to review the revenue cycle processing that pertains to a manual processing system. The appendix to this chapter contains background information concerning the accounting transactions in the revenue cycle as well as the processing steps and document flows.

---

*Certain data in the tables and sales invoice would be obtained from sources not shown. For instance, the quantities shipped would be found in shipping records and unit prices in a pricing reference file, while freight and sales tax would likely be computed by means of formulas in the application program or taken from other reference tables.

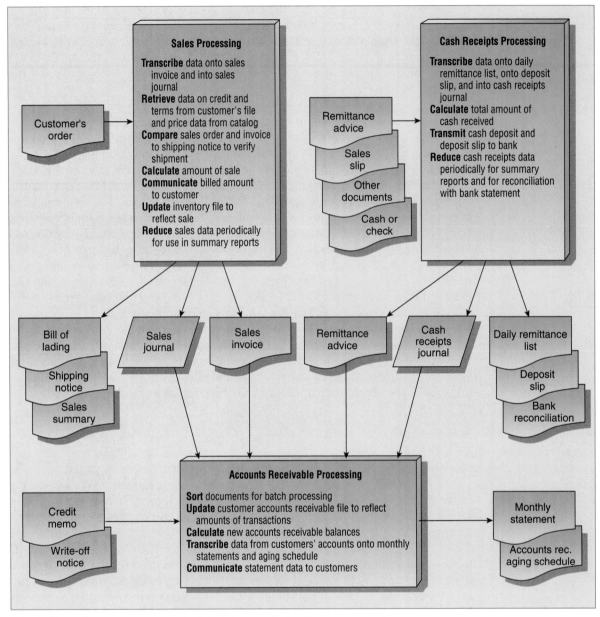

FIGURE 12-16   Processing steps and related documents for the revenue cycle.

CREDIT SALES PROCESSING SYSTEM

The proposed credit sales and receivables system for Infoage follows the processes of the data-flow diagram in Figure 12-17. It ties to the entity-relationship diagram in Figure 12-14 and the relational structure diagrams in Figure 12-15.*

*Figure 12-17 is somewhat more inclusive, in that it contains more data stores or files. For instance, it includes the following data stores not reflected in Figure 12-15: credit data, shipping data, pricing data, sales history, and general ledger data. These data were omitted from Figure 12-15 for the sake of simplicity.

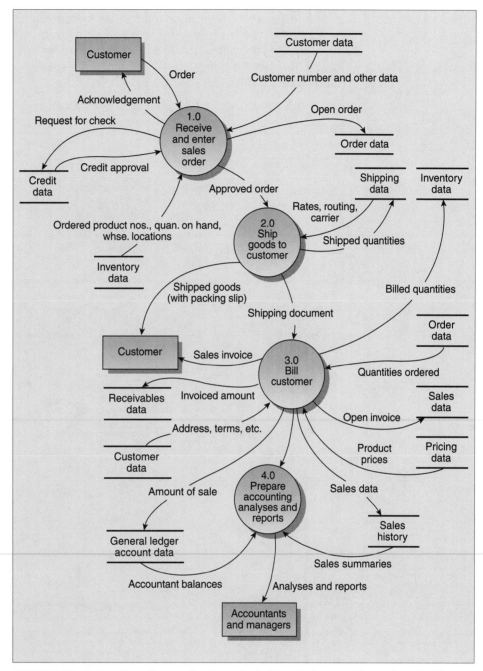

FIGURE 12-17   A data-flow diagram (level-zero) relating to Infoage's sales and receivables processing system.

In turn, Figure 12-18 displays a three-part system flowchart that corresponds to the three basic sales processes in the data-flow diagram. These processes are order entry, shipping, and billing. The files shown in the flowchart correspond to the data stores in the data-flow diagram. Note that the file symbol can represent tables if a relational data base is employed.

Order Entry Each customer's order is entered via an on-line terminal, as soon as received, by a sales order clerk in the marketing function. Entry may be from a sales

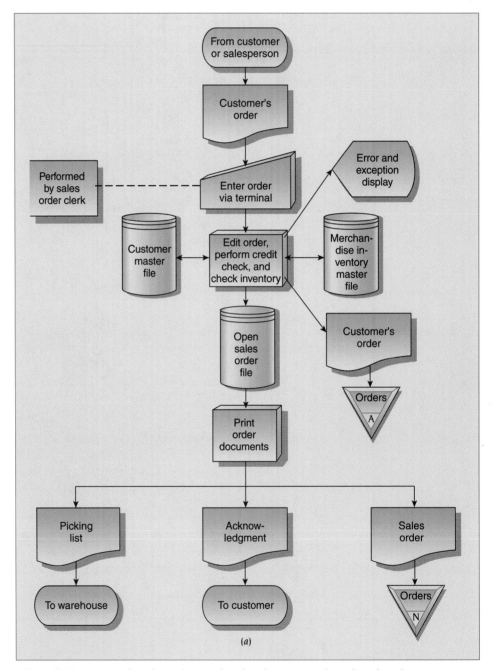

FIGURE 12-18   System flowchart of an on-line/batch computer-based credit sales transaction processing procedure proposed for Infoage. (*a*) Order entry.

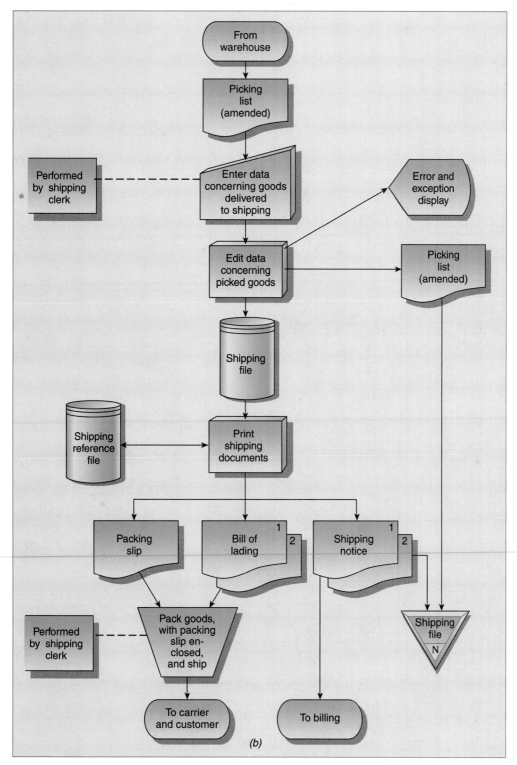

FIGURE 12-18   (*Continued*) (*b*) Shipping.

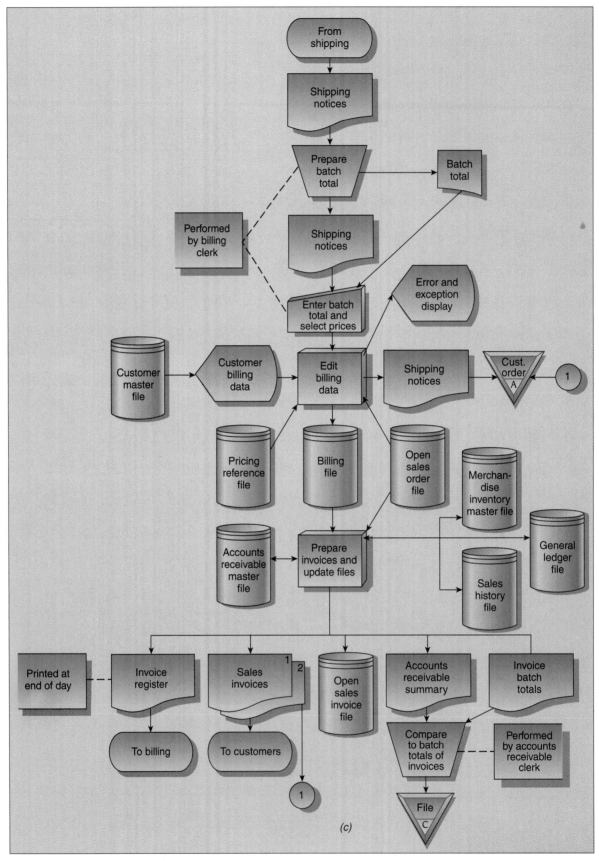

FIGURE 12-18 (Continued) (c) Billing.

order form, or from a phone call from a customer or salesperson. The edit program validates the accuracy of the data and verifies that adequate merchandise is on hand to fill the order. (If insufficient quantities of products are available, the sales order clerk may specify to the computer system that a back order is to be prepared. The back order procedure is discussed in the appendix to this chapter.)

Next, a credit-checking program determines if the customer is creditworthy. This check may consist of comparing the credit limit in the customer's record against the current balance plus the estimated sales amount of the order transaction. If the credit limit is not exceeded, the order is accepted and is placed in the open order file. If the credit limit is exceeded, the clerk may ask the credit manager to look at such credit data as past payments and to make a final determination.

If the order is accepted, then the order is ready to be filled. An order-entry program prints the acknowledgment to the customer, a picking list for the warehouse, and a backup file copy. The picking list, in essence an order for shipping, is transmitted directly to the printer in the warehouse, since it is linked to the computer system in the main office.

Shipping   After the ordered products have been picked in the warehouse, the picking list is initialed by the picker and amended to show any changes (e.g., items out of stock, substitutions). The products are moved to the shipping dock, where a clerk counts them and enters the quantities ready for shipment from the picking slip. A shipping program prepares the necessary documents for the shipment. When the products are weighed and packed, together with a packing slip, they are delivered to the carrier for shipment. A shipping notice (which is in effect a copy of the bill of lading) is generated on the billing clerk's printer concerning the shipment. It contains most of the data from the sales order, plus the quantities shipped, shipping route, shipping rates, freight charges, and other needed shipping data. The carrier delivers the shipment to the customer, accompanied by a copy of the bill of lading.

Billing   Upon receiving the shipping notices for the day, a billing clerk computes and enters batch totals (consisting of quantities shipped, number of shipments, and hashed customer numbers). The clerk also converts each order into an invoice by calling up the order on his or her screen, referring to the printed shipping notice for quantities shipped, selecting product prices from the pricing file, and entering needed data into a preformatted invoice screen. All entered data are validated by an edit program. Then the data for all the readied invoices are stored temporarily in a billing file until time for processing a batch. At that time, (1) the invoices are printed, (2) each customer's account is debited with its billed amount, (3) the inventory records are reduced by the quantities shipped, (4) the sales order is closed to the sales history file, (5) a new record is created in the sales invoice file, and (6) the total batched amounts affecting the sales and accounts receivable accounts are posted to the general ledger accounts. The sales invoices are usually mailed to the customers, although they will be transmitted electronically to those customers who are linked via an electronic data interchange network.

Preparing Analyses and Reports   At the end of each day, an invoice register and accounts receivable summary are printed. The invoice register is a sales transaction listing, in effect the sales journal; it contains the key data concerning each sales invoice prepared during the day. The accounts receivable summary shows the changes to the customer account balances that occurred via posting that day, plus the total amounts posted in the batches.

Accounting listings and analyses such as these are reviewed by accounting personnel. For instance, an accounts receivable clerk or accounting manager compares the batch totals listed on the summary with the precomputed batch total and with the postings to the general ledger. If they do not agree, the manager investigates, with the aid of the invoice register and shipping documents. The document numbers listed on the accounts receivable summary serve as an audit trail in this investigation.

Other listings, analyses, and reports can be printed as needed. For example, an accounts receivable aging analysis can be used by the credit manager for control over uncollectibles.

Modifications to the Procedure   Several changes to this credit sales procedure might be considered by Infoage. On the one hand, the billing data might be sorted by customer numbers, so that the postings to the customer/accounts receivable records are performed sequentially and thus more efficiently. On the other hand, the steps in preparing sales invoices may be performed more automatically by the billing program, thus removing this processing burden from the billing clerk. If this is done, the sales invoices should be reviewed carefully for correctness before they are sent to the customers. In still another modification, the sales returns and other adjustments to customer records may be processed together with sales, so that credit memos are produced as well as sales invoices. This will complicate the procedure, however, and probably should be performed as separate on-line transactions. Finally, the general ledger processing could be maintained as a separate application, as described in Chapter 11. If this is done, the billing application would generate a summary entry for later posting to the general ledger.

CASH RECEIPTS PROCESSING SYSTEM

The three-part system flowchart in Figure 12-19 shows the steps in the proposed on-line input batch processing cash receipts procedure. It is divided into three segments: entry of remittances, deposit of cash receipts, and posting to ledger accounts.*

Remittance Entry   Checks and remittance advices are received in the mail room in a batch each morning. One mail room clerk endorses the checks "For Deposit Only" and verifies that the amount on each check agrees with the amount on the remittance advice. This clerk then prepares batch totals from the remittance advices, including a total of all amounts received, a count of the remittances, and perhaps a hash total of customer numbers. Another clerk enters the batch total and lists such remittance data as cash receipt amount, customer number, and sales invoice number for each receipt, using a preformatted cash receipts screen. (See Figure 12-11.)

During this entry step, an edit program verifies that the entered data for each receipt are complete. It also performs edit checks on the entered data and lists errors on an exception and summary report. The edit program refers to the customer accounts receivable and open sales invoice files in performing certain programmed edit checks. However, it does *not* enter receipts data into these files. Instead, it writes receipts onto a temporary cash receipts disk file.

In addition to errors, computed batch totals are included on the exception and summary report. If the total of all the individual amounts entered (as computed by the edit program) is equal to the precomputed batch total, the batch is accepted. (If not, the totals must be reconciled before further processing.) Then the program prints a **remittance list** (also called a *prelist*) in three copies.

---

*No data-flow diagram accompanies the flowchart; however, a problem at the end of this chapter asks you to draw the data-flow diagram.

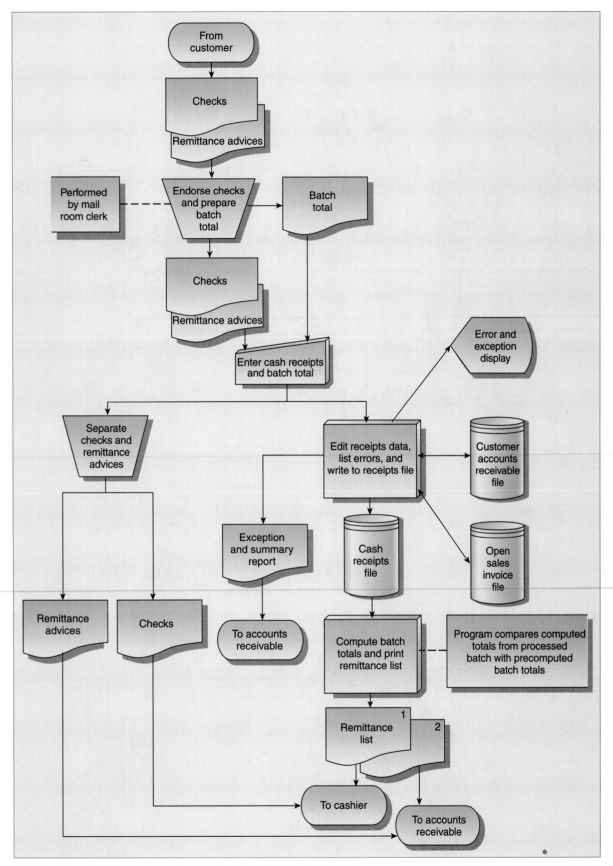

FIGURE 12-19 System flowchart of an on-line/batch computer-based cash receipts transaction processing procedure. (a) Remittance entry via mail room.

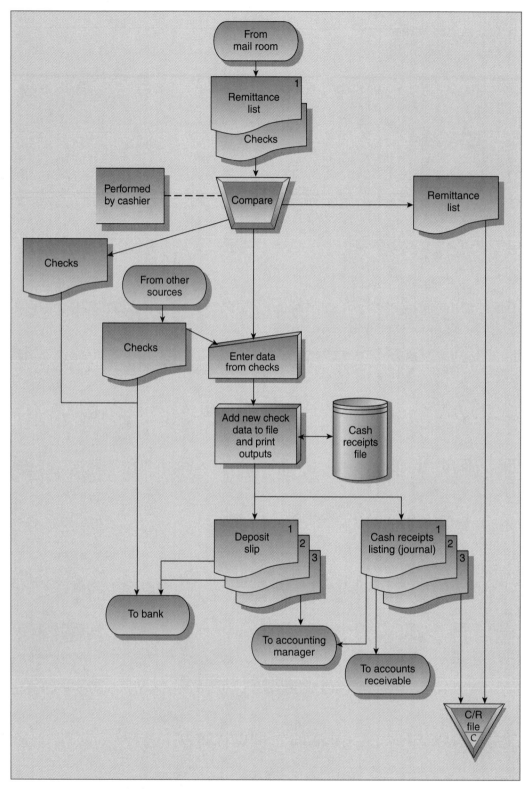

FIGURE 12-19 (Continued) (b) Depositing receipts via cashier. Note: The cash receipts file contains the receipts entered in the mail room.

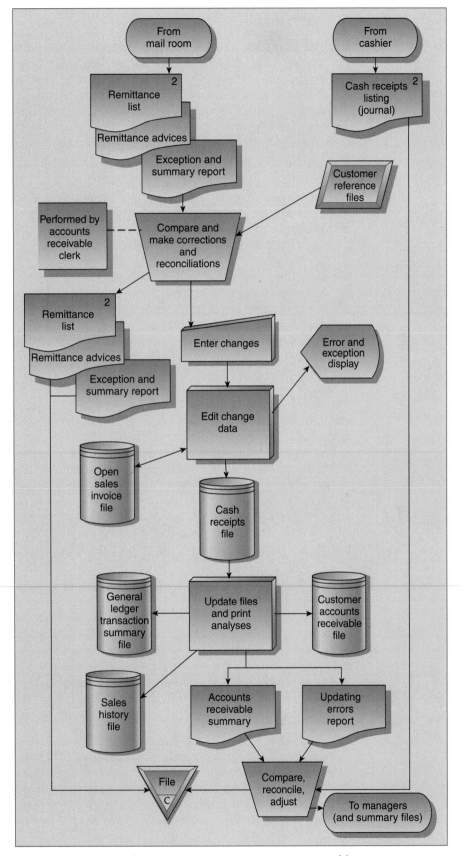

FIGURE 12-19 (*Continued*) (*c*) Posting receipts via accounts receivable.

Depositing Receipts   One copy of the remittance list and the checks are delivered to the cashier, who compares and reconciles. She then enters checks received from other sources than the mail room via her terminal. When the cashier is satisfied that all checks are accounted for, she notifies the cash receipts program to print a daily deposit slip (in three copies) and a cash receipts transaction listing (journal) in two copies. At a designated time the cashier takes two copies of the deposit slip to the bank, together with all the checks. The validated deposit slip is returned by the bank to an accounting manager, who reconciles the slip with a copy of the cash receipts listing.

Posting Receipts   The key processing step is to update the customer accounts. Before doing so, however, the accounts receivable clerk must enter needed corrections to cash receipts transactions listed on the exception and summary report. She may use a variety of references to make the corrections, including customer and sales printouts as well as on-line files. Hopefully, all corrections can be made during the day the cash is received, but if necessary they can be carried over to the next day.

As the clerk enters the corrections via the accounting area terminal, they are edited by reference to the open sales invoice file.* After all corrected transactions are validated, the updating run is performed. Direct posting is proposed, although the posting can be done sequentially if the cash receipts are sorted in a separate run by customer numbers. In order to post each cash receipt, the customer number on the transaction is matched with the customer number in the customer accounts receivable file. Since the open invoice method is employed, the next step is to match the invoice number in the remittance record with an invoice in the open invoice file and to flag that invoice as paid. Other checks are made, such as to verify that a cash discount taken is within the discount period. Any discrepancies are written onto an errors and exceptions file, which is printed at the end of the run.

In the updating action, the application program credits the accounts receivable records of the remitting customers with the amounts paid and closes the sales invoices to the sales history file. Also, the total of the amounts posted is computed and written on the general ledger transaction summary file. This total amount will later be posted to the cash and accounts receivable control accounts. (Alternatively, the posting could be performed at the end of this update run, as in the case of the sales total for the day.)

Preparing Analyses and Reports   At the end of the day, the summary of accounts receivable activity is printed. This may be combined with the accounts receivable summary mentioned in the credit sales procedure or may be a separate but related printout. It contains the computed batch totals pertaining to cash receipts for the day. An accounting clerk or manager compares these totals with those on the remittance listing and with the general ledger posting. Any differences are reconciled with the aid of the cash receipts transaction listing (journal).

BENEFITS OF THE ON-LINE INPUT BATCH PROCESSING SYSTEM

The proposed computer-based processing of sales and cash receipts transactions is logically sound. Capturing data on-line and maintaining data in network or relational data-base structures yields several benefits of modern technology. Processing sales and cash receipts in batches provides other benefits of proven practice. Batch processing is quite feasible when updating accounting records, since the added timeliness of immediate processing does not add much if any value.

---

*The customer accounts receivable file may also be employed in the editing step, although it is not shown on the flowchart.

Among the key benefits of the proposed computer-based systems are the following:

1. Sales are processed and shipped more quickly, so that customers should be better satisfied with the service and more likely to place orders in the future.

2. Sales data update records as soon as orders are received, thereby keeping key order and inventory information more up-to-date.

3. Data are validated upon entry, so that errors are detected more quickly and reprocessing delays due to undetected errors are reduced.

4. Paperwork flows are reduced, as when sales order data are entered from phone calls or orders are transmitted via electronic data interchange networks.

5. Accounting-related updating runs (i.e., billing, cash receipts) are efficient and better controlled, since sales and cash receipts transactions are handled in batches with control totals.

6. Accounting-related processing is also simplified, since transactions are posted without sorting and since the relevant files are on-line and integrated.

7. Information that is both current and integrated can be easily retrieved by clerks and managers; thus, inquiries (e.g., from customers) can be answered quickly and correctly, and control reports and summaries can be generated for managers as needed. For instance, the accounts receivable aging schedule and sales analyses can be viewed or printed as often as desired.

ACCOUNTING CONTROLS

RISK EXPOSURES

Transactions within the revenue cycle are exposed to all types of risks: unintentional errors, deliberate errors, unintentional losses of assets, thefts of assets, breaches of security, and acts of violence and natural disasters. Most are errors and losses, many of a fraudulent character. Figure 12-20 lists representative risks and consequent exposures due to these risks, roughly in the order as noted above.

Consider Risk 12 in the figure: the risk that payments from credit customers may be lapped when the accounts receivable records are posted. **Lapping** is a type of embezzlement that involves the theft of cash and its concealment by a succession of delayed postings to customers' accounts. A clerk who undertakes lapping first cashes a check from a customer and keeps the cash. Since the check cannot be recorded, the customer's account is in error. To cover his or her tracks, the clerk credits the customer's account upon receiving a check for an equal or larger amount from a different customer. Then the clerk credits the second customer's account with the proceeds from the check of still another customer. This falsifying process continues indefinitely, unless the clerk decides to return the embezzled funds. The major risk exposure to the firm from lapping is clearly a loss of funds received from customers. Another risk exposure, however, is that certain accounts receivable records will reflect overstated account balances; consequently, the accounts receivable total that appears in the balance sheet will be overstated.

CONTROL OBJECTIVES

In order to counteract such risk exposures, a firm must establish a variety of accounting controls. For instance, the risk of lapping can be reduced if the persons

Risk	Exposure(s)
1. Credit sales made to customers who represent poor credit risks	1. Losses from bad debts
2. Unrecorded or unbilled shipments	2. Losses of revenue; overstatement of inventory and understatement of accounts receivable in the balance sheet
3. Errors in preparing sales invoices (e.g., showing greater quantities than were shipped or showing unit prices that are too low)	3. Alienation of customers and possible loss of future sales (when quantities are too high); losses of revenue (when unit prices are too low)
4. Misplacement of orders from customers or unfilled back orders	4. Losses of revenue and alienation of customers
5. Incorrect postings of sales to accounts receivable records	5. Incorrect balances in accounts receivable and general ledger account records (e.g., overstatement of Mary Smith's balance)
6. Postings of revenues to wrong accounting periods, such as premature bookings of revenues	6. Overstatement of revenue in one year (such as the year of premature booking) and understatement of revenue in the next
7. Fictitious credit sales to nonexistent customers	7. Overstatement of revenues and accounts receivable
8. Excessive sales returns and allowances, with certain of the credit memos being for fictitious returns	8. Losses in net revenue, with the proceeds from subsequent payments by affected customers being fraudulently pocketed
9. Theft or misplacement of finished goods in the warehouse or on the shipping dock	9. Losses in revenue; overstatement of inventory on the balance sheet
10. Fraudulent write-offs of customers' accounts by unauthorized persons	10. Understatement of accounts receivable; losses of cash receipts when subsequent collections on written-off accounts are misappropriated by perpetrators of the fraud
11. Theft (skimming) of cash receipts, especially currency, by persons involved in the processing; often accompanied by omitted postings to affected customers' accounts	11. Losses of cash receipts; overstatement of accounts receivable in the subsidiary ledger and the balance sheet
12. Lapping of payments from customers when amounts are posted to accounts receivable records	12. Losses of cash receipts; incorrect account balances for those customers whose records are involved in the lapping
13. Accessing of accounts receivable, merchandise inventory, and other records by unauthorized persons	13. Loss of security over such records, with possibly detrimental use made of the data accessed
14. Involvement of cash, merchandise inventory, and accounts receivable records in natural or human-made disasters	14. Losses of or damages to assets
15. Planting of virus (e.g., logic bomb) by disgruntled employee to destroy data on magnetic media	15. Loss of customer accounts receivable accounts data needed to monitor collection of amounts from previous sales

FIGURE 12-20   Risk exposures within the revenue cycle.

who receive and handle cash are organizationally separate from those who record the receipts in the customer accounts.

As a foundation for establishing needed controls—both general and application—it is desirable first to clarify the objectives that the controls are intended to achieve. With respect to the revenue cycle, several key control objectives are to ensure that:

- All customers who are accepted for credit sales are creditworthy.
- All ordered goods are shipped or services are performed by dates that are agreeable to both parties.
- All shipped goods are authorized and accurately billed within the proper accounting period.
- All sales returns and allowances are authorized and accurately recorded and based on actual returns of goods.
- All cash receipts are recorded completely and accurately.
- All credit sales and cash receipts transactions are posted to proper customers' accounts in the accounts receivable ledger.
- All accounting records, merchandise inventory, and cash are safeguarded.

GENERAL CONTROLS

General controls concerning the revenue cycle can be categorized as organizational, documentation, asset accountability, management practices, data center operations, authorization, and access.

Organizational Controls   With respect to sales transactions, the units having custodial functions (i.e., warehousing and shipping) should be separate from each other and from those units that maintain responsibility for the records (i.e., billing, accounts receivable, inventory control, general ledger, and data processing). In the case of cash receipts transactions, the mail room and cashier should be separate from each other and from accounts receivable, general ledger, and data processing.

In computer-based systems the data entry and processing steps are controlled by application programs. These programs guide the human operators of the system, such as sales order clerks and accounting clerks. Built into the programs are the policies and procedures adopted by management, including those pertaining to checking credit and approving sales orders from customers. A vital segregation of functions, therefore, is between (1) the systems development personnel who write and modify the programs, and (2) the personnel who use and operate the system.

Documentation Controls   Complete and up-to-date documentation should be available concerning the revenue cycle, including copies of the documents, flowcharts, record layouts, and reports illustrated in this chapter. In addition, details pertaining to sales and cash receipts edit and processing programs should be organized into separate books or "packages" that are directed respectively to programmers, computer operators, and system users. Furthermore, management policies concerning credit approvals, account write-offs, and so forth should be in written form.

Asset Accountability Controls   An accounts receivable subsidiary ledger (master file) should be maintained and reconciled frequently with the accounts receivable control account in the general ledger. Also, merchandise inventory records should be maintained in a ledger and reconciled periodically to a merchandise inventory control account, as well as to physical counts of merchandise inventory on hand. A third type of reconciliation, a bank reconciliation, should compare the balance in the bank account with the cash account balance in the general ledger.

Other asset accountability controls include (1) the shipping clerk who acknowledges receipt of ordered and picked goods from the warehouse by signing the stock request (or shipping) order, (2) the mail room clerk who prepares a list of all received remittances, and (3) the customer who reviews the monthly statement of sales and payments for incorrect amounts.

Management Practice Controls Among the sound management practices that should be established and followed with respect to the revenue cycle are the following: Employees, including programmers and accountants, should be carefully trained; those that handle cash should be bonded. Systems development and changes should undergo a clear procedure involving prior approvals, testing, and sign-offs. Audits should be performed of the sales and cash receipts policies and procedures, including surprise counts of cash. Managers should review periodic analyses, control summaries, and reports concerning account activity and computer-approved transactions.

Data Center Operations Controls Computer processing schedules involving sales and cash receipts batches should be clearly established. Information systems and accounting personnel should be actively supervised and their work reviewed with the aid of computer processing control reports and access logs.

Authorization Controls All credit sales transactions (or service orders) should be authorized by a credit manager. In a computer-based system, this authorization may be performed by an application program into which the credit approval rules have been built. A manager not involved in the processing of sales or in accounts receivable, such as the credit manager, should authorize all sales returns and allowances, as well as write-offs of uncollectible accounts. A stock request copy of the sales order should authorize the picking of ordered goods from the warehouse and their transfer to the shipping dock.

Access Controls Among the needed access controls and security measures, especially in the presence of on-line computer systems and networks, are the following:

1. Assigned passwords that authorized clerks must enter to access accounts receivable and other customer-related files, in order to perform their strictly defined tasks.

2. Terminals that are restricted in the functions they allow to be performed with respect to sales and cash receipts transactions.

3. Logging of all sales and cash receipt transactions upon their entry into the system.

4. Frequent dumping of accounts receivable and merchandise inventory master files onto magnetic tape backups.

5. Physically protected warehouses (for storing merchandise inventory) and safes (for holding cash receipts).

6. A lockbox collection system, in those situations where feasible. (A **lockbox** is a postal address used solely to collect remittances, which are removed and processed by the firm's bank.)

APPLICATION CONTROLS

A wide variety of controls and control procedures are applicable to revenue cycle transactions and customer accounts. Figure 12-21 lists many of these controls, arranged by input, processing, and output categories.

Certain application controls are applicable solely to computer-based systems. Figure 12-22 lists a variety of programmed edit checks, critical to the validation of

Input controls

1. Prepare prenumbered and well-designed documents relating to sales, shipping, and cash receipts, with each prepared document being approved by an authorized person.

2. Validate data on sales orders and remittance advices as the data are prepared and entered for processing. In computer-based systems, validation should be performed by means of programmed edit checks. When data are keyed into a computer-readable medium, key verification is also appropriate.

3. Correct errors that are detected during data entry and before the data are posted to the customer and inventory records.

4. Precompute batch control totals relating to key data on sales invoices (or shipping notices) and remittance advices. These precomputed batch control totals should be compared with totals computed during postings to the accounts receivable ledger and during each processing run. In the case of cash receipts, the total on remittance advices should also be compared with the total on deposit slips.

Processing controls

1. Move ordered goods from the finished goods warehouse and ship the goods only on the basis of written authorizations such as stock request copies (i.e., picking lists).

2. Invoice customers only on notification by the shipping department of the quantities that have been shipped.

3. Issue credit memos for sales returns only when evidence (i.e., receiving report) has been received that the goods were actually returned.

4. Verify all computations on sales invoices (by a billing clerk other than the preparer or by a computer program) before mailing and postings to proper customers' accounts. Also, compare the sales invoices against shipping notices and open orders, in order to ensure that the quantities ordered reconcile with the orders shipped and back ordered.

5. Verify that total amounts posted to the accounts receivable accounts from batches of transactions agree with precomputed batch totals, and post the total amounts to the appropriate general ledger accounts.

6. Deposit all cash received intact and with a minimum of delay, thus eliminating the possibility of cash receipts being used to pay employees or to reimburse petty-cash funds.

7. Correct errors that are made during processing steps, usually by reversing erroneous postings to accounts and entry of correct data. The audit trail concerning accounts being corrected should show the original errors, the reversals, and the corrections.

Output controls

1. Prepare monthly statements, which should be mailed to all credit customers, especially if the balance forward approach is employed.

2. File copies of all documents pertaining to sales and cash receipts transactions by number, with the sequence of numbers in each file being periodically checked to see if gaps exist. If transactions are not supported by preprinted documents, as often is the case in on-line computer-based systems, assign transaction numbers to the transactions.

3. Prepare printed transaction listings (e.g., cash receipts journal) and account summaries on a periodic basis in order to provide an adequate audit trail and a basis for review.

FIGURE 12-21   Application controls pertaining to the revenue cycle.

Type of Edit Check	Typical Transaction Data Being Checked		Assurance Provided
	Sales	Cash Receipts	
1. Validity check	Customer account numbers, product numbers, transaction codes	Customer account numbers, transaction codes	The entered numbers and codes are checked against lists of valid numbers and codes that are stored within the computer system.
2. Self-checking digit	Customer account numbers	Customer account numbers	Each customer account number (e.g., 34578) contains a check digit (e.g., 8), whose value is based on an established mathematical algorithm involving the other digits of the number (e.g., 3, 4, 5, 7). When a customer account number is entered as a part of a sales or cash receipts transaction, the same computation is performed on the digits (e.g., 3, 4, 5, 7). If the value computed at this time (e.g., 2) differs from the attached digit (e.g., 8), the difference signals an input error (e.g., a transposition of 4 and 5) in entering the customer account number.
3. Field check	Customer account numbers, quantities ordered, unit prices	Customer account numbers, amounts	The fields in the input records that are designated to contain the data items (listed at the left) are checked to see if they contain the proper mode of characters (i.e., numeric characters). If other modes are found (such as alphabetic characters or blanks), an error is indicated.
4. Limit check	Quantities ordered	Amounts received	The entered quantities and amounts are checked against preestablished limits that represent reasonable maximums to be expected. (Separate limits are set for each product and class of customer.)
5. Range check	Unit prices	None	Each entered unit price is checked to see that it is within a preestablished range (either higher or lower than an expected value). To find the prestablished range, the edit program must first check the entered product number corresponding to the unit price and then look in a stored table of unit prices arranged by product numbers.
6. Relationship check	Product numbers	Amounts received	When two or more products are involved in a sales transaction, their numbers are checked to a stored table of reasonable combinations of products that appear on the same order; if the entered products do not appear in one of the combinations, the sales transaction is flagged by the edit program. When a payment amount is entered in a cash receipts transaction, together with the number of the sales invoice to which the amount applies, the amount in the sales invoice file is retrieved and compared with the entered amount. If a difference appears, the transaction is flagged.

FIGURE 12-22   Programmed edit checks that are useful in validating transaction data entered into the revenue cycle.

Type of Edit Check	Typical Transaction Data Being Checked		Assurance Provided
	Sales	Cash Receipts	
7. Sign check	Product on-hand balances	Customer account balances	After the ordered quantities of products for a sales transaction are entered and posted to the inventory master file (thereby reducing the on-hand balances of the affected products), the remaining on-hand balances are checked. If any of the balances is preceded by a negative sign, the transaction is flagged. After the amount of a cash receipts transaction is entered and posted to the account in the accounts receivable ledger (thereby reducing the account balance of the customer), the remaining balance is checked. If the balance is preceded by a negative sign (indicating a credit balance), the transaction is flagged.
8. Completeness check[a]	All entered data items	All entered data items	The entered transactions are checked to see that all required data items have been entered.
9. Echo check[a]	Customer account numbers and names, product numbers and descriptions	Customer account numbers and names	After the account numbers for customers relating to a sales or cash receipts transaction (and also the product numbers in the sales transaction) have been entered at a terminal, the edit program retrieves and "echoes" back the related customer names (and product descriptions in the case of sales transactions). The person who entered the data can visually verify from reading the names (or descriptions) on the screen that the correct numbers were entered.

[a]Applicable only to on-line systems.

FIGURE 12-22 (*Continued*)

input data in computer-based systems. Other application controls are applicable to both manual and computer-based systems. Figure 12-23 shows the application of batch control totals to transactions in the revenue cycle. While the figure illustrates the use of the batch totals in a manual system environment, a similar figure could show their use in a computer system.

REPORTS AND OTHER OUTPUTS

Reports generated as an integral part or byproduct of revenue cycle processing are needed to conduct a firm's operations and to aid in controlling and planning the firm's activities. Outputs generated by the revenue cycle include operational outputs and strategic outputs, financial reports and nonfinancial reports, sales-related and cash-related reports, scheduled (daily, weekly, monthly) reports and demand inquiries or reports, and hard-copy and soft-copy reports.

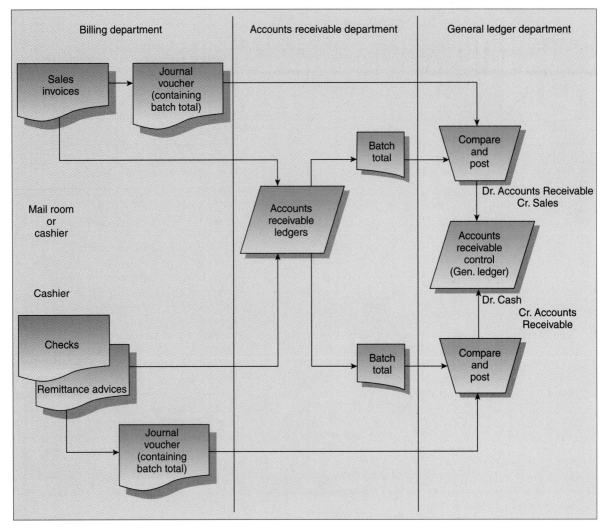

FIGURE 12-23   Diagram showing the use of batch totals for transactions affecting accounts receivable.

OPERATIONAL LISTINGS AND REPORTS

The **monthly statement** is a listing of all outstanding sales invoices for a customer. It is a financial output based on information in the customer, accounts receivable, sales invoice, and cash receipts files.

The **open orders report** lists those sales orders that are not completely shipped and billed. It may be arranged chronologically, by sales order numbers, or by customers. Figure 12-24 presents an open orders report by customer. Note that it also indicates back orders. This report thus provides operational control, since it helps to expedite the processing of sales orders. Related operational control reports include the *unbilled shipments report*, the *late shipments report*, and the *back order status report*. These reports are primarily nonfinancial in nature, since they emphasize the status of transactions.

Various registers and journals help to maintain the audit trail. Each lists specific transactions, with related documents and identifying numbers, pertaining to a particular event within the revenue cycle. The *sales invoice register* is a listing of all sales

OPEN ORDERS BY CUSTOMER
REPRESENTATIVE MERCHANDISING COMPANY

ORDER NO	ITEM NO		W/H LOC'N	ITEM CLASS	VENDOR NO	ORDERED QTY	U/M	UNIT PRICE	U/M	SOURCE SHIPMT	BACK ORDER
CUSTOMER-11111800		BOYER PLUMBING SUPPLY									
25137	7762000000000-1	ALUMINUM PAINT	L-147	07	1630VE	3	CS		CS	0	--
25137	8210000000000-1	RADIAL PIPE CUTTER 1-3	P-112	08	4155RR	2	EA		EA	0	--
25137	8960000000000-1	C12 L D CHAIN WRENCH 4CP	P-116	08	4115RR	1	EA	7.100	EA	0	--
CUSTOMER-11610000		FIELDS APPLIANCES									
80349	3325000000000-1	REFRIGERATOR-20.7 S/S COPPER	A-120	03	2010AB	1	EA		EA	0	--
80349	3341000000000-1	REFRIGERATOR-19 S/S GOLD	A-140	03	2010AB	2	EA		EA	0	--
80349	7890000000000-1	LATEX SEMI-GLOSS WHITE	L-169	07	9060LE	2	CS		CS	0	--
80349	7890000000000-1	LATEX SEMI-GLOSS WHITE	L-169	07	9060LE	3	GAL			0	--
CUSTOMER-11750000		FRIED & JONES SUPPLY CORP.									
25111	1111000000000-1	TWO-LIGHT WALL MOUNT	R-119	01	6000AR	10	EA		EA	0	--
25111	5681000000000-1	EVAPORATIVE COOLER	Q-190	05	7710JW	6	EA		EA	0	--
25111	6664000000000-1	BATHTUB FAUCET	F-100	06	7370UN	12	EA		EA	0	--
25111	8210000000000-1	RADIAL PIPE CUTTER 1-3	P-112	08	4155RR	6	EA		EA	0	--
CUSTOMER-11800010		WESTERNWIDE *STORE 1*									
77999	5789000000000-4	AIR FILTER 12 × 14 × 1	033	05	2250SS	32	EA	.900	EA	0	B
CUSTOMER-12780000		HEARN MANUFACTURERS									
78305	9120000000000-1	6 OZ COLD CUPS	X-380	09	7960BL	17	CS	6.900	CS	0	B
CUSTOMER-17640000		MADSEN CORPORATION									
75968	9502000000000-1	ROBOT-3FT	D-181	10	1180AB	27	EA	19.270	EA	0	B
CUSTOMER-21000000		QUINN & ASSOCIATES									
79219	7797000000000-1	CALUMET 750	L-160	07	1630VE	19	CS	88.960	CS	0	B
CUSTOMER-25000020		UNIVERSITY CONTRACTORS-APTOS									
80348	6836000000000-1	SINK-LAV	F-124			1	EA	42.500	EA	0	B
CUSTOMER-28000000		XAVIER HARDWARE & PAINT									
77996	2249000000000-1	U-BOLT FOOT MOUNT	M-115	02	6400IC	1	DZ	14.950	DZ	0	B

FIGURE 12-24 A status report of open orders. (Courtesy of IBM Corporation.)

499

Representative Merchandising Company
Journal - CJ001 Batch - 1

Cash receipts journal

Time 17:35:18 Date 5/31/97
Posting date 5/31/97

Page 1 35441

Date	Customer number	Customer name	Ref number	Inv number	1110 Accts rec CR	1010 Cash DR	8130 Cash disc DR	1150 Adjustment DR	General Ledger amount DR (CR)	number
5/31/97		Vending machine				15.60			(15.60)	8040
5/31/97		Pay phone				20.80			(20.80)	8040
5/31/97	10400	Anderson Inc.			100.00			100.00		
5/31/97	10700	Andrus Inc.	ck123		150.00	150.00				
5/31/97	10700	Andrus Inc.	adj90		(7.48)			(7.48)		
5/31/97	10800	Angeroth Incorporated			110.76	110.76				
5/31/97	11810	Westernwide *Store 1*		UN	66.76	66.76				
5/31/97	11810	Westernwide *Store 1*		20915	325.99	325.99				

Representative Merchandising Company
Journal - CJ001 Batch - 1

Cash receipts journal summary

Time 17:36:55 Date 5/31/97
Posting date 5/31/97

Page 1 35442

Account number	Debits	Credits
8040	.00	36.40
1010	6,917.67	.00
1110	.00	6,976.62
1150	92.52	.00
8130	2.83	.00
Totals	7,013.02	7,013.02

FIGURE 12-25 A cash receipts journal and summary. (Courtesy of IBM Corporation.)

invoices, arranged by sales invoice numbers. It is in effect the sales journal. The *shipping register* is a listing of all shipments, arranged by shipping date. The *cash receipts journal* is a listing of amounts received, arranged chronologically. Figure 12-25 shows a cash receipts journal, including a summary of debits and credits distributed to accounts. The *credit memo register* is a listing of all sales returns, arranged by credit memo numbers.

INQUIRY DISPLAY SCREENS

Inquiries from clerical personnel are often quite specific and involve relatively limited data. For instance, the Infoage sales order clerk may inquire with respect to the on-hand availability of a particular merchandise item such as a computer model. Figure 12-26 shows the display screen responding to a request for the status of a customer's account receivable. Other revenue cycle clerical inquiries might concern (1) the dates that certain orders are expected to be shipped, and (2) the details concerning a single cash remittance or a batch of remittances.

Inquiries from professional employees tend to be more analytical in nature. For example, an accountant may download sales and cost data for the past several years into a spreadsheet package on his microcomputer. He can use this data to compare the effects of direct costing and absorption costing methods.

Inquiries made by managers can be both analytical and decision-oriented. The data base they employ might be a specially assembled executive information system (EIS), which could draw from the revenue cycle data base as well as from other sources. Consider, for instance, a marketing vice-president who with her own EIS

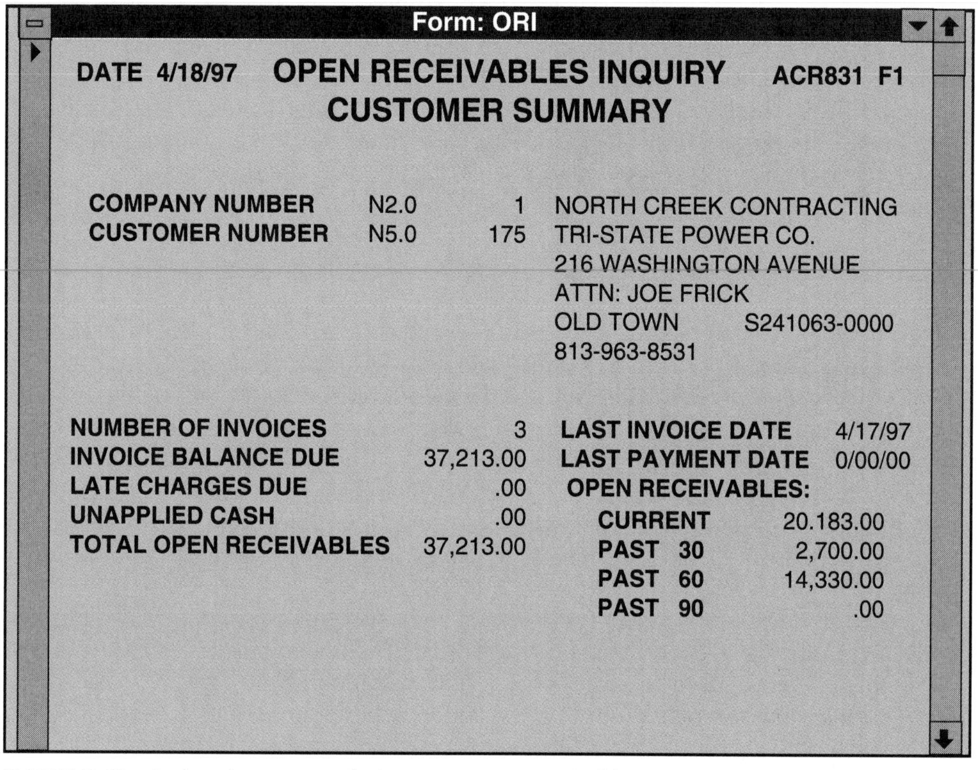

Form: ORI

DATE 4/18/97   OPEN RECEIVABLES INQUIRY   ACR831 F1
CUSTOMER SUMMARY

COMPANY NUMBER	N2.0	1	NORTH CREEK CONTRACTING
CUSTOMER NUMBER	N5.0	175	TRI-STATE POWER CO.
			216 WASHINGTON AVENUE
			ATTN: JOE FRICK
			OLD TOWN S241063-0000
			813-963-8531

NUMBER OF INVOICES	3	LAST INVOICE DATE	4/17/97
INVOICE BALANCE DUE	37,213.00	LAST PAYMENT DATE	0/00/00
LATE CHARGES DUE	.00	OPEN RECEIVABLES:	
UNAPPLIED CASH	.00	CURRENT	20.183.00
TOTAL OPEN RECEIVABLES	37,213.00	PAST 30	2,700.00
		PAST 60	14,330.00
		PAST 90	.00

FIGURE 12-26   An inquiry screen relating to an open receivable.

SPOTLIGHTING

SALESFORCE AUTOMATION
*at Campbell Soup**

Campbell Soup, the food giant headquartered in Camden, New Jersey, is investing $30 million to re-engineer its salesforce. At the heart of the redesigned sales and customer service support system is a *client/server architecture*, which links all sales representatives and sales administration personnel via a network of desktop and portable computers. According to the vice-president of management information systems, this automation platform adds the greatest value to the firm's sales promotion, customer order processing, and pricing activities.

The new sales support system enhances sales performance in a variety of ways. First, it consolidates data concerning product sales and customer preferences, so that product promotions can be targeted precisely. Second, the system captures the

sales orders from supermarket chains and other customers electronically and immediately validates the data. Validated orders become available for processing and filling. Customers can inquire about the status of orders and receive quick responses because of the on-line monitoring feature of the system. Third, shipping orders are billed by a centralized Customer Service System. Fourth, reports can be generated in a timely fashion concerning all aspects of sales activities and results.

Among the benefits expected from this new system are more effective returns from product promotions, shorter order cycle times, more accurate billings, and more satisfied customers. Overall sales costs are likely to be reduced. Also, salespersons can be more productive because they will have less administrative details to handle; thus, they can devote more time to selling.

---

*Emily Kay, "Selling Enters the Information Age," *Datamation* (May 1, 1995), pp. 38–42.

---

accesses the sales of each product for the past several months. In addition, she uses her EIS to retrieve from an external on-line information service (e.g., Dun & Bradstreet) the industry sales data for the same period. After having the EIS software compute the percentage gains, and observing that one of the firm's products has severely lagged behind the average, she decides to drop the product from the firm's line.

SCHEDULED MANAGERIAL REPORTS

A variety of reports are usually prepared on a scheduled basis for use by marketing managers. Several of the most popular will be briefly described.

The **accounts receivable aging schedule** is based on the same files as the monthly statement. However, it contains data concerning the status of the open balances of all active credit customers. That is, it arrays the overdue amounts by time periods. Through aging, those accounts urgently in need of collection are flagged. Consequently, the report provides operational control over the collection of open accounts and aids the credit manager in making collection and write-off decisions.

Critical factors reports reflect results in terms of such key performance measures as average dollar value per order, percentage of orders shipped on time, and the average number of days between the order date and the shipping date.

Sales analyses reflect the relative financial performances of individual salespersons, sales regions, product lines, customers, and markets. Figure 12-27 shows a sales analysis that compares the actual sales for three of the above segments against established quotas. It enables the chief marketing manager of Eastern Manufacturing

Eastern Manufacturing Co. Analysis of Sales by Salesperson, Product and Territory For the Month of August 1997 Central Massachusetts Territory (03)								
			Current Month			Year-to-date		
Salesperson		Product Line	Quota ($)	Actual ($)	Variance ($) Over (Under)	Quota ($)	Actual ($)	Variance ($) Over (Under)
Name	No.							
Comden, K. J.	325	A	4,000	5,000	1,000	32,000	34,600	2,600
		B	3,000	2,500	(500)	24,000	24,300	300
		C	1,000	800	(200)	8,000	7,100	(900)
		D	6,000	7,400	1,400	48,000	50,700	2,700
		E	10,000	12,100	2,100	80,000	83,200	3,200
		F	8,000	8,400	400	64,000	62,800	(1,200)
		G	2,000	1,700	(300)	16,000	15,300	(700)
		All	34,000	37,900	3,900	272,000	278,000	6,000
George, M. P.	381	A	5,000	4,800	(200)	40,000	39,200	(800)
		B	4,000	4,100	100	32,000	31,800	(200)
		C	1,000	900	(100)	8,000	6,900	(1,100)
		D	7,000	6,200	(800)	56,000	54,800	(1,200)
		E	12,000	11,800	(200)	96,000	96,500	500
		F	9,500	9,900	400	76,000	78,100	2,100
		G	2,500	3,200	700	20,000	25,300	5,300
		All	41,000	40,900	(100)	328,000	332,600	4,600
Totals		A	50,000	53,300	3,300	400,000	410,700	10,700
		B	35,000	34,700	(300)	280,000	281,500	1,500
		C	10,000	8,900	(1,100)	80,000	77,700	(2,300)
		D	65,000	69,100	4,100	520,000	528,100	8,100
		E	108,000	111,800	3,800	864,000	891,000	27,000
		F	86,000	84,700	(1,300)	688,000	679,300	(8,700)
		G	23,000	24,000	1,000	184,000	183,900	(100)
		All	377,000	386,500	9,500	3,016,000	3,052,200	36,200

FIGURE 12-27   A sales analysis report.

Co. to determine which salespersons, product lines, and sales territories are most effective in meeting their assigned quotas. This type of analysis provides managers with the basis for better control, perhaps by making decisions that further the meeting of desired objectives, i.e., the assigned quotas.

Cash-flow statements show the sources of cash, the operating uses of cash, and other special uses of cash for an accounting period. They provide the basis for developing cash forecasts and budgets. Hence, they aid financial managers in controlling and managing a firm's cash resources.

Figure 12-28 portrays most of the listings and reports described in the preceding paragraphs or earlier in the chapter. They are shown as outputs produced from data

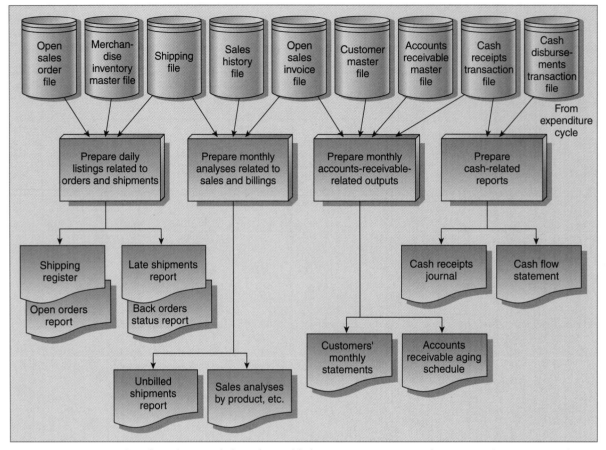

FIGURE 12-28   System flowchart showing daily and monthly listings, statements, and reports in the revenue cycle.

in the various files listed in an earlier section. Certain of the outputs shown were included as daily listings and reports in the illustrative computer system flowcharts.

DEMAND MANAGERIAL REPORTS

Demand reports are ad hoc nonscheduled reports. The information they contain is primarily used for managerial decision making and control. When also combined with decision-oriented modeling software and expert systems, the results can be quite powerful.

Consider a case in which Mike Barker, the marketing manager of Infoage, must decide on new products to market. The firm might employ a decision support system (DSS) that models the expected sales and costs for suggested products. The key output, in effect an ad hoc report, could show columns of expected revenues from sales, offset by expected direct and overhead costs, for three years. The expected contribution margins would appear below the revenues and costs. This format would be repeated several times, showing the effects of such "what if" scenarios as (1) What if sales volume were 10 percent less than in the base case? (2) What if the product unit cost increased by 15 percent in the second year?

An expert system is employed by IBM Credit Corporation to make decisions concerning the financing of large computer purchases by customers. The system processes all relevant credit and financing data to determine (1) whether the applying customer should be granted financing, and (2) on what terms the financing should be done. The demand report shows these decisions and provides the necessary paperwork (e.g., financing contract) to complete the deal. The time to process such financing requests has been cut from two weeks to four hours.*

---

*Teng et al., "Business Processing Reengineering," p. 21.

SUMMARY

The revenue cycle facilitates the exchange of products or services with customers for cash. Functions of the revenue cycle (for product sales) are to obtain the order from the customer, check the customer's credit, enter the sales order, assemble goods for shipment, ship the ordered goods, bill the customer, receive and deposit the cash payment, maintain accounts receivable records, post transactions to the general ledger, and prepare needed financial reports and other outputs. Related functions involve back orders and sales returns. These functions are achieved under the direction of the marketing/distribution and finance/accounting organizational units. Data generated during the processing of sales and cash receipts, together with externally oriented marketing and financial data, are needed in making marketing and financial decisions at all managerial levels.

Most of the data used in the cycle arise from customers. Documents typically employed are the customer order, sales order, picking list, packing list, bill of lading, shipping notice, sales invoice, remittance advice, deposit slip, back order, and credit memo. Preformatted screens may be used in on-line computer-based systems to enter sales and cash receipts data. The data base includes such files as the customer master, accounts receivable master, merchandise inventory master, open sales order, open sales invoice, cash receipts transaction, shipping and price data reference, and sales history files. In firms that adopt the data-base approach, these files would be converted into linked data structures. Data processing occurs upon the entry of data from sales transactions and cash receipts transactions. Usually it involves the updating of accounts receivable records. Processing may feasibly be performed by manual systems or computer-based systems. Computer-based systems with on-line inputs and batch processing are a suitable choice for many firms.

A variety of risks exist in the processing of sales and cash receipts transactions. Exposures due to these risks can be counteracted by means of adequate general and application controls. Among the outputs generated by the revenue cycle are customers' monthly statements, open orders reports, sales invoice registers, accounts receivable aging schedules, customer and inventory inquiry screens, performance reports, sales analyses, and demand reports.

APPENDIX TO CHAPTER 12

MANUAL PROCESSING WITHIN THE REVENUE CYCLE

This appendix provides a survey of manual processing procedures relating to credit sales and cash receipts. Narrative descriptions of the procedures are accompanied by document system flowcharts, which are keyed to the narrative by circled numbers. These numbers designate key control points within the sales and cash receipts procedures. The application controls described in the chapter are particularly needed at these points. The accounting entries pertaining to the revenue cycle are included at appropriate places in the narrative descriptions.

Credit Sales Procedure

Figure 12-29 depicts a document system flowchart of the manual credit sales procedure.

① **Receipt of the sales order.** The credit sales procedure usually begins when a customer's purchase order is received by the sales order department. After verifying that the order is valid and accurate, a sales order clerk prepares some type of sales order. In the case of the incomplete prebilling procedure (which is depicted in the flowchart), the prepared document is a sales order–invoice.

② **Check of credit acceptability.** A copy of the sales order is sent to the credit department for a check of the customer's credit. If credit is approved, the sales transaction is authorized by the sales order department. The customer is then sent an acknowledgment. Also, the order is entered for processing, with copies of the sales order–invoice being distributed to the billing department (to await notice of shipment), to the warehouse (for picking), and

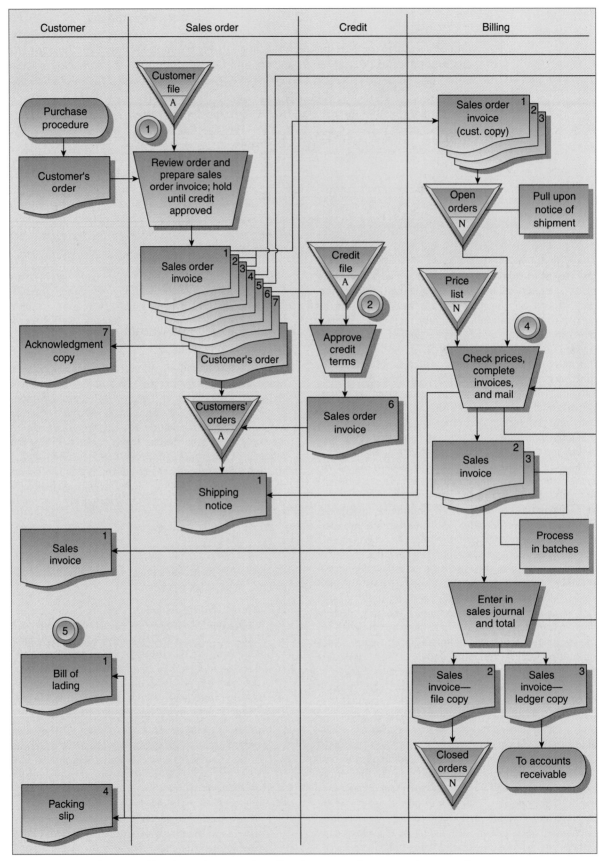

FIGURE I2-29 A document flowchart of a manual credit sales transaction processing procedure.

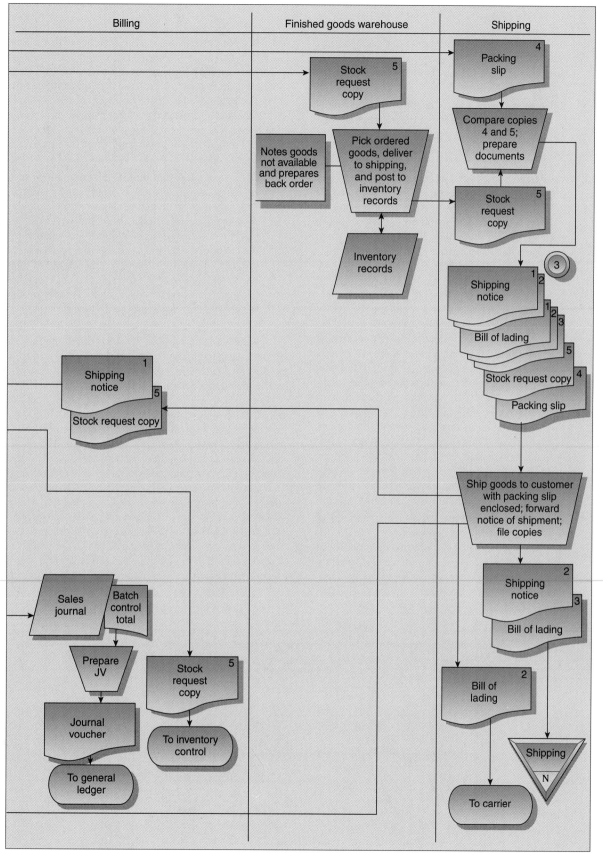

FIGURE I2-29   (Continued)

to the shipping department (as prior notification). A last copy is filed by customer name, so that it can be easily referenced to answer customer inquiries.

③ ***Shipping of ordered goods.*** The finished goods warehouse has physical custody of the merchandise inventory. When a stock request copy reaches the warehouse, an employee called a picker is assigned to assemble the ordered goods. He or she uses the stock request copy (or a picking slip) as a reference in picking the goods. If certain ordered goods are not in stock, this fact is noted on the document, which is also initialed by the picker. Then the assembled goods, together with the stock request copy, are delivered to the shipping department. There a shipping clerk pulls the packing slip copy from the file, checks the quantity of the physical goods against the copies, and prepares the shipping-related documents. The goods are packed for shipment, with the packing slip enclosed.

In some firms the warehouse keeps records of the quantities of goods on hand. If so, it is necessary to provide an added copy of the picking slip, which would be used to reduce the on-hand quantities in the records. By maintaining these memorandum records, the sales order clerk can check their status when orders are received. Customers can be informed more promptly when back orders are necessary. (Note that to provide adequate organizational independence, every firm should also maintain the "official" inventory records within an accounting department or in its computer system.)

④ ***Billing for goods shipped.*** Upon being notified of the shipment, a billing clerk compares the quantities shipped against the quantities ordered. He or she completes the sales order–invoice set, entering the quantities shipped from the shipping document and the unit prices from a current pricing file. A separate clerk verifies the accuracy of the billing. Other clerks in the billing department enter the invoice amount in the journal, accumulate sufficient invoices to form a batch, and compute batch totals. The batch of sales invoices is sent to the accounts receivable department for posting. A journal voucher is prepared for use in posting to the general ledger. These posting steps are discussed in a later section.

⑤ ***Delivery of goods and invoice.*** Shipped goods with enclosed packing slip are received by the customer. The customer, or an agent, signs for the shipment. If shipped by common carrier, the customer receives a copy of the bill of lading. Shortly thereafter the customer receives the sales invoice, usually via the postal service. Typically the customer will vouch the sales invoice by comparing it to a receiving report and purchase order. If errors are detected, the customer will then notify the firm.

Another copy of the sales invoice is distributed to the accounts receivable department for posting. Also, a copy of the sales invoice (or order document) should be sent to the inventory control department.

Record Sale in Inventory Records. Assuming that the perpetual inventory method is employed, the inventory control department maintains records for each merchandise inventory item. A document containing the quantities shipped of each item (either the sales invoice, shipping notice, or notated stock request copy) is used to update the inventory records. Figure 12-30 presents a merchandise inventory ledger card, one record in a subsidiary ledger. As the illustration shows, a quantity of 80 lawnmowers was shipped on December 5. This quantity is posted to the inventory ledger card.

As indicated in the figure, often the dollar amount of the on-hand balance is not maintained on inventory ledger cards. At the end of the accounting period, the cost

Merchandise Inventory Ledger Card

Item No.	Description	Location
L5862	Lawnmower	Row 8 Sector 15

Reorder point	Reorder quantity	Unit cost	Supplier No.
150	180	$120.00	8326

Date	Reference	Receipts	Sales	Ordered	Balances On order	Balances On hand
11-14-97	P.O. 768			180	180	0
11-24-97	R.R. 309	180			0	180
12-5-97	S.O. 2681		80		0	100
12-9-97	P.O. 797			180	180	100

FIGURE 12-30 A portion of a merchandise inventory ledger card.

value of the inventory sold is journalized and posted to the general ledger control accounts. The unit cost to apply to the quantity sold depends on the costing method adopted by the firm, e.g., average cost, first-in, first-out. A costing method must be chosen, since the unit cost of an item may change during the course of an accounting period. The posting to reflect the reduction of merchandise inventory due to sales is as follows:

Cost of goods sold	XXX	
Merchandise Inventory (control)		XXX

Cash Receipts Procedure

Figure 12-31 shows a document system flowchart of a procedure involving the receipts of cash related to credit sales. The principal control points involve the receipt of cash, the processing of the cash deposit, and the posting of cash amounts to the ledgers.

① **Receipt of cash.** The cash receipts procedure begins with the daily receipt of mailed cash and remittance advices from customers. An authorized person, such as a mail room clerk, compares the checks with the remittance advices (and prepares advices when none are received). Then the clerk endorses the checks "For Deposit Only," enters their amounts on a prenumbered remittance list, and computes a total of the batch received. One copy of the remittance list is sent to the cashier with the checks; a second copy is sent to the internal audit department (if any) for later reviews; the third copy is filed.

② **Processing of the cash deposit.** A person who is authorized to handle the cash, such as the cashier, prepares a deposit slip in triplicate. All checks from customers, plus cash received from other sources that day, are listed on the deposit slip. After the cashier compares the computed deposit total with that shown on the remittance list, he or she delivers the deposit to the bank intact. A cash receipts clerk then enters the total amount of receipts in the cash receipts journal. The clerk prepares a journal voucher, which is sent to the general ledger department for posting.

The internal audit department receives an authenticated copy of the deposit slip, which has been stamped and initialed by a bank teller and delivered direct by the bank. This deposit slip is compared to the remittance list, as well as to the deposit slip in the cashier's office and to the general ledger posting.

③ **Posting of cash amounts.** After preparing the remittance list, the mail room clerk forwards the remittance advices to the accounts receivable department for posting. The cashier sends a journal voucher to the general ledger department. Details

of the postings to the ledgers are discussed in the next section.

Accounts Receivable Maintenance Procedure

The accounts receivable subsidiary ledger is the link between the sales and cash receipts procedures. Figure 12-32 on page 512 illustrates the steps relating to posting sales transactions to the accounts receivable ledger and the general ledger, as well as those relating to sales returns and allowances and write-offs.

① **Posting to accounts receivable accounts.** Upon receiving copies of the sales invoices from the billing department, a clerk in the accounts receivable department posts the sales amounts to the customers' accounts. Another clerk verifies the posting and obtains a total of the amounts posted. This clerk then forwards the batch total to the general ledger department.

Upon receiving copies of the remittance advices from the cash receipts department, an accounts receivable clerk posts the payment amounts to the customers' accounts. As in the case of sales postings, another clerk verifies the accuracy and obtains a total of the amounts posted. The batch total is then forwarded to the general ledger department.

② **Posting to general ledger accounts.** In the general ledger department, a clerk compares (for each type of transaction) the total posted to the precomputed batch total amount, as shown on a summary journal voucher. If they agree, the clerk posts the totals to the general ledger accounts. If they disagree, the clerk locates discrepancies, corrects the errors, notifies the accounts receivable clerk of posting errors, and then completes the general ledger postings.

The posting to reflect sales is as follows:

Dr. Accounts Receivable	XXX	
Cr. Sales		XXX

The posting to reflect cash receipts is as follows:

Dr. Cash	XXX	
Cr. Accounts Receivable		XXX

③ **Processing of sales returns and allowances.** Upon requests from customers to return goods or to be given allowances, a manager must authorize the transaction. If a return is involved, the returned goods are received in the receiving department. There they are counted by a clerk and listed on a sales return notice (or special receiving report). If prior authorization was not obtained, the receiving department then forwards a copy to the credit manager for approval. The approved notice (or a return notification, if issued) is transmitted to the billing

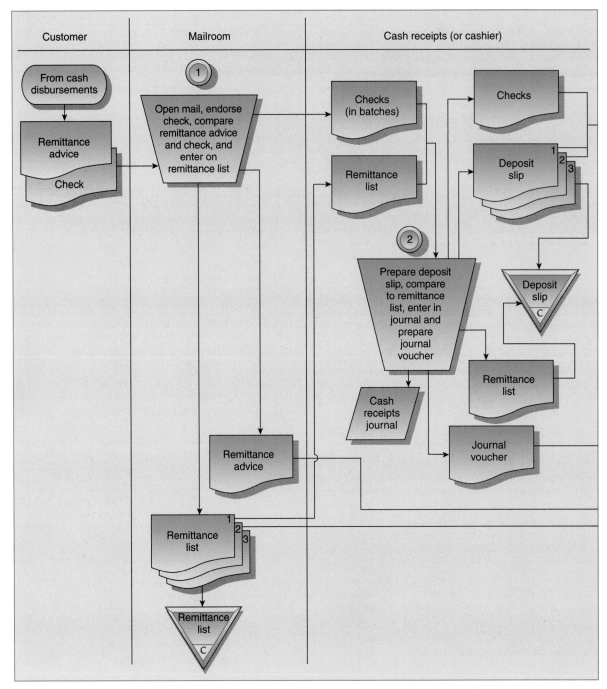

FIGURE 12-31   A document flowchart of a manual cash receipts transaction processing procedure.

department, where the prices are checked against the original sales invoice. Then a prenumbered credit memo is prepared, with copies being sent to the accounts receivable department for posting and to the customer. A clerk in the billing department also prepares a journal voucher for the gen-

eral ledger department, which posts the sales return transaction. Allowances on sales are granted for damaged goods, shortages, or similar deficiencies. In such cases the sales order department or salesperson settles the amount, which is then approved by the credit manager. Sales allowances are

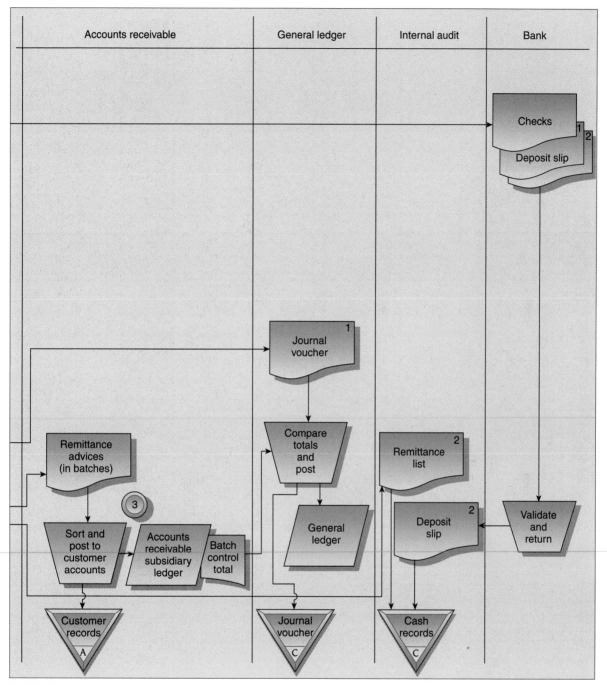

FIGURE 12-31 (*Continued*)

then processed in the same manner as sales returns.

Sales returns and allowances are posted to the general ledger accounts based on the following entry:

Dr. Sales Returns and Allowances XXX
    Cr. Accounts Receivable   XXX

④ **Processing of account write-offs.** Another type of adjustment is the write-off of customer account balances. Upon reviewing an accounts receivable aging schedule and other evidence, the credit manager makes a decision concerning which accounts are uncollectible. Then he or she prepares a write-off notice. After the treasurer or other designated manager approves the notice, it is

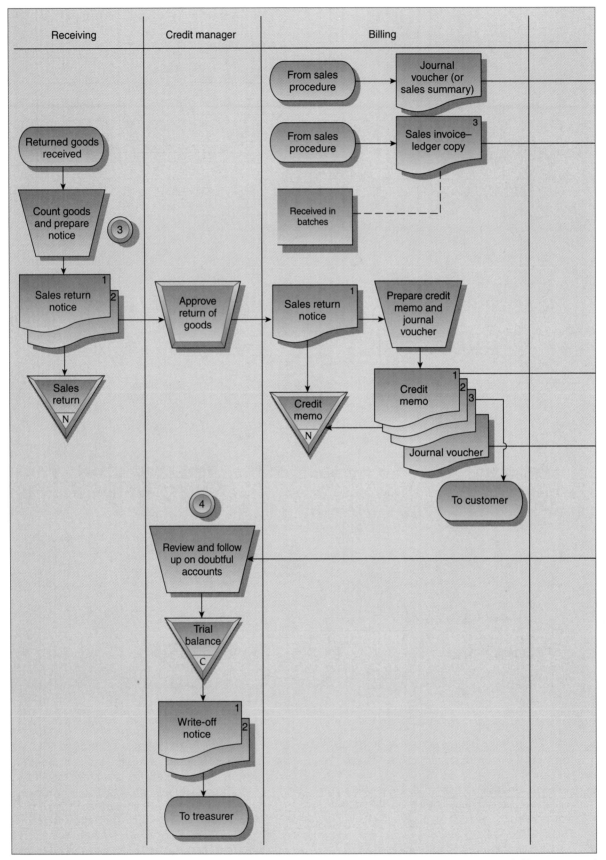

FIGURE 12-32 A document flowchart of procedures relating to accounts receivable, sales returns and allowances, and write-offs of accounts receivable.

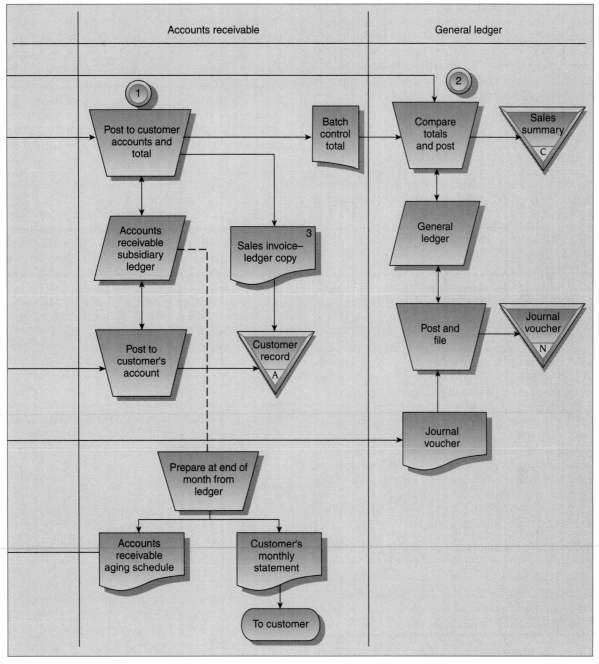

FIGURE 12-32 (*Continued*)

processed in the same manner as sales returns and allowances.

If bad debts have been anticipated by the prior establishment of an allowance account, the posting for written-off accounts is:

Dr. Allowance for Doubtful	XXX	
Accounts		
Cr. Accounts Receivable		XXX

REVIEW PROBLEMS WITH SOLUTIONS

CAMPUS BOOKSTORE, EIGHTH INSTALLMENT
Statement

The Campus Bookstore (described in the Review Problem at the end of Chapter 1) continues to add applications to its new minicomputer system. The central application, an on-line cash sales application, has been delayed because of its complexity. However, with the assistance of consultants from the public accounting firm, it is soon developed and successfully put into operation. The manager of the bookstore expects to gain immediate benefits from the new application, since it performs a number of integrated functions relating to sales and inventory.

Required

Describe the steps of the application involving the on-line processing of cash sales transactions, as well as the related functions.

Solution

A cash sales transaction on-line processing system would likely involve the following steps: As customers present their merchandise at the checkout stands, checkout clerks sweep their scanners across the bar codes on the merchandise packages. The captured coded data are entered via the terminals (to which the scanners are connected) and checked for errors and omissions. Each item of checked data is translated into the description of the merchandise item and its price and then is listed on a sales slip. When all merchandise items composing an individual sale have been entered, the clerk presses a key; then the sales tax and total are automatically computed and printed on the sales slip. The remainder of the transaction is handled in the same manner as it was by the former manual system.

The computer system performs several functions that are related to the sales transactions.

a. In addition to editing the captured data, it retrieves the sales prices from a stored file on one of the magnetic disks. Based on these sales prices, the system computes the sales amount for each merchandise item and for each sale, as already described. The system also lists the total amount of each cash sale in a cash receipts summary record (similar in purpose to the locked-in tape in the former cash register). This cash receipts summary record, or journal, is printed at the end of each day. It is broken down by point-of-sale terminal station so that a manager can reconcile the cash amounts in the drawers to the totals received for the day.

b. The computer system posts the quantities of merchandise sold to a merchandise inventory master file, which is stored on one of the on-line magnetic disks. (When on-hand quantities have been reduced by sales below a critical level, the purchasing department is notified automatically via a reorder report. It then places purchase orders for additional merchandise so that the shelves may be restocked. This procedure is an example of the integrated nature of on-line processing systems.)

c. At the end of each day, the computer system posts the total amount of cash sales to the general ledger accounts, which are maintained in a master file on an online magnetic disk, with a debit to Cash on Hand and a credit to Sales. (Also, when the cash is deposited in the bank, the system is instructed by the cashier to post the transaction to the appropriate general ledger accounts.)

EASY COMPANY

Statement

The cashier of the Easy Company intercepted customer A's check payable to the firm in the amount of $500 and deposited it in a bank account that was part of the firm's petty-cash fund, of which he was custodian. He then drew on the petty-cash-fund bank account a $500 check payable to himself, signed it, and cashed it. At the end of the month, while processing the monthly statements to customers, he was able to change the statement to customer A so as to show that A had received credit for the $500 check that had been intercepted. Ten days later he made an entry in the cash receipts book that purported to record receipt of a remittance of $500 from customer A, thus restoring A's account to its proper balance but overstating cash in bank. He covered the overstatement by omitting two checks, the aggregate amount of which was $500, from the list of outstanding checks in the bank reconciliation.*

Required

Identify the central control weakness in Easy Company's cash receipts procedure and specify control procedures that can improve the internal control structure.

Solution

The central control weakness in this situation is the inadequate division of duties and responsibilities. Not only does the cashier have access to cash as well as to the customers' records, but he is allowed to check on his own work and to handle the petty-cash fund in a very loose manner.

The internal control system can therefore be greatly strengthened if the following steps are taken:

a. Assign other persons not in the cashier's office to process the customers' records, to maintain the petty-

---

*Adapted from the May 1958 CPA examination. Copyright © 1958 by the American Institute of Certified Public Accountants. Reprinted by permission.

cash fund, to open the incoming mail, and to reconcile the bank account.

b. Do not allow the cashier to have access to incoming mail, to the customers' records, and to the petty-cash fund.

c. Instruct the bank to refuse to accept checks made payable to the firm for deposit in the petty-cash-fund bank account.

d. Require the person who opens the mail to make a separate listing in triplicate of all remittances received; one copy is to be sent to the cashier for entry in the cash records, another copy is to be sent to the accounts receivable clerk for posting to the customers' ledger accounts, and the third is to be sent to the treasurer or internal auditor for comparison with the deposit slip returned from the bank.

KEY TERMS

accounts receivable aging schedule (502)
accounts receivable master file (474)
back order (466)
balance forward method (464)
bill of lading (463)
credit memo (465)
customer master file (474)
customer order (460)
deposit slip (463)
incomplete billing procedure (462)
lapping (491)
lockbox (494)
merchandise inventory master file (474)
monthly statement (498)
open invoice method (464)
open orders report (498)
order acknowledgment (462)
packing slip (462)
picking list (462)
prebilling procedure (462)
remittance advice (463)
remittance list (486)
sales analysis (502)
sales order (462)
separate sales order and invoice procedure (462)
shipping notice (463)

REVIEW QUESTIONS

12-1. What are several objectives of the revenue cycle?

12-2. What are the major functions of the revenue cycle?

12-3. Contrast the three alternative procedures for billing customers.

12-4. Describe the back ordering procedure.

12-5. Describe the relationships of the marketing and distribution organizational functions to the revenue cycle.

12-6. Describe the relationships of the finance and accounting organizational functions to the revenue cycle.

12-7. Identify several decisions that must be made by the typical marketing manager.

12-8. What items of information are needed by a marketing manager when making decisions within his or her area of responsibilities?

12-9. Identify several decisions that must be made by the typical controller or treasurer, as well as information needed for making the decisions.

12-10. What are the sources of data used in the revenue cycle?

12-11. Identify the various documents used in the revenue cycle.

12-12. Describe a typical data-entry screen for use in the revenue cycle.

12-13. Identify the accounting entries needed to reflect the transactions within the revenue cycle.

12-14. Describe several relevant characteristics that may be reflected in codes for (a) sales transactions and (b) customers.

12-15. Identify the various files that are needed in the revenue cycle.

12-16. What are the entities that are involved in the revenue cycle?

12-17. Describe network and relational data structures that might be employed within a data base that supports sales processing.

12-18. What are the intersection records or relationship tables that are useful in data structures pertaining to sales processing?

12-19. Describe the credit sales procedure when an on-line input batch processing computer-based system is used. Contrast this procedure with one performed manually.

12-20. Describe the cash receipts procedure when an on-line input batch processing computer-based system is used. Contrast this procedure with one performed manually.

12-21. How does a sales return procedure differ from a sales procedure?

12-22. What are the benefits of processing sales and cash receipts transactions by means of an on-line input batch processing computer-based system?

12-23. What are exposures to risk that exist when processing transactions within the revenue cycle?

12-24. Identify the control objectives that should be achieved with respect to the revenue cycle.

12-25. Identify general controls that involve organizational independence, documentation, asset accountability, management practices, data center operations, and access within the revenue cycle. '

12-26. Identify the various input, processing, and output controls that pertain to the revenue cycle.

12-27. What are the different types of outputs that should be generated by the revenue cycle?

12-28. Describe three scheduled reports for use in managerial planning and control.

DISCUSSION QUESTIONS

12-29. What effects does a change within the revenue cycle from a manual system to an on-line input batch processing computer-based system have on the (a) form of inputs, (b) sources of inputs, (c) files, (d) processing steps, (e) internal controls, and (g) outputs?

12-30. What are the most useful sources of information for marketing managers, other than from revenue cycle processing, if the managers' firm has installed an on-line computer network?

12-31. In what ways does a cash sale differ from a credit sale, especially with regard to documents, files, procedure, and outputs?

12-32. Describe several programmed edit checks, such as the redundancy matching check, that can be applied by the posting programs used in processing sales and cash receipts transactions.

12-33. Figure 12-22 describes two relationship checks that may be applied during the revenue cycle. Describe another relationship check that involves dates.

Hint: Some firms that make credit sales have terms that allow a cash discount if the bill is paid within 10 days.

12-34. Why should a bank reconciliation be prepared periodically?

12-35. Which application controls that are needed in a revenue cycle procedure involving an on-line computer-based system are not suitable when a batch computer-based system is employed, and vice versa?

12-36. Discuss why a check received from a customer in payment of a previous credit sale should not be used as the medium for posting to the customer's accounts receivable ledger, rather than the remittance advices.

12-37. Do the information needs of the marketing manager at Infoage (a merchandising firm) differ from those of his counterparts at other types of firms, such as manufacturers and hospitals? If so, how?

PROBLEMS

Note: These problems include material presented in the Appendix to this chapter.

12-1. Go Co. is a retail grocer that sells its merchandise directly to individuals, who pay by cash only. Mo Co. is a distributor that sells to retailers and individuals from catalogs; customers place orders, are billed, and pay against their running balances monthly. Yo Co. is a manufacturer of specialty goods, whose salespersons call on distributors and retail chains to obtain orders; customers place orders, are billed, and pay within specified time periods.

Required

These three selling firms exhibit differences in their revenue functions. List these likely differences with respect to the following functions, providing as many differences as possible. (The first function is completed.)

a. Obtaining order from customer:
Go Co.—gives products to customer in person, who pays cash immediately.
Mo Co.—receives order by phone or in written form via mail.
Yo Co.—receives order via salesperson, who writes up order.

b. Checking credit of customer.

c. Entering sales order.

d. Assembling goods and shipping.

e. Billing customer.

f. Recording receivable.

g. Receiving and recording cash payments.

12-2. The Versatile Shopper sells a variety of parts and merchandise to credit customers ranging from manufacturing firms to individuals. Currently it employs manual sales and cash receipts systems to handle revenues, but it is considering a change to computerized processing. Explain how the various functions of the revenue cycle would be affected if the firm adopts the following:

  a. A point-of-sale system.

  b. Billing with turnaround documents.

  c. An electronic data interchange system.

12-3. Macon Merchandise is a medium-sized firm having the departments shown in Figure 12-7. Which of the departments is responsible for preparation (in the case of a document) or for recording (in the case of an accounting record)?

a. Sales invoice.

b. Shipping notice.

c. Sales order.

d. Credit memorandum.

e. Inventory records.

f. Deposit slip.

g. Customer records.

h. Remittance advice (if not submitted by the customer).

i. Cash receipts journal.

j. Write-off notice (of customer's account).

12-4. Motrol, Inc., is a manufacturer and global distributor of semiconductor products. Since almost all of its products are sold on a credit basis to about 30,000 firms around the world, its credit and collection policies and procedures are critical to the firm's well-being. Sandy Holm, the credit manager, therefore has been in the forefront in automating the activities relating to accounts receivable. Currently the firm has on-line receivables and credit management programs that are "state of the art." For instance, any customer's account can be accessed at any time. Also, as soon as payments are applied, they are reflected in the account balance. Moreover, the credit management software can generate ad hoc reports that pertain to credits and collections. These features are extremely useful to a global firm that services accounts in so many areas.

Required

a. Identify several decisions that the credit manager of Motrol would be involved in making.

b. Specify various types of displays and reports that would aid the credit manager in making decisions and conducting collection operations.

c. Identify several marketing decisions that must be made by Motrol. Explain which of these marketing decisions may affect the effectiveness of the credit and collections activities, especially those decisions that may have an adverse effect.

12-5. Sapphire Department Stores, Inc., has eight locations in a major eastern city. Sales are made on credit to customers who have applied for and received credit cards from Sapphire. All other sales are made for cash. Deliveries of purchased merchandise are made on request, whether the sale is for cash or on credit. Merchandise may be returned by customers, with refunds being made in the case of cash sales, and credits against account balances being provided in the case of credit sales. Credit customers are billed once a month, based on the accounts receivable records. Overdue balances are automatically assessed interest charges.

Required

a. List the data elements needed to record and process cash sales, credit sales, payments on account, and sales returns transactions.

b. List the files needed to store these data elements. For each master file identify the primary key and several secondary keys.

c. Design group codes for customer numbers and sales and cash receipts transactions.

d. Describe the formats of reports that would be useful to the firm's management in analyzing sales and cash receipts and the activities related to the credit customers' accounts. Note that the information available through such reports must be captured by the transactional codes designed in **c** above.

12-6. Antler and Horn, Consultants, bill their clients for services rendered. The invoices, which itemize the hours worked by the various classes of consultants in the firm, are sent at the end of each month. One invoice sent on September 30, 1997, to the Mover Construction Company showed the following billable hours: 4 hours for a partner, 10 hours for a manager, 85 hours for a senior staff consultant, and 230 hours for staff consultants. Hourly rates charged by the firm are $280 for partners, $200 for managers, $150 for senior staff consultants, and $100 for staff consultants. All taxes are included within the billing rates. Design and complete the invoice to be sent to the Mover Construction Company, whose offices are located at 50 Lark Lane, Prescott, Arizona 86301. The consultants are located at 1000 Woolshire Blvd., Los Angeles, California 90028.

12-7. The Tuffy Merchandising Company enters sales orders via on-line terminals as soon as received, and the computer system stores the orders in a file and then generates printed shipping orders. The Duffy Merchandising Company keys batches of sales orders onto magnetic tape and then enters these batches into its computer system, where the sales orders are stored and used at the end of the day to generate shipping orders and to provide data for later processing. Both firms employ the separate sales order and invoice procedure, and both store their sales order records on magnetic disks for reference and use in sales processing. Assume that the key-to-tape encoders used by Duffy's system do not perform any edit functions.

Required

a. List the data elements that should appear on the shipping orders of both firms.

b. List the programmed edit checks that should be performed by the computer edit programs of Tuffy's system; include with each check one or more key data elements from shipping transactions to which each check pertains.

Employ a controls matrix similar to Figure 8-13 to list these programmed checks.

c. List the programmed edit checks that should be performed by the computer edit programs of Duffy's system; include with each check one or more key data elements from shipping transactions to which each check pertains. Employ a controls matrix similar to Figure 8-13 to list these programmed checks.

d. Devise a transaction code that would pertain to sales and a variety of other transactions.

12-8. Omega's Specialties employs a turnaround document with respect to its monthly statement. Customers are expected to return these turnaround documents, the top portions of statements, as remittance advices that accompany their payments. A sample appears in Figure 12-3.

Required

Prepare a record layout of data from the remittance advice, which is to serve as a record in the cash receipts transaction file. Assign the number 3798 as the transaction number and CR as the transaction code. Include field sizes and data modes, based on the data shown in Figure 12-3.

12-9. At the end of each month, the Egress Corporation of Andover, Massachusetts 01810, prepares monthly statements for its credit customers, plus an accounts receivable aging schedule. The files on which these reports are based are the accounts receivable master file, the customer master file, the sales invoice file, and the cash receipts file. (The firm does not maintain a sales history file, but it does retain all sales and cash receipts data in related files for one year.) The files are all maintained on magnetic disk and can be accessed as needed during the end-of-month printing runs.

Required

a. Design the monthly statement, assuming that it is not intended to be used as a turnaround document.

b. Design the accounts receivable aging schedule, including such columns as customer account number and name, current balance, amount of the receivable balance that is not overdue, and amounts that are 31–60 days old, 61–90 days old, and over 90 days old. Terms are net 30 days.

c. Draw suggested record layouts, omitting field sizes and modes of data elements, for the listed files. Be sure that all the information in the two outputs can be derived from one of the files or can be computed or generated by the computer system. (For instance, the date may be computer generated.)

12-10. The Greek Company is a wholesaler that currently has three customers, Alpha, Beta, and Omega. It began business at the first of this year and sells on credit terms of net 30 days. Since it intends to grow significantly over the years, it has acquired a microcomputer and a relational data-base software package. Among the tables established within the data base are the accounts receivable master, customer master, sales invoice, and cash remittance tables. Data pertaining to the customers are as follows. (All customers have a credit limit of $6000, and are located in Minneapolis, and each has identical shipping and billing addresses.) Sales made since the inception of business (Jan. 1, 1998) are as follows:

Invoice Number	Customer Number	Billing Date	Invoice Amount
001	20	1/3	$2035.00
002	10	1/4	608.00
003	30	1/8	1300.00
004	10	1/17	460.00
005	30	1/23	1686.00
006	20	1/30	504.00
007	30	2/5	250.00
008	10	2/8	882.00
009	20	2/14	590.00
010	10	2/21	2304.00
011	30	3/3	773.00
012	20	3/11	1250.00
013	30	3/18	395.00
014	10	3/25	899.00
015	30	4/2	1400.00
016	20	4/9	714.00
017	30	4/11	300.00
018	10	4/17	1890.00
019	20	4/24	398.00
020	20	4/29	500.00
021	30	4/30	1030.00

Name	Account Number	Street Address	Zip	Phone
Alpha	10	235 Broad Street	55411	(612) 588-7421
Beta	20	3770 Local Avenue	55412	(612) 588-0093
Omega	30	7094 Orange Drive	55411	(612) 439-8666

Cash remittances have been as follows, identified by the remittance numbers assigned by the firm:

Remittance Number	Customer Number	Receipt Date	Remitted Amount
R001	20	1/30	$2035.00
R002	10	2/3	608.00
R003	10	2/15	460.00
R004	20	2/28	504.00
R005	10	3/6	882.00
R006	20	3/12	250.00
R007	10	3/19	2304.00
R008	30	3/23	1686.00
R009	20	3/31	340.00
R010	20	4/1	250.00
R011	10	4/24	899.00

Required

a. Design the relational data-base tables needed, including the keys necessary to provide adequate association among the tables. Enter complete data into the tables relating to customers, but only the first three rows (tuples) into those relating to transactions.

b. Prepare an accounts receivable aging schedule as of April 30. Be sure to include the totals of all columns in the schedule. Assume that there are no sales returns or other adjustments to the sales data, and that the open invoice method is employed in maintaining accounts receivable.

12-11. Refer to Figure 12-15, pertaining to Infoage's revenue cycle. Note that more than one payment may be received from a customer relating to a particular sale, while a single payment may span more than a single sale. Assume that each payment is associated with the one or more sales to which it relates.

Required

a. Prepare a data structure diagram for the cash receipts portion of Infoage's revenue cycle, assuming that a network structure will be employed.

b. Prepare a data structure diagram that shows the tables and their relationships for the cash receipts portion of Infoage's revenue cycle, assuming that a relational structure will be employed.

12-12. Visher Stores is a convenience store chain located in a southern metropolitan area. It serves 12 stores from a single warehouse, which maintains a complete inventory of merchandise items sold by Visher Stores. When a replenishment order is received from a store at the warehouse, the ordered items are picked and shipped the same day. At the store the received items

are stocked on the shelves. While the stores vary somewhat in the items they carry, each item is carried by more than one store. A listing of the items carried by each store, and the quantity on hand at the end of each day, is maintained. An on-line computerized system aids in maintaining the inventories at the warehouse and stores. Sales are made at each store to customers by sales clerks for cash only.

Required

a. Identify the entities in the inventory replenishment and sales procedure described above.

b. Prepare an entity-relationship diagram that spans the above procedure.

c. If Visher decides to acquire a relational data base, list the tables needed to contain data relating to the procedure described above.

12-13. The Overlord Company has just employed a new credit manager. Because the firm has an outstanding total of $3 million in accounts receivable (when last year's sales were $12 million), the credit manager realizes that her most urgent task is to reduce the level of accounts receivable. Credit customers are billed at the end of each month, based on individual accounts receivable records. The credit manager has been assured by the president that a new computer-based system is to be installed within the coming year.

Required

a. List the types of transactions that can affect the accounts receivable balances.

b. Show several transactions that might arise from a sale of $200. Assume that the firm allows 2 percent discount if paid within ten days.

c. Describe at least two reports that can aid the credit manager in controlling outstanding accounts receivable.

d. Discuss the relative advantages of processing the various daily transactions that affect the accounts receivable records by a computer-based system that (1) uses the periodic processing approach, and (2) that uses the immediate processing approach.

12-14. Refer to Figure 12-19. Prepare a data-flow diagram that reflects the processes relating to cash receipts.

12-15. The Jason Department Store of Ann Arbor, Michigan, sells a wide variety of merchandise for cash or credit. It mails account statements to credit customers monthly. Customers then return their payments, including in the envelopes the detached portions of the statements, which serve as remittance advices for the cash receipts procedure. These remittance advices are processed against the accounts receivable master file. Daily listings of cash receipts and monthly accounts receivable aging schedules are prepared.

Each remittance advice contains the customer account number, customer name and address, remittance advice code, type of account, payment date, and amount paid.

Each record in the accounts receivable master file contains the customer number, customer name and address, credit limit, sales amounts and dates for the past six months, cash payment amounts and dates for the past six months, adjustment amounts and dates and codes for the past six months, and current balance.

The daily listing of cash receipts (in effect, the cash receipts journal) reflects customer numbers, customer names, remittance advice codes, cash payment amounts, the daily deposit number, and the date.

The monthly accounts receivable aging analysis reflects customer names, total balances owed, plus portions of balances that are current, 31–60 days old, 61–90 days old, and over 90 days old.

Jason currently processes cash receipts manually, but it has decided to convert to computer-based processing.

Required

a. Specify the source of each item in the two output reports, assuming that the system has been converted to computer processing. Sources may be the master file, transaction document, or a "computer-generated" operation.

b. Prepare a system flowchart of a proposed computer-based cash receipts procedure. Assume that the firm adopts the periodic processing approach, that the remittance advices are converted to magnetic disk by means of an OCR device, and that the master file is stored on a magnetic disk.

c. Prepare a record layout of the remittance advice transaction record as it might appear on the magnetic disk medium. Include assumed field sizes and modes of data elements.

d. List the application controls that are suitable to the computer-based system. In the case of programmed checks indicate the data elements being edited.

e. Prepare a level-zero data-flow diagram of the cash receipts procedure.

12-16. Aqua Valves and Fittings Company of Laramie, Wyoming, sells plastic pipes, copper tubing, brass and cast-iron valves, and assorted other items to contractors. In addition to Sid Center, the general manager, the firm employs a salesperson (Nolan Kobb), a bookkeeper (Rita Records), and two yard workers (Phil Stone and Fred Bass).

Sales are made by phone, with later pickup. When a customer places an order, an unnumbered sales order is prepared. It lists the descriptions of the ordered items, the quantities ordered, and the unit prices, as well as a notation of whether the sale is for cash or credit. One copy of the sales order is filed in the office, and the second copy is taken to the yard. On the basis of the second copy, either Phil or Fred assembles the ordered items and tapes the copy of the sales order to the assembled order.

When a customer arrives to pick up an order, if the sale is cash and carry, he or she first stops in the office and pays. Otherwise, he or she goes directly to the yard and picks up the order. Whether the sale is for cash or on credit, the customer receives the second copy of the sales order.

At the end of each month, Rita prepares monthly statements from the file of open credit sales orders and mails them to the customers.

Each morning Rita or Nolan opens the mail and segregates the remittances from customers. Rita then removes the sales orders against which remittances have been received and files them in a closed orders file. She then prepares a deposit slip, listing cash received both from credit sales and from yesterday's cash sales, and carries the deposit to the bank. At the end of each month, she prepares the bank reconciliation.

Required

a. List the control weaknesses in the foregoing sales and cash receipts procedure and recommend improvements. Assume that Aqua cannot afford to hire any additional employees.

b. Prepare a context diagram and a level-zero data-flow diagram of the revenue cycle for Aqua.

c. Aqua decides to acquire a computer network, with linked microcomputers located in the general manager's office, on the desks of the bookkeeper and salesperson, and in an alcove of the yard. Prepare a system flowchart of an immediate processing computerized procedure for sales and cash receipts. Incorporate sound controls in the procedure.

12-17. O'Brien Corporation is a medium-sized, privately owned industrial instrument manufacturer supplying precision equipment manufacturers in the Midwest. The corporation is 10 years old and operates a centralized accounting and information system. The administrative offices are located in a downtown St. Louis building; the production, shipping, and receiving departments are housed in a renovated warehouse a few blocks away. The shipping and receiving areas share one end of the warehouse.

O'Brien Corporation has grown rapidly. Sales have increased by 25 percent each year for the last three years, and the firm is now shipping approximately $80,000 of its products each week. James Fox, O'Brien's controller, purchased and installed a computer last year to process the payroll and inventory. Fox plans to integrate the accounting information system fully within the next five years.

The marketing department consists of four salespersons. On obtaining an order, usually over the telephone, a salesperson manually prepares a prenumbered, two-part sales order. One copy of the order is filed by date, and the second copy is sent to the shipping department. All sales are on credit, F.O.B. destination. Because of the recent increase in sales, the four salespersons have not had time to check credit histories. As a result, 15 percent of credit sales are either late collections or uncollectible.

The shipping department receives the sales orders and packages the goods from the warehouse, noting any items that are out of stock. The terminal in the shipping department is used to update the perpetual inventory records of each item as it is removed from the shelf. The packages are placed near the loading dock door in alphabetical order by customer name. The sales order is signed by a shipping clerk when the order is filled and ready to send. The sales order is forwarded to the billing department, where a two-part sales invoice is prepared. The sales invoice is prepared only on receipt of the sales order from the shipping department so that the customer is billed just for the items that were sent, not for back orders. Billing sends the customer's copy of the invoice back to shipping. The customer's copy of the invoice serves as a billing copy, and shipping inserts it into a special envelope on the package in order to save postage. The carrier of the customer's choice is then contacted to pick up the goods. In the past, goods were shipped within two working days of the receipt of the customer's order; however, shipping dates now average six working days after receipt of the order. One reason is that there are two new shipping clerks who are still undergoing training. Because the two shipping clerks have fallen behind, the two clerks in the receiving department, who are experienced, have been assisting the shipping clerks.

The receiving department is adjacent to the shipping dock, and merchandise is received daily by many different carriers. The clerks share the computer terminal with the shipping department. The date, vendor, and number of items received are entered on receipt in order to keep the perpetual inventory records current.

Hard copy of the changes in inventory (additions and shipments) is printed once a month. The receiving supervisor makes sure the additions are reasonable and forwards the printout to the shipping supervisor, who is responsible for checking the reasonableness of the deductions from inventory (shipments). The inventory printout is stored in the shipping department by date. A complete inventory list is printed only once a year, when the physical inventory is taken.

The diagram on page 522 represents the document flows employed by O'Brien Corporation.

Required

O'Brien Corporation's marketing, shipping, billing, and receiving information systems have some weaknesses. For each weakness in the systems

a. Identify the weakness and describe the potential problem(s) caused by the weakness.

b. Recommend controls or changes in the systems to correct each weakness.

c. Prepare a level-zero data-flow diagram of the marketing, shipping, and billing procedure. Treat the receiving department as external.

(CMA *adapted*)

12-18. Thistle Co. of Berkeley, California, manufactures and sells 10 major product lines. About 25 items, on the average, are in each product line. All sales are made on credit, and orders are received by mail or telephone. The firm's transaction processing systems are computer based, with all active files maintained on magnetic disks.

All orders received during regular working hours are entered immediately by sales order clerks via video display terminals. Orders are first edited by an edit program. A second program (a) checks for credit acceptability by reference to the accounts receivable file and (b) checks for product availability by reference to the finished-goods inventory file. Outputs from this program for accepted orders are shipping notices and packing slips plus a sales order transaction file on magnetic disk. (If on-hand quantities are short of the ordered quantities, back-order cards are prepared. These cards are sent to the production planning department to initiate production of needed quantities.) The shipping notices and packing slips are sent to the warehouse.

After the products are shipped, with packing slips enclosed, the shipping notices are initialed (to verify shipments) and forwarded to the billing department. Billing clerks enter the data from the shipping notices via video display terminals. The shipping transaction data—consisting of the customer number, product number, and quantities shipped—are edited and stored temporarily.

At 7 P.M. that evening the shipping transaction data for the day are processed as a batch by a series of runs under the guidance of processing programs. First, batch totals are computed and printed on an exception and summary report. Next the data are sorted by customer number. Then the transactions are processed to update the records in the accounts receivable file. Sales invoices are generated during this update run; the originals are mailed to customers, and copies are stored in an on-line sales invoice file. Batch totals are verified on an exception and summary report. Next, the same data are resorted by product number and processed sequentially to update the records in the finished-goods inventory file. A listing of products shipped and on back order is also

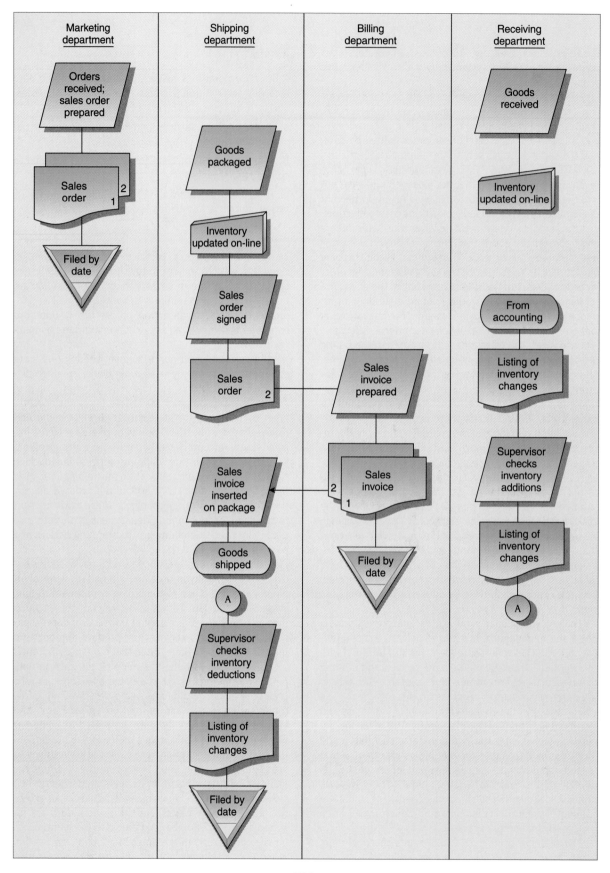

522

generated during this second update run for the sales manager. Batch totals are again verified, and a copy of the exception and summary report is sent to the general ledger clerk.

Inquiries concerning the quantities of products on hand and on back order, as well as those concerning the customers' current account balances, are frequently entered via their video display terminals by sales order clerks and accounting clerks.

At the end of each month a sales summary and analysis is prepared for the sales manager. Monthly statements are also prepared and mailed to customers. Furthermore, an aging analysis of accounts receivable is prepared for the credit manager.

Each record in the accounts receivable master file contains the customer's account number, customer's name and address, credit rating, invoice numbers and dates and amounts of all sales, remittance numbers and dates and amounts of all payments, and account balance.

Each record in the finished-goods inventory master file contains the product number, description, reorder point, units on back order, selling price, and units on hand.

Required

a. Prepare a computer system flowchart of the following portions of the above sales procedure:

(1) The on-line entry and initial processing of sales orders.

(2) The on-line entry and batch processing of shipping data.

(3) The on-line entry and processing of shipping data, assuming that the transactions are processed directly against the master files.

(4) The inquiries against on-line files.

(5) The monthly preparation of reports and statements from the master files.

b. Prepare a level-zero data-flow diagram of the sales procedure, omitting inquiries.

12-19. What error or fraudulent activity might occur if each of the following procedures is allowed?

a. The person who maintains the accounts receivable records also receives the cash payments from customers.

b. The person who approves the write-offs of uncollectible accounts also carries the cash receipts to the bank.

c. The sales invoices are not prenumbered (or if prenumbered, are not filed in a sequential file that is periodically checked for gaps in the numbers).

d. The accounts receivable ledger is not periodically reconciled to the control account in the general ledger.

e. Incompleted sales order–invoice copies are filed in the billing department but are not accounted for on a periodic basis.

f. After billing is completed the shipping notices are not marked in some manner, stapled to copies of the invoices, or filed.

12-20. What internal accounting control(s) would be most effective in preventing or detecting each of the following errors or fraudulent practices?

a. The amount of $380 is posted from a sales invoice to a customer's accounts receivable record as $308.

b. A customer is billed for all 100 units ordered, though only 80 units are shipped because of an insufficient quantity on hand to fill the order.

c. A customer is not billed for ordered merchandise shipped.

d. A general ledger clerk posts a debit to sales returns but does not post the credit to the accounts receivable control account.

e. A shipment never reaches a customer, even though it leaves the shipping dock via a common carrier.

f. Goods are shipped to a customer who is delinquent in paying for past sales.

g. Goods are taken from the finished-goods warehouse and knowingly shipped by the shipping clerk to a person who did not place an order.

h. A sale that is billed to a customer is not posted to the accounts receivable record.

i. Certain goods are never returned to the firm, in spite of the fact that a credit memo is issued and approved.

j. A cash receipt is stolen by the cashier.

k. A computer-prepared sales analysis is mistakenly sent to the personnel manager rather than the sales manager.

l. A computer operator mounts the magnetic tape containing the cash disbursements for the day, rather than the cash receipts, and incorrectly updates the accounts receivable master file.

m. A payment from a customer in the amount of $100.10, properly listed on a remittance advice, is keyed by a data-entry clerk onto the transaction tape as $101.00.

n. A sales order clerk accidentally omits the quantity of one of the ordered products when entering sales data via a terminal.

o. A sales order is coded with an incorrect and nonexistent customer number. The error is not detected until the file updating run, when no master is located to match the erroneous number.

p. A sales order clerk accidentally keys the letter o instead of 0 (zero) as a part of the quantity 30.

q. A mail room employee uses the mail room terminal to post a cash receipt against the balance of a friend's account receivable, even though the payment was made by a different customer.

r. A customer returns a payment of the balance less the purchase discount amount, even though the payment date is more than 10 days past the invoice date (the period during which discounts are allowed). Payments are entered via a preformatted screen into an on-line system by a clerk employee of the selling firm.

12-21. What internal accounting control(s) would be most effective in preventing or detecting each of the following errors or fraudulent practices?

a. An accounts receivable clerk issues fictitious credit memos to a customer (who is also a friend) for goods that were supposedly returned from previous sales.

b. Sales have been sharply rising since salespersons were placed on a commission basis, but uncollectible accounts receivable have risen even more sharply.

c. An accounts receivable clerk improperly writes off the balance in a customer's account to conceal the theft of cash.

d. A billing clerk correctly prepares a sales invoice in the amount of $3800.00, but the invoice is entered as $3008.00 in the sales journal and posted in the latter amount to the general ledger and accounts receivable ledger.

e. The magnetic tape containing the accounts receivable master file is accidentally used as a scratch (output) tape during a processing run for a separate application, with the result that the accounts are wiped out.

f. A mail room clerk accidentally omits the number of the customer when entering a remittance via a mail room terminal.

g. A sales order clerk accidentally enters the quantity 2000 when entering an order on her terminal for motorcycles from a small dealer.

h. The cashier, who enters over-the-counter payments from customers directly into the computer system, accidentally enters the name of a nonexistent customer on receiving a payment; when the cash remittances are later posted to the accounts by an updating program, the amount relating to the erroneously entered customer name cannot be posted.

i. The accounts receivable department prepares 100 remittance advices for transmittal to computer operations for processing; however, two of the advices are accidentally removed before the batch is transmitted, and thus the amounts of only 98 advices are posted to the accounts receivable records.

j. A warehouse worker takes merchandise from the warehouse for his personal use and covers the theft by deducting the quantities taken from the inventory records.

k. A programmer misunderstands the sales transaction processing procedure and makes several logic errors when modifying a sales invoicing program.

l. An employee in the cash receipts department accesses her personnel records via a terminal and increases her salary level.

m. A sales invoice is accidentally misplaced just after being prepared and thus not mailed to the affected customer; the omission is never detected.

n. Customers are often charged for merchandise items that they do not order and are not shipped.

o. A firm processes its sales transactions in batches and feels confident that all credit sales are properly billed to customers; however, the head of the accounts receivable department often has difficulty in tracing individual sales transactions.

p. The accounts receivable control account is generally out of balance with the total of the individual customer account records at the end of an accounting period.

q. An order-entry clerk prepares a credit memo relating to a sale made to her sister-in-law; thus, the sister-in-law's account balance is reduced by the amount of the credit, even though she kept the goods acquired through the sale.

r. A general ledger clerk forgets to post Wednesday's total cash receipts, amounting to $2397.

12-22. Fast Burger is a chain of fast-food establishments. List the control objectives to be achieved during cash sales transactions, as well as the internal accounting controls or security measures needed to achieve the objectives.

(CPA *adapted*)

12-23. Ajax, Inc., recently installed a new computer-based system to process more efficiently the shipping, billing, and accounts receivable records. During a review, an auditor determined the following information concerning the new system.

Each major application—that is, shipping, billing, cash receipts, and so forth—is permanently assigned to a specific computer operator responsible for making program changes, running the program, and reconciling the computer log. Responsibility for the custody and control over tape files and system documentation is randomly rotated among the computer operators on a monthly basis to prevent any one person from having access to the tapes and documentation at all times. Each computer programmer and computer operator has access to the computer room via a magnetic card containing an individual digital code. The systems analyst and the supervisor of the computer operators do not have access to the computer room.

The system documentation consists of the following items: program listing, error listing, logs, and record layouts. To increase efficiency, batch totals and processing controls are omitted from the system.

Ajax ships its products directly from two warehouses, which forward shipping notices to general accounting. There, the billing clerk enters the price of the item and accounts for the numerical sequence of the shipping notices. The billing clerk also prepares daily adding machine tapes of the units shipped and the sales amounts. Shipping notices and adding machine tapes are forwarded to the computer department for processing. The computer output consists of

- A three-part sales invoice that is forwarded to the billing clerk.
- A daily sales register showing the aggregate totals of units shipped and sales amounts that the computer operator compares to the adding machine tapes.

The billing clerk mails two copies of each invoice to the customer and retains the third copy in an open invoice file that serves as a detail accounts receivable record.

Required

Describe one specific recommendation for correcting each control weakness in the new system and for correcting each weakness or inefficiency in the procedures for processing and controlling shipping notices and sales invoices.

(CPA *adapted*)

12-24. Refer to Figure 12-30.

Required

a. Modify the form to show balances on hand in terms of amounts as well as quantities.

b. Reflect the following transactions concerning lawnmowers:

A receipt of 180 units on December 16, 1997 (R.R. 328)

A sale of 50 units on December 22, 1997 (S.O. 2729)

A sale of 90 units on December 24, 1997 (S.O. 2802)

A sale of 60 units on December 29, 1997 (S.O. 2857)

A purchase on December 31, 1997 (P.O. 831)

c. Design a computerized record layout of a merchandise inventory record that contains the data shown in the figure, as affected by the transactions in **b** above. Assume that the transactions pertaining to lawnmowers begin on 11-14-97, as shown in the figure, and end on 12-31-97.

12-25. An auditor's working papers include the narrative description below of the cash receipts and billing portions of the internal control structure of Rural Building Supplies, Inc. Rural is a single-store retailer that sells a variety of tools, garden supplies, lumber, small appliances, and electrical fixtures to the public, although about half of Rural's sales are to construction contractors on account. Rural employs 12 salaried sales associates, a credit manager, three full-time clerical workers, and several part-time cash register clerks and assistant bookkeepers. The full-time clerical workers perform such tasks as cash receipts, billing, and accounting and are adequately bonded. They are referred to in the narrative as "accounts receivable supervisor," "cashier," and "bookkeeper."

Narrative

Retail customers pay for merchandise by cash or credit card at cash registers when merchandise is purchased. A contractor may purchase merchandise on account if approved by the credit manager based only on the manager's familiarity with the contractor's reputation. After credit is approved, the sales associate files a prenumbered charge form with the accounts receivable (A/R) supervisor to set up the receivable.

The A/R supervisor independently verifies the pricing and other details on the charge form by reference to a management-authorized price list, corrects any errors, prepares the invoice, and supervises a part-time employee who mails the invoice to the contractor. The A/R supervisor electronically posts the details of the invoice in the A/R subsidiary ledger; simultaneously, the transaction's details are transmitted to the bookkeeper. The A/R supervisor also prepares a monthly computer-generated A/R subsidiary ledger without a reconciliation with the A/R control account and a monthly report of overdue accounts.

The cash receipts functions are performed by the cashier who also supervises the cash register clerks. The cashier opens the mail, compares each check with the enclosed remittance advice, stamps each check "For Deposit Only," and lists checks for deposit. The cashier then gives the remittance advices to the bookkeeper for recording. The cashier deposits the checks daily separate from the daily deposit of cash register receipts. The cashier retains the verified deposit slips to assist in reconciling the monthly bank statements, but forwards to the bookkeeper a copy of the daily cash register summary. The cashier does not have access to the journals or ledgers.

The bookkeeper receives the details of transactions from the A/R supervisor and the cashier for journalizing and posting to the general ledger. After recording the remittance advices received from the cashier, the bookkeeper electronically transmits the remittance information to the A/R supervisor for subsidiary ledger updating. The bookkeeper sends monthly statements to contractors with unpaid balances upon receipt of the monthly report of overdue balances from the A/R supervisor. The bookkeeper authorizes the A/R supervisor to write off accounts as uncollectible when six months have passed since the initial overdue notice was sent. At this time, the credit manager is notified by the bookkeeper not to grant additional credit to that contractor.

Required

Based only on the information in the narrative, describe the internal control weaknesses in Rural's internal control structure concerning the cash receipts and billing functions. Organize the weaknesses by employee job function: Credit manager, A/R supervisor, Cashier, and Bookkeeper. Do not describe how to correct the weaknesses.

(CPA *adapted*)

12-26. The Sunshine Housewares Company of Evansville, Indiana, is organized on a divisional basis, with each division having profit responsibility. The kitchenwares division has three product lines: utensils, ceramic cookwares, and cutlery. Each product line has a separate markup percentage. The division's 80 salespersons sell the three product lines to department stores, hardware stores, and other retail outlets. Groups of 10 salespersons are assigned to each of 8 branch offices. At the end of each day, the salespersons submit to their branch offices call reports that show, for each call, the type of outlet visited, the time involved, and the result of the call. At the end of each week, they submit a report of expenses based on mileage traveled, telephone calls made, and meals and lodging purchased.

Required

a. Design a salesperson's call report.

b. Design a weekly report for a branch manager that will enable him or her to evaluate the performances of all salespersons within the branch and the levels of expenses incurred. Each salesperson is assigned a weekly quota in terms of sales amounts and contributions to profits. Each branch office has an expense budget that includes office salaries, supplies, and miscellaneous expenses in addition to the expense budgets for the salespersons.

c. Design a monthly report for the general sales manager that will enable her to evaluate the performances of all branch offices, in terms of sales, contributions to profits, and expenses incurred. The general sales office incurs the same type of expenses as the branches.

d. Design for the marketing vice-president a monthly report that will enable him to evaluate the performances of all major subordinate units. In addition to the sales manager for the kitchenwares division, other managers reporting to the marketing vice-president are the sales manager for the patio division, the sales manager for the general housewares division, an advertising manager, and a manager of marketing planning. The vice-president's office incurs the expenses noted in **b,** plus office equipment expense.

e. Design a code by which to classify costs incurred by salespersons and organizational units within the marketing function.

12-27. Sullivan Sport is a large distributor of all types of recreational equipment. All sales are made on account with terms of net 30 days from the date of shipment. The number of delinquent accounts as well as uncollectible accounts has increased significantly during the last twelve months. Customers frequently complain of errors in their accounts. Management believes that the information generated by the present accounts receivable system is inadequate and untimely.

The current accounts receivable system was developed when Sullivan began operations in 1993. A new computer was installed 18 months ago. The accounts receivable application was not revised at that time because other applications were considered more important. Management has now asked the systems department to design a new accounts receivable system to satisfy the following objectives.

- Produce current and timely reports about customers that will
    aid in controlling bad debts.
    notify the sales department of delinquent customer accounts (those that should lose credit privileges).
    notify the sales department of customers with uncollectible accounts (accounts to be closed and written off).
- Notify customers on a timely basis regarding amounts owed to Sullivan.
    changes in account status (loss of charge privileges).
- Minimize the chance for errors in customers' accounts.

Input data for the system will be taken from four source documents—credit applications, sales invoices,

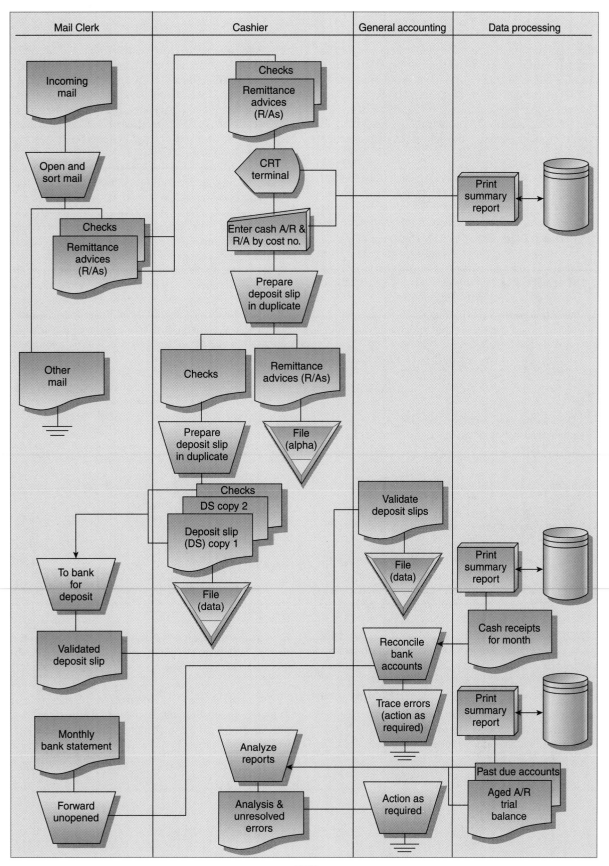

cash payment remittances, and credit memoranda. The accounts receivable master file will be maintained on a machine-readable file by customer account number.

The preliminary design of the new accounts receivable system has been completed by the systems department. A brief description of the proposed reports and other outputs generated by the system are detailed below.

1. **Accounts Receivable Register.** A daily alphabetical listing of all customers' accounts that shows the balance as of the last statement, activity since the last statement, and the current account balance.

2. **Customer Statements.** Monthly statements for each customer showing activity since the last statement and new account balance; the top portion of the statement is to be returned with the payment and serves as the cash payment remittance.

3. **Activity Reports.** Monthly reports that show
   a. customers who have not purchased any merchandise for 90 days.
   b. customers whose account balances exceed their credit limit.
   c. customers who have current sales on account but are delinquent.

4. **Delinquency and Write-off Register.** A monthly alphabetical listing of delinquent or closed customers' accounts.

Required

a. Identify the data that Sullivan Sport should capture and store in the computer-based accounts receivable file records for each customer.

b. (1) Review the proposed reports to be generated by Sullivan Sport's new accounts receivable system, and discuss whether these reports are adequate to satisfy the objectives designated by management.

(2) Recommend changes, additions, and/or deletions that should be made to the proposed reporting structure to be generated from Sullivan Sport's new accounts receivable system.

(CMA *adapted*)

12-28. VBR Company of Lubbock, Texas, has recently installed a new computer system that has on-line, real-time capability. Cathode-ray tube terminals are used for data entry and inquiry. A new cash receipts and accounts receivable file maintenance system has been designed and implemented for use with this new equipment. All programs have been written and tested, and the new system is being run in parallel with the old system. After two weeks of parallel operation, no differences have been observed between the two systems other than keying errors on the old system.

Al Brand, data processing manager, is enthusiastic about the new equipment and system. He reveals that the system was designed, coded, compiled, debugged, and tested by programmers utilizing an on-line CRT terminal installed specifically for around-the-clock use by the programming staff; he has claimed that this access to the computer saved one-third in programming elapsed time. All files, including accounts receivable, are on-line at all times as the firm moves toward a full database mode. All programs, new and old, are available at all times for recall into primary storage for scheduled operating use or for program maintenance. Program documentation and actual tests confirm that data-entry edits in the new system include all conventional data-error and validity checks appropriate to the system.

Inquiries have confirmed that the new system conforms precisely to the flowchart, part of which appears on page 527. A turnaround copy of the invoice is used as a remittance advice (R/A) by 99 percent of the customers; if the R/A is missing, the cashier applies the payment to a selected invoice. Sales terms are net 60 days, but payment patterns are sporadic. Statements are not mailed to customers. Late payments are commonplace and are not vigorously pursued. VBR does not have a bad-debt program, because bad-debt losses average only 0.5 percent of sales.

Required

a. Identify all control weaknesses and other defects in the new system, and propose how each may be corrected.

b. Redraw the computer system flowchart to reflect the design improvements and sound flowcharting technique.

(CMA *adapted*)

12-29. *Datacruncher Office Equipment, Inc. (Continuing Case)* Prepare a system flowchart and a data-flow diagram that pertain to the current procedure for the revenue cycle, as described in Case A.

CHAPTER 13

THE EXPENDITURE CYCLE

THE LEARNING OBJECTIVES FOR THIS CHAPTER ARE TO ENABLE YOU TO:

1. Describe the objectives, functions, organizational relationships, and decisions pertinent to the expenditure cycle.

2. Identify the expenditure cycle's data sources and forms of input.

3. Identify the files and data structures that are needed within the data base for the expenditure cycle.

4. Describe the steps and approaches employed in processing the transaction data flows through the expenditure cycle.

5. List the internal controls needed for the expenditure cycle.

6. Describe a variety of operational and managerial reports and other outputs that may be generated by the expenditure cycle.

INTRODUCTION

Infoage, Inc., Ann Strong, and all other organizations make expenditures for goods and services. Goods may consist of merchandise, raw materials, parts, subassemblies, supplies, and fixed assets. Services may include those provided by outside parties, such as telephone and legal services, as well as the labor provided by the organization's employees. Conceptually all of these goods and services may be encompassed by the expenditure cycle. Because this cycle involves the outflow of cash, it is the counterpoint to the revenue cycle, which provides inflows of cash.

Most acquired goods and services represent resources to a firm. Merchandise and raw materials and supplies are materials resources, fixed assets (also called plant assets or capital assets) are fa-

cilities resources, and hours worked by employees are human service resources. Outside services add value to all of these resources. Since most of the transaction activity involves materials and outside services, expenditures for materials and services are the subject of this chapter. Expenditures for facilities (fixed assets) and human resources (employee services), which have many similiarities to those for materials and services, are covered in Appendix 2 to Chapter 14.

OVERVIEW

OBJECTIVES OF THE CYCLE

The major purpose of the expenditure cycle is to facilitate the exchange of cash with suppliers (vendors) for needed goods (materials) and services.

Typical objectives within this broad purpose are (1) to ensure that all goods and services are ordered as needed, (2) to receive all ordered goods and verify that they are in good condition, (3) to safeguard goods until needed, (4) to determine that invoices pertaining to goods and services are valid and correct, (5) to record and classify the expenditures promptly and accurately, (6) to post obligations and cash disbursements to proper suppliers' accounts in the accounts payable ledger, (7) to ensure that all cash disbursements are related to authorized expeditures, and (8) to record and classify cash disbursements promptly and accurately. As by-products, the expenditure cycle captures information relating to purchases, suppliers, and payables.

FUNCTIONS OF THE CYCLE

When goods (i.e., merchandise, supplies, or raw materials) are purchased, the events or functions of the expenditure cycle consist of recognizing the need for the goods, placing the order, receiving and storing the goods, ascertaining the validity of the payment obligation, preparing the cash disbursement, maintaining the accounts payable, posting transactions to the general ledger, and preparing needed financial reports and other outputs. In the case of services, the functions of receiving and storing the goods are replaced by the function of accepting the ordered services. In the case of direct payments by cash (as is done through a petty-cash fund), the function of maintaining the payables records is unnecessary. Functions pertaining to the purchase of goods or services, pictured in Figure 13-1, are examined in the survey that follows.

Recognize the Need for Goods or Services   The need for goods is often triggered by inventory records, which show the on-hand quantity or balance of each inventory item (whether merchandise, supply, or raw material). These records are routinely checked by an inventory clerk or a computer program. When the current balance of an item falls below a preestablished reorder point, the inventory level is viewed as being below a safety stock level. Thus, according to the reorder point procedure, the time for reordering has arrived. The organizational unit assigned to reorder goods must be notified.

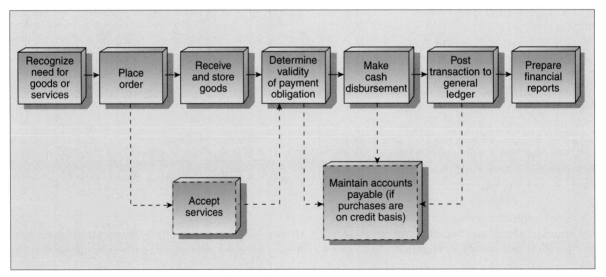

FIGURE 13-1   Typical functions of an expenditure cycle.

A written **purchase requisition** generally is employed to authorize the purchasing department to place an order for goods or services. Figure 13-2 shows a prenumbered requisition for goods that has been prepared by a clerk within Infoage's accounting function. Key data elements conveyed by a purchase requisition include the quantities and identifications of the goods to be purchased, plus the date needed, the name of the requestor and department, and the approver's name or initials. Optional data include the suggested supplier (vendor), unit prices, and shipping instructions.

Other means of recognizing needs are also employed by most firms. A back-order request from the sales procedure signals the need to place an order for a specific customer. A long-term procurement contract may specify that orders be initiated at regular intervals. Some firms employ materials requirements planning and just-in-time procedures, as discussed in Chapter 14.

Services may be acquired on a continuing basis (e.g., utilities), on a regular but noncontinuing basis (e.g., once-a-year audit service), or on an ad hoc basis (e.g., a systems consulting service). The need for a service is generally initiated by the manager of a department, division, or other organizational unit of the firm. Sometimes the need is brought to the attention of such managers by agents who represent the service, such as the salesperson of an office cleaning service.

Place an Order for Goods or Services   When a need is recognized, a legally binding **purchase order** must be placed with a supplier. Occasionally the order is placed by the person or unit that recognizes the need. For instance, a vice-president may sign an agreement with a management consultant concerning an organizational redesign project. Nevertheless, most orders for goods and services are placed through a central purchasing department. In merchandising firms buyers in this purchasing department who specialize in particular lines do the actual ordering.

The principal task in placing an order is to select the supplier (also called the vendor). Suppliers of goods are usually selected on the basis of such criteria as

INFOAGE, INC.				No. 11359
Purchase Requisition				

Deliver To: Receiving Dock		Requisition Date: 10/7/97
		Date Wanted: 10/16/97
Suggested Vendor: Databytes Co.		

Item No.	Description	Quantity	Unit Price
512364	Putz 500 Inkjet Printer	40	$200.00
586430	H-P High Capacity Inkjet Cartridge	300	20.00

Requested By: S. Swink	Approved By: J. Dyson	Department: Inventory control	Account No. 1114

FIGURE 13-2   A purchase requisition prepared by Infoage, Inc.

reliability, comparative unit prices, lead times required before goods are received, and after-sales services such as "hot lines." The quality level of goods is an increasingly important consideration in this age of international competition. In the case of consumer merchandise, styling is often a factor. After the supplier is selected, the specifications concerning unit prices, quality, and other matters are listed in writing on a purchase order.

The tasks of selecting suppliers and stating specifications can be relatively simple. On many occasions the buyers in the purchasing department may accept a supplier suggested by the requisitioning department. When the choice of the supplier is not clear-cut, the buyers may search through the current catalogs of approved suppliers, locate the best prices and styling, and complete the purchase order forms.

Complications can arise in a few cases, however. Consider the situation in which the needed goods are not routinely available and for which there are no established prices. In this situation competitive bids should be obtained. The bidding procedure, which should be set by management policy, usually involves sending a **request for proposal (RFP)** to each of several prospective suppliers. Upon receiving the bids or proposals from those suppliers who respond, the purchasing manager evaluates them by means of a rating procedure. If one of the bids is preferable, it is accepted and the order is placed; if necessary, a contract is also signed.

Figure 13-3 displays a purchase order prepared by an authorized buyer within Infoage, in response to the purchase requisition shown in Figure 13-2. The heading contains the supplier's name and address, shipping instructions, and reference items. The body contains one or more line items, with each line item pertaining to a single item of merchandise or material being ordered. Although unit prices for the various line items are included, cost extensions are not normally provided because the unit prices are tentative. If the supplier agrees to all stated terms and conditions of the order, it is binding on Infoage.

Several copies of the purchase order are needed. Two copies are mailed to the supplier. In the case of goods, additional copies are forwarded or made accessible to the inventory control department, receiving department, and accounts payable department.

The inventory control department adds the quantities of the items ordered to the inventory records, in order to show their "on order" status.

Receive and Store Goods or Accept Services Often a period of time elapses between the ordering date and the receiving date. This period is called the lead time. When incoming goods do arrive, they are directed to a receiving dock. There the packing slip with the goods is matched to the receiving department's copy of the purchase order, which authorizes the goods to be accepted.

Accepted goods are unloaded, counted, inspected for damage, and checked to see that all goods conform exactly to specifications in the order. The receiving clerk records the count and notes the condition of the goods on a receiving document—usually called a **receiving report**. He or she must count the goods, since the copy of the purchase order is a "blind copy"—with the ordered quantities and unit prices blacked out. Then the goods are moved, with the receiving document, to an inventory storeroom or warehouse.

If the received goods have been ordered but have certain deficiencies, such as lower-than-specified quality or breakage, they may be accepted on the condition that an allowance be granted by the supplier (vendor). However, if the goods vary so widely from specifications that they are unacceptable, they should be returned.

```
┌──────────────────────────────────────────────────────────────────────────┐
│                            INFOAGE, INC.                    No. 76531      │
│                           6000 Lakeshore Dr.                               │
│                           Seattle, WA 98195                                │
│                          Phone (206) 543-1217                              │
│                                                                            │
│                            PURCHASE ORDER                                  │
│                                                                            │
│        ┌  Databytes Co.                    Show purchase order             │
│        │  2020 Millbrae Rd.                number above on all             │
│   To:  │  Menlo Park, CA 94025             shipping documents              │
│        └                                   and invoices.                   │
└──────────────────────────────────────────────────────────────────────────┘
```

Order Date 10/9/97	Vendor No. 6810	Ship Via Common carrier—truck	FOB Shipping point	Terms 2/10, net 30

Expected Date 10/16/97	Requis. No. 11359	Requis. By S. Swink	Special Conditions Foam packing needed

Line	Quantity	Item No.	Description	Unit Price
1	40	512364	Putz 500 Inkjet Printer	$200.00
2	300	586430	H-P High Capacity Inkjet Cartridge	20.00

This order is not binding upon buyer unless accepted under the terms and conditions on the reverse side. Acknowledgment copy should be executed and returned promptly.

Melanie Powers

Authorized Buyer

FIGURE 13-3   A purchase order prepared by Infoage, Inc.

Figure 13-4 shows a prenumbered receiving report prepared by a clerk in Infoage's receiving department. The document pertains to the goods ordered on the purchase order in Figure 13-3.

Receiving reports may be used to reflect the receipt of goods on consignment or goods returned by dissatisfied customers as well as goods based on purchase orders. However, services do not require the use of receiving reports because they are intangible. If the service is provided over an extended period of time, or if quality is a factor, the receiving firm often prepares a written acceptance or evaluation. If the service is a routine one, such as electrical power service, the bill or invoice from the supplier is sufficient.

As a by-product of this purchasing and receiving procedure, appropriate postings are made to inventory records when goods are involved. Usually the quantities ordered as well as the quantities received are posted, so that the status is reflected in the inventory records. On the other hand, no postings are made to the ledgers as a result of ordering or receiving, since the dollar amounts of the transactions are not known.

Ascertain Validity of the Payment Obligation   In response to a purchase order, a supplier sends the acquiring firm a **supplier's (vendor's) invoice.** (To the supplier, an invoice is in effect a sales invoice, such as shown in Figure 12-6.) Each received

INFOAGE, INC.
RECEIVING REPORT

Date **10/15/97**   No. 15492

Vendor **Databytes Co.**		Purchase Order No. **76531**

Carrier **Simmons Trucking**	Shipping Weight **528 #**	No. Packages **2**

Freight Bill No. ———	Freight Charges $ **0.00**	Consignment? Yes ☐ No ☑

Item No.	Description	Quantity	Condition
512364	Putz 500 Inkjet Printer	40	Good
586430	H-P Inkjet Cart.	300	"

Received By **WF**	Checked By **GPD**	Delivered By **M. Toolson**

FIGURE 13-4   A receiving report or record prepared by Infoage, Inc.

invoice is first listed in a register. This register, or log, may be called an invoice register or purchase journal. Each invoice in the batch received is checked against supporting documents showing that the goods or services were duly ordered and received or accepted. This checking, called **vouching,** includes such steps as (1) tracing all data items (e.g., dates, unit prices, quantities) to the supporting documents (i.e., purchase order, receiving report), (2) recalculating extensions and totals, and (3) ascertaining payment terms. All questionable items and adjustments are settled with the supplier.

When the validity of a purchase transaction amount is determined, the amount must be recognized as a liability and an obligation to be paid when due. This amount is based on the supplier's invoice, which is in effect the posting medium to the accounting cycle. The various charges on an invoice are also distributed to the proper inventory or expense accounts. Then the invoice is approved for payment, by some type of notation, and filed in an open payables file according to the date on which it is due to be paid.

If the **voucher system** is employed, a payment voucher is also prepared. Called a **disbursement voucher,** this payment document accommodates one or more invoices from a single supplier. Figure 13-5 illustrates a disbursement voucher, together with the other components of a voucher system. A **voucher register**, which serves as a journal, records the disbursement vouchers. Totals of obligations are posted from the voucher register, rather than from an invoice register, to the general ledger accounts. A disbursement voucher provides an added measure of control, since it is prenumbered. Fewer checks need to be written, since multiple invoices can be accumulated on vouchers.

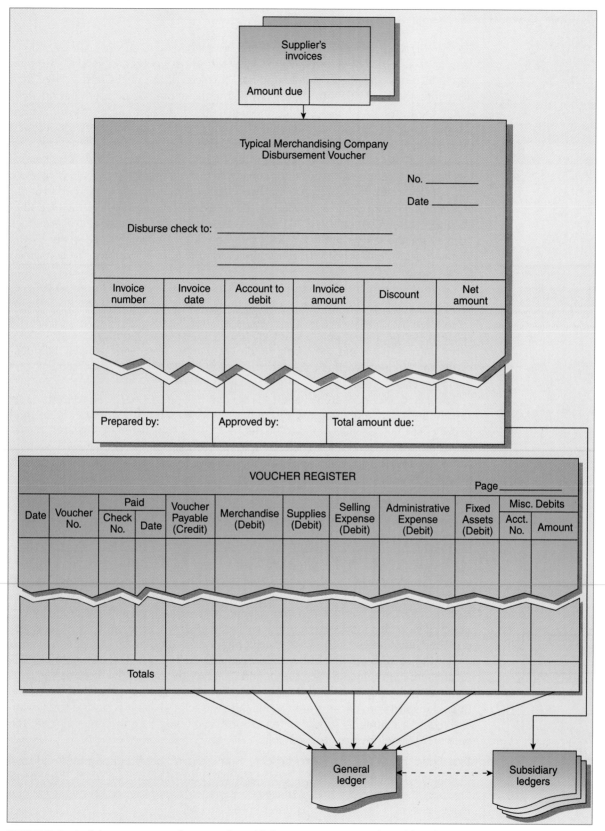

FIGURE 13-5   A disbursement voucher, together with key accounting records used in the voucher system.

Prepare the Cash Disbursement   In some cases goods and services are payable in cash upon receipt or even in advance. However, most goods and services are paid on credit terms specified on the suppliers' invoices. If the credit terms allow cash discounts, the acquiring firm should pay before the end of the discount period. Preferably the firm should also employ the net method of recording purchases. Under the net method the invoiced amounts are entered and posted *net* of the allowed purchase discounts; if discounts are missed, they are charged to a "Purchase Discounts Lost" account. By highlighting such losses, the account serves as a control mechanism. Goods and services not subject to discounts should be paid before the due dates stated on the suppliers' invoices. If goods and services are provided under contracts calling for progress payments, the conditions specifying the payment points should be carefully monitored. If goods are accepted on consignment, the firm does not pay for the goods until they are sold. Sometimes payments are made by the ultimate customers directly to the supplier, and the firm handling the consigned goods receives a fee.

Disbursement checks (known generally as checks) are prepared on the basis of approved suppliers' invoices. Each day a batch is prepared from those invoices (or vouchers) in the open payables file that have become due. The unsigned checks are given to the person or persons designated by management policy to sign checks. Often these persons are the cashier and/or treasurer. The signer reviews the documents that support each check, signs the check if it is a proper disbursement, and mails the check promptly.

Attached to checks are vouchers, as shown in Figure 13-6. The voucher portions specify the gross amounts and discounts, as well as the net amounts paid, and usually list the ledger accounts to be debited. Checks are listed in a cash disbursements journal, often called a **check register.** Copies of checks, known as check vouchers, are typically used as the posting media to the supplier accounts (if they are maintained as described next).

Maintain Accounts Payable   A firm must keep track of amounts owed to suppliers of goods and services. Two opposing approaches are currently in use.

In the first approach a separate record is maintained for each supplier with which the firm has a credit arrangement. The file containing these records is generally called the supplier or vendor file, although it is in effect the accounts payable subsidiary ledger. Each approved invoice in a batch is credited to the pertinent supplier's account. A variation of this approach is to prepare a disbursement voucher for one or more invoices, and to post from the voucher to the supplier's account in the ledger. In either case checks are entered in a cash disbursements journal or check register, and their amounts are debited to the suppliers' accounts.

In the second approach, the ledgerless approach, no formal accounts payable records are maintained during the period. Instead, the unpaid invoices or vouchers are filed and paid when due. At the end of each accounting period all remaining unpaid invoices or vouchers are totaled, and the total amount is posted to the general ledger accounts. A supplier file is kept, but it contains only copies of both the paid and unpaid invoices (or vouchers).

Post Transactions to the General Ledger   Summarized batches of payables and cash disbursements are posted to the general ledger. Journal entries on which these postings are based represent the interface between the expenditure cycle and the general ledger system. They are detailed later in the chapter.

Prepare Needed Financial Reports and Other Outputs   A variety of outputs are generated as by-products of the aforementioned expenditure cycle functions. Examples are summaries of purchases and disbursements, evaluations of suppliers, and sum-

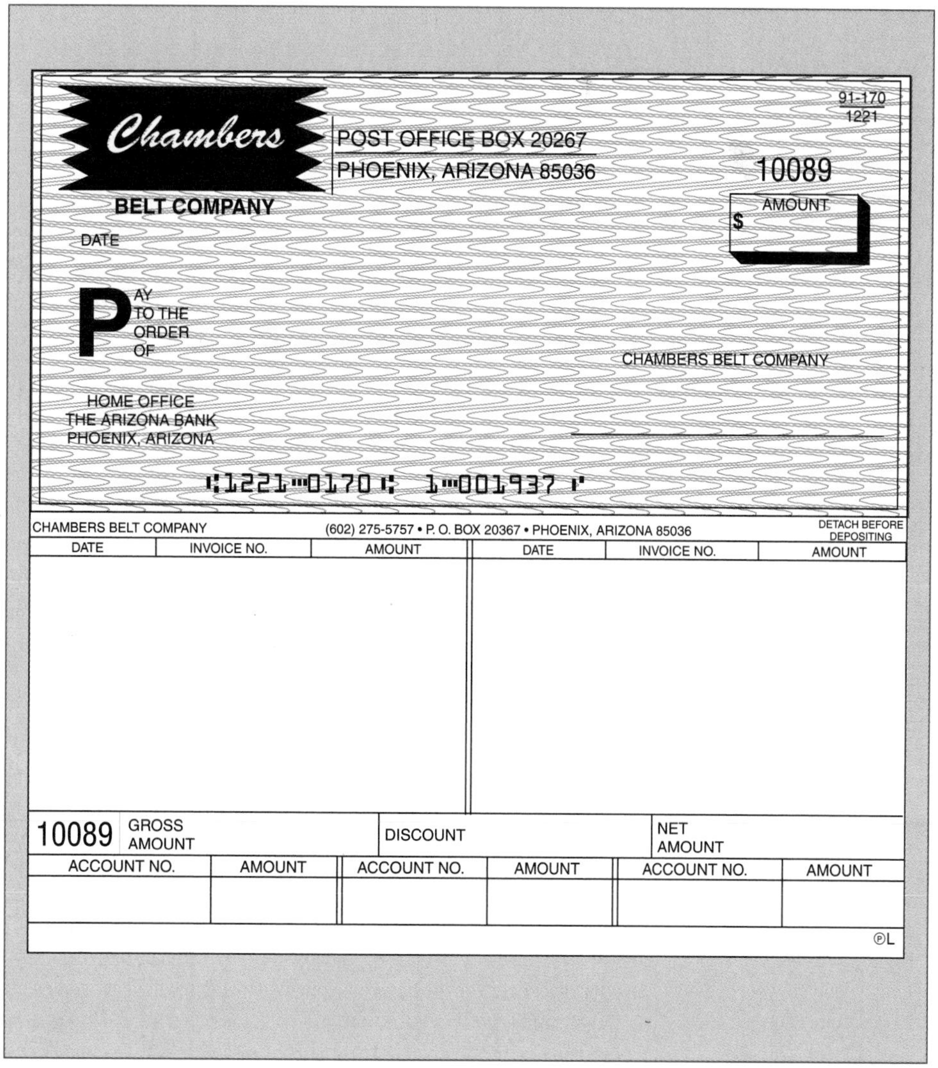
Chambers
BELT COMPANY
POST OFFICE BOX 20267
PHOENIX, ARIZONA 85036
91-170
1221
10089
AMOUNT
$
DATE
PAY TO THE ORDER OF
CHAMBERS BELT COMPANY
HOME OFFICE
THE ARIZONA BANK
PHOENIX, ARIZONA
⑆1221⑈0170⑆ 1⑈001937⑈

CHAMBERS BELT COMPANY (602) 275-5757 • P. O. BOX 20367 • PHOENIX, ARIZONA 85036 DETACH BEFORE DEPOSITING

DATE	INVOICE NO.	AMOUNT	DATE	INVOICE NO.	AMOUNT

10089 GROSS AMOUNT	DISCOUNT	NET AMOUNT

ACCOUNT NO.	AMOUNT	ACCOUNT NO.	AMOUNT	ACCOUNT NO.	AMOUNT

®L

FIGURE 13-6 A check with attached voucher.

maries of open payables. Displays of individual supplier accounts and other specific information are also available if an on-line computer-based system is employed.

Other Related Functions Additional functions of interest include payroll disbursements, capital expenditures, purchase returns and allowances, miscellaneous cash disbursements, and petty-cash disbursements. Payroll disbursements and capital expenditures are discussed in Appendix 2 to Chapter 14. The remaining functions are briefly discussed next.

- ***Handling purchase returns and allowances.*** Purchase returns arise when the purchasing firm is unsatisfied with ordered goods. Purchase allowances are adjustments in prices granted to the purchasing firm as compensation for damaged goods, overages (more goods delivered than ordered), or such specified deficiencies as overcharges. They may be triggered when the goods are received and inspected or when the suppliers' invoices are being vouched. The person who discovers the needed adjustment should notify the purchasing department. A buyer or purchasing manager prepares a prenumbered **debit memorandum**, which notifies the selling firm and the accounts payable department that the account balance is to be reduced by a stated amount. The accounts payable department clerk pulls the supplier's invoice and supporting documents. After comparing these documents, the clerk prepares a journal voucher to reflect the transaction. Other clerks (or the computer system) post the adjustment to the accounts payable ledger and general ledger.

In the case of a return, copies of the debit memorandum are also sent to the storeroom (or receiving department) and shipping department. The goods being returned are then released to the shipping department, which counts the goods, notes the count on the debit memorandum, and ships. The shipping department then forwards the debit memorandum to the accounts payable department, which performs the steps just described.

- **Disbursing cash for miscellaneous purposes.** In addition to acquiring fixed assets, miscellaneous cash disbursements include amounts paid to acquire investments, to repurchase the firm's own stock, and to discharge bank loans and mortgages. These disbursements are generally recorded in the cash disbursements journal, although some firms record them on journal vouchers.

- **Processing petty-cash disbursements.** Petty-cash funds are used to make currency payments for expenses involving small amounts. In effect a petty-cash disbursement is a type of miscellaneous disbursement. In order to control these amounts, an **imprest system** is normally used. It begins with the establishment of a petty-cash fund at some level (e.g., $500). The fund's balance remains fixed in the general ledger account at the established level. However, the currency itself, which is locked in a cash box or drawer, fluctuates in amount during use. One person, who has no other responsibilities related to cash, is assigned to administer the fund. This petty-cash custodian prepares in ink a petty-cash voucher for each disbursement from the fund, which the payee signs before receiving currency. At all times the total amount of the paid vouchers plus the cash remaining in the box or drawer should equal the established amount of the fund. When the remaining currency reaches a low point, the accounts payable department is requested to prepare a disbursement voucher. The petty-cash vouchers are attached to this voucher, together with a prepared check. The authorized check signer reviews the vouchers and signs the check. Then the custodian cashes the check and replenishes the fund. The replenishment check is listed in the check register. The imprest system allows small amounts to be disbursed conveniently, without the loss of effective control over the cash resource.

RELATIONSHIPS TO THE ORGANIZATION

The array of responsibilities within the expenditure cycle are typically under the direction of the inventory management and finance/accounting organizational functions, as Figure 13-7 portrays. The expenditure cycle therefore involves the interaction of the inventory management information system and the accounting information system (AIS). Moreover, the results attained and information generated by the expenditure cycle further the objectives of these organizational functions.

Inventory Management The organizational function known as **inventory management** has, in the context of a merchandising firm, the objective of managing the merchandise inventory that the firm acquires for resale. In merchandising firms, such as Infoage, it may be one of the principal functions reporting to the president. In manufacturing firms the activities involved in inventory management may be combined with production to form a broader logistics function. The distribution function

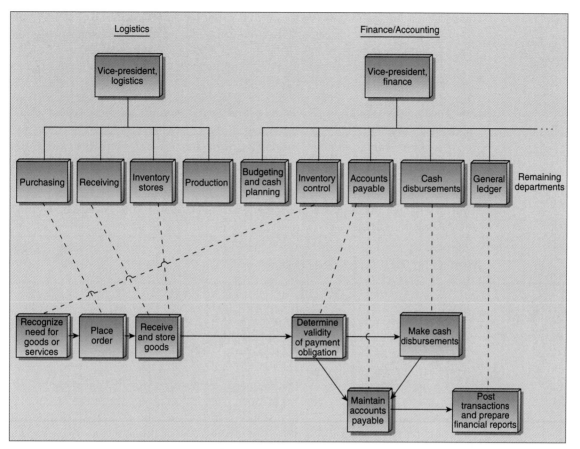

FIGURE 13-7   Relationships of organizational units to expenditure cycle functions.

might be included in this broad function or may alternatively be assigned to the marketing/distribution function. Besides planning responsibilities, inventory management includes purchasing, receiving, and storing.

Purchasing focuses primarily on selecting the most suitable suppliers or vendors from whom to order goods and services. It makes the selections on the basis of such factors as the unit prices charged for the goods or services, the quality of the goods or services offered, the terms and promised delivery dates, and the supplier's reliability. Together with inventory control (which is under the accounting function), purchasing ascertains the quantity of goods to acquire. The optimal order quantity is determined by a formula that includes such factors as the expected demand for the good, the carrying cost, and the ordering cost. However, this formula is normally applied only to the high-cost or high-volume goods. Order quantities for low-cost or low-volume goods are more likely to be determined on a rough basis that seeks to avoid stockouts. In some cases a good buying opportunity or a price break determines the quantities to order.

Receiving has the responsibilities of accepting only those goods that were ordered, verifying their quantities and condition, and moving the goods to the storeroom.

Storing has the responsibilities of safeguarding the goods from theft and loss and deterioration, and of assembling them promptly when proper requisitions or requests are presented.

Finance/Accounting   The objectives of financial and accounting management relate broadly to funds, data, information, planning, and control over resources. With respect to the expenditure cycle, the objectives are limited to cash planning and control, to data pertaining to purchases and suppliers' accounts, to inventory control, and to information pertaining to cash and purchases and suppliers.

The top financial manager in many firms is the vice-president of finance. Two managers often report directly to this top manager: a treasurer and a controller. The cashier is one important manager reporting to the treasurer. The treasurer's responsibilities include cash disbursements, whereas the controller's responsibilities include inventory control, accounts payable, and the general ledger. *Cash disbursements*, an arm of the cashier, prepares checks for disbursement and maintains the related records. *Inventory control* maintains the records pertaining to inventory balances and initiates the reordering of goods. *Accounts payable* maintains the records of individual suppliers and approves their invoices for payment. *General ledger* maintains control over all asset, equity, expense, and income accounts. (Other units, such as budgeting, are described in Chapter 12.)

MANAGERIAL DECISION MAKING

Inventory management and financial managers must make decisions that influence the effectiveness of purchasing and disbursing cash. The aims of their decision making are (1) to minimize the costs of inventory management and cash management to their firm while maintaining sound long-term relations with the suppliers, employees, and other affected parties, and (2) to optimize the use of the resources devoted to the expenditure cycle.

Among the decisions that must be made, especially at the tactical and strategic levels, are those listed in Figure 13-8. Much of the information needed to make such decisions derives from the AIS. For instance, information concerning costs of ordering and carrying merchandise aids in making decisions concerning inventory levels and reordering times. Additional information, however, must be obtained—such as in-

---

Inventory Decisions
1. What levels of merchandise inventory should be stocked?
2. When should particular inventory items be reordered?
3. What quantities of particular inventory items should be reordered?
4. When should long-term purchase contracts be obtained for particular inventory items?
5. Which suppliers should be established as long-term sources of merchandise and supplies?
6. From which suppliers should particular inventory items be ordered?
7. What procedures should be followed in receiving and storing merchandise inventory?
8. What organizational units are to be included in the inventory management and logistics functions?
9. What logistics plans and budgets are to be established for the coming year?

Financial Decisions
1. What policies concerning purchase terms and discounts should be established?
2. What level of services should departments be allowed to acquire?
3. What accounts payable records are to be maintained concerning amounts owed to suppliers?
4. What financial plans and budgets are to be established for the coming year?
5. What sources of funds are to be employed?

FIGURE 13-8 Types of managerial decisions pertaining to the expenditure cycle.

Decision support systems can aid in selecting suitable suppliers from whom to order. Firms such as Rockwell Incorporated have built models to compute performance indexes for all bidding vendor (supplier) firms. Input factors for the models include late deliveries, errors in paperwork, damaged products, and so on. The indexes help buying firms to rank the suppliers and to eliminate unsat-isfactory suppliers, as well as to select those that appear to perform best.

Associated Grocers, a wholesale and retail grocery chain in the Pacific Northwest, developed an expert system to aid in selecting merchandise to sell in its 400 member stores. The knowledge base contains consumer preference trends, price trends, seasonality, indicators of changes in product mix, product movement volatility, and distribution factors. The expert system has been successful in enabling buyers to make product buying choices quickly, and thus to keep pace with a rapidly changing marketplace.*

*Carol E. Brown and Mary Ellen Phillips, "Expert Systems for Management Accountants." *Management Accounting* (January 1990), p. 20.

formation concerning the performance of suppliers and estimated stockout costs. Examples of other useful information are described in Chapter 15.

In addition to relevant information, decision making is aided by specialized systems that incorporate decision-modeling capabilities. A nearby vignette presents several examples of real-world decision-oriented systems.

DATA ENTRY

SOURCES

Data used in the expenditure cycle are mainly based on inputs from the inventory records and from suppliers. The inventory records are the primary source of most purchase transactions, while supplier invoices are the source of payable/disbursement transactions. Other sources are department heads, buyers, supplier history files, receiving and stores departments, and (in the case of manufacturing firms) the production departments.

FORMS OF INPUT

Most of the source documents involved in the expenditure cycle have been identified in our discussion of cycle functions. Figure 13-9 summarizes the documents needed by merchandising firms, especially those that employ manual processing systems. Accountants are particularly concerned with the supplier's invoice, debit memorandum, and disbursement check, since these forms initiate entries into the accounting cycle.

Most of the above-mentioned hard-copy documents are also likely to be used in firms employing computer-based processing. Documents provide visible and tangible evidence and are necessary for certain users. For instance, purchase orders in hard-copy form represent understandable evidence of purchase transactions, especially to those suppliers who are not electronically linked to the buying firms.

Purchase requisition. The initiating form in the expenditure cycle that authorizes the placement of an order for goods or services.

Purchase order. A formal, multicopy form prepared from the purchase requisition that binds the acquiring firm.

Receiving report. A document that records the receipt of goods.

Supplier's (vendor's) invoice. A billing document from the supplier who provides goods or services.

Disbursement voucher. A document within a voucher system that accumulates suppliers' invoices for payment.

Disbursement check. The final document in the expenditure cycle that provides payment to a supplier for some goods or services.

Debit memorandum. A document that authorizes a purchase return or allowance.

New supplier (vendor) form. A form used in the selection of new suppliers, showing such data as prices, types of goods or services provided, experience, credit standing, and references.

Request for proposal (or quotation). A form used in a competitive bidding procedure, showing the goods or services needed and the comparative prices, terms, and so on.

FIGURE 13-9   Documents pertaining to the expenditure cycle.

As we observed in Chapter 5, transaction data may be transcribed onto magnetic media from hard-copy documents. Increasingly, however, transaction data are being entered on-line with the aid of preformatted screens. Many firms employ such screens to enter data concerning requisitions, purchases, receipts of ordered goods, payables, purchase returns, and cash disbursement transactions. These screens, like simplified entry forms, may be designed to handle individual transactions or batches of transactions.

Figure 13-10 displays a preformatted screen for entering receipts of goods. This screen would be available through a terminal located in the receiving area. Data would be entered on-line by reference to a hard-copy receiving report that has just been completed by the receiving clerk, based on counts of incoming goods. The receiving report could appear similar to Figure 13-4, or it could be a simplified user-friendly structured input form.

Figure 13-10 utilizes the data in Figure 13-4, except that the quantity counted of item number 512364 is 38 units rather than the ordered quantity of 40. By employing on-line entry, however, a firm such as Infoage can gain significant help from the computer system. When the data-entry screen is first accessed, the system (i.e., data-entry and edit program) automatically enters the current date and assigns the receiving report number. As the receiving employee enters the purchase order number, the system accesses the on-line open purchase order file and echoes back the name of the vendor (supplier). Likewise, as he or she enters the item numbers the system echoes back the descriptions, taken from the on-line merchandise inventory file. Also, by means of a relationship edit check, the system compares the quantities ordered with the quantities received. It notes in the right-most field that a shortage is detected for item number 512364. Finally, the system prints a hard copy of the prenumbered receiving report, roughly in the format shown in Figure 13-4, and puts a copy of the record in an on-line receiving report file.

TRANSACTION CODING

Codes can aid the entry of purchases and cash disbursements transactions. In addition to codes for general ledger accounts, codes can be entered for suppliers,

Form:rdes

RECEIVING DATA ENTRY SCREEN

R.R. NO. 15429

DATE: 4/10/97

P.O. NO. 76531

RECEIVED BY: WF

VENDOR: DATABYTES CO.

LINE	ITEM NO.	QUANTITY	DESCRIPTION	SHORT/OVER
1	512364	38	Putz 500 Inkjet Printer	Short
2	586430	300	H-P High Capacity InkJet Cartridge	OK

VOID

SAVE

PRINT

EXIT

FIGURE 13-10 A preformatted screen for the entry of received goods by Infoage, Inc., from suppliers. *Note:* The computer system automatically enters the date, receiving report (R.R.) number, purchase order (P.O.) number, and description. The last two data elements are "echoed" from on-line files.

purchase orders, products, buyers, purchase contracts, and so on. When such codes are employed, various purchase analyses can be performed.

Group codes are useful when recording such transactions as purchases, since they encompass several dimensions. They may also be used to represent such entities as products, suppliers, and buyers. A product code for a battery sold by a retail chain, for instance, might include such fields as the following:

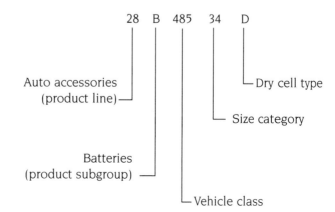

MASTER FILES

The *supplier (vendor) master file* contains records pertaining to individual suppliers or vendors. Each record contains such supplier data as supplier name, mailing address, phone number, and credit terms. The primary and sorting key of the file is the supplier number.

The *accounts payable master file* contains records that also pertain to suppliers, including at least the supplier identification (usually the supplier account number) and the current account balance.

The *merchandise inventory master file* contains the same data elements as listed in Figure 12-12. In addition, a separate file is maintained for supplies.

TRANSACTION AND OPEN DOCUMENT FILES

The *purchase order file* contains the purchase order number, the order date, the expected delivery date, the account number of the supplier, the requisition number, the shipping details, the name of the buyer, and data concerning each ordered item (i.e., inventory item number, description, and quantity ordered). The primary key is the purchase order number.

The *open purchase order file* consists of orders not yet approved for payment through vouching. The primary key of the file is the purchase order number. When an order is approved for payment, its record is transferred to a closed orders file.

The *supplier's invoice file* contains records providing the details of purchases transactions posted to the suppliers' accounts payable records. Each invoice may be given a number by the ordering firm, or the supplier's number may be used for reference. Generally they are organized according to those invoices not yet vouched and those invoices vouched but not yet paid (i.e., the open invoices).

The *open vouchers file* is used in a voucher system to replace the open invoices file. Data elements composing each voucher are similar to those shown in Figure 13-5, with the voucher number being the primary key.

The *cash disbursements file* typically contains data relating to the payments to suppliers and to others owed funds. As in the case of the other files, Infoage maintains the file on magnetic disk. Each record contains the check number (the primary key), the supplier's account number, related purchase order number(s), date of payment, and amount of payment. Copies of the hard-copy checks are filed by check number, although Infoage might maintain images of the checks on optical disk in the future.

OTHER FILES

A *supplier reference and history file* that contains reference and performance data concerning suppliers, so that buyers can make informed decisions when placing purchases. Included are such data as merchandise inventory items provided by each supplier, unit prices charged for each item, and summaries of all past purchases. In addition, evaluations based on these data and subjective opinions are included concerning such factors as quality of the merchandise, lead times to deliver ordered merchandise, comparisons of unit prices to average prices charged by competing suppliers, and overall reliability of each supplier.

A *buyer file* that contains the buyer number, buyer name, date hired, and types of merchandise for which responsible.

An *accounts payable detail file* that contains details of postings to each supplier's accounts payable record for the current accounting period. Its main purposes are to facilitate the preparation of purchases analyses and to enhance the audit trail.

FIGURE 13-11   Files maintained within Infoage's expenditure cycle.

DATA BASE

The data base supporting the expenditure cycle of a firm that buys merchandise for resale contains data pertaining to expenditure-related resources (merchandise inventory, cash), key events (purchase, receipt, vouching, cash disbursement), and principal agents (suppliers or vendors). It also reflects the relationships among these basic entities. Depending on the nature of a firm's procedure, additional data might be stored concerning associated events (such as requisitioning inventory and withdrawing cash from the bank) and agents (buyers and accounts payable clerks).

In a broader perspective, the data base would be inventory/logistics oriented. Beyond the categories of data just listed, the data base would contain much of the information needed for making inventory/logistics decisions—information pertaining to warehousing, inventory items that are alternatives to those carried, alternative sources of merchandise, and so on.

Data may be stored in files and/or data structures. Both forms will be surveyed.

FILES

Figure 13-11 lists the master, transaction, open document, reference, and other files required by a merchandising firm like Infoage, which currently employs a file-oriented approach for its expenditure cycle. The data elements contained in the records of such files will vary from firm to firm. While the size of the records in each file should not be unduly large, system designers must remember that the data contained therein determines the information that can be provided to management.

The master files for the expenditure cycle focus on suppliers. It is possible to consolidate all of the data elements concerning a supplier in a single master file. However, to reduce the size of records and thereby improve processing run times during updates, supplier-related data are often placed in two master files. The **accounts payable master file** contains such data elements as shown in Figure 13-12. The **supplier master file** contains such data elements as indicated in Figure 13-11.

If a firm sells products (merchandise), as does Infoage, it is necessary to include a **merchandise inventory master file**. This file should be identical to the file of the same name in the revenue cycle; data elements are listed in Figure 12-12.

DATA STRUCTURES

When a firm converts to the data-base approach, the contents of the expenditure cycle data base will be very similar to those in the above-mentioned files. However, there are significant differences. The data are organized as structured records or normalized tables (relations). Furthermore, these data structures are primarily focused on the key entities and relationships identified at the beginning of this section.

Supplier account number	Supplier name	Mailing address	Phone number	Credit terms	Year-to-date purchases, in total	Year-to-date payments, in total	Current account balance

Note: Although the lengths of fields and modes of data elements are necessary for complete documentation, they have been omitted for the sake of simplicity.

FIGURE 13-12   A layout of a supplier (vendor) accounts payable record for Infoage, Inc.

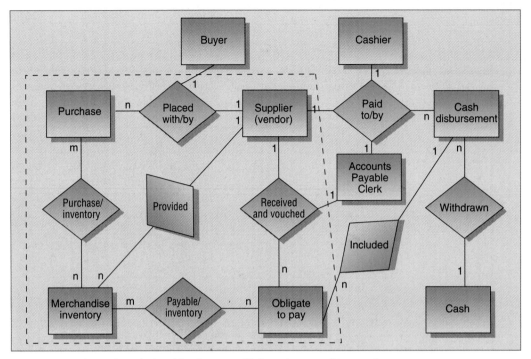

FIGURE 13-13   An entity-relationship diagram of Infoage's expenditure cycle.

In order to determine the specific data structures, system designers develop conceptual and logical views. You may find a review of the related material in Chapter 6 to be helpful before continuing.

Entity-Relationship Diagram of the Expenditure Cycle   The conceptual view of Infoage's expenditure cycle is depicted by the entity-relationship diagram in Figure 13-13. The diagram has been simplified, in that it combines the requisitioning event and purchasing event into a single purchase event and combines the receiving event and vouching event into a single obligate-to-pay (payable) event. It overlooks such adjustments as purchase returns and allowances.*

We will briefly examine the diagram, with an emphasis on the relationship among entities. Please keep in mind that the relationships reflected pertain specifically to Infoage's policies and procedures (sometimes called organizational rules and constraints). For convenience, the one-to-many relationships are first considered and then the many-to-many. Also, we will discuss only those relationships pertaining to purchases and payables, i.e., those within the dashed lines on the figure.

1. **One-to-many (1:n) relationships.** Replenishment orders for goods are placed by buyers in the purchasing area, based on requisitions. Each order is placed with

---

*As described earlier, the two key events of the expenditure cycle in a merchandising firm such as Infoage are the purchase/payable and cash disbursement. These events are accounting transactions that are reflected in accounting records such as journals and ledgers. (The purchase/payable event culminates with an obligation to pay, based on a sound vouching procedure.) Other events—such as placing the purchase order, vouching received suppliers' invoices, and receiving merchandise—are nonaccounting events that do not result in entries in accounting records. Some data modelers combine these events into the two key events. For instance, our example incorporates the receiving and vouching events into the obligate to pay (purchase/payable) event. However, certain nonaccounting events are sufficiently important to appear as separate entities in an E-R diagram. Our view is that the event concerned with placing a purchase order is particularly important when purchases are made for credit, since the status of open purchase orders is vital information to management.

one supplier, and more than one order may be placed with the same supplier over time; hence the relationship as shown is one (supplier) to many (orders). Suppliers can provide more than one item of merchandise (product), but each product is acquired from only a single supplier; hence, a one (supplier) to many (product) relationship is formed. Each payable event (called "obligate to pay" on the diagram) arises from the receipt of goods and the vouching of the related supplier's invoice. This payable pertains only to a single supplier; however, because repeat purchases are made from suppliers, one (supplier) can be involved in many (payable) events. Thus, three one-to-many relationships appear within the dashed-line borders.

2. **Many-to-many (m:n) relationships.** Each purchase order and payable can involve more than one item of merchandise (product), while each product may be involved in more than one purchase and payable. Hence, two many-to-many relationships exist with regard to the purchases and payables portion of the cycle. These relationships are signaled in two ways in Figure 13-13: (1) by the labels purchase/inventory and obligation/inventory in two diamonds, and (2) by the m:n notations between the entity boxes. In order to implement a sound data structure, it will be necessary to create records or tables that reflect these relationships.

Logical Views of Expenditure Cycle Data Structures   The logical view is determined by "mapping" from the entity-relationship diagram to a data structure diagram. If the network structure is selected, for instance, the mapping would yield records that correspond to the entities and relationships in the entity-relationship diagram. If the relational structure is selected, the mapping involves tables rather than records. Focusing on the portion of the entity-relationship diagram enclosed within the dashed lines, the following six entities and relationships (listed on the left) yield these nine tables or relations:

Supplier (vendor)	Supplier/accounts payable table
Merchandise inventory	Merchandise inventory table
Purchase	Purchase order header table
Obligate to pay	Receiving header table, disbursement voucher header table, supplier's invoice header table
Purchase/inventory	Ordered items table
Payable/inventory	Received items table, billed items table

Figure 13-14 depicts the logical view in the form of linked tables. Each table contains the attributes suitable to Infoage's purchases/payables situation. Dashed lines connecting the tables indicate the implied linkages that may be achieved via common columns. For instance, the primary or table key in the supplier/accounts payable table (i.e., supplier account number) allows the table to be joined to the purchase order header table, supplier invoice header table, and disbursement voucher table through foreign keys in those tables.* In turn, the ordered items tables, received items table, and billed items table (each containing line items) are linked to their respective header tables.

Let us focus for a moment on the ordered items, received items, and billed items tables. Because each purchase order and obligation can involve more than one product, the problem of repeating fields (product numbers and quantities) arises. To

---

*Since Infoage employs a voucher system, the tables relating to obligations include a disbursement voucher table as well as the supplier invoice table.

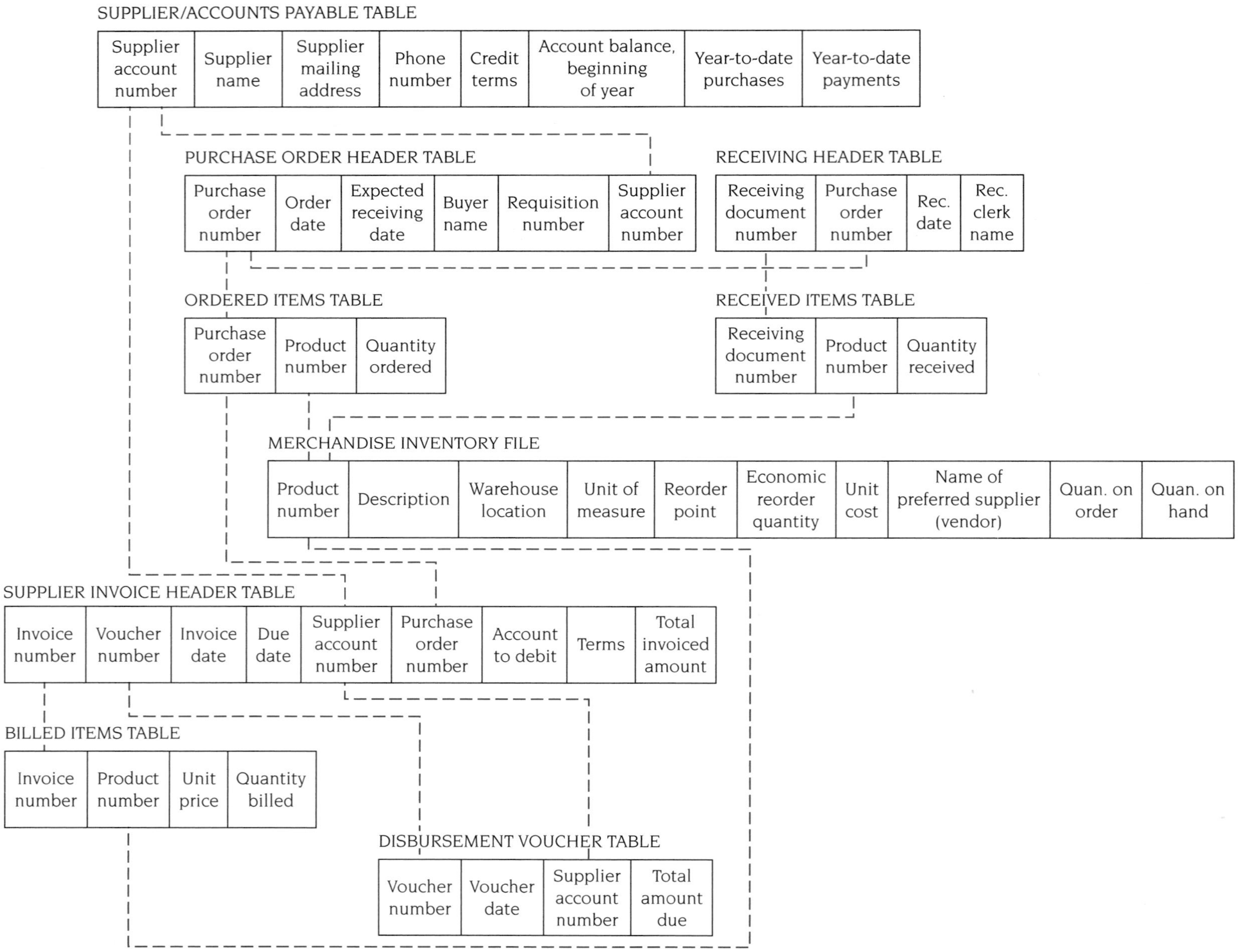

FIGURE 13-14 A relational data structure relating to Infoage's expenditure cycle.

normalize the purchase orders and obligations tables, it has been necessary to remove these repeating fields from their header tables and place them in line-item tables. Each line-item table can serve as a relationship table, since each contains two identifying numbers or keys. The ordered items table consists of the purchase order number and product (item) number, while for the other two tables the keys are receiving report number/product number, and supplier invoice number/product number. These multiple or concatenated keys provide a cross-referencing feature that facilitates the joining of tables in the structure. They also allow reports to be prepared quickly. For instance, by joining the merchandise inventory table and ordered items table, a data-base user could generate a report of all items ordered and their quantities. The report might include the description of each item as well as the extent to which it reduces the inventory on hand.

Given the attributes listed in Figure 13-14, we can observe how processing is performed. For example, assume that supplier (vendor) number 6810 is to be sent purchase order number 76531 (shown in Figure 13-3) pertaining to ordered products numbered 512364 and 586430. In order to print this document, Infoage's purchases application program would join (via the implied links) the table for supplier number 6810 with the purchase order header table. This latter table would in turn be joined with the ordered items records that show the ordered quantities to be 40 and 300 units, respectively. The resulting table would be joined with the merchandise inventory table to extract the merchandise product descriptions and to update the quantities on order.

Later actions in the cycle also involve the linked tables. For instance, to print a receiving report, the receiving application program first accepts data entered by the receiving clerk; then it extracts needed data from tables relating to the supplier, purchase order, receiving, and merchandise inventory. To vouch supplier's invoice PF3386, a vouching program joins the related purchase order header, ordered items, receiving header, and received items tables with the supplier's invoice header and billed items tables. It then compares the quantities of items ordered, received, and billed; compares the unit prices on the order and invoice; and so on. After the vouching has been completed and approved, a posting program (1) updates the year-to-date purchases with supplier (vendor) number 6810 in the supplier/accounts payable table and (2) adds the amount to the appropriate voucher in the disbursement vouchers table.

Although not shown in Figure 13-14, the cash disbursements table would be part of the linkage in an expenditure cycle data base. Thus, when payments are made to suppliers, they can be processed to reduce the current account balances in the accounts of affected suppliers. Through the linkage from the disbursements voucher table to the supplier invoice header table, they can also be matched to the appropriate invoices.

DATA FLOWS AND PROCESSING

Figure 13-15 presents an overview of the key processing activities and related documents for the expenditure cycle. The figure shows that the accounts payable processing activity serves as the connecting linchpin between the purchases and cash disbursements processing systems.

In this section we emphasize the computer-based processing of purchases and cash disbursements transactions. These types of transactions may be processed by the periodic (batch) approach, by the immediate (on-line) approach, or by some

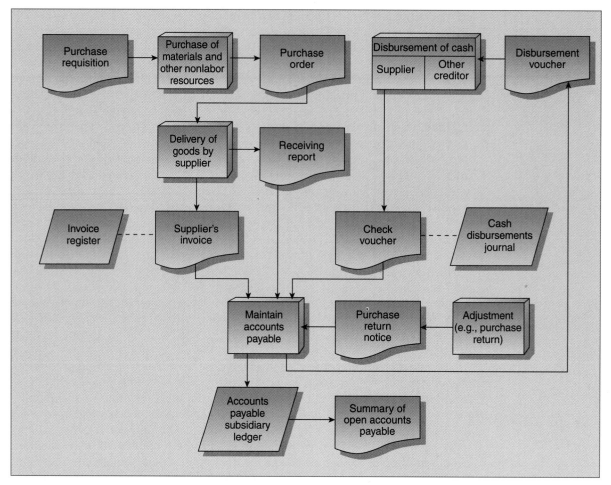

FIGURE 13-15   Relationships within the expenditure cycle.

variation of the two approaches. The procedural approach described in this section has been proposed for Infoage in processing its merchandise purchases and related cash disbursements. It essentially combines the immediate approach with the periodic approach and requires the presence of on-line files. Although other approaches are being employed by various firms, the described procedure (allowing for minor variations) is sound and in widespread use.

If you are not familiar with business procedures, it may be helpful to review the expenditure cycle processing that pertains to a manual processing system. The appendix to this chapter contains background information concerning the accounting transactions in the expenditure cycle as well as the processing steps and document flows.

PURCHASES/PAYABLES PROCESSING SYSTEM

The proposed purchases and payables system for Infoage follows the processes shown in the data-flow diagram of Figure 13-16. This diagram ties to the entity-relationship diagram in Figure 13-13 and the data structure diagram in Figure 13-14.*

*Figure 13-16 is somewhat more inclusive, in that it contains more data stores or files. For instance, it includes supplier and history data plus general ledger data, neither of which are shown in Figure 13-14.

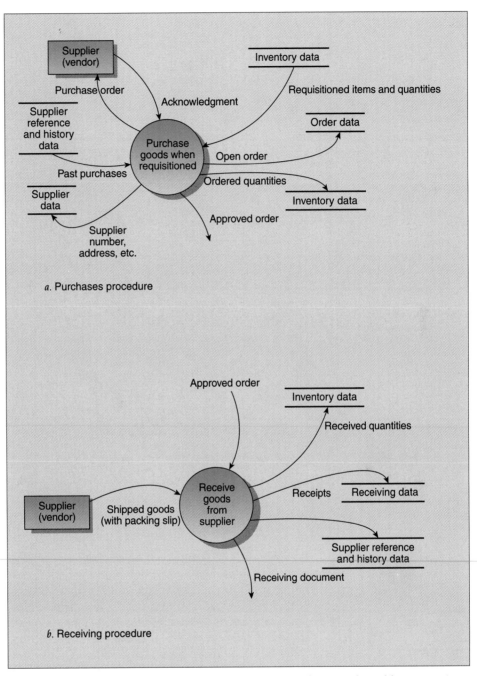

FIGURE 13-16   A data-flow diagram relating to Infoage's purchases and payables processing system.

Figure 13-17, beginning on page 553, depicts a three-part system flowchart that corresponds to the three basic processes in the data-flow diagram. Data are shown as being stored in files, but these can also represent tables.

Purchases   Figure 13-17a begins with the merchandise inventory file being checked for those products (items) whose on-hand quantities have been drawn below their reorder points. This step is performed by an inventory clerk who activates a search

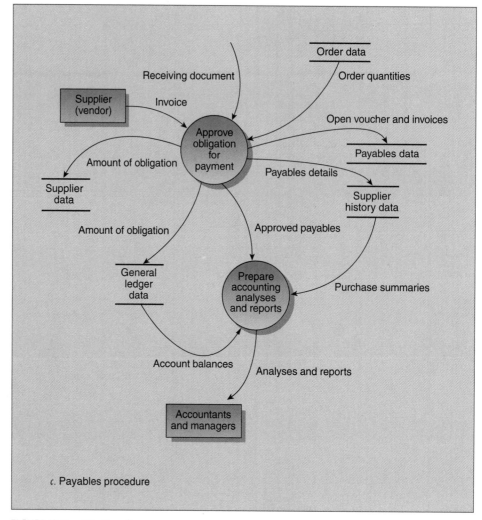

c. Payables procedure

FIGURE 13-16 (*Continued*)

program via an on-line terminal. When the program locates an item needing to be reordered, it stores the relevant data in a temporary requisition file, including the name of the preferred supplier (vendor), if any. After all items have been scanned, the program arranges the items by supplier and prints purchase requisitions. It also prints an inventory reorder list for the inventory manager, who uses the list to ensure that purchase orders are prepared for all requisitions. The manager approves the requisitions, adjusting for back orders, and delivers them to the buyers in the purchasing area. Requisitions for other than merchandise (e.g., for office supplies) are prepared by the responsible manager and delivered to the buyers.

Buyers review the requisitions that they are assigned, either by reference to the hard-copy forms or to the displays in the on-line requisition file. By making inquiries of an on-line supplier reference file, which contains evaluation data, the buyers either

FIGURE 13-17   A system flowchart of an on-line computer-based purchases payables system for Infoage.

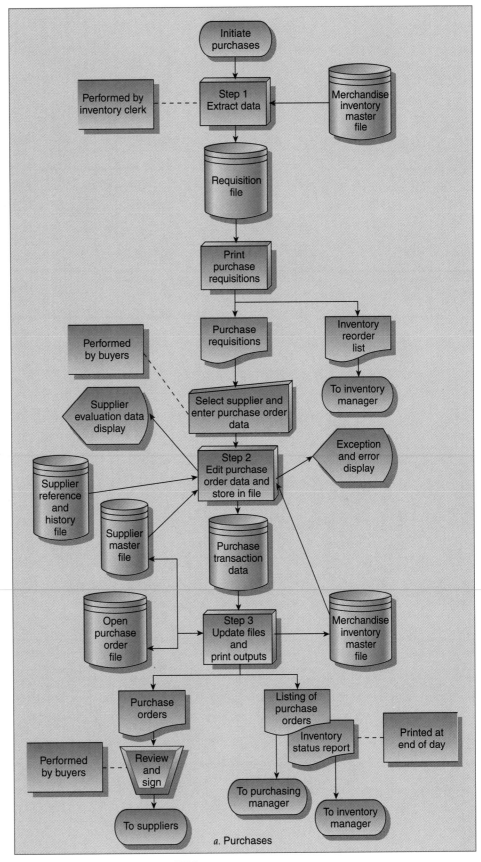

a. Purchases

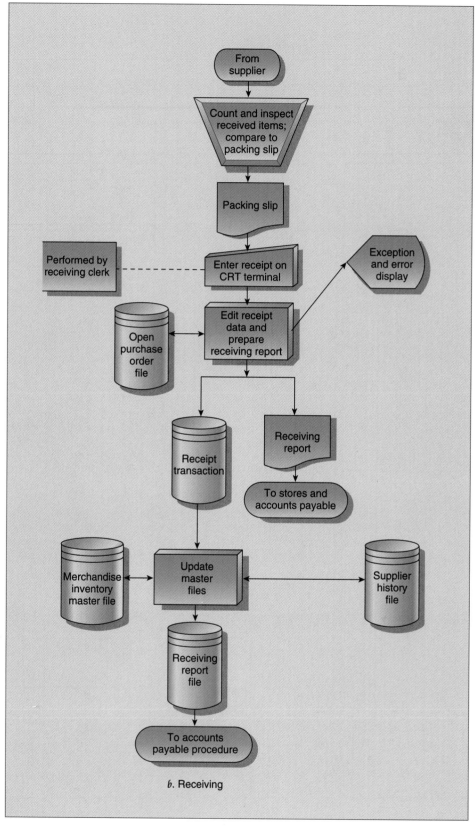

b. Receiving

FIGURE 13-17 (*Continued*)

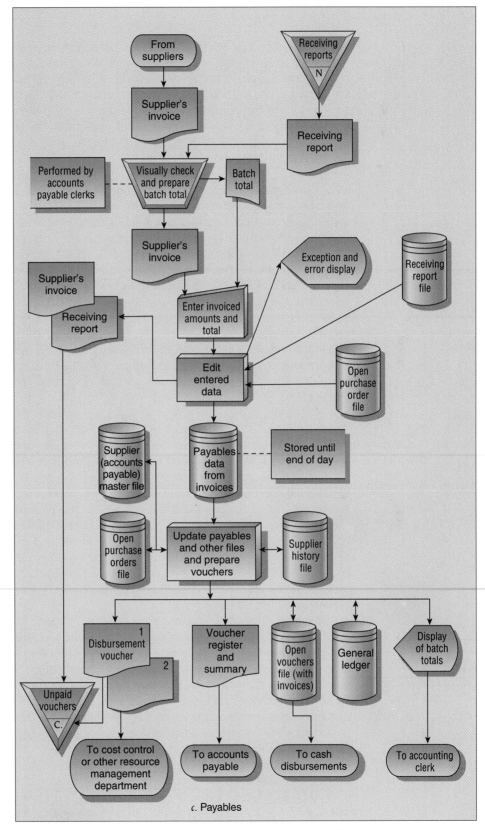

c. Payables

FIGURE 13-17   (*Continued*)

555

confirm the suppliers listed on the requisitions or select more suitable suppliers and enter their relevant data (e.g., names and numbers) into the system. Then they enter their approval of the purchase, any needed data not otherwise available (e.g., shipper), and activate the edit program related to purchase orders. The entered data from the buyers and the requisition file are edited by reference to the supplier and merchandise inventory files, with errors and exceptions being listed on the monitor screen. Validated and corrected data relating to purchase orders are temporarily stored in a purchase transaction file.

In step 3 purchase orders are printed, using data from the transaction file as well as needed data (e.g., suppliers' mailing addresses, product descriptions, unit prices) from the supplier and merchandise inventory files. The purchase order computer program automatically assigns numbers to the purchase orders and dates them. A copy of each purchase order is placed in the on-line open purchase order file, while the merchandise inventory file is updated to reflect the quantities ordered of the respective products. The buyer, or other authorized signer, reviews the printed purchase orders and signs. Then the purchase orders are mailed, faxed, or electronically transmitted to the suppliers. If revisions are necessary, the buyer retrieves the purchase transaction data via the terminal, makes the changes, and prints a revised purchase order.

At the end of each day, a listing of the day's purchase orders is printed and given to the manager who supervises purchasing (i.e., Ralph Cannon, Infoage's office manager). Other reports, such as inventory status reports, are provided to the inventory manager.

Receiving Figure 13-17*b* shows a system flowchart of an on-line receiving procedure. A receiving clerk first counts and inspects the received goods. Then he or she keys the count and inventory item numbers into a preformatted receiving screen on an on-line terminal monitor, together with the related purchase order number listed on the packing slip. Edit routines within a receiving program perform a variety of checks on the entered data. One important check is to compare the ordered quantities in the on-line open purchase order file with the counted quantities. Any differences are noted on the terminal screen. (Note that the receiving clerk cannot access the ordered quantities directly, since the receiving terminal is restricted to showing only a "blind" copy of the purchase order.) If no matching purchase order number is found in the on-line file, an alerting message is displayed. Figure 13-10 shows a completed receiving data-entry screen.

Assuming that the goods are accepted, the program prints a prenumbered receiving report. Data for the receiving report come from (1) the receiving clerk entries, and (2) the header data in the on-line purchase order file. In addition, the product descriptions are accessed from the merchandise inventory file, which is linked to the purchase order file. The hard-copy receiving report looks very similar to the form in Figure 13-4, except that most of the entries are printed. The condition of the goods is noted on the form and the delivery person signs a copy. The copy then accompanies the goods to the warehouse, where the quantities are checked and acknowledged (on the form in the "Checked By" box). Finally, the copy is forwarded to the accounts payable department.

The receiving program temporarily stores the validated receipts transaction data into an on-line file, which is the basis of updating actions. First, the merchandise inventory file is updated, increasing the on-hand quantities and reducing or eliminating the quantities on order for the affected items. Next, a summary of the receipt is added to the supplier reference and history file. (If a back order is involved, the back order record—not shown in the flowchart—is flagged.) Finally, the receiving data are added to a receiving report file.

Payables Figure 13-17c portrays a system flowchart of the combined on-line/batch payables system. As invoices are received from suppliers, an accounts payable clerk performs a visual check for completeness and pulls the related hard-copy receiving reports that had accompanied the goods to the warehouse. After all invoices have been visually checked, the clerk computes batch control totals (e.g., on the invoiced amounts). He or she enters the batch total, plus key data from each invoice, into an on-line terminal and activates the payables edit program. It validates the entered data, checks the quantities received (as shown in the receiving report file) against the quantities ordered in the open purchase order file, checks the unit prices in the open purchase order file with the unit prices that were billed, recomputes the batch totals, and displays any differences. After any detected errors and differences are corrected, the invoices are approved and the data stored on a temporary on-line payables file.*

At a designated processing time (e.g., the end of the day), a payables processing program accesses the payables file and performs several steps. First, it updates each account in the supplier file (in effect, the accounts payable subsidiary ledger) that is affected by an invoice, adding the amount of the invoice to the previous total owed to the supplier. Second, the program updates each affected item in the merchandise inventory file, adding the extended amount (quantity of units billed multiplied by the cost per unit) to the previous total.† Third, the purchase order giving rise to the invoice is removed from the open invoice file. (If all of the ordered quantities have not been received, the purchase order is flagged by a symbol placed in a field at the end of the record and left in the open order file.) Data concerning the purchase are transferred to the supplier reference and history file. Fourth, the total amount of invoices approved for payment is posted to the general ledger accounts. Finally, disbursement vouchers are established to incorporate the invoices from each supplier. They are put into an on-line file and linked to the invoice data (as shown in Figure 13-14). Each voucher is indexed by the due dates of its invoices.

Preparing Analyses and Reports At the end of the payables processing, a variety of outputs are generated for later use. Prenumbered disbursement vouchers are printed from the data stored in the vouchers file. One copy of the voucher is filed together with the supporting documents in an unpaid vouchers file arranged by due dates. A voucher register is printed to provide the accounts payable department and other accounting clerks with an audit trail. A total of the invoice amounts is also computed by the program and displayed for comparison with the precomputed batch total by an accounting clerk or manager.

Other listings, analyses, and reports can be printed as needed. For example, an accounts payable analysis can be used by the treasurer to verify that discounts are not being missed.

---

*Occasionally suppliers' invoices cannot be corrected immediately, perhaps because increased unit prices must be cleared with buyers. Data for those invoices are transferred to a suspended file (not shown), and the batch totals are adjusted to reflect their suspension. Also, the hard-copy invoices are put into a pending file or basket.

†The cost per unit is usually not the unit price shown on the invoice; instead, it may be a standard unit cost assigned by a firm such as Infoage, with the difference from the invoice price being carried to an adjustment account.

SPOTLIGHTING

REENGINEERED PAYABLES
at ITT Automotive*

ITT Automotive, a large automotive components supplier, found that 65 percent of its purchases involved only 30 percent of the dollar value. Many of these were small purchases (usually less than $1000). Also, most were for noninventoriable items, ranging from supplies and tools to varied services. The firm's accounts payable department processes each invoice from a supplier in the traditional way, that is, by comparing all relevant supporting documents and then entering data into the computer system to initiate payment. Each accounts payable clerk handled about as many invoices per year as his or her counterpart in similar organizations. For many invoices, especially those of very small value, the cost of processing exceeded the value of the purchases.

*Richard J. Palmer, "Reengineering Payables at ITT Automotive." *Management Accounting* (July 1994), pp. 38–42.

Through reengineering the payables process, ITT Automotive decided to make use of procurement cards—in effect, credit cards that allow designated employees to charge purchases. The vendors (suppliers) receive most of the purchase prices of items charged within a couple of days of the purchases. The using firm receives monthly statements that consolidate all of the charges of employees for a period; then the firm pays the full amount before a specified due date to the bank that issued the cards. The major benefit of the cards is due to cost reduction, arising from an array of nonvalue-adding activities that are eliminated. These activities include costs primarily incurred in purchasing, receiving, payables, and cash disbursements. For instance, the vouching of invoices against supporting documents is eliminated, as are the number of checks that must be written. Time is reduced in purchasing and receiving, and thus less stockpiling of supplies and other items is necessary.

Modifications to the Procedure   Numerous changes to this purchases/payables procedure might be considered by Infoage. The system could be made even more automatic and network based, as is described and illustrated in Chapter 17. Alternatively, the system could be more batch-oriented. Both the purchase requisitions and the purchase orders could be handled in batches and controlled by batch totals, rather than by means of reorder lists. Another modification concerns the merchandise inventory file, which in our illustration shows quantities on hand of the various inventory items. Instead, the merchandise inventory items could show dollar amounts as well as quantities, so that the account in the general ledger would be a control account. In still another modification, the degree of paper handling could be reduced in the entire procedure. For instance, received boxes of merchandise could be counted and recorded by means of bar scanners, and the receiving records could be maintained within the system with no hard-copy receiving reports. Finally, the general ledger processing could be maintained as a separate application, as described in Chapter 11. If this is done, the payables application would generate a summary entry for later posting to the general ledger.

Revolutionary approaches are being introduced into the purchases/payables processes. One approach involves the use of electronic data interchange (EDI) systems, with the purchasing data and billing data being transmitted electronically between the buying firm and the supplier. An application of an electronic data interchange system or network is described in a nearby vignette. Another approach involves reengineering the procedure and incorporating a procurement card to simplify the bulk of transactions. An application of this approach is also described in a vignette. Both approaches result in near-paperless systems.

SPOTLIGHTING

EDI NETWORKS
at Bedford Furniture Industries, Inc.*

Bedford Furniture Industries, Inc., manufactures and supplies bedding and upholstery products to more than 1000 Canadian retailers, using a single plant in Toronto. In the late 1980s the firm established an electronic data interchange (EDI) link with one of its major retail customers. Using the ANSI X12 message standard, the retailer began transmitting purchase orders via telephone lines with the aid of a value-added network. A year later, Bedford and the retailer installed a rapid delivery system to obtain faster response to orders.

Under this system, the retailer's sales department enters orders from its customers into the EDI network as received. Each evening the orders are transmitted to Bedford's electronic mailbox, with the expectation that the orders will be delivered to the ultimate customers within 48 hours. Bedford's order-entry program checks the mailbox periodically and retrieves any orders therein. It then summarizes the orders by customer, ship-to location, and type of product ordered. Production orders, based on these summaries and showing quantities to produce, are ready when production begins at 6

A.M. When products are completed and shipped, the details of shipment are entered on a bill of lading that accompanies the shipment. For most shipments, the bills of lading are also transmitted to the retailer via the EDI network, giving the retailer advance notice of the shipments and thus aiding it in verifying and reloading for shipment to the ultimate customers.

As the supplier, Bedford generates invoices for the retailer via the EDI network. Under an automated payment process called EDI/EFT, the retailer deposits funds directly into Bedford's bank account. The bank sends remittance advices reflecting payments, so that Bedford can post the payments against accounts receivable.

A few years after adopting the EDI approach, Bedford has established links with most of its major retail customers. Bedford, as supplier, has benefitted due to reduced paperwork, less administrative costs, more efficient production, and higher sales volumes from satisfied retail customers. The retail customers have benefitted through reduced inventory carrying costs and higher inventory turnover, as well as reduced paper flows and lower administrative costs.

*Allan Snow, "EDI: Made to Order." CMA *Magazine* (November 1994), pp. 22–24.

CASH DISBURSEMENTS PROCESSING SYSTEM

The key processes involved in Infoage's cash disbursements processing system appear as a part of Figure 13-7. Checks and vouchers are printed periodically. After the checks are signed, they are mailed to suppliers. The suppliers' accounts are updated to reflect the disbursements, and the general ledger accounts are posted.

Figure 13-18 shows a system flowchart of an on-line input batch cash disbursements procedure.* Periodically (usually daily) a disbursements clerk enters a request for disbursements that are due to be paid, especially to obtain discounts. A program searches through the open vouchers file for all that should be paid at that time, checking the due dates listed in the stored invoices. If more than one voucher is found for a single supplier, the vouchers are combined. All located vouchers are temporarily stored in a due disbursements file. Batch totals are computed based on the accumulated vouchers, and the totals are displayed on the terminal screen.

The cash disbursements program prints prenumbered checks based on the disbursement data. It also generates a check register listing the checks. Then the

*No data-flow diagram accompanies the system flowchart; however, a problem at the end of the chapter asks you to draw a data-flow diagram for a cash disbursements procedure.

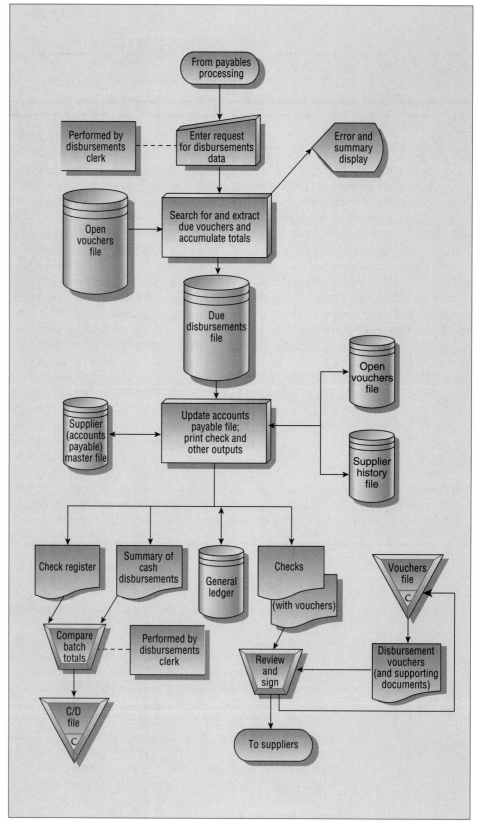

FIGURE 13-18   A system flowchart of a computer-based cash disbursements system for Infoage.

program updates the supplier accounts payable file, reducing the balance owed to each supplier by the amount of the check. Direct posting is proposed, although the posting can be done sequentially if the vouchers are sorted in a separate run by supplier number. Next, the paid vouchers are removed from the open vouchers file, and the data concerning disbursements are added to the supplier reference and history file. Finally, the program accumulates the total amounts disbursed and compares them with the batch totals that were computed before processing. If the totals agree, the cash and accounts payable accounts in the general ledger are posted. A summary of cash disbursements is printed, showing the accounts payable activity and the totals. A disbursements clerk compares the totals with the totals in the check register and investigates any differences.

The treasurer signs the checks, reviewing the supporting documents (purchase order, receiving report, and invoices) at least on a sampling basis. After signing she forwards the checks to the mail room. (If the volume of checks becomes sufficiently large, they may be signed automatically by the cash disbursement program, using a signature plate. If this is done, the checks are later reviewed to see that they pertain to authorized obligations. Also, if any suppliers are connected directly via an EDI network, the payments will be transmitted electronically rather than by paper checks.)

BENEFITS OF THE ON-LINE INPUT BATCH PROCESSING SYSTEM

The proposed computer-based processing of purchases and cash disbursements transactions is logically sound. Capturing data on-line and maintaining data in network or relational data-base structures yields several benefits of modern technology. Processing purchases and cash disbursements in batches provides other benefits of proven practice. Batch processing is quite feasible when updating ledger records, since the added timeliness of immediate processing does not add much, if any, value.

Among the key benefits of the proposed computer-based system are the following:

1. Needed purchases are automatically determined and requisitioned, so that merchandise inventory items should seldom be depleted in the warehouse stocks.
2. Purchases data update records as soon as orders are prepared and ordered goods are received, thereby keeping key order and inventory information up-to-date.
3. Data are validated upon entry, so that errors are detected more quickly, and reprocessing delays due to undetected errors are reduced.
4. Paperwork flows are reduced, as when receiving data are entered directly from counts or payments are transmitted via electronic data interchange networks.
5. Accounting-related updating runs (i.e., invoice payables, cash disbursements) are efficient and better controlled, since the related transactions are handled in batches with control totals.
6. Accounting-related processing is also simplified, since transactions are posted without sorting and since the relevant files are on-line and integrated.
7. Information that is both current and integrated can be easily retrieved by clerks and managers; thus, inquiries (e.g., from suppliers) can be answered quickly and correctly, and control reports and summaries can be generated for managers as needed. For instance, purchasing and accounts payable analyses can be viewed or printed as often as desired.

ACCOUNTING CONTROLS

RISK EXPOSURES

Transactions within the expenditure cycle are exposed to all types of risks: unintentional errors, deliberate errors, unintentional losses of assets, thefts of assets, breaches of security, and acts of violence and natural disasters. Figure 13-19 lists representative risks and consequent exposures due to these risks, roughly in the order as noted above.

Consider Risk 20 in the figure, the risk that checks may be kited. **Kiting** is a type of embezzlement that involves transfers of checks among bank accounts. The purpose is generally to cover cash shortages or to inflate the assets. Transfers typically take place near the end of a month, so that float (i.e., delay) causes the checks not to be recorded until the following month. At the least, the result of this kiting activity is an overstated cash balance for the end of the month. Another frequent occurrence is a loss of cash.

CONTROL OBJECTIVES

In order to counteract such risk exposures, a firm must establish a variety of accounting controls. For instance, the risk of kiting can be reduced if bank reconciliations are prepared with respect to all bank accounts as of the same date and compared.

As a foundation for establishing needed controls—both general and application—it is desirable first to clarify the objectives that the controls are intended to achieve. With respect to the expenditure cycle, several key control objectives are to ensure that

- All purchases are authorized on a timely basis when needed and are based on economic order quantity calculations.
- All received goods are verified to determine that the quantities agree with those ordered and that they are in good condition.
- All services are authorized before being performed and are monitored to determine that they are properly performed.
- All suppliers' invoices are verified on a timely basis and conform with goods received or services performed.
- All available purchase discounts are identified, so that they may be taken if economical to do so.
- All purchase returns and allowances are authorized and accurately recorded and based on actual returns of goods.
- All cash disbursements are recorded completely and accurately.
- All credit purchases and cash disbursements transactions are posted to proper suppliers' accounts in the accounts payable ledger.
- All accounting records and merchandise inventory are safeguarded.

GENERAL CONTROLS

General controls concerning the expenditure cycle can be categorized as organizational, documentation, asset accountability, management practices, data center operations, authorization, and access.

	Risk		Exposure(s)
1.	Orders placed for unneeded goods or more goods than needed	1.	Excessive inventory and storage costs
2.	Receipt of unordered goods	2.	Excessive inventory and storage costs
3.	No receipt of ordered goods	3.	Losses due to stockouts
4.	Fraudulent placement of orders by buyers with suppliers to whom they have personal or financial attachments	4.	Possibility of inferior or overpriced goods or services
5.	Creation of fictitious invoices and other purchasing documents	5.	Overstatement of inventory; losses of cash disbursed
6.	Lack of vigilance in writing down inventory that is aged or damaged	6.	Overstatement of inventory
7.	Omission of liabilities, such as material contingencies	7.	Understatement of liabilities
8.	Overcharges (with respect either to unit prices or to quantities) by suppliers for goods delivered	8.	Excessive purchasing costs
9.	Damage of goods en route to the acquiring firm	9.	Possibility of inferior goods for use or sale (if undetected)
10.	Errors by suppliers in computing amounts on invoices	10.	Possibility of overpayment for goods received
11.	Erroneous or omitted postings of purchases or purchase returns to suppliers' accounts payable records	11.	Incorrect balances in accounts payable and general ledger account records
12.	Errors in charging transaction amounts to purchases and expense accounts	12.	Incorrect levels (either high or low) for purchases and expense accounts
13.	Lost purchase discounts due to late payments	13.	Excessive purchasing costs
14.	Duplicate payments of invoices from suppliers	14.	Excessive purchasing costs
15.	Incorrect disbursements of cash, either to improper or fictitious parties or for greater amounts than approved	15.	Losses of cash and excessive costs for goods and services
16.	Improper disbursements of cash for goods or services not received	16.	Excessive costs for goods or services
17.	Theft of scrap proceeds	17.	Losses of cash
18.	Disbursement of checks payable to employees for unauthorized expenses or fraudulent claims	18.	Losses of cash
19.	Fraudulent alteration and cashing of checks by employees	19.	Losses of cash
20.	Kiting of checks by employees	20.	Overstatement of bank balances; possible losses of deposited cash
21.	Accessing of supplier records by unauthorized persons	21.	Loss of security over such records, with possibly detrimental use made of data accessed
22.	Involvement of cash, merchandise inventory, and accounts payable records in natural or human-made disasters	22.	Loss of or damage to assets, including possible loss of data needed to monitor payments of amounts due to suppliers within discount periods

FIGURE 13-19 Risk exposures within the expenditure cycle.

Organizational Controls With respect to purchases transactions, the units having custodial functions (i.e., the warehouse and receiving) should be separate from each other and from those units that keep the records (i.e., inventory control, accounts payable, general ledger, and data processing). (This separation is not always possible in the case of services, since every department requires some types of services.) In the case of cash disbursements, those who handle cash in the form of signed checks (i.e., the treasurer and cash disbursements clerks) should be separate from those units that have responsibility for the records (i.e., accounts payable, general ledger, and data processing).

In computer-based systems, the data entry and processing steps are controlled by application programs. These programs guide the human operators of the system, such as buyers and accounts payable clerks. Built into the programs are the policies and procedures adopted by management, including those that determine when and how many units of an item to reorder and which suppliers to order from. A vital segregation of functions, therefore, is between (1) the systems development personnel who write and modify the programs and (2) the personnel who use and operate the system.

Documentation Controls   Complete and up-to-date documentation should be available concerning the expenditure cycle, including copies of the documents, flowcharts, record layouts, and reports illustrated in this chapter. In addition, details pertaining to purchases and cash disbursements edit and processing programs should be organized into separate books or "packages" that are directed respectively to programmers, computer operators, and system users. Furthermore, management policies concerning purchase discounts, purchase returns, and so forth should be in written form.

Asset Accountability Controls   An accounts payable subsidiary ledger (master file) should be maintained and reconciled frequently with the accounts payable control account in the general ledger. Also, merchandise inventory records should be maintained in a ledger, with the on-hand quantities being reconciled periodically to physical counts of merchandise inventory on hand. Another type of reconciliation, a bank reconciliation, should compare the balance in the bank account with the cash account balance in the general ledger.

Other asset accountability controls involve (1) the receiving clerk who counts received goods and compares them to the ordered quantities, (2) the warehouse manager who acknowledges receipt of delivered goods by signing the receiving report, (3) the accounts payable clerk who logs all incoming invoices from suppliers and compares the invoices with supporting documents, and (4) the supplier who reviews the check payments for incorrect amounts.

Management Practices   Among the sound management practices that should be established and followed with respect to the expenditure cycle are the following:

- Employees, including programmers and accountants, should be carefully trained; those that handle cash should be bonded.
- Systems development and changes should undergo a clear procedure involving prior approvals, testing, and sign-offs.
- Audits should be performed of the purchases and cash disbursements policies and procedures.
- Managers should review periodic analyses, control summaries, and reports concerning account activity and computer-approved transactions.

Data Center Operations Controls   Computer processing schedules involving purchases and cash disbursements batches should be clearly established. Information systems and accounting personnel should be actively supervised and their work reviewed with the aid of computer processing control reports and access logs.

Authorization Controls All purchases transactions for goods or services should be authorized by designated managers, usually the inventory manager (for goods) or department managers (for supplies and services). In a computer-based system, the authorization for purchases of inventory may be performed by an application program into which the reorder rules have been built. A manager not involved in the processing of purchases or in accounts payable, such as the inventory manager, should authorize all purchase returns and allowances. Appropriate documents (i.e., requisitions, purchase orders, receiving reports) should authorize the acquisition of goods and their transfer to the warehouse.

Access Controls Among the needed access controls and security measures, especially in the presence of on-line computer systems and networks, are the following:

1. Assigned passwords that authorized clerks must enter to access accounts payable and other supplier-related files, in order to perform their strictly defined tasks.

2. Terminals that are restricted in the functions they allow to be performed with respect to purchases and cash disbursements transactions.

3. Logging of all purchases and cash disbursements transactions upon their entry into the system.

4. Frequent dumping of accounts payable and merchandise inventory master files onto magnetic tape backup.

5. Physically protected warehouses (for storing merchandise inventory) and safes (for holding stocks of blank checks).

6. Logs that monitor all accesses of data stored in files.

APPLICATION CONTROLS

The following controls and control procedures are applicable to expenditure cycle transactions and supplier accounts. Figure 13-20 lists a variety of application controls, arranged by input, processing, and output categories.

Certain of the application controls pertain only to computer-based systems. Figure 13-21, on page 568, lists several programmed edit checks that are critical to the validation of input data in computer-based systems.

REPORTS AND OTHER OUTPUTS

Reports generated as an integral part or by-product of expenditure cycle processing are needed to conduct a firm's operations and to aid in controlling and planning the firm's activities. Outputs provided by the expenditure cycle include operational and strategic outputs, financial and nonfinancial reports, purchases-related and cash-related reports, scheduled (daily, weekly, and monthly) reports and demand reports or inquiries, and hard-copy and soft-copy reports.

OPERATIONAL LISTINGS AND REPORTS

Various registers and journals help to maintain the audit trail. Each lists specific transactions, with related documents and identifying numbers, pertaining to a particular event within the expenditure cycle. The *invoice or voucher register* is a listing of

Input controls

1. Prepare prenumbered and well-designed documents relating to purchases, receiving, payables, and cash disbursements, with each prepared document being approved by an authorized person.

2. Validate data on purchase orders and receiving reports and invoices as the data are prepared and entered for processing. In computer-based systems, validation should be performed by means of programmed edit checks. When data are keyed onto a computer-readable medium, key verification is also appropriate.

3. Correct errors that are detected during data entry and before the data are posted to the supplier and inventory records.

4. Precompute batch control totals relating to key data on suppliers' invoices and vouchers due for payment. These precomputed batch control totals should be compared with totals computed during postings to the accounts payable ledger and during each processing run. In the case of cash disbursements, the precomputed total of vouchers should also be compared with the total of the check register and/or cash disbursements summary.

Processing controls

1. Issue purchase requisitions, purchase orders, disbursement vouchers, checks, and debit memoranda on the basis of valid authorizations.

2. Verify all data elements and computations on purchase requisitions and on purchase orders (by persons other than the preparers or by a computer program). Also, count the quantities received and compare the counted quantities against the ordered quantities.

3. Vouch all data elements and computations on suppliers' invoices; also, compare corresponding purchase orders and receiving reports (in the case of goods).

4. Monitor all open transactions, such as partial deliveries and rejected goods. Also, investigate all transactions in which one or more supporting documents are missing.

5. Issue debit memoranda only on the basis of prior approval of the purchasing or other appropriate manager.

6. Reconcile accounts in the accounts payable subsidiary ledger and expense ledgers (if any) with control accounts in the general ledger.

7. Verify that total postings to the accounts payable file accounts agree with the total postings to the general ledger accounts (when batch processing is performed).

8. Monitor discount terms relating to payment, in order to ensure that all purchase discounts are taken (if economical). Also, employ the net method for recording purchases.

9. Review evidence supporting the validity of expenditures and the correctness of amounts prior to the signing of checks.

10. Use check protectors to protect the amounts on checks against alteration before the checks are presented to be signed.

11. Require that checks over a specified amount be countersigned by a second manager.

12. Verify all inventories on hand by physical counts at least once yearly, and reconcile the counted quantities with the quantities shown in the inventory records. The inventory taking should be performed under close supervision, and differences should be made when necessary to reflect the actual quantities on hand.

13. Use imprest systems for disbursing currency from petty-cash funds, with the funds being subject to surprise counts by internal auditors or a designated manager.

14. Establish purchasing policies that require competitive bidding for large and/or nonroutine purchases and that prohibit conflicts of interest, such as financial interests by buyers in current or potential suppliers.

15. Correct errors that are made during processing steps, usually by reversing erroneous postings to accounts and entering correct data. The audit trail concerning accounts being corrected should show the original errors, the reversals, and the corrections.

FIGURE 13-20   Application controls pertaining to the expenditure cycle.

Output controls

1. Establish clear-cut receiving and payables cutoff policies, so that inventories and accounts payable are fairly valued at the end of each accounting period.

2. Establish budgetary control over purchases, with periodic reviews of actual purchase costs and such key factors as inventory turnover rates.

3. Compare monthly statements from suppliers with the balances appearing in the suppliers' accounts in accounts payable.

4. File copies of all documents pertaining to purchases and cash disbursements by number, including voided documents such as checks. The sequence of numbers in each file should be checked periodically to see if gaps exist. If transactions are not supported by preprinted documents, as often is the case in on-line computer-based systems, numbers should be assigned to stored records.

5. Print transaction listings (e.g., check registers) and account summaries on a periodic basis, in order to provide an adequate audit trail. Also, prepare various outputs that aid control, such as exception and summary reports.

FIGURE 13-20   (*Continued*)

invoices received from suppliers or a listing of the vouchers prepared from the invoices. The *check register* is a listing of all checks written. It may alternatively be called the cash disbursements journal. Each day's listing is accompanied by a summary of the gross amount of payables reduced, the discounts taken, and the net amount paid.

One class of operational reports aid in controlling operations by focusing on open documents. The **open purchase orders report** shows all purchases for which the related invoices have not yet been approved for payment. The **open invoices report** (also called the open payables report or the cash requirements report) lists all approved invoices that are currently unpaid. It may be arranged by invoice number, by expense account number, by due date, or by supplier (vendor) name. Figure 13-22, on page 569, shows a cash requirements report arranged by vendor name. It denotes special items, such as debit memos. This report is useful to the accounts payable department in determining which invoices should be paid in order to receive discounts, as well as the total amount of cash required to meet current obligations.

Other operational reports may emphasize inventory and receiving activities. The **inventory status report** contains quantities received, shipped, and on hand for the respective items of merchandise. This type of report can aid in determining when items should be reordered. The *receiving register* lists all incoming shipments from suppliers, including those that are rejected. It also contains comments based on the inspection of received goods. The **overdue deliveries report** pinpoints those purchase transactions whose requested delivery dates have passed without shipments having arrived from suppliers.

INQUIRY DISPLAY SCREENS

Inquiries from clerical personnel are often quite specific and involve relatively limited data. For instance, a warehouse clerk may inquire with respect to the status of a particular purchase order and obtain a screen display such as shown in Figure 13-23 on page 570. Other clerical inquiries might concern (1) the recent invoices for a particular supplier, and (2) a summary of open purchase orders.

Inquiries from professional employees tend to be more analytical in nature. For instance, an accountant may download purchases and inventory data into a

Type of Edit Check	Typical Transaction Data Being Checked		Assurance Provided
	Purchases	Cash Disbursements	
1. Validity check	Supplier account numbers, inventory item numbers, transaction codes	Supplier account numbers, transaction codes	The entered numbers and codes are checked against lists of valid numbers and codes that are stored within the computer system.
2. Self-checking digit	Supplier account numbers	Supplier account numbers	Each supplier account number contains a check digit that enables errors in its entry to be detected.
3. Field check	Supplier account numbers, quantities ordered, unit prices	Supplier account numbers, amounts paid	The fields in the input records that are designated to contain the data items (listed at the left) are checked to see if they contain the proper mode of characters (i.e., numeric characters). If other modes are detected, an error is indicated.
4. Limit check	Quantities ordered	Amounts paid	The entered quantities and amounts are checked against preestablished limits that represent reasonable maximums to be expected. (Separate limits are set for each product.)
5. Range check	Unit prices	None	Each entered unit price is checked to see that it is within a preestablished range (either higher or lower than an expected value).
6. Relationship check	Quantities received	Amounts paid	The quantity of goods received is compared to the quantity ordered, as shown in the open purchase orders file; if the quantities do not agree, the receipt is flagged by the edit program. When an amount of a cash payment is entered as a cash disbursement transaction, together with the number of the voucher or invoice to which the amount applies, the amount in the open vouchers (or invoices) file is retrieved and compared with the entered amount. If a difference appears, the transaction is flagged.
7. Sign check	None	Supplier account balances	After the amount of a cash disbursement transaction is entered and posted to the supplier's account in the accounts payable ledger (thereby reducing the account balance of the supplier), the remaining balance is checked. If the balance is preceded by a negative sign (indicating a debit balance), the transaction is flagged.
8. Completeness check[a]	All entered data elements	All entered data elements	The entered transactions are checked to see that all required data elements have been entered.
9. Echo check[a]	Supplier account numbers and names, inventory item numbers and descriptions	Supplier account numbers and names	After the account numbers for suppliers relating to a purchase or cash disbursements transaction (and also the product numbers in the purchase transaction) have been entered at a terminal, the edit program retrieves and "echoes back" the related supplier names (and product descriptions in the case of purchase transactions).

[a]Applicable only to on-line systems.

FIGURE 13-21 Programmed edit checks that are useful in validating transaction data entered into the expenditure cycle.

Representative Merchandising Company 1　　　Accounts Payable　　　Time 15:00:06　　　Date 4/23/97　　Page 1　　3948
Batch-6　Session 1　　　　　　　Cash requirements report　　　Expected payment date 4/29/97

Line number	Vendor name	Invoice number	Due date	Balance due	Payment amount	Discount taken	Net amount	Hold	Comments
1	Able Manufacturing Co.	000123	3/04/97	100.00	100.00	.00	100.00		
2		000789	2/26/97	600.00	600.00	.00	600.00		
3		004560	3/29/97	500.00	500.00	.00	500.00		
4		123457	4/29/97	100.50	100.50	10.00	90.50		
	Vendor A1011　Total			1,300.50	1,300.50	10.00	1,290.50		
7	Butler Supply Co.	112	4/29/97	1,567.98	1,567.98	235.20	1,332.78		
5		156710	4/29/97	400.00	400.00	.00	400.00		
	Vendor B2893　Total			1,967.98	1,967.98	235.20	1,732.78		
9	Bishop Brothers	2034	5/06/97	750.00	750.00	37.50	712.50		
	Vendor B4056　Total			750.00	750.00	37.50	712.50		
8	Sanford Stationery Store	10	4/29/97	12.00	12.00	.00	12.00		
	Vendor S3123　Total			12.00	12.00	.00	12.00		Debit memo
6	Doral, Inc.	32	4/29/97	7,200.00	7,200.00	800.00	6,400.00		Exceeds maximum check amt
	Vendor 0　Total			7,200.00	.00	800.00			

| Total debit memo amount | | | | 12.00 | 12.00 | .00 | 12.00 | | |
| Total check amount | | | | 11,218.48 | 11,218.48 | 1,082.70 | 10,135.78 | | |

```
Cash required           10,125.78
Number of checks            4
Number of debit memos       1
Summary totals check        1
Total number of checks      6
```

FIGURE 13-22　A cash requirements report. (Courtesy of IBM Corporation.)

spreadsheet package, in order to compare the effects on inventory valuations of assigning standard unit costs versus average actual unit costs.

Inquiries made by managers can be both analytical and decision oriented. The data base the managers employ might be specially assembled executive information systems (EISs), which can draw from the expenditure cycle as well as from other sources. Consider, for example, that Infoage's treasurer is concerned about the state of current liabilities. She could first obtain a screen showing comparative details of the outstanding bank loans and notes, with the interest rate on each. Then, she could retrieve from an external on-line information service (e.g., Dow Jones) the rates of interest charged by various banks for short-term loans. Observing that one outstanding bank loan carries a rate of interest well above a rate charged by a Chicago bank, for instance, she decides to pay off the bank loan and obtain a new loan at the lower rate.

SCHEDULED MANAGERIAL REPORTS

A variety of reports, such as the inventory status report, can be prepared on a scheduled basis for use by inventory and financial managers. Several others will be briefly described.

A **payables aging report** reflects the status of old unpaid invoices or vouchers, usually due to unresolved questions with suppliers or to liquidity problems. Unless action is taken to reduce large overdue amounts, the firm may jeopardize its relations with the suppliers and have difficulty in obtaining new merchandise.

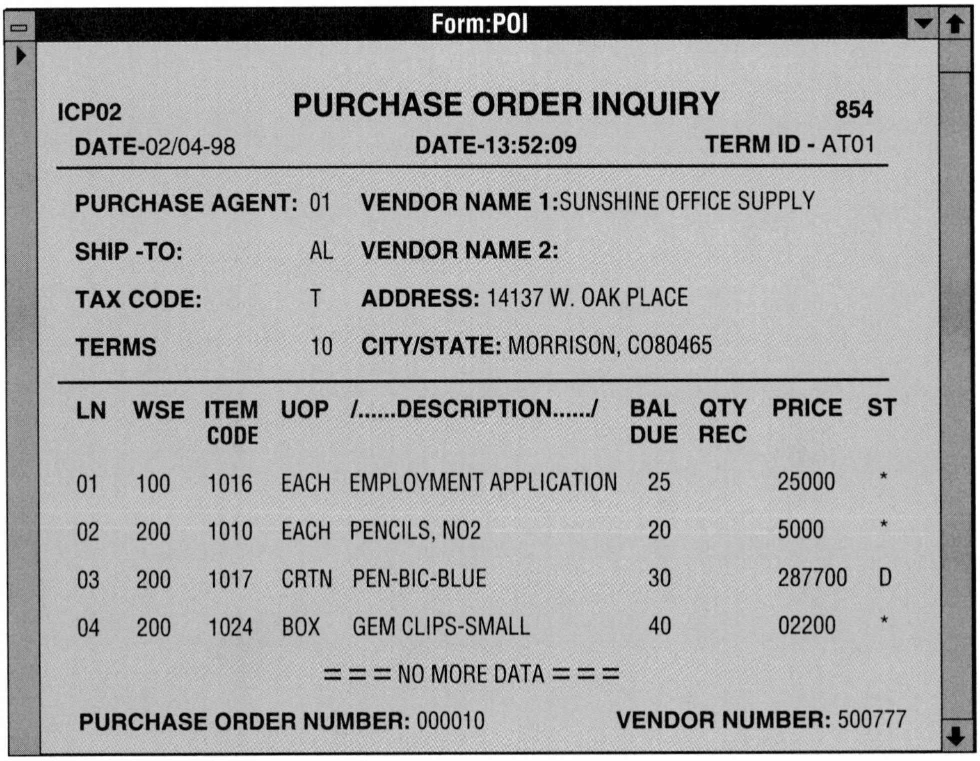

| | | | | Form:POI | | | | | |

ICP02   **PURCHASE ORDER INQUIRY**   854
DATE-02/04-98   **DATE**-13:52:09   **TERM ID - AT01**

PURCHASE AGENT: 01   **VENDOR NAME 1:** SUNSHINE OFFICE SUPPLY

SHIP -TO: AL   **VENDOR NAME 2:**

TAX CODE: T   **ADDRESS:** 14137 W. OAK PLACE

TERMS   10   **CITY/STATE:** MORRISON, CO80465

LN	WSE	ITEM CODE	UOP	/......DESCRIPTION....../	BAL DUE	QTY REC	PRICE	ST
01	100	1016	EACH	EMPLOYMENT APPLICATION	25		25000	*
02	200	1010	EACH	PENCILS, NO2	20		5000	*
03	200	1017	CRTN	PEN-BIC-BLUE	30		287700	D
04	200	1024	BOX	GEM CLIPS-SMALL	40		02200	*

= = = NO MORE DATA = = =

PURCHASE ORDER NUMBER: 000010   **VENDOR NUMBER:** 500777

FIGURE 13-23   A display screen in response to an inquiry.

| -----VENDOR----- | | | -----SHIPMENTS----- | | | --AVERAGE-- | | ---PRICE--- --VARIANCE-- | | VENDOR RATINGS |
NUMBER	NAME		TOTAL	PCT LATE	DEFECTIVE	DAYS LATE	PCT DEFECTS	AMOUNT	PCT	
AT3022	ANDREWS CO	THIS PERIOD	60	.9	11	3.5	5.0	7,364	8.0	IMPORTANCE MEDIUM
		THIS YEAR	222							QUALITY... AVERAGE
		LAST YEAR								SERVICE... GOOD
LM3021	LAWSONS CO	THIS PERIOD	30	50.0	4	3.4		118,245-	6.0-	IMPORTANCE HIGH
		THIS YEAR	97	12.1		4.6	.2	113,920-	3.0-	QUALITY... GOOD
		LAST YEAR	130	3.0	13	8.5	3.0	8,500		SERVICE... GOOD
RM3023	RIVERTON	THIS PERIOD	11	70.0	1	4.6		6	1.0	IMPORTANCE MEDIUM
		THIS YEAR	22	41.7	2	4.2	.1	436		QUALITY... AVERAGE
		LAST YEAR								SERVICE... AVERAGE
TF1028	TRIANGLE	THIS PERIOD	12							IMPORTANCE HIGH
		THIS YEAR	79							QUALITY... GOOD
		LAST YEAR	242							SERVICE... GOOD
VI3024	VOLMER IND	THIS PERIOD	2							IMPORTANCE HIGH
		THIS YEAR	12	5.0		.5	1.0			QUALITY... GOOD
		LAST YEAR								SERVICE... EXCELLENT

FIGURE 13-24   A supplier (vendor) performance evaluation report. (Courtesy of Data Design Associates.)

Purchase analyses show the levels of purchasing activity for each supplier, inventory item, and buyer. For instance, a typical analysis may show the number and dollar amount of purchases placed with each supplier this year, as well as the average dollar expenditure. This analysis would show the degree to which purchases are concentrated with certain selected suppliers. An analysis of the number of purchases placed by each buyer would indicate the relative productivity of the buyers.

A key report relating to suppliers is known as a **vendor performance report**. Figure 13-24 shows the relative performance of suppliers (vendors) in terms of on-time shipments, quality of goods, unit prices, level of service, and condition of goods delivered.

Still other reports include the cash-flow statement (discussed in Chapter 12) and a critical factors report, which includes such performance measures as the number of purchase discounts lost.

Figure 13-25 portrays most of the listings and reports described in the preceding paragraphs. They are shown as outputs produced from data in the various files listed in an earlier section. The check register, cash requirements report, inventory status report, and others were included in the computer system flowcharts.

DEMAND MANAGERIAL REPORTS

Demand reports are ad hoc nonscheduled reports. The information they contain is primarily used for managerial decision making and control. When also combined

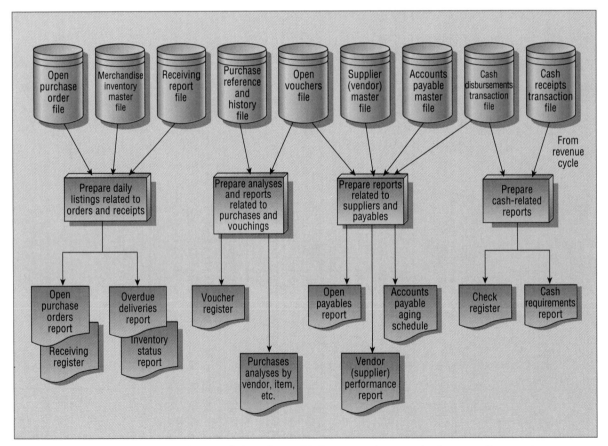

FIGURE 13-25   A system flowchart showing daily and monthly listings and reports in the expenditure cycle.

with decision-oriented modeling software and expert systems, the results can be quite powerful.

Consider a case in which Jack Dyson (Infoage's inventory manager) must decide on what levels of inventory to stock. The firm might employ a decision support system that models the expected demands for various items of merchandise, as well as the costs to carry merchandise and place orders. Other factors will include the cost of lost sales if inventory is not available, the lead times from suppliers, and the capacities of bins in the warehouse. The key outputs would be ad hoc reports showing the various costs for expected profiles of demand and levels of inventory. These reports would be repeated to show the effects of such "what if" scenarios as: What if the demands of all items were 10 percent less than expected? What if certain carrying costs were to increase by 15 per cent next quarter?

SUMMARY

The expenditure cycle facilitates the exchange of cash with suppliers for needed goods and services. Functions of the cycle (in the case of goods) are to recognize the need, place the order, receive and store the goods, ascertain the validity of the payment obligation, prepare the cash disbursement, maintain the accounts payable, post transactions to the general ledger, and prepare needed financial reports and other outputs. Related functions involve purchase returns and allowances and petty-cash disbursements. These functions are achieved under the direction of the inventory management and finance/accounting organizational units. Data generated during the processing of purchases and cash disbursements, together with externally oriented inventory and financial data, are needed in making inventory and financial decisions at all managerial levels.

Most of the data used in the cycle arise from suppliers and inventory records. Documents typically employed are the purchase requisition, purchase order, receiving report, supplier's (vendor's) invoice, disbursement voucher, and check (with voucher). Preformatted screens may be used in on-line systems to enter purchases and cash disbursements data. The data base includes such files as the supplier (vendor) master, merchandise inventory master, open purchase order, open voucher, cash disbursements transaction, and supplier reference and history files. In firms that adopt the data-base approach, these files would be converted into linked data structures. Data processing occurs upon the entry of data from purchases and cash disbursements transactions. Usually it involves the updating of accounts payable records. Processing may feasibly be performed by manual systems or computer-based systems. Computer-based systems that combine on-line inputs with batch processing are a suitable choice for many firms.

A variety of risk exposures exist in the processing of purchases and cash disbursements transactions. Exposures due to these risks can be counteracted by means of adequate general and application controls. Among the outputs generated by the expenditure cycle are the voucher register, check register, cash requirements report, open purchase orders report, open payables report, overdue deliveries report, purchase or supplier inquiry screens, payables aging report, purchases analyses, and supplier performance report.

APPENDIX TO CHAPTER 13

MANUAL PROCESSING WITHIN THE EXPENDITURE CYCLE

This appendix provides a survey of manual processing procedures relating to purchases, payables, and cash disbursements. Narrative descriptions of the procedures are accompanied by document system flowcharts, which are keyed to the narrative by circled numbers. These numbers designate key control points within the purchases, payables, and cash disbursements procedures. The application controls described in the chapter are particularly needed at these points. The accounting entries pertaining to the expenditure cycle are included at appropriate places in the narrative descriptions.

Purchases Procedure

Figure 13-26 depicts a document flowchart of the manual procedure involving the purchases of goods on credit. As just mentioned, numbers designate the control points within the purchases procedure, that is, the determination that goods are needed, the preparation of a purchase order, the receipt of ordered goods, and the receipt of the supplier's invoice.

① **Determination of the need for goods.** In the inventory control department, a clerk examines inventory records to locate those items whose on-hand quantities are below a preestablished reorder point.

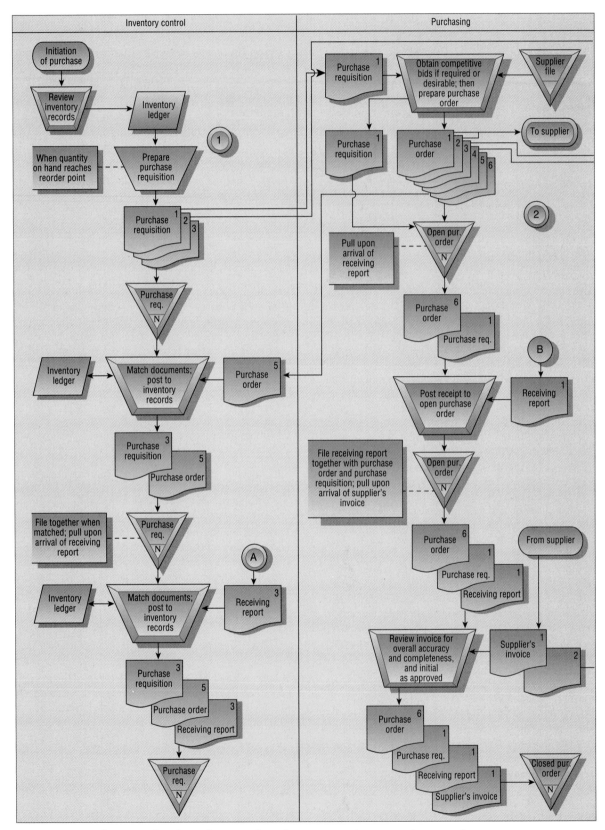

FIGURE 13-26 A document flowchart of a manual purchases transaction processing procedure.

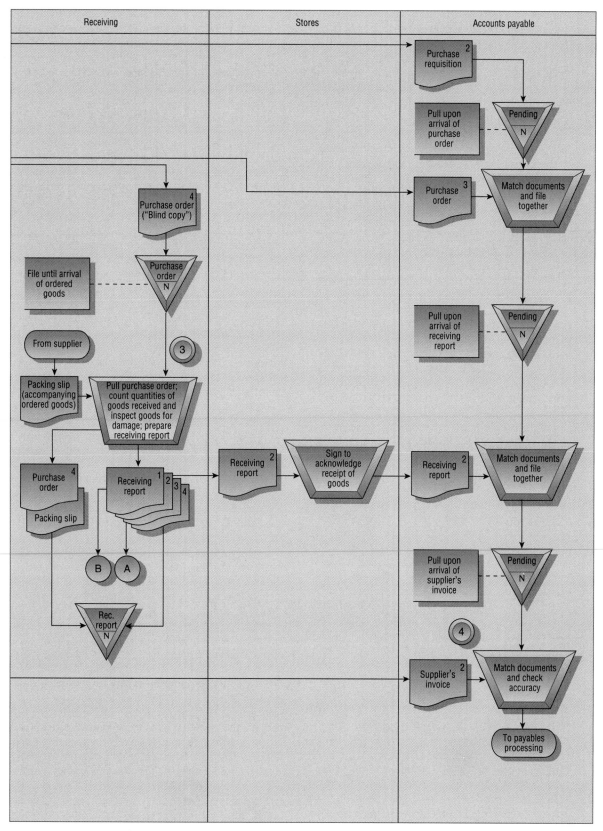

FIGURE 13-26 (Continued)

Those items that need to be reordered are listed on a prenumbered and well-designed purchase requisition form. For each item, the clerk specifies a precomputed economic order quantity. Upon approval of the requisition, perhaps by the inventory manager, copies are sent to the purchasing department and receiving department.

② **Preparation of the purchase order.** When the purchase requisition is received in the purchasing department, a buyer is assigned by the purchasing manager to handle the purchase transaction. If the goods or circumstances are nonroutine, competitive bids are obtained. If the needed goods are routine (or after bids have been evaluated), the buyer selects the most suitable supplier from an approved supplier file and prepares a prenumbered purchase order. When the purchase order has been checked for prices and terms and signed by an authorized person, such as the purchasing manager, the copies are distributed. Two copies are mailed to the supplier. Other copies are forwarded to the inventory control, receiving, and accounts payable departments. The copy sent to inventory control (which may actually be an amended copy of the requisition) is used to post ordered quantities to the inventory records. The copy for the receiving department (which has the quantities blacked out, i.e., is "blind") is used later to verify the authenticity of the received goods. The copy sent to accounts payable is to provide prior notification that an invoice is soon to be received. Also, the last copy is filed in the open purchase order file to await the arrival of the invoice.

③ **Receipt of ordered goods.** When the ordered goods arrive at the receiving dock, the "blind" copy of the purchase order is matched to the packing slip, in order to verify that the goods were ordered. Next the receiving clerk inspects the goods for damage and counts the quantities received. Then he or she prepares a prenumbered receiving report on which the findings are recorded. The original copy of this report accompanies the goods to stores, where the storeskeeper or warehouse worker signs the copy (to acknowledge receipt) and forwards it to accounts payable. Other copies of the receiving report are sent to the purchasing department (to update the open purchase order) and to the inventory control department (to update the inventory records).

④ **Receipt of the supplier's invoice.** When the supplier's invoice arrives soon after the ordered goods, it may first be routed to the purchasing department for comparisons with the documents relating to the purchase. If found to be proper and complete, the invoice is forwarded to the accounts payable department for more extensive processing. (Invoices pertaining to services are first routed to the using departments, where they are approved for payment by the managers responsible for incurring the expenditures. Then they are forwarded to accounts payable.)

Accounts Payable Procedure

Since accounts payable is an accounting department not directly involved in purchasing and receiving goods, it is the most suitable department to examine the supplier's invoice and to trace its contents to the supporting documents. As noted earlier, this examination process is called vouching.

Figure 13-27 presents the vouching step and the processing steps that follow. Upon receiving an invoice in the accounts payable department, a clerk pulls the supporting documents from a file and performs the various comparisons and checks that constitute vouching. These verifications are intended to determine that (1) the purchase has been authorized, (2) the goods or services listed in the invoice have been duly ordered, (3) the goods or services have been received in full, (4) the unit prices are in conformity with the purchase order or are satisfactory to the purchasing department, (5) the terms and other specifications are in agreement with the purchase order, and (6) all computations are correct. After finishing, the clerk initials an audit box (either stamped on the invoice or on another document such as a voucher) to acknowledge that the verifications have been performed and the supplier's invoice is approved for payment. Any differences must be settled, however, before a supplier's invoice can be approved for payment. For instance, if only part of the order is received, the purchase order should be so marked and returned to the file.

Assuming that the voucher system is used, a disbursement voucher is prepared on the basis of one or more approved suppliers' invoices. Then the voucher is entered in a voucher register. Batch control totals are computed from the columns in the voucher register, including the total amount of payables, the total merchandise cost, the total selling expense, and so on. A journal voucher is prepared from these totals.

A clerk posts the vouchers to the suppliers' accounts in the accounts payable subsidiary ledger. Batch totals are computed of the posted credits. Also, copies of the vouchers are forwarded to accounting departments that maintain the ledgers relating to the various expenditures (labelled in the flowchart as inventory/expense control). Clerks in these departments post debits to inventory, supplies, fixed assets, selling expense, and administrative expense ledgers. Batch totals are computed of the posted debits. Then the batch totals of the posted debits and credits are compared to the journal voucher

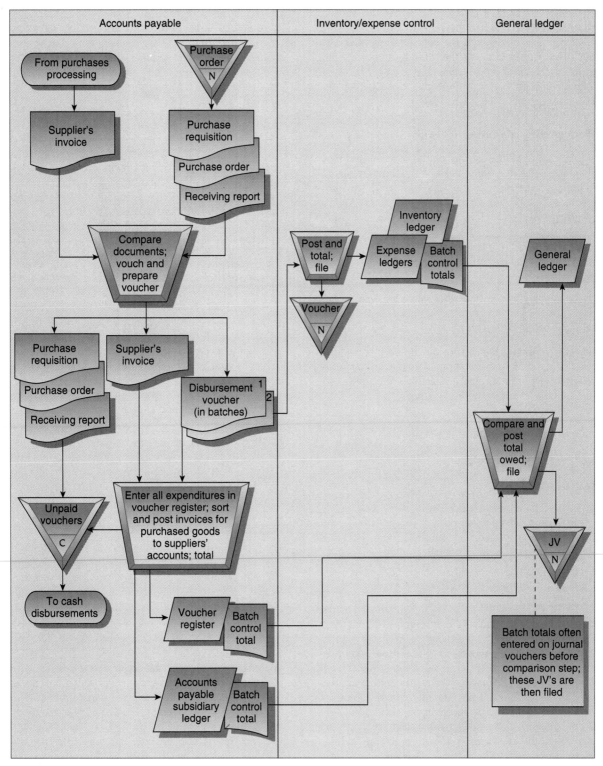

FIGURE 13-27 A document flowchart of a manual payables processing procedure.

previously prepared. If all amounts agree, the entry is posted to the accounts in the general ledger.

Finally, the originals of the vouchers, together with the supporting documents, are filed in a "tickler" file, which is a file arranged by payment due dates. There the unpaid vouchers remain until ready for use in cash disbursements processing.

Posting to General Ledger Accounts

The form of the entry concerning the purchases of merchandise depends on the inventory method employed. In the case of the periodic inventory method, the entry involves the following accounts:

Dr. Purchases	XXX	
Cr. Accounts Payable		XXX

In the case of the perpetual inventory method, the entry involves the following accounts:

Dr. Merchandise Inventory (or Raw Materials)	XXX	
Cr. Accounts Payable		XXX

Returns and allowances for purchased merchandise may be entered from debit memoranda onto journal vouchers. An entry would be as follows, assuming that the periodic inventory method is used:

Dr. Accounts Payable	XXX	
Cr. Purchases Returns and Allowances		XXX

When the periodic inventory method is used, the following adjusting entry must also be made at the end of each accounting period:

Dr. Merchandise Inventory, Ending	XXX	
Dr. Cost of Goods Sold	XXX	
Cr. Purchases		XXX
Cr. Merchandise Inventory, Beginning		XXX

Detailed Inventory Posting Procedure

Figure 13-28 presents a data-flow diagram of the activities relating to the merchandise inventory. It summarizes all of the postings to the merchandise inventory records, as follows: (a) when orders are placed, the quantities ordered are added to the Ordered column and the On Order balance is increased, (b) when ordered quantities are received, the quantities are added to the Receipts column, the On Hand balance is increased, and the On Order balance is decreased, (c) when sales are made, the quantities sold are added to the Sales column and deducted from the On Hand balance, (d) when purchases are returned, the quantities returned are deducted from the On Hand balance.

Inventory ledger records can include the dollar value of inventory items in addition to the quantities. However, it is necessary to determine the unit costs that will be used to calculate the dollar values of transactions. Actual unit costs based on suppliers' invoices have customarily been used, but they can vary from purchase to purchase and can also require adjustment to allow for freight and sales taxes. Thus, many firms use standard unit costs that are held constant for a year or more.

Cash Disbursements Procedure

Figure 13-29, on page 580, flowcharts a procedure involving the disbursements of cash related to purchases on credit. The principal control points involve the assembly of the unpaid vouchers, the preparation of the checks, the signing of the checks, the processing of the cash disbursement records, and the posting of cash amounts.

① **Assembly of the unpaid vouchers.** The cash disbursements procedure begins in the accounts payable department with the unpaid voucher file. Each day (or at specified periods) a clerk extracts the unpaid vouchers due to be paid that day. She or he reviews each voucher "package" to see that it contains all of the supporting documents, including the invoices. After computing the total amount to be paid and posting the payment amounts from the vouchers to the appropriate suppliers' accounts, the clerk forwards the vouchers and supporting documents to the cash disbursements department.

② **Preparation of the checks.** A cash disbursements clerk inspects each voucher for completeness and authenticity and then prepares a prenumbered check. When done, the clerk forwards the original checks to an authorized check signer, together with the supporting documents. Then the check copies are entered into the records.

③ **Signing of the checks.** In many firms the authorized check signer is the treasurer, although the cashier may be authorized to sign checks below a designated amount. The signer first reviews the supporting documents. Then he or she signs each check that is properly supported and routes the checks directly to the mail room. From the mail room the checks are delivered to the post office.

④ **Processing of the cash disbursement records.** The amounts and other key data concerning the checks are entered in a check register, and the total of the paid amounts is computed. One copy of the check (with voucher) is filed in the cash disbursements department numerically. The other copy of the check (with voucher) is stapled to the supporting documents, which are stamped as paid, and the package is returned to the accounts payable department. There the number of each check and the date are entered in the voucher register, and the package is filed alphabetically by supplier.

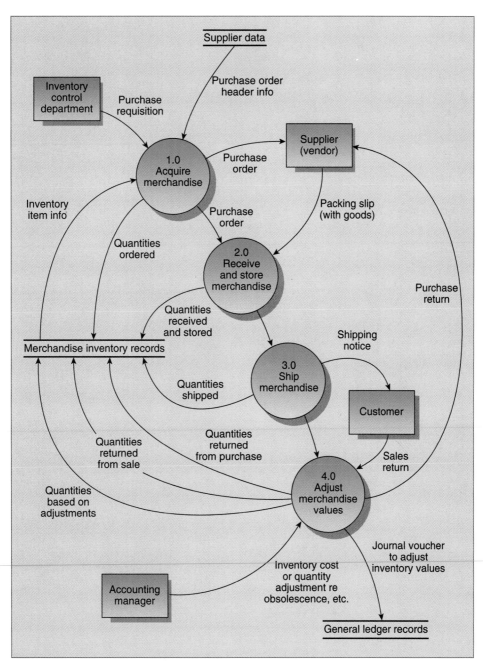

FIGURE 13-28   A data-flow diagram pertaining to merchandise inventory activity.

Firms that process large volumes of invoices often find that the bulky voucher packages consume much storage space and are awkward to retrieve. Thus they may decide to microfilm the documents after processing and then to destroy the documents. The microfilm images may be arranged by voucher numbers and cross-referenced to supplier names.

⑤ **Posting of cash amounts.** A journal voucher is prepared on the basis of the total of prepared checks and sent to the general ledger department. If the amount in the journal voucher agrees with the total debits posted to the accounts payable ledger, the entry is posted to the accounts in the general ledger as follows (assuming that the gross method of recording purchases is used):

Dr. Accounts Payable	XXX	
Cr. Cash		XXX
Cr. Purchase Discounts		XXX

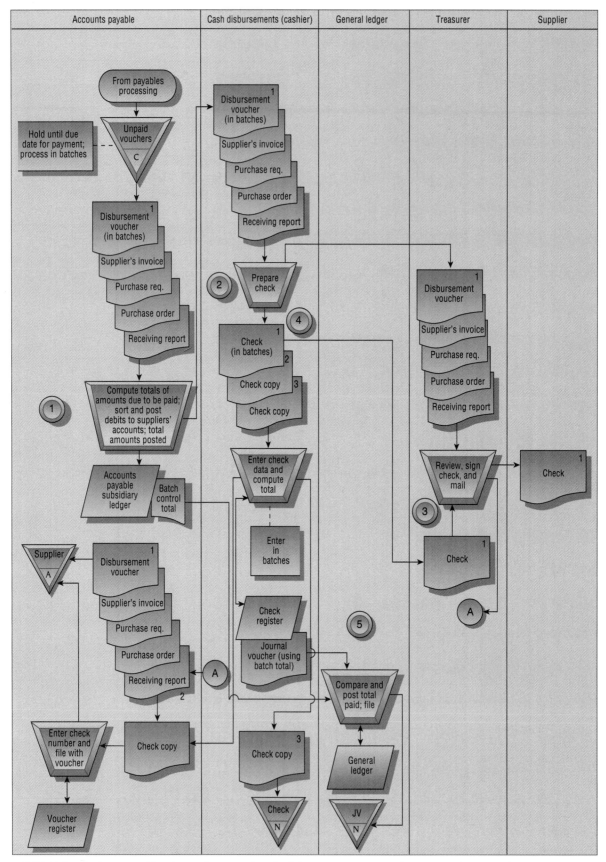

FIGURE 13-29   A document flowchart of a manual cash disbursements transaction processing procedure.

REVIEW PROBLEM WITH SOLUTION

HARTSHORN MANUFACTURING COMPANY

Statement

The Hartshorn Manufacturing Company of Wichita, Kansas, recently engaged a public accountant to review its various transaction processing procedures. During her review of the expenditure cycle, the public accountant made the following notes.

A production supervisor initiates a purchase by calling the purchasing department on the phone and stating his request. A buyer then prepares a letter concerning the requested materials, mails the letter to a supplier, and files his copy in the supplier's file folder. As the materials arrive, they are laid in any convenient area until the storeskeeper has an opportunity to store them in their bins or until the production supervisor carts them directly to the production line. When the supplier's invoice reaches the accounting department, an accounting clerk enters the invoice in the purchase journal. Near the end of each month the clerk prepares an unnumbered check for the amount of the invoice, has the treasurer sign the check, and mails the check to the supplier. Then the same clerk enters the amount of the check in the check register, posts the amount to the subsidiary ledger account sheet for the supplier, and files the check copy by supplier's name. Just before the trial balance is prepared, the same clerk totals the various special journals and posts the totals to the general ledger. When the workload is too heavy for this single clerk to perform, another clerk is assigned to handle those invoices from suppliers whose names begin with letters from N to Z. No one at any time counts the materials on hand, compares documents involved in a particular transaction, or reconciles accounting ledgers. When asked why such checks are not made, the accounting clerk replies that there is not enough time in a day and that the more urgent tasks have to be done.

Required

Analyze weaknesses in accounting control and suggest improvements.

Solution

Control Weakness	Suggested Changes
1. Verbal request for materials made by production supervisor.	1. Prepare a written request on a purchase requisition form; send the requisition to the purchasing department, with a copy to the accounts payable department; assign the preparation of the purchase requisition to the storeskeeper or to an inventory control clerk, who likely would have a better knowledge of inventory needs than the supervisor.
2. Letter prepared by buyer, with copy filed in supplier's folder.	2. Prepare a formal prenumbered purchase order, which is to be signed by the purchasing manager, and send to the supplier; send copies of the purchase order to a newly organized receiving department and to the accounting department as prior notification; also send a copy to the person who requested the order as verification and file a copy by number in the purchasing department. (*Note:* The copy to the receiving department should be blind. Also, consider requesting bids from suppliers before deciding on the supplier with whom to place the order.)
3. Arriving materials accepted without use of formal receiving procedure.	3. Require arriving materials to be formally accepted by a receiving department, organizationally separate from the stores department, which should perform the following steps: **a.** Verify that the materials were ordered by referring to its copy of the purchase order. **b.** Count the materials and note their condition. **c.** Prepare and sign a prenumbered receiving report, listing the quantities counted and the condition of the materials. **d.** Forward the materials with a copy of the receiving report to the storeskeeper, who should count the materials, sign the receiving report to acknowledge receipt, and then send the receiving report to the accounting department.

Control Weakness	Suggested Changes
	e. Send other copies of the receiving report to (1) an inventory control clerk for entry in inventory records and (2) the purchasing department for verification; also file a copy by number.
4. Materials laid in any convenient area accessible to the production supervisor.	**4.** Store materials promptly as received (see 3 above) in a stores area that is physically restricted to authorized stores personnel; issue to production supervisor on a prenumbered materials issue slip, which he should sign to acknowledge receipt.
5. Supplier's invoice inadequately verified and approved for payment.	**5.** Perform the following steps: **a.** Compare quantities shown to quantities listed on the receiving report. **b.** Compare unit prices shown to acceptable prices listed on the purchase order. **c.** Check the accuracy of the extensions and the totals. **d.** Initial and date the invoice, in a box stamped on its face, to indicate the completion of these actions. **e.** Prepare a disbursement voucher, attach supporting documents, and file by due date.
6. Cash disbursement not adequately controlled.	**6.** Prepare a prenumbered check and protect the amount; then forward the check to the treasurer, who should review the supporting documents, sign the check, and mail direct from his or her office (instead of returning to the accounting clerk for mailing); stamp "Paid" on all supporting documents and file by check number.
7. Inadequate separation of responsibilities in the accounting department.	**7.** Assign the responsibility for posting to the general ledger to another clerk in the accounting department, so that the work of the accounting clerk will be independently verified.
8. Tardy posting and lack of reconciliations.	**8.** Post daily from the journals to the general ledger and check the accuracy of posting by means of batch control totals; reconcile the accounts payable control account with the subsidiary ledger accounts on a frequent basis; count the materials on hand once or twice a year and reconcile with the perpetual inventory records maintained by an inventory conrol clerk.
9. Inappropriate assignment of duties during peak periods.	**9.** Assign a second clerk to particular tasks, such as making entries in the check register, filing copies of checks prepared for all suppliers, and totaling special journals. *Note:* This allocation of tasks is preferable to the assignment of a block of suppliers' invoices to the second clerk, since it enables one clerk to verify the work of the other.

KEY TERMS

accounts payable master file (545)
check register (536)
debit memorandum (537)
disbursement check (536)
disbursement voucher (534)
imprest system (538)
inventory management (538)
inventory status report (567)
kiting (562)
merchandise inventory master file (545)
new supplier (vendor) form (542)
open invoices report (567)

open purchase orders report (567)
overdue deliveries report (567)
payables aging report (570)
purchase analysis (572)
purchase order (531)
purchase requisition (531)
receiving report (532)
request for proposal (RFP) (532)
supplier master file (545)
supplier's (vendor's) invoice (533)
vendor performance report (572)
voucher register (534)
voucher system (534)
vouching (534)

REVIEW QUESTIONS

13-1. What are several objectives of the expenditure cycle?

13-2. What are the major functions of the expenditure cycle?

13-3. In what ways may the need for goods and services be established?

13-4. Describe the competitive bidding procedure.

13-5. How is the validity of a supplier's invoice established?

13-6. Describe the procedure for handling purchase returns.

13-7. Describe the imprest basis for handling petty-cash disbursements.

13-8. Describe the relationships of the inventory management organizational function to the expenditure cycle.

13-9. Describe the relationships of the finance and accounting organizational functions to the expenditure cycle.

13-10. Identify several decisions that must be made by the typical inventory manager.

13-11. What types of information are needed by an inventory manager when making decisions within his or her area of responsibilities?

13-12. What are the sources of data used in the expenditure cycle?

13-13. Identify the various documents used in the expenditure cycle.

13-14. Describe a typical data-entry screen for use in the expenditure cycle.

13-15. Identify the accounting entries needed to reflect the transactions within the expenditure cycle.

13-16. Describe several relevant characteristics that may be reflected in codes for (a) purchases transactions and (b) suppliers.

13-17. Identify the various files that are needed in the expenditure cycle.

13-18. What are the entities that are involved in the expenditure cycle?

13-19. Describe network and relational structures that might be employed within a data base that supports purchases processing.

13-20. What are the intersection records or relationship tables that are useful in data structures pertaining to purchases processing?

13-21. Describe the purchases/payables procedure when an on-line input batch processing computer-based system is used. Contrast this procedure with one performed manually.

13-22. Describe the cash disbursements procedure when an on-line input batch processing computer-based system is used. Contrast this procedure with one performed manually.

13-23. What are the benefits of processing purchases and cash disbursements transactions by means of an on-line input batch processing computer-based system?

13-24. What exposures to risk exist when processing transactions within the expenditure cycle?

13-25. Identify the control objectives that should be achieved with respect to the expenditure cycle.

13-26. Identify general controls that involve organizational independence, documentation, asset accountability, management practices, data center operations, and access within the expenditure cycle.

13-27. Identify the various input, processing, and output controls that pertain to the expenditure cycle.

13-28. What are the different types of outputs that should be generated by the expenditure cycle?

13-29. Describe three scheduled reports related to the expenditure cycle for use in managerial planning and control.

DISCUSSION QUESTIONS

13-30. What effects does a change within the expenditure cycle from a manual system to an on-line input batch processing computer-based system have on the (a) form of inputs, (b) sources of inputs, (c) files, (d) processing steps, (e) internal controls, and (f) outputs?

13-31. What are the most useful sources of information for inventory managers, other than expenditure cycle processing, if the managers' firm has installed an on-line computer system?

13-32. Describe several programmed edit checks, such as the redundancy matching check, that can be applied by the posting programs used in processing purchases, payables, and cash disbursements.

13-33. Figure 13-21 describes a relationship check that may be applied during the expenditure cycle. Describe at least one other relationship that involves dates. Hint: *Some suppliers offer terms allowing a cash discount if the bill is paid within 10 days.*

13-34. Which application controls that are needed in an expenditure cycle procedure involving an on-line computer-based system are not suitable when a batch computer-based system is employed, and vice versa?

13-35. Discuss why a check payable to a supplier for a credit purchase should not be used as the medium for posting to the supplier's account in the accounts payable ledger, rather than a copy of the check voucher.

13-36. Describe the differences in processing steps if Infoage employs batch input rather than on-line input for purchases and payables.

13-37. The illustrations in this chapter involving Infoage considered the purchasing of merchandise inventory to replenish the stocks in the warehouse. What additional processing steps and controls are needed to replenish the inventory in the retail sales outlets from the warehouse?

13-38. What are the benefits of employing electronic data interchange networks to link with major suppliers? How are cash disbursements handled under such arrangements?

....

PROBLEMS

Note: These problems include material presented in the Appendix to this chapter.

13-1. Po Co. is a merchandising firm that acquires its items from suppliers on consignment as its inventory grows low. Wo Co. is a merchandising firm that acquires merchandise for resale to specific customers; it employs a voucher system for handling invoices from suppliers. Both firms purchase services as well as merchandise.

Required

These two firms exhibit differences with respect to the functions associated in purchasing and paying for merchandise. In turn, the services that they purchase exhibit differences in the respective functions. List these differences with respect to the following functions in the expenditure cycle. (The first function is completed.)

a. Recognizing the need:
Po Co. merchandise—receives orders from customers for merchandise.
Wo Co. merchandise—determines when inventory items fall below their reorder points.
Services for both—receive requests from managers of departments in need of services.

b. Placing orders with suppliers.

c. Receiving merchandise or services.

d. Ascertaining validity of obligations.

e. Recording payables.

f. Preparing cash disbursements.

13-2. Rippon Manufacturing Co. is a medium-sized firm having the departments shown in Figure 13-7. Which of the departments is responsible for preparation (in the case of a document) or for recording (in the case of an accounting record)?

    a. Purchase order.

    b. Receiving report.

    c. Inventory records.

    d. Debit memorandum.

    e. Purchase requisition.

    f. Supplier records.

    g. Disbursement voucher.

    h. Cash disbursements journal.

    i. Disbursement check.

13-3. Sanford Electronics Co. is a wholesale distributor of electronic parts and products in Florida. It maintains a single warehouse, from which it distributes its inventory items to franchised dealers located throughout the state. The dealers place orders weekly, and Sanford delivers via a fleet of owned trucks.

The distributor has been profitable since it opened its doors, partly because it has carefully selected its dealers and partly because the electronics market has continually grown. However, the inventory and purchasing costs have grown faster, so that the profit levels have been shrinking. Jerry Sanford, the owner, has been surprised and disappointed each year by the declining profits when the financial statements have been prepared by the firm's accountants and presented to him. Upon investigation by consultants he has hired this year, the following conditions have been exposed: Among the 10,000 items carried in inventory, some have been excessively stocked and have aged; other merchandise items have been out of stock when ordered by the dealers. Apparently the inventory clerks do not order in a systematic manner, and the dealers vary their orders considerably based on the changing demands of their retail customers. Another problem is that inventory items are often difficult to locate in the warehouse, and in some cases items are stored in more than one place. Thus, the truck loading process is sometimes delayed and trucks cannot depart for their routes until two or three days have elapsed. With respect to purchasing, suppliers of merchandise are changed quite frequently, often on the whims of buyers. Partly because of these frequent changes, the accounts sometimes overlook purchase discounts when preparing disbursement checks. No long-term purchasing contracts are signed, although some parts and products have been consistent sellers in dealers' stores.

Required

Describe inventory and financial decisions that can apparently be improved. Explain what managerial actions and system changes are needed to aid in making these decisions.

13-4. The city of Rockrib is a southern city of 100,000 people. It has a centralized purchasing department, an accounts payable department, and a cashier's office, among other departments. Routine, widely used supplies are ordered on the basis of reorder reports, which are prepared daily by an inventory search program within the city's computer system. Nonroutine supplies and services are ordered on request by the various operating departments, such as the water department. Most of these nonroutine supplies and services are obtained after competitive bidding. Unacceptable receipts of supplies are returned to suppliers, with requests for refunds. Invoices from suppliers are approved via a voucher system. Checks are prepared on the computer system and mailed to suppliers within the discount periods. Balances owed and paid to suppliers are maintained in records on magnetic media.

Required

a. List the data elements needed to record and process purchases on credit, purchase returns, and cash disbursements transactions.

b. List the files needed to store the listed data elements. For each master file identify the primary key and several secondary keys.

c. Design group codes for supplier numbers and purchases and cash disbursements transactions.

d. Describe the formats of reports that would be useful to the firm's management in analyzing the purchases and cash disbursements and the activities related to suppliers' accounts. Note that the information available through such reports must be captured by the transactional codes designed in **c** above.

13-5. The National Industrial Corporation uses the form shown below as its purchase order.

Required

List added data items that should be included on the form and their locations, that is, in the heading, body, or foot. Also specify changes in the format of the purchase order to improve its usefulness.

(CPA *adapted*)

13-6. Mason Pharmaceuticals is a large manufacturer of drugs and other medical products. It receives numerous deliveries of raw materials and supplies at its central receiving dock. As each delivery arrives, a receiving clerk checks, via the receiving department on-line terminal, to ascertain that a related purchase order is on file. Then the clerk counts and inspects the received goods and lists the received items (and their condition) on a receiving form. Next the clerk transfers these receiving data to the computer system via the terminal. In doing so the clerk is aided by a preformatted receiving form that appears on the screen of the terminal. If the entered data correspond with the ordered data in the open purchase orders file, the transaction is accepted. This entry updates the inventory master file, makes a notation in the open purchase orders file, and creates a prenumbered formal receiving report.

Required

a. Draw a preformatted screen format that shows all the data elements to be entered by the receiving clerk

						PURCHASE ORDER

SEND INVOICE ONLY TO:
297 HARDINGTEN DR., BX., NY 10461

TO _____   SHIP TO _____

_____   _____

_____   _____

DATE TO BE SHIPPED	SHIP VIA	DISC. TERMS	FREIGHT TERMS	ADV. ALLOWANCE	SPECIAL ALLOWANCE
QUANTITY		DESCRIPTION			

PURCHASE CONDITIONS

1. Supplier will be responsible for extra freight cost on partial shipment, unless prior permission is obtained.
2. Please acknowledge this order.

3. Please notify us immediately if you are unable to complete order.
4. All items must be individually packed.

and that aids him or her in the data-entry process. Include in the screen format those elements that would be automatically entered by the computer program, either to identify the transaction or to aid in reducing input errors. Denote these system-generated elements by an asterisk (*).

b. Identify the programmed edit checks that should be incorporated into the data-entry program and the data element(s) that each is to check, plus all security measures that should pertain to the use and protection of this receiving department terminal.

13-7. Weepy Willows employs a voucher system for handling its disbursements. Checks that disburse funds, similar to the one shown in Figure 13-6, are mailed daily to suppliers and vendors of services. Among the files maintained in an on-line computer system are disbursement voucher and check files.

Required

Prepare a record layout of data from the disbursement check, which is to serve as a record in the cash disbursements transaction file. Include field sizes and data modes. Show sample data, for example, if the check number is 7690; the payee is Smith's Ceramics; the date is November 12, 1997; the check amount is $4300; the voucher against the check written is number 458; and the transaction code for disbursement checks is CD.

13-8. The Arrington Wholesaling Co. of Little Rock, Arkansas, services a number of retailers with several thousand grocery and sundry items. In turn it acquires merchandise from a wide range of suppliers across the country. Although it uses a computer system for billing, purchasing, and payroll processing, it has just recently turned to the application of cash disbursements.

Mary Brenner, a systems analyst, has been assigned the task of developing the processing procedure for cash disbursements. She begins by ascertaining the desired outputs from the procedure, as well as the file record layout and input document format. They are as follows:

Outputs

a. Check, which contains the check number, date, payee, accounts debited, invoice numbers, gross amount, discount, net amount.

b. Cash disbursements journal, which contains the date, check numbers, supplier numbers, supplier names, debits to accounts payable, credits to cash, purchase discounts.

Master File

Accounts payable, which contains in each record the supplier number, supplier name and address, invoice numbers, voucher number, date payment due, invoice amounts, discount, account balance.*

Input

Disbursement voucher, which contains the voucher number, date, supplier number and name, invoice numbers and dates, invoice accounts to be debited, discounts, net amounts.

Required

a. Indicate the source (i.e., the input document or master file) from which each item in the outputs is derived. If the item is produced by the computer system, state "system generated."

b. Prepare a computer system flowchart to reflect the batch processing of cash disbursements. Assume that the master file is stored on a removable magnetic disk pack.

c. Draw the outputs and the input, with all of the data elements being included within suitable formats.

d. List the accounting transaction controls that are suitable to a computer-based system for entering disbursement vouchers and processing cash disbursements by the batch approach. For each listed programmed check, also list the data elements to whch the check pertains.

13-9. The Teaneck Company purchases merchandise for resale from five suppliers. It maintains a trade accounts payable table in its relational data base, which lists the account numbers of these merchandise suppliers and their current balances. Other tables contain data concerning the suppliers, suppliers' invoices, open purchase orders, check disbursements, receiving reports, and merchandise inventory. (A separate accounts payable table also controls amounts owed for supplies and other expenses.) The firm assigns numbers to suppliers' invoices when received and prepares various records for control, such as invoice registers, open payables reports, and check registers. On September 1, the trade accounts payable table showed the following:

Supplier Number	Current Balance
20	4873.00
25	784.00
30	8310.00
35	1960.00
40	00.00

*This record layout reflects the assumption that only one voucher is unpaid at any time.

The open payables report on September 1 showed the following:

Invoice Number	Supplier Number	Purchase Order Number	Purchase Date	Payment Due Date	Invoice Amount	Discount Percent
276	30	568	8/3	9/14	5000.00	
277	20	569	8/6	9/18	4873.00	
278	30	570	8/13	9/24	2310.00	
279	35	571	8/17	9/3	2000.00	2
280	30	572	8/19	9/30	1000.00	
281	25	573	8/20	9/9	800.00	2

The open payables report on September 30 showed the following:

Invoice Number	Supplier Number	Purchase Order Number	Purchase Date	Payment Due Date	Invoice Amount	Discount Percent
282	20	574	8/25	10/5	2640.00	
283	40	575	8/31	10/12	950.00	
284	30	576	9/7	10/15	2350.00	
285	40	577	9/15	10/26	1400.00	
286	35	578	9/21	10/9	3000.00	2

Required

Using the transaction data provided, prepare the following tables as of September 30: trade accounts payable, supplier's invoice, and open purchase order. The tables should contain common columns where desirable. Assume that the discount period is 10 calendar days (where discounts are applicable) and that the firm takes all purchase discounts. For those suppliers who do not offer discounts, the terms are net 30 days. Also, the expected arrival date of ordered merchandise is always 8 calendar days later than the purchase date. No ordered items table is established in the case of purchase orders.

13-10. Regal Supply, Ltd., of Windsor, Ontario, maintains the following records pertaining to its vendors (suppliers) and outstanding (unpaid) accounts payable transactions. The general ledger account number refers to the type of expense incurred through the vendor: for example, purchases of new merchandise, purchases of used merchandise, or purchases of supplies, utility service, insurance service, and custodial service.

Required

a. Draw record layouts for both records.

b. Design a report listing the outstanding payables according to account numbers. Reported data concerning each payable should include the vendor name, city, prov-

Accounts Payable Transaction Record

Data Element	Field Size
Vendor number	7
General ledger account number	4
Invoice number	7
Voucher number	7
Invoice date	6
Due date	6
Invoice amount	10
Discount	5
Net amounts	10

Vendor Master Record

Data Element	Field Size
Vendor number	7
Vendor name	21
Street number	6
Street name	15
City	15
Province/state	15
Country	6
Postal/zip code	6

ince/state, invoice number, due date, and net amount due.

c. Key each element in the report to a field in one of the record layouts drawn in **a** above. For instance, enter a circled A under the account number column in the report, and also a circled A under the general ledger account number field in the transaction record.

d. Describe, with the aid of a computer system flowchart, the preparation of the report. Assume that the transaction records and the master records are on magnetic disk.

(SMAC *adapted*)

13-11. Refer to Figure 13-14, pertaining to Infoage's expenditure cycle. Although the figure indicates a one-to-many relationship between obligations and cash disbursements, assume that a many-to-many relationship exists. That is, more than one payment can be made with respect to a single obligation (e.g., a purchase of merchandise or a fixed asset), while a single payment may span more than one obligation (e.g., a purchase from a supplier, as reflected on an invoice).

Required

a. Prepare a data structure diagram for the cash disbursements portion of the expenditure cycle, assuming that a network structure will be employed.

b. Prepare a data structure diagram that shows the tables and their relationships for the cash disbursements portion of the expenditure cycle, assuming that a relational structure will be employed.

13-12. Bangles Products is a distributor that maintains 12 warehouses. It acquires the 2000 products it stocks from a variety of suppliers. Each supplier provides more than one product, while each product is acquired from more than a single supplier. In placing purchase orders the buyers usually request more than one product. Typically 100 purchase orders are placed each day, and in the course of a month usually a particular supplier receives more than one purchase order.

Each warehouse is headed by a manager and has several employees assigned to various warehousing duties. Each warehouse contains most of the products, while each product is stocked in more than one warehouse.

Required

a. Identify the entities in the purchasing and inventory situation described above.

b. Prepare an entity-relationship diagram that spans the above situation.

c. If Bangles decides to acquire a relational data base management system software package, list the tables needed to contain data relating to the above situation.

13-13. Bargains, Inc., a retail firm in Evansville, Indiana, purchases merchandise for resale. A wide variety of merchandise items are acquired from about 200 suppliers. The firm employs an on-line processing system, with terminals located in the purchasing and receiving departments (among others) to handle its purchases procedure.

Purchase orders are prepared by buyers, who select suitable suppliers from which to order needed merchandise specified on purchase requisition sheets received from the inventory control department. (To aid the selection process, they make on-line inquiries via their terminals and obtain displays of suppliers' records on their CRT screens.) A buyer next enters the necessary data into his or her terminal relating to each purchase, including the transaction code, the number of the selected supplier, the numbers of the merchandise items being ordered and corresponding order quantities and expected unit prices, the expected date of arrival of the merchandise, the terms, the method of shipment, the shipper, the code of the warehouse to which the merchandise is to be shipped, and the buyer's number. The computer system then generates a printed purchase order, which contains the foregoing data plus a computer-assigned order number, the order date, the supplier name and address, the merchandise descriptions, the units of measure, the shipping address, and so on. (The computer system also posts the number of the purchase order and ordered quantities, plus the expected date of arrival, to all pertinent records of the merchandise inventory master file.) After review, the purchasing manager signs and mails each purchase order.

When ordered merchandise arrives at the receiving dock, it is counted by a receiving clerk and entered on a simplified receiving report containing fields for the date, supplier number, related purchase order number, the merchandise item numbers and corresponding quantities, a space for comments concerning the condition of the received merchandise, and a box for the initials of the receiving clerk. After completing the form, the clerk keys the receiving data into his or her terminal. The computer system then posts the receipt of the quantities to the pertinent records of the merchandise inventory master file. It also posts the date of receipt to the pertinent record in the open purchase order file. Then it generates a printed copy of a prenumbered receiving report, containing the entered data plus the supplier's name and address and the merchandise descriptions. (It also adds a copy of this receiving report to a disk file.)

Required

a. Prepare a preformatted screen for inputting the purchase order data and enter assumed sample data.

b. Draw the simplified receiving report form used by receiving clerks and enter assumed sample data.

c. The firm employs a relational data base for storing the purchase-related data. Design the columns for four needed tables, based on the described procedure. Provide the common columns among the tables that facilitate the accessing of needed data.

d. Place circled POs by those data items within the foregoing table layouts that provide the sources of data for the printed purchase order (PO) (other than those provided by the screen).

e. Place circled RRs by those data items in the foregoing table layouts that provide the sources of data for the printed receiving report (RR) (other than those provided by the input form).

13-14. North Enterprises, Inc., has been experiencing increased difficulties in the accounts payable area. Numerous payments have been late, causing the loss of a significant amount in purchase discounts. A small minority of suppliers have been overcharging, either by raising their unit prices or by shipping larger quantities than appear on the purchase orders. In some cases it has been found that the same invoices have been paid two or three times. More errors than seem reasonable have appeared in the suppliers' accounts payable accounts. Many checks have been prepared for signing each day. In fact, often three or more checks are prepared for the same supplier during a day. These difficulties have led the accounts payable manager to press for a new computer-based system that will process accounts payable.

Required

a. List the types of transactions that can affect the accounts payable balances.

b. Show several transactions that might arise from a merchandise purchase of $400. Assume that the firm employs the periodic inventory method and that the supplier allows a 2 percent purchase discount.

c. Describe several reports that can aid the manager in assessing the extent of the difficulties and the success in overcoming them.

d. Describe one or more ways of correcting each of the difficulties raised, other than by installing a new computer system.

e. Assuming that a computer-based system is approved for installation, weigh the relative advantages between (i) a system that uses the periodic processing approach, (ii) a system that uses the immediate processing approach, and (iii) a system that uses on-line data entry but periodic processing.

13-15. Wooster Company is a beauty/barber supplies and equipment distributorship servicing a five-state area. Management has generally been pleased with the firm's operations to date. However, the present purchasing system has evolved through use rather than formal design. It may be described as follows: Whenever the quantity of an item is low, the inventory supervisor phones the purchasing department and provides the description and quantity of each item to be ordered. The purchasing department then prepares a purchase order in duplicate. The original is sent to the supplier, and a copy is filed in the purchasing department numerically. When the ordered items arrive, an inventory clerk (under the supervisor) checks off each item on the packing slip that accompanies the shipment. The packing slip is then forwarded to the accounts payable department. When the invoice arrives from the supplier, the packing slip is compared with the invoice by an accounts payable clerk. After any differences between the two documents have been reconciled, a check is drawn for the appropriate amount and is mailed to the supplier together with a copy of the invoice. The packing slip is attached to the invoice and is filed alphabetically in the paid invoice file.

Required

a. Prepare a level-zero data-flow diagram for the procedure described above.

b. Identify all documents that are needed to fulfill the requirements of an adequate expenditure cycle, and state the number of copies each form should have.

c. Prepare a document flowchart of the described procedure of Wooster's expenditure cycle. Include all departments needed to show the procedure and interfacing activities.

(CMA *adapted*)

13-16. Refer to Figure 13-18. Prepare a data-flow diagram that reflects the processes relating to cash disbursements.

13-17. The Old Missou Manufacturing Company is located in Columbia, Missouri. It has had many difficulties in materials control. Recently a raw materials inventory shortage was discovered. The resulting investigation revealed the following facts: Stock ledger cards are maintained in the storeroom and indicate the reorder point for each item. When the reorder point is reached, or when a special production order is received, the stock ledger clerk calls the purchasing agent and instructs him to order the item or items required. The purchasing agent prepares the purchase order in two copies, sending the original to the supplier and retaining the duplicate as the firm's record. All incoming materials are delivered direct to the storeroom. A receiving report is prepared; it is the basis for posting to stock ledger cards.

Invoices are received by the purchasing agent, who verifies price, terms, and extensions. He sends them to the stock ledger clerk, who verifies the receipt of the materials against stock-ledger-card postings. If the materials have been received, the invoice is sent to the cash disbursements section for payment. The stock ledger clerk verifies the balances shown by stock ledger cards with materials actually on hand as filler work. There has been little time recently to check ledger cards, since two clerks have been sick. No annual physical inventory is taken.

Required

a. List the control weaknesses in the foregoing procedures and recommend improvements.

b. Prepare a level-zero data-flow diagram that portrays the logical flows through the described activities.

13-18. The Acme Manufacturing Co. employs you as an internal auditor. Your current assignment is to perform an operational audit of the purchasing department, composed of 12 buyers and several secretaries and headed by a purchasing manager. "We run a fairly efficient operation here," the purchasing manager comments to you. "We have established purchasing policies and procedures. The buyers have an average of 12 years of purchasing experience, and all have long tenure with the firm. They have received on-the-job training, and a few have been sent to outside seminars for management training. Our main task is to get the right product in the right quantity to the right department. If you refer to the statistics on the number of purchase orders we handle each year, you will see that in recent years we have processed more purchase orders than ever with no increase in staff. I am pleased with my staff's performance."

During your review of operations you note the following:

    a. The firm is spending huge sums on microcomputers and related products. It acquires a variety of different makes from a variety of suppliers. The purchasing department orders the microcomputer that meets the capability requirements and has the lowest possible price. However, some of the suppliers have declared bankruptcy or have stopped producing the product lines the firm purchased.

    b. The purchasing department insists on ordering a certain chemical product from a supplier for the production department because the supplier is "stable and reliable and because the firm has always purchased from this supplier in the past." Some competing firms have successfully used a substitute product that has a much lower price.

    c. The firm normally purchases from local suppliers. By inquiries you determine that these local suppliers acquire their materials from two major producers in the East; any firm such as yours could order directly from these producers.

    d. One reason the number of purchase orders has increased is the increased frequency in gasoline purchases. It is possible to negotiate bulk purchases of gasoline.

    e. Only one quote is received from a supplier in the case of each product acquired, even though for most products ordered there are several suppliers available.

    f. Branch managers can order supplies in amounts less than $500 without following the purchasing department procedures. You note a few instances in which a purchase of an item costing more than $500 was made without the purchasing manager's approval by means of issuing several purchase orders for the item.

    g. One buyer is acquiring goods for Acme from a supplier owned by his wife and her brother.

Required

Identify each deficiency in the operations of the purchasing department, discuss the risk(s) related to the deficiency, and recommend controls to compensate for the exposures due to the risk(s).

(SMAC *adapted*)

13-19. The Alberta Company is a large research institute located in Calgary, Alberta. It employs a mainframe computer for transaction processing and research support. Magnetic disks provide all secondary storage, and on-line terminals are located in all the departments.

The institute allows managers in the various departments to acquire supplies, furniture, equipment, and other items needed and budgeted for. The purchases procedure begins with a requisition prepared by a department manager. Included on the purchase requisition are the description of each item to be purchased, the account number to be charged for the purchase, and the signature of the manager. On receipt of the requisition, a buyer in the purchasing department inserts the name and number of a suitable supplier and the estimated price of the item.

The buyer then enters the data from the requisition into the computer system via a video display terminal. First, the data are edited via an on-line program. Then a purchases program generates a prenumbered purchase order on a small impact printer in the purchasing department, with a copy of the purchase order being stored in an open purchase order file on magnetic disk. After the purchase order is signed by the purchasing manager, copies are distributed as follows: copy 1 to the supplier, copy 2 to accounts payable, copy 3 to receiving, and copy 4 to the requisitioner. However, if the amount of the purchase order exceeds the budget, as indicated by a message on the CRT screen, the buyer puts the purchase order in a hold file and notifies the requisitioner by preparing a hold notice.

When the ordered items arrive at the receiving dock, a receiving clerk pulls the purchase order (on which the quantities have been blanked out) from the file and counts the goods. Then the clerk enters the purchase order number, item numbers, and quantities counted via a video display terminal in the area. A receiving program edits the data, verifies that a purchase order exists, and updates the open purchase order file. It also updates either (1) the fixed-asset master file or (2) the expense control file, depending on the nature of the items received. The program then produces a prenumbered receiving report on a small printer in the receiving area, as well as a copy of the receiving report on a receiving report file (stored on a magnetic disk). The receiving clerk signs the receiving report and sends it, together with the items, to the requisitioning department. He refiles the purchase order copy by number, after stamping it completed.

The requisitioning department receives the items, signs the receiving report, and forwards it to accounts payable. When the supplier's invoice arrives, the payables clerk pulls the purchase order and receiving report from the file (where they have been filed by supplier name). Then the clerk enters the invoice number, purchase order number, receiving report number, item numbers, and quantities invoiced into a video display terminal. A payables program compares the data on the three documents and displays any differences. The clerk approves the invoice for payment if no differences appear (or puts it into a hold basket if differences must be reconciled) and enters the amount to be paid via the terminals. She files the documents by supplier name. The payables program (1) groups all payment data into an accounts payable file, (2) updates the open purchase order file by removing the completed purchase order, and (3) deducts the amount of the payable from the remaining balance in the department's budget.

At the end of each week the checks pertaining to all approved invoices are printed from the accounts payable file; data from the supplier file are also used in this run. A listing of the checks is generated during this run. In addition, a weekly report of open purchase orders is printed, arranged by order date. Finally, summary journal vouchers showing the total amounts of new payables and disbursements for the week are printed; these are sent to the general ledger clerk.

Required

a. Prepare a computer system flowchart of the following portions of the above procedure:

(1) The preparation of purchase requisitions and purchase orders, including the editing of requisition data.

(2) The processing of receipts of ordered goods.

(3) The processing of invoices and recording of accounts payable.

(4) The preparation of checks and weekly reports.

b. Prepare a level-zero data-flow diagram of the procedure pertaining to the expenditure cycle.

(SMAC *adapted*)

13-20. What error or fraudulent activity might occur if each of the following procedures is allowed?

a. The buyer in the purchasing department owns part interest in a supplier who provides merchandise of the type used by this firm.

b. The person who maintains the accounts payable records also prepares and signs checks to suppliers.

c. Suppliers' invoices are not compared to purchase orders or to receiving reports before payment.

d. Purchasing, receiving, and stores functions are combined into a single organizational unit.

e. Purchasing and accounts payable are combined into a single organizational unit.

f. The purchase orders are not prenumbered (or, if prenumbered, are not filed in a sequential file that is periodically checked for gaps in the numbers).

g. The accounts payable ledger is not periodically reconciled to the control account in the general ledger.

h. After checks are written, the suppliers' invoices are not marked in some manner, stapled to the supporting documents, and filed.

i. The bank statement is reconciled by the person who signs the checks or by the accounts payable clerk.

j. An accounts payable clerk prepares fictitious invoices from suppliers, who happen to be relatives, and approves them for payment.

k. A cashier signs checks to salespersons based on their oral statements that they incurred travel expenses and that the sales manager (who is on vacation) approved the travel.

13-21. What internal accounting control(s) would be most effective in preventing or detecting each of the following errors or fraudulent practices?

a. A supplier sends an invoice showing an amount computed on the basis of $10 per unit. However, the buyer in the purchasing department had listed the expected unit price as $7.

b. A supplier sends an invoice in the amount of $150. However, the goods were never ordered.

c. A supplier sends an invoice showing a quantity of 120 units shipped. However, only 100 units were actually received.

d. The cashier signs two checks, on successive days, to pay the same invoice from a supplier.

e. A firm's bank prepares a debit memorandum for an NSF (Not Sufficient Funds) check, but the bank clerk forgets to mail a copy of the memo to the firm.

f. A cashier prepares and submits an invoice from a fictitious supplier having the name of his neighbor, writes a check to the "supplier," and mails the check to his neighbor's address; the neighbor then cashes the check and splits the proceeds with the cashier.

g. A cashier prepares and signs a check that is not supported by an invoice. She cashes the check and conceals this theft by overfooting the columns of the check register (i.e., intentionally showing totals that are too large).

h. A petty-cash custodian removes $80 from the petty-cash fund to pay personal debts.

i. A truck driver who delivers goods to an electronics firm extracts for his use several small but expensive items from each delivery. On receiving one of these deliveries a receiving clerk signs a bill of lading that shows the number of items leaving the shipping dock and returns a copy to the driver.

j. A storeskeeper takes inventory items home at night; when the shortages become apparent, he claims that the receiving department did not deliver the goods to the storeroom.

k. When preparing a batch of disbursement vouchers for payment, a data-entry clerk keys the voucher number as 236544. (Voucher numbers in the firm in question are 5 digits in length.)

l. A purchasing department buyer requests a supplier (who happens to be a friend) to deliver ordered supplies directly to his home address, where he puts the supplies to personal use.

m. A prepared check voucher is accidentally lost; by the time the firm receives the following month's statement from the supplier, showing the continuing balance due, the purchase discount is lost.

n. A receiving clerk posts, via a terminal, the receipt of a quantity of goods that exceeds the quantity ordered.

o. A disbursement voucher is prepared in the amount of $3010, but it is incorrectly posted as $1030 in the accounts payable subsidiary ledger.

p. The expected unit price of a part is listed on a purchase order as $0.21, although the lowest unit price of any ordered part is $2.10.

13-22. What internal accounting control(s) would be most effective in preventing or detecting each of the following errors or fraudulent practices?

a. An accounts payable clerk, to whom a batch of signed disbursement checks is sent by the treasurer, abstracts one of the checks and cashes it after posting the amount to the payee's record.

b. A buyer enters, via her terminal, the number of a part being ordered as 54148, where the 1 is the letter l rather than the number 1.

c. An accounts payable clerk mistakenly enters, via her terminal, an account code for an expense as 333, although expense accounts begin at 500.

d. The actual quantity of a particular inventory item on hand in the storeroom is discovered to be zero, even though the inventory records show a quantity of 100 on hand.

e. A supplier's invoice is lost during the processing of a batch.

f. A purchasing department buyer orders unnecessary goods from a supplier firm, of which he happens to be an officer.

g. A receiving clerk posts the receipt of goods, via a terminal, to the incorrect inventory record.

h. During an inventory updating run, a receipt transaction is accidentally posted as an issue transaction, and so the on-hand balance in the computerized record is reduced to a negative quantity.

i. A buyer accidentally omits the unit price of one of the ordered products when keying the data for a purchase into a terminal.

j. A purchase order is coded with an incorrect and nonexistent supplier number. The error is not detected until the file updating run, when no master record is located to match the number.

k. Two supplier invoices are lost in transmitting the invoices to the data preparation room.

l. A check is written in the amount of $1000, whereas the disbursement voucher shows the amount to be paid as $100.

m. An error in an inventory transaction is referred by the data control group to the receiving department for correction. A week later the stores department complains that the weekly inventory status report is suspicious with respect to the inventory item in question. However, the data processing department cannot determine whether the error has been corrected and reprocessed.

n. Errors in posting and pilferage have led to a large difference for a particular item between the on-hand quantity shown in the inventory record and the actual physical quantity.

o. A posting error to the accounts payable control account has resulted in a large overstatement of the account.

p. A cashier of a firm prepares a check to a supplier that shows the amount to be net of the purchase discount allowed, even though the payment date is more than 10 days past the supplier's invoice date (the period during which discounts are allowed). Checks are prepared in batches via a check preparation program, based on data in an approved supplier invoice on-line file.

13-23. The following data pertain to vouchers that have been transmitted from the accounts payable department to the data processing department on May 18, where the data have been keyed onto a magnetic disk file. The vouchers represented by the data are to be used in preparing disbursement checks on this date.

Voucher No.	Supplier No.	Invoice Date	Disc. Pct.	Amount
6673	532	042098	0.00	540.00
6674	321	042098	0.00	892.00
6675	285	042098	0.00	1276.00
6676	502	042098	0.00	773.00
6678	477	042098	0.00	2343.50
6679	331	042098	0.00	390.00
6682	492	042098	0.00	3109.00
6723	294	050898	2.00	582.50
6726	439	050898	2.00	1500.00
6728	588	050898	3.00	668.00
6730	447	050898	1.50	800.00

Required

a. The preceding list of data constitutes a batch, for which control totals were precomputed in the accounts payable department. Identify all the possible batch control totals that might have been computed for this batch, and compute their values on the basis of the listed data.

b. Explain why gaps appear in the document voucher numbers.

c. Various edit checks may be applied to the preceding batched data during processing runs. For instance, the sequence of voucher numbers could be checked. If voucher number 6730 appeared ahead of 6728, an error would be listed on the exception and summary report.

Identify five additional edit checks that may reasonably be applied, and illustrate each by means of the listed data.

13-24. Lexsteel Corporation is a leading manufacturer of steel furniture. Although the firm has manufacturing plants and distribution facilities throughout the United States, the purchasing, accounting, and treasury functions are centralized at corporate headquarters.

While discussing the management letter with the external auditors, Ray Landsdown, controller of Lexsteel, became aware of potential problems with the accounts payable system. The auditors had to perform additional audit procedures in order to attest to the validity of accounts payable and cutoff procedures. The auditors have recommended that a detailed systems study be made of the current procedures. Such a study would not only assess the exposure of the firm to potential embezzlement and fraud, but would also identify ways to improve management controls.

Landsdown has assigned the study task to Dolores Smith, a relatively new accountant in the department. Because Smith could not find adequate documentation of the accounts payable procedures, she interviewed those employees involved. Descriptions of the current procedures are presented below.

The host computer mainframe is located at corporate headquarters with interactive, remote job entry terminals at each branch location. In general, data entry occurs at the source and is transmitted to an integrated data base maintained on the host computer. Data transmission is made between the branch offices and the host computer over leased telephone lines. The software allows flexibility for managing user access and editing data input.

Production orders and appropriate bills of material are generated by the host computer at corporate headquarters. Based on these bills of material, purchase orders for raw materials are generated by the centralized purchasing function and mailed directly to the vendors. Each purchase order instructs the vendor to ship the materials directly to the appropriate manufacturing plant. The manufacturing plants, assuming that the necessary purchase orders have been issued, proceed with the production orders received from corporate headquarters.

When goods are received, the manufacturing plant examines and verifies the count to the packing slip and transmits the receiving data to accounts payable at corporate headquarters. In the event that raw material deliveries fall behind production, each branch manager is given the authority to order materials and issue emergency purchase orders directly to the vendors. Data about the emergency orders and verification of materials receipts are transmitted via computer to accounts payable at corporate headquarters. Since the firm employs a computerized perpetual inventory system, physical counts of raw materials are deemed not to be cost effective and are not performed.

Vendor invoices are mailed directly to corporate headquarters and entered by accounts payable personnel when received; this often occurs before the receiving data are transmitted from the branch offices. The final day of the invoice term for payment is entered as the payment due date. This due date must often be calculated by the data-entry person using information listed on the invoice.

Once a week, invoices due the following week are printed in chronological entry order on a payment listing, and the corresponding checks are drawn. The checks and the payment listing are sent to the treasurer's office for signature and mailing to the payee. The check number is printed by the computer and displayed on the check and the payment listing and is validated as the checks are signed. After the checks are mailed, the payment listing is returned to accounts payable for filing. When there is insufficient cash to pay all the invoices, certain checks and the payment listing are retained by the treasurer until all checks can be paid. When the remaining checks are mailed, the listing is then returned to accounts payable. Often, weekly check mailings include a few checks from the previous week, but rarely are there more than two weekly listings involved.

When accounts payable receives the payment listing back from the treasurer's office, the expenses are distributed, coded, and posted to the appropriate plant/cost center accounts. Weekly summary performance reports are processed by accounts payable for each cost center and branch location, reflecting all data entry to that point.

Required

a. Identify and discuss three areas where Lexsteel Corporation may be exposed to fraud or embezzlement due to weaknesses in the procedures described, and recommend improvements to correct these weaknesses.

b. Describe three areas where management information could be distorted due to weaknesses in the procedures described, and recommend improvements to correct these weaknesses.

c. Identify three strengths in the procedures described and explain why they are strengths.

(CMA *adapted*)

13-25. Perky Sundries, a retail firm, has just installed an electronic data interchange (EDI) network that will be linked to its approved suppliers. Only the firm's purchasing agents can issue purchase orders via the EDI network. The total amount issued on purchase orders cannot exceed a budgeted amount specified by the marketing director. New suppliers will be added to the network only after thorough reviews by Perky's purchasing manager and marketing director.

All purchases go to the distribution center where they are electronically scanned into the computer system. All incoming items must reference a purchase order and any items that do not contain such a reference will not be accepted. Prenumbered receiving slips are not used, but all receipts are referenced to the purchase order. Price tags are generated per the purchase order and for the quantities indicated by the electronically scanned-in receiving report. The number of price tags generated is reconciled with the number of products received.

The supplier sends an invoice to the retailer. The invoices are keypunched and entered into the system. The computer software is programmed to match the vendor invoice, the purchase order, and the receiving report. If the three items are matched within a tolerance of 0.5 percent, the computer program schedules the items for payment at a time to take advantage of purchase discounts. A check is generated by the cash disbursements program and is electronically signed and mailed. If there is a discrepancy among the three documents, a report is printed and sent to the accounts payable department for investigation.

Required

a. Identify difficulties in maintaining adequate control over an EDI network, plus any control weaknesses in the described procedure.

b. Identify controls and security measures that should be taken with respect to the EDI network.

c. Describe audit procedures that are intended to determine

  (1) Whether the control relating to limiting the amount of purchases for a particular product line is functioning properly.

  (2) That the program for approving items for payment is functioning properly.

(CIA *adapted*)

13-26. The Wedge Manfacturing Co. of Cleveland, Ohio, processes purchases and inventory transactions as follows: The request for purchases begins in the plant operations department. That department prepares a two-part prenumbered inventory materials request, which indicates the description and quantity of inventory items and the date they are needed. The request must be approved by the plant manager. One copy of the request is forwarded to the manager of the purchasing department and the other copy is filed temporarily by inventory item name in the plant operations department.

On receiving its copy of the inventory materials request, the purchasing department prepares a six-part prenumbered purchase order. The distribution of the purchase order is as follows:

Original—supplier

Second copy—plant operations department

Third copy—receiving department

Fourth copy—accounts payable department

Fifth copy—filed temporarily with the inventory materials request by supplier name

Sixth copy—filed by number for two years

The plant operations department matches its copy of the purchase order to the inventory materials request and then files and retains for two years the two documents together according to the inventory materials request number.

The receiving department temporarily files its copy (the receiver copy) of the purchase order by supplier name until inventory materials are delivered. The receiving clerk indicates on the receiver the quantity of items received and the date. The clerk then photocopies the receiver and sends the original to the accounts payable department. The photocopy is sent to the purchasing department.

The purchasing department matches its supplier file copy of the purchase order with the receiver returned from the receiving department. When all items ordered are received, the purchase order, receiver, and the initial inventory materials request are filed by supplier name for two years.

The accounts payable department matches the receiver with its copy of the purchase order and files the documents by supplier name.

When a supplier's invoice is received, an accounts payable clerk compares the invoice and the related purchase order and receiver for description of material, quantities, and price. The three documents are then stapled together with a prenumbered two-part voucher ticket. The clerical accuracy of the invoice is verified and account distribution is assigned and indicated on the face of the voucher ticket. The voucher ticket also indicates the supplier name and number and the invoice number and date. This set of documents, called the voucher package, is filed by supplier name for seven years.

Before filing, however, the original copy of the voucher ticket is detached from the package and forwarded to another clerk in the accounts payable department, who verifies the clerical accuracy of the voucher ticket. Voucher tickets are accumulated and batched using a batch ticket, which indicates the date, the number of voucher tickets, and the total amount of invoices. From the batch ticket an adding machine tape is prepared of the daily total amount of invoices. The batch ticket and the related batch of voucher tickets are sent to the data processing (DP) department for processing.

On receiving the batch ticket and the voucher tickets, the DP department compares the documents for number of vouchers and the total amount of invoices. At this point, the batch ticket is assigned a number, and the batch is entered in the batch log (batch input control sheet). The voucher tickets are keyed to tape and forwarded for processing within the computer operations room. The voucher tickets are held in the DP department until all edit errors are corrected; then they are forwarded to the accounts payable depatment. The batch ticket is filed and retained in the DP department by batch number for two years.

Computer operations performs a report processing run that produces a daily voucher register, together with an error report. The accounts payable master file and the general ledger are the two disk files used in processing. The voucher tickets and error records from previous runs, on magnetic tape, serve as input.

The daily voucher register is returned to the same person in the DP department who prepared the batches for input. This person reviews the error report, accounts for the batches and control totals, and corrects errors. No approval is required for error corrections, which are processed the next day.

The accounts payable department receives the daily voucher register, together with the voucher tickets. The tickets and register are compared to ensure that each voucher ticket sequence number is in the daily voucher register. The voucher tickets are destroyed. The adding machine tape of the daily total amount of invoices on the batch ticket is compared to the total of the daily voucher register. The adding machine tape and the daily voucher register are filed separately by date and retained in the department for three years.

Required

a. Prepare a system flowchart that incorporates the manual and computer-based system operations described.

b. Identify any weaknesses in controls, indicate the possible errors or discrepancies that might occur because of such weaknesses, and recommend improvements.

c. Describe the voucher register, plus two reports that would be useful to the payables manager.

13-27. *Datacruncher Office Equipment, Inc.* (*Continuing Case*) Prepare a document flowchart and a data-flow diagram that pertain to the current procedure for the expenditure cycle, as described in Case A.

CHAPTER
14

THE CONVERSION CYCLE

THE LEARNING OBJECTIVES FOR THIS CHAPTER ARE TO ENABLE YOU TO:

1. Describe the objectives, functions, organizational relationships, and decisions that pertain to a firm's conversion cycle.

2. Identify the product conversion cycle's data sources, forms of input, and accounting entries.

3. Identify files and data structures that are needed within the data base for the product conversion cycle.

4. Describe the steps employed in processing flows of transaction data through a computerized product conversion cycle.

5. Discuss the components and benefits of computer integrated manufacturing systems within the product conversion cycle.

6. List needed internal controls for the product conversion cycle.

7. Describe the operational and financial measures needed for controlling the product conversion cycle, plus managerial reports and other outputs that are useful for planning and control.

INTRODUCTION

The conversion process consists of transforming resources into goods and services for sale. This chapter focuses on the **product conversion cycle,** in which raw materials and parts are converted into finished goods (products). However, conversion processes are found in a wide variety of firms and industries. Tangible goods are the outputs of conversion processes by construction, extraction (e.g., metals, oil), fishing, and repair organizations. Services are the outputs of conversion processes by health care, accounting services, systems consulting, transportation, and other professionally oriented organizations. Many of the operations and techniques employed in a product conversion cycle are applicable to the conversion processes in these varied organizations.

Currently the conversion cycle is undergoing highly significant changes. These changes, ranging from the integration of processing modules to the reporting of information for managers, affect the accounting information system (AIS) either directly or indirectly. Thus, these changes receive attention in addition to that given to the basic components of the product conversion cycle.

OVERVIEW

OBJECTIVES OF THE CYCLE

Within the essential purpose of transforming raw materials into finished goods, the objectives of the product conversion cycle are to ensure that

1. Adequate raw materials and other resources are available for production, while the investment in such resources is minimized.
2. Production costs are minimized through high labor productivity, full utilization of production equipment, low levels of scrap and rework, and optimal design of production layouts and procedures.
3. Work-in-process inventories are transformed into finished goods, which are warehoused or shipped on schedule.
4. Established levels of product quality and after-sales service are attained.
5. Costs for each order or process are accumulated fully and accurately.

FUNCTIONS OF THE CYCLE

The major functions involved in product conversion are shown in Figure 14-1. Each will be discussed in turn. The decisions that must be made concerning this cycle are incorporated in the discussion of the functions, rather than grouped within a following section.

Undertake Strategic Production Planning   Our view of product conversion functions is quite broad. Strategic planning extends years into the future and is primarily concerned with making critical decisions. Among these strategic decisions, which are typically made by higher-level as well as production managers, are the following:

• How much production capacity should be acquired and maintained?
• Which product components (e.g., parts, subassemblies) should be manufactured, and which should be purchased?

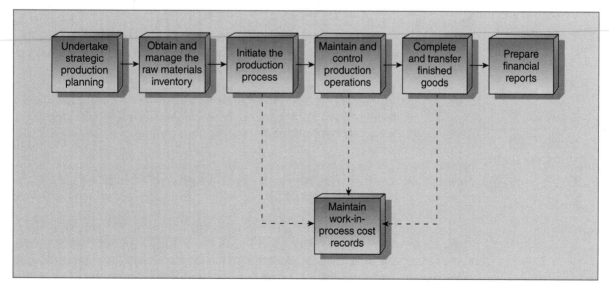

FIGURE 14-1   Typical functions of a product conversion system.

- How should the manufacturing process be laid out and what operations should be performed?
- What method of physical production should be employed?

A wide variety of information, gathered from numerous sources, will be required to make sound decisions. Production capacity depends on such factors as expected demands for the products, plus the availability of subcontractors and the costs of new construction. Determining which products components to manufacture is the classic "make or buy" decision, which depends on comparing the relevant costs of manufacturing versus purchasing. The manufacturing layout and operations are technically oriented decisions that involve engineering principles and techniques. The method of physical production depends on the nature of the products, with four major choices being available:

1. Process or continuous production of standardized products (e.g., petrochemicals, steel, cement).

2. Mass production of discrete and relatively similar products (e.g., automobiles, televisions).

3. Batch production of job lots of distinctly differing products (e.g., ball bearings in one batch, gears in another).

4. Make-to-order production of customized products (e.g., special equipment, ships, custom furniture).

After decisions such as these are made, long-range production schedules and budgets can be developed. The production schedules are affected by the way the production process is initiated. It may be initiated (1) to replenish inventory levels (if process or mass production methods are used) or (2) to fill customers' orders (if the custom method, and perhaps the batch method, is used).

Obtain and Manage the Raw Materials Inventory Raw materials consist of basic building materials (e.g., metal rods, wood boards, plastic screws), finished parts, and subassemblies used directly in finished goods. A basic material or part to one manufacturer, however, may represent a finished good to another. Like merchandise or fixed assets, raw materials traverse all the functions of the expenditure cycle. As described in Chapter 13, inventory management encompasses the receipt, storage, and disposition of all inventories (including raw materials). In a manufacturing firm the function of inventory management may be spread among several organizational units, such as inventory control and production planning.

A major aim of inventory management is to minimize the total cost of each type of inventory. In the case of raw materials, the total cost consists of the *sum* of ordering, storing, and out-of-stock costs for each raw material item. Ordering costs include the costs of processing purchase orders and freight on incoming orders; they vary with the number of orders placed. Storing (carrying) costs include interest on the investment in inventory, insurance, taxes, space utilized, and losses through spoilage and breakage. Out-of-stock costs for raw materials consist of losses in production efficiency and timeliness, which lead to higher unit costs for products and possible losses in customer goodwill.

Most of the decisions relating to raw materials are the same as those listed in Chapter 13. They include (1) when to reorder, (2) how many to reorder, and (3) whom to order from. These decisions are based on much of the same information needed when acquiring merchandise for resale. We may recall, for instance, that the decision of when to reorder involves a reorder point, and the decision of how many to reorder is often based on an economic order quantity (EOQ).

In certain manufacturing environments, however, the economic order quantity approach is modified for raw materials. Instead, raw materials are ordered to meet the requirements of planned production for the upcoming weeks or months. This alternative approach is called *materials requirements planning* (MRP). Even if quantities ordered under the MRP approach exceed those that are specified by the EOQ approach, the overall cost savings due to production efficiencies should outweigh the added costs of inventory management. An advanced manufacturing-related inventory approach is known as *just-in-time* (JIT). The objective of the JIT approach is to eliminate or at least minimize the need for raw materials inventory. Usually the needed materials are delivered in small batches and at fairly frequent intervals. The JIT approach provides such advantages as greatly reduced costs of materials storage and handling. MRP and JIT are discussed later in the chapter.

Initiate the Production Process The production process begins with a recognized need for finished goods. The need arises either when customers' orders are received or when items in the finished goods inventory reach replenishment levels. In the latter case the replenishment level is akin to the raw materials reorder point. It is based primarily on the expected future demands from customers and the production lead times.

However the need is recognized, two decisions must follow:

- What quantity of goods is to be produced?
- When should production of the goods be scheduled to start?

In the case of a custom order, the production quantity usually corresponds to the size of the order, of course. In the case of inventory replenishment, the quantity depends on such factors as setup costs, direct production costs, and the level of expected demand. The resulting quantity is typically called a *job lot*. The scheduled start date depends on the availability of production resources, which in turn is determined by production orders or jobs currently in production or previously scheduled, as well as by the relative priority of the pending order.

After scheduling the production order (or job), the next step is to determine the materials requirements. When the start date arrives, the materials are issued to the order (or job) and the following journal entry is prepared:

Dr. Work-in-Process Inventory	XXX	
Cr. Raw Materials Inventory		XXX
To issue raw materials into production.		

Then the labor and machines are assigned to the initial operation.

Maintain and Control Production Operations Each scheduled production order (or job) follows a physical flow through production operations. It moves either (1) from process to process (in the case of process production) or (2) from work center to work center (in the cases of batch, mass, or make-to-order production). As the order or job flows through the operations, it is monitored and controlled with respect to time, costs, and quality. The time control is based on the scheduled periods; cost control is based on standard product costs, as established by industrial engineers; and quality is based on specifications established by product design engineers. The actuals are compared to these bases and reported to those responsible for their control.

Maintain Work-in-Process Cost Records Product costs include those concerning direct materials, direct labor, and overhead. Included as overhead are costs of indirect labor, supplies, utilities, small tools, depreciation of machines, plant insurance, and other costs incurred within the production function. These product costs are accumulated to reflect the value of the orders or jobs flowing through production operations.

The direct costs are charged to the work-in-process inventory. As noted earlier, the raw materials costs are normally recorded at the time of issue. The direct labor costs are normally recorded at the end of each pay period by an entry such as follows:

```
Dr. Work-in-Process Inventory                          XXX
    Cr. Accrued Payroll                                        XXX
To accumulate the direct labor for the period.
```

The overhead, or indirect, costs are usually accumulated over a period of time and then allocated to the various orders and jobs. The accumulation of actual overhead costs would be recorded as:

```
Dr. Manufacturing Overhead                             XXX
    Cr. Accrued Payroll (for indirect labor)                   XXX
    Cr. Accumulated Depreciation (for machines)                XXX
    Cr. Accounts Payable (for utilities, etc.)                 XXX
    Cr. Miscellaneous Accrued Expenses                         XXX
To accumulate the actual indirect costs for the period.
```

The allocation is usually on the basis of an applied overhead rate, as follows:*

```
Dr. Work-in-Process Inventory                          XXX
    Cr. Applied Manufacturing Overhead                         XXX
To apply manufacturing overhead to jobs in process.
```

These entries are posted to work-in-process records; in total they should equal the work-in-process inventory control account balance in the general ledger.

Complete and Transfer Finished Goods   When a production order (or job) has flowed through all required production operations and is thus completed, the consequent finished goods are transferred to a warehouse or shipping dock. The related product costs are reflected in the following journal entry:

```
Dr. Finished-Goods Inventory                           XXX
    Cr. Work-in-Process Inventory                              XXX
To transfer completed production orders and jobs to
    finished goods inventory.
```

Prepare Financial Reports and Other Outputs   A variety of outputs are generated as by-products of the product conversion cycle. Examples are summaries of production status and costs, reports of quantities completed, and analyses of production delays and scrappage.

Other Related Functions   Quality control, scrap and rework, and excess materials are related matters of concern. Each deserves brief attention.

---

*Cost accounting systems and overhead allocation procedures vary widely. They are properly the subject of managerial or cost accounting, and alternative treatments may be found in any managerial or cost accounting textbook.

Quality control consists essentially of establishing product specifications and inspecting for compliance thereof. To ensure that quality is "built into" products, production employees should be adequately trained, machines maintained according to rigid schedules, and cutting tools frequently replaced. Inspections should take place as often as necessary to detect defective units. In the case of complex and critical components, such as computer processor chips, inspections are needed at every work center. For most products, one-time inspections are sufficient. These inspections normally occur as the completed units emerge from the last production operation. Inspections usually consist of sampling when job lots are in production. When more units than expected are found to be defective, the sample sizes are increased.

When units of product are found to be defective, they are either scrapped or reworked. *Scrappage* takes place when the units are so spoiled that they cannot be reworked. Scrap costs are usually charged as overhead to the work center that did the defective work, if this can be determined. *Rework* of units takes place when the units do not meet specifications but can be brought within specifications through additional efforts. Units to be reworked are returned to the work centers where the defective work was performed, and the added costs are charged to those work centers.

Excess materials are the units of raw material remaining in a work center after the work on an order or job has been completed. These excess materials should be returned to the storeroom, and the costs of the materials deducted from the work-in-process inventory. On the other hand, extra materials that are needed to complete an order or job are issued in the same manner as the original materials.

RELATIONSHIPS TO THE ORGANIZATION

The product conversion cycle functions are typically directed by the logistics management and finance/accounting organizational units of a manufacturing firm.

Logistics Figure 14-2 portrays the key units within the Precise Manufacturing Co., a hypothetical but typical manufacturer. Precise is involved in both custom and job lot (batch) production. In addition to the purchasing, receiving, and stores units found in a typical merchandising firm such as Infoage, the logistics function of Precise includes an array of production units plus engineering and sales units. The organizational structure shown in the figure reflects the view that **logistics management** concerns the planning and control of the materials resource and all its flows and transformations.

Figure 14-3 presents a broad-view diagram that depicts the relationships among the organizational units shown in Figure 14-2. Also included in the figure are key documents and several organizational units that interface with the logistics function.

Responsibilities of the production-oriented organizational units in the figures are as follows:

Engineering design determines the specifications by which products (either those specially ordered or those needed to replenish inventories) will be manufactured. It embodies these specifications in bills of materials and operations lists.

Production planning determines how many products are to be manufactured, when they are to be produced, and with what facilities they are to be produced. It generates production schedules and individual production orders.

Inventory management ensures that adequate quantities of materials are available to use in scheduled orders or jobs. In addition to materials requirements planning, this includes the purchasing and receiving of materials, the

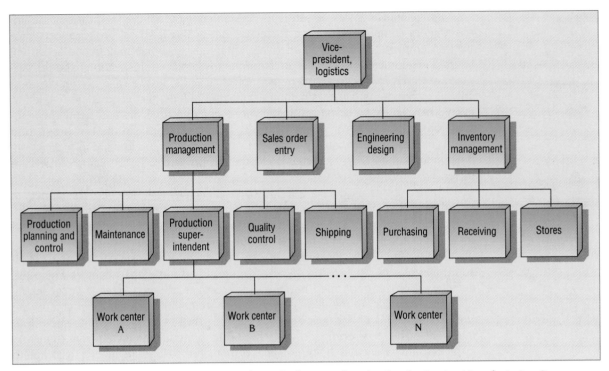

FIGURE 14-2   A partial organization chart that shows the logistics function for the Precise Manufacturing Co.

requisitioning of materials from the storeroom, and the assembly of the materials at the work centers.

Production control (a part of the production planning and control unit) dispatches orders or jobs and monitors actual flows and operations. It utilizes move tickets or documents for control.

Production operations, which includes all work centers, performs the actual production operations and rework.

Quality control conducts inspections and tests of the products and either accepts or rejects based on its evaluations.

Maintenance performs scheduled and nonscheduled repair and maintenance of production equipment and other facilities.

FINANCE/ACCOUNTING

The responsibilities of most of the units within the finance/accounting function have been discussed in Chapters 12 and 13. **Cost accounting,** however, is a unit that more often is employed by manufacturers than by merchandising firms. Cost accounting accumulates the costs incurred in the production process and provides cost analyses. It may also assist in preparing standard costs and developing cost accounting systems.

MANAGERIAL DECISION MAKING

The various decisions that must be made by logistics and production managers have been identified in the discussion of functions. Among the decisions that involve accounting are the following:

What type of costing system should be employed?

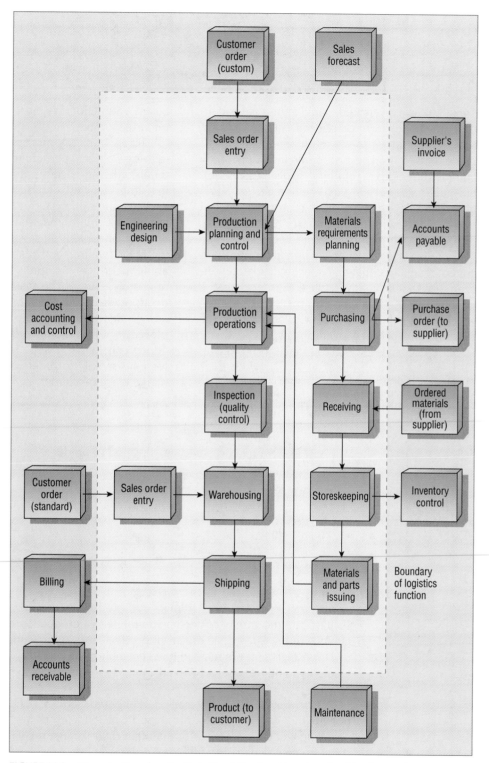

FIGURE 14-3   Organizational units that direct the functions involved in the product conversion cycle and the filing of customers' orders.

SPOTLIGHTING

KNOWLEDGE-BASED PRODUCTION
*at Indal Ltd.**

Indal Ltd. is a diversified manufacturer of residential construction, commercial construction, and automotive products, as well as aluminum and glass. These products can be customized in an apparently infinite array of configurations involving sizes, colors, materials, and add-ons. The firm needed a system that allowed it to meet customers' special needs, while reducing manufacturing cycle times with no loss in quality or cost-effectiveness. The system also needed to mesh with computer-integrated manufacturing and electronic data interchange systems already in place. Furthermore, the system had to be an improvement over MRP-II, which is not sufficiently flexible to deal with a true custom manufacturing environment.

The solution developed by Indal is a knowledge-based production system founded on expert systems technology. This system incorporates all of the firm's business processes and also the configuring elements pertaining to all its products. After an order-entry clerk enters the details concerning the desired product configuration, the knowledge-based system automatically generates a multilevel bill of materials, a manufacturing bill of costs, and a routing sheet. Through a link to the materials requirements planning system, the availability of critical materials can be determined immediately. Finally, the system links with the production scheduling programs to provide a schedule and promised delivery date. Although not yet employed for all of Indal's products, the system has added considerable value by enabling the firm to respond rapidly to orders as well as to changing marketplace demands.

---

*Kathleen M. Repath, "Knowledge-Based Manufacturing." CMA *Magazine* (May 1993), pp. 18–22.

How are overhead costs to be allocated to products?

If activity-based costing is to be employed, what will be the cost pools and cost drivers?

DATA SOURCES AND INPUTS

BASIC DOCUMENTS

Much of the data used in the product conversion cycle are based on inputs from documents generated by customers and production or other logistics departments. To illustrate the variety of documents related to production, we refer to the Precise Manufacturing Co., whose organization chart appears in Figure 14-2. This firm manufactures electrical products in batches, mainly for inventory. However, it also manufactures to fill orders, and it even designs new products to meet customer specifications.

Let us begin with a customer's order dated October 20, 1997, from Lipton Technology, Inc., for five generators, type PG21, 50 horsepower, including customized shielding and added devices to maintain tight voltage regulation. The following are the documents needed to fulfill the order:

A **bill of materials** specifies the quantities of parts, materials, and subassemblies to be used in specific products or assemblies. Figure 14-4 shows the bill of materials pertaining to the order just noted. This bill of materials must be modified by engineering design before production starts, since special features are specified.

BILL OF MATERIALS		
Product Name and No. Generator PG21	Authorization P D Q	Effective Date 1/1/97
Material or Part Number	Description	Quantity
18568	Casting for rotor shaft	1
32151	Salient poles	4
33592	Field windings	4
44276	Slip rings	2
98105	Ventilating fan	1

FIGURE 14-4   A bill of materials.

OPERATIONS LIST					
Product Name and Number Generator PG21			Authorization P.D.Q.	Effective Date 1/1/97	
Operation Number	Description	Work Center	Machine Requirement	Standard Time (Hrs)	
				Set Up	Operating
G100	Machine rotor shaft	A	Lathe 75P RPM: 900 Tolerance: .0005	0.3	3.0
G200	Attach slip rings	B		0.1	0.9
G300	Mount salient poles	B			2.5
G400	Wrap windings on poles	C		0.2	1.8
G500	Mount fan	C			0.3

FIGURE 14-5   An operations list.

An **operations list,** also called a *routing sheet*, specifies the sequence of operations to be performed in fashioning and assembling the materials and parts required for a product. As Figure 14-5 indicates, the list may include the work centers at which the operations are to take place, as well as machine requirements and standard time allowances.

A **production schedule** is the timetable for producing the orders and jobs. It shows the time durations of the various orders and jobs over a calendar period, enabling production planning to utilize available production capacity effectively and to avoid production "jams." Before an order is scheduled, the planners must determine that resources (e.g., machines, tools, materials, employees) are available. Formats of production schedules and periods covered vary considerably. Figure 14-6 shows a simplified schedule that emphasizes start and finish dates for the orders and jobs in process. More detailed schedules are usually developed, specifying the work dates for each operation and perhaps even the machines that have been assigned.

PRODUCTION SCHEDULE			
October 20–31, 1997			
S = start date			F = finish date
Prod. order number	Quantity	Type	20 21 22 23 24 25 26 27 28 29 30 31
8332	100	Inventory	--------F
8333	5	Make-to-order	S----------------------F
8334	500	Inventory	S------------------------F
8335	100	Inventory	S---------F
8336	200	Inventory	S---------F

FIGURE 14-6   A production schedule.

PRODUCTION ORDER

Cust. order no. __5658__   Product __Generator PG21__   No. __8333__

MRP no. ----------   Quantity __5__   Status __Routine__

Special conditions __See drawing # PS-47982__

Estimated added hours over standard __4__

Issue date 10/20/97	Start date 10/21/97	Completion date 10/28/97	Expected delivery date 10/30/97			
Work center	Operation	Description	Quantity	Start		Finish
A	G100	Machine rotor shaft	5	10/21	8:00 a	10/23	8:30 a
B	G200	Attach slip rings	20	10/23	9:00 a	10/23	2:30 a

FIGURE 14-7   A production order.

A **production order** incorporates data from sales orders (or sales forecasts, in the case of inventory replenishments) as well as from the relevant operations list and bill of materials. It authorizes the production of an order or batch. In addition, production orders provide the means of monitoring progress through the production process, since the scheduled dates for each operation can be compared to actual dates completed. Figure 14-7 shows the header portion of a production order related to our customer order, plus the first two operations in the routing through production.

A *work order* is often used in lieu of a production order by a service department, such as repair and maintenance, to authorize specified tasks within the production area.

A **materials issue slip,** also called a *materials requisition*, directs the storeskeeper to issue materials or parts to designated work centers or authorized persons. Figure 14-8 shows a materials issue slip for the five castings needed at work center A to produce the five generators on the customer's order. Additional materials and parts will be issued to work centers B and C. Normally the quantities issued are based on the bill of materials. Costs are entered later by the cost accounting unit.

```
                        Materials Issue Slip              No. 704

       Issued to   Work Center A                    Date   10/21/97

              Charged to production order number    8333
```

Material or part number	Description	Quantity issued	Unit cost	Extended cost
18568	Casting for rotor shaft	5	500.00	2500.00

```
         Authorized by   D. W. Munro

         Received by    T. J. Boswell

         Costed by     P. G. Johnson
```

FIGURE 14-8   A materials issue slip (requisition).

If materials are needed on a production order that exceed the quantities specified by the bill of materials, an *excess materials requisition* is issued. It is handled in the same manner as a regular materials issue slip, except that it is typically printed on a form of a different color. Conversely, if materials remain after an order leaves a work center, they are returned to stores via a *returned materials form*.

If materials and parts required for an order or job are not in stores, they must be purchased and received. These activities require the use of purchase requisitions, purchase orders, and receiving reports, as discussed in Chapter 13.

A **labor job-time ticket** records the elapsed time expended by a production employee on the work prescribed by the production order. Figure 14-9 shows that Bill Smarts spent 3.5 hours setting up and machining a rotor shaft under production

```
                      Labor Job-Time Ticket
```

Employee no. 1368	Employee name Bill Smarts	Production order 8333	Date 10/21/97
Work center A	Operation number G100	Operation description Set-up and machine rotor shaft	
Time started 8:30	Time finished 12:00	Elapsed time (hours) 3.50	
Pieces finished 1	Hourly rate 15.00	Labor cost 52.50	

```
         Approved:      D. W. Munro
```

FIGURE 14-9   A labor job-time ticket.

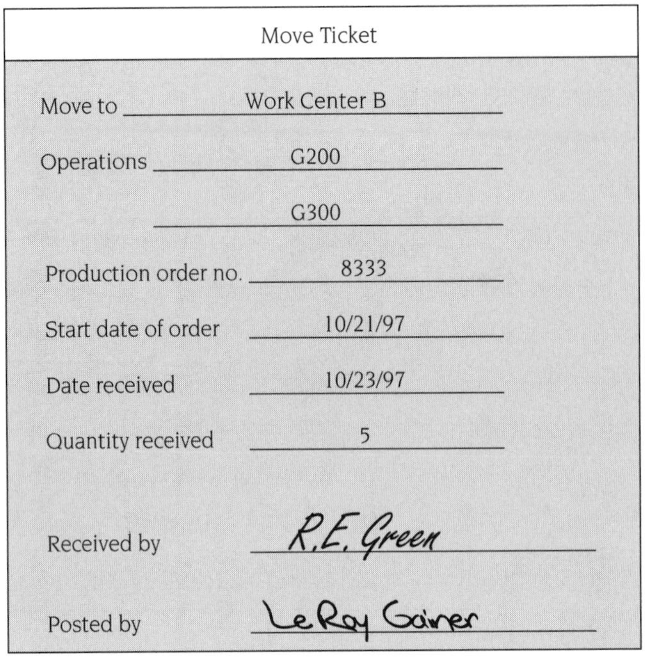

```
┌─────────────────────────────────────────────┐
│                 Move Ticket                   │
├─────────────────────────────────────────────┤
│                                               │
│   Move to _____ Work Center B _____     │
│                                               │
│   Operations _____ G200 _____       │
│                                               │
│              _____ G300 _____       │
│                                               │
│   Production order no. _____ 8333 _____     │
│                                               │
│   Start date of order _____ 10/21/97 _____   │
│                                               │
│   Date received _____ 10/23/97 _____    │
│                                               │
│   Quantity received _____ 5 _____   │
│                                               │
│                                               │
│   Received by _____ R.E. Green _____        │
│                                               │
│   Posted by _____ LeRoy Gainer _____        │
│                                               │
└─────────────────────────────────────────────┘
```

FIGURE 14-10 A move ticket.

order 8333. Numerous labor job-time tickets are necessary to reflect the hours and costs of direct labor for the various production orders during a typical week.

A **move ticket,** also called a *traveler,* authorizes the physical movement of a production order from one work center to the next. It also records the quantity of items on the production order and the date received at the incoming work center. A completed move ticket is used by production planning as the basis for posting work performed to production order records, so that progress can be tracked. Therefore, in effect move tickets are detailed transaction records relating to the flows of production work-in-process. Figure 14-10 shows the move ticket used to indicate the receipt of production order 8333 at work center B.

In lieu of separate move tickets for each work center, a move ticket having a series of stubs may be employed. One stub is removed at each work center when the production order arrives. The final stub is used to record the receipt of the production order at the warehouse or shipping dock.

Inspection reports record the results of inspections performed on products during or after the production process. If inspections are performed at every work center, inspection reports may be included as parts of move tickets.

COMPUTERIZED DATA ENTRY

A computer-based product conversion system needs all of the data contained in the above-mentioned documents. Instead of preparing the documents manually and in hard-copy form, however, a computer-based system

1. Captures the data via terminals or microbased work stations, using such techniques as keyed-in alphanumeric codes, inserted badges or cards, scanned bar codes, or touched monitor screens.

2. Automatically generates preformatted documents, using application software and on-line data bases.

3. Maintains electronic copies of the documents in on-line files, printing hard-copy forms only as needed and requested.

Computerized data entry can be illustrated by reference to the Lens Manufacturing Co., which has installed a client/server production system. Figure 14-11 provides a simplified view of the points of data entry and the supporting data bases and

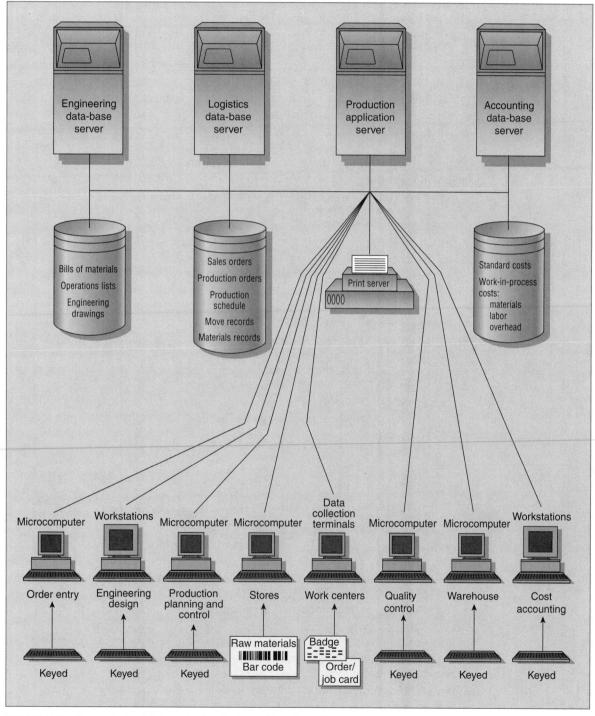

FIGURE 14-11 Computerized data entry for the Lens Manufacturing Co.

servers. Each designated point of entry leads to the generation of one or more electronic documents, similar in content to the hard-copy documents already described.

Our illustration begins with the receipt of an order from a customer for customized binoculars. The sales order clerk keys in the relevant data, which generates a sales order. Engineering design accesses the sales order and then retrieves drawings, operations lists, and bills of materials relating to binoculars. An assigned engineer uses a computer-aided design software package to modify the drawings and related documents according to the requested customization. Upon being notified of their completion by engineering, production planning retrieves the production schedule and enters the order for production. It then generates the production order, using the data from the modified operations list and sales order, and a materials issue slip that authorizes materials for the first work center.

At this point data are entered to initiate the production process. Stores draws needed raw materials and parts from their bins; then, the storeskeeper uses a hand scanner to read the bar codes attached to the needed raw materials and parts. Production control generates an order card to accompany the materials as they flow through the production process. At the first work center, the assigned employee inserts an identification card (or coded badge) into a data collection terminal, so that the system can record the time. When the employee completes the task, he or she reinserts the card; the system generates a labor time ticket record to reflect the elapsed time. Each time the employee inserts the identification card, he or she also inserts the order card, so that the system can read the number of the order. Also, when the order leaves the work center, the supervisor inserts the order card and enters a code to denote that work has been completed. Based on this data entry, the system posts the move to a record akin to a move ticket.

When inspections occur, quality control enters its evaluation by keying entries onto a preformatted screen of an inspection report. Finally, when the order is finished and transferred to the warehouse, an employee at the warehouse inserts the order card into a data collection terminal to record the receipt. (Instead of card reading devices, the data collection terminals can employ hand-held wand scanners if desired.)

Cost accountants monitor the progress of orders via a work station. While they do not normally enter data concerning specific orders, they retrieve data and generate various control reports.

DATA BASE

The data base supporting the conversion cycle of a manufacturing firm contains data pertaining to conversion-related resources (raw materials, work-in-process, finished goods), key events (dispatch production order, perform operations), and principal agents (work center personnel, production planners). The data base also reflects the relationships among these basic entities. Depending on the nature of a firm's procedure, additional data might be stored concerning associated events (such as issuing raw materials into production and shipping ordered products) and agents (cost accountants, inspectors).

In an even broader perspective, the data base would include data concerned with sales forecasting, production scheduling, purchasing of raw materials, and warehousing of finished goods. Data of these types are useful in production planning and inventory management, and their inclusion would create a more integrated data base. However, our focus in this chapter is primarily on the product conversion activity.

Data may be stored in files and/or data structures. Both forms of storage will be briefly surveyed.

FILES

Files in the conversion cycle can be classified by types as master, transaction, and others. As in the case of files in other cycles, the specific data contained in each will vary from firm to firm.

Master Files   The three major master files pertain to raw materials, work-in-process, and finished goods. They may be described as follows:

- The **raw materials inventory master file** contains records of the raw materials, parts, and subassemblies required by a manufacturer. Factory supplies are normally kept in a separate file. Each raw materials record reflects the receipts, issues, orders, and on-hand balances pertaining to a particular item. A hard-copy record, used in a manual system, appears in Figure 14-12. This particular record relates to one of the raw materials used in the bill of materials shown in Figure 14-4. The total of on-hand balance amounts for all such items should reconcile to the raw materials control account in the general ledger.

- The **work-in-process inventory master file** summarizes the materials, direct labor, and overhead costs pertaining to orders or jobs currently in production. Since each work-in-process inventory record ties to a production order, the primary key is usually the production order number. Figure 14-13 shows a hard-copy record for production order 8333, the key order in our early illustration. All of the work-in-process inventory records compose a subsidiary ledger.

- The **finished-goods inventory master file** is in effect the merchandise inventory or product file. The primary key is usually the product number or code, rather than the production order number.

Materials Record Card										
Material or part no. 18568					Description Casting for rotor shaft					
Stores location Row 10 Bin A5					Supplier Baker foundry				Unit cost (std.) $500.00	
Reorder quantity 40					Reorder point 16					
Receipts			Issues			On order			On hand	
Date	Ref.	Qty.	Date	Ref.	Qty.	Date	Ref.	Qty.	Qty.	Amount
									20	10000.00
			10/20	704	5				15	7500.00
						10/24	7581	40	15	7500.00
11/12	6213	40							55	27500.00

FIGURE 14-12   A raw materials record.

Work-in-Process Cost Record

Product _____ Generator PG21 _____   Production Order No. __8333__

Quantity _____ 5 _____

Date Started _____ 10/21/97 _____

Date Finished _____

Material costs			Labor costs				Overhead costs		
Date	Issue number	Amount	Date	Work center	Operation	Amount	Date	Applied level	Amount
10/20/97	704	2500.00	10/21/97	A	G100	120.00	10/21/97	8 hrs.	160.00
Total material cost			Total labor cost				Total overhead cost		

FIGURE 14-13   A work-in-process record (i.e., a job cost sheet).

Transaction Files   The key transaction file is the production order file, which is supported by the materials issues file and operations or routing file.

- The *production orders file* consists of records containing data similar to the elements shown in Figure 14-7. The **open production orders file** includes the data from the production orders file, plus postings from the move tickets. That is, it tracks the progress of orders and jobs as they move through the physical production operations.

- The *operations file* relates directly to the production orders in progress; in fact, each record in the file is the detailed portion of a production order record and is based on the operations lists maintained in an engineering data base.

- The materials issues file also relates directly to the production orders in progress. As we recall, the needed materials for a production order are prescribed in the bills of materials, which are usually maintained in an engineering data base. Together with the operations file, the bills of materials compose the product structure data.

Other Files   A *work center file* contains the status at each work center or department, especially pertaining to assigned machines and direct labor and completed work pertaining to specific production orders. Additional files concern standard costs (plus overhead rates) and inspection results. History files concerning past production orders, work center performances, and machine usage may also be maintained.

DATA STRUCTURES

When a firm converts to the data-base approach, the contents of the product conversion cycle data base will be very similar to those of the above-mentioned files.

However, the data will be organized as structured records or normalized tables, with the organization being centered around the key entities and relationships. We will develop conceptual and logical views that illustrate data structures for a relational data base.

Entity-Relationship Diagram of the Product Conversion Cycle   Figure 14-14 depicts an entity-relationship diagram for the Lens Manufacturing Co.'s product conversion cycle. Although simplified, the diagram shows the essential events, resources, and agents identified at the beginning of this section.

The relationships among the entities reflect these organizational rules and constraints established by Lens:

1. Each production order leads to a work-in-process inventory record.
2. Only one product can appear on a single production order.
3. Each operation can be performed at only one work center.
4. Each operation is performed by a single employee, who may be assigned to perform more than one operation in some cases.
5. Each type of raw material undergoes more than one operation, but no particular operation is performed on more than one type of raw material.

It should be emphasized that these rules and constraints are peculiar to Lens and may vary significantly for other manufacturing firms.

Based on the given rules and constraints, one-to-one relationships exist between production orders and work-in-process and finished-goods inventory. Similarly, one-to-many relationships exist between (1) work center employees and operations and (2) raw materials and operations. Several relationships are of the many-to-many type. They exist (1) between work centers and production orders, (2) between production orders and raw materials, (3) between production orders and operations, and (4) between operations and work-in-process. The relationships in product conversion therefore appear to be relatively complex in comparison to those found in typical revenue and expenditure cycles.

Logical View of Product Conversion Data Structures   Since Lens has decided to adopt the relational data structure, we need to map from the entity-relationship diagram to a set of tables. Focusing only on the portion of the diagram within the dashed lines, the described entities and relationships can yield nine tables or relations. However, two relationships (between operations and work-in-process and between production orders and work centers) can be omitted because the remaining two relationships provide adequate cross-references. Thus, the seven tables needed are the raw materials table, work-in-process inventory table, production order table, work center table, operations table, production order/operations table, and production order/raw materials table. Figure 14-15, on page 615, portrays these tables in normalized form.*

The relationship tables serve two purposes. In addition to providing cross-references between entity tables, they contain added data. For instance, the production order/operations table links the production orders with the detailed operations table, so that the complete operations list pertaining to each order can be printed.

---

*The production planner and finished-goods entities have been placed outside our example. If included, the table for the production planner would be the production schedule, while the table for finished goods would show the attributes of products, keyed on the product number. While necessary to complete the logistics data base, they are omitted for the sake of simplicity.

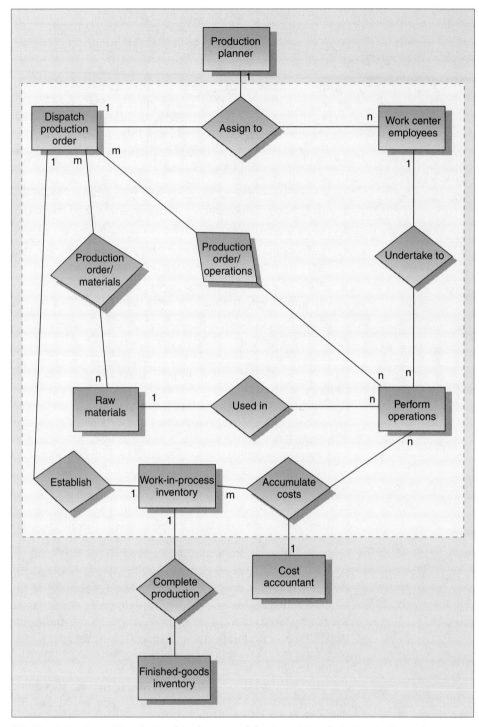

FIGURE 14-14   An entity-relationship diagram of the Lens Manufacturing Co.'s product conversion cycle.

PRODUCTION ORDER TABLE

Prod. order number	Product number	Cust. or MRP no.	Quantity ordered	Issue date	Start date	Completion date	Expected delivery date

OPERATIONS TABLE

Operation code	Description	Work center code	Standard set-up hours	Standard operating hours

WORK CENTER TABLE

Work center code	Title	Supervisor name

PRODUCTION ORDER/OPERATIONS TABLE

Prod. order number	Operation code	Date performed	ID no. of assigned employee	Hourly rate	Hours worked

WORK-IN-PROCESS INVENTORY TABLE

Prod. order number	Date started	Materials costs	Direct labor costs	Overhead costs

RAW MATERIALS TABLE

Material number	Description	Store location	Reorder point	Reorder quan.	Unit cost	Quan. on order	Quan. reserved for orders	Quan. on hand	Amount balance

PRODUCTION ORDER/MATERIALS TABLE

Prod. order number	Material number	Quantity issued or returned	Date of issue or return

FIGURE 14-15   A relational data structure pertaining to the product conversion cycle for the Lens Manufacturing Co.

Moreover, it contains the actual hours worked, so that they can be compared with the standard allowed hours for each operation. Furthermore, this table can transfer the labor cost to the work-in-process table through the linkage of the production order number. Similarly, the production order/raw materials table allows those two entity tables to be linked. In addition, it contains the quantities of materials issued to complete a production order, so that it serves as a surrogate for the bill of materials. These quantities issued can be posted to the work-in-process table, together with the standard unit cost from the raw materials table, so that the materials costs can be accumulated.*

*The overhead rate does not appear in any of these tables. Thus overhead charges must be added to the work-in-process table by a cost accountant or by the cost accounting application program.

DATA FLOWS AND PROCESSING

The product conversion cycle encompasses three major processing systems: production planning, production operations, and accounting for production costs. Our discussion will be focused on the conversion processing systems of the Lens Manufacturing Co., which essentially employ the immediate (on-line) approach. While the periodic (batch) approach is a possible alternative, it has serious disadvantages for the modern manufacturing firm. We assume that Lens does not yet have a relational data base. Instead, it employs a number of on-line but independent files. However, the data content is sufficient to meet the operational needs of production.

If you are not familiar with basic manufacturing procedures, it may be helpful to review background material before reading about computer-based processing systems. Appendix 1 to this chapter contains narrative descriptions and document flowcharts pertaining to a manual system.

PRODUCTION PLANNING SYSTEM

The processes involved in planning production, based on special orders from customers and other sales, are shown in the data-flow diagram in Figure 14-16. The flows of data and documents are also portrayed in Figure 14-17 on page 618, a computer system flowchart. The following description is tied to both figures.

Specifications relating to customized sales orders are received from customers. The engineering design department designs or modifies the appropriate bill of materials and operations list, in order to provide the plans for manufacturing the desired products. The production planning department then prepares a production order in accordance with these plans. Based on the requirements of the order, and taking into account the forecasted sales and back orders, production planning revises the production schedule.

The production planning system software then performs steps that consist of (1) printing prenumbered production orders needed to fill requirements, (2) adding the new production orders to the open production orders file, (3) printing multipart move tickets and materials issue documents to accompany the production orders, (4) printing make-to-order bills of materials and operations lists to accompany acknowledgements to customers who placed special orders, (5) updating the production schedules maintained in the on-line file and printing the revised schedules for use by planners, and (6) "exploding" the materials requirements needed to fill orders and replenish inventories and printing materials requirements reports. An example of an "exploded" materials requirements report, based on the special order for the five generators, would appear as follows:

Part or Material	Quantity per Product	Number of Products Ordered	Gross Requirements
Casting for rotor shaft	1	5	5
Salient poles	4	5	20
Field windings	4	5	20
Slip rings	2	5	10
Ventilating fan	1	5	5

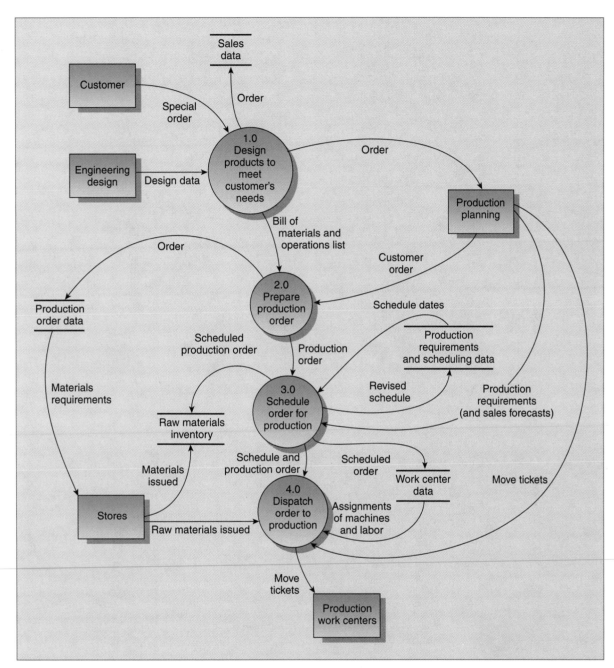

FIGURE 14-16 A data-flow diagram of the production planning processes of the Lens Manufacturing Co.

In addition to scheduling the orders, the production planning system reserves resources. That is, it updates the raw materials inventory file to place a "hold" on the quantities of items needed to be issued, and it updates the work center file to assign machines and labor to the scheduled orders on the days that they will be needed.

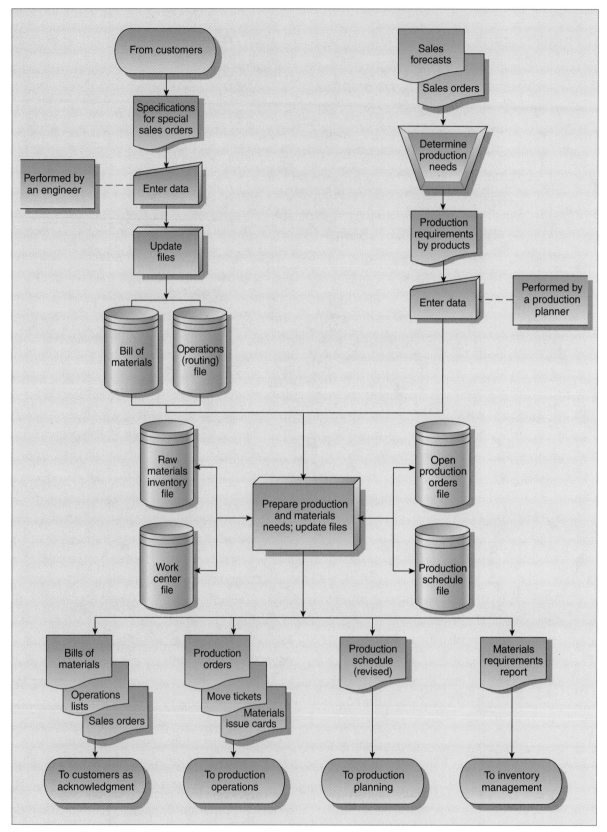

FIGURE 14-17   A computer system flowchart of the production planning system of the Lens Manufacturing Co.

PRODUCTION OPERATIONS SYSTEM

Orders are dispatched to the first work center to begin production operations. Figure 14-18 shows a computer system flowchart of the production operations. Since the production process consists of converting materials into products through operations, two resource inflows occur. Raw materials and parts are issued by the storeskeeper, who finds the items listed on the materials issue document and scans the bar codes on the items. Then the materials and parts are delivered to the production area where the first work center is located. The second resource inflow occurs when employees perform designated operations on the materials. As discussed under Data Entry, each employee records the time spent on an order by direct interaction with the system. He or she inserts an identification card or badge into a data collection terminal or alternatively uses a hand-held scanner to read the badge.

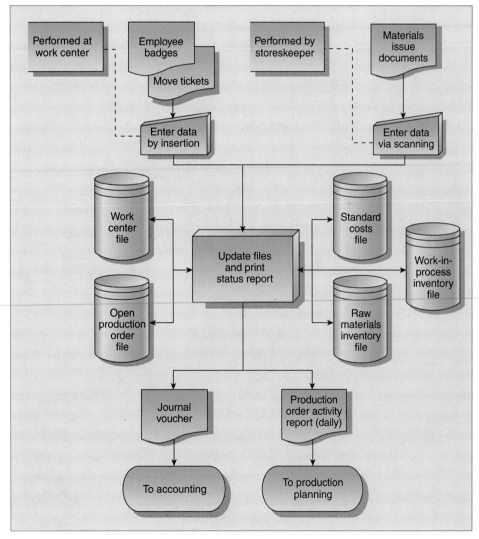

FIGURE 14-18   A computer system flowchart of the production operations system of the Lens Manufacturing Co.

Based on these entries, the production operations system software (1) updates the materials inventory file to record the issues and reduce the on-hand quantities, (2) updates the open production order file to reflect the work performed toward completing an operation, (3) updates the machine loading file to show that the machine is free for the next scheduled operation, and (4) opens a work-in-process

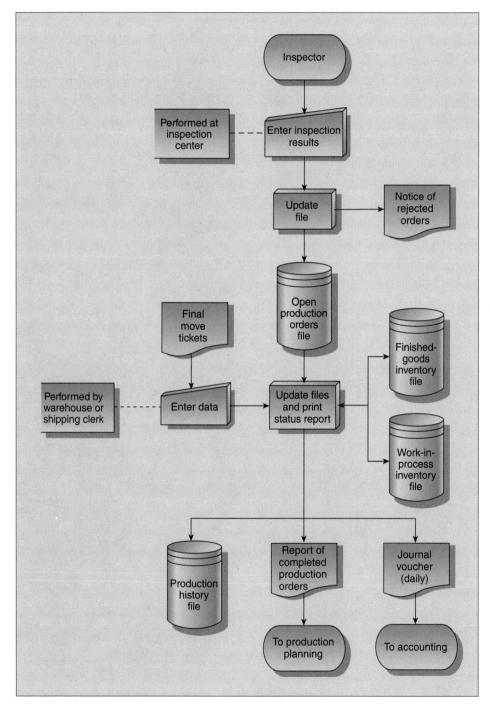

FIGURE 14-19   A computer system flowchart of processing steps at completion of production operations in the Lens Manufacturing Co.

record and records the materials and direct labor costs, using the standard costs file to obtain unit costs. At the end of each day, the system prints two outputs: (1) a journal voucher showing the costs accumulated that day for posting to the general ledger and (2) a production order activity report that shows the current status of all production orders.

Figure 14-19 contains a flowchart that shows the final production steps relating to an order. As work is completed on the last operation designated by a production order, the converted goods are inspected. The inspector enters the results via a terminal, and an inspection report is issued. Those orders that pass inspection are transferred either to a warehouse or to the shipping dock. (Those that do not pass must be reworked.)

At either point data are entered from the final segment of the move ticket via a terminal. This notification causes the production order to be closed and transferred to the history file. Final costs are posted to the work-in-process inventory file; then the work-in-process costs pertaining to the order are totaled and transferred to the appropriate record in the finished-goods inventory file. A journal voucher is prepared at the end of each day to reflect the total costs of all production orders completed and given to the general ledger department for posting. Also, a daily report is printed to show the production orders completed.

ACCOUNTING FOR PRODUCTION COSTS

Accumulating production costs and updating the various records with these costs are activities that occur in concert with the physical production operations. Since the cost and physical aspects are so interwoven, we have already noted several of the steps in the cost accounting system. However, since cost accumulation is so important to accountants, the procedure should be isolated and the cost-related steps repeated. Figure 14-20 portrays the key steps in the accounting for production costs, using a data-flow diagram to show the basic processes. The pictured cost accounting system pertains to the Lens Manufacturing Co., which applies manufacturing overhead on the basis of direct labor hours.

The first process is to accumulate materials and direct labor costs, as described earlier. These costs are recorded in the appropriate work-in-process inventory records based on standard unit costs. The next process is to accumulate and apply manufacturing overhead, with the amounts charged to work-in-process inventory on the basis of a standard manufacturing overhead rate.

It is next necessary to compute the variances for the three component costs. These variances are based on differences between the actual costs (as posted daily to the general ledger accounts from various invoices) and the standard costs charged to work-in-process inventory records. To compute the variances, the system draws on the standard labor hours that appear in the production orders (as taken from operations lists) and the standard unit costs in the standard costs file. While additional details concerning variances are beyond the scope of this text, we can note that the computed variances are posted to variance accounts in the general ledger. Also, cost variance reports are provided to managers, to aid them in controlling the costs.

The last process in Figure 14-20 shows the disposition of total costs that have been accumulated in work-in-process records relating to production orders. When the production orders are completed, the costs are transferred from the work-in-process inventory records to the finished goods inventory records. The costs are also posted to the inventory control accounts in the general ledger.

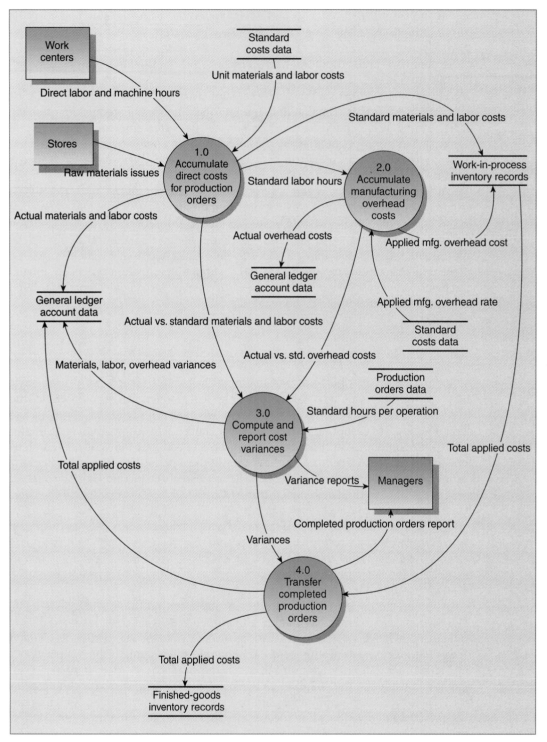

FIGURE 14-20   A data-flow diagram pertaining to the cost accounting system of the Lens Manufacturing Co.

COMPUTER INTEGRATED MANUFACTURING SYSTEMS

The on-line product conversion systems described for the Lens Manufacturing Co. provide a variety of benefits:

1. The materials requirements relating to demands for products are determined beforehand, so that the materials are transferred to the production areas in time for production starts.

2. Production orders are scheduled to accommodate the manufacturing capacity.

3. Data are validated upon on-line entry, so that errors are detected more quickly and reprocessing delays due to undetected errors are reduced.

4. Inventory and production order records are updated in a timely manner from materials requisitions, labor-time entries, and move tickets.

5. Accounting-related processing is simplified, since transactions are posted without sorting to on-line files.

6. Control reports such as cost variance analyses are prepared for managers.

Many manufacturing firms employ on-line systems similar to the one described for the Lens Manufacturing Co., although with numerous variations. The benefits listed above have yielded significant cost savings, production efficiencies, and useful information, especially in comparison with those available from manual and batch computerized systems. However, a system such as Lens's still can fall short in certain major respects:

1. The production planning and operations and the cost accounting systems are relatively unintegrated, thus leading to processing inefficiencies and time delays.

2. Although much data are stored on-line, the paperwork flows are still cumbersome and costly.

3. The materials inventories tend to be extensive, requiring costly investments in warehouse and production space as well as in the materials themselves.

4. The quality of the manufactured products is not likely to be consistently high, so that extensive reworking and scrapping may be necessary.

5. Changes in the production lines and setups of machines cannot be made quickly to accommodate make-to-order production, since the facilities are relatively inflexible.

6. Although certain operational and control reports are available, much needed information is not readily accessible.

These shortcomings are critical in the current-day manufacturing environment faced by many manufacturing firms. In this environment firms must compete on a global basis. They must cope with foreign competitors who have significantly lower labor costs, with ever-more demanding customers, and with increasingly changeable conditions. Manufacturing firms that desire to compete effectively must have world-class production information systems and outstanding production facilities. If they do, they can overcome the above-mentioned shortcomings and achieve significant and enduring benefits.

Manufacturing firms that aspire to world-class status are therefore incorporating information systems that attain much higher levels of effectiveness. These production/logistics systems are called **computer-integrated manufacturing (CIM) systems**—systems that provide an integrated and completely automated manufacturing

SPOTLIGHTING

COMPUTER INTEGRATED MANUFACTURING
at Caterpillar, Inc.*

Caterpillar, a global world-class manufacturer of heavy equipment, is installing computer-integrated manufacturing (CIM) via a massive project called Plants With A Future (PWAF). This project spans 32 manufacturing facilities in 12 countries and is expected to cost over $2 billion. The expected benefits include savings of 15 percent of manufacturing costs, improved product quality, shorter manufacturing cycle times, reduced inventory, and enhanced flexibility. In those plants where much of the CIM system is functioning, gains have been seen in improved materials handling, space-saving factory layouts, robotics, flexible-manufacturing cells, and just-in-time inventory handling. Electronically received orders drive the

*Wes Iversen, "Information Systems: Tying It All Together." *Industry Week* (August 20, 1990), pp. 26–28.

CIM processes, with MRP systems that draw inventory to the right place at the right time on the factory floor. Its communications network links its factories with more than 1000 dealers, customers, and suppliers. One result of this linkage is that Caterpillar can deliver spare parts to anywhere within 48 hours.

The new CIM system development is being accompanied by significant changes in the organizational structure. Organized around market-oriented profit centers, the structure has become flatter and leaner and more focused to customer needs. Its information systems groups, including the 600-person CIM Technology group, have become part of a corporate service division. With the new organization, these groups can better provide systems and software to the dealers and suppliers as well as to the plants within the firm itself.

---

environment. We will briefly survey the components that can be encompassed by a full-scale CIM system and the benefits that they provide.

COMPONENTS OF A CIM SYSTEM

A CIM system spans engineering, production, and cost accounting activities. In make-to-order situations, it also involves sales order entry. A CIM system includes machines, equipment, and other physical facilities as well as data bases and the other components of information systems. Furthermore, it may be viewed as a network or series of networks, since it usually includes interconnected mainframe, midsize, and microcomputers and terminals. In fact, an extended CIM network can incorporate the electronic data interchange networks of principal suppliers.

Figure 14-21 presents a simplified configuration of a comprehensive CIM system that the Lens Manufacturing Co. might install. This CIM system can be incorporated into the client/server architecture already installed by Lens. In addition, a relational data-base management system can be installed to merge and control the logistics and accounting data bases shown in the figure. Each of the components will be discussed in turn, starting with the left-most component in the figure. Certain components, such as MRP and JIT, may be installed apart from a CIM system. However, they enhance the overall effectiveness of production operations when included.

Computer-aided design (CAD) employs computerized techniques to create, modify, and document engineering designs. Using an interactive graphics workstation, a designer can develop three-dimensional models of products and automatically generate drawings. The results can also be stored in the logistics data base

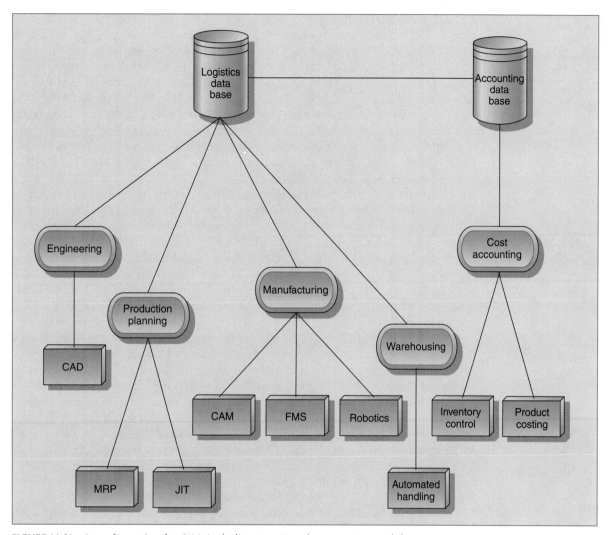

FIGURE 14-21 A configuration for CIM, including associated accounting modules.

and reviewed when desired. The CAD component enhances the productivity of engineers, improves the quality of products, and encourages complete documentation.

Materials requirements planning (MRP) schedules the production of ordered products and also arranges for materials and parts and subassemblies needed in the products. In preparing schedules it draws on the specifications already generated through the CAD system. When materials are to be purchased, the MRP system automatically prepares purchase requisitions for delivery to the purchasing department. (If an electronic data interchange network is attached, it triggers purchase orders to the suppliers.) An effective MRP system ensures that the acquisition of materials is synchronized with the production schedule.

Manufacturing resource planning (MRP-II) is a further development of MRP. It establishes master production schedules that extend as far as a year into the future, based on sales forecasts and expected production capacity. MRP-II also reviews capacity needs for each work center and in general considers the effective and efficient use of manufacturing resources.

Just-in-time (JIT), like MRP, focuses on the materials aspect of production planning. It has the objective of minimizing the need for raw materials inventory. In a perfect situation, the raw materials would arrive from suppliers just when a production order is scheduled to start and be delivered to the first work center. JIT is based on the *pull manufacturing concept,* in which each machine in the production process is viewed as "pulling" individual orders from one machine and center to the next as soon as operations are completed. Thus, there should be a minimum of idle time and handling in completing production orders. Because production cycle times are minimized, the quantities of work-in-process should be reduced throughout the entire production plant. For greatest effectiveness, JIT requires sound MRP and MRP-II procedures and very dependable suppliers.

Computer-aided manufacturing (CAM) involves the intensive application of automation to the physical production processes. At the heart of this component is *computer numerical control* (CNC), the replacement of skilled labor by computer-controlled machines that function by guidance from computer programs. One such machine can perform a series of operations as prescribed by a production order. Humans may only be needed to load, set up, and unload the machines in the case of individual machines. In a recent development, several types of CNC can be combined into single cells, or complex machine groupings, that can function without any human interaction.

Robotics involves the use of robots—programmable multifunctional devices that are designed to perform a variety of repetitive tasks. Robots consist of a series of assembled joints and links that are powered by electric, hydraulic, or pneumatic drives.

Flexible manufacturing systems (FMSs) are combinations of automated cells and robots, plus data collection terminals, that form complete production configurations or assembly lines. In addition to being automated, the major attribute of an FMS is flexibility. It can be modified from the production of one product to another very quickly—sometimes in a matter of minutes. Thus, an FMS allows a firm to accommodate rapidly changing customer demands. Due to the data collection terminals, the progress of the orders can be closely monitored.

Automated handling of materials involves the use of computers to aid in the movement and stacking of materials within the production area and warehouse. A prime example of automated materials handling is the automated guided vehicle system (AGVS), which uses self-propelled vehicles to move materials to points in the warehouse where they are needed. Then the vehicles are guided by the computer, or by built-in intelligent agents, to perform such tasks as moving goods to storage areas and loading pallets.

Cost accounting components include inventory control and product costing. As in other systems, these accounting activities consist of tracking the costs incurred in production, monitoring the levels of finished-goods inventory to alert the need for replenishments, and so on. As a part of a CIM system, they are closely integrated with such components as FMS and MRP.

BENEFITS OF CIM SYSTEMS

With the installation of a CIM system, a firm such as the Lens Manufacturing Co. can expect to achieve such added benefits as follows:

1. Greater flexibility in meeting the changing needs of customers.
2. Savings in the material inventory investment.
3. Increased quality in products, with less rework and scrappage.

4. Optimal scheduling of production, with dynamic adjustments as conditions change or new orders are received.

5. Shorter production cycle times.

6. Improved productivity of production employees and hence reduced labor costs.

7. Continuous monitoring of production operations, with immediate feedback of control problems as they arise.

8. Savings in paperwork costs, since most interactions are performed via computer and records are stored electronically.

9. Better utilization of all production facilities.

10. Greater accessibility of information, including the ability to provide ad hoc reports for planning and control.

ACCOUNTING CONTROLS

RISK EXPOSURES

Transactions within the product conversion cycle are exposed to all types of risks: unintentional errors, deliberate errors, unintentional losses of assets, thefts of assets, breaches of security, and acts of violence and natural disasters. Figure 14-22 lists representative risks and consequent exposures due to these risks.

Risk	Exposure
1. Incorrect costs charged to work-in-process inventory	1. Overstatement of inventory
2. Errors in recording quantitites of work-in-process or finished-goods inventory	2. Incorrect balances in inventory records
3. Release of wrong production order into production	3. Mix-up in production schedule, causing possible delays
4. Unauthorized release of production order into production	4. Mix-up in production schedule; added cost if product is unusable
5. Issuance of excessive or insufficient quantities of materials into production	5. Possibility of lost materials if excessive issue, or delay if insufficient issue
6. Fraudulent charging of labor hours to production	6. Excessive production costs
7. Fraudulent charging of excessive overtime for production employees	7. Excessive production costs
8. Theft of inventories or scrap	8. Losses of cash
9. Excessive delays of orders between production operations	9. Excessive production costs and possible revision in schedule
10. Falsification of finished-goods inventory records	10. Misstatement of inventory valuation
11. Improper use of cost-flow methods with respect to inventories	11. Misstatement of inventory valuation
12. Inflation of inventory values due to not writing down obsolescent items	12. Overstatement of inventory valuation
13. Undue delays in detecting items of product that have become defective during production operations	13. Excessive production costs
14. Involvement of inventories, production facilities, and ledger records in natural or human-made disasters	14. Loss of or damage to assets, including possible loss of data

FIGURE 14-22 Risk exposures within the product conversion cycle.

CONTROL OBJECTIVES

In order to counteract such risk exposures, a firm must first clarify the control objectives that are important to achieve. With respect to the product conversion cycle, several key control objectives are to ensure that

- All production orders are properly authorized and scheduled.
- All needed raw materials and other resources are assigned to production orders promptly and accurately, and the related costs are accumulated fully in accordance with the established system of cost accounting.
- All movements of production orders through the production process are reflected by acknowledgments at the various work centers.
- All finished goods are valued properly.
- All inventories are adequately safeguarded.

To fulfill these control objectives, the firm must then specify and incorporate adequate general controls and application controls.

Control Category	Specific Controls
Organizational	Separate production operations (i.e., work centers) from materials storeroom and warehouse, and also from accounting functions (i.e., cost accounting, inventory control). In the case of computer systems, separate systems development from computer operators and users of the information system.
Documentation	Maintain complete and up-to-date documentation concerning the documents, data base, controls, and reports affecting product conversion.
Asset accountability	Reconcile the records for the three inventories with physical counts and with the control accounts in the general ledger; reconcile actual usages of materials and labor with standards; reconcile completed production orders with transfers into finished goods.
Management practices	Train production employees fully; employ sound systems development and change procedures; perform periodic audits; provide adequate supervision of production operations; provide timely control reports and analyses to managers.
Authorization	Authorize all significant events, including initiation of production orders, issue of materials, and transfer of completed goods to the warehouse or shipping.
Access	Assign passwords to employees who access files; restrict terminal functions to those involving specified transactions (e.g., initiating production orders); log all logistics transactions on their entry; dump all production files frequently onto magnetic tape backup; physically protect production areas (where work-in-process inventories undergo operations) and warehouses (where finished goods are stored).

FIGURE 14-23 General controls pertaining to the product conversion cycle.

GENERAL CONTROLS

General controls concerning the product conversion cycle can be categorized as organizational, documentation, asset accountability, management practices, authorization, and access. Figure 14-23 lists several important controls in each category.

APPLICATION CONTROLS

A wide variety of controls and control procedures are applicable to product conversion cycle transactions and inventory accounts. Figure 14-24, on page 630, lists many of these controls, arranged by input, processing, and output categories.

REPORTS AND OTHER OUTPUTS

A wide variety of outputs are needed with respect to a firm's production activities. Information systems must be broad gauged if they are to provide adequate information for planning and control. Unfortunately, many systems are deficient in reporting, especially those involving cost and managerial accounting. Before surveying needed reports, we will briefly review the main deficiencies and the various measures that should be considered.

COMMON DEFICIENCIES IN REPORTING

The deficiencies in cost accounting and measurement systems have become widely recognized in recent years.* In essence, the typical system is based on manufacturing conditions in the early years of this century. Several of the more serious deficiencies are as follows:

1. Measures tend to be overly aggregated. Total costs of a production order is a common example.
2. Measures overlook such critical dimensions as product quality, productivity, and performance.
3. Measures are not responsive to automation and other rapidly changing conditions. For instance, most overhead rates are based on direct labor measures, even though direct labor may represent only a small percentage of the total product cost. Other factors, such as machine hours and materials costs, are not incorporated into the overhead cost allocation procedure.
4. Measures such as cost variances are often not computed in a sufficiently timely manner to provide effective control. For example, cost variance reports may be prepared weekly, even though most production orders require less than a week to complete.

NEEDED IMPROVEMENTS IN COST ACCOUNTING
AND MEASUREMENT SYSTEMS

In our discussion of production planning and control, we noted a variety of information needed by managers. However, we did not focus on information needed with

---

*See for instance Robert S. Kaplan, "Accounting Lag: The Obsolescence of Cost Accounting Systems," *California Management Review* (Winter 1986), pp. 174–199.

Input controls

1. Prepare prenumbered and well-designed documents relating to production orders, materials requisitioning, and moves through the work centers, with each prepared document being approved by an authorized person.

2. Validate data on production orders and other documents relating to production as the data are prepared and entered for processing. In computer-based systems, validation should be performed by means of programmed edit checks.

3. Correct errors that are detected during data entry and before the data are posted to the inventory and production order records.

4. Issue materials and parts into production on the basis of quantities shown on production orders, as taken from bills of materials.

Processing controls

1. Issue production orders, materials issue slips, and move tickets on the basis of valid authorizations.

2. Verify all computations on production orders and work-in-process inventory records.

3. Verify that all materials issued into production and all production orders are moved from one work center to the next and that all completed orders are moved from the last work center or inspection point into the warehouse or shipping dock. Also, ensure that all supervisors at work centers acknowledge the receipt of materials and production orders.

4. Monitor all open transactions, such as production orders that have been rejected and require rework. Also, investigate all transactions in which one or more supporting documents are missing.

5. Issue special excess materials issue slips when added materials are needed for a production order. Also, require the authorization of returned excess materials and disposition of scrap.

6. Require that labor-time records be approved by supervisors in the work centers.

7. Reconcile quantities on production orders placed in production with quantities of finished goods.

8. Correct errors that are made during processing steps, usually by reversing erroneous postings to accounts and entering correct data. The audit trail concerning accounts being corrected should show the original errors, the reversals, and the corrections.

Output controls

1. Establish clear-cut production cut-off policies, so that work-in-process inventory is fairly valued at the end of each accounting period.

2. Establish budgetary control over production, preferably with the aid of standard costs, and periodically review actual production costs and such key factors as scrap rates.

3. File copies of all documents pertaining to materials issues and production orders by number. The sequence of numbers in each file should be checked periodically to see if gaps exist. If transactions are not supported by preprinted documents, as often is the case in on-line computer-based systems, transaction numbers should be assigned to stored records.

4. Print transaction listings (e.g., production order lists) and account summaries on a periodic basis in order to provide an adequate audit trail. Also, prepare various outputs that aid control, such as cost variance reports.

FIGURE 14-24 Application controls pertaining to the product conversion cycle.

respect to the production process and products. Based on the experience of a few leading manufacturing firms, several proven improvements in needed product-oriented information can be offered.*

Improved Measures   A variety of measures, nonfinancial as well as financial, are needed to reflect such categories as customer satisfaction, performance, resource management, and flexibility. Figure 14-25 lists several examples in each category.

The number of measures employed does not need to be too large. In some cases only half a dozen have been employed with success. However, these measures should be viewed as *critical success factors*, which are to be tracked continually and on a very timely basis. Thus, an integrated on-line computer system is a necessary support for this expanded set of measures. On the other hand, the demands of financial accounting and generally accepted accounting principles should *not* be allowed to influence the measures.

Improved Overhead Cost Allocation   Instead of employing a single overhead cost driver, such as direct labor hours, a more useful approach is to allocate overhead costs according to activities. An **activity-based costing** approach assumes that activities cause the costs in a production process and that the products of a manufacturer cause the need for the activities. In applying the activity-based costing approach, a firm follows several well-defined steps. The first step is to establish the

Category	Examples of Measures
Customer satisfaction	• Quality (e.g., number of complaints) • Service (e.g., warranty periods) • Availability (e.g., percentage of back orders, percentage of on-time deliveries, lead time in days)
Performance	• Production cycle time • Product yield (percentage of items not requiring rework) • Percentage of scrap cost to dollars of product shipped • Employee productivity • Direct labor variance
Resource management	• Manufacturing cost as a percentage of dollar sales • Dollar sales per production employee • Raw materials inventory turnover • Production output per square foot of factory space • Average machine time in days per month
Flexibility	• Average cycle time per product • Number of days under production schedule • Changeover time

FIGURE 14-25   Measures relating to the product conversion cycle.

*Among the recent articles describing actual experiences in improving cost accounting measures and product information are K. V. Ramanathan and D. S. Schaffer, "How Am I Doing?" *Journal of Accountancy* (May 1995), pp. 79–82; Kim Constantinides and John K. Shank, "Matching Accounting to Strategy," *Management Accounting* (September 1994), pp. 32–36; George F. Hanks, Michael A. Fried, and Jack Huber, "Shifting Gears at Borg-Warner Automotive," *Management Accounting* (February 1994), pp. 25–29; Ronald B. Clements and Charlene W. Spoede, "Trane's SOUP Accounting," *Management Accounting* (June 1992), pp. 46–52; and Mark E. Beischel and K. Richard Smith, "Linking the Shop Floor to the Top Floor," *Management Accounting* (October 1991), pp. 25–29.

various activities—such as engineering design, machining a product, and assembling the product—and the cost drivers for each activity, such as engineering hours or machine hours. Next, the costs incurred during a period are measured for each activity cost pool. The third step is to divide these activity costs by the quantity of the cost driver for the activity, thereby determining the cost rate. Finally, the costs are applied to each product order by multiplying each cost rate by the quantity incurred. For instance, if the engineering design cost rate is determined to be $50 per hour, and the number of engineering design hours required by production order 8333 is 2, the overhead charge for that activity is $50 \times 2 = $100. The same procedure would be employed for every other activity in which order 8333 is involved.

Activity-based costing provides more realistic overhead values for products. This improved costing of products also aids in making decisions involving pricing of products and the mix of products to offer.

OPERATIONAL LISTINGS AND REPORTS

Most of the operational listings pertain to inventories and production orders. Apart from the materials requirements report, the *raw materials status report* shows the on-hand balance of all items in inventory, plus the issues and receipts during the past week or month, and the *finished-goods status report* shows the on-hand balances of all products in the warehouse, as well as quantities produced and sold. In addition, the *production activity report* lists all production orders outstanding and completed.

MANAGERIAL REPORTS

Reports for managers range from screen displays concerning current activity or status to analyses and control reports. Figure 14-26 shows a screen display concerning the current load at a particular work center. Other than cost variance reports, control reports include the following:

1. Employee productivity reports that compare the operations work center employees actually complete against standard levels of production.
2. Work center performance reports that reflect the efficiency of each work center.
3. Open production order status reports that show which orders are behind schedule and by how much.
4. Equipment utilization reports that show the percentage of downtime for each piece of factory equipment.
5. Waste reports that show the percentages of scrap, rework, and rejects for the production orders currently in process.

To be effective, these reports should be available to the responsible managers on a very timely basis. Certain reports that demand immediate attention, such as the breakdown of a computer-controlled machine or cell, should be triggered on a manager's screen as soon as they occur.

DECISION-ORIENTED REPORTS

Decision support systems and expert systems are being used to aid in making complex decisions in the production area. Decision support systems, for instance, can aid in developing production flows. A large steel manufacturer employs a model to simulate the flows of products through its steelmaking operations, in order to find

```
INQUIRY     WORK CENTER SHORT TERM LOAD W/C 4002-847 VERTICAL MILL   DAY 207
------      --------------------------- NO. OF MACH:  2  NO. OF SHIFTS: 2

TIME   START   PER   PLAN   * PRIMARY *   OVER    IDLE   * SETUP *
PER    DATE    LEN   CAP       LOAD       LOAD    TIME     TIME
               DAYS  HRS    HRS   PERC     HRS     HRS   HRS   PERC
- - - - - - - - - - - - - - - - - - - - - - - - - - - - - - - - -
 1     207      5    150   136.0  90.7              14   24.0  16.0
 2     212      5    150   139.0  92.7              11    8.5   5.7
 3     217      5    150   151.0 100.7      1            15.2  10.1
 4     222      5    180   199.0 132.7     49            25.4  16.9


ORDER    ITEM      OPER   OPERATION    ORDER  *SCHEDULED*  MACH   RUN    SETUP
NO.                NO.    DESCRIPTION   QTY   START COMPL   NO.   TIME    TIME
- - - - - - - - - - - - - - - - - - - - - - - - - - - - - - - - - - - - -
285510   003204    0020   MILL SLOT    1000   207   211     1    60.0    7.5
205530   220121    0080   MILL KEYWAY   500   207   209     2    36.0    2.7
205509   003204    0020   MILL SLOT    1000   211   215     1    60.0    7.5
205526   003210-A  0060   MILL FLAT     400   210   215     2    70.1    6.3
205501   220121    0080   MILL KEYWAY   100   215   216     2     7.2    2.7
205515   103216    0060   MILL FLAT     400   216   220     1    72.0    3.0
205516   103217    0090   MILL FLAT     800   217   225     2   120.0    2.6
205571   104718    0070   MILL FLAT     700   221   227     1   105.0    7.5
```

FIGURE 14-26   A screen showing the composition of the current load at a particular work center. (Courtesy of IBM Corporation.)

the most suitable routing. Carpenter Technology Corp., a specialty metals manufacturer, uses an expert system to schedule operations within its hot rolling mills. Because of the many variables, the schedule must be capable of adjusting dynamically as circumstances change and still achieve throughput efficiencies.*

---

*James D. Price, John C. Malley, and Phillip W. Balsmeier, "Expert Systems: Application to Inventory Control and Production Management," IM (September-October 1994), pp. 29–30.

SUMMARY

The product conversion cycle facilitates the conversion of raw materials into products or finished goods. Functions of the cycle are to undertake strategic planning, manage the raw materials inventory, initiate the production process, maintain and control production operations, accumulate work-in-process costs, complete and transfer finished goods, and prepare financial reports and other outputs. Related functions include quality control inspections, rework and scrappage, and return of excess materials. These functions are achieved under the direction of the logistics management and finance/accounting organizational units.

Most of the data used in the cycle arise from materials management, engineering design, and production planning and operations. Documents typically employed (either in hard-copy or electronic form) are bills of materials, operations lists, production orders, materials issue slips, labor job-time tickets, move tickets, and the documents involved in purchasing raw materials. The data base includes such master files as raw materials inventory, work-in-process inventory, and finished-goods inventory. It also includes the open production orders file and machine loading file. In firms that adopt the data-base approach, these files would be converted into linked data structures. Data processing consists of order entry (for make-to-order products), planning for production and materials requirements, production operations, disposition of finished goods, and cost accounting. Processing is performed by on-line computer-based systems in many firms, while a growing number of firms are installing computer-integrated manufacturing systems.

A variety of risk exposures exists in the processing of production-oriented transactions; these can be counteracted by means of adequate general and application controls. Cost accounting systems tend to be inadequate for modern production operations, in part because of insufficiently varied and relevant measures and in part because of simplistic overhead cost allocations to products. These inadequacies can be overcome through selective nonfinancial as well as financial measures and by adopting the activity-based costing approach. Among the outputs generated by the product conversion cycle are inventory status reports, production activity reports, production status and analysis reports, machine utilization reports, labor productivity reports, and material scrap reports.

....

APPENDIX 1 TO CHAPTER 14

MANUAL PROCESSING IN THE PRODUCT CONVERSION CYCLE

This appendix provides details concerning the flows of data through the product conversion cycle in a manual processing system. It should aid you in understanding the flows and processing of computer-based systems described in the chapter. With respect to each procedure, a narrative description is assisted through the use of document flowcharts.

Order Entry and Engineering Design

Figure 14-27 shows the document flows through the various organizational units composing the logistics function. Orders received from customers are first checked for accuracy and credit acceptability. Then formal sales orders are prepared in four copies. Two copies are sent to engineering design, where the appropriate bill of materials and operations list are pulled from the product file and modified to meet the specifications in the sales order.

Production and Materials Requirements Planning

After receiving the bill of materials and the operations list, plus a materials inventory status or reorder report as prepared by inventory control, production planning

(1) prepares a production order and distributes copies to production work centers and to cost accounting, (2) explodes materials requirements and prepares a list to reflect the requirements, (3) refers to the materials inventory status report to determine that sufficient materials are on hand, (4) prepares materials issue slips to request the issuance of the required materials and parts from stores, (5) prepares move tickets, (6) enters the production order on the production schedule, and (7) obtains approval from the customer for production specifications and scheduled completion date.

Production Operations

Up-to-date production schedules are issued to the respective work centers. A copy of each production order is dispatched to the initial work center listed in the order. Materials for each production order are issued to the production work centers according to the production schedule. Employees and machines are assigned in accordance with the schedule, unless departures are necessary because of employee absences, machine breakdowns, or other causes.

Certain paperwork actions occur as work commences and progresses on each production order. Labor jobtime tickets are prepared to record labor performed; these tickets are signed by the work center supervisors and forwarded to cost accounting. One copy of each materials issue slip is attached to the production order and accompanies the work in progress. Other copies of the materials issue slip are forwarded to inventory control for updating the raw materials inventory file and costing; the costed copy is then sent to cost accounting. Move tickets, previously issued by production planning, are signed to reflect the transfers of work in succeeding work centers; these signed move tickets are returned to production planning and control, which updates the open production order file to show the current status of work-in-process.

As each production order is completed, the work is inspected and an evaluation of the quality is expressed in an inspection report. This report is returned to production planning. Any units of work-in-process that do not meet inspection are returned for rework.

Disposition of Finished Goods

When production orders are satisfactorily completed, the resulting finished goods are moved out of the production area. If the goods are produced for inventory, they are sent to the warehouse. A move ticket signed by a warehouse supervisor signifies that the order is completed and notifies production planning to close the production order. The copy of the order that has accompanied the work-in-process is forwarded to inventory control, where the finished-goods inventory file is up-

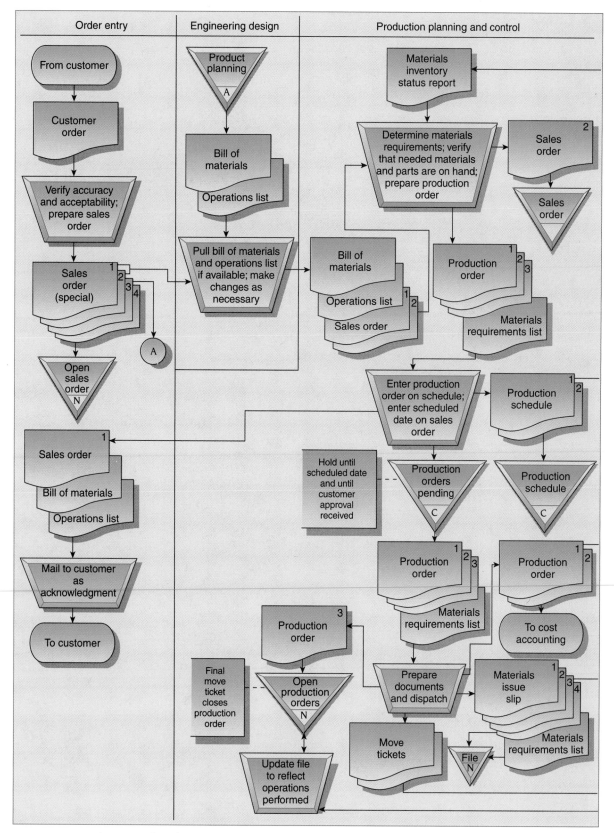

FIGURE 14-27 A document flowchart of manual processing within the logistics function.

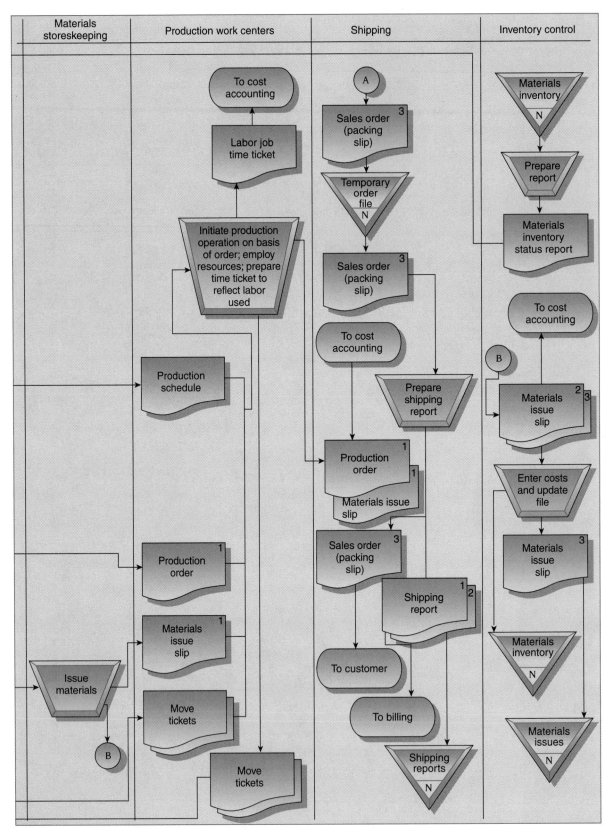

FIGURE I4-27 (*Continued*).

dated. Then the production order is sent to cost accounting, which pulls the cost sheet from the work-in-process inventory file. Periodically, cost accounting transfers, via a journal voucher, a journal entry to update the accounts in the general ledger.

If the goods have been produced in accordance with customers' special orders, the finished goods are transferred to the shipping dock. There a shipping clerk pulls the packing slip copy of the sales order from its pending file, ships the products, and prepares a shipping report. One copy of the shipping report is sent to billing and the other copy is filed. The final move ticket is returned to production planning, thus giving notice that the production order can be closed. The production order and materials issue slips are forwarded to cost accounting with a notation that the order is completed.

Cost Accounting

To back up in time, a new cost sheet was opened by cost accounting on first receiving each production order from production planning. Then, throughout the production process, the material and labor costs chargeable to the production order are posted to the cost sheet from materials issue slips and labor job-time tickets. Overhead costs are applied on some basis such as direct labor hours. Periodically, cost accounting transmits to the general ledger a journal voucher that summarizes the cost accumulations. Figure 14-28 portrays these processing steps.

When a production order is completed, the cost sheet is removed from the work-in-process inventory file. The costs are totaled and the cost sheet, together with the production order and materials issue slips, is forwarded to billing. Then the journal entry is transmitted, via a journal voucher, to the general ledger. Figure 14-29, on page 639, shows these final processing steps.

APPENDIX 2 TO CHAPTER 14

THE HUMAN RESOURCE, FIXED ASSETS, AND CASH MANAGEMENT CYCLES

As described in Chapter 5, the resources-management cycle includes business events related to personnel (human resources), fixed assets, and cash. This appendix surveys the management cycles pertaining to these three key resources, which are employed by every organization.

The Human Resource Management Cycle

The *human resource management cycle* spans the functions that involve services performed by an organization's em-

ployees. Traditionally the human resource giving rise to employee services has been labeled labor, manpower, or personnel. In certain organizations, such as service-oriented firms and governmental agencies, this resource consumes the greatest portion of the recurring expenditures. In other organizations, such as manufacturing firms, this resource is a key cost in the conversion of raw materials into finished goods. All types of organizations, however, encounter the same concerns and undertake the same functions with respect to employee services. From a systems point of view, the cycle that encompasses the human resource and related employee services is in essence a special version of the expenditure cycle.

Objectives of the Cycle

Several objectives of the human resource management cycle are to ensure that the status, pay rates or salaries, and pay deductions of employees are authorized; that payments are made for actual services rendered; and that employee-related costs are promptly and accurately recorded, classified, summarized, distributed, and reported. Payment for employee services is a critical objective; in fact, the human resource management cycle is often called the *payroll cycle* in recognition of this objective's importance.

Functions of a Payroll Cycle

Functions related to employees (the human resource) include hiring, training, transferring, terminating, classifying, adjusting pay levels, establishing safety measures, preparing payrolls, maintaining employee benefits programs, and reporting to governmental agencies. All of these are important concerns within the personnel information system; however, due to the focus on payroll, a more relevant listing of functions for our use is: establishing pay status, measuring the services rendered, preparing paychecks, issuing and distributing paychecks, distributing labor costs, and preparing required reports and statements.

Establish Pay Status Before an employee can be paid, his or her status should be clearly stated in writing. Status is a multifaceted concept. It first implies that the employee has successfully completed the hiring process, which usually consists of filling out a detailed application form and undergoing interviews. When the applicant is hired, the data from the application form becomes a part of the employee's personnel data record. Status also involves classification and type of remuneration. An employee may be classified as an accounting clerk, a salesperson, a production worker, a manager,

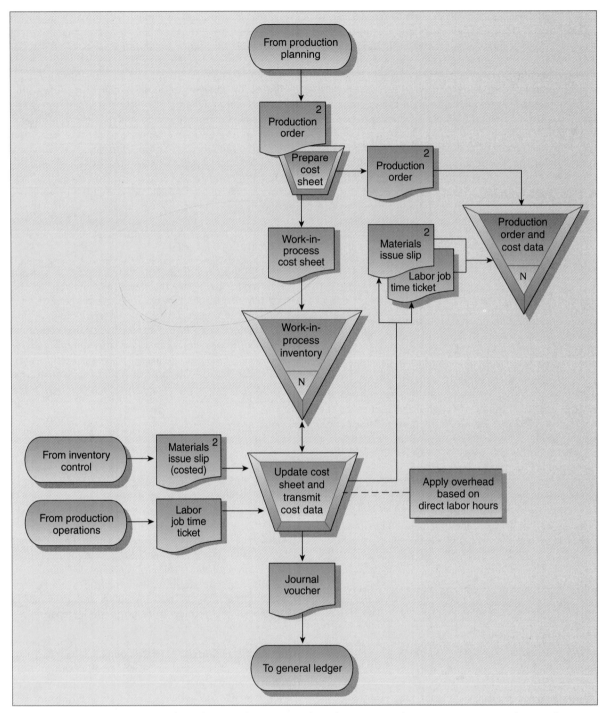

FIGURE 14-28 A document flowchart showing the posting of production costs by cost accounting and control.

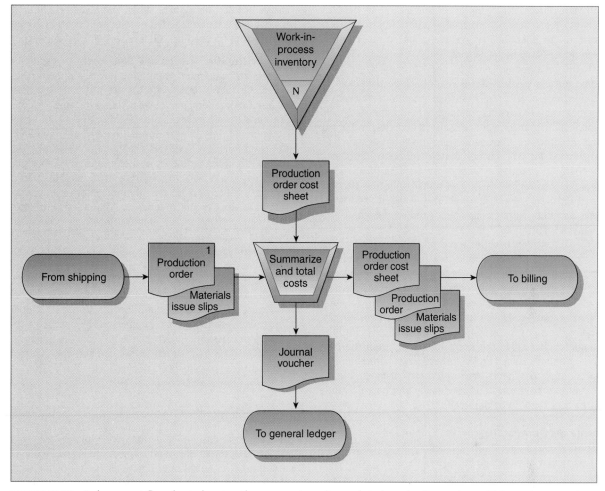

FIGURE 14-29 A document flowchart showing the processing of completed production orders within cost accounting and control.

and so forth. Production workers, other operational employees (e.g., truck drivers), and many clerks are paid according to hourly rates; professional and managerial employees and certain clerks are generally paid monthly salaries; and salespersons are often paid on a commission basis. Certain employee classifications are eligible for overtime rates and shift differentials, while others are exempt from such premiums. Finally, pay status depends on the types of and number of deductions that are to be offset against the amounts payable by a firm. Of two employees who were hired on the same day with the same job classification, one may have a higher "take-home" pay than the other as a result of fewer deductions from his or her pay.

Measure the Services Rendered The means by which employee services are measured vary according to the type of remuneration. Those employees on hourly wages are expected to record their times on the job rather precisely; each time they enter and leave the job locations, they enter the times on time cards. Salaried employees prepare attendance records of some sort (e.g., time sheets), showing attendance and absences during the various days composing the pay period. Commission employees prepare vouchers that reflect the amounts of sales made during the period for which commissions are to be computed. Each type of service-related document serves as the legal basis for payment when approved by the employee's supervisor.

Prepare Paychecks Employees are normally paid by checks, since they provide relative safety and written records of the amounts due. In some cases, however, hourly employees may be paid by currency.

The net amount of each paycheck is equal to the gross amount less all deductions. Certain deductions are required by law or contract, such as premiums or dues for social security benefits, unemployment benefits, group medical insurance benefits, pension benefits, and union representation. Other deductions are voluntary, such as payments for U.S. savings bonds and contributions to recognized charities. All approved deductions are withheld by the employees' firm, at which point they become accrued liabilities. These liabilities are removed when the amounts withheld are deposited in designated financial institutions.

As a control procedure, a special payroll-imprest bank account may be established to accommodate paycheck amounts. A firm that follows this procedure prepares a disbursement voucher when the total amount of the payroll is known. Next a check is drawn on the firm's regular bank account and given to the person who signs checks. He or she signs the prepared check and delivers it to the bank for deposit in the special account. Then the paychecks can be issued and distributed. A separate imprest account for paychecks improves control because the account can be reconciled more easily and payroll frauds are more likely to be detected.

Issue and Distribute Paychecks Employees are paid, according to law, on established schedules. A schedule for a particular pay classification may be weekly, biweekly, semimonthly, or monthly. After the paychecks are signed, they are either distributed to the employees at their job sites or at other designated places.

Paychecks may be replaced by other modes of payment. Hourly workers are sometimes paid in currency. In such cases the employees are generally expected to obtain their pay amounts at a cashier's window and to sign receipts. Salaried employees and managers are often encouraged to select a direct-deposit arrangement, under which the firm deposits their pay amounts directly into their personal bank accounts.

Distribute Costs for Employee Services An employer's costs for employee services include the gross amounts of pay for all employees. In addition, the employer incurs payroll-related expenses pertaining to such benefits as unemployment, pensions, vacations, sick leaves, and group insurance plans. Like costs of any type, these costs for employee services must be distributed in accordance with the organizational structure and/or activities. For instance, a merchandising firm may distribute employee costs to the marketing, finance, and other functions. A manufacturing firm will likely distribute employee costs related to production activities to direct labor or manufacturing overhead. In turn, these costs are absorbed in the values of the products. When employees are directly involved in activities related to the development of long-lived assets for the firm, their costs will be capitalized.

Prepare Required Reports and Statements A variety of reports and statements related to payrolls must be prepared. Certain of these outputs are precisely specified by a maze of federal and state regulations, since various amounts from paychecks are destined to flow into governmental funds. For instance, the Federal Insurance Contributions Act specifies the manner of computing and withholding employer and employee contributions for old age, survivors', disability, and hospital insurance benefits. State and federal unemployment compensation laws specify the manner of computing and withholding contributions by employers for unemployment benefits. These laws also detail the manner of reporting these withholdings at the end of each quarter and year. Furthermore, they state that the withheld amounts must be deposited, together with the employer's portions, in designated financial institutions.

Figure 14-30 shows a data-flow diagram of the functions just described. Each function in the diagram is in effect a process that links to the remaining functions and to entities and data stores. As we can see, the diagram highlights the parallel flows of paychecks and distributed costs for employee services.

Relationships to the Organization

The above-mentioned functions are typically achieved under the direction of the personnel and finance/accounting organizational functions (units) of the firm. The employee services management system therefore involves the interaction of the personnel information system and the accounting information system (AIS). In addition, every department or other organizational unit is involved since the employees are located throughout the organization. Figure 14-31, on page 642, shows the relations between key departments and the system functions.

Personnel Personnel management has the primary objective of planning, controlling, and coordinating the employees—the internally employed human resource—within an organization. The personnel function may be under the direction of a vice-president of personnel. Among the managers who might report to this top personnel manager are those in charge of employment and personnel planning, safety and benefits, industrial relations, employee development, and human resource administration. The employment and personnel planning unit is concerned with recruiting and testing prospective employees, hiring selected employees, ensuring sound promotion and termination procedures, and determining future personnel needs (in terms of both skills and levels). The safety and benefits unit is responsible for employees' safety and health, and for providing pleasant

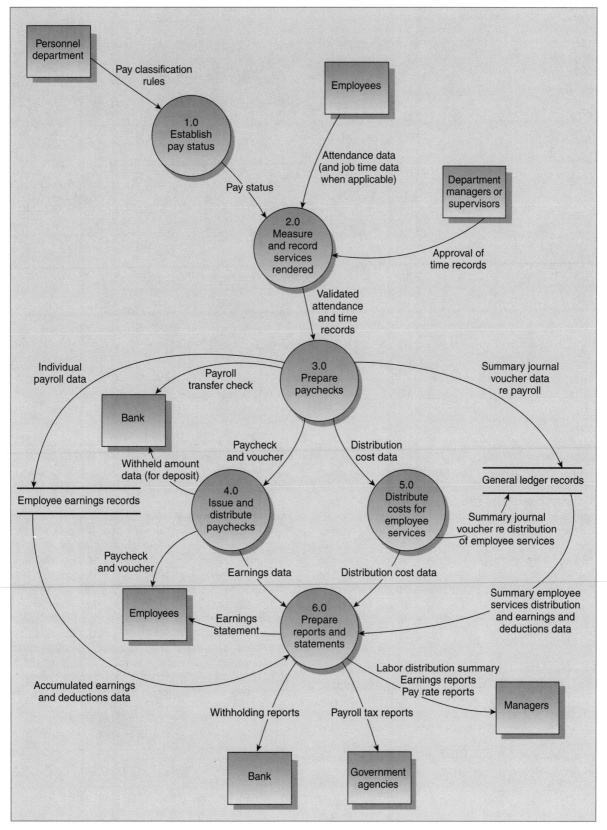

FIGURE 14-30   A data-flow diagram pertaining to the human resource management cycle.

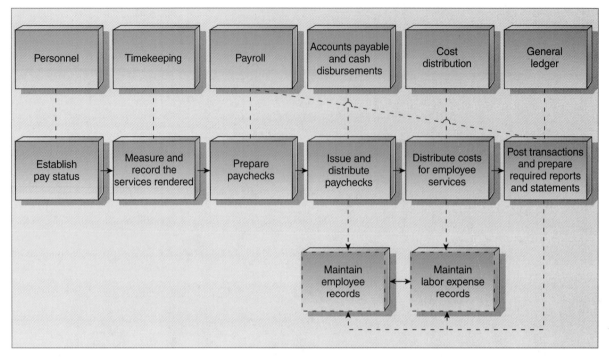

FIGURE 14-31   Typical functions and related organizational units of a human resource management cycle.

working conditions. The industrial relations unit is responsible for dealing with unions and other labor-related organizations. The employee development unit is concerned with the training of employees and the development of executive skills in managers. The human resource administration unit is responsible for salary compensation plans, group insurance and related programs; it also administers and maintains the records of all employees and related personnel actions. Thus, the human resource administration unit (also called personnel administration) is the most closely related to the payroll activity.

Finance/Accounting   The objectives of financial and accounting management relate broadly to funds, data, information, planning, and control over resources. Organizational units within this function and involved in the management of employee services include timekeeping, payroll, accounts payable, cash disbursements, cost distribution, and general ledger. Timekeeping maintains control over the time and attendance records of hourly employees. Payroll prepares paychecks, maintains the payroll records, and prepares required reports and statements. Accounts payable, in the context of employee services, approves the disbursement voucher pertaining to employee services. Cash disbursements, together with the cashier, signs and distributes the paychecks. Cost distribution maintains the records reflecting detailed costs of the products. General ledger maintains control

over all asset, equity, expense, and income accounts. Note that the timekeeping and cost distribution units are more typically found in manufacturing firms than in other types of organizations.

Managerial Decision Making   Three managers whom we have identified as having key responsibilities with respect to the human resource management cycle are the personnel manager, the treasurer, and the controller. They must make decisions that influence the effectiveness in acquiring, managing, and paying employees.

The personnel manager depends most heavily on the personnel information system to provide needed information for decision making. Many of the decisions are not based, even in part, on routine accounting transactions. However, some of the payroll-related decisions do draw on by-product information from the AIS. Several of the decisions most closely bound to employee services are the following:

1. What organizational units are to be included within the personnel function?

2. Which applicants should be hired as new employees?

3. Which employees should be promoted, transferred, given pay raises, or terminated?

4. What benefits of financial value (and hence cost to the firm) should be made available to employees?

PERSONNEL FORM 1174

Distribution:
White, Green, Canary: Personnel
Pink: Originator

PERSONNEL — PAYROLL ACTION NOTIFICATION

Name ______________________________

Effective Date ____________ Organization Unit No. ____________ Employee Number ____________

Address (*Change Only*) ______________________________

Enroll or transfer only — Overtime Exempt ☐ Overtime Non-Exempt ☐

ACTION TO BE TAKEN — CHECK APPLICABLE BOX(ES)

☐ Enroll ☐ Termination ☐ Vacation (Specify dates & pay request below)

☐ Transfer ☐ Leave of Absence ☐ Other (Explain)

☐ Rate Change ☐ Cross Charge

Present Status:

Job Title ____________ Salary ____________

Dept. & Div. ____________ Job Class ____________

New Status:

Job Title ____________ Salary ____________

Dept. & Div. ____________ Job Class ____________

If salary increase, give following information:

Amount of increase as % of present salary ____________.

Midpoint of salary range for job class ____________.

Date of last increase ____________ ; amount of last increase ____________.

(Guidelines per Sec. -0500 must be observed.)

Date of last appraisal ____________ summary evaluation ____________.

(Within 6 mos. of requested increase.)

Explanation: ______________________________

Originated by ____________ Transmittal date ____________

Management Approval ____________ Personnel Approval ____________

PAYROLL USE ONLY

Pay Period ____________ Permanent

Follow Up Yes ______ No ______ ______ hrs. $ ______

Action PR# ____________ Temporary

Action Type ____________ ______ hrs. $ ______

REMARKS: ______________________________

FIGURE 14-32 A document relating to personnel actions. (Courtesy of John Wiley & Sons, Inc.)

The controller and treasurer depend primarily on the AIS for needed decision-making information. Much of the information is a by-product of processing within the human resource management cycle. Among the decisions required of these managers (or their subordinates) are:

1. What employees' earnings records are to be maintained concerning amounts paid to employees?

2. Which payroll deduction plans (e.g., United Way) are to be made available to employees?

3. What type of payroll bank accounts are to be established?

4. Who is to sign paychecks, and how are pay amounts to be distributed to employees?

5. What pay periods (e.g., weekly, biweekly) are to be established?

Among the information items needed to make such decisions are qualifications and skills of applicants, evaluations of employees, wage and salary scales (both for the firm and for the industry), expected costs of benefit plans, and educational and work experience histories of employees.

Various human resource management system software packages have been developed by software development firms for use with different computer architectures. Currently most such systems are being developed for client/server environments. Certain of these systems provide decision support as well as operational efficiencies. For instance, Snelling International, a temporary employee service agency, acquired PeopleSoft HRMS (from PeopleSoft). It aids management in locating employees with job skills needed by clients, forecasts the need for and helps schedule training courses, accumulates information concerning employee performance for use in evaluations, and so on.*

Data Entry

Sources Data used in the human resource management cycle are mainly based on inputs from time records and from documents provided by the personnel department. Other sources are the payroll files and the departments in which jobs are performed requiring direct labor.

Forms of Input Source documents typically used in the management of employee services include the following:

1. **Personnel action form.** A *personnel action form* serves to notify interested parties of actions concerning employees. These actions may pertain to the notice of hiring, a change of status, an evaluation of job performance, and so on. Figure 14-32, on the previous

*Lee The, "HR App Meets Critical Needs," *Datamation* (June 15, 1995), pp. 69–72.

page, shows a personnel action form that notifies the payroll department of a situation or change affecting the status of an employee's pay. Another category of personnel actions concerns deductions. Some of these forms are issued by the firm and some by government agencies. An example of the latter is the W-4 Form, Employee Withholding Allowance Certificate, which is provided by the Internal Revenue Service. It specifies to the employer the number of exemptions to assign in computing the employee's withholding for income taxes.

2. **Time and/or attendance form.** The *time card*, also known as a clock card, records the actual hours spent by hourly employees at their work locations. It contains an employee's name and number, plus the dates of the applicable pay period. Each time the employee enters or leaves, he or she "punches" the card in the time clock. At the bottom of the card is a space for the supervisor's signature. Figure 14-33 shows a basic example of a time card. Other attendance forms, as noted earlier, include a time sheet for use by salaried employees.

3. **Job-time ticket.** In contrast to the time card, which focuses on attendance at the work site, the *job-time ticket* focuses on specific jobs or work orders. Each time an hourly employee, such as a production

Employee No. 45982			
Name Jacob Keeley			
Week ending 8/8/97			
First day	Aug 4 1997 7:52 A Aug 4 1997 12:01 P Aug 4 1997 12:58 P Aug 4 1997 5:03 P	Total regular hours	
Second day		Overtime hours	
Third day		Hourly rate	
Fourth day		Total earnings	
Fifth day		Total deductions	
Sixth day		Net pay	
Supervisor			

FIGURE 14-33 An attendance time card.

worker, begins and ends work on the job, he or she records the time on the card. As in the case of the time card, the means of entering the times may be a time clock or terminal. If appropriate to the employees' tasks, spaces are provided for entering the productivity in terms of pieces completed during the elapsed periods.

4. **Paycheck.** A *paycheck*, with voucher stub, is the final document in the human resource management cycle. Figure 14-34 presents a typical paycheck prepared by computer. The stub shows all necessary details, including overtime pay and deductions.

Accounting Entries Figure 14-35 shows the flow of payroll transactions through the accounting cycle. The transactions begin with records reflecting times worked by employees. These source documents, when expressed in dollar terms by applying rates of pay, are used in the two steps composing payroll processing.

As the first step, the data from these source documents are entered into a summary that distributes the costs for employee services to such activities as selling goods, performing administrative tasks, and manufacturing goods. The totals from this summary are posted to the general ledger accounts as follows:

Dr. Selling Expense Control	XXX	
Dr. Administrative Expense Control	XXX	
Dr. Direct Labor (or Work-in-Process Inventory)	XXX	
Dr. Manufacturing Overhead Control	XXX	
Cr. Wages and Salaries Payable		XXX

To record the costs of employee services for the period.

Details are also posted to appropriate expense subsidiary ledgers for manufacturing overhead, selling expense, and administrative expense, if such ledgers are maintained.

The second step consists of using time data to prepare payroll checks. Copies of these paychecks, together with attached earnings statements, are the source documents from which pay data are entered into the payroll register. They are also used as the basis for posting the same data to the earnings records of individual employees. Totals from the payroll register are then posted to the general ledger accounts as follows:

Dr. Wages and Salaries Payable	XXX	
Cr. Federal Income Taxes Withholding Payable		XXX
Cr. FICA Tax Payable		XXX
Cr. Other Accrued Deductions Payable		XXX
Cr. Cash		XXX

To record the payroll for the period.

A Payroll Clearing account may be used in place of the Wages and Salaries Payable account, since the effect is to clear the costs of employee services. Either account also serves as a control over the total of the gross amounts of pay for all employees.

Transaction Coding Codes are useful for identifying data needed in payrolls and labor cost distributions. In addition to codes for general ledger accounts, codes can be used to identify employees, departments, production jobs, and skills. Consider a code for employees. Many firms use the social security number, since it is unique and familiar to the employees. Other firms may use a group code that includes such factors as pay category (i.e., hourly or salaried), department number, skill, date of hire, and self-checking digit.

Data Base

Files Among the files needed in managing the human resource are the following:

1. **Employee Payroll Master File.** An *employee payroll master file* shows the personal attributes and earnings records of the employees. It is updated to show the amounts received from paychecks at the end of each pay period. Generally the primary and sorting key is the employee number. Additional data elements consist of the employee name, social security number (if not used as the employee number), department code, pay classification, pay rate or salary, overtime rate, marital status, data related to deductions (e.g., number of exemptions), year-to-date earnings withheld, year-to-date gross pay, and year-to-date net pay.

    An important concern with this file is keeping the records and their permanent data up-to-date. When an employee marries and obtains a new last name, for instance, this change should appear quickly in her record. When a new employee is hired, a record must be established before the end of the pay period. On the other hand, when an employee is terminated, the record should not be discarded until after the end of the year. Certain year-end reports require data concerning all employees who were active during any part of the year.

2. **Personnel Reference and History File.** As the main source of personnel data in the firm, the *personnel reference and history file* complements the payroll master file. It contains a variety of nonfinancial data as well as financial data concerning each employee. For instance, it might contain the employee's address, skills, job title, work experience, educational history, performance evaluations, and even family status.

3. **Skills File.** A related file is the *skills file*, which provides an inventory of skills required by the firm, and

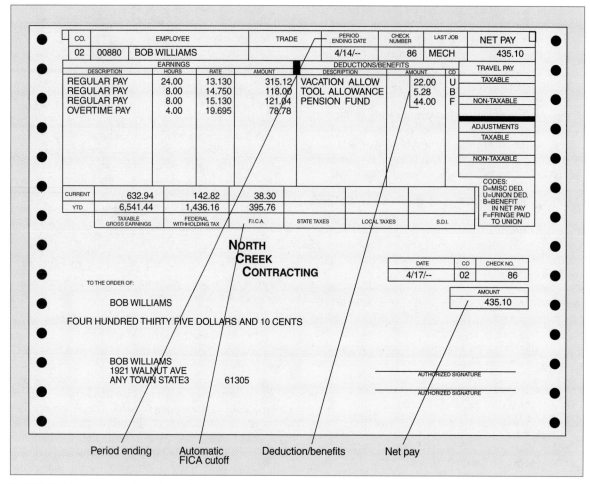

FIGURE 14-34   A paycheck and voucher stub. (Courtesy of IBM Corporation.)

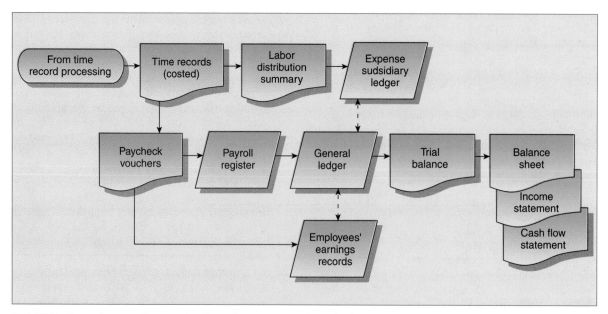

FIGURE 14-35   A diagram showing the flow of transactions through the payroll cycle.

the employees who currently possess each skill. This type of file enables a firm to locate qualified candidates when an opening or new need arises.

4. **Time Record Transaction File.** A *time record transaction file* consists of copies of all the time cards or sheets for a particular pay period. In computer-based systems they are likely to be stored on magnetic media for use in processing the payroll.

5. **Paycheck Transaction File.** In a manual system the *payroll transaction file* consists of a copy of each current paycheck, arranged in check number order. In a computer-based system the record layout on magnetic media may appear similar to a record in the check disbursements transaction file.

6. **Compensation Reference File.** A table of pay rates and salary levels for the various job descriptions serves as a *compensation reference file*.

7. **Personnel Planning File.** In order to provide the basis for planning for future personnel needs, a firm may maintain a collection of information relating to current and past trends as well as projections. It might show the number of employees in each department during the past ten years, for instance, as well as the turnover for each department.

Data Structures Integrated data bases are becoming more common in the human resource management cycle. They may include such key entities as employees, skills, personnel action events, service events, and pay-

roll payments. Figure 14-36 portrays an entity-relationship diagram that incorporates these key entities within a human resource data base.*

As the diagram portrays, employees are affected by such personnel actions as hiring and promotions, which are processed by clerks in the personnel or human resources department. The employees perform various services, which in the case of hourly employees are reflected in earned hours of pay. Each payday the employees are paid via disbursements from cash, with the payroll amounts being based on hours worked multiplied by hourly rates minus payroll deductions. Most of the relationships are likely to be of the one-to-many type. However, the relationship between employees and the services performed is shown to be of the many-to-many

---

*The entity-relationship diagram in this figure, applicable to Infoage, can be viewed as rather typical for the human resource management cycle. The resources consist of the skills of employees and the cash paid to them for their services. The events are the personnel actions, services provided, and cash disbursements. In addition to employees, the agents include the personnel clerk and cashier. Other agents involved in the human resource management cycle—such as timekeepers, payroll clerks, and supervisors—are not shown in order to keep the diagram from being too cluttered. It should be noted that the human resource cycle gives rise to a variety of possible situations and thus entity-relationship diagrams. Consider the changes that might be needed to reflect advances made to employees, the use of consultants, and so on.

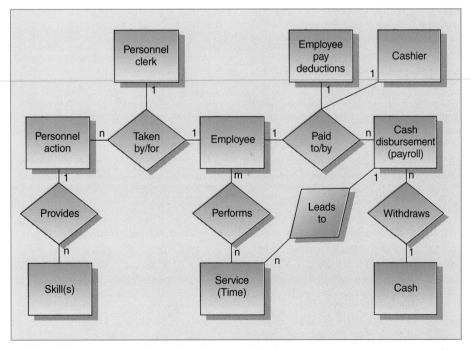

FIGURE 14-36   An entity-relationship diagram of the human resource management cycle.

type; each employee can perform more than one service, while each type of service can be performed by more than one employee.

Based on this diagram, the entities and relationships can be mapped to tables within a relational data base. The tables will contain such data elements as described for the above-mentioned files. Thus, the employee table will contain personal data concerning each employee, including accumulated earnings data. The services table will contain the time and attendance data, plus job time data for hourly employees who work on specific jobs.

Information such as the following can easily be obtained from the tables:

- An inventory of skills and the employees currently possessing each skill.
- The current pay status and history of each employee.
- The employees who performed each service or worked on each production job this pay period and the hours worked.

Data Flows and Processing

Manual Processing System   Figure 14-37 presents a document flowchart of a procedure involving the payment of hourly operations-type employees (e.g., production employees) who also work directly on specific jobs. The narrative discussion will be assisted through the use of reference numbers, which have been placed on the flowchart at key spots. These numbers designate the various control points within the procedure and parallel the functions described earlier.

1. **Establishment of pay status.** This beginning function takes place in the personnel department, where all of the personnel actions and changes are prepared and then transmitted to the payroll department.

2. **Measurement of the services rendered.** The time records are prepared in the operational (e.g., production) departments and timekeeping areas. Time cards are maintained in racks near the entrance to the work site. Employees clock in and clock out under the eye of a timekeeper. The job-time tickets are available right at the work site. Employees either punch the tickets on a clock or mark them manually under the eye of their supervisor.

   At the end of each day, the job-time tickets are collected and approved by the employees' supervisor. Then the supervisor forwards the tickets to the timekeeper. At the end of the pay period, the timekeeper compares the total hours shown on the job-time tickets for each employee with the total hours shown on his or her attendance time cards. If the two sets of total hours are approximately equal (allowing for breaks, lunch, etc.), the time records are said to be reconciled. Then the timekeeper sends the attendance time cards to the payroll department (to-gether with the total of hours worked) and the job-time tickets to the cost distribution department.

3. **Preparation of the paychecks.** In the payroll department, a clerk prepares a paycheck and voucher stub for each employee, based on data from the time card and from the employee's payroll reference file. Next the clerk enters the relevant information from the paycheck and voucher stub (i.e., gross pay, deductions, net pay, overtime premium) on the payroll register. Another clerk then posts the information to the employee's earning record (i.e., the payroll master). Still another clerk verifies that the hours used in preparing the payroll register equal the total hours on the time cards, and that the total payroll amount entered into the register equals the total amount posted to all employees' earnings records. The paychecks and attached voucher stubs are sent, in a batch, to the cash disbursements department (or cashier).

4. **Issuance and distribution of the paychecks.** On receiving a copy of the payroll register, an accounts payable clerk verifies its correctness and then prepares a disbursement voucher. A clerk in the cash disbursements department draws a check on the firm's regular bank account and gives it to the cashier for signing. The signed check is delivered to the bank and deposited in the special imprest payroll account. Then the cashier signs all the paychecks. A paymaster (a designated person not otherwise involved in personnel or payroll procedures) distributes the paychecks.

5. **Distribution of the labor costs.** Meanwhile, a clerk in the cost distribution department distributes the costs of services incurred by the operational personnel (e.g., production employees) to the various jobs in progress. The clerk next reports the costs, via a *labor distribution summary* or a journal voucher, to the general ledger department. Then the general ledger clerk debits the amounts to the various labor-related accounts (e.g., direct factory labor) and credits a payroll control account (e.g., wages and salaries payable).

   Subsequently, the general ledger clerk clears the payroll control account by reference to the disbursement voucher (or related journal voucher) prepared by accounts payable. That is, he or she debits the Payroll Clearing account and credits the Cash account plus deductions withheld accounts. Since the total from both sources (labor cost distribution and disbursement voucher) should be equal, the Payroll Clearing account will be cleared to zero if processing has been correct.

   Note that this clearing procedure is a partial substitute for the computation of formal batch totals in the timekeeping department. When attendance time records are not accompanied by time records related

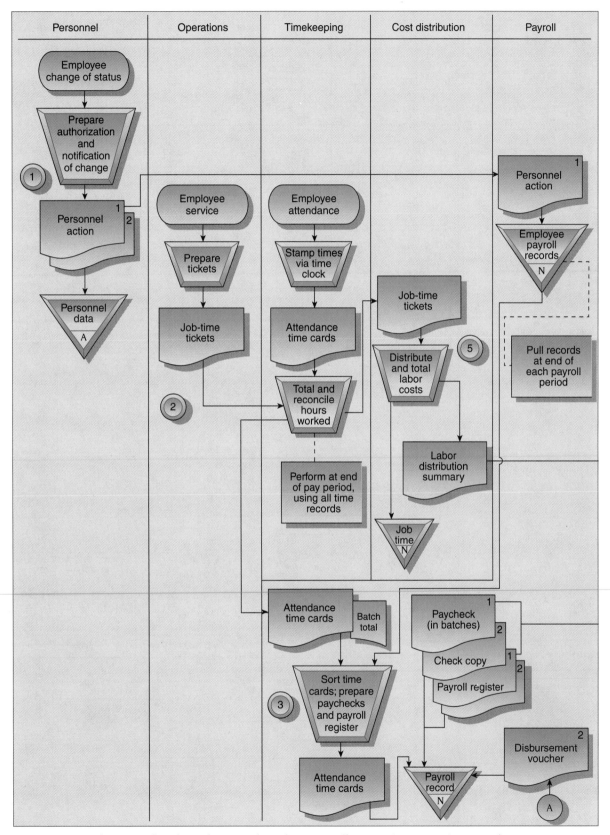

FIGURE I4-37   A document flowchart of a manual employee payroll transaction processing procedure.

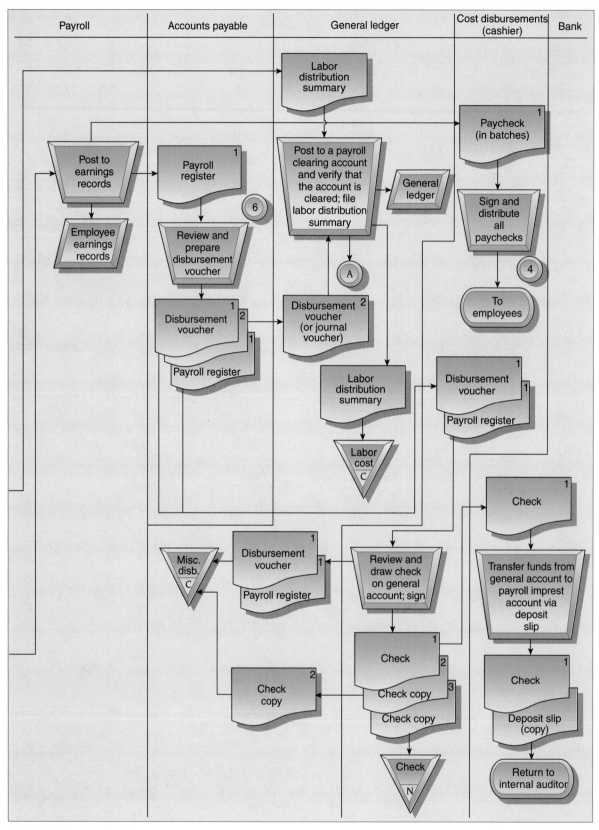

FIGURE 14-37 (Continued)

to jobs, it is highly desirable to compute batch totals at the point where the time records are assembled.

6. **Preparation of required reports.** Numerous reports and statements and other outputs are prepared. The only outputs shown in the flowchart are the labor distribution summary (mentioned in the previous step) and the payroll register. Additional reports are discussed in a later section.

Computer-Based Batch Processing System When a computer-based system is available, the batch approach is well suited to the payroll procedure. Since all of the records in the employee payroll master file are affected, sequentially accessing and updating the records is the more efficient alternative. Figure 14-38 therefore shows a system flowchart in which the batch approach is applied. The flowchart has three segments: time data entry, paycheck preparation, and pay status changes.

1. **Time data entry.** Attendance time cards are first gathered in a batch by the timekeeper and transmitted to the payroll department. In the system being described, the employees do not prepare job-time tickets. Therefore, to enhance control the timekeeper (or a payroll clerk) computes batch totals based on the time records. One total is based on the hours worked, a second total (of the hash variety) is based on the employee numbers, and a third total is based on a count of the time cards.

   In order to avoid manual keying in the next step, data collection devices may be employed to capture the time and attendance data. Employees enter their badges into these devices, usually called badge readers, which record the employee numbers, dates, and times. These data are accumulated throughout the pay period and the batch totals are calculated.

2. **Paycheck preparation.** The batch of time cards, prefaced by a batch transmittal sheet, is forwarded to the data processing department. There the time data are keyed onto a magnetic disk and edited. In the first computer processing run, the data are sorted by employee numbers. (If all programmed edit checks cannot be performed by the key-to-disk device, the remaining checks are performed prior to sorting.) In run 2 the time data are processed to produce paychecks (and voucher stubs). The program also updates the employee payroll master file and prints the payroll register. The paychecks and a copy of the register are sent to the cashier, where the paychecks are signed and distributed. (The transfer of funds from the regular account may be included, if desired.) The program in run 2 also adds a journal voucher concerning the payroll transaction to the general ledger transaction file.

3. **Pay status changes.** The left side of the flowchart portrays changes made in the pay status of employ-ees. Clerks in the personnel department enter all personnel actions via departmental terminals. Since the employee payroll master file is stored on-line on a magnetic disk, the actions (e.g., a change in pay rate) can be entered into the affected employee records promptly by direct access. Thus, all actions can be effected during the pay period and before the payroll processing begins.

On occasion it is necessary to process individual paychecks by the on-line approach. For instance, a terminated employee may desire the final paycheck before the end of the pay period. This can be done as simply as making changes to pay status, assuming that an integrated data base is accessible. However, when either type of on-line action is expected, the system should be designed to incorporate adequate on-line controls and security measures, as discussed next.

Integrated Computer-based Human Resource System As noted earlier, many firms are acquiring human resource management systems that integrate data structures and employee functions. The experiences of two firms should illustrate their usefulness.

- Newmont Mining Corporation found that its separate personnel and payroll systems could not handle the employee load due to brisk hiring trends. Also, it was spending too many hours compiling the many personnel and payroll reports that were being demanded. After reviewing the available software packages, it selected an on-line software system that integrates personnel, payroll, and employee benefits functions. The system is implemented on the firm's Denver mainframe computer and can be accessed via microcomputers located at the various mining sites. In addition to increasing productivity, the system has allowed the firm to generate a greater variety of managerial reports for planning and control.*

- Woodward Communications recently considered the acquisition of a human resource management information system. It did a thorough study of the possibilities, ranking all of the available software packages according to a variety of criteria—ranging from audit trails to ad hoc reporting capabilities. The decision has been delayed in part because the firm intends to move from a mainframe environment to a client/server architecture. However, it expects to achieve numerous benefits from a selected package, and to avoid unpleasant surprises, because it has employed a careful planning process.[†]

---

*Leila Davis, "On the Fast Track to HR Integration," *Datamation* (September 15, 1991), pp. 61–63.

[†]Steven A. Larson, "Selecting a New Payroll/Human Resources Information System," *Management Accounting* (October 1993), pp. 28–31.

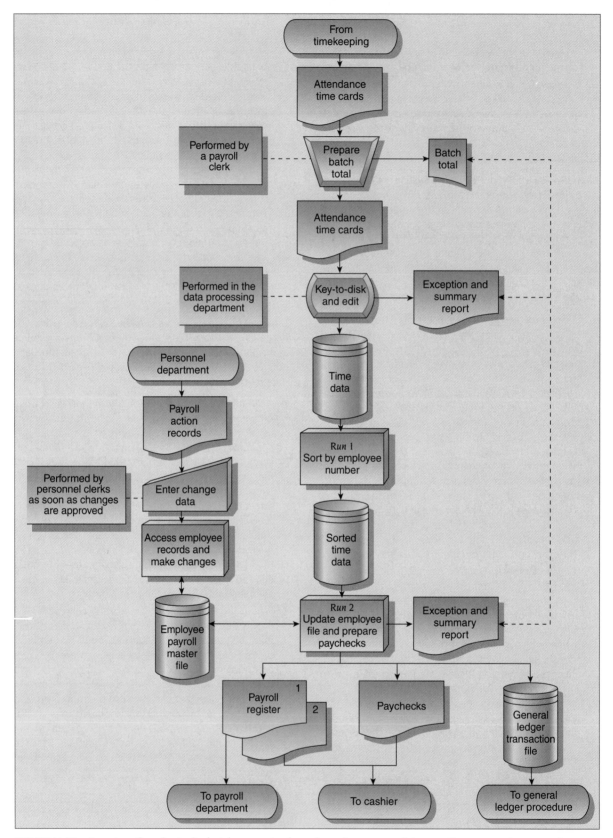

FIGURE 14-38   A system flowchart of a batch computer-based employee payroll transaction processing procedure.

Internal Controls

Risk Exposures Transactions within the employee services system are exposed to a variety of risks. Figure 14-39 lists representative risks and consequent exposures due to these risks.

Control Objectives With respect to the employee services system, several key objectives are to ensure that

- All services performed by employees, including hours worked on specified tasks, such as production jobs, are recorded accurately and in a timely manner.
- All employees are paid in accordance with wage contracts or other established policies.
- All paychecks are calculated accurately, with due allowance for authorized payroll deductions and approved benefit programs.
- All costs for employee services are disributed to accounts in accordance with clearly established accounting policies.
- All required reports are accurately and completely prepared in accordance with prescribed laws and regulations and submitted by their scheduled dates.

To fulfill these control objectives, the firm must then specify and incorporate adequate general controls and transaction controls.

General Controls General controls relate to organizational independence, documentation, asset accountability, management practices, data center operations, authorization, and access. Among those most relevant to the human resource management cycle are the following.

With respect to organizational independence, the persons and units that have custodial functions (i.e., the cash disbursements department, cashier, and paymaster) should be separate from those units that keep time records (i.e., timekeeping) and that prepare the payroll documents (i.e., the payroll department). The personnel department should authorize all personnel actions, while the departmental supervisors should approve the time records of their employees; both should be separate from all the above-mentioned units.

When on-line systems are employed, access should be restricted by requiring that clerks enter assigned passwords before accessing employee-related records and employing terminals with restricted functions for the entry of personnel actions. Other procedures that should enhance security involve (a) generating audit reports (access logs) that monitor accesses of system files, (b) dumping the employee files onto magnetic tape backups, and (c) storing stocks of blank paychecks and signature plates in safes.

Application Controls The following controls and control procedures are applicable to employee services transactions and employee records:

1. Preparing prenumbered and well-designed documents relating to payroll payables and cash disbursements. Also, preprinting time cards, and job-time tickets where applicable, with the employees' names and numbers.

2. Validating data on time records as they are entered for processing by means of such edit checks as (a) validity checks on employee numbers, (b) limit checks on hours worked, (c) field checks on key

Risk	Exposure(s)
1. Employment of unqualified persons	1. Lessened productivity and higher training costs
2. Employment of larcenous persons	2. Possibility of loss of assets and circumvented policies and controls
3. Errors or omissions in time records, including overtime abuse	3. Incorrect payroll records and labor distribution summaries
4. Errors in payments to employees	4. Possibility of overpayments and/or adverse effects on employee morale; erroneous quarterly statements sent to federal and state agencies
5. Incorrect disbursements of paychecks to fictitious ("ghost") or terminated employees, or diversions of valid paychecks to unentitled employees	5. Excessive wage and salary costs
6. Errors in charging labor expenses or in stating payroll liabilities	6. Incorrect levels for expense and liability accounts
7. Violation of government regulations and laws, with regard to payments or reporting requirements (e.g., withholding-tax schemes)	7. Possibility of penalties and fines being assessed

FIGURE 14-39 Risk exposures within the employee services management systems.

identification and amount data, and (d) relationship checks on employee numbers and related departments to which employees are assigned.

3. Validating the results as data are processed by means of such edit checks as the sign check and cross-foot balance check. Thus, the net-pay field of each paycheck should be verified by the former check to see that the sign is positive and by the latter check to see that the amount equals the gross pay less all deductions.

4. Correcting errors that are detected during data entry or processing as soon as possible by means of an established error correction procedure. A part of this procedure may involve the printing of suitable exception and summary reports during edit runs. Processing of paychecks should be delayed until all transaction data errors and discrepancies have been corrected.

5. Issuing personnel actions (such as new hires and pay rate changes) promptly on the basis of valid authorizations.

6. Reconciling the hours reflected on job-time tickets (when they are used) with the hours shown on the attendance time cards.

7. Precomputing batch control totals on hours worked, as reflected by time cards, and on net pay amounts, as shown in the payroll register; comparing these batch totals with totals computed during paycheck preparation and during postings to the employee payroll master file, respectively.

8. Drawing paychecks on a separate payroll-imprest bank account.

9. Retaining voided paychecks, in order that all paycheck numbers can be accounted for.

10. Tracing unclaimed paychecks back to the time records and employee payroll master file, in order to verify that they belong to actual current employees.

11. Reviewing a preliminary payroll register before the paychecks are printed, in order to determine that all errors have been corrected.

12. Printing payroll account summaries periodically to enhance the audit trail.

In addition, all controls pertaining to cash disbursements also apply to the issuance of paychecks.

Reports and Other Outputs

Operational Listings, Statements, and Required Reports
One of the most used outputs is the *payroll register*. It essentially lists the key payment data concerning each employee for a single pay period, ranging from gross pay to net pay. A related output is the *deduction register*, which provides a detailed breakdown of the deductions for each employee. The *cumulative earnings register* shows amounts earned year-to-date, and possibly quarter-to-date, for each employee and for all employees. Figure 14-40 provides an excerpt from an earnings register. Various control reports are also needed. One example is a report that shows the number of checks printed and the total amounts of the checks.

Required governmental reports include those pertaining to withholdings of social security and federal income taxes, plus a variety of others. Some are due at the end of each quarter, while others are due at the end of each year.

Inquiry Screens Most inquiries concern employees, so on-line systems usually enable personnel clerks and others to view the data in an individual employee's payroll or personal data record. Other inquiries may relate to departmental payrolls or to cumulative earnings.

Managerial Reports Various analyses are of interest to managers, such as those pertaining to absenteeism, overtime pay, turnover, sales commissions, and indirect labor costs. One useful analysis is a projection of salaries for the upcoming months of the year. Other reports that are often helpful include (1) surveys of average pay rates per occupational category, compared to similar firms, and (2) personnel strength reports, showing levels of staffing and changes during the past month.

The labor distribution summary can serve two purposes: as the basis for accounting entries, and as an analysis for management. In essence, the summary shows the amounts of employee service costs to charge to various accounts. However, it can also include details concerning the costs incurred by individual employees and departments on various tasks. For instance, it might show that Ray Valdez incurred $350 during one week on Production Job 301, and $420 on Production Job 318. In addition, it separates the costs between direct labor and indirect labor.

Fixed Assets Management Cycle

The facilities resource concerns the fixed assets, also known as plant assets, or property, plant, and equipment. Since the term fixed assets is more familiar to accountants than facilities, we shall employ that term throughout this appendix. Within the wide range of fixed assets are buildings, machines, furniture, fixtures, vehicles, and other items requiring capital expenditures. Because they have lives of longer than one year, fixed assets are subject to depreciation. Another feature of fixed assets is that their dollar value is often a relatively large portion of the total asset value of a firm. In spite of these distinctions, the acquisition of fixed assets involves most of the functions of the expenditure cycle. Moreover, the management of fixed assets extends beyond their acquisition. Therefore, our discussion also covers the

| NORTHCREEK INDUSTRIES | | | | | | | | | PAYROLL | | | | TIME 20:23:03 DATE 4/08/97 PAGE 2 41503 | | | | |
| JOURNAL-PR002 BATCH - | 1 | | 1 | | | | | YTD AND QTD EARNINGS REGISTER | | | | | PERIOD ENDING 4/04/97 | | | | |

EMP NUMBER	EMPLOYEE NAME	HOME DEPT		GROSS EARNINGS	GROSS TAXABLE	SICK PAY	TIPS TAXED	TIPS NOT TAXED	FIT	FICA	EIC	WEEKS WORKED
71500	THOMAS C. RYAN	DADM	YTD	4,500.00	4,500.00	.00	.00	.00	784.50	299.25	.00	16
			QTD	562.50	562.50	.00	.00	.00	107.39	37.41	.00	2
75000	RUSS A. STINEHOUR	DADM	YTD	13,800.00	13,800.00	.00	.00	.00	4,303.28	917.70	.00	16
			QTD	1,725.00	1,725.00	.00	.00	.00	511.66	114.71	.00	2
76000	VINCE J. TAVORMINA	DOFC	YTD	2,254.00	2,254.00	.00	.00	.00	234.80	149.89	.00	15
			QTD	304.00	304.00	.00	.00	.00	68.01	20.22	.00	2
	TOTAL YTD			84,472.77	84,472.77	520.98	.00	.00	18,847.16	5,582.81	.00	
	TOTAL QTD			10,844.60	10,844.60	63.28	.00	.00	2,551.13	716.97	.00	
	TOTAL PAY PERIOD			9,764.60	9,764.60	63.28	.00	.00	2,443.60	645.14	.00	

FIGURE I4-40 A cumulative earnings register. (Courtesy of IBM Corporation.)

transactions that occur during the economic lives of the fixed assets, and the disposals of such assets.

Objectives of the Cycle

The essential purpose of the *fixed assets management cycle* is to facilitate the acquisition, economic life, and disposal of needed fixed assets. Objectives within this broad purpose are (1) to ensure that all acquisitions are properly approved and recorded and exchanged for cash or equivalents, (2) to safeguard the fixed assets in assigned locations, (3) to reflect depreciation expense properly and consistently in accordance with an acceptable depreciation method, and (4) to ensure that all disposals are properly approved and recorded.

Functions

The three major functions of the facilities management cycle consist of acquiring the fixed assets, maintaining the fixed assets during their economic lives, and disposing of the fixed assets.

Acquire Fixed Assets   The capital expenditure process begins when a manager perceives that his or her department (or other organizational unit) needs an additional fixed asset, or needs to replace an asset. For instance, a shipping manager may learn from the drivers that certain delivery trucks need replacement. This need should be substantiated through formal capital investment analyses. As we recall from managerial accounting, this type of analysis requires that expected benefits and costs be gathered for the economic lives of the new fixed assets, as well as such factors as the expected disposal or salvage values of the assets. Furthermore, these benefits and costs must be discounted to the present time by a factor (i.e., desired rate of return or opportunity cost of capital) that management specifies.

The manager places a formal request for the needed fixed assets. Higher-level management must approve such a request. The larger the amount involved, generally the higher the request must ascend for approval. Upon receiving approval the request follows a procedure similar to the acquisition of merchandise. That is, a copy of the request is sent to the purchasing department (or in the case of highly technical equipment, the engineering department, if one exists). Bids are requested, a supplier is selected, and a purchase order is prepared. When the fixed asset arrives, a receiving report is completed, and the asset is delivered to the requesting organizational unit. Upon the receipt of the supplier's invoice, a disbursement voucher is prepared (if the voucher system is in effect). On the due date a check is written and mailed.

If a firm constructs its own fixed assets, the procedure is closely related to the product conversion procedure. That procedure is discussed in the next major section.

Maintain Fixed Assets   Fixed assets usually represent valuable property. In order to safeguard and maintain each acquired fixed asset, all relevant details are generally recorded. Included are all acquisition costs, the estimated salvage value, the estimated economic life, and the location. If the fixed asset is transferred to a new location, this move is recorded. If costs are incurred during the life of the asset that increase its value or extend its economic life, these costs are added to the asset's current value.

A fixed asset diminishes in value during use or the passage of time. An allocated portion of the asset's value, called depreciation expense, must be removed at periodic intervals. The amount of the depreciation expense is determined in part by the method of depreciation that is selected for the asset, and in part by the estimated economic life of the asset. These depreciation amounts are included in the record of the individual fixed asset, as well as in adjustments to general ledger accounts.

Dispose of Fixed Assets   When their economic lives have come to an end, fixed assets are either sold, retired, or exchanged for replacement assets. These disposals, like acquisitions, require the approval of management. They also lead to the removal of asset values from the general ledger accounts.

Relationships to the Organization

The facilities management system functions are mainly achieved under the direction of the finance/accounting organizational function (unit) of the firm. The key departments involved are budgeting, accounts payable, cash disbursements, property accounting, and general ledger. The budgeting department develops capital expenditures budgets and coordinates these budgets with the short-range and cash budgets. The accounts payable department approves the suppliers' invoices pertaining to fixed assets for payment. The cash disbursements department, an arm of the cashier, prepares checks for disbursement to suppliers of fixed assets. The property accounting department establishes and maintains the records concerning fixed assets. The general ledger department maintains control over all asset, equity, expense, and income accounts.

Other units of the organization are involved to a degree. Higher-level managers, from various organizational functions (e.g., production) in addition to the finance/accounting function, approve the acquisition and disposal of fixed assets. As in the case of the expenditure cycle, the purchasing and receiving departments are responsible for ordering and receiving the fixed assets. Figure 14-41 shows the relations between key departments and the system functions.

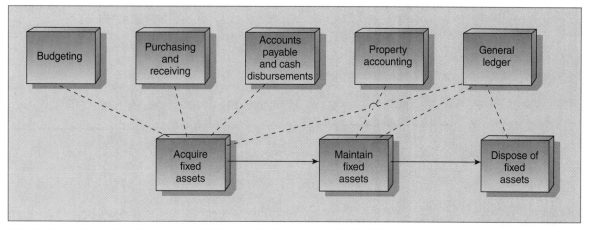

FIGURE 14-41 Typical functions and related organizational units of a facilities management system.

Managerial Decision Making The critical decisions, as the above paragraphs suggest, pertain to the acquisition and disposal of fixed assets. Lesser decisions concern the depreciation method and maintenance routine to employ.

Data Entry

Sources Data used in this system are mainly based on inputs from the managers in departments needing new fixed assets. Other sources are the fixed asset records maintained by accounting departments.

Forms of Input Source documents typically used in the management of facilities include the following:

1. **Capital investment proposal.** The initiating form is the *capital investment proposal*, also called the property expenditure request. This form describes and justifies the capital project, listing the items of capital equipment needed, the places they will be used, the fixed asset accounts to be charged, and the expected amounts. It may be accompanied by a capital investment analysis form. This latter form lists all future cost and benefit flows that are expected to accrue from the asset investment, with the net cash flows being discounted to present values. The proposal package, including both forms, is forwarded to higher-level managers, such as the controller and vice-president and president, for approval. Upon approval a copy of the proposal is sent to the purchasing department, where it serves as a requisition.

2. **Fixed asset change form.** A fixed asset change form is used as the basis for (1) transferring fixed assets from one department to another, or for (2) retiring, selling, or trading in fixed assets. It lists the asset net book value and the amount to be received (if

disposed of). It also provides spaces for justifying the disposal and for the approval signatures of higher-level managers.

3. **Other source documents.** Since expenditures are involved, additional documents include the request for quotation, purchase order, bill of lading, receiving report, supplier's invoice, disbursement voucher, check voucher, and journal voucher. See Chapter 13 for a description of these documents.

Accounting Entries The acquisition of fixed assets is recorded by an entry such as the following:

```
Dr. Machinery (or some other fixed      XXX
    asset category)
    Cr. Accounts Payable                        XXX
To record the acquisition of machinery
    having an estimated life of ____ years.
```

The depreciation of a fixed asset is recorded periodically by an entry such as the following (using Machinery as the example):

```
Dr. Depreciation Expense                 XXX
    Cr. Accumulated Depreciation–               XXX
    Machinery
To record the depreciation expense for the
    year.
```

The disposition of a fixed asset is recorded by an entry such as the following, assuming that machinery is sold for its book value:

```
Dr. Cash                                 XXX
    Cr. Accumulated Depreciation–               XXX
    Machinery
    Cr. Machinery                               XXX
To record the disposal of a machine
    acquired on _____.
```

Fixed asset number	Description	Asset type code	Location code	Supplier number	Date acquired	Estimated economic life

Estimated salvage value	Depreciation method	Depreciation annual rate	Cost basis	Accumulated depreciation

FIGURE 14-42   A layout of a fixed asset record. (*Note:* Although the lengths of fields and modes of data elements are necessary for complete documentation, they have been omitted for simplicity.)

Data Base

Files   The critical files needed are the fixed assets master file and the fixed assets transaction file. Other files are those used in all expenditure transactions, such as the supplier master, open purchase order, open voucher, and check disbursement files. See Chapter 13 for details of these other files.

1. **Fixed Assets Master File.** A key file is the *fixed assets master file*, a subsidiary ledger that supports the fixed

asset control accounts in the general ledger. Figure 14-42 portrays the layout of the contents of a typical record for a fixed asset. Included is the fixed asset number, a unique identifier that generally serves as the primary and sorting key. The asset type code identifies the major classification of fixed assets (e.g., buildings, equipment) to which the individual asset belongs. The location code refers to the department or physical site to which the asset is assigned.

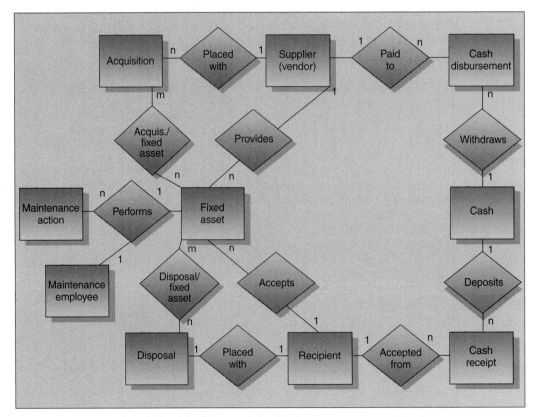

FIGURE 14-43   An entity-relationship diagram of the fixed assets management cycle.

An important concern is keeping the records and their permanent data up to date. When an asset is relocated, for instance, the location code should be promptly changed. When a new fixed asset is approved and acquired, a new record should appear in the file.

2. **Fixed Assets Transaction File.** A fixed assets transaction file contains transactions pertaining to new acquisitions, sales of currently held fixed assets, retirements, major additions to asset costs or to economic lives, and transfers between locations. This file is needed if fixed asset transactions are accumulated for a period of time (e.g., a week) and then processed in a batch. If the transactions are posted to the records as they arise, the file will likely not exist in a physical sense.

   Transactions that allocate depreciation expense for each fixed asset are not included in this file. Instead, they are included in the adjusting journal entries at the end of each accounting period.

Data Structures An integrated data base concerning the fixed assets management cycle includes such key entities as the fixed assets and the major events (i.e., acquisition, disposal, maintenance) concerning the fixed assets. Additional entities include the suppliers who provide the fixed assets, the recipients who accept the discarded fixed assets, and the cash-related events. Figure 14-43 presents an entity-relationship diagram that incorporates these entities.

As the diagram shows, the focus is on the fixed assets and the major events. The relationships between the fixed assets and the acquisition and disposal events are likely to be of the many-to-many type, while the remaining relationships are largely of the one-to-many type.

Based on this diagram, the entities and relationships can be mapped to tables within a relational data base. The data elements in the tables will be similar to those described in the above-mentioned files and input forms.

Data Flows and Processing

Two processing procedures are described. The first description emphasizes the logical sequence and the key source documents. The second focuses on the processing of the master file within a computer-based system.

Logical Flows and Documents Figure 14-44 presents a data-flow diagram of the fixed assets activity. In essence it follows the functions discussed earlier, although it includes an added process.

1. **Acquire fixed asset.** To begin the acquisition, a manager in a user department prepares a request. Together with a capital investment analysis, this form is forwarded to higher-level management. After the request is reviewed and approved, it is distributed to the purchasing and accounts payable depart-

ments. Then the regular purchasing, payables, and cash disbursements steps are followed. (These steps are not included in the data-flow diagram, so that we may focus on the distinctive steps involving fixed assets. Refer to Figure 13-16 for a data-flow diagram that shows the expenditure procedure.)

2. **Receive and install fixed asset.** On receiving the ordered fixed asset from the supplier, the fixed asset is sent to the requesting department and installed. The receiving report, which accompanies the fixed asset, is signed in the using department to acknowledge receipt. Then, a suitable department within the accounting function, such as the property accounting department, assigns a number to the new fixed asset, and prepares a record that shows the relevant details. A journal voucher is prepared and forwarded for posting to the general ledger accounts.

3. **Depreciate fixed assets.** At the end of each accounting period an amount representing the depreciation expense, determined in accordance with the specified depreciation method and economic life, is computed. An adjusting journal entry is prepared and posted to the general ledger accounts.

4. **Dispose of fixed asset.** The disposal procedure likewise begins with a request. After the request is approved, the fixed asset is shipped to the person or firm who has agreed to accept the fixed asset. Based on a copy of the approved request form, a property accounting clerk posts and removes the appropriate record from the fixed asset file. Then the clerk prepares a journal voucher that reflects the final depreciation expense, actual salvage value (if any), and the gain or loss on the disposal.

Computer-Based Processing System Figure 14-45, on page 661, shows a system flowchart of a procedure involving fixed assets transactions. The on-line approach is used because the number of fixed-asset transactions is relatively small in many firms and the records can easily be kept up to date. However, the batch method is suitable for firms that have numerous acquisitions.

The flowchart begins at the point when the property accounting department has been notified of an acquisition or disposal. A clerk uses the department terminal to enter data from each transaction document when received. The entered data are first validated by programmed edit checks. Then the data are immediately posted by an updating program to the appropriate record in the fixed asset master file. If the transaction affects general ledger accounts, the program also prepares a journal voucher and stores it on the general ledger transaction file. At the end of the accounting period (e.g., month), a print program generates useful reports. It also prepares journal vouchers that reflect depreciation entries.

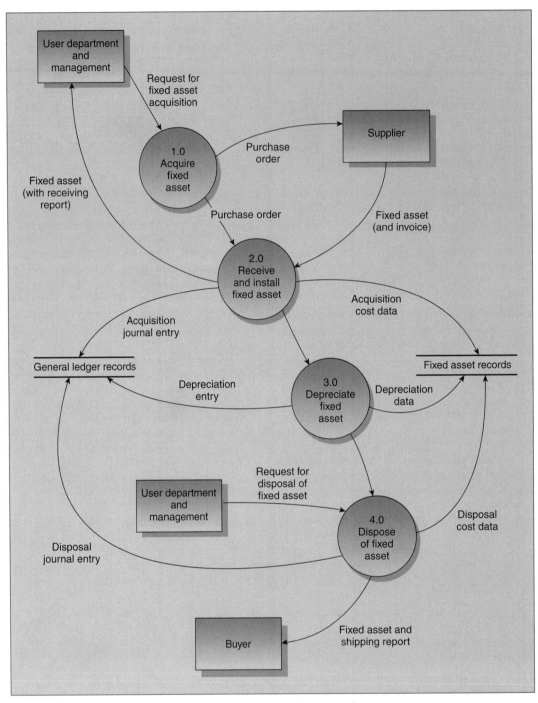

FIGURE 14-44   A data-flow diagram pertaining to the fixed assets cycle.

Accounting Controls

Risk Exposures   Figure 14-46, on page 662, lists representative risks to which the fixed assets management cycle is exposed, and the consequent exposures to these risks.

General Controls   Among the general controls needed to counteract risks due to the exposures are those involving organizational independence, documentation, asset accountability, management practices, data center operations, authorization, and access. Several of the

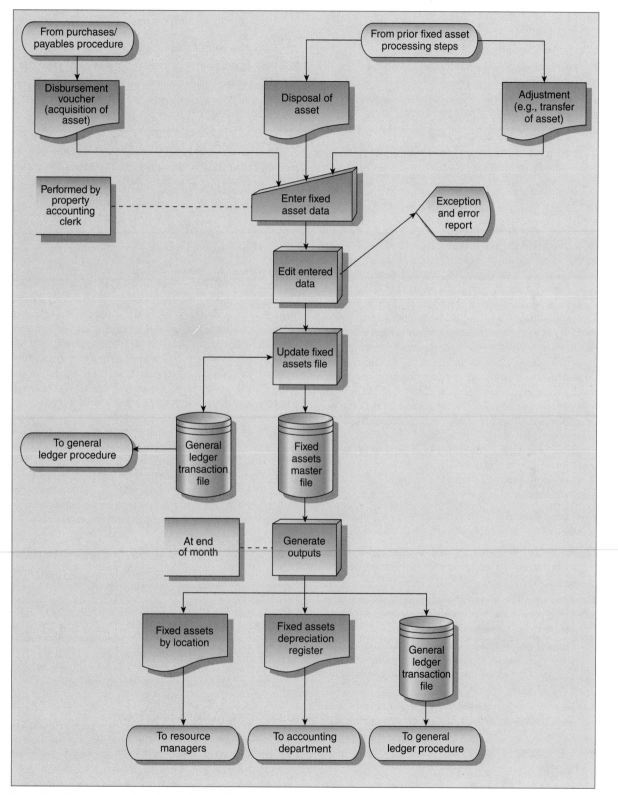

FIGURE 14-45 A system flowchart of an on-line computer-based fixed assets processing procedure.

Risk	Exposure(s)
1. Improper acquisition of fixed assets	1. Excessive costs for fixed assets
2. Improper disposal of fixed assets	2. Loss of productive capability; loss of disposal values
3. Theft or loss of fixed assets	3. Loss in fixed-asset values
4. Errors in billing for ordered fixed assets	4. Possibility of excessive costs for fixed assets
5. Misclassifying fixed assets as current assets	5. Undervaluation of fixed assets
6. Recording fictitious fixed assets	6. Overvaluation of fixed assets
7. Recording fixed assets at market value rather than at original cost	7. Overvaluation of fixed assets (if market value exceeds original cost) or undervaluation of fixed assets (if original cost exceeds market value)

FIGURE 14-46 Exposures to risks within the fixed assets management cycle.

most important, other than those described earlier (such as the authorization process), are as follows:

With respect to organizational independence, the managers who approve requests relating to fixed assets should be separated from the users of the fixed assets and from all units involved in the processing of expenditures and disposals. Otherwise, the organizational segregation described for the expenditure cycle pertains.

Access should be restricted by requiring clerks to enter assigned passwords before accessing fixed asset files, and by limiting the number of terminals that are allowed to enter changes to fixed assets. Also, audit reports (access logs) should monitor accesses of system files, and fixed asset files should be dumped periodically onto magnetic tape backups. Security of fixed assets should additionally be provided by managers who ensure that they are used properly and are not moved from their assigned locations.

Application Controls The following controls and control procedures are applicable to fixed asset transactions:

1. Preparing prenumbered and well-designed documents relating to requests for fixed asset acquisitions and disposals.
2. Requiring that acquisition and disposal documents are approved by responsible higher-level managers before being issued.
3. Requiring that fixed asset acquisitions follow the same purchasing, receiving, payables, and cash disbursements procedures employed for merchandise, raw materials, and supplies.
4. Assigning a unique identification number to each fixed asset, and affixing a tag bearing this number to the asset.
5. Maintaining detailed and up-to-date fixed asset records.
6. Reconciling balances in the fixed-assets subsidiary ledger at least monthly with the balances of the fixed assets control accounts in the general ledger.

Reports and Other Outputs

Operational Listings and Reports The *fixed asset register* is a listing of all fixed assets, arranged by fixed asset numbers, and showing book and/or tax values of the assets. The *fixed asset acquisition listing* shows all assets acquired during an accounting period, including capitalized values and estimated salvage values. The *asset retirement register* shows all assets disposed of during the accounting period. In addition, a fixed asset change register for an accounting period is very useful. It allows accountants to review all transactions that affect fixed assets and can serve as an audit trail. The *fixed asset depreciation expense report* lists depreciation expense for every fixed asset for the current accounting period, plus related costs and accumulated depreciation amounts. Certain reports are also needed to fulfill information requirements of the Securities and Exchange Commission, the Internal Revenue Service, and local property tax authorities. An example is a summary of all acquisitions, transfers, and retirements during a year.

Inquiry Screens Most inquiries concern individual fixed assets. Other inquiries may relate to specific fixed asset transactions or capital budgeting data.

Managerial Reports Various analyses are of interest to managers, such as those showing fixed assets reported by location or by department. Other reports show maintenance schedules and costs and projected depreciation expenses. Figure 14-47 shows a variety of reports that can be prepared from the files described earlier.

Fixed Asset Management Software

An increasing number of firms are selecting specialized fixed asset management software as the core of their systems. A number of packages are available from software vendors for use with stand-alone microcomputers and networks. To be most useful, a package should be user-friendly, flexible, and versatile. It should offer many

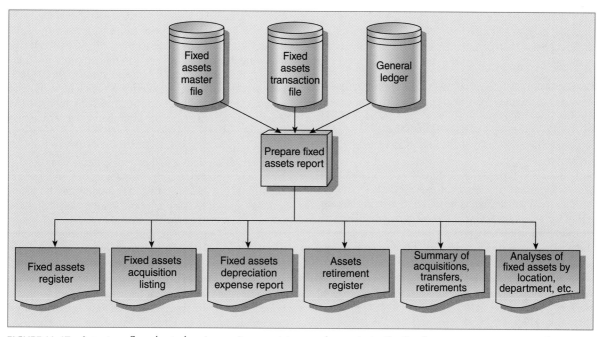

FIGURE 14-47   A system flowchart showing various registers and reports in the fixed assets management cycle.

capabilities related to fixed asset management, including the calculations of depreciation by several methods, the maintenance of fixed asset records, the calculation of property taxes, and the tracking of the physical locations of specific fixed assets. One of the most important capabilities is generating all required reports and a variety of managerial reports, such as those described in the previous section. An example of a comprehensive fixed asset manager software package is FAS2000 (marketed by Best Programs, Inc.).

The selection of a suitable package requires careful planning to meet a firm's particular needs. National Business Parks, a firm that manages commercial buildings, selected a package from Best Programs of Arlington, Virginia. A critical feature of the package is the ability to develop tailored reports, such as a breakdown of assets by building and tenant.*

Cash Management Cycle

Managing cash entails much more than receiving and depositing cash from credit customers. Thus, *cash management*, whose broad purpose is to facilitate the inflows and outflows of the cash needed to maintain a going concern, deserves more attention than cash was given in Chapters 12 and 13. As noted in those chapters, the top financial manager (often called the chief financial officer, or CFO) has the overall responsibility for cash manage-

*Bridgette A. Hobart, "Fixed Asset Management," *Management Accounting* (September 1991), pp. 57–58.

ment. In most sizable firms, a treasurer who reports directly to the CFO has specific responsibilities in this area. Together with the CFO, the treasurer is involved in such decisions as:

From which sources should needed cash be acquired, and when?

What dividends should be paid?

How should excess cash be used?

In this section we briefly discuss the sources of cash, uses of cash, techniques for effective cash management, and controls over cash. Although our discussion does not include the management of working capital, investments, and other broad measures of "funds," their management is closely tied to cash management.

Sources of Cash   In addition to receipts from customers, a firm's sources of cash include loans from banks, issues of bonds, sales of stock, sales of plant assets, dividends and interest from investments, sales of investments, factoring of accounts receivable, and delays in paying amounts due on accounts. When acquiring cash from any of these sources, a firm should follow established policies and procedures. Short-term and long-term planning should be performed, employing tools and techniques to be discussed later. All of the possible alternative sources should be investigated. For instance, if short-term borrowing is necessary, various banks should be compared with respect to borrowing rates and terms, reputation, service, and so on. Also, decisions involving cash should be made by managers who are clearly authorized, such as the treasurer. When large amounts are involved, more than one manager should sign off on the decision.

Uses of Cash Cash may be used to purchase goods and services (as discussed in Chapter 13), build plant assets, acquire investments, retire bonds, pay off bank loans, pay dividends on stock and interest on bonds and notes, reacquire the firm's own stock, and redeem stock rights or options.

Policies and procedures, fostered by careful planning, are as important to the sound uses of cash as are the sources from which cash is acquired. Consider this scenario, for example. A firm could set a planned level for its cash balance. When the actual cash balance exceeds the planned level, the excess could be automatically invested in money market funds or some other short-term instrument. When the actual balance drops below the planned level, the deficiency would be covered by selling an adequate amount of the short-term instrument. Furthermore, when the firm's stock price drops below the book value of the firm, excess funds in the short-term instrument could be employed to repurchase shares at the advantageous price.

Techniques of Cash Management A variety of techniques may be applied to aid in making effective decisions related to cash management. The scenario described in the previous paragraph incorporates two techniques: setting planned cash levels and monitoring key information. The monitoring devices may include executive information systems and outside information retrieval services. Other important techniques include scheduled reports, budgeting, modeling, and expert systems.

One of the most useful scheduled reports for cash management is the statement of cash flows, one of the three basic financial statements. It shows the inflows and outflows of cash over the past accounting period, usually a year. Other helpful scheduled reports include an analysis of changes in the cash balance, and registers of cash receipts and cash disbursements.

Since the above-mentioned scheduled reports look backward at past changes to cash, they are more useful for monitoring cash than for cash planning. Perhaps the most important vehicle for cash planning is the *cash budget*, a projected cash-flow statement. Because it looks to the future, often the coming year or quarter, the cash budget helps a firm to anticipate its cash needs. Because it is broken down by days or weeks or months, the cash budget can project the timing of (1) expected borrowings, when outflows exceed inflows, or (2) likely investment opportunities, when inflows exceed outflows. Furthermore, by matching inflows against outflows, the extent of the borrowings or investment opportunities

can be estimated. With an effective cash budgeting system, the financial managers can ensure that the cash balance remains adequate to meet all expected needs, including taking all cash discounts allowed on purchases. If a cash shortfall is forecasted by the budget, however, the manager should have sufficient warning to arrange short-term financing (e.g., a bank loan) at the lowest feasible rates. On the other hand, if a cash excess is forecasted, the manager can look for the most lucrative short-term investments.

Financial modeling and expert systems can be used for cash planning over longer time horizons or in special situations. For instance, financial models can be incorporated into a decision support system that simulates the firm's operations over the next couple of years. "What if" conditions can be tried within the DSS concerning changes in sales prices, economic factors such as interest rates, and so on. After a series of manipulations, the DSS would likely indicate when and how much long-term financing could be needed over the time horizon. An expert system could be developed and used to help decide which types of long-term financing (e.g., stocks, bonds, bank line of credit) might be most suitable.

Internal Controls over Cash The needed internal controls should ensure that all cash transactions are properly authorized, recorded, and processed; that cash is properly safeguarded and effectively used; and that the cash balance in the balance sheet is reliable. Among the specific needed controls (in addition to those listed in Chapters 12 and 13) are the following:

1. Appropriate separation of custodial, recording, and authorization functions with respect to cash.
2. Prompt endorsement and recording of all cash receipts, with the deposit of all cash received daily by an authorized person.
3. Issuance of prenumbered checks for all expenditures (except petty-cash items.)
4. Proper use of petty-cash funds under imprest procedures.
5. Use of separate imprest bank accounts for payroll expenditures.
6. Reconciliation of each bank account monthly by a person not otherwise involved in cash procedures.
7. Adequate physical security over cash (and blank checks), including the use of locked cash registers, lockboxes, safes.
8. Close supervision over and restricted access to cash and cash-related activities, including access to electronic transfers of cash.
9. Surprise audits of cash.

REVIEW PROBLEM WITH SOLUTION

SLICK SIGNPAINTERS

Statement

Stanley Fischer manages Slick Signpainters (SS), which comprises three painters and one secretary-bookkeeper. Customers consist of small business firms and other organizations, such as churches and towns, which place special orders. Since it acquires raw materials and supplies—boards, paints, brushes, turpentine—and produces finished signs, SS resembles a manufacturing firm. SS has a single microcomputer, which it uses to aid in processing its main transactions.

Required

Briefly describe the data sources and inputs, data base, procedures, controls, and reports that are likely to be involved in the process of converting the new materials into finished signs.

Solution

The process begins with a special order from a customer. Stanley plans the sign and determines the materials needed. If the materials are not on hand, he acquires the items from suppliers, either by preparing and mailing a purchase order or by calling the suppliers' stores and placing the orders. On receiving the materials and checking them in, he assigns the job to one of the painters and provides him or her the materials. Stanley also gives the painter the plan of the sign and provides notes (i.e., an operations list) concerning steps in completing and installing the sign. Stanley estimates the overall cost of the job and the expected completion date. If the painter is currently busy on another job, he schedules the job in question.

The secretary-bookkeeper maintains the schedule and records the costs of the materials and time spent on each job. When the job is completed, the sign is delivered to the customer. She then applies an overhead charge to the job (based on the hours spent on the job), adds a markup percentage, and computes the total amount. After Stanley reviews the figures, she prepares an invoice for the customer.

The main files maintained, in addition to the production schedule, are a raw materials inventory file (in quantities only) and a job-cost file of orders currently in progress. Since the completed signs are immediately delivered to customers, no finished-goods inventory file is necessary. Another file not directly related to production is an order-invoice file, consisting of records of each customer special order and open invoice. All of these

files are maintained on the hard disk of the microcomputer system and are updated via the microcomputer keyboard by the secretary-bookkeeper.

Many of the controls are maintained through the close supervision, planning, and reviews carried out by Stanley. He also keeps the raw materials locked in a storeroom, to which only he has a key. Only the secretary-bookkeeper and Stanley are allowed to use the microcomputer, which is located in her office. Order-invoices are assigned consecutive numbers and are reviewed by Stanley when he performs the monthly bank reconciliation.

At the end of each month Stanley receives listings of raw materials inventory and jobs in process, prepared by the secretary-bookkeeper. She also prepares reports that show actual costs for completed jobs versus the estimated costs, the jobs that were not completed on schedule, and the jobs currently in progress that appear to be behind schedule.

Note: This problem illustrates that many of the components of the product conversion cycle can be applied to a simple manufacturing situation. Even more could be added to this example. However, the problem also illustrates that the design should be adapted to the situation.

KEY TERMS

activity-based costing (631)
automated handling of materials (626)
bill of materials (604)
computer-aided design (CAD) (624)
computer-aided manufacturing (CAM) (626)
computer-integrated manufacturing (CIM) system (623)
cost accounting (602)
engineering design (601)
finished-goods inventory master file (611)
flexible manufacturing system (FMS) (626)
inventory management (601)
just-in-time (JIT) (626)
labor job-time ticket (607)
logistics management (601)
maintenance (602)
manufacturing resource planning (MRP-II) (625)
materials issue slip (requisition) (606)
materials requirements planning (MRP) (625)
move ticket (608)
open production orders file (612)
operations list (605)
product conversion cycle (596)
production control (602)
production operations (602)

production order   (606)
production planning   (601)
production schedule   (605)
quality control   (602)
raw materials inventory master file   (611)
robotics   (626)
work-in-process inventory master file   (611)

REVIEW QUESTIONS

Note: The questions include information pertaining to Chapter 14 and the appendices at the end of Chapter 14.

14-1. What are the key objectives of the product conversion cycle?

14-2. What are the major functions of the product conversion cycle?

14-3. What are several key decisions that must be made during strategic production planning?

14-4. What are four methods of physical production?

14-5. What are several key decisions that must be made with respect to the management of raw materials inventory?

14-6. What are several factors that determine the quantities of goods to be produced?

14-7. Briefly describe the steps in accumulating and recording costs during the production process.

14-8. How does the logistics management function relate to the product conversion cycle, and what are several organizational units within the function?

14-9. What documents are used in the production process?

14-10. What are the key files needed in the product conversion data base?

14-11. What are the entities that are involved in the product conversion cycle?

14-12. Describe a relational data structure that might be employed within a data base that supports production operations.

14-13. What are the relationship tables that are useful in data structures pertaining to production operations?

14-14. Describe the procedural steps employed in an online computer-based system that processes the conversion of raw materials into finished goods.

14-15. Briefly describe the various components and technologies that are included in computer-integrated manufacturing.

14-16. Identify the benefits of computer-integrated manufacturing.

14-17. What are the exposures to risk that exist in the processing within the product conversion cycle?

14-18. Identify various general and application controls that can help manage the risk exposures within the product conversion cycle.

14-19. What are the inadequacies of many current cost accounting and measurement systems?

14-20. What are a couple of significant improvements that can be made to cost accounting systems to enhance their effectiveness?

14-21. Identify various reports and other outputs that may be generated from information provided by the product conversion cycle.

14-22. What are several typical objectives of the employee services (payroll) cycle?

14-23. What are the major functions that pertain to payroll expenditures?

14-24. Which organizational units are involved in paying employees?

14-25. Identify several decisions that must be made by the personnel manager.

14-26. What are the key source documents used in the management of employee services?

14-27. Identify the accounting entries needed to reflect the transactions within the employee services cycle.

14-28. Identify the major files and/or data structures that are suitable to an employee services data base.

14-29. Describe the payroll procedure when a batch processing computer-based system is employed. Contrast this procedure with one performed manually.

14-30. What exposures to risk exist when processing transactions involving employee services?

14-31. Identify the control objectives that should be achieved with respect to the employee services cycle.

14-32. Identify general and application controls that pertain to the employee services cycle.

14-33. Identify various reports and listings that are required in connection with payroll processing.

14-34. What are several objectives and functions of the facilities (fixed assets) management cycle?

14-35. What organizational units are involved in transactions pertaining to facilities (fixed assets)?

14-36. What source documents are used in the management of facilities?

14-37. Identify the accounting entries needed to reflect the transactions related to facilities (fixed assets).

14-38. Identify the major files that relate to facilities (fixed assets).

14-39. Describe the processing of transactions related to facilities (fixed assets) when on-line processing is employed.

14-40. What exposures to risk exist in the facilities (fixed assets) management cycle?

14-41. Identify general and application controls that can counteract the exposures to risk within the facilities management cycle.

14-42. Identify several reports and listings that may be generated from transactions involving fixed assets.

14-43. What are the objectives and functions of cash management?

14-44. What are several internal controls that are critical with respect to cash management?

14-45. Describe several symptoms of poor cash management, and discuss practices that can improve the cash management of a firm.

14-46. What decisions must be made by the treasurer of a firm in managing the firm's cash?

DISCUSSION QUESTIONS

14-47. What changes are needed to adapt the product conversion cycle to a construction firm that engages in various projects for clients?

14-48. Contrast a computer-based processing system in a manufacturing firm using job-order costing with a system in another firm using process costing.

14-49. A number of measures were suggested in this chapter to improve the information from cost accounting systems. What are several other measures that might be considered?

14-50. In this chapter a relational data base is illustrated that focuses on production operations. Describe the various tables that would be needed to expand the data base to include inventory management of raw materials and sales to customers, plus the cash-related transactions that accompany these events.

14-51. A manufacturing firm decides to install a CIM system but to keep the cost accounting completely apart. What problems, if any, are likely to result?

14-52. What changes must be made to a CIM system if a firm decides to include electronic data interchange networks with its major suppliers, and what added benefits are likely to result?

14-53. What would be the effects on the duties of payroll clerks if a firm converts from a manual payroll system to a computer-based system?

14-54. Describe several programmed edit checks, such as the redundancy matching check, that can be applied by the posting programs used in processing payrolls.

14-55. Discuss the development known as human resource accounting (HRA), in which investments in employees are treated as assets in the financial accounts.

14-56. How would the managers of a firm benefit from periodic reports that evaluate the performances of the employees for whom they are responsible, and what specific information would likely be in such reports?

PROBLEMS

Note: These problems include material presented in the appendices to Chapter 14.

14-1. The Hardmon Manufacturing Company produces metal products for industrial customers. Although some of the products are standard items (e.g., pistons), many are made in response to special orders. The firm therefore maintains a number of work centers, each with a particular type of machine or assembling equipment. It puts each order into the production process via a production order and accumulates the related costs on a work-in-process inventory record. Standard unit costs are applied to material quantities and direct labor hours; standard work center overhead rates are applied on the basis of machine hours. When special orders are completed, they are delivered directly to the shipping area. Completed standard items are delivered to the finished goods warehouse.

Required

a. List the journal entries needed to record (i) the conversion of raw materials into finished goods, (ii) the application of raw materials, direct labor, and various indirect costs to the production of the finished goods, and (iii) the shipment of the finished goods. State how the actual costs for such items as indirect labor and equipment maintenance are recorded and disposed of.

b. Assuming that a computer-based system is approved for installation, describe the type of system (batch, on-line, or mixed) that appears most suitable for each of the following: (i) monitoring the production process, (ii) preparing payrolls for the direct production employees, (iii) managing the utilization and valuation records of the factory machines and equipment.

c. Identify the various decisions that Hardmon must make. Organize the decisions according to strategic, tactical, and operational.

14-2. Precise Manufacturing Co. is a medium-sized firm having the departments shown in Figure 14-2. Which of the departments is responsible for preparation (in the case of a document) or for recording (in the case of a document accounting record)?

  a. Move ticket.
  b. Production order.
  c. Work-in-process inventory records.

   d.   Materials issue slip.

   e.   Production schedule.

   f.   Bill of materials.

   g.   Inspection report.

   h.   Labor job-time ticket.

   i.   Operations list.

14-3. In the chapter, refer to the figures pertaining to the hypothetical manufacturer of electrical products. Note that several materials are used in the production of generator type PG21, including part number 18568.

   a.   The current code for materials and parts has five numeric characters, which have been assigned rather randomly to the various materials. Suggest a revised code for materials and parts based in part on the data provided in the chapter concerning the hypothetical manufacturer. Make assumptions as necessary, and add other dimensions to the code that could render it more useful. Do not use more than eight characters in the code.

   b.   Prepare the materials requirements report that is based on production order 8333, prepared on October 15, 1997.

   c.   Prepare a materials issue slip dated October 22, 1997, and prenumbered 705, and enter the materials needed at work center B for production order 8333. Unit costs are as follows: salient poles, $30 each; field windings, $55 each; slip rings, $68 each; ventilating fan, $84. Assume that all the parts except the casting are issued to work center B.

14-4. Refer to the hypothetical manufacturer of electrical products that has been used as an example in discussing the organization and input forms pertaining to the product conversion cycle. Figures 14-5 through 14-10 contain data pertaining to an order from Lipton Technology, Inc., for five generators, type PG21, 50 horsepower each. The date of the sales order was October 17, 1997, and the customer order number was 28662.

Required

a. Design a preformatted production order screen and insert the data just given and those provided on the various figures in the chapter. The date of the production order was Oct. 20, 1997. Assume that an order cannot be at a work center for less than a day, even though the work required at the center may not require more than an hour or two. Also, consider that an added day must be allowed for final inspection (Operation No. G600) at the QC center. The product is to be shipped the day following the inspection, provided that the quality is acceptable.

b. Design a record layout for an open production order file that is stored on magnetic disk. Insert the data pertaining to the order in **a** in the layout to reflect the progress of the order as of the end of October 22. Assume the start and ending times of operations; also assume that the record is variable in length.

14-5. The Gem Manufacturing Company of Waltham, Massachusetts, employs a job order cost accounting system to record the costs of products manufactured. It charges costs into production from three types of source documents: materials requisitions, job-time tickets, and expense vouchers. Entries are recorded on journal vouchers. Subsidiary ledgers are maintained for raw materials inventory, work-in-process inventory, manufacturing overhead expense, and finished goods inventory. Related control accounts appear in the general ledger.

Required

a. Prepare a diagram that shows the flow of production transactions through the accounting cycle.

b. Use sample journal-entry formats to reflect the flows of costs from source documents into the financial statements.

c. Describe the contents of each of the foregoing subsidiary ledgers.

14-6. Custom Woodcrafters is a small firm that manufactures custom-made home and office furniture. Its employees consist of 30 artisans (craftspersons), 7 master artisans, one scheduler, and several clerks. The owner is the sole manager. No salespersons are needed, since the quality of its products attracts more orders than the firm can handle. Each order is assigned to a master artisan, who designs the product, guides it through the production process, and approves the final result. At least two artisans are assigned by the scheduler to work on each order, depending on the complexity, requested date, and so on. After the product is completed, the price is determined by accumulating all related costs and then adding a percentage markup.

Required

a. List the data elements that are needed in order to be able to plan, manufacture, and monitor the progress of an order.

b. List the data elements that are needed to price an order.

c. Design a production order and enter data concerning order 3908 from OfficeFurn on January 8, 1998, for three desks, based on model 345J. The order is numbered 817 and is scheduled to be completed four days from the start date of January 12. Gary Thomson is the master artisan to whom the job is assigned, with his assistant being Jan Maples. Gary will customize the desks, based on the above-mentioned model. No operation list is needed, and photographs will be taken of the final products.

14-7. Draw the layout for a record of a work-in-process master file stored on magnetic disk. The file belongs to a manufacturing firm that accumulates costs by production orders. Enter data based on the following for production order 3569, started on February 16, 1998: direct materials issued, 40 units at $13 per unit; direct labor, 12 hours at $6.50 per hour and 20 hours at $8.30 per hour; overhead, applied on the basis of $7.00 per direct labor hour. Assume values for other data elements that you include in the record layout. Ignore the lengths of the data fields.

14-8. Refer to Problem 14-6 concerning Custom Woodcrafters.

Required

a. Prepare an entity-relationship diagram pertaining to the custom orders from customers and the manufacture of the ordered products.

b. Design the tables needed to reflect the entities and relationships, assuming that a relational data base will be acquired. Insert the data elements in each table that represent the needed attributes for the table, including primary and foreign keys.

c. Describe several reports that will be useful to the scheduler and master artisan in performing their duties. These reports should be based on data in the tables.

d. Design the format of a report that will be useful to the manager in controlling the production costs.

14-9. Refer to Figure 14-14, pertaining to the Lens Manufacturing Co.'s product conversion cycle.

Required

a. Expand the entity-relationship diagram to include the following:
  (1) Receipt of sales orders.
  (2) Production scheduling.
  (3) Purchasing of raw materials.
  (4) Warehousing of finished goods.
  (5) Shipping of finished goods.

Hint: *Make a copy of Figure 14-14 and add the above activities to the copy.*

b. Prepare a data structure diagram for the portion of Figure 14-14 within the dashed lines, assuming that a network structure will be employed.

14-10. The production and inventory managers of a fast-growing manufacturer of outdoor clothing recognize that they need a better system for tracking orders and maintaining raw materials inventory. The manual job order and inventory cards currently in use were adequate when the firm was smaller. However, now many orders are not completed by their promised dates, partially finished batches often wait several weeks for back-ordered raw materials, and substantial amounts of raw materials are often left over after production runs. These excess materials cannot be used and are eventually written off.

Job order and raw material inventory cards are updated only once a week and the updating process takes a week. When customers inquire about their orders, production expediting clerks estimate the percent of completion and a shipping date. These estimates are almost always wrong. Customers like the manufacturer's clothing but many of them are beginning to hint they will be reluctant to place further orders because the manufacturer can no longer provide reliable delivery dates.

Operating managers have unsuccessfully tried to convince the president and vice-president of the need to improve the timeliness of information flow between inventory and production. The president and vice-president are convinced that the key factor in their success is the creative design of the product line. They believe that customers will wait for the clothing because it is what individual consumers want to buy. As proof, the president notes that last year other manufacturers began imitating their designs. In fact, the president has commented that they ought to sue the "copycat" manufacturers for infringement.

The president was concerned that automating inventory and production control would simply cost too much and be too troublesome to convert.

Required

The production and inventory managers have asked you to help them prepare a last attempt to convince the president and vice-president that a new information system is essential to the continued success of the firm. Specifically you are to

a. Identify five problems associated with the existing system.

b. Identify the specific items of information that an improved and computerized system should provide, including nonfinancial as well as financial measures of performance.

c. Identify the relevant information that should be gathered in this case to support the decision of whether or not to automate.

(CIA *adapted*)

14-11. What error, loss, or fraudulent activity might occur if each of the following procedures is allowed?

a. The work-in-process inventory ledger is not periodically reconciled to the control account in the general ledger.

b. Production supervisors do not observe factory employees as they clock in and out on production jobs.

c. Scrapped materials are not maintained in a separate inventory and are not reported as they are generated during production.

d. Overhead costs charged to various production jobs are based on the actual allocation of indirect production costs incurred during the current period.

e. Products are manufactured at levels sufficient to utilize the production resources fully throughout the year.

f. Raw materials are issued in quantities requested by the employees who will actually perform the production operations.

g. Physical inventories of raw materials and finished goods are taken only when production activity is slow and factory employees are available to make the counts.

h. The valuations of the raw materials inventory items are adjusted only to reflect receipts and issues.

i. Production orders are started in production by production supervisors when they observe that machines and employees are temporarily idle.

j. Finished-goods records are maintained only in the warehouse.

k. Accounting clerks are allowed to value inventories on either the first-in, first-out or last-in, first-out methods from year to year.

14-12. What internal accounting control(s) would be most effective in preventing or detecting each of the following errors or fraudulent practices?

a. A cost distribution clerk makes an arithmetic error in calculating the total costs allocated to all production jobs.

b. An order that arrives at the final inspection station on the production line is missing 10 of the 100 units of product specified by the order; all of the work center supervisors protest that the units were missing when the order arrived at their centers.

c. A production order is coded with an incorrect and nonexistent product number. The error is not noted until the order begins moving through the production process.

d. The on-hand balance of a raw material shows a negative quantity.

e. The manager of a production work center questions the direct materials cost and asks to see the materials requisitions. Personnel from the production planning department search for hours to find the requested documents.

f. A raw materials storeskeeper takes certain expensive circuit boards home and covers the theft by submitting a write-off form to the accounting department that shows the boards to be obsolete and hence worthless.

g. A small production order is laid aside when a rush job must be accommodated by a work center; the small order is then forgotten and never completed.

h. As production orders are received, the production supervisor requisitions the materials that he believes are needed for completing the job. Often he overestimates the materials needed; the excess materials are then taken home by production employees.

i. A production planning clerk accesses the confidential salary file via an on-line terminal in the department.

14-13. What internal accounting control(s) would be most effective in preventing or detecting each of the following errors or fraudulent practices?

a. A production cost accounting program needs to be changed to reflect new standard costing procedures; however, the programmer who developed the program is no longer with the firm, and no one else understands the details of the program.

b. A production supervisor accesses the standard cost reference file and increases the standard overhead rate for her work center, so that the cost control reports will reflect favorable overhead cost variances.

c. A production employee enters a request for costly electronics parts on a materials issue slip, using a nonexistent production order number, and then keeps the parts he receives from stores for personal use.

d. When entering the times pertaining to a particular job via a data collection terminal at a work center, an employee forgets to enter the job number to which they pertain.

e. At the end of the month it is discovered that the amount shown in the work-in-process inventory control account significantly exceeds the total of accumulated costs for all jobs in process.

f. The quantity of a raw material posted to a work-in-process ledger record is 450 units rather than

540 units; posting is performed by a cost accounting clerk who posts all the materials issues once each day to the jobs in process.

g. The quantity of finished goods transferred into the warehouse for a production order was 100, but the warehouse clerk accidentally entered a quantity of 1000 into the computer system via the warehouse terminal.

h. A production employee keys an incorrect job number when entering his job hours, and the hours are posted to the wrong production order.

i. In entering data into an on-line terminal for a new production order, a production planning clerk keys a number for a product that is obsolete.

14-14. Munchen Manufacturing produces basic garden tools such as rakes and shovels. It maintains a large stock of raw materials in order to ensure that the production lines can operate at full capacity. Because the raw materials consist mainly of bulky wooden poles and steel plates, they are stacked next to the production areas as soon as they are received. No records are employed for their receipt. Production jobs are started each day on the basis of phone calls from the warehouse concerning which tools and sizes appear to be relatively low in stock. Since the warehouse supervisor keeps the only records concerning finished goods, he is the best qualified to make such recommendations.

Jobs are moved along the three production centers by an expediter. When completed, the finished goods are moved into the warehouse by a production employee. Then the warehouse supervisor estimates the quantity received and enters the rough count on the finished goods inventory records.

Management receives reports that reflect quantities produced and current levels (estimated) of finished goods on hand. The quantities produced have been gradually declining each month, even though the production lines are continually utilized. There often seem to be imbalances in the finished goods on hand, certain sizes of tools being in excessive supply and certain other sizes being quite low. Complaints are often received from customers (mainly garden shops) concerning inconsistent quality; when management investigates these complaints, it learns that all tools ruined during production are discarded immediately. Employees are allowed to take any ruined tools home for personal use.

Required

a. Discuss the problems in production management and the weaknesses in internal accounting control.

b. Identify specific improvements that should be made with respect to the production processes and reporting.

c. What benefits would be provided by an advanced computerized production information system?

d. Identify the specific items of information that an improved and computerized system should provide, including nonfinancial as well as financial measures of performance.

14-15. The Prescott Manufacturing Company employs a computerized processing system to track its production orders. Each production order is first issued by the production planning department after a clerk enters data from a customer's order. In addition to three copies of the production order, which is automatically prenumbered and dated, the issuing program generates a move ticket for the initial work center and a materials requisition. The production data file (containing the schedule, machine loadings, bill of materials, and product structures), open production order file, work-in-process inventory master file, and requisition file are accessed by this program.

The second step is to deliver a copy of the production order, move ticket, and requisition (the "package") to the initial work center. (The other copies of the order are filed numerically and sent to the sales order department.) Materials are delivered to the work center by the storeskeeper, who has received a copy of the requisition on his printer. The same program that generates the requisition for him reduces balances in the raw materials inventory master file to reflect their issuance. When materials are received, they are compared with the requisition already received.

Before and after the operation is performed at the initial work center, the involved employee enters the production order number and employee number into the work center terminal. The quantity completed is also entered on completion. The computer system automatically records the start and completion times and dates. The program generates a move ticket for the next work center and enters the costs in a general ledger transaction file. The work-in-process is moved to the next center, together with the production order package. The files accessed by this program are the production order file, employee payroll file, work-in-process inventory file, production data file, and general ledger file.

At the final work center, the employee who performs the last operation enters the same data as was entered at each previous center. The program recognizes, after accessing the production order file, that the order is completed. Then the program totals the work-in-process inventory record, transfers it to the finished-goods inventory file, and enters the journal entry into the general ledger transaction file. It also removes the production order from the open file, transfers it to a completed order file, and enters time data into the employee payroll file. The production order package is returned to the production planning department.

At the end of each day a program posts the production transactions to the general ledger file and prints a summary of all completed production orders.

Required

a. Prepare a level-zero data-flow diagram that reflects the five steps (processes) in the procedure described.

b. Prepare a separate computer system flowchart for each of the five major steps or processes described.

c. List programmed checks that should be performed by the computer program involved in each step described; indicate for each check one or more data elements on which the check should be performed.

14-16. Fluff-Down, a pillow manufacturer, produces about 1 million pillows in three plants. Pillows are made to order for large-volume customers. The firm tracks its production process by manual means.

Production at Fluff-Down begins with the receipt of an order from a customer. A blank production sheet is prepared based on the customer's order. As the order progresses through the production operations, each production employee manually records the quantity of raw materials and production labor hours added. Packers load finished pillows into cartons and update order sheets manually to show that orders are complete. When an order is shipped, its production order sheet is sent to the data-entry unit, where clerks key the data onto magnetic tapes. Then the magnetic tapes are read into the computer system to update inventory records maintained on magnetic disks.

Several problems exist due to this procedure. Often errors are made in data entry and processing. Even when the data are correct, a significant delay occurs between shipping an order and updating the inventory records. Thus, the inventory as well as production records do not reflect up-to-the-minute conditions. Since the firm does not know the quantities of raw materials needed for producing pillows, it maintains a surplus inventory level sufficient for 25 days of production *at each plant* in order to meet its delivery commitments.

Another problem is that the quality of raw materials often varies, thus affecting the quality control of raw materials. When the quality of raw materials is perceived by production employees to be below standard, they requisition additional raw materials from inventory in order to maintain desired levels of quality in pillows. Any unused raw materials are returned to inventory.

Because of the inaccuracies, delays, and excessive inventories, Fluff-Down has decided to implement an electronic data interchange (EDI) network within one year. The EDI network will involve both customers and its own suppliers. Purchase order data will be sent to suppliers, while customer orders will be received including shipping instructions. Confirmations of orders will be electronically dispatched to the customers, who will submit their payments electronically after receiving the ordered pillows. The EDI network should aid Fluff-Down in addition by facilitating the just-in-time inventory approach. A related improvement will be the affixing of bar codes to cartons and pillows, so that the receiving process can be simplified for customers.

Required

a. Identify the specific benefits of an EDI network to Fluff-Down, and relate each benefit to one or more problems if possible.

b. Identify problems that Fluff-Down will likely encounter in installing an EDI network, especially since the network ties to both customers and suppliers.

c. Identify controls relating to the EDI network that

    (1) Ensure authenticity of the electronic orders received.

    (2) Detect forged electronic messages.

    (3) Minimize the likelihood of unintelligible messages due to incompatible software.

d. Describe an automated production, receiving, and warehousing system for Fluff-Down that would aid in these activities and provide useful information to management. Include the use of the just-in-time inventory method and bar codes in your description.

e. Describe the best approach for reducing the variation in the quality of raw materials.

(CIA adapted)

14-17. Eileen Kunselman, president of Phoenix Electronics (PE), is concerned about the prospects of one of its major products. The president has been reviewing a marketing report with Jeff Keller, marketing product manager, for their 10-disk car compact disk (CD) changer. The report indicates another price reduction is needed to meet anticipated competitors' reduction in sales price. The current selling price for their 10-disk car CD changers is $350 per unit. It is expected that within three months PE's two major competitors will be selling their 10-disk car CD changers for $300 per unit. This concerns Kunselman because their current cost of producing the CD changers is $315, which yields a $35 profit on each unit sold.

The situation is especially disturbing because PE had implemented an activity based costing (ABC) system about two years ago. The ABC system helped them better identify costs, cost pools, and cost drivers and reduce costs. Changes made when adopting ABC reduced costs on this product by approximately 15 percent during the last two years. Now it appears costs will need to be reduced considerably more to remain competitive and to earn a profit on the 10-disk car CD changers. Total costs to produce, sell, and service the CD changer unit are as follows.

10-disk Car CD Changer		Per Unit
Materials:	Purchased components	$110
	All other materials	40
Labor:	Manufacturing, direct	65
	Setups	9
	Material handling	18
	Inspection	23
Machining:	Cutting, shaping, and drilling	21
	Bending and finishing	14
Other:	Finished-goods warehousing	5
	Warranty	10
	Total unit cost	$315

Kunselman has decided to hire Donald Collins, a consultant, to help decide how to proceed. After two weeks of review, discussion, and value engineering analysis, Collins suggested that PE adopt a just-in-time (JIT) cell manufacturing process to help reduce costs. He also suggested that using target costing would help in meeting the new target price.

By changing to a JIT cell manufacturing system, PE expects that manufacturing direct labor will increase by $15 per finished unit. However, setup, material handling, inspection, and finished-goods warehousing will be eliminated. Machine costs will be reduced from $35 to $30 per unit, and warranty costs are expected to be reduced by 40 percent.

Required

a. Determine Phoenix Electronics' unit target costs at the $300 competitive sales price while maintaining the same percentage of profit on sales as is earned on the current $350 sales price.

b. If the just-in-time (JIT) cell manufacturing process is implemented with the changes in costs noted above, will Phoenix Electronics meet the unit target cost you determined in requirement **a** above? Prepare a schedule detailing cost reductions and the unit cost under the proposed JIT cell manufacturing process.

(CMA *adapted*)

14-18. Design formats for two reports that will provide needed information to enable the responsible managers to achieve the stated purposes:

a. The first report should allow the evaluation of cost levels incurred in production. Costs relate to direct materials, direct labor, and overhead for the production orders that have been completed this month. The evaluation should consist of first comparing the actual (or applied) costs for these three elements with budgeted costs and then computing variances. No specific production numbers or cost values need to be entered.

b. The second report should allow the daily evaluation of the use of materials in production operations, in order to control waste caused by the carelessness and inefficiency of employees. The report should pinpoint individual employees, by name, as well as specific materials and operations. Enter onto the format the following identifying data: employees May Banks, Jerry Kimble, Robert Lambert, Judy Pierpoint, and Sandy Tempo; materials Delta and Omega; operations I, II, III, and IV. It is not necessary to enter numerical values for the actual quantities of materials used or for any comparative values.

14-19. Refer to Figure 14-15. Identify the tables from which data for the following reports should be drawn:

a. The production orders currently in the production process and the completion and expected delivery dates of each.

b. The costs accumulated to-date for all the orders currently in production, broken down by materials, direct labor, and overhead.

c. The raw materials issued to all the orders currently in production, identified by their descriptions and showing the quantities issued.

d. The operations completed for all orders currently in production, identified by their descriptions and work centers at which performed, showing the dates completed and the employees performing the work.

14-20. *Datacruncher Office Equipment, Inc.* (*Continuing Case*) Prepare a document system flowchart and a data-flow diagram that pertain to the current procedure for the production cycle, as described in Case A.

Note: The remaining problems in this set pertain to the material in Appendix 2 of this chapter. They are arranged so that problems related to human resource management (personnel/payroll) appear first, followed by problems concerning fixed asset management and finally cash management.

14-21. Refer to Figure 14-33. Design a job-time ticket for Jacob Keeley, a production employee who worked on job order 34 from 8:00 A.M. to 11:50 A.M.. on August 4, 1997. During this period, he produced 26 pieces of part B482 in a milling machine operation. His department is number 08 and his supervisor is William Killey. A time clock is employed to record his beginning and ending times.

14-22. Chambeers Clothiers of Princeton, New Jersey 08540, has 200 employees, including Ms. Peggy Ames

Gridley, No. 138. On Friday, April 17, 1998, she receives a weekly paycheck, which is prenumbered 7421. The check has been signed by Morton J. Bottom, treasurer, and is payable by the Tiger National Bank. Peggy worked 48 hours during the week and receives a regular hourly rate of $10, with time and one half for all overtime hours. Weekly deductions for Peggy are as follows: 8.50 percent of gross pay for FICA, $30 plus 20 percent of gross pay over $300 for federal income tax withholding (FITW), 3 percent of gross pay for state income tax withholding, $8 for group hospitalization plan, $5 for term life insurance plan, 5 percent for pension plan, and 1 percent for United Way contribution. Before being updated with this week's amounts, the employee payroll master record for Peggy showed year-to-date gross earnings of $6,450, net earnings of $4349.18, and FITW of $832. Assume that all deductions and withholdings have been computed every week in the same manner as this week. Other relevant facts concerning Peggy are as follows: social security number, 526-99-9966; department number, 04; pay classification, HR; marital status, S; number of exemptions, 1. The bank number on the paycheck (including the ABA transit code) is 18-170, the check routing code is 1001, and the firm's account number is 04-52365.

Required

a. Design a paycheck with attached stub or voucher for Chambeers Clothiers and enter suitable data from the problem statement.

Hint: Use a paycheck received by you or a friend, as well as the sample paycheck in Figure 14-34, to guide you.

b. Design a record layout for the employee payroll master file and enter suitable data for Peggy *after* the paycheck amounts for this week have been added to the record. Draw the fields in the record to scale, allowing sufficient lengths to accommodate data for employees with longer names and larger amounts than Peggy.

c. Design a payroll register (i.e., the journal or transaction listing) and enter Peggy's pay data for this week. The design should include such columns as employee name, number, department, hours worked, regular amount, overtime amount, all deduction amounts, and other relevant amounts.

14-23. Boone and Bower, CPAs, is a public accounting firm in the northeast. It has two offices and approximately 50 employees. The firm has been very progressive in its use of microcomputers. Recently it acquired a software package that manages the time records of its clerical and professional employees and that also prepares the payroll and related reports. Now the firm is also considering a software package to manage its various plant assets, such as furniture, office machines, fixed and portable microcomputers, and fixtures.

Required

a. List the data elements that are likely to be needed by the time management–payroll package in order to generate the outputs.

b. List the data elements that are likely to be needed by the fixed-asset package in order to manage the fixed assets and prepare outputs.

c. List the files needed by both of the packages.

d. Describe several listings and reports that can be provided by each of the packages and would likely be useful to the partners and office manager. (Do not include reports that are required by governmental agencies.)

14-24. Devise and illustrate a numeric group employee code that has fields to represent pay category, department number, year of hire, and sequential hire within the year. Use not more than eight numeric positions. Assume that 300 employees, on the average, are hired each year. Illustrate with employee Jerry Bell, who was the 57th person hired in 1997, is assigned to department 14, and is paid an hourly rate.

14-25. Roadrunner Casinos, Inc., with headquarters in Reno, operates five casinos in Nevada. The firm maintains its employee files on magnetic disks, since numerous personnel changes occur between pay dates. Personnel actions are entered via a video display terminal in the personnel department. To enter a personnel action, a payroll clerk chooses the Personnel Actions menu from the Main Menu. Next the clerk chooses the desired action (e.g., enter a new hiring, change an employee pay rate, add an employee deduction, display an employee record). A preformatted screen then appears, onto which the clerk enters the personnel action data.

    a. Design the Personnel Actions menu, which should list at least eight options and also allow for exit to the Main Menu.

    b. Design a preformatted screen for the Change an Employee Pay Rate option.

    c. Design a record layout for a skills file that Roadrunner Casinos maintains in order to select replacements quickly when employees resign. Include assumed modes for data elements and sizes of fields.

Note: Repeating fields will be needed, so the skill record will be variable in length.

14-26. Tempo Retailers of Durham, New Hampshire, processes its payroll by means of a small computer system. The following table presents sorted transaction data pertaining to the first several employees for a recent pay period.

Employee Number	Employee Name	Department Number	Hours Worked
13251	Smith, John	1	40
13620	Black, Charles	1	40
13543	Adams, Steve	1	48
13658	Br0wn, Rodney	1	40
13752	Jones, Paul	2	42
24313	Krause, Ken	2	44
25001	Tingey, Sharon	2	79

The first digit of the employee number indicates the employee's department, and the last digit is a nonzero self-checking digit.

Required

Assuming that the above data represent the entire group of employees to be paid:

a. Compute three types of batch control totals.

b. Identify errors in the data and the specific type of programmed check that should detect each error.

14-27. Manor Company of Orlando, Florida, operates several manufacturing plants on the East Coast. Its internal audit department performs operational audits of the various procedures in the plants on a regular basis. As an experienced internal auditor you have been assigned to head an audit team at the Galena plant. A major objective of the audit is to review the payroll procedures currently employed.

Various plant personnel were interviewed to ascertain the payroll procedures being used in the department. The findings were as follows:

- The payroll clerk receives the time cards from the various department supervisors at the end of each pay period, checks the employee's hourly rate against information provided by the personnel department, and records the regular and overtime hours for each employee.
- The payroll clerk sends the time cards to the plant's data processing department for compilation and processing.
- The data processing department returns the time cards with the printed checks and payroll register to the payroll clerk on completion of the processing.
- The payroll clerk verifies the hourly rate and hours worked for each employee by comparing the detailing in the payroll register to the time cards.

- If errors are found, the payroll clerk voids the computer-generated check, prepares another check for the correct amount, and adjusts the payroll register accordingly.
- The payroll clerk obtains the plant signature plate from the accounting department and signs the payroll checks.
- An employee of the personnel department picks up the checks and holds them until they are delivered to the department supervisors for distribution to the employees.

Required

a. Evaluate each finding of the audit team as either a weakness or a strength to the payroll procedures. In the cases of weaknesses, specify improvements that should be effected.

b. Prepare a level-zero data-flow diagram based on the described procedure.

(CMA *adapted*)

14-28. What error or fraudulent activity might occur if each of the following procedures is allowed?

a. Personnel and payroll are combined into the same organizational unit.

b. Departmental supervisors distribute paychecks to their employees.

c. The same person who prepares paychecks also signs them.

d. The paychecks are not prenumbered (or if prenumbered, copies are not filed in a sequential file that is periodically checked for gaps in the numbers).

e. Voided paychecks are destroyed.

f. A payroll clearing account, which should have a zero balance after payroll processing and distribution, usually reflects either a debit or credit balance. (The account is debited for the gross amount paid to employees and credited for the amount distributed to the work-in-process inventory and expense accounts).

14-29. What internal accounting control(s) would be most effective in preventing or detecting each of the following errors or fraudulent practices?

a. A payroll clerk computes 40 hours times $6 per hour to equal $250 gross pay.

b. An employee spends four hours in working on job order 782; however, he erroneously enters five hours on the labor job-time ticket.

c. A supervisor does not notify the personnel department when one of his employees quits; the supervisor turns in phony time cards for the employee each week and then keeps the paychecks for the employee when given the paychecks for distribution.

d. A computer operator enters a correction to a transaction via the console terminal and accidentally erases part of the employee payroll master file stored on magnetic tape.

e. A programmer obtains the employee payroll master file and increases her salary in her record.

f. Each week a computer operator is issued the check-signature plate the day before the paychecks are processed and signed by computer; one week the computer operator prepares a large check for himself, uses the plate to sign the check, and resigns before the malfeasance is discovered.

g. A computer programmer modifies the payroll programs so that the deduction for FICA is not made when preparing paychecks.

h. Ten time cards are accidentally lost in transmitting them to the payroll department.

i. A personnel clerk accidentally omits a deduction code when entering a personnel action change for an employee into an on-line terminal.

j. A data-entry clerk accidentally keys the letter l for the number 1 when entering time-card data onto a magnetic tape.

k. A data-entry clerk misreads a zero as a six when keying the employee number 12047 from a time card; as a result the entered times are processed for employee 12647 and a second paycheck is printed for her.

l. A payroll clerk increases the pay rate for a friend from $7 per hour to $9 per hour and then uses this higher rate to compute the friend's pay amount.

14-30. Arlington Industries manufactures and sells component engine parts for large industrial equipment. The company employs over 1000 workers for three shifts, and most employees work overtime when necessary. Arlington has had major growth in its production and has purchased a mainframe computer to handle order processing, inventory management, production planning, distribution operations, and accounting applications. Michael Cromley, president of Arlington, suspects that there may be internal control weaknesses due to the quick implementation of the computer system. Cromley recently hired Kathleen Luddy as the internal control accountant.

Cromley asked Luddy to review the payroll processing system first. Luddy has reviewed the payroll process, interviewed the individuals involved, and compiled the flowchart displayed on the next page. Additional information is listed below concerning payroll processing.

- The Personnel Department determines the wage rate of all employees at Arlington. Personnel starts the process by sending an authorization form for adding an employee to the payroll to the payroll coordinator, Marjorie Adams. After Adams inputs this information into the system, the computer automatically determines the overtime and shift differential rates for the individual, updating the payroll master file.

- Arlington uses an external service to provide monthly payroll tax updates. The company receives a magnetic tape every month that the Data Processing Department installs to update the payroll master file for tax calculations.

- Employees at Arlington use a time clock to record the hours worked. Every Monday morning, Adams collects the previous week's time cards from the card bin, leaves the new week's time cards, and begins the computerized processing of payroll information in order to produce paychecks the following Friday. Adams reviews the time cards to ensure that the hours worked are correctly totaled; the system will determine whether overtime has been worked or a shift differential is required.

- All the other processes displayed on the flowchart are performed by Adams. The system automatically assigns a sequential number to each payroll check produced. The checks are stored in a box next to the computer printer to provide immediate access. After the checks are printed, Adams uses an automatic check-signing machine to sign the checks with an authorized signature plate that Adams keeps locked in a safe.

- After the check processing is completed, Adams distributes the checks to the employees, leaving the checks for the second- and third-shift employees with the appropriate shift supervisor. Adams then notifies the Data Processing Department that she is finished with her weekly processing, and they make a backup of the payroll master file to magnetic tape for storage on the tape shelves in the computer room.

Required

By referring to the information above and the flowchart on the next page, identify and describe

a. Five different areas in Arlington Industries' payroll processing system where the system controls are inadequate.

b. Two different areas in Arlington Industries' payroll processing system where the system controls are satisfactory.

(CMA *adapted*)

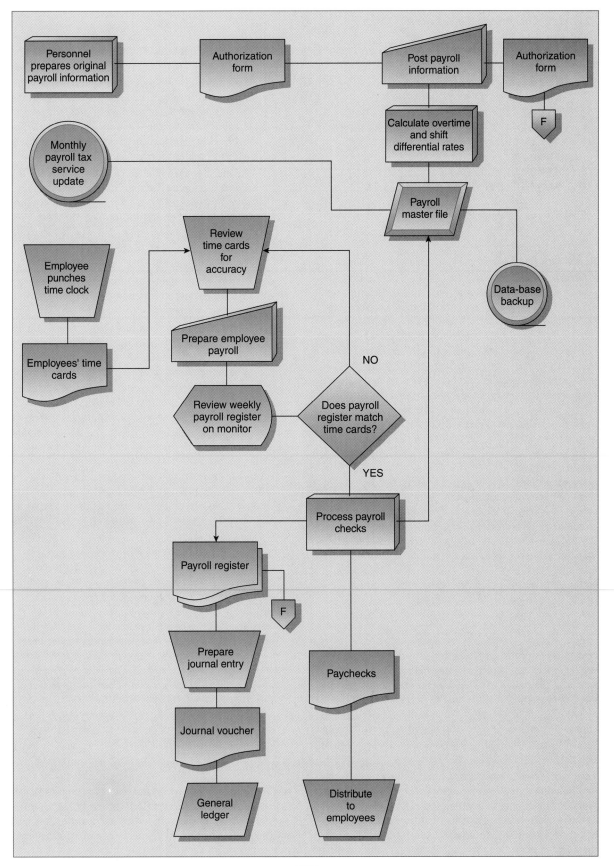

Personnel prepares original payroll information

Authorization form

Post payroll information

Authorization form

F

Calculate overtime and shift differential rates

Monthly payroll tax service update

Payroll master file

Review time cards for accuracy

Employee punches time clock

Data-base backup

Prepare employee payroll

Employees' time cards

Review weekly payroll register on monitor

NO

Does payroll register match time cards?

YES

Process payroll checks

Payroll register

F

Prepare journal entry

Paychecks

Journal voucher

General ledger

Distribute to employees

677

```
┌─────────────────────────────────────────┐
│       FIXED ASSETS MASTER MENU          │
│                                          │
│   1. ASSET DATA ENTRY                    │
│   2. ASSET ACQUISITION ENTRY             │
│   3. ASSET DISPOSAL ENTRY                │
│   4. ASSET ACCOUNT STATUS INQUIRY        │
│   5. INDIVIDUAL ASSET STATUS             │
│      INQUIRY                             │
│   6. REPORT DISPLAY                      │
│   7. DEMAND REPORT GENERATION            │
│                                          │
│   ENTER DESIRED NUMBER > _____          │
│                                          │
└─────────────────────────────────────────┘
```

14-31. The Shriver Computer Services Company of Pullman, Washington, uses an on-line processing system to keep its plant-asset records up to date and available for inquiry. It employs preformatted screens for the entry, modification, and retrieval of data pertaining to plant assets. To access the preformatted screens, a user first specifies the master menu shown above. When this menu screen is displayed on the user's CRT terminal, the user enters the desired number. The computer software then presents the requested screen or asks for additional information (e.g., the number of the desired asset). For instance, if the user needs to adjust the depreciation amount of an asset, he or she enters the number 1; the software then asks the number of the asset to be adjusted.

Assume that the user enters the number 2. A screen would appear that provides spaces for entering data concerning the acquisition of a plant asset. Among the data elements provided on the preformatted screen are date of purchase, manufacturer from whom purchased, class of asset, general ledger account number, assigned property number, description of asset, location of asset within firm, method of depreciation, estimated life, cost basis, and estimated salvage value.

Required

Design a preformatted screen that arranges the preceding elements in a structured manner, and simulate the action of the data-entry clerk by entering sample values for the elements. Include in the screen format those elements that would be automatically entered by the computer program, either to identify the transaction or to aid in reducing input errors. Denote these system-generated elements by an asterisk (*).

14-32. Deake Corporation is a medium-sized, diversified manufacturing firm located in Norman, Oklahoma. Frank Richards had been promoted recently to manager of the property accounting section. Richards has had difficulty in responding to some of the requests from individuals in other departments of Deake for information

about the firm's plant assets. Some of the requests and problems Richards has had to cope with are as follows:

a. The controller has requested schedules of individual plant assets to support the balances in the general ledger. Richards has furnished the necessary information, but always late. The manner in which the records are organized makes it difficult to obtain information.

b. The maintenance manager wants to verify the existence of a punch press that he thinks was repaired twice. He has asked Richards to confirm the asset number and location of the press.

c. The insurance department wants data on the cost and book value of assets to include in its review of current insurance coverage.

d. The tax department has requested data that can be used to determine when Deake should switch depreciation methods for tax purposes.

e. The firm's internal auditors have spent a significant amount of time in the property accounting section recently, attempting to confirm the annual depreciation expense.

The property account records that are at Richards' disposal consist of a set of manual books. These records show the date when the asset was acquired, the account number to which the asset applies, the dollar amount capitalized, and the estimated useful life of the asset for depreciation purposes.

After many frustrations Richards has realized that his records are inadequate and he cannot supply the data easily when they are requested. He has decided that he should discuss his problems with the controller, Jim Castle.

RICHARDS: *Jim, something has got to give. My people are working overtime and can't keep up. You worked in property accounting before you became controller. You know I can't tell the tax, insurance, and maintenance people everything they need to know from my records. Also, that internal auditing team is living in my area and that slows down the work pace. The requests of these people are reasonable, and we should be able to answer these questions and provide the needed data. I think we need an automated property accounting system. I would like to talk to the information systems people to see if they can help me.*
CASTLE: *Frank, I think you have a good idea, but be sure you are personally involved in the design of any system, so that you get all the information you need.*

Required

a. Identify and justify several major attributes Deake Corporation's computer-based property accounting system should possess in order to provide the data necessary to respond to requests of information from personnel.

b. Assume that Deake intends to install a relational data base for maintaining property records. Design the columns that should be included in the table for each asset included in the property account. Identify the primary key and several secondary keys. Also, design other tables that can logically be related to the property (plant asset) table, including the foreign keys needed to combine the tables.

c. Design a group code for a plant asset identification number and illustrate the code for a punch press assigned to one of the firm's production departments.

(CMA *adapted*)

14-33. What internal accounting control(s) would be most effective in preventing or detecting each of the following errors or fraudulent practices?

a. A department manager has a large fireproof vault installed in the department, even though firm policy is to maintain a centralized vault for use by all departments.

b. An employee is assigned a microcomputer for use in her job; however, she keeps it at home for personal use.

c. A property accounting clerk accumulates depreciation on a machine in an amount that exceeds the cost of the machine.

d. One fixed asset account in the general ledger reflects a considerable overstatement of asset value, since two posting errors were made earlier this year.

e. An engineering technician employed by a firm removes a complex testing machine from the premises and then reports to the property accounting department that it has been scrapped.

f. A computer-prepared fixed asset analysis is mistakenly sent to the storeskeeper rather than to the property accounting manager.

g. Certain fixed assets are misplaced and cannot be easily located.

14-34. The Superior Co. of Huntington, West Virginia, manufactures automobile parts for sales to the major U.S. auto makers. On the basis of a recent review of the procedures concerning machinery and equipment, the firm's internal auditors noted the following findings in a memorandum:

a. Requests for purchases of machinery and equipment are normally initiated by the supervisor who needs the asset. This supervisor discusses the proposed acquisition with the plant manager. A purchase requisition is submitted to the purchasing department when the plant manager is satisfied that the request is reasonable and when he determines that the balance in the plant's share of the total corporate budget for capital ac-

quisitions is adequate to cover the acquisition cost.

b. On receiving a purchase requisition for machinery or equipment, the purchasing department manager looks through the records for an appropriate supplier. A formal purchase order is then completed and mailed. When the machine or equipment is received, it is immediately sent to the requesting department for installation. This allows the economic benefits from the acquisition to be realized at the earliest possible date.

c. The property, plant, and equipment ledger control accounts are supported by lapsing schedules organized by year of acquisition. These lapsing schedules are used to compute depreciation as a unit for all assets of a given type that are acquired in the same year. Standard rates, depreciation methods, and salvage values are used for each major type of plant asset. These rates, methods, and salvage values were set ten years ago, during the firm's initial year of operation.

d. When machinery or equipment is retired, the plant manager notifies the accounting department so that the appropriate entries may be made in the accounting records.

e. There has been no reconciliation, since the firm began operations, between the accounting records and the machinery and equipment physically on hand.

Required

a. Identify each internal control weakness and describe the risk exposure due to the weakness.

b. Recommend improvements in control to counteract each weakness.

(CMA *adapted*)

14-35. Globrite, a major franchiser of video rental stores, experienced an explosion of growth. Over a two-year period, 2400 franchise stores opened around the country. Unfortunately, financial control systems lagged behind the growth in operations. While the franchisor's earnings grew in pace with its expanding operations, it experienced severe cash management problems. Cash receipts from franchise fees and product sales were habitually late. Creditors clamored for payment of past-due obligations, and some distributors of essential supplies would sell to the franchisor only on "cash on delivery" terms. Cash overdrafts were a daily occurrence.

Globrite processed all billings and disbursements at the corporate headquarters. Billing terms to franchisees for all product sales were net 30 days. The average collection period was 45 days. Payments by franchisees were remitted by check directly to corporate headquarters and deposited in the corporate general cash account. All payments to vendors were delayed as long as possible. Payroll checks were distributed every other Friday, and cash was transferred on each payroll distribution date from the general cash account to a special payroll account.

As a result of its cash flow problems and the adverse effects of a continuing national recession, Globrite filed for bankruptcy in late 1997.

Required

Describe the specific policies and controls that Globrite should have put into effect in order to maintain sound funds management and to avoid the unfortunate step of bankruptcy.

(CIA *adapted*)

14-36. Oakdale Inc. is a subsidiary of Solomon Publishing and specializes in the publication and distribution of reference books. Oakdale's sales for the past year exceeded $18 million, and the firm employed an average of 65 employees. Solomon periodically sends a member of its Internal Audit Department to audit the operations of each of its subsidiaries, and Katherine Ford, Oakdale's treasurer, is currently working with Ralph Johnson of Solomon's internal audit staff. Johnson has just completed a review of Oakdale's investment cycle and prepared a report containing the following paragraphs:

Throughout the year, Oakdale has made both short-term and long-term investments in securities; all securities are registered in the firm name. According to Oakdale's bylaws, long-term investment activity must be approved by its board of directors whereas short-term investment activity may be approved by either the president or the treasurer.

All purchases and sales of short-term securities in 1992 were made by the treasurer. In addition, two purchases and one sale of long-term securities were executed by the treasurer. The long-term security purchases were approved by the board whereas the long-term security sale was approved by the president. Because the treasurer is listed with the broker as the firm's contact, all revenue from these investments is received by this individual, who then forwards the checks to accounting for processing.

Purchase- and sell-authorizations, along with the brokers' advices, are maintained in a file by the treasurer. The certificates for all long-term investments are kept in a safe deposit box at the local bank; only the president of Oakdale has access to this box. An inventory of this box was made, and all certificates were accounted for. Certificates for short-term investments are kept in a locked metal box in the accounting office. Other docu-

ments such as long-term contracts and legal agreements are also kept in this box. There are three keys to the box held by the president, treasurer, and the accounting manager. The accounting manager's key is available to all accounting personnel should they require documents kept in this box. Documentation for two of the current short-term investments could not be located in this box; the accounting manager explained that some of the investments are for such short periods of time that formal documentation is not always provided by the broker.

Deposits of checks for interest and dividends earned on investments are recorded by the Accounting Department, but these checks could not be traced to the cash receipts journal maintained by the individual who normally opens, stamps, and logs incoming checks. These amounts are journalized monthly to an account for investment revenue. Checks drawn for investment purchases are authorized by the treasurer; checks in excess of $15,000 must be signed by both the treasurer and the president. When securities are sold, the broker deposits the proceeds directly into Oakdale's bank account by an electronic funds transfer.

Each month, the accounting manager and the treasurer prepare the journal entries required to adjust the short-term investment account. There was insufficient backup documentation attached to the journal entries reviewed to trace all transactions; however, the balance in the account at the end of last month closely approximates the amount shown on the statement received from the broker. The amount in the long-term investment account is correct, and the transactions can be clearly traced through the documentation attached to the journal entries. There are no attempts made to adjust either account to the lower of aggregate cost or market.

Required

To achieve Solomon Publishing's objective of sound internal control, the firm believes the following four controls are basic for an effective system of accounting control.

- Authorization of transactions
- Complete and accurate recordkeeping
- Physical control
- Internal verification

a. Identify an area in Oakdale's investment procedures that violates each of the four controls listed above.

b. For each of the violations identified in **a** above, describe how Oakdale can correct the weakness.

(CMA *adapted*)

CHAPTER 15

MANAGERIAL DECISION MAKING AND REPORTING

1. Describe the basic process by which effective managers make decisions, as well as the various types of decisions made by managers.

2. Discuss the information needed by the managers of firms to make decisions.

3. Identify types of reports and the impact of reports on management behavior.

4. Describe various financial reporting systems for management.

5. Discuss ways to improve the reporting process.

6. Describe emerging world-class organizations.

INTRODUCTION

As previous chapters have emphasized, transaction processing is an important purpose of a firm's accounting information system (AIS). However, an even more important role of accountants, especially management accountants, is to aid in the making of decisions. Providing managers with pertinent decision-making information to run and control the firm consists of collecting and storing relevant data, processing the data through decision models, and providing useful information outputs in varied forms. These decision-making functions are collectively called **information processing.** During the course of our discussion we recognize that managers, a very important group of decision makers, are fallible human beings. They tend to be biased and to employ distinctive cognitive styles in making decisions. Managers are

also quite limited in their information processing capabilities. With the advent of recent developments in information technology, firms can develop information systems to enhance the information processing capabilities of managers, thereby effectively aiding managers in their decision-making efforts.

ROLE OF ACCOUNTANTS IN MANAGERIAL DECISION MAKING

Accountants have traditionally provided financially oriented information for decision making. For instance, financial information generated by a firm's accounting information system (AIS) flows to users both inside and outside the firm. In recent decades accountants have continued to perform this information processing and interpreting role. With the flowering of the information age, however, other professionals have joined accountants in providing decision-making information. Computer information analysts, management scientists, knowledge engineers, financial modelers, and industrial engineers have all become increasingly involved in business information processing.

To retain their usefulness, accountants must become familiar with the key concepts discussed in the next three chapters. These concepts are decision making and reporting, emerging computer-based support systems and techniques, and specialized information systems and networks.

MANAGERIAL DECISION MAKING

In order to design effective information processing systems that produce useful information outputs, we must understand managerial decision making. Thus we begin this chapter with a discussion of the decision process and the specific types of decisions made in business firms.

DECISION PROCESS

The managers of a firm are responsible for setting its objectives and making decisions to achieve the established objectives. Each decision maker is unique. Also, problems vary widely and thus processes by which decisions are made vary considerably among decision situations. Some problems are defined very clearly and objectively, and a manager has complete information to examine all the alternatives with a great deal of certainty. Usually, for these types of problems, a manager makes what are called **optimal decisions.** Conversely, other problems, and hence decision process steps, are characterized by much vagueness, subjectivity, incomplete information, and uncertainty; due to time and processing constraints and other personal considerations, only a limited number of alternatives are evaluated. These problem situations are solved by making what are called "good enough" or **satisfactory decisions.**

Some decision makers employ a systematic or reasoned approach and seek to collect information to develop the most explicit decision model possible in each problem situation; others employ an intuitive or unsystematic approach to analyze problems and habitually depend on implicit decision models. Both approaches are recognized as effective in making decisions. Nevertheless, the process by which all decisions are made follows a relatively standardized series of steps. Although decision makers and problems requiring decisions differ greatly, a rational process for making effective decision choices can be generalized. Figure 15-1 shows the steps in this **decision process,** which is relevant to both individual and group decisions.

To accommodate a wide variety of problems and decision makers, however, each step within this process may

1. ***Recognize and define the problem.*** The problem may be an adverse change, as when the profits of a product are declining. Or it may be an opportunity, such as the opportunity to acquire a smaller firm with a complementary product line. Defining the problem consists of expressing the desired results (criteria), the key factors in the problem situation, constraints, assumptions, time horizon, and so on. This may be the most difficult step in the process. One of the most important tasks during this step is to choose the criteria and determine their weight. The *criteria* are the important factors used to evaluate the alternatives. Each criterion must be allocated a proper weight in relation to its importance compared to the other criteria. For example, the most important criterion can be given a weight of 100 percent and the other criteria are assigned weights against this standard.

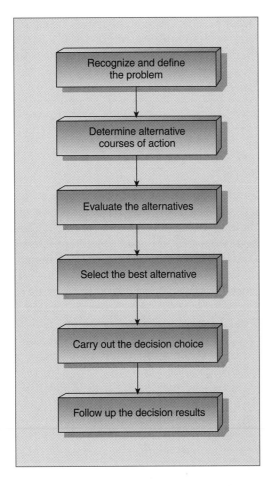

FIGURE 15-1 Steps in a decision process.

2. **Determine alternative courses of action.** Feasible solutions to the problem or courses of action should be listed, including the alternatives to "do nothing" and "continue as we are now."

3. **Evaluate the alternatives.** Each of the alternative courses of action must be compared to the others. To perform this step, a decision model must be employed. A **decision model** (a) describes the relationships and behaviors of all the significant factors and (b) provides a means of evaluating the alternatives in terms of the criteria. When data concerning each alternative are in turn fed into this model, the resulting criteria values enable each alternative to be ranked in relation to the others. It is not necessary, however, to develop a formal written or programmed model. As stated, in many situations the decision maker simply employs a "model" that is formulated implicitly within his or her mind.

4. **Select the preferred alternative.** This step consists of "making the decision." Normally the choice is based essentially on the results provided by the decision model. If the model is sound and all feasible alternatives are considered, the choice should focus on the best course of action. Often, however, qualitative factors enter the picture, especially when the decision situation is complex. In these instances, managerial judgment is necessary.

5. **Carry out the decision choice.** A decision is meaningless unless implemented. Thus the decision choice must be communicated to those persons who are to carry out the necessary activities.

6. ***Follow up the results.*** A decision maker should be clearly aware of the expected results (e.g., the payoff) from each decision choice. In addition, he or she should monitor the effects of each decision, comparing the actual results against those that are expected. If this control procedure is followed, corrective actions can be taken when necessary.

To reinforce your understanding of the decision process, you might study the first Review Problem at the end of this chapter before reading the following sections.

TYPES OF DECISIONS

The decision process described above is used by managers in making several specific types of decisions. These decisions may be classified according to resources (e.g., inventory), organizational functions (e.g., accounting decisions), and other dimensions. One very useful classification relates to the problems that the decisions are intended to solve. Thus a **structured,** or **programmed, decision** is routine, repetitive, and concerns a problem whose factors and relationships are very clear, simple, and well known to the decision maker. Since these decisions are common, they have well-established procedures for solving them. Therefore, precise sets of instructions can be provided to clerks (or programmed for computers) and clear-cut decision results will be derived. For instance, when Diane Varney, treasurer and controller of Infoage, approves a customer's credit application for purchasing a microcomputer, assigns one of her accountants to perform a particular task, or approves an adjusting journal entry, she is making structured decisions.

At the opposite end of the problem spectrum is the **unstructured,** or **nonprogrammed, decision,** which concerns an unusual or infrequently occurring problem situation whose factors and relationships are poorly understood. These complex and broad-scope problem situations require the exercise of considerable judgment, creativity, and logic. Many decisions fall into the semistructured category, which ranges between these two extremes. When George Freeman, president of Infoage, authorizes the construction of a new retail microcomputer outlet in another state or initiates a campaign to advertise the firm's line of microcomputers on the local television station, he is making unstructured decisions.

Perhaps the most useful way to classify decisions is in accordance with the key management activities of strategic planning, tactical planning, and operational control. These decisions are discussed in Chapter 2. An activity that is closely related to these three managerial decision-making activities, known as *management control*, extends through all the levels. Management control (discussed in Chapter 7) determines whether or not resources are effectively and efficiently utilized by operational units. For example, George Freeman makes a management control decision when he evaluates the performance of the treasurer/controller's department by studying a cost performance report that shows variances from the standard.

INFORMATION NEEDS

To make sound decisions, managers must be provided with valuable information. The value of information, and hence the soundness of decisions, can be affected by qualities that attach to the information. Unfortunately, these qualities are missing or deficient in many firms, leading managers to make suboptimal decisions.

Particularly useful **information qualities** are relevance, accuracy, timeliness, conciseness, clarity, quantifiability, and consistency. **Relevance** is the degree to which particular information directly makes a difference in the decision choice. Information is relevant, therefore, if it has specific content, it can be used in the decision process and leads to some action taken. For instance, the level of microcomputer sales forecasted for next month is relevant to the decision by Infoage concerning how many units to stock. In contrast, the production of mainframe computers worldwide last year is not relevant to the decision. In summary, all relevant information pertaining to a decision should be provided, while irrelevant information should be excluded.

Accuracy pertains to the reliability and precision of information. *Reliability* refers to freedom from errors or bias; *precision* refers to the degree of refinement during measurement. For instance, the actual sales made during the past year by Infoage may be determined reliably and precisely from sales records to be $2,589,376. The estimate of next year's sales cannot be stated as reliably and should not be stated precisely. Errors can be reduced by carefully checking input data and processing steps through a series of controls and security measures built into the AIS.

Timeliness concerns the currency and accessibility of information. With respect to currency, timeliness is measured by up-to-dateness. For instance, if a customer's account is posted as soon as a sale is made, the information is continually up-to-date. If postings occur once each day, the information is less up-to-date. With respect to accessibility, information is sufficiently timely if it can affect the process of the decision for which it is intended. One measurement of accessibility is response time, the length of time between the request for information and the receipt of information by the user. Computer systems allow the response times for certain information to be a matter of seconds.

Conciseness is the degree to which the quantity of information has been selectively reduced. Conciseness can be viewed as a quality, since it avoids excessively detailed and unnecessary information, and hence information overload. It is also related to the quality of relevance. For instance, a manager may be provided only the information needed for required decisions. So-called *exception reports*, in which only the information items requiring control decisions are included, are an example of conciseness. Conciseness can be a slippery quality. Thus, managers often need information that is summarized, such as sales summaries. However, if the information is aggregated, certain key trends or patterns may be hidden.

Clarity is the degree to which information is readily understandable by the users. For instance, information concerning the sales made by Infoage may be explained in three ways for the managers: in narrative terms, in analytical tables, and in graphs. Thus, clarity is enhanced by differing formats, as well as by completeness.

Quantifiability is the degree of measurability, or the extent to which numeric values can be assigned to items of information. In general, the quality of information is enhanced if it can be quantified in some manner. For instance, a level of customer satisfaction of 4.5 on a scale of 5.0 can be more useful than a statement that customers are "generally very satisfied."

Consistency is the degree to which information can be compared in a uniform and meaningful manner. For instance, the sales of one division of a firm may be viewed as consistent and hence comparable with the sales of other divisions. Sales reports for managers hence have greater value when division sales are shown in adjoining columns.

Other qualities of information may be briefly noted. *Verifiability* is the ability to independently generate the same information value, as when one person checks the calculations of another. *Scope* is the span of activities or responsibilities covered by an item of information. For example, a firm's overall sales cover a broader scope than the sales of one product line.

If a piece of information reduces a manager's uncertainty in making a particular decision it is considered useful. Useful information must be identified by conducting an information-needs analysis, which takes a variety of considerations into account, including the needs and desires of individual managers. Experience has shown that this analysis cannot be performed well alone, either by individual managers or by skilled analysts such as managerial accountants. Instead, determining information needs should be jointly undertaken by *both* individual managers and information analysts such as accountants. The procedure and concerns of an information-needs analysis are described in Chapter 19.

Although the decision *process* is reasonably uniform for all types of decisions, *needed* information varies widely from decision to decision. It also varies widely from manager to manager within the same firm. We can observe these differences by first looking at individual decision makers and decisions. Next, we provide a general profile contrasting the information needs of managers at the highest and lowest levels in an organization. Third, we examine specific information that can be furnished to managers and other employees for making a variety of long-term and short-range decisions. Then, we discuss the importance to employees of informal information flows. We conclude the section with an example illustrating these information needs, as well as the decision process.

INDIVIDUAL DECISION MAKERS AND DECISION MAKING

Personal characteristics have an impact on decision making and, hence, on information needs, since they determine each manager's cognitive style. **Cognitive style** refers to the manner in which a manager perceives and processes information in arriving at a decision. For example, Diane Varney of Infoage may have an analytical style; other Infoage managers may prefer an intuitive approach. An area of study known as **human information processing** reveals that cognitive styles vary widely among managers. Another personal characteristic affecting decision making is the attitude of the decision maker. While a manager believes that his or her own well-being is aligned with that of the firm's welfare, the manager is encouraged to make the best possible decision. This condition is known as **goal congruence.**

GENERAL PROFILE OF INFORMATION NEEDS

Top-level managers, such as presidents and vice-presidents and divisional heads, make strategic planning decisions. Thus their information needs are directly related to the qualities of information required by strategic decisions. As Figure 15-2 shows, the needed information should be (1) broad in scope, (2) relatively summarized or aggregated, (3) qualitative as well as quantitative, and (4) drawn mainly from external sources. Because strategic decisions pertain to the planning activity of a firm, the information is oriented toward the future and consists largely of estimates. Since top managers have a long-range time horizon, the needed information is not likely to be highly accurate or precise. Also, timeliness in making the decisions is not normally critical. That is, making a sound decision is usually much more important than making a quick decision. Top-level managers often bypass the formal manual or computer-based information processing systems and obtain much of their information from both verbal media, such as meetings, tours, and telephone calls, and written media, such as periodicals, letters, and reports.

Lower-level managers, like department heads or supervisors, make operational control decisions. As Figure 15-2 shows, the needed information tends to be (1) narrow in scope, (2) relatively detailed, (3) mainly quantitative, and (4) derived mainly

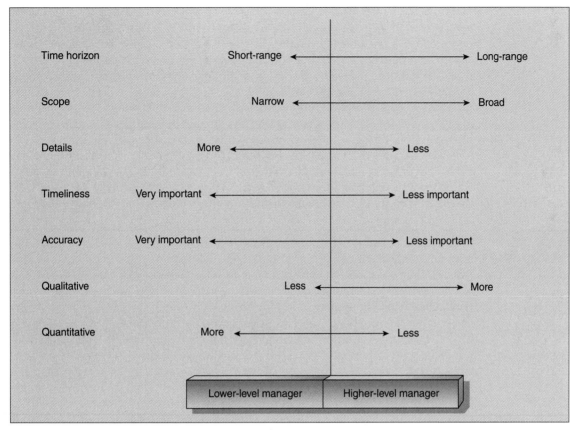

FIGURE 15-2   Information-needs profiles of two managers.

from internal sources. Since the decisions often facilitate control, the information pertains to the recent past or present and is compared against benchmarks. Because the time horizon of operational control decisions is short-range, the information can usually be quite accurate and precise. It should also be timely, so that corrective actions can be promptly taken. Often a large portion of the recurring information needs can be drawn from written media, such as reports, and can be generated by the computer-based transaction processing activities of the AIS. Tactical-level or middle managers' information needs range between those of top and operational managers.

SPECIFIC TYPES OF INFORMATION NEEDS

Employees (i.e., managers, key workers, and self-managed work teams) working for all types of firms,* including so-called emerging world-class organizations, require financial and nonfinancial information. World-class organizations and self-managed work teams are examined in a subsequent section of this chapter.

---

*The manufacturing sector includes mining, utilities, and most manufacturing and employs about 15 percent of the workforce. The services sector includes people-oriented services such as auto repair, banking, and hotels; most health care; state and local government; and elementary and secondary education. This sector employs about 70 percent of the workforce. The information sector includes information-oriented services such as advertising and entertainment, communications, publishing, software, computers, higher education, medical diagnosis, and the securities industry. About 15 percent of the workforce is employed in this sector. See "A New Way to Split the Economy," *Fortune* (November 7, 1994), p. 116.

Financial Information Responsible employees who are held accountable for the results of work achieved should be able to effectively follow their firm's financial performance. Consequently, financial reporting systems (described below) should convey to proper employees periodic **financial information** so that the firm's overall profitability can be evaluated. Such information includes income, earnings per share, key financial ratios, budgetary information, economic value added (e.g., income after taxes minus cost of capital), variances, product costs, activity-based costs, operating margins, cash flows, sales trends, and sales and operating profits by segments of the business. This financial information should be accompanied by analysis of the financial data, such as reasons for changes in the financial data, and the identity and past effect of key financial trends.* For example, a former CEO of Walmart Industries stated that the only way the employees (associates) can effectively and efficiently do their jobs is to share, on a regular basis, important financial information with them.†

Nonfinancial Information In addition to financial information, a wide variety of timely nonfinancial information should be reported to employees. Some firms only report nonfinancial information to employees on a need-to-know basis. However, the trend in many of today's organizations is to make nonfinancial information widely available to all accountable managers, key workers, and self-managed work teams. **Nonfinancial information** includes operational, customer, stockholder, general firm, and external information, examples of which are presented in Figure 15-3. Whereas financial information tends to be aggregated and summarized at regular intervals, nonfinancial information often is disaggregated, detailed, and reported less frequently than financial information. However, at the present stage of development, many firms' formal reporting systems cannot capture certain nonfinancial information. As firms improve their financial reporting process (described below), other types of nonfinancial information will be captured and communicated. In addition, some nonfinancial information is gathered by informal information flows, described below.

Operational information includes all information relevant to an employee's job, such as information about product defect rates, machine breakdowns, amount of rework, error rates, orders filled, worker productivity rates, quality of product, percentage of rejected parts, and on-schedule performance. Much of this information should be reported in a very timely manner, such as hourly or daily, so that key employees can make decisions about the organization of work, the allocation of resources, the evaluation of their performance, and how this performance affects the operations of the department and the firm.

A second category of nonfinancial measures focuses on **customer information,** such as number of customer complaints, percentage of revenues from new customers, percentage of products delivered on time, percentage of products returned, and number of major competitors. This information should be communicated as quickly as possible so that immediate actions can be taken to respond to customer inquiries, to prevent misunderstandings or to prevent lost revenues.

To keep them abreast of the latest developments within the firm, employees need nonfinancial stakeholder and general measures. **Stakeholder information** of interest includes market value of the firm, market price per share of common stock, and major shareholders. This data should also be accompanied by a commentary explaining the reasons for changes in the stakeholder data and key trends that the data reveals. **General firm information** includes information on market share, em-

---

*The AICPA Special Committee on Financial Reporting. *Improving Business Reporting—A Customer Focus.* Supplement to the *Journal of Accountancy* (September 1994), p. 4.
†Gerald M. Hoffman. *The Technology Payoff* (Burr Ridge, Ill.: Irwin Professional Publishing, 1994), p. 118.

absenteeism rates	new product ideas
amount of rework	number of customer complaints
back orders	number of customer visits
best sales performance	on-schedule performance
competitors' performance	on-time deliveries
competitors' plans	orders filled
core/noncore business	price comparisons
customer complaints	product defect rates
customer returns	production scheduling
customer sales	product quality
customer satisfaction levels	recruitment plans
customer survey results	rejected parts per hour
customer visits	sales by territories
defective goods delivered by suppliers	sales/orders
employee attitudes	sales trends
employee morale	scrap rates
general economic conditions	service response time
lead time to receive orders	staffing requirements
machine breakdowns	status of work orders
major competitors	units produced
management plans, objectives	vendor performance
market share	warranty claims
market trends	worker productivity rates

FIGURE 15-3   Examples of nonfinancial information.

ployee morale, employee attitudes, absenteeism rates, capital budgeting data, management plans, objectives and strategies, and core and noncore business activities.

External information pertaining to the firm's environment should also be reported. This type of information enables key personnel to evaluate the potential future impact of the many external influences on the profitability and competitiveness of the organization, particularly its ability to survive and adapt to the world beyond its borders. Relevant external information includes information about competitors' plans and performance, government regulations, legislation, market trends, and new technological developments.

INFORMAL INFORMATION FLOWS

In addition to formal information captured by a firm's reporting systems, employees also base decisions on information that they acquire through informal communication channels. Such **informal information** cuts across all functions and organizational units and moves horizontally, vertically, and diagonally. All firms can effectively use informal information. However, informal flows are more important in flattened organization structures.

Sources of informal information include networks of relationships among subordinates, colleagues, employees, and friends in other firms. Other important sources include magazines, newspapers, fax, E-mail, observation of processes, and suggestion boxes. For instance, George Freeman, president of Infoage, might have a casual conversation at a computer technology convention that yields otherwise unavailable data about a new development in laptop microcomputers. Or, Ann Strong, CPA and CMA, may read about a new type of consulting service that she can offer to clients.

Informal information items can be critical when making certain strategic, tactical, or operational decisions. For instance, the planned routes of freeways can be extremely important information to Infoage's managers when deciding where to locate a new retail outlet computer store (a strategic decision). Or, the number of complaints received from customers about a particular brand of microcomputer might influence George Freeman to drop the model from his product line (a tactical decision). Also, comments received from Ann Strong's clients may convince her to expand her offerings of income tax services (a tactical decision). Finally, observation of high scrap rates by a production supervisor may prompt him or her to recalibrate the machine generating the excessive scrap (an operational control decision).

Even though informal information often enables quick decisions, informal flows are not always useful or dependable. Often the information is unstructured, incomplete, imprecise, and misunderstood. It may be biased by the personal attitudes of the sources. For instance, information received from one of Infoage's accounting employees about possible wrongdoing by another accountant may be colored by the "whistleblower's" feelings about his or her supervisor, Diane Varney. Even information received from Diane Varney's subordinate manager, the assistant controller, may be distorted to make him or her "look good" or to keep unfavorable results from being exposed.

AN EXAMPLE

To illustrate information needs—both formal and informal—as well as the decision process, we will consider the strategic decision concerning the introduction of a product line and the tactical and operational decisions regarding inventory management. Assume that George Freeman is exploring the prospect of introducing a leading-edge microcomputer product line to the firm's existing line of products. The family of microcomputers is manufactured by a major computer vendor. Since the product life cycle spans several years, the decision is clearly at the strategic level. George's needed information includes expected sales during the product's life, costs of purchasing the laptop, amount of volume discounts, and expected unit prices that can be charged to customers. To aid George in developing this quantitative information, Diane Varney may also obtain information concerning competitors' unit sales and prices, as well as qualitative information concerning evolving customer preferences and satisfaction with the new product line. Much of this external information is likely to come from sources other than Infoage's computer-based MIS or AIS. Mike Barker, marketing manager of Infoage, may conduct surveys, interviews, and market demand studies to determine customers' preferences and satisfaction. He may also hire consulting marketing associations or polling services to assist him in obtaining the needed information.

The problems in the recurring inventory management decision are to have desktop and laptop microcomputers, printers, and peripheral devices available for Infoage's customers at the retail outlets when requested, while avoiding excessive inventory costs. Unsold units of microcomputers, particularly laptops, rapidly become outdated. Thus, if forecasted laptop sales are below expectation, excess inventory will accumulate and will force Infoage to incur a large loss on the marked-down units. Or, conversely, if Infoage underestimates the demand for laptops, significant lost sales and profits may result.* Dealing with these problems requires two decisions with respect to each merchandise inventory item: (1) how much inventory to order and carry in stock and (2) when to reorder.

The former decision can be classified as a tactical planning decision and is normally made by a middle manager like Jack Dyson, Infoage's inventory manager. To make this reorder quantity decision, Jack first considers two alternatives. One alternative is to maintain the inventory at a very high safety level, so that stockouts are unlikely to occur. This inventory system is sometimes referred to as *just-in-case* (JIC). Another alternative is to maintain the inventory at a moderate safety level, so that costs are reduced but stockouts may occasionally occur. Jack uses a decision model known as the *economic order quantity* (EOQ) *formula* to evaluate these alternatives. The EOQ decision model yields the optimal choice, since it takes into account the stockout costs, carrying costs, and reorder costs, as well as the expected demand for the inventory item. In fact, it specifies the exact quantity to reorder (which includes the needed safety stock). After being computed, the EOQ is stored in the inventory records for use as needed. However, even this model often results in carrying excess inventory. Recall that an alternate model employed by many firms, known as *just-in-time* (JIT), enables a firm to carry the minimum amount of inventory.

The decision when to reorder is a programmable operational control decision. It is usually made by an inventory control supervisor, a subordinate of Jack Dyson. The decision model used to implement this decision is called the reorder point formula, which computes the reorder point by multiplying the average daily demand for the inventory item by the expected lead time (the time between placing an order and receiving the item from the supplier). Since the reorder decision is of the control type, it is implemented by comparing the reorder point to the actual quantity on hand. The "corrective action" consists of Infoage's inventory control supervisor notifying the purchasing section that the EOQ quantity needs to be reordered. As the inventory example illustrates, the needed information is detailed, quantitative, and focused on individual inventory items; it also can be employed in a very timely manner.

IMPACTS OF REPORTS ON MANAGERIAL BEHAVIOR

Information needs of managers are often met by generating hard-copy reports and other outputs. In Chapter 4 we classified reports according to conciseness, occurrence, and main purpose. As discussed in Chapters 11 through 14, a large number of specific reports and output displays fitting into one or more of these three categories are generated by a typical firm. These specific reports aid in making the necessary planning and control decisions and in meeting the firm's other responsibilities.

Reports influence managerial behavior. Managers make decisions and take action on the basis of information in reports. If the information is reported effectively, the managers are likely to make sound decisions and take desirable actions. If the information is not reported effectively, the managers are inclined to act in undesirable manners.

Consider the common reporting deficiency of **information overload**—providing more information than busy managers can reasonably digest. For instance, an inventory manager may receive a thick listing of all materials, showing the quantities

*Both IBM Corp. and Compaq Computer Corp. lost tens of millions of dollars in microcomputer sales when both firms incorrectly forecasted demand for the 1994 Christmas season.

on hand and on order; a personnel manager may receive a report containing numerous comparisons of personnel needs and availabilities. Managers who receive such reports may act dysfunctionally by simply tossing them in a corner. Other reactions might be to use the information casually (thus, perhaps, making errors), to use only selected items, or to have an assistant boil the report down to digestible size.

FINANCIAL REPORTING SYSTEMS FOR MANAGEMENT

In this section we briefly examine differences between financial reporting systems outputs intended for external and internal users. Then we examine three types of firmwide integrated financial reporting systems that communicate useful information to the firm's managers. They are budgetary reporting systems, responsibility reporting systems, and profitability reporting systems. A fourth type—cost accounting systems—was surveyed in Chapter 14. Then, we clarify the relationships among reporting systems.

FINANCIAL REPORTING TO INTERNAL AND EXTERNAL USERS

To generate much of the above information, every firm requires a basic **financial reporting system** that produces a wide variety of financial reports and statements. This reporting system draws on the transactions collected and processed by the general ledger system described in Chapter 11. Numerous reports and statements, as noted earlier, are prepared according to financial accounting standards to serve users outside the firm. Certain reports may be highly summarized. Income statements provided to stockholders via annual reports fall into this category. Other reports for external users are relatively detailed and tailored. For instance, income statements required from some firms by the Securities and Exchange Commission provide revenue and cost information that is detailed by appropriate segment (products or services).

Nevertheless, significant differences frequently exist between financially oriented outputs intended for internal and external users, even when the outputs span the same scope. First, reports and statements for internal users tend to contain more details. For example, an income statement usually provides even more detail than the segment information required by the Securities and Exchange Commission. Second, reports and statements for internal users are not constrained by generally accepted accounting principles. Thus alternative forms of income statements are often provided to managers. One format will likely be prepared according to the full-absorption costing format used for externally directed statements. Another format may be prepared according to the direct-costing format, with the costs grouped into variable and fixed categories. Third, many firms have switched from traditional full costing to activity-based costing (ABC) to provide a more effective measure of profitability and competitiveness. Whereas full costing measures the total production cost as the total amount of the costs of all the operations a product passes through until finished, ABC measures the cost of a whole process, including receiving, manufacturing, assembling, testing, shipping, servicing, and installing costs. Fourth, financial reports and statements destined for internal users are mainly intended to serve managerial planning and control aims. Since budgets and budgetary control reports effectively serve both of these purposes, they constitute a major component of the typical internal financial reporting system.

In traditionally structured firms with functional departments, these financial reports are usually for use by managers. Most information is only communicated to other employees on "an as needed basis." However, many of today's organizations are striving to achieve "world-class status" by restructuring, downsizing, reengineering, outsourcing, and creating self-managing teams of empowered workers. To expedite these new decision-making processes, nonfinancial as well as financial information is provided to all employees.

BUDGETARY REPORTING SYSTEMS

A **budgetary reporting system** is a financial reporting system that is applicable to all types of firms. It consists of an integrated set of reports that aid in planning and controlling a firm's operations. Figure 15-4 portrays the composition of a budgetary

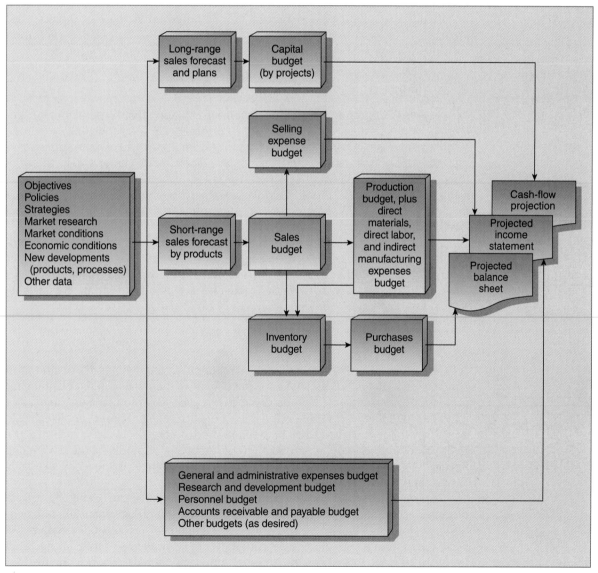

FIGURE 15-4   Composition of a budgetary reporting system.

reporting system. The budgetary process begins with the preparation of long-range and short-range sales forecasts. These sales forecasts are based on a variety of inputs, ranging from objectives set by top management to environment data concerning the markets and economy. After setting the firm's expected level of activity by reference to the sales forecasts, top management requests the various functions and departments to prepare component budgets. These component budgets have the purpose of allocating the firm's resources and providing detailed plans for every activity. On being reviewed and approved by management, the component budgets are condensed into summary statements of operating results, cash flows, and financial status. The component budgets and summary statements become the performance standards against which actual performances are to be evaluated. As the budget period unfolds, budgetary (management) control reports, reflecting variances from budgeted values, are issued periodically. When the time arrives for the next budgetary planning process, the results shown in the control reports become part of the input data affecting future expectations.

Results from the budgetary process can be improved by the use of proven approaches. For instance, participation by managers at all levels of the organization should be encouraged. Also, flexible budgeting techniques may be incorporated.

RESPONSIBILITY REPORTING SYSTEMS

The **responsibility reporting system** provides information that is useful for management control decisions. As we observed in Figure 11-23, a responsibility reporting system (also called a responsibility accounting system) consists of a set of correlated reports. Each report focuses on a particular responsibility center within the firm. Reports for each managerial level summarize the results of lower levels. From an overall point of view, the reports feed accountability information upward through the managerial levels of the organization. Thus the entire set links together all managerial levels and all organizational units.

Each report for a responsibility center contains budgeted amounts, which represent performance standards. If the center is cost oriented, the amounts represent controllable costs. If the center is profit oriented, the amounts may include revenues and profits as well as costs. In either case, only the amounts that are controllable by the responsibility center are shown.

PROFITABILITY REPORTING SYSTEMS

A **profitability reporting system** provides reports that parallel a firm's organization structure and span all of its segments and activities. It emphasizes the planning for profits through segments such as product lines, classes of customers, and sales regions. Profitability reports show the impact of each segment on a firm's fixed costs and overall profits. Hence, they help managers to make decisions concerning the retention of a segment (e.g., product line), the pricing of products, the advertising needed for each product, and the allocation of sales resources to the respective sales regions and classes of customers.

Because profitability reports emphasize profit planning, they generally consist of budgeted values that have been recast from the traditional financial statement formats. However, they may also be used to supplement responsibility reports. As such, they would show variances of actual profits from planned profits, segregated for each segment that serves as a profit center (e.g., a sales region). Figure 15-5 shows a profitability report for a manufacturing firm. The segments illustrated by this report are the three products sold by the firm. In the total column the costs are

	Total	Products		
		1	2	3
Net sales	$1,575,000	$500,000	$850,000	$225,000
Variable costs				
Direct materials	$525,000	$172,000	$290,000	$63,000
Direct labor	360,000	100,000	215,000	45,000
Variable indirect manufacturing expenses[a]	83,000	26,000	45,000	12,000
Variable selling expenses[b]	79,500	25,000	42,500	12,000
Variable administrative expenses[c]	5,500	2,000	2,500	1,000
Total variable costs	$1,053,000	$325,000	$595,000	$133,000
Contribution margin	$522,000	$175,000	$255,000	$92,000
Fixed costs				
Committed costs assignable to products	$160,000	$55,000	$80,000	$25,000
Managed costs assignable to products	158,000	50,000	85,000	23,000
Total assigned fixed costs	$318,000	$105,000	$165,000	$48,000
Planned operating margin	$204,000	$70,000	$90,000	$44,000
Operating margin percentage		14.0%	10.6%	19.5%
Unallocated joint fixed costs	44,000			
Planned net income	$160,000			
Income taxes	83,200			
Planned net income after income taxes	$76,800			
Planned return on total assets[d]	5.1%			

[a]Schedule A details expenses (not shown).
[b]Schedule B details expenses (not shown).
[c]Schedule C details expenses (not shown).
[d]Expected average total assets = $1,500,000.

FIGURE 15-5   A report of planned profits by product for a manufacturing firm.

separated according to their variable and fixed natures. In turn, the fixed costs are separated into (1) those costs that are directly traceable to individual products (e.g., product advertising expense), and (2) those that are joint or common to all products (e.g., factory indirect labor expense). In accordance with sound managerial concepts, the joint fixed costs are not allocated to the products. Thus the "bottom lines" for the products are planned operating margins, computed by subtracting the variable costs and direct fixed costs for a product from its planned sales amount. Planned returns on invested capital can also be computed for each product if desired.

In contrast to the control orientation of cost accounting and responsibility reporting systems, a profitability reporting system is not designed with the control objective in mind. Although cost and profit variance reports may be prepared within the formats of profitability reports, the reports are useful primarily for tactical and strategic planning.

RELATIONSHIPS AMONG REPORTING SYSTEMS

The reporting systems just described are closely related, including the cost accounting systems described in Chapter 14. Each provides reports that are (1) expressed in financial terms, (2) geared to a firm's chart of accounts, and (3) used to aid managers in fulfilling planning and control responsibilities. The financial reporting system is the most comprehensive in that it provides reports for external as well as internal users and serves the greatest variety of purposes. In fact, the financial reporting system can be viewed as incorporating the other four financially oriented reporting systems within the framework of the accounting information system.

Consequently, budgetary reporting, responsibility reporting, profitability reporting, and cost accounting systems represent specialized reporting subsystems designed to aid managers in coping with decisions related to planning and control. The budgetary reporting system focuses on informing managers of the amounts they are permitted to spend during the period and on establishing the firm's activity levels against which actual performance is to be evaluated; hence it provides reports useful for short-term planning and management control. The responsibility reporting system focuses on costs and revenues incurred by responsibility centers; thus it provides reports useful for management control. The profitability reporting system focuses on the profitability of products and other segments; hence it provides reports useful primarily for tactical and strategic planning. The cost accounting system focuses on the cost of operations and provides reports useful for operational control.

IMPROVING THE REPORTING PROCESS

Financial reporting systems are indispensable to all types of organizations. In most firms, enterprisewide transaction processing systems collect and process mission-critical accounting and operational applications. Accounting information systems (AISs) generate financial statements and reports. Operational systems, which overlap with AISs, generate a variety of information and reports to perform day-to-day tasks and to run the business. Currently, as mentioned in Chapter 4, most of a firm's transactional data is maintained in **legacy systems.** They are not intended to generate decision-making information. Thus, they produce only aggregated end-results reports from multiple transactional data bases that cannot be directly accessed by end users.

To supplement legacy systems, firms can develop a data warehouse that operates within a LAN-based client/server platform.

DATA WAREHOUSE

A **data warehouse** is a data base that organizes and stores copies of "informational" or decision support data. Before developing a data warehouse, firms often reengineer their legacy systems' business processes.* This reengineering procedure may involve rewriting outdated legacy accounting software, thereby retaining the mainframe architecture. Or, firms may purchase off-the-shelf accounting software packages specifically written for the client/server platform. A LAN-based client/server architecture may be preferred because it is usually a less expensive alternative, and it permits end users flexible and real-time access to constantly updated transactional database files.

The data warehouse contains relational data-base tables of integrated data derived from legacy systems and nonrelational data obtained from other diverse

---

*Transaction processes are interconnected systems that enable firms to complete day-to-day routine tasks, such as paying bills, filling orders, posting cash receipts, handling customer complaints, distributing mail, and scheduling production.

SPOTLIGHTING

A LAN-BASED DATA WAREHOUSE APPLICATION
at Shell Western Exploration and Production, Inc.*

Shell Western Exploration and Production, Inc., needed a more flexible way of generating financial reports based on mainframe data. End users, including the firm's business managers and engineers, were frustrated with the time and effort required to generate reports using mainframe data-base management systems reporting tools.

This division of Shell Oil developed a local-area network-based application that eliminates mainframe programming, saves money, and drastically reduces the effort needed to change the numerous reports reviewed by management each month. The application updates what had been a cumbersome manual process. Under the old way of producing decision support information, legacy data was printed out in tables and rekeyed into Lotus 1-2-3 or Microsoft Excel spreadsheets to produce graphs, charts, and reports. Not only was this time-consuming, but it also was terribly inflexible. If end users wanted to see numbers displayed in a different format, analysts had to go through the whole process again. But the old inflexible system has been replaced with a new system that automatically extracts important information from main-

frame and minicomputer data bases each month. This data is downloaded to a data warehouse that resides on a LAN.

The new system enables Shell employees to access information about the firm's financial performance by pointing and clicking. They can print out preset graphics and reports of current data or construct their own queries and import data into their personal spreadsheet, data base, or graphics tool of choice. The legacy data for the new system is kept on a corporate mainframe. After the books are closed each month and the legacy files are updated, a series of data-base queries are triggered to extract critical financial and production data and store it in a relational file on the mainframe. The data remains in this file until an employee manually triggers the download process to the data warehouse.

The LAN-based data warehouse application has done more than simply facilitate chart making for meetings. It has significantly improved the reporting process by enabling end users to make quicker and better business decisions. For example, a manager can view a division's financial results on-line and check if production is increasing. He or she can also drill down into the data in finer levels of detail to determine the region and particular oil field responsible for the increased production.

*Alice La Plante, "Shell Oil Develops a LAN-Based Data Warehouse." Infoworld (August 30, 1993), p. 58.

---

sources, such as market research, credit reports, or newspaper articles. As opposed to legacy systems, which store data by applications, warehouse data is stored by subject areas (e.g., customers, products, and vendors).

Developing a Data Warehouse At least three levels of data warehouses can be constructed:

1. **Local.** A distributed data warehouse is designed for individual employees, such as for sales personnel assigned to the St. Louis branch office, containing detailed customer and product information.

2. **Segmentwide.** A distributed data warehouse is constructed for a major subset of the firm, such as for sales managers of the Midwest region, comprising detailed and summarized sales and marketing information.

3. **Enterprisewide.** A distributed enterprisewide data warehouse is a combination of local and segment warehouses that are joined together in a network.

A data warehouse is built with an existing microcomputer-based relational database management system (DBMS) software package.* Then this repackaged data, as well as data from other sources, is copied to one or more data-base servers (e.g., mainframes, minis, and/or microcomputers) that are interconnected to other computers within a LAN-based client/server setup. End users' desktop computers, called clients, can readily access this data.

Accessing the Data Warehouse   Since the stored data are frequently updated, the data warehouse contains "views" of recent informational data and archives of informational data for a designated past time period. Data may be stored in both summarized and detail or "raw" form. By using graphical user interface (GUI) and report generator tools, such as decision support and executive information software, end users can easily generate daily, weekly, and monthly *predefined* reports. Also, by using DBMS query language commands, information consumers can quickly produce a variety of customized, innovative *one-time* reports and analyses. Finally, the data warehouse informational reporting system can be designed to automatically transmit relevant reports and analyses to designated end users.

ROLES OF ACCOUNTANTS IN EXPANDED REPORTING SYSTEMS

Accountants should be involved in the design of data warehouses and the reengineering of legacy systems. Important ongoing value-added activities include the following:

1. Educating and training workers to understand and use the information received. Accountants can provide explanatory comments—either written or incorporated into voice chips—and unbiased second opinions, thus expanding the information provided by the reporting systems.

2. Conducting short courses covering basic accounting concepts, as well as meeting with end users to answer specific questions. Internal auditors should determine how the expanded reporting systems affect risks, and how these risks may modify the five components of the internal control structure (discussed in Chapter 7). Figure 15-6 shows the functions of internal auditing in traditionally organized firms, and the changes to these functions generated by emerging world-class organizations. Internal auditors should also verify the validity of the important financial and nonfinancial information provided to end users.

EMERGING WORLD-CLASS ORGANIZATIONS

A recent American Institute of Certified Public Accountants (AICPA) committee concluded that

> "to survive and compete, companies are changing everything—the way they are organized and managed, the way they do work and develop new products, the way they manage risks, and their relationships with other organizations. Winners in the marketplace are the companies that are focusing on the customer, stripping away low-value activity, decentralizing decision

---

*An emerging approach to constructing a data warehouse requires a firm to purchase special purpose data warehouse management software. The data warehouse management software, which also resides on a data-base server, automatically extracts and cleans up the legacy data and downloads it to the data warehouse. These data warehouse management packages also offer generic entity-relationship models and generate generic entity-relationship informational data-base files that reside in the data warehouse.

The Functions of Traditional Internal Auditing

▼ *Providing independent assurance that internal controls are functioning as intended.*

Internal auditors traditionally have been assigned the task of providing an independent evaluation of systems to assure that internal controls are functioning as designed. Due to an assumed inherent bias in other performance reports, the auditors have offered a more objective assessment of performance with particular focus on well-controlled systems.

▼ *Helping management improve control systems.*

Internal auditors have sold themselves as internal control experts. At the same time that they have audited adherence to existing controls, auditors have evaluated the adequacy of the control systems. Many internal auditors argue that the primary aim of the internal auditing function is to improve internal control.

There has been an assumption that without controls, systems are automatically biased to do bad things. Machines break down and go out of adjustment and people make mistakes, for example. Internal audits have provided the mechanism to counter these tendencies. Internal audits identify where controls break down or are absent, and then make appropriate recommendations to management. Virtually all audits have produced recommendations since almost all systems have had a tendency to break down and do bad things, at least to some extent.

▼ *Exposing internal irregularities.*

Defalcations and other forms of fraud and irregularities have been common to most organizations. While many reasons may be cited for this situation, all such occurrences would seem to have one thing in common. The person, or persons, perpetrating an irregularity considers his/her welfare separate enough from the organization's welfare, and of a higher priority, that he/she is

Changes Generated by World-Class Organizations

▼ *Internal controls aren't what they used to be.*

The senior management of many organizations now pay less attention to traditional internal control principles. The perception is that traditional internal controls focus on comparatively small matters. Even a $1 million defalcation is tiny compared to the loss of hundreds of millions of dollars in the marketplace due to poor product quality. In addition, better systems and more loyal and better trained employees have reduced the need for traditional internal controls.

For example, instead of separating related duties among employees, cross-functional employee teams now may be encouraged to accept entrepreneurial responsibility for entire classes of activities and transactions. Instead of required authorization from superiors for individual actions, employees now may be empowered to make many of their own decisions and take significant actions without specific authorization from anyone else.

▼ *Many systems can now operate largely error free.*

Just-in-time production systems, poka yoke devices, statistical process control, total preventive maintenance, extensive employee training, certification of suppliers, and other new management techniques have resulted in greatly improved operations. Where errors might occasionally occur, systems are now designed to self-correct immediately so that the errors do not produce defects.

In this environment, weak internal controls are not the problem they once might have been, and internal auditors are no longer the only experts on internal control. Besides, the focus now is on designing systems that do things right, not on imposing controls on faulty systems.

▼ *Motivation for internal irregularities is decreased.*

World-class management empowers employees with far more responsibility. Line employees are integral to problem-solving teams, and they are cross trained to perform a wide variety of functions.

Employees are rewarded, like management, for good performance. Facilities are better and cleaner, more pleasant places to work. It is easy for employees in such organizations to understand that whatever harms the organization harms them. There is greater cooperation between labor unions and management, and among different management teams.

The Functions of Traditional Internal Auditing (continued)

willing to do it. Internal audits have provided a means to expose such irregularities. The regular performance of audits is even considered a preventive device, due to the threat of exposure.

▼ *Helping to keep a relatively isolated senior management better informed about operations.*

The isolation of management occurs in three ways. First, a bureaucratic organization has many layers and highly specialized staff functions. Highly specialized staff proliferates. Therefore, it is easy for members of management to be organizationally isolated from line operations and customers.

Second, the layout of most facilities physically isolates management in offices and even buildings that may be some distance away from operations. The design of offices and meeting rooms also isolates management in walled cubicles protected behind legions of secretaries and other staff. What is more, managers have tended not to stray very far, or very often, from these regions.

Third, management has been considered somehow functionally separated from operations, which are to be planned, organized, directed, and monitored from afar. This functional separation can create a psychological isolation from operations and customers.

An independent internal audit function can provide a window to operations for management that otherwise is likely to be absent. Internal audit reports provide details unavailable in other performance reports, and internal audit reports tend to contain information about organizational weaknesses and problems that otherwise would probably not reach management.

Changes Generated by World-Class Organizations (continued)

Leaner operations, with less waste, also provide fewer opportunities for employee fraud and easier detection when it does occur. What's more, jobs in today's economy are precious. Each job now must make a direct contribution to organizational success or face elimination. Workers are less mobile in such an environment, and therefore, less inclined to risk their jobs.

For similar reasons, management employees in these enterprises also are likely to be less inclined to commit irregularities against their own organizations. A significant reduction in motivation for such irregularities further reduces the need for traditional internal auditing.

▼ *Management is now less isolated.*

The function of management has been redirected from planning, organizing, directing and monitoring to leading, empowering, assessing, and partnering. It is no longer management's job to be the "boss," but rather to facilitate the success of individual operations and employees. This requires direct contact with employees, operations, suppliers, and customers.

World-class managers now spend relatively little time in their offices. One new term to describe this style of management is "MBWA," or management by wandering around. Many managers have actually moved their desks out of offices to the shop floor. Even executive dining rooms have been eliminated. Physical and psychological isolation of management in these organizations is disappearing.

The many layers of bureaucracy have been reduced to only a few, perhaps five from the top executive to the lowest supervisor. Managers and other employees in separate functions have been combined into cross-functional teams, thereby helping to eliminate organizational isolation. Rather than depending on the "window" of internal auditing, management has knocked down the walls that created the need for a window in the first place.

One tenet of world-class management is to provide immediate and relevant information to decision makers, be they line workers or managers. Consequently, everyone is better informed about individual, team, divisional, and corporate performance. Also, the term "performance" now is more broadly defined to include nonfinancial as well as financial measures. Simply put, traditional internal auditing reports now constitute mostly old news.

FIGURE 15-6 How world-class management has affected traditional internal auditing. Source: Richard L. Ratliff and Stephen M. Beckstead, "How World Class Management is Changing Internal Auditing," *The Internal Auditor*, December 1994, pp. 40–41. Used with permission of the Institute of Internal Auditors.

making, reducing the time required to perform key activities, and forming new alliances with suppliers and customers—even competitors. . . . In response to changes, companies also are changing their information systems and the types of information they use to manage their business."

Massive changes are altering the way information is communicated throughout the organization, who receives information, the format and types of information communicated, and the nature and types of reporting systems. Such changes are predicted to rapidly accelerate in all industries due to increased competition and rapid advances in information technology. Thus, to effectively compete in today's marketplace, a large number of traditional, functionally organized firms of all sizes are striving to change the way they bring products to market or provide services. Changes such as flattening organization structures by eliminating layers of managers and workers, reengineering legacy systems and developing data warehouses, and empowering self-managed work teams are made in an effort to achieve so-called **world-class status.** A major goal of such status is to develop quality products and services having defects and customer complaints approaching zero, respectively.

Managers and key employees working in world-class organizations need rapid access to both financial and nonfinancial information. The latter type of information is especially critical, chiefly operational and customer information. A data warehouse can significantly improve the decision-making process in world-class organizations by enhancing the types of information that end users receive. Instantly accessible, comprehensive information stored in the data warehouse can be shared with colleagues anywhere in the firm, thus facilitating collaborative decision making and empowering employees. The quality of customer service, a critical success factor in a world-class organization, is improved by providing real-time access to critical information.

A data warehouse also alters the traditional reporting process of decision makers by reducing the time necessary to generate and distribute financial and nonfinancial reports and analyses. Many reports can be distributed directly to users over the LAN-based client/server setup via E-mail attachments. This direct distribution eliminates mounds of paper documents and increases efficiency since accessing and manipulating information is made easier.

CHANGES AFFECTING THE ORGANIZATION

Although hierarchical organizational structures will not disappear, many are being modified or replaced with flattened structures, such as networked structures, which are a caveat for success in the information age. A flattened organization structure reduces the number of layers of managers between line workers and customers, modifies the role of managers, and gives line workers more authority to make decisions. Line workers are being empowered to take, with minimal supervision, all necessary actions to perform and supervise their own tasks. These actions include setting goals, allocating resources, interacting with customers, and building quality control into the processes. As a result, most of the financial and nonfinancial information that formerly went to supervisors now may be routed to the workers themselves.[†] Substantially autonomous work teams decide on the actions to be taken to improve results and therefore are held accountable for the results achieved. These self-managed teams of **empowered workers,** often accomplishing tasks in teams con-

---

*Adapted from *Client/Server Implementation*, by the AICPA Special Committee on Financial Reporting, p. 4.
[†]Gerald M. Hoffman, *The Technology Payoff* (Burr Ridge, Ill.: Irwin Professional Publishing, 1994), p. 117.

SPOTLIGHTING

EMPOWERED WORK TEAMS
at Duffy Tool and Stamping Company*

How does a firm increase efficiency and quality, cut costs, increase profits, and become more responsive to customer needs? Line employees often hold the answer to these key questions. That is why many firms are empowering line personnel to meet the challenges of a more demanding workplace.

Duffy Tool and Stamping Company empowered work teams to make a variety of decisions. One problem tackled by a particular work team improved operational efficiency. On two presses in one department, completed parts come down a chute and fall into a parts tub. Press operators had to stop production whenever a stock person removed a full tub and replaced it with an empty one. The work team solved the problem by fabricating dual chutes that allowed two tubs to be in place at the same time. Now as parts come off the press, they are routed into a tub using one branch of the chute. When that tub becomes full, the parts are sent into the empty tub using the second branch of the chute, allowing the full tub to be replaced with no machine downtime. Another team's project was purchasing a mechanical manipulator for handling heavy die inserts for a large press. Prior to the acquisition of the "robot," the inserts were placed manually—a difficult process. By reducing changeover downtime, the mechanical manipula-

tor has increased efficiency and job safety and comfort.

The benefits of Duffy Tool's work team program are not only financial in nature. Employees provide actual input into their day-to-day activities and maintain a degree of control over their work environment, thus improving morale. Managers have seen that given the opportunity, line employees can and will do their best to make the firm more competitive. At the same time, production workers know that management has given them the power to influence their daily workplace and improve the firm's effectiveness. This process results in mutual trust.

Because empowered work teams are simply applying a problem-solving methodology, it should apply to any size or type of firm. Employee empowerment presents the problem of developing a strategy for effectively evoking employees' inputs and channeling them into action. Without careful planning, the move to a more participative workplace could result in chaos. The chances for success, however, probably are best in firms that have a reasonable relationship between management and line employees. Perhaps the most critical factor for successful implementation is top-management support. If the program is initiated and endorsed strongly by top management, the prospects for success are great and the rewards, financial and non-financial, are likely to be far reaching.

*George F. Hanks, "Excellence Teams in Action." *Management Accounting* (February 1995), pp. 33–36.

sisting often or so workers, are able to develop multiple competencies and can significantly increase productivity. As reported, such teams typically deliver a 40 percent increase in output per worker hour.* Organizations utilizing self-managed work teams are often able to dismantle unneeded supervisory layers of management and communicate information directly to the team members, frequently bypassing the formal reporting systems.

ROLES OF MANAGERS

As firms flatten organization structures, the roles of managers change. Top managers become the leaders and visionaries responsible for developing the firm's overall

*"The Search for the Organization of Tomorrow," *Fortune* (May 18, 1992), p. 93.

strategies and objectives. Middle-level managers assume the roles of motivators, teachers, and coaches. Since work teams are responsible for making many of their own decisions, supervision by middle-level managers is kept to a minimum. Middle managers also determine strategies for their responsibility centers and for acquiring resources to allocate to the work teams. Finally, the roles of supervisory managers are primarily that of teacher and coach or facilitator. The teams themselves are responsible for measuring and evaluating each team member's efficiency and productivity levels, and for initiating any necessary corrective actions required to improve an individual's unsatisfactory performance.

Information technology (IT) is the "driver" that enables firms to build "information highways" of specialized interconnected information systems that improve the financial reporting process. Components of IT, including groupware, model-based software, and data communication networks, are discussed in Chapters 16 and 17.

SUMMARY

The managerial decision-making process consists of six steps that should result in the preferred alternative being selected, carried out, and followed up. Decisions may be classified as structured, semistructured, or unstructured. Alternatively, they may be classified in accordance with the management activities of strategic planning, tactical planning, management control, and operational control.

Information consumers (e.g., managers, key workers, and work teams) in a firm need information to aid in making a variety of decisions. In determining information needs, an information analyst attempts to maximize the value of information communicated to every information consumer in the firm. Information needs vary significantly along such dimensions as managerial activities, managerial levels, organizational structures, job responsibilities, and operational functions. By analyzing information needs along these dimensions, an accountant or systems analyst gathers clues concerning the information needs of individual information consumers. Specific information needs include financial and nonfinancial information. The latter category encompasses operational, customer, stakeholder, general firm, and external information. Managers also frequently rely on informal information sources, such as colleagues, employees, and professional acquaintances, to make important decisions.

Managerial reporting systems, which are supported by the management information system and the accounting information system, can provide a variety of information for planning and control and for meeting a firm's other responsibilities. Well-established managerial reporting systems include budgetary reporting systems, responsibility reporting systems, and profitability reporting systems. These reporting systems, which are closely related, are all designed to help various end users make more effective planning and control decisions.

To achieve an advantage in a highly competitive global marketplace, organizations' legacy reporting systems must be expanded to give key employees access to information that previously was made available only to management. This can be accomplished by developing a data warehouse that usually operates within a LAN-based client/server environment. A data warehouse separates mainframe legacy transaction processing data from decision support data. End users can navigate easily through the data with their flexible desktop analysis and reporting tools. Development of a data warehouse often results in the modification of the way tasks are completed, a flatter organization structure, and the disbursement of decision-making responsibilities throughout organizations. Such changes frequently result in the expansion of roles of key employees.

The roles of managers of many progressive organizations are changing to allow empowered workers to accomplish their work tasks with minimum supervision. Instead of commanding, managers assume the roles of visionaries, facilitators, coaches, and teachers.

Information technology enables firms to implement networks and specialized information systems. With these technologies in place, managers and members of work teams can use groupware and model-based software to support their decision-making activities.

REVIEW PROBLEMS WITH SOLUTIONS

Hippo Co.

Statement

Hippo Co. is a large department store in downtown Denver. Ms. Carlene Franks, the treasurer, receives a phone call from the president, who says, "We have a problem. Our fleet of delivery trucks is no longer adequate because of our continued growth in sales and the flight of many of our customers to outlying suburbs. Roger, our marketing manager, feels we should take prompt action. We've discussed the possibility of acquiring new trucks. I'd like for you to look into the problem, including the financing aspects."

Ms. Franks begins the definition of the problem by reviewing relevant objectives. The Hippo Co. stresses customer service. Part of this service consists of prompt customer deliveries. Another objective emphasizes economy in all activities, including the delivery of customer packages and the financing of capital acquisitions. She concludes, therefore, that the decision should (1) minimize total delivery costs while (2) ensuring prompt deliveries. These two measures represent the overall criteria by which the decision choice will be judged. (Note that she does *not* narrowly state the criteria to be the acquisition of funds promptly and at the lowest interest rate. Therefore, she widens the range of possible actions beyond the acquisition of new delivery trucks.)

Next Ms. Franks considers constraints, assumptions, and the planning horizon. The first constraint pertains to the decision deadline, which, because the matter is urgent, she sets at one week. Next she eliminates the possible solution of issuing common stock. Firm policy forbids this method of financing, since Hippo Co. is family owned. Then she ascertains that available garage space is limited to only one dozen more trucks. Any additional trucks would have to sit unprotected or would require additional garage space. Her assumptions are that sales will grow at the same rate as in recent years and that interest rates will remain at about the same level for the foreseeable future. Finally, she specifies the planning horizon to be three years, the estimated life of delivery trucks.

As the final aspect of problem definition, she gathers relevant data (with the aid of the accounting department). The gathered facts include the acquisition cost of each truck, the terms of sale, the operating costs of similar trucks, the availability of drivers in the labor market, the current financial status of the store, the current interest rate, the rates charged by commercial delivery services in the area, and so on.

Ms. Franks next lists the following courses of action:

a. To purchase trucks by borrowing funds from the local bank on a long-term note.

b. To lease trucks and pay out of current revenues.

c. To contract with a commercial delivery service.

She also considers briefly the alternative of factoring accounts receivable, but discards it as involving too high a cost for funds.

She then determines that a decision model can be developed in explicit terms, since most of the factors are quantitative in nature. Therefore, Ms. Franks sets to work and has a completed model in a matter of hours. Her model relates the financing costs, the initial and oper-

ating costs pertaining to the trucks, the costs of added garage rental, and other relevant costs. Although none of the alternatives will incur all of these costs, the model is sufficiently general to apply to all. That is, it enables all of the alternatives to be compared on the basis of the first criterion—minimized total delivery costs (expressed at present values).

Furthermore, it enables the second criterion, prompt delivery service, to be incorporated in the decision model via the values of key factors. That is, the operating costs of acquired trucks in the first and second alternatives and the contract price for a commercial delivery service in the third alternative can be computed under the assumption that one-day delivery service is provided.

Thus, Ms. Franks uses the newly developed decision model to determine the total delivery costs, at present values, for the four alternatives. She finds that contracting with a commercial delivery service involves the least cost over the three-year planning horizon. The purchase of trucks involves the next lowest cost. She then meets with the president and marketing manager, since all three managers must agree on the final decision choice. After considerable discussion, in which nonquantitative factors are added to the quantitative results, they reach this decision: The commercial delivery service alternative should be rejected and the alternative involving the purchase of trucks should be selected.

Their reasoning in reaching this decision is as follows. In spite of incurring the lowest cost and providing a contractual guarantee of prompt service, the commercial delivery service alternative is not suitable. Its acceptance would conflict with objectives relating to the store's public image and control over its activities. On the other hand, purchasing and using its own labeled trucks enhances both these objectives while incurring only relatively small added costs. By means of this latter alternative, the store preserves its image as a personalized messenger service as well as a merchandiser of goods. It also retains control over the truck drivers, so that instances of discourtesy and unreliability can be corrected easily.

With the concurrence of the president, Ms. Franks prepares a schedule of all required activities. For instance, the first activity she lists is to notify all managers and employees of the decision, the next step is to contact the bank officials, and so on. Beside each activity she notes the expected completion date. As each activity is executed, she inserts the actual date of completion.

After the delivery trucks are acquired, the appropriate managers receive periodic reports. Ms. Franks receives reports concerning loan repayments. The marketing manager receives reports indicating the level of operating costs and the number of complaints about delivery service. If the actual level of operating costs rises significantly above predicted costs, the marketing manager will investigate and take necessary cost-reduction steps.

Required

Identify the several steps of the decision process that are illustrated in this problem situation.

Solution

Step	Paragraph
1. Problem recognition and definition.	1, 2, 3, 4
2. Determination of alternative courses of action.	5
3. Evaluation of alternatives.	6, 7, 8
4. Selection of best alternative.	8, 9
5. Implementation of decision choice.	10
6. Follow-up of decision results.	11

TOLLIVER ELECTRONICS, INC.

Statement

George Morrill is the purchasing manager for Tolliver Electronics, Inc., an Amherst, Massachusetts, manufacturer of high-quality electronics products. Before becoming purchasing manager, he was an electronics technician and quality control supervisor.

Among decisions made by George are the following:

a. Selecting the suppliers from whom to buy parts and subassemblies (tactical planning decisions).

b. Establishing purchasing policies (strategic planning decisions, to be made together with higher-level managers within the firm).

c. Hiring and evaluating supervisors, buyers, and other purchasing department personnel (management control decisions).

d. Negotiating purchase contracts (tactical planning decisions).

Required

a. Describe briefly how George would determine his information needs.

b. For one of the foregoing decisions, list needed items of information and required properties.

c. Note any other information that should be provided to George.

d. Describe a key report that George should receive.

Solution

a. Together with one of the firm's accountants or systems analysts, George would first list the decisions that he makes. Then they would develop information specifications for each decision, add other information needs, and design suitable reports to provide the information.

b. With respect to the selection of suppliers, George needs such information concerning each potential supplier as the expected unit prices of the parts or subassemblies, the expected lead times (time periods between the order dates and receipt dates), the quality of the parts or subassemblies, and the current availability of the parts or subassemblies. He needs this information in a summarized form at least weekly. Although some of the items, such as unit prices and availability, are subject to change, they should be as reliable as possible and thus based on up-to-date facts. The quality of parts or subassemblies should be expressed quantitatively if possible; perhaps an index rating based on a top score of 10 could be used.

c. Because of George's technical background, he also might desire key technical information concerning critical subassemblies. For instance, he may want to know the allowable tolerances between the various parts within such subassemblies, as reflected in the manufacturer's specifications. If he has this kind of information for the subassemblies available for each potential supplier, he may feel that he has a better basis for comparing quality.

To help spot upcoming supplier problems, George should receive information that shows trends in (1) the unit prices charged by each supplier for critical subassemblies and (2) the expected lead time for each supplier.

d. One key report George might receive would be a weekly report that summarizes on a single page the important factors pertaining to each potential supplier of critical subassemblies. In addition to showing the up-to-date status of unit prices, lead time, quality, and availability, the report should reflect percentage changes in unit prices and lead times.

KEY TERMS

accuracy (685)
budgetary reporting system (693)
clarity (685)
cognitive style (686)
conciseness (685)
consistency (685)
customer information (688)
data warehouse (696)
decision model (683)
decision process (682)
empowered workers (700)
external information (689)
financial information (688)
financial reporting system (692)
general firm information (688)

REVIEW QUESTIONS

15-1.   Describe the several steps in the decision process.

15-2.   Distinguish between an optimal decision and a satisfactory decision.

15-3.   Contrast the several types of decisions.

15-4.   Provide examples of structured accounting decisions and unstructured accounting decisions.

15-5.   Contrast the characteristics of management control and operational control.

15-6.   Identify several problems requiring control decisions and classify each as either management control or operational control.

15-7.   How do information needs vary among managerial levels?

15-8.   How do information needs vary among types of decisions?

15-9.   Describe a suitable approach for developing the information needs of the managers within a firm.

15-10.   What are the five types of information that information consumers need to make a variety of decisions?

15-11.   How does operational information differ from customer information?

15-12.   What is informal information? How is it related to formal information generated by financial reporting systems?

15-13.   Why might two departmental managers who have identical responsibilities receive different sets of information?

15-14.   What are several differences between financial reports intended for external users and those intended for internal users?

15-15.   Describe several important reporting attributes.

15-16.   List the steps in the budgetary process of a firm.

15-17.   Describe the types of reports provided by a typical budgetary reporting system.

15-18.   Contrast the purposes of a responsibility reporting system and a profitability reporting system.

15-19.   Describe the types of reports provided by a profitability reporting system.

15-20.   In what ways are managers likely to react to information overload?

15-21.   What are the relationships among the financial reporting systems described in the chapter?

15-22.   What are production or legacy data bases? What are the limitations of these data bases?

15-23.   List the two options for expanding the financial reporting process.

15-24.   What is a data warehouse? How is it related to legacy systems? How can the creation of a data warehouse improve the financial reporting process?

15-25.   What are the options for creating a data warehouse? Once the data warehouse is developed, how is it accessed by end users?

15-26.   What are the main advantages of reengineering mainframe legacy transaction processing systems to a client/server platform?

15-27.   How would you define a world-class organization?

15-28.   What are the responsibilities of self-directed work teams?

15-29.   How do the roles of managers change in world-class organizations?

15-30.   "Information technology is the driver that enables firms to achieve world-class status." Do you agree or disagree with this statement?

DISCUSSION QUESTIONS

15-31.   What are suitable roles of accountants in managerial decision making?

15-32.   Discuss the extent to which a formal information system can be expected to provide information for making the typical strategic planning decision and for making the typical operational control decision.

15-33. How do the information needs of external users differ from the needs of managers?

15-34. What are the possible drawbacks of providing too much information to a manager? Too little information?

15-35. Managerial accountants generally are responsible for designing responsibility and profitability reporting systems. However, the technical accounting aspects underlying such reporting systems are only a part of the broader fabric, which includes organizational relationships, behavioral patterns, and corporate philosophies. Discuss the implications of these factors on the design approaches to be taken by accountants.

15-36. Do you think that client/server accounting software packages are more effective in developing financial reporting systems than traditional mainframe accounting software packages?

15-37. "Reengineering legacy systems opens up all of the data bases across an enterprise—from general ledger to production to decision support—providing new levels of analysis and reporting capabilities." Comment on this statement.

15-38. What are suitable roles of accountants in improving the financial reporting process?

15-39. Changes made by organizations attempting to achieve world-class status include eliminating layers of middle managers. Assuming that these managers are not replaced, how will their former job responsibilities be performed?

15-40. Infoage, Inc., is a relatively small information services firm. Its organization chart reveals that it is traditionally organized by functions. George Freeman, the president, has attended a seminar on world-class organizations. He wishes to bring about changes in his firm to become more competitive and responsive to customer needs. He has called you in as a consultant to recommend how the firm should accomplish its objectives. How would you proceed to carry out this assignment?

15-41. Assume that George Freeman forms self-directed work teams at his two retail outlet stores. What should be the duties of those empowered work teams? How should Diane Varney, the treasurer and controller, modify the financial reporting systems to meet the information needs of the work teams? Is the empowerment of these workers likely to have any effect on the firm's other managers and workers?

15-42. What types of nonfinancial information would be important to Ann Strong's consulting firm? Would her current financial reporting systems be able to generate these necessary measures? What modifications, if any, to the reporting systems would be in order to generate such information?

15-43. Assuming that Infoage decides to become more market driven and customer focused, why is it likely to modify its organization structure to be similar to the structure of a professional service organization?

15-44. Ann Strong's consulting firm is very small, employing only three persons. Five other small consulting firms operate within a 25-mile radius, as do three large regional public accounting firms. Suggest changes Ann can make within her firm to effectively compete with the eight firms and possibly become the largest firm in the region.

PROBLEMS

15-1. Name two or more alternative courses of action that should be considered during the decision process pertaining to each of the following problems:

a. How to establish a public accounting firm's billing policies.

b. How to expand plant capacity.

c. How to promote a CPA firm's products (services).

d. How to reduce costs in production operations.

e. How to generate a firm's growth.

15-2. Describe the steps in the decision process pertaining to each of the following problem situations:

a. Whether a local CPA firm should acquire the practice of another public accounting firm located in the same city.

b. Whether to open a second fast-food restaurant in a city of 75,000 residents.

c. Whether a national fast-food chain should discontinue a sandwich that mainly appeals to older, health conscious persons.

d. Whether a small firm should replace an accounting software package that it has used for the last 12 years.

e. Whether to replace a van that is part of a university's motor pool.

15-3. Use the following information to answer questions 1 through 8 on the next page.

A firm manufactures several lines of athletic footwear for many competitive sports including football, baseball, basketball, and tennis. Over the past three years, sales and market share have been declining for all major product lines. The president of the firm is deeply concerned and believes that improved planning and control could reverse this trend. The president has called in a management consulting firm. Statements numbered 1 through 8 below describe characteristics of different types of planning performed by different levels of management. Select the appropriate word or phrase from the following list to match each statement. Use each word or phrase only once.

Words and phrases

a. Operational planning.
b. Six months to two years.
c. Organizational mission.
d. Objectives.
e. One to ten years.
f. One week to one year.
g. Intermediate (tactical) planning.
h. Strategic planning.

1. Planning horizon for operational planning.
2. Planning horizon for intermediate planning.
3. A clear, formally written, published statement that is the cornerstone of any planning system.
4. Planning horizon for strategic planning.
5. The process of determining how to pursue the organization's long-term goals with resources expected to be available.
6. The process of determining how specific tasks can best be accomplished on time with available resources.
7. Specific commitments to achieve a measurable result within a given time frame.
8. The process of determining the contributions subunits can make with allocated resources.

(CIA adapted)

15-4. Arment Co. has sales in the range of $25 million to $30 million, has one manufacturing plant, and employs 700 people, including 15 national account salespersons and 80 traveling sales representatives. The home office and plant are in Philadelphia, and the product is distributed east of the Mississippi River. The product is a line of pumps and related fittings used at construction sites, in homes, and in processing plants. The firm has total assets equal to 80 percent of sales. Its capitalization consists of: current liabilities, 30 percent; long-term debt, 15 percent; shareholders' equity, 55 percent. In the last two years sales have increased 7 percent annually, and income after taxes has amounted to 5 percent of sales.

Required

List the strategic decisions that must be made or confirmed during the preparation of the annual profit plan or budget.

15-5. Determine whether each of the following decisions is structured, semistructured, or unstructured, and the managerial level most likely to make the decision—top, middle, or operational.

a. Preparing an adjusting journal entry to record the yearly depreciation expense.
b. The hiring of a new staff accountant. The new employee is a recent college graduate.
c. Determining the number of branch CPA offices to open for business during the next two years.
d. Evaluating the performance of the accounting department.
e. Evaluating the performance of the accounts receivable accountant.
f. Authorizing the construction of a seven-story office building to house a public accounting firm's partners, staff accountants, and nonprofessional staff.
g. Selecting the location of the office building in **f** above.
h. Selecting a vendor to provide office supplies to a Big-Six public accounting firm.
i. Controlling the costs of the data processing department.
j. Promoting a senior accountant working for a regional public accounting firm to manager.
k. Assigning a salesperson to the Mid-Atlantic region.
l. Determining the amount of the advertising budget for the next 10 years.
m. Determining the advertising media to employ to promote the firm's products for the coming year.
n. Selecting a repair service to fix the accounts payable accountant's microcomputer's hard disk drive.
o. Exploring the possibility of a large CPA firm merging with a regional CPA firm.
p. Determining the best source of financing to purchase the regional CPA firm mentioned in **o** above.

15-6. Determine whether each of the following decisions is structured, semistructured, or unstructured, and the managerial level most likely to make the decision—top, middle, or operational.

a. Determining the quantities of raw materials to purchase during the coming year.
b. Determining whether to add a new product to an existing product line.
c. Assuming that the new product in **b** above is introduced, determining if additional employees must be hired and another shift added.
d. Billing a customer for merchandise ordered.
e. Determining what additional manufacturing facilities to purchase.
f. Determining where to establish a new sales branch.

g. Determining whether to hire new staff accountants for a large public accounting firm.

h. Determining the amount of finished goods to produce during the coming month.

i. Determining which operational audits to conduct.

j. Determining the amount of product A to manufacture.

k. Determining the pay rate for a recently hired CPA. The CPA has seven years of experience with a Big-Six public accounting firm.

l. Determining whom to hire as the new controller.

m. Scheduling machines to produce special orders received from customers.

n. Approving a customer's credit application.

o. Setting the prices on products.

p. Issuing common stock to finance the purchase of a firm as a 100 percent wholly owned subsidiary.

15-7. The nurse-manager of the orthopedic ward of Barnes General Hospital of Memphis, Tennessee, is preparing a list of the most pressing problems to be faced in the coming week. The ward is open 24 hours a day, every day of the year, and employs 40 full-time nurses. The management team consists of the nurse-manager plus three shift-charge nurses. Vacations and sick leave are covered with part-time replacements.

The following is a list of tasks or problems facing the nurse-manager:

a. Decide what to do about a nurse on the 3–11 P.M. shift whose performance has declined in the past two weeks for no apparent reason.

b. Prepare salary increase recommendations for each of the shift-charge nurses.

c. Decide which computer to get for the nurse-manager's office. (A PC has been approved; central data processing has supplied a list ot those available.)

d. Set up a personnel schedule for next month (account for vacations and shift rotations).

e. Do something to improve the appearance of the ward. Patients are complaining it looks depressing.

Required

a. Discuss whether the nurse-manager is a top, middle, or lower-level manager.

b. Questions 1 through 6 concern decision-making theory. For each question, mark the letter of the item on the nurse-manager's list that *best* matches the description given.

1. An unstructured decision.

2. A structured decision under relative certainty.

3. An item best suited for a decision maker with an intuitive information processing style as opposed to one with an analytical style.

4. An item in the problem definition stage.

5. An item in the definition of alternatives stage.

6. An item in the evaluation of alternatives stage.

c. Questions 7 through 12 relate to the application of decision-making theory. For each question, mark the letter of the item on the nurse-manager's list that *best* matches the description given.

7. A decision where creativity is important.

8. A decision where acceptance by employees is important.

9. A decision that would be influenced most by input from the environment.

10. A decision the nurse-manager should delegate to the appropriate shift-charge nurse.

11. A decision the nurse-manager should not delegate.

12. A decision where brainstorming would be helpful.

d. Select one of the tasks or problems on the nurse-manager's list and discuss the type of information needed to make the decision.

e. What types of formal and informal information systems would satisfy the information needs of the nurse-manager?

(CIA *adapted*)

15-8. Contrast the qualities of information needed to make the following pairs of decisions:

a. A decision to locate a new warehouse versus a decision concerning which machine to assign a production employee tomorrow.

b. A decision concerning the possible elimination of a product line versus a decision concerning the possible promotion or reprimand of a department manager who has cost responsibilities.

15-9. What management level or levels—top, middle, or operational—can most effectively utilize the following reports or information to make decisions?

a. Information about long-term trends.

b. Mainly quantitative information, financial as well as nonfinancial.

c. Very detailed information.

d. Scheduled reports.

e. Management control information.

f. Gossip.

g. Largely external information.

h. More timely information.

i. Highly summarized information.

j. Real-time information.

k. Graphical reports.

l. Short-range historical quantitative information.

m. Exception reports.

n. Strategic planning information.

o. Short-range quantitative task-oriented control information.

p. Information to evaluate alternatives.

q. Very accurate information.

r. Broad information, often spanning several functions.

15-10. Assume the following categories of employees:

- Top management
- Middle management
- Operational management
- Line workers
- Self-managed work teams

Assume that the following specific types of information are generated and communicated to relevant employees:

1. Worker productivity rates.
2. Customer sales by region.
3. Production cost variances.
4. Earnings per share of common stock.
5. Key financial ratios.
6. Product defect rates.
7. On-schedule performance.
8. Percentage of products delivered on time.
9. Report of major shareholders.
10. Market value of the firm.
11. Customer complaints compared to a prior period.
12. Employee turnover.
13. Financial statements.
14. Responsibility accounting report on plant A.
15. Pending legislation.
16. Major competitors' plans.
17. Benchmarks on major competitors and noncompetitors.
18. Profit planning report.
19. Sales and operating profits by segments.
20. Narrative explaining the changes in the financial data.
21. General economic conditions.
22. Customer satisfaction levels.

Required

a. Which category or categories of the above employees can most effectively utilize each of the specific types of information to make decisions?

b. How frequently do you feel that each specific type of information should be prepared and communicated (e.g., hourly, daily, weekly, etc.) to the relevant employee(s)?

c. Recommend the best way to communicate each of the specific types of information. For example, information can be communicated in a formal report, informally, E-mailed over a network, etc.

15-11. For the following managers of a typical firm, describe (1) decisions for which each is primarily responsible, (2) suitable performance measures by which each decision may be evaluated, and (3) information needed by each to make decisions and to carry out assigned responsibilities:

a. President.
b. Controller.
c. Production manager.
d. Sales manager.
e. Personnel manager.
f. Treasurer.
g. Materials manager.
h. Advertising manager.
i. Credit manager.
j. Production supervisor.

15-12. Adler Harris has been treasurer of Varker College for two years. As treasurer, Harris manages the interrelationships between faculty, staff, and the board of directors, and also manages the college's finances. Harris has been notably effective in managing these relationships, and accordingly, was recently elected to the position of secretary to the board and informally designated as the board's liaison with faculty and staff.

Harris started a new practice of issuing a memorandum following each quarterly board meeting. The memorandum on the next page was issued following the most recent meeting of the board.

Required

a. (1) Referring to the memorandum issued by Adler Harris, identify and explain at least three characteristics of formal communication.

(2) Describe three other types of formal communication.

b. Review the memorandum that was issued by Adler Harris, and identify

(1) at least three positive aspects of the memorandum as a communication device.

(2) at least three weaknesses of the memorandum as a communication device, and provide a brief explanation why each item identified is a weakness.

To: Faculty and Staff
From: Adler Harris
Date: October 25, 1997
Subject: Board of Directors' Meeting

Listed below are some of the major actions taken during the October 1997 Varker College (VC) board of directors' meeting that was held this past week. These reported items are selected because they seem to be of general interest to the faculty and staff. This is not a total listing of all of the actions taken by the board nor do they represent a summary of the official minutes.

- Two long-time friends and avid VC supporters were elected to membership on the board. They are Dr. Kenneth Bussman, Professor of Applied Sciences at Eastern Technical University, and Ms. Anna York, chief executive officer of EMK Enterprises.
- A salary pool providing for a modest increase in faculty and staff salaries was set aside from the reserve fund.
- The tuition and fee charges for the 1998-99 academic year were set.
- Reports were received from each of the standing committees of the board as well as from the Alumni Association and the VC Guild.
- The financial report for the quarter ended September 30, 1997, was reviewed and a tentative budget for the 1998-99 academic year was approved.
- A report from Vice-President Marge Lemons, Academic and Administrative Computing Department, was received and acted upon.
- Ms. Susan Chester and Mr. Noel Dunes were installed as new members of the board while Mr. Garnett Dixon and Mr. Henry Foster were designated as honorary members of the board.
- The next meeting of the board is scheduled for January 25, 1998. This meeting will take place on the VC campus.

15-13. Wright Company of Princeton, New Jersey, employs a computer-based data processing system for maintaining all firm records. The present system was developed in stages over the past five years and has been fully operational for the last 24 months.

When the system was being designed, all department heads were asked to specify the types of information and reports they would need for planning and controlling operations. The systems department attempted to meet the specifications of each department head. Management specified that certain other reports be prepared for department heads. During the five years of systems development and operation, there have been several changes in the department head positions because of attrition and promotions. The new department heads often made requests for additional reports according to their specifications. The systems department complied with all of these requests. A report was discontinued only on request by a department head, and then only if it was not a standard report required by top management. As a result, few reports were in fact discontinued. Consequently, the data processing system was generating a large quantity of reports each reporting period.

The firm's management became concerned about the quantity of information that was being produced by the system. The internal audit department was asked to evaluate the effectiveness of the reports generated by the system. The audit staff determined early in the study that more information was being generated by the data processing system than could be used effectively. They noted the following reactions to this information overload:

a. Many department heads would not act on certain reports during periods of peak activity. The department head would let these reports accumulate, with the hope of catching up during a subsequent lull.

b. Some department heads had so many reports that they did not act at all on the information or they made incorrect decisions because of misuse of the information.

c. Frequently, action required by the nature of the report data was not taken until the department head was reminded by someone who needed the decision. These department heads did not appear to have developed a priority system for acting on the information produced by the data processing system.

d. Department heads often would develop the information they needed from alternative independent sources, rather than utilizing the reports generated by the data processing system. This was often easier than trying to search among the reports for the needed data.

Required

a. Indicate, for each of the observed reactions, whether they are functional or dysfunctional behavioral responses. Explain your answer in each case.

b. Assuming one or more of the foregoing were dysfunctional, recommend procedures the firm could employ to eliminate the dysfunctional behavior and to prevent its recurrence.

(CMA *adapted*)

15-14. WoodCrafts Inc. is a manufacturer of furniture for specialty shops throughout the Northeast and has an annual sales volume of $12 million. The firm has four major product lines—bookcases, magazine racks, end tables, and bar stools—each of which is managed by a production manager. Since production is spread fairly evenly over the 12 months of operation, Sara McKinley, controller, has prepared an annual budget that is divided into 12 reporting periods for monthly reporting purposes.

WoodCrafts uses a standard cost system and applies variable factory overhead on the basis of machine hours. Fixed production cost is allocated on the basis of square footage occupied using a predetermined plant-wide rate; the size of the space occupied varies considerably among product lines. All other costs are assigned on the basis of revenue dollars earned. At the monthly meeting to review November performance, Ken Ashley, manager of the bookcase line, received the report shown below.

While distributing the monthly reports at the meeting, McKinley remarked to Ashley, "We need to talk about getting your division back on track. Be sure to see me after the meeting."

Ashley had been so convinced that his division did well in November that McKinley's remark was a real surprise. He spent the balance of the meeting avoiding the looks of his fellow managers and trying to figure out what could have gone wrong; the monthly performance report was no help.

Required

a. (1) Identify at least three weaknesses in Wood-Crafts Inc.'s monthly Bookcase Production Performance Report.

(2) Discuss the behavioral implications of Sara McKinley's remarks to Ken Ashley during the meeting.

b. WoodCrafts Inc. could do a better job of reporting monthly performance to the production managers.

(1) Recommend how the report could be improved to eliminate weaknesses, and *revise it accordingly*.

(2) Discuss how the recommended changes in reporting are likely to affect Ken Ashley's behavior.

(CMA *adapted*)

15-15. Dartmoor Inc.'s main business is the publication of books and magazines. Alan Shane is the production manager of the Bridgton Plant, which manufactures the paper used in all of Dartmoor's publications. The Bridgton Plant has no sales staff and limited contact with outside customers, as most of its sales are to other divisions of Dartmoor. As a consequence, the Bridgton Plant is treated as a cost center for reporting and evaluation purposes rather than as a revenue or profit center.

Shane perceives the accounting reports that he receives to be the result of a historical number-generating process that provides little information that is useful in performing his job. Consequently, the entire accounting process is perceived as a negative motivational device that does not reflect how hard or effectively he works as a production manager. In discussions with Susan Brady, controller of the Bridgton Plant, Shane said, "I think the cost reports are misleading. I know I've had better production over a number of operating periods, but the cost

WoodCrafts Inc.
Bookcase Production Performance Report
For the Month Ended November 30, 1997

	Actual	Budget	Variance
Units	3,000	2,500	500F
Revenue	$161,000	$137,500	$23,500F
Variable production costs:			
Direct material	23,100	20,000	3,100U
Direct labor	18,300	15,000	3,300U
Machine time	19,200	16,250	2,950U
Factory overhead	41,000	35,000	6,000U
Fixed production costs:			
Indirect labor	9,400	6,000	3,400U
Depreciation	5,500	5,500	—
Taxes	2,400	2,300	100U
Insurance	4,500	4,500	—
Administrative expense	12,000	9,000	3,000U
Marketing expense	8,300	7,000	1,300U
Research and development	6,000	4,500	1,500U
Operating profit	$ 11,300	$ 12,450	$ 1,150U

reports still say I have excessive costs. Look, I'm not an accountant; I'm a production manager. I know how to get a good quality product out. Over a number of years, I've even cut the raw materials used to do it. The cost reports don't show any of this; they're always negative, no matter what I do. There's no way you can win with accounting or the people at headquarters who use these reports."

Brady gave Shane little consolation when she stated that the accounting system and the cost reports generated by headquarters are just part of the corporate game and almost impossible for an individual to change. "Although these reports are used to evaluate your division and the means headquarters uses to determine whether you have done the job they want, you shouldn't worry too much. You haven't been fired yet! Besides, these cost reports have been used by Dartmoor for the last 15 years."

From discussions with the operations people at other Dartmoor divisions, Shane knew that the turnover of production managers at the company was high, even though relatively few were fired. Typical comments of production managers who have left Dartmoor follow.

"Corporate headquarters never really listened. All they consider are those monthly cost reports. They don't want them changed, and they don't want any supplementary information."

"The accountants may be quick with numbers but they don't know anything about production. I wound up completely ignoring the cost reports. No matter what they say about not firing people, negative reports mean negative evaluations. I'm better off working for another firm."

A copy of the most recent cost report prepared for the Bridgton Plant is shown below.

Bridgton Plant
Cost Report
Month of November 1997
(in thousands)

	Master Budget	Actual Cost	Excess Cost
Raw material	$ 400	$ 437	$ 37
Direct labor	560	540	(20)
Overhead	100	134	34
Total	$1,060	$1,111	$ 51

Required

a. Discuss Alan Shane's perception of
  (1) Susan Brady, controller;
  (2) corporate headquarters;
  (3) the cost report; and
  (4) himself as a production manager.

Include in your discussion how Shane's perceptions affect his behavior and performance as a production manager and employee of Dartmoor Inc.

b. Identify and explain at least three changes that could be made in the cost information presented to the production managers that would make the information more meaningful and less threatening to them.

(CMA *adapted*)

15-16. Adult Recreation, Inc. (ARI) manufactures games for sale to the adult marketplace. This is a very competitive industry that continually requires modification to existing games and the introduction of new games to meet customer desires. Janice Hardy, vice-president of marketing, and Frank LeBlanc, vice-president of design, have been discussing the challenges facing ARI as a result of the continued worldwide recessionary climate.

Hardy and LeBlanc noted that the current economic conditions may present a unique opportunity if ARI could design and promote sales of games that meet expanded family recreational needs. The recession is causing customers to turn away from more expensive types of entertainment and spend their disposable income on less expensive entertainment.

These discussions then turned to the establishment of a work group of diverse firm personnel to coordinate customer input, identify new ideas, and make collaborative decisions. Questions were raised about who should participate in this work group and whether or not this should be an ongoing effort. Their discussions also revolved around the needs of this work group to ensure that it has the appropriate power and authority to be effective.

Required

a. In a business environment
  (1) Define what constitutes a work group, providing at least two examples.
  (2) Describe at least two advantages and two disadvantages of work groups.

b. Describe the general reasons why authority is delegated.

c. What groupware software should enable this work group to make collaborative decisions?

(CMA *adapted*)

15-17. In the last several years, as the global marketplace has been evolving, firms have had to react to meet changing customer demands and, at the same time, position themselves to meet the global competitive challenge. As part of their overall strategy, firms in the United States have aggressively eliminated several levels of management in order to achieve flatter organizational structures.

Required

a. Identify at least three benefits that U.S. firms expect to realize from flatter organizational structures in responding to changing customer demands.

b. (1) Identify at least three advantages to the organization from eliminating several levels of management.

(2) Identify at least three disadvantages to the organization from eliminating several levels of management.

c. Identify at least three steps that U.S. firms must take in order to successfully implement flatter organizational structures.

(CMA *adapted*)

15-18. *Datacruncher Office Equipment, Inc. (Continuing Case)* For the systems project you have selected or been assigned, specify a strategic or tactical decision that must be made by one of the managers. Determine the types of formal and informal information that the manager needs to make the decision.

CHAPTER
16

DECISION SUPPORT
AND EXPERT SYSTEMS

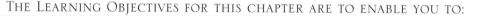

1. Contrast the various types of information processing systems and levels of decision support.

2. Discuss the characteristics, benefits, and suitable applications of decision support systems.

3. Discuss the characteristics, benefits, and suitable applications of expert systems.

4. Describe emerging developments in support systems, fuzzy logic, multimedia, and hypertext.

INTRODUCTION

This chapter continues our discussion of information processing. Our focus is on information systems that aid managers in making the variety of planning and control decisions needed to operate their firms.

IMPORTANCE OF SYSTEMS THAT AID MANAGERIAL DECISION MAKING

With the advent of computer technology, managers have been effectively supported in their decision-making efforts. Not only can they receive needed information more quickly and in customized form but also they are supported by powerful processing and model-based systems. These information systems enable managers to make decisions that lead to sounder plans and more effective controls over operations and performance.

ROLE OF ACCOUNTANTS IN SYSTEMS THAT SUPPORT MANAGERIAL DECISION MAKING

Accountants can retain their usefulness in the face of competition from computer information analysts, knowledge engineers, financial modelers, and other professionals, but only if they become familiar with computer-based support systems and techniques. Accountants have important roles to play with respect to decision support systems, expert systems, and neural networks. They should acquire a sound understanding of support systems so that they can help develop relevant accounting applications for their firms. Accountants can aid in developing appropriate decision models, knowledge bases, and other components of the support systems that are described in this chapter. Also, both internal and external auditors should be familiar with the risks associated with these intelligent systems and the internal control and audit implications of such systems.

TYPES OF INFORMATION PROCESSING SYSTEMS

As you may recall from earlier discussions, the information system of a firm is in reality a collection of systems. Each system has one or more purposes and serves certain users with needed information.

LEVELS OF SYSTEMS SUPPORT

Before introducing each type of information processing system, let us briefly survey the varied levels of support assistance, as well as the kinds of information, that a system can provide. Figure 16-1 portrays five degrees of support, designated by lines and numbered circles.

Support Level 1 represents the level at which the least degree of support is provided. Data are collected from internal or external sources and are stored in unprocessed form. An example would be when Diane Varney, treasurer and controller of Infoage, collects current interest rates from local banks.

Support Level 2 represents the level at which data are collected and processed or analyzed. For instance, Diane Varney might collect data concerning daily sales and prepare a monthly sales analysis report for Mike Barker, Infoage's marketing manager.

Support Level 3 represents the level at which a system employs a decision model to process data and to estimate the consequences of alternative courses of action. For example, Diane Varney may collect data related to product prices from the marketing department. She may incorporate the product prices into a pricing model, for the purpose of estimating the effects of several prospective prices on sales. From the resulting information, Mike Barker might be aided in selecting the most suitable price for a particular product.

Support Level 4 represents the level at which the system uses a decision model, as in Support Level 3. However, at this higher level of support, the system continues the decision process to the point at which it determines the best alternative course of action. For instance, a decision model prepared by Diane Varney might suggest the best possible location for a third retail outlet in the Seattle metropolitan area.

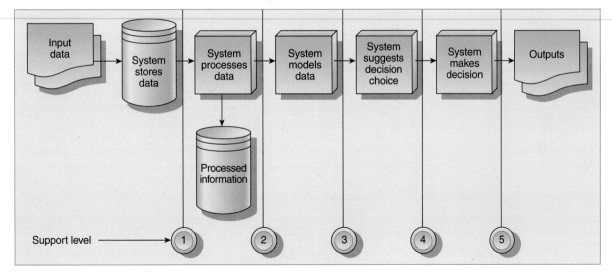

FIGURE 16-1   Levels of decision-making support provided by support systems.

George Freeman, president of Infoage, would most likely accept the recommended choice (location) and prepare the necessary instructions to carry out the choice.

Support Level 5 represents the highest level of support. The system employs one or more decision models to make one or more decisions, and the system then automatically puts the decision(s) into effect. The level of support may be labeled the **replacement level,** since the human decision maker has essentially been replaced by the system. An instance of the replacement level may be found in a system at Infoage in which Diane Varney constructs decision models to determine when inventory items need to be replaced, how many units to reorder, and which supplier to order from—after which the system actually prepares the purchase orders for mailing to Infoage's selected suppliers.

Each of these levels of support can be identified with specific types of processing systems. Assumptions concerning the systems underlie the several levels of support. Furthermore, the assumptions are cumulative, that is, each higher level of support includes all of the assumptions of the lower levels, plus one or more new assumptions. The set of assumed system capabilities for the various levels is summarized in Figure 16-2.

Now we shall contrast the types of processing systems arrayed in Figure 16-3 and examine the levels of decision support that they provide. As illustrated, data processing support systems are composed of transaction processing systems, and information processing support systems embrace operational support, decision support, and artificial intelligence systems. Another type of support system—executive information systems (EISs)—is separately described. Since EISs are similar to de-

Support Level	Assumed System Capabilities
1	Data concerning observations of actual events (e.g., sales) can be stored in an organized manner that allows easy retrieval of specified data elements or records
2	In addition to the capability of Support Level 1, data concerning actual events can be processed and analyzed and then be used to generate specified reports and/or analyses
3	In addition to the capabilities of Support Levels 1 and 2, data concerning projected events (e.g., sales forecasts) can be processed and analyzed via decision models; users can interact with the models to determine consequences of assumed alternatives or changes (e.g., "What is the effect on net profits if sales are 10 percent higher than forecasted?"); then the results from applying the models plus the responses to such assumed changes can be provided in the forms of model analyses or reports
4	In addition to the capabilities of Support Levels 1, 2, and 3, consequences of assumed alternatives can be compared against rules or criteria (which must be predetermined and incorporated into the system), in order to select the best alternative course of action; then this recommended alternative is provided to the user in the form of a statement
5	In addition to the capabilities of Support Levels 1 through 4, the recommended course of action can be fully carried out (which includes the capabilities of initiating actions, committing resources, and monitoring results *without* the aid of humans)

FIGURE 16-2 Assumed information system capabilities for five levels of suport.

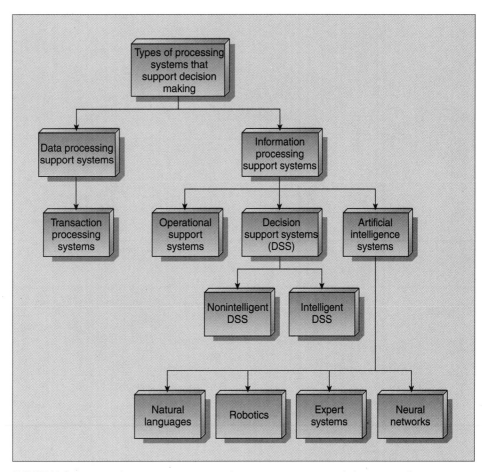

FIGURE 16-3   Types of processing systems that support managerial decision making.

cision support systems, they are omitted from Figure 16-3. Figure 16-4 represents the first three types of data and information processing systems as support layers within the overall information system. Since the data and information processing support systems mirror the organizational and physical features of a firm, the layers within the triangle also represent managerial and operational levels. In addition, these layers interrelate with operational, tactical, and strategic decisions that must be made by a firm's managers. (See Figure 2-13.)

TRANSACTION PROCESSING SYSTEMS

Transaction processing systems reside at the lowest, or operational, layer of a firm's processing systems. We have become quite familiar with these systems, which together make up the accounting information system (AIS) of a firm. Although the sole purpose of a transaction processing system (TPS) is not to aid managerial decision making, it does nevertheless generate useful information. This information, which is a by-product of the transaction processing activity, appears in scheduled reports and documents. For instance, a purchasing TPS generates outputs such as purchase orders, open purchase order reports, and analyses of purchases. Since such reports and documents are a result of processing, a TPS typically provides level 2 support.

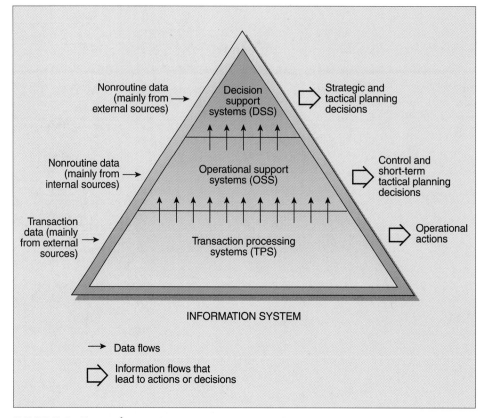

FIGURE 16-4   Types of support systems.

OPERATIONAL SUPPORT SYSTEMS

At the middle layer of the triangle are operational support systems. An **operational support system (OSS)** is an information processing system that aids the planning and control of operations. It focuses mainly on the short-range tactical planning and operational control decisions (although management control decisions may also be included). These relatively structured types of decisions are made by middle-level and lower-level managers.

As Figure 16-4 shows, an OSS uses both nonroutine data from internal sources and transaction data from external sources. It also may require nonroutine data from external sources. All of these data are processed before being stored or reported. An OSS may thus provide support ranging from level 2 through level 5.

The collected group of OSSs within a firm essentially composes the management information system (MIS) of a firm. Since the MIS can be subdivided into functional information systems, an OSS may be classified as a financial OSS, an inventory management OSS, and so on. The system that automatically provides purchase orders at Infoage, used as an illustration for level 5 support, is an example of an inventory management OSS. Most OSSs are dedicated to particular activities, which vary according to the type of firm. For instance, motels and airlines have dedicated reservations systems.

Information generated by an OSS will generally appear in periodic and routine managerial reports such as an operational budget report and a work-order status report. Information from an OSS may appear in other forms, however. For example, an automatic credit-checking system developed by Diane Varney may simply notify the firm's credit manager of approvals or rejections of credit orders via a video display screen.

Because of the variety of decisions that they may support, OSSs range widely in capabilities. Most OSSs possess the first two of the following attributes, and many possess some or all of attributes three through five.

1. Interactive processing and inquiries by users.
2. Concurrent, or time-shared, access by a variety of users.
3. Algorithmic and computational perspective toward decision making.
4. Real-time control over an ongoing process or operation.
5. One or more embedded decision models, which are applied automatically by the system in controlling a process or operation.

Most OSSs enhance the efficiency and timely control of operations. Some OSSs help to improve the quality of operational and short-range tactical decisions.

DECISION SUPPORT SYSTEMS

At the top layer of the triangle are decision support systems, another type of information processing system that requires its users to have relatively sophisticated computer expertise. A **decision support system (DSS)** aids higher-level and middle-level managers in making strategic and certain tactical planning decisions. It is therefore concerned with decisions usually involving relatively unstructured or semistructured problem situations that have long-range impacts. These types of problem situations have not been well supported by OSSs. Thus a DSS usually provides level 3 support and sometimes level 4 support. However, a DSS by definition cannot provide level 5 support. Because of their distinctiveness and increasing importance, nonintelligent and intelligent DSSs are explored more fully in a later section.

EXECUTIVE INFORMATION SYSTEMS

An **executive information system (EIS)** is a customized information support system. Originally designed for the chief executive officer of a firm, it is now often used by other executives as well. The purposes of an EIS are to provide rapid and easy access to critical information used to fulfill managerial responsibilities, such as making timely and well-informed strategic planning and management control decisions and overseeing firmwide operations.

Although they have many similarities, there are several important and noticeable differences between an EIS and a DSS. First, an EIS's most vital concern is to facilitate more effective control by key managers. A DSS primarily aids in the planning process. Second, an EIS is easier to learn than a DSS. Most executives can use the full features of an EIS after receiving very little instruction. Third, an EIS is data retrieval oriented, thereby allowing limited analysis of the data. A DSS is model oriented, allowing users to thoroughly analyze and manipulate data. This versatility makes the DSS more complicated to master than an EIS. Fourth, since an EIS is simple to run, top executives are hands-on users of the system. Due to the complexity of DSSs, few top executives work directly with the software. Subordinates or professional support staff, such as middle managers, accountants, or marketing researchers, report the information generated from the DSS to the senior executive(s). Finally, most EISs at present use a concept known as drill down. **Drill down** means that the EIS software can display information in several levels of detail, with each successively lower level displayed in more detail. On the other hand, DSSs rarely allow more than one level of detail to be visualized.

The heart of an EIS is a data base. The data base of an EIS usually includes data from both internal and external sources. Examples of internal data captured by an EIS include sales, budgets, trends, cash flows, variances on product quality, segment data, profitability figures, and other key business variables. External data often accessible via on-line commercial data bases include information about competitors, products, stock prices, economic data, projected legislative action, world news, and industry trends.

Data might be stored in multidimensional forms, with separate dimensions for the major income statement and balance sheet accounts, time periods, product lines, customer classes, and divisions of the firm. Thus, the amount sold of product line A to customer class 2 during the past three years would be accessible. Stored models might relate to the industry and economy as well as the firm itself. By using menus, prompts, and touch screens, an effective EIS aids the executive in accessing the EIS's data base. He or she can quickly display customized and easy-to-understand multi-colored tables, graphs, trend analyses, and comments interpreting the screen displays. Certain outputs could consist of analyses and trends presented in graphical forms. Consequently, an EIS can provide support ranging from level 1 to level 3.

ARTIFICIAL INTELLIGENCE

As shown in Figure 16-3, artificial intelligence systems are subdivided into natural languages, robotics, expert systems, and neural networks. However, we will limit our discussion of artificial intelligence to expert systems and neural networks, both branches of which have important implications for accountants. In a sense both expert systems and neural networks are variations of DSSs. However, expert systems and neural networks can be designed for problems that arise at any managerial level or even for some types of clerical applications of a firm. **Artificial intelligence (AI)** is the science of building computer devices and software applications that mimic many of the characteristics that we associate with human behavior, such as the ability to reason, see, learn, solve problems, understand language, and so on. In contrast to the other areas of AI, expert systems, neural networks, and robots process and analyze information. AI technologies are becoming increasingly adaptable; thus their use is expected to be commonplace and widespread with time.*

An **expert system (ES)** is a computer program that contains a knowledge base of one or more experts' rules. To a degree, the program can replicate the reasoning or thought processes of human experts by recommending solutions to specific but difficult problems. An expert system is essentially an interactive software package intended to enable nonexpert users to make decisions that are as sound as those of an expert. For instance, an expert system has been developed that enables an inexperienced investor to imitate experienced investment advisors in selecting sound stocks for his or her portfolio. Since expert systems recommend decisions, they provide level 4 support. Because expert systems have many applications in the accounting area, we will examine them more closely in a later section.

A **neural network (NN)** is an emerging tool structured in a manner similar to the parallel processing technique used by the human brain. A neural network com-

---

*Systems Auditability and Control Report, Module 11: Emerging Technologies (Altamonte Springs, Fla.: Institute of Internal Auditors Research Foundation, 1994), pp. 222 and 226.

puter software model is constructed to repeatedly analyze sample data. The sample data base contains examples of known output associated with each known input. The neural net learns the relationship between the output and input by constructing a mathematical model that recognizes patterns in the sample data, such as correlations between seemingly unrelated data. Since neural networks recommend decisions, they provide level 4 support. Because these emerging neural networks potentially have a significant number of applications in the accounting area, we will examine them further in Appendix 2 of this chapter.

DECISION SUPPORT SYSTEMS

The concept of a DSS is not new. Managers have always made strategic and tactical decisions. They have usually been assisted in doing so, typically by staff personnel who have collected and analyzed needed data for decisions. What is new is the array of capabilities that recent advances in information technology bring to decision making. Fifth-generation computer hardware and software, plus modeling techniques, have provided added dimensions of decision support.

The benefits that a modern DSS can provide to managers include the following:

1. Improved effectiveness in making strategic and tactical decisions.

2. Greater timeliness in collecting and processing the needed data that bear on unstructured and semistructured decisions.

3. Broader understanding by the decision makers of the array of factors involved in problems requiring complex decisions and their relationships to each other.

As illustrated in Figure 16-3, decision support systems may be subdivided into nonintelligent and intelligent DSSs. A **nonintelligent DSS** allows a decision maker to include relevant facts and data into a model that calculates a solution to a problem or that ranks alternatives. For example, assume that Diane Varney of Infoage designs a spreadsheet template to compare the costs of leasing versus buying a firm truck. The DSS's comparative calculations enable Diane to quickly evaluate the two alternatives. Her nonintelligent DSS does not provide advice in making the decision of which alternative to select. It provides a solution based upon the specified calculations. An **intelligent DSS,** on the other hand, is a hybrid DSS–expert system that not only makes basic computations but also inserts an expert's decision rules into the model. Thus, the intelligent DSS provides a higher level of support in making the decision. For example, assume that Ann Strong, CPA and CMA, has accepted a consulting assignment to select a suitable microcomputer for a family-owned farming operation located in Ft. Dodge, Iowa. She uses an intelligent DSS software package called Criterium (from Sygenex) that is loaded onto her laptop computer's hard disk to complete the engagement. She adds her alternatives—specific models of microcomputers—and criteria, such as cost, vendor support, and quality of documentation for each microcomputer, used to evaluate the alternatives into a model. In addition to the facts and data pertaining to each criterion, she adds several rules into the model obtained from an expert knowledgeable about microcomputers. A possible rule placed into the model might read as follows: "If vendor support is below average, then quality of documentation must be above average." This rule and others added into the model function as policies or guidelines that assist Ann in selecting a course of action. The Criterium package generates a graphical report showing the final ranking of the microcomputers, taking into account the decision rules incorporated into the model.

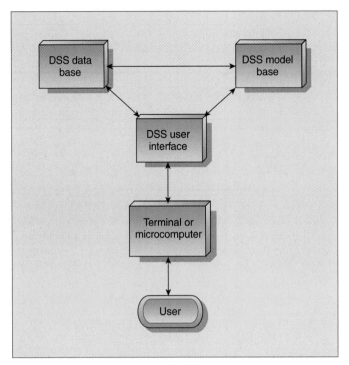

FIGURE 16-5   Key components of a decision support system.

Figure 16-5 shows the key components of a DSS. In the following paragraphs we will examine each component, as well as the nature of outputs from a DSS. Then we will survey applications of DSSs in a business firm.

DSS DATA BASE

Data used by managers in making strategic and tactical decisions will normally be drawn from varied sources. Some data may be acquired from managerial reports like those provided by the firm's profitability reporting system. Other data may be summarized from transaction processing systems. Still other data may be gleaned from informal systems, such as phone calls from friends and professional journals. Much of the data, however, will likely be obtained from an established data base.

A data base that suits the needs of a DSS must have several attributes. The data must be relevant to the decisions to be made. Thus, forecasts as well as actual results will be included. The actual data should be as up-to-date and accurate as possible. Also, the data base should be comprehensive, since a wide range of data are needed for decisions that affect strategic and long-range tactical planning. For instance, the data should include nonroutine data concerning the environment and drawn from external sources. It should also include much of the data used in operations, at least in summarized form. Figure 16-6 presents the contents of a comprehensive DSS data base.

DSS MODEL BASE

Decision Models   Because of the complexity of the problems with which a DSS must contend, the system employs various models within a model base. Figure 16-7 lists

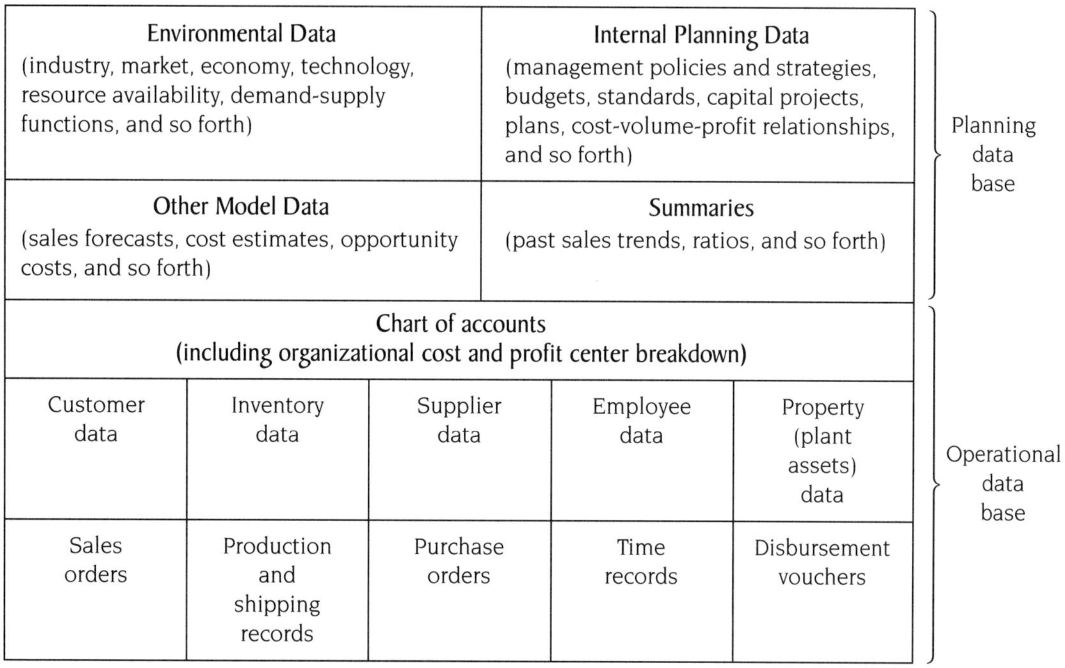

Environmental Data (industry, market, economy, technology, resource availability, demand-supply functions, and so forth)		Internal Planning Data (management policies and strategies, budgets, standards, capital projects, plans, cost-volume-profit relationships, and so forth)		Planning data base
Other Model Data (sales forecasts, cost estimates, opportunity costs, and so forth)		Summaries (past sales trends, ratios, and so forth)		
Chart of accounts (including organizational cost and profit center breakdown)				Operational data base
Customer data	Inventory data	Supplier data	Employee data	Property (plant assets) data
Sales orders	Production and shipping records	Purchase orders	Time records	Disbursement vouchers

FIGURE 16-6   A comprehensive data base that spans a firm's decision needs.

a variety of models that a firm might use with DSSs. Most of the models listed are called **decision models,** since they are directly related to the process for making specific choices among alternative courses of action. One or more decision models can be applied in exploring a problem involving a strategic or a tactical decision. The figure also suggests the functional nature of the decision for which each model is suited.

Many decisions involving a DSS require the assistance of more than one model. For instance, the economic order quantity model is an **optimization model** because it provides the optimal solution for a structured decision pertaining to inventory. Since a DSS by definition does not directly specify solutions, this model would be

Description of Model	Typical Function Aided
1. Regression model	Sales forecasting
2. Exponential smoothing model	Sales forecasting
3. PERT model	Engineering design
4. Linear programming model	Production scheduling
5. Line-of-balance model	Production routing
6. Economic order quantity model	Inventory control
7. Supplier evaluation model	Purchasing
8. Transportation model	Physical distribution
9. Discounted cash-flow model	Investment planning
10. Production cost-variance model	Cost analysis
11. Cash-flow model	Financing
12. Budget model	Accounting control
13. Manpower planning model	Personnel planning

FIGURE 16-7   A variety of models used by decision support systems.

used in conjunction with other models. It might, for example, be employed in exploring possible decisions relating to production and warehousing facilities.

Statistical models or procedures may be included in a DSS model base. Examples listed in Figure 16-7 are regression analysis and exponential smoothing, which aid in sales forecasting. Forecasted sales are often a key input to a strategic or tactical decision.

Firmwide Planning Models   After gaining experience and confidence in using a DSS, broader models might be developed. Two examples of broad-based models are corporate models and financial planning models. A **corporate model** reflects the physical and financial relationships of a firm. A **financial planning model** reflects a firm's formalized plans in financial terms. Both of these models provide frameworks that can aid managers in making a variety of strategic and tactical decisions.

The financial planning model is of particular interest to accountants, since it in effect models the budgeting process. Thus it produces outputs such as the income statement, balance sheet, and cash-flow statement. This financially oriented model can simulate the flows of transactions over a budget period. It therefore enables managers to perceive likely financial consequences of possible decisions. As a result, they can develop the most suitable financial plans for the coming year. A short-term financial planning model can also be integrated with a longer-range capital budgeting model.

Modeling Languages   Most of the decision models and broad-based models used by a firm must be tailor-made to fit the particular decision circumstances or the firm's planning structure. Fortunately, high-level modeling languages are available. They provide powerful, easy-to-use, concise, and versatile program instructions and features. Of particular interest to managers and accountants are the subset of languages known as financial modeling languages. They are sometimes called nonprocedural languages, since they enable developers to enter program statements without regard for sequence. Thus they allow developers to focus on the important aspects of the problems for which decisions are needed. Examples of financial modeling languages are IFPS (available from Comshare) and Express (available from Management Decision Systems).

One of the most important features of a modeling language is the capability that it provides for experimentation with the data. A list of several useful manipulative or analytical techniques offered by a financial modeling language appears in Figure 16-8. By means of these techniques—simulation, "what-if" analysis, sensitivity analysis, and goal-seeking analysis—a decision maker can gain greater insight into problem situations and the consequences of decision choices. Another technique is risk analysis. Also called *Monte Carlo analysis*, risk analysis involves the manipulation of data values expressed as probability distributions.

Model-Base Management Systems   A **model-base management system (MBMS)** is the modeling counterpart to a data-base management system. In effect, it is software that operates under the control of the operating system. Its functions usually consist of providing (1) links between models in a DSS, (2) a modeling definition language, (3) mechanisms for modifying decision models, and (4) a user-friendly means of executing and manipulating models.

Example of a Financial Planning Model   A real-world financial planning or budget model is being used by the Tanner Companies, a Phoenix-based construction firm. The model has improved the soundness of the budgeting process and has reduced the lead time. One of its major benefits is to aid managers in major financial deci-

1. The **time-based simulation** technique projects the states (values) of the key factors and criteria over future time periods, given current data values and expected rates of change.
   Example: A user might simulate the firm's budget over five years, with values of sales and net income being calculated each year.

2. The **"what-if" analysis** technique allows the user to ask "what-if" questions in order to determine how key factors will respond to assumed changes or conditions.
   Example: A user might ask, "What will be the increase in my firm's labor costs next year if we grant a $2.00 per hour average increase in wage rates on January 1?"

3. The **sensitivity analysis** technique, a special version of the "what-if" analysis technique, reveals the sensitivity of the decision model criteria to changes in the values of key factors.
   Example: A user might ask, "What will be the effect on my firm's net income (the model criterion) if unit sales decrease by 10 percent next year?"

4. The **goal-seeking analysis** technique allows the user to determine the levels of key factors needed in order to achieve a desired level in a model criterion.
   Example: A user might ask, "What volume (level) of sales units must my firm generate next year in order to achieve a 25 percent share of the market?"

FIGURE 16-8   Four model-manipulation or analysis techniques that may be used with a financial model.

sions. For instance, by means of "what-if" analysis the treasurer is able to evaluate the effects of refinancing a loan on the firm's net income and cash balance. He is confident that the model has led to improved cash management and reduced borrowing rates.

Constructing financial models by means of modeling languages like IFPS is quite straightforward. Essentially these models consist of statements that have the appearance of equations. For example, if the contribution margin percentage can be expected to remain at 30 percent of sales, this relationship is expressed as

$$\text{Contribution margin} = 0.30 \times \text{Expected Sales}$$

After all needed statements have been compiled into an income statement model, the user specifies the key estimates, such as the sales forecast. The model then computes the expected value of net profit. A review problem at the end of this chapter illustrates a model that computes expected net profit.

USER INTERFACE

The users of an effective DSS are offered several means by which to interface with the models and stored data. In our discussion of modeling languages, we noted that they allow users to perform manipulations. This **user interface** capability is provided through modeling and reporting modules that incorporate special manipulating commands. Other means of aiding decision makers to use a DSS (and other decision support tools) include query languages, information centers, and groupware. Groupware is examined in the next section.

Query Languages   Special **query languages** enable users to express requests for information in a user-friendly manner. They are similar to those mentioned in Chapter 6, since query languages generally access stored data through data-base software. Two of the most common approaches by which query languages facilitate requests are the command language approach and the menu approach.

The **command language approach** allows the user to communicate by means of English-like commands. Simple but descriptive words in the language can initiate reasonably complex processing sequences.

The **menu approach** displays listings of items on the screen. To select the desired item (e.g., record, report), the user simply enters the number beside the described item or uses an intuitive Windows-based graphical user interface (GUI) to point and click to logically organized, graphical icons.

Information Center   An **information center** is a physical location within a firm where users can receive computer system–oriented services. Among the services that may be offered are training in the use of computers (including microcomputers) and in system development tools, help in selecting computers and software, consultation on system development problems, and assistance in user development. Assigned to the information center may be system analysts, model builders, software specialists, and application specialists. These centers are likely to expand, both in numbers and in services offered, in coming years. With respect to DSS development, an information center can be a vital resource. Users are realizing that they should become actively involved in developing their own models. Otherwise, they will not be able to trust the results provided by the models used in a DSS.

OUTPUTS FROM A DSS

Most of the information obtained from a DSS will typically be tailored to the needs of the decision maker–user. Often the information will take the form of analyses and trends. The user may employ a query language to specify what he or she needs. However, it may be necessary to supplement a query language with a report generator. Examples of report generators are Easytrieve Plus (from Pansophic) and Comprehensive Report Writer (from Software International). Certain software packages, such as Focus (from Information Builders), combine a query language with a report writer.

Information in graphic form has become increasingly popular. Graphs aid managers in understanding quantitative data and in spotting trends. They are especially useful in helping nonaccounting managers to interpret accounting information. When displayed in color, and perhaps also in three dimensions, graphs can be very impressive and persuasive. Graphics output are available via terminals and microcomputers; graphs may then be printed in color or black and white on plotters or laser printers. Although much of the recent growth in graphics output results from the added availability of microcomputer graphics software, high-end graphics are also quite important to many firms. High-end graphics from mainframe computers or minicomputers are necessary when graphs must be of very high quality and/or in large volumes. An example of a popular high-end graphics package is SAS/GRAPH (from the SAS Institute, Inc.).

APPLICATIONS

Decision support systems have been applied in a wide variety of problem situations in the business world. Decisions resolved with the aid of a DSS include the ones shown in Figure 16-9. Accountants should take a more active role in developing many of these real-world DSSs that can be used (1) directly by accountants and (2) directly by middle- and upper-level managers. The management accountant may well be the person who is in the best position to facilitate the development of DSSs for at least three reasons. First, management accountants have the professional background and

- Should a newly developed product be marketed?
- Where should our new production facilities be located?
- Should a particular firm be acquired and merged into our operations?
- What should be the budgeted net income and return on investment for each of our operating divisions?
- How should we price our products for maximum sales and contribution to profits?
- Should our current computer system be replaced?
- Should we accept a firm's loan application?
- Which applicant should we hire?
- Which employee should we promote?
- What investments should we purchase for the employees' pension fund?
- What advertising media should we select?
- Should we purchase or lease equipment?
- What brand of PC should we select for the firm?
- Which vendors should we select?
- What is the optimal product mix?
- What products should we manufacture offshore?
- In what countries should we make foreign investments?
- What software package should we purchase?
- Who are our best sales prospects?
- What benefits package should we select?
- Where should we locate the new fast-food franchise?
- Should we relocate our manufacturing facilities in another country?
- Should we extend credit to the new vendor?
- How risky is the proposed computer project?

FIGURE 16-9   Examples of real-world applications of decision support systems.

experience to make a significant contribution in the area of DSSs. Second, they are familiar with the information and decision support requirements of managers. And third, they are well aware that traditional management accounting systems have not fully met these requirements.* A very powerful easy-to-use generalized DSS generator already mentioned is Criterium. Accountants can utilize Criterium to quickly develop a number of the real-world DSS applications illustrated in Figure 16-9 and numerous other DSS applications as well.

GROUP DECISION SUPPORT SYSTEMS

As the wave of interest in collaborative work groups, participative management, and self-directed work teams becomes more commonplace, group decision support systems or groupware tools will significantly grow in demand. An organization can employ **group decision support systems (GDSSs)** or **groupware tools** to share information and to support collaboration among two or more employees. With GDSS tools, information can be rapidly communicated among employees, enabling them to work together as if they were all in the same room, quickly arriving at a joint decision.

---

*Ciaran Murphy, et al., "Decision Support Systems and Management Accountants," *Management Accounting* (England) (February 1992), pp. 46–47.

One of the most widely used groupware tools is **electronic mail (E-mail) software,** which allows individuals who have access devices linked to networks to communicate with other individuals within the networks. Messages can be written when desired, routed to the appropriate destinations, stored in an on-line file, and easily retrieved by the addressees. Messages may assume formats ranging from stand-alone brief notes to E-mail attachments, such as formal letters, reports, and graphs. The heart of electronic mail is the "mailbox," an on-line storage area that is reserved for each user of the system. E-mail software sends a message to the address of the mailbox designated in the message; some E-mail systems can be set up to alert the addressee when a new message arrives at his or her mailbox. E-mail systems are easy for accountants and other employees and managers to understand and use. Significant advantages of E-mail include the elimination of communication barriers, the facilitation of work, and the sharing of information across the firm.

In addition to sending and receiving mail via a network, recently developed E-mail systems can also aid users in easily retrieving desired information from internal and external data bases. Called *mail-enabling*, these applications involve the use of software that automatically queries the data base on behalf of users and returns the information to the users' mailboxes. Other categories of GDSS, including Lotus Notes, are examined in Appendix 1 of this chapter.

EXPERT SYSTEMS

A paraphrase of the definition of expert systems may enhance your understanding of this important development in information systems. An expert system is a computerized software model that simulates the thinking process of one or more human experts in solving a complex problem or in making a decision. It utilizes a type of knowledge engineering to incorporate into a computer program the specialized knowledge and symbolic reasoning process of the human experts. As opposed to procedural programming languages like COBOL or FORTRAN, which solve numeric problems, expert systems computer programs solve problems requiring judgment; they emulate the way experts manipulate symbolic or nonnumeric information. Thus, they are electronic consultants able to advise, analyze, train, diagnose, explain, and justify their conclusions to a nonexpert user.

In the following survey of expert systems, we discuss the benefits of expert systems, the contrasts between an expert system and a DSS, the components of an expert system, methods to determine suitable expert systems applications, and design considerations.

BENEFITS OF AN EXPERT SYSTEM

Expert systems offer many benefits to the accountant and the firm. In addition to improving the quality, reliability, timeliness, and consistency of decision making, they preserve critical expertise. Furthermore, expert systems are inexpensive to operate, are available at any time, increase the productivity of less experienced employees, and can be employed as training tools for new staff.

CONTRASTS BETWEEN AN EXPERT SYSTEM AND A DSS

An expert system is similar to a DSS in certain respects. Both are normally designed to aid managers in making decisions relating to semistructured problem situations.

Both can best be developed by means of the top-down and prototyping approaches. That is, the objectives for a system are first established; a simple prototype system is developed next; then the system should be improved and enhanced in an iterative fashion.

On the other hand, an expert system differs in significant ways from a DSS. It is less flexible than a DSS, since it does not allow a manager or other user to interact with the model. For instance, a user cannot conduct a "what-if" or "sensitivity" analysis using an expert system. Instead, an expert system specifically recommends a solution to a problem or a specific choice for a decision along with an explanation and justification for its conclusions. Furthermore, expert systems typically pertain to problems of a narrower scope than those for which DSSs are developed. Problem situations most suitable for an expert system require a high degree of scarce expertise, entail frequent decisions with high payoffs, and remain relatively stable (unchanged).

Perhaps the differences between an expert system and a DSS can be clarified by reference to the game of chess. When a newspaper reports that a chess champion played the "computer," an expert system is involved. When the chess champion uses a computer program to aid him or her in learning chess or to suggest moves to be made against a human opponent, a DSS is involved.

COMPONENTS OF AN EXPERT SYSTEM

Figure 16-10 depicts the major components of an expert system. The user "consults" with the expert system by providing specific data via the user interface. In turn, the task-specific data base feeds the facts to the knowledge base, which then interacts with the inference engine in tracing the steps through the computer program. Recommendations resulting from this process are provided via the user interface. Let us examine each component more closely.

The **knowledge base** incorporates the knowledge of the experts pertaining to the domain of the problem situation. Two techniques for expressing the knowledge are (1) production rules (including "rules of thumb") and (2) semantic networks. Production rules are simple "if-then" rules that represent the specific consequences

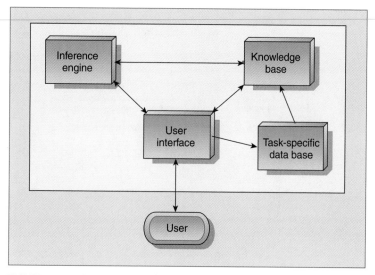

FIGURE 16-10   Components of an expert system.

of given conditions or actions. An instance is as follows: If (1) a patient has been exposed to cold germs, and (2) the patient has developed a fever, *then* the patient likely has a cold. Semantic networks are decompositions of facts, such as the breakdown of the parts composing a product. They have an appearance of hierarchies that are linked through word labels. Figure 16-11 shows a simplified semantic network pertaining to the broad object called ASSET. Each node in the lower levels represents an attribute of the broad object.

The **task-specific data base** contains the data relevant to a specific application of the expert system. For a tax planning expert system, it might contain dollar values and characteristics of the various assets and other accounts from a firm involved in tax planning. Figure 16-10 shows these data are fed into the knowledge base by the user at the beginning of the consultation.

The **inference engine** contains the logic and reasoning methods that simulate the thought processes of the experts in reaching conclusions. It "drives" the expert system; that is, it determines the sequence in which to apply the production rules or to trace through the semantic networks of the knowledge base. Two types of sequences are called forward chaining and backward chaining. **Forward chaining** consists of moving through the rules or networks to reach conclusions, that is, to develop specific recommendations. **Backward chaining** consists of beginning with a conclusion (recommendation) and moving back through the rules or networks to determine if the conclusion is valid.

The user interface, as in a DSS, allows a user to communicate with the expert system. An effective means of initiating a session is to have the expert system ask the user questions, via the interface.

An additional component not shown is the **development engine.** This component provides the means by which the knowledge and inference processes of the experts are encoded and embedded in the expert system. It also allows the rules or semantic networks to be modified.

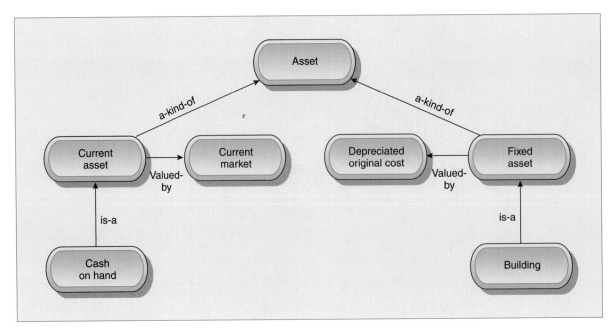

FIGURE 16-11   An example of a simplified semantic network making up part of a knowledge base.

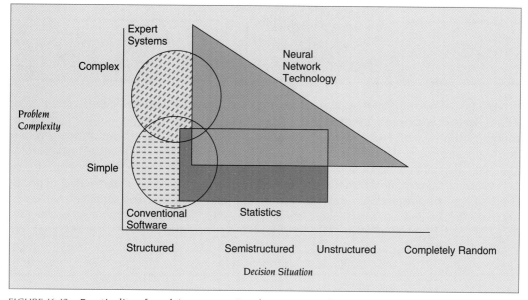

FIGURE 16-12   Practicality of applying conventional computer software, statistics, expert systems, and neural networks to solve a large class of problems. Adapted from *ModelQuest Manual* (Charlottesville, Va.: AbTech Corporation, 1996), Chapter 2, p. 3.

CONDITIONS SUITABLE FOR EXPERT SYSTEMS DEVELOPMENT

A firm must painstakingly single out potential accounting applications suitable for computerized expert systems development. Selection of ill-suited applications will result in improper allocation of scarce resources, low payoff, and systems that are never used or are used only very briefly. Figure 16-12 illustrates the practicality of applying conventional computer programs, statistical techniques, expert systems, and neural networks to solve problems. As shown, expert systems, represented by the top circle in the figure, are suitable for moderately complex to complex and structured to some semistructured problems. Indeed, a recent empirical study on real-world usage of intelligent technologies reported that 73 percent of the respondents' expert systems were being used to support operational problems, 19 percent to support tactical decisions, and only 8 percent to support strategic decisions.* An expert systems approach is likely to be successful if the factors stated in Figure 16-13 are given careful consideration when selecting potential applications.

APPLICATIONS

Expert systems in accounting and nonaccounting fields are rapidly being adopted by many types of organizations. For example, a nonaccounting expert system developed by Digital Equipment Company, named XCON, enables the manufacturer to specify the needed components and their arrangements for computer systems ordered by customers. Many of the expert systems in commercial use or in the process of being developed apply to accounting-oriented problems. All of the Big-Six accounting firms, the Internal Revenue Service, governmental agencies and other not-for-profit firms, manufacturing firms, and numerous other organizations are either using or

*Bindiganavale S. Vijayaraman and Barbara A. Osyk, "An Empirical Study on the Usage of Intelligent Technologies," *Journal of Computer Information Systems* (Fall 1994), pp. 37–38.

SPOTLIGHTING

AN EXPERT SYSTEM
at KPMG *Peat Marwick**

Loan Probe is the name given to an expert system developed by KPMG Peat Marwick, one of the Big-Six public accounting firms. Loan Probe is designed to aid banking clients in assessing the probable losses in their commercial loan portfolios, as well as to help bankers in calculating their loan-loss reserves. This expert loan evaluation system contains more than 6000 rules derived from those used by experts in KPMG's financial services department. It was tested with banking clients whose assets ranged between $200 million and $1 billion.

*Grace T. Chu, "Expert Systems in Computer-Based Auditing." EDP *Auditor Journal*, Vol. 1 (1989), pp. 31–32.

In order to use Loan Probe, a user gathers data concerning both the borrower and the loan. Relevant data include the loan amount, types of collateral guarantees, and the key financial facts pertaining to the borrower. By asking a series of questions, the expert system ensures that needed data are entered. When Loan Probe is satisfied that it has sufficient facts, it then produces a recommendation. It might suggest that the lending bank set aside a loan-loss reserve within a certain range. Alternatively, it might indicate that no reserve is necessary.

developing accounting expert systems. High-payoff areas of expert systems by branch of accounting are highlighted in Figure 16-14. Although all four branches have high potential for expert systems development, the majority of accounting expert systems are being used or developed in the audit and tax areas.* Figure 16-15, on page 734, indicates a sample of eight real-world expert systems that are in the prototype or commercial stage of use in the audit and tax areas. The knowledge base of if-then rules ranges from 25 for Auditor to 2000 for ExperTAX.

√ Moderately complex to very complex, well-defined or focused, procedural high-value problems or decisions requiring judgment.

√ Highly structured to somewhat semistructured, recurring, repetitive operational and tactical problems.

√ Expertise is difficult to acquire. Human experts are expensive and in short supply. Nonhuman expertise is available in the form of authoritative pronouncements, such as APBs, FASBs, and IRS tax regulations.

√ The accounting problem can be solved in a relatively short period of time.

√ The accounting problem is rule-intensive and can be solved with "if-then" rules.

√ Common sense or intuition is not required to solve the problem.

√ The accounting problem cannot be solved efficiently with traditional or conventional computer software programs, such as COBOL or FORTRAN.

√ The body of knowledge is being continually updated.

√ The problem's conversion to a computer-based expert system must result in a high payoff.

√ The expert system must produce clearly identified solutions with which most experts must agree among themselves.

FIGURE 16-13 Summary of factors to consider when selecting potential accounting expert systems applications.

*An on-line search of accounting expert systems articles in January 1996 revealed that about 60 percent pertained to auditing and tax applications.

AUDITING (INTERNAL AND EXTERNAL)
- Deciding whether to accept a prospective auditee
- Evaluating risks and the internal control structure in computer systems
- Reviewing prior years' working papers
- Issuing audit reports and forming audit opinions
- Writing audit programs
- Assisting in making a going-concern judgment
- Scheduling audit personnel
- Analyzing the adequacy of the allowance for doubtful accounts
- Analyzing unusual transactions

TAXATION
- Advising on potential acquisitions and mergers
- Claiming a dependent
- Auditing deferred tax accruals
- Determining corporate tax status
- Determing if a firm qualfies for Subchapter S tax status
- Offering personal and corporate tax planning advice

COST/MANAGERIAL
- Analyzing significant variances and explaining the variation
- Assisting in monthly closings
- Allocating revenue and expenses
- Analyzing performance of projects
- Reviewing trial balances

FINANCIAL ACCOUNTING
- Accounting for nonmonetary transactions (APB No. 29)
- Accounting for contingencies (FAS No. 5)
- Purchasing vs. pooling (APB No. 16)
- Accounting for futures contracts (FAS No. 80)
- Developing expert systems for other professional pronouncements
- Classifying financial transactions correctly
- Evaluating creditworthiness

FIGURE 16-14   High-payoff areas of expert systems by branch of accounting.

In some instances expert systems can be incorporated into the information systems of firms to aid with daily decision making. American Express has a very successful expert system that is being employed to detect fraudulent credit card activity. Each time an authorization request is received, the expert system "looks" in the data base to see the pattern of recent expenditures. If the previous requests this week relating to a particular card, for instance, have been entered from Paris, Hong Kong, and Chicago, the system would alert the credit clerk that the card might be stolen.*

DEVELOPMENT CONSIDERATIONS

Building an expert system can take from a few weeks to two or more years. For example, Digital Equipment's XCON and KPMG Peat Marwick's Loan Probe expert

*Harvey Newquest, "The Real Thing: How Artificial Intelligence Is Changing Business," *Business Software Review* (March 1988), p. 58.

Name	Purpose	Developer
Auditing expert systems		
Loan Probe	To aid banks in assessing commercial loan portfolios	KPMG Peat Marwick (see Spotlighting box)
Auditor	To aid in evaluating the adequacy of the allowance for bad debts	Dungan (University of South Florida)
EDP-XPERT	To aid audit specialists in evaluating the reliability of controls in computer systems	Hansen and Messier (University of Florida)
GC-X	To aid in making going-concern judgments	Biggs and Selfridge (University of Connecticut)
Audit Planner	To aid in making materiality judgments during the planning of audits	Steinbart (St. Louis University)
Tax expert systems		
TAXADVISOR	To aid tax specialists in rendering estate planning advice	Michaelsen (University of North Texas)
ExperTAX	To aid in tax planning and corporate tax accruals	Coopers and Lybrand
Taxpayer Service Assistant	To aid IRS agents in answering taxpayer questions on complex tax issues	Internal Revenue Service

FIGURE 16-15   Examples of expert systems applications in accounting.

systems, both large-scale systems, each required over two years to create and implement. Developing an expert system requires the services of experts, knowledge engineers, and users. As a rule, expert systems go through three major stages of development: knowledge acquisition, computer modeling and debugging, and validation.

Knowledge Acquisition   The **knowledge engineers,** akin to systems or information analysts, are the architects of the system's development engine. They first determine from users the purposes and applications of the proposed expert system. Then they extract relevant knowledge from the experts. Based on this knowledge, the knowledge engineers determine the rules (or semantic networks) of thumb or heuristics the expert uses to make decisions in the problem area being programmed. For example, assume that Diane Varney of Infoage has attended a two day training seminar on a widely used microcomputer-based expert system—VP-EXPERT (from WordTech Systems, Inc.). Shortly after returning from the seminar, she decides to develop an expert system of APB No. 29, *Accounting for Nonmonetary Transactions.* Its purpose is to prepare the journal entries for nonmonetary exchanges of similar and dissimilar assets. Diane, as knowledge engineer, obtains a copy of APB No. 29, the "expert" source she will consult to develop the expert system.

Computer Modeling and Debugging   Two approaches can be employed to develop an expert system. First, a programmer could write the program that embodies the reasoning to be incorporated in the inference engine and the user interface. The coding of the expert system might be done in a language like Prolog or Lisp. Both have the ability to analyze logical statements, determining whether they are true or false on the basis of the rules in the knowledge base. However, this approach is time consuming and costly. A programmer must write a complex computer program to create an inference engine and its user interface for each expert system application.

Alternatively, an expert system can be developed by using an **expert system shell,** that is, a commercial software development package. In effect, it is a preprogrammed inference engine generator containing an empty knowledge base.

Diane selected VP-EXPERT, an easy-to-use and powerful expert system shell, to develop her application. Other popular microcomputer rule-based expert system shells include 1st CLASS (from Progress in Motion), EXSYS (from EXSYS Company), Level5 (from Information Builders), and Personal Consultant (from Texas Instruments).

Figure 16-16a shows three representative rules that Diane extracted from APB No. 29. Diane's next step is to convert each statement extracted from APB No. 29 during the knowledge acquisition phase into a format that can be processed by the microcomputer. This format requires each statement to be converted into an

(a)	(b)

Rule 6

Assume this is a nonmonetary exchange and the assets exchanged are similar. Then, the earning process is not complete.

Rule 6

If   nonmonet = yes and assets = similar
then earning_process = not_complete;

Rule 8

Assume this is a nonmonetary exchange and the assets are dissimilar and that the fair market value of the assets surrendered is greater than the book value of the assets surrendered and that both of these values are greater than zero. Then, the gain is equal to the fair market value of the assets surrendered minus the book value of the assets surrendered.

Rule 8

If   nonmonet = yes and assets = dissimilar
and boot = received and
     fmv_surd_gt_bookval_surd = yes
and fmv_surd > 0 and bookval_surd > 0
then gain = (fmv_surd − bookval_surd);

Rule 24

Assume this is a nonmonetary exchange and the assets exchanged are similar and Infoage receives boot and the fair market value of the assets surrendered is greater than the book value of the assets surrendered. Further, the fair market value of the assets surrendered is greater than zero and the fair market value of the assets received is greater than zero. Then, the asset's basis is equal to [(book value of the asset surrendered plus (boot received divided by (boot received plus fair market value of the asset received) multiplied by (fair market value of the assets surrendered minus book value of the assets surrendered)] minus boot received.

Rule 24

If   nonmonet = yes and assets = similar
and boot = received and
     fmv_surd_gt_bookval_surd = yes
and boot_rec = 0 and fmv_surd > 0 and fmv_rec > 0
then basis = [bookval_surd + (boot_rec/ (boot_rec + fmv_rec) * (fmv_surd − book val_surd)] − boot_rec);

FIGURE 16-16 Developing rules for an expert system. (*a*) Three rules Diane Varney of Infoage extracted from APB No. 29, *Accounting for Nonmonetary Transactions*. (*b*) A partial knowledge base of if-then rules generated from the statements in (*a*). Note: This partial knowledge base is written in VP-EXPERT syntax.

English-like syntax of if-then rules. These rules are entered into the expert system shell to form the knowledge base. A knowledge base of three of the 41 if-then rules contained in the completed expert system, derived from the statements in Figure 16-16a, is illustrated in Figure 16-16b.

Before Diane can consult with the APB No. 29 expert system, she must develop a series of questions specific to the application that enables her to communicate with the expert system. For example, these questions will contain dollar values and facts about the various assets, including whether the asset is nonmonetary, similar or dissimilar; fair market values for the asset received and surrendered; amount of boot (cash) received; and cost of the asset surrendered.

Figure 16-17a shows the list of questions asked by Infoage's expert system to elicit from the user the necessary dollar amounts and facts. The dollar amounts and facts are shown within parentheses next to each question. Once all the data have been entered into the task-specific data base at the beginning of the consultation, it will generate an explanation and the journal entry shown in Figure 16-17b.

Validation   An expert system must be proven reliable before it is used by nonexperts to make real-world decisions. **Validation**—measured by the validity rate—is the process of determining and improving the reliability of an expert system. The **validity rate** is the percentage of time that an expert system gives answers that correspond to those of one or more human experts. The expert system's validity rate should be equal to or higher than the validity rate of its human counterparts. For highly structured recurring decisions with clear-cut rules and clearly focused problem domains, the validity rate may approximate 100 percent. As the problem domain becomes more complex and semistructured with less clear-cut rules, a validity rate of about 60 percent is more than adequate to place an expert system in operation.

(a)	(b)

• Is this a nonmonetary exchange?   (yes)
 	
• What kind of asset is being exchanged?   (Similar)
 	
• Is boot paid or received or neither?   (Received)
 	
• Is the fair market value of the asset surrendered greater than the book value of the asset surrendered?   (Yes)
 	
• What is the amount of boot received? ($10,000)
 	
• What is the book value of the asset surrendered?   ($29,000)
 	
• What is the fair market value of the asset surrendered?   ($40,000)
 	
• What is the fair market value of the asset received?   ($30,000)
 	
• What is the cost of the asset surrendered? ($55,000)
	At the completion of the consultation with Infoage's APB No. 29 expert system, the system will provide a brief explanation of the transaction and a journal entry to record the exchange, in accordance with generally accepted accounting principles, as follows:
	
	The earning process is not complete. The gain should be partially recognized.
	
	Journal Entry:
	Cash 10000
	Assets Received 21750
	Accumul. Deprec. 26000
	    Assets Surrendered 55000
	    Gain on Exchange 2750

FIGURE 16-17   Consulting with an expert system. (*a*) A list of questions asked to the user during a consultation with Infoage's APB No. 29 expert system. (*b*) Output generated by Infoage's APB No. 29 expert system based on the sample data provided.

EMERGING DEVELOPMENTS

The use of all types of systems that support decision making can be expected to significantly grow in popularity in the near future. Many new applications will be discovered, and more firms will reap the benefits.

INTELLIGENT AGENT SOFTWARE

Perhaps the most notable improvement in EIS software will be the development of intelligent EISs that work in conjunction with small, self-contained artificial intelligence programs known as intelligent agent software. **Intelligent agent software** are customized programs that travel across networks, act as experts by mimicking human behavior, and retrieve information on behalf of a principal. By learning what the executive requires, the agent can store a set of rules in its program that specifies how to procure the necessary information. The more the agent is utilized, the more it learns about the executive's behavior patterns and how he or she deploys the EIS. For example, an intelligent agent could be sent across a network to filter data bases for content and meaning. The agent would automatically inform the executive about unfavorable trends, such as when net income is materially under budget, and also subdivide the variation by responsible manager and provide possible reasons for the discrepancies. A final enhancement to EISs will include links to DSS software that enable senior executives not only to view data but also to analyze it.

INTEGRATING DSSs WITH OTHER SUPPORT SYSTEMS

Another emerging development is to use two or more decision support systems in combination. For instance a DSS may be used in concert with an expert system to aid bank managers in making investment and loan decisions. Still, another avenue of development is to integrate a neural network with an expert system to construct a hybrid system that extends the usefulness of both types of software packages, thus increasing the variety of problems that can be solved. To illustrate, neural networks should enable expert systems to combine rational problem solving with pattern recognition and other functions that involve intelligence.

FUZZY LOGIC

Fuzzy logic is a revolutionary form of artificial intelligence systems that extends the range of problems that can be modeled with expert systems and neural networks. Such systems attempt to model common sense by developing a mathematical model for dealing with inexact logic like "maybe" and "almost." The fuzzy logic model can interpret these subjective concepts that fall between absolute values, without fitting them arbitrarily into yes or no categories. Fuzzy logic makes use of imprecise or ambiguous if-then rules to define input and output values. Applications of fuzzy logic are slowly beginning to penetrate business organizations. For instance, FuziCalc (from Fuziware, Inc.) is a spreadsheet package that applies the principles of fuzzy logic theory to work with imprecise values. A user of FuziCalc has the option of plugging a single value or a range of high and low values in each spreadsheet cell. The range of values enables a decision maker to deal with ambiguity or uncertainty by formulating a number of possible outcomes that fall between exact values, thus making more effective decisions. Primary FuziCalc accounting applications include decision support applications such as forecasting, bidding, and other financial analyses.

DEVELOPMENTS IN MULTIMEDIA AND HYPERTEXT

Various technological developments should dramatically affect the support systems of the future. One development is **multimedia,** a computer-based presentation technique that allows users to associate information in multiple forms. Text, graphics, animated graphics, full-motion video, and sound can all be linked and mingled together and stored for later playback. Presenting information in a multimedia format should become the preferred method to provide training and instruction to new staff and ongoing training to employees. For example, accountants should find it useful to develop visually appealing multimedia presentations to train managers and self-directed work teams about accounting topics. Also, accountants can present many types of reports and information in a multiple media format. Such presentations should be quite effective, enabling employees to interact with the system and making complex accounting concepts easier to grasp and decision making more effective. Also, multimedia forms containing information on an accounting topic may be linked together. On retrieving a specific document pertaining to the topic, the user automatically has access to other related materials. **Hypertext** is similar to a data management software package that facilitates multimedia applications. For example, by highlighting words in a document such as "expert systems applications in accounting," any text, video clips, images, or sound about those words in other documents will be randomly retrieved, if any occurrences can be found.

SUMMARY

The purpose of an information system is to support decision making. To do so, it may employ a variety of systems: transaction processing systems, operational support systems, decision support systems, executive information systems, expert systems, and neural network systems. The transaction processing systems provide information relating to the operations; the operational support systems focus on short-range operational and tactical decisions made by the middle- and lower-level managers; and the decision support systems focus on long-range strategic and tactical planning decisions made primarily by the higher-level managers. Executive information systems provide information to higher-level managers for monitoring and controlling the firm's activities. Expert systems provide recommendations concerning a range of difficult decisions. Compared to expert systems, neural network systems give advice about a broader range of difficult problems.

A firm's set of decision support systems should consist of relevant, accurate, and up-to-date data in a comprehensive data base; decision models and statistical routines plus broad-based models (e.g., corporate models, financial planning models) in a model base; and a user interface that allows interactions via a command language that is powerful, easy to use, and versatile. The

language should also allow the user to perform manipulative techniques such as "what-if" analysis, sensitivity analysis, time-based simulation, and goal-seeking analysis. Outputs from a DSS usually include tailor-made hard-copy and soft-copy reports in graphical as well as tabular formats.

Many decision support systems tools can only be used by individual decision makers. Group decision support systems software or groupware tools allow two or more decision makers, who are connected to a computer network, to share information and make collaborative decisions.

Expert systems are knowledge-based computer programs that simulate the behavior of human experts. Like decision support systems, they aid in making decisions. However, they explicitly recommend decisions and they are adaptive. The components of an expert system are a knowledge base, task-specific data base, inference engine, and development engine. Expert systems of either the rule type or semantic type can be developed and implemented. An expert system can be developed using special languages that perform symbolic reasoning or by using an expert system shell. The major stages of development for an expert system are knowledge acquisition, computer modeling and debugging, and validation. The knowledge acquisition stage requires the services of knowledge engineers and experts. The computer modeling and debugging stage requires the writing of a computer program to convert the experts' knowledge to if-then rules. The validation process measures the reliability of the expert system. Technological developments that should improve the performance of support systems include fuzzy logic, multimedia, and hypertext.

APPENDIX 1 TO CHAPTER 16

GROUP DECISION SUPPORT SYSTEMS

In addition to E-mail (previously discussed), there are at least four other categories of group decision support systems (GDSS) software tools. They are electronic calendaring, group document management, workgroup utilities and development tools, and meeting/conferencing support tools.

Electronic Calendaring/Scheduling Software

Electronic calendaring/scheduling software will automatically arrange the activities of managers and other workers so that they do not conflict with one another.

Group Document Management Software

Group document management software permits documents to be scanned into a computer that is often part of a client/server network. The documents can be electronically filed, modified, and updated. They can be shared by any authorized person on the network, thus eliminating the need for making copies. Such systems reduce paper-handling costs, storage costs, and lost documents, and increase productivity of support staff who are freed to perform more important tasks.

Workgroup Utilities and Development Software

Workgroup utilities and development software include intelligent software agents (previously discussed); group information and collaborative development software, other than E-mail; and brainstorming utility software. **Group information and collaborative development software** allow persons to collaborate, share knowledge, and develop departmentwide and firmwide applications. An example of software in this category is Lotus Notes. **Lotus Notes** (from IBM Corporation) is used to develop applications that reside in separate data bases. A preformatted electronic form is used to enter data into the various data bases. For example, the receptionist at Infoage could develop an application that logs all customer complaints into a data base. The E-mail component of Lotus Notes would enable the complaints data base to be shared by all members of the marketing department, as well as by any other employees, including George Freeman, president. Anyone connected to the firm's computer network could log into the complaints data base, make comments, and add other information. A brainstorming session could be conducted in real-time by all members of the marketing department to generate ideas on possible reasons for the complaints, suggestions for reducing the complaints, and so on. Every change to the complaints data base is updated immediately so that every member of the discussion group has up-to-date information.

Electronic Brainstorming Utility Software

Electronic brainstorming utility software provides a structured approach designed to improve the problem-solving process. Brainstorming is a creativity catalyst that enables persons to set priorities and to generate new ideas. Studies have shown that electronic brainstorming groups evaluate more options and more quickly reach consensus compared to oral brainstorming groups. Microcomputer-based brainstorming software can be used effectively by both small and large firms. For example, Mike Barker of Infoage and his subordinates in the marketing department could use such software to develop a marketing plan and to write advertisements.

Meeting/Conferencing Support Tools

Meeting/conferencing support tools can be subdivided into electronic meeting systems, videoconferencing, and computer conferencing. An **electronic meeting system (EMS)** consists of a specially equipped conference room containing computer hardware and software designed to improve the quality of same time, same place face-to-face meetings. An EMS consists of a microcomputer for each participant that is interconnected to a local-area network, software, a file server, keypads for voting, and large-screen monitors. A facilitator is responsible for guiding management participants through the EMS process. An EMS provides anonymity to the management participants because comments and ideas are typed rather than expressed orally, and votes are recorded anonymously and displayed on the large display monitor. Of course, verbal discussion of the displayed comments and ideas is permitted. EMSs are more effective than traditional face-to-face meeting rooms since managers are less inhibited to contribute ideas, meetings are shorter, higher-quality decisions are made, and fewer meetings are required. **Videoconferencing** is used to conduct same time, different place virtual face-to-face meetings. A closed-circuit television system is installed at the sites, which may be separated by thousands of miles. Audiovisual signals are transmitted to all the interconnected sites. **Computer conferencing** enables participants at different locations to interact via on-line meetings. Participants can join the meeting at different places and times by logging on to an appropriate bulletin board. A participant adds his or her remarks on-line and the other participants make comments. Computer conferencing meetings may last for days since participants can reply to messages or make comments at their convenience.

APPENDIX 2 TO CHAPTER 16

NEURAL NETWORKS

Neural networks (NNs) process data the way the brain processes data—in a parallel processing mode. An NN consists of many processing elements joined together to form a network that can process multiple operations simultaneously. This multiple processing capability enables NNs to execute operations much faster than traditional methods, which process data serially one operation at a time. NNs solve problems by recognizing patterns in data that may be too subtle or complex for humans or other types of computer methods to discern. Basically, an NN creates a mathematical model from a data base of historical examples of input and output values. The NN system automatically adjusts its analyses until it learns the most probable relationships between the inputs and outputs.

Contrasts Between a Neural Network and an Expert System

A neural network differs in significant ways from an expert system (ES). An ES is developed from knowledge extracted from an expert, whereas an NN derives its knowledge from examples of historical data. Further, an ES has a strong user interface and an explanation facility to establish the reasoning for its decisions; an NN does not provide these options. Moreover, a large-scale ES may require two or more years to create and implement. Many NNs can be created and implemented very quickly, often in a matter of days or weeks. Also, a developer of an ES must write a computer program constructed of explicit if-then rules. For even simple ESs, this programming is often time-consuming and complex, particularly testing and debugging the program. An NN is trained by processing examples of historical data. The network constructs a model by recognizing patterns or correlations in these observations.

Applications

As indicated by Figure 16-12, an NN is suited for simple to complex and structured to unstructured problems. Thus, an NN can solve a much broader range of problems than an ES, including problems that are almost completely random in nature. Specific accounting applications suitable for development by using NN software are exhibited in Figure 16-18. Most of these problems can be categorized into prediction, classification, and pattern recognition problems. The first nine and last five applications displayed in the figure are more suitable for NNs than ESs for the following reasons:

1. Complex pattern recognition is necessary.
2. The size of the decision domain is large.
3. The applications are unstructured.
4. The problem situations are difficult to reduce to if-then rules.
5. The problems require intuition to solve.
6. A large number of variables are necessary to detect patterns or correlations.

The remaining applications, beginning with estimating inventory and ending with predicting earnings per share, require numeric variables to estimate, forecast, or predict a dollar value. Such applications are usually unsuitable for development by expert systems since symbolic knowledge is not required to represent the model. Traditionally, these applications have been solved using

- Detecting credit card fraud
- Detecting employee fraud
- Detecting management fraud
- Detecting weaknesses in internal control structure
- Interpreting audit evidence
- Interpreting audit quality
- Interpreting staff evaluations
- Predicting bankruptcy
- Predicting occurrence of risks
- Estimating inventory
- Estimating product costs
- Estimating sales
- Estimating selling prices
- Forecasting bond prices
- Forecasting budgets
- Forecasting earnings
- Predicting earnings per share
- Predicting employee performance
- Predicting loan risks
- Predicting stock prices
- Advising on decisions on mergers
- Advising on personal financial planning

FIGURE 16-18 Accounting applications suitable for neural networks.

a number of widely known statistical or other modeling techniques. However, unlike NNs, these techniques often cannot discern complex patterns with a large number of data items.

Development Considerations

As previously mentioned, developing and implementing an accounting NN application is often much easier and faster than developing an accounting ES application. Also, some NN software packages select the network structure automatically, making the developmental process much faster than other NN packages that do not offer this feature. As illustrated in Figure 16-19, the NN development process consists of creating a data base of examples, constructing a mathematical model of the relationships detected in the data values, evaluating the performance of the derived network, and implementing the model for its intended purpose. Each of these stages will be examined in turn.

Create Data Base

A data base of historical numerical examples, input into the NN software, is used to generate the mathematical models. The data base must contain both independent input variables and corresponding dependent output variables. Creating the data base is the most important step in the NN developmental process. Unrepresentative sample data or too few data observations will result

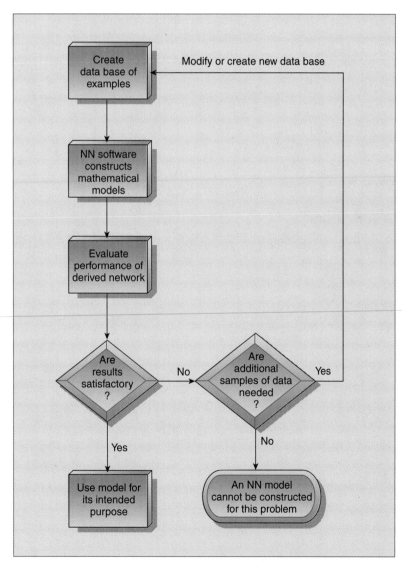

FIGURE 16-19 The neural network development process.

in a model that poorly estimates or predicts future values.

To illustrate these concepts, assume that Ann Strong has selected the ModelQuest (from AbTech Corporation) NN package. Other NN packages include Brainmaker (from California Scientific Software), and NeuralWorks Professional (from Neuralware). Ann has acquired a good working knowledge of the package and plans to use it in her financial audit and consulting engagements. Her first use of the NN package will be to aid in predicting bankruptcy during the preliminary analytical review phase of financial audits. The model developed by the NN software will enable her to predict whether a client will remain a going concern. After some preliminary research in the local library, she decides to use five financial ratios as the independent variables to predict pending bankruptcy, the dependent variable. Ann does an on-line search of national newspapers and finds eight firms that have declared bankruptcy and seven that have not. At the local library she does a search of the Compustat database to obtain the actual five ratios for the 15 firms. She develops the historical examples shown in

(a)

Sales to Assets*	Equity to Debt	Current Ratio	Inventory Turnover	Quick Ratio	Bankruptcy**
14.9	9.4	3.2	13.8	1.3	1
20.5	9.2	8.0	15.1	1.8	0
5.9	2.0	3.4	17.5	1.8	1
12.8	2.9	7.0	4.5	0.7	0
28.9	0.6	3.8	4.8	2.4	1
13.8	2.0	7.5	10.9	2.4	1
26.1	7.4	2.7	10.9	2.0	1
23.8	3.5	8.9	17.2	2.6	0
9.1	10.9	8.1	3.5	1.8	1
4.1	10.1	4.4	8.7	2.6	0
22.0	3.2	8.0	15.8	0.7	0
12.1	4.0	6.0	14.1	2.2	1
25.4	6.0	4.9	8.6	1.1	0
25.8	5.1	2.2	9.9	1.6	1
23.7	6.9	7.5	8.5	3.0	0

*In millions of dollars.
**A "1" means the firm has declared bankruptcy. A "0" means the firm has not declared bankruptcy.

(b)

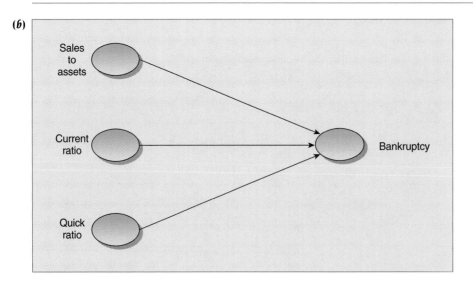

FIGURE 16-20   Predicting bankruptcy with a neural network. (a) Data base of examples used by Ann Strong to predict bankruptcy. (b) The model synthesized by the neural network software to predict bankruptcy.

Figure 16-20*a* for the 15 firms. Since symbolic values cannot be processed by the NN software, they must be converted to numerical values. As shown in the figure, a bankrupt firm is assigned a 1 and a nonbankrupt firm a 0.

Construct Model

Figure 16-20*a* is a table containing the historical ratio values and the bankruptcy status of each firm—a 0 or a 1. This table of input and output values is keyed into the NN package to construct a network depicting the relationships of the inputs to the output. Ann will have the software automatically split the table into a training file of 10 observations and a test file of five observations. The training file will be used by the NN software to synthesize a mathematical model to recognize patterns between the ratios (inputs) and the bankrupt-nonbankrupt firms (output). The model will be used by Ann to determine how well the trained network performs on the five test observations to predict which of the five firms, if any, may go bankrupt. The test data determines how well the synthesized network model is able to generalize on new, unseen data.

Evaluate Performance

The next step is to evaluate the performance of the network. Ann evaluates the first model constructed by examining the test data file, noting differences between the actual test value (a 0 or a 1) and the network estimate, and by evaluating summary statistics for the synthesized network. If the results are unacceptable, she synthesizes a second model by adjusting parameters within the software to fine-tune the model. This process is repeated until an acceptable model is generated. Figure 16-19 shows that if an acceptable model is not generated, Ann may increase the size of the first sample or obtain data that is more representative and begin the process again. If the results from running the modified data base through the NN software are still unacceptable, an acceptable network probably cannot be constructed for this problem.

Use Model

Assume that Ann gets satisfactory results after several models have been synthesized. Her network, depicted in Figure 16-20*b*, reveals that three input variables—total assets and current and quick ratios—are synthesized by the model to predict bankruptcy. The model can be implemented for its intended purpose of predicting bankruptcy by providing it with values for the three ratios. Assume that Ann uses the NN bankruptcy predictor model on an audit engagement of a medium-sized manufacturing firm. She computes the total assets and the current and quick ratios from the firm's financial records, and she inputs the three values into the network using the query function. The model immediately computes a 0 output value from the three inputs, which indicates that bankruptcy is unlikely for this firm.

REVIEW PROBLEM WITH SOLUTION

NIELSEN SALES COMPANY

Statement

The Nielsen Sales Company of Youngstown, Ohio, is interested in developing a financial planning model. It intends to begin with a very simple overall model and then progress to more detailed and complex versions. On analyzing the basic financial trends and relationships, it discovers the following:

  a. Sales have increased by about 10 percent each year for the past several years.
  b. The contribution margin percentage has remained rather constant at 30 percent.
  c. Fixed expenses consist of selling, administrative, and financial expenses. Selling expenses for a coming year are budgeted as 20 percent of sales for the first six months of the current year. Administrative expenses have remained constant. Financial expenses have averaged 15 percent of outstanding debt.
  d. Income taxes have averaged 18 percent of profit before taxes.

Required

a. Construct a financial planning model that generates the expected sales, contribution margin, total expenses, and net profit after income taxes for a standard planning period (i.e., the coming year).

b. Compute values for the foregoing factors if the following values are assumed for the current year.

Actual sales, first six months	$1,000,000
Estimated sales, second six months	900,000
Administrative expenses	217,000
Average outstanding debt	800,000

Solution

a. Expected sales = 1.10 × (sales, first six months + sales, second six months)

Expected contribution margin = 0.30 × expected sales

Expected total expenses = (0.70 × expected sales) + (0.20 × sales, first six months) + administrative expenses + (0.15 × outstanding debt)

Expected profit before income taxes = expected sales − total expenses

Expected net profit after income taxes = $(1 - 0.18)$ × profit before income taxes

b. Expected sales = $1.10 \times (\$1,000,000 + \$900,000) = \$2,090,000$

Expected contribution margin = $0.30 \times \$2,090,000 = \$627,000$

Expected total expenses = $(0.70 \times \$2,090,000) + (0.20 \times \$1,000,000) + \$217,000 + (0.15 \times \$800,000) = \$2,000,000$

Expected profit before income taxes = $\$2,090,000 - \$2,000,000 = \$90,000$

Expected net profit after taxes = $(1 - 0.18) \times \$90,000 = \$73,800$

KEY TERMS

artificial intelligence (AI)   (720)
backward chaining   (730)
command language approach   (726)
computer conferencing   (739)
corporate model   (724)
decision model   (723)
decision support system (DSS)   (719)
development engine   (730)
drill down   (719)
electronic brainstorming utility software   (739)
electronic calendaring/scheduling software   (739)
electronic mail (E-mail) software   (728)
electronic meeting system (EMS)   (739)
executive information system (EIS)   (719)
expert system (ES)   (720)
expert system shell   (735)
financial planning model   (724)
forward chaining   (730)
fuzzy logic   (737)
group decision support system (GDSS)   (727)
group document management software   (739)
group information and collaborative development
   software   (739)
groupware tools   (727)
hypertext   (738)
inference engine   (730)
information center   (726)
intelligent agent software   (737)
intelligent decision support system   (721)
knowledge base   (729)
knowledge engineers   (734)
Lotus Notes   (739)
meeting/conferencing support tools   (739)
menu approach   (726)
model-base management system (MBMS)   (724)
multimedia   (738)

neural network (NN)   (720)
nonintelligent decision support system   (721)
operational support system (OSS)   (718)
optimization model   (723)
query language   (725)
replacement level   (716)
task-specific data base   (730)
user interface   (725)
validation   (736)
validity rate   (736)
videoconferencing   (739)
workgroup utilities and development software   (739)

REVIEW QUESTIONS

16-1. Contrast the five levels of decision support provided by information systems.

16-2. Identify and contrast the five types of information processing systems.

16-3. Contrast the purposes of operational support systems and decision support systems.

16-4. What capabilities does a computer-based operational support system typically possess?

16-5. What capabilities does a computer-based decision support system typically possess?

16-6. Contrast the purposes of decision support systems and executive information systems.

16-7. How does an executive information system differ from a decision support system?

16-8. What types of outputs may be available from an effective executive information system?

16-9. Contrast a nonintelligent decision support system and an intelligent decision support system.

16-10. What are the benefits provided by a decision support system?

16-11. Identify the components of a decision support system.

16-12. What attributes should be possessed by the data base, model base, and user interface of a decision support system?

16-13. Describe the variety of models that are likely to be found in the model base of an effective decision support system.

16-14. Contrast a corporate model and a financial planning model.

16-15. Identify several attributes of a typical modeling language.

16-16. What are the functions of a model-base management system?

16-17. Contrast four data manipulation and analysis techniques.

16-18. Contrast the command language and menu information retrieval approaches.

16-19. What types of services may be provided by an information center?

16-20. What types of outputs may be available from an effective decision support system?

16-21. What are examples of decisions supported by decision support systems?

16-22. What are group decision support systems, and how do they differ from conventional decision support systems?

16-23. What is electronic mail?

16-24. What benefits are provided by an expert system?

16-25. Contrast a decision support system and an expert system.

16-26. What are the components of an expert system?

16-27. What are suitable applications of expert systems in the auditing area? Tax area? Managerial/cost accounting area? Financial accounting area?

16-28. Describe the development of an expert system, and identify the roles of knowledge engineers, experts, and users. Do expert systems have common sense?

16-29. How is an expert system validated?

16-30. What future developments are likely with respect to systems that support decision making?

16-31. What is fuzzy logic?

DISCUSSION QUESTIONS

16-32. Why are users increasingly involved in the development of decision support and related types of systems?

16-33. Should decision support systems be immediate processing systems?

16-34. Can Ann Strong, CPA and CMA, justify the use of a decision support system? What types of services can she provide to her clients with decision support systems?

16-35. What problems is Ann Strong likely to encounter in the development of a decision support system for a client?

16-36. Describe how Mike Barker, marketing manager of Infoage, Inc., might use decision support systems to more effectively manage his department. Who would likely develop any decision support systems used by Mike?

16-37. Can the accounting information system be viewed as a collection of integrated models?

16-38. What are the objections, if any, to providing "real-time" (say "hourly") financial reports to George Freeman, president of Infoage? To self-directed work teams of empowered employees in general?

16-39. Discuss difficulties that can occur in the development of expert systems. Do you feel that Ann Strong encountered these difficulties when she developed an expert system for APB No. 29, *Accounting for Nonmonetary Transactions*? Do you feel that her expert system will be used for a long duration? Why do you suppose many expert systems are used only for a short duration?

16-40. Discuss how decision support systems and expert systems might be combined in "expert support systems" to aid managers in making very complex decisions.

16-41. Describe how Infoage's key management team might use group decision support systems.

16-42. Assume that Ann Strong developed a tax planning expert system but improperly validates it. The expert system was developed from expertise provided in an authoritative tax planning textbook. She uses the expert system to provide tax planning advice to one of her clients. As a result of the advice, assume the client loses a substantial amount of money. What reaction is the client's management likely to have when they find out that an expert system was used to make the tax planning decision? What are the legal ramifications of this situation? Are there any ethical issues involved in this situation?

PROBLEMS

Note: Certain problems require knowledge found in the appendixes at the end of this chapter.

16-1. For each of the following situations, identify a suitable support system and the level of support that is required or can reasonably be expected:

  a. Checking pension plan provisions to determine if the plan meets federal regulations.

  b. Making of reservations by an airline.

  c. Checking of credit by a discount store.

  d. Providing assistance to a large fast-food chain in locating new restaurants.

  e. Maintaining of control over accounts receivable by a home appliance retailer.

  f. Maintaining of controls over the physical flows of job orders by a manufacturer that has a complex production process involving numerous parts and materials, labor inputs, machining operations, and inspections.

g. Detecting automatic teller machine fraud by a bank.

h. Maintaining of controls over its freight cars by a railroad that carries cargo across the country.

i. Maintaining of controls over the times and costs incurred on construction projects currently in progress by a contractor.

j. Providing of an electronic transfer of funds service by a statewide bank whose depositors can have bills debited directly from their accounts into the accounts of creditors such as utilities.

k. Providing assistance to an architect in designing a new special-purpose building.

l. Helping a manufacturer that has alternative uses for its available production space to decide whether to make or to buy parts.

m. Helping a public accounting firm decide whether to terminate a staff accountant.

n. Deciding whether to authorize construction of a new manufacturing facility to produce microcomputers.

o. Selecting a new plant site by a large microcomputer manufacturer.

p. Providing assistance to a hospital in selecting the most suitable capital expenditure projects to undertake during the next five years.

q. Providing assistance to a regional public accounting firm in establishing pricing policies for its services.

r. Assisting a consumer goods firm in evaluating proposals for new products.

s. Verifying of the validity of warranty claims by a large automotive manufacturer.

t. Providing assistance to a public accounting firm in determining whether to promote a manager to partner.

16-2. The Industrial Savings and Loan Association of Akron, Ohio, has 50 branches throughout Ohio. It has experienced several gradually worsening problems in recent years. One problem is obtaining daily prompt summary information concerning total transactions conducted at all branches. Another problem pertains to a check-cashing service provided by the association for the purpose of attracting new depositors; occasionally a "patron" will cash bad checks at several branches in a single day, and the fact will not be discovered until the next day. A third problem has been a difficulty in developing sound appraisal values quickly when potential borrowers apply for loans on real estate. A fourth problem pertains to a poor service pattern: almost twice as many customers are serviced at a typical branch between 10:00 A.M.

and 11:00 A.M. and also between 2:00 P.M. and 3:00 P.M., as during the noon hour.

Required

Describe the array of *support systems* that could help overcome these problems. Note that a single system will likely *not* be the best solution. Assume that the home office currently has a medium-sized computer and that each branch has terminals connected to the home office computer, and microcomputers.

16-3. Butler Machinery Co., with $10 million in annual sales, designs and manufactures complex machinery. To increase efficiency and to remain competitive, the firm has decided to install a computer-aided design and manufacturing system. Bob Talbot, vice-president of engineering, and George Jackson, vice-president of manufacturing, have been given the responsibility for selecting and installing the new system.

Only Talbot and Jackson have worked on this project, having spent a considerable amount of time in reviewing available systems and making on-site visits to see various systems in operation. They are still undecided about which system to select after several months of work.

During a steering committee meeting on the project status, the president suggested that Talbot and Jackson include selected members from the engineering and manufacturing staff in the decision-making process as system selecting will have significant impact on the way Butler designs and manufactures its machinery. The president added that this process may result in a better decision because there are many complex factors to consider.

Required

a. Explain how organizational complexity can affect decision making.

b. Identify and discuss advantages and disadvantages of group decision making.

c. What criteria should be used to determine if a group should be involved in a decision?

d. What types of groupware or group decision support systems (GDSS) software are available to make collaborative decisions?

(CMA *adapted*)

16-4. You are the sales manager of the recently formed Vega Corporation, which sells two products in three sales territories. The contents of two files of keen interest to you contain the up-to-date information shown on page 747. Vega has installed an interactive decision support system for use by you and the other managers. The system includes a command language, a relational data base, and a report generator.

Sales File

Date of Sale	Sales Invoice No.	Customer Name	Sales Territory	Product Name[a]	Quantity Sold	Amount of Sale
Jan. 2	1	D. Smith	B	Alpha	3	$30.00
Jan. 3	2	F. Brown	A	Omega	8	160.00
Jan. 5	3	M. Mosley	C	Omega	5	100.00
Jan. 8	4	G. Dane	C	Omega	10	200.00
Jan. 8	5	O. Lamm	A	Alpha	6	60.00
Jan. 9	6	P. Piper	A	Alpha	10	100.00
Jan. 10	7	S. White	B	Omega	7	140.00
Jan. 12	8	H. Rosner	C	Alpha	12	120.00

[a]Only one product may be recorded on a single invoice.

Product File

Product Name	Description	Unit Cost	Unit Price	Supplier Name	Quantity on Hand
Alpha	Whirl	7.00	10.00	Cody	150
Omega	Swirl	16.00	20.00	Barker	80

Required

Show the report that the system would provide if you enter each of the following command statements:

a. REFER TO SALES FILE
PRINT DATE AND NAME AND AMOUNT
BY TERRITORY

b. REFER TO SALES FILE
PRINT AMOUNT AND NAME
BY TERRITORY
RANKED BY AMOUNT
IF AMOUNT LESS THAN $100, OMIT

c. JOIN SALES AND PRODUCT FILES
PRINT CENTERED HEADING
"SALES SUMMARY"
SUM UNIT SALES AND AMOUNTS
BY PRODUCT
PRINT TOTALS AFTER NAME AND
DESCRIPTION AND SUPPLIER
PRINT GRAND TOTALS, UNIT
SALES AND AMOUNT

16-5. Note: *This problem can be solved on a microcomputer by means of an electronic financial modeling package such as IFPS/PC.*

Refer to the Review Problem. Solve for the expected net profit after taxes if each of the following changes is made. In each part return to the "base" model formula and values given in the Review Problem.

a. Sales are expected to increase by 20 percent in the coming year.

b. Actual sales for the first six months were $800,000.

c. Administrative expenses are expected to increase by $83,000 during the coming year.

d. Financial expenses are expected to average 20 percent of outstanding debt in the coming year (and debt is expected to remain at the present level).

16-6. Note: *This problem can be solved on a microcomputer by means of an electronic financial modeling package such as Javelin or IFPS/PC.*

For several years the Programme Corporation of Urbana, Illinois, has encountered difficulties estimating its cash flows. The result has been a rather strained relationship with its banker.

Programme's controller would like to develop a means by which he can forecast and plan the firm's monthly operating cash flows. The following data were gathered to facilitate cash forecasting and planning.

a. Sales have been increasing and are expected to increase at 0.5 percent each month.

b. Of each month's sales, 30 percent are for cash; the other 70 percent are on open account.

c. Of the credit sales, 90 percent are collected in the first month following the sale and the remaining

10 percent are collected in the second month. There are no bad debts.

d. Gross margin (profit) on sales averages 25 percent.

e. Sufficient inventory purchases are made each month to cover the following month's sales.

f. All inventory purchases are paid for in the month of purchase at a 2 percent cash discount.

g. Monthy expenses are payroll, $1500; rent, $400; depreciation, $120; other cash expenses, 2 percent of that month's sales. There are no accruals.

h. Ignore the effects of corporate income taxes, dividends, and equipment acquisitions.

Required

a. Construct a financial planning model that generates the monthly operating cash inflows and outflows for any specified month.

b. If sales for the current month are $10,000, compute the cash inflows and outflows for the next two months.

c. "What if" the sales are expected to increase at 1.0 percent per month in the future? Determine the changes in the amounts of the cash inflows and outflows for the next two months, assuming that sales for the current month remain at the level of $10,000.

d. "What if" monthly inventory purchases are changed to cover the average of one-half the current month's sales and one-half of the following month's sales? Show the change to the financial planning model and determine the changes in cash outflows for the next two months, assuming the conditions specified in **a** above.

e. Often a cash forecast is used to determine the expected level of cash at the end of each month. Assume that this model is expanded to include the calculation of the expected level of cash. Assume further that the forecast for a following month shows that the cash balance is $2000 lower than desired but that the firm prefers not to borrow money to raise the cash balance to the desired level. Describe a type of analysis that can aid in determining other means by which to raise the cash balance to the desired level.

(CMA *adapted*)

16-7. Advances in computer hardware technology and software design have enabled management information systems to evolve from systems that primarily process transaction data to systems that impart knowledge. One type of management information system, an operational support system, is used by managers and accountants to support the operational activities of the firm. These systems emerged in the late 1950s and supported short-term planning and control. Three examples of such systems are real-time, interactive, and communication-

based systems. However, managers required more flexible systems that could respond to less well-defined questions. With advances in hardware technology and software engineering, higher-level systems such as decision support systems, expert systems, and neural network systems evolved.

Required

a. Identify the purpose and characteristics of a management information system.

b. Describe the characteristics of the following operational support systems, and give a different example of each of these three systems.

   (1) Real-time system

   (2) Interactive system

   (3) Communication-based system

c. Describe the purpose as well as the characteristics and capabilities of a(n):

   (1) Decision support system

   (2) Expert system

   (3) Neural network system

d. Describe suitable accounting applications for each of the three systems described in **c** above.

(CMA *adapted*)

16-8. For each of the scenarios labeled *a* through *s*, select the best alternative from the following list of systems labeled 1 through 9, which can be utilized to effectively develop the automated system in question. Also defend the answer you selected:

   1. Procedural programming language (i.e., COBOL, FORTRAN)

   2. Accounting software package (i.e., DAC Easy, Real-World Accounting)

   3. Management information system

   4. Nonintelligent decision support system

   5. Intelligent decision support system

   6. Expert system

   7. Neural network

   8. Spreadsheet package

   9. None of the above

a. Screening accounting job applicants prior to an on-site interview.

b. Keeping track of inventory levels (perpetual).

c. Computing earnings-per-share computations per APB No. 15.

d. Aiding a manufacturing firm to make the decision of where to locate a new manufacturing facility.

e. Providing help in deciding whether a person can be claimed as an exemption on the preparer's tax return.

f. Providing personal financial advice to clients.

g. Deciding whether to develop a specific intelligent decision support system application.

h. Deciding whether to develop a specific expert system application.

i. Computing a firm's key financial ratios and then using the ratios to interpret the firm's financial condition.

j. Helping an accountant select a microcomputer.

k. Helping to determine the type of audit opinion to issue.

l. Providing advice on whether a condition is reportable.

m. Recording complex and unusual accounting transactions.

n. Providing a manager with a specific answer.

o. Preparing all necessary journal entries for monetary and nonmonetary exchanges of similar and dissimilar assets.

p. Preparing individual income tax returns.

q. Giving advice about the causes of complex manufacturing cost variances that are significantly over standard.

r. Accounting for fixed assets and calculating depreciation schedules.

s. Determining whether a firm should lease or buy equipment.

16-9. Long Island Financial Bancshares, a large bank-holding corporation located in New York City, is evaluating financially sound, small rural New England banks for acquisition. Jim Bennett, the assistant controller, has been appointed to a committee to develop a decision support model to analyze the alternatives and criteria related to the decision. The committee has identified six rural New England banks (the alternatives) for possible acquisition, designated as Bank A, Bank B ... Bank F. The table below shows the six criteria that will be used to evaluate each bank, along with the numerical and nonnumerical data for each criterion for each bank.

Required

a. One of Jim Bennett's first steps in constructing a decision model is to assign independent weights to each of the six criteria. The weights should range from 0 to 100 percent. What factors should be considered in assigning these weights? You are to "intuitively" assign weights to each of the six criteria, as best as you can, based on the limited information given in the case.

b. Taking into consideration the weights you assigned in **a** above, construct a structured decision model to rank the six alternatives, from low to high. Which bank would you recommend for purchase? What other factors should be taken into consideration, other than the derived numerical rankings?

c. List some other types of accounting applications that can be solved by constructing decision models, similar to the one you developed in **b** above.

d. *Optional*: If you have access to a decision support package, such as Expert Choice, Lightyear, or Criterium, which can rank alternatives based on criteria, use the package to generate a graphical solution to the problem. How does the solution in **c** above compare to the solution you derived in **b**? What do you feel are the limitations, if any, of these types of decision support software packages?

16-10. Identify which of the following problem situations are most suitable for the application of expert systems. Briefly describe the construction of the expert system in each such case.

a. Determining whether a person's application for a major credit card should be approved, and if approved, the appropriate credit limit.

b. Determining whether an order from a customer should be accepted.

			Criteria			
Alternative	Annual Sales	Management Quality	Price/Earnings Ratio[a]	Public Image	Financial Strength	Price in $ Millions[b]
Bank A	$400	Outstanding	11	Above Average	A	$800
Bank B	475	Good	17	Poor	C	750
Bank C	280	Fair	10	Average	B	600
Bank D	160	Very Good	9	Excellent	A	475
Bank E	510	Outstanding	18	Below Average	D	900
Bank F	450	Poor	42	Finest	B−	700

[a] The P/E ratio is computed by dividing price per share of common stock by earnings per share of common stock. The lower the ratio, the more desirable the bank for acquisition.

[b] The lower the purchase price, the more desirable the bank for acquisition.

c. Determining whether a person qualifies as a dependent on a tax return.

d. Determining whether the internal control structure of a firm is adequate.

e. Determining the variety of activities to be undertaken by a manager during the course of a workday.

f. Determining the type of audit opinion to issue.

g. Determining the stocks to select for an investment portfolio.

h. Determining the particular computer system to select for a firm's business data processing applications.

i. Determining the quantity of an inventory item to reorder.

j. Determining whether a mortgage loan applicant qualifies for a residential home mortgage.

k. Determining whether the financial position of a firm is sound, based on the financial statements.

l. Determining whether the balance of a general ledger account is material.

16-11. For each of the following audit problems, indicate whether an expert system, a neural network system, or some other type of system could effectively assist in solving the problem.

a. Estimating the allowance for doubtful accounts.

b. Sampling a master accounts receivable file on disk containing 57,500 customer accounts.

c. Detecting fraudulent credit card transactions.

d. Evaluating the internal control environment for a medium-sized retail organization.

e. Evaluating audit evidence.

f. Scheduling the accounting staff to client financial audits for the next three-month period.

g. Detecting purchasing fraud.

h. Evaluating a computer system flowchart of the cash receipts cycle.

i. Issuing an audit opinion on a firm's financial statements.

j. Determining whether a firm has properly selected the purchase or pooling of interest method.

k. Predicting current monthly sales and comparing the output to the firm's actual monthly sales.

l. Assessing the riskiness of large-scale computer projects whose costs may run into the millions of dollars.

m. Conducting analytical review procedures.

n. Evaluating whether or not imputed interest has been correctly computed.

16-12. As a Certified Public Accountant and Certified Financial Planner, you have been consulted about the construction of an expert system to aid in personal investing. You begin by investigating the variety of factors that influence the investment environment for individuals. Some of the factors you discover are income level, amount of savings, amount of insurance coverage required, amount of emergency funds required, marital status, and investment objectives. Then you consider the various investment options, such as money market fund, bond fund, stock fund, T-bills, gold, and real estate.

Required

Describe how you would continue in developing a rule-based expert system. Include in your description (a) typical questions that the system should ask the potential investor in order to develop the task-specific data base, for example, "Are you married?"; (b) typical rules that might be found in the knowledge base, for example, If the potential investor is married *and . . . and . . .*, *then* the investor should make an investment; (c) suggested recommendations that the expert system might offer, for example, If investing is indicated *and . . . and . . .*, *then* a bond fund is the best investment.

16-13. Liepsner and Associates, PC, a public accounting firm located in Newton, Iowa, is developing a tax expert system to aid in preparing tax returns. The tax expert system will assist the firm's tax preparers to determine whether clients' dependents qualify as an exemption on their individual tax returns. Five tests must be met before a person can be claimed as a dependent on the tax return:

1. Income level.
2. Amount of support.
3. Marital status.
4. Citizenship or place of residence.
5. Relationship of dependent to taxpayer.

Required

Hint: *You may wish to consult a current tax textbook or Internal Revenue Service publications. Refer to the section on claiming personal exemptions.*

a. List typical questions that the expert system should ask the firm's tax preparers, for example, "Did the dependent attend school full-time for any five months during 1998?"

b. List typical rules that might be found in the knowledge base, for example, "If the dependent is a citizen of the U.S. *or* is a resident of the United States *or* is a resident of Canada *or* is a resident of Mexico, *then* the citizen test is satisfied."

c. Is the tax exemption determinator a good choice for the development of an expert system? Explain. What are the limitations, if any, of developing an expert system for this application?

d. How would you validate this expert system? Other than validation, what other problems are likely to be encountered in auditing expert system applications? Decision support system applications?

16-14. You are a newly hired accountant working for Great Switzer Bank of Natick, Massachusetts. One of your first assignments is to develop a prototype expert system that approves residential loan applications and provides an explanation for accepting or rejecting each application. A major objective of using the expert system is to reduce loan processing time from 10 days to one day.

A study of the bank's procedures for accepting residential loans discloses the following information:

1. An applicant must have been with his current employer for at least one year.
2. The amount requested for the loan must not exceed 80 percent of the property's appraised value.
3. The monthly housing expenses, including principal, interest, taxes, and mortgage insurance, must not exceed 30 percent of the applicant's monthly income.
4. Anticipated total monthly expenses (including monthly housing expenses) must not exceed 42 percent of the applicant's monthly income.

If an applicant's application is rejected, he or she has seven working days to provide any additional information and to request an interview with one of the bank's senior vice-presidents.

Required

a. List the typical questions that the residential mortgage application evaluator expert system should ask the mortgage loan applicant.

b. List typical rules that might be found in the knowledge base, for example, "*If* an applicant has not worked for his or her present employer for at least one year, *then* reject the application."

c. List suggested recommendations that the expert system might offer, for example, if the application is rejected, the expert system might provide the following recommendation: "The application has been rejected because anticipated total monthly expenses exceed 36 percent of the applicant's monthly income."

d. Is the residential mortgage loan evaluator a good choice for the development of an expert system? Fully discuss. What are the limitations, if any, of developing an expert system for this application?

e. *Optional*: If you have access to an expert system shell, such as VP-EXPERT or 1st CLASS, develop the expert system for accepting or rejecting residential loan applications.

16-15. A regional public accounting firm has developed a prototype rule-based expert system to assist its director of recruiting to determine whether a job applicant should be invited to the firm's headquarters for an on-site interview. As shown in the diagram below, the three factors considered are a degree in accounting, grade point average, and campus interview. For example, one rule states that "*If* a job applicant has a degree in accounting *and* a GPA of at least 3.1 *and* an adequate campus interview, *then* invite the candidate for an on-site interview."

Degree in Accounting	GPA of at Least 3.1	Adequate Campus Interview	Invite for On-Site Interview
Yes	Yes	Yes	Yes
No	Yes	Yes	Yes
No	No	Yes	No
No	Yes	No	No
Yes	Yes	No	No
Yes	No	No	No

Required

a. The diagram reveals that a total of six rules are used by this expert system. Is the rule base complete? If not, what other rules would you add to the diagram?

b. What questions will the expert system ask the director of recruiting during a consultation?

c. Is this topic area a good choice for the development of an expert system? What are the limitations of the expert system as developed? What recommendations would you make for improving this expert system?

d. *Optional*: If you have access to an expert system shell, such as VP-EXPERT or 1st CLASS, develop the expert system for the interview process, including any rules you added to your revised decision table.

16-16. Big Sky Sports Company, a large sporting goods store with annual sales approaching $130,000,000, is headquartered in Provo, Utah. Big Sky has 110 retail outlets in Colorado, Idaho, Montana, Nebraska, Utah, and Wyoming. During the last five years, the firm's controller staff has developed 25 prototype expert systems applications in the areas of risk analysis, internal auditing, tax, and financial accounting. Twenty-four of these applications have progressed from the prototype to commercial stage and are used on a daily basis by the firm's accounting staff. During the coming year, the controller has decided to expand the number of expert systems in the financial accounting area. One of the first expert systems will be written for FASB No. 5, *Accounting for Contingencies*.

The staff accountant, Kate, who is responsible for developing this expert system obtains the following information from the assistant controller, Bill, who is the firm's expert on matters relating to contingencies:

Bill tells Kate that certain conditions, situations, or circumstances exist on the balance sheet date that involve uncertainty as to possible losses or gains that a firm may incur should some future event occur. Bill states that these events are known as loss contingencies or gain contingencies and may need to be included directly in the financial statements by establishing related accounts through a journal entry or disclosed in a note to the financial statements.

Kate asks Bill which events require journal entries and which require only footnote disclosure. Bill provides the following answer: "A *material* estimated loss from a loss contingency should be *accrued* (e.g., journalized as a debit to a loss account and a credit to a liability account) if it is *probable* that a liability has been incurred and the amount of the loss can be *reasonably estimated*." Bill further states that "if, on the other hand, it is only *reasonably possible* that a loss has been incurred, even though the amount can be *reasonably estimated*, footnote disclosure is necessary. No disclosure of any kind is required if the likelihood of loss is reasonably possible or remote and the amount of the loss cannot be estimated. If the possibility of loss is only remote, even though the amount of the loss can be estimated, no disclosure of any kind is necessary."

With regard to gain contingencies, Bill states that "gain contingencies are never recorded in the accounts because of the conservatism rule—account for all potential losses, but do not recognize gains before they are realized. If the gain contingency is material and probably will materialize in the future and the amount can be reasonably estimated, it should be disclosed in a footnote to the balance sheet. Otherwise, no disclosure is necessary if the possibility of materialization is remote, even if the amount of the gain can be estimated. Also, if the probability of gain is remote, whether the amount of the gain contingency can or cannot be reasonably estimated, no disclosure is necessary. Finally, no disclosure is necessary if the gain contingency is probable and the amount of the gain cannot be estimated."

Required

a. List typical questions the contingency advisor should ask a user of the expert system during a consultation.

b. List typical rules that should be found in the knowledge base, for example, *If* it is probable that a liability . . . *and* the amount of the liability . . . , *then* a loss contingency. . . .

c. Is the contingency advisor a good choice for the development of an expert system? Fully discuss. What are the limitations, if any, of developing an expert system for this application?

d. *Optional:* If you have access to an expert system shell, such as VP-EXPERT or 1st CLASS, develop the contingency advisor expert system.

16-17. Novak Jabouri Schmidt, PC, a small public accounting firm located in Littleton, Colorado, is developing a prototype expert system to provide advice regarding the type of audit opinion to issue at the completion of a financial statement audit. As their staff accountant specializing in the management consulting area, they ask you to prepare a prototype and report back on your progress in two weeks.

You decide to include in your working prototype only three factors that affect the issuance of audit opinions:

1. Limitations placed on the scope of the audit.
2. Departures from generally accepted accounting principles (GAAP).
3. The likelihood of a firm continuing as a going concern.

You plan to expand the expert system to include other factors after the senior partner has evaluated the prototype system and given you the authority to proceed further.

After interviewing the firm's audit partner, you develop the diagram on page 753. Your next step is to develop the rules by following the diagram's path. For example, one path indicates that "*if* the scope limitation is material *and* departure from GAAP is material *and* doubt about going concern is material, *then* the firm should issue an adverse opinion for any client meeting these conditions."

Required

a. Are there any rules that are missing from the diagram? If so, what other rules would you add to the diagram? (Prepare a revised diagram for any additional rules added.) Are all of these rules needed, or are some redundant? How many rules do you feel that the final version of the expert system should contain?

b. What questions will the expert system ask an auditor during a consultation?

c. Is the audit opinion advisor a good choice for the development of an expert system? What recommendations would you make for improving this expert system, other than adding additional factors that affect the issuance of audit opinions?

d. *Optional:* If you have access to an expert system shell, such as VP-EXPERT or 1st CLASS, develop the prototype audit opinion advisor expert system from your revised diagram, eliminating any rules that you feel are redundant.

16-18. As a result of recent advances in information processing and communications technology, a large manufacturing firm is proposing the following changes in its field sales operation:

1. All salespersons will be issued personal computers equipped with a modem. They will be trained to use an integrated software package that will give them data-base, word processing, spreadsheet, graphics, and communications capabilities.

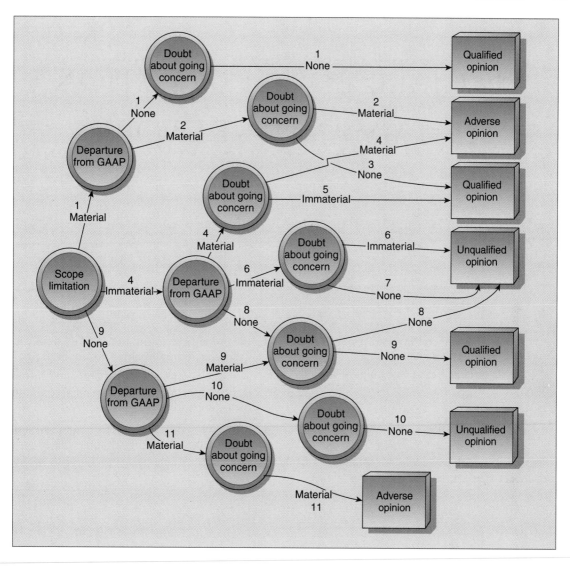

2. Regional sales managers will be housed at the home office. Teleconferencing will be used for communications between the sales managers and the members of the sales force should a group conference be required.

3. Regional sales offices will be closed and sales personnel will work out of their homes. All "office" work will be conducted using the concept of "telecommuting."

The firm is concerned about making such drastic changes in its operations and has asked you to evaluate the advantages and disadvantages of the changes.

Required

Identify three advantages and three disadvantages of the changes noted above in terms of the following concepts:

a. End-user computing.

b. Teleconferencing.

c. Telecommuting.

(CIA *adapted*)

16-19. *Datacruncher Office Equipment, Inc.* (*Continuing Case*) For the systems project you have selected or been assigned, describe the components and attributes of an executive information system (EIS) that can effectively aid one of the firm's managers in making a strategic decision. Also, describe the components and attributes of a decision support system (other than an EIS) that can effectively aid one of the firm's managers in making a strategic or tactical decision. Finally, describe the components and attributes of an expert system that can effectively aid one of the firm's managers in making a tactical or operational decision.

CHAPTER
17

••

SPECIALIZED INFORMATION
SYSTEMS AND NETWORKS

••

THE LEARNING OBJECTIVES FOR THIS CHAPTER ARE TO ENABLE YOU TO:

1. Describe the features, advantages, and drawbacks of wide-area computer-based communications networks.

2. Describe the features, advantages, and drawbacks of local-area computer-based communications networks.

3. Describe the components, advantages, and drawbacks of client/server computing.

4. Examine accounting and related applications of data communications networks.

5. Identify controls, security, and audit measures that pertain particularly to data communications networks.

6. Survey several specialized business information systems/networks that are based on data communications networks.

INTRODUCTION

PURPOSE AND NATURE OF DATA COMMUNICATIONS

A modern firm may conduct its affairs from two or more locations. For instance, a typical manufacturing firm may have several plants, warehouses, and sales offices—all at locations removed from a home office. Communications between these remote locations have traditionally been conveyed by letters, telephone calls, and interoffice messenger services. Currently, however, a geographically dispersed firm may electronically link its remote locations by means of a data communications system. This means of communication provides the managers and employees of a firm who happen to reside in remote locations with the same access to data, computing power, and guidance that they

would have if they were physically in the home office.

In a technical sense, a data communications system links together the data collection, processing, storage, and dissemination facilities into a computer network. Networks have become increasingly important for three reasons: (1) many firms have become geographically dispersed and need to transmit large volumes of data quickly and reliably; (2) data communications technology has become more sophisticated, versatile, and affordable; and (3) many firms are using groupware tools to share data and to facilitate collaboration among work groups, managers, and other employees. Currently, it is estimated that more than 90 percent of all computers (excluding microcomputers) in the United States are connected to data communications networks; for microcomputers, the estimate is about 70 percent and rapidly increasing.

TYPES OF COMPUTER NETWORKS

In the 1950s and 1960s data communications technology was in its infancy. Computer networks were scarcely feasible. Hence, geographically dispersed firms desiring to employ computers for data processing had three choices: (1) to subscribe to a computer service bureau; (2) to install a single large computer, usually at the home office; or (3) to install a variety of computers, usually at various locations. Those firms electing the second option employed centralized computer systems, whereas those choosing the third option created **decentralized computer systems**. Figure 17-1*a* illustrates a decentralized computer system for a firm having a home office and two remote locations.

In the early 1970s data communications networks became feasible options. Hence, many firms installed large computers at a central location and tied the centralized computer to terminals at various remote locations. For instance, Ramada Inns installed a large reservations computer at Omaha and tied each of its separate inns (motels) to the computer via terminals. This **centralized computer network** enabled Ramada Inns to accommodate reservations quickly; because the computer was placed at the approximate center of the United States, it was able to minimize the communication line costs. Figure 17-1*b* illustrates a centralized computer network for the same firm that earlier had a decentralized computer system.

Later in the 1970s the emergence of minicomputers opened a new option. A firm could link two or more minicomputers together or to a large computer (though the linked computers usually had to be of the same make, e.g., IBM). When the linked computers were located in different geographical locations, they formed a **distributed computer network**. Figure 17-1*c* illustrates this option for the same firm. The appearance of microcomputers has accelerated the trend toward distributed computer networks.

Because the two types of networks just described link together geographically dispersed points, they are called **wide-area networks**. Networks can also be formed of computers that are not geographically dispersed. A **local-area network** is a distributed network that functions within a single limited geographical area, such as a single building or cluster of buildings. In a few years, the distinctions between wide-area and local-area networks will rapidly diminish in importance as more firmwide networks evolve to include both types of networks. As discussed in Chapter 3, an evolving *logical* model of computing known as **client/server computing** processes applications within a *physical* local-area network or wide-area network or both. In the client/server computing model, processing of applications is optimally allocated to the network resources that can most efficiently handle the task. The three major types of computer networks and client/server computing will be discussed in later sections of this chapter.

ROLES OF ACCOUNTANTS WITH RESPECT TO NETWORKS

By their nature, computer networks are quite complex and technical creations. Accountants cannot be expected to understand fully the technical details or implications. However, networks are extremely significant to accountants for several reasons. First, a network is an integral part of an accounting information system (AIS), since it transmits data and information. For example, a firm may make sales at stores across the country. The marketing manager, located at the firm's headquarters in Chicago, needs summary reports concerning yesterday's sales by tomorrow morning. Only a computer network can easily and routinely provide the needed sales reports.

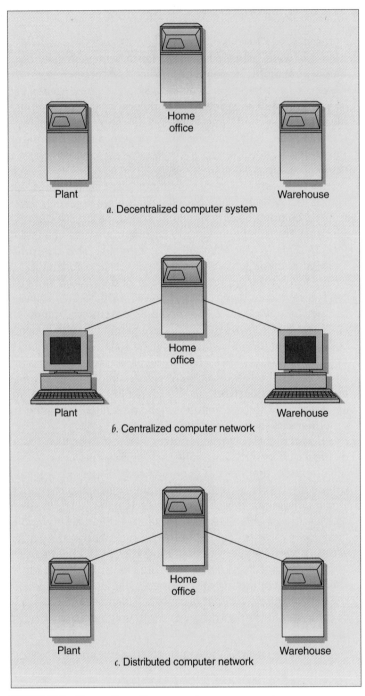

FIGURE 17-1   Three alternative computer arrangements.
(a) Decentralized computer system. (b) Centralized computer network.
(c) Distributed computer network.

Second, a network is exposed to high-level risks. Thus it requires special controls and security measures. Third, specialized networks are being developed that can serve users with a great variety of financial information. In some networks the users may be third parties.

Consequently, accountants should be actively involved in using and evaluating computer networks. They can help integrate data via these networks into useful financial information. They can also evaluate controls and security measures for networks. As key users of computer networks, they should be aware of ways to enhance productivity and effectiveness through using networks.

Our coverage in this chapter focuses on the needs of accountants. Thus we begin by contrasting the three types of computer networks. Next, we survey the client/server computing architecture. Then, we examine controls and security measures and basic design considerations that relate to computer networks. Finally, we explore several specialized information systems that incorporate computer networks.

WIDE-AREA NETWORKS

Data communications networks differ in so many respects that each specific network may be unique. Nevertheless, they can be classified in terms of service areas and basic hardware/software architectures. With respect to service areas, networks may be classified as wide-area and local-area. In this section we focus on the two major architectures of wide-area networks: centralized networks and distributed networks.

CENTRALIZED NETWORKS

A centralized network consists essentially of one central mainframe computer (or a cluster of centrally located computers), plus one or more physically remote terminals and the necessary communications devices and channels.

Configurations   A centralized network may be configured in various ways. Assume that a firm has a mainframe computer located at its home office in Kansas City. This central computer is tied directly by data communications lines to terminals at its four sales offices in Omaha, Wichita, Tulsa, and Little Rock. By altering the arrangements of the communications channels, three distinct configurations can be formed. These configurations or topographies are contrasted in Figure 17-2. Terminals are connected to the central computer by a "lightning bolt" symbol. This symbol is borrowed from the system flowchart set of symbols; it indicates that the terminals are located at significant distances from the central computer.

The **point-to-point configuration** links each terminal separately to the central computer. This configuration provides the best service, since no terminal user has to wait when interacting with the processor. It also is very reliable from a network point of view, since only one user is affected if a communication channel fails. The principal drawback to the point-to-point configuration is that it requires more miles of communication lines than alternative configurations and, hence, is the most expensive. This is especially true if private lines (rather than public or WATS lines) are used for the communication channels.

The **multidrop configuration** links the terminals, via "drops," to a single line that connects to the central processor. This configuration is economical, since the total communication line mileage is generally minimized. However, it has several drawbacks. A terminal user must typically wait for service, since only one terminal may transmit at a time. If a communication line fails, all terminals beyond that point will be out of service. Also, only private lines may normally be used.

A **multiplexed**, or line-shared, **configuration** links a cluster of terminals to the central processor by means of a multiplexor or other line-sharing device. In the example in Figure 17-2, the multiplexor might be placed somewhere between the

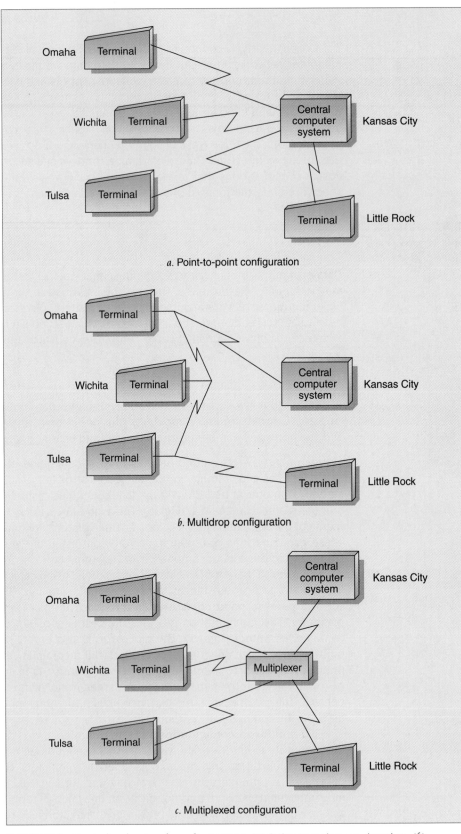

FIGURE I7-2 Centralized network configurations. (a) Point-to-point congiruation. (b) Multidrop configuration. (c) Multiplexed configuration.

Wichita and Tulsa locations. This configuration tends to be a compromise between the other two configurations. It generally reduces the total communication line mileage below that of the point-to-point configuration, but not as low as that of the multidrop configuration. However, the savings in overall communication line costs are offset somewhat by the cost of the line-sharing device and the single private communication line to the processor. Owing to the simultaneous transmission of messages over the shared line, it reduces the waiting time below that of the multidrop configuration. Also, public or WATS lines may be used to link each terminal to the line-sharing device.

Benefits   Centralized networks offer the concentrated computing power of a large processor, which can handle large volumes of transactions and the processing needs of large applications (e.g., computerized budget models). Also, because large processors can accomplish such processing at low operating costs per transaction, they may offer economies of scale. Because they can accommodate integrated data bases, centralized networks can facilitate the use of the data-base approach. Since the facilities are centralized, better security can be provided. Furthermore, standardized and professional planning and control of information-related activities are more likely to be achieved if the computing facilities are centralized.

Centralized networks are best suited for firms that have centralized organizational structures, homogeneous operations, and low processing activity at numerous remote sites. Examples are savings and loan institutions, banks with many automatic teller machines (ATMs) and branches, merchandising chains, motels, and airlines.

Drawbacks   Although centralized networks provide benefits in some situations, the single centralized computer approach creates severe drawbacks. It causes the network to be inflexible. Also, very complicated and costly system software is needed to move application programs in and out of their on-line library, to assign priorities to messages, to move data throughout the network, and so on. The network is quite vulnerable to disaster, since it is dependent on the functioning of a single central computer. Finally, a centralized network may not be responsive to the needs of users at the various remote points.

DISTRIBUTED NETWORKS

The concerns and varying needs of users at remote locations have become increasingly important in many firms. Although the users in decentralized computer systems have control over their own processing, they do not have easy access to centralized data nor can they transmit data and information rapidly. Thus user-oriented distributed networks have come into being. These networks share the overall processing load of a firm among linked computers, including minicomputers and microcomputers as well as mainframe computers.

Distributed networks allow a range of data entry and processing options. As in centralized networks, transactions may be entered in batches or individually at remote sites and transmitted in detail to the host computer system for processing. Alternatively, transactions may be processed by either the batch or on-line methods at the remote sites by **satellite systems**. Then the summary results may be transmitted to the host computer. Also, summary data may be obtained from the data base located at the host computer site.

Configurations   The two basic distributed network configurations are the star and the ring. Figure 17-3 contrasts these configurations (with the communications

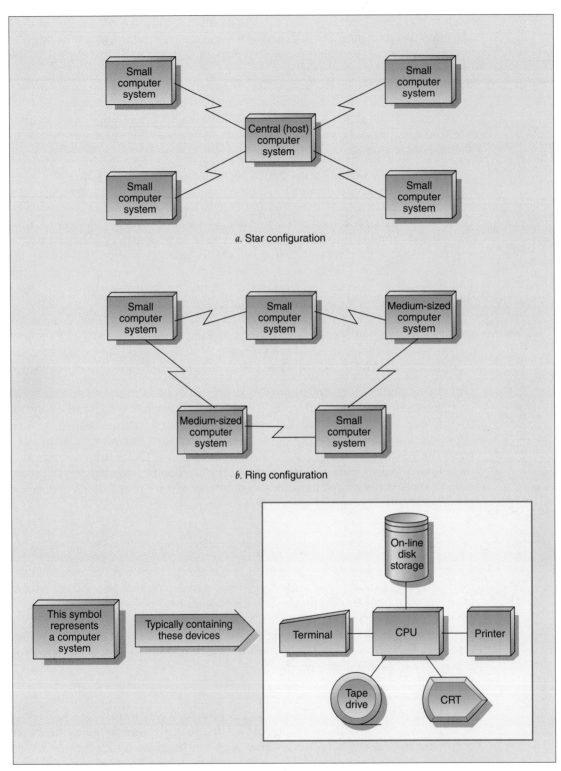

FIGURE 17-3   Two basic distributed network configurations. (*a*) Star configuration. (*b*) Ring configuration.

devices omitted). A third configuration, the bus, is mainly applicable to local-area networks.

The **star configuration** consists of a host computer system plus computer systems that radiate from the center of the network like spokes from a hub.* In Figure 17-3a the configuration is assumed to consist of four small computer systems connected to the host computer system. Each computer system is assumed to contain a processor with a terminal keyboard, video display (CRT) screen, disk storage unit, printer, and backup magnetic tape unit. The star configuration corresponds to the point-to-point configuration of centralized networks. Each computer system composing the network routes all messages through the host computer. This configuration has simplicity and flexibility, although it does not allow direct communication between remote locations.

The **ring configuration** consists of a closed loop of linked computer systems. No single computer system shown in Figure 17-3b is preeminent, in contrast to the dominant host computer system of a star configuration. Each computer system in a ring configuration can directly communicate with its neighbors; however, it cannot easily communicate with the other computer systems in the network.

If the star and ring configurations shown in the figure were combined, one of the many possible hybrid configurations would be formed. Such a hybrid configuration would enable each computer system in the network to communicate directly with every other computer system. Although the overall communication would be greatly improved, the overall cost of constructing the network would be greater.

Perhaps the most popular hybrid configuration is the **hierarchical configuration**. It consists of several levels of distributed computer systems, with a mainframe host computer system at the top level. Computer systems at each level download part of their processing tasks to lower levels and upload summary data to higher levels. This configuration is well suited to a manufacturing firm having a home office and remote plants, warehouses, and sales offices. Figure 17-4 pictures a simple hierarchical configuration for such a firm.

Distributed Data Bases   The term "distributed network" normally pertains to the distribution of data processing and is sometimes called *distributed data processing* (DDP) *networks*. However, the data base may also be placed at various locations throughout a network. Distributed data bases are particularly useful when (1) large volumes of data need to be processed at remote locations, or (2) managers and employees need very fast access to data on a frequent basis.

Data bases may be distributed by replication or partition. In the replicated approach, copies of files from the main data base are stored at remote locations. In the partitioned approach, segments of files are allocated to various locations within the network. The latter approach avoids data redundancy but increases the complexity of transmitting data throughout the network. At present most data bases are a hybrid of the two approaches. Nevertheless, the advantages of the partitioned approach are so great that it is likely to become the dominant approach as technology improves.

Benefits   A distributed network can be very responsive to the diverse needs of users. It also enables the facilities of the network to be used efficiently, since processing jobs can be routed to those unoccupied computer systems in the network that are

---

*In a "pure" centralized star configuration, the host computer system is replaced by a switching device. Few of these configurations exist in practice, however.

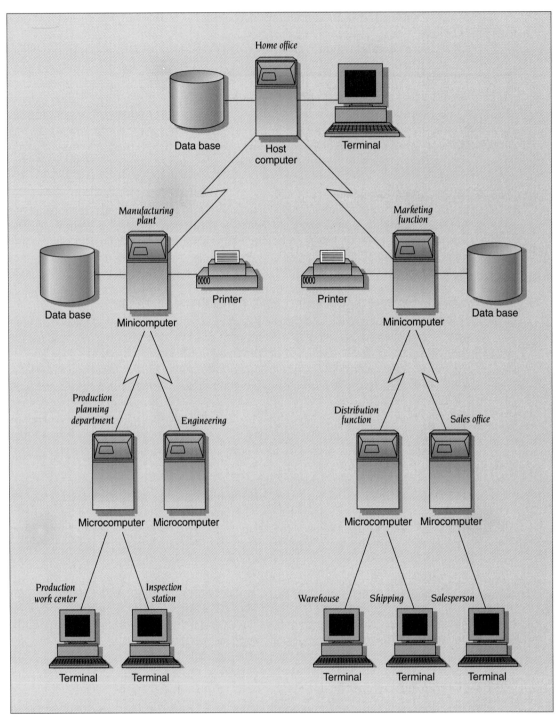

FIGURE 17-4   A distributed network having a hierarchical configuration.

most suitable. If a particular computer system fails, the remaining computer systems can generally handle its processing load with slight loss in service. Finally, the network is flexible and adaptable to change, since new computer systems can easily be added and present systems deleted.

SPOTLIGHTING

COMPUTER NETWORKS
*at Frito-Lay Inc.**

Frito-Lay Inc., a division of Pepsico, Inc., is headquartered in Purchase, New York. It currently operates a distributed wide-area network, with two mainframe computers located at the central site of the information systems function in Plano, Texas. A hierarchical configuration ties the mainframes to midrange (mini) computers at 40 manufacturing plants and 200 distribution sites throughout the country. Attached to the midrange computers at each site are basic microcomputers and terminals. A public data network called Systems Network Architecture (available from IBM Corporation) is used to transmit data to and from the mainframes.

Now the firm is in the midst of a changeover to a new network configuration and hardware. The replacement network is essentially of the ring type, with data being transmitted via a satellite to the 240 remote sites. The midrange computers are giving way to thousands of powerful microcomputer

workstations. Each remote site is established with an Ethernet LAN that is controlled by a network server. A token ring protocol manages the transmission of data within each LAN and from a LAN to the mainframe computer. One powerful mainframe computer, the ES/9000 IBM processor, replaces the two current mainframes.

Information concerning local operations will be gathered by the new network at two levels: the local plant or distribution site level and the corporate level. Plant managers will be able to monitor their operations, while top management will gain a composite view of all manufacturing and distribution activities. In addition, top management has already established an executive information system that combines information from remote site operations with comparable information concerning competitors' activities. Sophisticated graphics packages and a relational data-base package enable the information to be provided in the most readable formats.

*Bob Francis, "Frito-Lay's Network Recipe." *Datamation* (January 15, 1991), pp. 57–60.

Distributed networks are best suited for firms that have decentralized organizational structures, diverse operations or user groups, and clustered functions at various locations. Examples of firms using distributed networks are multiproduct manufacturing firms and firms that offer a variety of services. On the other hand, many firms with diverse activities and services find that both centralized and distributed networks are desirable. For instance, large airlines may use centralized networks for their reservations systems but distributed networks for their maintenance operations.

Drawbacks The most serious drawback of distributed networks is the difficulty in maintaining adequate control and security. Each of the distributed processing locations requires its own set of controls and security measures. Because each location is relatively small, organizational independence is not easily achieved. Also, certain managers are likely to sacrifice control and security for greater productivity. A related drawback is the difficulty of coordinating the relatively independent and sometimes incompatible computing systems. That is, computers made by one manufacturer and using a particular operating system will often not transfer data to hardware made by another manufacturer. An operating system such as Unix will not easily "talk" to the Windows 95 operating system. A third drawback is the relatively high overall cost of the network. Added costs are incurred for the multiple computers, other system components, and communications services. Some of the cost occurs in attempting to blend dissimilar computer systems. Figure 17-5 contrasts the advantages of centralized and distributed networks.

Centralized Networks

- Concentrated processing power for handling all processing needs
- Lower computer hardware costs, due to a sole large computer and likely economies of scale
- Better control, security, and coordination over processing and data storage functions
- Facilitation of the data-base approach, since complexities of distributed data are avoided
- Standardized planning, procedures, and documentation
- Availability of highly skilled information system professionals who are attracted to larger centralized installations

Distributed Networks

- User satisfaction due to control over local processing
- Better responsiveness to processing needs of users
- More efficient use of computer resources and balancing of their processing loads
- Built-in computer system backups, due to multiple computers
- Flexibility and adaptability to change

FIGURE 17-5 Comparison of relative advantages of centralized and distributed networks.

LOCAL-AREA NETWORKS

Microcomputers and terminals on a sea of desktops is becoming a common sight in many offices. Managers and employees are using these desktop devices to perform many of their daily tasks, from entering data for processing to retrieving information for decision making. Since the managers and employees of a firm are involved in related activities, communication via the microcomputers and terminals has become highly desirable. Localized communications are best achieved by means of local-area networks (LANs). A local-area network (LAN) for a particular firm might support two or more computing devices located within a relatively confined geographical area, such as its home office building. It might also include the warehouse located adjacent to the home office building. In this section we briefly survey the components, configurations, benefits, and drawbacks of LANs.

COMPONENTS

Being a computer network, a LAN incorporates hardware (e.g., terminals, computer processors, magnetic disks, printers), software (e.g., operating system, communications programs, application programs), and communications channels (e.g., fiber optics, microwave, cables).

At the heart of a LAN is the **workstation**, a desktop task-oriented area that consists generally of a processor and video display screen. Three levels of workstations can be identified: a microcomputer-based workstation, a traditional workstation, and a superworkstation. All three levels of workstations are used with LANs. In addition to providing relatively powerful microcomputer processors, these workstations often include features such as windows and graphics displays. They are typically linked to devices such as graphics printers, teleconferencing video screens and audio units, laser printers, and a variety of hardware devices known as servers.

In smaller LANs every workstation functions as both a client (e.g., a workstation that requests services from a server) and a server (e.g., a workstation that provides requested services to the client). Thus, all users can share data and files on all workstations in the LAN. This type of LAN is called a **peer-to-peer network** since no workstations are dedicated to performing only server functions. Compared to a server network (described below), a peer-to-peer network is less costly, easier to install, and performs about as well as a server network of the same size. As a result, the number of these smaller networks is expected to significantly increase in future years. For instance, the microcomputers at the home office of Infoage are joined together in a peer-to-peer LAN. This network connects the president's office with the departments shown in Figure 2-4. Within the treasurer/controller's department, several other workstations are also connected to the LAN. Infoage's LAN is not connected to the microcomputers located at the two outlets; thus their network is not wide-area.

Currently, most LANs found in larger firms are **server networks**, which may interconnect hundreds of workstations. Compared with peer-to-peer networks, server networks are more difficult to implement and manage, but provide users with a greater degree of security. Such networks require that at least one workstation be dedicated to performing specific server tasks. Examples of these server workstations include file servers, database servers, print servers, communications servers, and transaction processing servers. A large server network often contains multiple servers to efficiently run the network. These dedicated, centralized servers can only perform specific tasks and cannot act as client workstations. Client workstations may request services from one or more servers.

Another component vital to the functioning of a LAN is the network operating system (NOS). In a peer-to-peer network, the NOS software is installed in each user workstation. In a server network, most of the NOS is installed in a file server and a portion also resides in each user workstation. To run centralized LAN applications, the NOS installed in the file server interacts with the NOS and local operating system (e.g., DOS, Windows 95) installed in the user workstation. The client workstation NOS initiates a request to the file server NOS to load files and programs into the client's random access memory (RAM). In a peer-to-peer network, a client NOS initiates a request to another client NOS, which also functions as a server, to load the requested files or programs into RAM. (NOSs are described further in Appendix A.)

CONFIGURATIONS

A LAN can employ either the star or ring configuration. In a LAN star configuration, all workstations are linked to a centralized network server; this server replaces the host computer found in a distributed network. The ring configuration in a LAN does not use a network server, since it is a peer network. Each workstation in the LAN is connected to two other workstations. A third LAN configuration, the **bus configuration**, is a peer network with a break in the ring. That is, all network workstations are connected to a common cable or telephone line (the "bus") that stretches from end to end. Each workstation in a bus configuration is independent, in that failure of a single workstation does not disrupt the remainder of the network. By contrast, an inoperable workstation in a ring configuration causes the entire LAN to be inoperable.

As with wide-area networks, many combinations of stars, rings, and buses may be found in practice. For instance, a tree configuration is a combination of the star and bus configurations. Figure 17-6 portrays a simple tree configuration.

Most firms do not build their own LANs from "scratch." Instead, they purchase or lease predeveloped network configurations that reside in a network interface card

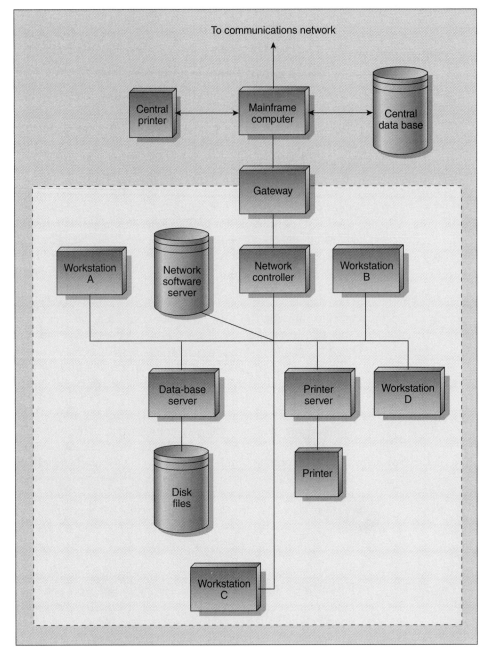

FIGURE 17-6   A local-area network configuration.

(NIC). Before data can be received or transmitted by the networked microcomputers, a NIC must be installed in each workstation. Examples of commercial LAN NICs, each one marketed by several different vendors, are EtherNet, Token Ring, and ARC-net. When acquired, the cabling for the LAN is usually installed within the walls of the buildings that are to house the LAN. The NIC enables the hardware devices that compose the workstations to be connected to the network cable by simply plugging them into wall sockets.

BENEFITS

A LAN is an effective means of enabling a variety of users to share information technology resources as well as information. It tends to be less costly than stand-alone systems. A well-designed LAN normally improves the productivity of employees; not only does the LAN provide easier access to the needed services but it allows the employees and managers to communicate more easily and quickly with each other. Finally, a LAN is quite flexible, since workstations can easily be added or removed.

DRAWBACKS

Since a LAN is akin to a distributed network, adequate controls and security are difficult to maintain, particularly in peer-to-peer networks. Also, some application software for workstations is lacking or inadequate. Furthermore, protocols and equipment have not been standardized for LANs. Hence, workstations and servers of one manufacturer are generally incompatible with those of another manufacturer. It should be noted, however, that standardization is likely to be achieved within the near future since most vendors support this concept. The International Standards Organization has issued a network model description called the **open systems interconnection (OSI)**. This model prescribes the open systems architecture (hardware, software, and protocols) for a LAN.

CLIENT/SERVER (C/S) COMPUTING

In this section we briefly examine the components, configurations, benefits, and drawbacks of the client/server computing model. You may want to review the discussion in Chapter 3 covering the basic concepts of client/server computing. In client/server (C/S) computing, application processing is split between a user workstation (called a client) and one or more other computers (called servers). Generally speaking, the client initiates a request for services from the server, and the server complying with the request returns the processing results to the client computer.

COMPONENTS

In a C/S setup a client uses an intuitive graphical user interface (GUI) operating system that provides a flexible way to find the most pertinent information. The GUI consists of pull-down menus, on-line help screens, icons, and prompts that link the client to the LAN-based C/S setup. From the displayed customized GUI icons, the client initiates (opens) an application by selecting the appropriate logical commands. The client uses a data communications program to transmit the commands to a server(s) that activates a program(s) residing at the server(s). The server(s) processes the request and returns the results to the client, where additional processing may be performed, if necessary. The user is often unaware of where the processing is occurring; all processing is invisible to the user and appears to be taking place locally.

Most of the other components unique to C/S architecture fall into the category of middleware, which is software critical to developing applications and supporting interactions among clients and servers. **Middleware** enables diverse multivendor standards, workstations, and software to seamlessly function as one integrated unit. Thus, different hardware devices and software joined in a network can exchange messages with each other, transfer data, update distributed data bases, process transactions, and provide security. (Middleware is further discussed in Appendix A.)

CONFIGURATIONS

Since the client/server model operates within a physical network environment, it can employ star, ring, and bus configurations. Within these configurations, a client can access one or more dedicated servers located in a department or distributed throughout the enterprise. The most prevalent client/server model is the **departmental dedicated single-server** platform. This platform usually supports 20 or fewer users and is found mainly in small firms, departments and branch offices of larger firms.*

The **departmental dedicated multiple-server** platform enables users to process applications on two or more servers. It supports 30 to several hundred or more clients and is found primarily in large firms.† In the **enterprisewide dedicated multiple-server** platform, communication takes place over linked networks that may be separated by large geographical distances. Users can access servers that are strategically located in departments, branch offices, divisions, and other geographically dispersed sites.

BENEFITS

Client/server computing offers flexible information processing. Since processing is split between two or more processors and only the requested results are returned to the users, traffic on the communication network is reduced. Also, a frequently cited benefit is the savings incurred from moving mission-critical AIS applications from a mainframe computer or *supermini* to less expensive microcomputer servers. These savings translate into lower hardware, software, systems maintenance, and personnel costs. Another advantage is that multiple servers, operating in parallel, often generate more computing power than a mainframe computer, as measured in millions of instructions per second (MIPS). Moreover, storing important software and data resources on centralized servers results in improved security, such as better monitoring of accesses to data.

DRAWBACKS

Client/server setups also have several potential drawbacks and risks. In the long run, hardware cost savings may be offset by a number of unanticipated hidden costs. Frequently unbudgeted or underbudgeted costs include additional applications software costs, middleware software costs, design and development costs, testing costs, implementation costs, systems maintenance costs, network management costs, end-user retraining costs, and security costs.

Also, it can be difficult to downsize mainframe applications to multiple servers because a large-scale application often requires splitting and partitioning among the hard disks of multiple servers. Technically competent personnel—staff or consultants—are needed to downsize the applications. Implementing a client/server system that delivers less than the promised benefits may cause disgruntled users. Client/server systems are built with multivendor hardware and software components that

---

*Robert Orfali, Dan Harkey, and Jeri Edwards, *Essential Client/Server Survival Guide* (New York: Van Nostrand Reinhold, 1994), p. 23.
†Ibid.

require additional support. Thus, it is often more difficult to manage and effectively operate these different platforms than originally anticipated. In addition, as more and more user workstations are added to the setup and applications increase in complexity, traffic between servers causes undue demands in the timely fulfilling of user requests. Finally, as client/server setups become more complex, unanticipated security and reliability breaches will often be encountered.

···

APPLICATION OF NETWORKS

In this section we focus on common LAN applications and representative wide-area network LAN-based client/server applications.

LAN APPLICATIONS

Currently, LANs can be used for a number of accounting and business-related applications, including E-mail, sharing data, sharing devices such as printers, and sharing network versions of applications software such as spreadsheets, data-base management systems, and accounting software packages. Both small and large firms generally employ LANs for similar types of applications, regardless of the number of workstations connected to the LAN.

Several current and proposed LAN applications are employed by Infoage, Inc. Infoage has implemented a peer-to-peer LAN, as opposed to the more complex, and costly, dedicated server LAN. As Figure 17-7 shows, the clerical staff, the warehouse stores clerk, the secretary, George Freeman, president, and his five managers are connected to the LAN. The firm uses the LAN version of the DAC Easy Accounting software package for performing other accounting duties not depicted in the diagram. The president, his five managers, and the secretary also utilize the LAN for nonaccounting applications, including E-mail, spreadsheet, graphics, desktop publishing, word processing, and groupware applications, such as electronic calendaring and scheduling. Recall that the warehouse is adjacent to the main office building. To keep the example simple, only part of Infoage's proposed expenditure cycle system is shown in Figure 17-7. Before continuing with the illustration, you may want to refer to Figures 1-5 and 5-1, which review Infoage's transaction processing cycles. Figure 1-5 illustrates the relationships among these cycles and Figure 5-1 lists included business events and accounting steps and key accounting records for each cycle. As portrayed in Figure 17-7, the partial expenditure cycle application includes the purchasing, accounts payable, cash disbursements, warehousing, and receiving systems. Software accounting modules for purchases, accounts payable, cash disbursements, and inventory reside on the hard disks of four microcomputers. Each module integrates with the general ledger package maintained on Diane Varney's (the treasurer and controller) computer's hard disk.

Accounting Applications The proposed expenditure cycle application begins when Jack Dyson, inventory manager, approves purchase requisitions received from employees, including the two outlet branch managers. The approved purchase requisitions are sent to one of the firm's secretaries. She uses the information in each purchase requisition to complete a preformatted purchase order (PO) displayed on her microcomputer's screen. The computer automatically fills in the price on each PO by scanning an up-to-date master supplier price list file. Using a fax/modem

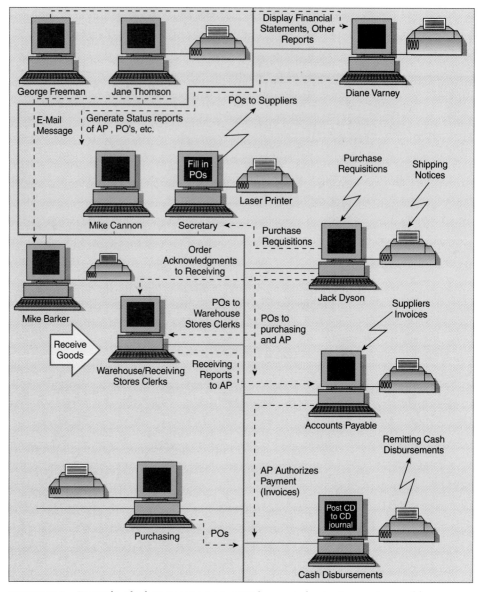

FIGURE 17-7 Example of a bus peer-to-peer LAN for a purchasing/accounts payable accounting system for Infoage, Inc.

installed on the secretary's computer, Jack faxes the POs to the appropriate suppliers.*

Jack sends via interoffice mail or E-mail a copy of the PO to the employee initiating the purchase requisition.† A copy of each PO is also transmitted over the network to the purchasing and accounts payable (AP) microcomputers and to the warehouse stores clerk.

---

*Any authorized employee can share the fax/modem on the secretary's computer. Thus, Infoage can save hundreds of dollars since this device is not needed by each LAN user.
†Infoage could implement a groupware system by installing an E-mail and electronic calendaring and scheduling package. This package could be installed on part of the secretary's hard disk. Space on her hard disk is also reserved to store and retrieve messages.

Some suppliers send acknowledgments to Jack via regular mail and others via fax. He sends these to the receiving clerk to inform him or her of when to expect shipment. When the goods are received, the receiving clerk counts the goods and enters the receiving data into the microcomputer server. The program compares the quantity on the PO with the quantity listed on the receiving report. Assuming the quantities match, the warehouse worker optically scans the proper inventory data into the computer, which automatically posts to all inventory accounts. He or she also optically scans the receiving reports into the computer and electronically transmits copies to the AP bookkeeper.

The payment process begins when the AP bookkeeper receives a supplier's invoice. She scans each invoice into her computer, and the invoice is automatically matched with the correct purchase order and receiving report. She notes on the invoice the amount authorized to be paid and electronically transmits each invoice to the cash disbursements (CD) bookkeeper. On the appropriate date, the CD bookkeeper enters the authorized amount to be paid to each supplier into the computer, and a check is automatically prepared by the software package. He or she sends the checks via regular mail to the suppliers in payment of the goods. The CD bookkeeper uses the microcomputer to automatically post all cash payments to the CD journal. Finally, he or she electronically transmits a batch of check vouchers to the AP bookkeeper. The AP bookkeeper uses this batch of check vouchers, which represent cash payments to suppliers, to update the AP subsidiary ledger.

Periodically, the general ledger package kept on Diane Varney's computer is updated by the three clerks and the warehouse worker. They post the summary amounts to the general ledger over the LAN. Financial reports and financial statements can be prepared on a regular basis. For example, Diane could produce relatively up-to-date reports, such as financial statements, cash-flow forecasts, inventory status information, sales reports by outlet and salesperson, and purchase order tracking. Diane can share the one strategically located laser printer connected to one of the secretaries' computers to print out these reports and send them to the president and other managers.* Alternately, whenever desired, any manager can access Diane Varney's computer to display the reports over his or her computer's monitor. They could also use the E-mail package to send a message to Diane asking her to elaborate on items requiring further explanation, and she could E-mail her responses.

Other Applications   A LAN version of a spreadsheet package is installed on Diane's computer and is shared by other authorized users needing to analyze key financial information. To illustrate, if one of her staff is using the spreadsheet to prepare a cash forecast, Diane can access the forecast file, copy it to her computer, and analyze it. Diane can E-mail a memo to the preparer suggesting changes to the cash forecast. The staff member could load the cash forecast on his or her computer, make the recommended modifications, and print out the forecast using the laser printer at a secretary's workstation.

George Freeman can E-mail a message to Mike Barker, marketing manager, to determine the status of Mike's pending graphics presentation to one of the firm's important microcomputer suppliers. Mike can send an E-mail message to George stating that the presentation, prepared using a desktop publishing package, is complete and transmit the presentation file over the network to George who can edit it and make suggestions for improvement. George can E-mail a memo to Jane Thomson, the systems services manager, to draft a letter to one of the firm's consulting

---

*If Infoage's microcomputers were stand-alone units, one or two additional laser printers would be needed to adequately meet the firm's high-quality printing needs.

SPOTLIGHTING

A CLIENT/SERVER PLATFORM
*at Bankers Trust**

In order to stay competitive and profitable, Bankers Trust management recognized the need to completely revamp the commercial loan process. The firm replaced its many disconnected mainframe legacy loan transaction processing systems with a fully integrated, client/server C/S-based application called LS2. The LS2 C/S system revolves around customer data and deal data. These data are stored in many transaction processing servers. The LS2 system integrates a number of major business functions; two that will be looked at are the origination and sales and trading systems.

In the origination system, information on the customer is entered only once, and is immediately available to both authorized servicing and sales personnel. The system is flexible at establishing

fees and pricing schedules. Compliance with laws and regulations is tracked and reminders for renewals are sent out automatically. A document checklist automatically tracks and reports the status of required documentation. In the sales and trading system, all relevant information entered during the origination process is also immediately available to the sales and trading group.

The LS2 cooperative C/S processing application enables salespeople and traders to store information about salability, offering terms, and lender profiles. With this more timely information, deals are distributed faster than before, increasing the fees collected and improving customer service. Also, trading opportunities are quickly identified, providing an additional source of revenue.

The LS2 is one of the most successful projects undertaken by Bankers Trust. This real-time application emphasizes the value that can be provided by deploying C/S technology to radically enhance the processing of loans.

*Adapted from *Client/Server Implementation: A Management Case Study.* A Supplement to the Systems Auditability and Control Report (Altamonte Springs, Fla.: Institute of Internal Auditors, 1994), pp. CS-3–CS-17.

---

clients. Jane can draft the letter using the word processing package kept on a secretary's computer and transmit the draft to George who can view and edit it. Because of the letter's importance in soliciting potential new business, George E-mails a request to meet with Jane. The secretary can use electronic calendaring and scheduling software to finalize the meeting time. Both George and Jane can access the calendaring software and post the times they are free to meet with one another. The secretary can access both George's and Jane's calendars, finalize the meeting time, and post it on each calendar. Thus, at their convenience, George and Jane can access their electronic calendars and learn the meeting time. Major duties of Ralph Cannon, the office manager, include supervising the office staff, hiring new employees, training the staff, and so on. He can use the LAN to review reports pertaining to the staff's performance and E-mail messages scheduling training sessions and other meetings. He can also review on-line resumes of applicants for positions and electronically send to the other managers resumes of promising applicants and receive their comments via E-mail. Examples of other LAN applications implemented at Infoage and at Ann Strong's consulting firm are described in Appendix 1 of this chapter.

WIDE-AREA NETWORK LAN-BASED CLIENT/SERVER APPLICATIONS

In client/server computing, client workstations exchange information with one another and request services from server workstations. Also, recall that this platform

SPOTLIGHTING

A CLIENT/SERVER TRACKING SYSTEM APPLICATION
*at Nordstrom Company**

Before implementing the client/server (C/S) system, Nordstrom used 1000 stand-alone microcomputers to automate several applications. Three strategically located mainframes executed processing of accounting and operations applications. The 1000 micros gained access to the mainframe-based E-mail, purchase order management, and credit systems. The 2270 IBM terminal emulators were on-line to the IBM mainframes. The terminal emulators activated programs residing on the mainframe; the mainframe executed the processing and returned the results to the terminals. The C/S application replaced all the terminals with PCs. The 1000 client microcomputers were upgraded with modems, communications software, and an easy-to-use Windows graphical user interface.

Nordstrom implemented the new C/S application in one of its geographical regions. The application, known as the Merchandise Check Express, is being used in women's clothing departments in 10 Nordstrom stores in Washington state. As im-

plemented, the application enables a salesperson to use a PC workstation next to the cash register to poll other Nordstrom stores to locate a specific piece of merchandise for a customer. The PC workstations located in the stores access data files on a dedicated data-base server located at Nordstrom's Seattle data center. Each PC client workstation communicates with the data-base server, enabling the client to access the tracking system files located on the data-base server. The salesperson (i.e., the client) can describe what he or she is looking for by keying in information that identifies the item by style, color, and size, and send that message to all PCs on the network.

Meanwhile, at the local client PCs, lists of items that other salespeople are looking for are also displayed at the workstations. Thus a salesperson can check for the item, confirm that a particular store has it, and then drop the item from the active list. Salespersons can also indicate the method of delivery—shipping to the customer's home or store transfer—or whether the customer wants the item held at the original store so that he or she can pick it up. So far the Merchandising tracking system is working well.

---

*Adapted from Christine Strenlo, "Nordstrom Pilots In-Store Tracking System." *Infoworld* (August 17, 1992), pp. S66 and S68.

---

splits the processing of applications between the client and one or more servers. However, in a LAN the entire application is processed at the client workstation and only simple tasks, such as sharing a file stored on a hard disk and printing reports, are distributed to the servers.

Most firms are evaluating or increasing the number and types of client/server applications as a way to deliver more flexible computing power to the end user. Currently, the most often encountered client/server applications employ dedicated single or multiple data-base servers to facilitate access to a variety of relational data bases containing primarily financial information. An example of a firm that has successfully implemented a strategic transaction processing application via a wide-area LAN-based client/server computing platform is Bankers Trust, one of the largest U.S. banking institutions. The specifics of the application are discussed in the nearby vignette. Another example of a firm that has "upsized" a major mission-critical tracking system transaction processing application from stand-alone microcomputers to a wide-area LAN-based client/server platform is Nordstrom Company. This application is also described in a nearby vignette.

SECURITY, CONTROL, AND AUDIT OF NETWORKS

A distributed data communications network of any type introduces complexity and control problems. A network consists of a mixture of sophisticated hardware devices, many of which represent open points of access. Without the discipline provided by a centralized installation, controls and security measures are often de-emphasized. Instead, managers at the various localized computing sites focus on productivity and profitability. As a consequence, accountants (preferably the internal audit function, if one exists) need to evaluate the elements of the internal control environment relevant to the network. After identifying the specific objectives of the network, a risk assessment should be completed. A firm using such a network will not avoid any of the risks discussed in Chapter 7. In fact, certain risk exposures are likely to be heightened. Among the specific risk exposures to be assessed on a periodic basis are the following:

1. Loss of capability of transmitting and processing data because of equipment and software breakdowns, including bridge failure, cabling problems, or network operating system failure.

2. Loss of capability of transmitting and processing data due to power outages, viruses, theft, loss of key personnel, or natural disasters.

3. Unauthorized access of data through tapping of communications lines by vengeful ex-employees or hackers.

4. Unauthorized access of data by snooping employees via terminals and microcomputers in open and unprotected areas.

5. Numerous errors in data entry, such as accidental file deletions, owing to unsophisticated users who access the network at a variety of remote locations.

6. Errors in the main database due to uploading of unverified data from terminals and microcomputers to the host computer.

7. Fraud and errors as a result of weaknesses in controls at various remote locations within the network.

Once the risk assessment is finished, specific control and security activities designed to eliminate or minimize the individual stand-alone microcomputers' and the computer network's risk exposures should be assessed, evaluated, and tested. Controls for stand-alone microcomputers are covered in Appendix 2 of this chapter. The specific information processing control and security activities to be considered for the computer network are these:

1. Appointing a part-time or full-time administrator who is responsible for establishing a network security plan that addresses security issues.

2. Encrypting messages that contain confidential data, or using special cables or high-speed transmissions, so that the data cannot be intercepted and read by unauthorized persons. Since coding/decoding data can be annoying and complex to execute, the process can be automated by using combination hardware-software systems, such as the Network Security System (from Semaphore Communications Corporation). This product automatically encrypts/decrypts all data without human intervention as it travels over the network and requires a password to decode the data.

3. Employing highly reliable and compatible channels and devices, as well as error-detecting and correcting devices, so that errors and malfunctions are minimized.

4. Ensuring availability of data by preparing continuous or regularly scheduled backups. Backups should be written to devices such as magnetic disks, optical disks, magnetic tape, or digital audio tape. At least one copy of backups should be stored off-site. Either full or incremental backups can be prepared. The incremental approach only backs up files that have been modified since the last backup. Where continued processing is vital, a **disk mirroring** approach might be installed to provide real-time data protection. This technique simultaneously writes data to a second hard disk drive maintained on the same server. A higher level of disk mirroring is called server duplexing. **Server duplexing** involves concurrently duplicating the contents of an entire server to a second remotely located server. A network having an added server can switch automatically to the second server when the main server fails or is down for maintenance.

5. Employing transmission controls such as echo checks, dual transmission of messages, and standardized protocols.

6. Placing network devices in protected and restricted locations, so that they are not likely to be damaged or stolen.

7. Using system software that is write protected and that performs parity checks, echo checks, and other verification checks to ensure that the software is not altered and that data are transmitted accurately.

8. Using passwords to keep sensitive data safe from unauthorized access and alterations. As large networks emerge and more workstations are placed in remote, unsecured locations, a dedicated password server, using a security software utility known as Kerberos, may be deployed. This centralized, trusted *Kerberos server* has become the de facto standard used to store and validate passwords, thereby providing secure, authenticated access between workstations in a network. Also, a small credit-cardlike device, such as the SecurID card (from Security Dynamics, Inc.) can provide a high degree of network security when used in conjunction with Kerberos. The SecurID card device, which is connected to a workstation, discloses a randomly generated numerical password that changes every minute. To gain access to the network, the user enters his or her Kerberos password and the currently displayed SecurID password, both of which must be authenticated. An intruder would find it almost impossible to purloin the SecurID card password since it is altered so frequently.

9. Using a *network audit system* (NAS) or *network management system* (NMS) software package to monitor network resources, compile reports on network performance, detect systems breaches, monitor the network administrator, and assign message numbers to create adequate audit trails.

10. Validating input data to detect and prevent errors from being transmitted.

11. Maintaining standardized documentation and procedures (e.g., connectivity standards) throughout the network, including all remote sites.

12. Providing proper training, preferably by a centralized systems group, to users throughout the network.

13. Providing close supervision at each remote location.

14. Limiting access to vulnerable network entry points. Provide a point of centralized control, known as a *firewall*, to provide secure access to these entry points. A *router*, for example, can be configured to isolate two or more networks from unauthorized access.

Finally, ongoing monitoring activities and periodic evaluations of the network should be performed by the accountant or internal auditor. Ongoing activities include reviewing the reports and logs prepared by the network management or accounting system and tracking the activities performed by the network administrator. Important network administrator tasks to monitor include methods of resolving user complaints, evaluating day-to-day security monitoring tasks, and appraising the system of assigning and maintaining passwords. Periodic monitoring activities to be included in a network operational audit are the following:

1. Evaluating the effectiveness of the network administrator.
2. Evaluating the skill levels of network personnel in running and maintaining the network.
3. Analyzing long-term plans for expanding the network.
4. Determining from network diagrams if the network appears to be well conceived.
5. Evaluating the backup methods.
6. Testing the system plan to restore data.
7. Evaluating the methods of educating and training users in network fundamentals.
8. Ensuring that policies are in place to reprimand or prosecute employees who wrongfully misuse the network.
9. Evaluating change procedures to the network operating system.
10. Conducting reviews for unlicensed network software.
11. Conducting a physical inventory of the network resources.
12. Determining violations of software site-licensing agreements.

SPECIALIZED SYSTEMS AND NETWORKS

A variety of specialized computer systems and networks are in use and are discussed in this section, including those pertaining to points of sale, electronic funds transfers, and electronic data interchanges. Also, a firm's computers or networks can be connected to external network services. Several major external networks are the focus of the last part of this section.

POINT-OF-SALE SYSTEMS/NETWORKS

Today, computer-based **point-of-sale (POS) systems/networks** are revolutionizing the information systems of retailing firms, especially those having numerous retail outlets. As customers, we have encountered these systems in grocery chains (e.g., Safeway Stores), department stores (e.g., Mervyn's), discount stores (e.g., Home Depot), and even university bookstores. Manual and electromechanical cash registers have disappeared in such retailing businesses. In their places have appeared electronic cash registers, which in reality are intelligent terminals containing microprocessors. Such POS systems enable organizations to speed service, cut costs, accurately and efficiently process orders, and significantly improve decision making.

Figure 17-8 shows a POS terminal at a check-out station within one store of a grocery chain. The POS terminals capture sales transactions as they occur, either through keying the product data or by optically scanning the Universal Product Code (bar code) on the products. Thus, it is a real-time transaction processing system. In the diagrammed system the terminal then transmits the sales data via a centralized

POINT-OF-SALE SYSTEMS/NETWORKS
at Acme, Acme Supercenters, and Y-Mart Stores*

Fred W. Albrecht Company, a grocery chain, is installing a new point-of-sale system in all 36 of its Acme, Acme Supercenters, and Y-Mart stores. Management implemented the new system out of competitive necessity. It is especially crucial for taking the necessary strategic steps toward managing product pricing, monitoring inventory, and gathering customer data for marketing purposes.

The system will help provide the chain with enhanced scanning ability, and ultimately the transmission of data in a speedier and more accurate fashion, which is critical for competing successfully in today's marketing environment. The POS system will also allow store inventory levels to be constantly monitored and updated, making it possible to implement an expanded direct-store-delivery system.

Another key benefit of the new system will be an enhanced ability to develop and take advantage of electronic marketing programs, including card-based frequent-shopper programs. Such card-based scanner-driven programs will enable the chain to gather information for identifying key market segments and shopping habits. That information could then be used to target specific consumer groups via telemarketing campaigns, direct mailing and special coupons. The system will tell management which departments are being shopped, and who is shopping them. If a customer is not shopping a particular department, management can call the customer and find out the reason, which could lead to positive changes. The system will also allow the firm to target specific demographic consumer groups. For example, the system can determine which age groups are not shopping in the stores, and management can develop a marketing campaign to attract their business.

---

*Jonna Crispens, "Albrecht Is Rolling Out Updated POS Systems." *Supermarket News* (April 25, 1994), pp. 11–12.

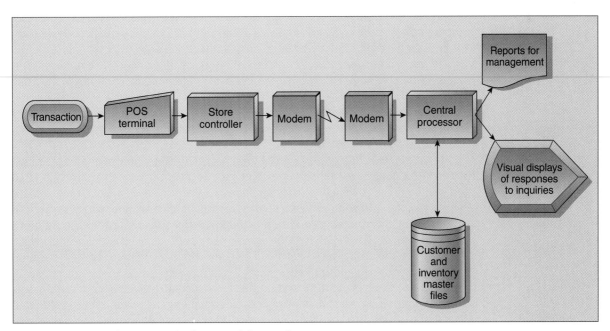

FIGURE 17-8   An on-line point-of-sale network for retailers.

network to a central processor. Through a communications device called a store controller, all of the terminals in the branch are connected to the central processor.

In fact, the most important benefits derived from POS systems are the various support functions that they perform, such as

1. Checking the credit of customers via an on-line connection to the credit center. Credit approvals take about four to ten seconds to complete.

2. Applying prices, stored in a data base, to the scanned merchandise items and then listing the amounts and item descriptions on the sales receipt slips.

3. Updating the inventory master file to reflect sales of the various merchandise items. To pinpoint what stock is selling, a number identifying every transaction indicates an item's size, style, color, and vendor. By tracking these identifiers, the buyers improve the stock purchasing and inventory management functions to attain just-in-time delivery.

4. Reordering merchandise for stores based on predetermined reorder points. Retailers can keep shelves full of fast selling goods, thus minimizing shortages. Also, by showing product sales by time of day and week, product mixes can be fine-tuned and store layouts can be revamped according to demand patterns.

5. Preparing daily sales analyses for store managers, as well as timely information such as sales during the past hour or day, the average sale per customer today, the volume of customers today, sales total by employee, and credit card transactions by terminal.

ELECTRONIC FUNDS TRANSFER SYSTEMS

Financial institutions, such as commercial banks and savings and loan associations, have pioneered the application of computer-based networks. Increasingly the networks are being employed as **electronic funds transfer (EFT) systems/networks**, which transmit and process the funds-related transactions of customers. EFT systems/networks differ from traditional banking systems in that the transfers of funds are handled electronically rather than by means of paper checks. Not only can customers make deposits and withdrawals electronically but they can also have their paychecks transferred directly to the bank via direct deposits.

The transactions accommodated by EFT systems/networks can be made via terminals located at the teller windows of a bank. Alternatively, customers may use ATMs at bank locations or at supermarkets and convenience stores. Accessing the system via an ATM requires the depositor to insert a bank card and to key in a PIN (personal identification number); these precautions provide considerable security against accesses by unauthorized persons.

POS systems are integrated with EFT systems/networks when payments are made for purchases at retail establishments. When a customer buys merchandise at a retail establishment, he or she gives the merchant a bank debit card. The customer's identifying data are read from the card, either by means of a scanner or by keying the data into a POS terminal. In addition to entering the sales data into the retailer's data base, the retailer's POS system transmits the debit to the customer-depositor's account. Thus the entire transaction and cash transfer are completed during the time that the customer is checking out.

The advantages of an EFT system/network—added convenience to customers and reduced transaction costs for banks and retailers—have led many banks to install ATMs and to issue debit cards. However, EFT systems/networks have created several problems. They require high initial costs, and they also introduce difficulties with respect to security. In addition, customers resist the immediate transfer of funds that debit cards entail, since they lose the benefit of bank "float."

ELECTRONIC DATA INTERCHANGE SYSTEMS/NETWORKS

An **electronic data interchange (EDI) system/network** facilitates the near instantaneous interchange of business transaction information from the computer system of one firm to the computer system of another. The parties involved in the exchanges are called trading partners. Even though any size firm can conduct some form of EDI with its trading partners, EDI is predominantly utilized by large firms. Many smaller firms can become involved in EDI by conducting document transfers via E-mail and by using fax/modem devices. EDI trading partners store and retrieve common documents, such as purchase orders, invoices, shipping notices, and bills of lading, as opposed to mailing hard copies of the documents. Special EDI software is used to translate one firm's paper documents into a standard, electronic equivalent format that can be read by its trading partners' computers. Some EDI systems are expanding to become comprehensive management tools that will allow true extended enterprise systems among independent organizations. In addition to sharing documents, expanded EDI systems will enable trading partners to integrate their applications. Such integration allows the exchange of text, voice messages, images, graphics, data bases, and production plans and schedules, with E-mail and electronic conferencing systems.

As noted previously, a network that integrates the POS system of a retailer with the EFT system of a bank is an EDI system/network. However, a large percentage of EDI systems/networks still focus on *order entry*; that is, they involve electronic interchanges of data between ordering firms and key suppliers. An EDI system/network of this type can also be integrated with a POS system and/or an EFT system. Figure 17-9 shows how such an integrated, private point-to-point network might be configured. When a customer makes a purchase, the amount is debited to his or her bank account and credited to the account of the retailer. The POS system reduces the inventory balances by the quantities sold. When the stock of a merchandise item falls below its reorder point, the system notifies the EDI system/network. This system then prepares the data for a purchase order and transmits the data electronically to the appropriate supplier. After shipping the ordered merchandise, the supplier's EDI system/network prepares the data for a sales invoice and transmits the data electronically back to the retailer. Then the EDI system/network of the retailer transmits the amount to the EFT system, which debits the bank account of the retailer and credits the bank account of the supplier. Finally, the EFT system confirms the payment transactions, so that the correct balances will be reflected in the retailer's and supplier's records. Note that the EFT system can involve as many as three separate banks (and a clearinghouse) in these transactions.

Instead of directly sending and receiving documents from one trading partner to another, a large number of firms use EDI value-added networks, such as those operated by AT&T or General Electric Information Services. Value-added networks enable trading partners to overcome the incompatibility, scheduling problems, and high costs associated with private point-to-point networks. Other firms are beginning to use public data networks, such as CompuServe or the Internet, to link them with their trading partners. These value-added or public networks furnish communications services and act as clearinghouses for the trading partners by providing electronic mailboxes and translation software that enable participants to store and retrieve the EDI files or messages.

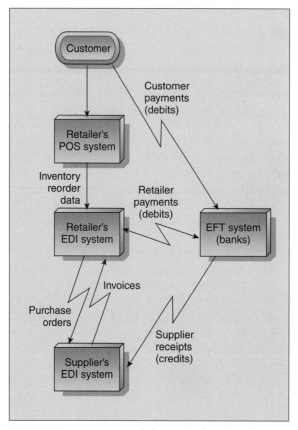

FIGURE 17-9   An integrated electronic data interchange system.

EDI systems/networks are growing rapidly among automobile manufacturers, retailers, pharmaceutical firms, hospitals, transportation firms, and grocery chains. They not only reduce the paper flows, document storage, and filing costs, but also can reduce lead times by providing quicker delivery on orders, reducing inventory to just-in-time levels. This latter advantage can strengthen a firm's competitive position, since it enhances the speed with which the firm delivers products and reacts to changing conditions. However, EDI systems/networks do require extensive arrays of network controls, as discussed earlier.

EXTERNAL ON-LINE SERVICES

Whether the microcomputer is part of an internal firmwide computer network or functions as a stand-alone microcomputer, equipped with a modem and communications software, users can connect to the vast world of external on-line network services. Such services offer an array of data and information that can be utilized to support managerial decision making and other activities. Although many external on-line services are available, this discussion will be limited to national external networks offering an array of accounting and business services. As illustrated in Figure 17-10, the largest external on-line national service providers can be categorized as:

1. General business services

2. Specialized business services

3. The Internet

Figure 17-10 also presents the major features of each of the three categories of external on-line services. A fourth category not shown in the figure, that of other external on-line services, will be briefly discussed.

On-Line National General Business Services   The **on-line national general business services** allow huge numbers of subscribers to be on line simultaneously. All offer their subscribers excellent E-mail services. Depending on the type of services used, subscribers can very rapidly accumulate a large monthly bill. Typically, *CompuServe Information Service* provides more comprehensive and in-depth services than Dow Jones News/Retrieval and GEnie. CompuServe is a business-oriented service, providing subscribers with the latest news, stock quotes, general references, business board forums, data bases, and full text of numerous newspapers, magazines and journals, as well as many other business-related services. *Dow Jones News/Retrieval* (DJN/R)

Name of On-Line Service	Features
General Business Services:	
CompuServe Information Service	A very comprehensive, in-depth service—news, stock quotes, general references, bulletin board forums, data bases, full text of numerous newspapers, magazines, and journals.
Dow Jones News/Retrieval	Excellent source for general information, business news, and financial data, including stock quotes and corporate reports. Full text of *The Wall Street Journal*. Its key-word searchable data bases include over 1000 trade and business publications, general magazines, and major newspapers.
GEnie (General Electric Network for Information Exchange)	Large number of business and financial data bases. Numerous bulletin board forums, including many computer forums covering most major hardware and software topics.
Specialized Business Services:	
Ziff-Davis Interchange	A computer-oriented service. Provides full text of its line of computer magazines, including PC *Magazine*.
Ziffnet	A computer-oriented service also provided by Ziff-Davis. Thousands of software programs can be downloaded, many for a nominal fee. Computer forums enable subscribers to get answers to technical questions and to interact with the firm's editors.
Dialog	Its numerous data bases cover an assortment of topics. The business data base enables users to conduct key-word searches of about 1000 business journals, including numerous accounting journals. In addition, hundreds of general purpose magazines and major newspapers can be searched.
The Information Highway:	
Internet	A loosely configured web of tens of thousands of interconnected computer networks. There are tens of millions of users worldwide in almost every country. Provides access to virtually any type of information for every type of user. Can be frustatingly difficult to navigate. There is no central authority to oversee the Internet. The three most popular services are E-mail, discussion groups, and downloading files to a user's computer. Security of information is a continuing problem.

FIGURE 17-10   Major national on-line services.

provides a variety of in-depth financial and business information, such as stock quotes, information data bases, and full text of articles from *The Wall Street Journal*. It is perhaps the most expensive of the national on-line general business services. GE*nie* subscribers have at their fingertips a large number of business and financial data bases and numerous bulletin board forums. Although these forums cover a variety of topics, the variety of computer bulletin boards dealing with most computer subjects is very well respected.

On-Line National Specialized Services   The three major **on-line national specialized services** are Ziff-Davis Interchange, Ziffnet, and Dialog. *Ziff-Davis Interchange* is primarily a computer-oriented service provider. It provides the full text of its line of computer magazines. *Ziffnet* focuses on the microcomputer industry, providing a large selection of downloadable software, many for a nominal fee. It also maintains a listing of thousands of shareware and freeware computer products that can be ordered and paid for on-line. It also has technical support bulletin boards enabling users to converse on-line with well-known computer experts about almost any computer-related topic. *Dialog* is best known for its large number of data bases covering a wide variety of topics. For example, the business data base enables users to conduct key-word searches of about 1000 business publications, including numerous national and international accounting journals.

The Internet   The **Internet** (called *the* Net for short), by far the world's largest and fastest growing network, is a loosely coupled web of tens of thousands of interconnected corporate, government, and education computer networks. These computers store all kinds of information on several million servers that can be accessed by anyone with an Internet account. About 75 million to 100 million persons residing in almost every country have Internet accounts, and the number of users increases every day. The three most popular services are E-mail, discussion group bulletin boards, and downloading of files. The Net is especially known for its huge number of bulletin board forums, covering almost all subjects. For instance, numerous accounting bulletin boards related to public accounting, internal auditing, information systems, government accounting, academic accounting, and other specialized accounting topics can be found on the Net. Almost every conceivable type of information can be found in a server that may be located almost anywhere in the world. A very small sampling of the types of information accessible include research reports, magazines, newspapers, various data bases, key-word searches on almost any subject, article abstracts, SEC filings, weather reports, stock market quotes and information, software reviews, census data, Library of Congress holdings, and economic statistics. In addition, the Internet offers organizations the opportunity to establish a relatively inexpensive electronic data interchange system through its Enterprise Integration Network (EINet).

Although millions of pages of documents and other types of information are stored on Internet servers, much of it cannot be easily accessed unless a subscriber employs effective software as navigational aids. Three frequently used Internet subnetwork servers are File Transfer Protocol, Gopher, and the World Wide Web. These three types of subnetwork servers operate similarly to client/server computing systems. That is, the more effective a client's graphical user interface (GUI) software, the easier the search process. They are examined further in Appendix 2 of this chapter.

Other On-Line Services   America Online, Apple Computer's e.World, Delphi, and Prodigy are national general on-line services that target personal users. The breadth and depth of services provided is not as extensive as that offered by the national on-line services. For an additional fee, they all offer limited- or full-access privileges to the Internet. **Lexis** and **Naars** are national specialized on-line services that provide keyword searches of legal and accounting articles, respectively. Nexis displays the entire text of most major newspapers. In addition to the national on-line service providers, thousands of local on-line service providers offer an abundance of general or specialized services. Listings of these local on-line providers by state are available in the Computer Shopper (from Ziff-Davis Publishing).

SUMMARY

The two major types of wide-area networks are centralized and distributed. Centralized networks offer concentrated computing power, an integrated data base, possible economies of scale, large processors, plus all the advantages of centralized management and security. Distributed networks offer responsiveness to user needs, optimal use of facilities, less vulnerability to total failure, and flexibility. The basic centralized network configurations are point-to-point, multidrop, and multiplexed. Distributed networks have two basic configurations, star and ring, but many hybrid configurations (including the hierarchical configuration) are built from these two basic configurations. Distributed networks may distribute their data bases as well as providing processing capabilities; two methods of distributing data are by replication and by partitioning. An alternative type of network is the local-area network. It offers the same two basic configurations, plus the bus configuration. A LAN consists of workstations, servers, network controllers, and other familiar hardware.

LANs are used for a wide range of accounting and related applications. LANs enable users to share a variety of common resources, such as printers, files, accounting software packages, spreadsheets, and modems. The most prevalent wide-area LAN-based client/server applications include relational data-base applications that automate transaction processing and operational systems.

Among the controls and security measures suited to networks are encrypted transmissions, reliable communications channels and devices, protected communications devices, continuous or periodic backups, varied system software checks, passwords, documentation, training, and network audit systems software. A part-time or full-time network administrator should be appointed to manage the network. An accountant, preferably an internal auditor, should be involved in ongoing and periodic monitoring activities.

Computer-based systems/networks have been installed to meet a variety of specialized needs. Among the currently available specialized systems/networks are those involving points-of-sale, electronic funds transfers, and electronic data interchanges. In addition to the specialized networks, users can connect to a variety of third-party on-line network services. Third-party on-line services include general and specialized national business providers, the Internet, and numerous other national and local on-line services.

APPENDIX 1 TO CHAPTER 17

OTHER LAN APPLICATIONS AT INFOAGE, INC., AND ANN STRONG, CPA/CMA

Figure 17-11 presents other applications of LANs implemented at Infoage and at Ann Strong's consulting firm.

APPENDIX 2 TO CHAPTER 17

THREE SUBNETWORK SERVERS FOUND ON THE INTERNET

Client workstations connecting to a *file transfer protocol* (FTP) server can use a Windows-based GUI to access computer software by title and key word, and download the results to the workstation.

Client workstations accessing *Gopher* servers can display mostly text, and not graphics; this is a significant limitation to using Gopher. A Gopher search can be conducted by also using a graphical user interface (GUI) to access *Veronica* software, which allows easy-to-use key-word searches. For example, assume a user employing the Veronica key-word search tool is researching instances of "fraud" in Germany, and decides to search the libraries of the University of Cologne. After connecting to the University of Cologne, the user enters the search string key word fraud, and in a few seconds is provided with the number of citations on the topic; he or she can

Infoage could also use remote access software, such as Norton pcAnywhere (from Symantec) to dial in to each microcomputer installed at the two retail outlets. The remote access software must be installed on each computer to be accessed. Since the store managers will be transmitting primarily financial and related data to the home office, the remote software could be installed on Diane Varney's computer. The managers can use the fax/modem installed in each of their microcomputers to dial in to Diane's computer, thereby operating as if they were another workstation connected to the home office LAN. Each manager sends the daily sales files and other operating files to Diane's computer; accesses financial reports, files, and data-base files within the LAN; and exchanges E-mail. Thus the home office gains access to the resources of the retail outlets, and the retail outlets share the resources of the home office LAN, all without paying for a costly coaxial cable hookup.

Even Ann Strong may be able to use a LAN in her office, as well as in her consulting practice. She could implement a two-workstation peer-to-peer bus LAN, with the workstation in her office connected to her secretary's workstation. Many of the same accounting and office automation applications performed with Infoage's LAN could be accomplished by Ann Strong's LAN, except on a smaller scale. In addition, she will come in contact with a number of LANs in her consulting practice and should be able to interact with them in several ways. To illustrate, Ann can bring a laptop computer into the field to aid in her audit engagements. She can attach a pocket LAN adapter to her laptop and to a client's LAN, log into the network, and perform a number of auditing-through-the-computer tests on the client's internal controls, such as the preparation of test data. She can also use a general audit software package, such as Audit Command Language (ACL), to perform substantive tests of account balances and analytical tests of key relationships. Ann can also use remote access software to connect to her home office computer to exchange mail, documents, and files. At her home office, after the completion of an audit, she can connect the laptop to her LAN and transfer the client data to her desktop computer, thereby freeing valuable space in the laptop's hard disk. As she gains experience with the peer-to-peer bus LAN, which is becoming the LAN of choice in smaller firms, Ann will be able to implement this type of LAN for smaller clients about to interconnect their stand-alone microcomputers.

FIGURE 17-11   Examples of other LAN applications implemented at Infoage and at Ann Strong's consulting firm.

browse through each citation. However, since there are thousands of citations on fraud, the user may decide to limit the search by looking for specific instances of particular frauds, such as computer frauds committed in hospitals. A major disadvantage of using Veronica is that a hypertext-linked search of related documents on other servers around the world cannot be performed.

One of the fastest growing and most popular sub-network servers on the Internet is the **World Wide Web (WWW)** or simply the *Web* for short, which can display graphics and text, and if certain conditions are met, video, sound, and animation. Web servers are among the most frequently visited because of the availability of excellent, intuitive Windows-based GUI navigational aids or "browsers," which are required to conduct searches. The most widely used browser is **Netscape Navigator** (from Netscape, Inc.). Some versions of Netscape Navigator can be downloaded free from various Internet servers or purchased for a nominal fee from many software

vendors. By typing in a specific subject or address, it electronically takes a user to Web sites called "home pages" or Usenet newsgroups set up by individuals and organizations. Clicking on key words displayed on a home page or Usenet newsgroup initiates a hypertext-linked search of similar and related subjects found on other Web servers throughout the world. If a user does not have access to the specific Web address desired, but knows generally the nature of the subject, he or she can use a "search engine," such as Yahoo!, Infoseek, or Lycos. These search engines send out intelligent software agents to cull the information contained in the Web servers. By keying in the desired subject or topic, a list of related Web sites or Usenet newsgroups will appear on the screen; this list can be searched until the specific Web site is found. Frequently used sites can be "bookmarked." Clicking on a stored bookmarked site quickly connects the user to the site, without having to retype the site's address.

REVIEW PROBLEM WITH SOLUTION

MERTZ WHOLESALING COMPANY

Statement

The Mertz Wholesaling Company maintains a home office and two warehouses (A and B). It has decided to install a computer-based network that links the home office to the warehouses. The distances from the home office to warehouses A and B are 300 and 500 miles, respectively, and the distance between the two warehouses is 400 miles. The following cost data are available.

a. The monthly cost of leasing a suitable multiplexer is $500.

b. The monthly cost of leasing switching hardware for multidrops is $300.

c. The costs per minute for phone calls from the home office to warehouses A and B are $0.40 and $0.50, respectively.

d. The hours of message traffic between the home office and warehouses A and B are expected to be 40 and 30 hours, respectively.

e. The monthly rates for private lines of a suitable grade are $5 per mile through the first 100 miles, $4 per mile for the next 100 miles, $3 per mile for the next 100 miles, and $2 per mile for all distances above 300 miles.

Required

If each of the two warehouses is provided a video display terminal,

a. Describe four alternatives, involving various network configurations and types of service, that may be employed in the network.

b. Compute the total monthly cost for each alternative in **a**.

c. Comment on the results obtained in **b**.

Solution

a. and b.

Alternative 1 A point-to-point configuration that links the home office to each warehouse by separate private lines.

Monthly cost from home office to A:

$$(100 \text{ miles} \times \$5) + (100 \text{ miles} \times \$4)$$
$$+ (100 \text{ miles} \times \$3) = \$1200$$

Monthly cost from home office to B:

$$\$1200 + (200 \text{ miles} \times \$2) = \$1600$$

Total monthly cost = $1200 + $1600 = $2800

Alternative 2 A point-to-point configuration that links the home office to each warehouse by separate public switched lines.

Monthly cost from home office to A:

$0.40 per minute

× 40 hours

× 60 minutes per hour = $960

Monthly cost from home office to B:

$0.50 per minute

× 30 hours

× 60 minutes per hour = $900

Total monthly cost = $960 + $900 = $1860

Alternative 3 A multidrop configuration that links the home office to warehouse B through warehouse A by private lines, as follows.

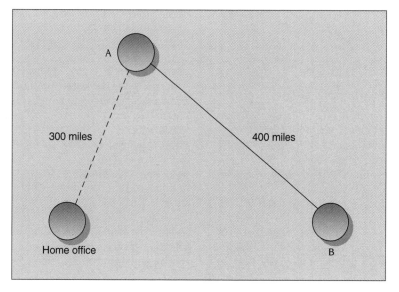

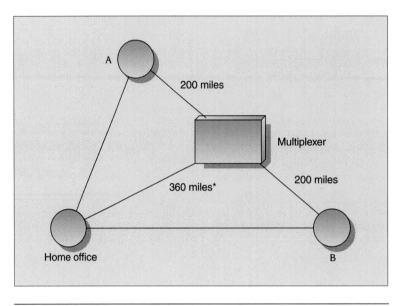

*Since the distances among the home office, warehouse A, and warehouse B form a 300–400–500 right triangle, the distance to the midpoint of A and B is $\sqrt{300^2 + 200^2} = \sqrt{130,000} = 360$.

Total monthly cost:

$1200 + (400 miles × $2)

+ $300 for hardware = $2300

Alternative 4 A multiplexed configuration that links the home office to each warehouse via private lines and a multiplexer located at the midpoint between warehouses A and B, as shown above.

Monthly cost from home office to multiplexer:

(100 miles × $5) − (100 miles × $4)

+ (100 miles × $3) + (60 miles × $2)

= $1320

Monthly cost from multiplexer to A and B:

2(200 miles × $2) = $800

Total monthly cost = $1320 + $800

+ $500 for multiplexer = $2620

c. The computations show that the point-to-point configuration using private lines is the most costly alternative, followed by the multiplexed and multidrop configurations. The point-to-point configuration using public-switched lines is the least costly. However, since a configuration employing public switched lines suffers the disadvantages of longer waiting times and less accurate transmissions than private lines, this least costly alternative may not be the best choice. Furthermore, if the hours of usage increase significantly in the future, public switched lines may become more costly. In other words, there is a break-even volume above which private lines become less costly than public switched lines.

KEY WORDS

bus configuration (765)
centralized computer network (755)
client/server computing (755)
decentralized computer system (755)
departmental dedicated multiple-server (768)
departmental dedicated single server (768)
disk mirroring (775)
distributed computer network (755)
electronic data interchange (EDI) system/network (779)
electronic funds transfer (EFT) system/network (778)
enterprisewide dedicated multiple-server (768)
hierarchical configuration (761)
Internet (782)
Lexis (783)
local-area network (LAN) (755)
middleware (767)
multidrop configuration (757)
multiplexed configuration (757)
Naars (783)
Netscape Navigator (784)
on-line national general business services (781)
on-line national specialized services (782)
open systems interconnection (OSI) (767)

REVIEW QUESTIONS

17-1. Why have data communications networks grown in recent years?

17-2. Distinguish among decentralized, centralized, and distributed networks.

17-3. Why do accountants have significant roles with respect to computer networks?

17-4. Contrast the three configurations that are suited to centralized networks.

17-5. What are the benefits and drawbacks of distributed networks?

17-6. For what types of firms are centralized and distributed networks best suited?

17-7. Identify the key hardware components of a LAN.

17-8. Identify three configurations that may be employed by LANs.

17-9. Distinguish between a peer-to-peer and server network.

17-10. What is the function of a network operating system?

17-11. What are the benefits and drawbacks of LANs?

17-12. What are specific risks to which a firm may be exposed because of the use of a computer network?

17-13. Identify several controls and security measures that are particularly suited to communications networks.

17-14. Identify several activities to be included in a periodic network operational audit.

17-15. Describe several accounting applications of LANs.

17-16. Contrast a point-of-sale system, an electronic funds transfer system, and an electronic data interchange system.

17-17. Identify the major on-line national general business service providers.

17-18. What types of services do on-line national general service providers offer?

17-19. Identify the major on-line national specialized business service providers.

17-20. Compare and contrast the Internet with the other on-line service providers.

17-21. Identify the major Internet servers.

17-22. What types of services are offered by Lexis and Naars?

DISCUSSION QUESTIONS

17-23. Discuss the likely impacts of a firm's communications network on data inputs, data base, reports, decision making, and organizational structure.

17-24. Contrast a communication network for a university having a single campus with a communications network for an automobile insurance firm having regional offices and agents.

17-25. To what extent does the configuration of a communications network affect decision making? For instance, does a centralized network require centralized decision making?

17-26. A centralized network requires a very lengthy design and implementation period. What difficulties may be encountered because of this lengthy period, and how might they be minimized?

17-27. Discuss the information that can be captured during the operation of such computer networks as those involving credit card verifications (e.g., American Express) and automated ticket selling.

17-28. What types of accounting information can Diane Varney, treasurer and controller of Infoage, Inc., obtain from CompuServe? Dow Jones News/Retrieval? The Internet?

17-29. Assume that Ann Strong has acquired a working knowledge of the major on-line service providers, including the Internet. Armed with this knowledge, what additional consulting services can Ann offer to her clients?

PROBLEMS

17-1. A group of three small community hospitals within the San Antonio, Texas, metropolitan area decide to establish an on-line computer system to serve their data processing and retrieval needs. A centralized mainframe IBM AS/400 processor and on-line disk devices containing hundreds of gigabytes of storage are located in a building in the downtown section of San Antonio. The hospitals are in the surrounding suburbs. Each is 15 miles from the mainframe computer site. The middle hospital is five miles from the other two of the three small hospitals.

Required

a. List the data communications components needed to connect the central processor to the middle hospital, assuming that the other two hospitals are not included.

b. Identify all the options available when selecting the communications channel in **a**.

c. Describe three possible configurations by which the three hospitals may be linked to the central processor. Which configuration do you feel is most feasible for the three hospitals to implement?

17-2. A firm maintains a home office and six remote locations, geographically situated as follows.

A mainframe computer is installed in the home office; each remote location houses a single terminal. The firm intends to establish a computer-based network.

Required

a. Connect the locations to form a centralized network having each of the following configurations.

(1) Point-to-point.

(2) Multidrop.

(3) Multiplexed, with the multiplexer located at ④.

(4) Point-to-point for three locations; multidrop for the remaining three locations.

(5) Point-to-point for one location; multidrop for two locations; multiplexed for the remaining three locations. Select the points for each configuration, with an eye toward designing the most suitable combinations.

b. Assuming that microcomputers are placed in the remote locations, connect the locations to form a distributed network having each of the following configurations.

(1) Star.

(2) Ring, including the home office.

(3) Combined star and ring.

17-3. The directors of Colorgraph Printing of Buffalo are reviewing a proposal to acquire Puball Publishers. Puball's operations are located in an urban area about 300 miles from Buffalo. Colorgraph's success in recent years, according to its management, is attributed in large part to its computerized information system. Puball, however, has used a computer only for financial accounting applications, such as payroll and general ledger records.

In considering the acquisitions, Colorgraph's board of directors focuses on the possibilities of two options for expanding its information system to include Puball: (a) a centralized network, or (b) a distributed network.

Required

a. Can terminals having only the capabilities of collecting, editing, transmitting, and receiving data be employed with both types of networks, or are they restricted to one of the types?

b. Compare the degree of detail likely to be transmitted from a remote location to headquarters by each of the two types of networks.

c. Explain briefly why Puball's management would be more likely involved in and concerned with data processing if a distributed network were installed. Assume that Puball would be organized as an independent profit center if acquired.

d. Explain why a distributed network would be less subject to a complete system breakdown.

(CIA *adapted*)

17-4. Which type of network—centralized, distributed, local—would likely be most suitable in each of the following situations?

a. A bus firm headquartered in a large city coordinates its numerous bus stations located throughout all states.

b. An airline reservation system with local offices in most larger cities.

c. An integrated consumer-goods manufacturer that maintains close coordination among its plants, distribution centers, warehouses, and home office.

d. A savings and loan institution with numerous branch offices throughout the cities of a state.

e. A public utility that establishes automated offices throughout its headquarter's facility.

f. A railroad coordinates the movement of all its rolling stock scattered throughout many states.

g. A New York stock exchange that maintains communications with brokers on the exchange floor and brokerage offices in several northeastern cities.

h. A department store chain that allows individual stores to handle credit sales and inventory, but that distributes paychecks from the home store.

i. A specialty retailer and supplier of women's and men's clothes, with numerous retail outlets in several states.

17-5. Electra Enterprises, Inc., is based in Los Angeles, where it maintains a relatively powerful minicomputer. At present it is considering the establishment of a centralized network that will tie its field offices to the main office. Its plans are to install video display terminals as follows: two in San Francisco, one in Denver, two in San Diego, and one in Phoenix. Three configurations are under consideration: (1) individual leased lines to each terminal; (2) point-to-point leased lines to each location, with concentrators used at those locations having two terminals; and (3) a multidrop leased line to the four locations, with a concentrator used at each remote location.

The leased lines for each of the alternative configurations may be voice-grade communications lines, which have a monthly pricing schedule as follows: $4 per mile for the first 25 miles, $3 per mile for the next 75 miles, and $2 per mile for all miles over 100 miles. (This schedule applies separately to each link.)

The mileages between affected cities are given below.

To From	San Francisco	Denver	Phoenix	San Diego
Los Angeles	379	1059	589	125
San Francisco		1235	763	504
Denver			792	1108
Phoenix				353

The devices needed for the three alternative configurations are (a) 12 fax/modems; (b) 8 fax/modems, one front-end processor, two data concentrators; (c) 5 fax/modems, one front-end processor, four multidrop concentrators. Purchase price for each fax/modem is $140. Monthly lease costs are $300 per front-end processor, $100 per data concentrator, and $150 per multidrop concentrator.

Required

a. Calculate the total communications costs for each of the three alternative configurations.

b. Draw a hardware configuration diagram for each of the three alternatives.

17-6. For each of the following situations, describe desirable networks or combined networks. Identify the types of networks by name, and describe the characteristics of the data base where pertinent.

a. A nationwide brokerage firm, headquartered in New York City, has offices in most cities. In addition to providing prompt stock market information to its representatives and processing transactions at each office, the firm desires to allow its clients to access its securities data base.

b. A regional speciality retailer and supplier of automotive parts, tools, supplies, equipment, and accessories currently operates 167 retail stores in five midwestern states. The firm employs an automated inventory system that links its 167 outlets to a centralized 250,000-square-foot distribution center. The distribution system allows the firm's retail stores to maintain optimal inventory levels and to provide every store same-day or overnight access to more than 150,000 items.

c. An integrated steel manufacturer needs to coordinate the operations of its mills with those of its sales and service centers and with its headquarters. In addition, it desires to have close links to its key suppliers of raw materials and to its major customers, in order to reduce inventories and provide faster service.

d. A large grocery chain with numerous retail stores needs to check out its customers quickly and to maintain control over its pricing and stocking of merchandise. In addition, it desires to perform prompt credit checks on customers when necessary and to obtain payments from customers as quickly as possible.

e. A nationwide electronics products firm, with several plants and office complexes in separate cities, needs to maintain control over production and to increase efficiency in office operations. In addition, it desires to send memoranda from one site to another and to conduct videoconferences on a regular basis.

17-7. Barbara Applestein is an internal auditor with Phoenix Consulting Company, a large consulting firm located in Athens, Georgia. Annual billings from consulting services for the current year are $125 million. The top management committee of Phoenix recently made the decision to downsize their accounting and management information systems, migrating applications processing from two centralized mainframes to a local-area network (LAN). Barbara is the internal audit department's representative on the systems steering committee that is designing and implementing the new system.

Required

a. Describe the reasons why Phoenix Consulting Company would choose a distributed LAN over the centralized mainframe computers.

b. Define the term "local-area network (LAN)" and describe its major components and configurations.

c. Before making a decision, Phoenix considered the benefits and risks of information systems downsizing. Identify and explain

    (1)   several of the benefits.

    (2)   several of the concerns/risks.

(CMA *adapted*)

17-8. Mercybrite, a large hospital in an eastern metropolitan area, has installed a large mainframe computer to support its patient systems. Connected to this computer by coaxial cable are serveral dozen video display terminals, on-line disk files, and three printers. From the time a patient enters the hospital, he or she is monitored by means of the network. Terminals located in the admitting room, labs, operating rooms, central supply, nursing stations, and elsewhere record all actions and progress. When necessary the network triggers actions, such as the administering of medications. Reports and documents are printed as needed from the patients' files.

Required

a. Identify the type of computer network described in this case and specify the benefits that it provides.

b. What risks does such a network entail with respect to hospital operations and the patients?

c. Draw a hardware configuration diagram of the described network. Include all needed types of hardware. Identify the assumptions that you make.

17-9. Vincent Maloy, director of special projects and analysis for Milok Company, is responsible for preparing corporate financial analyses and projections monthly and for reviewing and presenting to upper management the financial impacts of proposed strategies. Data for these financial analyses and projections are obtained from reports developed by Milok's systems department and generated from its mainframe computer. Additional data are obtained through terminals via a data inquiry system. Reports and charts for presentations are then prepared by hand and typed. Maloy has tried to have final presentations generated by the computer but has not always been successful.

The systems department has developed a package utilizing a terminal emulator to link a microcomputer to the mainframe computer. This allows the microcomputer to become part of the current data inquiry system and enables data to be downloaded to the microcomputer's disk. The data are in a format that allows printing or further manipulation and analyses using commercial software packages, for example, spreadsheet analysis. The special projects and analysis department has been chosen to be the first users of this new computer terminal system.

Maloy questioned whether the new system could do more for his department than implementing the program modification requests that he has submitted to the systems department. He also believed that his people would have to become programmers.

Lisa Brandt, a supervisor in Maloy's department, has decided to prepare a briefing for Maloy on the benefits of integrating microcomputers with the mainframe computer. She has used the terminal inquiry system extensively and has learned to use spreadsheet software to prepare special analyses, sometimes with multiple alternatives. She also tried the new package while it was being tested.

Required

a. Identify five enhancements to current information and reporting that Milok Company should be able to realize by integrating microcomputers with the firm's mainframe computer.

b. Explain how the utilization of computer resources would be altered as a result of integrating microcomputers with the firm's mainframe computer.

c. Discuss what security of the data is gained or lost by integrating microcomputers with the firm's mainframe computer.

(CMA *adapted*)

17-10. World Insurance Group, Ltd., is an old, established insurance firm, located in Elsmere, Delaware. It employs 4500 employees and operates 150 regional sales offices scattered throughout the Midwest. The firm has been using the same large IBM mainframe system for 10 years to support the regional offices and firm analysts with low-speed terminal links. The firm sells individual and group life and health insurance policies, automotive insurance policies, and a line of investment products. Because data transfer charges are high and the transmissions are slow, not everyone who needs it has had access to the mainframe system.

Management views the lack of a responsible system as especially troublesome, given its desire to increase the firm's market share by 15 percent over the next three years. Management believes its growth goal is realistic if the firm could respond more quickly to the needs of policyholders and new customers.

Everyone agrees that users need faster access to policy information, but hardly anyone agrees on how to achieve this goal. The two most popular approaches to improving access and supporting new applications are (1) to integrate existing separate data bases on an upgraded mainframe and (2) to install local-area network (LAN)-based PCs with communications software for formatting data-base queries and sending them to headquarters. Even the firm's 250 information systems professionals are evenly divided in their support for the two alternatives.

Required

a. Why are data transfer charges high in the existing mainframe system?

b. What are the advantages and disadvantages of maintaining policy information only in a single mainframe computer?

c. What are the advantages and disadvantages of maintaining policy information only on LANs at regional offices?

d. What type of data communications configuration would you recommend to connect the regional LANs to the headquarters' IBM mainframe computer? Draw a hardware configuration illustrating at least two options.

e. Assume that all updates occur on the data base on the central mainframe computer, and no data-base segments may be downloaded for local use. What are the advantages of this type of arrangement?

(CIA *adapted*)

17-11. Tulsa-based clothing retailer McCormack Department Stores, Inc., uses a ring LAN for purchasing and receiving applications and a bus LAN for billing and sales applications. The specific configuration for each LAN is shown below and on the next page. However, not all documents flowing into and out of the system, represented by arrows, are identified.

Required

Hint: Refer to the Application of Networks section of this chapter, to Figure 17-7, and to appropriate sections of Chapters 12 and 13 regarding the revenue and expenditure cycles. A review of these materials should enable you to complete the document flows and assist you in deriving a satisfactory solution for this problem.

a. Complete the documents flow in figure *a*.

b. Based on the completed figure *a*, explain how McCormack Department Stores can use the ring LAN for processing its purchasing and receiving applications.

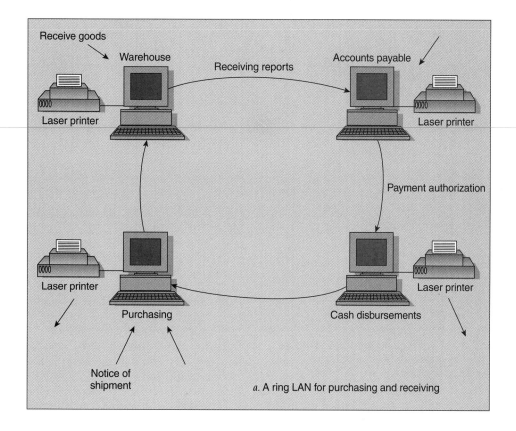

a. A ring LAN for purchasing and receiving

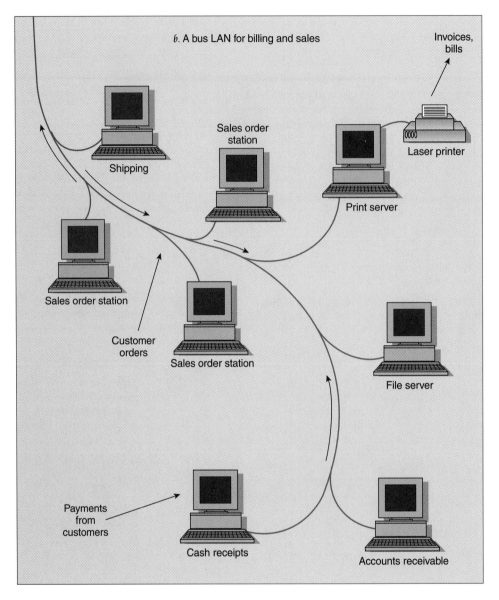

b. A bus LAN for billing and sales

c. What are the disadvantages, if any, of using a ring LAN to process purchasing and receiving applications?

d. Complete the documents flow in figure b above.

e. Based on the completed figure b, explain how Mc-Cormack Department Stores can use the bus LAN for processing for its billing and sales applications.

f. What are the disadvantages, if any, of using a bus LAN to process billing and sales applications?

17-12. For each of the case situations described below, determine whether you would recommend a client/server computing setup. Be sure to state any assumptions you make when justifying your answer.

a. A manufacturing firm with revenues in excess of $600 million processes all accounting applica-

tions on a mainframe computer. The firm's accounting staff batch processes payroll every two weeks for its 37,500 employees.

b. Infoage, Inc. (refer to Figure 1-4), has installed a LAN at its home office to process accounting and other applications. Automated accounting applications include general ledger, accounts receivable, accounts payable, and cash receipts/disbursements. The LAN is not currently connected to the firm's two retail outlets.

c. The Port of New York is one of the busiest in the world. The Port is concerned with keeping track of ship schedules, truck schedules, refrigeration requirements, union negotiations, weights, legal problems, and many other variables. The Port's objective is to provide "timely" information on these variables to keep the Port running effectively and efficiently. The Port uses a large IBM mainframe computer.

d. A large restaurant chain based in Denver has 197 eateries located in the states of Colorado, Nebraska, Wyoming, Utah, and New Mexico. Among the mainframe applications processed at the Denver administrative offices is a fixed asset accounting packaged system, which keeps track of 65,000 fixed assets. This packaged application was written by a software vendor decades ago and needs to be completely rewritten. However, the software vendor no longer supports the package, since its programmers are writing software packages exclusively for the client/server environment.

17-13. For each of the case situations described below, determine whether you would recommend a client/server computing setup. Be sure to state any assumptions you make when justifying your answer.

a. A small retail firm with sales of $2,000,000 uses five stand-alone microcomputers to process its accounting applications. It wants to develop automated decision-making applications to support its two key managers in making a variety of decisions.

b. A military defense agency in charge of national security employs several of the largest supercomputers manufactured. Its annual information systems budget is in excess of $45 million. An in-house study revealed that a client/server system could process the same applications as the mainframes, except at a cost of $15 million. Also, critical information needs could be generated in two days instead of five days. However, the agency requires zero downtime and very secure information systems.

c. An auto parts manufacturer located in the Southeast sells its parts at 226 outlet stores. Annual sales are $265 million. Within the firm, a LAN has been implemented in the budget department that employs 30 management accountants. The annual master budget is prepared using a popular spreadsheet package. A network version of the package has been installed on the LAN and is accessible to all analysts, enabling them to share the spreadsheet files and jointly modify the spreadsheets. In addition, the department's accounting manager can load one of his staff's spreadsheets, review it, and make suggestions for modifications.

d. With annual sales approaching $150,000,000, a distributor of women's fine clothing has installed LANs at its 73 retail outlets scattered throughout the Southwest. All LANs can communicate with one another, as well as with the home office LAN. LAN applications include general ledger, cash receipts/disbursements, inventory management, order entry, accounts payable, purchase order tracking, and cash forecasting. Recently, the firm's top managers have complained that most of the information received from the system is outdated by the time they receive it.

17-14. For each of the case situations described below, determine whether you would recommend a client/server computing setup. Be sure to state any assumptions you make when justifying your answer.

a. A railroad has developed a system that runs on a mainframe to track its rolling stock, such as locomotives. The current monitoring system is slow and requires at least 20 screen displays to monitor the locomotives and railroad cars. It often takes 10 or more hours to generate the data required to monitor the railroad's operations.

b. A large manufacturer of electronic devices processes approximately 6.5 million accounting and business transactions annually on a large parallel processing mainframe computer. The firm currently manufactures 126 different lines of electronic products.

c. A large national rental car agency with over 700 outlets uses a centrally located mainframe to process reservations for its customers. The time to process reservations is seven minutes, which management deems unacceptable.

d. A large pizza franchisor with 1100 delivery-style outlets located in all 50 states uses a mainframe computer to process transactions and provide decision-making information to the managers of the eateries. As recently as one year ago, the pizza franchisor did not own one microcomputer. Presently, it is implementing a wide-area network whose goal is to provide the 1100 managers with up-to-date information that is relatively easy to access.

17-15. Seaton Industries of Groton, Connecticut, manufactures large cargo ships for the U.S. and foreign merchant marines. Its annual revenues are approximately $16 billion. It is in the first year of implementing a LAN-based client/server computing platform to replace its three mainframe computer systems. The project is expected to take another six years to complete. All accounting, human resource, decision support, and manufacturing/distribution applications will be moved to 2500 client workstations.

The firm formed a client/server steering committee made up of representatives from a large consulting firm and in-house information systems staff members to develop and implement the client/server system. The annual costs of the current system, including hardware, software, personnel, supplies, maintenance, and so on are $7 million. The projected annual costs of the client/server system are $4 million, resulting in an annual savings of $3 million.

One member of the board of directors recently came across an article titled, "Client/Server Costs: Don't Get Taken for a Ride." Since reading the article, he has become somewhat concerned about the estimated annual savings from the client/server system. As a result, the chairman of the audit committee asks Mr. Robert Burden, CIA and director of Internal Audit, to look into the matter. Mr. Burden asks Ms. Pamela Salvaggio, senior auditor, to independently estimate the total annual costs of implementing the client/server system. Pamela completes some background study on the project and decides to use the Gartner model, which is used to accurately estimate client/server costs. After several weeks on the project, Pamela estimates annual client/server hardware and software costs to be close to the $4 million original estimate. However, she also has uncovered a number of so-called hidden costs that were not included in the original budget of estimated costs. These costs include end-user operating costs, administration, capital investment, and technical support, and amount to additional annual costs of $4 million. Instead of a $3 million annual savings, Ms. Salvaggio projects an annual loss of $1.5 million. She presents the report to her supervisor, Mr. Bob Burden, who in turn presents it to the Corporate Audit Committee. Three months pass and Mr. Burden still has not heard anything from the Corporate Audit Committee pertaining to Ms. Salvaggio's report.

Required

a. Why do you think the original annual savings were underestimated?

b. What should have been the role of internal audit in the original client/server project?

c. What are the ethical implications of not hearing from the Corporate Audit Committee?

d. What action should Mr. Burden take?

17-16. Gackle Remanufacturing Company is a remanufacturer of truck engines, located in Norwood, Ohio. Gackle has over 200 microcomputers with full processing capabilities linked into an integrated local-area network with a file server that in turn is fully connected to the central mainframe computer. Data entry, comprehensive processing, and inquiry routines are possible at all microcomputers in the LAN.

Required

a. Assume that highly confidential files need to be properly deleted from several microcomputers. What is the best way to accomplish this task?

b. To achieve the highest degree of control within this distributed network, how should versions of critical software application programs on the server be stored?

c. What type of backup system should Gackle implement for the LAN? Be specific.

d. What control(s) within the network would determine if any data have been changed during a transmission to another microcomputer in the network?

e. If the system did not have the mainframe computer or a file server, what is the type of network that would process applications within the linked microcomputers?

f. Assume that in the future Gackle intends to implement a client/server setup within the local-area network.

(1) What type of client/server network would probably be implemented?

(2) What applications would be processed on the client/server setup?

(3) What problems is Gackle likely to encounter as it implements the client/server system?

(4) What additional control and security measures are necessary for a client/server environment?

(CIA *adapted*)

17-17. Pinta Company is a regional discount chain headquartered in Montgomery, Alabama. Its stores, scattered throughout the Southeast, sell general merchandise. The firm is considering the acquisition of a point-of-sale (POS) system for use in all its stores. Of the various models available, the president believes that the type using a light pen to scan the universal product code on merchandise is the most suitable. However, it is quite expensive, so Charles Brenski, the president, asks the systems staff to prepare a report answering several questions.

Required

Prepare a report to the president that

a. Explains the functions and operation of a POS system, including its extension into credit checking and electronic transfers of funds.

b. Identifies the advantages and disadvantages of the extended POS system described in **a.**

c. Identifies the special control and security problems that the extended POS system could present, together with suitable controls and security measures that should effectively counteract these problems.

Hint: Look for a recent article describing POS systems.

(CMA *adapted*)

17-18. Tucker Productions, a manufacturer of fashion apparel, has just opened its first large retail store for selling in-season clothes at regular prices. The firm's competitive strategy depends on a comprehensive point-of-sale (POS) system supporting on-line, up-to-the-minute sales totals, day-to-day tracking of stock information, and quick checkout of customer purchases. Management installed an advanced microcomputer-based POS system. Because cashiers were already familiar with electronic cash registers, management decided that only minimal training was required.

Cashiers enter four-digit stock tracking numbers (STNs) into the microcomputer, which retrieves price and description data, computes the tax and total amount due, accepts the type of payment, and controls the cash drawer. A unique STN identifies each of the 9500 pieces of merchandise. The microcomputer maintains stock information.

In the first month of operation new cashiers were awkward in their use of the PC. They eventually became proficient users and chafed at the perceived slow response for printing sales tickets and the unpredictable action of the cash drawer.

Required

Identify several problems that exist in the current POS system/network. Suggest an improvement for overcoming each identified problem.

(CIA *adapted*)

17-19. Fastcar Parts, a small manufacturer of automobile parts, has just learned that its primary customer is requiring all of its suppliers to accept orders via electronic data interchange (EDI). The primary customer uses EDI instead of paper forms for transactions with its largest suppliers. The customer is expanding its use of EDI and intends to drop all suppliers who cannot participate in EDI within a year. Along with using EDI for orders, the customer also requires daily reports of the status of work-in-process for each of its orders so that it can modify orders by giving notice at least 48 hours before production begins.

Currently, the manufacturer maintains manual records for receivables, payables, materials inventory, order entry, work-in-process, and finished-goods inventory; it uses a service bureau for payroll. Finished-goods inventory is very small, as the manufacturer produces mostly "to order" for its larger customers and ships the parts immediately on completion. The manufacturer wants to continue producing for its primary customer, even if it involves implementing EDI.

Required

a. Describe the objectives of an EDI system/network for Fastcar Parts that is responsive to the requirements of the primary customer.

b. Describe the steps in developing the EDI system/network.

(CIA *adapted*)

17-20. Use the following information to answer multiple-choice questions 1 through 11.

A pillow manufacturing firm tracks its production manually. That process results in continuing inaccuracies in inventory and production records on monthly production of about 1 million pillows in three plants. Not knowing how much raw materials inventory is needed, the firm maintains surplus inventory of about 25 days production usage at each plant so it can meet its delivery commitments.

The firm makes pillows to order for large-volume customers that have given it one year to (1) implement electronic data interchange (EDI) for sending and receiving business data for orders, shipping instructions, confirmations, and payments and (2) affix bar codes to each carton and pillow. The firm believes it would also be advantageous to implement EDI with its suppliers as a means to facilitate just-in-time inventory. The firm is fully aware that its automation plan is ambitious, but management senses that the firm really has no choice if it is to remain in business.

Production begins with the receipt of an order, when a blank production sheet is prepared. As the order progresses through production, each worker writes in the quantity of raw materials and production hours added at each stage. Packers load finished pillows into cartons and update the order sheet to show that the order is complete. When an order is shipped, its production sheet goes to data entry where clerks key the data to update inventory records. Often, there are errors, but even when there are none, there is a significant delay between shipping an order and updating inventory records. Consequently, the firm never really knows how much inventory it has or the quality of individual shipments still in inventory.

The quality of raw materials matters because customers expect their shipments to be of uniform quality. The quality of the final product varies in direct proportion to the quality of its raw materials. Consequently, when the quality of raw materials varies, production workers requisition more materials from inventory to maintain consistent quality. The unused materials go back into inventory.

1. After the firm implements electronic data interchange (EDI) to communicate with its customers, an appropriate control for ensuring authenticity of the electronic orders it receives is to:
   a. Encrypt sensitive messages such as electronic payments for raw materials received.
   b. Perform reasonableness checks on quantities ordered before filling orders.
   c. Verify the identity of senders and determine whether orders correspond to contract terms.
   d. Acknowledge receipt of electronic payments with a confirming message.

2. A control the firm could use to detect forged EDI messages is to:
   a. Acknowledge all messages initiated externally with confirming messages.
   b. Permit only authorized employees to have access to transmission facilities.
   c. Delay action on orders until a second order is received for the same goods.
   d. Write all incoming messages to a write-once/read-many device for archiving.

3. Although the firm and its largest customers will invest in the trading relationships, there is still the potential for disputes over the contents of messages. The best practice for ensuring that the firm will be able to substantiate its version of events in the case of a disagreement over the contents of a customer's order is to:
   a. Write all incoming messages to a tape file.
   b. Mail the customer a confirmation for large orders.
   c. Write all messages to a write-once/read-many device.
   d. Agree to submit all disagreements to arbitration.

4. Before sending or receiving EDI messages, the firm should:
   a. Execute a trading partner agreement with each of its customers and suppliers.
   b. Reduce inventory levels in anticipation of receiving shipments.
   c. Demand that all its suppliers implement EDI capabilities.
   d. Evaluate the effectiveness of its use of EDI transmissions.

5. The best approach for minimizing the likelihood of software incompatibilities leading to unintelligible messages is for the firm and its customers to:
   a. Acquire their software from the same software vendor.
   b. Agree to synchronize their updating of EDI-related software.
   c. Agree to use the same software in the same ways indefinitely.
   d. Each write their own version of the EDI-related software.

6. Regardless of whether the firm develops, buys, leases, or pays for the use of the software for EDI transmissions, internal audit should be responsible for evaluating whether the software:
   a. Was developed in a controlled environment.
   b. Is backed up adequately to permit recovery.
   c. Was acquired with adequate review by legal counsel.
   d. Meets business objectives.

7. After implementing EDI with suppliers, the firm discovered a dramatic increase in the prices it paid the single supplier of some special materials for its primary product line. After consulting with the supplier, the firm determined that the supplier had assumed the risk of not having inventory and raised its prices accordingly since the firm was the only buyer for the special materials. The best approach for managing inventory in this situation is for the firm to:
   a. Give the supplier more information about expected use of the materials.
   b. Demand that the supplier reduce the prices of the materials.
   c. Find another supplier to replace the one charging higher prices.
   d. Change its product line so the special materials are no longer needed.

8. If the cycle time for manual purchase orders is 25 days, composed of 4 days preparation, 3 days in the mail, 14 days in process at the supplier, and 4 days for delivery of raw materials, the shortest possible cycle time if the firm fully implemented EDI with suppliers would be:
   a. 21 days.
   b. 18 days.
   c. 14 days.
   d. 1 day.

9. If implementing EDI with suppliers permitted more frequent orders and more frequent communication about them, the firm could be more effective by using EDI to:
   a. Reduce costs by reducing raw materials inventory.
   b. Ensure that it always maintained a 25-day buffer stock.
   c. Track materials through production to completed orders.
   d. Schedule production to reduce the number of setups required.

10. Suppose a major supplier responded to the firm's request to implement EDI by asking the firm to share raw materials usage data so it could smooth its production. The most effective response to this request would be for the firm to send the supplier:
    a. The requested data daily via EDI.
    b. Usage data via weekly reports.
    c. Monthly production reports.
    d. No data at all because it is confidential.

11. Suppose the firm begins bar coding raw materials and production, implements EDI with suppliers and customers, and invests in new automated equipment for production. A risk associated with these changes is that:

a. The firm will be less able to respond to customers' inquiries about their orders.

b. Having less raw materials inventory will increase the likelihood of stockouts.

c. The firm will be less responsive to customers because it has less finished-goods inventory.

d. Employees may fail to modify their efforts consistent with the new approaches.

(CIA *adapted*)

17-21. Taco-Juan's Mexican Restaurants, Inc. (TJs for short), operates 840 fast-food restaurants throughout the West, Midwest, and Southwest regions of the United States. TJs is a privately held firm. One hundred percent of the stock is owned by the founder and CEO, Mr. Juan Rapheal. The home office is located in Kansas City, Missouri. Total annual firm sales are $1.1 billion. Same store sales are growing 5 percent annually. TJs is expanding at the rate of 50 to 75 new fast-food restaurants per year.

The firm is currently leasing an IBM mainframe for $165,000 per month. Other monthly data costs are $350,000. The mainframe is primarily used to automate legacy operating and accounting information system (AIS) applications, including accounts receivable and billing, purchasing, accounts payable, payroll, inventory, and fixed assets. All applications are run using a batch processing mode. TJs uses a central warehouse inventory distribution system to distribute food items to its 840 operating units. The firm operates a warehouse in Denver, Colorado, to receive, store, and distribute food products. Restaurant managers use an economic order quantity (EOQ) model to forecast product demand and reorder food items by faxing their orders to the Denver warehouse. Orders are shipped within 24 hours of receipt and are received at the individual restaurants within one week of ordering.

Future versions of the fixed asset accounting software will no longer run on TJs IBM mainframe computer. The fixed asset system currently keeps track of 375,000 fixed assets—everything from deep fryers to stools. However, the batch data-entry process for keeping track of these assets and entering data for the other applications results in many errors. Systems analysts use a mainframe data-base management system and structured query language to generate decision-making information and reports to management.

The 840 fast-food restaurants, which are firm owned, are located as follows:

- St. Louis and vicinity: 50 units.
- Wisconsin, Minnesota, North Dakota, Indiana: 100 units.
- Los Angeles: 10 units.
- San Francisco: 20 units.
- Seattle, Spokane, Portland, Coos Bay: 35 units.

- Denver and vicinity: 300 units.
- Cheyenne, Casper, Laramie, Gillette: 100 units.
- Phoenix: 100 units.
- Tucson, New Mexico, southern Colorado, western Texas: 125 units.

The firm maintains a centralized data processing network. No data communication links connect Denver to any of the 840 operating units. The restaurants are open seven days a week, from 6 A.M. to 12 P.M. The manager on duty at closing faxes the gross sales figures and other operating statistics to the Denver headquarters. Monthly, each manager receives from the home office a set of financial statements and cost performance reports disclosing significant operating variances for materials, labor, and overhead. Mr. Rapheal has recently established a computer steering committee made up of three general managers, the controller, the assistant controller, the internal auditor, five restaurant managers, the data processing manager, several other key data processing employees, and the marketing manager. Mr. Rapheal is concerned about the type and timeliness of information he is receiving from the 840 operating units. He is also concerned about the fact that the operating units only receive scheduled monthly reports that are faxed from the home office. He has charged the steering committee to recommend a new reporting system for the firm, making extensive use of data communications networks.

Required

a. Recommend a telecommunications network for Taco-Juan's Mexican Restaurants, Inc. Present at least two alternative designs. Provide a diagram of each alternative, showing proper placement of all hardware and data communication devices recommended. List the software requirements of the proposed alternatives.

b. Discuss key security and control measures for your proposed network.

c. Discuss audit implications of your proposed network.

CONTINUING CASE.

With respect to the small firm that you selected in Chapter 1, complete the following requirements:

a. If the firm uses a computer system and has implemented a local-area network, draw a configuration diagram, and state the expected benefits. If a LAN has not been implemented, determine the reasons why one has not been implemented.

b. If the firm uses a computer system and has implemented an electronic data interchange (EDI) network, draw a configuration diagram, and state the expected benefits. If an EDI network has not been implemented, determine the reasons why one has not been implemented.

c. State how the firm is using external networks, such as CompuServe or the Internet. If the firm is not currently using these types of networks, state how such networks can be employed in the firm.

d. If the firm employs a client/server system,

(1) Specify the types of applications the firm automates.

(2) State the benefits it derives from the system.

(3) Identify any problems the firm is having operating the system.

e. If the firm has plans to implement a client/server system, specify the types of applications the firm will automate and the advantages of the proposed applications.

f. Determine the specific types of internal control and security measures that have been implemented in the networks described in **a** through **d** above.

CHAPTER 18

SYSTEMS ORGANIZATION, DEVELOPMENT, AND MANAGEMENT

1. Survey the organization of the information systems function, including its location within the overall organizational structure as well as its internal structure.

2. Describe the need for and major phases in the systems development life cycle.

3. Contrast several approaches to systems development.

4. Identify important steps in the systems planning phase.

5. Describe issues and techniques for managing and controlling a system during its operational phase.

INTRODUCTION

Accounting information systems (AISs) are becoming larger, both in size and in numbers. They also are becoming more complex, due to the emerging information technologies and techniques. To cope with such growth and complexity, firms are giving greater attention to systems organization, development, and management. They begin by establishing a sound organizational structure for the information systems function. They plan and develop the AIS and related systems by following proven approaches. Finally, many firms employ effective management techniques that extend from the development phases into the operational phase of the AIS.

IMPORTANCE OF INFORMATION RESOURCE MANAGEMENT

We emphasized as early as Chapter 1 that information is a valuable resource. In Chapter 3 we observed that recognition of this fact, plus the rise of information technology, has led to the idea of **information resource management (IRM).** Essentially, IRM has the purpose of assuring the effective acquisition and use of information. Conceptually it stresses that information cuts across all organizational boundaries, in order to knit together a firm's objectives and activities. By following the purpose and concepts of IRM, a firm increases the odds that it will succeed in achieving its basic objectives.

IRM can be furthered through a well-organized information systems function and continual attention to systems development. In turn, new systems development implies the need for a carefully established systems development life cycle. Finally, IRM points to the need for effective management and controls during the operational phase of a system's life, including accounting for systems-related costs and evaluating the performance of systems-related resources.

IMPORTANCE TO ACCOUNTANTS OF SYSTEMS DEVELOPMENT AND MANAGEMENT

Accountants have been closely involved in developing and managing the AIS from its beginning. In the days before the information age, in fact, persons with accounting backgrounds were usually the sole developers of information systems. With the rise of management information systems and information technology, information systems specialists (e.g., systems analysts) have become the principal group with systems development responsibilities. They are directly concerned with analyzing current systems, designing new applications for computer-based systems, and implementing these systems according to the design specifications. However, accountants and auditors often are and should still be actively involved in development activities.

Accountants are continual users of the AIS. Every transaction has an accounting implication. Outputs of the AIS, such as financial reports and listings, provide information needed for verifying the reliability of financial statements or to aid managers in their decision-making responsibilities. Furthermore, accountants are concerned with the underlying models that generated the information, since many are based on accounting principles. For instance, accounting principles are involved in the analysis of future capital investments, including investing in new information technology.

Accountants also may be involved with systems development as members of project teams. Accounting expertise is particularly needed in evaluating the internal controls for new systems. It is critical when designing accounting applications that incorporate accounting principles. In addition to aiding in the analysis and design aspects, accountants can participate in systems implementation. For instance, accountants can help to test the controls and to train clerical employees in using accounting applications. They may be of help to managers who use expert systems that involve accounting concepts.

The challenge for accountants is to actively seek such roles and to assert their participative responsibilities. This challenge requires that accountants become more knowledgeable in systems development techniques and communicate effectively with systems analysts and managers. Accountants must overcome their "bean counter" image.*

Management of the AIS and other information systems has become more important in recent years. Budgets for information systems have mushroomed in many firms, mainly because of expanding information technology. Accountants are clearly the most appropriate professionals to control these activities. Most control techniques are based on accounting concepts. Thus, the role related to managing the AIS should be at least as apparent to accountants as the roles pertaining to its development.

---

*William M. Baker, "Shedding the Bean Counter Image," *Management Accounting* (October 1994), pp. 29–31.

ORGANIZATION OF THE INFORMATION SYSTEMS FUNCTION

The information systems function has steadily grown in many firms. Its responsibilities include operating and maintaining the accounting and other information systems, plus developing and installing new systems.

Four major questions must be answered concerning the organization of the information systems function:

1. To whom should the information systems manager report within the organization?
2. What should be the nature of the information systems function, with respect to size, structure, and responsibilities?
3. To what extent should the organizational structure of the information systems function be centralized or decentralized?
4. What should be the interactions between the information systems function and groups such as the accounting function and outside consultants?

LOCATION OF THE SYSTEMS FUNCTION

Before the computer era, systems responsibilities were traditionally assigned to the accounting function. Often they were handled by a department whose head reported to the controller. With the advent of computers and the emergence of new information systems, the systems function has been relocated in many firms. Instead of being a department within the controller's area, it has been placed under the jurisdiction of a nonaccounting manager.

Figure 18-1 indicates three of the more likely locations to which the systems function has been moved. At each of these three locations, it is positioned higher in the organization than when it reported to the controller. Thus the function has generally gained status and hence "clout."

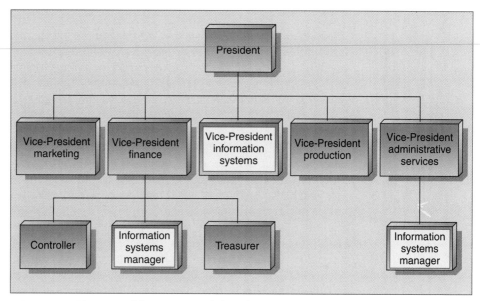

FIGURE 18-1   Three possible overseers of the information systems function.

The most conservative move has been to place the function under the vice-president of finance and on the same managerial level as the controller. This move can be defended on the bases that many reports generated by the information system are financial in nature and that the function maintains a close association with its former accounting roots. On the other hand, the location under the finance function may be viewed with concern by such functions as marketing and production. Managers of those functions may perceive that financial and accounting reports receive favored treatment under such an arrangement.

Another move has relocated the systems function under a vice-president of administrative services. This move allows the systems function to be truly independent, and to be perceived as such. As a consequence, the systems function has greater freedom to cross organizational boundaries and to develop integrated information systems. It also can resist pressure tactics by any function.

Some firms, however, have not established an administrative services function. Other firms may feel that the systems function deserves full recognition as a major function within the organization. In such firms the systems function may report directly to the president (or an executive vice-president).

INTERNAL STRUCTURE OF THE INFORMATION SYSTEMS FUNCTION

As discussed in Chapter 8, the responsibilities of the information systems function must be segregated in a manner to effect sound internal control. Since the function is charged with the tasks of managing the information resource, its organizational structure is particularly affected with the introduction of information technology. Figure 8-3 presented an organization chart that provided effective segregation between data processing and systems development responsibilities. Figure 18-2 also presents a hierarchical organization chart; however, it emphasizes the responsibilities that pertain to systems development and to user and staff support. The figure is suggestive only, since innumerable variations are found in practice. For instance, the systems analysis and programming functions could be in separate units.

Each manager or group shown in Figure 18-2 has assigned responsibilities such as follows:

Information Systems Manager   As the head of the information systems function, the **information systems manager** provides overall leadership. He or she helps to set the objectives for the function, takes part in long-range systems planning, and directs both the systems development and operations activities of the function. The information systems manager also (1) supervises and evaluates the performances of the key managers and staff personnel within the function and (2) hires and trains new managers when needed.

A number of firms, especially those endorsing the IRM view, have appointed a **chief information officer (CIO),** normally at the vice-presidential level. In such firms the information systems manager reports to the CIO, or the two positions may be combined in some manner. A key responsibility of the CIO is to develop policies that govern the standardization, generation, and dissemination of information throughout the firm. In addition, the CIO usually develops and justifies budgets for the function, keeps abreast of new technological developments in information technology, and stays alert for new ways of improving the information system. Accountants, who have been trained in the generation and use of information, are well suited for the position of CIO—especially if they have acquired a sound understanding of information technology.

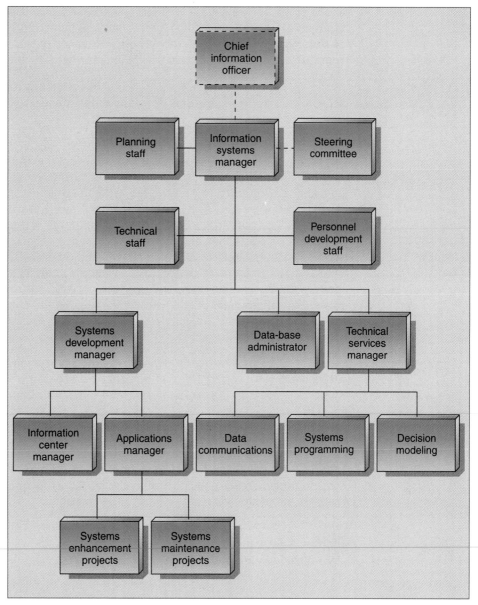

FIGURE 18-2 A partial organizational structure of the information systems function, with emphasis on systems development.

Staff   Various staff groups are needed in larger organizations. A *planning staff* aids in developing long-range systems plans, in coordinating with the corporate strategic planning group, and in establishing information-related policies. A *technical staff* aids in monitoring technological developments, evaluating the potential for applying new technologies within the firm, and planning the diffusion of new hardware and software throughout the firm. A *personnel staff* aids in recruiting and training systems professionals.

Steering Committee   An information systems development group, typically called a **steering committee,** provides overall guidance in systems development. It reviews and approves the long-range systems plans and hardware/software acquisitions, establishes priorities concerning systems development projects, controls the progress of systems projects, and monitors the performance of the function. It is generally composed of the major users of the information system.

Systems Development Manager   Direct line responsibility for systems development activities rests with the **systems development manager,** who provides overall direction of new systems projects, information systems management, user-support activities, and hardware and software maintenance.

Applications Manager   The primary responsibility of the **applications manager** is to develop information systems applications. Work concerning these applications may be organized according to ongoing projects. Typical purposes of projects are to develop new or enhanced systems applications. Projects are headed by **project managers,** who take part in overall project planning, obtain needed resources, and direct and control the activities of systems project teams. Project teams are composed of systems analysts, application programmers, and other personnel who represent the users and understand the project areas. **Systems analysts** analyze the present system, devise the broad design, and provide specifications to the programmers. **Application programmers** prepare structured program flowcharts or other logical diagrams and then write the computer programs used to direct the applications.

Information Center Manager   Since the position is a relatively recent addition in most firms, the responsibilities of an **information center manager** are not uniformly established. However, in a typical firm they may consist of providing internal consulting services and support facilities for end-user applications. For instance, services may involve assistance to users in developing special applications and acquiring an understanding of microcomputer-based software packages.

Technical Services Manager   A variety of specialized development responsibilities may be assigned to a **technical services manager,** including data communications, systems programming, and decision modeling. If the organization includes a security manager, he or she could also report to this manager.

Data-Base Administrator   As noted in Chapters 6 and 8, a data-base administration function is responsible for the design and control of a firm's data base. Headed by a **data-base administrator (DBA),** the function manages all aspects of the data and information resource. One primary responsibility is to establish and define the schema of the data base. Fulfilling this responsibility consists first of assigning standardized names to elements and records; specifying their contents, formats, primary keys, and their relationships; and compiling the results into an on-line data dictionary. A second responsibility is to control the use of the data base by assigning user codes and maintaining other security measures. A third responsibility is to control all changes in data and in programs that use the data base. Fulfilling these responsibilities is critical to the success of the data base, although the DBA is not likely to be popular with users who desire easy access to all data.

Internal Auditor   Although not shown in the organization chart, an internal auditor has an important relationship to the information systems function. An internal auditor heads a group of auditors who ensure that the controls are being implemented as designed. One key type of control, as we know, is the appropriate segregation of responsibilities within the information systems function, as well as the separation of that function from user groups.

INFORMATION SYSTEMS ORGANIZATION AND DEVELOPMENT
at Merrill Lynch*

Merrill Lynch is a securities brokerage and financial services firm. Its two major divisions are consumer markets and capital markets. Merrill Lynch is a huge international firm; in fact, it is the largest underwriter of debt and equity securities in the world. The firm places great importance on the use of information technology, since it has assigned the executive vice-president to head the operations, systems, and telecommunications functions. The sector that he heads has a three-pronged mission: to deliver the highest-quality service, to be the low-cost producer and distributor of these services, and to upgrade the firm's technology. Under the executive vice-president are top-level managers—the first vice-president and director of information systems and the senior vice-president of global information services. The yearly budget for all systems activities, plus accompanying technology, is about one billion dollars.

To continue into the 1990s, an applications productivity task force has been established. This task force has been charged with an objective of improving productivity by 100 percent within three years. To achieve this objective, the task force has adopted the strategy of integrating and simplifying a diverse collection of information systems. It has decided that this strategy can best be implemented by means of several systems-related "platforms."

The most crucial of these is a data platform, consisting of common access to all the major data bases (e.g., customer data base, product data base). Other platforms will relate to the array of consumer market transactions, global trading, and banking and trust activities. Concurrently, the information systems will also be enhanced by new technology. For instance, image processing technology will be added for processing new account applications. Workstation technology will be added to the trader desks in the capital markets division of the firm. Through these workstations the traders will be able to access account information, market quotes, news stories, and other data. Trades will be processed more efficiently.

As a result of the integrated systems architecture represented by these platforms and new technologies, the firm should greatly increase end-user computing. By making available easy-to-use and more effective systems to the various end-users, costs are expected to be reduced and productivity should be dramatically increased.

To reap these benefits, of course, the system must be soundly designed and carefully implemented. In addition, the end users will need intensive training, with annual training costs expected to average 15 million dollars. Only time will tell how effective the new system will be. As the senior vice-president of global information systems states: "This tends to be a very technology-intensive business from a user perspective."

*Elaine M. Koerner, "Integrating Information Systems for Competitive Advantage at Merrill Lynch." Long Range Planning (April 1990), pp. 27–34.

CENTRALIZATION VERSUS DECENTRALIZATION

Centralization consists of grouping all systems-related activities in one central location under the line authority of an information systems manager. Figure 18-2 by implication portrays a centralized organizational structure. Decentralization consists of dispersing the systems personnel and activities throughout the organization. For instance, systems analysts and programmers and technical specialists may be attached to each division and production plant of a large manufacturing firm, and some may be assigned to various departments and functions throughout the home office and regional offices. Decentralized personnel are generally under the line authority of the local managers, whereas the information systems managers maintain only functional authority.

Each type of structure has benefits. A centralized structure requires fewer systems personnel overall, can usually attract highly qualified personnel more easily, and can provide better overall control and standardization. It also tends to be less expensive, especially with respect to hardware and communications costs. A decentralized structure, however, allows the dispersed systems personnel to provide faster service that is more attuned to localized needs. It therefore fosters greater enthusiasm from users.

Decentralization is a matter of degree, of course. Even firms with highly decentralized systems functions retain central groups of managers and specialists. Normally the decision concerning the degree of decentralization is related to the type of computer network employed. Those firms with highly distributed networks tend to decentralize systems personnel to a significant degree.

INTERACTION WITH ACCOUNTANTS AND OTHER KEY USERS

The information systems function interacts with a wide variety of parties, both inside and outside the firm. In addition to individual managers and employees, these parties include user groups such as the accounting function, suppliers of hardware and software, and consultants.

Accounting Function   One of the largest and most significant user groups is the accounting function. Because it is so dependent on information products, it must maintain extremely close ties with the information systems function.

Several ways to maintain these close relationships are

1. Assigning both the controller and information systems manager to the steering committee.

2. Assigning accountants to systems project teams.

3. Assigning persons who are knowledgeable in both accounting and information technology to serve as coordinators between the accounting and information systems functions.

4. Establishing an internal audit group, staffed by accountants and systems-oriented auditors.

5. Establishing data control groups within accounting departments.

Suppliers   When acquiring and updating its computer system, a firm must deal with the representatives of various suppliers or vendors of hardware and software. Most of the day-to-day interactions are conducted by the technical staff or the systems manager. Ideally, all such contacts are friendly and professional. However, close personal relationships should not be encouraged, in order to maintain an objective viewpoint between competing suppliers. Moreover, the sales representatives should not be used as consultants; they are biased toward particular brands of hardware and software. Also, they are typically not as well informed about information needs as are trained consultants.

Consultants   Many firms do need professional outside assistance with their systems development activities. They should acquire such assistance from reputable consulting firms, such as the large public accounting firms. These consultants may aid in any phase of the systems development life cycle. By using such consultants, a firm receives objective viewpoints and the benefits of accumulated experiences gained from prior engagements. On the other hand, a firm should not lean unduly on consultants. For instance, consultants should not be allowed to make decisions or to perform detailed systems development tasks.

SYSTEMS DEVELOPMENT LIFE CYCLE

Assume that a newly established firm hires consultants to design and install the information system that exactly meets its needs, and that the consultants do so. Can this firm's management then ignore further systems development? The answer is a resounding NO. Systems planning and development is necessary throughout the life of a firm.

NEED FOR CONTINUAL SYSTEMS DEVELOPMENT

Three major reasons dictate the need for continual systems development:

1. Changes inevitably occur, both within a firm and in its environment. The firm may grow and/or market new products and services. New competitors may come into being; new government regulations may be promulgated. These changes affect the information system and organization as well as the firm's physical operations.

2. Shortcomings arise or become apparent. New managers may be hired who demand better information for making decisions. Customers may begin pressing for speedier answers to inquiries and on-time deliveries. Certain key factors, such as the bad debts ratio and product unit costs, might develop adverse trends. These shortcomings can only be overcome through improvements to the information system.

3. Information technology improves, thereby obsoleting currently installed computer hardware and software. Examples of recent technology developments include more powerful multitasking microcomputers and optical scanners.

If a firm's information system does not adapt in response to these changes and shortcomings, the firm is likely to lose its competitive edge. In addition to becoming more inefficient and ineffective, the firm will be less able to take advantage of opportunities as they arise. Thus, in spite of the fact that systems-related costs are absorbing ever-larger shares of many a firm's resources, progressive firms must continually undertake systems development activities.

PHASES IN THE SYSTEMS DEVELOPMENT LIFE CYCLE

The **systems development life cycle (SDLC)** describes the development and post-development periods of one cycle in the life of an information system. As Figure 18-3 indicates, this life process consists of several phases that follow a sequence. Although no two authorities seem to agree totally concerning the exact phases, all essentially agree concerning the broad process and the key results or outputs. Each phase in our view of the process—planning, analysis, design, selection, implementation, and operation—involves several activities and concludes with a tangible output called a *deliverable*.

Systems Planning Phase　The initial phase merges with planning for the overall information system, which culminates with a deliverable called a *strategic systems plan*. The planning phase then involves initial investigations or feasibility studies, which search for feasible projects that will develop new or improved systems within the overall information system. This portion of the phase ends with project proposals for those systems areas found to be feasible. We discuss the systems planning phase later in this chapter.

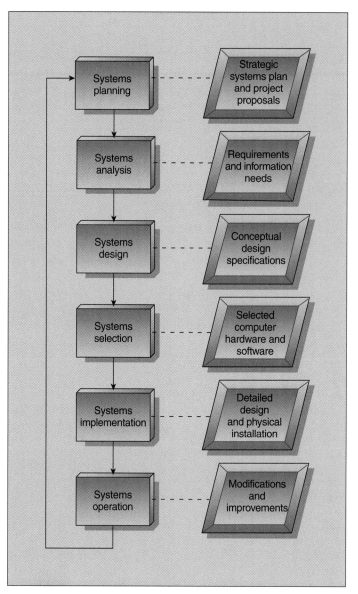

FIGURE 18-3   The phases in a systems development life cycle.

Systems Analysis Phase   With respect to each proposed project, several analytical steps are taken. The current system is surveyed and analyzed, the information needs of managers and other users are identified, and the requirements for a new or improved system are determined. These requirements and needs are stated in a deliverable called a *systems analysis report*.

Systems Design Phase   With the analysis completed, the systems analysts can proceed to design a system that meets both the functional system requirements and the information needs of users. Since more than one design will often meet these needs, it may be necessary to evaluate alternative designs for the system. After the preferable design alternative has been chosen, the various system components are specified at a conceptual level. These system specifications—pertaining to inputs, procedures, outputs, controls, and data base—are stated in the design deliverable.

Systems Selection Phase   The first step is to determine that the conceptual design is feasible—economically, technically, and operationally. This step confirms the early determination of feasibility during the planning phase. Then proposals are obtained from vendors concerning information technology resources. After evaluating the proposals, the most suitable computer hardware and software are selected. A report of the selected resources, supported by calculations showing that their benefits exceed the costs, becomes a deliverable to management. Note that if the project does not involve new hardware or software, this phase is not necessary.

Systems Implementation Phase   If management agrees that the newly designed system and selected resources are suitable, the final development phase begins. This implementation phase involves numerous activities, some of which are conducted simultaneously. One of the most important activities consists of preparing the detailed sets of specifications that lead to computer programs and specific controls and procedures. (This detailed design activity is so important that some authorities award it a separate phase.) Other phases include installing computer hardware, training affected employees, and testing the software.

Systems Operation Phase   During this postimplementation phase, the newly installed system begins and continues its operating life. The system is evaluated with respect to its performance and acceptability. When deficiencies are found, they are corrected. Modifications are also made, as warranted, to improve system performance and security.

APPROACHES TO SYSTEMS DEVELOPMENT

A variety of approaches to developing an AIS are widely used. All function within the framework of the SDLC, although certain approaches modify it severely. They have become popular because systems development projects have often disappointed their users and sponsors. Sometimes the systems development periods have stretched out too long; sometimes the resulting systems have not met the users' needs or have been too inflexible. Among the approaches that have successfully overcome one or more such disappointments are the following: top-down, bottom-up, modular, prototyping, user-developed, reengineering, outsourcing, and vendor-developed. Although certain of these approaches overlap to some degree, each offers a unique perspective bearing on systems development. In general, the approaches are complementary, rather than mutually exclusive.

TOP-DOWN APPROACH

The **top-down approach** begins at the top of the organization. First, the overall objectives and strategies are clearly defined, both for the organization and the information system. Knowing the objectives and strategies, the next steps are (a) to identify the decisions and (b) to determine the information needed to make the decisions. Then the approach leads from needed information to the needed reports, data bases, and other system components. In essence, the top-down approach is a refined application of the *integrated systems approach*. The focus is on the overall organization and its information needs for decision making. Thus, the top-down approach is well suited as an approach for developing decision-oriented systems such as decision support systems, executive information systems, and expert systems.

BOTTOM-UP APPROACH

The **bottom-up approach,** in contrast to the top-down approach, begins at the bottom of the organization. It focuses on the individual operations and applications. After each application is fully designed and operational, the approach looks at the possibilities of tying together two or more applications. This approach can continue the integrating process to form massive interlocking applications. For instance, purchasing and accounts payables applications may first be developed separately, then joined, then combined with production and shipping applications that form a large logistics application. Information generated as a by-product of transaction processing may be available for decision making.

MODULAR APPROACH

The information systems of most firms are too large and complex to be developed as single monolithic projects. In recognition of this reality, the **modular approach** treats the AIS as a network of interconnected building blocks or modules. Figure 18-4 presents a set of modules for a hypothetical manufacturing firm. Each module can be viewed as a separate project area, to be opened like a "black box" and subjected to the phases of the SDLC.

The modular approach has three benefits. First, it reduces the scope of a development project to manageable proportions. Second, it allows a design to be devised that is tailored to the characteristics of the module. For instance, if the primary purpose of the module is to support managerial decision making, such as in the case of the strategic planning module, a design can be developed that emphasizes deci-

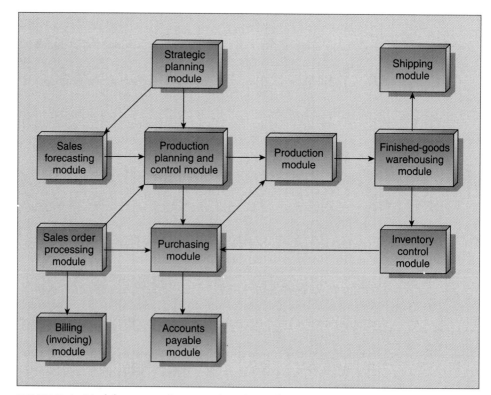

FIGURE 18-4   Modules composing a portion of an information system.

sion effectiveness. If the primary purpose is to perform transaction processing, as in the case of the purchasing module, a design can be developed that emphasizes efficiency. Thus, the modular approach functions easily with either the top-down or bottom-up approach. Third, the modular approach provides greater flexibility when maintenance of the system is required during the operational phase.

PROTOTYPING APPROACH

The **prototyping approach** is evolutionary in nature. It incorporates a learning process into systems development. Prototyping consists of devising a preliminary design within a relatively short time period as an initial iteration. This prototype design, which represents a crude approximation of the expected final design, is then put into use. As experience is gained with the prototype, the design is refined. This fine-tuning usually continues through several iterations. One benefit of this approach is that a newly designed system can be put into use much sooner than in the case of a fully sequenced development. Besides being less costly, it is likely that errors will have been detected early and eliminated. Furthermore, the prototyping approach is quite flexible, in that additional needs can easily be incorporated into later iterations. While it may be employed in developing transaction processing applications, the prototyping approach is especially suited to decision support systems, expert systems, and other nontransactional systems.*

USER-DEVELOPED APPROACH

Systems development has traditionally been performed by information systems professionals. In many development situations, this traditional modus operandi is very sensible. Software, for instance, requires the professional touch when developing accounting application packages. High-volume transaction processing applications, such as those involving accounts receivable processing, are most feasibly developed by professionals.

However, traditional systems development has exhibited disturbing trends and problems in recent years. One major problem is the increasing cost of systems development. An accompanying problem is the lengthy period, usually months or years, between the time that a user requests a system and the time a new system has been implemented. These cost and time problems are partly attributable to the fact that several labor-intensive phases are required by the SDLC. Because of the scarcity of qualified systems analysts, their salaries have steadily risen during the past decade.

Consequently, the **user-developed approach** has gained in popularity. In this approach, also called *end-user computing*, the users develop and operate their own systems. They are usually guided by trained professionals, often through information centers that have been established within the users' firms. The users are also aided by computerized software system development tools and user-friendly fourth-generation programming languages. Several such tools and languages are discussed in Chapter 19.

Joint applications development (JAD) is an adaptation of the user-developed approach that employs computer-based tools and the prototyping approach. JAD may involve a coordinator who stimulates interaction between the users and systems professionals, in order to facilitate the systems development process.

---

*Prototyping involves a variety of strategies that are beyond the scope of this textbook. A good survey article is Reinhard Budde et al. "What is Prototyping?" *Information Technology & People* (1992), pp. 89–95.

The types of systems best suited to user development include decision support systems, specialized reporting systems, and specialized transaction processing systems. These systems would normally be intended to serve only the user-builders and their immediate staffs or units.

REENGINEERING APPROACH

The **reengineering approach** focuses on the operational (business) processes of a firm. It takes a revolutionary view, in that it is concerned with *why* a process is necessary, rather than with the details of *how* it is done. By taking this view, systems analysts often can eliminate entire processes or portions of processes that do not add value. Even when processes are determined to be essential in toto, the ways they are performed may be radically changed. For instance, Cigna Corporation designed new underwriting processes in its reinsurance division, with cross-functional customer service teams to handle applications. As a result, it reaped such benefits as reduced operating costs (by 40 percent), shortened underwriting cycle times (from two weeks to 15 minutes), lessened errors (by 50 percent), and improved customer satisfaction.*

Reengineering does not represent a true alternative to the SDLC, since it employs the various phases. However, it reduces the effort spent in analyzing the current system and emphasizes the conceptual design phase. It is similar in spirit to the IDEALS approach, advocated in earlier years by Gerald Nadler, which suggested that system design should not be impeded by the current system. Several guiding principles of reengineering are as follows:

1. Organize a process around a team, which has the responsibility for the entire process and the outcomes. Apply this principle to information processing as well as physical processing, as Cigna did.

2. Simplify the organizational structure, reducing the number of managerial levels and giving the employees more decision-making responsibilities.

3. Apply information technology to the greatest extent possible, in order to reduce the number of needed employees and the errors in processing, as well as to be more responsive. Client/server systems and various networks, such as electronic data interchange networks, are very suitable for implementing reengineering concepts.

OUTSOURCING APPROACH

The **outsourcing approach** consists of a firm employing an outside firm to handle information system activities. Outsourcing may involve all of the activities, with the outsourcing organization even acquiring the needed hardware and software and systems employees. A full-service outsourcer such as Electronic Data Systems has outsourcing contracts with a variety of client firms. More often, however, outsourcing involves basic or specialized applications, such as payroll and telecommunications. Outsourcing can be an attractive approach, since it eliminates the frustrating problems that information systems management can cause. Instead, it turns these problems over to firms that have specialized knowledge and experience. It also can eliminate or reduce the capital outlays for computer facilities, and in some situations it can lower the costs of operating information systems. On the other hand, out-

---

*J. Raymond Caron et al. "Business Reengineering at CIGNA Corporation: Experiences and Lessons Learned from the First Five Years," MIS *Quarterly* (September 1994), pp. 235–236.

sourcing causes a firm to lose a degree of control over its information system. A firm also does not develop in-house expertise in information systems management. Long-term outsourcing contracts also may not be responsive to changed conditions and can be difficult to break.

VENDOR-DEVELOPED APPROACH

Traditionally firms have employed their own programmers to develop application programs for their information systems. In recent years, however, firms have increasingly been acquiring software from outside vendors. That is, they have employed the **vendor-developed approach.** Vendor-developed software consists of canned or off-the-shelf software packages. These packages are developed by a wide variety of commercial vendors and range broadly in the tasks they perform. Many of the packages pertain to accounting applications such as general ledger and accounts receivable. Some packages are specialized, such as those described as computer-aided manufacturing (CAM) systems. Although most software packages are provided by specialized software firms, some are developed and marketed by outsourcing firms and computer manufacturing firms. Certain of these developers combine software with hardware and market them as **turnkey systems**—so named because the vendors install the combined systems and the accepting firms only have to "turn the key" to start operations.

The vendor-developed approach provides such benefits as well-tested software packages at reasonable costs. They also drastically reduce the time required to develop software in-house, following the phases of the SDLC. The main drawback is that software packages must be generalized. Thus they cannot meet the precise needs of a particular firm to the degree that they can be met by in-house developed systems. In fact, it may be necessary to modify an acquired package extensively to render it usable. This necessity of course increases the costs, while invalidating the warranties offered by the software vendor.

CONCLUSIONS CONCERNING SYSTEMS DEVELOPMENT APPROACHES

Combinations of approaches are often useful in developing specific systems. Thus, decision-oriented systems are best developed by a combination of the top-down, prototyping, and user-developed approaches. Transaction processing systems are best accommodated by the bottom-up, modular, and traditional SDLC approaches, often with the judicious use of the vendor-developed approach. All types of systems can be improved by the application of reengineering. Firms that have little experience in systems development, or have cash-flow problems, are likely to lean toward outsourcing and vendor-developed approaches. In the last analysis, however, each firm must carefully consider its own situation. A surprisingly large number of firms may find that all or most of the approaches may have applicability to their situations.

SYSTEMS PLANNING

The first phase of systems development involves planning. It begins with long-range strategic planning and then leads into the planning of systems projects.

STRATEGIC PLANNING FOR INFORMATION SYSTEMS

Strategic systems planning provides the overall guidance within which systems projects are planned and developed. Although not actually a part of an SDLC, strategic systems planning enables a firm to avoid piecemeal, haphazard, and costly development of its information system. By looking ahead several years and spanning all of a firm's activities and functions, strategic systems planning attempts to

1. Integrate the information system development with the firm's overall planning processes.

2. Ensure orderly development of systems projects, making efficient use of available resources.

3. Recognize changing priorities and newly arising conditions as well as increasing informational demands.

4. Incorporate improvements in information technology as they become relevant to the firm's needs and promise greater benefits than the cost outlays.

Figure 18-5 lists five steps that compose sound strategic systems planning. The first, and most critical, step is to obtain vocal and enthusiastic support of top management, beginning with the president. Managers at the middle and lower levels take their cues from the top. This support is becoming easier to obtain, since computer knowledge and skills have steadily moved up the management ladder in recent years.

The second step is to form a *steering committee* if one is not already in existence. As noted earlier, this committee might consist of major users, such as the vice-presidents of the various organizational functions. It might be headed by the chief

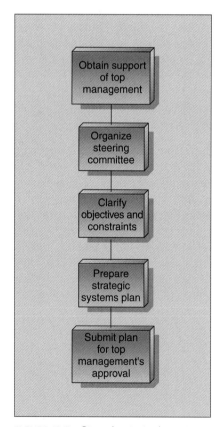

FIGURE 18-5   Steps in strategic systems planning.

information officer or even the president. Outside parties, such as auditors and consultants, may be engaged to provide advice. For example, Infoage has decided to establish a steering committee headed by Ralph Cannon, who has responsibility for the firm's overall information system. Working with Ralph on the committee will be Diane Varney, Mike Barker, Jack Dyson, and Jane Thomson.

A steering committee usually has key responsibilities, ranging from setting information systems policies to approving systems projects. By serving as a high-level coordinating body, it provides guidance and reduces conflicts among competing interests.

A third planning step is to clarify the objectives of the information system and to align these objectives with the firm's objectives. To be operationally useful, the system objectives should be identified with the firm's critical success factors, which reflect the firm's objectives in specific terms. For instance, one critical success factor might be to improve customer service. A system objective related to this success factor could be to provide the on-line capability to answer all customer inquiries within 15 minutes.

Systems policies should also be reviewed and developed where necessary. For example, an objective of reducing processing costs might be translated into a policy that requires all purchases of new computer equipment to be approved in advance. Furthermore, constraints on systems planning should be identified. Examples are ceilings on systems expenditures and limitations on changes to the organizational structure.

Preparing a strategic systems plan follows the clarification of objectives and policies, as the fourth step. A **strategic systems plan** is in effect a blueprint for systems development in the coming years. It provides a means for coordinating systems planning with other strategic plans. In addition, it serves as a standard against which to measure performance of the information systems function.

In order to prepare the strategic systems plan, a firm may appoint a planning team to gain an overall view of such aspects as

1. A model of the organization structure and key functional areas.
2. The key entities and objects, plus their relationships and the basic application architectures.
3. The current information systems and ongoing projects.
4. A strategy for integrating and developing projects in future years.[*]

The strategic view can be quite broad, taking into account outsourcing and other development approaches, financial budgets relative to the allocation of information system resources, information technology platforms, and cultural and behavioral issues. Latin Bank employed a consultant to aid the CEO by developing a strategy; it took a full year to complete but was extremely beneficial in guiding the bank toward sound system development.[†]

Often the written strategic systems plan is divided into two parts: a one-year operational plan and a multiyear plan. The short-range plan provides adequate details for budgetary control, while the long-range plan provides the broad perspective. Both parts of the plan include data concerning the planned projects that are to lead

[*]Albert L. Lederer and Veronica Gardiner, "Meeting Tomorrow's Business Demands Through Strategic Information Systems Planning," *Information Strategy: The Executive's Journal* (Summer 1992), pp. 20–25.
[†]Antonio Kovacevic and Nicolas Majluf, "Six Stages of IT Strategic Management," *Sloan Management Review* (Summer 1993), pp. 77–87.

INFOAGE, INC.
Strategic Systems Plan
for the five years from 1998 through 2002

I. Summary of the plan
II. Objectives of the redesigned information system
III. Assumptions and constraints
IV. Schedule of personnel requirements (person-months)
V. Schedule of cost requirements (dollars)
VI. Schedule of equipment requirements (dollars and units)
VII. Systems projects
    a. Title
    b. Problems and objectives
    c. Scope and relationship to other projects
    d. Estimated time schedule
    e. Estimated personnel, equipment, and other needed resources
    f. Justification, or expected benefits versus costs
Appendix A. Summary of data processing equipment currently in use
Appendix B. Forecast of hardware and software developments

FIGURE 18-6   An outline of the strategic systems plan for Infoage.

to developed system modules. Figure 18-6 presents an outline of a five-year strategic systems plan that Infoage has devised under the direction of Ralph Cannon.

Top management's approval of the plan is the fifth and final step. Approval serves two purposes: (1) it signals the future direction of systems development, and (2) it ensures that only those systems-related expenditures that are desirable will be made.

PLANNING OF SYSTEMS PROJECTS

In accordance with the modular approach, systems development typically proceeds through a series of systems projects. These **systems projects,** which apply resources to specific areas within the information system, are established through strategic systems planning.

Prior to its undertaking, a systems project must be clearly defined and approved. After approval gives life to a project, several initiating steps are necessary before project work really begins. Figure 18-7 diagrams the various steps in project definition and initiation.

Project Definition   An important aspect of strategic planning is surveying the various modules that make up an AIS, in order to identify needed project areas. Likely prospects include those areas that are either (1) greatly in need of improvement, due perhaps to changes in the environment, or (2) severely lacking in the quality of the information products. For instance, Infoage's sales transaction processing module may not contain needed accounting controls nor process orders promptly; its inventory management module may be capable of managing the inventory resource much more effectively and providing better decision-making information.

While a number of needed systems projects are likely to be detected through such surveys, others may not. Lower-level managers not on the steering committee are often first aware of problems. Anyone in the firm should be allowed to request that a systems project be initiated.

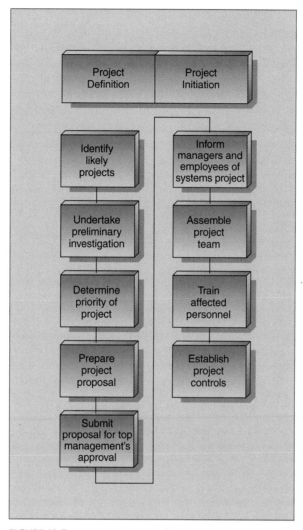

FIGURE 18-7 Steps in project definition and initiation.

Upon identifying a likely project, the steering committee begins a preliminary investigation. In the space of a few days or weeks, certain facts and estimates are developed—including such essentials as the work necessary to carry out the phases of a project, and the expected benefits and costs and time spans. Figure 18-6 lists under heading "VII. Systems projects" the types of facts and estimates to include in the strategic systems plan.

The preliminary investigation may serve as a **feasibility study,** a study whose purpose is to determine whether a prospective project is feasible to undertake. Alternatively, a separate feasibility study may be conducted with respect to a collection of prospective projects. For instance, feasibility studies are often conducted to determine if the AIS, with its collected modules, can feasibly be converted from a manual system to a computer-based system. Regardless of its scope, a feasibility study considers the benefits versus the costs (economic feasibility), the acceptability of a changed system by the users (operational feasibility), and the availability of the technology needed by a changed system (technical feasibility). If a prospective project is not likely to meet these feasibilities, it will probably be discarded after the feasibility study. Even if it does appear to meet the feasibilities at this point, the prospective project must still undergo a series of approvals during the course of the project. Thus, we will return to these feasibilities in Chapter 19.

Armed with the facts and estimates from investigations of the identified prospective projects, the steering committee can then assign priorities. These priorities are important, since they determine the order for undertaking the array of prospective projects. They are necessary, since most firms do not have the personnel to carry out all prospective projects concurrently. To illustrate, Infoage's steering committee may assign top priority to an inventory management project, due mainly to the cost savings and added information that an improved system should provide. It may assign the next highest priority to a data-base project, due to such expected benefits as more timely and higher quality information for decision making and answering inquiries. The major criteria for assigning priorities to systems projects include (1) the expected economic return, (2) the competitive advantage that is gained, (3) the extent to which the firm's objectives are achieved, (4) the degree of improved information, and (5) the freedom from adverse impacts on the firm's organization and technological infrastructure.*

The key document supporting a systems project is the **project proposal.** Also called a *problem definition statement*, the project proposal provides a detailed description of a prospective project that appears to be feasible. It links the objectives of the system area to be developed with the objectives of the firm. The content of the project proposal is a detailed version of the summary data provided in the strategic systems plan. In addition to a statement of the problems and scope of the project area, it presents the details of a work plan, expected resources that the project will require, and so on. These details would normally be developed through the preliminary investigation and often through a separate feasibility study.

Before a project can proceed, the project proposal should be approved by the managers at the highest level of the firm. This high-level approval represents a necessary control, since it often authorizes the expenditures of considerable time and money.

Project Initiation   Before rushing to work on a project, other preliminary steps are necessary. All those who will be affected by the project should be notified immediately. Employees and managers will thereby have an opportunity to adjust mentally to the impending changes. Otherwise, they will become victims of a "rumor mill" and react negatively. (We will discuss these behavioral reactions at more length in Chapter 20.)

Another preliminary step is to assemble the team that is to conduct the project. **Project teams** enable persons with differing areas of expertise and experience to pool their ideas. Members of project teams usually include computer systems analysts and programmers. Users, who are familiar with the operations within the project area, also should be represented on the teams. In addition, managerial accountants often can make significant contributions with respect to accounting controls and reports.

For some projects, the team members can consist of a variety of managers as well as information systems professionals. For instance, United Parcel Service established a team of 12 members for its automated package-tracking system project. The

---

*A. Rebecca Reuber, "Planning for Information Resource Management," CMA *Magazine* (April 1991), p. 20, as extracted from M. M. Parker and R. J. Benson, *Information Economics: Linking Business Performance to Information Technology.* Englewood Cliffs, N.J.: Prentice-Hall, 1988.

project was personally approved by the president and CEO and was headed by the vice-president for customer automation. In 16 months the team acquired and installed $150 million of cellular communications, networking, and legacy system improvements that aided in providing better service to its customers.*

Prior training of project team members usually enhances the results achieved by teams. Members who represent the users can gain from basic training in systems analysis and design. Systems analysts can receive advanced technical training in systems techniques, as well as briefings concerning the operations within the project area. Managers who will be affected by newly developed computer-based systems might also benefit from training in basic systems technology. Although they will not likely become technically proficient, the training should prevent them from acquiring "computeritis," an affliction that causes the sufferers to be blinded by the mystique and glamour of computers.

One last step might be to establish project controls. Controls over time and costs may be exercised through such techniques as Gantt (bar) charts and PERT networks, plus progress reports.

MANAGEMENT OF SYSTEMS-RELATED RESOURCES

Upon the completion of a systems project, a new or improved system module achieves full operational status. That is, the systems operation phase begins. Although the major development activities will have been completed, post-implementation evaluations will commence and continue. Modifications and improvements will be made as needed. The various operational activities and system-related resources require careful management and control.

Figure 18-8 shows the framework for generating information needed to control and thus to manage the resources employed by the AIS and other information systems. It begins with measurements of the times and other factors that reflect the usage of resources and services. These measurements then feed into chargeback and performance evaluation systems. In turn the systems provide reports pertaining to chargeback costs and performance. Each of the components of this control framework is discussed in the following sections. Since the framework is based on accounting concepts, accountants should contribute significantly during the installation and maintenance of control techniques.

MEASUREMENT OF RESOURCE USAGE

Effective control begins with the collection of relevant data. Thus, the times that systems personnel and computer facilities and personnel perform needed tasks are measured. Measurement data may be collected by either manual or automated methods. **Personnel time reporting systems** usually produce time sheets that have been prepared manually by systems personnel. Each completed time sheet reflects hours worked during a period. Times may be coded according to either or both of the following breakdowns:

1. By task, such as programming, testing, preparing documentation.
2. By projects, such as developing a new general ledger system.

---

*Jeff Moad, "Can High Performance Be Cloned? Should It Be?" *Datamation* (March 1, 1995), pp. 44–46.

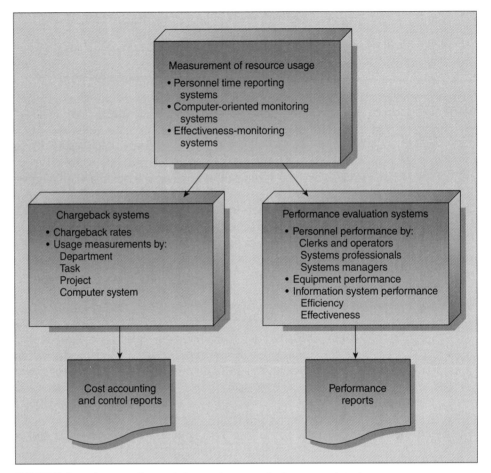

FIGURE 18-8   A framework pertaining to the control of system-related resources.

Derivative measurements may be computed from recorded times. Examples are number of documents typed per hour and number of debugged instructions written per day.

Computer-oriented measuring systems involve such methods as the following:

1. **Computer logs,** which are manually kept records of productive and nonproductive uses of computer facilities. A separate log, such as shown in Figure 18-9, may be prepared by each computer operator during his or her shift. In addition to showing data pertaining to the various jobs processed, a computer log reflects time periods required for preventive maintenance, program testing, and other necessary activities.

2. **Hardware monitors,** which are electronic or electromechanical devices having probes that attach to various components of computer systems. They count the signals emitted by the components and record these counts on some medium such as magnetic disks. A particular monitor, for instance, may count the number of times that disk accesses occur and the duration of each access.

3. **Software monitors,** which are programs or software packages residing within computer systems. They can record the same signal counts as hardware monitors; however, they can perform such additional actions as taking "snapshots" of internal conditions and indicators at designated times.

COMPUTER LOG									
Date 11/23 Shift 2 Operator B.P.									
Job No.	Usage Code	User Charge No.	Program No.	Equipment			Operation Time		
				Tape Drives	Disk Drives	Printers	Start	End	Elapsed
268	01	10	756-5	1, 4	3		7:56	8:10	14 min.
268	01	10	783-4		3	1	8:12	8:14	2 min.
269	10	06		1, 2, 4			8:16	8:20	4 min.
269	02	06	825-3	1, 2, 4	1, 2	1, 2	8:21	8:58	37 min.
	12						9:00	10:00	60 min.

FIGURE 18-9   A computer log of data processing operations.

Measurements may be taken that do not focus on specific personnel or facilities. For instance, software that monitors the effectiveness of systems may measure the time delays in correcting particular systems problems. Effectiveness measures may also consider other factors than time. Thus a survey of users may elicit the number of complaints concerning the level of service provided by the information system.

ACCOUNTING FOR SYSTEM-RELATED COSTS THROUGH CHARGEBACK SYSTEMS

One reason for measuring resource usage is to allocate the costs needed to provide services via the information systems to the users. These costs related to operating an information system can be very expensive. Among typical costs are leases of computer hardware and software, maintenance of computer and communications equipment, and salaries of professional systems personnel. In large firms the yearly costs may easily range into the millions of dollars, and the overall budget for information services tends to increase by several percent each year. Most of the costs for information services are fixed in nature. Those costs that are variable in nature tend to be for consultants, outside computing services, overtime, supplies, and utilities.

Information services costs represent a type of overhead. In previous decades most firms simply absorbed all such costs into general overhead accounts. This practice avoided sticky problems, such as how to allocate the costs easily and fairly to users. (In fact, most firms still do not allocate those costs for services that jointly serve multiple users, e.g., costs related to data-base administration). However, by not allocating any information services costs to users, they treated the services as a "free good." Not surprisingly, systems-related costs grew rapidly in such firms and much waste occurred. Consequently, many firms have or are considering the use of **chargeback systems**—procedures by which the costs are allocated to the users.

Several decisions must be made with respect to systems-related costs. Figure 18-10 displays a decision tree with five branches. Assuming that the decision (in the first branch) is to use a chargeback system, the next decision concerns the type of rate to use. Then decisions concerning the activity base and the costing approach must be made. In the following discussion we will first review the benefits of a chargeback system. Then we survey chargeback rates and methods of allocating costs.

Benefits of Chargeback Systems   A soundly developed chargeback system is essentially an accounting procedure, in that it carefully assigns costs to organizational

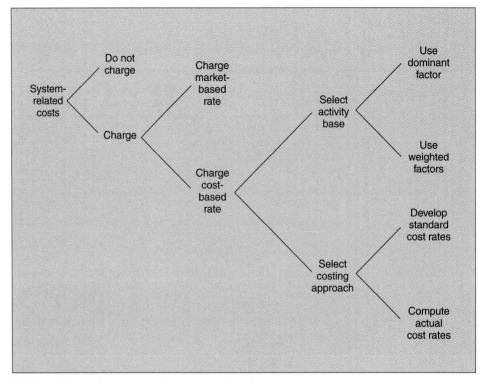

FIGURE 18-10   A decision tree for system-related costs.

units (i.e., users). However, it is also a planning and control system for management, since it does the following:

1. Ensures that the systems-related resources will be shared efficiently and effectively in accordance with each user's needs.
2. Stimulates the involvement of the benefiting users in developing the information system.
3. Provides cost data by which to evaluate the efficiency and effectiveness of the information systems function.
4. Provides reliable usage and cost data by which to plan future expansions in information services.

Chargeback Rates   The heart of a chargeback system is the **chargeback rate** used to charge users for information services. To the greatest extent possible, the chargeback rate should be

1. Fair, in that it reasonably reflects the value of resources used.
2. Understandable, in that it is or can be expressed in terms familiar to users.
3. Consistent, in that similar services under similar circumstances are comparably priced.

The chargeback rate is multiplied by the measured usages to assign the costs to users. As Figure 18-10 indicates, the two major classes of chargeback rates are market-based rates and cost-based rates.

1. **Market-based rates.** Most of the services provided by a firm's information system may alternatively be acquired from an outside commercial data processing service bureau. For instance, a bureau may process a firm's payroll on a large computer and charge so much per minute for the processing time required. A **market-based rate** is a transfer price that is directly related to the average rate charged by such commercial bureaus. When a firm establishes its information systems function as a profit center, a market-based rate should be considered. It would seem to be the most reasonable rate, since a manager with profit responsibility is viewed as competing in an open market environment. In fact, if users are allowed to acquire information services from any source, the use of a market-based rate should motivate the information systems function to be highly efficient. If it is less efficient than commercial sources, it may lose business to outsourcing and incur a loss.

   Although market-based rates seem appealing, their use can pose dangers for a firm. Determining average rates in the marketplace is difficult. As a consequence, the information systems function might attempt to substitute a negotiated transfer price or rate. Animosity might then develop between the systems function and users. Due to such practical difficulties relatively few firms have adopted market-based rates.

2. **Cost-based rates.** A **cost-based rate** is directly related to the costs that are or should be incurred by the information systems function. In essence, cost-based rates are intended to provide sufficient returns to enable the systems function, as a cost center within the firm, to recover its costs. The allocated costs are then absorbed by the various user departments as elements of their overhead.

The system-related costs to be allocated may be specified as the full amount budgeted to the information systems function. However, it is often adjusted to remove joint costs that cannot reasonably be allocated. Also, in accordance with the activity-based costing concept, the information systems function may be split into several cost pools. Examples of cost pools are data entry, operations, and systems development. If more than one pool is recognized, a separate cost driver could be designated for each. Then separate cost-based rates would be computed.

Cost-based rates are either of two types: actual cost rates or standard cost rates. *Actual cost rates*, also known as average cost rates, are computed by dividing the system-related costs for a period (e.g., a month) by an activity base such as actual processing hours. Although actual cost rates are understandable to users, they will vary from month to month. When total activity is high, the rate is low, and vice versa. Actual cost rates also do not provide a means for evaluating the efficiency of the systems function. *Standard cost rates* are determined on the basis of careful studies. Instead of reflecting actual costs and activity levels, they express attainable levels, given reasonably efficient operations. They are also held constant for a reasonably lengthy period, such as a year. Thus, they are fairer and more consistent. They provide the basis for computing efficiency variances. Figure 18-11 contrasts the computations of the two types of cost-based rates and the market-based rate, assuming the activity level to be measured by computer processing hours.

Charging Algorithms and Cost Allocations   Most information systems provide a variety of services. In addition to computer processing, they print reports, access data from on-line storage devices, and provide software consulting services. Thus rates should reflect more types of activity than computer processing. A *charging algorithm* is a formula that in effect combines several rates. To illustrate a charging algorithm, we assume that a particular computer system consists of a central processor, a disk

	RATE	× USAGE	= CHARGED COST TO USER
Actual cost rate	$\left[\dfrac{\text{Actual total systems-related costs}}{\text{Actual processing hours}}\right]$	× Actual hours of processing	= Prorated actual cost
Standard cost rate	$\left[\dfrac{\text{Estimated systems-related costs}}{\text{Estimated processing hours (at standard)}}\right]$	× Actual hours of processing	= Prorated cost at actual
	Market rate	× Actual hours of processing	= Computed market price

FIGURE 18-11   Three methods of computing chargeback costs.

drive, a terminal, and a printer. A suitable charging algorithm, which encompasses standard cost rates, might be as follows:

$$\text{Charge} = (Cr + Pr + Tr + Dr)$$

where

C is the central processor time used in minutes.

P is the number of lines of printed output.

T is the terminal connect time in minutes.

D is the number of kilobytes of disk used.

ri is the individual chargeback rate of the ith component.

Assume that a particular user—such as Ralph Cannon (and the office activities at Infoage that he manages)—required the following services for a month: C = 50 hours, P = 10,000 lines, T = 100 hours, and D = 200 kilobytes. If the rates are $2 per minute of central processor time, $.002 per line of printed output, $.01 per minute of terminal connect time, and $.05 per kilobyte per month of disk storage, the amount charged to Ralph Cannon's office activities would be:

$$\text{Charge} = [(50 \times 60 \times 2) + (10{,}000 \times .002) + (100 \times 60 \times .01) + (200 \times .05)]$$
$$= \$6{,}090.$$

Cost accounting reports would be prepared monthly for both the user areas and the information systems function. Thus, Ralph Cannon in the above example would receive the computations that support the $6,090 charge. The information systems function would receive a report that shows the variance between its actual costs and the costs charged to user areas for the month. For instance, if the costs charged by the algorithm to all users in the current month total $208,000, and the actual costs total $231,000, the report would show a $23,000 unfavorable variance.

PERFORMANCE EVALUATION SYSTEMS

In addition to chargeback systems, a control framework for systems-related costs should include performance evaluation systems. Their mission is collectively to aid the management of systems resources, ensuring that the resources are employed efficiently and effectively. The major resources are the systems personnel and computer equipment, both individually and collectively.

Two key aspects of performance evaluation systems are standards of comparison and measurements of usage. Performance standards are generally established through engineering studies. Then, the measured usages are compared against the standards and reported.

Personnel Evaluation   Standards with respect to personnel focus mainly on productivity. Examples of performance measures range from keystrokes per hour to instructions written per day. Reports that reflect the performances of systems-related personnel may thus include:

- A report that compares the performances of data-entry clerks, measured by keystrokes per hour, against standard output rates.
- A report that compares the actual processing times of jobs handled by computer operators against scheduled processing times.
- A report that compares performances of programmers, measured by number of instructions written per day, against standard daily quotas.
- A report that compares the actual progress of systems analysts who are assigned to systems projects against milestones established for those projects.

Equipment Evaluation   Systems managers are vitally concerned with the proper utilization of computer-related equipment. Inadequate utilization can result in operational ineffectiveness and degraded levels of service. Thus answers are needed to such questions as: How many hours of computer time were employed in productive uses last month? Were sufficient hours devoted to preventive maintenance, so that the equipment will avoid undue downtime? To answer such questions, performance standards are needed as well as actual measurements. In the case of equipment

Equipment Utilization Report					
Month: March					
Usage Code	Use	Actual		Standard		Variance in hours Favorable (Unfavorable)
		Hours	%	Hours	%	
01	Production runs, regular	260	43.1	255	43.3	(5)
02	Production runs, special	4	0.7	5	0.8	1
03	Reruns	10	1.7	15	2.5	5
04	Compilations	42	7.0	40	6.8	(2)
05	Tests	80	13.3	85	14.4	5
	Total chargeable hours	396	65.8	400	67.8	4
10	Setups	120	20.0	100	17.0	(20)
11	Equipment failure	10	1.7	15	2.5	5
12	Preventive maintenance	40	6.7	40	6.8	—
13	Idle time	12	2.0	10	1.7	(2)
14	Training	15	2.5	15	2.5	—
15	Other	8	1.3	10	1.7	2
	Total nonchargeable hours	205	34.2	190	32.2	(15)
	Total hours	601	100	590	100	(11)

FIGURE 18-12   An equipment utilization report.

utilization, a suitable performance measure is the number of hours devoted to each type of activity.

Figure 18-12 shows an **equipment utilization report.** This report is useful because it provides a detailed breakdown of types of equipment usage, separated between chargeable (productive) and nonchargeable (nonproductive) tasks. It also reflects the variances of actual hours from standard hours for each usage. Thus the report aids planning and control by identifying problem areas and providing information for scheduling next month's processing operations and estimating future needs for additional capacity.

Other reports pertaining to equipment performance should reflect performance with respect to throughput (e.g., jobs processed per hour), response times, and multiprogramming levels.

System Evaluation Many aspects of the performance of the information system, apart from specific resources, need to be evaluated. Thus systems performance information should be developed and reported. Examples of needed performance information are costs per transaction processed, project cost overruns or underruns, number of complaints from users, and number of applications developed by users.

SUMMARY

When establishing an information systems function within the organizational structure of a firm, it is necessary to decide (1) where it will be located within the structure, (2) how the responsibilities will be structured and divided, (3) whether the structure will be centralized or decentralized, and (4) what the interactions with other groups and functions will be. Three likely locations are within the finance/accounting function, within an administrative services function, and as one of the equally independent major functions of the firm. Responsibilities of the information systems function are generally divided among systems development and data processing activities, with a variety of projects and specialized units being located within the systems development activity. Both centralization and decentralization offer advantages. Some firms attempt to achieve the advantages of both by blending a central group with decentralized units. Continuing relationships must be maintained by the information systems function with key users, such as the accounting function, and with hardware and software suppliers; occasional relationships with consultants are also desirable.

All firms should plan and develop their information systems carefully and with a long-range point of view. Changes occur, shortcomings arise, and information technology improves. After a need for development is recognized, the firm must select from among such developmental approaches as top-down, bottom-up, modular, prototyping, user-developed, reengineering, outsourcing, and vendor-developed approaches.

The development life cycle consists of such phases as systems planning, systems analysis, systems design, systems selection, systems implementation, and systems operation. Systems planning involves three subphases: strategic planning, project definition, and project initiation.

Systems in the operational phase require postimplementation evaluation and management, including the control of system-related resources. The process of controlling such resources includes measurement of resource usage, accounting for system-related costs through chargeback systems, and evaluation of the performance of systems personnel and equipment.

REVIEW PROBLEM WITH SOLUTION

PRECISE MANUFACTURING COMPANY, FIRST INSTALLMENT

Statement

The Precise Manufacturing Company is a Chicago-based firm that has been producing and selling quality light machine tools since 1950. Although Precise's sales have continued to grow, the rate of sales growth has been declining for the past couple of years. Its net income has also sharply dropped, since both the cost of sales and operating costs have been rising faster than sales. Also, the average time to fill a sales order has become so lengthy that many promised delivery dates are being missed. These problems are due in part to the fact that an average of 500 sales orders are received each day. Clerks are so busy that they make errors in processing sales orders. Other problems include rising inventory levels, increasing numbers of back orders, and poor sales forecasts.

The firm's president has become so concerned by these problems that he engages a consultant from a public accounting firm. On surveying the situation, the consultant reports that the underlying problems are mainly traceable to an inadequate and antiquated manual AIS. After considerable discussion among the higher-level managers of the firm, the president decides that the AIS should undergo a long-term development process. Thus he hires the consultant as the new information systems manager who, in turn, appoints two persons from the accounting function as systems development manager and data processing manager.

A newly organized steering committee, composed of the six vice-presidents plus the information systems manager, begin by defining the objectives and policies of the new AIS. The president issues the memorandum shown in Exhibit 1, specifying the objectives, to all managers of the firm. During several additional meetings the steering committee drafts a strategic systems plan, whose outline was similar to Figure 18-6 within the chapter. Included in the plan are summaries for potential systems projects pertaining to areas such as inventory management, financial management, and sales order processing and management. The president approves the plan and agrees that the project concerning sales orders should have the highest priority.

If approved, the sales order processing and management project would be scheduled to begin April 1, 1997, and to be completed on November 30, 1998. It is expected to cost a total of $271,000, consisting of supplies and equipment as well as salaries for the members of the project team, programmer, typists, and clerks. Added

---

PRECISE MANUFACTURING CO.

Memorandum

To: All Managers
From: John Curtis, President
Subject: Objectives and Policies Pertaining to the Information System
Date: October 1, 1996

As our firm grows over the years in size and complexity, it is necessary that the information system grow and adapt to provide the information needed for planning and control purposes. This statement lists the objectives that the firmwide information system should meet in the years ahead and issues the initial policies that are to aid in implementing the objectives. The objectives and policies are the result of considerable thought on the part of our Information System Steering Committee and should lead to a greatly improved information system.

Objectives:

1. To foster continued growth in sales by providing information regarding product demand, market trends, competitors' actions, new products, state of the economy, and technological developments.

2. To develop and maintain a high level of customer service by providing appropriate information that enables shipments to be delivered when promised and in good condition.

3. To conserve resources and reduce operating costs by providing information for controlling the productivity of employees, the levels of inventories, the utilization of equipment, and the percentage of production-line rejects.

4. To maintain financial soundness by providing information regarding the flow of and need for working capital and long-term funds.

5. To adapt the information system to future changes encountered, in order to continue to provide managers at all levels with all the information that they need, when they need it, for making effective decisions.

6. To incorporate new techniques and equipment into the information system when they show promise of providing information benefits that exceed their costs.

EXHIBIT 1

costs will be necessary for computers and systems support personnel during the period of operations through 2002. Benefits are estimated to be $164,000 for each year of operation.

A formal proposal for the sales order project is prepared and presented to the president, who approves it in March 1997. All employees to be affected by the project are notified immediately. A project leader is appointed and three members are assigned to the team. One member is a section head in the sales order department, another is an internal auditor, and the third is a recently hired MBA. The team receives training in a basic systems analysis course and begins work on the project on April 1, 1997.

Required

a. Prepare a project summary page for the sales order project, using the facts in the problem statement. Include benefits that might be reasonably expected and define the scope of the project based on a typical manufacturing organization.

b. Prepare a comparison of expected benefits and costs for a five-year life of an improved sales order system.

Solution

a. Project Summary for the Sales Order Project:

Precise Manufacturing Co.
Strategic Systems Plan
Page 25

Project: Sales Order Processing and Management Module
Problems: Rising clerical costs, numerous billing errors, and complaints about delayed deliveries.

Project Scope: Survey the present procedures and reports relating to sales orders, shipping, and billing; analyze the operating, planning, and control needs related to branch sales offices, sales order section, finished-goods warehouse, credit department, shipping department, and billing department; develop a detailed design of an improved sales information system; integrate the designed system with such other systems as the inventory management system, the production planning system, and the accounts receivable system; install, test, and put into operation the designed information system.

Project Objectives:

To improve the sales order processing and management system so that it provides needed information regarding sales levels and flows to other systems and to managers; to enhance sales processing efficiency with respect to processing and shipping times and costs; to improve accuracy of processing and billing.

Estimated Time Schedule: Beginning on April 1, 1997, and ending on November 30, 1998.

Estimated Resources:

Person-Months: 80.   Cost: $271,000.
Equipment: Purchased servers and leased computer workstations.

Expected Benefits:

1. Shortened average time between the receipt of a sales order and the shipping of the ordered products, so that at least 99 percent of promised delivery dates are met.
2. Reduced average time to respond to customer inquiries concerning the status of orders, so that 100 percent of inquiries are answered within one minute.
3. Reduced billing error rate to one error per 1000 transactions (from a current rate of one error per 12 transactions).
4. Reduced costs of processing sales orders and billing, by at least 25 percent.
5. Improved up-to-dateness of information regarding the status of any particular sales order and the availability of finished goods, so that no record is out of date by more than eight hours.
6. Better information for making decisions concerning sales.

b. A comparison of expected benefits and costs appears in the table below.

	1997	1998	1999	2000	2001
Benefits	0	0	$164,000	$164,000	$164,000
Costs	$105,000	$166,000	50,000	58,000	66,000
Net, yearly	($105,000)	($166,000)	$114,000	$106,000	$ 98,000
Net, cumulative	**($105,000)**	**($271,000)**	**($157,000)**	**($ 51,000)**	**$ 47,000**

KEY TERMS

application programmer (804)
applications manager (804)
bottom-up approach (810)
chargeback rate (822)
chargeback system (821)
chief information officer (CIO) (802)
computer log (820)
cost-based rate (823)
data-base administrator (DBA) (804)
equipment utilization report (826)
feasibility study (817)
hardware monitor (820)
information center manager (804)
information resource management (IRM) (799)
information systems manager (802)
joint applications development (JAD) (811)
market-based rate (823)
modular approach (810)
outsourcing approach (812)
personnel time reporting system (819)
project manager (804)
project proposal (818)
project team (818)
prototyping approach (811)
reengineering approach (812)
software monitor (820)
steering committee (803)
strategic systems plan (815)
systems analyst (804)
systems development life cycle (SDLC) (807)
systems development manager (804)
systems projects (816)
technical services manager (804)
top-down approach (809)
turnkey system (813)
user-developed approach (811)
vendor-developed approach (813)

REVIEW QUESTIONS

18-1. Why is the management of information systems important to an organization in this information age?

18-2. How can accountants be involved in the development and management of information systems?

18-3. What are three likely locations of the information systems function in a modern firm having a computer-based system?

18-4. Describe the internal organizational structure of the systems development group within the information systems function.

18-5. What are the key responsibilities of a steering committee?

18-6. What are the advantages of a centralized information systems function?

18-7. What are the features and advantages of a decentralized information systems function, and in what circumstances is it likely to be found?

18-8. How may close relationships be maintained between the accounting and information systems functions?

18-9. Why should a firm continue to conduct systems planning and development throughout its existence?

18-10. Describe the several phases within a systems development life cycle.

18-11. Identify and describe several alternative approaches to the systems development life cycle.

18-12. What problems in traditional systems development have led to an increase in the user-developed approach?

18-13. Which of the alternative systems development approaches are better suited to the development of decision-oriented systems? To the development of transaction processing systems?

18-14. What are the benefits of strategic systems planning?

18-15. What are the key steps in strategic systems planning?

18-16. What are the essential contents of a strategic systems plan?

18-17. What steps are necessary to define a systems project that is to lead to an improved information system?

18-18. What are the purposes of a feasibility study?

18-19. What steps should be taken to initiate a systems project?

18-20. What skills should be included within a project team?

18-21. What are the deliverables from the systems planning phase?

18-22. Identify several manual and computer-based measurement techniques that can be employed during the systems operation phase.

18-23. Why should systems-related costs be charged to users?

18-24. What decisions must be made in establishing a chargeback system?

18-25. Contrast three basic types of chargeback rates.

18-26. Describe the use of a charging algorithm and the reporting of the allocated costs.

18-27. Briefly describe several reports that can serve as the means of controlling the performances of system-related resources.

DISCUSSION QUESTIONS

18-28. Why is the accounting function decentralized in many firms? Does this situation parallel the decentralization of the information systems function?

18-29. Discuss the trade-offs involved in deciding the extent to which the information systems function of a large firm should be decentralized.

18-30. A consultant comments to the president of a manufacturing firm, "Your firm's financial health is declining because your picture of your business has become blurred." What are the implications of this comment with respect to the information system of the firm?

18-31. Should a small business firm emphasize the bottom-up or the top-down systems development approach?

18-32. Identify several pitfalls of systems planning and development, and indicate how each may be circumvented.

18-33. Discuss difficulties that can arise when one module of an information system has been newly designed and installed, while the remainder of the information system is relatively obsolete and problem-ridden.

18-34. An accountant can be involved in systems development. In which of the phases can the accountant have the greatest impact? The least impact?

18-35. Representatives of computer vendors can provide detailed knowledge concerning how their computer systems can solve the problems that a firm is experiencing. Discuss the limitations of such advice, as well as the appropriate initial steps that a firm considering the in-

stallation of a computer system might take to obtain help and advice.

18-36. Why would a giant firm like General Motors choose to outsource some of its information system operations? Discuss the drawbacks as well as the benefits of doing so.

18-37. North American Lighting, a manufacturer of lighting products for the automotive industry, reengineered its manufacturing and distribution processes. The current data-related processes in these areas mainly involved manual operations, required large investments in inventory, and were unintegrated. What benefits would possibly be achieved through reengineering?

18-38. Infoage, Inc., has decided to consider the implementation of a new data base and modernized on-line computer system, with particular emphasis on marketing, distribution to its sales outlets, and sales through the outlets. What steps should it take and what approaches should it employ in developing the new system?

18-39. Is it possible for any except the smallest firm to achieve "fully realized" information systems that are completely up-to-date and sound throughout? What approaches are likely to be most helpful in attempting to achieve this state?

18-40. Discuss the relationship of strategic systems planning to the overall budgeting process of a firm.

18-41. Discuss activities likely to be undertaken during the operations phase of an information system, other than those discussed in the chapter.

18-42. Discuss the problems that a poorly established and administered chargeback system might create for the information systems function and the firm of which it is a part.

18-43. Compare the use of a chargeback rate based on standard costs with a predetermined manufacturing overhead rate.

18-44. In what situations might the use of chargeback rates be unsound?

PROBLEMS

18-1. Stephanie Booster is a professional accountant who has worked for several years since graduation in a medium-sized industrial firm, primarily as an internal auditor and internal systems accountant/consultant. Now she is interested in beginning her own consulting firm, with an announced specialty of consulting in information resource management. She believes she can provide considerable assistance to growing firms that are interested in applying information technology, especially those firms that are too small to afford full-time systems personnel.

Required

a. Discuss the relationship between information resource management and information technology.

b. Do small firms need assistance in "information resource management" to the same degree as large firms?

c. What types of specific services can an accountant such as Stephanie provide with respect to information systems development?

18-2. The Chem Products Corporation of Lafayette, Indiana, has employed automated data processing for a number of years. Furthermore, the manager of data processing, Mike O'Dell, has headed the data processing activities since the days when punched-card equipment was in use. Now he supervises an information system that incorporates the latest-model Burgen computer. As in the days of punched-card equipment, he reports to the controller (who in turn reports to the vice-president of finance).

Mike O'Dell has organized his department so that three managers report directly to him: the manager of data preparation, the manager of systems analysis and design, and the manager of operations and programming.

Susan Hazelbaker, the manager of data preparation, supervises the data entry clerks. In addition, she maintains the data library and documentation books.

Doug White, the manager of systems analysis and design, supervises five systems analysts. They are each assigned systems design tasks, pertaining either to new systems or to systems maintenance, that they are expected to undertake on their own. In the case of most assignments, their outputs consist of flowcharts and forms layouts, from which the programmers are expected to develop new or modified programs. Often, however, the systems analysts must coordinate their efforts with the procedures and reports section, which has the responsibility of developing procedures, forms, reports, the chart of accounts, and documentation pertaining to noncomputerized operations. This procedures and reports section is headed by Dorothy Hines, who reports to the chief accountant, a manager on the same level as Mike O'Dell.

Bill Ferrell, the manager of operations and programming, has responsibility for three activities: computer operations, computer programming, and data control. However, the computer operators and programmers in effect form one group, since they assist each other in their respective duties and even substitute for each other when an employee is sick or on vacation. Also, of course, the computer programmers work closely with the systems analysts, since the latter provide the specifications from which the former must prepare programs. The data control clerks and the computer operators also assist each other; for instance, a computer operator may check the control totals to the batch input control sheet or may distribute the outputs to the user departments.

Required

Critique the organizational structure of the Chem Products Corporation.

18-3. The Bryan Trucking Company of Newark, Delaware, has four major functions: operations, sales, finance, and administration. Each function is headed by a vice-president. Three managers report to the vice-president of finance: the controller, the treasurer, and the budget director. In turn, four managers report to the controller: the chief financial accountant, the tax manager, the cost analysis and reports manager, and the data processing manager.

Recently the president has received several complaints. The operations and sales vice-presidents have complained that they do not receive adequate reports to help them in planning trucking operations or in analyzing sales trends; they also say that the reports they do receive are often a week or so late. In fact, they say, the financial statements and accounting reports always seem to take precedence over other reports. They feel that this situation is not only unfair; it is also hazardous to the firm's financial health, since sales and operations are the primary contributions to the firm's profits. The data processing manager complains (more softly and indirectly) that she is short of staff and hardware, since the systems budget is too restrictive. She must contest with the other accounting managers for budget resources; after all, she has been told by the controller, there are only so many dollars available for finance and accounting activities. Currently the dollars available to her are being used to maintain generally sound transaction processing systems and financial reporting; as a result, few dollars are available to provide other key management information.

The president is concerned about these complaints. He feels that relevant, adequate, and timely information is vital to the firm's well-being. Therefore, he calls on a consultant from a local management consulting firm to aid him in resolving this problem.

Required

Prepare a report from the consultant to the president of the Bryan Trucking Company. The report should identify and weigh the alternative courses of action available to him and suggest a preferable course of action.

18-4. Marshall Associates, a sports gear manufacturer, is planning to install a new computer system to integrate

Marshall's marketing, accounting, and customer information. At a recent meeting of Marshall's management, there was discussion about how to proceed with this project as well as questions about the project's economic feasibility. The roles of management and users in the development of this project were also discussed. Marshall's management identified the four phases of the systems development life cycle as

- Systems Analysis.
- Systems Design.
- Systems Acquisition.
- Systems Implementation.

Required

a. Identify the benefits that the new computer system should provide to Marshall Associates.

b. Describe the following roles with respect to the above-mentioned phases of the systems development life cycle of

    (1) The management of Marshall Associates.

    (2) The accounting users within Marshall Associates.

    (3) Internal auditors within Marshall Associates.

    (4) The systems analysts within Marshall Associates.

    (5) The outside consultants who are engaged to aid in the development.

c. Describe the phase that precedes the four phases listed, as well as the phase that follows the four phases.
(CMA *adapted*)

18-5. Marvin Grey is the president of the Grey Manufacturing Company, a firm located in St. Paul, Minnesota. After returning from a business equipment convention, he calls in Denise Ballard, the director of information systems, and expresses his enthusiasm for what he has just seen. He further states that he has decided the Grey Manufacturing Company should have the most advanced equipment and systems concepts available. All the warehouses, plants, and sales offices are to be tied by a communications network to the home office and to each other. Each remote site will maintain its own microprocessors that can perform remote processing and also transmit data to the home office and to all other remote sites. A sophisticated data base with a firmwide schema, plus distributed data bases at the remote sites, will store all active data.

Denise Ballard mentions in response that she has not been associated with system development programs involving the features mentioned by Grey. In fact, the present system at Grey is a basic computer-based system that focuses on the more routine accounting transactions.

Marvin Grey responds that the system he described is essentially simple and straightforward. Thus, it should not be unduly difficult to design and implement. Denise can learn whatever else she needs to know on the job. He, for one, wants to "get the jump" on his competitors. Denise is therefore to present a systems development plan in three weeks.

Required

a. Discuss the pros and cons concerning the attitudes of and actions taken by Mr. Grey.

b. Describe the most suitable approaches to systems development that should be taken in order to help ensure the success of the new system.

c. Describe the phases that should be taken by Denise in developing the computer network desired by Mr. Grey (assuming that she retains her job).

18-6. Kids Incorporated is a medium-sized toy manufacturer headquartered in Oakland, California. The firm manufactures three lines of toys: plastic, metal, and electric. Each line consists of approximately 30 individual toy products. Although all the toys are manufactured in the same plant, each line is separated organizationally from the others. However, all three lines are sold by all members of the sales force, who are assigned to the five regional sales territories covering the continental United States.

The president of Kids Incorporated, Ms. Uno, has become increasingly dissatisfied with the firm's information system. She and her fellow managers can obtain information from the system only at the end of the month. Because of the present highly competitive conditions in the toy-making industry, such infrequent reports put the firm at a disadvantage. On questioning the controller, the president learns that the information system also has serious weaknesses at the operational level.

Thus, Ms. Uno informs Mr. Moni, the controller, that he is to study and develop a redesigned information system. She states that the only constraint is "to leave the organizational structure untouched. Otherwise, you have free rein." However, she insists that the study must be completed within four months, as conditions have become intolerable.

Mr. Moni realizes that he does not have the time or expertise to undertake such a systems study. Therefore, he hires Berry Low, a recent MBA graduate, as a special staff assistant. Berry is assigned the system study as his first project; he is to report to Mr. Moni when the study is completed and again when the revised system design is prepared.

Berry Low goes to work. He researches what other firms are doing and talks to computer manufacturers. He follows their ideas and approaches as closely as possible. He designs forms to aid in maintaining better control over production and marketing operations. He designs reports to provide more timely sales and competitive information to managers. He chooses a computer that is the most modern version available. In fact, it will not be on the market for another two months, although he is assured that it can be delivered within the four-month deadline.

At the end of four months, Mr. Moni, together with Berry Low, attends a meeting of the president and top managers of the firm. Berry presents the design for the new system. All of the managers are impressed. They enthusiastically approve the acquisition of the computer system and the entire system design.

One month later the new computer-based information system is in place, thanks to the efforts of Berry Low and several sales engineers from the computer manufacturer. The employees, operating managers, and supervisors then see the system for the first time. They had not been told about it earlier, so that they would not become upset. Some respond to this surprise with grumbles and mumbles; some are even overheard to say that they had guessed something like this was in the works. The grumbles, mumbles, and comments are suppressed, however, when Ms. Uno announces that no one will be fired because of the new system.

Three months pass. To the surprise of the managers, as well as of Ms. Uno and Berry Low, the complaints come rolling in. More time goes by, and the complaints become a crescendo. Finally, when it is evident that the system is not working but instead is causing dissatisfaction, the computer and system are scrapped. The firm returns to the old way of doing things. The only feature retained is the more timely preparation of managerial reports.

Required

a. Critique this systems development project undertaken by Kids Incorporated.

b. Describe the phases and steps that should have been taken, from the planning phase through the implementation phase.

18-7. The Molte Company plans to develop a decision support system that will be used in strategic planning through the analysis of varied and often complex alternatives. Potential users are directed to specifically identify their information requirements in a manner similar to that utilized for recently developed general ledger and accounts payable applications. However, responses to this new request are vague and the project appears to be stalled. User comprehension is incomplete and developer proficiency is low due to lack of applicable prior experiences. The nature of these problems leads management to conclude that a prototyping approach would

be preferable to the system development life cycle approach, which was used for the recently developed general ledger and accounts payable applications.

Required

a. Identify the steps for prototyping an application system.

b. Identify several advantages of prototyping in development of applications having a high degree of uncertainty as to requirements.

c. Identify the disadvantages of prototyping.

d. Decide whether prototyping should have been used to develop the general ledger and accounts payable applications and explain your response.

(CIA *adapted*)

18-8. Mammoth Bank has 24 major application systems supporting more than 200 different kinds of customer accounts ranging from standard checking and savings accounts to sophisticated trust accounts. The systems have been developed over two decades in several languages and data base systems. Individually, the systems work as intended with minimal errors. However, different systems have different user interfaces, and that increases both the training time for new account representatives and the likelihood of misuse of the systems.

Ten years ago, account representatives were generally familiar with all the account types and could make good recommendations to customers regarding which accounts to select. Now, however, only a few account representatives are familiar with most of the account types, and even they have trouble helping customers select the best portfolio of accounts for their individual financial situations. Management became concerned that the quality of customer service was dependent upon which account representative was contacted by the customer. The customer received good service if the account representative was familiar with the account types most suitable for the customer.

After extensive discussions with the account representatives, the management of Mammoth Bank has become convinced that the bank is falling behind its competitors in customer service. It therefore decides to develop a new computerized account management system. However, after a preliminary investigation it is apparent that the new system will be quite extensive. It also will be complicated due to uncertain requirements and unstructured tasks related to customer relations. Thus, the approach to systems development must be carefully considered before getting underway.

Required

a. Is prototyping a sound approach to employ with respect to this system development? What are its benefits?

b. Describe three other possible systems development approaches that might be considered with respect to a new account management system. Can any of these approaches be used together with the prototyping approach, and if so, how?

c. Does the use of the prototyping approach preclude any of the phases in the systems development life cycle?

d. Assume that a new account management system is successfully implemented. Later the bank's management decides to add another type of account, which would involve revision of the user interfaces, the addition of data fields, and the addition of a master file. Describe the approaches and phases needed to revise the system to incorporate this new account.

(CIA *adapted*)

18-9. In each of the following situations, describe the one or more systems development approaches that appear to be the most suitable, and explain your choices. Assume that all of the approaches function within the framework of the systems development life cycle (SDLC) and hence it should not be a choice.

a. Wilson's Grocery Chain needs a computerized inventory replenishment system that aids it in reducing inventory levels in its warehouses, and in providing merchandise items to its retail stores promptly to replenish the store shelves. The inventory process is well understood, and inventory replenishment systems have been successfully installed in other grocery chains.

b. Idaho Instruments, a computer peripherals manufacturer, is dissatisfied with its capital investments procedure. It is very time consuming, since numerous documents must be compiled, and the decisions often lead to poor selection of equipment and other investments. Hence, management has decided to develop an expert system, which should aid management in making better decisions. The system should also reduce the time in preparing documents, since the data will be entered online and computations will be performed by the computerized system.

c. Terry Makins, the treasurer of Makins Materials, has heard of executive information systems. She decides that such a system would be very useful to her in carrying out her responsibilities. As she envisions the system, it will be computerized and provide a variety of informational outputs for her exclusive use. In addition to hard-copy financial analyses, the system will be expected to provide graphical and tabular displays on her office microcomputer.

d. Highlighting, Inc., a manufacturer of vehicle lighting systems, is dissatisfied with its manufacturing and distribution process. It appears to be unintegrated and to involve unnecessary activities. The production and delivery times, as well as inventory levels, are excessive. Many of the operations are performed in batch mode. If

feasible the firm would like to consider scrapping such steps as inventory storage and warehousing of finished products. The possible use of a client/server architecture has been mentioned.

e. Schluss Corporation manufactures skis and related equipment. Due to the increasing popularity of skiing, the firm's sales have grown very rapidly during the past 10 years. During the busy season, each employee averages several hours of overtime per week. However, during the slow season some of the employees must be laid off. One of the problems is that some of these employees are involved in maintaining and operating the information system, which is critical to the success of the firm. When a busy season begins, new systems employees must be hired, which leads to inefficiencies and errors in the information system and hence the needed information. Management feels that some alternative to the present information system operation must be found. One approach might be to automate the present system more highly by means of newly developed information technology. However, it is concerned that the costs of further automating the system may add too much debt to the firm's financial condition.

18-10. State one or more quantitative objectives that might pertain to each of the following systems projects undertaken by a manufacturing firm.

    a. Payroll processing system.

    b. Accounts payable—cash disbursements processing system.

    c. Accounts receivable—cash receipts processing system.

    d. Cash management system.

    e. Production management system.

    f. Personnel management system.

    g. General ledger—financial reporting system.

18-11. PWR Instruments is a manufacturer of precision nozzles for fire hoses. The firm was started by Ronald Paige, who has an engineering background and who serves as PWR's president. This closely held corporation has been very successful and has experienced steady growth.

Reporting to Paige are six vice-presidents representing the firm's major functions—marketing, production, research and development, information services, finance, and personnel. The Information Services Department was established during the fiscal year just ended when PWR began developing a new computer-based information system. The new data-base system employs a minicomputer as a central processing unit with several terminals and microcomputers in each of the six departments connected to the central processing unit. The microcomputers are capable of both downloading data from and uploading data to the main computer. For example, analysts in the Finance Department are able to access the data stored on the main computer through the microcomputers and use the microcomputers as smart terminals on a stand-alone basis. PWR is still in the process of designing and developing new applications for its computer system.

Paige has recently received the management letter that was prepared by the firm's external audit firm at the conclusion of the annual audit, and has called a meeting with his vice-presidents to review the recommendations. One of the major items that Paige wants to discuss with his management team is the recommendation that PWR form an information systems steering committee.

Required

a. Explain why the external auditor would recommend that PWR Instruments establish an information systems steering committee, and discuss the specific responsibilities of an information systems steering committee.

b. Identify the individuals at PWR Instruments who would most likely serve on the information systems steering committee.

c. Explain several advantages that PWR Instruments might realize from the establishment of an information systems steering committee.

d. An information systems steering committee must be familiar with the general system life cycle. Identify the steps in a system life cycle.

(CMA adapted)

18-12. Spiffy Wares, a large manufacturing and distribution firm currently serving the U.S. market, has decided to expand on a global basis. Consequently, it selects 30 countries in which to locate plants and distribution centers during the next several years. The countries into which it will expand range from Great Britain and Germany to the Philippines and Nigeria. As an integral part of its expansion, the firm intends to establish a worldwide information system that will handle a variety of transactions (e.g., sales orders, purchasing, cash disbursements, payrolls), operations (e.g., manufacturing, warehousing, shipping), and management activities (e.g., planning new facilities, controlling inventories).

Required

a. Describe the steps in strategic planning that Spiffy Wares should undertake in developing its worldwide information system.

b. What strategic objectives should Spiffy Wares establish in order to ensure success in its global expansion?

c. What should be the attributes of its worldwide information system?

d. What pitfalls should be avoided in its global expansion, especially with respect to developing its information system?

e. How will the information system be affected by the fact that such diverse countries as sophisticated Great Britain and the developing Philippines are included in the expansion effort?

18-13. The Malone Corporation of Corvallis, Oregon, installed a computer-based information system several years ago. The quality of information has improved and growth in transaction volumes has been handled with ease, but system-related costs have also risen in an alarming fashion. Consequently, the president recently asked the firm's public accounting firm for assistance in pinpointing the problems. In response to this request, a specialist in management advisory services (MAS) from the public accounting firm visited the Malone Corporation and observed the activities within the systems department.

In her report, submitted today, the MAS specialist offers these observations:

a. No written policies or procedures concerning information systems development or operations can be found.

b. Systems projects are assigned verbally, with target completion dates being suggested casually. Projects are undertaken only on requests of users and the concurrence of the systems manager.

c. Jobs from users are processed as received. Turnaround time for an average job is three days; however, jobs marked "rush" are given top priority and processed within one day, even if overtime is required.

d. Systems personnel are evaluated casually. Personnel turnover is high, partly because the job market is excellent but also because many employees feel that the systems manager plays favorites.

e. Reports concerning equipment utilization and personnel performance are nonexistent.

f. Documentation is scant, consisting primarily of manufacturers' publications.

Required

a. Describe the relationships between the observations by the MAS specialist and the problem of high system-related costs.

b. Discuss the likely state of relationships between the systems manager and (i) systems personnel and (ii) users.

c. Describe what steps should be taken by the president.

18-14. Wagstaff Pharmaceuticals of Milwaukee is a drug manufacturer. Its several divisions are served by a corporate headquarters and staff functions that are centralized and located at the home office. Information System Services (ISS) is one of these staff functions. Its services range from the data processing of routine transactions to the development (i.e., analysis, design, implementation) of information systems at the department, division, or functional level.

ISS provides its services on request to the various departments and functions within the several divisions, as well as to other corporate staff functions. The systems manager assigns priorities to the various requests, usually on a first-come, first-served basis.

However, he tries to give due consideration to rush requests. The users are not charged for these services; instead, all costs related to the system are absorbed as corporate overhead.

Despite the simplicity of this approach, many managers within the firm have complained about it. They say, for instance, that often they must wait for quite a while before their requests are filled. Also, they complain, other managers seem to receive service before they do, even though they (the complaining managers) had entered their requests earlier.

Because such complaints have been increasing, the president of the firm has decided to change the approach. Henceforth, he states, the recipients of services from ISS will be charged for services they receive. At the end of each month the systems manager will compute a chargeout rate, based on actual costs for the past month and the actual number of hours the central processor was in use. This chargeout rate will then be multiplied by the number of hours required by each user's job; the resulting amounts will then be charged against each user's budget. If the services requested by a user are quite sizable or are expected to be of long duration, however, the systems manager will have authority to negotiate a lower chargeout rate for that user. On the other hand, if any user is dissatisfied with the services provided by ISS or with the rates, that user has permission to utilize outside commercial processing services.

The systems manager's performance will be evaluated according to the extent that the charges to users "cover" his budgeted costs. Thus, he is expected to be energetic in stimulating usage for the services provided by ISS. (Currently, the systems manager is evaluated according to the extent that actual costs compare with budgeted costs. He prepares his budget semiannually on the basis of his estimate of user demand; this budgetary procedure will remain unchanged under the new approach.)

Required

a. Discuss the weaknesses of the current approach for accounting for system-related costs.

b. Discuss the advantages of the proposed accounting approach over the current approach.

c. Discuss problems that the proposed approach will likely create and describe means of overcoming these problems.

18-15. The Lagoon Company of Gainesville, Florida, utilizes a centralized computer installation to provide data processing and information services to its various operational functions. It treats the computer installation and all system-related activities as a single cost center. Once each year a budget is prepared and a single chargeback rate is computed. This chargeback rate is then used to allocate system-related costs to users for services provided.

At the beginning of this year the system-related costs for the coming year were budgeted as follows:

Payroll (including salaries, benefits, and taxes)	$210,000
Equipment rental (including maintenance)	350,000
Supplies (variable)	24,000
Utilities (includes a variable component of $10 per hour)	70,000
Miscellaneous (including insurance and security)	30,000

The time of computer operations during the current year was expected to total 3000 hours.

During the year, four functions utilized system-related services for the following time periods:

Accounting-finance	1000 hours
Marketing	800 hours
Administrative services	600 hours
Purchasing	500 hours

Required

a. Compare the chargeback rate for the year, if all of the system-related costs are fixed in behavior except for those explicitly designated to be variable.

b. Determine the amounts to be charged each of the four functions during the year.

c. If actual system-related costs during the year are $700,000, compute a cost variance that can help higher-level management to evaluate the performance of the systems manager.

Hint: Apply flexible budgeting concepts in computing the cost variance.

18-16. Tyler Enterprises, Inc., of College Park, Maryland, charges its operating and staff departments for computer-based processing and information services. The chargeback rate is determined by the total budgeted costs for the information systems department, divided by the available hours for processing productive jobs on the central processor. For the current year the total costs have been budgeted at $2 million, and 5000 hours of central processor time have been projected.

In recent months, however, the systems manager has received complaints from the market research and production planning departments. They feel that they are being treated unfairly by the current chargeback rate. A substantial portion of the budgeted costs of $2 million includes rental costs for printers, terminals, and disk storage units. However, their jobs essentially require the use of the central processor alone; the other hardware is primarily available for such jobs as processing accounting transactions.

As a result of these complaints the systems manager proposes that the charges to users be computed on the basis of a chargeback algorithm. (The algorithm that she proposes is identical to the one appearing on page 824.)

The following month the systems manager's proposal is put into effect. Two of the first jobs processed under the new charging scheme exhibit the following usages according to the monitors:

	Job #761	Job #762
Central processor time	2 hours	1 hour
Number of lines of printed output	200	5000
Terminal connect time	0	1 hour
Disk time	30 minutes	1 hour

Job #761 involved the preparation of the monthly production schedule by the use of a linear programming model.

Job #762 involved the processing of sales orders, with shipping notices being printed on the terminal at the remote warehouse and sales invoices being printed at the home office.

Required

a. Compute the charges for jobs #761 and #762 by using the chargeback rate based solely on central processor time used.

b. Compute the charges for jobs #761 and #762 by using the chargeback algorithm. Assume that the rates established for the various components are as follows:

$$r_1 = \$300 \text{ per hour}$$
$$r_2 = \$1 \text{ per 25 lines}$$
$$r_3 = \$25 \text{ per hour}$$
$$r_4 = \$30 \text{ per hour}$$

c. Compare the results obtained in **a** and **b** above, and comment on the apparent desirability of each charging approach.

18-17. *Datacruncher Office Equipment, Inc. (Continuing Case)*

Required

a. Prepare a brief memorandum from the president announcing the need for a systems development program and the composition of the steering committee. (Do not include information system objectives or policies in this memorandum.)

b. Outline a strategic systems plan and include the details of the following:

(1) Objectives of an improved information system.

(2) Proposals for system projects, including for each project the objectives, scope, and suggested priority. Justify the priority rankings of the projects.

CHAPTER 19

SYSTEMS ANALYSIS
AND DESIGN

INTRODUCTION

At the heart of the systems development life cycle are two complementary phases: systems analysis and systems design. In this chapter we examine the major steps composing the phases, plus the techniques and approaches by which they can be conducted both efficiently and effectively. An entire information system is usually too large and complex to tackle in a single system development project. Thus, in this chapter the term *information system* refers to a module of the system on which an approved systems project is to focus.

NATURE OF SYSTEMS ANALYSIS AND DESIGN

Systems analysis follows systems planning. On gaining approval for a systems project, as requested by a user and confirmed during systems planning, the systems analysis phase begins. The primary purposes of a systems analysis phase are to survey the current information system and to define what is required to create an improved system. Tangible results of these steps—deliverables—are requirements relating to a new system and listed information needs of the users. These

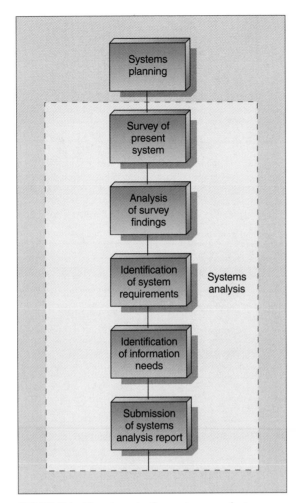

FIGURE 19-1   The steps in the systems analysis
phase.

requirements and needs are submitted for acceptance by management. Figure 19-1
diagrams these steps.

In the systems design phase, the task of the designers is to consider the features
of an improved system that will satisfy the requirements. Since more than one set
of features may be satisfactory, they must specify the particular set that appears to
be *best* suited to the firm's circumstances, both present and future. The *deliverable* from
the systems design phase, therefore, is a set of specifications that pertain to this
best design. These design specifications are also subject to approval by the firm's
management. Figure 19-2 lists these steps.

The analysis and design phases are closely interrelated, both with each other
and with the systems planning phase. In fact, most authorities disagree to some
extent with respect to which steps belong in which phase. Some would say, for instance, that the preliminary investigation and feasibility study form a part of the
systems analysis phase. All authorities agree, however, that the functions of analysis
and design must be performed early during the development process. They must also
be performed carefully, since any mistakes and omissions will be very costly to correct
in later systems development phases.

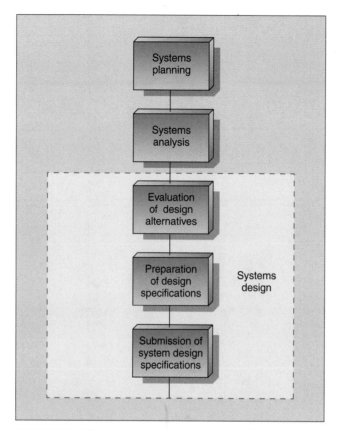

FIGURE 19-2   The steps in the systems design phase.

Systems analysis and design are especially compatible topics for an academic course. The activities involved in analyzing and designing a system are conceptual in nature, with the requirements and specifications appearing in lists, diagrams, flowcharts, and so on. Our study of these phases has been deferred to a relatively late chapter, since their processes integrate many of the concepts related to an information system. By first acquiring the basics of information systems, you will be better able to understand and apply the analytical and creative aspects of these phases.

MAJOR ACTIVITIES DURING SYSTEMS ANALYSIS

As the systems analysis phase opens, the project team has an approved systems proposal in hand. A summary of Infoage's proposal for the inventory management module, based on a preliminary investigation, appears in Figure 19-3.

Before looking in detail at the systems analysis phase, we need to ask an obvious question. If a preliminary investigation or analysis has already been performed, and the results have been prepared in writing, is it necessary to spend more time and money in further analysis? The answer is *yes*, and the reasons are as follows:

1. The systems analysts and others constituting the project team are generally not familiar with the detailed data and information flows and operations within the system module.

2. The current problems are not likely to be fully or clearly defined in the project proposal, nor are their causes usually understood; also, other problems and weaknesses may exist that are only detectable through thorough study.

3. Detailed cost data for the present system are needed, in order that they may be compared against estimated costs for an improved system.

4. Aspects worth keeping can be detected, and likely improvements are often generated by studying the present system operations.

5. Users of the system are more likely to accept a changed system if their cooperation is solicited, that is, if they are asked about the present system and its problems and the changes that are needed.

6. The requirements for an improved system can only be developed via thorough fact gathering and thoughtful analysis.

SURVEY OF THE PRESENT SYSTEM

A **system survey** essentially has the purpose of documenting all relevant aspects of the current system. In doing so the project team must confirm the scope of the project and gather a wide variety of data. Since these tasks bring the team members in close

---

Project: Inventory Management Module
Problems: Increasing investment in inventories, accompanied by frequent out-of-stock conditions.

Project Scope:
  Survey the present procedures, forms, and reports relating to the various inventories maintained and controlled by the firm; analyze the operating, planning, and control needs related to inventories; develop a detailed design of an improved inventory information system; integrate the designed system with such other systems as the purchasing system and the distribution system; install, test, and put into operation the designed information system.

Project Goal:
  To improve the inventory information system so that it provides needed information regarding inventory levels and flows to other systems and to managers; to maintain inventories at those levels that minimize total costs related to inventories and their management.

Estimated Time Schedule: Still undecided; possibly beginning in 1997 and ending in 1998.

Estimated Resources:

  Person-Months: 75. Cost: $100,000. Equipment: Testing facilities.

Expected Benefits or Objectives:

1. Savings from a 25 percent reduction in inventory investment.
2. Reduction in the error rate from one error per 15 transactions to one error per 1000 transactions.
3. Reduction in lost sales caused by product shortages from 7 percent of net sales to less than 1 percent of net sales.
4. Reduction of product shortages in the warehouse, resulting in more reliable delivery schedules.
5. Better information for making inventory decisions.

FIGURE 19-3   A likely project as identified in the strategic systems plan of Infoage.

contact with the current and prospective users of the system, the success of the endeavor depends on sound behavioral approaches.

Scope   Although the project proposal outlines the scope of the project area, the project team should verify the stated scope and provide greater clarity and depth. Otherwise, the team may overlook important data or waste time gathering data that cannot be used. If Infoage's inventory management system is the focus of the project, for instance, it is necessary to raise questions concerning its boundaries and levels. Is the purchasing activity included? Also, is the project limited to the operational level, or does it extend upward to include managerial reporting? Generally a project's scope will encompass not only data and information flows, but also the physical operations and resource flows and organizational structures. Moreover, it may range outward to the interfaces with adjoining modules. Thus, in Infoage's inventory management project, the survey should gather data concerning the links with purchasing and distribution, even though those activities are not included within the scope of this project.

Data Types and Sources   After clarifying the scope, the systems analysts must consider three questions: (1) What types of data should be gathered? (2) What sources should be tapped? (3) Which techniques should be employed in fact gathering? Fact-gathering techniques—interviews, observations, questionnaires, and document reviews—are discussed in a later section, so our focus at this point is on the first two questions.

Facts should be gathered concerning the inflows of data and outflows of information, the ways that data are processed and stored, and the controls built into both the manual and computerized portions of the information system. Certain data will usually involve measurements, such as volumes of transactions processed, times of key processing operations, costs of resources, numbers of errors made in processing transactions. Other data appear in format or model forms, such as formats of source documents and managerial reports, layouts of records, and flowcharts of transaction processing applications. Still other data are mainly qualitative in nature, such as policy statements, corporate minutes, charts of accounts, job descriptions, organization charts, procedures manuals, and budget guidelines. Finally, some data may be expressed in narrative forms and pertain to such matters as historical developments, informal and social relationships, and corporate philosophy.

The sources for such data are found both inside and outside the firm. Internal sources include file drawers and magnetic media, paperwork and physical operations, and managers and employees. External sources include customers, industry trade associations, government agencies, and trade journals such as *Moody's*. Another useful source is a firm that has an information system similar to the one being surveyed.

In-depth studies may be necessary on the part of the systems analysts and others who form the project team. For instance, with respect to the external operations, they may trace source documents, observe operational activities, locate control points, spot problem areas, and talk with all affected employees as well as managers.

Behavioral Approaches   During the survey the project team interacts with the employees and managers who will be affected by a systems change. Some if not most are likely to be concerned and worried. They may fear the loss of their jobs or at least the status they have achieved. In addition, the affected employees and managers may be uncertain concerning the social and other informal relationships they have developed. Thus, they may resist any change, even if they understand that it will be advantageous to the firm with which they are associated.

Resistance takes various forms. Some employees (and managers) may *blame* the changed system for all the problems and errors that arise, even those that may be due to human causes. Certain employees may show *aggression*, perhaps causing deliberate slowdowns, disruptions, and even acts of sabotage. Other employees may *avoid* the changed system as much as possible. For instance, a manager may avoid using a financial model package on the system for preparing next year's budget, preferring his hand calculator instead.

Since systems developers are agents of change, they must be aware of the expected resistance and the adverse effects it will have on the success of a newly designed and installed system. Therefore, sound approaches are needed to cope with and counteract negative behavioral reactions. These approaches are grounded in principles of human relations, which emphasize showing respect for the welfare of the affected employees and managers. If the principles are applied skillfully, the changed system is likely to receive greater acceptance, thereby helping to ensure its success.

The following concrete actions, taken by the project team, have been found to minimize dysfunctional behavior and motivate the effective and intensive use of a new system:

1. Communicate openly with the persons to be affected by the system project. They should be told of the project's purpose, scope, and expected duration as soon as the project is approved. Preferably top management should communicate this information, expressing its full and enthusiastic support. Those affected are less likely to resist when support comes from the top.

2. Encourage participation by the affected persons throughout the survey. Not only does participation build the self-esteem of those affected and gain their commitment to the project, but it can lead to useful suggestions. Good suggestions should be incorporated into the systems design, with full credit given to the suggestors. In the cases of suggestions not used, the suggestors should be thanked and told why their suggestions could not be applied.

3. Emphasize the positive aspects of the project and explain that the resulting system can better meet the users' needs. Thus, the purpose could be announced as "helping employees to be more effective in their jobs" or "providing a more user-friendly system." Such expected benefits as "cutting clerical costs" should be minimized.

4. Reduce the fears of employees and managers by establishing and publicizing fair personnel policies. An example is the policy that no employee will lose his or her position due to a change in the system. Furthermore, the policy should state that employees will receive adequate training to handle the new system or will be transferred to new positions at no loss in pay or status.

Aetna Life & Casualty, a large investor-owned insurance and financial services institution, employed an innovative approach with respect to its newly established automated offices.* It created a unit called People Technology Programs, which has the responsibility of handling issues that overlap personnel and data processing systems. This unit focuses on four areas of concern: (1) the ease of using automated office hardware and software, (2) the impact of the automated office environment (e.g., lighting, furniture) on the health and comfort of the affected employees, (3) the involvement of managers in systems development, and (4) the considerations by the

---

*Richard J. Telesca, "Aetna Plans for 'No-Fault' OA," *Datamation* (April 15, 1984), pp. 93–98.

project team of human factors when designing the automated office systems. During the implementation of the automated office, this unit realized that people must be handled differently than computers. Employees prefer challenging and interesting tasks, variations in duties, participation in decisions affecting them, and freedom to adopt individual working styles. Employees also want ample assistance in learning their new duties and the accompanying jargon, as well as assurances that they will not be replaced by the computer.

ANALYSIS OF SURVEY FINDINGS

A survey consists essentially of asking such questions as: What is done? How is it done? Where is it done? An analysis attempts to answer such searching questions as: How well is it done? Should it be done at all? If so, is there a better way of doing it? Why is it being done? In effect, this portion of the systems analysis phase resembles a reengineering effort.

Sound analysis depends in part on carefully documented findings derived from the survey. It can also be aided by fact-organizing techniques and checklists of specific questions.

Fact-organizing techniques provide models of various aspects of information systems. Several of the techniques—such as the data-flow diagram, system flowchart, and entity-relationship diagram—were described and illustrated in Chapter 4. Since the techniques are increasingly important to systems analysis, we will discuss the major categories in a later section.

Figure 19-4 lists a number of specific questions that are analytical in nature. Each question focuses on an aspect of the information system in terms of one of the concerns stated in the preceding paragraph. Consider the question: Are redundant processing operations being performed? The straightforward part of the answer can be provided by referring to the studies made during the survey and perhaps reflected in flowcharts. The analytical aspect can be answered by thoughtful analysis. In the case of Infoage's project, if the former answer is that a redundant operation takes place in the inventory function, the systems analysts must then consider the merits of the operation. Perhaps the redundant operation is to have the warehouse keep separate inventory records, which are posted each time products are received and sold. In a manual system this redundancy may be acceptable, so that the warehouse clerks can respond quickly to requests from salesclerks concerning quantities on hand. However, the project team may consider that the redundancy may not be necessary, especially if inventory records are maintained in on-line computer files that can be accessed directly by the salesclerks.

On performing a complete analysis with the aid of such questions, the systems analysts should discover the severity of the underlying problems, deficiencies, and weaknesses in the system module. They should also have begun to consider what needs to be done and thus to develop likely requirements.

IDENTIFICATION OF PHYSICAL SYSTEM REQUIREMENTS

The requirements relating to the physical system are determined in part by reference (1) to the analysis of the present system and its problems, and (2) to expected future conditions. They also are strongly affected by the objectives stated in the strategic systems plan and project proposal.

System Objectives   The objectives in the strategic systems plan are broad in nature and related to the objectives of the firm. Examples of such objectives are as follows:

- To foster continued growth in sales by providing information regarding product demand, market trends, competitors' actions, technological developments, and so on.

- To develop and maintain a high level of customer service by providing appropriate information that enables shipments to be delivered when promised and in good condition.

- To incorporate new information technology on a cost-effective basis.

The objectives in a systems project proposal are more specific and quantitative. Objectives for a sales order project may include the following:

- To shorten the average time between the receipt of a sales order and the shipping of the ordered products, so that at least 99 percent of promised delivery dates are met within two years.

- To reduce the average time of responding to customer inquiries to less than one minute.

- To reduce the costs of processing sales orders and of billing by 25 percent within one year.

1.	Are tasks and responsibilities clearly defined and assigned?
2.	Are tasks and responsibilities distributed effectively among employees and organizational units?
3.	Are the policies and procedures understood and followed?
4.	Does the productivity of clerical employees appear to be satisfactorily high?
5.	Do the various organizational units cooperate and coordinate well in maintaining smooth flows of data?
6.	Does each procedure achieve its intended objective?
7.	Are redundant processing operations being performed?
8.	How necessary is the result accomplished by each operation?
9.	Do unnecessary delays occur in obtaining and/or processing data?
10.	Do any operations cause bottlenecks in the flow of data?
11.	Are the number of errors that occur in each operation minimized?
12.	Are physical operations adequately planned and controlled?
13.	Is the capacity of the information system (in terms of personnel and equipment and other facilities) sufficient to handle the average volumes of data without large backlogs?
14.	Are the peak volumes of data handled adequately?
15.	How easily does the system adapt to exceptional occurrences and growth in use?
16.	How necessary is each document?
17.	Is each document suitably designed for efficient use?
18.	Are all the copies of documents necessary?
19.	Can reports be prepared easily from the files and documents?
20.	Do unnecessary duplications occur in files, records, and reports?
21.	Are files easily accessible and kept up-to-date?
22.	Are sound performance standards developed and kept up-to-date?
23.	Is data processing equipment being used effectively?
24.	Is the system of internal control adequate?
25.	Do the informal flows of data and information harmonize with the formal flows?

FIGURE 19-4   A checklist for analyzing information systems.

- Efficient and hence economical operations.
- Adequate capacity for expected growth.
- Timeliness in responding to inquiries and providing reports.
- Reliability of system hardware and software.
- Accurate, up-to-date, and relevant information.
- Security of the data and system facilities.
- Flexibility and adaptability to changes and new demands.
- Simplicity and hence user-friendliness.

FIGURE 19-5   A list of information system capabilities.

Underlying the objectives for a specific systems project are the overall capabilities that the information system should exhibit. Figure 19-5 summarizes the capabilities that are essentially applicable to any firm's information system.

Typical Requirements   A list of requirements for the physical aspects of an information system provides more specifics concerning the capabilities needed by a typical information system. Figure 19-6 shows a preliminary list that Infoage prepares with respect to its planned inventory management system. Actual values will be assigned to the requirements in the final list that the project team prepares.

System requirements, such as illustrated in Figure 19-6, fall into several categories. One group of requirements states how an information system should perform in measurable terms; these are called performance requirements. Another group relates to the content of the applications, rather than to their performances. A third group constrains the nature and features of needed computer hardware and/or software. For instance, requirements might state that optical scanning devices are to be used, that client/server architecture is to be employed, and that all newly installed equipment must be compatible with current computer hardware and operating systems. In general, requirements should be stated in functional terms—that is, in terms of what the system is to be able to do—rather than in terms of particular physical devices, persons who are to perform the tasks, or system component details. Specifications concerning the physical makeup of a system should be deferred until the design phase.

- Required processing capability, expressed in terms of transactions per time period
- Required storage capacity, expressed in terms of kilobytes
- Required response time in number of seconds or minutes
- Maximum allowable number of errors per 1000 transactions
- Required number of file accesses per time period
- Maximum allowable delay in preparing reports after an event, such as the end of an accounting period
- Required frequency of reports, such as daily or weekly
- Required applications, including key inputs, processes, and outputs
- Required hardware capabilities, such as interactive processing, graphics displays, multiprogramming, specialized servers
- Required controls, such as programmed checks and passwords at several security levels

FIGURE 19-6   A list of system requirements prepared by Infoage.

IDENTIFICATION OF INFORMATION REQUIREMENTS

Most system modules generate reports for managers and key employees, as well as outside parties. Thus, an added part of the requirements usually consists of needed information. Determining the information needs involves a special analysis.

An **information needs analysis** consists of the several steps shown in Figure 19-7. This type of analysis involves the top-down approach described in Chapter 18. Thus it should be preceded by a review and overhaul of the objectives and strategies for the firm. Then the objectives and strategies of the function within the scope of the systems project should likewise be examined. With respect to Infoage's project, the inventory management's objectives and strategies would be scrutinized by the steering committee.

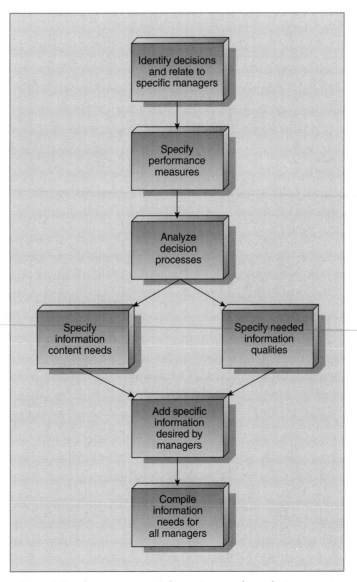

FIGURE 19-7 The steps in an information needs analysis.

Identify Decisions Made by Managers Each manager within the project area has responsibilities that are intended to further the objectives and strategies. When the responsibilities are clarified, it is possible to identify the specific decisions that each manager must make. For instance, Jack Dyson, the inventory manager for Infoage, has the responsibility for inventory and warehousing. One of his decisions concerns what level of inventory to carry with respect to each product. As the various decisions of each manager are identified, they can be arrayed in a matrix. Decisions that are the joint responsibility of two or more managers should be specially noted.

Specify Performance Measures After pinpointing the decisions to be made, performance measures are needed to reflect the effectiveness of the decisions. In most cases the performance measures are critical success factors, since effective decisions help achieve the objectives of the function and firm. Examples of performance measures (and hence critical success factors) related to inventory management include amount of inventory investment, average inventory turnover, average age of inventory, and number of times inventory items are out of stock when requested by the sales outlets. Many of the performance measures and critical success factors should have been identified during strategic planning, and thus would be known before a project begins.

Analyze Decision Processes Through interviews, a systems analyst and manager should jointly analyze the array of identified decisions. By "walking through" each step in the rational decision process (described in Chapter 15), they can determine much of the information needed for making each decision. Although this approach is useful for all decisions, it is most satisfactory for structured decisions in which the process is clearest. Unstructured decisions cannot be as satisfactorily analyzed on a joint basis. It will often be necessary for the manager to scan a spectrum of information from an executive information system or to employ a decision support system.

Different types of decisions also require somewhat differing approaches. With respect to planning-type decisions, the systems analyst could focus on the decision models and make them explicit to the manager whenever possible. If a decision relates to a control responsibility, the analyst could ask: What factors need to be investigated to see if the situation is under control?

Specify Information Needs Through such analyses the needed items of information gradually emerge for each decision (at least of the structured variety). This decision-oriented information should pertain both to content and to qualities, as discussed in Chapter 15. For instance, information for deciding on inventory levels would include carrying costs, reorder costs, stockout costs, expected sales in coming weeks, and related items of content. The information should possess suitable qualities; that is, it should be quantified, accurate (including realistic forecasts), timely, and so on.

To this decision-oriented information should be added the specific information that managers say they will find useful. However, managers should be told of the costs and difficulties in obtaining such information, so that the requests are kept in bounds.

Finally, the array of information needed by each manager within the project area should be compiled. Duplications should be culled, and items of questionable worth should again be called to the attention of managers. In addition to information needed internally for managerial decision making, the analysts should determine the information needed by such outside parties as government agencies and banks. For certain systems project areas, such as payroll, this added analysis may be as important as the internal information needs analysis.